ON A SEA OF GLASS

ON A SEA OF GLASS

THE LIFE & LOSS OF THE RMS TITANIC

TAD FITCH
J. KENT LAYTON &
BILL WORMSTEDT

INTRODUCTION BY GEORGE BEHE

AMBERLEY

Frontispiece: Titanic *departs White Star Dock on her maiden voyage.*

Above: Titanic *departing Southampton, April 10, 1912. The photo was taken from the* Beacon Grange. *On the right, a photographer can be seen preparing to snap his own photo of the event.*

*To the memory of all who were intimately connected with the Titanic …
in commemoration of a century's passing since her life and loss.*

For my wife, Jackie, my father Jerry, and my brother Jason. ~ Tad Fitch
To my friends and family for their support in these endeavors. ~ J. Kent Layton
For my kids, Tom and Tavia, and my wonderful wife Nancy. ~ Bill Wormstedt

First published 2012; Third Edition 2015

Amberley Publishing
The Hill, Stroud
Gloucestershire, GL5 4EP

www.amberley-books.com

Copyright ©Tad Fitch, J. Kent Layton & Bill Wormstedt 2012, Third Edition ©2015

The right of Tad Fitch, J. Kent Layton & Bill Wormstedt to be identified as the Authors of this work has been asserted in accordance with the Copyrights, Designs and Patents Act 1988.

ISBN: 978 1 4456 4701 2 (Print)
ISBN: 978 1 4456 1439 7 (E-book)

British Library Cataloguing in Publication Data. A catalogue record for this book is available from the British Library.

Typeset in 9pt on 10pt Crimson Text
Typesetting and Origination by Amberley Publishing.
Printed in the UK.

CONTENTS

To purchase other copies of this book,
or for the interactive experience, please visit:
www.atlanticliners.com

INTRODUCTION

By George Behe

The year 2012 marked the hundredth anniversary of the sinking of the passenger liner *Titanic*, and the centenary saw the publication of a host of books that (with several notable exceptions) were written very quickly utilizing the usual well-known stories for the sole purpose of cashing in on public interest in the anniversary. (Indeed, one grows tired of reading the silly claim that the *Olympic* and *Titanic* were secretly switched prior to the maiden voyage, and the equally silly claim that the steamer *Californian* was not within easy sight of the sinking *Titanic* and that multiple 'mystery ships' lay between them.) The present book is decidedly different, and the reader will become aware of that happy fact before he or she has delved into it for more than a dozen pages.

The study of history does not consist merely of assembling a collection of facts for their own sake. Rather, the proper study of history requires two separate and distinct activities, one of which must take place before the second can be attempted. The first of these requirements is that a historian must research his subject very thoroughly and assemble sufficient 'raw material' to enable him to move on to the second activity – which is to utilize that raw material in telling the complete story of the historical event in question. In other words, proper historical methodology requires the proper *interpretation* of historical data and the putting of raw facts in their proper historical context in order to get an accurate overview of the 'big picture.' One need only look at the detailed footnotes and list of sources contained in the present book to recognize the depth of research that its three co-authors accomplished prior to the day when they began to write down the fruits of that research in a form that made sense of the information in question. Kent Layton, Tad Fitch and Bill Wormstedt have gone out of their way to fill their book with accurate historical information and rare, little-known survivor statements that have been arranged in such a way as to let the story of the *Titanic*'s maiden voyage unfold in a logical chronological manner.

Readers of this book will learn about the background of the White Star Line and the reason behind the construction of the *Titanic* and her older sister *Olympic*. The reader will 'watch' as the *Titanic* is being built at the Harland and Wolff shipyard in Belfast and as she is taken out for her trial voyage prior to her delivery to the White Star Line. The reader will learn what it was like for passengers to take the boat train to Southampton and experience the hustle and bustle on the quayside as they prepared to board the great vessel for her first voyage to America. The subsequent four days of the maiden voyage are described in exquisite detail, and the reader will get to know many passengers and crewmen who – for all practical purposes – have previously been regarded as just 'anonymous names' that appeared on the ship's yellowing passenger and crew lists. The *Titanic*'s collision with the iceberg and the subsequent partial-evacuation of the great vessel are described with meticulous accuracy and vivid realism, and the heart-shaking events that took place during the minutes, hours and days that followed the sinking of the big passenger liner are presented with sensitivity and with an acute awareness of the fact that the *Titanic* disaster was a human tragedy that affected not only her passengers and crewmen, but devastated the lives of the thousands of family members and friends whose lives were intimately intertwined with those of the loved ones who sailed on the ill-fated maiden voyage of the largest ship in the world.

An added bonus to the present work is a fine collection of appendices, each of which addresses a specific historical topic that has puzzled and mystified *Titanic* researchers ever since the ship went down. The authors have carefully and dispassionately examined the existing evidence pertaining to each individual topic and have then offered their objective opinion regarding possible answers to the mysteries in question. The reader will now be able to evaluate the very real possibility that a *Titanic* officer shot a couple of passengers before taking his own life with his own revolver during the final stages of the sinking; the reader can impartially investigate the question of whether or not the *Titanic*'s band really played the hymn, 'Nearer, My God, to Thee' before they and their instruments were swallowed by the ever-rising sea; the reader can examine evidence pertaining to the way in which the *Titanic*'s Captain Edward Smith and her designer Thomas Andrews met their individual fates during the ship's final moments; the reader will also be able to read the cold, hard facts about the infamous '*Californian* affair' and dismiss the revisionist claim that the latter vessel lay far beyond visual range of the sinking *Titanic*.

The three co-authors of this book have been very judicious in selecting the most accurate and most descriptive historical source material with which to tell the story of the *Titanic*, and their acuity has resulted in one of the best books about the *Titanic* disaster that I have ever read. I was honored when Kent Layton, Tad Fitch and Bill Wormstedt asked me to write the foreword to this marvelous book, and I sincerely hope that the reader will be as impressed with their work as I am.

George Behe
Mount Clemens, Michigan

Opposite: Titanic *casts off from her Southampton pier.*

A CENTURY AND COUNTING

The *Titanic* has passed from living memory ... even so, it seems impossible to believe that more than a century has elapsed since that great liner set forth on her maiden voyage, filled with hopes, and since her loss shocked the world less than a week later. The story of that five-day voyage into destiny has haunted the public consciousness ever since the terrible news broke on the morning of Monday, April 15, 1912. It has remained a never-changing 'moment' in time that seems as relevant and fascinating today as it did back then, in spite of the earthshaking and turbulent century which separates us from the sinking.

In the last century, dozens of books have been written about the infamous events of the *Titanic*'s life and loss. Thus, many – when hesitantly reaching for this volume and turning to the first pages – will inevitably pose the question: 'Why another...? Hasn't everything about the *Titanic* been told already?' The answer to that question is a resolute: 'No.'

The truth is that the picture of history is never complete, especially once events pass from living memory. With a subject as popular, and often so hotly debated, as the story of the *Titanic*, the importance of telling historic events well, and as they really happened, is a great challenge. Why?

The challenges begin with the survivors – our only link to the events of that night. Of all those who were aboard, only one third managed to reach New York safely; two thirds were lost. That tremendous death toll means that we have enormous gaps in the historical record of what happened as the great ship steamed into an ice field and sank. That incomplete picture is all we have to reconstruct a chain of events. Additionally, there are now no living survivors to interview for fresh thoughts and input.

Already it begins to look like an uphill battle, but it gets worse. As one studies the existing survivor accounts, it becomes clear that not all the pieces of the puzzle fit together cleanly. Sometimes, survivors forgot to mention everything they did ... Occasionally, when they gave more than one account of their experiences, the different accounts do not agree with each other; among these are the various recollections of some of the best-known survivors, including Archibald Gracie, Lawrence Beesley and Jack Thayer. At times, they simply add a detail in one account that they omit in another, but sometimes they changed the order of what they did during the sinking, periodically even contradicting themselves. At other times, there are significant contradictions between different survivors on what order events happened in. The problems become so thorny that only a majority of the evidence can be used to determine the most likely chain of events.

At other times, the problem lies with those who have tried to re-tell the story. The earliest of these were newspaper reporters, swarming over the lower Manhattan wharves, jockeying to get stories from exhausted and grieving survivors. Notes were often taken in shorthand or in some other condensed manner, and then filled back in before going to press. Stories sometimes got jumbled; names were misspelled or recorded wholly incorrectly; and at times, reporters felt that the accounts needed 'tarting up' in order to make them more marketable to the public.

At the formal inquiries, the situation was more controlled and carefully recorded; even so, confusion arose, sometimes even from those who were conducting the investigations. Reading the transcripts, it is clear that there were times when investigators did not understand testimony, the working technicalities of ocean liners, and even basic nautical terminology. Even the accent or style of expression that a witness used was misunderstood. Simple mistakes during the proceedings were sometimes compounded and affected the investigators' final judgments on matters.

In the years since, the whole matter has come into the purview of enthusiasts, researchers and authors. Because the subject of the *Titanic* always evokes strong feelings, and certain events have long been thought either open to interpretation or resoundingly unsolvable, differences of opinion and even bitter arguments have erupted time and again. Commendably, some researchers and authors follow the available evidence like a trail of bread-crumbs, letting facts guide them to conclusions in the best 'Sherlock Holmes-ian' style. Others seem to have made up their minds that things had to have happened a certain way; then they have gone to find evidence to support their preconceived conclusions.

In a market which has become increasingly glutted with all sorts of books on the subject, attempts have been made by some to carve out a niche where they can specialize in a certain area of the *Titanic*'s history. This has at times produced astounding works. For other authors, the niche has become finding conspiracy theories surrounding the liner: that the steel used to build the ship was too weak ... that the shipyard and perhaps personnel from White Star colluded to build and equip the liners to a knowingly substandard level ... that the *Olympic* and *Titanic* were switched in order to accomplish some sort of insurance scam ... the list of such conspiracy theories goes on and on.

Another issue is the recent micro-dissection of *Titanic* information spread across dozens of books, research papers in quarterly journals, and online articles. While help-

---

Opposite: This view shows Second Class passengers strolling on Titanic's port Boat Deck on Thursday, April 11, 1912.

ful in certain areas – much like zooming into a scene with a telephoto lens camera to pick out a certain detail – some three-dimensional perception can and has been lost. Additionally, not everyone within the *Titanic* community or with an interest in her story has access to all this material. Even if they do, it can be very difficult for them to put it all back together again properly so that the larger picture emerges with accuracy.

In this book, we have attempted to reconstruct the entire story of the ship in a scholarly manner, documenting everything as we worked, and ending up with about 2,600 endnotes – most of them to cite original source material. We have included as much information as was available to us – including previously unpublished or rare accounts – as well as all of the research done on even the smallest details. Then we have taken all of this aggregate evidence to create a large-scale re-telling of the *Titanic's* history in a running narrative that we hope is as engaging as it is educational.

Where multiple retellings of the story from a single survivor are available, they have been compared with each other and with the testimony of other survivors that touch on similar, nearby, or corresponding events. Where differences arose among all available evidence, credence was given to the testimony that best fit the overall larger picture that was compiled from numerous lines of parallel evidence. Forensic research from the wreck itself was added to this, as well as any other piece of information which might have a bearing on the matter.

One of the things that we have seen the need for is to draw upon a wide range of expertise in the field when embarking upon a project of this magnitude. Our expertise ranges from a broad knowledge of the *Titanic's* technical construction through to individual stories. In the course of our work, however, we have also tapped the experience of a large number of other *Titanic* and *Olympic*-class liner researchers, and these other individuals have been very important in providing perspective and in playing 'devil's advocate' with our findings.

Overall we are stunned by the clarity that an impartial investigation of original sources can provide; like the interlocking pieces of a jigsaw puzzle, we have managed to piece much of the story back together. In a number of cases, the way two or more completely different accounts came together was absolutely stunning. At other times, seemingly contradictory accounts offered a small yet vital clue which helped us to understand what most likely happened.

Despite all of the progress we've made, we are also careful to note that certain details of events that night may never be established with finality. Our desire is, not to try to 'one-up' other researchers, but to present the most accurate picture of those events that can be compiled with the evidence that is now available to us. Since the first edition of this volume went to press, we have found a few errors, which we have put to right in this volume. If future evidence comes to light that helps us to understand that some of our findings and conclusions need to be revised in light of new information, we will happily make these findings available to other researchers and the public alike, initially through an accompanying web site.

The reader will no doubt notice that in several chapters – particularly the chapters focusing on the disaster – we have included subheadings to indicate that the events in that section happened during the listed range of times. These have been placed as 'guide-posts' to help readers stay oriented as they go through the lengthy narrative. However, they should be used merely as guide-posts, and a small range for variance should be allowed for.

We hope that you enjoy reading this volume, and that it makes the events which unfolded on that cold, dark night a century ago come back to life for you. We hope that this helps to bring into sharper focus the picture of what happened to what was then the world's greatest ship, and what it was like for the passengers and crewmembers who sailed aboard her … perhaps most importantly, we hope that this work will help to preserve the memory of the *Titanic* and those who participated in those events for generations to come.

Bon voyage.
J. Kent Layton, Tad Fitch, and Bill Wormstedt

PROLOGUE

The night of Sunday, April 14, 1912 was rapidly coming to a conclusion. Aboard the Cunard steamship *Carpathia*, it had been a rather ordinary day. In the ship's Marconi Shack, her sole wireless operator, 21-year-old Harold Thomas Cottam, was just winding down for bed. He had already removed his jacket, and was listening through his headset, awaiting a response from another liner, the *Parisian*.

Cottam had worked for the Marconi Company for about three years. Nearly half of that time had been spent in their shore-based stations. Then he had been assigned to the White Star liner *Medic*, on the Australian run. After two round-trip voyages on that vessel, Cottam had transferred to the *Carpathia*.

The *Carpathia* was an intermediate-sized liner of some 13,500 gross registered tons, and with a maximum speed of about fourteen knots. The little Cunarder was engaged on the Mediterranean run, and had just departed New York bound for Gibraltar. Cottam was aware that the ship was not, perhaps, the most prestigious; her wireless set was not the most up-to-date, being an older-style 1 1/2-kw design with a range of about two hundred and fifty miles. But it was a good job, which paid £4 10s per month[1] ... the hours were flexible ... there was the excitement of travel ... and it was stable employment.

Throughout the day, Cottam had received a number of wireless transmissions warning of ice. These had come in from the *Caronia*, the *Californian*, the *Baltic* and the *Mesaba*. He had dutifully sent these messages up to the Bridge. At about 10:00 p.m. New York Time, Cottam was awaiting confirmation of a previous transmission to the *Parisian*. He was almost ready to turn in.

While he waited, Cottam listened to the nightly news bulletins being transmitted from ashore, wrote down a few pieces of correspondence and took them up to the Bridge. When he returned to the Marconi Room, he put the headphones back on. Almost on a whim, he called up the new White Star liner *Titanic*, which was on her maiden voyage to New York. Cottam had been in touch with the *Titanic* earlier in the day ... what a job she must have been! Now, however, he thought to ask *Titanic*'s wireless operators if they were aware of the fact that there were a good many messages coming through for them from ashore.[2]

The response, when it came through at 10:35 p.m. New York Time, was stunning: 'Come at once. We have struck a berg. It's a CQD OM [old man]. Position 41° 46' N, 50° 14' W.'[3]

Cottam was stunned. A CQD meant that the *Titanic* – the largest and newest ship in the world – was in grave distress. Was it even possible? He replied, asking if he should inform his Captain. The response from the *Titanic* was a

definite 'yes'! At this, Cottam bolted for the Bridge. There he found First Officer Dean standing an icy cold watch. He quickly conveyed the information to Dean, and then he hurried down toward the Captain's cabin, with Dean following hard on his heels.

Carpathia's Captain, Arthur H. Rostron, had already turned in for the night and was in bed. He had not yet fallen asleep when the two men arrived with the shocking news. Rostron remembered that the ...

> ... Marconi Operator came ... right up to me and ... told me he had just received an urgent distress signal from the '*Titanic*' that she required immediate assistance; that she had struck ice, and giving me her position.[4]

Rostron asked Cottam if he was sure about the whole thing ... twice.[5] Cottam replied in the affirmative.

Carpathia's Second Officer, James Bisset, had already turned in for the night. He was just dozing off to sleep when he heard Captain Rostron's response to the news:

> Suddenly I heard the Captain's voice, singing out orders up to the bridge. 'Stop her. Send for the Chief Engineer. Send for the Chief Officer. Call all the Officers. Call all hands on deck and get ready to swing out the boats.'

This last order, in particular, motivated Bisset to full alertness. He jumped out of bed, quickly donned his clothes, overcoat and boots, and headed up to the Bridge to find out what was going on. He found First Officer Dean, the Officer of the Watch, had returned there.

'The *Titanic* has struck a berg and has sent out the distress signal,' Dean informed Bisset in a terse and highly excited voice.

By that time, Captain Rostron was in the Chart Room, working out the *Titanic*'s position, comparing it with his own, and figuring out what course he would need to take to intercept the stricken liner. Once he had made his calculations, he returned to the Bridge and said to the helmsman: 'North 52 West! Full ahead!'

'Aye aye, sir, North 52 West!' came the automatic response.

By that point, the ship's officers and department heads – such as the Chief Purser, the Chief Steward, the English doctor – had begun to congregate on the Bridge, and Rostron moved them inside, out of the cold. Once inside, he gave them the astounding explanation in a clear and steady tone of voice: 'The *Titanic* has struck a berg and is in distress fifty-eight miles from here on the bearing N. 52 W. We will make our utmost speed in going to her rescue. Call out an extra watch in the engineroom and

Carpathia's *Marconi Operator, Harold Thomas Cottam.*

brewed and ready to serve to all crew members to keep them alert. Coffee, tea, soup and everything of that nature would be supplied to each saloon ... blankets were to be brought to the saloons, the gangways, and some were to be readied for the boats.

All of the rescued were to be cared for and their immediate wants attended. Rostron and 'all officials' were to give up their cabins, while the public rooms would also be utilized to accommodate the survivors. All spare Third Class berths were to be utilized for *Titanic's* passengers ... all of *Carpathia's* Steerage passengers were to be grouped together. Stewards would be placed in each alleyway to reassure the Cunard vessel's own passengers, should they inquire about the noise in getting the lifeboats out or the high-speed working of the engines. Rostron charged all with 'the necessity for order, discipline and quietness and to avoid all confusion.'

To the Chief and First Officers, he ordered that all the hands were to be called, some coffee gotten into them, and then that they should prepare and swing out all the lifeboats. All the gangway doors were to be opened. Electric sprays, or lights, were to be placed in each gangway and over the sides of the ship. A block with line rove hooked was to be rigged in each gangway ... also a chair sling at each gangway, for getting up sick or wounded, as well as Boatswain's chairs, pilot ladders and canvas ash bags, with the canvas ash bags for children.

Rostron also ordered: 'Cargo falls with both ends clear; bowlines in the ends, and bights secured along [the] ship's sides, for boat ropes or to help the people up.' Heaving lines should be distributed along the ship's side, and gaskets were to be handy near the gangways for lashing people in chairs, and the like. The forward derricks were to be topped and rigged, with steam on the winches. Also, he gave different officers orders to maintain different stations and to be ready for 'certain eventualities.' Lastly, beginning at 2:45 a.m., Rostron would fire company rockets every fifteen minutes to help reassure those on the *Titanic* that they were coming.[7]

When Rostron had finished with this steady stream of orders, Bisset recalled that not one of the formerly-groggy men in the room were sleepy. They all turned out double-quick to carry out the Captain's instructions.[8]

As the *Carpathia* began to charge northwest toward the distress position of the *Titanic*, Rostron could do little but pace the decks of his Bridge, maintaining a careful watch for icebergs and praying that he would arrive in time to render assistance to those aboard the stricken White Star liner.

The road which paved the way to the *Carpathia's* mad dash to the *Titanic* in the dark of night was a long one, one which had begun years before. She was to have been a triumph for her owners, her builders, and for the shipbuilding industry as a whole. Instead, something had gone dreadfully wrong. ... This is the story of her life and loss. ...

raise every ounce of steam possible. We may reach her in four hours. We may have to pick up 2,000 or more people.'[6]

Then Rostron began to give an incredibly detailed set of orders for coping with the situation. The English doctor, and his assistants, would remain in the First Class Dining Room; the Italian doctor and his assistants were assigned to the Second Class Dining Room; the Hungarian doctor and his assistants would take the Third Class Dining Room. Each doctor was to have 'supplies of restoratives, stimulants, and everything to hand for immediate needs of probable wounded or sick.' The Purser, with his assistant and the Chief Steward, would 'receive the passengers, etc., at different gangways, controlling our own stewards in assisting *Titanic* passengers to the dining rooms, etc.' They were also ordered to 'get Christian and surnames of all survivors as soon as possible to send by wireless.' Meanwhile, the Inspector, Steerage stewards, and Master-at-arms were to control *Carpathia's* own Third Class passengers and keep them out of their Dining Room and 'out of the way and off the deck to prevent confusion.'

To the Chief Steward, Rostron ordered all hands to be called out, and that a steady supply of coffee should be

CHAPTER 1

A LEGEND IS BORN

In the first decade of the twentieth century, competition on the North Atlantic was at a near-frenzy. The second half of the nineteenth century had seen tremendous advances in technology in what later became known as the Industrial Revolution. This had allowed for greater worldwide communication, the emergence of a global economy and international trade, and also increased opportunities for world travel. There was a need for businessmen on both sides of the Atlantic to travel back and forth in caring for various responsibilities. There were also a large number of people who took passage across the ocean for leisure. For Americans with ample time and funds, there was little more exciting, more cultured, than a season abroad. For many Europeans, there was the attraction of great cities like New York or Chicago, as well as the wide open scenery of the American West and the Gold Coast. At the same time, a mass migration was in progress, with hundreds of thousands of people immigrating to the Americas to start a new life in the hopes of increased prosperity.

Any number of steamship lines were busily engaged in transporting these individuals to and fro across the Atlantic. The liners – so termed because they steamed upon fixed routes, or lines – were a matter of company, and national, pride. Britain had long dominated the waves not only militarily, but also with its merchant fleet. During the second half of the nineteenth century, Britain almost exclusively had the world's largest, fastest and most prestigious ships at hand between their two premier steamship lines, Cunard and White Star.

Beginning in 1897, however, a pair of German steamship companies unexpectedly trounced their British competitors by unleashing a stream of super-large, super-luxurious, and super-fast liners onto the North Atlantic shipping lanes. In this endeavor, they were backed by the Emperor of Germany, Kaiser Wilhelm II. Young, energetic and dubiously ambitious, he foresaw in his country a nation that could – and would, if he had anything to do with it – surpass Britain in every conceivable way. Since ocean liners were such a powerful symbol, it was determined that the German liners had to outdo the British liners in every regard. Their ships quickly gained prestige on the Atlantic. The ability to boast of having taken passage on the 'world's largest' or 'world's fastest' liner was unbelievably attractive to prospective passengers, and so the German ships enjoyed great success.

The British press and public veritably howled over 'foreign' liners having bettered their own. Personnel at the British White Star Line were not particularly happy with this development, either. The responsibility of their plan to respond to this development settled squarely upon the shoulders of the company's founder, Thomas Henry Ismay.

The White Star Line had a fascinating history. The company name 'White Star' was first used by a shipping line engaged in the Australian run, which had its origins in the early 1850s. Originally, they ran clipper ships, but eventually began to introduce steam power to their fleet. Unfortunately, the company became quagmired in financial distress and went bankrupt. The company's assets, house flag and goodwill were purchased by Thomas Ismay and registered under the formal title of the Oceanic Steam Navigation Company, with a capital of £400,000, in 1869. Shortly thereafter, Ismay began to engage in direct competition on the Atlantic with the Cunard Line. Although Cunard was nearly thirty years White Star's senior in the Atlantic trade, the newer company had quickly gained ground on the established one. By the end of the century the two companies shared the pride of the British Empire's mercantile industry.

The first major ship to appear in White Star's fleet after the German threat emerged in earnest was the *Oceanic* of 1899. She was a truly remarkable vessel, but on her own she was not enough to regain British supremacy on the Atlantic. Then, in November of 1899, Thomas Ismay died at the age of 62. After his death, the company came under the watchful eye of his son, Joseph Bruce Ismay. Frequently referred to as Bruce, the younger Ismay would lead the White Star Line in its bid to recapture British supremacy on the waves – and to keep a wary eye on developments from the Cunard Line, as well. By the time Thomas Ismay had died, plans to proceed with another great liner were already under way, but more would be needed ... much more.

In 1899 and 1900, Cunard put two new intermediate-class ships into service, the *Ivernia* and the *Saxonia*. Granted, a pair of liners was better than a single ship, such as the *Oceanic*, but they, too, were not a suitable response to the German threat. Both White Star and Cunard began to hatch bold plans for a more proper return salvo to their Teutonic neighbors across the North Sea.

First up came White Star's *Celtic*, which entered service in July of 1901. At 20,904 tons, she was the largest vessel in the world, and the last vision of Thomas Ismay. Even more exciting was that she was but the first of a quartet of great liners that White Star would put into service, which would become known as the 'Big Four'. Each of these ships – the 21,035-ton *Cedric* of 1903, the 23,884-ton

---

Opposite: *The* Olympic (background) *and* Titanic (foreground) *meet at the Harland & Wolff shipyard in October of 1911.* Olympic *has returned for repairs following the* Hawke *collision. A single funnel, No 2, stands in place on the* Titanic*. Work can clearly be seen progressing on the configuration of* Titanic's *B Deck windows, but her fitting out is far from complete.*

Far left: *Thomas Henry Ismay.*

Near left: *The* Oceanic *of 1870.*

Right: *Joseph Bruce Ismay.*

Lower left: *White Star's* Adriatic *of 1907, seen here in New York Harbor.*

Bottom left: *Far larger than the* Adriatic, *the Cunard liner* Lusitania *entered service in September of 1907. She is seen here in Liverpool on April 23, 1908.*

Below right: *The luxury and spaciousness of the new Cunarders is amply demonstrated in this 1907 photo of the* Lusitania's *First Class Dining Saloon.*

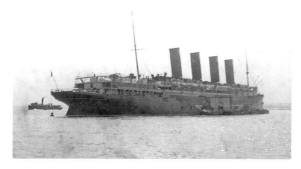

Baltic of 1904, and the 24,541-ton *Adriatic* of 1907 – were the largest in the world when they entered service. All of them were comfortable and noteworthy for their great size, and they were successful, but they were not exactly swift vessels; even the fastest of them only managed seventeen knots.

Meanwhile, in 1902, the White Star Line had been bought out by American financier J. P. Morgan and rolled into his international steamship combine, the International Mercantile Marine. Shortly thereafter, Bruce Ismay became President of the IMM, taking the helm of a very large company with White Star clearly in the forefront in terms of prestige.

As the new century got under way, Cunard had not been sitting still, either. In 1901, they had an English shipbuilding firm draw up plans for a proposed new vessel of some 700 feet in length, and with a remarkable speed of 24 knots. However, with a rate war under way among the great steamship companies, and their own coffers far from full, Cunard needed financial assistance in order to come

up with a proper response to the German threat and, in the eventuality, White Star's 'Big Four'. Eventually, they were able to secure a loan and additional financial assistance from the British Government to build a pair of liners the likes of which the world had never seen. They would become the world's first true superliners, and their names would become legendary: they were named *Lusitania* and *Mauretania*.

The *Lusitania* was built on the River Clyde in Scotland by John Brown & Company. Her keel was laid on August 17, 1904, and she was launched on June 7, 1906. The *Mauretania* was built on the River Tyne in England by Swan, Hunter & Wigham Richardson. She was laid down on August 18, 1904, and launched on September 20, 1906. The two ships were built from a single concept, but the two shipyards were given leeway in a number of details which in the end gave each of the liners their own personal identity. Both ships were remarkable in a number of ways. When they entered service, they were simultaneously the longest, the tallest, and the largest moving objects ever built. The *Lusitania* was some 787 feet in overall length, while the *Mauretania* was three feet longer; at the same time, they were the first vessels to top 30,000 gross registered tons, again with the *Mauretania* having the slight advantage in enclosed volume. Their unprecedented size gave more space over for the use of their passengers, and thus they were every bit as luxurious as – and in many ways far more luxurious than – any other ships in service.

Whereas all previous Atlantic liners had been content to use one or two – and in some rare instances three – propellers to drive them through the sea, the two new Cunarders sported a four-screw setup which would be copied on many

in a decade. The *Mauretania* entered service before the year was out, and not only did she take the records for size and length, but she also engaged her sister in a friendly game of one-upmanship, with the two ships taking the speed prize from each other over and over again. Even in this regard, however, the *Mauretania* had a narrow but clear margin over her older sister; after the summer of 1909, and despite repeated attempts, the *Lusitania* could not best her sister's average speed for an entire voyage.

All of these little details about which ship was faster, larger, or better were really for the true enthusiasts, however. The most important detail was that the pair of new Cunard-

successive liners. Yet even with all the previously noted distinctions, the *Lusitania* and *Mauretania* had one more – and perhaps their most stunning – feature, which set them apart from everything else on the sea: their powerplants. Instead of reciprocating engines, each of the new liners boasted no less then six turbine engines, four for ahead thrust, each geared to its own propeller, and another pair for use in being driven astern. These turbines gave a nominal 66,000 horsepower to each ship, with the capacity for even more under ideal circumstances. Dumping that much raw energy into the water through the screws, and having hulls built with fine lines to cut cleanly through the water, the pair was bound to set world records for speed – and this they did with relish.

When the *Lusitania* entered service in early September of 1907, it was clear she was a ship for a new era, a bold step forward in liner design. The *Lusitania* returned the world records for speed to British hands for the first time

ers was eminently successful. With bragging rights in every conceivable category, they were tremendously popular and proved to be fantastic sources of revenue. They instantly eclipsed every other ship on the Atlantic, and any other crack shipping line wishing to stay competitive was going to have to match, or preferably better, them.[1]

No one knew this better than Bruce Ismay. A long-lived legend has sprung up that Ismay dreamed up his next move at a dinner party at the home of Lord Pirrie, the man who was then at the helm of the Belfast, Ireland, shipbuilding firm of Harland & Wolff. As the story goes, Ismay and his wife dined at the Pirries' home one evening during the summer of 1907; after dinner, over cigars and brandies, Ismay and Pirrie discussed the *Lusitania* and *Mauretania*, and came up with a plan to best Cunard in the great trans-Atlantic game.

In truth, the legend is utterly impossible as it is so often retold. For one thing, many details about the new Cunarders

Above: Lusitania's *slightly larger, marginally faster sister* Mauretania *entered service in November 1907.*

had been available for years before 1907. The provisions of the 1902 loans from Parliament to fund their construction were a matter of public record, and included therein were many of the pertinent particulars about the ambitious project. Many other details had also become progressively clear to those 'in the know', or could have been easily surmised by shipping men who knew what sort of specifications the new vessels were being built to. There were also numerous press reports which gave some of the new liners' specifications. Finally, Harland & Wolff was allied, to some extent, with the shipbuilding firm constructing the *Lusitania*, John Brown & Company, and thus it is possible that Harland & Wolff personnel were able to acquire additional details on the vessels. In short, it is the height of absurdity to believe that Ismay would have waited until the summer of 1907 – mere weeks before the new liners' maiden voyages – to come up with a plan to counter the Cunarders' corporate threat.

Finally, and most importantly, on April 30, 1907 – some months before the dinner allegedly took place at Pirrie's home – White Star had gone ahead with a formal request to Harland & Wolff to plan their next move. They had asked the shipbuilders to design a pair of new liners that would counter the threat posed by the *Lusitania* and *Mauretania*.

In response, Harland & Wolff had begun work on two new slipways specifically for White Star's new ships, as well as a graving dock large enough to accommodate them – all long before the summer of 1907.[2] This meant that the dream to build the greatest ocean liners the world had ever seen was conceived earlier than is so often supposed; the tale as it is so often told is nothing more than romanticized fiction.[3]

Exactly how the plan to counter the soon-to-debut *Lusitania* and *Mauretania* evolved thus remains a mystery, yet proceed it did. White Star had long since eschewed the concept of building speed-competitors in favor of building comfortable, spacious, luxurious liners. So there would be

no need to follow Cunard's lead and build ships with such ground-breaking powerplants. On the other hand it was also clear that with the Cunarders coming in at roughly twenty-five knots, ships that had a maximum speed of only seventeen knots – like the 'Big Four' – were not going to be enough. It was also clear that a single-ship response simply wouldn't do; White Star opted to build two new liners, and they left the option open to build a third ship of the same class at a later date, if the first two were deemed successful.

However the concept for the next two White Star liners had its beginnings, it is clear that Ismay and Pirrie would have consulted closely on the matter. As Chairman of Harland & Wolff, Pirrie was very much accustomed to working with Ismay. Starting with White Star's first Atlantic liner, the *Oceanic* of 1871, Harland & Wolff had built all of White Star's new tonnage. Indeed, Thomas Ismay's financial backing to break into the Atlantic trade had come from a Liverpool businessman, Gustav Schwabe, whose nephew Gustav Wolff was a partner in the Belfast shipbuilding firm. Schwabe had arranged the deal on the proviso that Ismay ordered White Star's ships from his nephew's yard. By 1907, the arrangement had worked well for nearly forty years, and during that entire period, there had not been a single day that Harland & Wolff had not been engaged in building at least one White Star vessel.

While the collaborative team working on the initial concept was thus not by any means unique, the ships that they were planning to build were going to be unprecedented on a grand scale. Between 1906 and 1908, Harland & Wolff set about modernizing their yards to deal with the upcoming construction project. Three major slipways were demolished and replaced by two new ones, which were then covered by a gantry which housed electric cranes and which would greatly facilitate the work to be undertaken. Work on a new graving dock to accommodate the liners had begun even earlier, in 1904.

Above left: *J. P. Morgan and Lord Pirrie at the Harland & Wolff shipyard on October 20, 1910, just prior to the* Olympic's *launch.*

Above right: *Construction on the new slips and 'Great Gantry' had begun well before the* Olympic *and* Titanic *were laid down. Clearly, the dream for the two new superships was not conceived in the summer of 1907.*

Opposite: *General arrangement plans of the* Titanic.

THE WHITE STAR TRIPLE SCREW STEAMER
RMS TITANIC

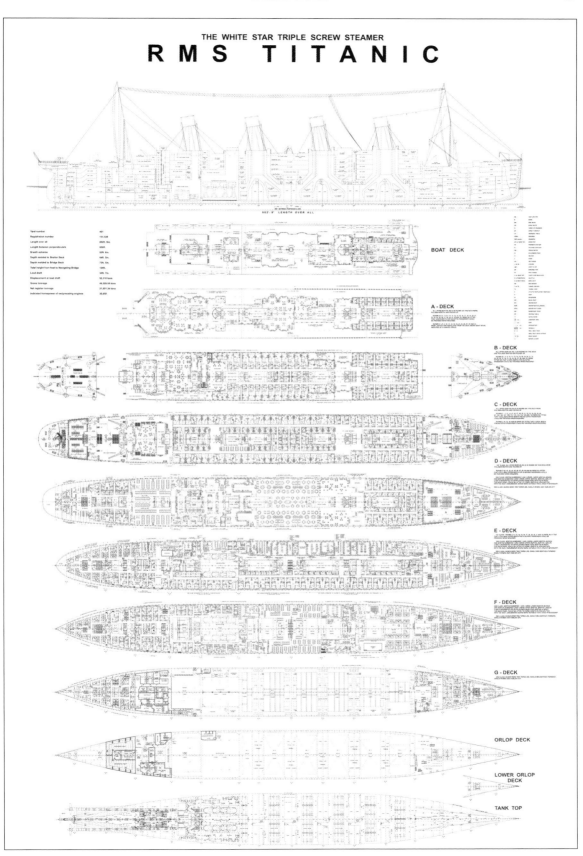

Far left: *This photograph, taken in early May of 1909, shows work to plate the forward end of Olympic's double bottom. Titanic's double bottom is clearly seen on the other slipway.*

Left: *Titanic's stern frame and some of her after frames stand in place in this view.*

The two new ships would be built nearly simultaneously on the new side-by-side slips. The first to be laid down, on Wednesday, December 16, 1908, was Harland & Wolff Yard No. 400. She would be named *Olympic*. The second ship laid down, on Wednesday, March 31, 1909, was Harland & Wolff Yard No. 401. This vessel was named *Titanic*.[4] When all was said and done, the two sisters would both be a breathtaking 882 feet 9 inches in overall length, nearly one hundred feet longer than the *Lusitania* and *Mauretania*, while they would be some 92 feet 6 inches in maximum breadth. They would, like the Cunarder speed-queens, bear four proud funnels, but at a projected 45,000 tons, they were nearly half again as large in enclosed volume. This gave a tremendous amount of space over to the ships' passengers, particularly in First Class, where there would be amenities, public rooms, and staterooms like there had never been before. They would also sport a competitive service speed projected at 21 knots – not quite as fast as the Cunarders, but certainly much faster than any of the 'Big Four', and also faster than most of the other ships on the Atlantic at the time.[5]

During 1909 and 1910, the hulls of the *Olympic* and *Titanic* began to take shape on the ways in Belfast, and it quickly became clear that they would be truly astonishing vessels. Although the Great Gantry towered over almost everything else in Belfast, by the time their twin hulls had been completed, they all but filled the monstrous enclosures. Work continued at a tremendous pace, with a peak of about 15,000 workers employed while the two ships were being constructed side by side. The yard was a hive of activity, with workers crawling over the hulls of the vessels like Lilliputians crawling around the giant form of Gulliver.

Work in the yard continued at full speed six days out of the week. Yard managers were expected to be at their stations before 6:00 a.m., so that work could begin smoothly under their watchful eyes. Many workers in the shipyard had joined as premium apprentices and were thus guaranteed a day's employment when they arrived at the yard's gates. The remainder of the workforce, however, had to go through the morning ritual of the mass hiring, and thus might or might not end up obtaining work.[6] For those who gained employment, they were in for a long day. The shift continued until 5:30 p.m., with only a half-hour lunch break. On Saturdays, the shift was short, last-ing just through the morning. Workers only had Saturday afternoons and Sunday off.

The work itself was physically demanding, and conditions were often dangerous. Heavy loads of material, not to mention the enormous hydraulic riveting machines, were often moving about from cranes overhead while workers toiled on scaffolding around the ultra-tall hulls of the ships being formed below. Materials could be dropped, people could – and sometimes did – fall from scaffolds. The work was also incredibly loud. Rivet gangs and the hydraulic riveting machines pounded rivet after rivet into the frames and hull plates, and steam-powered pieces of hoisting machinery hissed and whined as they moved heavy loads of material through the yard. Men shouted information to each other through the clamor. Ear protection was quite literally unheard of, and men were said to have come out of their day's work either deaf or nearly so. Even if their hearing began to return during the evening, the constant, day-after-day exposure to such incredible levels of noise would have left many with permanent hearing damage. If all of these hazards sound offensive to modern sensibilities of workplace safety – and rightly so – it must be remembered that those were very different times. Jobs at Harland & Wolff were considered highly desirable, and the company was considered by and large quite a fair employer. There were always plenty of workmen hoping to find employment with the prestigious firm.

Harland & Wolff did not provide housing facilities for their employees, but the workers did tend to choose housing in certain areas of the city. Newtownards Road in East Belfast was one such area, and it was within easy walking distance from the shipyard. There were also workers who lived on the west side, in County Antrim. To a large extent workers were segregated according to religion. For the most part, Catholics lived on the west side in County Antrim, with most Protestants residing on the east side in County Down. Although it was not a rule and there were areas where members of the two religions lived in the same areas, this was certainly a portent of more unpleasant chapters in Belfast's history that would follow a few decades after the *Titanic*'s construction.[7]

Despite low wages, dangerous working conditions, long shift schedules, and physically demanding labor, it was clear that the workers at Harland & Wolff viewed the *Olympic* and *Titanic* as more than just the means to another

Left: This photo shows the end of a day's shift at Harland & Wolff. Hundreds of workers walk down Queen's Road. The bow of the tender Nomadic *can be seen at the extreme left.*

Above: *Thomas Andrews.*

Below: *Alexander Carlisle.*

paycheck. Most of these individuals took great pride in the quality of their work, and in the vessels they built.

While up to 15,000 of these laborers moved throughout the various departments of the shipyard during the construction of the *Olympic* and *Titanic*, there were several key figures who were guiding the workforce in their endeavors. Foremost among these was, naturally, William James Pirrie. Pirrie was born in May of 1847 in Quebec, Canada. He joined Harland & Wolff in 1862 as an Apprentice Draughtsman, and worked his way up through the ranks until he eventually became a partner in the company in 1874. After Sir Edward Harland died in 1896, and Gustav Wolff retired in 1906, Pirrie was left as the Controlling Chairman of Harland & Wolff. He was also quite active in local politics, and served as Lord Mayor of Belfast (Liberal Party) between 1896 and 1898. From that point forward, he bore the title of Lord Pirrie, and throughout the remainder of his life, he would hold a number of other honorary titles, as well.[8] Pirrie was an excellent businessman, and once he became Chairman of the shipyard, he continued the close relationship established so many years earlier between his company and the White Star Line. Since the concept for the *Olympic* and *Titanic* was most likely first dreamed up between Ismay and Pirrie, it is probable that Pirrie himself made the first preliminary drawings for the new behemoths.[9]

At the earliest stages of development, during the critical months between April of 1907 and July of 1908, there was another key figure in the development of the concept for the *Olympic* and *Titanic*. His name was Alexander Montgomery Carlisle, and he was in point of fact Lord Pirrie's brother-in-law. This relationship was formed through Carlisle's sister, Margaret Montgomery, who had married Pirrie in 1879. Carlisle was born in 1854, and had joined Harland & Wolff as a premium apprentice in 1870, when he was sixteen years of age. By 1890, he had risen through the ranks to become the yard's General Manager, and by 1907, he was the Chairman of the Managing Directors. He was an outspoken man of robust health, later telling someone that he had never really known true illness in the whole of his life. He loved riding his bicycle, which he did every day, and he also said that he enjoyed the thrill of cycling through heavy

traffic. He also never wore an overcoat, no matter how cold the day was.[10]

Carlisle was intimately involved in the designs for the new vessels, and took particular care in making sure that their general arrangement, their scheme of internal decoration, and their equipment were all of top-notch quality.[11] Carlisle remained with the shipyard through the design phase of the two new liners, and saw construction begin in earnest on both. He eventually retired from the company on June 30, 1910,[12] and moved to London. There, in 1911, he became a member of the Merchant Shipping Advisory Committee on Life-Saving Appliances.

When Carlisle departed the shipyard, his position was filled by one of Harland & Wolff's true rising stars. This man could typically be seen in the yard offices, or making his way through the shipyard wearing a paint-smeared bowler hat, as well as a blue linen jacket, the pockets of which were invariably stuffed with plans. At nearly six feet in height and weighing two hundred pounds, he was well built and bore broad shoulders, with the figure of a man accustomed to athletic exertions such as cricket. Despite his athletic build, it is likely that he walked rather stiffly at times, especially after a long day on his feet in the yard.[13] This figure – with dark brown hair, a clean-shaven face, and brown eyes – was none other than Thomas Andrews, Jr, nephew of Lord Pirrie.

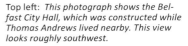

Top left: *This photograph shows the Belfast City Hall, which was constructed while Thomas Andrews lived nearby. This view looks roughly southwest.*

Lower left: *Wellington Place, looking west, with the grounds of City Hall on the left. Andrews' residence in 1901, Number 11, is on the right side of the street in the distance.*

Lower right: *Standing in front of the new City Hall, looking north, shows a magnificent view of Donegall Place. If Thomas Andrews walked to work from his residence, he would have crossed the street here moving from left to right. The building on the east side of the street – also visible on the right side of the previous photo – still stands today.*

Born on February 7, 1873, Andrews was only running through his mid- to late-thirties during the construction of the *Olympic* and *Titanic*.[14] Despite his relative youth, his sharp wit and penchant for hard work had long-since brought him prominence within his uncle's company. Andrews had been with the yard since 1889, when he had joined as a premium apprentice at the tender age of sixteen. During his five-year stretch as an apprentice, there wasn't the slightest hint that he was loafing along, expecting to be shown some sort of favor because his uncle was, at the time, gaining prominence in the firm.

In those years, Andrews worked tirelessly during the day and continued his studies in the evening hours. As of March, 1901, he was boarding at 11 Wellington Place by Donegall Square, just down and across the street from the Belfast City Hall building, which was then under construction.[15] The residence was also quite close to Queen's Island and the Harland & Wolff yards.[16] Every day on his way to and from work, Andrews would have passed the splendid new City Hall, watching the workmen climb about the scaffolding which enshrouded its outer structure, and no doubt he followed its progress with interest. Of course, that eight-year construction project must have, in some ways, paled in comparison with the tremendous projects that Andrews was involved in bringing to life at the shipyard – and the massive structures that he helped to design and build braved the rugged elements of the North Atlantic.

At the time, Andrews was deeply involved in the construction of White Star's 'Big Four' ocean liners, and was serving as Assistant Shipyard Manager.[17] Before the year was out, he would be appointed Manager of the Construction Works.[18] By 1907, he had been appointed Managing Director of Harland & Wolff. At that time, he was intimately connected with the design of the *Olympic* and *Titanic*, as the formal order from White Star to proceed with work on the new giants had been given on April 30 of that same year. By that point, Andrews had earned a well-deserved reputation as a genius in the field of ship design, and a bright future was ahead of him within the company.[19]

Interestingly, Andrews usually referred to his position as that of a 'Shipbuilder' or a 'Director' of the shipbuilding firm he worked at, rather than claiming the more formal title of 'Naval Architect'. This was despite the fact that he was a Member of the Institution of Naval Architects, the Institution of Mechanical Engineers, the Society of Naval Architects and Marine Engineers, as well as an Honorary Member of the Belfast Association of Engineers.[20]

If his work was going well, things in his personal life certainly were, as well. On June 24, 1908, when Thomas Andrews was aged thirty-five, he married Helen Reilly Barbour. Helen was then aged twenty-seven, and was a member of a prominent Irish family. The couple honeymooned in Switzerland, and upon their return moved into Dunallon, 12 Windsor Avenue, Belfast.[21] Dunallon House was a comfortable, detached, two-floor brick home located in the very desirable Malone area of southern Belfast; it was just a few blocks from the prestigious Queen's University of Belfast, and was located only about four miles from Queen's Island and the Harland & Wolff yards. This meant that the location could hardly have been more ideal for Andrews' work and for his family. The house was large enough that by 1911, the Andrews employed four servants – a cook, a housemaid, a parlormaid, and a general servant – in its upkeep.[22]

Just over a month after the wedding was another momentous day in Andrews' life. On Wednesday, July 29, 1908, representatives from the White Star Line traveled to Belfast and gave their formal approval for Harland & Wolff's design variant 'D' of their new steamships, *Olympic* and *Titanic*. For Andrews, it was an incredible and exciting period of life: a new wife, a new home, and a new project of unprecedented proportions to begin construction on.

Apparently lacking nothing in his personal and professional lives, Thomas Andrews was a tireless worker. He was not content to be an 'office man', as it were. Although he had much paperwork and designing to oversee, he could – and frequently did – show up anywhere within the shipyard at any given time. From the Draughting Offices to the Boiler Shop, then to the Engine Works and even up to the Moulding Loft, then on to the Joiner's Shop and out onto the various slipways to climb over and inspect every square inch of the ships, he was everywhere at all times, it seemed, throughout the vast shipyard complex. His daily travels through the yard would have exhausted most other men, but it was routine for him.

However, his visits were never unwelcome ones to the workers. He was always willing to pitch in and lend a hand at some physically demanding task as the need arose. He was known to have shared his lunch with fellow workers when the need came up. Even so, Andrews was not afraid to correct workers when he saw them doing something the wrong way or breaking shipyard rules. It was said afterward that while he wouldn't fire a worker when he found him in the middle of some such nonsense, he would give the worker 'the rough side of his tongue and a friendly caution.'

He also enjoyed it when workers did more than just mindlessly plug away at their tasks – he encouraged them to put their minds into it. If workers thought that they had a better way to do something, Andrews was willing to listen to their input. In fact, everyone seemed to describe him as cheery, optimistic, and generous. One yard foreman recalled that it 'seemed his delight to make those around him happy. His was ever the friendly greeting and the warm handshake and kind disposition.'

Such a friendly, personable attitude is something rarely found in people possessing great talent and abilities, as Andrews unquestionably did. He was always interested in seeing how work was progressing on the ships he had played such an important role in designing. He was passionate about his work – a perfectionist in every form of the word. Indeed, one of his co-workers described him as 'diligent to the point of strenuousness'. He was always willing to acknowledge the hard work of other people, and his wife recalled that he had 'of himself the humblest opinion of anyone I ever knew'.[23]

Andrews rose very early every morning and frequently worked late into the evening. Although he lived only a few miles from the shipyard, he had a Renault motorcar at his disposal. This allowed him to bypass the city's not wholly reliable system of public transportation and travel to and from the yard at any time of day, whether early in the morning or late at night.

Even as the forms of the *Olympic* and *Titanic* took shape on Slips Nos 2 and 3, Andrews and his wife had begun their own building project: the construction of a family. When the *Olympic* took to the water for the first time on October 20, 1910, Helen Andrews was about eight months preg-

nant. She would give birth to a daughter, named Elizabeth, on November 27.[24]

One wonders how Andrews could have juggled the responsibilities of family and work so, but he was not the only incredibly talented or hard-working individual in the shipyard as the *Titanic* was taking shape. Beyond the thousands of individual workers – most of whom were diligent, hardworking men who were every bit as proud of the ships they built as Andrews was – there were others who held key positions of oversight.

For example, one of the senior Naval Architects within Harland & Wolff was a man named Edward Wilding. Aged 35 in April of 1911, he was recently married to a woman named Marion Emily. The newlyweds lived in the Jordanstown area of suburban Belfast, on the west side of the Belfast Lough, and had two servants – Housemaid Margaret Glynn and Cook Julia Stewart.[25] Apart from his family life, however, Wilding would have been kept quite busy with long days spent at the shipyard. He worked very closely with Thomas Andrews, and had been a friend for some time, attending Thomas and Helen's wedding in the summer of 1908.

Wilding worked very closely with Andrews and other members of the design staff, and he knew the ship nearly as well as Andrews did. Indeed, later on he would be able to pull many facts and figures regarding the ship's technical construction directly from his memory, and he almost infallibly knew where to find anything he didn't know offhand. Beyond Wilding, there were over four dozen various department heads at Harland & Wolff. Each was responsible for the division under their watch, and each consulted daily or nearly daily with Thomas Andrews.

Another person who had oversight of the unprecedented construction project that was the *Olympic* and *Titanic* was a man who actually did not work for Harland & Wolff. His name was Francis Carruthers, and he was employed by the British Board of Trade as an on-site surveyor; his job was to ensure that both ships were meeting Board of Trade requirements for design, strength and safety. By 1912, the 54-year-old Carruthers had some thirteen years of experience as a sea-going engineer, and he had been in the employment of the Board of Trade for sixteen.[26] In all, by mid-1912, he had been surveying ships for twenty years. Carruthers lived in Ballybeen, Dundonald – which was just east of Belfast proper – with his wife Mary and son William.[27]

Over a period of about two and a half years, during the construction of the *Olympic* and *Titanic*, Carruthers made careful inspections, nearly every day, of the progress being

This view, looking south across Victoria Channel, shows Slips Nos 2 and 3 and the Great Gantry.

Top left: *This photograph shows the* Titanic's *bow on the slip during May of 1911. Her anchors have not yet been put in place, but the anchor cable for her center anchor has recently been attached and remains unwound, dangling from the hawsepipe. The ship's name was written in after the photograph was taken, and inaccurately at that.*

Top right: *Forging the massive anchor chains, which were referred to as 'anchor cables'.*

Right: Titanic's *center anchor was shipped across the Irish Sea to Ireland, where it was eventually fitted in place aboard the liner.*

made on the vessels.[28] He also served as an intermediary between the Board of Trade and Harland & Wolff, regularly corresponding with Board of Trade representatives and discussing technical details of the new liners in order to ensure the highest standard of build quality; he was also to furnish answers to any questions Board representatives in London might have had regarding their design.

When the London representatives had questions, they would send them to Carruthers, who would obtain the information directly, or pass on the requests to Harland & Wolff personnel like Thomas Andrews. When he was able to get the answers directly, he would submit them back to the Board of Trade; at other times, the shipyard personnel would personally respond to the Board's inquiries.

Carruthers' job was at times a delicate one. The laws always needed to be complied with, and of course that was nothing extraordinary. However, where the ships were breaking new ground – and this was quite frequent on ships half again as large in enclosed space as anything previously built – both the Board of Trade and the shipyard needed to come to agreements on such technical details. At the same time, Carruthers was privy to highly sensitive, cutting-edge information that was not to be shared with others, because some of the finite details of the ships' construction were very advanced, and competition between shipyards was so keen. Looking through the correspondence between the Board of Trade, Carruthers, and shipyard personnel, it seems that – just as could be expected on any modern building project – there were any number of opportunities for annoyances between the shipyard and the Board of Trade, each with the potential to catch Carruthers in the middle. Yet it seems that Carruthers was able to strike a good balance, as is indicated by the length of his tenure.

As one particular example, there was a point in April of 1910 when Carruthers was not certain that the design of the collision bulkhead on the *Olympic* and *Titanic* was sufficient; existing plans called for it to be 'stepped' forward some six frames on E Deck. Harland & Wolff's team was certain this would prove no issue, and contended 'that they were right', but Carruthers was not entirely convinced. So he forwarded the dilemma to the London offices, requesting instructions. The Board of Trade's Principal Ship Surveyor, Mr Archer, initially thought that Carruthers' objection was correct. Harland & Wolff explained to the Board of Trade in great detail the methodology behind their design, and provided them with highly specific flooding calculations. After a great deal of correspondence spanning several months, Principal Ship Surveyor Alfred J. Daniel was able to write on September 15 that he had confirmed Harland & Wolff's calculations. With the ships' second watertight bulkhead carried right up to D Deck, both the Board of Trade and Harland & Wolff felt confident in the safety of this particular area of the designed watertight subdivision. Carruthers was able to report on June 2, 1911 that 'all requirements of the Board' on the subject had been 'satisfactorily carried out'.[29]

Carruthers was also very busy inspecting every other feature of the ships' design and the quality of their construction. In the course of Carruthers' daily inspections, he saw the double bottom filled with water to test for watertightness, and he also saw the Forepeak tank filled with water to ensure that it would withstand the pressure of any flooding.[30] Although none of the ship's other watertight compartments were tested by flooding to ensure watertightness, Carruthers satisfied himself that each one was watertight by a thorough inspection of the riveting quality and the quality of the caulking. Just a few days before the ship was finished, he also made a careful inspection of each bulkhead piercing – for steam piping, conduit, or electrical wires and the like – to make sure that it would be watertight in an emergency situation.[31]

From these few simple examples, it can be seen just how involved Carruthers was in the day-to-day activity in the shipyard as the *Olympic* and *Titanic* were both constructed. Indeed, between Carruthers and the other Board of Trade Surveyors who visited the ship in the course of construction, they made an estimated two to three thousand visits for inspections of the vessels.[32]

Another familiar face at the Harland & Wolff shipyard as the *Olympic* and *Titanic* were constructed was the man who would eventually serve as the first Chief Engineer of each ship: Joseph Bell. Bell had served his engineering apprenticeship as a youth at the Tyneside works of Robert Stephenson, and had become one of the White Star Line's most trusted engineers. He was so trusted, in fact, that he had been sent to Belfast to oversee the construction and installation of the engines of a number of new White Star liners, including the *Laurentic* and *Megantic* in 1908 and 1909.[33] He had subsequently taken each of those liners out for their first few voyages, serving as Chief Engineer.

The *Laurentic* and *Megantic* had been unique for the company's fleet, as they were nearly identical in every respect except their powerplants. While the *Megantic* had been bestowed with a pair of traditional reciprocating engines operating twin screws, the *Laurentic* had also been given a low-pressure turbine, operated from exhaust steam from the reciprocating engines, which drove a third, central propeller. It was this hybrid powerplant which was subsequently adopted on the *Olympic*-class liners, and so Bell was one of the most experienced engineers in the world on that type of powerplant. Subsequently, Bell had remained 'in Belfast during the whole of the time [*Olympic*] was being built, superintending her construction, making any suggestions which he thought would lead to improvements.'[34]

Such a large segment of Belfast was focused on the construction of the *Olympic* and *Titanic* that a large portion of the city came to depend on them. Their construction provided employment and a means of providing for thousands of families for a period of about three-and-a-half years. Beyond merely providing jobs, however, the entire city came to take the new liners into its collective heart. The *Olympic* and *Titanic* were 'Belfast's own', the pride of the great city.

Progress on the ships was steady and, considering their size, surprisingly quick. The *Olympic*'s construction was advanced by some months over that of her sister, and work on her proceeded more quickly than it did on the *Titanic*. Work did advance on *Titanic* at a good pace, however; the process of setting her frames in place was finished by April 6, 1910, just over a year after her keel was laid. The process of installing individual hull plates to the frames followed immediately thereafter, and continued until October 19, 1910. The following day, all attention was focused on the launch of the *Olympic*, and her subsequent tow to the fitting out basin for completion. As the *Olympic* entered this new phase of her construction, work on the *Titanic* progressed rapidly toward the time when she, herself, would be launched. That event was scheduled to take place on Wednesday, May 31, 1911.

Left: *Joseph Bell, Chief Engineer of the* Olympic, *and subsequently the* Titanic.

Below: *This photograph was taken in July of 1911. It shows the aft end of* Titanic's *port reciprocating engine, looking forward, in the engine assembly shop at Harland & Wolff. The* Titanic's *yard number, 401, is clearly seen marked in numerous locations on the engine itself.*

As the date of launch neared, the hull of the *Titanic* assumed its finished form. Atop the hull, some portions of the superstructure – including A and B Decks – were already built and in place. When the *Titanic* was ready to take to the water for the first time, she was nearly a carbon copy of her slightly older sister. Her Promenade Deck was open for its entire length, just as *Olympic*'s was. Even the windows along her B Deck were configured as *Olympic*'s were, in several large clusters along each side. However, there was one marked difference in the two ships' appearance at the time of their respective launches: Whereas the *Olympic*'s hull had been painted 'virgin white' with dark red anti-fouling paint applied below the waterline on the day she was launched, the *Titanic* was painted in her White Star service colors – white superstructure, black hull, and dark red anti-fouling below the waterline.[35] Excitement around Belfast over the second *Olympic*-class liner's forthcoming launch was at an all-time peak. That Harland & Wolff had built the largest ocean liner in the world, which

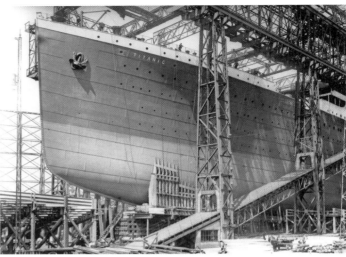

Above left: Titanic *stands on the ways, nearly ready for launch.*

Above right: *This is one of the best-known* Titanic *photographs. The grandstands have been erected for spectators to view the launch from; yard workers are dwarfed by the towering hull. The anchors are in place. The ship's name was artistically enhanced on the plate-glass negative, but the 'improvement' at least closely matches the actual letters' shape and size.*

was then nearing completion, was a tremendous feat in and of itself. To have produced two such liners side by side, and constructed nearly simultaneously, was a remarkable accomplishment.

Preparations for the event also included the erection of grandstands to accept members of the public who had purchased tickets, and also for the various dignitaries who would be on hand. Yard workers who had tasks to perform in connection with the launch would, of course, be allowed to remain on hand to witness the event. On May 30, 1911, a flurry of request forms would have been presented to yard foremen by various employees. As of the spring of 1910, all Harland & Wolff employees who wished to watch a launch event, and who were not actively involved in it, were required to submit a request for permission to be present. As there would have been no pay for the time that they would not have worked, some would no doubt have felt that it was just as important to stick with their assigned tasks elsewhere in the yard. Many others, however, were proud of the ship and their accomplishment in her construction, and made arrangements to be present.[36]

Two years and two months to the day after *Titanic*'s keel was laid, the morning dawned when she would take to the water for the first time. The shipyard was a hive of activity. The weather was clear and fair, with a cool southerly breeze. Twenty-one tons of tallow and soap had been spread on the 772-foot sliding ways, in a coating one inch thick, to facilitate the movement of the vessel's massive 26,000-ton bulk into the water. That morning, workers crawled around the ground beneath the towering hull, making final preparations for the launch. Support timbers which steadied the hull while it stood perched atop the ways were knocked out, one after another, leaving the vessel balanced ever more precariously on the ways.

The task was dangerous, as many tasks were in the construction of the *Titanic* and other vessels of the day. One worker, James Dobbin, was crushed by a falling timber on

that morning. He was seriously injured and died the next day. He was not the first, nor would he be the last to die in building the great liner. In the full course of the ship's construction, up to the time of her delivery, some eight people died building the *Titanic*. Twenty-eight others were seriously injured, and a further 218 slight injuries were noted.[37]

Despite the injury to – and eventual death of – James Dobbin, the launch preparations continued to progress that morning. Eventually, the ship was standing poised atop the ways, held in place only by the hydraulic launch triggers. Lord Pirrie & Bruce Ismay were photographed in the shadow of the *Titanic*'s hull, walking along the floor of Slip No. 3 underneath the Great Gantry. It was Pirrie himself who made a final inspection of the preparations before signaling that all was ready.

Throughout the morning, crowds had built steadily, and eventually, some 100,000 were present. An atmosphere of anticipation slowly began to build as the set launch time of 12:15 p.m. approached. J. P. Morgan, the driving force behind the IMM, and Bruce Ismay's wife – along with some others from their family – were present. There were a great number of other important personages present, as well. It was noted:

> Ladies formed a considerable proportion of the aggregate attendance, and even if their picturesque frocks appeared a trifle incongruous when contrasted with the surroundings of the shipyards itself they were unmistakably in harmony with the glow of the soft turquoise sky, from which the piercing rays of the sun descended, making the heat exceedingly trying… The weather was glorious, a multitude of people assembled to bid the vessel 'God speed', and it would be impossible to conceive of a launch for which the whole of the conditions could be more ideal.[38]

Top left: *This photograph seems to have been taken on the mid- to late-morning of May 31, 1911, and looking to the north. Titanic's bow stands beneath the Great Gantry, awaiting launch. The White Star Line pennant flutters from the center of the gantry. Queen's Road, in the foreground, is a busy scene; many of the people visible are doubtless headed to view the special event.*

Top right: *Spectators stream into the yard.*

Above left: *Two women – a rare sight in the shipyard – make their way toward the grandstands. A young man, also visible in the preceding photograph, stands behind a lengthy makeshift fence. It is possible that he was stationed there to help make sure non-employees did not cross into dangerous areas of the shipyard.*

Above right: *A throng of special invitees wends its way through the shipyard toward the towering bow of the Titanic. Careful inspection of the photo shows another yard employee standing behind a makeshift fence, perhaps to keep the human traffic flowing smoothly through designated areas.*

Right: *This photograph emphasizes the Titanic's great size, even as the crowd begins to swell in her shadow.*

Top left: *The bow of the* Titanic *retreats down the ways, and the crowd begins to rush after her.*

Top right: Titanic's *stern plunges into the water for the first time.*

Left: *Taken only a couple of seconds after the previous photo, the stern continues to glide backward, while the liner's bow has not yet left the ways.*

Bottom left: *This photographer has moved onto the newly-vacated ways to snap a unique photo of the liner bobbing in the water.*

ing, she did not in that moment become the largest moving object ever made at the time. She and her sister *Olympic* were identical in dimensions, and by that point, the *Olympic* had been completed and formally held the title. That small detail, however, did not dampen the spirits of the crowd as they saw her begin her journey.

> It was a wonderful and awe-inspiring sight and a thrill passed through the crowd as their hopes and expectations were realised. The ship glided down to the river with a grace and dignity which for the moment gave one the impression that she was conscious of her own strength and beauty, and there was a roar of cheers as the timber by which she had been supported yielded to the pressure put upon them. She took the water as though she were eager for the baptism, and in the short space of 62 seconds she was entirely free of the ways.[39]

A mad cacophony of whistles and sirens from river steamers followed the cheering. Then there came the great clatter as the drag chains began to slow the ship's progress before she simply careened into the opposite bank. At last, the knife-edge of the prow slid from the ways and into the water. The ship was afloat for the first time, and she came to a stop 'in less than one half of her own length', bobbing serenely on the surface of the River Lagan. The launch was a complete success.

The men on board took off their caps and cheered lustily after the launch had been consummated,

In the end, the *Titanic* was given no special attention or greater ceremony than was bestowed upon the *Olympic* the previous fall. Contrary to popular belief, and at least one cinematic depiction, the *Titanic* was not christened with a bottle of champagne broken over the prow and a formal invocation for divine protection. Typical of all Harland & Wolff launches, the hull was simply 'let go'. Two foremen turned the release valve, the hydraulic triggers canted over, and the monstrous hull began to slide inexorably down the ways and toward the water.

It was two minutes before her official launch time, 12:13 p.m., when the *Titanic* began to move. Technically speak-

and the thousands of people in the yard and on the banks of the river promptly followed their example. For two or three minutes there were scenes of great enthusiasm. The tugs which were waiting close at hand to convey the vessel to the deep water wharf, where she will receive her engines, sent up shrill sounds from their sirens, the ladies waved their handkerchiefs excitedly, and the men shouted themselves hoarse. But gradually the noise of the sirens and the cheers of the spectators died away, and a quarter of an hour after the vessel had been pulled up the crowd had melted away, and the yard was left in possession of the workmen who had for months been devoting their energies and talents to the building of the mighty leviathan.[40]

Slowly, as the ship was towed away to the fitting-out jetty, the excitement and crowds began to thin. It was later said that 'the spectacle was one which can never fade from the memory of those who witnessed it', and that 'if the circumstances under which the launch took place can be accepted as an augury of the future, the *Titanic* should be a huge success'.[41] Belfast celebrated heartily that night, and with good reason. Not only had the *Titanic* been launched successfully, but the *Olympic* – largest ship in the world – had left and would soon set out on her maiden voyage. Things were going very well for White Star and for Harland & Wolff.

Yet an enormous task still lay ahead of the workers at the Belfast shipyard. The *Titanic*'s enormous hull was an engineless, function-less shell. Her cavernous steel interior spaces needed to be transformed into finished, comfortable – and in First Class, luxurious – accommodations for her passengers and crew. Carpenters and joiners would now take their place beside riveters and steel workers in bringing the ship to life. The interior spaces that they were creating would be truly breathtaking.

On the Boat Deck, behind the Bridge and Officers' Quarters, was the First Class Entrance, which housed the Grand Staircase. On all Atlantic liners, the main First Class staircase was a high traffic area, but the *Titanic* was graced with arguably the most beautiful First Class staircase ever built; in fact, she was endowed with two of them. The main, forward Grand Staircase ran from the Boat Deck down to E Deck. Made from solid oak with intricately hand-carved panels, columns, and accents, it was topped off by a 19 foot by 26 foot wrought iron and white glass dome that allowed daylight to illuminate the First Class Entrance. At night, the dome was electrically illuminated. There were lights within the outer skylight casing which backlit the dome itself at night. There were also lights in the carved wood molding around the interior of the dome's base, which were concealed from the view of those below. Finally, a fifty-light fixture was installed in the center of the dome; with a gilt metal frame, a cut-glass bowl, and glass-bead

Top left: *Yard tugs begin to take the hull of the* Titanic *to the fitting out jetty to commence the next phase of work.*

Top right: *A unique view of the newly-launched vessel's starboard side.*

Lower left: *A ferry filled with spectators passes the* Titanic *as tugs move her toward the fitting out jetty.*

Lower right: *This photo was taken in early June, 1911, and shows the fitting out in its earliest stages. The two structures on the Forecastle are lavatories, and the tail pipes help direct sewage away from the ship's hull.*

Top left: *Looking forward, and slightly to port, from the A Deck landing of* Olympic's *forward First Class Grand Staircase.*

Top centre: *Olympic's 'Honour & Glory Crowning Time'. A similar carving was installed in this location on* Titanic.

Top right: *Olympic's Grand Staircase, seen here flowing into the Reception Room on D Deck. A special candelabra stands at the foot of the center balustrade. This photo was taken while the room was still under construction – notice the tarp at the lower-right corner of the image.*

Left: *Olympic's First Class Reception Room, looking from starboard to port, gives an idea of how the same space on* Titanic *appeared.*

Bottom left: *Olympic's First Class Dining Saloon, on the port side, looking forward toward the Reception Room. The tables are set and appear ready to take passengers.*

panels, it was the perfect centerpiece to an already magnificent setup.[42]

Against the forward wall of the half-landing between the Boat Deck and A Deck was an ornate wood carving meant to represent 'Honour and Glory Crowning Time', which was similar if not identical to that gracing *Olympic*'s staircase. In the center of this carving there were plans to install a clock. This clock, like many others in various public spaces aboard the ship, would help passengers keep track of correct ship's time as it was adjusted each day. To prevent the necessity of sending stewards through the ship adjusting each clock, and making sure that they all agreed with each other, these devices were operated on what was called a Magneta system. Two 'master' clocks located inside watertight cases in the Chart Room recorded the time to the second. They were tied in to nearly fifty 'slave' clocks located in various areas all over the ship. This included the Wheelhouse clock, one of the two Marconi Operating Room clocks – the second one being set to New York Time

– and various public rooms throughout the ship. Thus, as the *Titanic*'s time was adjusted at sea, these 'slave' clocks automatically updated to reflect that change.[43]

On every level of the Grand Staircase, there was a large foyer, the largest of which was on D Deck, and formed the First Class Reception Room. The Reception Room, which ran the full width of the ship, was the area where passengers could gather for tea during the day, and where they gathered prior to entering the adjacent First Class Dining Saloon for meals, as well as for after-dinner music. A Steinway grand piano[44] and a space where the orchestra could play completed the elegant atmosphere. The Reception Room and most other public rooms closed at 11:00 p.m., meaning that any passengers who wanted to extend their evening's activities beyond that hour would have to do so in the Lounge – open until 11:30 – or Smoking Room.

The Dining Saloon, just astern of the Reception Room, was an immense public space. It ran the full width of the ship, like the Reception Room, and was 113 feet long. While the Reception Room deck was covered in a dark Axminster carpet, the Saloon's deck was covered in 'lino' tiles. The color of this tiling seems to have been red, ocher and blue.[45]

While the Dining Saloons on many previous Atlantic liners, including the *Lusitania* and *Mauretania*, took up two or more decks and were often capped with elaborate domes, the new White Star ships' Saloons were only a single deck in height. Many were critical of this decision, notably Leonard Peskett from Cunard when he toured the *Olympic*.[46] For one thing, multi-deck Saloons allowed stifling warm air – always a bane in those times before fully air-conditioned

Above: A fine view of Olympic's *First Class Restaurant on B Deck.*

Below: A March 1912 photo of Titanic's *Gymnasium on the Boat Deck.*

liners – to rise away from both diners and frazzled Saloon Stewards. For another thing, Saloons encompassing more than one level gave a great sense of roominess. *Titanic*'s admittedly lost some points on both accounts. However, no one could complain about the room's tasteful Jacobean décor; neither could anyone find fault with the fact that those dining in the Saloon found themselves ensconced in comfortable, leather-padded chairs that were freed from all restraints to the deck. Every other Atlantic liner, including the *Lusitania* and *Mauretania*, retained the old-fashioned bolted-to-the-deck Saloon chairs, and they were all instantly dated with the introduction of the *Olympic*-class ships.[47]

On B Deck just astern of the aft Grand Staircase, an extra tariff, or *à la carte*, First Class Restaurant was installed.[48] This facility would cater to First Class passengers who wished to dine in more intimate surroundings than the Dining Saloon, or who wished for more flexibility in their meal times. The concept of seagoing extra tariff restaurants had been conceived by the enterprising head of the German Hamburg-Amerika Line, Albert Ballin, when his liner Amerika was being built by Harland & Wolff in 1904–1905. On the way to check in on the progress of her construction, he had dined at the new London Ritz-Carlton Restaurant, and had been absolutely taken with the experience. He had subsequently hammered out a deal whereby actual Ritz Restaurants – run by Ritz-Carlton directly,

with a separate kitchen facility, employing Ritz–Carlton staff, and bearing Ritz insignia on their menus – could be installed on his liners.

Ballin's concept had been such a fantastic success that White Star had decided to follow Hamburg-Amerika's lead. However, the *Titanic*'s Restaurant was not directly affiliated with the Ritz-Carlton, and its menus did not bear Ritz insignia. Despite this, for any seasoned trans-Atlantic travelers who had previously taken passage on German liners, the terminology tended to stick. Passengers on the *Olympic* – and eventually *Titanic* – frequently if incorrectly referred to these facilities as the 'Ritz Restaurant.'

The *à la carte* Restaurant itself was paneled in French walnut with 'richly carved and gilded' mouldings and ornaments, and a vieux rose, or old rose, colored Axminster carpet. The overall style was Louis XVI, and seemed to be quite a success with those who reviewed the room's décor. White Star selected 37-year-old Gaspare Antonio Pietro Gatti, previously of the Oddonino Imperial Restaurant in London, to run *Titanic*'s establishment.[49] His staff was drawn from top-end London restaurants, and was largely Italian and French. The Restaurant's personnel were not formal members of the ship's victualling crew, and they did not report to the ship's Chief Steward, but rather functioned as a wholly separate entity.

Directly aft of the First Class Entrance, on the starboard side of the Boat Deck, was a Gymnasium intended solely for the use of First Class passengers. Here, the more athletically inclined could while away the hours on rowing machines, stationary bicycles, or even enjoying the novelty of a ride on an electric camel. The use of all of this equipment was free of charge.[50] However, ladies could only use the Gymnasium between 10:00 a.m. and 1:00 p.m. Children could only use the room between 1:00 p.m. and 3:00 p.m. Gentlemen could use the facility from 2:00 p.m. to 6:00 p.m. There was also a map that could be used to track the progress of the *Titanic* as it plowed its way across the Atlantic. Adding to the atmosphere, the Gymnasium was illuminated by natural light thanks to seven large arched windows. Thirty-four-year-old Thomas W. McCawley served as the Gymnasium Instructor; he provided, to passengers who needed such, both fitness advice and directions on how to use the equipment.[51]

Below, in the forward portions of F Deck, was the First Class Swimming Bath. Although located deep within the ship, it was very easily accessed from E Deck – at the foot of the forward First Class Grand Staircase – by a secondary staircase that descended to F Deck. Passing through a watertight door, passengers would then walk down a corridor toward the starboard side of the ship. A door on the left, or forward side of the corridor, would then lead them into the Swimming Bath. Here the passengers could use the adjacent dressing rooms to change from their Edwardian splendor into attire more befitting a plunge in the bath. The pool itself was filled with seawater which was heated to a comfortable degree. Use of the facility was free to gentlemen between 6:00 and 9:00 a.m., and ladies also had a period of time where admission was free; during other times of the day, however, admission to the Swimming Bath was 1s or \$.25.[52]

Surprisingly, the Swimming Bath was a utilitarian space, resembling more a Steerage portion of the ship. Only a coat of whitewash covered over the ship's steel hull and structure. While Swimming Baths were a new feature on the

Top: Olympic's *First Class Swimming Bath, nearly identical to that found on* Titanic.

Middle: *The Cooling Room of* Olympic's *Turkish Baths. Although the arrangement and exact location of this space differed on* Titanic, *the décor and furnishings were very similar.*

Bottom: Olympic's *First Class Reading and Writing Room, after it was reduced in size. This same space on* Titanic *included an L-shaped section which extended forward.*

Directly astern of the Swimming Bath were the Turkish and Electric Baths. Use of these novel facilities cost 4s or $1 per person, and tickets were obtainable from the Enquiry Office. Again, strict sex segregation was enforced; ladies could use these baths between 10:00 a.m. and 1:00 p.m., and gentlemen could between 2:00 p.m. and 6:00 p.m.[53] The Turkish and Electric Baths were luxurious and elegantly decorated – exotically Moorish in their feel and very chic for the period.

The Squash Racquet Court – also intended for the more athletically inclined – was located on G Deck. It was two decks high, with a spectator's gallery on F Deck. Entry to the playing court was only obtained by descending a set of stairs from the Spectator's Gallery on F Deck, as there was no entrance on G Deck itself. Use of this facility could be arranged through the on-board Racquet Professional for 2s or $.50 per half hour, and included the services of the Professional if his assistance was needed. Equipment such as racquets or balls could also be rented for additional fees. If other passengers were awaiting a turn at the game, players could not use the court for more than two consecutive half-hour sessions.[54]

The remaining First Class public spaces were centered on A Deck. Abaft the Entrance, there was a corridor which led astern. On the port side of this corridor was a door that led into the Reading & Writing Room. This room was primarily designed as a space for ladies to spend their time during each crossing, and decorated with their delicate tastes in mind. However, it was open to the use of both sexes, and was available for use up to 11:30 p.m. With a rose-colored carpet, white-painted paneling, and large windows looking out upon the port side Promenade Deck, the room's décor was quite soothing. The ceiling of the room was extended above the level of the Boat Deck, and small windows were set in to the portion of wall extending above the deck level, giving additional access to sunlight during the day.

At the aft end of the corridor which gave access to the Reading & Writing Room, there was a door that led into the Lounge. The Lounge was a large and impressive space; it was designed as a place for men and women to spend time with one another listening to music, playing cards, or simply socializing. Like the Reading & Writing Room, the Lounge's ceiling was taller than other public rooms, extending beyond the constraints of the Boat Deck itself, and giving it a particularly spacious feel. Afternoon tea was served in the Lounge, which was fitted in the Louis XV-style. Details were taken from the Palace at Versailles, and paneled in the finest English oak. The paneling was embellished by detailed relief in floral, shell, and musical themes.

At sea, the Lounge was open for passengers' use between 8:00 a.m. and 11:30 p.m. By special arrangement with *The Times* Book Club, a selection of the latest works was also made available for passengers to choose from. Any of these volumes were obtainable direct from the bookcase upon application to the Steward in charge. Passengers were 'respectfully' asked 'not to leave volumes lying about the deck, and to return them when done with.'[55] The Lounge was also serviced by a small bar, accessed through a vestibule on the starboard aft side of the room. This bar was directly connected, through a small service window, to a Deck Pantry immediately astern. That Deck Pantry serviced not only the Lounge, but also the decks immediately

Atlantic, just over a year after the *Titanic* was due to begin her maiden voyage, the German liner *Imperator* would boast of a luxurious Pompeian-style Swimming Bath. Encompassing two decks, with a spectator gallery and stunning décor, the baths aboard *Imperator* – and her two sisters to follow – trounced the appearance of the Swimming Baths aboard *Olympic* and *Titanic*. Despite its Spartan feel, the bath was very popular aboard *Olympic*, and would prove to be so on *Titanic* as well.

Right: Olympic's *First Class Lounge, looking forward and to port.*

Below left: *Looking aft along the starboard side of the* Olympic's *Lounge.*

Below right: *This view shows* Olympic's *First Class Smoking Room, looking forward and to starboard.*

adjacent, which were usually filled with passengers lounging in deck chairs.[56]

On the aft port side of the Lounge, a corridor ran aft, through a revolving door, and beyond to the aft First Class Grand Staircase and a good-sized Entrance. The aft stairs descended from the Promenade Deck down to B Deck. Remaining on A Deck, moving aft of the aft staircase, one arrived in the Smoking Room. As this space was the sole preserve of male passengers, it was decorated in a decidedly masculine manner. There were backlit stained-glass windows along the inner walls, giving the illusion of eternal day. Paneled in rich, dark mahogany with inlaid mother-of-pearl, there were numerous small tables for playing cards and the like, and there was a working fireplace set into the aft wall. Over its mantle hung a portrait by Norman Wilkinson: 'The Approach to the New World' on the *Olympic*, and 'Plymouth Harbour' on the *Titanic*. The floor tiles covered the deck in an interesting pattern, and were blue and red in color.[57] Like the Reading & Writing Room and Lounge forward, the Smoking Room's ceiling was extended above the level of the Boat Deck, giving extra access to light from the deck above and also making the room feel more spacious. The Smoking Room Bar was open from 8:00 a.m. to 11:30 p.m., and lights in the Smoking Room were turned out at midnight.[58]

Aft of the Smoking Room, on each side of the ship, were the Verandah Cafés. These comfortable spaces were designed as places where passengers could spend time enjoying the ocean vista outside, a close parallel to the idea behind similar spaces on the *Lusitania* and *Mauretania*, although infinitely superior in execution. The cafés installed

on the *Olympic* and *Titanic* had an advantage over those on the Cunard sisters as they were completely enclosed and protected from the elements, while still retaining an outdoor feeling complete with a trellis covering the walls for climbing plants. The port side café was for the use of patrons who wished to smoke; the starboard café, meanwhile, was restricted to non-smokers, and thus turned out to be quite popular with mothers and those looking after young children. Light refreshments could be obtained in the Verandah Cafés, but not full meals. The rooms were officially open between 8:00 a.m. and 11:00 p.m.[59]

While *Olympic* and *Titanic's* sumptuous First Class appointments may have garnered the lion's share of attention in the press and White Star publicity, the majority of their passengers would actually book in Second and Third Classes. As such, a great deal of thought and attention was also given to providing comfortable accommodations for these two groups. Second Class public rooms were quite luxurious for the period. It was said that 'it would have been difficult a few years ago to conceive such sumptuous apartments as have been provided on the *Olympic* and *Titanic.*'[60] Indeed, when compared with the First Class accommodations of many other liners then in service, particularly the smaller ones, Second Class on these newer ships was generally considered far superior.

The Second Class Dining Saloon was located on D Deck, abaft the Galley, which also serviced the First Class Dining Saloon. Like its First Class counterpart, the Second Class Dining Saloon spanned the full width of the liner, but was somewhat shorter. Whereas First Class passengers reveled in unprecedented mobility with movable chairs, Second

Class passengers' Saloon seats remained bolted resolutely to the deck. Most of the tables could accommodate eight persons, but in the busy season, the room's capacity was boosted by inserts which connected the tables, creating long, uninterrupted rows. There was thus very little of the intimacy that First Class passengers enjoyed in their Dining Saloon alcoves, or in the Restaurant on B Deck. However, the Second Class Dining Saloon was considered a very efficient use of space, and many passengers were able to make new and interesting acquaintances during the voyage.

A well thought out pair of Second Class stairs and Entrances gave access not only to Second Class cabins, but also to the Dining Saloon and – in the case of the forward set – up to the Boat Deck. Directly above the Dining Saloon, on C Deck, was the Second Class Library. Here, passengers could socialize with each other, read, or write letters to friends and family ashore. Six windows to port and six to starboard, all graced with silk curtains, overlooked the Second Class Covered Promenade. That Promenade ran along just inside the ship's hull. There, passengers could enjoy a stroll and overlook the sea through large sliding windows, all without being unnecessarily exposed to the elements.

Directly above, on B Deck, was the Second Class Smoking Room. Like the same space in First Class, this was the sole preserve of gentlemen. Beyond the tasteful oak paneling, six windows on either side overlooked the Second Class Open Promenade. The Second Class Lounge and Smoking Room were closed at 11:30 p.m.[61]

The Smoking Room itself was connected directly to the forward Second Class Entrance. However, anyone utilizing the aft Second Class Entrance, which did not continue past B Deck, would have been forced to exit to the outer elements, walk forward to a midships door leading directly into the Smoking Room, or along either side of the Smoking Room on the Promenade, to doors leading into the Forward Second Class Entrance.

The Forward Second Class Entrance continued up through A Deck, sandwiched between the First Class Verandah Cafés, but gave no external access on that deck. Finally, passengers arrived at the Boat Deck level Entrance, which was housed in a small rectangular deckhouse. Here, passengers could egress to the open Boat Deck, where they were given virtually free rein to stroll and promenade over a large section of open and unencumbered deck. Their deck space ran from the stern rail at the Boat Deck all the way

---

Top left: Olympic's *port side Verandah Café, looking toward the revolving door which led into the smoking Room.*

Top right: Titanic's *starboard Verandah Café.*

Above left: *The* Olympic's *Second Class Dining Saloon, showing the room's appearance with the tables interconnected.*

Above right: Olympic's *Second Class Library.*

to the railing denoting the start of the Engineer's Promenade, which extended out from the deckhouse enclosing the Reciprocating Engine Hatch, Tank Room, and Engineers' Smoke Room.

Third Class passengers were much less luxuriously housed. Instead of the intricately carved paneling in the First and Second Class rooms, Third Class had to make do with a whitewashed steel hull, exposed frames, and rivetheads. Even so, these passengers – primarily immigrants or working-class individuals – would by and large have been thoroughly impressed with their accommodations. Third Class service was considered of great importance to steamship companies; even if these same individuals never took trans-Atlantic passage again, it was hoped that they would tell friends and relatives what a wonderful trip they had made, and that this positive 'word-of-mouth' would generate future customers. Passengers accustomed to using outhouses, or who had never tasted refrigerated milk or sampled the delights of ice cream, found themselves partaking of such wonders in a significantly upgraded standard of living.

Most Third Class passengers were accustomed to working with their hands – often in appalling conditions – or had previously been employed in the service of others. But in their Dining Saloon they were treated to full-service attention by stewards who did their best to provide for their needs and wishes. The Saloon itself was located amidships on F Deck, and was comprised of two rooms separated by a watertight bulkhead with two interconnecting watertight doors.

On C Deck, astern, Third Class passengers could promenade on the after Well Deck, or they could climb two sets of stairs to the B Deck level and walk around the Poop Deck. Promenading on the forward Well Deck was also available to Third Class passengers, but in rough weather, that location was not likely to be fit 'for man or beast.' Beneath the Poop Deck were the Third Class General Room and Third Class Smoking Room. Both of these spaces had portholes to the outside and seating consisted primarily of robustly-built benches, along with a number of tables and chairs. While the Smoking Room was intended for use only by men, the General Room was available to both sexes, and it even had an upright piano for passengers to use during the voyage. On D Deck, beneath the Well Deck forward, was the Third Class Open Area, which was larger than the

General Room and Smoking Room combined, although it was fitted up similarly to those spaces. One bar serviced the Open Area forward, while another served both the Smoking Room and General Room. Third Class passengers were requested to turn in at 10:30 p.m.

When *Titanic* was launched, however, all of these spaces were nonexistent – blank sheets of canvas for the workmen to transform into completed masterpieces. Months of work lay ahead for them. In light of all this labor, one question was foremost on the minds of everyone involved, or who had even a passing interest in the subject: exactly when would all of this work be complete?

In the days immediately after the *Titanic* was launched, it seemed logical to conclude that her fitting out would take about the same amount of time that it had taken to fit out the *Olympic*: about seven-and-a-half months.[62] This would have placed the *Titanic*'s maiden voyage somewhere around mid- to late-January of 1912. As she was on a Wednesday sailing schedule, this may have fallen somewhere around January 17, 24, or 31.

Beyond simple mathematics, there is actually evidence that, initially at least, the yard was pushing to have the ship complete by that time. For example, many of the *Olympic* and *Titanic*'s fittings and furnishings had to be ordered many months in advance. In the process of *Olympic*'s fitting out, a good number of these items were scheduled for delivery only about a month before her maiden voyage, as they were wholly unneeded before that point. With *Titanic*, similar or identical items – including some of her special-order sets of china – were scheduled for delivery in December of 1911.

Additionally, some of *Titanic*'s special suites – which were completed by a subcontracting firm rather than the builders directly – were actually finished and furnished by January of 1912. At that point, most of the ship's interiors were still a tangled web of confusion, with joiners, carpenters and others vying for space to work in order to have the spaces completed on schedule. Indeed, even by the time the ship sailed, some of the work on her interior spaces was still incomplete. Yet those suites were finished long in advance and sat gathering dust.

However, any plans for a January of 1912 maiden voyage for the *Titanic* quickly came to a screeching halt. During the

Above left: *The Third Class Entrance of the* Olympic, *underneath the Poop Deck. Looking through the door on the left, or starboard, side, the General Room is visible; the door on the right, or port, side, led into the Smoking Room.*

Above right: *The Olympic's Third Class Smoking Room.*

summer of 1911, the official date for the *Titanic*'s maiden voyage was announced as Wednesday, March 20, 1912 – some two months later than originally anticipated. It seems that shortly after *Titanic* was launched, something was found that would require more time to handle. What was this alteration? What could have intruded upon such a delicately choreographed schedule? Simply put, it was the maiden voyage of the *Olympic*.

Overall, Bruce Ismay was so pleased with the *Olympic*'s performance that before she had even reached New York, the option was exercised to order a third ship of the class: the *Britannic*. In other words, *Olympic* was overall a resounding success. However as she steamed west, Bruce Ismay, Thomas Andrews and others connected with White Star and Harland & Wolff were going over things with a fine-tooth comb. A few details began to come to light that could be improved upon on *Titanic*. Some of these were quite small in the overall scheme of things, but others would be far more involved in implementing. The minor upgrades to *Olympic* would be made within a few crossings' time; the more involved of them were slated for integration during her next major overhaul. All of them, however, would be put to right on the *Titanic* from the start.

sported long enclosed promenades between the First Class cabins and the ship's hull. When combined with an even longer open promenade on A Deck just above and large amounts of space on the Boat Deck as well, it all seemed a bit excessive. An idea was thus conceived to utilize otherwise redundant space: installing new cabins outboard in place of the promenades.

More First Class passengers could be carried as a result of these alterations. The opportunity was also taken to install, among these new cabins, two special Parlour Suites. Each of these suites would be comprised of three interconnecting cabins and included two bedrooms, a private bathroom, and a sitting room. Each suite would also boast a 48-foot long and 13-foot wide private promenade. Windows from within the suite's bedrooms and sitting rooms looked out over this space, and could be opened. The promenades also had large square windows which overlooked the sea beyond, and which could be opened in good weather, giving not only a private vista, but also fresh sea air. There was nothing like these spacious, ostentatious Parlour Suites anywhere on the Atlantic at the time, and they would give *Titanic* the distinction of having the most luxurious First Class accommodations available.

A number were minor matters. Some of the mattresses in First Class on the *Olympic* were found to be too springy, a detail which tended to enhance the minor vibration from the working of the ship's engines. The problem would be solved by fitting lath bottoms to the beds on *Olympic*, and would not be repeated on *Titanic*. There was a need to fit cigar holders in the First Class bathrooms. It was also necessary to remove some of the wardrobe door mirrors in certain C Deck cabins. Apparently if a passenger was inside the cabin dressing or undressing, and the entrance door was ajar, the mirror on the wardrobe door could under certain circumstances allow anyone in the passage outside to see them. It was also found that some of the ship's interior spaces could grow uncomfortably warm during the summer months, and improvements in ventilation were needed.[63]

Perhaps the most complex changes, however, were highly involved alterations to *Titanic*'s B Deck. *Olympic*'s B Deck

While this change might at first seem a rather simple one, it was actually quite complicated. Not only did new plans need to be drawn up and the location of many vital features juggled about, but then all of the changes needed to be transferred into cold steel. The changes actually meant re-configuring the large windows and shell plating of B Deck.

This work took nearly two months, and on its own would almost certainly have necessitated the postponement of the maiden voyage from late January to late March.[64] Yet there were other extensive alterations that were to be incorporated aft on B Deck. Due to the popularity of the First Class Restaurant on the *Olympic*, the decision was made to enlarge *Titanic*'s Restaurant so that it could accommodate more patrons. This would have the effect of cutting the port Second Class Promenade in half. Additionally along the starboard side of the Restaurant, a French 'sidewalk' restaurant, named the Café Parisien,[65] was slated for installation, similarly cut-

---

Above left: *Titanic*'s port side Private Promenade, for rooms B-52, -54 and -56, looking forward. This suite was occupied by J. Bruce Ismay and was not found on Olympic.

Above right: The starboard Private Promenade, for rooms B-51, -53 and -55, looking aft from the First Class Entrance. This suite was occupied by Charlotte Cardeza during the maiden voyage, and like its port side counterpart was not found on Olympic.

ting the length of the starboard Second Class Promenade. Although the expansion of the Restaurant and the Café Parisien would shorten the Second Class Promenades, at least Restaurant clientele would no longer have to worry about Second Class passengers staring in at them through the windows from their open promenade deck, as was sometimes the case on the *Olympic* during her first year of service.

In for a penny, in for a pound… still further changes on B Deck were quickly settled upon. Since more cabins had been added along the edges of the deck, this meant that a number of cabins directly adjacent the Aft Grand Staircase could be done without. This alteration allowed for the Entrance on B Deck to be enlarged and converted into a special Reception Room for the Restaurant. Very late in the fitting out of the *Titanic*, two more staterooms were installed just above the Restaurant Reception Room, on A Deck's Entrance. These two cabins – which did not even appear on December 1911-issued deck plans of the *Titanic* – were eventually numbered A-36 on the port side, and A-37 on the starboard.[66]

There would be other changes, as well. On the *Olympic*, the First Class Reception Room on D Deck proved enormously popular. It was agreed that additional seating was called for, and the Entrance vestibules to port and starboard

would be reduced in size aboard *Titanic* to allow for an expansion of the Reception Room. It was also agreed that the Dining Saloon, directly aft, could be increased in capacity, from *Olympic's* 532[67] to 554.[68]

During the maiden voyage of *Olympic*, it was also seen that there was room for improvement forward on the Boat Deck. *Titanic's* Officers' Quarters would be expanded forward slightly, making room for a few new First Class cabins just forward of the Grand Staircase; this also required re-arranging the layout of individual officers' cabins, the Marconi rooms, the Chart Room, and a number of other things. The shape of *Titanic's* enclosed Wheelhouse, which was located within and at the aft side of the open Bridge, was also changed from *Olympic's* arrangement. The face of *Titanic's* Wheelhouse was to be flat, as opposed to the curved face of *Olympic's*. Captain Smith also suggested adding protective windows with bull's eye lights to the square windows forward on the Bridge, for protection against breakage in foul weather.

As the *Olympic* continued her service through the fall and winter of 1911–1912, it was also found that her A Deck Promenade was far too exposed to the elements. Passengers who had paid a fortune for their passage, particularly finely-dressed ladies, had to suffer as wind howled down the

Below left: Titanic's *Café Parisien, looking from aft to forward. A similar but non-identical room was not installed on* Olympic *until after her winter 1912–1913 layup.*

Bottom left: *An artist's rendering of the First Class Restaurant Reception Room on* Titanic, *another dramatic difference between the layout of* Titanic *and her sister.*

Right: *This photo, taken in September 1911, shows work progressing on removing the B Deck windows along* Titanic's *starboard side. Much work still lay ahead in completing the task.*

Switched at Birth?

One of the more bizarre theories surrounding the *Titanic* suggests that she and her older sister *Olympic* were switched, and that it was the *Olympic* which actually sank on April 15, 1912. It is suggested that the *Olympic*'s collision with the cruiser HMS *Hawke* in September of 1911 caused far more significant damage than White Star acknowledged; according to the theory, this damage was so extensive that it rendered the £1.5 million-liner beyond repair – technically, fiscally or both.

According to this theory, *Olympic* and *Titanic* were so similar that with a few modifications to the *Olympic*, she could pass for the *Titanic*. The theory goes on to suggest that the *Olympic* was sent out into the North Atlantic to be deliberately sunk under the second ship's name in a large-scale insurance scam.

At first blush, the theory seems to be quite intriguing, and sounds eminently plausible. The two liners have often been called nearly-identical ... the damage from the *Hawke* incident to the *Olympic* was quite extensive. Further damage – enough to render the *Olympic* irreparable – could theoretically have been concealed by White Star and Harland & Wolff. The two sisters were together on two documented occasions after the Hawke collision. Perhaps the White Star Line and Harland & Wolff managed to pull off the greatest cover-up in maritime history?

When were there opportunities to carry out this switch? We know that *Olympic* was at Harland & Wolff between October 6 and November 20, 1911, and again from March 2–7, 1912. We know that the switch could not have been carried out during the lengthier early stay, since the ship that returned to service afterward was clearly the *Olympic*. Also, a photograph taken on March 3, 1912 is clearly of the *Olympic* and not the *Titanic*. There is no way that in the subsequent four days the two liners could have been switched. The switch would have to have been made at some point later in March or the first few days of April, 1912. No documented evidence has ever been brought to light that the two ships again met to carry out the necessary technical alterations.

While some circumstantial evidence has been brought to light over the years which could be interpreted as evidence of a switch, no absolute proof has ever been presented to back up these claims. No 'smoking gun' in the form of photographic evidence, either from the wreck or in period pictures; nothing in the way of authentic, original letters or correspondence from White Star or Harland & Wolff personnel; no direct first-hand reports, testimony, newspaper interviews or deathbed confessions by individuals involved in or aware of the alleged cover-up. Not a shred of direct, ironclad evidence. Instead, support for this theory has been based upon a string of coincidences and supposition.

At the other end of the spectrum, there is a great deal of evidence against such a switch and cover-up. For one thing, the insurance did not cover the construction cost of either vessel, fully equipped. It cost £1,500,000 sterling, or about $7,500,000 to build *Titanic*. At the time of the accident the vessel carried insurance of £1,000,000 sterling or about $5,000,000, the remaining risk being carried by the company's insurance fund.

Furthermore, the technical and thus visual differences between the two sister ships were far more numerous than has been previously allowed for. These were both external and internal differences. The alterations to *Titanic*'s B Deck were far more involved both internally and externally than they might seem at first mention.

Externally, the alterations included the widespread changes in *Titanic*'s window configuration. This work originally took quite a long time on *Titanic*, and could not have been duplicated on the *Olympic* in just a couple of days' time; nor could it have been put back to its original configuration on *Titanic* in a

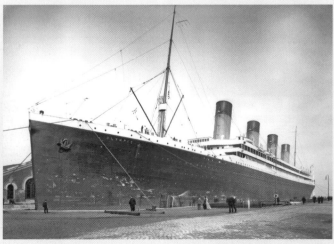

similarly short period. The internal configuration of *Titanic*'s B Deck had also received significant alterations.

Perhaps, to save time, the internal alterations were simply skipped, proponents of the theory might suggest. Would not this also explain why some passengers suffered from apparent deck-letter confusion in their accounts, saying that they were on B Deck promenades? Unfortunately for the conspiracy-theorists, many of these internal B Deck alterations are still visible on the wreck today. Ismay's port side suite, B-52, -54, -56 – new and very luxurious accommodations which had not been installed on *Olympic* – was thoroughly explored with ROVs in 2001.[69] The design of these new B Deck cabins did not match either *Olympic*'s 1911-1912 design or many of the modifications later made to that ship's B Deck.

The enclosing of *Titanic*'s A Deck Promenades were a very late-stage alteration to the *Titanic*, but this work still took a period of two or three weeks to carry out – more time than was available to do the work when the two liners were together. *Olympic* never subsequently received such a modification. There were also differences between the two ships' C Deck porthole arrangements, some of which never changed on the *Olympic*.

There is also evidence that the interiors of the two ships differed more than was previously thought. The coloring of the 'lino' tiles of *Titanic*'s First Class Dining Saloon and Smoking Room are known to have represented a significant departure from those on the *Olympic*. These color-palette changes on the floors of such prominent rooms would probably have necessitated color changes in the furniture, as well. There were a number of additional variations in layout, fittings and furnishings throughout the two ships, both in passenger and crew spaces.

A great many of the *Olympic*'s crew were transferred to the *Titanic* for that ship's maiden voyage. Some of these individuals reported differences

between the two liners' interior and fittings; the switch would either have had to be so complete that it fooled all of them, or all of them subsequently remained silent on the subject. The same level of effective deception or crew complicity would have been required of the second ship's crew, as well.

Additionally, for the conspiracy theory to be accurate means that everyone involved in the switch and cover up – including nearly 15,000 laborers at Harland & Wolff, all White Star and Harland & Wolff management personnel, and the crews of both ships – kept the secret perfectly for the rest of their lives. Not one of the yard's general employees shared the secret after a few rounds down at the local pub; no one connected with White Star ever shared the secret, even after the company went out of existence as a standalone entity in the 1930's; none of those proven to have been members of either crew ever spoke up about it.

Finally, when *Olympic* – purportedly *Titanic*, after a long and successful career masquerading as her old sister – was scrapped, her interior fittings and furnishings were auctioned off. On the reverse side of every panel was stamped the *Olympic*'s original Harland & Wolff Hull Number: 400. Clearly, every last documented item had come from the *Olympic*. Unless every scrap of the *Olympic*'s interior had been disassembled, moved, and reinstalled aboard the *Titanic* in the space of a couple of days' time – a resoundingly preposterous concept – then the ship that sank was definitely not the *Olympic*.

Despite the evidence against it, proponents of the switch theory will doubtless continue to try and raise doubts and claim to have found 'new evidence' supporting their claims. Each new claim will, in turn, have to be thoroughly investigated by technical and visual historians and researchers, but the simple truth is that this alleged switch never happened.[70]

Opposite left: *Damage to* Olympic's *starboard-aft quarter from the* Hawke *collision.*

Opposite right: *This photo shows the* Olympic *in the Belfast Graving Dock on March 3, 1912. Certain features of the ship visible in the photo prove beyond a shadow of a doubt that this is Olympic, and that the two liners had not been 'switched' up to that point. Members of the public are clearly in evidence beside the Olympic.*

Right: *This photo was taken as the* Olympic *arrived in New York on April 10, 1912. Not only is her forward A Deck Promenade open, but clearly visible behind the outer B Deck windows is Olympic's open First Class Promenade. Titanic's B Deck in this vicinity featured new cabins; similar but non-identical changes were not made on Olympic for years. Clearly, the two sisters were not switched.*

Promenade Deck. In rough conditions, things quickly deteriorated; bow spray even shot onto the deck. Something had to be done to shelter the passengers a bit more.

It was thus decided to enclose the forward half of the Promenade Deck on the *Titanic* with 37-inch by 31-inch

rectangular windows of the same type which were previously installed all along *Olympic* and *Titanic*'s B Decks.[71] Each of these could be opened by means of a removable crank, which operated a set of gears fitted into teeth on the glass pane's frame. When the crank was inserted into the

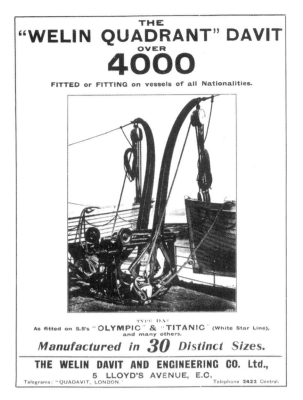

THE "WELIN QUADRANT" DAVIT
OVER
4000
FITTED or FITTING on vessels of all Nationalities.

As fitted on S.S's "OLYMPIC" & "TITANIC" (White Star Line), and many others.

Manufactured in **30** *Distinct Sizes.*

THE WELIN DAVIT AND ENGINEERING CO. Ltd.,
5 LLOYD'S AVENUE, E.C.

Telegrams: "QUADAVIT, LONDON."   Telephone **2422** Central.

Left: An advertisement for the 'Welin Quadrant' davit fitted aboard the Olympic *and* Titanic. *The photo was undoubtedly taken on* Olympic.

Opposite page: This period illustration shows workers building lifeboats like those used on the Titanic.

receptacle and turned, the windows would slide down into a protected slot between the outer side plating and an inner steel plate. Finally, a bulkhead with a door was erected across the front end of each side of the Promenade to prevent winds from funneling down the length of the enclosed deck. These alterations were not made until very late in *Titanic's* fitting out. Yet, once all of these modifications had been completed on the *Titanic*, they ended up increasing her gross registered tonnage over the *Olympic's*. This gave her bragging rights as 'the largest liner in the world.'

Despite the many differences between the two ships, one thing that would be identical on both sisters was their arrangement of lifeboats. At the time that *Olympic* and *Titanic* were taking rough shape on the drawing boards at Harland & Wolff, the Merchant Shipping Act of 1894 was in effect for ships under British registry. Its rules required that ships of over 10,000 tons carry sixteen lifeboats. However, ships were growing in size, and quickly. Even White Star's *Oceanic*, which entered service in 1899, was measured at 17,272 gross tons, or nearly double the maximum tonnage considered by the standing regulations. *Lusitania* and *Mauretania*, of 1907, more than tripled that tonnage. *Olympic* and *Titanic* would each best that regulation by four and a half times. There was some concern among members of the Board of Trade, and in certain other circles, that the regulations needed to be updated in order to more closely reflect the actual passenger capacity of newer ships.

At Harland & Wolff, in mid-1909, Alexander Carlisle fully 'expected' that the Board of Trade regulations for lifeboat capacity could be raised significantly by the time the *Olympic* and *Titanic* entered service. If more boats were required, this meant that strides would also need to be made in the design

of their storage and launching gear. Current lifeboat davits, then in use on just about every ship on the North Atlantic, were of the radial round-bar type; they had significant drawbacks, both for storage and launching purposes. Because of this, Carlisle began work on an idea for new davits and storage solutions. He then took his rough concept and submitted it to Lord Pirrie and 'the directors of the White Star'. They believed Carlisle's plan was a very good one under the circumstances, and gave authorization for him to proceed with the concept. Harland & Wolff's own draughtsmen 'made a rough design' for the new davits, and Carlisle then forwarded that concept to the Welin Quadrant Davit Company for final design and recommendation.[72]

Initially the idea was for each set of davits to accommodate up to four boats. With sixteen sets of davits, this would have allowed for up to sixty-four lifeboats each to be installed on the *Titanic* and her older sister. If the expected changes to the Board of Trade regulations did not require that many boats, however, the davits could also accommodate two or three boats per station, for a total of thirty-two or forty-eight boats. Welin worked up final designs for the davits in short order.

By October of 1909, Carlisle and Pirrie had enough material on hand to discuss that they undertook a journey to England to meet with Bruce Ismay and Ismay's right-hand man, Harold Sanderson.[73] The meeting lasted all day,[73] and during much of it, there was detailed discussion of the ships' elaborate fittings and decorations. The discussions were very involved, and there was a lot of ground to cover, some 'two or three thousand things'.[74] It had been previously agreed that the conversation would really be between Pirrie and Ismay only, and that neither Sanderson nor Carlisle would do much talking; this, it was felt, would expedite the meeting's progress greatly.[75]

When the subject eventually turned to the matter of lifeboats, Pirrie suggested that in light of uncertainty over changes to the Board of Trade regulations, it would 'be a good thing to make preparations for supplying the larger number of boats'. Ismay fully agreed.[76] There was no mention of needing to carry more than sixteen lifeboats, merely that it would be good to install davits that could handle more lifeboats if it was required of them. In all, the conversation took five to ten minutes, and nothing specific was settled at the time, other than a general approval for the concept.[77]

In January of 1910, there was a similar meeting, with the same participants, which lasted about four hours.[78] At this second gathering, the subject came up again. The Board of Trade still had not come to a decision on whether to raise the regulations, and things were still rather up in the air on the subject. On this occasion, conversation on the subject lasted only five or ten minutes, as Carlisle later recalled.

The discussion proceeded very similarly to the first, although this time things were a bit more technical in nature. The advantage of using the new Welin davits was clear: by installing them right from the start, there would be 'no expense or trouble' in case the Board of Trade imposed new

regulations 'at the last minute'.[79] Then the conversation turned once more to other matters. There had never been any discussion about the number of boats that the ships would actually carry[80] – that was being left entirely to what requirements the Board of Trade had in place when they entered service.

Carlisle placed the formal order with Welin for the new davits that same month.[81] Personally, he felt that *Olympic* and *Titanic* should carry forty-eight boats each – or three lifeboats to each set of davits.[82] He put the plans on paper showing as much, but later claimed that he did not recall whether he verbalized this sentiment to anyone else at Harland & Wolff.[83] When Axel Welin submitted the new davit design for the approval of the Board of Trade, in March 1910, the Assistant Secretary, Marine Department – one Alexander Boyle – noted:

> The '*Titanic*' and '*Olympic*' are each to be fitted with 32 boats, which are to be carried under 16 sets of double acting davits, 8 on each side. Sixteen of the boats will be placed inboard of the others, and all the davit frames are to be double ones.[84]

Despite the certainty of this statement, the Board of Trade was still not entirely sure what to do on the point. Up to the time of Carlisle's departure from Harland & Wolff on June 30, 1910, the matter had not been settled. The Board of Trade had yet made no final decision – and would not for some time – and so both Harland & Wolff and White Star remained in something of a 'wait-and-see' mode.[85] Carlisle and Pirrie could have recommended to White Star that they go ahead and install more boats than were required, but it seems that they showed no specific initiative in this regard. Although the builders had 'a very free hand' with many matters, Carlisle did not think that they 'could possibly have supplied any more boats to the ship without getting the sanction and the order of the White Star Line.'[86]

Looking back, one must at this point wonder why there is no record of Carlisle or others at Harland & Wolff pressing Ismay or upper management at White Star to add more lifeboats. Carlisle suggested a possible answer when he said that White Star had 'to consider their other fleet and their other steamers'.[87] In other words, if they made changes in the lifeboat capacity of the *Olympic* and *Titanic*, then they would also have to make similar changes to the *Adriatic* and the other liners in their fleet. Since the Board of Trade was seriously considering revising then-standing regulations on the subject, perhaps it was felt that subject was better settled by them. So, perhaps they simply concluded that if the Board of Trade did not feel it necessary to change the regulation, there was very little reason to suggest that White Star implement the changes on their own – changes that would require costly upgrades to their other steamers, as well.

At the time that Carlisle retired from Harland & Wolff, there was still nearly a year before the maiden voyage of the *Olympic*, and so there were still some months before a final decision would need to be made on how many boats to supply. This was not the end of Carlisle's involvement in the subject, however. When he was working with the Merchant Shipping Advisory Committee – which had been set up to advise the Board of Trade on whether to increase the lifeboat regulations – the subject had by necessity come up again.

The committee met then less than a month before *Olympic* made her maiden voyage, on May 19 and 26, 1911. Even at that late moment in the fitting out of the massive new White Star liner, the final decision on whether her size and carrying capacity would force new lifeboat regulations had not yet been reached. On those dates, plans of *Olympic* and *Titanic*'s lifeboat arrangements were passed around the table, and in the course of their meeting Carlisle flatly told the committee that he did not think the ships had enough lifeboats.[88] However, the committee eventually decided not to recommend that the existing regulations be raised, submitting its report to that effect in July of 1911.

What was more, Carlisle signed off on the report, even though he thought its recommendation incorrect. When later asked why he would sign off on the report if he did not agree with it, Carlisle responded: 'I do not know why I did. I am not generally soft … But I must say I was very soft the day I signed that.'[89] Nine others signed the report as well, even though Carlisle believed that at least one of others felt as he did.[90] The committee's report carried great weight with the Board of Trade, and in the end the Board allowed the standing regulations to continue without alteration.

When all was said and done, *Titanic* was supplied with some twenty boats. There were fourteen 30 foot by 9 foot wooden lifeboats, each capable of carrying 65 persons, for a total capacity of 910; there were an additional two 25 foot by 7 foot emergency cutters, each capable of carrying 40 persons, with a combined capacity of 80; finally, there were four Engelhardt collapsible boats, with a total capacity of 188 persons. These latter craft were 25.5 feet in length, with wooden bottoms and collapsible canvas sides. All twenty lifeboats were certified to hold an aggregate total of some 1,178 persons in the event of an emergency.[91]

At the same time, the *Olympic* was certified to carry 3,511 passengers and crew, and the *Titanic* would be certified to carry some 3,547.[92] The 2,369-person disparity between *Titanic*'s registered capacity of passengers and crew and the number who could be accommodated in her lifeboats has shocked the world ever since the morning of April 15, 1912.

However shortsighted this series of decisions was, such a lifeboat complement was simply the standard practice of the time; it was less evidence of unscrupulous disregard for passengers' safety than it was of simple complacency. If the Board of Trade did not require more boats, it was felt that there was very little reason to supply them independently.

The lifeboats themselves were actually built in May of 1911 by Harland & Wolff, and were specifically designed with strength in mind. Their construction was described so:

> Keels of elm, stems and stern posts of oak, all clinker built of best selected well-seasoned yellow pine, double fastened with copper nails clinched over rooves; the timbers were of elm spaced about 9 inches apart, and the seats pitch-pine secured with galvanised iron double knees.[93]

As the sixteen primary lifeboats were being built in the Harland & Wolff boat builder's shop, Board of Trade Ship Surveyor William Henry Chantler was instructed to visit the shop and inspect the boats carefully. Chantler did so on May 30, 1911, and again ten days later.[94] He found that they were 'well made and of good material',[95] and that they would hold not only the requisite sixty-five people with ease, but that they would even hold as many as seventy.[96] He calculated that with a load of sixty-five individuals, the boats' strength would only be tested to about half of their capacity before suffering structural failure.[97] When filled with sixty-five people and hanging from the davits above the water, he reckoned that the stress at the boats' gunwales would have been about 224 lb per square inch, while pressure at the boats' keels would have totaled about 252 lb per square inch.[98] After noting that the lifeboats' capacity, air cases, and equipment were all in order in the shop, he issued a certificate to that effect.

When these sixteen craft and the four collapsible lifeboats were brought aboard *Titanic*, they were quickly mated with the new-style Welin davits in an arrangement identical to that found on the *Olympic* the year before. The davits themselves had been made of cast steel. Test pieces had been cut from them during the manufacturing process for tensile and bending strength tests. The results of those tests were then submitted and approved by the Board of Trade Engineer Surveyor.[99]

Massive as the boats were, as well built as they were, and as well-designed and built as the Welin davits were, the whole setup might have looked harebrained enough to anyone standing on the Boat Deck over sixty feet above the water peering warily over the edge. So on *Olympic*, very careful tests had been carried out to ensure that the arrangement was safe, and would work according to plan if called upon. These tests upon *Olympic's* lifeboats were carried out in early May of 1911. On May 5, Francis Carruthers noted that the boats …

> … worked smoothly + well. The time taken to swing a boat out of the chocks + into the water a depth of about 58 feet averaging from 1 minute 40 seconds to 1 minute 55 seconds.[100]

Simply lowering them into the water was not enough however. These tests had to be far more thorough. On May 9, one of the *Olympic's* lifeboats was lowered empty into the water. Then it was filled with 'half-hundredweight weights[101] distributed so as to represent a load equal to about 65 people', and then the boat was raised and lowered six times. Not only did this prove that the electric boat winches were capable of raising and lowering fully-laden craft – which was the actual purpose of the test – but it also physically proved that the boats and davits themselves were strong enough to be fully loaded before they were raised or lowered. Harland & Wolff's Edward Wilding was present for the test. He said that after the weights had been removed, the boat was still quite watertight and showed no evidence of distress at all. In his mind, there wasn't a shadow of a doubt that the lifeboats were strong enough to be lowered when filled with their designated complement of passengers.[102] Similar tests would be carried out upon *Titanic's* lifeboats the following March. Francis Carruthers thought that the boats were 'well made and satisfactory'.[103]

Meanwhile, the fitting out of *Titanic* had continued at a breakneck pace. In Harland & Wolff's engine works, the *Titanic's* two massive reciprocating engines had been fabricated, assembled, and tested. Then they were disassembled, the components were hoisted into the hull, and the engines were re-assembled. The low-pressure turbine was also shipped out to the wharf, lifted aloft, and carefully lowered into place. Each of *Titanic's* 29 boilers was also brought from the shops out to the wharf, where the enormous crane picked them up and deposited them in their correct compartments for seating. Once all of the major machinery was aboard, then the uptakes, which would vent the combustion gases from the boilers, had to be erected. With three uptakes leading to the operational funnels, and six boiler rooms, each funnel would vent

Opposite bottom left: *This photo was taken in the Reciprocating Engine Room of* Titanic's *younger sister* Britannic *on April 29, 1914. It shows the engines in the midst of re-assembly. The photo looks aft and to starboard and gives an excellent idea of the same process on* Titanic.

Opposite bottom right: *This photo shows* Titanic *with only her forward three smokestacks in place. It was most likely taken in December of 1911. Notice that scaffolding is still in place around the B Deck windows.*

This page, top: *This spectacular photograph appears to have been taken in January 1912. The fourth funnel has been put into position, and workers' scaffolds surround both after smokestacks. Although all of the new B Deck windows are in place, scaffolds are still in place.*

Middle: *This photo was taken at a very similar time to the preceding one, perhaps even on the same day.*

Bottom: Titanic *as seen on February 3, 1912, as she entered the Belfast Graving Dock for the first time. Coaling outriggers are visible along the outer hull between B and C Decks. Smoke is billowing from the No. 3 funnel.*

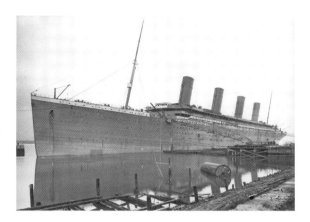

the smoke from two boiler rooms; like a giant jigsaw puzzle on a nightmarish scale, the flues vented from each boiler, and then these individual conduits converged to the primary vertical uptake above the watertight bulkhead separating the two boiler rooms. Once these uptakes were in place, and the surrounding deckhouses were complete, the ship's funnels were lowered gently into place and seated. The final funnel that was attached to the *Titanic* was the after-most one. Although envisioned primarily to create a powerful profile, it would also serve several useful ventilation functions aboard *Titanic*.

Meanwhile, work continued on completing her magnificent interior appointments. Vast open spaces on each deck had to be partitioned off into separate areas by wooden walls. Once the basic partitions were in place, then came the task of installing the paneling – some of it basic in crew or Third Class quarters, some of it exquisitely ornate in Second and First Class sections. Next there came the installation of tiling, carpeting, painting, furniture, lights, and a nearly uncountable array of other furnishings and fittings. The Grand Staircases were turned from basic shells into arguably two of the most beautiful and easily recognized staircases ever placed on an ocean liner.

In the Joiners' Shop, workmen carefully crafted the intricate pieces of paneling and molding, and then would take them in for installation aboard the liner. One of the most interesting stories of something which ran amok during the fitting out was recalled by Joiner Hugh McRoberts; he was about twenty years of age when the event took place. One day, one of McRoberts' fellow joiners finished carving a piece of hardwood trim that would be installed on the base of one of the staircase newel posts. Then he took it aboard the ship to install it; shortly thereafter, the worker returned to the Joiners' Shop, nearly frantic, and told McRoberts that as he had been fitting the piece, it split. To many today, such an unfortunate situation would not seem worth worrying over. However the cost of damaged materials was typically deducted from workers' wages, meaning that the situation could be quite expensive for the hapless worker. Together, the two men thought about the situation for a while, and then they struck upon an idea: they took sawdust and glue and filled the split, and then polished it in such a way that, it was hoped, it would not be noticeable upon installation. The clever idea worked, the split piece of trim was put back in place, and no one seems to have noticed the issue.[104]

The *Titanic*'s maiden voyage was originally scheduled for Wednesday, March 20, 1912, nearly ten months from the date of her launch, and under ordinary circumstances, it would not have been an issue for Harland & Wolff to complete on schedule. After all, this sort of project – turning the *Titanic* into a finished liner – was not unprecedented for Harland & Wolff. Not only had they built many grand ocean liners, but they had also finished the nearly-identical interior spaces of the *Olympic* just a year before. So in this particular instance, one might have

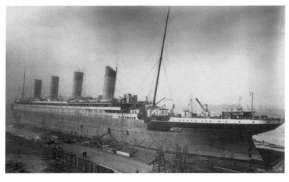

Opposite, top: This photo is of Olympic's *stern props, as seen in October or November of 1912, during the onset of her 1912–1913 refit. Often used to portray* Titanic's *propeller configuration, it now seems certain that* Titanic's *center prop was 3-bladed, rather than 4-bladed.*

Middle: Titanic *(right) has been removed from the Graving Dock, and now sits astern of* Olympic *(left).* Olympic *was still in the Graving Dock on March 3, as seen in the photo on page 38.*

Below: March 6, 1912: Olympic *(right) and* Titanic *(left) are together at the Harland & Wolff shipyard.*

Bottom left: Titanic *in the Belfast Graving Dock on March 6, 1912. Steam is emitting from her after funnels, indicating signs of life within the vessel. All 16 lifeboats are in position. The paint work is still incomplete, and fresh paint is being applied to the hull below the aft Well and Poop Decks. This photograph was taken from the* Olympic.

Bottom right: This photograph was taken on or after March 8, 1912. Titanic *has been returned to the wharf. It shows that the scaffolding has been removed from B Deck. A new layer of paint is being applied to the hull starting from the bow and moving aft.*

---

expected things to go more easily for the yard than they had even on the *Olympic*. However, *Titanic's* older sister was about to throw two cogs into the gears at the shipyard.

On September 20, 1911, at the beginning of the *Olympic's* fifth voyage, she was involved in the first major incident of her career; it caused a delay in the fitting out of *Titanic*. While clearing Southampton waters, with over 1,300 passengers aboard, she encountered the 7,350-ton Admiralty cruiser HMS *Hawke*. The courses of the two ships converged until they were steaming parallel with one another. The *Hawke* began to overtake the *Olympic* on the liner's starboard side. Then the *Olympic's* speed was increased to sixteen knots. As the engines ramped up to meet this new order, the suction between the starboard side of the *Olympic* and the port side of the *Hawke* increased. The result was startling: quite suddenly, the bow of the *Hawke* veered to port, right toward the enormous ship. On the Bridge of the *Hawke*, her commander ordered the helmsman to port the helm, to turn his ship away to starboard. But the burbled waters effectively jammed the helm of the cruiser, and before anything else could be done, she slammed into the liner's aft-starboard quarter. The *Hawke's* reinforced bow was crumpled like tinfoil; two huge gashes were cut in the side of the *Olympic*, one above the waterline and one below. Damage was also done to the liner's starboard propeller as debris in the water was sucked through the still-turning blades. Two of the *Olympic's* watertight compartments began to flood immediately, and her starboard propeller shaft was badly mangled.

Amazingly, neither vessel was in danger of sinking after this shocking event, and remarkably, nobody was injured. The *Hawke* limped away to Portsmouth for repairs, and the *Olympic* anchored in Osborne Bay off the Isle of Wight. Unable to continue the voyage to New York, she off-loaded her passengers by tender and her crew made temporary damage repairs through the course of that night. The following day, she returned to Southampton where Harland & Wolff's local works carried out still further temporary repairs. Once these had been completed, *Olympic* was guided cautiously back to Belfast, and Harland & Wolff's main shipyards, where full repairs were made between October 6 and November 20. In the course of this work, *Titanic's* starboard propeller shaft was utilized to help return *Olympic* to service quickly; a replacement shaft for the second liner would have to be fabricated as her fitting out continued.

At this time, *Titanic* was still being fitted out at the Alexandra Wharf. Upon *Olympic's* arrival, she was placed in the Graving Dock, and then the two vessels swapped location, with *Olympic* entering the drydock. While *Olympic* was being repaired, work on the *Titanic* was nearly halted, but the pace picked back up when *Olympic* resumed her schedule. The *Olympic* again returned to Harland & Wolff on March 1

because she had thrown a blade from her port propeller. This repair took six days, making an already bad situation worse by causing further delay in work on *Titanic*. Additionally, it seems that in order to return *Olympic* to service more quickly, one of the blades from *Titanic's* port propeller was utilized to replace the lost blade from the *Olympic*.[105]

On March 6, the *Titanic* was placed in the Thompson drydock again, in order to give the *Olympic* enough room to swing around to make her departure and subsequent return to service. Carruthers took the opportunity to make a third inspection of the *Titanic's* lower hull to ensure its integrity, and found it quite satisfactory.[106]

In both of these incidents, White Star felt it was more important to have the *Olympic* back on the Atlantic again than it was to proceed with work on the *Titanic* without interruption. Indeed, these two delays caused Harland & Wolff to fall so far behind on the *Titanic* that they had to postpone her delivery. White Star, in turn, had to postpone the ship's maiden voyage from March 20, 1912 to the date originally scheduled for the start of the liner's second round trip voyage: Wednesday, April 10, 1912.[107] Even so, it was still going to be a close shave, and everyone knew it.

It was into this chaos that three of the *Titanic's* senior officers blithely steamed. All three – Chief Officer William Murdoch, First Officer Charles H. Lightoller, and Second Officer David Blair – arrived together. These 'three very contented chaps' had taken 'the midnight boat for Belfast', arriving on March 20, 1912. They would take the coming days to familiarize themselves with the new ship.[108] Despite the frenzy surrounding their new charge, there is no doubt that they glowed with pride that they, out of the entire officer corps of the White Star Line, had been chosen to crew the flagship of the line – even if she was at that point a chaotic and incomplete mess. These three officers knew each other, even though they were arriving from three different ships. Lightoller had previously served with both Murdoch and Blair.[109]

Lightoller was quick-thinking and cool-headed. He was a good 'company man' and an able officer who had already enjoyed a wide and varied career. Serving on four-masted barques, clipper ships, and other sailing vessels early on, he had already survived being shipwrecked. For a time he had even left the sea to prospect for gold in the Yukon, and to work as a cowboy in Alberta, Canada. He had put in time on the White Star Line's Australian run, and among other ships, had served aboard the *Medic*, *Majestic* and the *Oceanic*. He had met his future wife while serving on the *Majestic*.[110]

Lightoller had been transferred to the *Oceanic* in 1907, initially serving as her Third Officer. His performance aboard that vessel allowed him to be promoted from Third to Second Officer, and eventually to First Officer. In March of 1911, while serving as *Oceanic's* First Officer, Lightoller had been

Top left: *Charles Lightoller, c. 1919.*

Second from left: *William Murdoch in a photo probably dating to June of 1911, when he served aboard* Olympic.

Centre: *Herbert Pitman, Third Officer of the* Titanic. *At the time of the White Star liner's maiden voyage, Pitman was the only one of the senior officers sporting facial hair other than Captain Smith.*

Second from right: *This photo shows Fourth Officer Joseph Boxhall between the years of 1919 and 1923.*

Top right: *Fifth Officer Harold Lowe.*

aboard when the liner's foremast was struck by lightning in a gale. He was standing on the Bridge at the time, and had just narrowly avoided being seriously injured by falling splinters.[111]

When he wasn't dodging lightning bolts and mast splinters, Lightoller had a rather playful side and something of a penchant for practical jokes. Playing pranks on his fellow officers – while off-duty, of course – had nearly gotten him into trouble on more than one occasion in the past. So did his playful side. For example, while on the *Oceanic*, with the Bridge decking wet and the ship rolling, he liked to amuse himself 'by trying to slide from one side of the bridge to the other, without touching anything'. This particular diversion had been cut short one day when the Captain, Herbert James Haddock, showed up unexpectedly.[112]

There would be no sliding across the bridge on the *Titanic*, that was for sure. Although Lightoller had loved the *Oceanic*, this transfer was a tremendous promotion for him; every officer in the fleet wanted a post on the newest ship – she was almost three times the gross tonnage of the *Oceanic*. When he turned 38 years old on March 30, 1912, he was still trying to find his way around the behemoth:

> I was thoroughly familiar with pretty well every type of ship afloat, from a battleship and a barge, but it took me fourteen days before I could with confidence find my way from one part of that ship to another by the shortest route.[113]

Lightoller's old shipmate and friend, 39-year-old William Murdoch, was a happily married man. Not long before, he had shaved the large mustache that he had previously sported, apparently at his wife's prodding. Murdoch – who had served as a Lieutenant in the Royal Navy Reserve – hailed from Dalbeattie, and was the *Titanic's* only Scottish officer. The Chief Officer had served on sailing vessels, as well as the Australian run aboard White Star's *Medic* and *Runic*. He then plied his trade on the Atlantic aboard, among others, the *Arabic, Oceanic, Adriatic* and finally the *Olympic*.

A sensible and well-seasoned officer who was a quick thinker, Murdoch had proven himself willing and able to take action in a crisis on previous occasions. In 1903, while serving as Second Officer of the *Arabic*, he had narrowly averted a collision with another vessel by countermanding the helm

orders of a superior officer, shoving the Quartermaster out of the way, and taking control of the ship himself.[114] As he was just transferring from the *Olympic*, *Titanic's* size probably did not impress him; however, it would make sense that his experience on *Olympic* came in handy in assisting Lightoller and Blair to familiarize themselves with the ship, as he was the only one of the three with experience on the class.

Thirty-seven-year-old Second Officer David Blair had transferred from the Dominion liner *Teutonic*.[115] *Teutonic* was a legendary ex-White Star liner which had been in service since August of 1889. One of the last White Star ships built for speed, she had the ability to steam at over twenty knots. Yet, at nearly twenty-three years of age, she was showing her years, and her waning prestige on the Atlantic had prompted the IMM internal transfer from White Star to Dominion. Blair must have been dumbstruck at the upgrade *Titanic* represented from his previous ship. *Teutonic* had grossed only some 9,984 tons, whereas *Titanic* was over four-and-a-half times that size. The older vessel was only 582 feet in length, but *Titanic* bested her by three hundred feet. The scale of the *Titanic* must have been hard for Blair to grasp, but he seemed quite pleased at the promotion.

At noon on Wednesday, March 27, 1912 – a week after the three senior officers had stepped aboard, and precisely two weeks from the scheduled start of the ship's maiden voyage from Southampton – the *Titanic's* four junior officers arrived in Belfast. Theirs had been a rather grueling trip, leaving Liverpool at 10:00 p.m. the previous night for the cross-Channel voyage. The group of men made their way aboard the great liner and immediately reported to Chief Officer Murdoch.[116] They were young, but they were already quite experienced and they were full of promise.

There was 34-year-old Third Officer Herbert J. Pitman. Pitman, though rather short in stature, cut an imposing figure with his large mustache. He was also an extremely capable officer with some sixteen years of experience at sea. Like several of the other officers, he had served on vessels in the less prestigious Australian and Japanese routes. He had previously served aboard the White Star vessels *Delphic* and *Majestic*, and was just transferring from the *Oceanic*, where he had served as her Fourth Officer.[117]

Twenty-eight-year-old Fourth Officer Joseph G. Boxhall had already been at sea almost thirteen years, having

Top left: *Sixth Officer James Moody.*

Centre: *Doctor William O'Loughlin* (right) *seated with Captain Smith* (left) *on the* Olympic.

Top right: *This very rare photo of Harold Bride in his Junior Marconi Operator's uniform was most likely taken when he first joined service with the Marconi Company.*

Above left: *Jack Phillips.*

joined a steel-hulled barque with the William Thomas Line in 1899. He had entered service with the White Star Line in late 1907,[118] and in the preceding years had become another veteran of the Australian run, also serving on White Star's *Oceanic* and *Arabic*. He would prove a valuable officer during *Titanic*'s maiden trip. Pitman and Boxhall were both single.

Twenty-nine-year-old Fifth Officer Harold G. Lowe had been at sea since he ran away from home at age 14. Although born in Wales, his mother was from Liverpool, England, and his father was also from England. While Lowe could speak Welsh fluently, when he spoke English he did not have a trace of Welsh accent.[119] The young officer was new to the North Atlantic service, as he had served on the Australian run aboard the *Belgic* and *Tropic* prior to his transfer.[120]

Lowe was a no-nonsense man, a self-described teetotaler, and he was occasionally a little strong with his language.[121] He was still young, but his youth and the experience he had already gained in his years at sea were two of his best assets, making him a most promising officer. Lowe felt like something of an outsider aboard the *Titanic*, as he was the only officer who did not know and who had not previously served with any of the liner's other officers.[122]

Sixth Officer James P. Moody also had a lot of promise. The youngest of the officers, he was twenty-four years old, and like Pitman, Boxhall, and Lowe, was still single. Moody had only received his Master's License the previous April, but he had a broad base of knowledge and decades of experience to look up to in his senior officers and Captain. Among others, he had previously served on sailing vessels, on the Navy training vessel HMS *Conway*, and the *Oceanic*. He would certainly gain much experience on this voyage,

and was no doubt very pleased – in light of his junior status – to have been posted to the line's flagship.

A number of other crewmen were also beginning to arrive on board the *Titanic*. Among these was 62-year-old Ship's Surgeon Dr William O'Loughlin, who signed on March 24. O'Loughlin, who was from Tralee, County Kerry, Ireland had been at sea since he was 21 years of age. He had studied at Trinity College in Dublin, and looked very distinguished with graying hair and large mustache.

At some point in early 1912, Captain Smith had met up with O'Loughlin and another famed White Star Ship's Surgeon, J. C. H. Beaumont, at the South Western Hotel in Southampton. At the time, Smith was aware that he would be transferring to command the *Titanic* on her maiden voyage. During the meeting of these three men, O'Loughlin had mentioned that at this stage of his life, he 'was tired' of 'changing from one ship to another'. In response, Captain Smith had good-naturedly 'chided' O'Loughlin 'for being lazy, and told him to pack up and come with him.'[123]

O'Loughlin was much loved by just about everyone who knew him.[124] It was said that he 'regarded life with a twinkle in his eye but kept clear of the whirlpools'. He was so engaging that many of the stewardesses he worked with wondered how he had managed to remain a bachelor all those years. His typical response to the question was given in his lilting Irish brogue: 'Sure, haven't I worn all the knees out of me pants proposing to ladies and sure they won't have anything to do with me at all.'[125]

Two others who arrived early aboard the *Titanic* worked, not for the White Star Line or Harland & Wolff, but for the Marconi International Marine Company.[126] John George 'Jack' Phillips, aged 25, had been in service with the company since the summer of 1906, sailing on ships such as the *Teutonic*, *Lusitania* and *Mauretania* before taking a land-based station in 1908. He had returned to the sea in late 1911, and finally in March of 1912 he was tapped to report to the *Titanic* at Belfast to serve as her Senior Operator.

Phillips met his assistant for the first time in Belfast when the two men converged on the mighty new liner.[127] That assistant was Harold Sydney Bride, then aged 22. Bride was rather a newcomer to the Marconi International Marine Company, having received his first posting only in July of 1911. However, in that time, he had managed to make three round-trips to Brazil, one to Philadelphia, and two to New York aboard the *Lusitania*.[128]

Both men must have been enthralled with their new ship as they boarded her for the first time. The shipyard was an absolute hive of activity … the liner was still clearly incomplete … workmen scrambled around trying to get the ship prepared in time for her departure. The sights, the sounds, the absolute kinetic energy of those final days in Belfast – this was the introduction of Phillips and Bride to the *Titanic*.

They were very likely also enthralled by the Marconi equipment that they were going to be working with, a 5kw generating set with a rotary spark gap. As far as Marconi sets went, this was quite a space-age design, far advanced over the older 1½-kw sets.[129] Whereas most sea-going Marconi sets of the period produced an electric rasping sound as it formed the 'dot' and 'dash' of Morse code, *Titanic*'s set actually produced a musical tone. This musical tone, or voice, was not entirely unique at the time; the *Olympic*, although originally slated to receive a lesser system, had in the end been endowed with a similar set.[130] Even so, it was quite a rare installation.

Just as automobile enthusiasts love nothing more than to open their vehicles' engine compartments and discuss every little feature with fellow aficionados, and train buffs compare the vital statistics of various locomotives, so the Marconi wireless sets were to enthusiasts of the time. When the *Lusitania* had made her maiden voyage just four-and-a-half years before, one newspaper reporter was able to pop in to the Wireless Shack; his report made for a near adventure story. Yet, the technology was rapidly advancing, and there were new features to fuss over and be enthralled by. Phillips and Bride must have gazed in open astonishment at their new instrument.

The set's guaranteed daytime range was conservatively placed at 350 miles, but it was thought that it would manage more, perhaps up to 500 miles. Beyond that, it was expected that at night, when the atmospherics were more conducive to transmissions, the set's range would be far more impressive, with reception from high-powered stations up to 1,500 miles away.[131] The concept of contacting people in far-flung corners of the globe in real time was still a novel one, and no one knew that they were on the 'cutting edge' of technology better than Phillips and Bride.

The Marconi rooms were conveniently located on the Boat Deck, just astern of the uptake for the No. 1 funnel, within the structure of the Officers' Quarters. The shipboard domain of these two men consisted of three separate rooms: the actual Marconi office, where the key was located, sat amidships; a door on the starboard side of the operations center led to their sleeping quarters,[132] which had an upper and a lower berth, a settee, and other typical fittings; on the port side of the Marconi Room, through another door, was the Silent Room, which contained the alternator and the motor and spark gap. This room had special insulation so that the noise from the sparks wouldn't disturb anyone nearby.[133]

Once Phillips and Bride had become familiar with their suite's general layout, the next order of business would have been to set up house. Since the *Titanic* was to have a 24-hour constant watch, it was up to the two operators to decide how they would break their duties up to achieve that. Four watches of six hours each would cover the complete period.[134] In the end they decided that during the night, Phillips would keep watch from 8:00 p.m. through 2:00 a.m. Bride would take the next six hours on watch, from 2:00-8:00 a.m.[135]

During the day, however, they decided to keep the schedule a little more pliable, relieving each other 'to suit each other's convenience'[136] while still dividing the watches fairly.

Until the *Titanic* put to sea, however, things were far more chaotic, far more hectic. While the ship was at Belfast, the operators' time as well as the rooms housing the Marconi set were not their own. Marconi Company engineers were on hand, setting up the complicated equipment in those final days before the ship was to depart Belfast. Numerous tests needed to be performed, and adjustments made, for the equipment to work properly when the liner took to sea for the first time.[137] Fortunately, the two men seemed to get along very amiably – something not always guaranteed between workmates, but particularly valued in such a close-quarters working environment – and they quickly started to become friends.

Meanwhile, inspections were being made to ensure that the ship was thoroughly equipped. Chief Officer Murdoch ordered Fifth Officer Lowe and Sixth Officer Moody to inspect the starboard side lifeboats and to make sure their equipment was complete; he ordered Third Officer Pitman and Fourth Officer Boxhall to do likewise with the port side lifeboats.[138] It is likely that this was done as a preliminary to the formal inspections, which would be performed by Board of Trade Inspectors such as Francis Carruthers, among several others.

First Officer Lightoller personally accompanied Carruthers through some of his surveys.[139] A few days before the ship was finished, Carruthers inspected the bulkheads for watertightness.[140] Lightoller also went through the watertight bulkheads, although he later could not remember whether it was with Carruthers or whether he did so independent of the Board of Trade Surveyor.[141] Lightoller was also with Carruthers as the Surveyor formally examined the lifeboats, had them swung out, lowered down and hauled up, and as he thoroughly scrutinized their equipment. These tests were probably very similar to those Carruthers had performed on the *Olympic* the previous year. Carruthers also had the 15¾-ton[142] auxiliary anchor – normally stowed in a well at the tip of the Forecastle – hooked up to the crane, swung out and back again in order to test the entire setup.[143]

On March 25, 1912, 51-year-old Herbert James Haddock took command and became *Titanic*'s first official Captain. Haddock had just transferred over from the *Oceanic*, which he had commanded since April 1907. As such, he was First Officer Lightoller's previous commanding officer.[144] Haddock had also commanded the *Cedric*, *Britannic*,[145] *Germanic* and *Celtic* for White Star. His tenure as Captain of the *Titanic* was to be short-lived, however, as he would soon be taking command of *Titanic*'s sister *Olympic*. His time aboard was doubtless spent familiarizing himself with the sheer scale of the *Olympic*-class ships – his former command, *Oceanic*, had less than forty per cent of the *Olympic* and *Titanic*'s interior registered space.

Another individual who was very much present as the *Titanic* neared completion was her first Chief Engineer, 50-year-old Joseph Bell.[146] Although Bell did not formally sign on to the ship until the morning of April 2, it was only natural that he was boarding the *Titanic* as her Chief Engineer. Not only had he overseen the installation of *Olympic*'s powerplant, but he had then served on *Olympic* as Chief Engineer during her maiden voyage. During that early period with *Olympic*, Robert Fleming – another of White Star's senior engineers[147] – was at Bell's side, gaining experience with the *Olympic* and getting 'accustomed to her'.[148] Then Bell had returned to Belfast, and Robert Fleming was promoted to Chief Engineer on the *Olympic*. Back in Belfast, Bell was present as the *Titanic's* own engines – nearly identical to her older sister's – were constructed and assembled at the yard Engine Works, then disassembled, and finally installed and tested in their final positions aboard *Titanic*.[149] Very likely, Bell was planning to return to Belfast after *Titanic's* maiden voyage, in order to oversee the *Britannic's* engines as they were constructed and installed.

Other crew members were also joining the ship. Among them were a number who would not only sail during the trials and brief trip on to Southampton, but who would continue with the ship on her first voyage to New York. A number of these signed on in Southampton on March 25, with the understanding that they would muster at Southampton's West Station at 2:30 the following afternoon for passage to Belfast. Among those listed from this group were Quartermaster Arthur J. Bright, Lookout Frederick Fleet, Lamp Trimmer Samuel Hemming, Lookout Archie Jewell, Quartermaster Alfred Olliver, George Rowe – although listed as a Lookout for this brief trip, he would eventually serve as a Quartermaster during the maiden voyage – Purser Reginald Barker, Chief Steward Andrew Latimer, Steward Edward Wheelton, Gymnasium Instructor Thomas W. Mc-Cawley, and many, many more.

In amongst this group of *Titanic's* first crew forming at Belfast was 33-year-old Deck Engineer Thomas Millar. Millar had worked at Harland & Wolff, and had assisted in the construction of both the *Olympic* and *Titanic*. His wife had died just recently, however, and he had left Harland & Wolff for work with IMM and the White Star Line.[150] As the *Titanic* was nearing completion, Millar was planning to find a new home in America before having his two young sons sent over, so that they could all begin a new life. Just a few days before the ship's trials, Millar had taken his boys on a tour of the great *Titanic*. When the boys' Uncle Bob, with them for the tour, had scoffed that the ship was just too big, Thomas had retorted: 'Nonsense, she's as safe as houses, in fact they say she's unsinkable.'[151]

Millar's tour must have been carried out amidst quite a chaotic scene as work continued aboard the great ship. So much yet needed to be done before she would be ready to sail on her maiden voyage. Fortunately, work on enclosing the A Deck Promenade was finished … so too were most of the various pieces of equipment in the Gymnasium … the engines were operational … most of the major decorations and wall coverings were in place. Yet paint crews still swarmed over the ship, touching up her internal and external paint … carpet still needed to be laid, and trimmed … many light fixtures were not yet installed. The story was the same with draperies, many of the mattresses, the linens, the china and cutlery … even the ship's Steinway pianos did not arrive until mid-March.[152]

It must have seemed that Thomas Andrews was needed at all times everywhere to help sort things out. Clearly not everything could be finished at Belfast, and much would need to be done in the days before the ship sailed from Southampton. There must have been concerns within some circles at Harland & Wolff over whether everything was going to come together in time on this, the Firm's greatest accomplishment.

In June 1911, prior to her maiden voyage, the *Olympic* had made a stopover in Liverpool, England, the location of White Star's Company headquarters. For years, Liverpool had been the primary English terminus of White Star ships, as it was for the prestigious Cunard Company. However, in 1907, White Star had transferred its terminus to Southampton, which was far more favorable for large ships because of its double tide and the lack of a shallow bar at the entrance of Southampton water. This shift had left many in Liverpool disgruntled, and *Olympic's* stop at her registered, if only honorary, home port had been part of an attempt to ease public relations. A stop on the part of *Titanic* would doubtless have been intended to have the same effect; due to the terrific crush of time, however, this post-trials stop was canceled.

As the date set for the trials to commence – Monday, April 1, 1912 – arrived, much work still needed to be done. However, the important things were complete, and the trials could proceed as scheduled. On Saturday, March 30, 62-year-old Captain Edward John Smith, White Star's senior Captain and unofficial Commodore,[153] left the *Olympic* at Southampton, and set out for a quick trip up to Belfast. He arrived there in time to take command of the new *Titanic* on Monday, April 1. Captain Haddock's 'command' of the *Titanic* – more of an on-paper position since the ship did not move under her own power while he was in charge – had spanned less than a week. After he was relieved, Haddock rushed down to Southampton to take Smith's place on the *Olympic* and command that liner for her next departure on Wednesday, April 3, 1912. When Captain Smith left the *Olympic*, so did quite a number of that ship's officers and crew, well over two hundred of them, all told.

The *Titanic's* officers held Captain Smith in very high esteem. Smith, a long-term White Star veteran, had been a Commander in the Royal Navy Reserve, and had served in the Boer War in South Africa. As such, he had received an Admiralty warrant that allowed the ships he commanded, including *Titanic*, to fly the blue ensign of the Royal Navy Reserve, rather than the red ensign of the merchant marine. During his career Smith had served on or had commanded, among other ships, the *Republic*, *Coptic*, *Majestic*, *Baltic*, *Adriatic* and *Olympic*. Second Officer Lightoller had served with him for many years, including a stint on the *Majestic*. He described the Captain as follows:

'E.J.' as he was familiarly and affectionately known, was quite a character in the shipping world. Tall, full whiskered, and broad. At first sight you would think to yourself, 'Here's a typical Western Ocean Captain. Bluff, hearty, and I'll bet he's got a voice like a foghorn.' As a matter of fact, he had a pleasant, quiet voice and invariable smile. A voice he rarely raised above a conversational tone – not to say he couldn't; in fact, I have often heard him bark an order that made a man come to himself with a bump. He was a great favorite, and a man any officer would give his ears to sail under.[154]

By 4:00 a.m. on the morning of Monday, April 1, the firemen who were to bring the liner's new furnaces to life boarded and set to their task. Seamen engaged for the trial trip arrived by 6:00 a.m.[155] The trials were set to commence at 10:00 a.m. However, as the day began, it was clear that the weather was not going to cooperate, with high winds and a heavy chop to the water. It was prudently decided

Left: *April 1, 1912: Titanic's trials are delayed due to high winds. This photograph shows that her port side white paintwork had only just been re-touched.*

Below: *Proud Harland & Wolff employees posing beside the hull of the* Olympic *in 1911. Most of these same individuals would have been involved in completing* Titanic *the following year.*

not to risk maneuvering the *Titanic's* immense bulk about the confines of shallow waters under such circumstances. It was said:

> Hundreds of spectators made the journey to the new deep water wharf where the *Titanic* is lying, with the object of witnessing the departure, and if disappointed at not seeing her leave, they had the satisfaction of obtaining a good view of the vessel, which presented a magnificent spectacle.[156]

The stokehold crew and seamen were released for the remainder of the day. According to the terms of their sign-on agreement, they would be paid 5s each per day for any unforeseen detention in Belfast, starting from midnight of Monday, April 1. Eventually, the spectators who had turned out to see the ship's departure dispersed. It was hoped by everyone that on the following morning, the weather would be better and the trials could be carried out.

The weather the next day, Tuesday, April 2, indeed proved a marked improvement. Yet again, the ship's crewmen were aboard early – the firemen by 4:00 a.m., and the seamen by 6:00 a.m. In the early hours of that morning, it was rapidly becoming clear that with the weather's moderation, the greatly-anticipated event would actually

come to pass. In the ship's galleys, the victualling staff was beginning to prepare the first meal that would be served aboard the liner in open water. The ship's machinery was humming, as if in anticipation of taking to the sea for the first time.

Workmen from Harland & Wolff were still aboard that morning, yet engaged in the task of finishing the ship. Thirty-three-year-old First Class Dining Saloon Steward Frederick Dent Ray, who had just transferred from the *Olympic*, was wandering the corridors between the First Class staterooms on C Deck. He happened across a carpet layer installing carpeting in one of the staterooms. Noticing some small remnants in the corner, he asked the man if he could bring a piece home with him. Apparently, the piece was too small to be of use elsewhere, and the workman agreed. Ray took a scrap and brought it back to his home in Reading.[157]

Other details of the ship's fittings were also incomplete. It would seem that as the ship prepared to leave Belfast on her trials, the iconic clock due to be installed on the wall paneling of the top half-landing of the Forward Grand Staircase was still absent. According to Charles Wilson – carver of the central portion of the 'Honour and Glory Crowning Time' panel on *Olympic*, and a similar panel on *Titanic* – there was not enough time to set the clock, and a

Above left: The weather on April 2 shows a marked improvement. Titanic's funnels belch large quantities of coal smoke. The liner is about to begin her trials, but the boarding ramp has not yet been removed.

Above right: With the boarding ramp now taken away, Titanic is about to venture from her place of birth for the first time.

mirror was temporarily substituted in its place.[158] It is thus quite possible that the clock still had not been installed when the ship left Southampton on her maiden voyage.[159] Work on the ship's as-yet incomplete details would continue through the trials and, if they were successful, the trip to Southampton and her subsequent stay in that port prior to the maiden voyage.

Thomas Andrews was certainly busy that Tuesday morning, since he had been assigned to head up the builder's delegation during the trials. It was a weighty responsibility, but one that he was eminently well-qualified to handle. He was accompanied by Edward Wilding and a contingent of yard employees, all working to finish and test every possible feature of the ship and ensure that all of her systems were working flawlessly. Foremost among these employees of Harland & Wolff were eight men who would be accompanying Andrews on the maiden voyage. A special 'guarantee group' was typically sent with new deliveries on their maiden voyage, to make sure everything was working efficiently, and to see if any improvements could be made with the ships. Andrews would be heading up this group during the trip to Southampton, and on the subsequent maiden voyage; including him, the group would total nine men.

Andrews was booked in First Class, and would occupy cabin A-36, on the port side of the aft Grand Staircase's top level. Also booked as First Class passengers were 40-year-old Chief Draughtsman Roderick Robert Crispin Chisholm[160] and 29-year-old Electrical Department Assistant Manager William Henry Marsh Parr. The remaining men were booked in Second Class. They were 21-year-old Apprentice Joiner William H. Campbell; 21-year-old Apprentice Fitter Alfred 'Alfie' Fleming Cunningham; 37-year-old Foreman Fitter Anthony 'Artie' W. Frost; 39-year-old Fitter Robert Knight; 18-year-old Apprentice Plumber Francis 'Frank' Parkes; and 18-year-old Apprentice Electrician Ennis Hastings Watson. No matter what class the members of this group were booked in, they would have free reign of the entire ship throughout the crossing. Whether old or young, each of these individuals showed great promise within Harland & Wolff, for being selected as a member of the 'guarantee group' was a very special privilege.

Amongst those who did not board the ship that morning were Bruce Ismay and Lord Pirrie, the men who had first imagined the concept of the *Olympic* and *Titanic*, and who were ultimately unable to attend. Ismay was busy with other company matters, while Pirrie was having health issues at the time. As the final personnel climbed the gangplank, the time to depart had arrived. At around six o'clock that morning, the *Titanic* cast off and was shepherded down Victoria Channel and the Belfast Lough by a bevy of escorting tugs.

Belfast was a city accustomed to early mornings, and just as on the previous day many spectators turned out to see the liner off. They lined the banks of the Lough to watch, and photograph, the great ship as she ventured from the nest for the first time. Once the liner had entered the open water of the Irish Sea, the tugs cast off, and it was time for the *Titanic* to be put to the test.

The trials would run through the remainder of the morning and the afternoon. They would not be as long in duration as those of the *Olympic* the year before. This was in part because of the shortness of time, and in part because it was rightly expected that she would behave nearly the same as her older sister. Even so, the tests had to meet certain requirements so that Board of Trade Surveyor Carruthers could sign off on her passenger certificate. He later said:

> The trials consisted of running from slow up to full speed ahead, manoeuvring with the turbine cut out, going astern and swinging the vessel at full speed ahead with the helm hard over to test the steering gear.[161]

Carruthers was not the only one paying attention to the results of the various tests. Edward Wilding of Harland & Wolff recalled that the ship made two full turning circles, one of them with both engines at 'Full Ahead' and the helm thrown to starboard, turning the ship's bow to port. In the second circle, the helm was put to port, and the ship's starboard engine was then reversed and put 'Full Astern' to aid the maneuver. The ship entered each of these two turns at speeds between 18 and 20 knots.

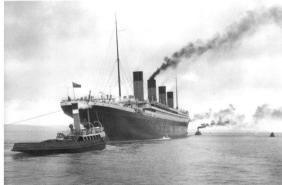

Top left: *Tugs shepherd the enormous liner through the confined waters of the Victoria Channel. The ship is moving northeast, and will soon reach less restricted waters.*

Top right: Titanic *steaming through the Belfast Lough.*

Above: *A splendid broadside view of the liner in the Lough.*

Left: *The ship threads a carefully marked route through the Lough as she moves toward open water.*

Further circles were also made at various speeds under starboard helm, at 11, 19½ knots, and 21½ knots. A full-stop test was also conducted. With the helm amidships, and the ship moving forward at 18 knots, both engines were reversed. It took the liner 3 minutes and 15 seconds to come to a complete stop, covering just over 3,000 feet in the process. Although this may seem like a positively enormous distance, the reality is that in accomplishing this, *Titanic* proved that she was able to stop in less than three-and-a-half times her own length; this is quite a swift reaction for a liner weighing over fifty thousand tons and slicing through

the water at high speed.[162] Fifth Officer Harold G. Lowe thought that the *Titanic* 'behaved splendidly and maneuvered very well' throughout the course of her trials.[163]

It took hours to carry these tests out. In the middle of the tests, lunch was served in the Dining Saloon. The menus were printed bearing the White Star Line house flag, as well as the logo of White Star's parent company, the Oceanic Steam Navigation Company. Despite the fact that the ship had not yet been formally handed over to White Star, it was clear that she would be. Options on the menu included salmon, sweetbreads, roast chicken, lamb with mint sauce, baked ham, and a variety of vegetables, sides and desserts. Doubtless those who attended the meal enthusiastically chatted about the liner's performance, comparing her results with those of other ships, including her sister, trying to guess how she would perform during the post-lunch tests. This meal really gave a glimpse of what life for First Class passengers would be like on her maiden voyage. It was the first hint of what lay just ahead on the horizon.

Throughout the day, Jack Phillips and Harold Bride had been virtually sequestered in their Marconi cabin. They were busy putting the liner's Marconi installation through its paces.[164] The Marconi engineers had only just finished with it before the ship was ready to leave, yet the results they obtained were very good. As the two men felt the great liner being maneuvered and tested in various ways beneath their feet, they were in communication with the Liverpool and Malin Head wireless stations.[165] Bride felt that their own tests were very satisfactory, and the set worked very well.[166]

Having passed her trials with flying colors, the *Titanic* returned to the Belfast Lough at about 6:00 p.m. that evening,[167] arriving in Belfast at about 7:00 p.m., or shortly after dusk.[168] Board of Trade Surveyor Carruthers was thoroughly pleased with her performance, and after testing both the port and starboard anchors and hauling them back up again to ensure the machinery worked as intended, he granted her 12-month certification as a passenger-carrying vessel.[169]

What came next was a bittersweet moment for everyone from Harland & Wolff who had worked so hard to bring this great ship to life. Many would not be proceeding with the ship to Southampton, and for these individuals, the time came to bid workmates, friends, and the ship herself a fond farewell.

Thomas Andrews was undoubtedly pleased with the liner's accomplishment that day, but he was sad to be leaving behind his family; his father was ill at the time, and his wife Helen had not been well, either.[170] He would doubtless also miss his daughter Elizabeth. Yet, he had much work ahead to keep his mind focused. Even as his friends and colleagues departed the *Titanic's* decks, Andrews and the rest of the builder's delegation still had much to do before the liner could actually depart Southampton on her maiden voyage. Although she had been granted a certificate for carrying passengers, she was far from a finished liner. Andrews wrote a quick line to his wife:

> Just a line to let you know that we got away this morning in fine style and have had a very satisfactory trial. We are getting more ship-shape every hour, but there is still a great deal to be done.[171]

Charles Lightoller noted that prior to *Titanic's* departure for Southampton, crewmembers and workers were busy bringing aboard materials and items that were 'required for the completion of the ship'. Amongst other things, these materials included 'requisites down in the galley, cooking apparatus, a few chairs, and such things as that'.[172]

Despite the ship's unfinished state, that evening one individual actually boarded the *Titanic* as a passenger. He was 61-year-old Wyckoff Van der Hoef, and he had booked passage not only to Southampton, but also right straight through to New York in First Class. Van der Hoef was returning to his home in New York, and it seems that he had decided that taking the *Titanic* would be an interesting way of concluding his trip despite the extended layover in Southampton.[173]

Once the last-minute supplies and equipment had been brought aboard, and after those not proceeding with the ship disembarked, the *Titanic* turned and departed Belfast, bound for Southampton and the start of her new career. It was about 8:00 p.m., April 2, 1912.[174] As the liner slowly steamed away down the Belfast Lough, her brilliant lights reflecting on the surface of the water, the throb of her engines began to fade in the distance. Finally, she vanished from the sight of those left behind in the great shipbuilding city. *Titanic* had ventured from the nest.

At that point, there was very little evidence that the *Titanic* had ever been present, that so many laborers had toiled and sacrificed – that some had even given their lives – in the construction of the great ship. She was now her own entity, even as the *Olympic* was. For those left behind who were intimately connected with the *Titanic*, however, there was more work at hand: her younger sister *Britannic* lay on the ways, her construction yet in its earliest stages. It would take years of labor before she, too, would steam from Belfast to begin her own career.

That Tuesday night, although they had been quite insulated from the action with the ship's trials, the wireless operators learned just how well the battery of tests had gone. The news broke when a number of telegrams addressed to the White Star offices at Liverpool and Southampton – including some sent specifically to Bruce Ismay – came through for transmission. Through these messages, the operators learned that the 'trials of the ship were very favorable'.[175] Impressively, as the ship steamed toward Southampton that night, Phillips and Bride were able to make direct contact and exchange messages with stations at Tenerife, in the Canary Islands, and Port Said, Egypt.[176]

Through that night and the following day, April 3, the *Titanic* steamed south in overall good weather, although there was some fog between two and six in the morning on Wednesday.[177] Yet when the fog dispersed, it turned into a 'fine and bright' day, all in all 'quite presentable'. The sea was fairly smooth, at least for liners of *Titanic's* ilk, and quite favorable for making good time. For several hours that day, the liner reportedly achieved a speed of about 23¼ knots – two full knots over her originally-intended speed.[178]

Edward Wilding, Thomas Andrews' right-hand man, had stayed aboard the liner with a number of other Harland & Wolff employees beyond the 'guarantee group' that would sail on the maiden voyage. They busied themselves carrying out 'further trials' and tests on board, to make sure that the liner's equipment would be fully ready to accept her first load of passengers in just seven days' time. There was a 'still further electrical trial, trials involving the sanitary arrangements and various other matters of that sort', Wilding recalled. Indeed, these trials included 'trying everything in the ship, and there [were] a good many things to try'.[179] Thomas Andrews must have been a consistent blur of activity. It was said:

> During the whole of Wednesday, the 3rd, until midnight, when the ship arrived at Southampton, Andrews was ceaselessly employed going round with representatives of the owners and of the Firm, in taking notes and preparing reports of work still to be done.[180]

Andrews did find time to eat, however. Saloon Steward Frederick Ray remembered that he was assigned to wait on

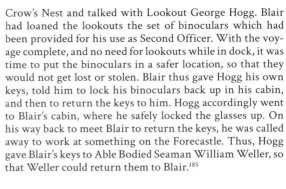

Crow's Nest and talked with Lookout George Hogg. Blair had loaned the lookouts the set of binoculars which had been provided for his use as Second Officer. With the voyage complete, and no need for lookouts while in dock, it was time to put the binoculars in a safer location, so that they would not get lost or stolen. Blair thus gave Hogg his own keys, told him to lock his binoculars back up in his cabin, and then to return the keys to him. Hogg accordingly went to Blair's cabin, where he safely locked the glasses up. On his way back to meet Blair to return the keys, he was called away to work at something on the Forecastle. Thus, Hogg gave Blair's keys to Able Bodied Seaman William Weller, so that Weller could return them to Blair.[185]

Above: *A summer 1911 view of the new London & South Western Railway docks, where the* Titanic *would tie up.*

Right: *The inside of the pier building's upper floor, still under construction.*

Andrews' table during the trip down to Southampton. Ray was already acquainted with Andrews, having served him previously on the *Olympic*.[181]

Eventually, the *Titanic* turned east, entering the English Channel and steaming along the southern coast of England. That Wednesday, *Olympic* had departed her berth in Southampton, west-bound for New York via Cherbourg and Queenstown. As the *Titanic* passed the island of Portland, the two ships were in communication with one another via wireless.[182] As the sunlight began to fade in the western skies, *Titanic* began to near her new English center of operations: Southampton. The Trinity House Harbor Pilot, most likely George Bowyer, boarded the brilliantly-lit ship and guided her up the dark waterways toward her berth.[183]

Eventually the great liner reached the vicinity of the White Star Dock, Berth 44, and she was maneuvered in stern-first by a half-dozen tugs. Apparently, Pilot Bowyer and the tug commanders had learned from the difficult time they had bringing the *Olympic* out of the same berth on her maiden voyage the previous year, when she had been docked bow-first and had to be turned prior to departure, and they were determined not to have a repeat performance. The *Titanic* tied up at about midnight that Wednesday night-Thursday morning, her trip from Belfast having encompassed approximately 570 miles.[184] The arrival was without any formal salutes or fanfare, no visiting dignitaries to be formally welcomed aboard, or anything of the sort. In fact it was quite a quiet scene, very different from the noisy welcome *Olympic* had enjoyed nearly a year before. When *Titanic* tied up, Second Officer Blair went up to the

The *Titanic* arrived in Southampton in the middle of an absolute nightmare, both for the port, for all steamship lines, for railway travel – indeed, for all of the United Kingdom. This nightmare had come in the form of a nationwide coal strike; some estimates said that the strikers amounted to a million men. The strike was centered upon the workers' desire for a minimum wage. Coal was the fuel of the day, powering ships, locomotives, industry, and heating private homes as well. Liners were nothing short of ravenous for the bituminous black substance. Everything in the nation's economy depended on a steady supply of coal being handy, and without it, everything began to grind to a halt.

The strike had begun on February 29, 1912, and initial optimism that it would pass quickly began to fade. The coal unions had in their coffers about $10,000,000 when the strike started,[186] and paid the workers a strike pay. As deliveries of coal began to fall off, ships were laid up, causing thousands of men and women employed on those ships to similarly become unemployed; however, they did not benefit from strike pay.

White Star needed to find enough fuel for the *Titanic's* maiden voyage, and so they canceled upcoming passages of some of the smaller White Star and IMM ships, and laid the ships up in Southampton. Then the coal from those ships – along with some leftover fuel from the *Olympic's* previous coaling – was transferred to *Titanic's* cavernous bunkers. As a result of these cancellations, dock space in Southampton was at such a premium that some liners were tied up side by side in sets of two or three, instead of with each ship being given their own berth. Among the vessels laid up were the famous White Star liners *Majestic* and *Oceanic*. So, too, were the famous American liners New York, *Philadelphia*, *St Louis* and *St Paul*. Some of the passengers booked on the smaller ships had their passages transferred to the new White Star vessel.

Meanwhile, the British economy as a whole began to show signs of strain. The miners' unions had spent the equivalent of $6 million in a little over a month. Towards the end of March, it was said:

> The coal strike appears to have settled down into a test of endurance between the miners and operators. Gloom pervades the country, with all classes suffering from the effects of industrial war.
>
> The confidential reports of the operators because of which they refused all concessions stated that the miners generally were at the end of their resources. Facing starvation, it was asserted, they would be forced to give in, and it was pointed out by the leading operators that if they stood firm they would utterly wreck the unions.
>
> The miners deny, however, that they are in such shape financially and that further resistance is hopeless. They have reduced strike benefits and claim they can hold out for another fortnight, by which time they say the operators will have been forced to concede their demands.[187]

While there were still funds remaining in the union coffers for strike pay, soon a growing number of the workers – some 30,000 by April 3, with another 10,000 more the following day – had begun to break the lines and return to work. It was clear that the strike would not last much longer.

Finally, on Saturday, April 6, the Miners' Federation ended the strike by a vote of 440 to 125. The loss of coal output from the mines was estimated at 28 million tons during the five-week ordeal – a monetary loss of over £11.2 million, the equivalent of about $56 million at the time. It was said that the strike had paralyzed 'half the trade of the United Kingdom for a month, causing misery to millions of persons'. The railway companies alone, estimates ran, had suffered losses of some $12.5 million as a result, although it was also said that 'the full extent of the mischief' would 'never be known'.[188] However, even with the strike's end, it was going to take quite some time before things would return to normal:

> In Scotland the miners will return to the collieries on Monday [April 8], but as that day is a holiday in England and Wales, the strikers there will not return to the coal fields until Tuesday. In many mines two or three days more will elapse before repairs can be completed. By the end of the week, however, it is expected that every colliery will be in full swing ...
>
> In North Wales the miners in general have returned to work, but many pits are blocked with debris and several days must pass before coal can be produced from them.[189]

After work had resumed in the mines, it was going to take still longer for the coal to reach the waterfronts in Southampton. Thus, although news of the strike's end was welcome to many in Southampton, it was clear that unemployment in the shipping-oriented city would still be rife when the *Titanic*

departed on her maiden voyage. Consequently, demand for employment as a member of her crew was very high. Most of the crew who would be joining the *Titanic* signed on during Saturday, April 6 – the same day that the coal strike had ended.

The maiden voyage of a new ship was always a trying time for her crew – particularly for those in the victualling department who had to cater to passengers' needs and wishes. One of *Titanic*'s First Class Stewardesses, 24-year-old Violet Jessop, remembered that the first trip of the *Olympic* had been 'somewhat of an education'.[190] *Olympic* was so much larger than any previous White Star liner – indeed, any previous ship in the world – that it took quite a bit of time for her crew to become accustomed to her scale, her facilities, and to simultaneously attempt to keep service for the passengers as smooth as they were on any other ship. Eventually, Jessop – who stayed with the *Olympic* through March of 1912 – and the other members of that liner's crew, had grown comfortable with the ship.

The maiden voyage of the *Titanic*, it was hoped, would prove less unfamiliar to the crew. When the *Olympic* had departed Southampton on Wednesday, April 3, she had left behind nearly two hundred and fifty of her nearly nine hundred-person crew, who would subsequently join *Titanic* on her maiden voyage. It was hoped that these individuals, highly experienced in the operation of her similar sister, would ensure a smooth transition into service for *Titanic*. Happily, the auburn-haired, blue-gray-eyed Jessop, who spoke with a trace Irish brogue, would find many familiar faces from the *Olympic* among *Titanic*'s crew members. Jessop was also well acquainted with Thomas Andrews, who she admired for his kindness to the crew.

Andrews was a busy man during the six-day stretch while *Titanic* was in Southampton. He was up early on Thursday, April 4, left the South Western Hotel where he was staying, and spent the day 'with managers and foremen putting work in hand'.[191] When White Star had moved its primary English terminus from Liverpool to Southampton in 1907, they had soon asked Harland & Wolff to set up facilities in that port to help maintain and service their liners. This branch of the Belfast shipbuilding firm was actually quite extensive, situated upon a two-acre site. Included in the works was a boiler shop, platers' shed, joiners' department, electrical shop, and more. There was also a suite of offices.[192]

It was with these local facilities and employees that Andrews and the other members of the 'builder's delegation' coordinated in order to help finish the *Titanic* by the following Tuesday night. Things must have gone fairly well in the course of that Thursday, for in the evening he wrote to his wife:

> I wired you this morning of our safe arrival after a very satisfactory trip. The weather was good and everyone most pleasant. I think the ship will clean up all right before sailing on Wednesday.[193]

Andrews went on to mention that Lord Pirrie's doctors had refused to allow him to make the maiden voyage. From that point on, Andrews was constantly busy. Andrews' secretary, Thompson Hamilton, wrote this account of Andrews' activities at the English port:

> Through the various days that the vessel lay at Southampton, Mr. Andrews was never for a mo-

ment idle. He generally left his hotel about 8.30 for the offices, where he dealt with his correspondence, then went on board until 6.30, when he would return to the offices to sign letters. During the day I took to the ship any urgent papers and he always dealt with them no matter what his business. He would himself put in their place such things as racks, tables, chairs, berth ladders, electric fans, saying that except he saw everything right he could not be satisfied.[194]

As energetic as this activity might at first sound, they may have seemed a nearly leisurely set of hours compared to those that Andrews was accustomed to keeping in Belfast.

Certain issues were identified with the ship. These would need to be taken care of, but there would only be time to do this after the maiden voyage. There was some sort of serious trouble with the Restaurant Galley hot press. Andrews also considered and advanced a design to reduce the number of screws in stateroom hat hooks. He agreed with the owners that the coloring of the pebble dashing on the Private Promenades was too dark. There was also a plan in motion to stain the wicker furniture on one side of the ship green.[195]

Beyond the actual technical problems – and considering the enormity of the task Harland & Wolff had accomplished despite setbacks, there were remarkably few of them – there still remained the small matter of finishing the ship. There were a number of details still being seen to, and as it turned out some would still be incomplete when she departed on the morning of Wednesday, April 10. Some of the Second Class areas were not fully furnished, including the lavatories. In one such section, it was reported that only about half of the fixtures had been put in place, and that some of the fixtures were sitting in crates, waiting to be installed.[196] Some of the staterooms themselves had also not been finished by the time she left Southampton.

Much of the ship's china, glassware and cutlery were not brought aboard until the liner was in Southampton. Crate after crate of the items were carried up the gangplanks and carefully unpacked. Location-specific items – the china for the First Class Dining Saloon, for example, was quite different than that used in the First Class Restaurant – had to be brought to the correct area before they could be unpacked and finally stored.

In addition to attempts to have the ship ready in time for the start of her maiden voyage, there was a full list of all of the things that usually had to be done to prepare a ship for trans-Atlantic passage. This included coaling the vessel. By early in the morning of Thursday, April 4, the ship had been 'boomed out' about twenty feet from the pier; as odd as this process might sound, it actually was quite simple in execution. By placing booms against the sides of the ship and pushing her away from the dock, and then making the mooring lines quite fast to keep her from drifting further out, this provided a stable gap between the side of the ship's hull and the dock wall. The opening allowed coal barges, commonly known as 'coalies,' from the R. & J. H. Rea Company to slide along not only her starboard side, but also her port side – an important consideration for simplifying the process of loading fuel aboard.

The coaling process was notoriously gritty, grimy and back-breaking, but the Rea Company had things down to quite a science. Once the coaling barges were alongside, Titanic's thirty-five coal ports – eighteen along her port side, and seventeen on the starboard side – were opened. These coal ports, located just above the waterline, led to chutes that permitted coal to tumble down into the bunkers, where it was subsequently distributed to prevent the ship from listing one way or another. Coaling outriggers, mounted along the sides of the Promenade Deck far above, would then be swung out. Lines were then attached to the outriggers, which would then be used to haul buckets of coal from the barges up to the coal doors, and dump each bucket down the chute.[197] It was a tremendously messy and noisy job, but Rea was said to be able to load over 4,000 tons of coal in 15 working hours by 1911. This was a world record, but quite naturally had to be split up, thus translating into a good two working days.[198]

For Titanic, the coaling process would thus have encompassed not only Thursday, April 4, but Friday, as well. In all, she took on some 4,427 tons of fresh coal, including what had been transferred from the bunkers of other White Star and IMM ships laid up in port. With some 1,880 tons of coal left in her bunkers when she arrived in Southampton, and burning a total of 415 tons during her six-day stay in port, upon departure she had some 5,892 tons of coal aboard. This was not a capacity load for her bunkers, but considering the coal shortage, it was quite respectable, and would probably have left her with about one thousand tons of spare coal at the crossing's end.[199]

The Olympic had been opened for public inspection three times before her maiden voyage: once, on May 27, 1911, in Belfast; again, on June 1, 1911 in her registered home port of Liverpool; and finally on June 10, 1911, in Southampton. The proceeds from the small admission prices benefited local charities. However, because the Titanic was so thoroughly behind schedule in completion, there had been no public inspection in Belfast, and the stopover in Liverpool had also been canceled. Similarly, White Star had to extend their apologies to local Southampton residents: the Titanic would not have a public inspection during her first stay in the port. Only later, after the maiden voyage, would there be time for the public at large to become thoroughly acquainted with the ship. As a sort of salute to the city, however, Titanic was dressed in a dazzling array of multi-colored flags from early in the morning of Thursday, April 4.

That same morning, a local photographer went down to the much disorganized Berth 44, which appeared to be strewn with rubble. He snapped a bow-on picture of the liner with Rea's 'coalies' alongside, and the celebratory flags fluttering from her rigging. By the end of the day, the photo had been reproduced in post card format and made available to the public for purchase. A proud Fourth Officer Boxhall picked up a copy of the post card and wrote upon it before the day was out, mentioning that the photo had been taken earlier on that same Thursday.[200]

In addition to the coaling process, there was a considerable amount of cargo to load aboard. There was also bedding and other linens to be brought on to the ship and stored; there were beds to make, pillows to fluff, and a good deal of other work to do to make the ship presentable for her first batch of passengers. Yet, for many of the ship's crew who had come down from Belfast and would be continuing on the maiden voyage, the six days their ship would spend in Southampton meant time to spend seeing the sights of the local area.

Top left: *This photo was taken on Thursday, April 4. The ship is already being coaled for her maiden voyage; she is dressed as a salute to the city of Southampton. This photo, in postcard form, was printed, distributed, sold, and posted before the day was out.*

Top right: Titanic *remains dressed, and coaling continues.*

Above right: *This view of* Titanic *was likely taken from a passing harbor vessel or the Hythe ferry in the River Test.*

Left: *Although somewhat grainy, this photograph of* Titanic's *Bridge and Forecastle shows men on the ratlines for the foremast.*

For Marconi Operators Jack Phillips and Harold Bride, there was very little to do. As employees of the Marconi Company, and not the White Star Line or Harland & Wolff, it was not their job to pitch in and help finish the ship, load her cargo, or tend to the malfunctioning Restaurant Galley hot press. Their business was the wireless, and as the ship was in port, there seems to have been a notable absence of work to accomplish. Apparently, they went ashore pretty much every day. Phillips even made an excursion to Cowes, on the Isle of Wight, on Friday, April 5, and noted that the weather was glorious.[201]

Naturally the ship's officers needed to maintain their standard in-port watches. There was always a senior officer – either Chief Officer Murdoch, First Officer Lightoller, or Second Officer Blair – on duty during the day, alongside one of the junior officers. At night, two of the junior officers maintained the watch, although Second Of-

ficer Blair stood watch on the night of April 4.[202] However, in their off-duty hours even the officers were free to go ashore.

Yet almost as soon as the *Titanic* had tied up in Southampton, there came news of a significant change in the ranks of her senior officer corps. *Olympic's* Chief Officer, 39-year-old Henry T. Wilde had been kept ashore when the *Olympic* departed Southampton on April 3, and was assigned to make the *Titanic's* first round-trip voyage. Lightoller later recalled that Wilde had stayed ashore because he was to receive 'command of another of the White Star steamers, which, owing to the coal strike and other reasons was laid up'.[203]

The news was not entirely welcome to the senior officers who had already been attached to the ship. Then Chief Officer William Murdoch was forced to step back to First Officer; First Officer Lightoller likewise stepped back to fill the role of Second Officer. Second Officer David Blair found that he had become superfluous, and was to be left behind.

On Thursday, April 4, David Blair got to spend the day at his home. Having picked up a picture post card of the liner, he took the opportunity to dash off a note:

Top left: *The stern Boat Deck on the port side, looking forward.*

Top right: *This photo shows that the photographer has likely turned to face aft. Crates of supplies and material have been brought aboard and sit on the Well Deck.*

Left: *A stern view of the liner at her berth.*

4th, Southampton
Arrived on 'Titanic' from Belfast today. Am afraid I shall have to step out to make room for [the] Chief Officer of the Olympic who was going in command but so many ships laid up he will have to wait. Hope eventually to get back to this ship ... Been home all day and down on board tonight on watch. This is a magnificent ship, I feel very disappointed I am not to make the first voyage.[204]

He posted the note to a Miss Mackness of Broughty Ferry, Scotland. Interestingly, although Blair was disappointed not to be able to sail with the *Titanic* on April 10, he stayed with the ship during the entire time she was in Southampton. The note quoted above mentioned that he would stand watch on the night of Thursday, April 4, and other officers from the liner recalled that Wilde did not formally join the ship until the evening of Tuesday, April 9.[205] Thus throughout the stay in Southampton, officer designations – with Murdoch as Chief Officer, and so forth – remained officially unchanged.

Henry Wilde was a good officer, accomplished and highly able. He had served as a Lieutenant in the Royal Navy Reserve, and had also seen service aboard the White Star liners *Republic, Coptic, Majestic, Baltic, Adriatic* and *Olympic*. He was a widower supporting four children since his wife's untimely death a year and a half before. Not unexpectedly, he had some difficulty overcoming the tragic loss. Her passing had hit him so hard that an acquaintance heard him remark that 'he didn't care particularly how he

went or how soon he joined her.'[206] Despite this, there is no evidence that Wilde was anything but ready and willing to serve when he returned to work, although he was a bit apprehensive about the switch to *Titanic*.[207] Lightoller called Wilde 'a pretty big, powerful chap, and he was a man that would not argue very long.'[208]

Understandably, the other officers were somewhat dissatisfied with the alteration in officer positions, although there is no direct evidence that they harbored any resentment toward Wilde for his presence. Lightoller recalled the change-up, however, as 'unfortunate'. He felt that it was a 'doubtful policy' which 'threw both Murdoch and me out of our stride; and, apart from our disappointment of having to step back in our rank, caused quite a little confusion.' Although he recalled that they settled into their new positions quickly, events on sailing day and thereafter would prove that there was still some lingering confusion.[209] A sort of ship-board game of 'musical cabins' subsequently ensued within the Officers' Quarters. Murdoch and Lightoller had to leave their own quarters, in which they had been settled since before leaving Belfast, and move: Murdoch to Lightoller's, and Lightoller to Blair's old cabin. Meanwhile, Wilde moved into Murdoch's cabin, and Blair had to make sure he had cleared out of his quarters.

In another interesting twist, it would seem that the decision to bring Wilde aboard was so last-minute, and in all likelihood so temporary, that Lightoller did not have time to change his uniform insignia or the number of stripes on his sleeves that reflected his rank. It is also quite likely that Murdoch did not alter his uniform.[210] Naturally, there would have been no need for Wilde to alter his uniform, as he had already been serving as the Chief Officer of the *Olympic*. Confusion continued to linger among many members of the crew, as well, with some using the term 'chief officer' to refer to Murdoch, and so forth.

The coaling process had most likely been finished by the end of Friday, April 5. The ship was pulled back in close to the dock's edge. By Monday, April 8, at the latest, the ship's dress flags had been put away. That same day, workmen perched precariously in bosun's chairs above the Boat Deck

Top left: *This photo was likely taken on Monday, April 8. The coaling process is complete and the ship has been placed back against the wharf.*

Bottom left: *Also taken on April 8, this beautiful view shows the White Star pennant fluttering from the mainmast. Paint crews touch up the funnel paint.*

Above: *Chief Officer Henry T. Wilde. He is seen here in his Royal Navy Reserve Lieutenant's uniform, c. 1911.*

Above right: *Lightoller's sleeves on April 11 still show the two stripes of a First Officer, even though he was then serving as Titanic's Second Officer.*

touched up the paint on the ship's quartet of smokestacks. The ship's white upper works on the port side had already received some 'touching up' just before leaving Belfast; rust, the bane of all steamships, had to be thoroughly tended and covered with fresh paint even in the newest of ships.

On Tuesday, April 9, Board of Trade Emigration Officer Maurice Clarke came aboard the *Titanic*. Clarke's responsibility was to make sure that the ship adhered to all Board of Trade safety regulations, and if she did, to clear her to depart the following day. Apparently, Clarke was a stickler for making sure that ships were properly equipped before

he signed off on clearance for their departures. First Officer Lightoller was very familiar with him; he recalled that, he and the other officers referred to him as a 'nuisance' because he made them 'fork out every detail'. Lightoller recalled that Clarke insisted on inspecting everything that contributed to the ship's life-saving equipment. 'Life preservers throughout the ship, all the boats turned out, uncovered, all the tanks examined, all the breakers examined, oars counted, boats turned out, rudders tried, all the davits tried – there was innumerable details work.'[211] Lightoller later said that during Clarke's work aboard the *Titanic*, he 'certainly lived up to his reputation of being the best cursed B.O.T. representative in the South of England at that time.'[212]

Among the more exotic tests carried out that day was the ship's stability test. Then First Officer Lightoller described it thus:

> The builders knowing the exact weights on board, additional weights are placed on each side of the ship. A pendulum is suspended in the most convenient place in the ship with a plumb on the end of it, and a method of registering the difference with the plumb line; a number of men then transfer the weights from one side of the ship to the other, bringing all the weight on one side and transferring the whole of it back again; and with this, I believe the builders are able to draw up a stability scale.[213]

In this particular instance, the test was carried out on C Deck, not quite amidships. In all, Lightoller was with Clarke for about four hours that day; he then passed Clarke on to the care of Chief Officer Murdoch – no doubt with a measure of relief.[214] Eventually, Clarke had completed as much of his work as he could for the day and departed; he would return early the next morning to finish the job.

During that same Tuesday, Second Officer Blair had enough time to take his sister aboard the ship for a tour. *Titanic* was so big that it took several hours for Blair to lead her throughout the vessel. Even at this late stage, the ship was still a 'hive of activity', as carpets were still being laid and decorators were hard at work trying to finish up the last few details.[215]

Although not specifically mentioned by Blair's sister, we know that much interior painting had been carried out during the stay in Southampton, and some may even have been done on the day before sailing, as it seems that not all of it had completely cured by sailing time. Several passengers, upon boarding on April 10, recalled that certain sections of the ship smelled strongly of fresh paint.

The presence of this strong chemical smell may partially explain why the *Titanic* was remembered by at least one of her passengers as a 'ship full of flowers.'[216] Although floral arrangements for ships like the *Olympic* and *Titanic* were always quite extensive, steamship companies habitually provided more flowers on board a ship which had just received fresh paint in her interior spaces, in an attempt to mask the smell.[217] Such a provision seems to have been made in *Titanic*'s case, for the sheer number of flowers aboard seemed to stand out even to seasoned First Class travelers during the voyage.

The flowers themselves were brought aboard on Tuesday evening by a local florist, Frank Bealing, his son Frank, Jr., and the Bealings' foreman, W. F. 'Bill' Geapin. The Bealings had the contract to supply all flowers for White Star liners calling in Southampton, and were very proud to have such an illustrious client. They arrived at Berth 44 in a mule-driven cart loaded with hundreds of potted plants, large and small. A tarpaulin was spread out on the floor in one of the ship's foyers, and the plants were carried aboard and placed on the tarp. Then the flowers were distributed to the individual cabins and public rooms. Some even went into cool storage so that they could look fresh as they were

Top left: *This photograph was apparently taken on April 9, and shows the Bridge and forward superstructure from the Forecastle, just forward of the breakwater.*

Top right: *Left to right, the* Majestic, Philadelphia *and* St Louis *are berthed on the opposite side of the LSWR docks.* Titanic's *stern can be seen on the right edge of the photograph.*

Above left: *A stern view of the* Titanic *in her dock, with the hull of the* St Louis *on the extreme right.*

Above right: *A large consignment of bottled beer inside the upper level of the pier building, waiting to be loaded aboard the liner.*

brought out and placed in various locations, such as the tables of the First Class Dining Saloon, during the course of the crossing.[218]

By that night, it was becoming clear that things were actually going to come together for the scheduled sailing time of noon the following day. Thomas Andrews wrote to his wife: 'The *Titanic* is now about complete and will I think do the old Firm credit to-morrow when we sail.'[219] Former Second Officer David Blair made his last departure from the liner, no doubt still wishing he could have remained aboard for the trip.[220] That night, Fourth Officer Boxhall returned to the *Titanic* from his last shore excursion at about 11:00 o'clock.[221] He and the other officers of the ship would stay aboard for the last night in port. Senior Wireless Operator John 'Jack' Phillips and his assistant, Harold Bride, spent their last evening before the maiden voyage ashore, but they eventually found their way back aboard by 11:30 that night.[222]

Meanwhile Captain Smith went ashore and stayed overnight at his red brick, twin-gabled home – which was named Woodhead – on Winn Road. It was his last opportunity to spend time with his wife Sarah Eleanor and their 12-year-old daughter Helen, before an anticipated two-week round-trip voyage. It seems likely that Smith was going to retire after this prestigious round-trip voyage on the *Titanic*. He may very well have looked forward to spending more time with his family in the months and years ahead. But there was one last task at hand, and it was to be the crowning achievement of his career: he would be commanding the world's largest, newest and greatest ship on her maiden voyage.

Through that night, the *Titanic* sat at Berth 44, White Star Dock. Her dark shape dwarfed the pier-side structure, her size only given away by the amount of horizon that she blocked out, and the number of her windows and portholes which stood out at her side. A slight whiff of coal smoke might have been in the air, as her auxiliary equipment was providing electrical power to the ship. Every now and then, an officer could have been seen walking back and forth on the Bridge and Bridge wing. Overall, the scene would have been quiet.

There must have been an aura of anticipation surrounding her presence. One wonders how many of her crew, her officers, and of the Harland & Wolff personnel who had come down to take passage aboard her had trouble sleeping from excitement. What would the morning bring with it? Only time would tell, but one thing was for sure: all of the hustle and bustle of sailing day was coming quickly, and activity would begin very early the next morning.

The Last Voyage?

Over the years, there has been extreme controversy over whether or not the maiden voyage of the *Titanic* was slated to be Captain Smith's last round-trip before a quiet retirement at the pinnacle of a long and largely uneventful career. While many have simply reported that this was to be Smith's final voyage, others find the story unlikely. Those who fall into the latter category cite two press stories published in a Halifax newspaper just a few days after the disaster.

These papers reported that Smith would have remained in command of the *Titanic* until such time as 'a larger and finer steamer' entered service with the White Star Line. Such reports could only have been referring to the *Britannic*, third of the *Olympic*-class ships. Although the information purportedly came from White Star officials, the reference to the new steamer was quite vague, particularly as the ship had already been laid down four months before, and was well known to be under construction in Belfast. Yet no connection to the *Olympic* and *Titanic* was made, despite the fact that the new liner was the third of the class. The reference seems so vague, in fact, that it begins to cast a shadow of suspicion on exactly who the sources were.

Based on experience with the first two ships of the class, from the *Britannic*'s status in April of 1912 it would have been expected to take at least two to two-and-a-half full years before she would be ready to enter service. In fact, delays in the third ship's construction, due to a number of factors, would delay her delivery even further. When he took command of the *Titanic* in April of 1912, Smith was already 62 years old. This means that he would have been no less than 64 years of age when the White Star Line anticipated the *Britannic* to enter service, and possibly older. In 1910, the Cunard Line had placed a 60-year-old age limit for skippers of their crack liners *Lusitania* and *Mauretania*. To expect Smith to stay in service until 64 or 65 years of age for the third ship of the class would, on its own, seem an unreasonable delay in retirement for him.

Interestingly, the *New York Times* of June 6, 1911 reported:

> Capt. E. J. Smith, R.N.R., the Commodore [*sic*] of the White Star Line, who is to command the new mammoth liner *Olympic*, will retire at the end of the present year, it is understood, as he will have reached the age limit. He will be relieved by Capt. H. J. Haddock of the *Oceanic*.

This well-put-together report was circulated well before the *Titanic* disaster, instead of shortly after when press stories were at times playing fast and loose with the facts. Interestingly, we have yet to find a retraction or correction on this retirement story between June of 1911 and April of 1912.

So although far more ironic in hindsight, it seems that Captain Smith's career was extended for a few months past the end of 1911 in order to give him the honor of taking out the *Titanic*. Not only would this have been a wonderful 'thank you' from a grateful company, but it would have served the dual purpose of ensuring that a skipper experienced with ships of *Titanic*'s ilk would be at her helm during the maiden voyage.

CHAPTER 2

AN AUSPICIOUS CROSSING

Day One – Wednesday, April 10, 1912.

Dawn arrived in Southampton, England, at 5:23 a.m.[1] The day was rather overcast, but every now and then the sun poked brilliantly through the clouds.[2] The temperature during the morning stood at about 48° Fahrenheit.[3] *Titanic* towered over the Southampton waterfront. The *Majestic*, *St Louis* and *Philadelphia* – all tied up astern of the *Titanic* on the opposite side of the new London & South Western Railway Dock facility – looked positively diminutive by comparison. The swallow-tailed White Star house flag fluttered from the peak of the *Titanic*'s mainmast.[4] The mighty liner sparkled in all her resplendent newness.

At 6:00 a.m., Thomas Andrews boarded the *Titanic*, having stayed one last night in his room at the South Western Hotel. Immediately upon boarding, he began a thorough inspection of the ship. He was pleased with what he found, it was said.[5] It was also at 6:00 a.m. that many of the *Titanic*'s crew members began to gather aboard.[6] The number of crew boarding the ship began to increase as time passed, as all had to be on hand in time for the crew muster.

Those who hadn't already been aboard during the ship's stay in Southampton made their way to their quarters to drop off their kits and get settled in. How many of them managed to find their way to the proper quarters quickly is anyone's guess. Certainly, most of those who had come over from the *Olympic* could have found their way around easily enough – although there were some differences between the two ships that no doubt confused even those crewmen. Those who reported aboard from other, smaller liners were no doubt stunned by the ship's size. Once they found their accommodations, there were many old shipmates to catch up with, and some new faces to meet, as well. For the most part, however, things were all business that morning.

Captain Smith left his home on Winn Road, which was about two and a half miles north of White Star Dock, at about 7:00 a.m. As he came out his front door, the local paperboy, 11-year-old Albert 'Ben' Benham, was at the house next door. The young lad caught up with Smith, and the Captain said: 'Alright son, I'll take my paper.'[7] Smith then proceeded to Berth 44, arriving at about 7:30 a.m. By 8:00 a.m., a 15-foot long Blue Ensign was raised at the ensign staff on the stern. There were two British Ensigns, one red and one blue. The Blue Ensign could only be flown upon Admiralty warrant aboard a ship whose Captain, as well as at least 10 ratings or officers, were members of the Royal

Naval Reserve. Hoisting this particular ensign was thus another special honor for the world's largest ship.[8]

Like Captain Smith, British Board of Trade Immigration Officer Captain Maurice Clarke also boarded at about 7:30 a.m.[9] In the limited time available to him that morning, Clarke had to oversee the crew muster and the lifeboat drill. White Star's Southampton Marine Superintendent, Captain Benjamin Steele, also boarded early that morning. His responsibility was to ensure that all of the proverbial ducks were in order as far as the Company was concerned.

The crew members began to assemble for the formal muster at about 8:00 a.m.; as the ship's crew was so large, they had to congregate in a number of different locations. The firemen were mustered in one area, the seamen in another, and the stewards in a third. One by one, every member of the ship's crew had to assemble and pass in a line before Captain Smith, the ship's officers and surgeons, Captain Clarke, Captain Steele, and the Board of Trade Doctor.[10] The sign-on sheets were produced, roll-call taken, and a firm head count was also taken. A medical examination was made – an important detail, although probably rather cursory in nature considering the somewhat limited time available that morning – to make sure that the crew members were all in good health. As could be expected, there were a few crewmen who had signed on but who had not actually shown up for duty. Replacements were on hand and quickly signed aboard. It took about an hour for this task to be completed.[11]

The crew dispersed from the muster; firemen not on duty were free to go ashore as long as they returned before the ship sailed. Many of those who disembarked for the remainder of the morning did so to visit the local pubs for a last pint. In the meanwhile, stewards, stewardesses and others in the victualling department could not go ashore, as they had to prepare for and tend to arriving passengers.

After the muster, almost the entire Deck Department – which was comprised of some sixty-six men – headed up to the starboard Boat Deck for the ship's lifeboat drill.[12] By about 9:00 a.m.,[13] Chief Officer Wilde, First Officer Murdoch, Second Officer Lightoller, Third Officer Pitman, Fifth Officer Lowe, and Sixth Officer Moody were assembled along with the rest of the men.[14] Lowe and Moody were selected to take charge of the two lifeboats chosen for testing, Boats Nos 11 and 13.[15] Lowe took Boat No. 11, and Moody took No. 13.

The two lifeboats were uncovered, swung out, and lowered until level with the deck. Eight crewmen – quar-

---

Opposite: *This bow view of the* Titanic *gives a good idea of what she looked like to those standing on the wharf on the morning of April 10, 1912. The photo was taken earlier during* Titanic's *stay, however; workers can be seen touching up the ship's white paint amidships.*

Top: *In this photo,* Titanic *glistens. A careful inspection shows that much of her starboard hull had recently received fresh paint along its length.*

Above left: *Captain Smith standing on the Bridge of the* Titanic *on the morning of April 10, 1912.*

Above right: *This photo is of* Titanic's *A Deck Promenade. The photographer is looking forward on the port side. Judging from the angle of the sun and shadows, the photo was taken at about 9:30 in the morning of the departure. The weather that day was only partly sunny.*

Left: *A typical crew muster on the* Olympic.

termasters and Able-Bodied Seamen – were placed into each of the boats.[16] They tied on lifebelts, and then they were lowered away under Captain Clarke's watchful eye.[17] White Star Marine Superintendent Captain Steele was also present and overseeing the test. Usually, the boats would have had their sails raised and tested once in the water, but on that morning the winds were a bit gusty, so that part of the drill was canceled.[18] Instead, the boats were rowed around the waterfront for 'a couple of turns', before returning to the ship and being hoisted back up to the deck.[19] In all, the drill had lasted about a half-hour.[20] Captain Clarke and Captain Steele were both satisfied with the results. Next, Fifth Officer Lowe and some of the other men headed off for a quick bit of breakfast before the ship departed.[21]

Meanwhile, the ship's passengers were beginning to converge on Southampton, and things at the dock were beginning to get rather busy. Two 'Titanic Special' Boat Trains had been scheduled to depart London's Waterloo Station that morning. One was for Second and Third Class passengers, while the other was for First Class passengers only. These Boat Trains would whisk passengers conveniently from London directly to the new London & South-Western Railway facilities at Southampton's Berth 44, directly adjacent to the towering side of the *Titanic*. If there were no delays, the exact length of this railway passage could run from about an hour and a half to an hour and three quarters.[22] First Class passengers nearly unanimously remembered that their Boat Train departed the London station at 8:00 a.m., but it would not arrive in Southampton until about 11:30.[23]

Boarding the First Class Boat Train at Waterloo that morning were 48-year-old Elmer Zebley Taylor and his 49-year-old wife, Juliet. Taylor later wrote:

> The boat train from Waterloo was scheduled to leave about 8:00 A.M. We took a 'growler' [a slang term for a four-wheel hansom cab] from Whitehall Hotel, 8 Montague Street, W. C., and when we arrived at Waterloo, three people were getting out of another 'growler' just ahead of us. I took a look, and said to my wife, 'What oh! John D. is going along with us.'
>
> Securing a porter, we moved along the platform without luggage, to find every compartment marked 'Engaged' or 'Occupied'. Finally, I dropped a half-crown in the conductor's hand, and asked him to find us seats. Much to my surprise, he unlocked the door of a compartment in which were seated, next to the corridor, the two ladies we saw getting out of the 'growler'. The old gentleman finally came along with a half dozen roses, the kind with long stems and single buds at the top. As soon as he entered, mother said (Mid-West twang) 'I thought you reserved a compartment for us.' 'So I did,' was his reply. Well, it was not long before we began to move along.[24]

Also boarding the First Class Boat Train that morning was 32-year-old[25] Francis 'Frank' M. Browne, a student at the Belvedere College, which was a Jesuit school in Dublin, Ireland.[26] Browne was only traveling to Queenstown, Ireland, aboard the *Titanic*, but he was quite excited about the trip, as it was to be his first time at sea on a large liner. Browne was traveling with a group of friends: brothers Richard and

Passengers board the special First Class Boat Train to Southampton at London's Waterloo Station. Although frequently identified as such, the man looking at the photographer was neither John Jacob Astor or his cousin, William Waldorf Astor. The photo was taken by Francis Browne. As of this writing, there is no certain identification for anyone in the photo.

Stanley May, their sister Mrs Lily Odell, and her children Jack and Kate Odell.[27] Browne had traveled from Dublin to Holyhead, Wales, and thence overland to London; apparently, he stayed that Tuesday night in London with his brother James, who was an eye specialist.

Francis Browne was a budding amateur photographer, a hobby heartily encouraged by his Uncle Robert, who had even bought a camera for him. That morning, as the First Class Boat Train was preparing to depart, he walked out on the platform, turned back and photographed the scene. He then walked back and took a closer photograph of the group on the platform. Although it would be a beautiful day, the early morning temperatures still had quite a chill, and top coats and hats were quite in evidence.[28] Once aboard, and as the train pulled out of the station, Browne daringly held his camera out the window, snapping a photo as they rounded a curve in the tracks.

Meanwhile, Elmer and Juliet Taylor were getting settled into their compartment on the Boat Train. It turned out that they were sharing the space with the Crosby family of Milwaukee, Wisconsin. The father was 70-year-old Captain Edward Crosby, a veteran of the Civil War and a Great Lakes shipping magnate. His wife Catherine, then aged 64, was born in Waterloo, New York, and the couple was just eight days shy of their forty-fourth wedding anniversary. They were traveling with their daughter Harriette, who was then thirty-nine years of age. Harriette was divorced from her first husband, and just that February had given birth to a daughter, the result of an affair with another – and already married – man. The trio was traveling without the infant, and had made special plans in order to be able to sail to the United States aboard the *Titanic*.[29] Elmer Taylor recalled:

> The old gentleman seated opposite me on the window side fumbled with a cigar in his waistcoat pocket, anxious to have his morning smoke, and as we were in a 'No Smoking' compartment, I said, 'Go ahead, my friend, and light up, and if you don't mind I will join you.'

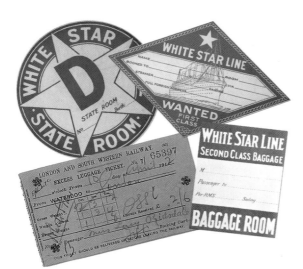

A selection of three White Star Line baggage tags. Top left and right: First Class tags. Lower right: Second Class Baggage tag for luggage not wanted on the voyage. Lower left: A LSWR ticket for the Second Class Boat Train from London's Waterloo Station to Southampton. The ticket belonged to Miss Lucy Ridsdale. Unfortunately, no specific time of departure is marked on the ticket.

They had many small parcels – last minute shopping, I thought. As we rolled along, I began to point out places of interest, Houses of Parliament, Lambeth Palace, Doulton's Pottery Works, this and that. Breaking the ice in this informal way, the ladies softened, became friendly, and long before we reached Southampton, we were a family party.[30]

Many stood on the White Star Dock beside the cliff-like sides of the *Titanic* that morning, staring up in awe at her size, her grace, her majesty. When he arrived dockside at 9:30 a.m., however, one man must have beamed more than anyone else: J. Bruce Ismay.[31] The Chairman and Managing Director of the White Star Line – and, since 1904, President of J. P. Morgan's International Mercantile Marine – must have felt a thrill at seeing the second of the *Olympic*-class liners in her berth, nearly ready to sail. It was not the first time he had seen the liner, and she was only the second of three ships in the class. However her entry into the North Atlantic route was a tremendous step forward in equaling the express service then offered by Ismay's chief rival, Cunard, with their liners *Lusitania* and *Mauretania*. She was an improvement over her older sister, *Olympic*, in many small ways, and she even held the title of 'world's largest ship'. She was a tremendous liner in her own right, and she was his company's greatest achievement.

Ismay's wife, Julia Florence, his three youngest children, his valet Richard Fry and his secretary William Henry Harrison, all boarded *Titanic* with Ismay. They had stayed the previous night at the South Western Hotel, within sight of the enormous liner.[32] Although Ismay's family had accompanied him on the *Olympic*'s maiden voyage the previous June, they would not be making the maiden voyage of the *Titanic*. Ismay himself made a habit of taking the maiden trip of all his new liners, to see how they worked, and what could be improved upon them and in their successors, so

the trip was not an unusual one in that sense. Once Ismay had settled in to his port side suite – rooms B-52, B-54 and B-56 – with its private promenade, and after his family saw some of *Titanic*'s interior spaces, the remainder of the Ismay family disembarked.

As the morning wore on and sailing time approached, the First Class Boat Train was making its way toward the Southampton docks. In every multi-stage trip, there are moments of excitement as well as lulls, moments when the traveler can catch his breath and relax before the next burst of activity, perhaps even to feel quite comfortable in his new if temporary surroundings. Yet invariably as the next junction is approached, the sensation of excitement builds again: all of the accompanying luggage needs to be re-gathered; a nose count done of friends and family to make sure everyone in the group is sticking together; and a quick double- or triple-check to make sure that the tickets are still on hand. The more grounded individuals – likely seasoned travelers, or perhaps the sort that simply are rather at ease no matter where they are, familiar surroundings or not – tend to take the whole thing in stride, as if they are doing nothing more exciting than coming down the stairs of their own home for a relaxed breakfast.

A second category of traveler compulsively worries and frets to make sure everything is taken care of. Still others, roiling within, create a heavy-lidded, 'ho-hum' sort of façade – as if giving in to the excitement or worry was somehow beneath their dignity. They try, with varying degrees of success, to look as cool and collected as those who really are calm.

Finally, there are those who are seemingly oblivious to the details of luggage and what-nots, and are instead visibly excited about spotting the actual mechanical marvel that they would next board: 'Didn't you know', they might ask their unflappable companions, hoping to instill some sense of excitement and elicit an enthusiastic response, 'that *Titanic* is fifty per cent bigger than the *Mauretania*?' Perhaps if the ship they were about to board was an older, smaller liner, their enthusiasm could be dismissed as passé. But on this morning, even the most incorrigibly under-whelmed seemed to be caught up in the anticipation of climbing aboard the largest and newest ship in the world.

As the hour-and-a-half rail passage began to come to its inevitable conclusion, many strained to catch their first glimpse of the *Titanic*. Francis M. Browne peered out of the First Class Boat Train windows as it chugged its way through the city of Southampton. Frustratingly, he could only manage fleeting glances of the enormous White Star liner as the train moved through city streets, between buildings, and toward the docks. Finally, the train pulled in and stopped just a stone's throw from the ship's sides.

When the Boat Train came to rest and the time came to disembark, Elmer Taylor noticed that the trio sharing their compartment might have trouble getting all their parcels and other bits and pieces out and to the ship. So he obligingly offered to lend them a hand in carrying their things to the ship, and they accepted his kind offer. Taylor picked up every item he could possibly hold, carried them to the towering side of the steamer, and there he amiably parted company with the Crosby party.[33]

Although the scene at the Southampton waterfront was already busy, with the arrival of the Boat Trains and their human cargo, the workload increased still further. For Third Class passengers, cursory medical examinations

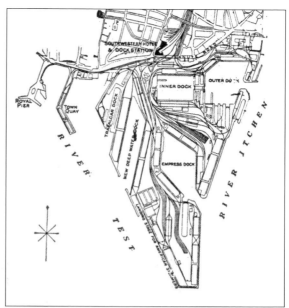

Above: *This c. 1911–12 photo shows the* Olympic *in the LSWR docks, near where* Titanic *was berthed. The view gives an excellent idea of the many rail lines and heavy traffic in the vicinity.*

Right: *A period map of the Southampton waterfront, showing the location of the South Western Hotel, the Dock Station, and the new LSWR docks where* Titanic *was berthed.*

had to be made; luggage from all passengers had to be sorted and brought aboard – some of it tagged 'Not Wanted' and bound for the holds for the journey, and some of it marked 'Wanted' and bound for passenger cabins.

The scene at Berth 44, although no more hectic or greater in scale than a typical *Olympic* departure during the previous ten months, was still rather epic. The new pier-side cargo sheds, built by the London & South Western Railway, were nearly as large as the *Titanic* herself, at 700 feet in length and 120 feet in width. There were waiting rooms and lavatories at the southern end of the shed – closest to the *Titanic's* bow – as well as cages for bonded cargo, offices for the Medical Examiner, Foreman and clerks. Porters moved rapidly back and forth within the shed, straining to carry numerous pieces of luggage aboard the ship.

It was from the upper level of the Berth 44 shed that passengers could walk out onto a verandah, some eighteen feet above the ground, which ran parallel with the dock wall. It faced not only the dock below but also the towering side of the *Titanic*, the fresh paint of which gleamed in the morning sun that occasionally decided to peer out from behind the clouds. It was also from this upper level that passengers could make their way to the boarding gantries. Each of these gantries, steel framed but covered with timber shelters, was 40 feet high and 20 feet wide. They had two levels so that passengers could board or disembark the *Olympic* or *Titanic* no matter what the state of tide.[34]

The northern gantry – for the use of Second Class passengers – was attached to the Second Class shell doors on C Deck, astern, and passengers embarked the ship via that gantry's lower level. The southern gantry was for the use of First Class passengers; from its upper level, they entered the ship through the B Deck shell doors, landing in the special B Deck Entrance area, just forward of the Parlour Suite with its private promenade. Just inside – through two sets of double doors – was the forward First Class Entrance and Grand Staircase, which led either up or down, depending on what deck passengers' cabins were on. Considering

their exertions in boarding the ship, it is also possible that a number of them found their way to the trio of elevators just forward, which could smoothly and effortlessly carry them up to the Promenade Deck, or down to the lower decks of accommodation.

Doubtless some of the First Class passengers were familiar with the *Olympic's* similar interior decorations, but at the same time, many others remembered being nearly flabbergasted by the ship's beauty, splendor, newness, and sheer size. Francis M. Browne, for example, had met an old friend – Tom Brownrigg – after disembarking the Boat Train. Brownrigg decided to accompany his friend aboard and get a peek at the new ship before she sailed. Browne recalled:

> Together we started; but it was not till, having ascended three flights of stairs, we stood on the little gangway that gave admission to the Saloon entrance lobby, that we could form any adequate idea of the size of the 'largest ship in the world'.
>
> Left and right stretched a wall of steel that towered high above the roof of the station that we had just left. We were about forty feet above the quay level, and yet scarce more than half way up the side of the ship. Below us the people looked tiny, while some hundred and twenty yards aft we could see the Second-class passengers crossing the gangway into their portion of the ship.[35]

Browne paused about two-thirds of the way out to the ship on the boarding gantry, and snapped a picture looking to the north, along the ship's cliff-like sides, capturing the scene he described. Once aboard, the next order of business for Browne and Brownrigg was to proceed to the Purser's Enquiry Office, which was one deck below on the starboard side of the forward First Class Entrance.

The Enquiry Office was the focal point of much activity on sailing day. Passengers proceeded there for information on how to find their cabins, deposit valuables for safekeeping, exchange money, arrange for table assignments

Above: *As Francis Browne walked across the gangway, he turned to photograph the cliff-like sides of the* Titanic. *Three of the windows to Bruce Ismay's private Promenade, on the left, are open. Many of the C Deck portholes are also open. In the distance, Second Class passengers can be seen boarding on C Deck, and several crew gangways are visible at the wharf level.*

Left: *Chief Purser McElroy on the* Olympic *mere months before his transfer to* Titanic.

in the Dining Saloon, to rent steamer chairs or rugs for the voyage, or to arrange for their rebate if taking all meals aboard ship in the *à la carte* Restaurant rather than the main Dining Saloon. Here, Browne had only to produce a 'letter of introduction', which 'served as a passport to the genial friendship' of 37-year-old Chief Purser Hugh McElroy.

McElroy had been with the White Star Line since 1899, when he had joined the *Majestic*. He had married in 1910, and had been promoted to the prestigious position of *Olympic's* Chief Purser in June of the previous year. Now he had been promoted again, to Chief Purser of the *Titanic*.[36] Being a ship's purser was a demanding job. Being Chief Purser of the company's flagship was a tremendous responsibility, as the Chief Purser ran the entire Victualling Department of the ship. All passenger interaction went through him, and keeping even the fussiest of passengers happy dur-

ing a crossing they had paid a great quantity of money for was entirely his responsibility. Was the meal in the Saloon for some reason not up to par? Had one of the stewards or stewardesses been perceived as boorish? Perhaps the passenger's beds were too springy, or there weren't enough pillows, or the temperature of their cabin was too warm, or too cold, or ... well, the list of potential complaints during any crossing just went on and on.

Everything in caring for passengers' needs and wants had to be seen to by the Chief Purser, and every situation had to be handled with graciousness, delicacy and tact. Good pursers befriended their passengers, got to know their likes and dislikes, even made special arrangements to cater for their every whim. It was his job to know his passengers' needs and wants before they knew them, whenever it was possible to do so. Some of the finest Chief Pursers were even followed by passengers, who would literally make their travel arrangements around his sailing schedule.

It is obvious, then, just how important Chief Purser McElroy's role was in making passengers happy during *Titanic's* maiden voyage. The maiden sailing day of the world's largest and most luxurious liner must have been particularly demanding for him, but he seemed to take it all in stride. Francis Browne and his friend certainly seemed to be quite pleased with McElroy's amiable service. Soon they were happily on their way – camera, bags, and other paraphernalia in hand – to find Browne's cabin: A-37. The Enquiry Office was on C Deck, so the cabin would logically have been up two decks, but ... where from there? Browne admitted that he and Brownrigg were 'really "at sea"' as they hunted for the elusive stateroom.

Far left: *First Class passenger Frederick Hoyt c. 1920.*

Left: *First Class passenger Jane Hoyt c. 1920*

Below: *A publicity pamphlet to show the wonders of the* Olympic *and* Titanic, *which were both still under construction at the time it went to press. The final statement on the back cover (in the lower left corner) specifically mentions that 'as far as it is possible to do so, these two wonderful vessels are designed to be unsinkable'.*

White Star ticketing agents liberally used the term 'unsinkable' to reassure potential passengers who were nervous about sailing on such a new ship. However, definitive claims about the unsinkability of crack liners of the period were not uncommon.

Waylaying a steward, the pair asked where A-37 could be found. The steward also seems to have been rather perplexed, and could only reply, 'That's somewhere aft, Sir.' Heading aft, the two men finally found the cabin on the starboard side of the aft First Class Entrance, at the top of the aft Grand Staircase on the starboard side. Thomas Andrews' own stateroom, A-36, was just across the foyer on the port side. Interestingly, Browne's early-date deck plans, issued in December of 1911, did not show either A-36 or A-37, which had been late additions; Browne later had to mark them in on his copy.[37]

Browne thought the stateroom was 'large and very prettily furnished'. It even had a private bathroom attached, some-

thing of a novelty even on the world's grandest ship. Once all of Browne's accoutrements had been deposited in the cabin, the two men decided to head out to explore the ship together, at least until such time as the 'All ashore who's going ashore' warning was sounded and Brownrigg had to disembark.[38]

One of the married couples embarking that morning was 38-year-old Frederick Hoyt and his 31-year-old wife Jane. The couple hailed from New York, New York, but had departed for an extended holiday the previous November. During the course of their trip, they had visited Mediterranean ports, and then traveled on to Paris and eventually London. They had decided to sail home on the *Titanic*, but 'not solely because of the fact that it was the maiden voyage

Above left: *First Class passenger Henry B. Harris.*

Above right: *First Class passenger Irene Harris.*

Below left: *Second class passenger Sidney Collett.*

Below right: *This photo, taken about 1920, shows the* Olympic's *Second Class gangway open. Passengers line the windows of the Enclosed Promenade on C Deck.*

of the empress of the seas'. Instead, it was 'because Captain Smith was a personal acquaintance, as was also Dr William F. N. O'Loughlin'.[39]

Other passengers boarding that morning were a bit nervous about taking passage on the *Titanic*. Among these was thirty-five-year-old May Futrelle, who climbed aboard that morning with her husband, 37-year-old Jacques. The couple had not initially planned to take the *Titanic*, having booked passage on the *Adriatic*. But when they were delayed, they were forced to cancel passage on the smaller White Star liner. Then they decided to take the *Mauretania*, but Mrs Futrelle 'had heard that the turbines of those fast boats made a disagreeable vibration. The *Titanic* was sailing on her maiden trip. We thought it a good adventure to go on her.' However, on Tuesday afternoon, as they were finishing their packing, Lily was seized with nervousness. 'I'm a little afraid,' she told her husband. 'This boat is new. She has never been tried out.'

'Don't you ever worry about that,' Jacques replied. 'She'll never be so safe again as on this trip. They're out for a re-cord in every way. Besides, those big boats are practically unsinkable.'

On sailing day, however, Mrs Futrelle's nerves were still a little edgy. 'In case of trouble', she asked her husband, 'whom do they save first?'

Mr Futrelle responded humorously, 'They save the first-class passengers.'

'Just after' boarding the *Titanic*, however, Jacques and May made a pleasant discovery – one which may have helped to distract May from her worries. They bumped into Henry and Irene Harris, a married couple with whom they were previously acquainted. Forty-five-year-old Henry Harris was a theater manager from New York. His wife was then 35 years old. While the Harrises occupied cabin C-83, Mrs Futrelle was 'delighted to find that they had a stateroom in the same entry with ours – amidships on the starboard side of C deck.' Over the course of the voyage, the Futrelles and the Harrises 'were much to-gether'.[40]

Another couple boarding as First Class passengers was Edwin and Susan Kimball. Forty-two-year-old Edwin was the President of the Hallet & Davis Piano Company of Boston, Massachusetts. The company traced its roots all the way back to 1835, and was one of the most prestigious American piano companies of the period.[41] His wife, Susan Gertrude, was then 45 years old. The Boston couple was returning from a nearly five-week vacation to some of the most interesting places in Europe.

The Kimballs were acquainted with a number of other First Class passengers who also boarded that morning. Among these were 37-year-old Richard L. Beckwith and his wife, 46-year-old Sarah 'Sallie', as well as Sarah's 19-year-old daughter Helen Newsom. Sarah had been previously married and actually had two children, but when her first husband passed away, she had married Richard. Sarah's son William was not traveling with them. At the time, young Helen Newsom was being pursued by 26-year-old tennis star Karl Behr. Helen's mother had been trying to throw a bit of cold water on the budding relationship, and had taken Helen with them on a tour of Europe. Behr, however, was most determined, and had concocted a 'business trip' to Europe. He would be joining the *Titanic* in Cherbourg and was determined to continue his relationship with Helen during the trip home.

The Second and Third Class Boat Train had left Waterloo Station before that for First Class. Twenty-five-year-old Sidney Clarence Stuart Collett was on this earlier train, as he was booked in Second Class aboard the *Titanic*. The young man's family hailed from North London, but little by little had begun to emigrate to other areas. His brother Thomas left first, moving to Syracuse, New York, in 1904. His parents, Reverend and Mrs Mawbey Collett, moved to Port Byron, New York – slightly west of Syracuse – six years later. By 1912, only Sidney and his brother Ernest were left behind in London.

Collett had made arrangements to attend a theological seminary in Liberty, Missouri, and was planning to pay a visit to his parents in Central New York before completing his journey. After attempting to book passage aboard the *St Louis* and *Philadelphia*, both of which had been laid up due to the coal strike, he had happily found that he could book on the *Titanic* for the same price. As he boarded the Boat Train from Waterloo, he carried in his hand a brand new walking stick; he had just purchased it the previous day as a sort of final souvenir of England. He was being accompanied by his paternal uncle for the journey down to Southampton. Of the train trip, he recalled a brief delay: 'At the very start there was trouble. The train stopped because somebody had interfered with the brake valve.'[42]

Second Class passenger Ellen Walcroft remembered that the special train to Southampton departed London at 8:30 that morning, and arrived at the Southampton Dock at 10:15.[43] Meanwhile, 42-year-old Second Class passenger Father Thomas Byles took this same Boat Train, and wrote that evening that he had arrived at Southampton at 11:30 a.m., only about a half-hour before sailing time.[44]

Nineteen-year-old William John Mellors was also traveling as a Second Class passenger. Mellors was from London, and had been serving as the valet for Sir Frederick Schuster.

confirmed when the steward opened their cabin door. Mrs Shelley and Mrs Parrish were deeply disappointed to find that the cabin was significantly smaller than what they had thought it would be. Imanita said it was 'a cell, I cannot call it a cabin'. She said that there were two bunks and a washstand, no carpeting, and 'no room to open my steamer trunk at all. If we were outside of our berths, one of us had to go out into the passage in order to allow the stewardess to come in.'

Imanita complained to the steward, saying that they 'had not purchased any such accommodation at all', and that their ticket called for the best Second Class cabin on the ship. The steward retorted that the ticket said no such thing, but Imanita insisted that he check with the purser to see if there had been a mistake. The steward spoke with Chief Purser McElroy, who sent Imanita a message saying that this was the cabin their ticket called for, but that if there had been a mistake, 'he would be unable to rectify it until after the ship had reached Queenstown and the passengers from that port had been taken aboard. Then he could check up the list and find out.' Imanita and her mother begrudgingly made due in the meantime.[46]

Another group traveling in Second Class was the Hart family. Forty-seven-year-old Benjamin Hart was a talented carpenter from the London suburb of Ilford whose business had fallen on hard times. He had decided to move his family – comprised of his 48-year-old wife Esther and 7-year-old daughter Eva – to Winnipeg, Manitoba, in Canada to make a fresh start. The move was rather hastily plotted out, and they had bid a tearful farewell to their friends and family, having booked passage on the *Philadelphia*. However, the ongoing coal strike had caused the cancellation of a number of sailings, including the sailing of the *Philadelphia*. Many travelers' plans were disrupted as a result. However, the Harts were reassigned passage aboard the much larger

From left: *Second Class passengers Imanita Shelley, Lutie Parrish, and Lawrence Beesley.*

In 1912, having saved up some money, he was emigrating to New York, for better work and opportunities at a country club on Staten Island.[45]

Also boarding that morning were 25-year-old Imanita Shelley and her mother, 59-year-old Lucinda 'Lutie' Parrish, who were also traveling home to the United States as Second Class passengers. Imanita was from Deer Lodge, Montana, and her mother was from Woodford County, Kentucky. Mrs Shelley had taken ill while overseas, and had just left a hospital in London prior to the voyage. She was still not feeling well.

Unlike most passengers who boarded the *Titanic*, Imanita and her mother were far from impressed with their accommodations. Both believed that they had booked 'the best second [class] cabin' but when the steward led them down below 'what seemed to be thousands of feet to the bowels of the ship', they began to have concerns. Their fears were

Titanic. Benjamin Hart, for one, was not about to complain, as he was very keenly interested in the *Titanic*. Esther Hart, however, had been apprehensive about the trans-Atlantic voyage from the start, and found no comfort in their upgrade.

The family arrived at the docks on the Second Class Boat Train that morning, and Benjamin Hart led them toward the ship. He stood there, looking up at her proud, confidence-inspiring profile, and beamed as if he owned the liner. 'There! old girl', he said, trying to ease his wife's nerves, 'there's a vessel for you! You're not afraid now.' Esther tried to squelch her nerves and summon her confidence as the family boarded the ship.[47]

Lawrence Beesley was a 34-year-old former teacher from Dulwich College. Beesley had been married in 1901 to Gertrude MacBeth; at the time, he was 23, and she was five years his senior. The couple had a son, Alec, in 1903. Sadly,

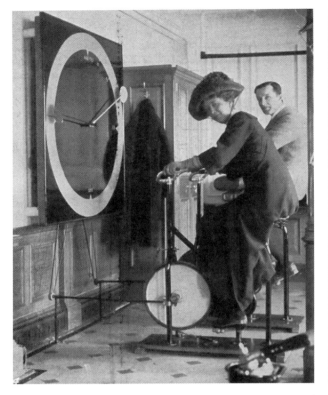

Gertrude had died in 1906 from a form of tuberculosis. Beesley had booked into Second Class aboard the *Titanic*, and was on his way to visit his brother in Toronto, Canada. Some of his friends had taken passage on the *Olympic* within the past year, and they had heartily recommended her as 'a most comfortable boat in a seaway'. Knowing that some improvements over *Olympic* had been incorporated into the *Titanic*, Beesley had decided to indulge in the 'novelty' of taking passage on the 'largest ship yet launched'.

Beesley had stayed overnight in a Southampton hotel, and as he had eaten breakfast that morning, he could see 'the four huge funnels of the *Titanic* towering over the roofs of the various shipping offices opposite, and the procession of stokers and stewards wending their way to the ship.' Beesley boarded the liner at 10:00 a.m., along with a couple of friends from Exeter who had come to see him off.

The barriers between First and Second Class areas of the ship were open at the time, and Beesley and his friends spent time inspecting 'the various decks, dining-saloons and libraries; and so extensive were they that it is no exaggeration to say that it was quite easy to lose one's way on such a ship.' While they were in the Gymnasium on the Boat Deck, Beesley hopped on to one of the stationary bicycles. Just then, Gymnasium Instructor Thomas W. McCawley came in with a pair of photographers from the *Illustrated London News*. McCawley insisted that the group stay on the equipment while they were photographed using it; just then still other passengers entered the Gymnasium. McCawley 'ran here and there, looking the very picture of robust, rosy-

cheeked health and "fitness" in his white flannels, placing one passenger on the electric "horse" and another on the "camel", while the laughing group of onlookers watched the inexperienced riders vigorously shaken up and down as he controlled the little motor which made the machines imitate so realistically horse and camel exercise.'[48]

Another Second Class passenger who boarded that morning was Miss Susan Webber, aged 37. Traveling with six individuals from her home town of Holsworthy, Devonshire, Miss Webber was traveling to Hartford, Connecticut, to visit her nephew Charles and his wife. Once she had boarded the liner that morning, the seasoned trans-Atlantic traveler was thoroughly impressed with the *Titanic*'s luxurious Second Class accommodations. 'I have been on beautiful boats', she said, 'but never one so beautiful.' She remembered seeing 'thousands' of people gathered at the waterfront to witness the steamer's first departure. 'Never was there a crowd more merry, or a ship which seemed so proud', she said of the scene.[49]

Also traveling in Second Class was 48-year-old Miss Ellen Toomey. When she boarded that morning, Miss Toomey was bound for her home in Indianapolis, Indiana. Originally born in Kilcornan, Limerick Ireland, she had eventually immigrated to Indianapolis, where she found work as a servant. Both of her sisters, one of whom was married, also lived in Indianapolis.

Just before the Christmas holidays of 1911, Ellen Toomey had obtained a leave of absence from her employers, and returned to Ireland to visit her mother – a trip that her sisters

---

Top left: Lawrence Beesley rides a stationary bicycle in Titanic's *First Class Gymnasium. The lady beside him has been identified as a friend who came down to see Beesley off, but who was not taking passage. The pair pose gamely for photographers.*

Top right: Nineteen-year-old Second Class passenger Lillian Bentham demonstrates one of Titanic's *pieces of gym equipment.*

made several times before. Once her stay with her mother was complete, Ellen toured through England, and intended to sail back to America on the *New York*. However, when the *New York*'s voyage was canceled due to the coal strike, she transferred her passage to the *Titanic*. She found herself in a cabin with three other women: 32-year-old Mrs Rosa Pinsky, originally from Poland but then living in Brooklyn; also 40-year-old Elizabeth 'Bessie' Watt and her 12-year-old daughter Robertha 'Bertha' Watt. Mrs Watt's husband, James, had preceded the family in moving from Aberdeen, Scotland, to Portland, Oregon.[50]

Also boarding was Miss Elizabeth Dowdell. She had booked passage as a Third Class passenger aboard the *Titanic*. The 30-year-old housekeeper from Union Hill, New Jersey, had in her care 5-year-old Virginia Emanuel. Young Virginia was the daughter of opera singer Estelle Emanuel, who had recently signed a six-month performing contract in England. As a result, young Virginia was being sent back to stay with her grandparents in New York, and had been placed in Elizabeth's care for the trip. Their morning was a bit stressful. Elizabeth recalled:

> We were delayed on [the] special train to reach the *Titanic* in the time we had planned, and feared we would miss it. However, we arrived just in time for the gateman to remark, "You're lucky to have caught it."

Olympic's trio of First Class Elevators. Olympic *and* Titanic *were not the first liners to offer this feature, but they were still quite the novelty at the time, and very much impressed Ernest Townley.*

Once they were aboard, they found that they would share a cabin during the voyage with 24-year-old Amy Stanley. Amy had worked as a servant in Wallingford, Oxfordshire. She was on her way to New Haven, Connecticut, to take up new work as a children's maid.[51]

Among the actual passengers, there were also a number of visitors who – although they were not there to see friends or relatives off – took the opportunity to come aboard, as well. For most of the public, this was the first such opportunity since the vessel had docked in Southampton a week before. There were plenty of people enthused enough about the ship to make the trip to the waterfront, or perhaps even up the gangplank.

In amongst the visitors was noted marine artist Norman Wilkinson. Since he was acquainted with Captain Smith, he reasoned that he might just be able to obtain a tour of the ship, and he brought a friend aboard with him. They asked a Quartermaster at the top of the gangway about Captain Smith's whereabouts, and the crewman obligingly took them to the Captain, who was then in his cabin. Captain Smith gave Wilkinson a warm welcome, but had to admit that he was too busy to conduct them on a personal tour of the liner. Instead, he asked one of the pursers to show them around. Wilkinson thought the tour was 'thorough', but perhaps the highlight of the expedition came in the First Class Smoking Room. There he paused to admire the artwork over the mantelpiece in its finished location. Entitled 'Plymouth Harbour', it was his handiwork, one of a pair of commissions; the other, a scene of New York Harbor, was in the same location over the Smoking Room fireplace of the *Olympic*.[52]

Another non-passenger visiting the ship that morning was a man named Ernest Townley, and he engaged in a couple of hours' tour of the liner. He said that:

> … on board the *Titanic* one felt as safe as if one were sitting in the Savoy or the Cecil Hotel, with thousands of tons of concrete for foundations. She was so much

larger than one even expected; she looked so solidly constructed, as one knew she must be, and her interior arrangements and appointments were so palatial that one forgot now and then that she was a big ship at all. She seemed to be a spacious regal home of the princes.

In the First Class Smoking Room, he sat on a leather-covered settee, toasting his feet by the fire under Norman Wilkinson's painting. Perhaps Townley and the artist even passed each other in the crowd as Wilkinson himself toured the ship? The spacious Smoking Room 'spoke of wealth, refinement, luxury. It was a place for millionaires of taste and millionaires of beauty.'

From the Boat Deck Townley looked down at the trio of liners lying tied up at the north end of the dock, which looked like mere toys compared to the great ship he stood upon. He went below to the Dining Saloon on D Deck:

> There were scores of tables for parties of from two to eight. I recall a sensation of thick pile carpets, spotless napery, glittering silver, and countless flowers; and you entered by wide door-ways from the large crush room [Reception Room] where the guests gathered before and after meals.

He watched passengers writing letters to friends and family in the Reading & Writing Room on A Deck, and watched as 'women in beautiful clothes, who moved with a conquering air of possession' also sampled the ship's wonders. Not to be missed was a ride in the electric lifts. Townley even had a peek at Second and Third Class portions of the ship.

The degree of comfort in the third-class quarters was as surprising as were the more luxurious surroundings of the millionaires. Most of the third class passengers I saw on board were fair-haired, happy looking Scandinavians. The first and second-class seemed all to be English or Americans, and I was told that many more Americans would be picked up at Cherbourg.

Perhaps most exciting – and perhaps late in his tour, since the ship was positively buzzing with noise and activity – he even managed to get a peek inside the cutting-edge technology in the Marconi shack:

You entered by a cool, white passage, closed the white door behind you, and there you sat in a quiet, white enameled Marconi cell, seemingly as much cut off from the rush of the world as if you were in a Trappist monastery.

Then the young operator placed his hand affectionately on a mysterious apparatus, and said, 'This will send a message five hundred miles across the Atlantic in daytime and fifteen hundred miles at night.' He opened another white enameled door and showed me the dark inner room where the marvelous boxes of Marconi wizardry were compactly arranged. He had some new piece of wonder-working mechanism which, I think he said, the *Titanic* alone among ships possessed.

He pulled a handle, and the bluish sparks cracked and spat fire.

'At night', he said, 'we shall only be out of touch of land for a few hours. Soon after we lose touch with Europe we shall gain touch with America.'[53]

Meanwhile, an Irish newspaper correspondent for *The Irish Times* had also found his way aboard the ship, and he – like Townley – toured the First and Third Class spaces. He was thoroughly impressed with the Gymnasium on the Boat Deck, where he watched Instructor McCawley fuss over passengers who happened to stop by about an hour before sailing time:

On one side a lady was having a camel ride and recalling the delights of the Pyramids; in another corner there was a bicycle race; many passengers took their own weights on the automatic chairs, and some had a spin on the mechanical rowing machines.[54]

Just forward of the Gymnasium, on the Bridge, the *Titanic's* senior officers met with Captain Smith, Captain Clarke, and Captain Steele. The ship's officers made their official status reports to the effect that the ship was ready to sail. Captain Smith and Captain Clarke finished their paperwork up tidily. Within these documents, it was shown that the *Titanic* was then drawing 33 feet 8 inches of water forward, and 34 feet, 4 inches of water aft, giving a mean draft of 34 feet 0 inches.[55] Captains Clarke and Steele then went ashore, their jobs complete.

As the morning progressed, Pilot George Bowyer stepped back aboard the decks of the *Titanic*. As soon as the ship was completely ready, he would be taking charge of the task of bringing her out of Southampton waters and to the open sea. Coal smoke was beginning to waft from the funnels –

Top: Titanic's Gymnasium. This was a busy scene on that Wednesday morning.

Above left: *First Class passenger Major Arthur Peuchen.*

Above right: *First Class passengers Bess and Trevor Allison.*

the stokers were building a full head of steam in the Boiler Rooms below – and it was obvious that the ship would be departing quite shortly. Charles Lightoller recalled that as '"zero" hour drew near, so order could be seen arriving out of chaos.'[56]

At about 11:30–11:40 a.m. on that 'fine day',[57] 52-year-old Major Arthur Godfrey Peuchen boarded the liner. Although married and with children, Peuchen was traveling without his family. He was a seasoned Atlantic traveler, with business interests on either side of the ocean. Peuchen lived in Toronto and at his mansion on Lake Simcoe; he owned a yacht, which he named *Vreda*, and was closely involved with the Royal Canadian Yacht Club in Toronto. His family came from railroad interests, but Peuchen was the President of the Standard Chemical Company.

On this day, he was boarding with several prominent individuals from Montreal, Canada. There was 55-year-old Harry Markland Molson, great-grandson of the John Molson who had founded the Molson Brewing Company; Peuchen had convinced Molson, who was finishing up a business trip, to delay his departure from England and take passage on the *Titanic*. There were also 30-year-old Hudson

J. C. Allison and his 25-year-old wife Bess. The Allisons' two children, 2-year-old Helen Loraine and 11-month-old Trevor, were closely in tow. The children were being looked after by 22-year-old Alice Cleaver, and the Allisons' maid, 33-year-old Sarah Daniels, was close at hand.

Peuchen had several other friends aboard for the trip, as well, including 55-year-old Charles M. Hays of Montreal. Hays was the President of the Grand Trunk Railway; he was involved in building a number of crack hotels in Canada, including one in Ottawa named Château Laurier, which was set to be opened on April 26, just over two weeks hence. Also acquainted with Peuchen were Hugo Ross and Thomson Beattie of Winnipeg, as well as Thomas McCaffry of Vancouver, and several others. For Peuchen, this trip was nothing unusual, as this was to be his fortieth crossing of the Atlantic. Once he had boarded on the morning of that 'fine day', he found his way to his cabin, C-104. Most of his friends, he discovered, had cabins on A Deck.[58]

At 11:45 a.m., fifteen minutes before the scheduled sailing time, the bells clanged, and there came cries of, 'All ashore!' throughout the ship. Streams of visitors said their good-byes and descended the gangplanks. Ernest Townley disembarked the liner and stared up at her enormous bulk, towering over the quay. 'Her size suggested rock-like safety', he thought, and he abstractly wondered how she would behave in a gale. Francis Browne's friend Tom Brownrigg bade farewell and returned to the quay, while Browne himself ascended to the starboard side of the Boat Deck amidships to watch the departure play out.

Thomas Andrews took the opportunity to say goodbye to Thomas Hamilton and others who were not to be accompanying the ship on the maiden voyage. His spirits were high, and he said: 'Remember now and keep Mrs Andrews informed of any news of the vessel.'[59]

Most of the off-duty stokers who had decided to go ashore after the muster were back on board already, many of them not daring to cut things too fine. There were a few stragglers, however. When Able-Bodied Seaman William Lucas boarded at ten minutes to twelve – he was cutting things a mite close – he saw that 'all the gangways were up' except for the one that he used.[60]

Second Class passenger Sidney Collett had found his way safely aboard the liner. He had been met in Southampton by his aunt on his mother's side of the family. Collett was standing at the port side rail, looking down at his aunt and uncle in the crowd on the dockside, and he noticed that his aunt was 'beckoning vigorously' to him. A little confused, he turned in the direction she was indicating, and saw a young lady looking at him. She turned out to be a friend of his extended family, 26-year-old Marion Wright.[61] Miss Wright was on her way to the United States to be married to her longtime sweetheart, Arthur Woolcott, who had immigrated to the State of Oregon, in the United States. Collett considered this long-distance 'introduction' by his aunt as a charge to keep Miss Wright under his protective care during the upcoming voyage.[62]

The Titanic's officers made their way to their departure stations. Chief Officer Wilde was at the head of the Forecastle, overseeing the crew working the mooring lines. Second Officer Lightoller was a bit further aft on the Forecastle, working under Wilde's direction. At the opposite end of the ship, First Officer Murdoch was on the Poop Deck, in charge of the mooring lines there. Assisting him was Third Officer Pitman, who stood by the telephone and telegraphs on the

Stern Docking Bridge. Fourth Officer Boxhall was on the Bridge, seeing to giving orders on the telegraphs and keeping the ship's log filled in. Fifth Officer Lowe was inside the Wheelhouse, working the telephones. Sixth Officer Moody was below, at the head of the last gangway connecting ship with shore. It was astern on E Deck, located just off the main crew thoroughfare, Scotland Road.[63]

Just after noon, the massive triple-toned whistles atop the forward two funnels sounded their breathtakingly-loud cry three times, signaling that the Titanic was about to depart. A last knot of straggling firemen rushed along the pier toward their ship. Among these was Leading Fireman Percy Pugh and his brother, Steward Alfred Pugh, who both managed to make it up the gangplank in time.

Another group of six crewmen were also rushing down the docks. Fireman John Podesta and his friend William Nutbean were with Alfred, Bertram and Tom Slade, three brothers, and a trimmer named Penney. The group had gone to the pub at Newcastle Hotel, leaving there at 11:15 a.m.; they next proceeded to a second pub, called The Grapes, for another round. However, the group had ended up staying there for a little too long, leaving at only 11:50. They were coming down the pier when a train approached, about to cross their path. Podesta and Nutbean decided to cross the tracks before the train passed, but the Slades and Penney held back until it had passed.

Podesta and Nutbean made it up the gangway and past Sixth Officer Moody; Moody then ordered the gangplank withdrawn from Titanic's side, and it had gotten about a foot from the side of the ship when a 16-year-old R. C. Lawrence turned up. Lawrence had been sent aboard that morning to deliver typewriters to the Purser's Office; he had ended up staying to tour the ship, and couldn't find his way to a gangway when the 'All ashore' bells were sounded. 'Amid protestations on my part and vocabulary which was unprintable, the officers instructed the ABs to pull in the gangway', he said.[64] Once the gap had been closed, Lawrence hurried down the gangplank to shore.

It was about then that the Slades and Penney arrived, having waited for the lengthy train to pass before crossing the tracks. By this time, Moody had apparently had enough nonsense for one day. Lawrence Beesley watched the ensuing scene unfold from his vantage point, most likely from the Second Class Open Promenade on the port side of B Deck, where a large number of Second Class passengers had gathered to watch the departure. He observed as a …

> … knot of stokers ran along the quay, with their kit slung over their shoulders in bundles, and made for the gangway with the evident intention of joining the ship. But a petty officer guarding the shore end of the gangway firmly refused to allow them on board; they argued, gesticulated, apparently attempting to explain the reasons why they were late, but he remained obdurate and waved them back with a determined hand, the gangway was dragged back amid their protests, putting a summary ending to their determined efforts to join the Titanic.[65]

Perhaps Moody believed that being left behind from a good berth would teach the men a lesson in punctuality that they would not soon forget, and that they would not repeat their mistake. Maybe he felt that the men were not reliable enough to wait for; after all, there were a number

Top: *The tugs begin to ease the* Titanic *away from Berth 44. A single line connects the liner to shore, and it is about to be cast off. The port side Emergency Boat, No. 2, has been temporarily cranked in. It is possible that this was done to increase visibility aft from the port side Bridge wing.*

Above left: *A detail view of the previous photograph, showing Chief Officer Wilde on the Forecastle. He is just to the right of the anchor crane, with his hands clasped behind his back.*

of standby crewmen already aboard the ship who could be engaged in their place, and some of these were signed on. Whatever Moody's thinking, the tardy crewmen were left high and dry as the last gangway was pulled ashore.[66]

A bevy of tugboats approached the *Titanic* and were made fast to help ease her away from the pier and into the main channel. With the final gangways disconnected, but the two shell doors on E Deck astern not yet closed, the order came down from the Bridge to cast off, separating the ship from shore completely. Men on the docks were informed of the order via megaphones and whistle signals. At least one of the men on the dock held a megaphone with which to call back to the departing liner. The men on the dock slipped the mooring lines off the bollards and cast them into the murky water between the dock and the ship's side one by one.

The tugs began to ease the liner away from Berth No. 44. The crewmen aboard the ship – working under the supervision of Chief Officer Wilde at the bow and First Officer Murdoch at the stern – began to haul up the lines, which would not be needed again until the liner had reached New York and the time came to tie up at Pier 59. Chief Officer Wilde stood by the anchor crane at the bow. With his hands clasped behind his back, he watched the crewmen kneeling on the deck next to him, coiling the lines neatly for storage. Finally, only one lengthy line connected the port side Forecastle to the pier, and soon it was cast off and hauled aboard, as well.

Francis Browne, standing on the starboard Boat Deck amidships, had no idea that the ship had cast off until he looked down and saw one of the tugs on the starboard side straining at the line, pulling the ship straight away from the berth. He snapped a photo of the tugs and then crossed over to the port side of the Boat Deck, taking a photo of the crowds on the dock below.

Top left: *Francis Browne stood on the starboard Boat Deck, just aft of Boat No. 7, and snapped this photograph looking toward the liner's bow. It is interesting to see that Emergency Boat No. 1, like its counterpart on the port side, was cranked in during these docking maneuvers.*

Top right: *As* Titanic *pulled away from the wharf and moved forward toward the River Test, Francis Browne walked to* Titanic's *port side Boat Deck. Looking back toward the wharf, he took this view. Although in shadow, a close inspection shows that the state of the tide is well below peak.*

First Class passenger Elmer Taylor recalled:

> We sailed about noon. That 45,000 ton steamer … was a huge mass to move. Lines were cast off, and tugs pulled us away from the quay until we were fairly in the clear.[67]

The tugs slowly maneuvered the *Titanic* forward until she was clear of the docks, and gently turned her to port until she was pointed down the River Test. The maneuvers needed to be made cautiously to avoid an incident. As the *Titanic* was drawing an average of 34 feet 0 inches of water, and four further inches beyond that at the stern, and as the tide was not anywhere near its peak, there was very little room between the *Titanic*'s hull and the bottom of the river.

Although no band had been engaged to play from the docks, as had been the case with the *Olympic*'s maiden departure the previous year, there was music being played that afternoon. Turkish Bath Stewardess Annie Caton remembered the scene as the ship cast off:

> A large crowd had gathered on the pier to watch the ship leave her moorings, and as she began to move cheers rolled out across the waters.
> The ship's band was playing a lively tune on deck. Passengers leaning over the rails waved farewell greetings to their friends, and gave answering cheers.[68]

Second Class passenger Lawrence Beesley recalled that as the *Titanic* moved slowly down the dock, it was …

> … to the accompaniment of last messages and shouted farewells of those on the quay. There was no cheering or hooting of steamers' whistles from the fleet of ships that lined the dock, as might seem probable on the occasion of the largest vessel in the world putting to sea on her maiden voyage; the whole scene was quiet and rather ordinary, with little of the picturesque and interesting ceremonial which imagination paints as usual in such circumstances.[69]

Second Class passenger Susan Webber remembered things a little more festively, saying, 'Steamers and tugs tooted goodbye.' One observer on shore that morning remembered:

> It is doubtful whether the *Olympic* has ever cleared the new dock in such a splendid manner as did the *Titanic* on this occasion. From the moment she began to move from her berth in that dock she was under absolute control, and she passed out of the dock not only majestically, but also smoothly and calmly. If anything she was proceeding more slowly than the *Olympic* usually does, and she turned her nose towards the sea with the greatest of ease.[70]

Ernest Townley was among the spectators on the quay watching the *Titanic* depart. He said that 'the great vessel moved in slow majesty down Southampton water … She looked so colossal and so queenly.'

> Passengers waved fare-wells from her decks and windows – she has large, square windows high up, as well as portholes lower down – and a mob of jolly stokers yelled from the forecastle side. One of these – he must have been a Cockney – played a mouth organ and waved his old cap. He seemed a merry soul then …[71]

Stewardess Sarah Stap recalled that she and the other members of the crew 'were all so radiantly happy together when we left Southampton … There was no ceremony whatever when we moved off from the pier.'[72] Stewardess Violet Jessop recalled that the *Titanic* cast off gently, and then slipped away gracefully and full of hopes 'over the din of send off – goodbyes, fluttering flags and handkerchiefs.' As the tugs escorted the ship, they tooted their whistles, while simultaneously the farewells from the dock grew fainter.[73]

The tugs turned *Titanic* around the knuckle at the pier's edge, and then the liner was pointed southeast in the main body of the River Test, more or less parallel with the Berths 38–41, which were numbered in descending order from

Above: *This spectacular photo from the wharf shows* Titanic *beginning her turn into the River Test. Her helm is 'hard to starboard' in order to help aid the tugs in the maneuver.*

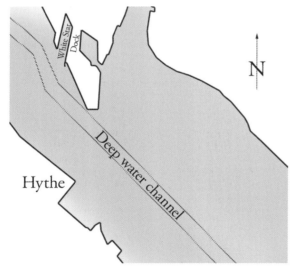

Left: *This map shows the approximate location of the deep water channel in the River Test.*

Below left: *The* Titanic *turns into the River Test.*

Below right: *The tugs guide the ship further into the River Test.*

north to south. The quay which housed Berths 38–41 ran roughly south-southeast, while the opposite shore of the river, across from Berth 38, moved roughly east-southeast. These two land formations formed a tapering gap, just over a half-mile wide at its narrowest point, through which the river flowed. The deep water channel was located closer to the northern shore than to the southern shore, meaning that *Titanic* needed to 'hug' the line of quays to a certain extent. Meanwhile, smaller traffic moving up river would pass along *Titanic*'s southern, starboard side.

In order to see the *Titanic* pass, quite a few individuals had assembled farther on down the 2,000-foot long face of the quay. A number had even scrambled aboard the idled liners *Oceanic* and *New York* – which were tied up alongside one another at Berth 38, at the very end of the quay – hop-

Far left: *First Class passenger Colonel Archibald Gracie.*

Centre: *First class passenger Isidor Straus.*

Left: *First Class passenger Rosalie Ida Straus.*

ing to get a front-row view of the new White Star liner as she passed. *Oceanic* was tied up directly to the dock, and *New York* was tied to the White Star liner, with both ships pointing down-channel. The *Titanic* and her escorting flotilla began to approach the *Oceanic* and *New York*.

Standing together on the *Titanic's* decks as the liner moved parallel to Berths 38–41 was a pair of First Class passengers: 54-year-old Colonel Archibald Gracie IV, and an elderly gentleman, 67-year-old Isidor Straus. Straus's 63-year-old wife Rosalie Ida had already left the deck, but the two men remained together, watching the departure.[74] Colonel Gracie was from an old Southern family, and his father had died during the Civil War, fighting for the Confederacy. Gracie was independently wealthy, and lived in Washington, D.C. Only a few months before, he had a book published; entitled *The Truth About Chickamauga*, it told of a Civil War battle that his father had played a role in. Gracie was married, and the couple had four daughters. Two of the girls had died very young, and a third had perished in an elevator accident in 1903. The fourth daughter, Edith, was alive and well, then about eighteen years of age. Edith was a very attractive young woman who had made her debut in Washington Society the previous fall, along with five other Washingtonian young ladies.[75]

Gracie's health was poor; he was a diabetic and had fought the disease for eight years. The years of constant work on his first book had taken a toll on his health, and he had undergone an operation several months before. He had decided to take a trip to Europe, partly to recuperate, and partly to delve into research for an article about the War of 1812. He was traveling without his wife and daughter, and it was his first extended separation from them.[76]

The Strauses were also very interesting individuals. Both were originally from Germany, Isidor from Bavaria, and his wife from Worms. During the Civil War, he had engaged in blockade running while working as an agent for the purchase of supplies with the Confederate Government Commissioners. He had played a role in the founding of a New York importing firm called L. Straus & Sons.[77] Isidor and his brother Nathan had become involved with the R. H. Macy's department store – which had been established in 1858 on New York City's Sixth Avenue between Thirteenth and Fourteenth Streets – in the year 1874. Isidor had become a partner of the company in 1888, and by 1896, he had become its owner.[78] When not running a department store, Straus had served in the House of Representatives for the Fifty-Third United States Congress, and had a personal friendship with President Grover Cleveland. Additionally, he and Ida had seven children, one of whom had died in infancy; the pair was virtually inseparable, and even after so many years of marriage, it was obvious that they were very much in love.[79] The couple was just returning from a trip to Jerusalem.

Colonel Gracie was speaking with Mr Straus when the *Titanic* began to near the *New York* and *Oceanic*. Isidor Straus was pointing the *New York* out to Gracie, telling her that he had been on that vessel's maiden voyage in 1888, when she was known as the *City of New York* and flew under the flag of the Inman Line. Back then – it seemed to him that it was just a few years before – the *New York* was known as the 'last word in shipbuilding'. What progress had been made in the last twenty-four years, Straus observed.[80]

First Class passengers Jacques and May Futrelle were watching the departure with interest. May recalled:

> Because this was the *Titanic's* maiden trip our departure was a great occasion. The wharves and the decks of the *Olympic* [sic, *Oceanic*] and *New York*, which lay in port, were crowded with people, who had come to see us off. They cheered and saluted as we pulled out: our band played: a band from shore answered.[81]

At that point, not all of the attending tugs had cast off, but some – like the tug *Vulcan* – had let go, and Captain Gale was maintaining a close proximity to the ship as she moved parallel to the quay. He was about to move in to pick up the few remaining standby crewmen who had not disembarked at Berth No. 44.

From the Bridge, Pilot Bowyer had ordered the *Titanic's* engines engaged at 'Slow Ahead'. Chief Engineer Joseph Bell, down on the Starting Platform in the Engine Room, had promptly opened up the steam lines. The engines, powerless up to that point in the departure, began to come to life, turning the two outboard props – but not the central propeller driven by the turbine – with gathering momentum.[82] Their building force was immediately obvious to everyone on board the liner and ashore. Passenger Elmer Taylor recalled:

> The signal was then given to go ahead. Those powerful engines began to pile water up astern, creating a swift current, more than the entire length of the steamer, without perceptibly overcoming the inertia of the great mass.[83]

The correspondent for *The Irish Times* had watched the liner depart, standing amid the crowds gathered on the quay.

Suddenly, among 'the crowds still waving handkerchiefs there was a sudden silence. The gigantic triple expansion engines had begun to work.' So far, things had proceeded much better than with *Olympic*'s maiden voyage the previous year, when that liner had to be brought out stern-first and then turned down the River Test. However, what happened next nearly ended the maiden voyage before it began.

'Directly the huge screws of the *Titanic* began to revolve',[84] the reporter from *The Irish Times* recalled, they began to build up a powerful and complex series of forces in the confined waters on the northern side of the deep-water channel. The force began to exert an irresistible influence on the American liner *New York*, and the result was both immediate and shocking. Lawrence Beesley said that …

… as the bows of our ship came about level with those of the *New York*, there came a series of reports like those of a revolver, and on the quay side of the *New York* snaky coils of thick rope flung themselves high in the air and fell backwards among the crowd, which retreated in alarm to escape the flying ropes. We hoped that no one was struck by the ropes, but a sailor next to me was certain he saw

a woman carried away to receive attention. And then, to our amazement the *New York* crept towards us, slowly and stealthily, as if drawn by some invisible force which she was powerless to withstand … On the *New York* there was shouting of orders, sailors running to and fro, paying out ropes and putting mats over the side where it seemed likely we should collide.[85]

May Futrelle recalled:

Jacques and I stood by the rail nearest the *New York* as we got headway. Suddenly we saw the *New York* shiver and move, then her cable nearest us snapped, and the stump whipped back on deck, knocking over some people. I saw her begin to swing toward us. Jacques shouted: "Hold fast for the shock!" I gripped the rail.[86]

First Class passenger Major Arthur Peuchen said:

There was considerable excitement on those boats on account of the snapping of their mooring lines, but there was no excitement on ours, the *Titanic*. There was also excitement on the wharves when the larger ship commenced to snap one or two of her moorings.[87]

Up on the port Boat Deck of the *Titanic*, Francis Browne heard five sharp reports of the *New York*'s hawsers snapping 'like thread'. From his right, up forward on the Bridge, there came the sound of the telegraph handles jangling. In response, the throb of *Titanic*'s engines ceased completely. However, the dominoes were already set in motion, and the

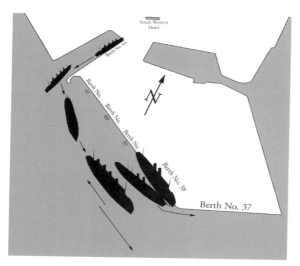

Left: *This three-dimensional map shows the stages of* Titanic's *departure and her near-collision with the* New York. *The arrows indicate the reversal of* Titanic's *engines and then the resumption of her course after the crisis had passed. The* New York *was warped into Berth No. 37.*

Below: *The stern of the* New York, *having broken loose from its moorings, is drawn toward the stern of the* Titanic.

New York's stern continued its arc toward the *Titanic*'s after port flanks.

The *Irish Times*' correspondent, standing on the quay, watched as the American liner's stern, loosed from its moorings, began to swing around into the channel, directly toward the stern of the *Titanic*. Ernest Townley had started to leave the waterfront once the *Titanic* had turned the corner and begun to proceed downstream. He hadn't made it a hundred yards before 'the magic of the *Titanic*' drew him back. He began to walk down the quay, and saw 'with great amazement' as the suction of *Titanic*'s propellers dragged the *New York* from her berth. Her 'stout hawsers ... [had] snapped like string under the strain.'

One of the two officers at the stern of the *Titanic* called out to Captain Gale of the tug *Vulcan* via megaphone. He ordered Gale to proceed to the port side stern of the *Titanic*. Meanwhile, the engine order telegraphs on the Bridge of the *Titanic* rang out again, and the liner's port engine was reversed. Captain Gale saw that the port engine was engaged in reverse as he came around the port side. Someone, he never knew who, called out to him to get between the onrushing stern of the *New York* and the stern of the *Titanic*, and to push the powerless American liner back. Gale immediately dismissed this idea as madness, preferring not to have his tug crushed into kindling between the giant steel hulls. Instead he proceeded to get a line on the port stern of the *New York*. Although that line immediately parted under the strain, he quickly got a second one attached, and began to drive his tug at full power, trying to slow and then stop the American vessel's stern-first dash at the *Titanic*.

Up on the Boat Deck of the *Titanic*, the man standing beside Francis Browne said: 'Now for a crash.' Browne ignored the remark, held his camera far over the bulwark rail, pointed down and aft, and snapped a photo of the *New York*'s stern closing on the *Titanic*. To Second Officer Lightoller, who was then forward, a collision looked 'inevitable'.[88] To May Futrelle, standing braced for whatever would happen next, 'it seemed certain' that the two vessels would collide.[89] Thomas Andrews thought that the 'situation was decidedly unpleasant.'[90]

However, all was not lost. Between the reverse wash from *Titanic*'s port propeller and the frenzied attempts of the tug *Vulcan*, the *New York* stopped its forward advance. Captain Gale later swore that by that point there were only four feet separating the two hulls. *Titanic* Saloon Steward John 'Jack' Butterworth thought that the two ships were so close that one could have tossed a penny onto the *New York* from the *Titanic*.[91] Meanwhile, the *Titanic* herself began to move astern, and a delicate ballet of enormous steel vessels and tugboats ensued, with the *Titanic* backing straight up the channel, and the tugs trying to make sure that her motion did not cause the *New York* to start toward her afresh.

Beesley remembered watching the *New York*, with the *Vulcan* trailing behind, as she 'moved obliquely down the dock, her stern gliding along the side of the *Titanic* some few yards away.' May Futrelle watched this turn of events, being 'only a little frightened' as the *New York*'s counter stern passed alongside and then out ahead of the *Titanic*'s bows. Francis Browne ran over to the starboard side of the Boat Deck, and took a photo looking forward, showing the *New York*'s stern swinging out ahead of the *Titanic*'s bow, her hawsers trailing limply in the water. Meanwhile, Major Peuchen recalled that the *Titanic* had come to rest, and was 'simply standing still'.[92]

Above: *This photo, taken by Francis Browne, looks aft along the port side of the* Titanic *from the Boat Deck. The stern of the* New York *is perilously close to striking the White Star liner. Passengers and crew on the larger vessel lean out over the rail or through Promenade Deck windows to watch the scene unfold. To take this picture, Browne held the camera over the midships bulwark rail.*

Below: *The* Vulcan *begins to pull the* New York *away from the* Titanic.

The whole thing had been a tremendously close shave. Pilot Bowyer and Captain Smith – the same men who had been in command of the *Olympic* the previous fall during the affair with the *Hawke* – no doubt breathed a particularly deep sigh of relief at avoiding similar unpleasantness on this day. Ashore, Ernest Townley said that the incident was 'astounding. It gave one an eerie fear of the greatest steamer in the world.'[93] Indeed, some aboard the ship took the event as a very bad sign. First Class passenger Norman Chambers recalled it as an 'evil omen'.[94] Others took it completely in stride. Second Class passenger Charlotte Collyer said that the incident 'didn't frighten anyone, as it only seemed to prove how powerful the *Titanic* was.'[95] Jacques Futrelle turned to his wife and laughed, now that the danger was behind them. 'Well', he said jocularly, 'she got that out of her system, anyway!'[96]

Two tugs took the errant *New York* under their lead, and 'between the two of them they dragged her round the corner of the quay which just here came to an end on the side of the river', Beesley recalled. The *New York* was tied up at the extreme southern edge of the Eastern Docks. This was only a temporary berth for her, as the strip of dock was only about 470 feet in length, and the *New York* was nearly a hundred feet longer than that. This meant that her clipper-style bow protruded from the eastern edge of

the dock. Meanwhile, further hawsers were made fast to the *Oceanic*, to make sure that she did not decide to follow the *New York*'s example when the *Titanic* resumed her trip down the river.

Once the *Oceanic* and *New York* were squared away, the *Titanic* resumed her down-river journey. Then she paused, and the tug *Vulcan* nudged along the after port quarter of the liner. It took some minutes for the standby crewmen, who had not disembarked earlier, to board the tug through the after gangway on E Deck. Once this task had been completed, the *Titanic* resumed her forward progress for the second time that afternoon. Elmer Taylor recalled:

> When the mild excitement of a collision ceased and the consequent delay was over, we were finally moving with the engines barely turning, but it wasn't long before we were in Southampton water with enough leeway to safely proceed at full speed.[97]

Ahead of the liner lay a course of about twenty-five land miles of water before she reached the Nab Light. This navi-gational aid, which sat off the eastern shore of the Isle of Wight, marked the endpoint of Southampton Water and the starting point to the open waters of the English Channel. Although *Titanic* had only just begun her maiden voyage, she was already behind schedule.

Passing from the White Star Dock and steaming south-east down the River Test was a relatively straightforward affair. It encompassed about an hour's steaming once the *New York* incident had been resolved and the ship's engines were restarted.[98] For this journey, the ship was brought up to a speed of about 20 knots, and the central turbine was engaged.

Shortly after the liner's trip down the Test had resumed, Ship's Bugler Peter Fletcher began to play 'The Roast Beef of Old England,' signaling that lunch was being served. Francis Browne recalled that this, the first meal served aboard the liner, was a very brief affair, as everyone was 'anxious to be on deck while we steamed down the channel between England and the Isle of Wight'.[99]

At the bottom of the River Test, the channel diverged to the east and southwest, around the Isle of Wight. Although

With the Titanic *backing up the river, the stern of the* New York *swung out in front of the White Star liner, still trailing her broken lines into the water. Two tugs carefully maintain the* Titanic's *orientation in the channel, while many of* Titanic's *passengers lean over the Well Deck bulwark to see the* New York.

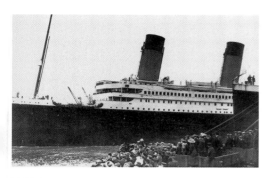

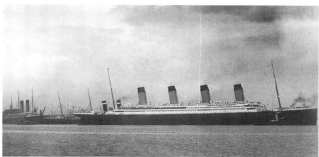

Top left: *With the* New York *tied off at Berth No. 37,* Titanic *resumes its departure. The bow of the White Star liner* Oceanic *can be seen at the extreme right of the image.*

Top right: *Titanic* continues to move forward, with the *Oceanic* and *New York visible at left. One of the tugs maintains a position off the liner's starboard bow.*

Second row, left: *This heavily re-touched photo is of the* Titanic, *although one could hardly discern this through the artist's 'improvements'. The tug remains at the liner's bow.*

Second row, right: *Looking aft from* Titanic's *decks, the* New York *hardly fits at Berth No. 37. Her clipper bow overhangs her temporary dock by quite some distance. The* Oceanic, *beside which* New York *had been moored prior to the incident, can be seen behind the American liner.*

Third row: *This photo was taken from the edge of the wharf.* New York, *being pushed into Berth No. 37, can be seen at the right side of the photo.* Titanic *has moved forward some distance, but is again stopped. The tug* Vulcan *is alongside her aft-port quarter, ready to offload the last standby crewmen.*

Left: *Another view of the* Titanic *during her second stop in mid-river, offloading unneeded standby crew to the* Vulcan.

Top left: *A wide-angle shot of the River Test as the* Vulcan *paused alongside the* Titanic.

Top right: Titanic *resumes her course down the Test. Lifeboat No. 1 remains cranked in, and the starboard anchor dangles nearly to the water.*

Above: *This photo, taken near Cowes, shows that the liner has decelerated from her pace down the Solent. The anchor remains low to the water, but Boat No. 1 has now been cranked out into its normal position over the water.*

Left: Titanic *steams down the Solent in this similarly-timed view. A large number of Third Class passengers still line the Poop Deck. A knot of Second Class passengers can be seen aft on the Boat Deck and B Deck, as well.*

the western passage was a more direct route to open water and Cherbourg, which was west of their current position, that channel was not dredged deeply enough to accommodate the White Star liner's draught. *Titanic* was thus forced to take the eastern passage, which was known as the Solent. However, the 'reverse-S' curve to enter the Solent was tricky, taking about ten minutes to execute from beginning to end. As the ship was decelerated to a speed of about 11–12 knots preparatory to entering the bend, the central turbine was disengaged, and Pilot Bowyer would have sounded the ship's whistles to indicate to other traffic that the liner was about to make a turn.

The maneuver began at Calshot Spit, when the ship was steered on to a course of about South 65° West, or west-southwest.[100] After slowing, and then reversing the ship's port engine while turning the helm, the *Titanic* would have made the turn into the Solent in about two minutes' time. Swinging to a course of South 59° East,[101] or southeast by east, the ship's engines would then have been engaged again together, and the turbine re-engaged. Although the telegraphs were set to 'Full Ahead', that speed was limited to 20 knots in confined waters. From that point, it took about three-quarters of an hour for the ship to reach the Nab Light, and the open water of the English Channel.[102]

Second Class passenger Lawrence Beesley recalled a truly picturesque trip down Southampton Water to the Channel:

> We dropped down Spithead, past the shores of the Isle of Wight looking superbly beautiful in new spring foliage, exchanged salutes with a White Star

Below left: *This photo – forward on A Deck, looking to port – was taken by Francis Browne as the* Titanic *steamed through Southampton water. A lone crewman, possibly Quartermaster Alfred Olliver, stands vigil. Browne's young friend Jack Odell leans against the forward bulkhead. In the distance, one of the three men standing in the distance was identified as Archibald Butt.*

Below right: *This Browne photo, looking aft on the port side Promenade Deck, near the time* Titanic *made her turn into the Solent. The steamer visible in the water was reportedly named* Tagus, *and was about to take the western channel around the Isle of Wight to open water. The figure walking aft is not Captain Smith, as is commonly thought; he would still have been on the Bridge during this series of maneuvers.*

Bottom: Titanic *off Cowes on the Isle of Wight, moving east through the Solent.*

tug lying-to in wait for one of their liners inward bound, and saw in the distance several warships with attendant black destroyers guarding the entrance from the sea.[103]

Francis Browne had a rather odd experience while the ship was steaming down the Solent, with the Isle of Wight visible off the starboard side. A fellow passenger not known to Browne, but who he later discovered was Jacques Futrelle, asked him: 'Could you tell me, Sir, why is the Channel so narrow here?'

A few moments of confusion followed. Browne at first thought that he was referring to the forts guarding the entrance to the Spithead, and managed to respond with: 'I suppose when they built these forts they never calculated on having ships as big as the *Titanic*.'

'Oh, I did not mean that', Futrelle clarified. 'Why is the land so near here?'

The clarification only added to Browne's confusion. 'Well, I suppose, Sir, that they could not shift the Isle of Wight back any further than it is.'

Futrelle was still unsatisfied. 'How far would you say it is from shore to shore here, Sir?'

Browne hazarded a guess. 'I should say about ten or twelve miles.'

'Well, how far is it from Dover to Calais?' Futrelle pressed.

'Twenty-one', Browne was able to respond smartly.

'Why then don't you English cross here?' Futrelle asked.

It was at this point that Browne began to understand what all the confusion was really about. This gentleman with the loud, penetrating voice, believed that the Isle of Wight visible to the south was actually France, and that the Solent was the English Channel. 'Oh that's not France', Browne said, 'that's the Isle of Wight.'

'I see', Futrelle replied. 'I thought it was France.' Then he walked off.[104]

At the Nab Light, *Titanic* stood poised to begin the first open-water stage of her crossing. Her mighty powerplant was brought up to a reading of 68 revolutions on the reciprocating engines, indicating a speed of about 20.2 knots through the water. Sixty-five nautical miles away lay the breakwater which shielded the harbor at Cherbourg, France: her first port of call.[105] The liner set her bow south-southwest, making a bee-line for that port as she tried to make up for lost time. The weather on that short journey was splendid, calm and clear if cool and overcast. The cool temperatures, as well as the breeze on decks, prompted many passengers to procure a good steamer rug for themselves while sitting in their deck chair; however, the conditions were not by any means inclement or unpleasant.

Francis Browne recalled a picturesque cross-Channel passage that afternoon. He and a number of others on board were surprised at just how good a *ship* the *Titanic* was. Easily visible from the liner's decks were four-masted sailing vessels and packet boats, all of which were 'tossing in the choppy sea, while on the *Titanic* there was no indication that the ship was at sea save the brisk cool breeze blowing along the decks, and the swiftly moving panorama of distant coast line.'[106]

Many others were impressed with her behavior, as well. Just after clearing the Isle of Wight, one passenger on the Boat Deck overheard as a lady nearby pointed out a small three-masted sailing vessel and said: 'Look how that ship is

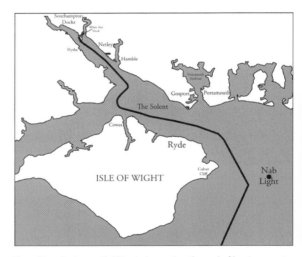

Top: *Near Portsmouth,* Titanic *is nearing the end of her journey to open water. She is framed nearly perfectly by a pair of Royal Navy warships. Doubtless, these were the same warships noticed by Lawrence Beesley.*

Middle: *This Browne photo, looking aft along the port side, shows Boat No. 10 behind two Second Class passengers. The liner is near Portsmouth, and is making good speed; her wake can clearly be seen and she has recently made a turn to port. Although the small craft is the Pilot Boat, the photo does not actually show Pilot Bowyer being disembarked. Astern, the No Man's Land fort can be seen.*

Bottom: *This map shows the approximate course of* Titanic *in leaving Southampton water before setting a course for Cherbourg.*

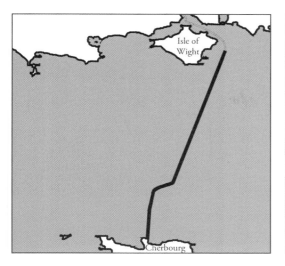

Top left: Titanic's *approximate course for Cherbourg.*

Top right: *This photo was taken by Francis Browne. Frequently cited as dating to Thursday, April 11, it was more likely taken on Wednesday afternoon, as is clear from the largely overcast weather. The view looks forward along the aft A Deck Promenade. The sliding doors to the starboard Verandah Café are open. Above, on the Boat Deck, Second Class passengers enjoy the panorama astern.*

Left: *This photo was also apparently taken on Wednesday, judging from the overcast weather. Here two First Class passengers walk on the aft Promenade of A Deck. Since the location of the photo was very close to the preceding one, it may have been taken at around the same time. A great quantity of deck chairs has been stacked on the Boat Deck above. The photo is a double exposure; a very faint view of the starboard Private Promenade can be seen.*

rolling. I never thought it was so rough.' The man turned and watched the tiny little vessel, noticing that she 'rolled and pitched so heavily that over her bow the seas were constantly breaking'. Up on the decks of the *Titanic*, however, 'there was no indication of the strength of tossing swell below. Were it not for the brisk breeze blowing along the decks, one would have scarcely imagined that every hour found us some 20 knots farther upon our course.'[107]

Some passengers, particularly those who were disembarking at Cherbourg or Queenstown, made the most of their time aboard, exploring every nook and cranny of the ship that they could find. Others took a more leisurely approach to the afternoon's activities. The ship's band played at tea in the D Deck First Class Reception Room in the mid-afternoon, and many took the opportunity to wind down from the excitement of boarding and departure, sip some tea, and listen to soothing music.

Nearly everyone who heard the band play recalled that they were very good. Even Bandmaster Wallace Hartley himself believed that their little orchestra was a nice ensemble – and he certainly would have had reason to complain if he did not think them up to par. Hartley was very much looking forward to making a good amount of money during the voyage ahead – not just from his wages, but also from the collection that was typically taken up for the orchestra members on each crossing.[108]

Among those who were taking refreshment in the Reception Room that afternoon was Elmer Taylor. He had just entered the room when he ran across a friend, Fletcher Fellows Lambert-Williams; Taylor referred to him simply as 'Williams.'[109] The two men fell into conversation. Apparently, Taylor found Miss Harriette Crosby to be quite an attractive girl; Williams was then traveling alone, and Taylor offered: 'I'll introduce you to a nice looking girl,

The *Titanic*'s Band

The *Titanic*'s band was comprised of eight men. However, in point of fact the band was divided into two separate groups. The first was a quintet led by Bandmaster and lead violinist Wallace Hartley, who was then aged 33. There was also a separate musical trio, who played for patrons of the First Class *à la carte* Restaurant. Each of the two groups had their own list of selections from which to play. Under normal circumstances, they did not play together; however, Hartley had direct oversight over all of the musicians.

The remaining musicians were 24-year-old pianist Theodore Brailey,[110] 20-year-old cellist Roger Bricoux, bass player John Clarke,[111] violinist John 'Jock' Hume,[112] violinist George Krins, cellist Percy Taylor,[113] and 32-year-old cellist John Woodward.

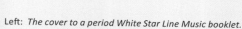

The five-man band led by Hartley played daily in both First and Second Class areas of the ship. From 10:00–11:00 a.m., they played in the Aft Second Class Entrance Foyer on C Deck. Then they proceeded to the First Class Entrance on the Boat Deck, and played from 11:00 a.m. to noon. At 4:00 p.m., they re-assembled in the First Class Reception Room on D Deck to play for tea for an hour. Then they returned to the Second Class Entrance on C Deck between 5:00 and 6:00 p.m. After dinner, they went up to the Reception Room and played from 8:00–9:15 p.m. Finally, they went down to the Second Class Entrance again, playing from 9:15–10:15 p.m. In all, this made for about six and a quarter hours of performing on a daily basis, with plenty of time for meals between stretches of performing.

We know that violinist John 'Jock' Hume and cellist John Woodward played in the five-man orchestra with Wallace Hartley. It would also seem that cellist Roger Bricoux played in the trio for the Restaurant, and his Continental roots would have lent itself to the Continental ambiance White Star was trying to create there. We also know that a pianist would not have been needed in the First Class Restaurant trio, since unlike the *Olympic*, no piano had been provided for *Titanic*'s Restaurant.

Beyond that, however, we have very little to go on. More than that, there is some evidence that things were a bit flexible in their composition. For example, Second Class passenger Juliette Laroche wrote a letter in which she mentioned that the

Left: *The cover to a period White Star Line Music booklet.*

First row, left to right: *Bandmaster Wallace Hartley, Theodore Brailey, Roger Bricoux, John Clarke.*

Second row, left to right: *John 'Jock' Hume, George Krins, Percy Taylor, John Woodward.*

2			
38 Dear Little Denmark	...	...	*Rubens*
39 The Fair Co-ed	...	...	*Luder*
40 The Grand Mogul ...	...	...	"
41 The Gay Musician	...	*Julian Edward*	
42 A Trip to Japan	...	...	*Klein*
43 His Honour the Mayor	...	*Julian Edward*	
44 The Red Mill	...	...	*V. Herbert*
45 The Prima Donna ...	...	...	"
46 The Three Twins	...	*Karl Hoschna*	
47 The Prince of Pilsen	...	...	*Luder*
48 It Happened in Nordland	...	*V. Herbert*	
49 Neptune's Daughter	...	...	"
50 Faust ...	...	...	*Gounod*
51 Carmen	...	...	*Bizet*
52 Il Trovatore	...	...	*Verdi*
53 Rigoletto	...	...	"
54 La Traviata ...	...	...	"
55 Puritani	...	...	*Bellini*
56 La Sonnambula	...	...	"
57 Lucia di Lammermoor	...	*Donizetti*	
58 La Favorita ...	...	...	"
59 Tosca	...	...	*Puccini*
60 La Bohéme ...	...	...	"
61 The Mikado...	...	...	*Sullivan*
62 Pirates of Penzance	...	...	"
63 Iolanthe	...	...	"
64 A Princess of Kensington	...	*E. German*	
65 Merrie England	...	...	"
66 Tom Jones	...	...	"
67 Manon Lescaut	...	...	*Puccini*
68 Les Contes D'Hoffman	...	*Offenbach*	
69 Mefistofele ...	...	...	*Boito*
70 Tannhauser	...	...	*Wagner*
71 Lohengrin	...	...	"
72 The Girls of Gottenburg ...	*Caryll & Monckton*		
73 Haddon Hall	...	...	*Sullivan*
74 The Gondoliers	...	...	"
75 Recollections of Gounod ...	...	*Godfrey*	
76 Sullivan's Melodies	...	...	"
77 The Maid and the Mummy	...	*A. Aarons*	
78 Love's Lottery	...	*Julian Edwards*	
79 M'lle Modisté	...	...	"
80 Miss Dolly Dollars	...	...	"
81 Wonderland	...	...	"

3			
82 The Princess Beggar	...	...	*A. G. Robyn*
83 The Geisha ...	...	...	*Jones*
84 San Toy	...	...	"

Suites, Fantasias, etc.

85 Peer Gynt Suite	...	...	*Greig*
86 Three Dances : " Henry VIII " ...	*E. German*		
87 Three Dances : " Nell Gwyn " ...	"		
88 Three Dances : " Tom Jones " ...	"		
89 The Rose	...	...	*Myddleton*
90 The Thistle ...	...	...	"
91 The Shamrock	...	...	"
92 American National Airs ...	...	*Tobani*	
93 Plantation Songs	...	...	*Clutsam*
94 Canadian Songs	...	...	*Retford*
95 Tosti's Popular Songs	...	...	*Godfrey*
96 Popular Songs	...	...	*S. Adams*
97 Reminiscences of the Savoy	...	*M. Moore*	
98 Reminiscences of Wales	...	...	*Godfrey*
99 Reminiscences of All Nations	...	"	
100 National Anthems, Hymns, etc., of all Nations.			

Waltzes.

101 Love and Life in Holland	...	...	*Joyce*
102 Partners Galore	...	...	*G. V.*
103 The Druid's Prayer	...	...	*Davson*
104 Vision of Salome	...	...	*Joyce*
105 Remembrance	...	...	"
106 Beautiful Spring	...	...	*Lincke*
107 Wedding Dance	...	...	"
108 Comedie d'Amour	...	...	*G. Colin*
109 Valse Septembre	...	...	*F. Godwin*
110 Mondaine	...	...	*Bosc*
111 Réve d'Artiste	...	...	"
112 Swing Song	...	...	*Hollaender*
113 Sphinx	...	...	*Popy*
114 Songe d'Automne	...	...	*Joyce*
115 La Lettre de Manon	...	...	*Giliet*
116 Cecilia	...	...	*Pether*
117 Apach's Dance	...	...	*Offenbach*
118 Verschmähte Liebe	...	...	*P. Lincke*
119 Lysistrata	...	...	"
120 Luna	...	...	"

Selections 38–120 of a later White Star Line songbook.

band was playing nearby at the time. This would normally have been the duty of the five-man band; instead, she specifically mentioned only four players: one violin, two cellos and a piano.[114]

There is no reason to doubt this report, so where was the second violin player or the violist at the time? Had Hume or Krins been shifted on to the trio? Was Krins seasick, perhaps? We know that three of the players – Clarke, Krins and Taylor – had never played on a liner before. Who was the second cello player she mentioned? We know that Woodward was the cellist most regularly seen in Second Class, according to Kate Buss. Was the second cellist Mrs Laroche mentioned Roger Bricoux? Possibly not. Pianist Brailey could also play the cello, but in that case, Percy Taylor would have been playing the piano.

Another interesting report comes from First Class Stewardess Violet Jessop, who reported that Sunday evening, she saw Scottish cut-up Jock Hume leading the main orchestra and playing first violin. He spoke to her 'during the interval' – probably a reference to the time when they finished playing for tea in the First Class Reception Room at 5:00 p.m., and as they were headed down to do the Second Class performance immediately thereafter.[115] Young Hume told Jessop with a laugh that the band

was 'about to give them a "real tune, a Scotch tune, to finish up with".' Perhaps he was merely kidding with the pretty stewardess, as Hume was notoriously witty, or perhaps he was thinking of something in particular he had in mind for the Second Class concert. It is impossible to tell. Yet the sighting leaves the question: unless Jessop was wholly mistaken in this recollection – which would not be an impossibility – where was Wallace Hartley?

Perhaps the composition and number of the two musical ensembles was not wholly fixed, and there was some variance between the different performances or days of the crossing. While one could hardly imagine that some of the eight performers would normally have changed positions, perhaps some of the members were unable to play during portions of the voyage due to illness or seasickness. In the end, we are left with more questions than answers regarding the composition of the *Titanic*'s two bands.

What we do know is that each of them was an accomplished musician, and that some of them were even able to play more than one instrument. Their work during the voyage was favorably mentioned by many passengers, and their performances added materially to the pleasant atmosphere aboard the ship as the crossing progressed.[116]

and if you play your part, you will have a companion for the entire voyage.'[117]

'Oh yes, how come?' was Williams' response.

Accordingly, Taylor walked over to the Crosbys, who were sitting not far away, and he asked if he could introduce a friend. The Crosbys responded in the affirmative, and suggested that they join them for tea. The conversation over tea seemed to go very well, and the entire party was quite convivial. They thus asked the purser for a table for six at dinner, so that they could continue their social interaction as the evening, and the voyage, progressed.[118]

Even as passengers began to get acquainted with one another, the crew was beginning to try and settle into some sort of a routine. There were a lot of things that needed to be seen to before the crew could become a single, cohesive entity that could perform its duties efficiently.

The ship's lookout men were struggling with one particular curiosity. During the trip down from Belfast, then-Second Officer David Blair had supplied the lookouts with a pair of binoculars to use, but once the liner had departed Southampton, it became evident that the set of binoculars had not been made available for them again. Binoculars were not an absolute essential in lookouts' work of spotting things to report to the officers on the Bridge, but the lookouts were unsure why they were suddenly doing without. Accordingly, Lookout George Symons made a trip up to the Bridge after departure to ask if they could have a pair; Second Officer Lightoller made some inquiries, but did not find a pair that had been set aside for their use.[119]

There were other behind-the-scenes things that needed to be tended to, as well. For example, wholly unknown to the *Titanic*'s passengers, and most of her crew, there was a problem brewing below decks: a fire in one of the coal bunkers. In point of fact, this fire did not threaten to cause the ship to go up in one giant plume of smoke, fricasseeing passengers while they slept; it was wholly confined to the starboard coal bunker at the forward end of Boiler Room No. 5.[120] Bunker fires were a rather common problem on coal-fired ships.[121] Coal stored in a bunker near a source of heat was well known at the time to be susceptible to spontaneous combustion. In the case of the *Titanic*, the fire had begun at Belfast, over a week before the liner departed on her maiden voyage.[122]

While not unheard of, leaving a coal fire unattended simply wouldn't do. As soon as the ship cleared Southampton, Chief Engineer Bell approached Leading Fireman Frederick Barrett, and ordered him begin the task of extinguishing it. By using the coal in that bunker as quickly as possible, it was hoped that the actual source of the fire could be exposed and removed sooner rather than later. By way of explanation, Bell said to Barrett: 'Builder's men want to inspect that bulkhead.'[123] Accordingly, a hose was run into the bunker, and it was 'going all the time' under the watchful eye of Barrett and a team of between eight and ten stokers.[124] Unfortunately for the men, getting to the bottom of the pile was going to take some time. Meanwhile, the ship proceeded across the Channel to her very first port of call …

The port of Cherbourg was located at the northern tip of a large peninsula of the French coast which jutted north toward England. Its location was thus ideal for cross-Channel steamships to stop over and embark or disembark passengers. One period reference book said:

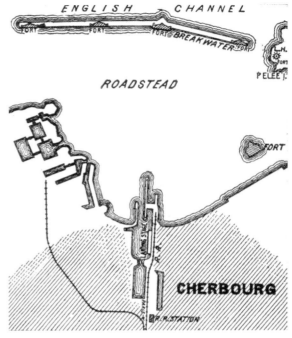

Above: *A period map of Cherbourg Harbor.*

Right: *First Class passenger Edith Rosenbaum.*

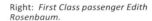

This important port is a great French naval base, and the steamer passes the forts and anchors inside the breakwater … Cherbourg has become the most important gateway for Americans planning a trip to the Continent, and the principal trans-Atlantic lines include this port now in their itineraries. The great Continental metropolis, Paris, is only a few hours distant and lines radiate from it to all parts of Europe.[125]

The port was not without drawbacks, however. Passengers disembarking there were advised that under '*no circumstances*' should they 'ever stop at a hotel in Cherbourg'. It was also noted that the 'train service to Paris is abominable, and one steamship company threatened to abandon it as a port of call, if conditions were not improved. It is a shame that such an ideal port should be so badly served.'[126]

Passengers intending to take passage on the *Titanic* that evening began to congregate in Cherbourg. The Boat Train from Paris arrived at about 4:00 p.m., bringing with it most of those who were planning to take passage on the liner.

Among them was 33-year-old Edith Rosenbaum, a journalist with *Women's Wear Daily*. Later known as Edith Russell, she also designed her own line of clothing for the Lord &

Above: *A splendid view of* Titanic *entering Cherbourg Harbor.*

Second row, left to right: *First Class passengers Margaret Brown, John Jacob Astor IV, and Madeleine Astor.*

Taylor department store of New York.[127] She had booked passage to America on the *George Washington*, which was scheduled to sail on April 7, but had switched her ticket to the *Titanic*. Not only did this decision net her three extra days in Paris, including Easter weekend, but it also gave her the opportunity to take passage on the new flagship of the White Star Line. Edith noticed that everyone was quite merry on the Boat Train, and excitement was high over boarding the great liner and seeing her wonders – so ably described in the press during the previous months – first-hand.[128] Upon arrival, however, the intended passengers were disappointed to learn that the ship had been delayed in leaving Southampton.

Forty-four-year-old Mrs Margaret Brown, a wealthy socialite from Denver, Colorado, also arrived in Cherbourg aboard the Boat Train from Paris. She was returning to the United States rather suddenly, having received word that her grandson was ill. Margaret – she would only become known as 'Molly' many years later – recalled boarding the *Nomadic*, 'the tender that was waiting to convey the hundreds of passengers to the master palace of the sea', shortly after leaving the train. Unfortunately, the group then had to wait for 'an hour or more … in the cold, gray atmosphere' aboard the little vessel. Only then did the funnels of the mighty *Titanic* – 'the world's greatest masterpiece of modern ocean liners' – appear on the other side of the harbor breakwater. With the appearance of the vessel, there was a murmur of excitement which ran throughout the First Class passengers aboard the tender …

… *Titanic* had finally arrived.

As the liner approached the Cherbourg breakwater, passenger Francis Browne and a number in his traveling party took the opportunity to bid farewell to some of their acquaintances from that day who were to disembark at the French port. They were still saying their goodbyes when the ship's bugler sounded the call to dinner.[129] A number of individuals, Browne recalled, had to ask him for directions on how to find the Dining Saloon.

Eventually, at about 6:30 p.m., the *Titanic* dropped anchor inside the breakwater, with her starboard side facing south, toward the city of Cherbourg. The sky was still quite light, as sunset would not take place for another twenty minutes, at around 6:50 p.m. The White Star tender *Traffic* tied up alongside first, taking the cross-Channel mails, depositing mails bound for Queenstown or New York, and transferring 102 Third Class passengers to the liner.

Elmer and Juliet Taylor watched as the French port tender, apparently the *Traffic*, disembarked its human cargo into the enormous *Titanic*. They watched, amused, as sailors on the tender were 'handling, or shall I say smashing luggage and moving continental mails'. Then the couple proceeded to dinner.

Among those boarding from the *Traffic* were two young Lebanese siblings bound for Jacksonville, Florida. They were 11-year-old Master Elias Nicola-Yarred and his 14-year-old sister Jamila. Their family had begun a staged migration from Lebanon to the United States in 1904, and the two youngsters and their father were the final members to make the crossing. They had purchased tickets aboard the *Titanic* in Marseilles, but unfortunately their father had failed to pass a physical examination due to an eye infection. As a result, the two children were traveling alone.[130]

Meanwhile, the First and Second Class passenger tender *Nomadic* was steaming out to meet the *Titanic*. Margaret Brown, who was aboard the *Nomadic*, recalled:

> The tender put on steam, and after half an hour in a running sea we were alongside the keel of the *Titanic*. The tossing of the small craft in the

choppy sea caused most of the passengers to be uncomfortable and actively ill. All were chilled through.[131]

Among the chilled and queasy passengers on the *Nomadic* with Mrs Brown were many of the most prestigious individuals booked for the upcoming Atlantic crossing. It may have seemed as if boarding from Cherbourg, rather than Southampton, was the ultimate execution of being 'fashionably late', but in reality it was simply a matter of convenience, as many were returning from excursions to the Continent or even Africa.

Margaret Brown, for example, had been traveling through Egypt. While there, she had met up with 47-year-old John Jacob Astor and his second wife, 18-year-old Madeleine. Astor was undoubtedly the richest man taking this trip on the *Titanic*; the couple was returning from an extended honeymoon, during which they had seen Egypt and Paris. Their wedding had become something of a scandal in their American social circles, and their choice of honeymoon travel arrangements could not have been more ideal. Not only was an extended European and North African honeymoon extremely fashionable at the time, but its protracted length would also – hopefully – have allowed for the scandal to calm in their absence.

As the *Nomadic* steamed out across Cherbourg Harbor, darkness began to envelop the great ship and *Titanic*'s lights all began to flicker to life, until she looked like a city afloat. She was truly a magnificent spectacle. Edith Rosenbaum watched her as the *Nomadic* approached the liner. She recalled:

In the dusk, her decks were 11 tiers of glittering electric lights. She was less a ship than a floating city, pennants streaming from her halyards like carnival in Nice. Colonel and Mrs John Jacob Astor were standing near me at the rail. I had made the eastern crossing with them the previous spring. The colonel pointed out some of the vital statistics of the mammoth ocean liner ...

'She's unsinkable', Colonel Astor said, 'a modern shipbuilding miracle'.[132]

Sixty-five-year-old Engelhart Ostby and his daughter, 22-year-old Helen, had been traveling through Europe. Hailing from Providence, Rhode Island, Ostby was a jeweler; Mrs Ostby had, unfortunately, passed away just over twelve years before. Since 1906, he had taken his daughter with him on his regular business trips to Europe. On this occasion the pair had been vacationing in Egypt and southern Europe. While they were in Nice, they had caught wind of the *Titanic*'s upcoming maiden voyage. After discussing the matter, father and daughter decided to take the new liner back to the States, obtaining reservations in First Class. Helen recalled:

We went up to Paris and while there we met two acquaintances, Mr and Mrs Frank Warren of Portland, Ore., whom we had met in Egypt, and who also had reservations for the *Titanic*.

On the 10th of April we took the boat train to Cherbourg. The *Titanic* remained out in the harbor, lighted and beautiful in the night.[133]

Shortly after sunset, or at about 7:00 p.m., the *Nomadic* tied up alongside the towering hull of the *Titanic*. In short

Top: *A mid-1930s view of the* Nomadic *at work in Cherbourg Harbor.*

Middle: *A heavily-retouched starboard side view of the* Titanic *in harbor. The original photograph was taken in daylight, and can be seen at the top of the preceding page, but it was rendered to show the ship after darkness had fallen.*

Bottom: *Another heavily-retouched view of the* Titanic *in Cherbourg Harbor; like the preceding photo, it was taken in daylight, but retouched to show the ship after dark.*

order, the passengers began to board the great liner via a gangplank into the D Deck Entrance and Reception Room, but the process would take quite some time. Among those climbing that gangplank was 71-year-old First Class passenger Ramon Artagaveytia. Artagaveytia was an Argentinean businessman returning from visiting his nephew in Berlin. 'When we approached ..., surrounded by the steam, it [*Titanic*] seemed like "Rio de la Plata".' Looking up, he thought that she looked like a five-story house. 'At the entrance', he recalled, 'there were like fifty butlers. One of them took my luggage, and through an elevator (there were three) we went up to my stateroom on floor B.'

Another trio of First Class passengers boarding that evening consisted of 49-year-old Sir Cosmo Duff Gordon, his 48-year-old wife Lady Lucy Christiana Duff Gordon, and her secretary, 30-year-old Miss Laura Francatelli.[134] Sir Cosmo Duff Gordon was a member of a prestigious Scottish family, and was the fifth Baronet of Halkin. He was an athletic man, and was revered for his fencing talents. At the 1906 Summer Olympics in Athens, he had led the English to pick up a silver medal in the four-man Team Épée. In so doing, he was hit only once, and came out top in scoring.[135]

Lady Duff Gordon, born Lucy Christiana Sutherland, was the daughter of a Toronto civil engineer, and the older sister of authoress Elinor Glyn. Lucy had married James Wallace in 1884, and had a daughter, Esme, the following year. The marriage was not a happy one, however, with both husband and wife regularly seeking solace in extramarital affairs. They were divorced in 1893, and this situation – being a divorcée with a young daughter – forced Lucy to find a way of supporting herself. As she had always had a penchant for fashion, she became a dressmaker, working from her home. She was so successful that she eventually opened a shop in London, and became known as 'Lucille'. She had married Sir Cosmo in 1900, adding an air of old-world respectability to her personal reputation. Her business continued to expand, becoming 'Lucille, Ltd', and she had just recently opened branch shops in New York City and Paris. 'Lucille' lingerie, tea gowns and evening wear became quite popular with the stars of the stage, and of the emerging 'silver screen'.

Sudden and pressing business in New York had prompted Lady Duff Gordon to book passage on the first available ship. A couple of days before the sailing, she had traveled down to the White Star offices to see what offerings they might have. The booking clerk had told her that the only berths he had were on the new *Titanic*.

'Oh, I should not care to cross on a new ship. I should be nervous', she replied, though the seasoned trans-Atlantic traveler wasn't exactly sure why the idea made her uneasy.

The clerk laughed at her trepidation. 'Of all things, I should imagine you could not possibly feel nervous on the *Titanic*', he said. 'Why the boat is absolutely unsinkable. Her water-tight compartments would enable her to weather the fiercest sea ever known, and she is the last word in comfort and luxury.' Finally, he added: 'This first voyage is going to make history in ocean travel.'

Still unconvinced, Lady Duff Gordon did not immediately book passage. Instead, she returned home and told her husband of her unease. At first he laughed at her, thinking that she was joking. Then he had realized that she was in earnest, and so he offered to join her on the voyage. Her fears somewhat soothed, she had returned to the ticket office and booked passage for them both – under the name Mr & Mrs Morgan – as well as for her secretary, Miss Francatelli.[136]

After the trio boarded, they found their way to their accommodations. Sir Cosmo was booked into cabin A-16, while his wife would be staying across the passageway in A-20. Miss Francatelli – or 'Franks', as Lady Duff Gordon referred to her – would be staying below in E-26. While at first strike one as unusual for the Duff Gordons to have been staying in separate rooms, each of the cabins was listed as a single-berth room, with only a narrow bed. Although each

could accommodate a second passenger on a sofa berth if necessary, booking two cabins directly across the passageway from each other would give each of the Duff Gordons much more room to get comfortable. Each of their cabins had a pair of windows overlooking the enclosed port side Promenade Deck. Lady Duff Gordon was particularly pleased with her stateroom. 'My pretty little cabin, with its electric heater and pink curtains, delighted me,' she later recalled.[137]

For others who boarded from the *Nomadic*, there was less trepidation about the voyage than there was excitement, as well as thoughts of returning home after an extended absence. The Thayers, from Haverford, Pennsylvania, were another notable family boarding that evening. Forty-nine-

---

Below left: *First Class passenger Sir Cosmo Duff Gordon.*

Below right: *First Class passenger Lady Lucy Duff Gordon*

Bottom: *Olympic's stateroom A-16, a near duplicate of the room Sir Cosmo Duff Gordon had during* Titanic's *voyage. His wife's room, although laid out differently, would have been of similar style.*

Top row, left to right: *First Class passengers John B. Thayer, Marian Thayer, Jack Thayer, and George Rheims.*

Second row, left: *A 1917 view of First Class passenger Karl Behr.*

Second row, right: *First Class passenger R. Norris Williams in 1918.*

year-old John B. Thayer was the Second Vice-President of the Pennsylvania Railroad; his wife Marian was 39 years old, and the family had four children: John B. III, Frederick, Margaret and Pauline. Young John 'Jack' Thayer was then only 17 years old, and had been attending school in England. When he graduated, his parents and Mrs Thayer's maid Margaret Fleming had crossed to England to meet up with him; the family had done some traveling through Europe, and were headed for their Pennsylvania home.

George Alexander Lucien Rheims, 36, and his brother-in-law Joseph Loring, 30, also boarded from the *Nomadic* as First Class passengers. Rheims, who was president of an importing company in Paris dealing with millinery and silk goods, was traveling to New York City. Rheims' business required him to travel to America and back twice a year. Loring had originally been booked to sail to America on the *Carmania*, but Rheims had convinced him to change his ticket to the *Titanic* at the last minute.[138]

Twenty-eight-year-old Edgar Meyer and his 25-year-old wife Leila were also boarding the liner at Cherbourg. Edgar Meyer was a graduate of Ithaca, New York's Cornell University. After college, he moved to New York City, and had become a successful businessman. About two and a half years previously, he had married Leila Saks, daughter of Andrew Saks, founder of Saks & Co. – known more widely today as Saks Fifth Avenue. They had a one-year-old daughter, Jane, who had not made the European trip with them. In a strange twist, Andrew Saks had died on Monday, April 8, 1912, and the couple was hurrying home to attend his funeral.[139]

Twenty-six-year-old tennis star Karl Behr was joining the *Titanic* for happier reasons. He had quite literally chased young Helen Newsom – who had sailed on the *Titanic* with

her mother and stepfather, Richard and Sarah Beckwith – across the Atlantic. Behr fully intended to continue his courtship of Helen Newsom during the crossing.

Another tennis star boarding the *Titanic* at Cherbourg was Richard Norris Williams II, then 21 years old. The Geneva, Switzerland, native had intended to travel to the States for a summer of tennis, and then to see if he could get into Harvard. He was making the trip with his father, 51-year-old Charles D. Williams, a lawyer.

Forty-three-year-old First Class passenger Isaac Frauenthal was a lawyer from Wilkes-Barre, Pennsylvania, with a practice in New York City. He was boarding the liner with his brother, 49-year-old Dr Henry Frauenthal, and the doctor's 42-year-old wife Clara. Isaac Frauenthal was a little trepidatious as he boarded the *Titanic* that evening. He had a dream shortly before sailing which had disturbed him. In the dream, he seemed to be on a 'big steamship which suddenly crashed into something and began to go down'. He didn't pay much attention to the dream, as he was 'not at all superstitious or given to belief in the supernatural.' However, when the dream was repeated before he boarded the ship, it gave him pause for thought, and he became 'a little worried'. Frauenthal hadn't told his brother or sister-in-law about the dreams by the time the trio boarded the ship, perhaps thinking himself a little foolish for his nervousness. Still, he couldn't shake the unsettled feeling.[140]

Few others boarding that evening felt so apprehensive. Elmer Taylor recalled:

> Sailing day is usually given over to unpacking, making the cabin homelike, getting the lay of public rooms, trying to determine fore and aft, port and starboard, studying the passenger list, getting the feel of the ship, picking out landmarks and shipping as we sailed …
>
> The first day out, many passengers are so exhausted with farewell parties and preparations for the voyage they do not dress for dinner.

The Taylors remembered their dinner companions with fondness. Elmer wrote:

> It was an agreeable party. The Crosbys had been traveling through Europe, making London their last stop. They were Milwaukee people. He [Captain Edward] owned and operated the Crosby Line steamers on Lake Michigan. We had much in common, and I was not disappointed to learn that he was not John D., as I thought, when I first saw him. He was interested in Diesel engines, in mechanics and business. The young lady [Harriette] had been abroad to finish her musical education – a perfect model for a magazine cover, attractive, vivacious,

with a good modulated voice. Mother [Catherine] was rather "high hat", I thought – one of those tourists who flaunt their social position.[141]

Sitting not far away from the Taylor and Crosby clans in the Dining Saloon that night were Francis Browne and his companions. Sitting at a table for eight, Browne recalled that they were able to watch through the windows overlooking the Reception Room as the new arrivals boarded from the *Nomadic*; it was quite an active scene, and occasionally he could hear the 'busy hum of work as the luggage and mails were brought on board'.[142]

Edith Rosenbaum, who had stepped aboard from the *Nomadic*, recalled boarding an elevator and speaking with a young Lift Steward who was operating the equipment. The young man said that he felt very honored to have such a position on the mighty *Titanic*, particularly so because of his age.[143]

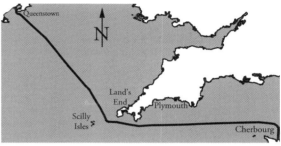

Meanwhile, Thomas Andrews was watching the *Nomadic* and *Traffic* at work. He wrote to his wife that night:

> We reached here in nice time and took on board quite a number of passengers. The two little tenders looked well, you will remember we built them about a year ago. We expect to arrive at Queenstown about 10.30 a.m. tomorrow. The weather is fine and everything shaping for a good voyage. I have a seat at the Doctor's table.[144]

After the commotion of new passengers boarding from Cherbourg had died down a bit, someone at Francis Browne's dinner table remarked: 'I wonder have we started yet.' Everyone around the table stopped their conversation, intently listening for any sound of engines, but there was no apparent vibration or throb indicating that they were operating, so they all agreed that the ship could not have started yet.

Just then, a Saloon Steward, who had overheard their conversation, leaned in and informed them: 'We have been outside the breakwater for more than ten minutes, Sir.'[145]

In all, some 172 First and Second Class passengers had boarded at Cherbourg, in addition to 102 Third Class passengers, for a total of 274. At the same time, some fifteen First Class and nine Second Class passengers disembarked at the French port. Many items of mail, cargo and luggage were also moved off the ship and onto the tenders. The process had taken quite some time – about an hour and a half from when the ship had first stopped. She finally weighed anchor at about 8:10 p.m. and steamed past the breakwater, bound for her next port of call: Queenstown, Ireland.

Thirty-six-year-old Mrs Eleanor Cassebeer had just boarded from the *Nomadic* as a First Class passenger. She was traveling without her husband, but was a veteran Atlantic traveler with ten crossings under her belt. After boarding, she proceeded to the Purser's Office on C Deck. Her first order of business was to see if she could upgrade her cabin. She had originally booked the cheapest First Class accommodations, as she was taking the trip on something of a budget.

As she got into line at the Enquiry Office, she apparently wasn't paying much attention to her surroundings, for she nearly ran into a fellow First Class passenger, 30-year-old Benjamin Foreman. Foreman stepped back and graciously told Mrs Cassebeer to go on ahead of him. They got behind a Jewish passenger who, Mrs Cassebeer thought, was taking an interminable time getting his seat assignment in the Din-

This page, from top: *The* Traffic.

This map gives an approximate idea of Titanic's *course from Cherbourg to Queenstown.*

The Olympic's *Enquiry Office on C Deck later in her career.*

First Class passenger Eleanor Cassebeer.

ing Saloon. She whispered back to Foreman: 'I hope I don't get next to that Jew.' Foreman smiled but didn't say anything.

When she finally arrived at the counter, Chief Purser Hugh McElroy was ready to help her. First order of business: she asked if the accommodations couldn't be improved for a few pounds. McElroy did a little digging, and upgraded her

Above: *First Class passengers Elmer and Juliet Taylor.*

Left: *A 1915 photo of First Class passenger Mahala Douglas.*

to a D Deck stateroom near that of Henry S. Harper and his wife Myna.[146] Mrs Cassebeer also inquired about her seat assignment in the Dining Saloon. She playfully asked McElroy if she couldn't get a seat at the Captain's table – a highly coveted spot on all trans-Atlantic liners.

McElroy affably told her: 'I'll do better than that', and assigned her to his own large table for ten or twelve.[147]

Newly-embarked passengers in all three classes began to get themselves settled in for the night. They began to familiarize themselves with the ship's layout even as passengers boarding in Southampton that morning had. Many of them headed for the Dining Saloons for a late supper.

Among those who had just boarded the ship from the *Nomadic* as First Class passengers were 50-year-old Walter Douglas and his 48-year-old wife Mahala. Mrs Douglas remembered:

> We left Cherbourg late on account of trouble at Southampton, but once off, everything seemed to go perfectly. The boat was so luxurious, so steady, so immense, and such a marvel of mechanism that one could not believe he was on a boat …[148]

First Class passenger Arthur Gee had spent some time looking over the ship since boarding that morning. He wrote in a letter that night:

> In the language of the poet, "This is a knock-out." I have never seen anything so magnificent, even in a first class hotel. I might be living in a palace. It is, indeed, an experience. We seem to be miles above the water, and there are certainly miles of promenade deck. The lobbies are so long that they appear to come to a point in the distance. Just finished dinner. They call us up to dress by bugle … Such a dinner!!! My gracious!!![149]

After dinner, the ship's band sprang into action in the D Deck Reception Room, which many passengers simply referred to as 'the lounge'. Among those present was Francis M. Browne and members of his party. As they and other passengers …

> … sat in the beautiful lounge listening to the White Star orchestra playing the "Tales of Hoffman" and "Cavalleria Rusticana" selections more than once we heard the remark: "You would never imagine you were on board a ship."[150]

No matter how enthused passengers were over the ship and its wonders, eventually the exertions of the day caught up with everyone. Many were tired; beyond that, a number

of the passengers later said that they were completely exhausted. Eventually, the concert wound down, passengers began to drift off to their cabins and staterooms throughout the ship, and sailing day officially began to wrap up.

Overnight, the *Titanic*'s engines were built up, from the 68 rpm made during the trip to Cherbourg up to 70 rpm; this indicated a speed of about 20.7 knots through the water.[151] As the ship had been late in departing Cherbourg, it is clear that the trip over to Queenstown had to be made at a very good speed; considering the fact that the she was then working on steam from only twenty of her twenty-nine boilers, this was quite a respectable showing.[152] Overnight, the liner steamed generally west and north-west. At midnight, the ship's clocks were set back 25 minutes from Greenwich Mean Time to match Dublin Mean Time (DMT). Dublin Mean Time encompassed Queenstown, the *Titanic*'s next port of call.[153]

Day Two – Thursday, April 11, 1912.

Dawn came at about 5:40 a.m. Greenwich Mean Time, or 5:15 a.m. Dublin Mean Time, the time to which *Titanic*'s clocks were then adjusted.[154] At about that time the *Titanic* was steaming between Land's End, in Cornwall, England, and the Scilly Isles, having turned approximately north-northwest on her course toward Queenstown. The weather was good, if windy, and the seas were spirited. Yet it was recalled:

> After a windy night on the Irish Sea, when the sturdy Packet boat tossed and tumbled to her heart's content … the lordly contempt of the *Titanic* for anything less than a hurricane seemed most marvelous and comforting.[155]

During the morning …

> … when the full Atlantic swell came upon our port side, so stately and measured was the roll of the mighty ship that one needed to compare the moving of the side with the steady line of the clear horizon.[156]

Francis Browne recalled getting up early to make his way around the ship with his camera in hand. He captured a lovely view of the sky as the sun rose through broken cloud cover. Then he took photos of passengers engaged in their morning activities aboard the ship: the wake washing out from the liner's starboard side as the liner sliced through the seas; Jacques Futrelle on the Boat Deck outside the Gymnasium; Thomas McCawley at the rowing machine just inside; even a snap of Harold Bride hard at work in the Marconi Room.

Lawrence Beesley recalled that the passage across the channel was 'most enjoyable … although the wind was almost too cold to allow of sitting out on deck on Thursday morning.'[157] Some people preferred to explore the ship's interior spaces, which were warmer. Jacques and May Futrelle were among these; they 'went over the whole ship', exploring the liner's amenities. One thing that May noticed is that some workmen were still installing the doors to the First Class Café Parisian on B Deck.[158]

Elmer Taylor also took the opportunity to explore the ship with his friend Fletcher Williams:

Left: *This photograph was taken Thursday morning by Francis Browne. Titanic is steaming in the vicinity of Land's End, and it is clear from the S-shaped wake that she has made a serpentine course.*

Lower left: *This photograph shows Frederic Spedden looking on as his son Robert Douglas Spedden spins a top on the aft Promenade Deck on Thursday morning.*

Lower right: *Francis Browne spent only one night in this cabin, A-37, which was on the opposite side of the aft First Class Entrance from Thomas Andrews' cabin, A-36. He took this photograph on Wednesday before sailing time; his friend Tom Brownrigg can be seen in the mirror.*

Bottom left: *Francis Browne held his camera over the A Deck bulwark rail on the starboard side to get this photograph. Looking forward, the ship is slicing powerfully through the sea toward Queenstown.*

Bottom right: *This photo shows Harold Bride hard at work in the Marconi Room Thursday morning.*

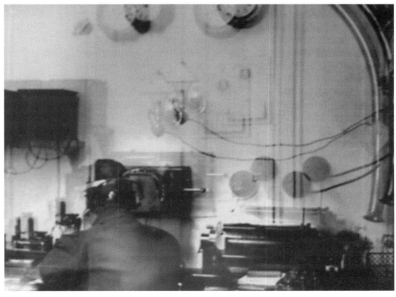

Top left: *A Thursday morning photo of* Titanic's *Gymnasium. Instructor McCawley demonstrates the rowing machine. Behind McCawley, William Parr – a member of Harland & Wolff's Guarantee Group – tests another piece of equipment.*

Top right: *Outside the Gymnasium, Browne runs across writer Jacques Futrelle on the Boat Deck. Behind Futrelle is Boat No. 7.*

Far left: Titanic's *Café Parisien, looking forward.*

Near left: *First Class passenger May Futrelle in 1918.*

The ship, as a whole, revealed the result of generations of skill, labor, and ingenuity ... By one means or another, engineering skill had stepped up travelers' comfort to an a la carte restaurant, Turkish electric and swimming baths, gymnasiums, squash racquet courts, clothes pressing, cleaning and laundry, lounge, reception rooms, passenger elevators, palm court, electric heaters, real beds (not bunks), hot and cold running water, paneled white walls and ceiling, custom-made upholstered armchairs, wardrobes – well, what else could one want?

The brother of my esteemed friend Clarissa Smith had suggested it might be interesting to scrutinize the woodwork, paneling, carvings, etc., throughout the public rooms, the disposition of interior space and disguises used to create a homelike feeling, a hotel life atmosphere, while getting away from steamer consciousness inside the ship and enhancing life at sea on decks.

Williams and I nosed about ... We were particularly impressed with a new type davit, the apparent ease of launching life boats accommodating as many as eighty people by simply turning a crank until the life boat was level with the deck, an additional assurance of efficiency in emergencies – a really great improvement over that old type davit which made it necessary to lift the life boat by rope tackle and shuttle it back and forth until it was in position to lower to the edge of the deck.

We admired the especially designed custom-made furniture, the floor coverings, wall decorations, palms and semi-tropical plants, the huge fat green pillows in the Music Room ...[159]

Edith Rosenbaum, who had just boarded the ship the night before, was a seasoned Atlantic traveler, and the *Titanic* impressed even her. From the Squash Court and Gymnasium to the Turkish Bath and Swimming Bath, the ship seemed to offer everything imaginable. 'There was a lounge larger than that of the Grand Hotel, a complete hospital with operating rooms, bedrooms larger than any Paris hotel room, suites with private promenades ...' The amenities seemed endless to her.[160]

Thirty-year-old Philipp Mock was similarly impressed. He and his sister, 35-year-old Emma Schabert, had boarded the previous night in Cherbourg. Mock thought that the *Titanic* was 'without question the finest boat that ever was afloat and that she was so large passengers almost lost the idea that they were on board ship. She was so huge that there was no rolling or pitching, she seeming to keep an even keel all the time.'[161]

Forty-six-year-old Mrs Margaret Swift was traveling in First Class. She had boarded the ship at Southampton with her friend, 49-year-old Dr Alice Leader – who, like Mrs Swift, was traveling without her husband. In an era when female doctors were not extremely common, Mrs Leader worked in a practice in New York City, with her husband John. The pair was also traveling with a married couple, the Kenyons, 41-year-old Frederick and 31-year-old Marion. Margaret Swift and Alice Leader shared cabin D-17, while the Kenyons occupied the cabin directly across the hall, D-21. To Mrs Swift, their stateroom was 'a magnificent room with two four-poster beds'. Beyond how much she liked their stateroom, she was also thoroughly impressed with the *Titanic*, recalling that the vessel 'was one of the finest I ever saw; so solid, so large, and so luxurious in every appointment.'[162]

By late morning, the coast of Ireland appeared on the horizon ahead of the great steamship. Lawrence Beesley recalled:

> The coast of Ireland looked very beautiful as we approached Queenstown Harbour, the brilliant morning sun showing up the green hillsides and picking out groups of dwellings dotted here and there above the rugged grey cliffs that fringed the coast.[163]

Ramon Artagaveytia took the opportunity to write to his brother Adolfo of his experiences aboard. He thought his B Deck stateroom was 'very good'. It had an electric heater, which he had left on all night to ward off the cold. 'I visited what I could of the steamer: its different rooms, and today to find this room to write in – there were more than two, it cost me to know. The dining rooms are painted in white, and some rooms like this one have carved wood (I think it's oak) with lounges and chairs covered in rich and elegant jade green velvet.' He recalled that the 'food is very good with an abundance of dishes'. Looking out through the window, he realized time was short if he was to post the letter and have it taken off with the other mails at Queenstown. 'Now I see land close by, Ireland, so I end this letter leaving you all my memories and hugs.'[164]

Artagaveytia wasn't the only one to drop a line to family with the Queenstown mails. Chief Officer Wilde, who had only reluctantly accepted the post of Chief Officer of the *Titanic*, wrote in a letter to his sister: 'I still don't like this ship … I have a queer feeling about it.'[165]

When the *Titanic* reached the entrance to Queenstown Harbour, between Roches Point on the east and Church Bay on the west, the ship paused to rendezvous with the Harbour Pilot, and he clambered aboard. Under his careful direction, the ship 'ran slowly towards the harbour with the sounding-line dropping all the time, and came to a stop well out to sea, with our screws churning up the bottom and turning the sea all brown with sand from below.'[166] It was at about 11:30 a.m. according to *Titanic*'s shipboard clocks when the liner finally ceased her forward progress and dropped anchor.[167] She was about two miles from shore at the time.

From the wharf at Queenstown, the two tenders *Ireland* and *America* had already taken their cue and begun their short journey to meet the *Titanic*. As the *Titanic* was slowing to a stop, the *America* was already approaching her from the starboard side. A gangway door on E Deck forward on the starboard side had been opened to facilitate the movement of passengers and mail; another door on the port side forward as also opened.

Top: *A 1920 photo of First Class passenger Philipp Mock.*

Centre: *The White Star wharf at Queenstown.*

Bottom: *The tender* Ireland *at the wharf.*

The *America* circled around the ship and tied up along the liner's port side, while the *Ireland* tied up to starboard. Aboard the tenders were many sacks of mail bound for America, and a number of passengers set to board the liner: three First Class passengers, seven Second Class, and one hundred and thirteen immigrants traveling in Third Class. There were also a number of local port officials, journalists and photographers who boarded the *Titanic* from the tenders. Crew and postal employees were also aboard to aid in the off-loading of the Irish mails from the liner, and to help load her with mail bound for America.

Second Class passenger Lawrence Beesley was watching the two tenders with interest as they disembarked their human cargo to the *Titanic*. Nothing ...

Top: *The* Titanic *entering Queenstown Harbour. She is decelerating, but has not yet stopped. The E Deck gangway door has already been opened.*

Above left: *This photograph was taken from the tender* America *as it approached the* Titanic. *Third Class passengers line the Poop Deck rails. At the top of the fourth funnel a stoker's head can just barely be discerned. He was covered in soot, and some of the more superstitious believed his appearance was an ill omen.*

Above right: *With the* America *tied alongside the* Titanic, *a lady leans tentatively over the port side rail to get a better view. Behind her, on the deck, is Boat No. 8, while Emergency Boat No. 2 can be seen swung out over the water.*

... could have given us a better idea of the enormous length and bulk of the *Titanic* than to stand as far astern as possible and look over the side from the top deck, forwards and downwards to where the tenders rolled at her bows, the merest cockleshells beside the majestic vessel that rose deck after deck above them. Truly she was a magnificent boat! There was something so graceful in her movement as she rode up and down on the slight swell in the harbour, a slow, stately dip and recover, only noticeable by watching her bows in comparison with some landmark on the coast in the near distance; the two little tenders tossing up and down like corks beside her illustrated vividly the advance made in comfort of motion from the time of the small steamer.[168]

One of Beesley's fellow Second Class passengers, Miss Susan Webber, said that 'crowds stared in admiration' of the great ship, even as similar crowds had done the night before in Cherbourg.[169]

While all of the passengers, luggage and mails were being transferred, a photographer from *The Cork Examiner* swarmed over the liner, snapping photos of everything he

could. He caught Captain Smith and Chief Purser McElroy on the starboard side of the Boat Deck, beside the Officers' Quarters, and the two men obligingly paused for a photo. From aft, he took a photograph looking forward along the port Boat Deck, and then took another up the starboard Boat Deck, making for a nearly-identical set. He then turned and, from his vantage point on the aft Boat Deck, photographed emigrants lounging on the Poop Deck astern.

While the photographer snapped away, Third Class passengers were boarding the ship and getting settled in. Amongst the Irish Third Class passengers who came aboard that afternoon were Eugene Daly of Athlone, and his cousin Maggie Daly. Along with them was Bertha Mulvihill, a mutual friend from Coosan, a village three miles outside

Top left: *Captain Smith and Chief Purser McElroy pause on the starboard Boat Deck and obligingly pose for a photo.*

Top right: *Second Class passengers stroll along the port Boat Deck. Boats 10, 12 and 14 are visible at the left, with the edge of No. 16 just barely peeking through the edge. A stack of deck chairs has been placed against the raised roof over the First Class Smoking Room.*

Above left: *The starboard Second Class Boat Deck, showing Boats Nos 9, 11 and 13 at the right.*

Above right: *A photograph overlooking the stern. Third class passengers line the rail. Barely visible nearly amidships, aft of the Stern Docking Bridge, an enterprising individual has managed to acquire a deck chair to relax on.*

Bottom left: *Third Class passenger Eugene Daly and his uilleann pipes.*

Bottom right: *Third Class passenger Maggie Daly.*

of Athlone. Eugene was a hard-working 29-year-old man. His father, a policeman, had been killed in the line of duty when Daly was just twelve years old. From that point on, Daly became the head of the household, going to work in the woolen mills in Athlone as a weaver and a mechanic.

Daly's 17-year-old sister Maggie was frail, and his mother and siblings depended on him for financial support. In 1912, Eugene decided to seek out better opportunities to support his family in America. Daly, a fierce believer in Irish independence, played the uilleann pipes,[170] and was traveling to New York City. A member of the Athlone Gaelic League band, he timed his journey to coincide with a War Pipes competition that was to be held on May 19, 1912, as part of a Gaelic Feis in Celtic Park, Queens. While aboard the tender, Daly played lively Irish airs.[171]

Bertha Mulvihill, who had been living in America since 1906, was recently engaged to Henry Noon of Providence, Rhode Island. She had traveled back to Ireland aboard the *Lusitania* in the autumn of 1911 to announce her engagement to her family, and to attend the wedding of her sister Kitty. Arriving in her native country unannounced, she rode home on a jaunting cart, waving and yelling out to everyone that she was back. She spent her spare time gathering linens and laces for her wedding dress. In early April, 1912, Bertha was returning to her family's home from a funeral, when she passed by a White Star Line ticket office. On

Top left: *Third Class passenger Bertha Mulvihill (second from left) with some friends and coworkers in front of the Perry House in Newport.*

Top right: *The starboard anchor being raised. This photo was taken by Francis Browne as he disembarked on the tender* Ireland.

Right: *Second Officer Lightoller (centre) and First Officer Murdoch (right) in the E Deck gangway, with several crewmen on the left behind them.*

Far right: *From the tender, this photograph was taken on the starboard side of the ship, looking up toward the starboard Bridge wing. Boat No. 1 is clearly visible, A number of First Class passengers and crew are visible along A Deck, while Third Class passengers are visible at the Well Deck. From the Bridge wing, Captain Smith peers down at the tender.*

a whim, she went in: 'I went in and bought a ticket … without saying a word to anybody … Friday I told my folks that I was going back to America … and I was going to Queenstown the next morning to go aboard the boat.' She had not contacted her fiancé in America to let him know she was returning, as she was hoping to surprise him.[172]

When they learned that Eugene was going to America, the families of Maggie Daly and Bertha Mulvihill placed the two girls under his protection; he made a vow to look after their safety. Bertha was a long-term friend of Eugene and his family. Joining the trio on their journey to America was Margaret Rice, a widow originally from Athlone; she was returning home to Spokane, Washington with her five children: Albert, 10; George, 8; Eric, 7; Arthur, 4; and Eugene, 2.[173]

With the arrival of these Third Class passengers on that afternoon, there was a fundamental shift in the makeup of the steerage passengers as a whole. Those who had embarked from Southampton were primarily comprised of English, French, Dutch, Italian and other rather exotic nationalities. This made for an eclectic melting pot of languages and cultures. There was an Interpreter Steward aboard, but on sailing day, he had been only one man

faced with a large crowd of confused people trying to find their way around an enormous ocean liner. As the Irish emigrants boarded the liner, they brought with them their own unique culture. One of the ship's stewards recalled – no doubt with a measure of relief – that 'at least this lot spoke English'.

Francis Browne, the Odells and the Mays all knew that the end of their brief journey was at hand. Even so, Browne had his camera ready. Looking down from the port side of the Boat Deck, he took a splendid snap of the tender *America* alongside the ship's bow. Eventually, however, the time came for him and the other members of his party to disembark. As he went down the gangway to the *Ireland*, which was along the liner's starboard side, he ran across Purser McElroy and one of the liner's five-man team of Postal Clerks. 'Goodbye', Browne said, 'I will give you copies of my photos when you come again. Pleasant voyage.' Then he disembarked.[174]

He was one of seven First Class passengers who left the ship; in addition to the Odells and Richard and Stanley May, Emily Nichols from First Class also disembarked. Unbeknownst to nearly everyone, one of *Titanic*'s crewmen, Stoker John Coffey, decided to 'jump ship' at that point. He snuck onto the tender and hid among the sacks of mail until the tender had left the liner's side. Also disembarking were the visiting dignitaries, port officials and members of the press.

When all was said and done, after the exchange of passengers and the desertion by the single crewman at Queenstown, there were some 2,208 men, women and children aboard the *Titanic* for the trans-Atlantic trip. This number was divided among 891 members of the crew and officers, 324 First Class passengers, 284 in Second Class, and 709 in Third Class.[175]

The entire process of debarking and embarking passengers, cargo, and mail at Queenstown had taken about two hours. Shortly after 1:30 p.m. the liner raised anchor, telegraph bells from the Bridge jangled, and her engines sprang to life once again. As the tenders pulled away, and the *Titanic* resumed her voyage, Eugene Daly, dressed in his kilt and full regalia, stood on the Third Class Promenade and played 'A Nation Once Again' and 'Erin's Lament' on

time. New York Harbor lay over two thousand miles to the southwest. The giant reciprocating engines were engaged at 'Full Ahead', and soon the central turbine-driven propeller was also spinning away.

Once the *Titanic* passed the Daunt's Rock Light Vessel at 2:20 p.m. Greenwich Mean Time, or 1:55 p.m. ship's time, she had reached the official starting point of the trans-Atlantic crossing. The *Titanic* then steamed parallel to the southern coast of Ireland for the next 55 nautical miles of her track. Soon, she was making 70 rpm on the reciprocating engines, indicating a speed of about 20.7 knots.[178] Fireman John Thompson recalled: 'From Queenstown out, all the firemen had been talking of the orders we had to fire her up as hard as we possibly could. We were to make as quick a passage as possible.'[179]

While the firemen toiled in hellishly hot conditions below in the boiler rooms, Second Class passengers Lutie Parrish and Imanita Shelley were still trying to extract an improvement of their cabin from the ship's personnel. The

his uilleann pipes. He had mixed emotions about leaving his homeland. Bertha Mulvihill also felt melancholy as the ship got underway. She was excited to be reunited with her fiancé, but was sad to leave her family behind, particularly her baby brother Brian, since she had just met him. There was no telling when she would see him again.[176]

Second Class passenger Lawrence Beesley recalled of that moment that …

> … the tenders cast off, and at 1.30 P.M., with the screws churning up the sea bottom again, the *Titanic* turned slowly through a quarter-circle until her nose pointed down along the Irish coast …[177]

The *Titanic* slowly, majestically moved back out to the open sea, and paused one more time to allow the Queenstown Pilot to disembark. Once he was clear, it was time for the *Titanic* to make her way to the Atlantic Ocean for the first

previous day, Purser McElroy had told them that they had received the cabin their ticket called for; however, he had also said that if there had been a mistake, then after leaving Queenstown, it was possible that they might be able to do something further for them.

The two ladies were unhappy with the room's size, and also with its fittings. The 'lower of the two berths was so high from the floor that my mother had to stand on two suitcases in order to climb in', Mrs Shelley recalled, and there was another problem as well. 'Oh, how cold it was in that cell', Mrs Shelley complained. Having 'just come from under the doctor's care in England, I came down with an awful chill and had to crawl in between the blankets. When not waiting on me my mother had to go to bed in self-defense.'

Thus, hardly had the ship cleared Queenstown when Lutie Parrish set off to find McElroy to discuss their keen dissatisfaction in person, and to see if they could be trans-

Above left: As the tender moves away from the Titanic, *a bumboat is visible in the foreground.*

Above right: The Titanic *steams off toward open water.*

Above: *Two women confer with an obliging steward in this publicity photo from the* Olympic *during the 1920's.*

Far left: *Stokers hard at work in a coal-fired boiler room of the period.*

Near left: *First Class passenger Alfred Nourney.*

ferred to the cabin they felt their ticket called for.[180] Apparently not content with McElroy's response, she returned to the Purser's Office eleven more times as the day progressed. By the time of the twelfth visit, if not long before, these two ladies must have seemed a matching set of proverbial pebbles in the Chief Purser's shoes. How would he handle this sticky situation?

Unfortunately, this wasn't the only pair of dissatisfied passengers that McElroy had already needed to deal with on this voyage. The previous evening, one 'Baron Alfred von Drachstedt' had boarded at Cherbourg, as a Second Class passenger. The 20-year-old young man, traveling alone, was actually named Alfred Nourney, and he was traveling under a pseudonym. Nourney had acquired an extensive wardrobe befitting a Baron before departing on the trip; between his cash, jewelry and wardrobe, the value of his effects was some $2,320.50. One is forced to wonder, with such lavish tastes, why Nourney had decided to book passage in Second Class to begin with.

Whatever his reason, once he had boarded the liner, he had shown intense dissatisfaction with his Second Class cabin, and complained to the pursers about it. For a £38 surcharge, the staff allowed him to upgrade to First Class, and he was assigned cabin D-38. Located nearly all the way forward in First Class spaces of D Deck, this was an inside cabin. Even so, the upgrade seemed to pacify the 'Baron', and he socialized amongst First Class travelers with wardrobes of comparable tastes.

While McElroy struggled to keep passengers content, the *Titanic* continued to steam along the picturesque coast of Ireland. At about 2:30 p.m. ship's time,[181] or some thirty-five minutes after passing Daunt's Rock Lightship, she passed the Old Head of Kinsale at a distance of about three miles. Then she proceeded another 41 nautical miles to Fastnet Light, which marked the southwestern-most point of the Emerald Isle. Once she had passed this famous landmark, at about 4:30 p.m., the Irish coastline began to fade into the distance astern. *Titanic* had reached the open Atlantic Ocean.[182]

Second Class passenger Sidney Collett was watching the Irish coast grow fainter in the distance astern. As part of a family moving from the Old World to the New, he knew that it might be some time before he returned to his homeland in England; this could be his last sighting of the Old World for some time to come. That Thursday afternoon 'I took my last look and bade farewell to the old country. Everything was going finely.'[183]

Lawrence Beesley recalled:

> All afternoon we steamed along the coast of Ireland, with grey cliffs guarding the shores, and hills rising behind gaunt and barren; as dusk fell, the coast rounded away from us to the northwest, and the last we saw of Europe was the Irish mountains dim and faint in the dropping darkness.[184]

As the sun began to set ahead of the liner's bow, the ship was aglow with light from stem to stern. The haunting strains of the ship's orchestra, playing cheerful music in a pre-dinner concert, drifted across the sea.[185] The reciprocating engines throbbed steadily away, driving the ship forward in the smooth seas. The sound of convivial social intercourse filled the ship, and the smell of fine cuisine wafted from the galleys.

Thirty-six-year-old Second Class passenger Kate Buss was traveling alone. She was on her way to San Diego, California, to marry her fiancé, and was fighting feelings of loneliness. Fortunately, she had become acquainted with another young lady, Marion Wright, at her table in the Dining Saloon. On Wednesday, the pair had even shared a steamer rug on deck and discussed where they were headed. Miss Buss learned that Miss Wright was traveling to Oregon, and was to meet her fiancé in New York for the wedding. On Wednesday night, Kate had not slept very well, 'owing to the vibration. There is a good deal of it,' she recalled, 'and I fancy they travelled at a pretty good speed last night to make up for lost time.' Happily she was able to report not a hint of seasickness, and that she had 'eaten anything and everything'.

One of the events that Miss Buss soon came to love were the daily concerts given by the ship's orchestra. In Second Class, they performed in the aft Second Class Entrance Foyer on C Deck between 5:00 and 6:00 p.m., and then again from 9:15 to 10:15 p.m. Kate recalled:

> The 'cello man [32-year-old John Woodward] is a favorite of mine, every time he finishes a piece he looks at me and we smile. It's a real Liberty Hall. Everyone seems to be as happy as sandboys for the time being.

She also recalled, perhaps with a little less enthusiasm, that fellow passenger Stuart Collett 'tries to teach us all religion'.[186]

Now that ports of call were falling ever farther behind the ship's wake, and there were no cross-Channel passengers to disembark, or fresh passengers to embark, the normal shipboard routine began to set in. Every morning, Captain Smith and his officers made a thorough inspection of the ship, according to White Star Line's policy. The senior officers also began to settle in to their daily 'at sea' watches. Chief Officer Wilde had the 2:00–6:00 watch every morning and afternoon; Second Officer Lightoller followed him with the 6:00–10:00 watch every morning and night; finally, First Officer Murdoch took the 10:00–2:00 watches every mid-day and night. Meanwhile, the ship's six lookout men were divided into three two-man teams, and each team served four two-hour watches in the Crow's Nest. Throughout all of the other areas of the ship, the various crewmen formed up their watches and began to get into their routine.[187]

Passengers also began to fall into a routine. Although the three main meals were served to passengers every day – breakfast between 8:00 and 10:00 a.m., lunch at 1:00 p.m., and dinner at 7:00 p.m. – it was really dinner that stood out as the centerpiece of daily activity. Before dinner, First Class passengers would gather in the Reception Room on D Deck, at the foot of the Grand Staircase. Dressing for dinner was not required on the first night after the voyage began. However, on Thursday night and all subsequent nights, formal attire was always – as Colonel Archibald Gracie later recalled – 'en regle'. After socializing with friends or new shipboard acquaintances in the Reception Room, this throng of hungry individuals would next proceed through one of the two sets of double-doors and enter the Saloon itself.

Once in the Saloon, the passengers would make their way to their individual tables. As on all ocean liners, passengers were given table assignments in the Saloon that

Above: *The* Olympic*'s band plays in the Second Class Entrance during the 1920s.*

Below: *A Third Class menu from the* Olympic, *dating to some six weeks after* Titanic's *maiden voyage, shows a broad variety of selections for her passengers.*

WHITE STAR LINE.

R.M.S. "OLYMPIC."   MAY 30, 1912

THIRD CLASS.

BREAKFAST.

OATMEAL PORRIDGE & MILK
BROILED CAMBRIDGE SAUSAGES
IRISH STEW
FRESH BREAD & BUTTER
MARMALADE   SWEDISH BREAD
TEA   COFFEE

DINNER.

BARLEY BROTH
BEEF A LA MODE
LIMA BEANS   BOILED POTATOES
FRESH BREAD
RICE PUDDING
ORANGES

TEA.

LEICESTER BRAWN
PICKLES
FRESH BREAD & BUTTER
COMPÔTE OF APRICOTS & RICE
TEA

SUPPER

GRUEL   CHEESE

Any complaint respecting the Food supplied, want of attention or incivility, should be at once reported to the Purser or Chief they would maintain throughout the crossing; when the table companions consisted of old friends, mealtimes were sure to be convivial. Occasionally, passengers were dismayed to find themselves seated with fellow passengers whom they considered dull, irksome, or outright dimwitted. Under such circumstances, many simply labored through each meal while praying for a quick, merciful end to the crossing. Another alternative, at least aboard *Titanic*, was to take as many meals as possible in the First Class à la carte Restaurant on B Deck.

More often than not, however, passengers found their company pleasant and the dinner conversations at the very least cordial. If they did not know each other directly, table companions would frequently find that their social circles intertwined and they had mutual acquaintances. Indeed, it was not unusual for good shipboard friendships to be formed over mid-Atlantic meals. Elmer Taylor recalled:

> We were mildly interested in the passenger list; many of the names were internationally known – Colonel John Jacob Astor, Isidor Straus, C. M. Hays, W. T. Stead, and men equally or better known in commercial and literary life. There were many lovely women to blend with the rich furnishings; the prevailing style of apparel and "hair-do" were studies for artists. Day dresses were not too short to be attractive, extra long evening gowns, fur coats, jewelry and all that goes to make glamour was the spirit of the time.[188]

Purser Hugh McElroy had kindly given Mrs Eleanor Cassebeer a seat at his own large table in the Dining Saloon, which was for either ten or twelve people. She found herself dining not only with McElroy, but also with Ship's Surgeon Dr William O'Loughlin, Assistant Surgeon John Simpson, 47-year-old New York stockbroker Harry Anderson, Harland & Wolff's Thomas Andrews, Frederick and Jane Hoyt, and Albert and Vera Dick.[189] She sat on Dr O'Loughlin's left side, and directly across from Thomas Andrews.

During the course of their mealtime conversations, Andrews mentioned that in certain ways, *Titanic* really wasn't ready to sail on this trip; yet, they had to proceed because the prescheduled sailing date of April 10 arrived, and the ship simply had to sail on time. This made sense to Mrs Cassebeer, as she had noticed that none of the standard printed notices were in her cabin, although the frames were in place.[190]

By this point, Isaac Frauenthal was beginning to feel better over his misgivings about the voyage aboard *Titanic*. Once he had boarded, he told his brother and sister-in-law about the dream, and 'they laughed' at his fears. As Frauenthal became acquainted with the others aboard, he said:

> I don't suppose any ship that ever took an Atlantic track had a happier, more confident crowd of passengers than the *Titanic*. The novelty of having a part in the maiden trip of the world's greatest ship appealed to everybody. Then, too, nearly all of us felt that there was no reason to be alarmed or apprehensive about anything.[191]

The previous evening, a trio of First Class passengers from Zurich, Switzerland had boarded at Cherbourg. There was 60-year-old Maximilian Frölicher-Stehli and his wife,

48-year-old Margaretha Frölicher-Stehli, and their daughter, 22-year-old Miss Hedwig Margaritha Frölicher, who was frequently referred to as Marguerite.[192] Mr Frölicher-Stehli was involved in silk manufacturing and importing, and as such he was a frequent trans-Atlantic traveler. As Miss Marguerite had done quite well in her school examinations, this trip was something of a reward for her. On the first night aboard, the family had been settled in nicely and, fortunately, there was no trace of the dreaded *mal-de-mer*.

On Thursday evening, Marguerite recalled that 'everyone was gay and happy. But that night I became seasick. So did my mother. We were in adjoining cabins and … we just lay in our bunks, knocking occasionally to each other through the wall.' Marguerite suspected that she was 'the most seasick girl on the *Titanic*'.[193]

In Second Class, Lutie Parrish and Imanita Shelley were still discontent with their accommodations. Their cabin was slightly more expensive than the Second Class cabin that they had enjoyed onboard the *Mauretania* when traveling from New York to England, and in their opinion it was not furnished nearly as nicely. A dozen trips to see Chief Purser McElroy had netted no response favorable enough for their finicky tastes.

When 9:00 p.m. came and went without anyone addressing their situation, Imanita was incensed. Still feeling quite ill and thoroughly chilled, she undertook to write a personal, and pointed, note to Purser McElroy. She stated therein that McElroy was 'obtaining money under false pretenses', as she 'had paid for the best second cabin on the ship'. She even sent him the receipt for her ticket indicating how much she had paid for the cabin.

Then she played her final card, telling the purser that she 'had just left the hospital in London and on account of the intense cold and lack of any facilities for heat in this cell' that she was in mortal danger. Furthermore, she threatened, if he did not do something to redress their intolerable conditions, she 'would appeal to the captain direct'. If the Captain did nothing, then she would handle things when she reached shore – if, she pointed out, she 'lived to reach America'. She sent the note on via her Cabin Stewardess.

McElroy received the note from the stewardess and read it. He then asked the stewardess, perhaps with exasperation, if Mrs Shelley was 'really so very ill'. Perhaps to his surprise, the stewardess replied that there was 'no doubt about that part of it'. McElroy then asked, perhaps rhetorically, 'if it was true that there was such a cell on board the *Titanic*, where a steamer trunk could not be opened at all, and where only two women could stand up at one time.' Apparently, the stewardess confirmed to him that the room was rather small.

McElroy was finally sure that this particular problem was not going away unless drastic action was taken. 'Well, we must act at once or we will get the company into trouble', he said to the stewardess. It seems clear that although he still was not convinced that the ladies were due for some sort of upgrade, there were other Second Class cabins available and unoccupied at the time. So, the ever-tactful Purser that he was, he sent four stewards down to the offending 'cell' in question.

The stewards carried Mrs Shelley, as well as all of the two ladies' belongings, up to the room that Mrs Shelley believed she had paid for. Before they left, Mrs Shelley recalled that the stewards offered '10,000 apologies'. The new cabin was 'spacious, with a high ceiling', but Imanita and her mother still believed that their quarters on the *Mauretania* had been better furnished. Mrs. Shelley was also told that she could 'choose any stewardess I desired, so I had the little woman who had waited on me so faithfully in the cell promoted.'

Besides being moved to a larger cabin, Assistant Surgeon John Simpson began checking in on Mrs. Shelley three to four times a day for the remainder of the voyage; he ordered her to stay in the room on bed rest. He was concerned that she might have diphtheria, and had meals served to her in her room. Unfortunately, despite the cabin upgrade, Mrs Parrish and Mrs Shelley found that the new room was no warmer than the previous one. In fact, Mrs Shelley recalled that when Dr Simpson called upon her, 'his teeth could chatter and rattle although he always denied he was cold.'

Imanita continued to complain to her Cabin Steward about the rooms being so cold. The steward responded: 'Young lady, I don't think they ever will be on this ship until they change the heating system. There is a system of hot air flues through which the warmth is supposed to pass, and it does not get around. Three passengers who have second cabins, where the hot air enters the system, are complaining that they are smothered and cannot stand the heat. All the rest are freezing, so there is something radically wrong.'[194] Apparently, this was a bug that would need to be worked out following the maiden voyage, and it was no doubt proving something of a stress for Mr Andrews and the other members of the Guarantee Group from Harland & Wolff.

That same Thursday, Third Class Steward John E. Hart recalled that at some point during the day, there was a general bulkhead inspection. He saw Chief Officer Wilde and Thomas Andrews together, and they were checking to make sure that the crew could close the watertight doors manually. Hart was ordered to attempt to do so, and he 'closed them with a big spanner'.[195] The test went well, and at least Andrews didn't have to worry about any serious issues in that regard.

Thomas Andrews' Bedroom Steward, Henry Etches, had known the *Titanic's* designer for some time, having met him several times in Belfast while serving on the *Olympic*. He noticed that Andrews 'was working all the time'. In his cabin he 'had charts rolled up by the side of the bed, and he had papers of all descriptions on his table during the day ... He was making notes of improvements; any improvements that could be made ... Anything that was pointed out to him, he was making notes of it.' Etches pointed out to Andrews a few details that might be improved, and Andrews kept careful record of the suggestions.

During the days of the trip, Etches recalled seeing Andrews 'in all parts, with workmen, going about ... The whole of the day he was working from one part of the ship to the other.' Etches also noticed that he 'was very late in going to bed', but not because he was socializing in the Smoking Room or the Lounge. Rather, it was because he was hard at work. Etches saw Andrews 'at different parts of deck E more often than anywhere else.' For times that Andrews was going down into the grimy engineering spaces, he would put on a blue surveyor's suit; when he came back up, Etches noticed that the ship's designer would cast the suit onto the bed in his room.[196]

First Class Stewardess Violet Jessop remembered that every now and then through the voyage, she came across the 'beloved' Thomas Andrews. No matter how busy he was, she recalled that Andrews 'never failed to stop for a cheerful word, his only regret that we were "getting further from home".'[197] Doubtless, Andrews' business helped keep his mind off thoughts of home and how far he was from it.

As was the usual custom aboard ship, every night after dinner there was a pool to bet on the ship's run for the next day. Male passengers would congregate in the Smoking Rooms and purchase one number from a range of mileage estimates for the next day's run, which was calculated every day at noon. This pastime was a highly popular one aboard ocean liners of the period; the betting was particularly keen on high-speed vessels which were out to take the Blue Riband. Before placing their wager, passengers were eager to obtain 'inside information' on the subject from stewards, engineers and officers that they came into contact with, all in the hopes of purchasing the most accurate figure. Although the *Titanic* was not capable of making a Blue Riband-winning crossing, it was expected that she would make a swift passage, and interest in the daily mileage runs was thus quite high.

Eventually, passengers began to drift off to their cabins; Saloon Stewards set about the nightly task of cleaning up the Dining Saloons and setting the tables for breakfast. Bakers worked through the night to prepare fresh bread and other goods for consumption the next day. Cabin Stewards on night duty monitored their charges, waiting for the least sign that their assistance was required. Up on the Bridge, the ship's officers and lookouts strained their eyes into the clear night ahead, ever vigilant despite the routine nature of their watches. *Titanic* steamed west through the night, her engines throbbing away with a reassuring constancy ... the wind whistled through the rigging ... everything was quiet on the ship's first night on the Atlantic Ocean.

At midnight that night, the ship's public area clocks on the Magneta circuit were set back to 11:01 p.m.[198] This 59-minute adjustment was made in order to agree with local time at the ship's anticipated position at noon the following day. In order to share the time change between the various crewmen, the setback was further divided between two watches – 29 minutes in the first watch, and 30 minutes in the second watch.[199]

Day Three – Friday, April 12, 1912.

Activity around the ship started early Friday morning, as it usually did on liners at sea. Breakfast was served beginning at 8:00 a.m. Lady Duff Gordon recalled:

> Like everyone else I was entranced with the beauty of the liner. I had never dreamt of traveling in such luxury. I remember being childishly pleased on finding strawberries on my breakfast-table.
> 'Fancy strawberries in April, and in mid-ocean. The whole thing is positively uncanny,' I kept saying to my husband. 'Why you would think you were at the Ritz.'[200]

Throughout the day, the problems with the ship's internal heating system continued. First Class passengers were less susceptible to this issue, as the cabins had individual electric heaters and there were many similar electrical heaters throughout the public rooms – not to mention the heat generated from thousands of incandescent electric lights.

However, things were still quite cold in Mrs Shelley's replacement Second Class cabin. Her steward told her on Friday that the three overheated passengers that he had mentioned the day before 'had kicked so that the heat had all been turned off', and so the issue continued to persist. Down in Third Class areas of the ship, a number of Steerage passengers also said that their heating apparatus, while present, 'did not work'.

Mrs Shelley was also experiencing a new problem. Dr Simpson, truly concerned about her health, would not allow her to get out of bed, so he arranged for her meals to be brought in. 'The food was excellent', Mrs Shelley allowed, 'but it seemed impossible to get it to me. My stewardess could not even get a tray to serve on and had to bring the different articles one at a time in her hand. There seemed to be no one in charge and no one to whom to turn for orders. The stewards and stewardesses were so willing, but could not get any action from their superiors.'[201]

turn a steward was called and then another and another, and no one could make the thing stop running. Finally, after much confusion and red tape, a ship's plumber was sent for.' When the man arrived, he 'instructed' the confused passengers and ship's personnel 'in the mysteries of that patent faucet'.[202]

Lawrence Beesley was impressed with the ship's size, and the fact that Second Class spaces were so large that they needed an elevator to help passengers get around:

> Whatever else may have been superfluous, lifts certainly were not: old ladies, for example, in cabins on F deck, would hardly have got to the top deck during the whole voyage had they not been able to ring for the lift-boy. Perhaps nothing gave one a greater impression of the size of the ship than to take the lift from the top and drop slowly down past the different floors, discharging and taking in passengers just as in a large hotel … [The liftboy] was quite young, – not more than sixteen, I think,

There just seemed to be no pleasing Mrs Parrish and Mrs Shelley. By that point, perhaps Purser McElroy and other members of the *Titanic*'s staff secretly wished that the two ladies had instead booked passage on the *Mauretania*, in the cabin that they had loved so much … or, indeed, that they had booked passage on *any* liner other than the *Titanic*. If they did nurse such feelings, however, they were far too professional to reveal their irritation.

Passengers were still growing accustomed to their surroundings all over the liner. With growing confidence, they were able to find their way around the *Titanic*'s cavernous interior spaces. However, there were still some things that no one seemed to be familiar with: the special lavatory faucets in Second Class, for example. While some of the fixtures were still in their crates, uninstalled, at least some of these special patent lavatory faucets were in operating order. However, their operation was not exactly intuitive.

Passenger interaction with these baffling faucets resulted in at least one rather comedic situation. One day during the voyage, a 'passenger went to wash and started to fill the basin, but was unable to stop the flow of water. She called the stewardess and she did not know the combination; in

– a bright-eyed, handsome boy, with a love for the sea and the games on deck and the view over the ocean – and he did not get any of them. One day, as he put me out of his lift and saw through the vestibule windows a game of deck quoits in progress, he said, in a wistful tone, "My! I wish I could go out there sometimes!" I wished he could, too, and made a jesting offer to take charge of his lift for an hour while he went to watch the game; but he smilingly shook his head and dropped down in answer to an imperative ring from below.[203]

Far below Beesley and the Second Class lift, the stokers fired up another one of the double-ended primary boilers; *Titanic* was then steaming on twenty of her twenty-nine boilers, and would continue to do so until the new boiler was brought up to pressure some hours later. In the meanwhile, the ship's speed was increased to 72 rpm on the reciprocating engines, indicating 21.2 knots through the water.[204] By noon, the ship had reached a position of about 50° 06' north latitude, 20° 43' west longitude. She had steamed 484 miles since leaving Daunt's Rock, at an average speed

Above left: *The* Olympic's *Second Class elevator on C Deck.*

Above right: *First Class passengers Doctor and Mrs Washington Dodge.*

of 20.98 knots … Not bad for a ship designed for only 21 knots, and only operating on twenty of her 29 boilers.[205] Once calculated, the ship's run was posted for the passengers to view, enjoy and discuss.

Fifty-two-year-old Doctor Washington Dodge was traveling in First Class with his 34-year-old wife Ruth, and their 4-year-old son Washington, Jr. The Dodge family was from San Francisco, California. Although a medical doctor, Dr Dodge was the Property Tax Assessor for the City of San Francisco. He worked hard at his job, and the family was returning home after an extended vacation in Switzerland. Master Dodge recalled:

> I remember walking the decks of the *Titanic* during the early part of the voyage … I had a toy animal ox that ran a bell as I pulled it. My father scolded me. Said I was waking up people trying to take naps.[206]

Miss Helen Ostby and her father …

> … spent the first few days exploring the ship, or should I say, the areas reserved for passengers in the first class. There were great distinctions and the different classes were kept apart.
>
> Mostly we just wandered around between meals, enjoying the luxury and newness of it all. We always traveled on the White Star Line, so we could compare the *Titanic* with other ships of the company.[207]

Eleanor Cassebeer was walking on the Promenade Deck that day when she met Benjamin Foreman again. On Wednesday evening, she had nearly collided with him as they went to get in line at the Purser's Enquiry Office on C Deck. On that evening, she had whispered to Foreman that she had not wished to get a seat in the Saloon beside a Jewish man who, she believed, was being a little too fussy about his seat assignment. On Friday, when she bumped into Foreman, she asked if he would like to take a walk with her. Foreman laughed and, perhaps teasingly, told her: 'You don't want to walk with me. You said you didn't like Jews and I'm one too.'

This caught Mrs Cassebeer off guard, since she believed that her prejudice against Jewish people was very typical of the period. She and Foreman went into one of the alcoves in the Lounge, where they sat and talked for a little while. They talked a bit about his background, and how he had been abroad for two years working in his father's textile company in Switzerland. They discussed the subject of Jews in general, and Foreman told her that his feeling on the subject was that, just like every other national group, there were good Jews and bad Jews, and that it all depended on the individual. The two became fast 'shipboard friends'.[208]

In Second Class, Kate Buss was enjoying the fine day, although she recalled that it was 'much more choppy' than the previous day and several people were seasick. She had slept well the night before, and was enjoying watching a pair of three- or four-year-old 'Japanese' girls walking around the decks and looking 'like dolls'.[209] Much of her time that afternoon was taken up with reading. At the concert that afternoon, she sat on the stairs and was again charmed by cello player John Woodward, saying he was a very 'superior bandsman, and he always smiles his parting to us'. And while some of the passengers had been having

trouble figuring out how to operate the ship's amenities, Kate was fascinated by one convenience in particular. She said that when …

> … you go into the lavatories and bedrooms they are in darkness until you close the door, which is connected with a clip to the electric light, you open the door and the light goes off.
>
> I have two clips to the one light in my cabin, one at the head of my bed and the other at the door.[210]

In the wireless office, just behind the Bridge, things were busy. Wireless Operators Jack Phillips and Harold Bride were kept very occupied with the general messages passing between ship and shore. Among these ordinary messages, a few other communications began to come in that hinted there might be something unusual ahead. It all began rather auspiciously on Friday afternoon.

At 5:46 p.m.,[211] the *La Touraine* sent a wireless message to the *Titanic*. It started with the prefix M.S.G., which meant: 'Master Service Message.' This was the title given to official messages between one Master and another regarding important navigational matters.[212] The message read:

> To Capt. 'Titanic.' My position 7 p.m. GMT [Greenwich Mean Time] lat. 49.28 long. 26.28 W. dense fog since this night crossed thick ice field lat. 44.58 long. 50.40 'Paris' saw another ice field and two icebergs lat. 45.20 long. 45.09 'Paris' saw a derelict lat. 40.56 long. 68.38 'Paris' please give me your position best regards and bon voyage. Caussin.[213]

The message was brought to Captain Smith, and he formulated a response, which was sent at 6:21 p.m.:[214]

> M.S.G. To Capt. 'La Touraine,' Thanks for your message and information. My position 7 p.m. G.M.T. Lat. 49, 45; long. 23, 38 W. Greenwich; had fine weather; compliments. – Smith.[215]

The message from the *La Touraine* was overall congratulatory in its tone. The offhand mention of ice – which lay ahead of the *Titanic*'s general track – was not unusual for an April crossing, either.

Just before this message came in, there was a muster held on the Bridge. The two Emergency Cutters, Boats Nos 1 and 2, were kept swung out so that if anyone fell overboard, they could be lowered away quickly to help carry out search and rescue operations. The boats could not be sent away quickly, however, without crews. Thus, at 6:00 p.m. every evening, an officer, a Quartermaster, and six seamen gathered for a muster, to make sure that the men would be ready in the event of an emergency.[216]

Another routine occurrence aboard the ship was the posting of the boat list for the crew members. It was First Officer Murdoch's responsibility to draw up the list of boat assignments, and he followed through on this promptly after departing Southampton.[217] Seaman Archie Jewell saw a boat list posted 'right in front of our forecastle'.[218] Seaman George Symons saw the same list on 'Thursday night or Friday morning early', and was even more specific in saying that there was 'one [list] in the forecastle, what they call the emergency boat list, and also on the forecastle door [at the top of the companionway] was a general boat list.'[219]

An Account of Wages for the Olympic in 1914 shows how carefully crew wages were recorded.

Leading Fireman Charles Hendrickson remembered that rather than a single list of the entire crew, there were several lists broken down by various departments, and that the pertinent list was posted in a place where crewmen of that department were likely to see it. Hendrickson saw the list for the firemen, trimmers and greasers.[220] Bathroom Steward Frank Morris saw a boat list posted in the First Class Pantry on Thursday, April 11;[221] Bathroom Steward Samuel Rule saw this same list.[222] On the same day, Chief Baker Charles Joughin saw the boat list for the kitchen staff posted on the wall of the Galley.[223] Posting the boat lists that early on in the voyage would make for a smoother time of things on Sunday, during the typical at-sea lifeboat muster for the crew. It was all a matter of routine – so routine, in fact, that many of the crewmen did not bother to read the list to see what boat they were assigned to.

That same evening, First Class passenger Philipp Mock noticed that there was another routine beginning to develop. He recalled that dinner 'was served at 7 o'clock and by 8:30 the people were gathered in the big saloon, sitting around the tables or on the lounges, talking, the men smoking, and everyone happy and interested.'[224]

As Thomas Andrews was headed down the Grand Staircase to dinner in the Dining Saloon that night, 28-year-old First Class Stewardess Mary Sloan saw him and the two paused to converse. Miss Sloan hailed from Belfast, and she was 'proud' of Andrews. She said:

He came from home and he made you feel on the ship that all was right. It was good to hear his laugh and have him near you. If anything went wrong it was always to Mr Andrews one went. Even if a fan stuck in a stateroom, one would say, "Wait for Mr Andrews, he'll soon see to it," and you would find him settling even the little quarrels that arose between ourselves. Nothing came amiss to him, nothing at all. And he was always the same, a nod and a smile or a hearty word whenever he saw you and no matter what he was at.

However, on this night, Miss Sloan thought that he was not quite himself. Dr O'Loughlin was waiting for him on the stair landing, 'calling him by his Christian name, Tommy'. Even then, the young stewardess thought that Andrews …

… seemed loth to go, he wanted to talk about home; he was telling me his father was ill and Mrs Andrews was not so well. I was congratulating him on the beauty and perfection of the ship; he said the part he did not like was that the Titanic was taking us further away from home every hour. I looked at him and his face struck me as having a very sad expression.[225]

For a man like Thomas Andrews, juggling the responsibilities of a work that he adored and a family that he loved and who needed him was not an easy thing. As good-natured and happy as he was, the strain apparently still wore at him from time to time.

Elmer Taylor recalled that at their dinner table, conversations among his party …

… were usually in a serious mood. Williams, like myself and my wife, had been regularly attending Christian Science services … and the Crosbys had attended C. S. lectures and meetings in their home town. At times, we were almost the last people to leave the dining room, discussing perhaps man's greatest engineering skill and contemplating future developments. …

… Our discussions and conversations sometimes continued as we took coffee in the Reception Room adjoining the dining room.[226]

Lady Duff Gordon said that everything …

… aboard this lovely ship reassured me from the captain, with his kindly, bearded face and genial manner, and his twenty-five years of experience as a White Star commander, to my merry, Irish stewardess, with her soft brogue and tales of the timid ladies she attended during hundreds of Atlantic crossings. …

The time passed happily enough. I had my secretary, Miss Francatelli, with me, as well as my husband, and we both found several friends on board. Mr and Mrs Thayer, the former was President of the Pennsylvania Railway, were among them.[227]

Despite the pleasant atmosphere, the kindly Captain, the merry Irish stewardess, and the presence of friends, Lady

Duff Gordon simply couldn't shake the uneasiness that she had felt before boarding the ship. As a result, every night when she went to bed, she did not completely undress. She also kept a warm coat and wrap, as well as a little jewel case with a few of her most treasured possessions in it, handy by her bedside through the night.

On that evening, Captain Smith dined with Bruce Ismay in the First Class *à la carte* Restaurant on B Deck. After dinner, the Captain left Ismay and their dining companions in the First Class Restaurant. Ismay, however, stayed on with the others. Eventually, Ismay invited everyone back his spacious suite, B-52, B-54 and B-56, and the group played bridge.[228]

As Friday came to a conclusion, the twenty-first boiler, fired earlier that day, was brought online and added its steam pressure to the engines. At midnight, the ship's public clocks were set back by a total of 49 minutes. Throughout the day on Saturday, *Titanic*'s clocks would be running 2 hours and 47 minutes ahead of New York Time, and 2 hours and 13 minutes behind Greenwich Mean Time.[229]

Day Four – Saturday, April 13, 1912.

During Saturday morning, Kate Buss finally had an opportunity to chat with her favorite cellist, John Woodward. She had wanted to ask him to play a solo, but up to this point had not had the chance. She took the opportunity on this morning, he agreed, and they began chatting. It turned out that he had been on the *Olympic* the previous September when she had been involved in the collision with the cruiser *Hawke*. He told her that the *Olympic* had been struck 'just where their berths were, and he said that had they been in there, they must have been killed.'[230]

At noon, the ship was located at about 47° 22' North, 33° 10' West; since noon the previous day, she had covered some 519 miles at an average speed of 20.91 knots in terms of 'speed made good'. Once the run had been calculated, it was again posted for passengers to see, and quickly became a hot topic of conversation. Lawrence Beesley recalled that over lunch that day, the subject came up. He was dining with Assistant Purser Reginald Barker in the Second Class Dining Saloon, and Barker told the table's occupants that this latest run was 'a disappointment, and we should not

dock until Wednesday morning instead of Tuesday night, as we had expected.'[231]

All hope of docking early was not lost to those really in the know, however. Word was soon passed to increase the revolutions from 72 to 75 rpm on the reciprocating engines. Leading Fireman Fred Barrett recalled receiving the order directly from the Second Engineer, and he passed word along to all of his own men. The stokers put their backs into it, and the revolutions increased. Barrett knew this because, although he never checked to see what revolutions they were making – something that would necessitate traveling from Boiler Room No. 6 all the way aft to the Engine Room – the phone never rang with a complaint, either. The next day's run was sure to show an improvement.[232] Bruce Ismay was also informed of the improved speed on the engines.[233]

At about 1:30 that same afternoon, 50-year-old passenger Mrs Elizabeth Lines strolled into the First Class Reception Room on D Deck, where she ordered some after-lunch coffee. She had chosen one of the small tables on the port side of the room, near the bow; the atmosphere was very quiet, and she lingered over her coffee for quite some time. Mrs Lines had boarded *Titanic* at Cherbourg, along with her 16-year-old daughter Mary. Mrs Lines' husband Ernest, who was not aboard for the crossing, was the Medical Director of the New York Life Insurance Company. Although the family members were American citizens, when Mr Lines had been placed in oversight of the company's interests in Europe, Asia and Africa, they had moved to Paris. Elizabeth and Mary were making the westward trip to visit relatives, and to attend the graduation of Mrs Lines' son from Dartmouth College. They were very excited to have booked passage across the Atlantic on the new *Titanic*.

While Mrs Lines absorbed the restful atmosphere of the Reception Room, she noticed Bruce Ismay and Captain Smith come in. She had been able to identify the two men previously during the course of the voyage, and so she easily recognized who they were on that afternoon. They chose to sit just two tables away from her; apparently they were creatures of habit, since Mrs Lines had also noticed them sitting and talking at the same table the previous day. On Friday, she had paid no attention to their conversation, since she had only been passing by them. To begin with, she was not inclined to pay attention on this afternoon either, since she was occupied with something else. Eventually, however, she noticed that they were dis-

Far left: Olympic's *First Class Reception Room.*

Upper right: *First Class passenger Elizabeth Lines.*

Lower right: *First Class passenger Mary Lines.*

This stokehold scene comes from the USS Massachusetts *just a few years before the* Titanic's *maiden voyage.*

cussing the ship's daily runs – a popular topic amongst passengers. Now her attention was fully arrested; she had plenty of time on her hands, and found the room was quiet enough to overhear their discussion quite clearly without obviously eavesdropping.

Ismay was visibly excited over the success of his new ship. *Titanic* was clearly making better time than her sister, *Olympic*, had made on her maiden voyage. The boilers were standing the pressure of full-steam quite nicely, he noted; the ship would certainly make a better run up to noon on Sunday than they had made this day. Mrs Lines noticed Captain Smith nodding in the affirmative to Ismay's enthusiastic comments, but observed that the conversation was not much of a conversation at all, since Smith was saying nothing. Ismay wasn't coming up for air, and neither was he asking any questions … Smith merely continued to nod in agreement with his statements. Later, she couldn't recall hearing the Captain speaking at all during the *tête-à-tête*.

The White Star Chairman, she thought, 'was very positive, one might almost say dictatorial'. He was so excited that he was repeating himself a great deal. 'You see they are standing the pressure, everything is going well, the boilers are working well', Ismay said. 'We can do better tomorrow, we will make a better run to-morrow.' Ismay thought that they could put a little more steam on, and increase the ship's speed still further. Then she heard Ismay say: 'We will beat the *Olympic* and get in to New York on Tuesday.'

Eventually, Ismay was satisfied. The two men rose and went to depart the Reception Room. Mrs Lines recalled hearing Ismay say to Smith: 'Come on, Captain, we will get somebody and go down to the Squash Courts.'[234]

This conversation shows that Ismay was apparently fully informed on the ship's navigation up to that point. Unquestionably, he expected the *Titanic* to perform better than her older sister on her first voyage the previous summer.[235] It is also very clear that Ismay – like many others aboard the ship throughout the crossing – hoped that *Ti-*

tanic would arrive in New York on Tuesday evening rather than Wednesday. Captain Smith, for his part, seemed to show no reservation on the point.[236]

In the meantime, another troublesome situation which had plagued the ship right from Belfast was finally being put to bed. During Saturday, the fire which had been burning in the forward coal bunker of Boiler Room No. 5 was finally extinguished. Leading Fireman Charles Hendrickson recalled that the 'fire was not out much before all the coal was out'.[237] He and the three or four men that were working with him 'finished the bunker out'.[238]

Only then, with the fire out and the bunker wholly emptied of coal, could anyone get a look at the fire's effects. Hendrickson and Leading Fireman Fred Barrett had a look for themselves. Barrett recalled that the bulkhead which ran through the bunker 'was damaged from the bottom … The bottom of the watertight compartment was dinged aft and the other part was dinged forward.'[239] Hendrickson said that he 'could see where [the bulkhead] had been red hot; all the paint and everything was off. It was dented a bit.' He recalled that it was 'warped'. So he 'brushed it off and got some black oil and rubbed over it'.[240]

That same day, Walter and Mahala Douglas were strolling along the Promenade Deck, enjoying the fine weather and the 'fresh favoring winds' which had seemed to caress their entire crossing. They noticed a nearby seaman lowering a weighted pail toward the sea so that he could retrieve a sample and take the temperature of the water. Curious to view this bit of shipboard routine, Mrs Douglas watched from one of the open Promenade Deck windows. She wondered if the pail would manage to reach the water or if it would simply be buffeted about in the breeze. The bucket, in the end, did not make it to the water, and the seaman drew it back up, 'filled it with water from the stand pipe, placed the thermometer in it, and went with it to the officer in charge.'[241]

Colonel Archibald Gracie was a seasoned trans-Atlantic traveler, but on this particular trip, he found himself straying from his typical shipboard routine:

> In the various trips which I have made across the Atlantic, it has been my custom aboard ship, whenever the weather permitted, to take as much exercise every day as might be needful to put myself in prime physical condition, but on board the *Titanic*, during the first days of the voyage, from Wednesday to Saturday, I had departed from this, my usual self-imposed regimen, for during this interval I had devoted my time to social enjoyment and to the reading of books taken from the ship's well-supplied library. I enjoyed myself as if I were in a summer palace on the seashore, surrounded with every comfort – there was nothing to indicate or suggest that we were on the stormy Atlantic Ocean. The motion of the ship and the noise of its machinery were scarcely discernible on deck or in the saloons, either day or night.[242]

The majority of the passengers aboard the ship were very much enjoying the crossing. Elmer Taylor recalled:

> Thursday, Friday, and Saturday on this voyage passed quickly. Everyone was speculating on [the]

No. 659

WHITE STAR LINE.

R.M.S. "TITANIC."

This ticket entitles bearer to use of Turkish or Electric Bath on one occasion.

Paid 4/- or 1 Dollar.

figure would have made them noticeable in any circumstances. She was wearing a pretty ermine cap, and we used to spot it all over the ship, for they moved about among us very freely. They were all alone most of the time. Perhaps they would have been rather glad to scrape up a few acquaintances. I used to think so when I saw her glance up from her reading at every one who passed. But, of course, the rest of us felt that it would have been rather presumptuous to make the first move.

Unfortunately, Irene Harris suffered an unusual accident on Saturday. While descending the Grand Staircase, she slipped on a damp spot where something had been mopped up. She broke her arm in the fall, and was initially tended to by Dr O'Loughlin; then, at her request, her arm was set by First Class passenger Dr Henry Frauenthal. To everyone in First Class, this was the event of the crossing, and word spread quickly. A number of passengers sent notes to the Harrises cabin, conveying their hopes that she would get better soon. May Futrelle, a friend of the Harrises, stayed with Irene 'a great deal' after that. At dinner that evening, a good number of fellow First Class passengers came up to the Harris's table and wished Irene a swift recovery.[244]

Eleanor Cassebeer had become fast 'shipboard friends' with Benjamin Foreman. During the trip, she lent him a small book of epigrams that she was reading. Things were so comfortable between the two that he began to tease her over her somewhat sternly-tailored suits. 'Is that the only thing you have?' he would say with a laugh. 'Come on, I bet you've got a real knockout hidden away somewhere.'[245]

On one of the nights, after dinner, Elmer Taylor, his wife and his friend Fletcher Williams were in the Reception Room listening to music from the ship's orchestra. Taylor recalled:

> Williams was a democratic sort of chap, [and] did not hesitate to move among the high, the less high or lowly, so after dinner he selected a table for coffee in the Reception Room next to a table at which Captain Smith was entertaining a party.
>
> We were close enough to hear Captain Smith tell his party the ship could be cut crosswise in three places and each piece would float.[246]

Isaac Frauenthal, who had been so disturbed by two dreams of disaster before boarding the *Titanic*, seemed to finally be relaxing:

> The notion that the *Titanic* was unsinkable had taken hold everywhere. The crowd contained many women and men of delightful personality. The days and evenings were charmingly spent. Capt. Smith and his officers seemed to be at pains to make everybody comfortable and gay. If anybody ventured an opinion that we might sink that person would have been hooted down.[247]

mileage of the maiden voyage, the behavior of the great ship, indulging in gossip, inside information and time of arrival.[243]

First Class passenger Irene Harris, wife of theatrical producer Henry B. Harris, recalled that there was a 'spirit of camaraderie unlike any I had experienced on previous trips. No one consulted the passenger list, to judge from the air of good fellowship that prevailed among the cabin passengers. They met on deck as one big party.'

May Futrelle, who spent much time with the Harrises during the voyage, recalled being particularly curious about the Astors during the crossing:

> Someone had pointed out the Astors to us. Of course I, with every other woman on board, was curious about them. His height and her smart little

Second Class passenger Lawrence Beesley recalled:

> There is very little to relate from the time of leaving Queenstown on Thursday to Sunday morning. The sea was calm, – so calm, indeed, that very few were absent from meals: the wind westerly and southwesterly, – "fresh" as the daily chart described it, – but often rather cold, generally too cold to sit out on deck to read or write, so that many of us spent a good part of the time in the library, reading and writing. I wrote a large number of letters and posted them day by day in the box outside the library door …
>
> Each morning the sun rose behind us in a sky of circular clouds … It was a beautiful sight to one who had not crossed the ocean before (or indeed been out of sight of the shores of England) to stand on the top deck and watch the swell of the sea extending outwards from the ship in an unbroken circle until it met the sky-line with its hint of infinity; behind, the wake of the vessel white with foam where, fancy suggested, the propeller blades had cut up the long Atlantic rollers and with them made a level white road bounded on either side by banks of green, blue, and blue-green waves that would presently sweep away the white road, though as yet it stretched back to the horizon and dipped over the edge of the world back to Ireland … while along it the morning sun glittered and sparkled. And each night the sun sank right in our eyes along the sea, making an undulating glittering pathway, a golden track charted on the surface of the ocean which our ship followed unswervingly until the sun dipped below the edge of the horizon, and the pathway ran ahead of us faster than we could steam and slipped over the edge of the skyline, – as if the sun had been a golden ball and had wound up its thread of gold too quickly for us to follow.[248]

One of the things that Beesley enjoyed doing was to stand on the Boat Deck …

> … in the angle between lifeboats 13 and 15 on the starboard side … and watch the general motion of the ship through the waves resolve itself into two motions – one to be observed by contrasting the docking-bridge, from which the log-line trailed away behind the foaming wake, with the horizon, and observing the long, slow heave as we rode up and down … The second motion was a side-to-side roll, and could be calculated by watching the port rail and contrasting it with the horizon as before.

Beesley also noticed the goings-on with the Third Class passengers, who 'were enjoying every minute of the time: a most uproarious skipping game of the mixed-double type was the great favourite, while "in and out and roundabout" went a Scotchman with his bagpipes playing something that Gilbert says "faintly resembled an air".' A couple of people in particular stood out to him:

> Standing aloof from all of them, generally on the raised stern deck above the "playing field," was a man of about twenty to twenty-four years of age,

A splendid view of Olympic's *stern decks in September of 1920 gives a good idea of how this same area on* Titanic *would have looked as Lawrence Beesley watched his fellow travelers.*

well-dressed, always gloved and nicely groomed, and obviously quite out of place among his fellow-passengers: he never looked happy all the time. I watched him, and classified him at hazard as the man who had been a failure in some way at home and had received the proverbial shilling plus third-class fare to America: he did not look resolute enough or happy enough to be working out his own problem. Another interesting man was travelling steerage, but had placed his wife in the second cabin: he would climb the stairs leading from the steerage to the second deck and talk affectionately with his wife across the low gate which separated them.[249]

As Beesley observed, things in Third Class were quite convivial. In fact, the Irish among Third Class even managed to start some impromptu parties with musical accompaniment.

Late Saturday evening, the east-bound Furness Withy vessel *Rappahannock* emerged from 'a heavy rain squall' and found herself 'abeam of the *Titanic*, which, with all her lights glowing, made a splendid picture as she passed'. *Rappahannock's* Chief Officer Smith estimated that *Titanic* was then making 'about twenty-one knots', and it did not take long before she disappeared into the darkness astern of the smaller ship.[250]

At 8:00 p.m. that night, Senior Marconi Operator Jack Phillips sat down at the key for his six-hour shift, and his assistant Harold Bride turned in. At 11:00 p.m., just three hours into his watch, Phillips began to have significant trouble with the wireless apparatus. Soon, he roused Bride from his slumber so that the junior operator could help Phillips get to the bottom of the problem; only if they could find the trouble could they, perhaps, put it to right.

At first, Phillips thought the issue was that the condensers had broken. The pair rummaged around the inner workings of the set until they had pulled out the condensers and examined them for signs of damage. It turned out that Phillips' first instinct was off the mark, however, as the condensers were in perfect shape. Phillips and Bride then had to find the real cause of the problem, and they were put to a 'deal of trouble' before discovering the source of the difficulty. It turned out that the leads from the secondary of the transformer had burned through inside the casing and made contact with some of the iron bolts which held the woodwork and frame together, 'thereby earthing the power to a great extent'. With the problem found, the solution was not long in coming: 'After binding these leads with rubber tape', Bride recalled, 'we once more had the apparatus in perfect working order'. However, the repairs had taken quite some time, and the system was only working once more by 'half-past four or five'.[251] Throughout the day on Sunday, the two exhausted men would be forced to deal with a backlog of messages, and it must have seemed they would never catch up.

While Phillips and Bride toiled to repair the wireless set, at midnight, the ship's clocks were set back. The clocks in the public spaces were set back by 45 minutes to 11:15 p.m. As was the typical custom, the first night watch took a portion of the adjustment, in this case 23 minutes, and the second watch took 22 minutes.[252]

Meanwhile, Benjamin Hart was not having a very good night's sleep, either. His wife Esther had been concerned about the dangers of the voyage before they even boarded the ship. Throughout the crossing, however, she had gradually become more accustomed to the voyage, although she recalled that she was 'still far from easy' in her mind about their safety.

After the family had turned in to go to bed, Esther had just dozed off when she was awakened by 'a feeling as if some gigantic force had given the ship a mighty push [from] behind'. The sensation was repeated a second and third time, she thought. She struggled to full alertness, but was terrified, and decided to wake her husband. 'Ben, Ben wake up, get up, something dreadful has happened or is going to happen.'

She remembered that her husband 'was a little cross, as a man naturally is when he is woke from a sound sleep by the ungrounded fears (as he thinks) of a woman.' When he saw how upset she was, however, he went up to the Boat Deck, had a look around, and soon returned. He told her that the sea was calm and the ship was traveling smoothly.[253]

Day Five – Sunday, April 14, 1912.

It was a picturesque Sunday morning, bright and sunny. Elmer Taylor thought that it 'was one beautiful day – clear skies, smooth sea, perfect in every respect.'[254] Lady Duff Gordon said that the day 'dawned calm and bright; the sea was exceptionally still.'[255] Colonel Archibald Gracie recalled that on 'Sunday morning, April 14th, this marvellous ship … had, for three and one-half days, proceeded on her way from Southampton to New York over a sea of glass, so level it appeared, without encountering a ripple brought on the surface of the water by a storm.'[256] Seventeen-year-old Jack Thayer recalled that Sunday morning 'dawned bright and clear. It looked as if we were in for another very pleasant day.'[257]

The Titanic lived, teemed with life, seemed a vibrant entity all her own. As the great liner had been gradually increasing her speed ever since noon on Saturday, she was then charging through the ocean at a speed faster than she had ever attained and maintained for a long period of time.[258]

Colonel Gracie had spent the voyage up to Sunday morning relaxing, and without any form of physical activity beyond socializing. However…

> … when Sunday morning came, I considered it high time to begin my customary exercises, and determined for the rest of the voyage to patronize the squash racquet court, the gymnasium, the swimming pool, etc. I was up early before breakfast and met the professional racquet player in a half hour's warming up, preparatory for a swim in the six-foot deep tank of salt water, heated to a refreshing temperature. In no swimming bath had I ever enjoyed such pleasure before …
>
> The racquet professional, [Fred] Wright, was a cleancut, typical young Englishman, similar to hundreds I have seen and with whom I have played, in bygone years, my favorite game of cricket, which has done more than any other sport for my physical development …
>
> To the swimming pool attendant I also made a promise to be on hand earlier the next morning …

Gracie also made an appointment with Gymnasium Steward T. W. McCawley – whom the Colonel described as one 'of the characters of the ship, best known to us all' – for Monday morning. McCawley, a 'sturdy little man in white flannels' and with a 'broad English accent', showed passengers 'the many mechanical devices under his charge and urged us to take advantage of the opportunity of using them, going through the motions of bicycle racing, rowing, boxing, camel and horseback riding, etc.' Gracie said that the rigorous physical activity gave him 'an appetite for a hearty breakfast.'[259]

Over breakfast in the Second Class Dining Saloon, Benjamin Hart was regaling their shipboard friends and table companions with the story of his wife's scare the night before, and how she thought that the ship had been in trouble when nothing had happened. He told those around the table that on Sunday night, he was going to insist upon Esther's having a 'strong glass of hot grog' to keep her quiet and make sure she stayed asleep.[260]

While passengers were lingering over breakfast, at 9:12 a.m. a wireless message from the Cunarder Caronia came in. Addressed to Captain Smith by title as well as by the prefix MSG, or 'Master Service Message', it warned:

> [MSG] Captain Titanic. West-bound steamers report bergs, growlers, and field ice in 42° N, from 49 to 51 W. April 12. Compliments. [Captain] Barr.[261]

This message was delivered directly to Captain Smith. Smith's brief personal acknowledgment to this message was sent at 10:28 a.m.:

> Thanks for message and information. Have had variable weather throughout – Smith.[262]

Very shortly after giving this acknowledgment, Sunday services were held at 10:30 a.m. Captain Smith personally conducted the services in the First Class Dining Saloon, and Elmer Taylor thought that they were 'well attended'.[263]

First Class passenger James Clinch Smith.

Smith concluded his service with the hymn 'O God, Our Help in Ages Past', also known as the 'Prayer For Those at Sea' or 'Eternal Father, Strong to Save'. Gracie later recalled that this particular hymn was a favorite of his shipboard friend, 56-year-old James Clinch Smith.[264] It seems that this service was concluded at around 11:15 a.m.[265]

The services in Second Class were conducted by Assistant Purser Reginald Barker. Miss Susan Webber recalled that 'everyone turned out to church'.[266] Sydney C. Stuart Collett recalled that the service was Episcopalian and that Barker, whom he referred to as 'the chaplain', read from 'the 13th Corinthians'.[267] Additionally, 42-year-old Second Class passenger Thomas Byles – a pastor of the Headingly Hill church in Leeds, England – conducted a Catholic mass in the Second Class Lounge; he also conducted services for members of Third Class afterward.

Shortly after the main religious services had concluded in First and Second Class, there came another series of noteworthy communications via wireless. At 11:47 a.m., another message came in, this one from the *Noordam*, relayed from the *Caronia*:

[MSG] Captain SS *Titanic*. Congratulations on new command. Had moderate westerly winds, fair weather, no fog. Much ice in lat. 42° 24' to 42° 45' and long. 49° 50' to 50° 20'. Compliments. [Captain] Krol.[268]

Miss Helen Ostby recalled the scene when Captain Smith most likely received this message from the *Noordam*:

Late Sunday morning, as I was sitting on deck, Captain Edward Smith was talking nearby to a few passengers when a steward came out and handed him a message. Captain Smith looked at it, but then continued talking for a while with the passengers.[269]

At 12:31 p.m., Captain Smith's response was sent:

Captain *Noordam*. Many thanks. Had moderate variable weather throughout. Compliments. Smith.[270]

At noon, the ship's run was calculated at 546 miles, making for an average speed of 22.06 knots. As Ismay had expected on Saturday afternoon, Sunday's run was better than the previous day's, and stood as the best of the voyage so far. Ever since the *Titanic* had left Southampton, there was discussion among certain members of the passengers and crew that the ship would be arriving in New York on the night of Tuesday, April 16 rather than Wednesday morning.

Although the point had been in some doubt on Saturday, Sunday's run renewed those hopes – and with good reason.

The trans-Atlantic route which *Titanic* was following encompassed 2,891 nautical miles from Daunt's Rock Light to the Ambrose Light, and of that total, she had covered 1,549 nautical miles, with only 1,342 left to cover. Even if the ship had only maintained her speed carried from noon Saturday to noon Sunday, she would cover about 1,100 further miles by noon on Tuesday, giving her only about 240 further miles to steam before she reached the Ambrose Light and entered New York waters. So unless the great liner had been slowed significantly after noon on Sunday, she would almost certainly finish her trans-Atlantic passage late Tuesday night rather than her officially-scheduled arrival time of 5:00 a.m. Wednesday.

Yet *Titanic* was not only due to maintain her speed from Saturday to Sunday … she still had more to give. There was talk among the passengers and crew alike that she would make an even better run on Monday or Tuesday, and this was more than idle gossip. Ismay had been kept well apprised of his new liner's progress throughout the voyage. While anchored in Queenstown, the White Star Managing Director had called Chief Engineer Joseph Bell to his cabin, and discussed the matter of *Titanic*'s performance. Ismay later said that it was 'our intention if we had fine weather on Monday afternoon or Tuesday to drive the ship at full speed … for a few hours.'[271] Second Officer Lightoller and some of the other officers also discussed the subject of the ship's top speed, and they were 'interested' in seeing what she could do.[272]

As *Titanic* was a new ship, among their typical at-sea duties the officers were engaged in an additional task: computing and recording what was called a slip table. Fifth Officer Lowe described it as a…

… table based upon so many revolutions of engines and so much per cent of slip; and you work that out, and that gives you so many miles per hour. This table extended from the rate of 30 revolutions a minute to the rate of 85 and from a percentage of 10 to 40 per cent slip; that is, minus. We were working it all out, and of course it was not finished.[273]

Once this slip table had been worked out, the ship's officers would have a very good idea of what speed the ship was traveling, not accounting for current or other weather conditions, just by reading the speed of her engines. When complete, this would prove a very useful tool for the purposes of dead reckoning the ship's position. A good showing of high speed on Monday or Tuesday would have aided the officers in completing the higher end of this slip table.

Since a high-speed run was completely dependent upon the weather, which is notoriously finicky off the Grand Banks, it would have been preferable to carry out the run sooner rather than later. On Sunday morning, the last three main boilers were lit, and their steam would gradually be built up and then applied to the engines as the day progressed. By Sunday evening, the ship would be steaming under full pressure from all twenty-four of her primary boilers, at a greater speed than she had ever attained before.

It also seems likely that for this run, the ship's five auxiliary boilers, located in Boiler Room No. 1, would have been employed. Although they were not lit at any point on Sunday, they most likely would have been fired afterward; it would have taken about twelve hours for them to build

From left: *First Class passenger C. E. Henry Stengel.*

First Class passenger Annie Stengel in 1919.

A 1916 photo of First Class passenger Norman Chambers.

pressure before they could be applied to the engines.[274] If they were fired soon after midnight that night, then they would have been ready to contribute to the ship's speed shortly after noon on Monday. Starting the high speed run shortly after noon would also have given the *Titanic's* officers fresh data to calculate the speed trials with a fresh sighting of the sun, for precise computations afterwards.

Fifty-four-year-old First Class passenger Charles E. Henry Stengel had boarded the *Titanic* at Cherbourg, France, along with his 44-year-old wife Annie. He recalled of Sunday:

> As is usual in these voyages, there were pools made to bet on the speed that the boat would make, and at 12 o'clock, after the whistle blew, the people who had bet went to the smoking room, and came out and reported she had made 546 knots. I figured then that at 24 hours to a day we made 22¾ knots; but I was told I was mistaken; that I should have figured 25 hours … on account of the elapsed time, I believe, which made it almost 22 knots an hour. At the same time a report came – this was the report that came from the engine room – that the engines were turning three revolutions faster than at any time on the voyage.[275]

Lunch was served at about 1:00 p.m. With the impressive run having just been posted for passengers to see, this was sure to be a hot topic of conversation around the various tables. In the Second Class Dining Saloon, as Beesley and others conversed with Assistant Purser Reginald Barker, the subject of the ship's daily run naturally came up. Everyone was glad to see that a better run had been made, 'and it was thought we should make New York, after all, on Tuesday night', Beesley recalled.

Barker ventured: 'They are not pushing her this trip and don't intend to make any fast running: I don't suppose we shall do more than 546 now; it is not a bad day's run for the first trip.'

The conversation then continued to the subject of *Titanic* being 'the most comfortable boat', far superior to the Cunard speedsters, which 'bore through the waves with a twisted, screw-like motion instead of the straight up-and-down swing of the *Titanic*.'

Beesley pointed out to the others at his table something that he had noticed before, while watching the ship's motion in his favorite spot between lifeboats 13 and 15: *Titanic* was listing slightly to port. Everyone turned and watched the horizon through the portholes on either side, and it was immediately clear how accurate Beesley's observation was. On the port side, the horizon and sea were 'visible most of the time' from their seated vantage point, while on the starboard side they could see 'only sky'.

Purser Barker said that it was most likely that the coal supply had been used more from the starboard side. In light of the fact that the starboard coal bunker at the forward end of Boiler Room No. 5 had been emptied to douse the fire, Barker's observation was spot on.[276]

Twenty-seven-year-old First Class passenger Norman C. Chambers, who lived in New York, New York, was traveling with his 32-year-old wife, Bertha. Like Beesley, Chambers noticed this odd orientation of the ship, recalling that 'all day long [*Titanic*] had a slight list to port'.[277]

The list was certainly slight, for it did not alarm any of the passengers, and only the most observant among them seemed to notice it. It did nothing to spoil the trip. Indeed, Second Class passenger Nora Keane recalled that the 'voyage was one of the finest I have ever taken'.[278]

That afternoon, the temperature had reached a high of about 48°.[279] However after lunch, many passengers from all three classes emerged from their Dining Saloons to find an unpleasant change in the weather. The temperatures had begun to drop. There was also a stiff wind blowing all that day. Although the wind was tolerable before lunch, the falling temperatures combined with the wind caused the decks to be so chilly and breezy that not many people cared to remain outside.[280] Second Class Passenger Lawrence Beesley recalled that it was a 'bitter' wind.[281] Because of the chill, the interior spaces of the ship were heavily populated all afternoon. Beesley went to the Second Class Library on C Deck, and although he found that it was quite crowded, he remained there throughout the afternoon.[282]

Benjamin Hart, one of Beesley's fellow Second Class passengers, was a man who never seemed to have a problem with extremes of heat and cold. He was cool in the summer, and warm in the winter. That afternoon, however, Mrs Hart saw him rubbing his hands together. 'How cold it has turned', he said to Esther and little Eva. 'I feel as if there was not a warm drop of blood in my body. Come and have a romp with daddy,' he offered to Eva. Together, they went up to the Boat Deck and romped around for a while.[283]

Miss Helen Ostby noticed that while the first few days of the voyage 'were fairly mild', on Sunday it had 'begun to get quite chilly'.[284] Elmer Taylor remembered:

> About 4:00 P.M., it began to grow quite cold. The temperature dropped so suddenly that it was generally accepted that we were approaching icebergs.
>
> After tea, it was bitterly cold outside, but comfortably warm in all public rooms. Our little party exchanged impressions, gossiped and otherwise wasted time until we parted to 'clean up' for dinner.[285]

Assistant Saloon Steward Walter Nichols.

Philipp Mock and his sister Emma Schabert had been enjoying the trip thoroughly. On Sunday, they also noticed the drop in temperature, although they recalled things a little differently from Taylor:

> In spite of the fact that the weather was clear, the boat was cold throughout. People sat around in the lounging rooms with their coats and furs on, and complained a good deal about the cold ... [P]eople talked about the low temperature and wondered why the boat was not heated more comfortably.

Mock overheard a woman near him ask a steward why the boat was so cold. The steward replied that the ship would soon 'be surrounded by ice'.[286]

First Class passenger Margaret Brown remembered that everyone was 'restlessly searching for a warm place. The comfortable chairs in the lounge held but a few, as a shaft of cold air seemed to penetrate every nook and corner, and chill the marrow. Heavy furs and warm clothing were donned.'[287] It seems that the ship's heating system was still not functioning entirely properly, even as late as Sunday, and that some public rooms were colder than others.

Thirty-five-year-old Assistant Saloon Steward Walter Nichols had been busy that morning, but he was not too busy to notice the cold:

> All day Sunday it was very cold, although the weather was fine ... There were services on board ... in the first and second cabins. I was busy with my work and didn't go ... I didn't go on deck. On a big boat like that a man working inside doesn't go on deck often. Sometimes you don't get a peep at the water for days at a time. It's just like working in a big hotel. But I knew that it was mighty cold outside, and I knew what the reason was, too. I've crossed enough to know that when it gets cold like that at this season it's because there's icebergs around. And if we fellows down below knew it I guess the navigating officers knew it, too.[288]

Indeed, the officers were well aware of the proximity of ice – and they grew more aware of it as the day passed. First Officer Murdoch had the 10:00 a.m. to 2:00 p.m. watch on the Bridge. However, the officers' lunch was served at 12:30. Lightoller returned to the Bridge at that time to relieve Murdoch and let him grab a quick bite to eat. Murdoch did not return until 1:00–1:05 p.m.

At about 12:45 p.m., Captain Smith came on to the Bridge. Lightoller recalled that in his hands, the Captain held 'a wireless message, a Marconigram'. Spotting Light-

oller, he crossed the Bridge, 'and holding it in his hands told me to read it ... [He] held it out in his hand and showed it to me.' Lightoller looked at it, particularly making 'a mental note of the meridians – 49 to 51' degrees west longitude. It was the *Caronia*'s ice message, received at 9:12 a.m., that Smith had showed him.

This was the first that Lightoller recalled hearing anything about icebergs ahead of the ship. When Murdoch returned from his lunch, the Second Officer mentioned the encounter with Captain Smith and the message regarding ice. Murdoch showed no overt surprise, but Lightoller was under the impression that the subject was new to the First Officer, just as it had been to him. Then Lightoller headed off to grab a bite of lunch for himself.[289]

Even as most passengers were enjoying their lunch, two more important messages were received in the Marconi Room. The first came in at 1:49 p.m.,[290] and was from the German steamer *Amerika*:

> To the steamer 'Titanic' [MSG] via Cape Race to the Hydrographic Office, Washington, DC 'Amerika' passed two large icebergs in 41° 27' N 50° 8' W, on the 14th April. [Captain] Knuth.[291]

Titanic's operators dutifully passed this message on to other ships. Since it was concerning navigation, and specifically tagged as a Master Service Message, it should also have been taken to the Bridge, but there is no evidence that this was done. In fact, no one knows what happened to it after the operators relayed the transmission.

Only five minutes later, at 1:54 p.m., the White Star liner *Baltic* sent another message containing warning of ice ahead.

> [MSG] Captain Smith, *Titanic*: Have had mod[erate] var[iable] winds and clear fine weather since leaving. Greek steamer *Athinai* reports passing icebergs and large quantities of field ice today in lat. 41.51' N, long. 49.52' W. Last night we spoke [with] German oil-tank steamer *Deutschland*, Stettin to Philadelphia, not under control, short of coal, lat. 40.42 N, long. 55.11' W. Wishes to be reported to New York and other steamers. Wish you and *Titanic* all success. Commander [Ranson].[292]

This message was delivered to Captain Smith. Shortly afterwards, he ran across Bruce Ismay walking with some other passengers on deck. Ismay was about to head down for a late lunch. Without saying a word, perhaps because passengers were present, Smith handed Ismay the Marconigram. On previous voyages, Smith had occasionally given Ismay a telegram to read; Ismay took the message and 'glanced at it very casually', reading it silently. No words passed between the two men, and Ismay put the message in his pocket, before proceeding down to lunch.[293]

At 2:57 p.m., an hour after this latest warning had arrived, Captain Smith's response was sent out:

> Commander *Baltic*. Thanks for your message and good wishes. Had fine weather since leaving. Smith.[294]

The *Baltic*'s message was the fourth ice warning of the day, although one of the four does not seem to have been delivered to anyone on the Bridge. It was the fifth ice warning received during the crossing.

First Class passengers Mr & Mrs Edward Crosby were strolling along the Promenade Deck about mid-afternoon that Sunday, when they spotted a scene similar to that noticed by Walter and Mahala Douglas the previous day. They saw at least two seamen lowering a bucket to take the water's temperature. Mr Crosby was a seasoned sailor, and he explained the process to his wife as they watched. They must have been quite close to the seamen, as they overheard them mention to one another that the water temperature was colder, indicating that the boat was in the vicinity of ice fields.[295]

As Lady Duff Gordon and her husband Sir Cosmo walked about the open decks that afternoon, she was impressed with the fineness of the day. However, she was also a bit taken aback at how, as the day continued…

… the cold increased. The wind was the coldest I ever felt… As we walked round the deck I shivered in my warmest furs.

'I have never felt so cold', I said to Cosmo. 'Surely there must be icebergs around.'

He made fun of my ignorance, and Captain Smith, who happened to be passing, assured me that we were right away from the ice zone.

Miss Francatelli, my secretary, and I went into my cabin and shut up all the portholes and lit the electric stove to try to get warm, but it was no use, and when we all three went down to the restaurant we kept on our thick clothes instead of dressing for dinner.[296]

Despite the cold, many passengers were thoroughly enjoying the day. Mrs Mahala Douglas recalled that on Sunday…

… we had a delightful day; everyone in the best of spirits; the time the boat was making was considered very good, and all were interested in getting into New York early.[297]

Similarly, May Futrelle remembered:

All that afternoon and in the evening, everyone was discussing the probability of arriving in New York on Wednesday [sic, Tuesday]. It was regarded as certain that the Titanic would make her trip in record time…

The sea was so calm and the motion of the boat so slight that it was hardly noticeable.[298]

John Thayer, his wife Marian and son Jack spent much of the day walking the ship's decks. In the course of their walks, they came across Bruce Ismay, Thomas Andrews, Charles Hays and a number of others. They spent quite a lot of time talking to these people. But that afternoon, Jack noticed that it was getting much colder. He recalled bumping into Ismay after lunch. Ismay showed them 'a wire regarding the presence of ice', and remarked that they would not reach that position until about nine o'clock that night.[299] The White Star Chairman also told the Thayers: 'Two more boilers are to be opened up today.'[300]

Down in Second Class, Lawrence Beesley was still seeking shelter from the cold. Through the port and starboard windows of the Second Class Library – a half-dozen of them were located on either side of the room – Beesley and the other occupants of the Library could watch people walking by on the Second Class Enclosed Promenade to port and starboard. Among these, a number of young children could be seen playing or walking with their families.

Beesley specifically recalled seeing a man who had previously identified himself as Louis Hoffman, along with his two children, aged two and three. The 32-year-old Hoffman, however, was in actuality named Michel Navratil, and he was a tailor from Nice, France. Navratil and his wife, Marcelle, were separated; Navratil's business was in trouble, and he also claimed that Marcelle was having an affair. The boys, 3-year-old Michel and 2-year-old Edmond, had gone with their mother when the couple separated. When the two children had stayed with their father for the Easter weekend, Michel decided to take them with him to America; apparently, he hoped that his wife would follow them, and that they would reunite and be able to make a new life in the 'Land of Opportunity'. He took the two boys, traveled to Monte Carlo and thence to England, stopping over at the Charing Cross Hotel in London. Then they had traveled on to Southampton, where Navratil had purchased their tickets under the alias of 'Hoffman'.

It is unlikely, on that Sunday afternoon, that Beesley knew Navratil's real name or the family's startling story. However, he had already become acquainted with the trio well enough to recognize them by sight as the children played. He would only find out more about their story later on. Among the others Beesley saw were a man and wife and their two children – the father was an avid photographer who took his camera wherever he went on board; there were also two American ladies who seemed to be friends, one of them returning from India, the other a graceful, distinguished looking school teacher wearing a pair of pince-nez; also their acquaintance, who hailed from Cambridge, Massachusetts; a couple playing patience, with the husband frequently dropping strategy suggestions to his wife; a pair of Catholic priests, one reading while the other with an open Bible was 'earnestly' explaining a verse to a friend in German …

Beyond the outer Promenade windows, Beesley could see the clear blue sky and brilliant wash of sunlight which 'seemed to augur a fine night and a clear day to-morrow, and the prospect of landing in two days, with calm weather all the way to New York, was a matter of general satisfaction among us all.'

At the notice-board where the ship's run was posted, Beesley chatted with a fellow Second Class passenger, 54-year-old Reverend Ernest Carter. In the course of their conversation, Carter mentioned to Beesley that there was no evening service planned. He asked Beesley if he 'knew the purser well enough to request the use of the saloon in the evening where he would like to have a "hymn sing-song".' Beesley made the request, and the Purser agreed at once. Mr Carter asked everyone that he came across that afternoon to come down to the Dining Saloon at 8:30, shortly after dinner had ended. He was assisted in this endeavor by Sidney Collett, who 'went about and announced that if anyone was interested in a song service to come into the saloon.'[301]

Once Beesley had taken the opportunity to liaise this 'hymn sing-song', he returned to the Library. There he decided to tackle the scintillating task of filling out United States Customs Declarations Forms, which had been distributed by the Library Steward just that afternoon. 'Form for nonresidents in the United States. Steamship Titanic: No. 31444, D', the form began …[302]

Imanita Shelley thought that everyone on board realized that the ship was in the 'ice belt', because of the dramatic

Far left: Olympic's *Second Class Library* in a publicity photo from the 1920's. The scene gives an idea of how Titanic's *Library* looked on Sunday afternoon.

Left: Olympic *stationary, as well as a White Star envelope and playing card.*

drop in temperature. She also was aware that wireless messages with ice warnings had been received. Interestingly, she later heard that some First Class passengers had asked Captain Smith if the ship would slow down while traveling through the ice. The Captain's response – she was told – was that, on the contrary, the ship 'would be speeded through'.[303]

In Third Class, Elizabeth Dowdell thought that the voyage up to that point had been a delightful one. The weather had been 'very fine' and 'the sea was quite calm'. Indeed her cabin-mate, Amy Stanley, 'had not suffered from seasickness at all during the voyage. Many of the passengers seemed to enjoy the sun's rays that Sunday afternoon.' However, she noticed that as the afternoon passed, it grew progressively colder. By that night, she thought that 'it was almost too cold to be out on deck at all'.[304]

The usual custom on every crossing was to have one lifeboat drill for the crew, generally on Sundays. Many of the crew expected that this Sunday would be no different. However, Lookout Archie Jewell recalled that the boat drill for that day was canceled because the wind was so strong. Putting men on the deck and practicing with a lifeboat, even on the lee side of the ship, would probably have been more dangerous than if the weather was calmer. As a boat drill had been carried out in Southampton before departure – which included lowering the lifeboats to the water, rowing around, and re-shipping them – it was probably felt that an at-sea lifeboat drill in high winds was simply not worth the risk.[305]

The rather crowded nature of many of the ship's public rooms led to a lot of socializing among passengers. This scenario created a prime conduit for an interchange of information. All over the ship that Sunday afternoon, there was a lot of talk that the ship was going to speed up on Monday. Some passengers heard information to this effect directly from various members of the crew.

Edith Rosenbaum had found the day 'brilliantly clear but icily cold'. As a result, she stayed in her stateroom, A-11, until 4 o'clock. During that day, her Bedroom Steward, 36-year-old Robert A. Wareham, informed her that 'the *Titanic* was making a record run. She was expected to dock in New York by Tuesday.' Miss Rosenbaum remembered that the ...

... sea was extraordinarily calm, and the great engines had not yet been pushed to their capacity. Anchor pools were taken up as passengers wagered on the exact time we would berth at the ... dock in New York.

Later that afternoon she took a walk on the deck, and then she began to get ready for the 'gala dinner' that evening.[306]

Martha Stephenson remarked to her Bedroom Steward, John Penrose, about the 546-mile run posted that noon. Penrose replied that that run was nothing to what they would do the following day. He thought that they might even achieve a run of 580 miles, which would have meant an average speed of 23.4 knots. This was perhaps a rather high expectation considering *Titanic*'s mechanical capabilities, but if the weather held the next run would certainly be better than any previous run of the crossing.[307]

Another pair of First Class passengers received similar news, but this time it came from a fellow passenger rather than a member of the crew. Their story began between five and six o'clock, when Marian Thayer invited her friend Emily Ryerson to walk around the decks with her. Emily and her husband Arthur were traveling under a dark cloud; their son had been killed in an automobile accident in Pennsylvania the previous week. Up to that point in the voyage, Emily Ryerson had refrained from going on deck during the day, but had instead stayed in her cabin. She had only gone out with her husband at dinner time. On this evening, however, Emily Ryerson decided to accept the invitation for a walk. The two friends strolled around the Promenade Deck for a while. The weather was 'very cold', but 'perfectly beautiful'. At around six o'clock, the sky was becoming colorful as sunset approached, and the pair finally decided to rest on a nearby set of deck chairs near the doors that led to the aft Grand Staircase. These particular chairs were not specifically assigned to Mrs Ryerson, but as no one was sitting in them, there was no harm in resting here for a few minutes.

As they watched the sea pass by and the sky began to turn 'quite pink', Bruce Ismay happened across the two women. Mrs Ryerson knew Ismay by sight, as they had been introduced on a prior trip, and they had a number of mutual acquaintances. Ismay had been made aware of the tragic circumstances of their voyage, and when they had boarded in Cherbourg, he had offered an extra stateroom and steward to the traveling party, and they had accepted. When Ismay, wearing a dark blue suit, stopped, he said to Mrs Ryerson: 'I hope you are comfortable, and are all right.'

Ismay was a man of 'striking personality', and it was said that in any group, he 'arrested attention and dominated the scene'. People who were not well acquainted with him generally found him a rather grating personality, and came off with the impression that he was austere, taciturn, or hard. Meanwhile, Mrs Ryerson felt emotionally overwhelmed at the time, still grieving the loss of her son. She carried on a conversation 'merely to keep the ball going', even though she did not particularly feel like talking. Yet Ismay stayed, even choosing to sit down upon an adjacent deck chair.

Beneath his jarring personality, however, Ismay cared deeply about people; it seems very likely that his entire reason for stopping to talk with Mrs Ryerson and Mrs Thayer was that he was genuinely concerned about how Mrs Ryerson was coping with her loss. The conversation continued for perhaps five to ten minutes, touching on a couple of different subjects, but the whole thing seems to have been a bit awkward. Perhaps sensing this, Ismay eventually fell back on a favorite subject of passengers during a trans-Atlantic voyage: the crossing itself. 'We are in among the icebergs', he said rather off-handedly. As proof of the statement, he fished around in his pocket and produced the *Baltic*'s Marconigram – which Captain Smith had handed him earlier in the day – and showed it to the two women without handing it to them. 'We are not going very fast, 20 or 21 knots, but we are going to start up some extra boilers this evening.'

This particular tidbit, about firing extra boilers, was beyond the full technical grasp of Mrs Ryerson, but she knew that it meant that the ship would be speeding up. However, she did notice that within the message was the mention of another vessel, one that seemed to be in trouble. She asked: 'What is the rest of the telegram?'

'It is the *Deutschland*, wanting a tow, not under control,' Ismay replied.

'What are you going to do about that?' Mrs Ryerson asked.

Ismay replied that they weren't going to do anything about it, but that instead, they were going to 'get in and surprise everybody'.

Just then, Arthur Ryerson and John Thayer, Sr approached their wives and Mr Ismay. In response, Ismay rose, and went in through the nearby Entrance doors. As Mr & Mrs Ryerson went down the aft Grand Staircase together, headed for their stateroom, Mrs Ryerson spied Ismay standing at the foot of the stairs on B Deck, in the *à la carte* Restaurant Reception Room. As the couple made their way to their rooms, they discussed what they would do if the ship got in to New York on late Tuesday night rather than early Wednesday morning. They need not have worried so much about how they would handle such a situation, however, for White Star clearly outlined to their passengers that, should the steamer arrive at the wharf in New York after 8:00 p.m., they were welcome to stay overnight and disembark after breakfast the following morning.[308]

On the Bridge as the afternoon progressed into evening, the senior officers were becoming more and more aware of the fact that there was ice ahead of the *Titanic*. Third Officer Pitman, who was standing the 12:00–4:00 p.m. watch with First Officer Murdoch, remembered that while he was on duty, he saw two actual Marconigrams regarding ice ahead – one of which was this message from the *Caronia*.[309]

Fourth Officer Boxhall was the junior officer on duty during the First Dog Watch, which ran from 4:00 p.m. to 6:00 p.m. During that span of two hours, he proceeded to the Officers' Chart Room, which was just on the port side of amidships, directly abaft the Wheelhouse. In this Chart Room, which was separate from the Captain's personal Chart Room, there was a chest of drawers, where all the charts were placed. Lightoller recalled that they were 'nec-

The Bridge of the Olympic *in a photo taken by Francis Browne.*

essarily big drawers, to contain the charts fully laid out, and also drawers for navigational books, instruction books, and so on … A track chart is always lying on that chart room table … There are little pads, position pads, and deviation pads, and it is customary to tear off one of these chits and write on the back.' Such notes were 'left on the chart room table, lying on top of the chart', Lightoller said.[310]

This is precisely what Fourth Officer Boxhall proceeded to do. He saw the *Caronia*'s 9:12 a.m. Marconigram on the notice board over the table, 'copied it on a chit and took it into the Captain's chart room', where he 'put it on the chart'.[311] He copied the position out so that he would not have to take the original down from the notice board in the Officers' Chart Room.

At some point during the afternoon, Captain Smith made out what was called the night order book. Therein, he ordered the next major course change to be carried out at 5:50 p.m. It seems likely that it was at this same time that he made a footnote in the night order book, mentioning that a sharp lookout for ice needed to be kept overnight. Every Officer of the Watch was required to consult the night order book for any special instructions, and then to initial it as proof they had received the orders, as well.[312] By placing this note in the night order book, rather than relying on word of mouth, Captain Smith was efficiently ensuring that all the senior Officers of the Watch remained vigilant with regard to the ice ahead.

On the southern steamer track, which the *Titanic* was then using, the ship was due to make her last major course correction when she reached the position 42° north latitude by 47° west longitude. This course correction, called 'turning the corner', would take her from a southwesterly course to a more westerly one which would very closely line her up with the entrance to New York harbor. When the ship made this course change at 5:50 p.m., she had traveled about 129 miles from her noon location at an average speed of about 22.3 knots through the water, or about 22.12 knots in actual speed made good.[313] Thus, when she made the turn, *Titanic* was about three nautical miles from the actual location of The Corner. When the turn was made, the officers intended to settle her on a new course of approximately 265° true, lining her up almost perfectly with the entrance to New York Harbor.[314]

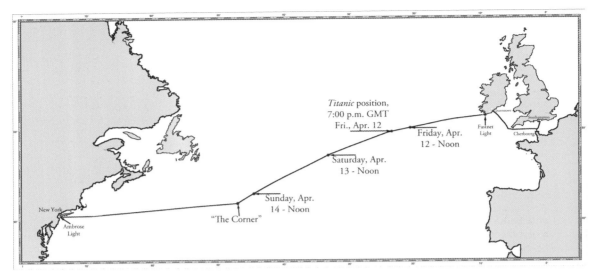

This map of the North Atlantic shows Titanic's intended route, and all of her known positions from Southampton through to when she turned 'The Corner' on Sunday evening.

Did They Turn the Corner Late?

On the *Titanic*'s route, after steaming roughly southwest from Ireland for about 1,600 nautical miles, she would reach the location where she needed to make the final major course change. This point was located at 42° N, 47° W, and was commonly referred to as 'The Corner'. Upon reaching these coordinates, the ship was turned to starboard, falling onto a nearly due-west course, which more or less lined up with the entrance to New York Harbor at the mouth of the Ambrose Channel.

Titanic's noon position on Sunday, April 14, was 43° 02′ N, 44° 31′ W, a distance of 1,549 nautical miles from Daunt's Rock Light over the route that the *Titanic* was steaming on. According to Fifth Officer Lowe, the ship steamed on a course of 240.6° true from noon until she turned the corner at 5:50 p.m.[315] The Corner was located some 126 miles from the *Titanic*'s noon position.[316] During the afternoon, Captain Smith left written instructions in the night order book to make this course correction at 5:50 p.m.

According to Third Officer Pitman and Fourth Officer Boxhall, in ordering the course correction to be made at 5:50 p.m., Captain Smith was delaying 'turning the corner' by a significant distance, allowing the ship to steam southwest of her typical route before turning for New York. In fact, Boxhall recalled that at some point between 4:00 p.m. and 6:00 p.m., he brought the matter up with Chief Officer Wilde, who was then serving as Officer of the Watch. Boxhall told Wilde that he thought that 'the course ought to have been altered some considerable time before 5.50 – that is, if it was meant to be altered at the corner. Whether we spoke to the Captain about

it or not I do not know ... I consider that the ship was away to the southward and to the westward of [the corner] when the course was altered.'[317]

If this was the case, one is forced to ask: why would Captain Smith have deviated from his regular route in such a manner? After the fact, it has been suggested that this divergence was an attempt to steam further south, so as to avoid the ice which was reported ahead of the ship. On the surface, this all seems to fit together nicely, and it has been reported in many books and documentaries on the subject. However, there is no evidence that Captain Smith ever said anything of that sort to any of the officers; rather, this seems to have been a conclusion made by others based upon supposition. More than that, as with so much else with the *Titanic*'s history, there is a great deal of evidence that suggests that this story is inaccurate. What kind of evidence? First, let's see why the ship's officers believed that the course change was made late.

After midnight that night, Fourth Officer Boxhall computed the ship's position as being 41° 46′ N, 50° 14 W. This position was some 146 miles beyond 'The Corner'. Boxhall arrived at those coordinates via dead reckoning, working with an estimated speed of 22 knots. Working backward from those coordinates for 5 hours and 50 minutes from 11:40 p.m. at 22 knots ostensibly placed the *Titanic* some 18 nautical miles west and slightly south of 'The Corner' when she made that turn at 5:50 p.m. It was based upon this dead reckoning position that everyone believed that the ship steamed past the corner before changing course.

So far, the pieces fit together nicely. At the time, there seemed little reason to doubt the accuracy of Boxhall's dead reckoning position. Thus there seemed little reason to doubt that the *Titanic* had turned the corner late. However, today we know – as no one did in 1912 – that Boxhall's dead reckoning position was actually some 13 miles off. If the dead reckoning position was inaccurate, then that threw off all reverse-engineered estimates about the ship turning the corner late.

Some might argue, however, that Boxhall believed – between 4:00 and 6:00 p.m. – that the course change should have been made prior to 5:50 p.m. However, what Boxhall thought that afternoon – assuming he was remembering the situation accurately – is not necessarily firm evidence of a delay. For example, we know that although the *Titanic*'s speed through the water was very high through the day on Sunday, her forward progress was being impeded somewhat by the effect of the currents. A full set of stellar observations would not be taken until after the course change at 5:50 p.m., so throughout the day, the officers were running off the ship's noontime position.

If, between 4:00 and 6:00 p.m., Boxhall felt that the ship had been making better progress than she actually was, this could easily explain why he surmised that they would be turning the corner late at 5:50 p.m. Interestingly, when he brought this matter to Chief Officer Wilde's attention, it seems that nothing was done about it. This could be evidence that no one wished to question the veracity of Captain Smith's computations. However, it may also suggest that Boxhall was mistaken in his belief that the ship was steaming beyond The Corner, and that the senior officers – aware of the retarding effect of the current – saw no need to discuss the matter with the Captain.

Looking at things from Captain Smith's perspective that afternoon, and working out the mathematics, it would seem that the Commander was apparently allowing for a 'speed made good' of about 21.6 knots from the noontime position, rather than the roughly 22.11 knots the ship was actually managing. In other words, Captain Smith had roughly accounted for the currents' effects when he wrote the order to change course at 5:50 p.m. However, he slightly under-estimated the rate of the ship's actual forward progress. The difference between his estimated geographic speed of what the liner was making, and her actual speed made good put the liner about three miles southwest of The Corner when she made the turn.

Looking at the location of the wreck, and working backward from that point, and working forward from the ship's noon position on Sunday, and then factoring in the exact time that the ship made her course correction that evening, it is not difficult to see that Captain Smith was really sticking quite close to the ship's standard route. In reality, the *Titanic* was only about three miles southwest of The Corner when her course was actually adjusted.[318]

At six o'clock, Second Officer Charles Lightoller became Officer of the Watch, relieving Chief Officer Wilde; Lightoller was set to remain in command until ten. Third Officer Pitman and Fifth Officer Lowe were the junior officers on duty during the 6:00 p.m. to 8:00 p.m. Second Dog Watch.

For at least part of the time he was on duty that evening, Lowe was in the Chart Room directly abaft the Wheelhouse, continuing work on the slip table. During his watch, he recalled that the barometric pressure was 29.80 inches, and he thought that it did not seem particularly cold during his watch. It 'could not have been less than 45', he felt.[319]

'Shortly after 6' o'clock, Lowe happened to casually notice something else. There 'was a slip that showed the position of the ice, the latitude and longitude', which was 'stuck in the angle of [the] frame' of the 'Chart Room table'. This was the same '3 x 3' chit of paper that Boxhall had shortly before transcribed from the *Caronia*'s Marconigram. Although the sighting's source was not given in the note, and there was no signature of who had written it out, Lowe did know that the note had only just been placed there, because he had not noticed it before. However, the Fifth Officer believed that the coordinates were 'to the northward of our track', and that they 'would not come within the limits of the ice regions' during his watch. Thus, he didn't pay any further attention to the note.[320]

Third Officer Herbert Pitman was on duty simultaneously with Lowe. When he began his watch, at 6:00 p.m., Pitman noticed that several coordinates – denoting the position of wireless ice sightings – had been clearly marked on the chart. Pitman assumed that they had been made by either Fourth Officer Boxhall or Sixth Officer Moody.[321]

In the beautiful, crisp air, the sun began to sink on the horizon ahead of the mighty *Titanic*. Second Officer Lightoller, standing on the Bridge, would have had a spectacular view of the sunset, which took place at about 6:52 p.m.[322] As night began to envelop the *Titanic*, the stars began to appear in the sky – initially in the darker eastern sky, and then in an ever-expanding canopy which would eventually meet the western horizon ahead of the ship. Lightoller recalled that at about 7:00 p.m., the outside temperature was 43°F.[323] At the same time, a great stillness began to set in. While a fresh breeze had been blowing all day long, as the sun set, Lookout Archie Jewell noticed that the wind began to abate.[324]

Dinner for the officers had been served at 6:30 p.m. in the Officers' Mess, which was located aft on the Boat Deck, on the starboard side of the deckhouse below the No. 3 funnel. First Officer Murdoch, then off duty, had taken the opportunity to have his meal. Then he headed up to the Bridge, arriving there at about 7:05. Upon arrival, he took the watch for a half-hour so that Lightoller could have his own dinner.[325]

CHAPTER 3

THE EVE OF DISASTER

Dinner for First Class passengers was set to be served at around seven o'clock. Bruce Ismay had been planning to dine in the Restaurant. Since he was alone, he decided to ask Ship's Surgeon Dr William O'Loughlin to join him. He must have made the decision rather late, because it was only at about seven o'clock that Dr O'Loughlin found out about Ismay's invitation. It was at about that time that the doctor was visiting with Mr & Mrs Frederick Hoyt in their stateroom, C-93; 'a steward came to the door and announced that Mr Ismay wanted the surgeon to take dinner with him.' The Hoyts and O'Loughlin were seated at the same table in the Dining Saloon, and were old friends; at least the Hoyts would not have to hear about the reason for the doctor's absence at dinner second-hand.[1]

As was his custom, just before dinner Major Arthur Peuchen headed for his cabin, C-104, to change from his day clothes to his more formal dinner attire. As he did so, he passed Captain Smith in one of the companionways. It would seem that very shortly thereafter, Captain Smith made his way to the First Class Smoking Room, where he came upon Bruce Ismay at about 7:10-7:15 p.m.[2] Smith took the opportunity to ask Ismay for the *Baltic's* iceberg warning, which he had handed him earlier in the day. The Captain explained that he wished to post it in the Chart Room for the officers to see.[3] Ismay retrieved the Marconigram, handed it to Smith, and the two men parted ways without further conversation.[4]

At 7:00 p.m., the last three primary boilers, which had been heating up throughout the day, were connected to the engines.[5] When they were hooked in, the results were immediate, and the ship's revolutions began to increase – as did the speed with which she cut through the water.

At about 7:15, Lamp Trimmer Samuel Hemming arrived on the Bridge and reported to First Officer Murdoch that all the lights had been set for the evening. He turned to leave, but Murdoch called him back and said: 'Hemming, when you go forward get the fore-scuttle hatch closed, there is a glow left from that, as we are in the vicinity of ice, and I want everything dark before the bridge.' Hemming promptly went down onto the Forecastle and closed the hatch himself.[6] Murdoch was keenly aware that ice was near, and he was being particularly careful to ensure that nothing interfered with the night vision of the lookouts and officers.

At 7:22 p.m.,[7] Harold Bride was on duty in the Marconi Room. He was working on the accounts with the headset on when a message came in from the Leyland liner *Californian*. It was a warning about ice in the area. Bride did not stop to acknowledge the transmission, or to take it down, and instead resumed his work. Fifteen minutes later, at 7:37 p.m.,[8] Bride heard the *Californian's* operator send the same message to the *Antillian*:

MSG to Captain *Antillian*, 6:30 p.m. in apparent ship's time; lat. 42° 3' N., long. 49° 9' W. Three large bergs five miles to the southward of us. Regards. [Captain] Lord.[9]

This time, Bride jotted it down on a scrap of paper, and acknowledged to the *Californian* that he had received the message. Then he went up to the Bridge, handing it to the Officer of the Watch 'about two minutes' after the message had been received.[10]

Around that time, Second Officer Lightoller returned from dinner to resume his watch. Murdoch remarked to him that in the half-hour that Lightoller had been eating, the temperature had dropped another four degrees. It was then just 39° Fahrenheit.

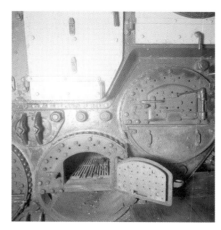

Opposite: *This publicity photograph was taken aboard the* Olympic *in the 1920s. It shows men and women enjoying dinner in the First Class Dining Saloon. The scene on* Titanic *would have been very similar on Sunday evening.*

Right: *The furnaces of a boiler in the USS* New York *give an idea of what the* Titanic's *furnaces looked like.*

Far right: *Lamp Trimmer Samuel Hemming.*

Indications of Ice?

During the day on Sunday, April 14, particularly beginning in the late afternoon, the air and sea temperatures were steadily declining. Aboard the *Titanic*, there was a great deal of discussion among both passengers and crew to the effect that the dropping temperatures were an indication of ice in the vicinity. In the years since, this general impression has often been repeated in books and documentaries on the subject of the voyage. But were declining sea and air temperatures really indications of ice?

Thus, when he was asked how he determined the proximity of ice or icebergs, Captain Lord replied: 'With my own eyesight.' He also said that in clear weather, there were really no tests other than actually sighting a berg, with which he would determine proximity to ice.

Titanic's Second Officer Lightoller went even further. He said that the decline in temperatures that night gave 'absolutely no indication whatever' to him that icebergs were in the vicinity ... not the

A period photograph of a small steamship sailing very close to a large iceberg.

During the two formal inquiries into the disaster, many witnesses were asked about the matter, and time and again, their responses showed that they would not depend upon a correlation between the two things.

At the Senate Inquiry, for example, Captain Lord of the *Californian* was asked about the drop in sea and air temperatures that he encountered that night, and whether that would indicate to him whether ice was in the vicinity. Lord replied:

I suppose it would, if you were close enough. But in the Arctic current you always get cold water, even if there is not any ice. I always take the temperature of the water in fog about every 5 or 10 minutes, if we are anywhere near the ice track. But still if we got the Arctic current we would have very cold water, but if we got within half a mile of an iceberg, I suppose it would not drop more than another degree or two degrees.[11]

The fallacy of relying on temperature indications to detect icebergs becomes clear in Lord's wording. If a ship was within a half-mile of an iceberg, traveling at full speed, by the time the sample of water was read and the report made to the Officer of the Watch, the vessel would already have covered the distance. At any rate, in good weather, the lookouts should already have spotted the iceberg.

slightest.'[12] More than a simple denial – which could be dismissed as trying to give cover for the officers' actions that night – Lightoller further offered the very reasonable explanation that ...

... though the temperature was very low, it was no indication of ice, because you might be approaching ice and the fact of the wind coming round from the southward would give you a warmer temperature, not necessarily fog, and therefore you would have a warmer temperature and still be approaching ice.[13]

Famed Arctic explorer Sir Ernest Shackleton was also called to give testimony, to draw upon his experience on the matter. He was asked: 'Is there any indication of the proximity of ice by the fall of temperature?' To this, he replied:

Unless the wind is blowing from a large field of ice to windward there is no indication at all by the methods that are used now, and it is a very poor thing to go upon, is the change of temperature. The film of fresh water that covers the sea is so thin that by dipping in a bucket you do not pick up that thin cold water; and if the temperature of the air is approximately the temperature of the sea there is practically no haze; it is only when the water is warmer or the air is warmer that the haze occurs. There are no methods that I have heard of before this that can really give you an indication of approaching ice by ordinary temperature methods.[14]

Shackleton went on to say that only 'if there was no wind and the temperature fell abnormally for the time of year' might he consider that he was approaching an area of ice.[15] If he 'knew what the mean temperature of that locality was for that month of the year and there was a great variation, then I would certainly think there was some abnormal disturbance in the ice to the North.'[16] He was pressed further on the matter:

> You would not say, I suppose, that a fall in temperature was anything like a certain indication of the presence of ice? – No, I would not at all.
> Not at all? – Excepting under very definite conditions, such as a dead calm and a sudden fall in the temperature, because if you are in colder water, and as I said before you have not an equal temperature of the air, then you have a haze. If both the air temperature and the water temperature are the same the effect is that the weather is clear.[17]

Shackleton finally said that 'all those methods such as dipping up water in buckets to get the temperature are no good' for the purposes of detecting ice.[18]

Hugh Young, a retired Captain from the Anchor Line said that he did not believe a drop in temperature was 'any indication' of ice. 'The temperature indicates a colder current and no more ... [The] change in temperature tells you you are getting into a colder current. There may be ice and there may not be.'[19]

Gerhard Apfeld, Marine Superintendent of the Red Star Line, was also asked about such indications. He said that he had tried to detect ice through temperature on previous occasions, and found it of absolutely no use. 'I have gone across the banks, where I had the temperature down to 28 or 31 bright clear weather, night and day, and absolutely no ice. At other times I have been close to ice ... Sometimes we took the temperature, and on passing a mile and a half or two miles from a mile of icebergs, we found a temperature up to 55 and 56 degrees.'[20]

The logbook of the steamship *Finland* was produced, with a very interesting record. 'At 2.50 p.m. to 4 p.m. passed nine large icebergs between latitude 41° 28' N. and 40° 58' N., and longitude 46° 7' W. and 46° 42' W. We were nine miles off the iceberg when we had a temperature on one occasion of 42 degrees,' the log stated. When the ship closed the icebergs to one mile's distance, the temperature again read 42 degrees. That same night, the ship passed a number of other bergs when the water temperature read 56 degrees – at 12 miles from the icebergs and at one mile, the temperature was the same. Apfeld concluded: 'Absolutely, you cannot tell by that.'[21]

So where did the correlation between a drop in air and sea temperature and the presence of ice come from, then? Icebergs and ice fields from the Arctic were usually carried south by the Labrador Current, which carried very cold water. Thus, an observed drop in water temperature would correlate more with entering cold water from the Labrador Current than it would the presence of ice.

In other words, some crew members were accustomed to noticing or hearing about a drop in water temperature – one which was the result of entering the Labrador Current – at about the same time that they might happen across any ice that had floated down in that same current. Thus, some of the crew believed that there was a direct correlation between the two. What they did not account for, when formulating that hypothesis, was that whether ice had actually floated down on that current or not, the same drop in temperature could be expected.

Similarly, the drop in air temperature on Sunday, April 14, was not an indication of ice. The most precipitous decline in air temperature really began after sunset. On a clear evening such as that one, when there was no insulating cloud cover, such a steady drop was to be expected once the warmth of the sun had vanished from the horizon. However, it should also be recalled that a fresh wind from the north or northwest – which had been blowing all day – subsided at sunset, around 7:00 p.m.[22]

The calm conditions and the temperature drop indicate that a high-pressure weather system had developed south of the Grand Banks of Newfoundland, and was then moving eastward. As the *Titanic* crossed the frontal boundary at around sunset, the liner entered the highly stable but very cold arctic air behind the front, which was then apparently being pulled down from the north or northwest.[23] As such, the drop in air – and sea – temperature that evening was by no means hard evidence of ice in the vicinity; however, it was certainly a reminder of its proximity.

After Murdoch and Lightoller exchanged any necessary information, Lightoller resumed his watch, which would continue for just under two and a half more hours. Murdoch departed the Bridge, having the same amount of time to while away before his own watch began at 10:00 p.m. Despite the lack of any weather-related wind after sunset, the 'wind' created as the ship moved forward through the atmosphere, combined with the frigid ambient air temperatures, would have been an unpleasant combination. Murdoch could be certain of only one thing as he made his way from the Bridge: his watch was going to be a bitterly cold one.

After changing for dinner, Major Peuchen left his cabin and descended the forward First Class Grand Staircase a single deck. He emerged from the landing into the Reception Room, and then proceeded aft to the First Class Dining Saloon, arriving there at about 7:15 p.m.[24]

First Class Stewardess Mary Sloan thought that Thomas Andrews had been a little down when she had talked to him on Friday evening. On this night, however, she spied him on his way to dinner, and noted that not only was he 'in good spirits', but that he also 'looked splendid'.[25]

While Andrews was going down to dine in the main D Deck Saloon, Captain Smith would not be found there

Above: *A 1911 photo of* Olympic*'s B Deck Restaurant, looking forward and to starboard.*

Left: *The cover of an* à la carte Restaurant *menu.*

was extremely well patronized. That evening played out for those in the Restaurant while a trio of musicians played 'in the corridor outside'.[26]

Bruce Ismay and Dr O'Loughlin arrived in the Restaurant at 7:30 p.m. and were given a table in the middle of the room on the starboard side.[27] During the two men's private conversation, Dr O'Loughlin mentioned to Ismay that the ship had already 'turned the corner', making her final turn to line up with the entrance to New York Harbor. This final major course correction had been carried out at 5:50 p.m., nearly two hours earlier. Ismay himself was aware that the ship had turned the corner; he also knew that the ship was nearing the vicinity of ice, but this knowledge did little to dampen enthusiasm over what was turning out to be a tremendous maiden voyage; indeed, the atmosphere was festive at their table. At one point, Dr O'Loughlin 'stood up, and raising a glass of champagne, cried "Let us drink to the mighty *Titanic*",' which met with cries of approval.[28]

Jacques and May Futrelle dined in the company of Henry and Irene Harris.[29] May Futrelle, not unlike Elmer Taylor, recalled that there was something special about the dinner that evening:

It was a brilliant crowd. Jewels flashed from the gowns of the women. And oh, the dear women, how fondly they wore their latest Parisian gowns. It was the first time that most of them had an opportunity to display their newly acquired finery. The

that night; this was because he had accepted an invitation to dine in the *à la carte* Restaurant on B Deck. While the Restaurant was always a popular fixture during the *Olympic*'s first season in service – and had proved to be similarly popular during *Titanic*'s maiden voyage – on this night it

Top row, left to right: *First Class passenger George Widener.*

First Class passenger Eleanor Widener.

First Class passenger William Thornton Carter II several years after the sinking. Young William did not dine with his parents Sunday evening in the Restaurant.

First Class passenger Lucile Carter was described as a 'young and beautiful Philadelphia society woman noted for wearing extreme-fashion garments'.

Second row, left to right: *First Class passenger Archibald Butt.*

First Class passenger Harry Anderson.

soft sweet odors of rare flowers pervaded the atmosphere. I remember at our table was a great bunch of American Beauty roses. The orchestra played popular music. It was a buoyant, oh, such a jolly crowd. It was a rare gathering of beautiful women and splendid men. There was that atmosphere of fellowship and delightful sociability which make the Sabbath dinner on board ship a delightful occasion.[30]

She remembered thinking that it would have been 'hard to find gathered in one place a crowd which would better typify the highest type of American manhood and womanhood … We were all filled with the joy of living.' Members of the group remarked that they 'might have been in a hotel ashore for all the motion we felt. You had to look out of the portholes to realize that you were at sea.'

Only one thing sounded a discordant note in the gaiety of the evening: the identification of a professional gambler among their ranks. He sat at another table in the Restaurant with a 'cold-blooded smile' plastered across his face as he surveyed the passengers in the room – perhaps sizing up his next potential victim. The men warned each other not to become involved in a game with this person, and spread the word as best they could.

Another subject of conversation between the Futrelles and the Harrises was more positive. As Jacques Futrelle was a writer who had some background in the New York theater scene, and Mr Harris was a prestigious New York theater manager, it was only natural that the conversation would drift toward the subject at their table. Jacques Futrelle and Irene Harris took the opportunity to engage in a discussion of some of the newest plays on the American stage.[31] At one point, they even turned and toasted the individuals sitting at the next table over.[32]

The focus of all attention in the Restaurant that night, however, was a rather large dinner party. This group was located in the forward starboard corner of the Restaurant; although partially concealed in a private alcove, the table was large enough that part of it extended beyond the privacy screen. Bruce Ismay, who was sitting with his back to this party, recalled that he could not see everyone in the group because some were within the alcove.[33] This special gathering had been arranged by First Class passengers George and Eleanor Widener.

George Widener, then aged 50, was a banker and financial advisor who lived in Elkins Park, just outside of Philadelphia, Pennsylvania. He was the son of Peter A. B. Widener, streetcar magnate and co-founder of the Philadelphia Traction Company. His wife Eleanor, also 50 years of age, was the daughter of William Elkins – his father's business partner. Their son, 27-year-old Harry, was an avid bibliophile; their daughter Eleanor was to be married on June 19, and as a result of the necessary planning for that event, she had not joined her family. The three Wideners had traveled to England on the *Mauretania* in February; Mrs Widener had proceeded on her own to France at some point during the trip. George and Harry had boarded the *Titanic* at Southampton, and had been reunited with Eleanor at Cherbourg, when she boarded the ship.

The Wideners were a very prominent family, and they had invited quite a number of the super-elite among First Class to dine with them in the Restaurant that evening. The meal was apparently being held in Captain Smith's honor.[34] In addition to the Captain, other participants included John and Marian Thayer, William and Lucile Carter, and military advisor Major Archibald Butt. Saloon Steward Thomas Whiteley stated that the atmosphere at the table was gay, that Captain Smith 'talked and joked with Mr Astor'; he reported that while wine was served at the table, he 'did not see the captain drink anything; I do not think he ever indulged.'[35] First Class passenger Harry Anderson – the New York stockbroker who typically dined with Thomas Andrews and Eleanor Cassebeer – also remembered dining at the Wideners' party. He said that even 'with a friend like me' Captain Smith 'refused to drink that … night. When I insisted, he had a small glass of port, sipped once and left it.'[36]

Captain Smith was apparently seated at the inboard side of the table, and was visible to many individuals within the Restaurant, including Bruce Ismay;[37] Major Butt sat more within the alcove, directly beside Mrs Marian Thayer. The 39-year-old Mrs Thayer had never met the 46-year-old Major Butt before, but as soon as they were introduced they bonded like old friends. Both of them marveled over the instantaneous bond they formed, and Mrs Thayer remembered that they never moved from each other for the remainder of the evening.

They discussed the Major's close friend President William Howard Taft, as well as his personal fondness for former President Theodore Roosevelt. Major Butt, Mrs Thayer recalled, was enjoying the trip very much; like many passengers facing the end of a relaxing crossing, he was unsure how he was going to dive back into the fast-paced life that awaited him ashore. Mrs Thayer promised that on Monday, she would teach him a method of controlling the nerves – something she had recently learned from a Swiss doctor. Major Butt said that she was just like his own mother.[38]

Forty-six-year-old George Rosenshine and his 38-year-old mistress, Gertrude Maybelle Thorne – both of whom were traveling as Mr & Mrs Thorne to avoid detection – were also dining in the Restaurant. 'Mrs' Thorne later told fellow passenger Charles Stengel that she was at the Captain's dinner party, and that he 'did not drink a drop'.[39] Mrs Widener also agreed, stating that the Captain had not consumed 'intoxicating liquor of any kind whatever' at the meal,[40] although it was readily available at the table.

Not all of the parties in the Restaurant were so large. Adjacent to the Wideners' group, there was also a table for three populated by Dr & Mrs William and Lillian Minahan, and William's younger sister Daisy. Daisy recalled that they had arrived in the Restaurant at about 7:15 p.m. They were seated so close to the Wideners' party that Daisy could actually hear snatches of conversation from their group. After several days aboard the ship, becoming familiar with the names and faces of her fellow passengers, she was able to identify the Thayers, Major Butt, and Captain Smith seated at the table with the Wideners. She was also able to pick out other noteworthy passengers: the Duff Gordons, Edgar Meyer and his wife Leila, and others.

By that point in the crossing – with shipboard gossip always traveling with legendary speed – many may have known of the death of Mrs Meyer's father, Andrew Saks, just six days before. What might not have been generally known to other passengers that night was that on Friday, Mr Saks' will had been read. Mrs Jennie Saks had received a life estate and his personal effects. However his daughter Leila, Mrs Meyer, was to receive $100,000 and a substantial share of the estate. Leila's one-year-old daughter, Jane, had been designated to receive another $10,000.[41]

Lady Duff Gordon, seated with her husband Sir Cosmo, painted the scene that evening very vividly:

I remember that … meal on the *Titanic* very well. We had a big vase of beautiful daffodils on the table, which were as fresh as if they had just been picked. Everybody was very gay, and at neighboring tables people were making bets on the probable time of this record-breaking run. Bruce Ismay … was dining with the ship's doctor next to our table, and I remember that several men appealed to him as to how much longer we should be at sea. Various opinions were put forward … Mr Ismay was most confident, and said that undoubtedly the ship would establish a record.

Further along the room the Wideners and the Thayers (American multi-millionaires both of them) were dining with the Captain and others, and there was a great deal of laughter and chatter from their table … At another table sat Colonel [John] Jacob Astor and his young bride. They were coming back to New York after a honeymoon in Europe, and I thought how much in love they were … They were joined by Isador Strauss [sic, Isidor Straus], the multi-millionaire, and his wife. These two so openly adored one another that we used to call them 'Darby and Joan' on the ship.[42] They told us laughingly that in their long years of married life they had never been separated for one day or night.[43]

Although her memories of the Astors dining with the Strauses on Sunday night must have been mistaken, since Steward William Burke testified that the Strauses dined in the Saloon at 7:15 that evening, her recollections of the Strauses' devotion to one another is unquestionable. Meanwhile, at another table located close to the Wideners' soirée sat Lucien and Mary Smith. They had arrived for their meal at about 7:30 p.m., or very close to the time that Ismay and Dr O'Loughlin had arrived. The Smiths did not pay much attention to the Wideners' dinner party, but the group did not strike Mary Smith as overly boisterous.[44]

Nearby were Walter and Mahala Douglas. As they entered, they noticed Sir Cosmo and Lady Lucy Duff Gordon dining close by; they also spotted Mr Ismay at his table with Dr O'Loughlin; naturally, they were also quick to spy the Wideners' dinner party. The Douglases came into the Restaurant fashionably late, arriving at about 8:00 p.m., and staying later than almost everyone else.[45] The Futrelles and the Harrises enjoyed their meal and their conversation so much that they lingered quite late over dinner.[46]

While dinner in the First Class Restaurant was under way, it was all business-as-usual on the Bridge. As soon as Lightoller returned from his dinner, the time had arrived to take a set of stellar observations, in order to help fix the ship's position with certainty.[47] Lightoller and Pitman did this together between about 7:30 and 7:40; Lightoller made the actual observations, while Pitman recorded the time for them.[48] However, once the observations had been taken and the data recorded, the fix was not complete. Next, the raw data needed to be worked out, and that task now fell to Pitman. For approximately twenty minutes, from about 7:40 until he went off duty at 8:00, Pitman was holed up alone in the Chart Room, buried in mathematical computations.[49] Pitman believed that the *Titanic* was only making about 21½ knots at the time, and was rather disappointed that she wasn't doing better, since he and the other officers felt that she could reach 24 knots under favorable circumstances. As it turned out, *Titanic* was making better speed than Pitman had thought when he began his computations. They would know for sure, however, when the 7:30 fix was worked out.

At 8:00 p.m., Fourth Officer Boxhall arrived to come on watch, and found Pitman still in the Chart Room. Perhaps

Above left: This photograph shows Olympic's First Class Dining Saloon. On the left, closest to the photographer, is a table for ten – one of the few tables in the saloon which could accommodate that many or more.

Above right: Saloon Steward Frederick Dent Ray.

happy to be relieved of the task of finishing all the computations, Pitman said to Boxhall: 'Here is a bunch of sights for you, old man. Go ahead.' Then he left and turned in, knowing that he would have to go back on duty at midnight.[50] Boxhall picked up where Pitman had left off, and later recalled spending much of the watch working on the calculations.[51] At the same time, Standby Quartermaster Robert Hichens – who was also just coming on duty – looked at the thermometer, and noticed that it read 31.5°.[52]

Meanwhile, in the main Dining Saloon on D Deck, a resplendent display of the Gilded Era was playing out. Elmer Taylor recalled:

> When we again assembled at table in a beautifully lighted dining room, we started a sort of mutual admiration competition in which the ladies always win. A smooth sea, clear skies and low temperature outside gave women passengers an opportunity to get out their latest Parisian gowns, their most brilliant jewels, transformation (a hairdo of the time), facial treatments, etc. It was a brilliant assembly – contentment and happiness prevailed. Conversations were perhaps animated by a social cocktail or two.[53]

Philipp Mock had thought that the scene at dinner every night of the crossing was a very interesting one. On Sunday evening, however, he felt that the women seemed 'more vivacious than usual and the men merry and contented.'[54]

Eleanor Cassebeer made a splendid entrance to the Dining Saloon. Having endured some teasing from her shipboard friend Benjamin Foreman over her rather severe looking suits, she had decided to put on a truly stunning gown that evening. The dress had white lace and she put an ermine stoll over the whole ensemble. When she showed up and arrived at the Purser's table, which she shared with Dr O'Loughlin and Thomas Andrews, a chipper Andrews let out a friendly

little cheer for her choice. Then he leaned over to her and said: 'Now that's the way a lady should look!'[55]

On this night, their table was a little emptier than usual, as Dr O'Loughlin was dining in the Restaurant with Bruce Ismay, and Harry Anderson was also in the Restaurant at the Wideners' dinner party. Two of Andrews' other table companions, 31-year-old Albert Dick and his 17-year-old wife Vera,[56] were from Calgary, Alberta. They had been married on May 31, 1911 – the very day that *Titanic* had been launched in Belfast. Over the course of the voyage, the couple had grown attached to Andrews for his character and his pride in the ship. They noted that 'upon every occasion, and especially at dinner on Sunday evening, he talked almost constantly about his wife, little girl, mother and family, as well as of his home'.[57]

Saloon Steward Frederick Dent Ray was busy tending to tables on the starboard side of the First Class Saloon. His section was usually occupied by Major Archibald Butt, Clarence Moore, Francis Millet, and Mr and Mrs Walter and Virginia Clark, but on this night, Ray recalled that it was emptier than usual. Mr Moore and Mr Millet dined between 7:30 and 8:15, but Major Butt was not down because he was in the Restaurant. Mr & Mrs Clark were also absent from dinner that evening, and it is possible that they, as well, dined in the Restaurant.[58]

Seventeen-year-old Jack Thayer, son of John B. Thayer and Marian Thayer, was eating in the Saloon that evening; his parents had been invited to the Wideners' special dinner function in the Restaurant on B Deck, but the invitation had apparently not included him. As a result, he was eating alone at his family's regular table.[59]

Mrs Martha Stephenson was traveling without her husband. However, her sister, Miss Elizabeth Eustis, was with her. The two ladies dined together, and remembered that the dinner that night was quite delicious. Their Saloon Steward even gave them a number of souvenir menus.[60]

Helen Ostby and her father sat at another table and discussed the reception that would be awaiting *Titanic* and her

10

278	Powder Rag "	Birch
279	You made me love you	Pether
280	When the midnight Choo-Choo	Berlin
281	Alexander's Ragtime Band	Irving Berlin
282	Ginger	Wurm
283	Ghosts	Penso
284	Red Pepper	Lodge
285	Red Wing	L'Estrange
286	Interruptions	Godin
287	Gnats	Rodger Eckersley
288	Niggers Birthday...	Lincke
289	L'Amour Qui Rit	Christine
290	Mosquitos Parade	Whitney
291	Ma Dusky Maid	Smith
292	Policeman's Holiday	Ewing
293	Bohemian Ladies...	Fall
294	The Bogey Walk...	Gallatly
295	Paddling Puddles...	Dix
296	Pearl Feather	Amelia Scott
297	Kwang Hsu	Lincke
298	Siamese Patrol	"
299	The Ladybird's Review	Moret
300	The Coons' Patrol	Lotter
301	The Cadet	Haines
302	Buy Jingo	Thurban
303	Paris à New York	Detrain
304	Strauss	Mezzocapo
305	A Bunch of Roses	Chapi
306	Cherries	Cremieux
307	The Baby Parade	Pryor
308	Marche de Madrid	Valverde
309	Le Prophête	Meyerbeer
310	Tannhauser	Wagner

11

311	Pomp and Circumstance, No. 1	Elgar
312	" " No. 2	"
313	" " No. 4	"
314	Marche Algérienne	Bosc
315	Le Pére La Victorie	Ganne
316	The Peace Maker	Lotter
317	The Light Horse	Von Blon
318	With the British Colours	F. Von Blon
319	Rakoczy	S. V. Balfour
320	Le Regiment Favori	D. Ertl
321	Castaldo	R. Novacek
322	Under the Double Eagle	F. Wagner
323	The Last Stand	W. H. Myddleton
324	Through Night to Light	E. Lankien
325	Sounds of Peace	Von Blon
326	Viscount Nelson	W. Zehle
327	Manuella	Lotter
328	Entry of the Gladiators	Fucêk
329	La Petite Tonkinoise	Scotto and Christine
330	Hobomoko	Reeves
331	Yankee Grit	Holzmann
332	Berliner Lüft	Lincke
533	Hail, Spirit of Liberty !	Sousa
334	Hands Across the Sea	"
335	The Bride Elect	"
336	The Invincible Eagle	"
337	The Charlatan	"
338	Stars and Stripes for Ever	"
339	El Capitan	"
340	Manhattan Beach	"

Waldteufel Polkas.

A set of pages from a period White Star Line songbook, showing numbers 278-340. No. 281 is 'Alexander's Ragtime Band'.

passengers in New York. Their friends, Mr & Mrs Frank and Anna Warren, had spent much time with the Ostbys that Sunday. Mrs Warren remembered that the 'general impression prevailing aboard the vessel' was that the ship's speed was going to be increased again on Monday, and that the New York arrival would take place sometime on Tuesday afternoon, rather than on Wednesday morning.[61]

Major Arthur Peuchen dined in the Saloon, as well. He was at the same table as his friends Harry Markland Molson, and Hudson and Bess Allison. For a brief time the group was even joined by little Helen Lorraine Allison. Peuchen recalled that the dinner was 'exceptionally good', and that it 'seemed to be a better bill of fare than usual', even though all of them were of a high caliber.[62]

The quality of the food at dinner didn't matter very much to 22-year-old Marguerite Frölicher-Stehli. Despite the noteworthy stability of the *Titanic*, she and her mother Margaretha had been horrifically seasick ever since Thursday evening. Finally, on Sunday evening, she had begun to feel better. Dressing in a warm wool suit and sweater, she managed to make it out of her stateroom and down to the Dining Saloon for the first time in days. After eating some dinner, however, she 'immediately became nauseous again', and was forced to return to her room.[63]

Colonel Archibald Gracie was in the Dining Saloon, as well, but he was having a better time than Miss Frölicher-Stehli. Gracie was seated with his usual companions, James Clinch Smith and Edward Kent. As the dinner itself began to wind down, many of the passengers started to drift out into the First Class Reception Room, where they sat for coffee and the usual evening concert by the five-man main orchestra led by Wallace Hartley. Gracie and his companions were among those who began to make their way to the Reception Room. As they did so, they marveled at the sheer number of beautiful women who were present that evening, and made remark to each other on the point.

Nearby, the Countess of Rothes had dined with her cousin, Miss Gladys Cherry. The pair felt 'very gay', obviously swept up in the nearly euphoric atmosphere that evening.[64]

At 8:00 p.m., a number of diners were still socializing in the Saloon when Wallace Hartley and his four fellow bandsmen assembled in the Reception Room and began to play their nightly after-dinner concert. Martha Stephenson and her sister Elizabeth Eustis moved from the Saloon to the Reception Room, listening to the excellent selections and noting a number of friends sitting nearby.[65] Major Peuchen and his dining companions also drifted from the Saloon to the Reception Room to enjoy the music of the orchestra.[66] Helen Ostby and her father Engelhart Ostby stayed for the concert, as well. Elizabeth Shute recalled that it was a ...

... beautiful concert, just as one might sit in one's own home. With never a realizing sense of being on the ocean, why should not one forget? – no motion, no noise of machinery, nothing suggestive of a ship.

Happy, laughing men and women constantly passing up and down those broad, strong staircases, and the music went on and the ship went on …[67]

Dinner in the Third Class Dining Saloon had gone just as well as – albeit somewhat less glamorously than – the dinner in First and Second Classes. Eighteen-year-old Emily Badman was on her way from Clevedon, England, to Skaneateles, New York, where her sister, Mrs Ernest Arthur, and her husband lived. During the course of the voyage, Emily had befriended 26-year-old Sarah Roth, who was on her way to New York for her wedding. Over dinner that night, she commented to her friend, a man from Kent, England, that she wished she could see such a big boat from a small one.[68]

After dinner in Second Class, at 8:30 p.m., the time arrived for Reverend Ernest Carter's 'hymn sing-song'. Despite the fact that the event had only been planned that afternoon, the gathering was quite robust – Lawrence Beesley thought there were about a hundred passengers present.[69] Nineteen-year-old Lillian Bentham, an American whose family lived in Rochester, New York, was traveling with a group of ten other individuals returning from a visit to Europe. She and some of her friends were among the attendees for this event.[70] So was Sidney Collett, who had helped Carter to invite people to the gathering. He was accompanied by his family friend and charge, Marion Wright. Marion had 'playfully suggested' to Collett that she should invite a friend – apparently referring to Kate Buss – so that Collett 'might not make love to her'.[71]

Douglas Norman, a young Scottish engineer immigrating to the United States, sat at the Steinway upright, ready to lead the group with the appropriate music. Carter announced each hymn, in turn, and gave a little background behind its composition before it was sung. The group sang hymns such as 'Now the Day is Over'. Marion Wright sang a number of solos, such as 'There Is A Green Hill Far Away', and 'Lead, Kindly Light'. As she sang 'For Those in Peril on the Sea', the others joined in what Beesley thought was a 'hushed tone'.

In the Marconi Room, Bride and Phillips had been engaged in conversation for 'a long while'.[72] Wireless traffic had already been 'very heavy' all day, as Bride recalled.[73] Both men had suffered a very short night's sleep on the preceding night, with the Marconi set acting up so badly. Phillips seemed very tired. Bride offered to relieve him at midnight rather than 2:00 a.m., to help the Senior Operator get caught up on his rest. Phillips agreed, and Bride turned in between 8:30 and 9:00 p.m. Just as he was headed off to catch a few hours of sleep, the *Titanic* came within range of the wireless station at Cape Race, Newfoundland.[74] Bride could 'hear the make and break of his key' as Phillips sent 'preliminaries' to the operator at Cape Race.[75] These preliminaries consisted of their 'distance and bearing from Cape Race, and the number of messages he had for Cape Race'.[76]

While Bride tried to drift off to sleep, the night wore on and the exquisite dinner in the First Class Restaurant began to wind down. When Bruce Ismay had finished his meal with Dr O'Loughlin there, at about 8:00–8:15 p.m., he got up to leave. As he did so, he noticed that the Captain was still seated at the Wideners' table. After departing the Restaurant, Ismay moved forward into the Restaurant Reception Room and socialized with other passengers.[77]

Lucien and Mary Smith departed the Restaurant for the adjacent Café Parisien at about 8:45 p.m. To reach this room they would have moved forward into the corridor that led to the Restaurant Reception Room, and then passed through the doors to starboard that gave entrance to the Café. As Mr & Mrs Smith left, they saw that Captain Smith and the rest of the Wideners' group were all still at their table in the Restaurant.[78] The Captain smoked two cigars that evening,[79] and he also enjoyed a cup of after-dinner coffee. At almost the same time that the Smiths left for the Café, Daisy Minahan was mentally preparing herself to turn in. Her brother had suggested that she do so just a few minutes before, but she wanted to hear the orchestra play one more piece before calling it a night. As they listened to that next selection, she saw Captain Smith finally rise from the Wideners' table, bid the ladies good night, and depart.[80]

Captain Smith headed directly to the Bridge, arriving there at 8:55 p.m. As he knew that the ship was in the vicinity of ice, he was without a doubt keen to check in on conditions. Fourth Officer Boxhall was then in the Chart Room, which was accessed by a door on the aft bulkhead of the Wheelhouse. Apparently the door was left at least partially open at the time, because Boxhall remembered seeing Captain Smith come onto the Bridge.

The Captain found Second Officer Lightoller maintaining watch, and the two men greeted each other with a typical, 'Good evening'.[81] Smith took the opportunity to confer with Lightoller about the weather. He remarked that it was quite cold.

'Yes, it is very cold, Sir,' Lightoller replied. 'In fact it is only one degree above freezing. I have sent word down to the Carpenter and rung up the Engine Room and told them that it is freezing, or will be during the night.'

'There is not much wind,' Smith noted.

'No, it is a flat calm as a matter of fact.'

'A flat calm,' Smith repeated.

Lightoller said: 'Yes, quite flat, there is no wind.' The Second Officer then remarked that it was rather a pity that the breeze hadn't kept up with them while they were going through the vicinity of the ice. This was because any wind-driven waves would have shown a 'dog's bone of foam' as they broke along a berg's base, making an iceberg infinitely more detectable in the dark.

The Captain was now getting his night vision pretty well, and said: 'Yes, it seems quite clear.' Lightoller agreed. As time passed, they unhurriedly discussed whether they would be able to see any icebergs lurking in the area 'at a good distance'. They agreed that they would certainly be able to do so. Captain Smith added that if it became 'in a slight degree hazy there would be no doubt we should have to go very slowly.'[82]

In all, their conversation lasted between twenty and twenty-five minutes. At some point, apparently during this conversation, Boxhall emerged from the Chart Room to report on his progress with the calculations on the fix. While there, he saw that the Captain was still present. As the conversation between Lightoller and Captain Smith wound down, at about 9:25 p.m., Smith said: 'If it becomes at all doubtful let me know at once; I will be just inside.' Then he left the Bridge.[83] Boxhall remembered that the Captain paid a visit to the Chart Room, passing through the Wheelhouse, as well; this may have been right after the Captain had departed Lightoller's direct company on the Bridge.[84]

It was now about 9:30, and Lightoller had roughly a half-hour left in his watch. He decided to take one further precaution. He asked Sixth Officer Moody to use the telephone to call up the lookouts in the Crow's Nest; he wanted to have them 'keep a sharp lookout for ice, particularly small ice and growlers', and to 'pass that word on until daylight', as each successive shift took its turn on duty.[85]

Moody dutifully went to the phone connecting to the Crow's Nest which was located within the Wheelhouse. Once Moody was connected to the lookouts, Lightoller overheard him order them: 'Keep a sharp look out for ice, particularly small ice.' Then he hung up.

Lightoller noted that Moody's order differed somewhat from the wording that he had specified, as the Sixth Officer had not mentioned 'growlers.' Lightoller thought the detail was important enough to have Moody call the lookouts again, and to clarify that they should keep a sharp lookout for 'small ice and growlers'. Moody carried the order out, ringing the Crow's Nest a second time, and conveying the order correctly this time.[86]

The lookouts didn't need much reminding, however, as they already had the feeling that ice was really close. About a half-hour before the phone had rung with Lightoller's order, Lookout Archie Jewell had turned to Lookout George Symons and said: 'It is very cold here.'

Symons had agreed, and replied: 'Yes; by the smell of it there is ice about.'

Jewell curiously asked what Symons meant.

Symons had responded: 'As a rule you can smell the ice before you get to it.'[87]

Meanwhile, Second Officer Lightoller decided to take up a position on the Bridge that gave him the most distinct visibility ahead – 'a view which cleared the back stays and so on' – and he remained there for the remainder of his watch. In his hand he held a set of the binoculars which were left on the Bridge at all times for the use of any officers; occasionally he would raise them to his eyes to get a detailed look at something of interest.[88]

Shortly after 9:30, Lightoller asked Standby Quartermaster Hichens to find the deck engineer and have him bring the key that would open up the heaters in the corridor of the Officers' Quarters, the Wheelhouse, and the Chart Room, as the cold was so intense. Hichens had time to do this before 9:45 p.m., because he was back on the Bridge by that point in time to give Murdoch the customary 15-minute warning that his watch would soon begin.[89] Hichens also took readings from the thermometer and the barometer, as well as a reading of the water temperature, and recorded these in the ship's log.

After dinner, Thomas Andrews made his way aft 'to thank the baker for some special bread he had made for him'. Then he returned to his stateroom, A-36, to do some more work. Steward Etches, who cared for Andrews' room, recalled that the cabin was 'full of charts', and that Andrews 'would sit for hours, making calculations and drawings for future use'. Throughout the voyage, Andrews had also been hard at work outside his stateroom. With the other members of the Guarantee Group, 'he went about the boat all day long, putting things right and making note of every suggestion of an imperfection.' This night was to be no different. There were things to do, and Andrews was not a man to leave work unfinished.[90]

Young Jack Thayer had been eating alone in the Dining Saloon that night, as his parents had been guests of the Wideners' group in the Restaurant. When he finished his meal, Jack had a cup of coffee. While he was sipping at it, 'a man about twenty-eight or thirty years of age drew up, and

introduced himself as Milton C. Long, son of Judge Charles M. Long, of Springfield, Massachusetts. He was traveling alone.' The two fell into conversation for about an hour.[91]

One Third Class passenger who might have been expected to feel festive that Sunday evening was Anna Sjöblom; the young lady from Munsala, Finland, was turning 18 that day. Although traveling with a rather sizeable group from Finland, she felt 'homesick alone', and was 'surrounded by immigrants of every nationality'. She did recall that 'there were dancing and festivities' among her fellow Third Class passengers during the day and in the evening. However, she did not feel much like participating, and retired early.[92]

Overall, however, things in Third Class were quite cheery. With a general optimism for better lives in America among the steerage passengers, spirits were high, and the mood was festive. There was an impromptu party in the Third Class General Room that evening, with a lot of music and dancing. Eugene Daly moved about the room, playing lively tunes on his uilleann pipes. Katie Gilnagh later said that 'the trip over was a delight', and that 'the girls all loved' Daly's pipe playing. She recalled seeing a rat scurry across the room during the party, with the boys giving chase, and the girls squealing with excitement.[93]

While most Third Class passengers thoroughly enjoyed their evening, Second Class passenger Imanita Shelley and her mother were still not entirely happy with their trip. During the evening, they noted the sharp drop in temperature, and guessed that this meant they were near ice. By 9:00 p.m., the lack of working heat in their cabin had allowed ice to form thickly outside of their windows. 'It was so very cold', Mrs Shelley recalled. Half-frozen, the pair retired early.[94]

At about the same time – 9:00 p.m. – First Class passengers Mr & Mrs Hoyt saw their friend Dr O'Loughlin 'making his rounds and visiting patients who were ill'. Although they weren't half-frozen, like Mrs Shelley and her mother, the Hoyts decided to turn in early.[95]

Sir Cosmo and Lady Duff Gordon had dined in the Restaurant on B Deck. Lady Duff Gordon recalled that once they had finished their dinner ...

> ... we went down into the lounge [Reception Room], where we met Mr and Mrs Edgar Meyer. I had my little autograph book with me, and got them to write in it. It was one of the 'Confession' books, which were so popular just then. Mr Meyer filled in his 'likes', 'abominations', etc., and then came to the column marked 'madnesses'. He laughed as he said: 'I have only one – to live', and wrote it down.

After this, the Duff Gordons went up to their staterooms on A Deck. Sir Cosmo went to his room, and turned in early. Lady Duff Gordon and her secretary, Miss Francatelli, 'sat chatting by the [electric] stove' for a while before turning in.[96]

As the clock advanced from 9:00 toward 10:00 p.m., things began to wind down in many of the areas of First Class. It was at about nine o'clock that Major Peuchen finally parted from his dinner companions and headed up to the First Class Smoking Room aft on the Promenade Deck. As time passed, he chatted and smoked with several friends.[97]

The Countess of Rothes and her cousin, Gladys Cherry, were enjoying their evening greatly as they listened to the concert wrap up in the First Class Reception Room. Typically, these concerts wrapped up at about 9:15 p.m., so that the band could go down to Second Class and play in the after

This 1920s publicity view shows people enjoying the comforts of the Olympic's *First Class Reception Room after dinner. The scene would have been nearly identical aboard* Titanic *after dinner on Sunday night.*

C Deck Entrance foyer for an hour, and it seems that the concert that night ended at the same time as usual. The Countess recalled that the orchestra played a selection from 'The Tales of Hoffman', by Jacques Offenbach, for the 'last piece of after-dinner music' that night. Although she did not specify exactly which piece was played, she most likely referred to 'Barcarolle', which was the most famous selection from that opera, and which appeared in the White Star Line songbook.[98]

However, even with the concert's conclusion and the departure of the band, many passengers remained in the Reception Room, talking and enjoying each other's company. A few began to prepare to turn in, but still others drifted off to other public rooms for further activities.

At about 9:30, Martha Stephenson and her sister, Elizabeth Eustis, left the Reception Room and ascended to the Lounge on the Promenade Deck. The fireplace against the aft wall was throwing off a welcome wash of warmth, a stark contrast to the chilly decks outside. For about a half hour, she read the Library copy of Sir Ernest Shackleton's *The Heart of the Antarctic*, looking at all the pictures of icebergs that were contained therein.[99]

Colonel Gracie was used to spending a lot of time in the Smoking Room with others from among First Class every evening. Usually he stayed up until around midnight. During those nights of the voyage, he would hear …

… Major Archie Butt, President Taft's Military Aid, discussing politics; Clarence Moore, of Washington,

D. C., relating his venturesome trip some years ago through West Virginia woods and mountains, helping a newspaper reporter in obtaining an interview with the outlaw, Captain Anse Hatfield; Frank D. Millet, the well-known artist, planning a journey west; Arthur Ryerson and others.

During these evenings I also conversed with Mr John B. Thayer, Second Vice-President of the Pennsylvania Railroad, and with Mr George D. Widener, a son of the Philadelphia street-car magnate, Mr P. A. B. Widener.

However, Gracie's 'stay in the smoking-room on this particular evening for the first time was short'; he returned to his cabin, C-51, early – probably by around 9:30 p.m. He asked his Cabin Steward, Charles Cullen, to awaken him early enough the next morning to prepare for another round of physical exercises.[100]

At 9:52 p.m., there was another noteworthy message received in the wireless room. It originated with the *Mesaba*, and it was addressed specifically to *Titanic* and all eastbound ships:

Ice report. In lat. 42 N. to 41.25 N. long. 49 W. to long. 50.30 W. Saw much heavy pack ice, and great number large icebergs, also field ice. Weather good, clear.[101]

Although the message concerned navigation, it was not preceded by the letters MSG, and was not attributed personally to the *Mesaba*'s Captain. Senior Operator Phillips heard the message, and replied: 'Received, thanks.' At the time, however, he was busy working away at a backlog of messages, and Bride was taking a nap before coming on duty. Perhaps because the message did not have the correct prefix, Phillips never made sure that this message was taken to the Bridge.

Down in Boiler Room No. 4, Trimmer George Cavell was on the 8:00–12:00 watch. He happened to look at the steam-pressure gauge, which was right alongside one of the boilers, and noticed that it was reading 225 lbs. The ship's steam system was ordinarily designed to work at a pressure of 215 lbs. The liner's steam-generating plant was being fired hard.[102]

Up on the Bridge, it had taken Boxhall some time to work out the calculations from the stellar observation taken between 7:30 and 7:40 p.m. At around 10:00 p.m., Boxhall and Captain Smith went to the Chart Room together. Boxhall had given the Commander the ship's position at the time of the observation, as he had calculated it. He stood close by while the Captain took the result and marked that position on the chart directly.[103]

At 10:00 p.m., the officers' and lookouts' watch changed.[104] First Officer Murdoch arrived on the Bridge to relieve his old friend Lightoller as Officer of the Watch. The two officers chatted for a few minutes, and Lightoller conveyed to Murdoch 'items of interest' such as the ship's course and speed, as well as a number of other typical tidbits. As their conversation continued, in the Wheelhouse, standby Quartermaster Hichens took the wheel from Quartermaster Olliver. Olliver told him that their course was North 71 West at the time, and Hichens repeated the course back to Olliver. Then Olliver went out to the officers on the Bridge, and one of them repeated the course back; this typical watch-change procedure was repeated until everyone was sure to be on the same page regarding the ship's course.[105] Hichens remembered that although the temperature was only 31.5° when he took the air temperature at 8:00 p.m., by 10:00, it had fallen further still during the two hours since then.[106]

At about 'half a minute to ten', Hichens called up Quartermaster George Rowe, who was then on the Stern Docking Bridge. From him, Hichens obtained a reading off the Cherub log, which trailed in the sea and gave a reading on the ship's speed. It read 45 nautical miles traveled since 8:00 p.m., meaning that the ship had traveled at a speed through the water of 22.5 knots in those same two hours.[107] Considering the fact that she was operating on only her twenty-five main boilers, and that none of the five auxiliary boilers had yet been lighted, this was a very good showing. Although the current was slowing her forward progress somewhat, her average 'speed made good' was still over 22 knots.

Meanwhile, Lightoller was conveying information to Murdoch about the ice field that they were approaching. At the time, Lightoller expected that they would be in the vicinity of the ice 'somewhere about 11 o'clock'. He mentioned his recent conversation with the Captain. They remarked on how calm and clear the weather was; indeed, it seemed that they could see an extraordinary distance on this night. They could actually see the stars setting right down to the horizon.[108] Then Lightoller wished Murdoch 'joy of his Watch' and started off on his rounds.[109]

Making the rounds may have sounded simple, but Lightoller recalled that it meant covering 'a mile or more of deck, not including a few hundred feet of ladders, staircases, etc.' Since the ship was on her first voyage, it was especially important to make sure that 'everyone was on the top line'. He covered several decks right fore and aft; he also went down to Scotland Road, made his way to the stern, and eventually emerged on the after decks. He made sure that Quartermaster Rowe, was at his station on the Stern Docking Bridge. By that point, Lightoller was thoroughly chilled. He remembered that the 'temperature on deck felt somewhere around the zero of Canada.' He was quick to make his way back to his own cabin, and crawled gratefully underneath the blankets for a few hours' rest before the vicious cycle started all over again on Monday morning.[110]

At 10:00 p.m., Quartermaster Rowe was almost half-way through his four hour and twenty-three minute watch on the Stern Docking Bridge. He had already been on duty for two previous watches that day – between 8:00 a.m. and 12:00 noon, and then a spell at the ship's wheel between 4:00 and 6:00 p.m. He was doubtless looking forward to turning in for the night when his relief showed up. Out there on the Stern Docking Bridge, however, there was plenty of quiet time to think.[111]

At about the same time, Charles Stengel and his wife Annie were headed to their cabin, C-116. Mr Stengel was 'familiar with engines in the manufacturing business', as his company had 'bought a great many engines in 28 or 29 years, and we generally take the speed of the engine. We want to buy an engine that will run a certain speed and do a certain amount of work.' So it was almost second nature to him to notice that the ship's engines were 'running faster than at any other time during the trip', and he commented on the point to his wife.[112]

Isaac Frauenthal recalled that he talked with his brother Henry and his sister-in-law for a while after dinner, and that all three had 'retired about the same time.' Isaac 'undressed, slipped into pajamas and lay down to read a book until I got sleepy.' He was still awake as midnight approached.[113]

Elmer and Juliet Taylor were still spending time with their dinner companions. Elmer Taylor said that shortly ...

> ... after 10:00 P.M., our party seemed to have had sufficient for the day. We arose from the table in the Reception Room, went through our [stereotyped] form of adieus, parted and proceeded to our cabin on 'D' Deck.
>
> Our cabin was rather cold, so we turned on an electric heater and prepared for a good night's rest.[114]

Lucy Dyer-Edwards – better known as the Countess of Rothes – and her cousin Gladys Cherry began to tire as the evening progressed. They finally decided to call it a night, and proceeded to their cabin, C-77 – which was an outboard cabin located on the starboard side, aft of the Nos 1 and 2 Boiler Casing – at 10:00 p.m.[115]

When the Futrelles and the Harrises had finished their dinner, someone in the group suggested that they go up on deck for a breath of fresh air. However, some who had already gone up returned saying that it had become freezing cold outside. Mrs Futrelle stalwartly went up and poked her nose out of the door to feel the cold for herself. She remembered that it felt like there was a 'death chill' in the air. She shivered involuntarily, happened to hear a nearby group of passengers casually discussing 'icebergs', and then she darted back to the inviting warmth inside. Unfortunately, her husband Jacques had been taken with a headache shortly after dinner. While May very much wanted to sit up for a while, she felt that she should go back to their cabin with her husband, try to soothe his discomfort, and help him to fall asleep.[116]

At ten o'clock, the lights in the Third Class public rooms were extinguished. This was done to encourage the passengers to retire, and it effectively ended the party that so many had enjoyed that evening. Eugene Daly and his fellow Third Class passengers began turning in for the night.

Assistant Saloon Steward Walter Nichols' shift ended at 8:00 p.m. that evening. He 'fooled around for a couple of hours', and then at about 10:00 p.m. went to his bunk to turn in. His berth was located amidships on the port side of E Deck, just off the main crew thoroughfare, which was known as Scotland Road to the crew, and Park Lane to the officers.[117]

In the Second Class Dining Saloon, the hymn singing had gone on for a bit longer than anticipated. Susan Webber said that the 'group did not break up at the appointed hour, but sang until 10 o'clock.'[118]

Sidney Collett recalled that the last hymn that they sang was 'Stand Up, Stand Up For Jesus', and it was sung without piano accompaniment since they did not have the music for that particular piece.[119] Lawrence Beesley recalled that by that point, the Saloon Stewards were standing around, waiting to serve light refreshments before finishing out their long day of work and turning in. Noticing this ...

> ... Mr Carter brought the evening to a close by a few words of thanks to the purser for the use of the saloon, a short sketch of the happiness and safety of the voyage hitherto, the great confidence all felt on board this great liner with her steadiness and her size, and the happy outlook of landing in a few hours in New York at the close of a delightful voyage.

Collett was sure, as the meeting closed, 'that everybody enjoyed it'. Beesley stayed behind, talking with Mr & Mrs

Carter over a cup of coffee for a little while. Then he finally bid them good night, returning to his cabin 'at about quarter to eleven'.

Susan Webber also stayed for the refreshments that 'were served in the dining room'. Finally 'late that evening', she broke away from the others and returned to her stateroom to go to bed.[120]

Martha Stephenson and her sister Elizabeth Eustis sat in the Lounge on A Deck for a while. Martha had enjoyed looking at the pictures of icebergs in Sir Ernest Shackleton's book, *The Heart of the Antarctic*. At 10:00, the two women had started down for bed in their cabin, D-20, forward of the Reception Room on the port side. On the way, however, they had encountered John and Marian Thayer, and ended up chatting for about three-quarters of an hour, reminiscing over what a wonderful trip they were all having. Finally, the two ladies retired, lamenting that they only had two more nights before arriving in New York.[121]

It seems that the same thought was beginning to intrude upon the minds of many of the passengers that night. There came a point on any happy crossing when passengers began to realize that there was less of the trip ahead than there was behind; that all too soon, the voyage would come to an end. What none of the passengers could have imagined as they drifted off to their staterooms, however, was just how close the end of their crossing really was – and what a bizarre ending it would have.

Walter and Mahala Douglas had arrived late in the First Class Restaurant aft on B Deck, and they were also among the very last to leave. They stayed until after the remnants of the Widener dinner party had broken up. Then they decided to head off for bed themselves, and made their way toward their stateroom, C-86. To get there, they went forward to the Restaurant Reception Room and then headed a single flight down via the aft First Class Grand Staircase. As they went down the stairs, they both noticed that the vibration of the ship's engines was 'very noticeable'. They remarked to each other 'that the boat was going faster than she ever had.'[122] Arriving on C Deck, they moved to the port corridor and walked forward a short distance before arriving at their stateroom door.

Mrs Mary Smith stayed in the Café Parisien for about an hour and three quarters after leaving the Restaurant at 8:45 p.m. While she had been in the Café, her husband stood just outside in the Restaurant Reception Room, chatting with some friends. Finally, Mrs Smith rose and asked her husband what time it was. He told her it was 10:30, and she then headed off to bed. As she passed through the Restaurant Reception Room she noticed that Bruce Ismay was still chatting with fellow passengers. Ismay did not remain for long, however; he later recalled that he headed off to his cabin and turned in at about 10:30 p.m., as well.[123]

After the concert in the D Deck Reception Room, some gentlemen moved along to the First Class Smoking Room for some after-dinner conversation, a brandy or a nightcap, and perhaps to play a hand or two of cards. The Café Parisien was quite chilly, and only the stoutest and most determined of patrons stayed there; others, less able to withstand the cold, eventually drifted off in search of warmer surroundings.

Thirty-six-year-old William E. Carter was traveling with his 36-year-old wife Lucile, and their two children, 13-year-old Lucile and 11-year-old William, Jr. William had broken off from his family after dinner, and spent the next 'several hours' in the Smoking Room. He remembered being joined by 'Major Archie Butt, Colonel Gracie, Harry Widener, Mr Thayer, Clarence Moore of Washington, William Dulles and several other men.'[124]

Even though Gracie had left the group early, there were still many others who were willing to stay up late on this wonderful night – another drink, another hand of cards, another cigar, and another story with fellow travelers. Major Arthur Peuchen, for example, was thoroughly enjoying himself there. He was chatting with a pair of fellow Canadians, 36-year-old Thomson Beattie and 46-year-old Thomas McCaffry.[125]

Around 10:40 p.m. or so, First Class passengers George Rheims and Joseph Loring were in the First Class Smoking Room, having a spirited discussion. They were trying to figure out what the ship's run would be the following day, since there was a pool on it. A steward, possibly Chief Steward Andrew Latimer, came up to them and said that they 'might figure on a bigger run'.

They asked why, and the steward said: 'Because we are making faster speed than we were yesterday.' Loring was skeptical, and asked him what he knew about it. The steward said that he had gotten that 'from the engine room'.

Loring scoffed at this, so the steward said: 'Gentlemen, come out and see for yourself,' and led them out into the hallway. He pointed out that the vibration from the engines was greater then than it had been thus far during the voyage.

This convinced Loring, and he said: 'I never noticed this vibration before; we are evidently making very good speed.'[126]

Before going to bed, Jack Thayer decided to go up for a turn on the deck. He put on an overcoat, and made a few rounds. He remembered:

> It had become very much colder. It was a brilliant, starry night. There was no moon and I have never seen the stars shine brighter; they appeared to stand right out of the sky, sparkling like cut diamonds … I have spent much time on the ocean, yet I have never seen the sea smoother than it was that night; it was like a mill-pond, and just as innocent looking, as the great ship quietly rippled through it. I went onto the boat deck – it was deserted and lonely. The wind whistled through the stays, and blackish smoke poured out of the three forward funnels … It was the kind of night that made one feel glad to be alive.[127]

At 11:07 p.m.[128] Jack Phillips was still working in the Marconi office when a deafening message burst into his headset:

> MGY [*Titanic*] [this is] MWL [*Californian*]. I say, old man. We are stopped and surrounded by ice.[129]

It was from Wireless Operator Cyril Evans on the Leyland liner *Californian*. As with the ice warning from the *Mesaba* an hour and a quarter earlier, this message was not a Master Service Message. Beyond that, the wording of the transmission came off as informal, perhaps even chatty. The extreme loudness of the message was due to the proximity of the *Californian*.

An annoyed and exhausted Phillips replied: 'Shut up, shut up, I am busy. I am working Cape Race.' The brush-off succeeded, and discouraged Evans on the *Californian* from trying again. Phillips failed to relay this – the seventh and last known ice warning to be received that day – to the Bridge.

Above left: *A 1923 photo of First Class passenger William Sloper.*

Above right: *First Class passenger Dorothy Gibson c. 1921.*

Right: *Able Bodied Seaman Thomas Jones* (left) *and Quartermaster George Thomas Rowe* (right).

First Class Stewardess Violet Jessop had found the maiden voyage of the *Titanic* enjoyable so far – apparently quite a bit less stressful than the maiden voyage of the *Olympic* the year before. Once she had gone off duty, she stepped out on deck, a daily habit before bed, and she found that it had grown 'penetratingly cold' outside. She also noticed little 'wisps of mist like tiny fairies', which wafted in from the sea and left her face feeling clammy.

Quartermaster George Rowe, then on duty on the Stern Docking Bridge, had also noticed this odd phenomenon. He recalled that they first appeared at about 11:00 p.m. Rowe and other seamen referred to these as 'whiskers 'round the light', because as they would get caught in the glow of any of the deck lights, they would give off a prism of color.[130]

Jessop shivered, and then retreated to the warmth of her upper berth, where she engaged herself in reading some English magazines that the Library Steward had brought by for her. Just then, she remembered a special prayer translation which an old Irish woman had given her; she had promised to read it, but had not yet found the time during the voyage. First she gave it to her cabin-mate, who was still awake in the lower berth. Then she began to read the prayer, as well, comfortably drowsy after a long day of work.[131]

At around 11:20, or perhaps just a little after, Major Arthur Peuchen decided to turn in; he bade good night to his acquaintances, and then started off in the direction of his stateroom, C-104, by the forward Grand Staircase.[132]

Margaret Swift had been enjoying the wonderful, 'successful' voyage. She and her traveling companions, Dr Alice Leader, and Frederick and Marion Kenyon, had 'sat late at dinner' that night, Mrs Swift recalled. Finally, she had turned in at about 11:00 p.m. Her cabin-mate, Mrs Leader, 'came in at about 11:30, I should think, and I was still awake'. The pair 'chatted for about fifteen minutes'.[133]

Fifty-year-old First Class passenger William B. Silvey was traveling with his wife, 39-year-old Alice. They were returning home to Duluth, Minnesota, and Mrs Silvey recalled that the night 'was cold and extremely clear and bright'. The couple retired to their starboard side cabin amidship, E-44, quite late, but they did not go to sleep immediately.[134]

Up in the Lounge on A Deck, a quartet of First Class passengers was playing a game of bridge. This group consisted of 34-year-old Frederic Seward, a New York lawyer; 28-year-old Connecticut stockbroker William T. Sloper;

44-year-old Pauline Gibson; and her 22-year-old daughter, actress Dorothy Gibson. Sloper recalled that at 11:30 p.m., the Lounge Steward came by and asked them to finish their game up, as the lights would soon be put out and everyone else had already gone to bed.[135]

After the hymn singing in the Second Class Dining Saloon, Sidney Collett remembered that over dinner, his table companion – 'a young fellow from Guernsey' – had told him that it was very cold on deck. Curious, he decided to go out to see for himself, and when he did so he found that the man had not been exaggerating at all, for it was 'very cold'. Collett recalled that there 'was much joviality before we went to our berths'. Safe in his cabin, he 'recited prayers, and it was so quiet you could have heard a pin drop'. One of his cabin-mates overheard the prayer and thanked him for saying it. It was about 11:30 p.m. when Collett crawled into his berth.[136]

Steward Alfred Theissinger was summoned to one of the cabins in his care, E-66, at about 11:30. The room was occupied by Arthur Gee, a First Class passenger en route to Mexico. When Theissinger arrived, Gee asked him go 'to the working passage', or Scotland Road, which was just on the other side of the ship, 'and have some firemen, who had just been relieved, cease their racket'. Theissinger did so, and then went to have a chat with George Brewster, one of his fellow stewards.[137]

Seaman Walter Brice was relaxing outside the Seaman's Mess Room on the port side of C Deck, underneath the Forecastle, just after 11:30 p.m. As he was on duty between 8:00 p.m. and midnight, on an ordinary night he would have been washing the decks down at that time. However, as it was Sunday, he and the men he was chatting with were relieved from that duty. On a frigid night like that one, it was one task that Brice must have been very glad that he didn't have to perform.[138] At about this time, the air temperature nearby was recorded as being only 27°, while the water temperature was only a single degree warmer, standing at a frigid 28°.[139]

Even at this late hour, the Smoking Room was well-populated. Alfred Nourney, who had upgraded from Second Class after boarding the ship in Cherbourg, and who was traveling under the pseudonym 'Baron von Drachstedt', was 'playing bridge in the smoking salon'. Two of his partners in the game were 39-year-old Henry Blank, a jeweler from Glen Ridge, New Jersey, and 23-year-old William Greenfield of New York, New York. Nourney recalled: 'The sea was calm, like a lake. I said to my bridge partner, "I wonder when there will be some waves".'

Major Arthur Peuchen had left his friends in the Smoking Room shortly after 11:20. On the way to his cabin, he 'probably stopped, going down', but eventually made it to his room, where he began to undress for bed.[140]

It had taken a few minutes for William Sloper, Pauline Gibson, Dorothy Gibson, and Frederic Seward to finish up their game of bridge in the Lounge. Sloper then bid them all good night, and started down the stairs to his stateroom.[141]

Seventeen-year-old Jack Thayer was still awake, and both he and his mother Marian were about to climb into bed in their respective staterooms. The Thayers had adjoining cabins C-66 and C-68, roughly amidships on the port side, with an adjacent bath. At the time, Jack's father John was already asleep. Having just called over to say 'good night' to his parents, Jack had opened the porthole of his cabin, and the breeze was coming in with a 'quiet humming whistle'. Far below, he could feel the 'steady rhythmic pulsation' of the ship's engines. It had been a long and exciting day for Jack, and he was quite tired. He concluded that it would be 'a fine night for sleeping'. The young man began to undress for bed...[142]

Even after Jacques Futrelle had slipped into the bliss of sleep, where his wife hoped he would find relief from his headache, May Futrelle still found that she wanted to go back up on deck. In the end she decided against it, as she believed her husband might still need her for something. After undressing, she climbed into bed, pulled out a novel, and started reading until she began to doze off. The novel was quite engaging, however, and she was nearing the end. She shook herself awake and kept on reading; this process played out a couple of times before she dozed off yet again...[143]

Meanwhile, Norman and Bertha Chambers had 'left the restaurant and went to their stateroom' at some point after 11:00 p.m. They had not gone to sleep immediately, however, and were still awake after 11:30.[144]

Third Class passenger Elizabeth Dowdell was in her cabin with little Virginia Emanuel and Amy Stanley. Elizabeth had already put Virginia to bed, and was preparing to climb into her berth. Amy had also retired for the night.[145]

Standby Quartermaster Alfred Olliver had been busy 'running messages and doing various other duties' since 10:00 p.m., when he had relinquished the wheel to Quartermaster Hichens. Then he was ordered to head aft, to the Compass Platform located on the roof of the First Class Lounge. Once he arrived and climbed up the platform, he began to check 'the lights in the standing compass', and 'was trimming them so that they would burn properly'.[146]

Minutes before 11:40 p.m. Jack Phillips was still busy sending private messages to the Cape Race station. Aboard the

Above left: *Lookout Frederick Fleet.*

Above right: *Lookout Reginald Lee.*

Californian, stopped for the night nearby, Marconi Operator Cyril Evans heard *Titanic*'s signals as she transmitted the messages.[147] Evans turned in and went to bed within a few minutes. For Phillips, however, things were starting to look up, as he was beginning to thin out the pile of traffic for Cape Race. Perhaps things were going to begin quieting down...

Up to that point, Sunday had been an ideal day for many of the *Titanic*'s passengers. At almost exactly the same time that Evans was overhearing Phillips working Cape Race, or just before 11:40 p.m., the *Titanic* was forging ahead at twenty-two-and-a-half knots through the water ... faster than she had traveled at any other point in the voyage. From noon that day, she had traveled about 258 miles in eleven hours and forty minutes, at an average 'speed made good' of 22.11 knots.[148]

From the time that the *Titanic* had been launched to the time she had left Belfast on her trials two weeks before, things had been an absolute frenzy of activity about the liner. It was beginning to seem that things were starting to settle into a routine.

Although he was on duty, Fourth Officer Boxhall had gone aft and was sitting in his cabin having a cup of tea. To do so, Boxhall would have needed to obtain permission from First Officer Murdoch to leave his post. It seems that the Fourth Officer sought this break because he may not have been feeling well.[149]

At 11:39 p.m., Lookouts Frederick Fleet and Reginald Lee were still standing watch in the Crow's Nest. It was bitterly cold, and they had already served about an hour and thirty-nine minutes of their two hour and twenty-three minute watch.[150] Perhaps they were looking forward to the end of their shift, and thawing out properly in their bunks.

Just then, Fleet spotted a 'black mass' in the water, right in the ship's path. In that instant, there was no question about what had been spotted ... They had been warned to keep a sharp lookout for ice, and there it was. As Lightoller and Captain Smith had feared, there was no breaking water at its base to outline its presence.[151]

All of this took only a moment to absorb, and then Fleet opened his mouth to say, 'There is ice ahead.' He simultaneously reached across the Crow's Nest and rang the brass bell three times, audibly signaling that there was something in the ship's path. Then Fleet went to the starboard side of the semi-circular nest and picked up the telephone that connected to the Bridge...[152]

First Class — Lounge — Promenade

Corridor — Private Suite — Promenade

Bath Rooms

First Class — Dining — Saloon

Companion way 3 pairs — Second Class — ← Starboard port holes

Class Dining Saloon

ICEBERG
From 50 to 100 fe
according to varie
accounts

Water Line

Boiler Room

Chapter 4
Rendezvous With Destiny

Collision: 11:39 – 11:40 p.m.

Standby Quartermaster Alfred Olliver was still working on the compass on the roof of the First Class Lounge when he 'heard three bells rung' up in the Crow's Nest. He immediately recognized what that three-bell signal meant, and looked out to see if he could see anything ahead, but he could not; the forward funnels were blocking his view. Then he started off for the Bridge ...[1]

In the Wheelhouse, Quartermaster Robert Hichens also heard the warning bells sound. The Wheelhouse was completely enclosed, so he was suddenly placed in a rather unpleasant position: he could not see what the lookouts had sighted, and had no idea what posed the danger ... but at the same time, he had to be prepared for whatever order came next from First Officer Murdoch.

First Officer Murdoch and Sixth Officer Moody heard the warning bell, as well. 'Immediately afterwards',[2] one of

the telephones mounted on the aft wall of the Wheelhouse began to ring. It was the call from Fleet in the Crow's Nest. Moody picked up the phone 'straight away' as soon as it began to ring.[3]

Moody did not say anything when he lifted the receiver, however. An anxious Fleet asked through the line: 'Is someone there?'

'Yes', Moody confirmed. 'What did you see?'[4]

Fleet responded with a crisp: 'Iceberg right ahead!'[5]

Moody's response was almost automatic: 'Thank you', he said politely.[6] Then he turned and relayed the warning to Murdoch: 'Iceberg right ahead!'

It is likely that Murdoch had already seen the iceberg by that point; alerted by the sounding of the warning bell, he would have been searching for and closely scrutinizing the water ahead of the ship, even while the report was being phoned to Moody and passed on ... Before beginning an evasive maneuver, he needed to be precisely sure that his next order was the best option available, and would not make the situation worse.[7] As soon as Moody shouted the warning out to him, Murdoch 'rushed', apparently from the wing, on to the Bridge.[8] As he went, he shouted: 'Hard a starboard!' Once he reached the engine order telegraph, the First Officer grabbed the twin handles – one handle giving orders for each of the main reciprocating engines – and swung them around until they came to rest ordering 'Stop' on both engines.[9]

For about thirty seconds from the time the Crow's Nest warning bell was rung, Hichens had been waiting for an order, and here it was.[10] He immediately threw his weight into the wheel, and began turning it in order to comply with the command.

In giving an order to turn hard to starboard, Murdoch was actually intending to turn the ship's bow to port. This was because helm orders were always reversed, in a hold-over from the times of using tillers rather than wheels to steer ships. The correct action for Hichens to take in response to this order was to turn the wheel counter-clockwise, and this is precisely what he did. Sixth Officer Moody was standing right beside him, watching carefully to make sure that the helm order was carried out properly.

Opposite: *A period illustration of the* Titanic *showing how it was thought to have struck the iceberg.*

Top left: *This sketch was made by a passenger aboard the Cunard liner* Carpathia, *Colin Campbell Cooper. Reportedly, it was a representation of the iceberg which sank the* Titanic, *although the accuracy of that claim is unclear.*

Above left: *This 1920s photo shows the Captain of the* Olympic *on the starboard Bridge wing. This was where First Officer Murdoch first spotted the iceberg.*

Far left: *This 1920s photo shows a Quartermaster at the Bridge wheel of the* Olympic. *It gives some idea of Quartermaster Hichens' stance in the enclosed Wheelhouse that Sunday night; the Wheelhouse windows were shuttered, however, meaning that Hichens could see nothing outside of the control center.*

Left: *Quartermaster Robert Hichens.*

Fourth Officer Boxhall was just coming out of the Officers' Quarters behind the Bridge, on the starboard side of the Boat Deck. He, too, had heard the three clangs of the warning bell.[13] As Boxhall began to make his way forward, he clearly heard Murdoch's order to turn the helm, as well as the jangling of the telegraph bells.

Down below, the engineers raced to follow Murdoch's orders, but it would take time to take the steam off the engines. In the meanwhile, the ship continued to charge toward the berg. The liner was so close to the ice that it was clear the engines were going to have little or no effect on the outcome of events ... everything now fell to the ship's rudder to do its job properly.

The rudder followed Hichens' command from the wheel and turned all the way to port until it came to rest against its stops. The effect was almost immediate. Back in the Crow's Nest, Lookout Lee overheard Moody's 'Thank you', and then Fleet clicked off the receiver and turned forward again to see what was happening. He noticed that the ship's head was already beginning to go to port.[14] Lee similarly remembered that as ...

As Hichens turned the wheel, he would have felt increasing resistance from the hydraulic system, which controlled the tiller. It took four complete revolutions, and perhaps ten seconds, for him to bring the wheel to its furthest extremity and jam it against its stops.[11] As soon as it did, Moody called out to confirm to First Officer Murdoch: 'Hard a-starboard. The helm is hard over.'[12]

... soon as the reply came back 'Thank you,' the helm must have been put either hard-a-starboard or very close to it, because she veered to port, and it seemed almost as if she might clear it ...[15]

Was Her Rudder Too Small?

Over the years, it has periodically been asserted that the *Titanic*'s rudder was too small for a ship of her size, thus contributing to the collision. However, this allegation does not hold up under scrutiny. The turning radius and maneuverability of both the *Olympic* and *Titanic* were well known to the British Board of Trade from tests made during the ships' trials in 1911 and 1912. Both vessels passed these tests with flying colors, and were well within the acceptable specifications of the Board of Trade.

The two White Star Liners compared favorably with other large ships, such as the *Lusitania* and *Mauretania*, both in the size of their rudder surface compared to the underwater surfaces areas of their hull, and in respects to their known maneuvering characteristics. This is noteworthy because the two Cunarders were designed to comply with the most

stringent British Admiralty specifications for potential use as auxiliary cruisers in time of war.[16]

Quartermaster Robert Hichens, when asked if the *Titanic* was a good steering ship, responded: 'Fairly well, yes.'[17]

Additionally, no changes were made to the rudder size of the *Britannic*, the third ship of the class, when that liner was re-designed in the wake of *Titanic*'s loss. If there had been any question about the turning characteristics of the *Olympic* or *Titanic*, there is no doubt that such an alteration would have been implemented on the *Britannic*.

By any accurate reckoning, there was no deficiency in the size of the *Titanic*'s rudder. Indeed, according to even the most rigorous of today's maritime standards, the *Titanic*'s rudder was only fractionally smaller than a modern ship's would need to be in order to obtain certification.

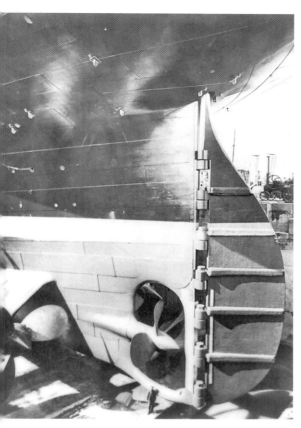

A view of Olympic's *stern, props and rudder.*

The problem had nothing to do with the ship not being maneuverable enough, but had everything to do with the fact that the iceberg had simply been spotted too late ... For such a large ship, with a mass of fifty thousand tons, to begin turning as quickly as Lee noticed, demonstrated that she was responding quite brilliantly to the maneuvering orders. To those on the Bridge, however, those next few seconds must have seemed an absolute eternity.

Finally the liner's stem shot into the clear. As the berg began to glide by the side of the prow, it seemed as if a collision had been avoided – but only by a hair's breadth. However, down below, there came a strange scraping, bumping, grinding noise as the starboard hull collided with the berg, denting plates and popping riveted seams.[18] The damage extended intermittently from the bow to a point just past Boiler Room No. 5's forward bulkhead. Above, as the berg passed the forward Well Deck, chunks of ice broke off and cascaded down onto the pine decking with a loud noise.

On the Bridge, it was obvious that the ship was colliding with the berg; Murdoch couldn't have helped but feel the collision, and he would also have seen the ice tumbling down onto the Well Deck. Fourth Officer Boxhall – almost to the Bridge by that point – felt it, as well. Murdoch raced toward the watertight door controls, which were located on the open Bridge ...

Quartermaster Olliver also heard the 'long grinding sound' of the collision. Entering the open Bridge from the port side, he saw the top of the iceberg glide past as he looked through the control center to the starboard side. Just then, he heard Murdoch order: 'Hard to port!' Olliver watched as Sixth Officer Moody ensured that this order was carried out promptly.[19] He also noticed that the collision – as evidenced by the continuous sound – had ceased by the time the berg was 'just abaft' the Bridge.

Boxhall arrived on the Bridge about this time, and later claimed that the Engine Room telegraphs then indicated 'full speed astern, both.'[20] Boxhall turned his attention from the telegraph to Murdoch, who had just arrived at the control for the watertight doors; it was located in the main Bridge rather than the Wheelhouse. Murdoch had already begun to signal the alarm below. Moody and Olliver then watched as the First Officer 'turned the lever over' which closed the doors to seal the compartments.[21]

Although there was no indicator panel on the Bridge or Wheelhouse to show whether the watertight doors were opened or closed, there was little question that the system had operated effectively and that the doors were closing.[22] Next Murdoch ordered Olliver to 'take the time, and told one of the junior officers to make a note of that in the logbook. That was at 20 minutes of 12.'[23]

As the ship struck the berg, the men working below in the Boiler Rooms were quite shaken up; the noise alone was cacophonous and disorienting. Fireman John Thompson described the impact as a 'terrible crunching sound'. Thompson had been shoveling coal, but dropped his shovel and clambered to the upper deck, where he found everything was quiet.[24] Trimmer George Cavell had it worse. He was working in the aft coal bunker of Boiler Room No. 4, and as the ship collided with the berg, an avalanche of coal buried him, and he 'had a job to get out' of the pile.[25]

But without a question, the most startled crewmen of all were those working in Boiler Room No. 6, the forwardmost Boiler Room. Leading Fireman Barrett was on the starboard side of that boiler room, conversing with Second Engineer John Hesketh, when he heard the telegraph bell ring and saw the red warning light indicating 'Stop' flash on. Barrett yelled, 'Shut all dampers', and almost immediately thereafter he actually *saw* the iceberg damage occur in this section. As the iceberg stove the starboard hull plates in, the Leading Fireman saw water come 'pouring in two feet above the stokehold plate'. Barrett and Hesketh immediately headed aft, and made for Boiler Room No. 5; they were just barely ahead of the closing watertight door that separated the two compartments.[26] On the port side

Above left: *Leading Fireman Fred Barrett.*

Above right: *Second Engineer John Hesketh.*

Above: *The fire room on the USS* Massachusetts *gives an idea of the scene as Barrett and Hesketh were enveloped by a torrent of icy water.*

Below: Titanic's *Poop Deck and Stern Docking Bridge.*

of Boiler Room No. 6, Fireman George Beauchamp also noticed the telegraph from the Bridge ringing 'Stop', and heard Barrett's order to shut the dampers. However, he stayed behind to see to his duty, despite the water which was clearly pouring in.[27]

As the iceberg passed along the ship's side, Quartermaster George Rowe was still on watch at the stern. He was standing underneath the Docking Bridge, about eight to ten feet from the edge of the deck, when he felt a 'jar'. Moving to the starboard edge of the Poop and looking over, Rowe saw the towering iceberg gliding along less than ten feet from the side of the ship. It was so close that he felt it was going to hit the edge of the Docking Bridge. However, Murdoch's order of 'Hard a port' following the initial contact with the berg had swung the stern out of the way, preventing additional damage to the hull or to the propellers.

Rowe stared up at the berg and watched it brush past. Then he ran up the ladder to the Stern Docking Bridge, and over to the port side, where the patent log was still reading the distance the ship had traveled since noon. 'About half a minute' after the collision, he read the log: 260 nautical miles traveled since noon. Then Rowe began to feel vibra-

tions as if the ship's engines were reversing, so he pulled the log in to prevent the line from fouling the propellers.[28]

In his quarters on the port side, aft of the Bridge, Second Officer Lightoller had not yet fallen asleep. His room lights were off, and he had laid there thinking about things for a bit when he noticed a 'slight jar and a grinding sound'; to him the noise seemed very faint. One of the first things that occurred to him was that it may have had something to do with ice, but he continued to lay in his berth. Then he felt that the engines had stopped.[29]

Immediately aft of Lightoller's cabin was that of Third Officer Herbert Pitman. He was asleep at the time the ship hit the iceberg, and was awakened by a noise which made him think that 'the ship was coming to anchor'. It didn't seem to be anything serious, just 'a little vibration' like that of 'the chain running out over the windlass'. He lay in his bunk for a while, trying to put together in his mind just what had happened.[30]

Many passengers also felt the collision. First Class passenger Edith Rosenbaum had just reached her stateroom, A-11, to turn in for the night. Just as she was switching on the light, 'the first tremor shook the ship. A second, then a third – much more violent – jolted me off balance.' Running to her window to look out over the enclosed Promenade Deck outside, she noticed that 'the cabin floor seemed slightly tilted'. She also noticed the absence of 'the rhythmic throbbing of the engines'. Through the outer Promenade Deck windows, she could see 'a ghostly wall of white' as it passed.[31]

Most passengers on the upper decks thought that the collision was less noticeable than what Miss Rosenbaum recalled. First Class passenger George Rheims was just coming out of a bathroom on A Deck at 11:40 p.m. As he closed the door, he felt only a slight shock. The bump was not strong enough to imbalance him, but he turned just in time to see – even as Edith Rosenbaum did – a white shape glide rapidly past the windows. He didn't know what the shape was at the time, however, and simply returned to his cabin.[32]

Frederick and Jane Hoyt, in cabin C-93 on the starboard side, had a similar experience. They had retired early, and 'were roused by a noise ... which seemed to indicate that the engines of the ship had reversed. I looked out of the stateroom window and saw something white passing by. I first thought it was steam but Mr Hoyt, who had seen icebergs before at sea, told me what it was.' The Hoyts decided to go up on deck to investigate the situation.[33]

First Class passenger Edwin Kimball had no doubt what the collision was ... having just returned to cabin D-19, which he shared with his wife Susan, the Boston native had a rather shocking experience:

> I had just gone down from the smoking-room to my stateroom and removed my coat and was standing in the middle of the room when the ship struck the iceberg. It seemed to me like scraping and tearing, more than a shock. It was on the starboard side of the ship under our room, and the ice came in our port hole.

His wife was quite unnerved by this unexpected development. He had to assure her 'that it was simply an iceberg,' and that they had 'probably just scraped it.'[34]

In port side stateroom A-20, Lady Duff Gordon had been in bed for what she believed was 'about an hour' when she

Above left: *The Sitting Room, B-51, of the* Titanic.

Above right: Titanic*'s bedroom B-59. It was in luxurious rooms such as these that many sleeping First Class passengers felt the collision.*

was awakened by 'a funny rumbling noise. It was like nothing I had ever heard before. It seemed almost as if some giant hand had been playing bowls, rolling the great balls along.' It was 'not a tremendous crash', she recalled, but more like 'someone had drawn a giant finger all along the side of the boat'. Then she felt the engines stop.[35]

Just a little further astern, stateroom A-34 was located right off the port side of the First Class Entrance. There, Dr Washington Dodge, his wife Ruth and their son Washington, Jr, were sleeping. Doctor Dodge and his wife were both awakened by the collision, even though it was slight, but young Washington slept through it. Perhaps the parents' perception of 'slight shocks' in the middle of the night was finely-honed from living in earthquake-prone San Francisco. Almost immediately afterward, they felt the engines stop.[36]

Twenty-two-year-old Helen Ostby had 'just dropped off to sleep' in stateroom B-36. Suddenly, she 'was awakened by a jar that felt about as it would if you were in a car that scraped the side of a tree'. Miss Ostby 'sat up straight in bed, trying to make out what happened'.[37]

In stateroom B-39, Marguerite Frölicher was having a miserable night. Seasick for most of the crossing, and then again after dinner, she had finally slipped into the bliss of sleep. Suddenly, through the wall between her room and her parent's room, B-41, she heard her mother cry out: 'A collision!'[38]

Twenty-four-year-old John Snyder and his 23-year-old wife Nelle were newlyweds from Minneapolis, Minnesota. They had been married for only seven weeks, and were finishing up their honeymoon. Snyder's grandfather, John Pillsbury, was the cofounder of the C. A. Pillsbury Company and a former Governor of Minnesota. John and Nelle were asleep in their stateroom, B-45, when she was 'aroused by a grating sound at the side of the boat'. Mrs Snyder called out to her husband to wake him up.[39]

On the port side, in suite B-52, -54 and -56, Bruce Ismay was asleep when the collision occurred. He was awakened by 'a jar' but 'stayed in bed a little time', perhaps 'a moment or two', not realizing exactly what had happened.[40]

Gladys Cherry and her cousin Lucy Noël Martha, the Countess of Rothes, were asleep in stateroom C-77. They were awakened by what seemed like an awful bang. Then they felt the engines stop, leaving a terrible silence behind. It seemed to the two women that something horrible had happened.[41]

Seventeen-year-old Jack Thayer was still awake in stateroom C-66, getting ready to turn in for the night. When the collision came, Jack was about to climb into bed, and it didn't seem very serious to him. 'I was on my feet at the time, and I do not think it was enough to throw anyone down,' he later recalled. 'I seemed to sway slightly. I immediately realized that the ship had veered to port as though she had been gently pushed … Almost instantaneously the engines stopped. The sudden quiet was startling and disturbing.'[42]

In cabin C-104, Major Arthur Peuchen was in the process of undressing for bed when he felt something unusual. It was 'as though a heavy wave had struck our ship. She quivered under it somewhat.' If the sea had not been so perfectly calm, Peuchen would have thought nothing of it. But on a calm night, this was something unusual. He immediately put on his overcoat and went up on deck.[43]

Charles Stengel and his wife Annie were in stateroom C-116, and were both sleeping. Annie was trying to wake Charles, as he was moaning in his sleep. 'Wake up', she said, 'you are dreaming.'

Charles woke up, and just then, he heard 'a slight crash'. However, he paid no attention to it until he also heard the engines stop. Then he said, 'There is something serious; there is something wrong. We had better go up on deck.'[44]

At that time, Elmer and Juliet Taylor were in their stateroom, C-126. Juliet was still reading and warming her feet by the electric heater, while Elmer had dozed off. Then he was …

> … aroused by a very slight lift of the bed, followed by the engines stopping. I did not get up immediately, but speculated on the cause of the stopping of the engines.[45]

Karl Behr and Richard Beckwith had left the Smoking Room only a few minutes before the collision. Beckwith was the man that Behr hoped to one day call his father-in-law; he liked Beckwith's step-daughter Helen Newsom very much. Behr had reached his cabin, C-148 aft on the port side, and started to undress. Then he felt 'a distinct jar, followed by a quivering of the boat.' He understood immediately that they had struck something, and began to reverse the dressing process, putting on the clothes he had just taken off.[46]

May Futrelle had dozed off over her novel when she felt a 'shock and a kind of shiver of the ship. It was so slight that it did not disturb anything, but I sat up in bed. I heard the engines pounding below – reversing. For about twenty seconds, I should say, this pounding continued. Then followed another shock, scarcely heavier than the first.' She sat up, a bit frightened; she also thought she heard some sort of 'gong' sounding below.[47]

Isaac Frauenthal was still reading a book in cabin D-40, trying to wind down so that he could get to sleep, when he heard a noise that puzzled him:

> It was a long-drawn out, rubbing noise, much the same as you hear when a ferry boat bumps into her slip and rubs slowly along its walls. There was nothing specially alarming about it, but it seemed out of place somehow ...[48]

Fifty-nine-year-old Philadelphian socialite Mrs Emma Bucknell had wintered in Rome, visiting her daughter Margaret, now the Countess Pecorini. Her husband William – the man who had saved Bucknell University from financial ruin in 1881 – had died in 1890, but she was not traveling alone. She was sharing her cabin – D-15, on the starboard side of the ship – with her maid Albina Bazzani. To Mrs Bucknell, it seemed 'at that moment of jar and thunder and shock that the very bottom of the boat had been torn out'. Looking out through their porthole a moment later, she 'saw something rise against the window which was white. At first I thought it was a spray of water, but it was the ice.'[49]

Next door, in cabin D-17, Margaret Swift and Alice Leader were still chatting when they heard 'an awful crash'. However, Mrs Swift noticed that 'the vessel stood up well after it and we did not think much about it'.[50]

In outside First Class cabin D-28, just forward of the First Class Reception Room and Entrance on the port side of the ship, Elizabeth and Mary Lines had retired for the night. It had been so cold that afternoon and evening that there was little else to do but go to bed, Mary later recalled. The teenage girl was just dozing off when she felt 'a jarring crash'.[51]

Eleanor Cassebeer, in her D Deck stateroom, had just finished asking a stewardess if it would be all right to leave her heater on overnight. The stewardess assured her that it would. 'Immediately after she had left my cabin the shock of the collision came. It sounded as if something were grinding and tearing away the very entrails of the monster liner,' Mrs Cassebeer recalled. Certain that something was 'radically wrong', she poked her nose out to ask a nearby steward about it. He said nothing was wrong, and that she could go back to bed. Instead, she decided to head up on deck, and began to slip on a kimono and a pair of slippers.[52]

Philipp Mock had been sound asleep before the collision. He awoke – curiously enough – 'standing in the middle of his cabin floor' and was not at all sure how he had arrived there. Hearing 'a series of "booms",' he immediately headed out of his cabin to find out what was happening. His sister, Emma Schabert, was asleep when 'a mighty crash' woke her up.[53]

Forty-seven-year-old First Class passenger Carrie Chaffee and her husband, 46-year-old Herbert, were asleep in their cabin, E-31. The jar of the collision awakened Mrs Chaffee, but 'was not violent'. There was 'a noise as if a chain were being dragged along the side'. She commented to her husband that it sounded as if 'something were being done with the anchor chains'. Feeling no alarm, they 'turned the electric button to see if the lights were still on and found that they were'.[54]

Just aft of the Chaffee's, in cabin E-44, Mr & Mrs William and Alice Silvey were still awake 'when the shock came. If I had not been awake, I do not believe I would have noticed it, it was so slight.' Her husband looked out of their starboard side porthole and told her that 'nothing appeared to be wrong'.[55]

Margaret Brown was reading in her cabin when she felt the collision. She didn't think much of it, but poked her nose out into the corridor outside her room. She saw a few passengers there, the men in pajamas and the ladies in kimonos. They kidded with each other about being ready to swim in their nightclothes. Margaret noticed that the ship's engines had stopped, but nothing serious seemed to be happening, so she returned to her room and to her book.[56]

Norman and Bertha Chambers were in their cabin, E-8, when they 'noticed a curious grinding rumble, as though a heavy chain had been dragged the length of the ship in the hold'. Then they heard the engines stop.[57]

Antoinette Flegenheim was a wealthy forty-eight-year-old widow traveling for a visit to America. Formerly a resident of New York, she had gone to live in Berlin after the death of her husband, who was from Germany. Mrs Flegenheim was bound for New Windsor – just outside Newburgh – New York. There she was to stay with her friends, Mr & Mrs William Walker. The socialite widow was sleeping in her cabin when she was awakened 'by the scraping of the boat against the ice. The noise and the movement of the vessel indicated that something was wrong', and she immediately arose, determined to ascertain what the trouble was.[58]

William Sloper was by the forward Grand Staircase on the way to his stateroom, which was only a few feet from the Washington Dodge's stateroom. Just then he felt a lurch and a 'creaking crash; the boat seemed to shiver and keel over to port'.[59] At the same time, the frivolities in the First Class Smoking Room aft on the same deck were suddenly interrupted. Hugh Woolner said that everyone present in the room at the time felt ...

> ... a sort of stopping, a sort of, not exactly shock, but a sort of slowing down; and then we sort of felt a rip that gave a sort of slight twist to the whole room. Everybody, so far as I could see, stood up ...[60]

William Carter, also in the Smoking Room, remembered that the impact occurred 'exactly 17 minutes of 12 o'clock'.[61] Alfred Nourney had just remarked to his bridge partner that he was wondering when there would be some waves when the ship 'was shaken slightly'.[62]

A number of Second Class passengers felt the impact, as well. Lillian Bentham was just disrobing for bed when the *Titanic* struck the iceberg. Something about the ship's motions caught her off guard, and she went sailing into the wall of her cabin. Other than some bruising, however, she was happily uninjured.[63]

Such recollections of being thrown off balance due to the collision, however, were very rare. Because Second Class accommodations were aft, to most of the Second Class passengers it was not so much the collision as it was the stopping of the engines that made an impression. Sidney Collett had been in bed 'about 10 minutes' when he felt 'two heavy throbs, just as if we had hit something, rebounded and then hit it again by going forward'.[64]

Lawrence Beesley felt something very similar. While reading in his upper berth – which was against the starboard wall of his cabin, D-56 – he 'felt a slight jar, and then soon after a second one, but not sufficiently large to cause any anxiety to anyone, however nervous they may have been. However, the engines stopped immediately afterward and my first thought was "She has lost a propeller."' He also remembered a 'more than usually obvious dancing motion of the mattress on which I sat'.[65]

Nora Keane, Susan Webber and Edwina Troutt were roommates in Second Class cabin E-101. Miss Webber recalled that at about '20 minutes of 12' she was 'awakened by a slight shock'.[66] Nora Keane also described the impact as a 'slight shock', and didn't think anything of it.[67]

Ellen Toomey was still awake in her cabin, which she shared with Elizabeth Watt and her daughter Bertha, as well as Mrs Rosa Pinsky. Toomey said that at 'about 11:45 p.m.', she 'felt a slight shock, and then the steamer's engines stopped'.[68]

Twenty-year-old Second Class passenger Dagmar Bryhl was in her berth at the time of the collision. The pretty Swedish girl was traveling to Rockford, Illinois, to visit her uncle; she was traveling with her brother Kurt, and her fiancé Ingvar Enander. She noticed a 'jar', but it didn't seem pronounced to her.[69]

William Mellors was asleep when the collision happened. He 'did not take any notice' of the slight shock, only stirring slightly before turning over and going back to sleep.[70]

Twelve-year-old Ruth Becker was not awakened by the sensation or sounds of a collision, either. What she did recall was that the engines stopped. 'Everything was silent, and it woke us up.'[71]

Esther Hart was still awake at the time of the collision, and she remembered it as 'the most awful' sound she had ever heard. She jumped to her feet and shook her husband awake. 'Daddy', she called to him, 'get up at once. We have hit something I am sure and it's serious.'

This wasn't the first time during the trip that she had thought there was trouble afoot, and all of the previous 'events' had come to naught. As Benjamin struggled to a state of semi-alertness, he groused: 'Oh woman, again! I really don't know what I shall do with you.' Eventually, he got up and went on deck in bare feet and a nightshirt.[72]

Mrs Mary Hewlett 'was not awakened by the shock of the collision with the iceberg'. However, she did awaken 'when the ship's engines stopped pounding'.[73]

Charlotte Collyer was talking with her husband in their cabin when the crash came. To her, the sensation seemed like 'a long backward jerk, followed by a shorter forward one'. Her husband was standing at the time, and only swayed on his feet. Then they noticed that the engines had stopped running.[74]

Imanita Shelley and her mother were 'startled out of their dreams' by the collision and the 'dreadful sensation caused by the stopping of the engines'. Imanita asked: 'What can be the matter, mother? The engines have stopped and a ship never stops until it gets into port unless there is an accident.' Just then they overheard several women 'talking excitedly outside and then a man's voice saying the ship had struck an iceberg'. Imanita Shelley 'rang the bell for the steward and rang and rang and rang'.[75]

Third Class passengers were housed both forward and aft, and most were in the lowest passenger accommodations on the ship. Many of them felt the collision, as well – and to most, it registered more strongly than it did with those on higher decks.

Third Class passenger Emily Badman and her three female cabin-mates were housed up in the forward sections of the ship. She recalled:

> I had gone to bed about half past 10 Sunday night. My birth [*sic*, berth] was in the third cabin, up near the front on the right hand [starboard side] of the *Titanic*. I was awakened by some jar, which sounded as if the boat were scraping land. There were four of us in the cabin.
>
> One of the girls looked out of the porthole and said she could see nothing.[76]

Not sure what was happening, the four girls started to dress. Anna Sjöblom, who had just turned eighteen on Sunday, was also in a cabin near the ship's bow. She, also, was awakened by the crash, and remembered that 'everyone became excited at once'.[77]

Mrs Rhoda Abbott was an American woman traveling with her two teenaged sons, Rossmore and Eugene. Mrs Abbott had separated from her husband about a year before, and the previous summer, the three had moved from Providence, Rhode Island in order to live with her mother in England. However, the two boys were homesick for Providence, and so they were traveling back to America. Mrs Abbott had been sleeping, but she 'was awakened by the crash of the liner'. Quickly 'becoming alarmed', she sent her son Eugene on deck to investigate what had happened.[78]

Elizabeth Dowdell was in the cabin she shared with her ward, Virginia and Miss Amy Stanley. She was about to get into bed when she felt the 'crash'. Elizabeth looked out into the corridor outside their room and asked a nearby steward what was wrong. He assured her that everything was all right, so she climbed into bed. Amy Stanley, however, decided to investigate matters further.[79]

Eleven-year-old Master Elias Nicola-Yarred and his 14-year-old sister Jamilia were asleep in their Third Class quarters at the time of the collision. The two children were traveling without their father, as he had failed to pass a physical examination. Elias recalled that it was at 'approximately 11:45' that night that he and his sister were awakened 'with a jolt'. She was in the upper berth at the time, and cried out: 'Something's wrong!'

'Go back to sleep,' her little brother told her. 'You worry too much.'[80]

Sixteen-year-old Laura Cribb, a fellow Third Class passenger, was traveling with her father John. She remembered that she 'suddenly awoke and with a slight shiver sat bolt upright in my bunk. I feel sure I sat there for a full three minutes. Suddenly the ship gave a violent jerk and the engines stopped.'[81]

Following the conclusion of the music playing and festivities in the Third Class General Room, Eugene Daly and the two men who were sharing the cabin with him had all returned to their room in the bow.[82] They did not undress, and laid on their bunks, talking about their prospects in America. Daly had just fallen asleep when 'a sound like thunder' jarred him awake. He leapt out of his bunk and went to the door. A steward in the hallway assured him that 'there was nothing serious' and that he 'might go back'.[83]

Percival and Florence Thorneycroft were also in a Third Class cabin. Florence was still awake at the time, as she was 'rather seasick'. Suddenly she felt a 'jar and noticed the stopping of the engines'. Her husband told her that the boat had struck something, but he did not think that the accident was of any real consequence.[84]

Concurrently, many members of the crew had also felt the collision. Lookout George Hogg was sleeping in his berth forward, and was awakened at 'about 20 minutes to 12'. He remembered that there was 'confusion in the forecastle'. He quickly got up to find out what was going on.[85]

Seaman Walter Brice was relaxing near the Seamen's Mess on C Deck, underneath the Forecastle. Although he was on watch, there was little to do, since on Sunday nights they were not required to wash the ship's decks. When he felt the collision, he recalled that it was not some sort of violent shock that threw him off his feet; rather, it 'was like a heavy vibration' and a 'rumbling noise' which continued for about '10 seconds'.[86]

First Class Stewardess Violet Jessop was lying in her top berth, not quite asleep but 'comfortably drowsy'. Then she heard a 'crash', followed by a 'low, rending, crunching, ripping sound'. The ship 'shivered a trifle', and the throb of her engines began to cease. Quiet followed, and Jessop could hear nearby doors opening and voices making discreet enquiries. She looked down at her cabin-mate, who was also awake in the lower berth.

'Sounds as if something has happened', Jessop's cabin-mate said.

Jessop felt the urge to laugh at the understatement, and replied: 'Something has happened!' The two women began to dress.[87]

At around 10:00 p.m., Steward Walter Nichols had turned in to his bunk amidships on the port side of E Deck. He remembered:

> At 11:40 I was awakened by feeling a bit of vibration. The ship went on for a bit and then the engines stopped. Nobody was frightened and some of the men in the room with me didn't want to trouble to get up to look out and see what had happened.[88]

Saloon Steward Frederick Dent Ray was asleep in his berth, also amidships on the port side of E Deck. The space was large enough to accommodate twenty-eight men, most of them Saloon Stewards. All of them, including Ray, were awakened by the collision. Ray sat up in his bunk, but did not get up. Eventually he turned over and started to try to get back to sleep.[89]

Saloon Steward William Ward felt the collision, as well. He got up out of his berth – which was in one of the three side-by-side rooms for accommodating Saloon Stewards amidships on the port side – and went over to the porthole. Opening it, he felt a blast of 'bitterly cold' air, but saw nothing but darkness outside. So he climbed back into his warm bunk.[90]

Mess Steward Cecil William Norman Fitzpatrick was just settling down to sleep in his E Deck cabin, not far from the Engine Room. He and his mates 'were aroused by a sudden lurch of the vessel' and the stopping of the engines.[91]

Bedroom Steward Alfred Theissinger was awake talking to fellow Bedroom Steward George Brewster in their E Deck quarters. As the two men talked, there came 'a noise, as is made by a rowboat running over a gravel beach. There was a slight shock, but absolutely no severe jolt.' Then the two men felt the ship's engines stop. Brewster and Theissinger looked at each other. Brewster spoke first: 'What do you think that is?'[92]

11:40 p.m.–12:00 midnight

Back up in the First Class Smoking Room, everyone had leapt to their feet with the sensation of the collision. Almost as if unified by some sort of collective consciousness, they raced aft, through the revolving door that led to the port side Verandah Café … past the tables and wicker chairs in the Café … and then out through the sliding doors onto the Promenade Deck astern, near the base of the Mainmast. Hugh Woolner recalled:

> I stood hearing what the conjectures were. People were guessing what it might be, and one man called out, 'An iceberg has passed astern', but who it was I do not know.[93]

William Carter, who was also standing in the group on the deck, similarly recalled being told 'that the ship had struck an iceberg'. After learning what had happened, many of the men in the group returned to the Smoking Room and to their card games.[94] Alfred Nourney went back inside with the others, and resumed his own card game.[95]

William Carter happened to come across some officers, and they informed him 'that the accident was not a serious one'. There was 'little excitement at the time.' However, Carter had a family to look after, so he decided to head below to his two adjoining staterooms, B-96 and B-98, where his family was sleeping. He woke his wife up, and told her about what had occurred. He then told her that she and the children should dress.[96]

William Sloper was still by the top of the stairs headed for his cabin. He saw about a half-dozen room stewards go by, and they all rushed out onto the Promenade Deck, where they peered into the darkness. 'We could see what appeared to be a sail or something white standing out off our starboard side, astern.'[97]

As the ship's engines were stopped, her momentum gradually began to slacken. On the Bridge, there had only been a few moments of stunned silence since the iceberg passed, and since Murdoch had signaled down to close the watertight doors. Murdoch and Boxhall did not even have

Left: Olympic's Smoking Room, looking aft and to port toward the fireplace.

Lower left: The port side Verandah Café of the Olympic in 1911, looking toward the revolving door to the Smoking Room, which is open in this photo.

Lower right: The sliding doors which led aft from the Verandah Café to the open Promenade.

the opportunity to speak before Boxhall turned, and found Captain Smith standing at his side.[98]

'What have we struck?' Smith asked his First Officer.

According to Boxhall, Murdoch replied: 'An iceberg, sir. I put her hard-a-starboard and run the engines full astern, but it was too close. She hit it. I intended to port around it, but she hit before I could do any more.'[99] Hichens and Olliver were close enough that they also overheard this exchange.[100]

'Close the watertight doors,' Smith ordered instinctively. 'The watertight doors are closed, sir.'

'And have you rung the warning bell?' Smith asked, to which Murdoch replied in the affirmative.[101]

Since the ship's head was still turning to starboard, as the tiller remained hard over to port, Smith, Murdoch and Boxhall walked out onto the starboard wing of the Bridge, trying to spot the iceberg.[102] Boxhall was not sure whether he could discern the berg's form, as his eyes were not yet adjusted to the dark. Then – either at an order from the Captain, or with his express permission – Boxhall left the Bridge to head below and look for any sign of damage.[103] He elected to use the emergency stairs just behind the Bridge wing to get down to B Deck ... then he walked forward and to port, beyond the ship's centerline, to take the staircase down to the open Well Deck ...

Even as Boxhall started off on his inspection, the Titanic continued to move forward and the iceberg gradually vanished into the darkness from which it had appeared. Even so, there were still many passengers and crew who were curious to find out what had happened.

Bruce Ismay had stayed in his bed for a few moments after the collision. His first thought was that the ship had dropped a propeller blade. Curious, Ismay got up, opened the door to his cabin, and walked along the passageway. He met a steward, and asked him: 'What has happened?'

The steward replied: 'I do not know, sir.'

Ismay was not satisfied. He returned to his room, and could feel that the ship was slowing down. Something was definitely wrong. Ismay put an overcoat over his pyjamas and set off for the Bridge to find out what had happened.[104]

On the port side of the Promenade Deck, Dr Washington Dodge heard some 'hurried footsteps' on the Boat Deck directly above their cabin. He partially dressed and slipped out onto the 'forward companionway', almost certainly a reference to the Forward First Class Entrance directly adjacent his cabin, by the top flight of the Grand Staircase. There the doctor found about a half-dozen men, all of whom were speculating about what had happened. Then, 'an officer passed by somewhat hurriedly,' and Dodge asked him what the trouble was. The 'officer' replied that 'he thought something had gone wrong with the propeller, but that it was nothing serious.'

Dr Dodge left the group of men and returned to his stateroom. There, he found his wife was a bit uneasy. She was about to get up and get dressed. Dodge informed her of what the officer had told him, that something had gone wrong with the propeller. Yet that explanation didn't make sense to either of them; they both agreed that it felt more like something had struck the ship on its side. However, they were not alarmed, knowing just how large and safe the *Titanic* was. Dr Dodge decided to investigate things more thoroughly.[105]

Meanwhile, Major Arthur Peuchen started out of his room, and began to head up the forward Grand Staircase. As he did so, he bumped into a casual acquaintance who told him: 'Why, we have struck an iceberg. If you will go up on A deck, you will see the ice on the fore part of the ship.' So Peuchen headed up to see for himself.[106]

In his Second Class cabin on D Deck, Lawrence Beesley 'felt the engines slow and stop' only 'a few moments' after the collision. The 'dancing motion and the vibration ceased suddenly after being part of our very existence for four days, and that was the first hint that anything out of the ordinary had happened ... But the stopping of the engines gave us no information.' His first conclusion was that the ship had dropped a propeller blade, but he was determined to find out more.

I jumped out of bed, slipped on a dressing-gown over pyjamas, put on shoes, and went out of my cabin into the hall near the saloon. Here was a steward leaning against the staircase, probably waiting until those in the smokeroom above had gone to bed and he could put out the lights. I said, 'Why have we stopped?' 'I don't know, sir,' he replied, 'but I don't suppose it's anything much.' 'Well', I said, 'I am going on deck to see what it is,' and started towards the stairs. He smiled indulgently at me as I passed him, and said, 'All right, sir, but it is mighty cold up there.' I am sure at that time he thought I was rather foolish to go up with so little reason, and I must confess I felt rather absurd for not remaining in the cabin: it seemed like making a needless fuss to walk about the ship in a dressing-gown. But it was my first trip across the sea; I had enjoyed every

minute of it and was keenly alive to note every new experience; and certainly to stop in the middle of the sea with a propeller dropped seemed sufficient reason for going on deck. And yet the steward, with his fatherly smile, and the fact that no one else was about the passage or going upstairs to reconnoiter, made me feel guilty in an undefined way of breaking some code of a ship's régime – and Englishman's fear of being thought 'unusual', perhaps!

I climbed three flights of stairs, opened the vestibule door leading to the top deck, and stepped out into an atmosphere that cut me, clad as I was, like a knife. Walking to the starboard side, I peered over and saw the sea many feet below, calm and black; forward, the deserted deck stretching away to the first-class quarters and the captain's bridge; and behind, the steerage quarters and the stern bridge; nothing more: no iceberg on either side or astern as far as we could see in the darkness.[107]

Not far away from Beesley's cabin, Sidney Collett had felt the collision, and his impression of it was very much like the one Beesley had formed. He jumped out of bed, 'put on light clothing' and then went up on deck.[108]

Second Class passenger Mary Hewlett had been awakened by the stopping of the ship's engines. She went to the door of her cabin, and found a stewardess in the hall. She asked 'if there had been an accident'. The stewardess replied that 'she did not believe there was any trouble', but that Mrs Hewlett could go up on deck to see for herself, if she wanted to. Curious, Mrs Hewlett went up on the deck and found them nearly deserted. She said that men were lazily sauntering around the deck, and some were inside playing cards. Many 'seemed to treat the matter as a joke', and everyone thought that the 'boat was absolutely unsinkable'.[109]

Lillian Bentham was curious about the collision which had thrown her off balance. She 'looked out into the corridor', and a nearby steward told her that 'they had struck a Newfoundland fishing-boat'. He reassured her that there was no danger. Miss Bentham was not easily alarmed, so she took the steward at his word, crawled into bed, and fell fast asleep.[110]

Philipp Mock left his cabin very quickly after the collision. He made his way toward his sister's cabin, which was further forward on the starboard side. When he met Emma, the pair made a few inquiries as to what had happened. However, they couldn't obtain much in the way of details, so they decided to return to their respective cabins and get dressed. As he returned to his cabin, Mock heard some of the stewards telling people that nothing was the matter, and advising them to return to bed. Many took that advice, he noticed. Meanwhile, Emma started dressing. She did not bother to put on a blouse, but rather donned a knitted jacket, and also placed a scarf over her head for protection from the cold.[111]

Helen Ostby remembered that after the collision, the engines were stopped, and everything was completely silent for a minute or two. She heard a few voices in the corridor outside her cabin, including one woman who asked a steward what had happened. She overheard the steward reply calmly: 'Everything will be all right.' Miss Ostby got out of bed and pulled on a dress, coat and shoes. However, as she dressed, the abstract idea occurred to her that she might

Chief Electrician Peter Sloan.

not want to have too much clothing on if she had to be in the water.[112]

William and Alice Silvey had felt the collision, but they did not believe that anything was really wrong. Shortly thereafter, they noticed that the engines stopped. Even this development did not alarm them, since when they had crossed previously on the *Olympic*, the engines had stopped on account of an accident. They thought something similar had happened. However, Mr Silvey suggested that they dress and go up on deck.[113]

Far below and aft, in the Electric Workshop above the Turbine Engine Room, Greaser Thomas Ranger had been mending a fan when he felt 'a slight jar' as the iceberg scraped the bow. About two minutes after the jar, he was able to see that the changeover valves had come up, indicating that the turbine engine was stopped. Chief Electrician Peter Sloan went down and stood by the main lighting engines.[114]

After the crash, Eleanor Cassebeer had slipped on a kimono and slippers, convinced that something was 'radically wrong'. She hurried from her cabin on the starboard side of D Deck, forward of the Reception Room, and moved up to the Promenade Deck, probably by way of the forward Grand Staircase. She found no sign of anything wrong at all, just two long stretches of empty deck.

Then she came across one of her table companions, stockbroker Harry Anderson. Together, the pair made their way 'to the bow of the boat', probably a reference to the forward bulwark rail of the A Deck Promenade, which overlooked the Well Deck below. Looking down, they 'found a litter of small particles of ice which had been torn from the iceberg by force of the impact'. From their vantage point, they 'could see the berg towering some 75 to 100 feet out of the sea'.

While they stood there, they bumped into another of their table companions, Thomas Andrews. Since Andrews' cabin was astern on A Deck, by the aft Grand Staircase, Andrews and Cassebeer had probably left their respective staterooms at roughly the same time, almost immediately after the collision. Mrs Cassebeer recalled that in ...

> ... answer to many questions he [Andrews] assured everybody that we were absolutely safe, and that the *Titanic* was absolutely unsinkable. He said that she could break in three separate and distinct parts and that each part would stay afloat indefinitely.

If Cassebeer and Anderson could see the iceberg and the ice on the Well Deck below, Andrews almost certainly saw it, as well. Then Andrews moved on. Cassebeer and Anderson stayed behind.[115]

Albert Dick and his wife Vera had been sleeping in their B Deck stateroom when the collision came, and were awak-

ened by the shock. Together, they made their way out on deck, and soon discovered that they had struck an iceberg. Vera recalled being able to see the berg.[116]

Major Peuchen arrived at the forward rail of A Deck and peered down onto the Well Deck. As his friend had told him, there was ice down there. It had 'fallen inside the rail, probably 4 to 4 ½ feet. It looked like shell ice, soft ice. But you could see it quite plainly along the bow of the boat.' Peuchen stood there for 'a few minutes', talking to some of his other friends, none of them thinking that anything was seriously wrong.[117]

Edith Rosenbaum had seen the iceberg pass the window of her A Deck stateroom, and had immediately 'slipped on a coat and ran out on deck'. She recalled:

> There were no more than five passengers standing at the rail when I got there. Publisher William Stead stood frowning at the ice fragments which littered the deck. Artist Francis Millet came down the companionway from the bridge. 'What do they say is the trouble?' Stead asked.
>
> 'Iceberg,' Millet answered.
>
> We all turned to the great floating mountain of white with new interest. It had drifted some distance to starboard and loomed indistinct and mysterious in the velvet dark.
>
> 'Well, I guess it's nothing serious,' Mr Stead said. 'I'll go back to my cabin and read. Cheerio, all.'
>
> The rest of us made our way forward, gathering up ice chips and balling them in our hands. Someone suggested a snow fight, but it was too cold for that.

With the excitement fading, Rosenbaum returned to her stateroom, undressed, and prepared to climb into bed.[118]

Immediately following the collision, First Class passenger Margaretta Spedden partially dressed and went up on deck. Though she herself wasn't told to go back to her room and go to bed, she heard some other passengers being given such direction.[119]

Isaac Frauenthal thought that the stopping of the engines was 'out of place', and so he got up 'to call for a steward and inquire what was wrong'. Just as he did so, he ...

> ... heard a furious pounding on the door of a stateroom near mine, and when I put my head out, a man whom I didn't know was doing his best to awaken his friends in that room. He said something about the ship hitting something, but was so incoherent I couldn't make head nor tail out of his explanation.

Something wasn't right, that much was for sure. To Frauenthal, it 'looked like a good time to take precautions', so he returned to his room and began to dress.[120]

Edwin Kimball left his ice-littered cabin and stepped out into the companionway outside, where he 'spoke to some friends who were located in the same section'. Then he went on deck to see if he could see the iceberg. He remembered that there were 'very few people out around the ship'. To those few who were milling about, stewards and officers were assuring them that everything was alright, and all were advised to return to bed.[121]

First Class passenger James R. McGough, a buyer with Strawbridge & Clothier, had a starboard side cabin on E

Far left: *First Class passenger James McGough.*

Left: *Trimmer Patrick Dillon.*

Deck. He was awakened by the collision, and left his stateroom to see what the matter was. He came upon Second Steward George Dodd, who told him there was no danger, and advised McGough to go back to bed – something that McGough did not do.[122]

George Rheims had felt the collision and seen the iceberg glide past. He encountered his Bedroom Steward just as he was entering his stateroom on A Deck. Rheims asked if he knew what had happened. The steward 'said he didn't know but thought that something might have happened to the machinery'.[123]

Lookout George Hogg had run up 'on the deck', probably a reference to the open Forward Well Deck. He found that there 'was not much confusion' there, so he soon decided to return to his quarters.[124]

Able Bodied Seaman Joseph Scarrott had reacted similarly to Hogg. Scarrott was having a smoke just below the Forecastle; he actually heard the three soundings of the Crow's Nest bell, and shortly thereafter had felt the impact. 'It seemed as if the ship shook in the same manner as if the engines had been suddenly reversed to full speed astern, just the same sort of vibration, enough to wake anybody up if they were asleep.' He also placed the time at 'about twenty minutes to twelve o'clock'. Scarrott quickly headed down to his mate, who was then in the Seaman's Wash Place on E Deck. His friend told him to 'give him a call if anything was doing'. Then Scarrott 'rushed on deck with the remainder of those that were in the forecastle … to see what was the cause of the vibration.' He recalled:

> We found the ship had struck an iceberg as there was a large quantity of ice and snow on the starboard side of the fore deck. We did not think it very serious so we went below again cursing the iceberg for disturbing us.[125]

On the Bridge, at around 11:43 p.m., Captain Smith rang the Engine Room telegraphs to 'Stop', followed by 'Slow Ahead'. He then ordered Quartermaster Olliver below to find the Carpenter, and to instruct him to 'take the draft of the water'.[126] In the Engine Room, Trimmer Patrick Dillon observed the engines starting to go ahead slowly.[127]

Simultaneously, Fourth Officer Boxhall was hurrying on his inspection trip, moving down to the Well Deck via the emergency stairway, and then forward to a staircase under the Forecastle. He moved down through the lower passenger areas in the bow, all the way down to F Deck, and found no damage. Then he turned back and started to make his way up again …[128]

Lawrence Beesley had gone up on deck in his dressing gown after the collision. The air was cold, but he noticed that there …

… were two or three men on deck, and with one – the Scotch engineer who played hymns in the saloon [Douglas Norman] – I compared notes of our experiences. He had just begun to undress when the engines stopped and had come up at once, so that he was fairly well-clad; none of us could see anything, and all being quiet and still, the Scotchman and I went down to the next deck.

There, through the windows of the Second Class Smoking Room, Beesley and Norman saw some men playing a game of cards, and several others watching them. As these men had been up at the time of the collision, the pair went inside to inquire if the card-players knew anything more than they did. None had bothered to go out on deck or try to find out what had happened, even though 'one of them had seen through the windows an iceberg go by towering above the decks. He had called their attention to it, and they all watched it disappear, but had then at once resumed the game.' They asked how high it was, and got a range of estimates, with one passenger saying he thought it was 'between eighty and ninety feet' high.

The next question was: what had happened to the ship? The 'general impression was that we had just scraped the iceberg with a glancing blow on the starboard side, and they had stopped as a wise precaution, to examine her thoroughly all over.'

One of the men ventured: 'I expect the iceberg has scratched off some of her new paint, and the captain doesn't like to go on until she is painted up again.' Everyone laughed. Another man looked up from his hand of cards, pointed to the glass of whiskey at his elbow, and turned to an onlooker, saying: 'Just run along the deck and see if any ice has come aboard: I would like some for this.' The laughter continued, and finally Beesley decided to return to his cabin, where he started reading again.[129]

While young Robertha Watt had slept through the collision, her mother Elizabeth 'Bessie' Watt had felt the impact. Their cabin-mate Ellen Toomey had been awake, and felt it, as well. She remembered that Elizabeth Watt 'went at once to the deck to learn what was wrong'. However, she did not return 'for quite awhile', and eventually Ellen got up to dress herself.[130]

In her Third Class cabin, sixteen-year-old Laura Cribb had felt the collision, and felt the engines stop. Then she 'dressed quickly and hurried out into the main passage which was rapidly filling with passengers'. Everyone was asking the same question: 'What has happened?' A moment later, she heard her father, 44-year-old John Cribb, calling out for her. Laura remembered that she 'answered as loudly as I could and he soon located me. He asked me if I was dressed and I replied that I was.' Then the two set off to the 'end of the passage' to talk with some other passengers and see what they could find out.[131]

Tennis player Karl Behr had put his clothes back on after the collision. His first thought was to find Helen Newsom, who was in stateroom D-47, forward on the starboard side. Upon reaching the area of her room, he found her in the passage outside the cabin; she had been awakened by the collision. Together, the pair went 'to the very upper deck', where they found it was bitterly cold.[132]

Margaret Brown had returned to her reading after the impact. Then she heard the occupants of the next room say something about getting up to see what was going on.

Thus, she got up, as well, and looked back out into the corridor. She saw about a half-dozen stewards and an officer, 'forcing an auger through a hole in the floor, while treating the whole thing with levity'. When she returned to her book a second time, she noticed that her curtains were moving, apparently because the ship was again under way, but at reduced speed.[133]

Although the appearance up on deck led one to believe that everything was all right, and that the accident had been minor, to seasoned crewmembers there were ominous signs of trouble. Lamp Trimmer Hemming was asleep when the accident occurred. Leaving his quarters, he put his head out a porthole and saw nothing amiss, but then he heard a loud hissing noise.

Investigating, he bumped into Storekeeper Frank Prentice. Curious to see if the ship was taking on water, they took the hatch off the Storeroom under the Forecastle head, which was located directly over the Forepeak Tank. Then they went right down to the top of the tank, which was located on the Orlop Deck.[134] At the very bottom of the store room, there was no indication of water or damage. Still hearing the hissing, Hemming and Prentice proceeded up to the Forecastle head, just forward of the anchor crane. By that time, it was nearly 11:45 p.m., and they found air hissing out of the vent pipe with considerable force, indicating that the Peak Tank was flooding rapidly.

Just then, Boatswain's Mate Albert Haines and Chief Officer Wilde came along. Wilde heard the hissing noise, as well, and asked: 'What is that, Hemming?'

Hemming replied: 'The air is escaping from the Forepeak Tank. She must be making water there, but the storeroom is quite dry.'

Wilde replied, 'All right,' and quickly proceeded on his way.

Hemming and Prentice then returned to their bunks, obviously unalarmed. There was no other evidence of damage, to their knowledge; if the Forepeak tank was flooding, it only had a capacity of 190 tons of water – hardly enough to endanger the ship's safety. Meanwhile, Haines headed off to do some more investigating.[135]

Second Officer Lightoller had just been drifting off to sleep in his port side cabin when he felt the collision. Although it didn't feel overtly serious, he waited about two or three minutes, and then rose and decided to have a quick look around; he didn't bother to dress at all. He first went out onto the port side of the Boat Deck, and moved forward a few feet until he could see the Bridge clearly. He observed First Officer Murdoch on the port wing.[136] Lightoller crossed to the rail and saw that the ship was proceeding ahead slowly again, at 'perhaps six knots'.[137] Third Officer Pitman – who had turned out of his cabin right after Lightoller – joined the Second Officer briefly on the deck. The two men conferred on what had happened. There wasn't much to go on, however … Clearly it seemed that they had struck something, but there was nothing in sight … ice was the prime candidate for the trouble, at least in Lightoller's mind. However, nothing seemed to be seriously wrong. So the two men went back inside where it was warm.

Pitman immediately retired to his cabin, and Lightoller's thinking was the same; he reasoned that he should be where everyone expected him to be if they needed to find him. Before he actually returned to his cabin, however, he crossed over to the starboard side of the Officers' Quarters,

opened the door that led back out onto the starboard Boat Deck, and looked forward toward the Bridge. He could discern Captain Smith on the wing on that side, but he did not see the iceberg. Then Lightoller returned to his room.[138]

Still at the helm, Quartermaster Hichens watched as the Captain came back into the Wheelhouse and looked at the inclinometer in front of the compass. Approximately five minutes had elapsed since the collision, and the ship already had a 5° list to starboard.[139] Following this observation, Captain Smith rang 'Stop' on the telegraph, Titanic's engines stopped for the last time, and the ship began slowing its forward momentum.

Just about then, Bruce Ismay arrived on the Bridge and asked the Captain what had happened. Smith told him that they had struck ice. White Star's Chairman asked whether the Captain believed the damage was serious. Although he apparently had not yet received a full damage report, Smith had seen enough to reply that 'he thought it was'. Ismay turned to leave the Bridge and head back below to his room …[140]

With the Titanic's engines stopped, she had drifted to a final halt with her bow facing north-northwest.[141] Since steam was no longer feeding into the engines, the pressure in the ship's boilers began to rise quickly. Soon it had reached safety tolerances, and automatic safety valves, which were fitted to each boiler, began to lift to vent the steam and reduce the pressure. This excess steam was carried up the steam escape pipes on the forward and aft ends of the funnels, where it began to 'blow off' with a tremendous racket.[142] Second Officer Charles Lightoller recalled:

> The ship had been running under a big head of steam, therefore the instant the engines were stopped the steam started roaring off at all eight exhausts, kicking up a row that would have dwarfed the row of a thousand railway engines thundering through a culvert.[143]

This thunderous roar could be heard all throughout the ship. In their stateroom, Elizabeth and Mary Lines heard the collision, and they knew that something was wrong – just not what. Shortly after the collision, the pair heard 'a tremendous noise of escaping steam'. A 'few seconds' passed, while they wondered what was wrong, but they did not think there was any danger. Just then, their steward came by and said to them: 'Captain's orders: stay in your stateroom and don't panic.' Then he disappeared, and the two women obediently settled in to wait.[144]

William Sloper and the stewards who had rushed out onto the Promenade Deck had managed to catch a glimpse of the iceberg. It was so cold on deck, however, that they soon returned to the companionway, where it was warmer. By that point the engines had stopped, and a number of people began to show up, many of them obviously concerned, and most of them not dressed. Sloper watched as the stewards reassured them that nothing serious was wrong. He was not entirely sure of that, however, so he went down to his room to get some warmer clothes on.[145]

Charlotte and Harvey Collyer had felt the collision in their Second Class cabin. They also had heard the engines stop. A few minutes later, they heard the engines re-start, but after only a short bit, they stopped again. Neither of them were alarmed, assuming it was a minor mishap in the Engine Room. At first, Harvey was not inclined to go on deck and investigate, but eventually he decided to do so. Charlotte lay back in her berth with her daughter, 8-year-old Marjorie.[146]

By this time, Lookout Hogg had returned to his quarters, having already gone out onto the Well Deck to see what had happened. He asked his mate, Lookout Alfred Evans, what time it was. Evans replied: 'It is a quarter to 12. We will get dressed and get ready to go on the lookout.' The two men started to get ready. Apparently, the idea was to head up to the Crow's Nest early, as their sleep had already been disturbed.[147] They also told Lookout George Symons – who had previously refused to get up and investigate like everyone else had – that he should get out of bed and start getting dressed. Symons, perhaps begrudgingly, did so.[148]

In contrast to the confusion and sense of urgency already unfolding in the bowels of the ship and among some members of the crew on deck, many of the First Class passengers had not even felt the impact. Arthur Ryerson slept right through the collision. His wife Emily had been awake and noticed the engines stop, but she had not even felt a jar as the ship ground along the iceberg. Not wanting to wake Arthur, she rang the steward to see what had happened. When Bedroom Steward Walter Bishop came to the door, he told Emily: 'There is talk of an iceberg ma'am, and they have stopped, not to run into it.' She asked Bishop to keep her informed if there were any orders.[149]

Lady Duff Gordon had previously felt the engines stop, and 'immediately there was the frightful noise of escaping steam'. Then she heard people ...

> ... running along the [Promenade] deck outside my cabin, but they were laughing and gay. One said to another: 'We must have hit an iceberg. There is ice on the deck.'

At this, Lucy crossed the passageway to her husband's cabin. He was still asleep, not having heard the collision, and was 'very annoyed' at being awakened. 'Don't be so ridiculous,' he told her. 'Even if we have grazed an iceberg it can't do any serious damage with all these water-tight compartments. The worst that can happen is that it will slow us down. Go back to bed and don't worry.' Lucy was not convinced, however. She went and ...

> ... looked over the side of the boat. I could see nothing unusual, and it was pitch black. Several people hurried up on deck, but on hearing from the ship's officers that it was 'nothing but temporary trouble' they went quietly back to bed.[150]

Everything on deck appeared quite normal, and Lady Duff Gordon started back for her stateroom. However, she was still uneasy about their situation.

Colonel Archibald Gracie had been sound asleep at the time of the collision. He woke up and turned on the light in his cabin. He had been awakened by a slight jar, and it also seemed to him that the engines stopped. Almost immediately after that, he also 'heard the blowing off of steam'. Gracie got up and looked out into the companionway, but didn't see anyone there. Still, he 'did not like the sound of it', and decided to dress.[151]

Meanwhile, Jack Thayer was more curious than alarmed. 'Almost instantaneously' after the collision, he had heard

and felt the ship's engines stop. Then he heard the 'distant noise of running feet and muffled voices, as several people hurried through the passageway.' Next he heard and felt that the engines had re-started, but slowly ... 'not with the bright vibration to which we were accustomed, but as though they were tired. After very few revolutions they again stopped.'

This was all irresistible to a 17-year-old ... Something had happened – serious, no, he thought ... but definitely exciting. Jack threw an overcoat over his pajamas and put slippers on. He called over to his parents 'that "I was going up on deck to see the fun." ' He heard his father say that he was going to dress and join him in a minute. Then Jack was gone ...[152]

Eleanor Cassebeer and Harry Anderson had remained on the forward end of the A Deck Promenade after receiving early reassurances from Thomas Andrews. They watched as Steerage passengers came out onto the Well Deck to play with the ice. Eleanor remembered a few passengers from First Class calling down to them, and asking for a bit of it. The Steerage passengers joined the fun and threw a few snowballs up in response. Just then, steam began roaring out of the funnels, creating a deafening racket and making conversation nearly impossible. Eventually, Eleanor and Harry Anderson moved inside, apparently to the forward Entrance Foyer on A Deck. A number of other people had begun to gather there, as well. They sat down and waited for further developments.[153]

In stateroom C-77, the Countess of Rothes and her cousin, Gladys Cherry, had been awakened by a bang and the stopping of the engines. Then they began to hear steam being blown off from far above. They could also hear some people walking up and down the corridor outside. The two ladies got up and found a steward nearby. He told them that the ship had struck an iceberg. The two ladies were a bit worried, so they put on their dressing gowns, and then donned fur coats. Then they went up on deck.[154]

Helen Ostby met her father, Engelhart Ostby, in the corridor between their B Deck staterooms. She remembered that everything was quiet as 'when a train stops in a station and you can hear everyone's voice'. She remembered seeing a few 'anxious looking faces', and that people looked rather outlandish, having thrown on anything they could think of over their nightclothes. Together, the father and daughter headed out on deck. They wandered around the corridors, and soon learned that the ship had hit an iceberg. Even so, no one knew exactly how much damage had been done, and no one thought it was really anything serious.[155]

May Futrelle was concerned by the collision, but she was more concerned by a rush of feet on the decks as people got up to investigate what had happened. She shook her husband Jacques and woke him up. He got up and peeked out the door, then walked into the passageway and came back. His conclusion was that the ship had just changed course for some reason, and that they should go back to bed.[156]

In Second Class, Dagmar Brhyl heard a knock on the door of her cabin. It was her fiancé Ingvar Enander; he called through the door: 'Get up, Dagmar. The ship has hit something.' Dagmar got up and put a skirt and coat on. Then they hurried up to the deck together. Soon, however, they encountered 'officers' who told them: 'Get back, there is no danger; you go to your cabins.' Dagmar went back to her room, undressed, and got back into bed.[157]

Second Class passenger Imanita Shelley rang for her steward multiple times. Finally, a different steward came to the door. She asked him what was wrong, and he replied: 'Nothing, madam. We had a slight collision, but it is all right now and the orders are for you to return to your beds and rest content.' He then 'went on down the line delivering the same message' to a number of others.[158]

In Third Class, Percival and Florence Thorneycroft had felt the collision, but didn't think much of it. Not long after, however, a young man they knew knocked on their door, and told them that 'the boat had run into a berg'. Even so, 'no one thought it was anything serious', and there were no indications to the contrary from the officers.[159]

Mess Steward Cecil Fitzpatrick had decided to get up and find out why the engines had stopped. He was told that the ship had struck an iceberg and that she was not seriously damaged. So Fitzpatrick returned to his berth and settled in to go back to sleep.[160]

Assistant Saloon Steward Walter Nichols remembered that some of the other stewards in his E Deck quarters didn't want to get up and see what had happened after the collision. Nichols, however, simply could not suppress his curiosity. He put his coat on and 'took a run out to look'. He apparently used the crew's working staircase which was just forward of the Reciprocating Engine Room. He remembered that it 'was all black outside' and that he 'couldn't see anything except that there was some ice on the deck forward. Half of the men went back to bed. Nobody believed anything could be wrong. They had such faith in the ship. Everybody believed in her.'[161]

Charles and Annie Stengel had dressed quickly after the collision. Charles had put on only what clothes he could grab, while his wife put on her kimono, and the two had gone up 'to the top deck and walked around there. There were not many people around there.'[162]

Bruce Ismay was proceeding from the Bridge down toward his suite of rooms on B Deck. He met Chief Engineer Joseph Bell at the top of the staircase, and asked him if he believed the ship was seriously damaged. Bell told him 'he thought the damage was serious, but that he hoped the pumps would be able to control the water.' Hearing this news, Ismay returned to his room briefly.[163]

Elsewhere, Major Arthur Peuchen left the forward rail on A Deck and went to see his friend, Hugo Ross, 'to tell him that it was not serious; that we had only struck an iceberg.' He went to try to call on his other friend, Harry Molson, to convey the same message. He found that Molson had already left his stateroom.[164]

By this time, Lady Duff Gordon had returned to her stateroom on A Deck from her excursion to investigate the situation. She had found no apparent reason for concern. It was only after she had felt the ship's engines stop, and the sound of rushing steam, that she felt cause for alarm. 'Something in the cessation of this busy, homely sound filled me with panic,' she recalled.[165]

Forward, Boatswain's Mate Albert Haines had discovered that the Forepeak Tank was flooding. He then moved aft, and 'went down to look' at the No. 1 Hold. He found the tarpaulin stretched out over the hatch, but was surprised by what he saw happening to it. Water was entering the No. 1 hold so fast that the tarpaulin 'was bellying up, raising', as the air escaped. Haines started to head for the Bridge to report this rather disturbing find.[166]

Seaman Edward Buley was on duty at the time of the collision, and he, too looked down the No. 1 Hatch after hearing water coming in at the bottom. He also remembered that the tarp was 'bending' up from 'the pressure of air underneath'.[167]

Back in Boiler Room No. 6, Fireman George Beauchamp was still working to draw the fires in his area. Because of the list to starboard, which the ship had developed almost immediately after the collision, Beauchamp's work on the port side was on the high, and therefore the more shallowly-flooded, side of the room. As the water continued to rise, he stuck to his post until someone shouted 'that will do'. Beauchamp estimated that this took place about a quarter of an hour after the collision. Accordingly, he headed up the escape ladder into the working alleyway – or Scotland Road, as it was frequently referred to – and then proceeded to the Boat Deck.[168]

After darting aft to Boiler Room No. 5 to escape incoming seawater, Leading Fireman Fred Barrett heard Second Engineer John Hesketh give the order, 'All hands stand by your stations.' For Barrett, this meant returning to Boiler Room No. 6. With Junior Assistant Second Engineer Jonathan Shepherd, Barrett went up the escape ladder in No. 5, forward, and then back down the ladder into No. 6. They had to take this laborious route because the watertight door in between the compartments was closed. When they went down the ladder into No. 6, they found that there was now eight feet of water on the starboard side of the compartment. In the ten minutes that had elapsed since they left, the water level had risen six feet there.

Having no chance to do anything, Barrett and Shepherd left the flooding compartment and headed back to Boiler Room No. 5. There, they found Senior Assistant Second Engineer Bert Wilson and Junior Assistant Second Engineer Herbert Harvey attending to the pumps. Water was pouring into the forward, starboard side coal bunker of No. 5 from a seam in the hull located two feet above the deck plates; even so, the stokehold itself was completely dry. Since the damage to Boiler Room No. 5 was less significant than in No. 6, the pumps were keeping up with the flooding.[169]

After failing to see any damage during his trip below, Fourth Officer Boxhall emerged onto the forward Well Deck again, eager to return to the Bridge with his bit of good news. When he came back out into the cold night air, he saw a man holding a piece of ice 'about as large as a small basin'. Boxhall took it from the man's hand and walked across the deck to see where he had gotten it. He found that there was 'just a little ice … covering a space of about three or four feet from the bulwarks', along the Well Deck. It was not really a lot, just some 'small stuff'.[170]

At around 11:50 a.m., the Fourth Officer arrived back on the Bridge. He reported that he had seen no damage whatsoever. With the delivery of this report, however, the good news had ended for Captain Smith. The Captain seemed unconvinced by Boxhall's preliminary findings. A 'couple of minutes' after he had arrived to make his report, the Captain told Boxhall: 'Go down and find the carpenter and get him

Right: *Junior Assistant Second Engineer Jonathan Shepherd.*

Far right: *Junior Assistant Second Engineer Herbert Harvey.*

Above: *The Forecastle and forward Well Deck of the* Olympic *in New York. The Crow's Nest is visible on the foremast. During the collision, ice fell down onto the starboard side of* Titanic's *Well Deck, just visible on the extreme right of the photo of her sister.*

to sound the ship.'[171] Apparently, Quartermaster Olliver had not yet returned from his own search for the carpenter.

Very shortly after Boxhall left to carry out this order, Olliver arrived back on the Bridge; he had delivered Smith's earlier order to the Carpenter for him to take a draft of the water. No sooner had Olliver gotten there, however, than Captain Smith handed him a folded-up note for Chief Engineer Joseph Bell, with orders for him to deliver the message right away. Olliver proceeded below once again ...[172]

Albert Dick and his wife Vera had gone on deck after the collision, and had seen the berg. They also ran into Thomas Andrews very shortly after the collision:

> He was on hand at once and said that he was going below to investigate. We begged him not to go, but he insisted, saying he knew the ship as no one else did and that he might be able to allay the fears of the passengers. He went.

With the departure of Andrews, the Dicks suddenly felt uncertain. Andrews was such a reassuring figure ... All they could do was to wait for further information.[173]

Saloon Steward James Johnstone was stationed as the night watchman in the First Class Dining Saloon.[174] His quiet shift had been interrupted by the slight jar of the collision. Shortly after, Greaser Alfred White came up asking for some hot water. Johnstone did not know White, but sent him below to find out what was going on. When White returned, he said that things looked 'a bit hot'.[175]

Around 11:50 a.m., Johnstone walked forward to the Grand Staircase in the Reception Room. He was just in time to see Thomas Andrews race down the working stairs to E Deck and turn aft, apparently heading toward the Engine Room.[176] A small knot of First Class ladies had gathered by the staircase, and they spotted Andrews as he went by; since he was pretty well-known among many of the First Class passengers, they looked to him for information and reassurance as he passed. Johnstone overheard Andrews telling the ladies, 'Be easy, it will be all right.' Johnstone piped in and also inquired, to which Andrews replied: 'All right.' Then he hurried off to dig into his inspection. Johnstone felt quite reassured by Andrews' statements.[177]

Down below, in the lowest crew areas of the ship, the damage was beginning to show, even in sections that had

Saloon Steward James Johnstone.

not immediately been inundated with water, as Boiler Room No. 6 had been. More and more members of the crew began to discover that water was entering different areas of the bow, and at an alarming rate. Just one example of this came as the five postal clerks were hard at work in the Post Office. This facility was set up with a sorting room on G Deck, and a hold for the mail just below on the Orlop Deck. Within ten minutes of the collision, water began entering the Orlop Deck level, and the postal clerks desperately began lugging the sacks of mail up the stairs to the upper level to escape the rising water. Hardly had this been accomplished when the water began to climb the staircase toward G Deck.

Bedroom Steward Henry Etches was still asleep in his berth in the Steward's Quarters, amidships on the port side of E Deck. He was awakened 'by something', but he didn't know what it was. A few minutes after the collision – he estimated that the time was then 'between 25 minutes and 20 minutes to 12' – Etches called down to his mate in the berth below: 'What time is it that they are going to call us next?'

Etches' neighbor steward replied: 'I don't know.' So Etches decided to go back to sleep again. Just then, there came a loud shout from their Boatswain – probably Alfred Nichols – out in the hall: 'Close water-tight bulkheads!' Etches got up and looked out into the companionway, noticing that the Boatswain and another seaman were running from fore to aft.[178]

About this time, after being awakened by the collision and hearing that the *Titanic* had hit an iceberg, Saloon Steward Alexander Littlejohn had gone up on deck, and saw about 'two feet' of ice lying in the scuppers on the starboard side of the forward Well Deck. Unalarmed, he returned below deck. Once there, he saw that the 'carpenters sounding the forward well'; he 'noticed there was a quantity of water in it as the line was pulled up'. Littlejohn went back to his room and told his fellow stewards that they might be called on shortly to assist the passengers. Still, he did not expect they would have to leave the ship. As he said, 'we all thought she was unsinkable.'[179]

In the First Class Smoking Room, Alfred Nourney had continued to play cards with Henry Blank and William Greenfield for a few minutes after the collision. But something, 'perhaps instinct', he thought, made Nourney decide to investigate the situation. The three men left the Smoking Room together, and 'went on deck to meet a few men and women, also making inquiries'. Nourney then walked forward on the Promenade Deck, and saw ice on the Well Deck below. 'There were huge chunks on the hatches,' he recalled.[180]

Honeymooning couple John and Nelle Snyder were in their B Deck cabin when the collision came. Nelle was concerned, and asked her husband to go up on deck to investigate. John wanted to go back to sleep, but his bride insisted; the new husband acquiesced and 'dressed hurriedly.' On his way out on deck, he ran across 'some of the crew', and he asked them what had happened. They informed him that the ship had 'scraped against an iceberg'. Fact-finding mission apparently accomplished, John returned to their stateroom. Yet Nelle was still nervous, and told him that 'he had better go on deck and make sure' of their safety.[181]

Meanwhile, Karl Behr and Helen Newsom had gone on deck. In addition to the cold, they found that the ship was listing to starboard, the side where Behr believed the collision had occurred. This was enough to tell Behr that she was 'dangerously injured', although he had no thought that the ship was actually 'doomed' at that point. They began to head below to the stateroom of Helen's parents, Richard and Sarah Beckwith.[182]

William and Alice Silvey had dressed after the collision and the stopping of the engines, and then they headed up on deck. When they left their E Deck cabin, there seemed to be a little confusion, with other passengers poking their noses out into the hall to see what had happened. However, no one was expressing fear. When the Silveys made it up on the deck, they found nothing more than 'a beautiful night, clear, still and cold. The water was like glass.' Mrs. Silvey saw no icebergs, but one of their friends, who had been on deck at the time of the collision, told them that the berg passed 'so close that he could have touched it.' The couple walked around the deck, and noticed that 'the ship had listed somewhat', but still no one thought there was any serious danger. 'The officers' told them to return to their cabin and put on some very warm clothing, so they headed back down to their room.[183]

About 'five or ten minutes' after the collision and the stopping of the engines, Elmer Taylor said to his wife: 'I think I will go on deck, nose about and see if I can be of any assistance.' Then he leisurely put on the clothes he intended to wear the next day, picked up a cigar from the table, lit it, and left the cabin.[184]

Margaret Swift and Dr Alice Leader were still in their cabin. They had felt the crash, but didn't think it was serious, as the ship had 'stood up well' after the collision. After a while, however, they got up, each threw a wrapper over herself, and they went out to investigate. The two ladies were 'assured that there was no danger', however.[185]

Emma Bucknell and her maid Albina Bazzani had seen the iceberg pass the window of their stateroom on D Deck. Without waiting for further information, Emma dressed partially, and then she opened her cabin door. The passageway from which the cabin was accessed ran down to the outboard side of the ship on the starboard side. There was a porthole at the end, and Emma discovered that there were pieces of ice on the floor which had 'been forced through' the 'broken port hole'.

At about that time, a man who seemed to be one of the stewards came through saying 'that there was no danger as a result of the collision'. However, Emma noticed that 'while his voice was calm and he delivered his message easily, his face belied the confidence of his words, expressing the fear he had in his mind.'

Emma was not convinced, and returned to her cabin to dress warmly. She told her maid to do the same. She 'anticipated that there would come greater difficulties', and fully intended to be prepared for anything.[186]

First Class passenger Martha Stephenson, in stateroom D-20, had remained in her cabin. Shortly after the impact, a steward came in to close the open porthole. When asked, the steward said it was too cold to get up, that it was nothing at all, and that she should go back to bed. Another First Class passenger, Martha Stone, was also awakened by the crash, but got up lightly dressed and went into the corridor with other passengers. A nearby ship's officer told her there was no danger, and to go back to bed and sleep.[187]

Down in Second Class, the same thing was happening. Twelve-year-old Ruth Becker's mother Nellie got up and asked a steward what the matter was. He said, 'Nothing', and advised that they should go back to bed. Marie Jerwan, sharing a cabin with Mrs Ada Ball, went on deck where an officer told her that 'there was no danger, that one could go back to bed.' Alice Phillips heard the crash and felt that the engines stopped. She rang up her steward to find out what was going on, but was told it was nothing serious and to go back to sleep. Edwina Troutt got as far as the corridor before being told to go back to bed, since they had 'only' struck an iceberg. Another Second Class passenger, Ellen Wolcroft, rooming with Clear Cameron, remained in her cabin, but a steward came down to tell them: 'Go back to your beds. No danger!'[188]

Shortly after Harvey Collyer had gone up to investigate the situation, he returned to his Second Class cabin. There he told his wife Charlotte that they had struck an iceberg, but that an officer had told him there was no danger.[189]

Third Class passenger Amy Stanley had gotten out of bed, thrown a coat on, and gone up on deck to investigate what had happened. Her roommates Elizabeth Dowdell and little Virginia Emanuel stayed behind, reassured by a steward in the hall outside their cabin that nothing was wrong. On deck, Amy encountered another steward, and asked him what was the matter. The steward told her it was only that the engines had stopped, and he ordered her and other women who were nearby back to bed.[190]

During the minutes directly following the collision – in First, Second, and Third Classes, both above and below deck – not only were the passengers being assured nothing serious had happened, but they were also being told to go back to their staterooms, and to go back to sleep. It is possible that for some of those who went back to sleep – particularly those in Third Class sections of the ship forward – this delay subsequently allowed them to become trapped by incoming water, or without enough time to save themselves.

Eugene Daly had returned to his cabin for a little while after being told everything was OK. Soon, though, he put on his lifebelt and stepped out into the passage, which was already 'thronged with excited men and women'. The assurances of the crew calmed the crowd, and Daly became the subject of laughter, as he was the only one who was wearing a lifebelt. Embarrassed, he returned to his cabin, pulled his overcoat on over his lifebelt, and shoved his rosary beads, watch, and some coins into his pocket.[191] Daly then proceeded up on deck, and found some of the stewards joking around with each other and smoking cigarettes, apparently unalarmed. This did little to calm his nerves, so he quickly returned below with the intention of arousing Maggie Daly, and Bertha Mulvihill.[192]

Third Class passenger August Wennerström.

Third Class passengers August Wennerström and Gunnar Isidor Tenglin were also awakened by the collision. They had returned early from the party in the General Room that night. Both men were Swedes traveling to America from their homeland, and shared a cabin during the voyage. Carl Jansson had joined them on the voyage, although he was berthed in a separate cabin. A steward knocked on the door and told them to get up and dress, but assured them that there was no danger. The two men grabbed their things and headed aft to the Third Class Smoking Room. Tenglin left so quickly that he did not even grab his shoes.[193]

After the collision, Bertha Chambers had asked her husband to find out what had happened, as she was 'rather alarmed'; Norman, on the other hand, had concluded that 'something had gone wrong with the engines on the starboard side', and would gladly have stayed in bed reading. However, to please his wife, he 'threw on sufficient clothes' and an overcoat, and leisurely went up to A Deck, emerging on the starboard side. He only noticed 'an unusual coldness of the air'. Looking over the side, he was unable to see anything in any direction, and returned to his cabin. He found that his wife had already dressed completely and warmly. Then he and Bertha started out together for a more thorough investigation.[194]

Sidney Collett emerged on the deck to find that 'steam was blowing with a deafening noise.' He heard quickly that the ship had struck an iceberg, but he could not see it himself. Collett turned and headed down again after being ordered by officers 'to get the ladies'.[195]

Just then, young Jack Thayer was rushing up to the deck on the port side.[196] He could see nothing from there, however. So he 'then went forward to the bow' on A Deck, eventually reaching the bulwark rail overlooking the Forecastle and Well Deck.[197] He could see the ice below on the Well Deck, but as he had just come out of the ship's brightly lit interior, he could not see very far ahead. Then he returned to his cabin on C Deck.[198]

By then, Colonel Archibald Gracie had dressed and left his cabin on C Deck. He ascended to the Boat Deck, emerging on the port side by the First Class Entrance. There, he found only one other 'young lad, seemingly bent on the same quest as myself'.[199] Gracie found that it was a 'beautiful night, cloudless, and the stars shining brightly'. It was very cold, but there was no indication of what might have hit them; Gracie's first conclusion was that it was a small boat. Whatever it was, however, it wasn't visible from the port side.

Gracie wasn't satisfied, so he set off aft. When he ran up against the railing designating the end of the First Class deck, he nimbly leapt over it, completely disregarding the 'not allowed' notice sign. He looked around to see if he had been caught entering Second Class areas, but found no sign of any officers nearby to reprimand him. So he completed his circuit on the deck, coming back up the starboard side, all without finding anything more exciting than a middle-aged couple out for a stroll on the Second Class Boat Deck. He decided to head down to the port side of the Promenade Deck next. There, he looked over the railing to see if he could tell whether the ship was on an even keel or not, but he could not tell anything that way. So far, it had been a thoroughly disappointing investigation.[200]

Before Fourth Officer Boxhall could get very far on his second trip below deck, he ran into Carpenter Hutchinson, who said that the ship was making water fast. Boxhall told Hutchinson to report it to the Bridge, and as Hutchinson proceeded topside to inform the Captain, Boxhall continued below. Next Boxhall encountered British Postal Clerk John Smith, who reported that the Mail Room was flooding.[201] Boxhall sent Smith along to report this to the Bridge as well, and then the Fourth Officer headed for the Mail Room to see this for himself. When he got there, sometime around 11:52 a.m., Boxhall could actually hear the water rushing in, and saw bags of mail floating about on the surface. The water was now within two feet of G Deck.[202]

Earlier, First Class passengers Albert and Vera Dick had seen Andrews go below, and following that, they 'did not know what to do or which way to turn'. Soon, they saw the Captain, and recalled that he 'was everywhere doing his best to calm the rising tide of fear', apparently as he headed below. The Dicks were not particularly reassured, however, and were waiting for further word from Andrews.[203]

Back in the First Class Reception Room, just minutes after Thomas Andrews passed through on his way below, Steward Johnstone and Saloon Steward Mackay saw Captain Smith proceed down the same working staircase to E Deck, presumably towards Chief Engineer Bell's room. Carpenter Hutchinson had just informed Smith on the Bridge that Cargo Holds 1, 2 and 3 were all flooding, and the Captain was likely going below to personally check in with Bell, Thomas Andrews, or both.[204]

Down on E Deck, Steward Theissinger had seen a fireman who was reporting that there was flooding forward; he had also heard an order to close the watertight doors. 'Just after' that, Theissinger passed Captain Smith. The Steward assumed, because of where the Captain was coming from, that Smith had been 'in a portion of the ship near the main salon', probably a reference to the Dining Saloon. Although Theissinger had not been alarmed by the collision, he headed forward along E Deck, since most of the cabins in his care were on that deck, near the aft-most passenger accommodations on the starboard side.[205]

At that time, in the Engine Room, a call came down for all of the stokers to be sent up on deck. Then the electric lights went out in the stokeholds, impeding the efforts of crewmembers who were fighting to control the flooding. Second Engineer Hesketh ordered Leading Fireman Barrett to go get lamps for Boiler Room No. 5.[206]

Greaser Thomas Ranger had remained at his station after the collision, repairing a fan, for about fifteen minutes. Then Chief Electrician Peter Sloan came back up and ordered him to go and stop all the electrical fans, starting with the ones for the stokeholds. It was an enormous task, and it took Ranger quite some time.[207]

Up on the Bridge, Boatswain's Mate Haines arrived and found Chief Officer Wilde, whom he had seen just a few minutes before at the exhaust vent for the Forepeak Tank. Haines reported to the Chief Officer that he had seen evidence of flooding in the No. 1 hold. Wilde told him to get his men up, and then to get the boats out. Haines hurried back down to awaken his hands.[208]

Back in First Class, Isaac Frauenthal had dressed after the collision, and then he left his cabin, D-40, which was all the way forward on that deck. He proceeded aft, then up the stairs to C Deck, and aft along the port corridor to just forward of the Aft Grand Staircase and Entrance. His brother and sister-in-law's room was there on the port side, cabin C-88.[209] When he arrived, Isaac Frauenthal 'rapped on the door', and his 'brother answered sleepily'. Isaac told Henry that 'he had better get up'. Henry was unconvinced, and said that 'he guessed he wouldn't' get up, and that 'any story about the ship being ready to sink was all nonsense'. Henry Frauenthal seems to have been in quite a sleep-induced fog, and later did not even remember this visit by Isaac.

Meanwhile, to Isaac, it was clear that Henry was going nowhere soon. Still uncertain about the ship's safety, Isaac decided to try to find out more ...[210]

Herbert and Carrie Chaffee were in their cabin on E Deck when the collision came. After trying the lights and finding the ship's electricity was still on, they heard movement in the hallway. The daughter of an Englishwoman, who was in the cabin across the hall, was leaving to go up on deck. The Chaffees waited until she returned, and she informed them that the passengers were to get on deck.[211]

'Oh, that's nothing to get excited about,' Mr Chaffee said. 'It's probably a precautionary measure, in case anything has happened.' The couple began to dress, but did so at a rather leisurely pace. Opening his trunk, Herbert took out and then donned a heavy suit. Carrie dressed fully, and when they left their cabin, she even remembered to take a small grip with her.[212]

Frederick and Jane Hoyt had left their C Deck cabin very quickly after the collision; they remained on deck for some time, even though Jane had followed her husband up 'wearing only a light dressing gown'. While they were on deck, the couple bumped into their friend, Ship's Surgeon Dr William O'Loughlin. Frederick asked O'Loughlin if anything serious had happened. O'Loughlin replied that he didn't know, and moved on.[213]

Meanwhile, Lucy Duff Gordon had been uneasy since the collision. She had already tried to wake her husband once, without success. However, with the stopping of the engines, she was nearly panic-stricken, and wanted her husband go on deck and make a proper investigation of the situation. She 'rushed' from her cabin, A-20, and went across the passageway to her husband's cabin, A-16. She hurried in to the cabin and over to the bed. Shaking Sir Cosmo's still-sleeping form, she cried: 'I beg you to go up on deck and see what has happened.' Sir Cosmo got up out of bed, 'rather unwillingly', and headed out on deck.[214]

Third Class passenger Emily Badman and the girls in her cabin had felt the collision. However, they had been unable to see anything out of the porthole of their forward, starboard-side cabin. When Miss Badman – who had just turned eighteen on Sunday – started out into the corridor just outside their room, she saw that it was 'filled with foreigners going up on deck loaded with luggage'. She went on one of the upper decks, where she met a young man from Kent, England, with whom she had become acquainted during the voyage. He told her to 'go back down and put on heavier clothing'. Although she did not want to, she returned below, also thinking to put on a lifebelt.[215]

Elsewhere, Bedroom Steward Alfred Theissinger stuck his nose out into the corridor in time to see a fireman running past 'carrying a bag of clothing'. As the man rushed by, he shouted: 'There is water forward!' Just then someone else shouted out: 'All watertight doors shut!'[216]

Assistant Saloon Steward Nichols thought it so 'bitter cold' on deck that he 'was glad enough' to get back to his quarters, which were not far forward of the entrance to the Engine Room. Within a few minutes of the collision, he could hear 'the engineers passing along the order to close the watertight doors. One man would tell it to the next and he would pass it on to someone else.' There was little for Nichols to do about this, though, so he 'stayed up and sat around talking with some of the fellows' for what he thought was 'three-quarters of an hour after the collision'.[217]

Anna Sjöblom was in a Third Class cabin near the ship's bow. She remembered that after the collision, she had gotten up and started to put on some clothes. However, water 'began coming up where I was in a short time', and she was literally chased from her cabin by it. She hurried above deck.[218]

Jack Thayer returned to his cabin, and he and his parents decided that they should all head up top together to obtain further information on the situation. Once they reached the deck, they went over to the starboard side, and noticed that the ship was listing.[219] Although Jack could not see anything of interest, his father thought he saw pieces of ice floating in the sea. Neither of them, however, saw any evidence of a large iceberg. They walked around the decks for a few minutes, and began to notice the list increasing.[220]

Bruce Ismay had met up with Chief Engineer Bell, and Bell had told him he was hopeful that the pumps could keep ahead of the flooding. Then Ismay had returned briefly to his stateroom. While in his suite, the Chairman only took the time to throw a suit over his nightclothes, and then left again, headed back up toward the Bridge.[221]

Colonel Gracie was just coming into the forward First Class Entrance from the Promenade Deck when he saw Bruce Ismay 'with a member of the crew hurrying up the stairway'. He noticed that Ismay …

> … wore a day suit, and, as usual, was hatless. He seemed too much preoccupied to notice anyone. Therefore I did not speak to him, but regarded his face very closely, perchance to learn from his manner how serious the accident might be. It occurred to me then that he was putting on as brave a face as possible so as to cause no alarm to the passengers.[222]

At the foot of the stairway, Gracie saw a number of male passengers, and went to join them.

Second Class passenger Lawrence Beesley had returned to his cabin to read after an initial investigation. After a few minutes, however, he could hear people 'walking about in the corridors'. Beesley looked out, and saw a number of people talking to a steward in the hallway, while others were going upstairs. He listened, and …

… found everyone wanting to know why the engines had stopped. No doubt many were awakened from sleep by the sudden stopping of a vibration to which they had become accustomed during the four days we had been on board. Naturally, with such powerful engines as the *Titanic* carried, the vibration was very noticeable all the time, and the sudden stopping had something the same effect as the stopping of a loud ticking grandfather's clock in a room.

Beesley put on a 'Norfolk jacket and trousers' and ascended to the Boat Deck. He walked from one side of the ship to the other. Looking over the edge, he had at one point noticed 'a little white line of foam on each side' of the hull as the ship sloshed slowly through the water. Initially he assumed that the ship had resumed her course. Depending on when he arrived on deck, this is possible; it could also have been the last gasp of forward momentum after the engines had been stopped by Captain Smith. In either case, Beesley had felt a little reassured by this, concluding that forward progress was better than being stopped dead in the middle of the ocean, and he stayed on the deck for 'some minutes'.[223]

Boatswain's Mate Albert Haines told the men up in the Forecastle Head that all hands should stand by, adding: 'You may be wanted at any moment.' Even though the official order for 'all hands' had not yet been given to crew members of all departments, Chief Officer Wilde had told Haines to get these men ready, because experienced seamen would be those most needed in order to prepare the lifeboats and begin to swing them out, if the worse came to the worst.[224]

Lookout George Symons had finally gotten out of his berth and gotten dressed, after Lookouts Hogg and Evans had suggested that he do so. He heard the Boatswain's order to stand by, and headed into the Seamen's Mess on the port side of C Deck to see if there was any coffee to be had. While he was there, he heard a strange sound.

Poking his nose back out of the Mess, he went to the other side of the passage and looked down the No. 1 Hatch. The tarp was off the wooden gratings, and he could see down the hatch all the way to G Deck. There, Symons spotted the source of the strange sound: water was pouring into the No. 1 Hold 'in a pretty good rush'. The water was already washing around the hatch coamings on G Deck, and it looked to be coming from the forward starboard side, in his estimation.[225]

At 11:55 a.m., Steward Johnstone watched Thomas Andrews come back up to D Deck; Johnstone believed that the ship's designer had already been to the Engine Room. Andrews moved forward before heading down another set of stairs toward the Mail Room. Johnstone waited for 'a minute', and then his curiosity got the better of him and he followed Andrews down. From E Deck, forward, he could look down the stairs straight through to G Deck. There he could see that the First Class Baggage Room on G Deck was flooding.[226]

Next Johnstone met up with Steward Joseph Wheat, who had come out of his berth to investigate what was going on. Wheat asked Johnstone, 'What is it?'

Johnstone replied: 'I think it is a bit serious.' Then Johnstone went to his berth and got dressed … in his shore suit. Steward Wheat, for his part, looked down the stairwell to G Deck and saw for himself the water in the Mail Room. Transfixed, he went down and watched the Mail Room flood …[227]

At that time, Edwin Kimball was just coming back from a trip up above decks to find out what had happened. He was returning to his D Deck stateroom, No. 19, which was near 'the stairway which went down to the deck below to the squash courts and mailroom'. Just then, he saw 'a mail clerk go down the stairs', and he apparently followed him down to E Deck.[228]

By then, Gladys Cherry and her cousin, the Countess of Rothes, had arrived on the deck. They went all the way forward on the Promenade Deck, and found ice collected on the well deck. They could not see any iceberg, but decided to stay on deck for a bit, talking and watching as things occurred there.[229]

Meanwhile, when Philipp Mock and Emma Schabert met back up after dressing, they went on deck to investigate the situation. Walking forward, probably on the Promenade Deck, they could look down on the ice that had fallen onto the Well Deck. They watched 'people below moving their belongings', probably referring to Third Class passengers coming up from their water-logged cabins below who were carrying their personal effects. Still, no one 'thought very much about' the collision. Mock thought that the concept of the situation being serious did not seem to have entered anyone's mind. Mock said:

The night was starlight, bright as could be above, the stars shining …, but was very dark along the water. There was no fog and no ice to be seen. Some men who were in one of the lounges said that they saw the berg immediately after the collision, as the ice rushed aft past the window.

Mock looked out from the Boat Deck on the starboard side, but he could not discern the outline of an iceberg.[230]

May Futrelle was not convinced by her husband's initial explanation of the collision; it was obviously something more than a simple change of course. She was nervous, and when it was clear that people were still up on deck, Jacques became unsettled, as well. He got up, dressed, and looked out into the corridor just as their friend Henry Harris did the same thing. Harris asked Futrelle: 'What's happened?' Futrelle replied: 'Oh, nothing I guess, but I suppose we'd better get out and see what's doing.' The two men then turned to May, and told her to go in to sit with Irene Harris in the Harris' cabin until they got back.

While the men were gone, the two women began to dress themselves. Mrs Harris was very nervous, and her broken arm was also in a sling, making the task of donning clothes difficult. May found that she had to cut the sling free before she could get Irene into a heavy fur coat.[231]

Elsewhere, Quartermaster Olliver saw the stokers coming out onto E Deck as he proceeded below to find Chief Engineer Bell. Entering the Engine Room, he noticed that the engines were stopped. He found Bell hard at work, and handed him the Captain's folded message. Bell looked at the note, and went back to work. Olliver waited 'two or three minutes', and finally, the Chief asked what he wanted. Olliver stated that he was waiting for a response to Captain Smith's message. Bell told him to tell the Captain that 'he would get it done as soon as possible.' Olliver never learned the content of the note he had delivered, but quickly proceeded up on deck to relay the information.[232]

Meanwhile, Washington Dodge had left his stateroom again, and this time ventured out onto the Promenade Deck. He found a group of six to eight men who were 'gaily conversing' about the incident. One man mentioned that it had been due to ice. Another in the group didn't believe him. In response, the man said: 'Go up forward and look down on the poop deck [sic, Well Deck], and you can see for yourself.' Hearing this, Dr Dodge went forward, through the door, and out to the forward bulwark rail overlooking the Well Deck and Forecastle. Looking down he could see, 'just within the starboard rail, small fragments of broken ice, amounting possibly to several cartloads.'

Just then, Dr Dodge saw two stokers standing near him. Stokers were almost never seen on the Promenade Deck, and the pair had apparently 'slipped up' without permission. They asked Dodge: 'Do you think there is any danger?' Dodge replied: 'If there is any danger it would be due to the vessel having sprung a leak, and you ought to know more about it than I.'

They replied, in what Dodge thought was an 'alarmed' tone: 'Well, sir, the water was pouring into the stoke 'old when we came up, sir.'

This encounter made the San Francisco doctor think that the situation was a bit more serious than he had before. After this brief chat with the pair of stokers, Dodge looked back down to the Well Deck, and saw 'quite a number of steerage passengers … amusing themselves by walking over the ice, and kicking it about the deck.' Dodge noticed that no one around was displaying 'any sign of apprehension'. There didn't even seem to be that many people out and about. Dodge decided to return to his stateroom to tell his wife what he had seen and heard.[233]

Having seen ice covering the Well Deck, Alfred Nourney had decided to go below and look for signs of damage. He 'raced' from the forward end of the Promenade Deck down to the Squash Racquet Court. The two-deck space had a Spectator's Gallery on F Deck, with the players' court on G Deck, below. The G Deck court was the furthest-forward and lowest area of First Class territory on the ship; it was directly inboard from the Post Office Sorting Room, and just aft of the First Class Baggage Room.[234] Nourney hurried down to the court, and was stunned to find three to six feet of water there. He turned and headed back up.[235]

About a quarter hour after the shock George Rheims was informed, perhaps by a passing steward, that the ship had collided with an iceberg, but that there was no danger and everyone should go back to sleep. 'Soon afterwards' Rheims was joined 'at the top of the stairway' by his brother-in-law, Joseph Loring. This location apparently referred to the Boat Deck First Class Entrance, at the top of the forward Grand Staircase. The two men stood around discussing the situation.[236]

William Carter went down to his two adjoining staterooms, B-96 and B-98, where his family was sleeping. He woke his wife up, and told her about what had occurred. He then told her that she and the children should dress.[237]

Norman Chambers and his wife Bertha had gone on deck after the collision. Earlier in the day, Norman had noticed that the liner had been listing slightly to port. But 'within a few minutes', he noticed that she had begun to list to starboard. There was also a slight pitch toward the bow. Although there was no confusion on the decks around them, and everything seemed under control, this list convinced Chambers that the ship was taking water, and taking it on rapidly. He decided to stay awake until the situation was

Above left: *First Class passenger George Rheims.*

Above right: *Second Class passenger William Mellors.*

resolved, 'in spite of a feeling of perfect safety'. Next, the couple started back down for their E Deck cabin.[238]

Second Class passenger William Mellors had fallen back to sleep for about ten minutes after the collision, having no reason to suspect anything was wrong. Suddenly, his roommate, also an Englishman, barged into the cabin and 'began to yell out that the ship had struck an iceberg and he thought we were going down. I really thought he was joking and told him so, but was soon convinced of the fact by hearing people running about and shouting on the deck and the engines being stopped.'[239]

Also in Second Class, Miss Susan Webber had gotten up out of bed after the collision. After wrapping herself in a robe, she left her E Deck cabin – which she shared with Edwina Troutt and Nora Keane – and went up on deck to investigate. In the course of her probe, she was informed by 'officers' that 'it was nothing', so she returned to her cabin and went back to bed. However, she found that she was having trouble getting back to sleep ...[240]

12:00 midnight–12:15 a.m.

At around 12:00 a.m., Fourth Officer Boxhall returned to the Bridge from his second trek below and confirmed to Captain Smith that the Mail Room was taking on water. At that point, the Captain had just returned from a trip down at least as far as E Deck aft. When Boxhall made his report, the Captain responded with a terse, 'All right,' and left the Bridge. Presumably, Smith was headed below for his own personal inspection of the flooding forward.

By the time Captain Smith departed from the Bridge, the order had already been given for 'all hands' to turn out, and Boxhall heard the order come down for the crewmembers to begin uncovering and clearing the lifeboats.[241] Bruce Ismay had by then returned to the Boat Deck, and 'heard Capt. Smith give the order to clear the boats'.[242] This order was proactive, as Captain Smith had not yet learned the full extent of the damage, and did not yet know that the ship was mortally wounded.[243]

Seaman Buley remembered an order from First Officer Murdoch for the 'seamen to get together and uncover the boats and turn them out as quietly as though nothing had happened'.[244] It was clear from all of this that the ship's officers were keen to do two things: first, to be fully prepared for any eventuality; and second, to prevent any panic on the part of nervous passengers as this work was done.

Around this time, Sixth Officer Moody told Quartermaster Olliver to go get the muster list for the lifeboats.[245] Boxhall was ordered – possibly by Chief Officer Wilde – to wake Second Officer Lightoller, Third Officer Pitman, and Fifth Officer Lowe. The Fourth Officer later recalled that this took place 'approximately 20 minutes to half-an-hour' after the collision, or about midnight.[246] Sixth Officer Moody was sent on his way to start preparing the aft port lifeboats.

A Weak Leader?

For many years, the public's perception of Captain Smith was that he was a weak leader, hopelessly ill-prepared for the startling circumstances in which he found himself after the collision. Why did it take him so long to give the orders to load the lifeboats? Why did he not make sure that every officer was fully informed as to the severity of the situation?

In fact, Captain Smith was not the weak leader so long assumed. Consider a summary of his actions after the collision: he was on the Bridge within moments of the impact, and immediately began an investigation into the nature and extent of the damage. He was seen heading below not once, but twice after the collision, coordinating his investigation with Thomas Andrews and also making two trips to the wireless office. In the course of his trips below, Albert and Vera Dick

recalled that he was 'everywhere doing his best to calm the rising tide of fear'.[247]

During the course of these investigations – even before he had received the grim news that the *Titanic* was doomed – Captain Smith had ordered his crew to begin preparing the lifeboats, and to get the passengers into their lifebelts. All of these were proactive orders that, in the end, wound up saving lives, since time was a far more precious commodity than could have been imagined before his bleak conference with Thomas Andrews at about 12:25 a.m.

By that point, Smith was confronted with a conundrum ... his officers and crew were spread out across the Boat Deck, engaged in the enormous task of preparing the lifeboats for loading and lowering. Calling these men, even if it was only the officers, to the Bridge for a confab would

Captain Smith in his summer whites.

By about 12:30, he had given Lightoller permission to fill the port side boats; at about 12:40, he was seen ordering passengers down to the Promenade Deck to begin boarding Boat No. 4; he personally assisted in the loading of Boats Nos 8, 6, and 2; a number of times he checked in on the Bridge with Boxhall about the firing of the rockets; he checked in with the wireless operators to see how things were going there, as well. Right up to the end of the disaster, he was seen giving orders to his men before heading to the Bridge. Indeed, for a man of his age, his physical exertions during the disaster seem to have been great.

Instead of supporting such claims, the historical record tends to disprove the popularly held concept that Captain Smith was a weak leader in a time of crisis. In retrospect, it seems that Captain Smith's actions probably saved many lives.

have wasted precious time. It seems that he believed it was better to let them do their work without interruption, and that he planned to take each step forward as the opportunities presented themselves.

Meanwhile, Isaac Frauenthal, who had been unable to rouse his brother, had decided to look for Captain Smith or any other officer who could tell him what had really happened. Eventually, he emerged on the deck, in search of further information. He recalled:

> There were few people on deck and none of them seemed to be agitated. Presently I saw the captain appear, apparently from the bridge, and several men approached him.
>
> One of these was Col. Astor, and I heard him say to Capt. Smith: 'Captain, my wife is not in good health. She has gone to bed, and I don't want to get her up unless it is absolutely necessary. What is the situation?'
>
> Capt. Smith replied quietly: 'Col. Astor, you had better get your wife up at once. I fear that we may have to take to the boats.'
>
> Col. Astor never changed expression. He thanked the captain courteously and walked rapidly, but composedly, toward the nearest companionway.

In overhearing this conversation, Frauenthal began to realize that there was some significant danger.[248]

As Astor began to head down to his staterooms, C-17 and C-21, to wake Madeleine, he bumped into Sir Cosmo Duff Gordon. Astor told Sir Cosmo that he was going to get his wife up and dressed, and suggested that Sir Cosmo do the same.[249]

Helen Ostby remembered seeing Captain Smith 'and one or two other officers' coming down the Grand Staircase, apparently just after Frauenthal saw him talking with Astor. She believed that he was on his way 'to explore the ship and see what damage had been done. The officers looked very sober. They didn't stop to talk to the passengers at all.'[250]

In stateroom C-78 on the port side, Daisy Minahan was awakened by the sound of a woman crying in the passage-

way outside. Daisy got up and awakened her brother William, and his wife Lillian. It took them about five minutes to get themselves put together before they turned out of their cabin.[251]

After the collision, Marguerite Frölicher, her father Maximilian and her mother Margaretha had gone up to the Promenade Deck. Young Marguerite was so seasick through the entirety of the voyage that her presence on the deck attracted attention. A Swiss banker who was a friend of her family came up and joked, 'Ah, Miss Frölicher, it takes an iceberg to get you on deck.'[252]

Below, the lights came back on in the stokeholds just as Barrett was returning to Boiler Room No. 5 with lamps. It was still clear of water at the time. Since the firemen had been called up a short while before this, and none were then in No. 5, Barrett was ordered to go get some of them and draw the fires in the boilers. This was necessary because the ship's engines had stopped, and most of her steam-generating plant was still providing steam at high pressure, which in turn was being vented from the funnels far above the ship. He returned with about 15 men, and got to work on this task …[253]

Elsewhere, Assistant Second Steward Joseph Wheat had watched for a few minutes as water came onto G Deck by the Mail Room. He noted that the water 'was rising rapidly'. Then it struck him that it would be a good idea to see if anyone had closed the watertight doors by the Turkish Baths. At the time, he was on F Deck, so he had to cross up to E Deck, where there were no watertight bulkheads, and move aft to the First Class staircase, where he descended to F Deck again.

At the bottom of the stairs, there was a small foyer just aft of watertight bulkhead F. The Swimming Baths were located forward of the bulkhead, while the Turkish Baths were located aft of it. A non-watertight door on the starboard side of the foyer led directly into the Turkish Bath suite, which was nestled against the starboard hull;

a watertight door also led from the forward side of the foyer, and through the bulkhead. It entered upon a corridor which ran along the bulkhead's forward face and out to the starboard side of the ship. On the forward side of that corridor, a non-watertight door led further forward into the Swimming Bath; opposite that door, a second watertight door passed aft, back through the bulkhead and into the Turkish Baths.[254]

Wheat closed the watertight door that led forward through the bulkhead, noting that there did not seem to be any water on F Deck at the time. However, the starboard of the two watertight doors – the one between the Turkish Baths and the Swimming Bath – had to be closed from E Deck, above. So Wheat climbed the stairs again. On E Deck, he met up with Second Steward George Dodd and Turkish Bath Attendant James Crosby. Someone produced the key which operated the watertight door control, and they succeeded in closing that watertight door, as well.[255]

By that time, Lookouts Hogg and Evans had dressed to relieve fellow Lookouts Fleet and Lee. They arrived in the Crow's Nest at about 12:00 a.m. Fleet and Lee were no doubt pleased to have the relief watch turn up a bit early. As Fleet and Lee left the nest, Hogg and Evans would have found that they had little to do, as the ship was stopped.[256]

Fleet and Lee descended the ladder within the Foremast, emerging on C Deck just beneath the Forecastle. Just then, Lookout Symons was looking through the open No. 1 hatchway at water entering that Cargo Hold below. Reginald Lee remembered seeing firemen and greasers coming up to C Deck with their kits, because their quarters were beginning to flood. Lee then joined Symons, and looked down through Hatch No. 1; he also could see the water coming into the hold. At about this time, Symons and Lee heard the Boatswain give an order. Symons recalled it as: 'All hands on the boat deck.' Fleet and Lee followed Symons and the other men up toward the Boat Deck.[257]

Bedroom Steward Etches decided to get up, partially dress, and see if he could figure out what was going on. He saw Third Class passengers 'coming along from forward with their portmanteaus'. Etches left his room, and had gotten 'about 30 yards' down the corridor when he encountered one Steerage passenger who was carrying a good-sized chunk of ice. Etches had no idea who this passenger was, but the man singled Etches out, apparently believing he was a steward who had not believed the ship struck an iceberg, and said to him: 'Will you believe it now?' Then he chucked the ice down on to the deck. After this rather bizarre conversation, of a sort, Etches returned to his quarters and finished dressing.[258]

Saloon Steward William Ward had waited for 'about 20 minutes' from the time of the collision. During that time, 'two or three people' had come by and said that the ship had struck an iceberg. Some even 'brought pieces of ice along in their hands' as proof. Ward's initial impression had been that 'it was the propeller gone'. At about this time, Ward – like Etches – heard steerage passengers coming aft from the bow along Scotland Road, 'carrying life belts with them. Some of them got their grips and packages and had them with them, and some were wet.' Still, he did not think it was anything particularly serious, so he lay there for a little while longer.[259]

Up on deck, Boxhall was carrying out his latest assignment. The Fourth Officer found Pitman awake and dressing at a rather leisurely pace. After stepping out to investigate the vibration that he had felt earlier, the Third Officer had returned to his cabin and lit his pipe, and decided to dress since he had to go on duty soon. When Boxhall came by he told the Third Officer that they had struck an iceberg, and that the Mail Room was flooding. As he moved on, Pitman finished dressing with greater haste.

Boxhall did attempt to wake Fifth Officer Lowe, but the exhausted and groggy Fifth Officer did not completely wake up and get out of bed. Instead, he fell back to sleep for a while longer. When Boxhall went to rouse Lightoller, though, he found him already awake and quietly remarked: 'You know we have struck an iceberg.'

Lightoller responded, 'I know we have struck something.' Then Boxhall told him that the Mail Room was flooding, and Lightoller found that information enough to move him into immediate action, realizing the damage to the ship was significant. Despite the obviously serious nature of the liner's injuries, Lightoller did not conclude that there was any danger of her actually sinking.[260] As Boxhall moved on and closed the door behind him, Lightoller 'slipped into some clothes as quickly as possible, and went out on deck'.[261] When he left his room, he left his watch behind.[262]

Meanwhile, Second Class passenger Sidney Collett had gone to his cabin to put more clothing on. Then he went to Miss Wright, and found that she had already gotten up and was out on the deck.[263]

Harvey and Charlotte Collyer were in their cabin when they heard a rush of people about the decks outside. Although Harvey had shortly before received reassurances that there was no danger, they decided to get up, get their daughter Marjorie up, as well, and find out what was wrong. Mrs Collyer tied her hair back in a ribbon, wrapped young Marjorie in a White Star Line blanket, and they all left their cabin together. Harvey even left his watch on his pillow … they all expected to return to their cabin soon.[264]

Bedroom Steward Alfred Theissinger passed the steps which led down toward the Mail Room. He 'saw water pouring into a room filled with mail bags', which would have been the Sorting Room on G Deck.

At that time, Second Steward Dodd was standing there. He caught sight of Theissinger, and shouted: 'All stewards, call your people. Warn them to go on deck.' Theissinger 'rushed' toward the passengers who were in his care, aft on E Deck.[265]

By then, Archibald Gracie had joined his friend Clinch Smith and a number of other male passengers at the foot of the forward First Class Grand Staircase on A Deck. Smith had informed Gracie that 'an iceberg had struck us'. Then he opened his hand and showed Gracie a piece of ice, 'flat like a watch', and deadpanned that Gracie should take it home for a souvenir. Gracie and the others stood there chatting for a time, getting some details about the collision, and hearing about how someone from the Smoking Room had rushed out in time to spot the iceberg.

Another tidbit of information soon came to Gracie's attention. The Mail Room was flooded, and 'the plucky postal clerks, in two feet of water, were at their posts. They were engaged in transferring to the upper deck, from the ship's post-office, the two hundred bags of registered mail containing four hundred thousand letters.'

It was at about that time that Smith and Gracie 'noticed a list on the floor of the companionway'. This development was somewhat sobering; the situation was obviously serious. However, the two men kept their observation between themselves, not wanting to cause any undue anxiety to others, particularly the ladies who had just begun to appear on the scene. Smith and Gracie promised then and there to 'stick together in the final emergency', helping each other to get through whatever lay ahead. Gracie recalled:

I recall having in my mind's eye at this moment all that I had read and heard in days gone by about shipwrecks, and pictured Smith and myself clinging to an overloaded raft in an open sea with a scarcity of food and water.[266]

The two men parted company, and headed to their respective staterooms to make further preparations.

Meanwhile, Third Officer Pitman had finished dressing and left his cabin. He went out onto the port side Boat Deck, and moved toward the aft quarter, where he came across Sixth Officer Moody and some of the crew uncovering the boats there. When Pitman asked, Moody told him that he had not seen the iceberg, but that there was ice up forward on the Well Deck. From his position inside the enclosed wheelhouse next to Quartermaster Hichens at the time of the collision, Moody would have been unable to see the iceberg as it passed by. Upon hearing the junior officer's news, Pitman decided to investigate for himself.[267]

By that point, Alfred Nourney had made it back topside after having seen the Squash Racquet Court flooding on G Deck. He informed his friends that the *Titanic* was in danger, but nobody believed him. Someone said to him: 'It doesn't matter because the *Titanic* cannot sink.'[268]

When William Sloper finished dressing and started to return to the deck, he noticed that the ship was listing toward the starboard bow. He met Pauline and Dorothy Gibson, as well as Frederic Seward, on the stairs; the quartet went up to the deck together. As they walked forward from the stern, Sloper's heart sank as he observed that 'there was really quite a pitch downward of the deck under our feet'. Just then, someone came by and told them that the Squash Court was filling with water. This news frightened Miss Gibson, despite reassurances from stewards that the watertight doors had been closed and the ship was safe. The group returned to the forward First Class Entrance.[269]

The Hoyts were still on deck, and had not yet returned to their cabin. Not long before, they had asked Dr O'Loughlin if the accident was serious, and he had replied that he didn't know. A 'few minutes afterward', O'Loughlin returned and told Frederick Hoyt that they should return to their stateroom and dress fully. Then the doctor leaned in and whispered to Frederick that the damage was 'serious', and that 'the squash court ... was rapidly filling with water at the time'. By that point, Mrs Hoyt had noticed 'a slight listing to the boat'. The couple then returned to their cabin to dress.[270]

Major Arthur Peuchen had bumped into Harry Molson and chatted for a bit. At this point, Peuchen came across Charles Hays on C Deck. Rather jocularly, he said: 'Mr Hays, have you seen the ice?'

'No,' Hays responded.

'If you care to see it,' Peuchen offered, 'I will take you up on the deck and show it to you.' Peuchen led Hays up to the forward rail on A Deck. It was then that the Major noticed the ship had taken on a list. Suddenly, all traces of levity were gone; the yachtsman knew something was wrong.

'Why, she is listing; she should not do that, the water is perfectly calm, and the boat has stopped.'

Hays confidently replied: 'Oh, I don't know; you can not sink this boat. No matter what we have struck, she is good for 8 or 10 hours.'[271]

The Thayers had been on deck for a while, looking to find more information on the ship's situation. While there, they began to notice not only the ship's list, but the fact that the list was steadily increasing. They also had seen some of the ship's officers, Bruce Ismay and even Thomas Andrews all pass by as these men investigated the damage to the ship. It seems to have been at about this point that Mrs Thayer decided to go below to their staterooms and begin to dress. John and Jack stayed behind on the deck for a little while longer.[272]

Elmer Taylor had also left his cabin to investigate what had happened. After leisurely dressing and leaving his cabin, he ...

... went up through the companionway [referring to the Aft Grand Staircase] adjacent to the restaurant, or Café Parisian, to 'B' Deck.

The orchestra was playing, and many people were sitting at tables playing cards as I passed through. There was scarcely anyone on deck. I said to a sailor, 'Why have we stopped?' 'Struck an iceberg,' he said.

I walked forward, saw nothing peculiar except for crushed ice which had been shivered from the iceberg. Picking up a piece of ice about the size of an egg, I went below, stopped at my cabin, told my wife we struck an iceberg and then went along to Williams' cabin [C-128].

He was sitting up in bed in a dressing gown, reading a book, smoking a huge cigar and sipping a highball which was beside him. 'Well, Williams,' I said, 'we have struck an iceberg and I have brought you a piece of it to put in your highball, so here goes.' Williams asked, 'Is there any cause for alarm?' and I again assured him that this ship was unsinkable.[273]

Taylor chatted with Williams for a few minutes more.

Meanwhile, Isaac Frauenthal had overheard Captain Smith telling John Jacob Astor that they might have to take to the boats, and that he should awaken Mrs Astor. 'From the captain and stewards,' Frauenthal recalled, 'I quickly got an inkling of the peril we were in so I went back to brother Henry's room in a hurry and began pounding on his door again.'

His brother Henry, Isaac recalled, 'had hardly paid attention to the fuss that was beginning all around, people running to and fro, men calling out everywhere, a general confusion of unfamiliar sounds, but finally I made him understand that the *Titanic* had been mortally hurt.'[274]

Dr Henry Frauenthal remembered that both he and his wife had been 'sleeping soundly', and that 'at about twelve o'clock', Isaac came pounding at their cabin door, insisting they get up. Henry was so groggy that he thought he 'had overslept and was late'. He asked what the matter was, and through the door, Isaac told him that something had happened to the boat.

This was enough to get Henry up to go to his cabin door and open it.[275] Isaac informed him that 'he had overheard the captain informing Colonel Astor that something serious had happened to the boat, and advised that everyone put on life preservers, and they were lowering the lifeboats.' This may have been a slight exaggeration of Captain Smith's words to Astor, but Isaac Frauenthal was doubtless desperate to get his brother to wake up and prepare for whatever lay ahead. Henry concluded 'that the trouble was with the machinery', and decided to go up to the Boat Deck to have a look for himself.[276]

Edwin Kimball had been out to see what all the fuss was about. As he returned to his stateroom forward on D Deck, he had seen one of the Mail Clerks head down below, taking the staircase from E Deck down toward the Mail Room and Squash Court. Kimball apparently followed him down to E Deck, for when he saw the Mail Clerk come back up from the Mail Room …

… he had one mail bag in his hands and was wet to the knees. I asked him how bad it was. He seemed very serious and said it was pretty bad and that he would advise the women to dress, as they might have to go on deck, and it would be cold.[277]

Kimball headed back up toward his cabin. On the way, he began to spread the news, almost word for word what the Mail Clerk had told him:

We instructed the other women in our party to dress and everyone else in our corridor, including a number of women who were traveling alone.

In his own cabin, he found that Mrs Kimball had already started dressing. Kimball told her 'to dress warmly, as we probably would be on deck for some time.'[278]

Karl Behr and Helen Newsom had already returned to her parents' room at that point. They were well acquainted with the Kimballs, and this was probably the group that William Kimball remembered instructing to dress. Behr and Helen Newsom agreed, and Behr waited while the Beckwiths and Helen began to dress warmly.[279]

Shortly after their first reassurance that there was no danger, Margaret Swift and Dr Alice Leader had a visitor who told them that they had struck an iceberg, and who held in his hand some of the ice that was 'thrown all along the passageway' under the porthole. At that time, Mrs Swift thought that no one seemed alarmed; the lights were all on, and there were no signs of panic. So she went back to bed, but soon got back up and got dressed 'as a mater of precaution'.[280]

Next door, Mrs Emma Bucknell was dressing in her warmest clothes, as was her maid, Albina Bazzani. Although they had already received reassurances, Emma was not convinced of their accuracy. As they dressed, a man came through the hallways 'crying out that everyone should dress immediately and go on deck'.[281] Emma asked Albina to fasten her gown, and then she grabbed a heavy fur coat and stepped out into the corridor.

Just then, Mrs Bucknell noticed a young woman nearby, telling another young woman that they had struck an iceberg. The second woman replied that it could not be possible.[282] Emma went to the end of the corridor, picked up the pieces of ice that still littered the floor, and then held them out to the two ladies. 'Here is ice. It is an iceberg,' she said. Then she went back inside to her cabin. Just

then, Emma recalled that her maid was becoming slightly unhinged. She 'pleaded' with Emma not to go on deck, and 'cried' that they would 'surely be lost' if they didn't stay in the safety of their room. Emma's reply was firm: the only thing to do was obey orders implicitly and their orders were to proceed immediately to the deck. The last thing she did before leaving the cabin was to take a drink of water. They also took the opportunity to gather up all the valuables that they 'could collect in a hurry'.[283]

Shortly after midnight, Norman and Bertha Chambers reached E Deck forward. Although they were headed toward their cabin, E-8, to fully dress, Mr Chambers 'looked at the starboard end of our passage, where there was the companion leading to the quarters of the mail clerks and farther on to the baggage room and, I believe, the mail-sorting room.' It was at the top of these stairs that the Chambers found 'a couple of mail clerks wet to their knees, who had just come up from below, bringing their registered mail bags. As the door in the bulkhead in the next deck was open,' Mr Chambers was able to 'look directly into the trunk room, which was then filled with water, and was within 18 inches or 2 feet of the deck above [F Deck].'

The Chambers stood there, 'joking about our baggage being completely soaked and about the correspondence which was seen floating about on the top of the water'. Norman Chambers still thought that there was no pressing danger, however, since the water was 'forward of the bulkhead'. He recalled:

While we were standing there three of the ship's officers – I did not notice their rank or department – descended the first companion and looked into the baggage, coming back up immediately, saying that we were not making any more water. This was not an announcement, but merely a remark passed from one to the other.

Then the Chambers returned to their stateroom, only 'a few yards away'. They encountered their Bedroom Steward in the companionway, and he told them that they could go back to bed again, as there was no danger. Mr Chambers thought that they probably could, as well. However, he decided to dress more completely.[284]

Third Officer Pitman was walking forward from the aft port quarter of the Boat Deck, where he had bumped into Sixth Officer Moody. Moody had told Pitman that there was ice on the Well Deck, forward. Pitman was not convinced that there was anything significantly wrong, but headed forward to see for himself. He descended to the Well Deck and saw the ice. Then he headed all the way forward underneath the Forecastle, but could see no sign of damage.[285]

While Pitman was forward, back on the Boat Deck, work was progressing under the watchful eye of Captain Smith's officers. First Officer Murdoch took charge of the starboard side boats. On the port side, Chief Officer Wilde took charge, and Second Officer Lightoller would assist him. At first, with Smith, Pitman and Boxhall occupied elsewhere, Lowe still in his cabin, and Murdoch working on the starboard side, Sixth Officer Moody did not have much assistance in overseeing the preparation of the port boats.

When Lightoller emerged from his cabin onto the Boat Deck, he had found that the noise of escaping steam made it very difficult to communicate with anyone. He met Chief

Officer Wilde right away, just outside the door to the Officers' Quarters, and Wilde ordered him to get the covers off the boats. He asked if all hands had been called, and Wilde replied in the affirmative. Lightoller found that none of the covers had been stripped off the regular lifeboats at that point.[286] There was a lot of labor ahead ...

Elsewhere, Sidney Collett had found Marion Wright. Then he headed back up to the Boat Deck, and saw that the crew was 'getting the lifeboats ready'. He went back down and told 'many women' that the accident was serious, but they did not seem to believe it.[287]

Second Class passenger Lawrence Beesley, still standing on the Boat Deck, noticed the same thing that Collett did ... just as he was about to go back inside he saw 'an officer climb on the last lifeboat on the port side – number 16 – and begin to throw off the cover'. He noticed that not many people seemed to be paying attention to the officer, perhaps Sixth Officer Moody, as he worked. Beesley turned to go below, and noticed something rather unusual:

> As I passed the door to go down, I looked forward again and saw to my surprise an undoubted tilt downwards from the stern to the bows: only a slight slope, which I don't think anyone had noticed, – at any rate, they had not remarked on it. As I went downstairs a confirmation of this tilting forward came in something unusual about the stairs, a curious sense of something out of balance and of not being able to put one's feet down in the right place.

The observant former school teacher concluded that 'some of the front compartments had been filled and weighed her down'. On his way down, Beesley found three ladies who were alarmed that the ship's engines had stopped. 'Oh! why have we stopped?' they asked.

Beesley replied: 'We did stop, but we are now going on again.'

'Oh, no,' one replied. 'I cannot feel the engines as I usually do, or hear them. Listen!'

Beesley listened for a moment with the ladies, and was forced to admit to himself that 'there was no throb audible.' Yet to reassure them that all was well, and perhaps to reassure himself, as well, Beesley took them into a nearby bathroom. Previously he had noticed that the vibration of the ship's engines was most noticeable while in the bath, and so he had them feel the vibrations of the ship's machinery on the side of the bathtub.

These vibrations made everyone feel much better, reassuring them that the ship was once again underway. In reality, however, the ladies were right. The ship's main engines had already been stopped; the vibrations Beesley showed them were almost certainly the result of some of the ship's auxiliary machinery, which was not far from their location on D Deck.

His good deed done for the night, Beesley returned to his cabin. Near his room, he ran across another man who asked him: 'Anything fresh?'

Beesley responded that there wasn't much to tell ... the ship was 'going ahead slowly' and that she was 'down a little at the bows', but he added that he didn't think that it was anything serious. The man then showed him his room mate, lying in his top bunk. Beesley asked if this man was asleep.

'No,' the other man said, laughing as he started to dress, 'he says –'

The aft port lifeboats on the Olympic. Pictured, from right to left, are Boats Nos 10, 12, 14 and 16.

Just then the man in the top berth grunted: 'You don't catch me leaving a warm bed to go up on that cold deck at midnight. I know better than that.'

Beesley suggested lightheartedly that he might as well get up, but the man refused. Beesley went back to his own cabin, put on some underclothes, and settled in to read.[288]

Second Class passenger Benjamin Hart had returned to his wife and daughter in their cabin, and told them that there was nothing to worry about. 'All the men are at the lifeboats, it's only a lifeboat drill,' he said. Esther was thoroughly unconvinced, responding that ship's crews did not hold lifeboat drills in the middle of the night. She was sure that something terrible was wrong with the ship, and eventually she managed to convince her husband of the trouble, as well. The three turned out and headed topside.[289]

Third Class passengers Percival and Florence Thorneycroft had waited another twenty minutes or so from the time their friend had informed them they had struck an iceberg. Only then did the word come down for them to 'get on their lifebelts and go to the second deck'.[290]

Elias and Jamilia Nicola-Yarred had felt the collision in their room in Third Class. Fourteen-year-old Nicola had been concerned by the collision, but her eleven-year-old brother had told her to go back to sleep, that she worried too much. A little while later, an elderly man who had taken a fatherly interest in the siblings during the voyage came into their room. He said very calmly: 'Come out of your cabin and go to the upper deck. Don't bother about taking your belongings for now. You'll get them later.'[291]

Bedroom Steward Alfred Theissinger eventually reached the stretch of cabins which were in his charge.[292] He proceeded to cabin E-67, where Emil and Tillie Taussig were berthed. This cabin was located on the starboard side of E Deck, just astern and outboard of the uptake for the No. 3 funnel. He knocked on the cabin door, and called out: 'You had better put on your lifebelts and rush to the deck.'

Emil Taussig responded from within the cabin: 'Is it as serious as all that?'

'Yes,' Theissinger replied. 'Hurry.'

From within, the steward was sure that he heard Tillie begin to cry, and he also heard her husband reassure her: 'Don't cry. Be brave. All will surely be all right.'

The steward moved across the hall to the door of their daughter's room, E-68. Just as he approached it, 18-year-old Ruth opened the door of her own accord; she had been awakened by 'the uproar'. Theissinger 'urged her to put on a coat; not to stop to dress.' Ruth said that she wanted to dress, but at this, Theissinger put his foot down. 'To hell with the clothes. Slip into this great coat. If you stop to dress you'll drown.' He made sure to adjust her lifebelt properly, and then he moved on to other cabins in his section.[293]

Elsewhere, Sir Cosmo Duff Gordon returned to his wife, Lucy, after being gone for about 'ten minutes'. Lucy had needed to beg him to go out and find out what the trouble was, a trip which he had set off on most unwillingly. However, it seemed that he had found something serious while he was gone; he was 'looking rather grave' as he came in. He said: 'I have just been up on the bridge and seen Colonel Astor. He told me that he was going to ask his wife to dress, and I think that you had better do the same.' He also informed her that they had 'hit some ice, apparently a big berg, but that there seemed to be no danger'. Lady Duff Gordon began to look for the warmest clothes that she could possibly find so that she could begin to dress.[294]

May Futrelle and Irene Harris had dressed while their husbands were out on deck investigating the situation. While the men were gone, another passenger came by, a young man who was a friend of the Harrises. He came into the cabin with the two ladies, and he looked pale. May asked him to tell them what had happened.

'I don't believe it's serious,' he said, 'but we seem to have brushed against an iceberg.'

Just then Jacques and Henry returned. They affirmed that they had heard the iceberg story. However, they also said that they had heard that the officers had closed the watertight doors, and done an investigation of everything below, and that they had been told there was no danger.[295]

Mrs Swift and Dr Leader had decided to dress 'as a matter of precaution'. Once they were decent, they 'went out into the passageway'. There, 'one of the officers' told them: 'We've struck a berg Madame, but there is no danger.'[296]

When Emma Bucknell and her maid Albina Bazzani finished dressing, they went up on deck, and found that there was 'no excitement' there among the passengers. 'They were in groups talking to one another.' She saw Colonel John Astor and his wife Madeleine, the Wideners, and a number of others talking about the collision with 'what was said to have been a submerged iceberg'.

However, Emma knew that it couldn't have been a submerged berg they had collided with, as there was too much ice in the hallways by the porthole. She then heard another woman passenger 'declare that it had been higher than deck D', which fitted very well with Emma's own sighting of the berg.

Emma 'stayed for a time on the starboard side, where the ship had struck. A man passing through declared that the bow had only been slightly damaged and that they were then lowering the bulkhead doors.'[297]

Margaret Brown had gotten up twice since the collision, and each time had found nothing particularly worrisome. It was probably at about this time, however, that she decided to get up and look out into the corridor again. When she did, she found a man who looked absolutely terrified.

He told her to get her lifebelt before he moved on. Margaret grabbed all of the lifebelts in her room, put on a fur coat, placed a silk capote over her head, and then hurriedly ascended to the Promenade Deck.[298]

When Daisy Minahan, her brother William and his wife Lillian arrived on deck, they found that the ship was listing. 'The frightful slant of the deck toward the bow of the boat gave us our first thought of danger,' she recalled.[299]

Below deck, Captain Smith was on his own inspection tour. Stewardess Annie Robinson saw him on E Deck, heading towards the Mail Room with a mail clerk and Chief Purser Hugh McElroy. Smith must have met Thomas Andrews there, for at around 12:10 a.m., Robinson saw the two men come back from the Mail Room together. She overheard Andrews telling the Captain: 'Well, three have gone already, Captain,' undoubtedly a reference to the first three watertight compartments. Her curiosity piqued, Robinson went to see what they had been looking at, and saw water within six steps of coming onto E Deck, near the stairs leading down to the Mail Room.[300]

Following this, Captain Smith and Andrews separated, with Smith heading back up to the Bridge, while Andrews stayed below to continue his inspection. At that point, it looked like a bad situation, to be sure, but not one that seemed uncontrollable. In fact, previously, the 'officers' inspecting the Mail Room were overheard saying something to the effect that 'we were not making any more water.'[301]

Captain Smith did not stay below long, and Saloon Steward Mackay saw him come back up the working staircase from below, and head towards the upper decks.[302] What Smith saw or was told during his first trips below is unknown, but between that knowledge, and the earlier reports that the Carpenter and the mail clerk had given him on the Bridge, he would have known that there was rather serious flooding below. While none of this information would necessarily have meant that the ship was actually in danger of sinking, he would have known that the situation was very serious.

Antoinette Flegenheim had gone up on deck quickly after the collision. She had only paused long enough to put on a pair of stockings and slippers. When she had arrived topside, 'there were comparatively few people there. There was no confusion, and as there did not seem to be anything to become excited over, no one was excited.' However, after a little while, she remembered that the order came through for passengers to board the lifeboats. Even so, there seemed no reason for excitement, and *Titanic* seemed safe for hours yet. At this point, she decided to head back down to her cabin and dress fully – and warmly – so that she would be fully prepared 'for the emergency if it came'. Just then, 'an officer detained' her, and told her that she had to get into the boats without going back below.[303]

In the Saloon Stewards' Quarters on the port side of E Deck, Frederick Dent Ray was just getting back to sleep. He estimated roughly that it was somewhere 'around about 12 o'clock' when he was suddenly brought back to consciousness. It was 'the saloon steward', apparently a reference to First Dining Saloon Steward William Moss.[304] He was followed in short order by 'Mr Dodd, the second steward'. They told everyone to get up and head for the lifeboats. Ray began to dress.[305]

William Moss was also spotted by Saloon Steward William Ward. Moss told Ward and those in the room that they 'were all to go on deck', and that they should 'put on some warm clothing' as they were 'liable to be there some time'. At that, 'most everybody' in the Ward's Glory Hole got up and began to dress. Ward was still not convinced that anything was significantly wrong.[306]

Steward Nichols had stayed up for a while after the collision talking to his mates. After this, Nichols recalled that 'the second steward in charge of our cabin came in and gave us the orders to report upon deck. That meant that we were to report to the positions assigned to us in the life boat drill.' Nichols' assigned lifeboat was No. 15, and he began to head up to the Boat Deck.[307]

Around this time, First Class Stewardess Violet Jessop had come back in from the Boat Deck, where she had seen crewmen working at the lifeboats; she was looking for something to throw over her shoulders, since it was quite cold outside. On her way back up, she ran into a group of officers, which included Captain Smith and Chief Purser McElroy – fresh from their inspection of the damage – along with Bruce Ismay, and Doctor O'Loughlin. They smiled at her, and she waved back. They did not seem overly concerned about anything at that point. She turned and ran into 21-year-old Scottish violinist John 'Jock' Hume, and the bandleader, Wallace Hartley. Hartley's 'crowd' – the other members of the ship's band – was close in tow, all holding their instruments. Hume smiled as he passed Jessop, and he said: 'Just going to give them a tune to cheer things up a bit.' Then he passed her and continued up.[308]

Charles and Annie Stengel had walked around the Boat Deck for a while, noticing only a few people were up and about. Then they turned and went back into the Entrance, and began descending to the Promenade Deck. Just then, they saw Captain Smith coming up. Charles Stengel's impression of the Captain's emotions was a bit different from that of Violet Jessop. He recalled that the Captain showed 'a very serious and a very grave face'. Stengel turned to his wife and said: 'This is a very serious matter, I believe.' They also noticed a couple, whom Charles Stengel thought was the Wideners, following the Captain up the stairs. He assumed they were returning to their staterooms.[309]

12:15 a.m.–12:25 a.m.

As Third Officer Pitman was headed aft from the extremity of the Forecastle, but before he emerged onto the Well Deck, he noticed 'a whole crowd' of firemen coming up from below with their kits. This was an unusual development. 'What is the matter?' he asked the men.

'The water is coming in our place,' they replied.

Above: *The Boat Deck level of the* Olympic's *First Class Entrance, looking forward and to starboard. It was at the top of* Titanic's *nearly identical twin that Bruce Ismay encountered Chief Engineer Joseph Bell. The space grew quite crowded as passengers began to arrive on the decks to investigate the collision, and it was in this room's near twin that they watched through the Palladian windows as the lifeboats were prepared on the Boat Deck.*

Above left: *First Class passenger Lucy Noël Martha, the Countess of Rothes.*

Above right: *One of Olympic's crewmen dons a lifebelt. He is standing just in front of the raised roof over the First Class Smoking Room on the port side.*

'That is funny,' Pitman replied. Then he went to the No. 1 hatch, just near the Seamens' Mess. There he – like Symons and a number of others before him – was able to look down and see water flooding the hold. He thought that it was 'quite a little stream, both sides of the hatch', and that it was coming 'mostly from the starboard side'. At this, Pitman turned and began to head back up to the Boat Deck.[310]

Captain Smith had arrived back on the Bridge sometime around 12:12 a.m. At around 12:15 a.m., Quartermaster Hichens, still standing at the ship's helm, overheard Smith give the order to swing out the lifeboats, and to begin getting the passengers up on deck with lifebelts on.[311] This was another proactive measure on Smith's part, as nobody yet knew that the ship was sinking.

It seems likely that Smith worked out the ship's approximate position, using dead reckoning, at about this time.[312] After giving the order to swing out the boats and begin getting passengers on deck, the Captain next headed off to the Marconi room. With some rather weighty information in hand, but without all the details at his disposal, the Captain was leaving nothing to chance. When he arrived there, he put his head in the cabin and said that they had struck an iceberg, and that an inspection was then being made to tell 'what it had done for' the ship. 'You better get ready to send out a call for assistance. But don't send it until I tell you.' Then he was gone ... [313]

By that point, Major Arthur Peuchen had proceeded to the First Class Entrance and was waiting by the Grand Staircase for '10 minutes or more' when he noticed 'ladies and gentlemen all coming in off of the deck looking very serious'. He spied Thomson Beattie, and asked him: 'What is the matter?'

Beattie replied: 'Why the order is for life belts and boats.'

Peuchen was stunned, hardly believing his ears. 'Will you tell Mr Ross?' he asked.

Beattie replied: 'Yes; I will go and see Mr Ross.'

Peuchen headed down the Grand Staircase to return to his own cabin. He was then in evening dress, and did not feel that his attire was equal to the frigid cold on the deck.[314]

'Shortly after' Charles and Annie Stengel had seen Captain Smith ascending the Grand Staircase with a 'very serious and a very grave face', the orders came through 'to have the passengers all put on life preservers'. The couple left and returned to their cabin.[315]

Gladys Cherry and the Countess of Rothes had stayed up on deck. They were talking about perhaps returning to bed when Captain Smith came by, appearing rather suddenly. He said: 'I don't want to frighten anyone, but will you all go quietly and put on your life belts and go up on the top deck?' The two ladies, along with a number of others nearby, did as they were asked without rushing and with the utmost calmness.[316]

Karl Behr was just then proceeding up the stairs from D Deck. He was with the Kimballs, and as his party and he were headed up the stairs, they ran across Captain Smith. Smith was 'on the main stairways and he was telling everyone to put on life belts'.[317]

Eleanor Cassebeer had gone up on deck quickly after the collision, not having taken the time to dress. She had bumped into a then-optimistic Thomas Andrews, who had told her that the ship could be cut into three parts and not sink; while he had gone below and was inspecting the damage, Cassebeer and Harry Anderson had stayed on the deck, and then proceeded to the First Class Entrance. While she and Anderson sat there, however, Eleanor noticed a change in the general mood ...

Chief Purser McElroy, in tandem with a number of his men, approached and 'started to go among the passengers ordering them to go below and put on warm clothing and be prepared to embark in the lifeboats'. He also mentioned that they should put on their lifebelts, and should bring all of the blankets in their cabins up to the Boat Deck with them. Harry Anderson asked Eleanor if she was frightened, and she replied that she was not. Then they parted, agreeing to meet back up right where they were. Eleanor 'hurried below' to her cabin to get dressed.[318]

It seems that right after Mrs Cassebeer spotted Chief Purser McElroy, McElroy started to go below via the Grand Staircase. Assistant Second Steward Joseph Wheat was then coming up the same stairs from E Deck to C Deck. Before he reached the C Deck landing, he saw McElroy 'looking over the banisters'. When McElroy spotted Wheat, the Purser told him 'to get the men up and get all lifebelts and all passengers'. Wheat turned back around and headed below to help rouse all of the stewards; when he got there, however, he found most of them were already awake, so he turned around and headed back up, pitching into the effort to help passengers get dressed and get their lifebelts on.[319]

Meanwhile, John and Jack Thayer were still on deck when they heard the stewards passing word, at 'about 12:15', for 'every one to get fully clothed and put on life preservers, which were in each stateroom'. Jack was still in his pajamas with a coat over them. He and his father descended to their rooms, where they found Marian Thayer and her maid, Margaret Fleming, already fully dressed. Jack 'hurried' into his own clothes, dressing warmly. Then they all put on their lifebelts.[320]

William Sloper heard the order for everyone to get their lifebelts on as he stood with Pauline and Dorothy Gibson and Frederic Seward in the First Class Entrance. As he watched people near him tying on their lifebelts, Sloper was consumed with an indescribable and horrible feeling. They headed below to get their belts from their respective rooms.[321]

Shortly after 'one of the officers' had come through and informed Mrs Swift and Dr Leader that everything was safe, he returned. This time, he advised them to go on deck and get into the lifeboats. He added, however: 'It is simply to be on the safe side.'[322]

Edwin Kimball and his wife had taken the time to dress warmly. When they eventually left their cabin, they still felt that everything was all right. Just a few steps on, however …

… a young lady of our party came back from the upper deck and we asked her what was going on up there. She said the order had been given to put on the life belts. We returned to our staterooms, which were only a few feet away, got our life belts and notified all the women in the corridor to do the same and come with us. None of us knew how to put on the belts, but I saw an officer in the companionway and he showed us how to put them on, telling us that there was no danger and that everyone would be all right.[323]

Karl Behr, the Beckwiths, and Helen Newsom joined the Kimballs, apparently in the hallway. Behr remembered that they put their lifebelts on calmly.[324]

Henry Harris and Jacques Futrelle had just returned to the Harris's cabin from their trip up on deck to investigate what had happened. Upon returning, they explained to the ladies what they had heard. Just then, Harris came across someone in the hallway outside their cabin. May Futrelle thought he might have been an officer. The two men conversed in low tones. She couldn't hear what the officer told Harris. However, she did hear Harris respond with the word, 'Really?' in a tone that she did not like.

Then Harris returned to the room. May noticed he had gone pale. He said: 'I think you'd better get over to your own cabin and dress. I don't like the looks of this very well.'

May Futrelle was frightened, and had scarcely risen from the bed when she heard knocking on cabin doors down the corridor, a sound which was coming steadily nearer. As she opened the door, she saw a steward in the opposite entry call out: 'Every one put on life-preservers and come on deck.'

As May crossed the corridor to their own room, she saw 'men rushing down the passageway trying on life-preservers'. Her inward 'terror seemed to grow'. Jacques tried to reassure her that all of this was just a precaution, and she wanted to believe him, but she was not entirely sure.[325]

Meanwhile, Colonel Archibald Gracie had returned to his stateroom and packed his bags. Then he had put on his long Newmarket overcoat, which reached below his knees, to ward off the frigid cold outside. This accomplished, he left his cabin and headed back up toward the First Class Entrance forward. As he came into the Entrance from the corridor, he spied Bruce Ismay standing next to a ship's officer – perhaps one of the very men that Violet Jessop had just seen standing with the Captain and Ismay. Gracie noticed that Ismay was smiling serenely. By this point, the well-known Chairman of the White Star Line knew that the ship was seriously damaged; one can only conceive that his unruffled smile was the putting on of a brave face for the sake of other passengers.

Incongruous to this rather reassuring sight, however, Gracie noticed something else, and something that only served to confirm his 'worst fears'. He saw that 'men and women were slipping on life-preservers, the stewards assisting in adjusting them. Steward Cullen insisted upon my

returning to my stateroom for mine.' Gracie headed back down to his cabin yet again.[326]

Earlier, Dr Henry Frauenthal had been awakened out of a deep sleep by his brother. Now convinced that something wasn't quite right, he had gone up to investigate matters. Upon reaching the Boat Deck, he noticed that 'there were a few people there, but no confusion'. He saw the crew lowering the boats down, and decided to go below and get his wife ready for whatever lay ahead.[327]

Within minutes of arriving on the Promenade Deck, young Marguerite Frölicher succumbed to another bout of violent seasickness. Her father was furious with her, pointing out that she couldn't be sick at a time like that. The young girl's response, fed by the miserable way she had felt for so many days, was equally tart: 'I don't care, I'm going back to my cabin.' Then she started off for their B Deck cabin, and her parents followed after her.

When they reached B Deck, they found a stewardess standing in the hall. Maximilian Frölicher-Stehli paused to ask her if there was any danger. The English stewardess replied: 'Yes, sir, there is. Take your lifejackets and go to the boat deck.'[328]

John Snyder had, at his wife's request, made one trip out on deck to investigate the situation. Reassured by crew members that nothing was wrong, he returned to his wife, who told him to go back out and make sure they were really safe. A second trip out on deck ensued, after which he returned to his cabin with further reassurance that nothing was wrong. Again Nelle sent him out to investigate the situation, and finally he returned to his room, B-45, with a third reassurance that 'nothing serious had happened'. This time, enough was enough. Just as he was preparing to climb back into bed, 'a steward came running along the aisle telling everyone not to be alarmed but to dress hurriedly and go on deck.' The couple began to dress.[329]

French singer Madame Léontine Aubart and her maid Emma Marie Sägesser had rushed on deck in their nightclothes after the collision. They took nothing with them; back in the cabin, Madame Aubart – mistress of Benjamin Guggenheim – had left many valuables, an expensive Paris wardrobe, and 'jewels worth £4,000'. As they passed up on deck, they were assisted into lifebelts.[330]

Steward Henry Etches turned out of his E Deck quarters and began heading up on deck. On the way, he met Steward Stone, who was the one of the E Deck Bedroom Stewards.[331] Etches asked Stone: 'What is the time?'

Stone replied: 'Never mind about that; there is something else for you to do. I saw them pull up bags of mail, and the water running out of the bottom of them.'

Just then, the steward who was to relieve Stone called out to him, and Etches left Stone and the other steward behind so that he could proceed topside. His first thought was apparently to stop by the stateroom of one of his charges, Benjamin Guggenheim, in stateroom B-84. He awoke Guggenheim and his valet, Victor Giglio, and told them to get dressed, but he told them that he would return, and that there was plenty of time. Then, perhaps because he was worried about being late to report for his night watch on A Deck, he left to find the steward he was supposed to relieve.[332]

Philipp Mock remembered 'a man' passing among the passengers, 'notifying them to put on life preservers'. His sister Emma remembered the same man as a 'tall, dark figure', and remembered his exact words as: 'Get on your life preservers right away.' This order surprised both Mock and Emma, but they started downstairs to get theirs. Emma recalled seeing 'pale-looking, silent stewards' putting life preservers on passengers. Mock remembered that 'there was no indication of uneasiness', and indeed many of the passengers were commenting humorously 'on the oddity of the figures that their fellow passengers made with the life preservers around their bodies'.[333]

By that time, Edith Rosenbaum had returned to her cabin and undressed for bed again. She was about to climb under the covers when there came a knock on her door. She opened it, and discovered that it was a man she had known in Cannes. 'There's an order to put on lifebelts,' he said. 'I didn't think you'd heard.'

'What in the world for?' Edith asked.

'I haven't an idea,' he replied.

Miss Rosenbaum closed the door, 'wondering why people in their right minds would choose such a ridiculous hour to hold some sort of silly boat drill'. She pulled off her nightgown and 'slipped on a dress, over absolutely nothing'. Then she wrapped a fur coat about her, took one of the lifebelts from her room, and slung it over her arm. She started off for the Lounge, amidships on the same deck.

As she walked, she ran across her Bedroom Steward, Robert Wareham, 'who came running toward me down the carpeted hall'. He was 'usually the picture of British correctness and reserve,' but seemed more like an 'agitated mother hen' as he said: 'Thank God you're here, Miss.'

Edith was distressed at this whole exercise. 'Well, Wareham,' she lit in to him, 'let me tell you what I think about your ridiculous British regulations. Imagine getting people ...' Her words choked off in mid-sentence. She thought she had caught sight of something deep in Wareham's eyes, and that his voice sounded unusual. 'What's the matter, Wareham? Is there really any danger?'

Wareham began helping her into her lifebelt. 'Danger, Miss? It's a rule of the Board of Trade that even in the threat of danger lifebelts will be donned by the passengers. Not that I think this ship can sink,' he added. 'She's an unsinkable ship. Everybody knows that.' Then he allowed, 'But if she does go down, I'm sure we can cheat the drink for about 48 hours.'

Edith Rosenbaum suddenly thought about the 'trunkloads' of Paris fashions she had in the hold. 'If the Titanic sinks, will they transfer the luggage?'

By this point, Wareham had finished with the last strap on her belt. 'Miss,' he said solemnly, 'if I were you, I'd go back to your room and kiss your lovely things goodbye.'

'Then you think this boat is going to sink, Wareham?'

'No one thinks anything at a time like this,' Wareham dodged. 'We can only hope – and pray.'

Miss Rosenbaum thought of the toy pig which her mother had given her which was back in her cabin. When the pig's tail was turned, a music box inside played Maxixe. She told Wareham where it was in her cabin, and he agreed to bring it to her in the Lounge.

When Edith Rosenbaum reached the Lounge, she realized that people were smiling. She began to feel better when she saw 'that few shared Wareham's apprehensions', and recalled:

The lounge filled with passengers in various stages of undress, many of them indignant at being routed out of bed after midnight. I listened to Col. Washington Roebling, the builder of the Brooklyn Bridge [sic].[334] 'Whatever the trouble is,' he said, 'I

doubt there's any real emergency. The Titanic has 15 watertight bulkheads which make her unsinkable. A leak might slow her speed a few knots, but it wouldn't do much more than that.'

Eventually Bedroom Steward Wareham caught up with Miss Rosenbaum in the Lounge. He gave her the little mascot pig which she had treasured so dearly.[335]

Alfred Nourney had taken the opportunity to dash off a few lines to his mother, and then he returned to his cabin. Once there, he changed from his evening dress into other clothes, remembering to don a sweater and a vest for protection from the cold; he put his lifebelt on, as well. Then he packed a little food and a bottle of whiskey, and headed back off toward the upper decks.[336]

William and Alice Silvey had gone up on deck shortly after the collision. There, they had been advised to return to their cabins for warmer clothing. They had done so, and while below Mrs Silvey had gathered up her valuables. Her husband tucked a 'nice, red apple' into her pocket without her knowledge. However, they did not bring their lifebelts with them when they left. When they returned to the deck, they were asked to return to their cabin yet again for their lifebelts.[337]

Twenty-two-year-old Helen Ostby remembered that it had been 'a good part of an hour' from the time of the collision until word came for everyone to get their lifebelts on. She and her father went down to their staterooms to follow the order. She thought that the lifebelts 'were very awkward to get on, since there had been no boat drill and nobody had even thought of trying on the lifejackets'. However, she recalled that the stewards were very helpful in getting them into the lifebelts.[338]

While Norman Chambers dressed, his wife stood in the doorway to their cabin, anxious to hear of any further developments. Mr Chambers still did not believe there was any great danger, but he did take the time to retrieve their valuables after he dressed. It wasn't long before she heard a passenger come down and pass by, saying that orders had been given for passengers to get their lifebelts on and proceed on deck. Mrs Chambers passed this disturbing tidbit on to her husband, who was already fully clothed and had his heavy overcoat on, with 'certain necessities' placed into the pockets.

Chambers poked his nose out into the passageway just in time to see their Bedroom Steward coming down the hallway – the same steward who had shortly before said that they could return to bed. He asked the steward if this rumor about needing to don lifebelts really was true, and the steward confirmed it.

Bertha Chambers was 'rather alarmed', but had the presence of mind to pick up a lifebelt for herself. Norman Chambers opened their steamer trunk and grabbed 'a small pocket compass'. Then, sending his wife ahead, he opened his bag and pocketed his automatic pistol. He followed immediately after her, and together the couple started up the stairs for the deck.[339]

Second Class passenger Dagmar Bryhl had already gone up with her fiancé Ingvar to investigate the situation. Told that there was no danger, however, she had returned to bed. After a short time, her fiancé returned to her door, knocking and yelling: 'Get up, Dagmar, we are in danger! I don't care what the ship's officers say, I tell you we are in danger of our lives. The boat is sinking!'

Far left: *Third Class passenger Rhoda Abbott.*

Left: *Third Class passenger Rossmore Abbott.*

Dagmar again got out of bed, put on her skirt and coat, and ran up on deck. As they began to interact with some of the others around, she remembered that someone told them that the ship had hit an iceberg. At some point, the couple ran across Dagmar's brother Kurt.[340]

Third Class passenger Emily Badman had returned to her cabin to dress, and to put on a lifebelt, on the advice of a fellow Third Class passenger. However, she 'took the whole thing as a joke', and even put her heavy coat over the lifebelt so that no one could see that she was wearing it. Next she turned out and went back up to meet her friend. The pair then hurried up to 'one of the upper decks'.[341]

An alarmed Rhoda Abbott had sent her son Eugene on deck after the collision to find out what had happened. He returned and told her that people were putting on lifebelts. The family then got up and began to dress fully. Once they were dressed, they headed up on deck.[342]

Not far away from Rhoda Abbott, Amy Stanley had returned to her cabin, where Elizabeth Dowdell and Virginia Emanuel were in bed. While on deck, Amy had received assurances that everything was all right, and had been told to go back to bed, but she was not about to go back to sleep. Then someone, probably a steward, came down their hallway, knocking on the doors and advising passengers to get up. 'Get hold of a life belt, ladies,' Elizabeth heard him say.

Another voice asked the man: 'Is there any danger?'

Elizabeth heard the response: 'I fear there is, madam.'

This was quite enough. She got up out of bed and started to dress Virginia. Amy helped in the effort. However, Elizabeth did not rush, as she did not think that the situation was serious. 'I firmly believed the *Titanic* was unsinkable', she later said. Young Virginia was dressed in her outfit from Sunday, and Elizabeth made sure to put on a heavy gray sweater in addition to her other things. Then she and Amy turned out of the cabin, with young Virginia in tow.[343]

Laura Cribb and her father John had gone on deck together to talk to some of their fellow passengers. She remembered:

> My father turned to me and said, 'We will probably have to go out in the lifeboats for a half hour or so as we have had an accident and they want to lessen the weight of the ship ...'

She also remembered that the 'captain and some officers came on deck shouting, "Women and children must get lifebelts on at once, then on deck." ' Laura accordingly returned to her cabin and got her lifebelt, and then went to meet her father again.[344]

Lady Lucy Duff Gordon was in her A Deck stateroom dressing in the warmest clothes that she could find. Before long her secretary, Laura Francatelli, veritably burst into her room, nearly hysterical. She was wearing only her nightclothes, a sweater and a long wool motoring coat. She had a cabin amidships on E Deck, and told her employers that she had seen water in the corridor as she had come up. 'And they are taking the covers off the lifeboats on deck,' she added.

This news upset Lucy greatly, but her husband told them to remain calm, and tried to keep them focused by making jokes about how terrible the two ladies looked in such a hodgepodge of clothing. Lucy apparently gave up on taking the time to dress warmly. She had on her nightdress and silk kimono. She put a scarf over her head, and then a squirrel-fur coat over the jumbled ensemble.

Just then a steward knocked on the door. 'Sorry to alarm you, Madam, but the Captain's orders are that all passengers are to put on lifebelts.' Lucy recalled that the steward 'laughed and joked' as he helped them to put on their lifebelts. Then they followed him out into the corridor, Lucy snatching her handbag up on the way out. She took a last look around her ...

> ... lovely, little room, with its beautiful lace quilt, and pink cushions and photographs all around, and with a big basket of lilies of the valley that my 'Lucile girls' had given me when I left Paris, on the table. It all looked so homely and pretty, just like a bedroom on land, that it did not seem possible there could be any danger.

Then she closed the door. Still left behind in the cabin were all of Lucy's jewels and pearls. The trio went aft, toward the First Class Entrance and Grand Staircase. There they found a throng of people; the group was noisy, obviously uneasy, but everyone was trying to reassure themselves with chatting, joking and laughing. They went to move up to the Boat Deck level, but found a large crowd at the top of the stairs.[345]

Colonel Gracie had returned to his room, C-51 on the starboard side. Once there, he grabbed the two lifebelts provided, and Steward Cullen fastened one of them on him. Then he brought the other one with him so that it could be used by someone else. Gracie next headed up toward the Promenade Deck.[346]

At about 12:15 a.m. or so, orders were passed down from the Boat Deck to begin provisioning the lifeboats. The boats already had hard biscuits and water in them, but Chief Baker Charles Joughin sent thirteen men up on deck with four surplus loaves of bread apiece, or roughly '40 pounds of bread each'; then he left the bakery and headed below to his room for a drink.[347]

At about 12:20 a.m., Third Officer Pitman joined First Officer Murdoch in the work on the starboard side lifeboats. Pitman had already seen the ice on the forward Well Deck, as well as water flooding into the holds through the hatch forward. These things had been enough to convince the Third Officer that the situation was very serious. When Pitman arrived, Murdoch ordered him to start working on Boat No. 5; at that point, the men had just started to strip the canvas cover off that boat, and Pitman dug into the task at hand.[348]

Along both sides of the Boat Deck, the men were hard at work: covers were torn off of boats, grips holding the lifeboats in their positions on the deck were released, and cranking handles were turned and turned, swinging the davit arms out into their extended position some sixty feet – no, not quite that much now for the forward boats as the bow began to settle – above the black, beckoning

Right: *Chief Baker Charles Joughin.*

Far right: *Crewmen work on Olympic's starboard Boat Deck. The view looks aft from the vicinity of the crew staircase down to the Promenade Deck. On the deck, closest to the photographer on the left, is Collapsible C. To the left, Emergency Boat No. 1 has been swung out in over the bulwark rail. Aft of No. 1, receding into the distance, are Boats Nos 3, 5 and 7. A crewman works to remove the cover of Boat No. 5. On the deck in the foreground is a collapsible that was not present on* Titanic. *The photo gives a good idea of the scene on* Titanic's *Boat Deck shortly after midnight.*

Interestingly, the davit arms which shared a single frame – in other words, all sets situated between lifeboats – could only be swung out one at a time. This was because there was only a single shared crank for turning the two arms to each set out; a switching lever on the frame would have allowed the crewman operating the crank to select which davit to turn out. However, both could not be cranked out simultaneously.

sea. There was still no order to load the lifeboats, but the officers were going to be sure that if it was necessary for them to do so, the boats would be ready. Second Officer Lightoller recalled of the effort on the port side, which had been hampered by the racket of venting steam:

It was an utter impossibility to convey an order by word of mouth; speech was useless, but a tap on the shoulder and an indication with the hand, dark though it was, was quite sufficient to set the men about the different jobs, clearing away the boat coves, hauling tight the falls and coiling them down on deck, clear and ready for lowering.

The passengers by this time were beginning to flock up on the boat deck, with anxious faces, the appalling din only adding to their anxiety in a situation already terrifying enough in all conscience. In fact it was a marvel how they ever managed to keep their heads at all. All one could do was to give them a cheery smile of encouragement, and hope that the infernal roar would soon stop. My boats were all along the port side, and by the time I had got my Watch well employed, stripping the covers and coiling down, it became obvious to me that the ship was settling ... Soon the Bosun's Mate came to me and indicated with a wave of his hand that the job I had set him of clearing away was pretty well completed. I nodded, and indicated by a motion of my hand for him to swing out ...

By the time all the boats were swung out she was well down forward, and the water was practically level with the main deck [E]. Even so I still had no thought that she was actually going to founder. There had been no chance or time to make enquiries, but I figured up in my own mind that she had probably struck the berg a glancing blow with the bluff of the bow and opened up one or perhaps two of the forward compartments, which were filling and putting her down by the head; also that she would go so far, until she balanced her buoyancy,

and there she would remain. Bulkheads were all new and sound and should be able to carry the pressure, and there was no reason to suppose they would not be equal to their task.[349]

However comfortable Lightoller was in his estimation of the ship's overall safety, Thomas Andrews was even then below deck. As he assessed the extent of the damage, a disturbing picture was beginning to emerge for the man who had helped to design and construct the great ship.

On his way down to his cabin, C-88, Dr Henry Frauenthal passed Harry Widener, who was in stateroom C-80. As he passed ...

... I informed him that I had learned the boat was in danger, but he said that it was ridiculous. This answer probably describes the mental state of nearly everyone on the boat, thinking that it was impossible for anything serious to happen to this paragon of modern ship architecture. I returned to my cabin, and insisted on my wife putting a life preserver on.[350]

Herbert and Carrie Chaffee had gone on deck after dressing leisurely. They found no excitement among the passengers there, Mrs Chaffee recalled. However, she thought that the crew was completely disorganized as they worked. The couple was soon instructed to put on their lifebelts, and they headed back below.[351]

Doctor Washington Dodge had returned to his stateroom, A-34, after seeing ice on the forward Well Deck. He had explained everything that he had seen and heard to his wife, but noticed that the ship was still stationary. It was clear that something was wrong, so he left their cabin for a third time. On this trip, he found their Bedroom Steward standing in the center of the First Class Entrance. Dodge asked the steward if he had heard anything, and the steward replied that 'the order had just come down' for all passengers to don their lifebelts. Dodge asked the steward 'if he really meant it', perhaps thinking it was some sort of joke. However, the steward replied that he really did mean what he had said. The steward's 'manner' suggested to Dodge that the order really had been given. The doctor 'sprang' to his stateroom door, just a few steps away, and told his wife that she needed to dress warmly. It was at that point that they roused their son, young Washington Dodge, Jr.[352]

Above: *Board of Trade Surveyors and crewmen prepare one of* Olympic's *lifeboats.*

Below: *Crewmen on the* Olympic *prepare Boat No. 13, working with a block and tackle.*

Saloon Steward Frederick Dent Ray and a number of other Saloon Stewards had been awakened and told to head to the lifeboats. Ray had dressed, and had even taken the time to put on his lifebelt. Then he left his quarters, went aft along Scotland Road, and encountered about twenty others waiting to head up 'the back stairway'. He patiently waited his turn, and then headed up the stairs to C Deck. There he bumped into Second Steward Dodd. Dodd asked Ray to get a lifebelt for him, so Ray set off in search for one.[353]

Norman and Bertha Chambers climbed the forward First Class staircase, 'passing, at the various landings, people who did not appear to be particularly frightened', until they arrived on the Promenade Deck. Then they went to the port side, and not long afterwards they bumped into the Deck Steward. They joked with him 'about opening his little office room', and managed to procure their two steamer rugs.[354]

After coming up from Benjamin Guggenheim's cabin, Steward Etches went forward on A Deck to talk to the steward he was supposed to relieve at midnight. He found the steward busily assisting passengers; most of the cabin doors were open at the time. Etches asked the other steward: 'Have you called all of your people?' The steward replied: 'Yes, but I can't get them to dress.' Etches noticed that many of the passengers were, indeed, standing in the corridors only 'partly dressed'. Since this steward was hard at work where Etches was due to come on duty for the night watch, Etches told the other steward that he was going to head down to his own regular section of passengers. In addition to returning as promised to help Mr Guggenheim, there were others in his section that he had to see to.[355]

Sidney Collett had been trying to tell people that the accident was rather serious, as he had seen men working at the lifeboats. However, no one had really believed him. Not long afterwards, however, he saw people putting their lifebelts on. Word was beginning to spread that the situation was rather serious, after all.[356]

Frederick and Jane Hoyt had gone back to their cabin, and they 'both dressed as warmly as possible'. When they left the deck, they had not heard any order for passengers to don their lifebelts. However, Jane Hoyt recalled that 'a man came up to us just as we were leaving the stateroom and asked us if we had an extra life preserver.' Although the couple had not thought about donning lifebelts before, this convinced Mr Hoyt that they should put their own lifebelts on. Once they had done this, they headed back up toward the deck.[357]

Captain Smith had personally asked both the Countess of Rothes and Gladys Cherry to put on their lifebelts. They

Left: *First Class passenger Mauritz Håkan Björnström-Steffansson.*

Below: *This photo, looking forward along* Titanic's *port side Promenade, was taken at about quarter to ten in the morning of Wednesday, April 10, 1912. This gives a tremendous idea of Gracie's view as he awaited orders for what to do next.*

returned to their stateroom and looked for their lifebelts, but could not find them. A man passing by came to their aid, and then a steward lent a hand. Finally they found the belts under the bed. The steward told them that there was time to dress, and so they did. Once they were done, they proceeded up to the Boat Deck. Still, no one believed that there was any real danger.[358]

When Margaret Brown arrived on the Promenade Deck, she bumped into her friend Emma Bucknell. Emma was still there, and had been told not long before that everything seemed to be under control. Still, she couldn't resist leaning over to her friend and whispering: 'Didn't I tell you something was going to happen?'[359]

Mrs Margaret Swift and her friend Alice Leader had thought that it would be 'just as safe to remain on board', even after hearing from an officer that they should go up on deck and board the lifeboats. While on deck, however, a man had pointed out that the ship was listing to starboard; Mrs Swift did not notice it, however, and she heard someone say that 'a ship always listed a bit when one struck anything'. She was still not convinced that leaving the ship was the better choice.[360]

It was probably between 12:15 and 12:20 a.m. that the first strains of music began to drift throughout the ship. It was apparently coming from the First Class Entrance forward on the Promenade Deck. The ship's band now set to a task that would take a mere two hours, but which would forever exalt them to the status of heroes. The beat was lively, the tunes consisting of popular ragtime and waltzes.

Colonel Archibald Gracie had returned to the Promenade Deck after donning his lifebelt. He found that out 'on Deck A, port side, towards the stern, many men and women had already collected.' He looked around for, and eventually found, the four ladies that he had promised to care for soon after departing Southampton: Mrs Charlotte Appleton, Mrs Caroline Brown, Mrs Malvina Cornell, and Miss Edith Evans. He also found John and Madeleine Astor, as well as Clinch Smith, Hugh Woolner and Mauritz Håkan Björnström-Steffansson. Just then, Gracie remembered, 'the band began to play ... We considered this a wise provision tending to allay excitement.' Gracie continued to stand in the group on the Promenade Deck.[361]

A crowd of First Class passengers in all stages of dress and undress, from the curious to the nervous, from the jovial to the annoyed, were gathering in the Lounge. The atmosphere was almost party-like, and the music lifted everyone's spirits. It was, as later termed, a 'fancy dress ball in Dante's Hell.'

One Last Performance

Sometime between 12:15 and 12:20 a.m., concerned and confused passengers in First Class spaces of the ship began to hear the refrain of cheerful music from the band drift through the corridors of *Titanic*'s upper decks. The work that the bandsmen did for the remainder of the night has elevated them to the status of heroes. Even a century on, the valor they displayed – particularly late in the disaster, when hopes for a rescue had faded into the icy night – stirs the emotions. It was to be their last performance, and it was one the world has never forgotten.

Even so, questions surround their final performance. To begin with, how did it come about that they began playing? First Class passenger Pierre Maréchal reported that they were ordered to play, and to keep playing to avoid a panic.[362]

Perhaps the word 'order', as Maréchal used it, comes off a bit strong, however. The musicians were not directly employed by the White Star Line; they were actually engaged by the Liverpool-based company of C. W. & F. N. Black, the exclusive agency for the major steamship lines. Furthermore, the musicians were members of the Amalgamated Musicians' Union. And while they were aboard the *Titanic* as employees of the Blacks, they were actually categorized as Second Class passengers. As such, they were not crewmen who were required to follow orders. Stewardess Sarah Stap thought that they 'were not asked to play, but did it absolutely of their own initiative.'[363]

Most likely, the truth lies somewhere in between Maréchal and Stap. It is probable that to begin with, Chief Purser McElroy – or perhaps even Captain Smith himself – thought that it would be wise to have the orchestra play in order to keep passengers calm, and asked them to come up and set to the task.

If this is the way their final performance began, it must have taken some minutes for word to be sent down to the musicians in their staterooms, for them to turn out with their instruments, and to make their way topside and forward. It seems to have been just after 12:10 a.m. that Stewardess Violet Jessop spotted violinist Wallace Hartley, John Hume and other members of the band headed up the forward Grand Staircase with their instruments.[364]

This would indicate that the request to have them come up and begin playing had been made as early as midnight. At that point, it was clear that the ship was damaged; steam was blowing off from the boilers; concerned and anxious passengers were beginning to wake up and come on deck in growing numbers; the crew was also given the preemptive order to start uncovering and preparing the lifeboats in case they would be needed. With the ship not getting under way any time soon, it would have been paramount to keep passengers calm while the crew investigated the damage and worked on the boats, in order to quell any signs of panic.

If the request was actually made of them, Hartley and his men most likely felt that pitching in would be the best thing that they could do under the circumstances. When they started to play, there was no obvious indication of impending doom. Later on, when the ship's peril was more obvious, they would certainly have known that they had every right to try to save themselves, to cast their instruments aside and make a break for it. However, there is no record that they did so.[365]

One passenger, Algernon Barkworth, said that he had seen the place where the band had been playing empty, their instruments left behind.[366] However, there is evidence that at some point after they had begun to play, the bandsmen took a break and went below to get their lifebelts, and perhaps to don warmer clothing. Very likely when they did this, they left some or all of their instruments behind – the piano, obviously, would be a fantastic candidate for this – as well as their music stands and sheet music, in order to make the trip more easily. It is possible, then, that Barkworth made his observation during this break.

Lawrence Beesley said that he saw one of the cellists come up to the Boat Deck through the Second Class Entrance, with his cello, at about 12:40 a.m. Beesley then watched as the cellist ran down the deck toward the bow with the instrument's spike dragging on the deck. Perhaps this was a sighting of a musician who was late to join his friends, since he was carrying his cello. Yet if he was going up for his first rendezvous with his fellow musicians, and the timing of Beesley's sighting was correct, then this would mean that he was nearly a half hour late to the performance. Another possibility is that this cellist was returning from the trip to get his lifebelt; however, it seems unlikely that a cellist would have taken his bulky instrument with him while going below to put on warmer clothes and perhaps fetch or put on a lifebelt.[367]

Whether they all went to get their lifebelts at the same time, or whether they did so in shifts, we know that they reconvened and began playing again. Many statements suggest that they continued playing right up until the final minutes of the disaster. They were not required to do so, yet they continued to play – it must have simply seemed to them to be the right thing to do, the best way they could contribute in a positive way to the situation.

Should They Have Kept Playing?

Shortly after the musicians began their performance, or at about 12:25 a.m., it became clear to Captain Smith that the *Titanic* was going to founder. At this point, he could have ordered Chief Purser McElroy to have the musicians stop playing; while he had no authority to compel them to keep playing, he certainly could have requested that they stop doing so. Such a move might have impressed the seriousness of the situation to passengers, prompting them to enter the lifeboats when asked by the officers; theoretically, this move might have maximized the carrying capacity of the boats, while not unnecessarily delaying the launching of the boats on a restricted timetable.

If such a thought ever occurred to Captain Smith or anyone else in authority, it was never followed through on, for the musicians would never have disobeyed such an order. In light of the half-empty boats which left the ship early on, it has in recent years been suggested that having the band continue playing was a poor decision. Because the music of the ship's band lulled passengers into a false sense of security, the argument goes, many passengers chose not to leave the ship, thus adding to the death toll.

However, the Captain and others who were in charge of the evacuation were also painfully aware of a dreadful fact: there was no room in the lifeboats for over a thousand of those aboard. Preventing a panic was thus even more important than it had been at around midnight, when the situation did not seem so desperate. Lives were on the line, time was short, and order had to be maintained. The ship's officers were all very concerned with preventing panic; whether they knew the ship was sinking or did not, loading lifeboats at night is a dangerous process, and disorder could easily lead to injuries or deaths.

Overall, things stayed relatively calm during the first portion of the evacuation. However, as early as the loading of Boat No. 5, officers were heard threatening to get their guns in order to keep the situation under control. Boat No. 5 was the second boat to leave the liner, at 12:45. This was only twenty-five to thirty minutes after the band began to play, and only about twenty minutes after Captain Smith discovered that his ship was doomed. Toward the end, things became even more critical. It was then becoming clear that there were not many lifeboats left and that the ship would sink soon. At that time, there were numerous reports that the officers in charge had trouble maintaining control and order.

In short, the band's music was extremely helpful in allaying a panic which would almost certainly have resulted in deaths or injuries. Simultaneously, many of the ship's officers were giving similar signals of reassurance to passengers. They told many passengers that the launching of the lifeboats was all 'only a precaution'. If at any point, while they were hunting for passengers to fill the early boats, Captain Smith or the officers felt that the band's music was lulling the passengers into an apathetic state that would cost lives, they could easily have asked them to stop playing, but they did not. They were all working toward a common goal – maintaining calm – via different methods.

It is also clear that the ship's officers were more concerned, as they loaded those early lifeboats, with getting the boats clear of the deck and into the water than they were with actually filling them. If passengers were handy and willing to get in, fine; if not, the boats were lowered anyway. There was still a method behind the madness, though. A number of times, these same officers ordered boats to come around and take off additional passengers from lower deck gangways. Although these plans later fell apart when time ran out, that was through no fault of the ship's bandsmen. It was instead symptomatic of the short amount of time the officers had in which to carry out their work.

So how did those present that night feel about the band's efforts? Colonel Archibald Gracie considered the music of the ship's band to be 'a wise provision tending to allay excitement'. Many other survivors expressed similar sentiments of gratitude for the results of the band's work. But perhaps the final word on this should come from the senior surviving officer, Charles Lightoller. He wrote in his autobiography that at about the time he was loading one of the early lifeboats ...

> ... I could hear the band playing cheery sort of music. I don't like jazz music as a rule, but I was glad to hear it that night. I think it helped us all.[368]

Although the terminology Lightoller used later on was incorrect – jazz did not emerge as a style until a number of years after the *Titanic*'s sinking – his sentiment was clear.

Who Played, And Where Did They Play From?

Another question about the band's efforts that night presents itself: how many played, and where did they play from? As there were really two separate ensembles, did they all play together? The most likely answer is yes. Yet how did two pianists work at a single instrument at the locations where they played? This conundrum is easily solved; perhaps the pianists traded off for different numbers. However, even more important is the knowledge that some of the musicians were able to play different instruments, and it is known that some of them carried one or more extra instruments with them. Thus it is possible the extra piano player may have played a different instrument instead. As the men had spent much time together during the voyage, there seems to have been a spirit of camaraderie among them even before the disaster. Even if there were more players than were needed, it seems likely that they tried to stick together.

This leaves the other portion of the question: Where did they play from? It has been suggested that they played in the Lounge on A Deck to begin with. In one account, Emma Schabert said that after the order was given for passengers to don their lifebelts she and her brother saw the band playing in 'the drawing room'.[369] There was no room officially called the 'drawing room' on the *Titanic*, so perhaps this was a reference to the First Class Lounge. We know that the Entrance on the Boat and Promenade Decks became quite congested as more passengers began showing up and were waiting for the lifeboats. So it is possible that for a time the Lounge seemed to be the better place for them to play. However, there was no piano in the Lounge on A Deck.[370] Also, when Gracie made his complete tour of the public rooms on A Deck, sometime after 12:40, he did not mention seeing the band there. Neither did he mention hearing them elsewhere as he passed up to the Boat Deck.[371]

Pierre Maréchal also reported that the band was first stationed 'on the deck, that is to say, between the decks [on A Deck]'.[372] Stewardess Katherine Gold saw them shortly before she left the ship in Boat No. 11; at the time, she noticed that 'men were sitting on A deck ... tapping time with their feet to the music of the band. These passengers and the bandsmen, too, had their lifebelts beside them, and I was specially struck by a glimpse of a violinist playing steadily with a great lifebelt in front of him.'[373]

However, the band was also spotted playing on the Boat Deck level of the First Class Entrance. A Steinway upright piano was supplied at that location, and it was an excellent place from which to play so their music would be heard by those outside. May Futrelle recalled that just before the launch of Boat No. 9 at 1:30 a.m. the ...

> ... orchestra had come out on the Boat Deck, where there was a piano, at about the time when they launched the fourth boat [Boat No. 4, which she nearly boarded]. As we made our way across the deck they were playing 'Alexander's Ragtime Band' – to keep us moving, I suppose.[374]

The initial wording of this statement might indicate a position on the open Boat Deck. However, upon closer inspection, she also said there was a piano where the band was then playing. The only piano on the Boat Deck was inside the Entrance. Her reference could only have referred to the Boat Deck level of the Entrance.

In one of her interviews, Second Class passenger Elizabeth Nye reportedly claimed to have seen the band playing in water up to their knees at the end.[375] However, Nye was in Boat No. 11, about a quarter-mile from the starboard-aft quarter of the *Titanic* at the time.[376] In other words, she was probably too far away to make out much detail about individual forms on the liner's decks; she was also in completely the wrong quarter of the ship to have seen the band playing where they are traditionally alleged to have played from.

Trimmer Thomas Patrick Dillon gave one newspaper account in which he said that a solo bandsman kneeling and playing 'Nearer, My God, to Thee' was the last thing he saw before jumping from the ship. Yet other evidence that Dillon gave indicates that he remained on the Poop Deck well after the ship broke up. So if he timed the sighting accurately, this meant that a single bandsman ran to a point aft of the break on the decks, held on to his instrument through the stern's gyrations, and then began or resumed a tune in those final few seconds – all a very unlikely possibility.

Other, similar statements which appeared in the papers shortly after the disaster must be treated with a measure of skepticism. Conclusions can only be drawn if the passengers were close enough and also in a position to see what they reported, and when multiple statements also seem to form some sort of consensus.

If all of this sounds confusing, it certainly is. Even the 'fact' – repeated time and again in books, documentaries and films – that the band played outside on the port Boat Deck, outside the First Class Entrance, suffers a curious lack of first-hand documentation.

Indeed, this legend is fraught with complications. First, the change in temperature from the ship's interior spaces would have required a re-tuning of all of the stringed instruments, and perhaps more than one tuning as the instruments and strings continued to cool. Second, the piano would not have been available on the Boat Deck. There was no way to get the piano on the Boat Deck level of the Entrance out onto the deck. It was well fastened down to prevent it from moving in bad weather, there was also a high sill in the doorway leading in from the deck, and also a ninety-degree turn to negotiate in the small vestibule. On a sloping deck in the freezing cold, moving the piano outside seems an absolute absurdity.[377]

Added to that, there would have been no place for the cellists to sit. Perhaps, it has been suggested, chairs were found and brought out? Possibly, but then again playing these strings instruments required complex fingering; the freezing cold would not have lent itself to a lengthy performance, since fingers would quickly have grown numb and senseless. Beyond that, there was not much light on the deck; enough to make out who someone was talking with, perhaps, but not much more. There were at least two lights on the bulkheads in the vicinity, and some diffuse lighting coming out from the Entrance windows. Still, it was not very much, and would not have been evenly dispersed. If the bandsmen stood with their backs to the light so the light could shine on their music, shadows would also have been a problem. In this scenario, is the band supposed to have squinted at their sheet music through dim lighting and shadows? Or did they play from memory? The latter would be more likely, but in light of all of the other complications a move out onto the Boat Deck would have entailed, placing the band there for any length of time simply does not seem viable.

We do know that passengers in the lifeboats and on the decks on both sides of the ship said that they could hear music playing; that alone might suggest that they were somewhere on an open deck. But there is a direct lack of first-hand accounts referring to them in their traditionally-named location. Beyond that, the acoustics were tremendously good that night – the air was still and cold, and sounds could carry across the water clearly, at least over short distances. When the venting of steam ended, there was very little screaming or crying on the decks, at least until late in the sinking, and little in the way of machinery or equipment noise. Knowing these factors, even if the band was inside they could most likely have been heard in the lifeboats on both sides of the ship for some distance.

On the other hand, there is evidence that the band remained inside. The testimony of Steward Edward Brown is very enlightening. Brown was on the starboard side Boat Deck helping in efforts to launch Collapsible A; he said he saw the Captain walk by with a megaphone in his hand, telling the crewmen to do their 'best for the women and children'. Only 'a very few seconds' later, the ship took her plunge. Brown was next asked about what the band was doing 'at the last'. He replied: 'I do not remember hearing the band stop playing. They were playing for a long time, but I do not remember hearing them stop.' When asked where the band was gathered, he said: 'Right on the forward companion on the very top – on the boat deck forward companion.'

In nautical parlance, a 'companion' has to do with a stairway leading down below within a ship. Many other survivors called the First Class Grand Staircase and Entrance Foyers the 'companionway'. Brown's choice of words in this sentence speaks volumes. He says that they were 'on the very top' of the 'forward companion'. This would make little sense if they were outside on the deck. The phrase 'on the very top' likely means the top of the Grand Staircase, also known as the 'forward companion'.

When the Solicitor-General added that that location was 'between the first and second funnels', he was correct. However, that statement does not necessarily imply that they were outside on the deck. If they were outside the Entrance on the deck, that location was actually beside the No. 2 funnel, not between the two forward funnels. However, the Grand Staircase and First Class Entrance was between the two funnels; it seems that the Solicitor-General understood the reference to mean the top of the staircase in the First Class Entrance.

So far, there may have been some room to debate the time of this sighting. Yet Brown added that the band was playing while he was working on getting Collapsible A down from the Officers' Quarters Roof, just a few seconds before his final sighting of Captain Smith. This was only moments before the ship took its downward plunge.[378]

The bodies of three of the musicians were later recovered, and this may indicate their final movements were to turn out of the First Class Entrance, probably through the port doorway. If this hypothesis is correct, it is unknown whether they brought their instruments out onto the deck with them and, if so, if they played in those final moments on the open deck at about 2:15 a.m.

When the ship took its forward plunge, it sent a wave of water up the deck which engulfed anyone forward of midships. It is likely that some or all of the musicians went into the sea with the first plunge. The deck's incline grew quickly from that point on, making progress toward the stern after the plunge difficult, if not impossible. As the bandsmen went into the sea, their final and most famous performance had come to a sudden and tragic conclusion.

In his D Deck cabin, Lawrence Beesley's reading was interrupted yet again by a 'loud shout from above: "All passengers on deck with lifebelts on." '

Beesley placed the two books he was reading in his jacket pocket, picked up his lifebelt and his dressing gown, and then walked upstairs, tying his lifebelt on as he went. As he headed up, he saw …

> … the purser's assistant, with his foot on the stairs about to climb them, whisper to a steward and jerk his head significantly behind him; not that I thought anything of it at the time, but I have no doubt he was telling him what had happened up in the bows, and was giving him orders to call all passengers.

Beesley didn't have much time to think about this, however, for just then two ladies were coming down the stairs. One of them grabbed Beesley's arm and told him that she had no lifebelt. She asked if he would go to her cabin with her to help find it. Beesley agreed, and went down to F Deck with her, amused as the lady continued to cling to his arm 'in a vise-like grip' all the way. Finally, they found a steward in her gangway who took them in and found their lifebelts. His services no longer required, Beesley turned around and headed back up the stairs.[379]

Meanwhile, Lookouts Hogg and Evans had been on watch in the Crow's Nest for about twenty minutes. Although there was very little to do while they were on this watch, it must have been a peculiar start to their duties that night: a collision … ice on the Well Deck … going up to the Nest … hearing steam blow off from the engines …

The two men were understandably curious about what was going on. They couldn't hear any of the activity over the sound of escaping steam. Nor could they simply turn around and look aft to the decks below, as the canvas weather screen was in place. Finally, the two of them 'lifted up the back cover of the nest, the weather cover', and Hogg noticed that there were 'people running about with life belts on'.

Something serious was going on, and they were being completely left out of the loop. Hogg recalled:

> I went to the telephone then, to try to ring up on the bridge and ask whether I was wanted in the nest, when I saw this. I could get no answer on the telephone.

That they received no answer is not at all surprising, for the ship's officers were very busy at the time. Unsatisfied, the two lookouts decided to leave their post and go to the Boat Deck.[380]

Down below, Greaser Fred Scott had been stationed on the starboard side of the Turbine Engine Room. He had felt a 'shock', and then heard the engine telegraph order change to 'Stop'. He had subsequently noticed a number of further orders for the engines before they were finally rung off for good.

A little while after the engines were stopped for the last time, Scott and another crewman headed aft. They opened up the individual watertight doors astern of the Turbine Engine Room to free a Greaser who had been caught in the after tunnel when the watertight doors were closed. The man in the tunnel could not have been terribly alarmed at being shut in the tunnel behind the doors, however; there

were escape ladders leading from the tunnel up to E Deck, and he does not seem to have used them. Scott estimated that the effort to open the doors took about ten minutes, and that he then returned to the Turbine Room.[381]

It was at about this time that the full, grim picture of what was really happening to the *Titanic* came into focus for Thomas Andrews. He was still observing the extent and rate of flooding in the forward compartments. Andrews had already been aware that the second, third, and fourth compartments starting from the bow – Cargo Holds Nos 1, 2 and 3 – were flooding uncontrollably. Forward of those, while the Forepeak Storeroom was undamaged, the Forepeak Tank below it – with a capacity of 190 tons – was also flooded, adding critical forward weight. Finally, Boiler Room No. 6, the fifth compartment starting from the bow, was also flooding fast and was a lost cause.

It all added up to an absurdly simple yet absolutely horrifying mathematical conclusion: the ship was doomed. Andrews turned and headed above quickly, no doubt looking for Captain Smith. Inquisitive passengers and crew had by this time gathered in the public spaces of their respective classes, in various stages of dress and undress. Some were alarmed, while others merely believed that it was the most exciting event of an otherwise unremarkable maiden voyage. Some of these spotted Andrews as he came up.

Around 12:22 a.m., First Class passenger Anna Warren saw Andrews rushing up the Grand Staircase on D Deck, taking the steps three at a time, with 'a look of terror' on his face. Just after this, First Class passenger William Sloper – who had gathered with Pauline Gibson and Frederic Seward in the First Class Entrance – saw Andrews rushing up the Grand Staircase on A Deck, hurrying towards the Bridge. Although Andrews said nothing, 'one look at his face' convinced Sloper that the ship's designer was 'worried'.[382] Albert and Vera Dick saw their table companion coming up from below as well. They had seen him go down on his inspection, and waited for him to return:

> As the minutes flew by we did not know what to do or which way to turn … and we waited for Mr Andrews to come back.
>
> When he came we hung upon his words, and they were these: 'There is no cause for any excitement. All of you get what you can in the way of clothes and come on deck as soon as you can. She is torn to bits below, but she will not sink if her after bulkheads hold.'
>
> It seemed almost impossible that this could be true … and many in the crowd smiled, thinking this was merely a little extra knowledge that Mr Andrews saw fit to impart.[383]

Andrews certainly seemed far less willing to answer questions as he came up from below than he had been in going down to inspect the damage. Earlier, he had even stopped to try and calm people's nerves. With the exception of the Dicks, as he made his way up the stairs it seems that he almost universally brushed past people and ignored their queries; he was intent on getting to Captain Smith as quickly as he could. As he went up the stairs and moved forward along the deck, Andrews must have wondered how, exactly, he was going to break the bad news to the Captain.

By that time, the bow had settled noticeably into the sea; the water had reached portholes that were originally twenty feet above the waterline on the bow. At about 12:25 a.m., the Seamen's Quarters on E Deck, some forty-eight feet above the keel, flooded. Seaman John Poingdestre was in the quarters at that time. He had been up on deck clearing the covers off the lifeboats, but went below to put his boots on. While there, the wooden bulkhead separating the Seamens' Quarters from Third Class passenger space collapsed, and water flooded the compartment to a depth of three feet. Poingdestre had to wade through freezing water up to his waist in order to escape, getting out in 'a matter of half a minute'. He quickly made his way back to the Boat Deck.[384]

Somewhere around 12:25 am, Smith and Andrews apparently conferred on the Bridge …[385] the situation was grave: the sea was filling the forward six watertight compartments. Fortunately, the water was still being kept down in the aft-most of these, Boiler Room No. 5, but as Andrews had seen first-hand, the forward five compartments were flooding uncontrollably. The *Titanic* had been designed to survive with the forward four compartments flooding – but not all five. The water in the forward five compartments would pull the ship's bow down until it would spill over the top of the next bulkhead. Once that compartment had flooded, she would settle by the head enough that the next compartment, too, would flood. This process would continue until the ship had sunk.

The conversation must have been grim; both men knew only too well that the *Titanic* didn't have enough lifeboats for everyone aboard. In fact, of the 2,208 passengers and crew on board, there was only enough room in the lifeboats for 1,178. Smith asked Andrews how long the *Titanic* could stay afloat, and was presented with another problem. After some quick calculating, Andrews told Smith that he believed she could last for an hour, perhaps an hour and a half, but not much longer.[386]

This last statement, in particular, must have been earth-shattering for the Captain. Perhaps his initial hope was that she would last as long as the *Republic* had three years before … maybe he had hoped to have a day, but at least if the ship could have held out until morning, the situation would be much improved. By then a veritable flotilla of nearby vessels would have had time to arrive and aid in the evacuation. But an hour to an hour and a half …?

What might have seemed absurd only an hour before was now a ghastly reality. The problems of carrying out a full evacuation in the time left were evident, but the situation was inescapable and there was no time to lose … The conversation must have ended quickly. Captain Smith gave the order to begin loading the women and children into the boats.[387] Able Bodied Seaman John Poingdestre made his way back to the Boat Deck just in time to hear this order being given.[388]

Although it may seem like this was an unconscionably long period of time for Captain Smith to have waited before ordering passengers to board the lifeboats, there were some good reasons for waiting until he was certain of the ship's fate. First of all, the crew had only had about twenty-five minutes to prepare the lifeboats for loading up to that time; some of the boats were still sitting on the deck at that point. It was a loud, rather dangerous bit of work, and keeping the passengers from getting under the crew's feet as they worked might have prevented injuries and perhaps have expedited the process.

However, whatever the condition of the boats, it would have been foolish for the Captain to have ordered the passengers to begin boarding the lifeboats before he knew for sure just how hopeless the situation was. As Second Officer Lightoller later recalled:

> Although the boats and falls were all brand new, it is a risky business at the best of times to attempt to lower a boat between seventy and eighty feet at night time, filled with people who are not 'boat-wise'. It is, unfortunately, the rule rather than the exception for some mishap to occur in lowering the boats loaded with people who, through no fault of their own, lack this boat sense.[389]

Only after this dreadful conversation between Andrews and Captain Smith was it clear that this risk was going to have to be faced. The only thing to do then was to try to get as many people off the ship as they could in the time available. Even as Captain Smith got this project under way, Andrews left the Bridge. The ship's designer seems to have proceeded below deck in order to help prepare the passengers for evacuation.

Captain Smith immediately moved aft to the Marconi room. Barely putting his head in the door, Smith told Jack Phillips and Harold Bride to 'send the call for assistance.' Phillips asked, 'What call should I send?' Smith told him 'the regulation call for help. Just that.' Then he left again, leaving the two men with a startling order, very little explanation, and a weighty responsibility to discharge.

Phillips, being the Senior Operator, naturally took the key from his assistant. At 10:25 p.m. New York Time, or 12:27 a.m. according to the *Titanic*'s clocks, he began tapping out the fateful message.[390] It was the international call for distress and the wireless call letters assigned to the *Titanic*, and the simple message that Phillips sent would soon become famous:

'CQD…CQD…CQD…CQD…CQD…CQD…MGY….'

About a half-dozen times the signal rasped out of the key, up through the aerials suspended far above the funnel tops, and out into the cold, black night. This was followed by the position: 41° 44' N, 50° 24' W.[391]

An illustration of a Marconi Operator at work on a set of the period.

CHAPTER 5
THE LOSING BATTLE

12:25 a.m. – 12:40 a.m.

By the time the first distress call was sent at 12:27 a.m., things were beginning to move forward on the *Titanic's* Boat Deck.[1] All of the officers were by then up and about and ready to assist; crew members were also beginning to show up on the deck in growing numbers. As a team, they began to move purposefully toward the lifeboats. However, it was like trying to get a steam locomotive started from a dead stop; the momentum of getting the ship's sixteen standard lifeboats ready had to build, even as more and more men showed up to pitch in and the officers began to take charge of what was going on. Hindering the efforts was the fact that many crewmembers, even after turning out and being told that there was an accident, were not aware of the urgency of the situation, and had not been told that the ship was doomed.

After Fourth Officer Boxhall had awakened the remaining officers, he went out onto the Boat Deck and helped to unlace some of the canvas covers on the lifeboats. He noticed men turning out on the stern section of the port side as well, and was about to head aft to see how they were doing when he heard 'someone report a light, a light ahead'. This information seemed to catch his attention, and he turned back toward the Bridge to investigate.[2] Before he was able to do so, he ran across Captain Smith, and the two men conversed briefly. Boxhall asked the Captain: 'Should I send a distress signal?'

Smith replied: 'I've already sent a distress signal.'

At this, a concern cropped up in Boxhall's mind. 'What, what position did you send it from?' he asked hesitantly.

'From the eight o'clock DR [dead reckoning fix],' Smith replied.

Boxhall replied that the celestial fix had indicated that 'she was about twenty miles ahead of' the dead reckoning position.

Smith suggested that Boxhall check the position he had worked out.[3] Before the two men parted, the Captain asked Boxhall how the work was progressing on the boats. Boxhall told him: 'Yes, they are carrying on all right.' Then he asked the Captain directly: 'Is it really serious?'

Smith responded just as directly: 'Mr Andrews tells me he gives her from an hour to an hour and a half.'[4]

With this stunning news fresh in mind, Boxhall headed directly into the Navigating Room just aft of the Bridge; there, he used the stellar observation taken around 7:30 p.m. to work out their location.

In the meanwhile, the first distress messages – sent from the *Titanic* starting at 12:27 a.m. ship's time – were immediately overheard by the Cape Race, Newfoundland, sta-

tion, as well as by the ships *La Provence* and *Mount Temple.* At 12:30, the *Ypiranga* overheard a series of about ten calls of 'CQD', followed by the position and the words: 'Require assistance.'[5] Word was beginning to spread, but it was difficult for anyone to comprehend the reality of what was taking place.

In the First Class Lounge, Edith Rosenbaum had just been listening to Washington Roebling tell her that the *Titanic* was entirely unsinkable. Right afterward 'a deck officer' came to the Lounge door: 'Women and children will kindly proceed to the boat deck,' he called out. Just to make sure he was understood, he repeated: 'Women and children only.'[6]

'When the order came for women and children to take to the lifeboats', William and Alice Silvey had realized for the first time that the situation was serious. Even then, 'the probability that the ship would sink was incredible.' At that point, she thought that putting the women and children off in the lifeboats was only a precautionary measure. However, Mrs Silvey objected to leaving her husband. He told her that 'to obey orders was the only course'. He also said that while there was no danger, if it became necessary, he would follow her in another lifeboat after the women and children were taken off.[7]

Helen Ostby and her father Engelhart had bumped into their acquaintances from Portland, Oregon, Frank and Anna Warren, after putting their lifebelts on. Together, they ascended the Grand Staircase to the Boat Deck, also having heard the order to proceed to the lifeboats. Helen recalled that everyone thought that they 'would be just going off in the lifeboats for a short time, as a precaution, [and] then would probably come back to the ship.' When they got out onto the deck, 'the noise of the ship blowing off steam from all four funnels was a deafening roar. You could hardly hear anyone speak to you.' They watched as the crew prepared the lifeboats.[8]

Back in their stateroom, Jacques and May Futrelle had dressed quickly but thoroughly. Jacques put on all of his clothes and his eyeglasses, while May took the time to

---

Opposite: *This detail view of the cover painting from this volume shows the scene at 1:50 a.m. Titanic's bow is mostly awash, and work is proceeding at Boats Nos 4 and 10 on the port side, while Boat No. 2 has just reached the water.*

Above right: *First Class passenger Washington Roebling.*

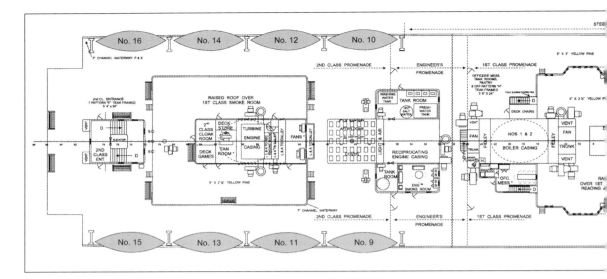

fasten all of her clothes properly, don a fur coat and gloves, and then put a blanket over her arm. Then they were ready to leave … May had heard of people in lifeboats at sea going nearly mad from thirst, so she took a drink of water just to be on the safe side. When she asked her husband if he wanted one, he told her he had just done so. Then they turned out to the hallway and started forward.

Upon reaching the First Class Entrance by the Purser's Office, May could feel, rather than see, that the ship 'was not riding the water as before', and they could hear talk of the lifeboats. This was too much for May, and she 'broke down' for a moment. Her husband tried to reassure her, and took her to the nearby notice-board. He pointed to all of the daily bulletins and showed her that they had 'sighted seven ships that day'. Then he said: 'Someone will come to secure us, of course.'

'But if we have to take to the boats we'll go together, won't we?' May asked.

'I suppose so,' he said quietly.

By that point, they could hear the creaking of the lifeboat davits overhead … Then they began heading up toward the Boat Deck.[9]

Mrs Bucknell had been on deck for some time; not long before she had heard the rumor that the damage was only minor, and that the watertight doors were being closed. Since then, she had moved across to the port side of the ship. Now she heard the order 'for the women and the men to separate'. Just then, she saw Mr and Mrs Astor; at the time, they were standing together on the port side. When the order came through, however, they left for the starboard side. She saw that the Colonel was 'bending over her as they walked'. She also saw the Wideners leave the area with the Astors.[10]

Meanwhile, things were beginning to move very quickly for many of the crew. The stewards and stewardesses from all three classes, including First Class Stewardess Violet Jessop, were called upon to find the passengers in their care and to make sure they were sent topside wearing warm clothing. They also had to help passengers into their lifebelts – something quite unexpected on this maiden voyage. To aid this effort, some were stationed at various high-traffic areas such as the forward Grand Staircase, to make sure

that errant passengers – if they had somehow escaped the assistance of their own cabin stewards and stewardesses – were cared for before reaching the upper decks.

George Rheims and his brother-in-law Joseph Loring were still talking when someone – apparently Thomas Andrews – came by and told them to put their lifebelts on. The two men parted company to return to their respective cabins. Rheims 'went down' to his A Deck cabin, 'put on some warm clothing' as well as his lifebelt, and then he returned to the Boat Deck, where he re-joined Joseph Loring. The two men decided that they were going to stick together from that time forward.[11]

Thomas Andrews had just come from his sobering conversation with the Captain when he seems to have come across Rheims and Loring; then he continued down on to A Deck. There, he helped crewmembers who were trying to get the passengers roused, dressed and up on deck with their lifebelts on. He came across Stewardess Annie Robinson, who had just finished getting the extra blankets and lifebelts out of the unoccupied rooms at the foot of the staircase. Andrews told her: 'Put your lifebelt on and walk about and let the passengers see you.'

The stewardess protested, saying, 'It looks rather mean.'

Andrews' reply was firm. He said: 'No, put it on.' Then he added: 'Well, if you value your life put your belt on.'[12]

The shipbuilder had already told Stewardess Mary Sloan that an accident had happened, and that she should get her passengers' lifebelts on, get one for herself, and then get everyone up on deck. At around the same time that Andrews came across Annie Robinson, Miss Sloan recalled seeing him again. He was 'here, there and everywhere, looking after everybody, telling the women to put on lifebelts, telling the stewardesses to hurry the women up to the boats, all about everywhere, thinking of everyone but himself.'[13]

Elmer Taylor had certainly had an interesting time of things since the collision. He had waited ten or fifteen minutes after the impact and the engines' stopping before he bothered to put on some clothes. After dressing, he had gone forward on A Deck, where he saw the ice on the forward Well Deck. Scooping up a piece, he returned to his cabin to show it his wife Juliet. Next, he went to

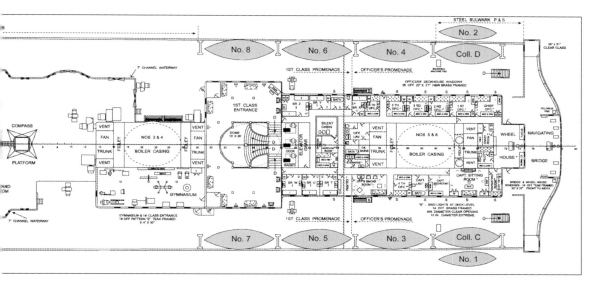

Above: *This plan of* Titanic's *Boat Deck shows the location of eighteen of her twenty lifeboats. Collapsibles A and B were located on the roof of the Officers' Quarters, abreast of the No. 1 funnel.*

Left: *Third Class passenger Eugene Daly.*

his friend's cabin, and talked with him for a few minutes before returning to his own cabin again.

As he walked 'along the corridor, an officer came from the opposite direction', and told him: 'Go to your cabin, put on your life belt and proceed to the Boat Deck.' Taylor thought that this was 'sheer stupidity', and told his wife so when he got back to their stateroom. Then he 'hesitated, thought again', and told his wife to dress and to put on her fur coat.[14]

Elsewhere, when William Mellors reached deck, he found crowds of passengers already there, putting on their lifebelts. Mellors 'had about 15 mins [sic] hard work tying the women's belts on'.[15]

Things were far less organized in Third Class regions of the ship. By this point, many Third Class men in the bow section of the liner had quite literally been chased out of their cabins by rising water. In response, they either moved aft, to higher and drier areas of the ship, or up to the forward Well Deck. As they migrated up and aft, many of them were carrying all of their belongings.

However, not everyone had such a great sense of urgency. In the Third Class Smoking Room aft, beneath the Poop Deck, August Wennerström and Gunnar Tenglin arrived and found the bar closed and nothing for them to do. August and some of the other passengers got someone to play the piano, and started to dance. Just then, a group of 'Italian' passengers arrived, presumably from the bow, carrying their belongings and acting 'crazy, crying and jumping, calling upon their Madonna'. Thinking them panicked for no reason, Wennerström and the others poked fun at them, forming a ring dance around them. Some stewards, annoyed at the panicked passengers, told them to take off their lifebelts, as nothing was wrong. When the passengers showed no sign of complying because of the language barrier, Wennerström said that the crewmembers physically removed the lifebelts from these poor, frightened people. Some of the Third Class passengers who had been joking with them joined in and also started to remove the lifebelts from off their backs.[16]

Similarly, Saloon Steward Littlejohn and his crewmates laughed at the steerage passengers when they saw them lugging their belongings aft along the corridors. They thought

they were unnecessarily scared, but then they noticed their clothes were wet, indicating that their quarters were flooding.[17]

Carl Olof Jansson was one of the passengers who had been forced to escape aft. He was initially awakened by the collision with the iceberg, which he described as a 'slight jar'. Hearing no panic or alarm, he had gone back to sleep. Now, he and his companions were awakened for a second time by a knock on the door; they were told to dress and come on deck – there had been an accident, but 'there was no danger'. As Jansson started to dress, water began coming into the cabin, and 'creeping up' around his feet. As he threw on his clothes, the water began rushing in, and was soon up to his ankles.[18]

Meanwhile, after navigating his way through the crowds beginning to mill about in the Steerage passageways, Eugene Daly arrived at Maggie Daly and Bertha Mulvihill's cabin. Pounding on the door, he shouted for them to wake up. The water was 'coming up and up rapidly', so there was a great sense of urgency on his part. The two girls, already awake from the collision, were annoyed by Daly's pounding, a fact which they made apparent to him. However, both realized that something serious had happened, and it didn't take much persuading to convince them to leave their cabin.[19]

Maggie quickly got dressed and went to wait in the hallway, while Bertha slipped her coat on over her nightgown and put on her shoes. Before leaving the room, Bertha grabbed her gold bracelet, cross, rosary beads, and prayer book, and slipped them all into her coat. Fortunately, her

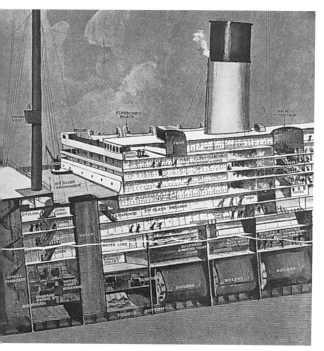

Top left: This period cutaway illustration shows passengers making their way through and out of the flooding interior of the Titanic.

Above: Olympic's aft Well Deck just before her maiden voyage in June 1911. This gives a wonderful idea of the perspective of Third Class passengers who gathered astern as the ship was sinking.

Below left: Looking forward from the forward edge of the Olympic's Poop Deck during the 1920's. This view shows the layers of open decks astern. Second Class passengers occupied the Boat Deck and B Deck; First Class passengers A Deck, and Third Class passengers the open Well Deck. The open door in the lower right corner leads forward into the enclosed Second Class Promenade. The stairs from the Well Deck up to B Deck existed on Titanic. *However, the staircase from B Deck to A Deck was a later addition to* Olympic *not present on* Titanic.

inscribed timepiece was already pinned inside the coat. The watch had been an engagement present from her husband Henry, and bore great sentimental value. Bertha then joined Margaret and Eugene in the hallway. Stewards were now telling everyone to put their lifebelts on. Bertha went back into her room, stood up on the washstand, and grabbed her lifebelt, before returning to the hallway.[20]

Around this time, the stewards in Third Class had begun to organize their efforts. Steward John E. Hart had assumed charge of working with a group of passengers in the stern sections of Third Class. He busied himself at helping them with getting their lifejackets on and, dichotomously, reassuring them all at the same time. At about 12:25 or 12:30 a.m., he recalled, word had been passed down: 'Women and children to the Boat Deck.' Instead of leaving them to their own devices in finding their way through unfamiliar territory to the lifeboats, Hart began to assemble a group of about thirty women and children; once they were all organized, he set off, personally leading them to the lifeboats.[21]

Third Class passengers Laura Cribb and her father John had also heard an order for women and children to get their lifebelts on and proceed to the deck. Laura went back to her cabin and grabbed her lifebelt without putting it on. Then she and her father went up on deck, where they were apparently among the first Steerage passengers to reach the open deck. They 'ran swiftly across the iron stairway' that led up to the Second Class deck.[22]

Elsewhere in Third Class, Eugene Daly and his charges had already begun climbing the stairs to escape the incoming water, perhaps with the intention of reaching the forward Well Deck. As they headed up, other people pushed past them, and a man that Bertha Mulvihill described as a 'fireman' knocked her down several steps, injuring her ribs. As she was in pain, Eugene had to help her up, and he led the girls up to the next deck. Suddenly, Maggie Daly realized that in the rush to leave her cabin, she had left her lifebelt and some personal items of sentimental value. She asked if she should go back below, but Eugene urged her not to. She ignored his advice and proceeded down the stairwell. After several minutes, she returned, saying that her cabin was now 'under five feet of water'.[23]

Around 12:25 a.m., a steward burst into Imanita Shelley and her mother's cabin saying: 'All on deck with life belts on.' Both women hurriedly dressed, and then put their lifebelts on over their clothes. As they readied themselves to go on deck, Imanita asked her mother, 'Can it be that the ship is sinking? Is it possible that this great leviathan of a ship can go down?'

Imanita had toured the battleship USS *Kentucky* when the American fleet was in Los Angeles, and had been 'shown how modern ships were built and how almost impossible it was for them to sink'. 'Half way up to the upper deck', the two women encountered First Class passengers Isidor and Rosalie Ida Straus, who were apparently aware that she was ill, and feeling week. Shelley recalled that Mrs. Straus wrapped her own cloak around her, and Isidor helped her to a nearby deck chair.[24]

Meanwhile, Assistant Saloon Steward Nichols made his way up to the Boat Deck.[25] On his way, he 'noticed some of the passengers about, but no one seemed to be worried or excited'. He passed by the Gymnasium on his way to his assigned lifeboat, which was No. 15. Glancing inside, he saw that there 'were a number of passengers amusing themselves. One man was riding the bicycle, one of those exercise machines, and another was punching the bag.'[26]

First Class passengers Charles and Annie Stengel had returned to their stateroom on C Deck once the order for passengers to put their lifebelts on had come through. Charles had helped his wife into one of the belts, and she tied his own on. Then they began to return to the Boat Deck.[27]

Lookout George Hogg had left his post in the Crow's Nest after seeing people on the decks in lifebelts; he went 'straight to the boat deck'. When he got there, he 'assisted in starting to uncover the boats'.[28]

Around this time, Saloon Steward William Ward bumped into Second Steward Dodd on D Deck. Dodd told Ward and some of the other Saloon Stewards who were with him to 'go forward to the saloon and see if there was anyone about, and if there was to order them up on deck.' He also told them to collect the lifebelts and bring them up to the Cloakroom on deck.[29]

Steward Etches was headed directly to his section of rooms, to make sure everyone was proceeding up on deck. He had under his care eight B Deck staterooms aft on the port side; he was also assigned Thomas Andrews' cabin, A-36, on the deck above. The cabins between B-86 and B-94 were empty. As he was proceeding from forward on A Deck, Etches first came upon B-84, which was occupied by First Class passenger Benjamin Guggenheim and his Valet, Victor Giglio.

Guggenheim answered the door on the first knock, leading Etches to conclude that the magnate had only just retired and undressed for bed. Etches entered the room, pulled their three lifebelts out, and placed one on Guggenheim. 'This will hurt', the mining magnate complained.

Etches helped to pull heavy sweaters over them both. Giglio and Guggenheim stayed together as they left the cabin and went out on deck.

Etches saw them on their way, and was about to move on to the after cabins in his section when he bumped into Thomas Andrews; the shipbuilder was coming through the area after talking to George Rheims and Annie Robinson about getting their lifebelts on. Andrews stopped and asked Etches if he had awakened all of his passengers.[30] Just then – and before Etches had the opportunity to respond – passenger William H. Harrison 'came up' right near him. Harrison was Bruce Ismay's Secretary, and his cabin, B-94, was one of the after cabins from Etches' section.

Etches replied to Andrews: 'No; I am going to see if the Carter family are up.' The Carter family was booked in cabins B-96 and B-98, while Mr Carter's Valet Alexander Cairns was in B-86. The Carters' cabins were just astern of Harrison's cabin.

Harrison overheard the conversation and interjected then, saying to Etches: 'I can tell you they are up. I have just come out of my cabin.' With Guggenheim gone, that accounted for all of Etches' charges.

Andrews responded to this news by telling Etches to follow him down the Pantry stairs to C Deck. As they descended, Andrews began to instruct the steward to 'be sure and make the passengers open their doors, and to tell them the life belts were on top of the wardrobes and on top of the racks,' as well as to assist them in every way that the steward could, which Etches endeavored to follow through on. Andrews also mentioned, before they parted, that Etches should be sure that no lifebelts were left in the cabins.

The steward moved to the cabin 'at the foot of the pantry stairs', and he went inside. There, he opened a drawer to stand on so that he could reach the lifebelts. Pulling them off the wardrobe, he took them with him and started to leave the cabin. As he came into the corridor, a stout gentleman, who Etches thought was English, was passing by. Etches gave him a lifebelt. 'Show me how to put this on,' the man requested. Etches demonstrated how, but then the passenger asked the steward to tie it for him. Etches told him: 'Pull the strings around to the front and tie it,' and as the passenger began to comply, Etches moved on, opening other nearby cabin doors until 'most of the doors were opened along C deck'.

Etches found the door to cabin C-78 shut, so he pounded on it with both hands. A man's voice answered: 'What is it?' A lady's voice added: 'Tell me what the trouble is.' Etches explained: 'It is necessary that you should open the door, and I will explain everything, but please put the lifebelts on or bring them in the corridor.'

The door remained closed; the passengers inside were obviously unconvinced. Etches said: 'Kindly open the door,' and continued to bang on it, but to no avail. He eventually concluded that he had given enough warning there. He moved on, finding the next cabin empty, and proceeded to the third cabin, where an American couple stood in the open doorway. They were swinging lifebelts in their hands. Since it was obvious that no warning was necessary there, Etches moved on.[31]

On the Boat Deck, Lookout George Hogg had been assisting in the efforts to uncover the lifeboats when the Boatswain ordered him to find a Jacob's ladder.[32] He set off to find the ladder, acquired one, and then returned to

Olympic's forward starboard lifeboats in 1911. From bow to stern, Boats Nos 1, 3, 5 and 7.

the starboard Boat Deck. When he got there, First Officer Murdoch ordered him in to Boat No. 7 in order to begin preparing the boat.[33]

By now, Fifth Officer Lowe was assisting in the efforts to get the boats loaded. Lowe never recalled Boxhall's attempt to wake him around midnight. When he was eventually roused by the commotion outside his port side cabin, he opened the door to the hallway and looked out. To his surprise, he 'saw ladies in [the Officers' Quarters] with lifebelts on.' Something was wrong for sure, and he had somehow managed to miss the boat ... He hastily dressed and then went out onto the port Boat Deck. There he found more passengers in lifebelts, and discovered that the crew was 'clearing' the lifeboats, preparing them 'to go overboard'. He ran across someone who told him that they had struck an iceberg. Lowe's senses had confirmed that something was, indeed, very wrong. He could feel the deck listing under his feet.[34]

Convinced of the severity of the situation, Lowe had next returned to his quarters and retrieved his personal revolver, which was a Browning automatic; he did this because he did not know what lay ahead, and whether he might need it. Then he had returned to the port Boat Deck and crossed over to starboard via the roof over the First Class Reading & Writing Room and Lounge. When he arrived, he found Murdoch working at Boat No. 7, and lent a hand there first.[35]

Second Officer Lightoller had moved all around the Boat Deck as work proceeded at getting the boats ready. He visited lifeboats on both sides of the deck, making sure that the seamen were uncovering the boats, but he did not spend much time at the forward starboard boats, as matters were well in hand there under Murdoch's watchful eye. When he returned to the port side, Lightoller asked Wilde if they could swing the boats out, but Wilde did not seem to want to just yet. When Lightoller ran across Captain Smith and asked him the same question, however, Smith gave permission and Lightoller got to work.

After the boats had been swung out, Lightoller once again went back to Smith. Cupping both hands over the Captain's ears to communicate over the racket of escaping steam, he shouted: 'Hadn't we better get the women and

children into the boats, sir?' The old Captain turned and nodded: 'Yes. Put the women and children in and lower away.'[36]

While Henry Frauenthal was below getting his wife ready to go up on deck, his brother Isaac was on the Boat Deck watching the scene play out there. He remembered that it ...

> ... was a jewel of a night, clear as crystal. Pretty cold, but not uncomfortably so. The stars gleamed brightly, and in their light I could see the iceberg we had hit. I estimated it stood about 100 feet above the water, although it seemed much smaller than the ship herself. I glanced over the side, and I tell you it looked pretty dark out beyond the radiance of the ship's lights. It made a man feel uneasy about what was going to happen.
>
> Right away it was apparent that the stewards were having trouble getting passengers on deck. The stewards were reporting constantly to their officers that they couldn't make people believe anything serious had happened. Some of them had been ridiculed and laughed at for saying the ship might sink.[37]

When fellow First Class passengers Charles and Annie Stengel returned from their stateroom to the starboard side of the Boat Deck, they were wearing their lifebelts. Just then, Charles heard an officer give the order 'to put all the women and children in the boats and have them go off about 200 yards from the vessel'. By that point, Stengel was 'a little bit agitated', but he recalled that 'the officers or men who had charge of loading the lifeboats' reassured the passengers that: 'There is no danger; this is simply a matter of precaution.'[38]

Edwin Kimball and his wife Susan were by this time already on deck with their lifebelts on. When they had been ready to head topside from their staterooms, they went up together with their friends, the Beckwiths, Helen Newsom and Karl Behr. Behr remembered leading them all up from below since he remembered exactly where the lifeboats were.[39] When the group arrived topside, there were only a few people there. Eventually, they saw the officers attempting to load Boat No. 7. Edwin remembered that 'the officers were having great difficulty in getting the people to go into the lifeboats, assuring them at the same time that it would not be a long while before they probably would be back on the big boat.'[40]

Below deck, Saloon Steward Ray was searching for a lifebelt for Second Steward Dodd. Ray 'went through five staterooms and saw nobody there in either of them'. Finally, he found a lifebelt in the fifth room and took it back to Dodd. With this accomplished, he decided to go to his assigned lifeboat, No. 9, on the Boat Deck.[41]

Meanwhile, Saloon Steward William Ward had searched through the forward First Class areas on D Deck. He didn't find anyone to send up to the Boat Deck, but he did collect seven lifebelts before he left the area. He donned one himself, and then began heading up. Ward found that most of the people he encountered had already been supplied with lifebelts, but he busied himself with fastening them to those who had not already put them on. Then he went to the Boat Deck to find out what the situation was at his assigned lifeboat, No. 7.[42]

First Class passenger Eleanor Cassebeer had returned to her D Deck stateroom to dress. She rummaged through her steamer trunk for the warmest clothes she had brought with her. As she lifted the lid, she noticed that it felt odd as it moved … then she realized it was because the ship was down by the head. She took the time to don a sealskin coat and hat, as well as a big sealskin muff.

While she was there, she also grabbed a blanket; then she hunted around for a lifebelt, which she only 'found with some difficulty'. Only then did she head off for the upper decks again. The beautiful dress and stoll which she had worn that night at dinner – which had caused such a stir among those at her table – were left behind. When Eleanor arrived at the upper decks, she recalled that 'stewards and pursers' were taking the time to pin steamer rugs around their waists, to help defend them against the cold.[43]

Following the collision, Second Class passenger Susan Webber had returned to bed, but found that she could not sleep. After some time had passed, she heard 'a ship's officer' shout: 'All hands on deck – put your life belts on.' She got back out of bed, put a traveling coat over her nightdress, and then donned stockings and shoes. When she emerged from her cabin, the steward fastened a lifebelt around her and then sent her packing topside.[44]

It seems that Second Class passenger Nora Keane had stayed in the cabin with Susan Webber following the collision; she remembered that she 'was ready for bed' when an officer came by and told them both to put their lifebelts on. She then left with Miss Webber. Even then, Nora thought that there was no particular danger, as they had been expressly told that the ship was unsinkable. People had said that 'it was an impossibility' for the ship to go down.[45]

When Lawrence Beesley reached the Boat Deck again, he found a somewhat different scene than when he had first come on deck. There was steam blowing off from the 'large steam pipe reaching high up one of the funnels: a harsh, deafening boom that made conversation difficult and no doubt increased the apprehension of some people merely because of the volume of the noise: if one imagines twenty locomotives blowing off steam in a low key it would give some idea of the unpleasant sound that met us as we climbed out on the top deck.' Beesley thought that

the time was about 12:20 a.m., and the ship still felt steady and secure.

> The ship was absolutely still and, except for a gentle tilt downwards, which I don't think one person in ten would have noticed at that time, no signs of the approaching disaster were visible. She lay just as if she were waiting the order to go on again when some trifling matter had been adjusted.

Yet a few moments later, crewmen began to work on all of the starboard side aft lifeboats, Nos 9 through 15. He noticed that they were lifting the covers from the boats. Some were …

> … inside arranging the oars, some coiling ropes [falls] on the deck … others with cranks fitted to the rocking arms of the davits. As we watched, the cranks were turned, the davits swung outwards until the boats hung clear of the edge of the deck.[46]

As this scene played out, Beesley watched intently.

By then, Bedroom Steward Alfred Theissinger had met up with fellow Bedroom Steward George Brewster on D Deck; their meeting was apparently after Theissinger had awakened a number of passengers below deck. The two stewards then went back up past the Purser's Enquiry Office on C Deck. Theissinger remembered that just then, 'passengers were running to and fro and as we passed the purser's office there were scores of men and women demanding and receiving their valuables.'[47]

In the meantime, Colonel Gracie had been standing on the port side of the Promenade Deck for quite some time, along with a group of others. Gracie realized that the four ladies he was with were 'somewhat disturbed' by the situation. However, there was some good news which came along just then:

> Our hopes were buoyed with the information, imparted through the ship's officers, that there had been an interchange of wireless messages with passing ships, one of which was certainly coming to our rescue.[48]

Gracie also reassured the ladies by showing them the …

> … bright white light of what I took to be a ship about five miles off and which I felt sure was coming to our rescue. Colonel Astor heard me telling this to them and he asked me to show it and I pointed the light out to him. In so doing we both had to lean over the rail of the ship and look close in towards the bow, avoiding a lifeboat even then made ready with its gunwale lowered to the level of the floor of the Boat Deck above us and obstructing our view.[49]

On the Bridge, Fourth Officer Boxhall had finished his own calculation of the ship's position. He then gave it to Captain Smith. Smith, in turn, ordered him to take this revised position to the Marconi room. When he arrived, however, the Fourth Officer could not verbally tell the two operators what the position was because of the racket of escaping steam. Instead, he wrote it on a slip of paper without interrupting Phillips and left. Just afterwards, at 12:37

Olympic's port side Boat Deck, looking forward from the vicinity of the No. 3 funnel. On Titanic, *the Chamberses emerged onto the Boat Deck from the door on the right hand side, and moved forward to the vicinity of the lifeboats, where they encountered Captain Smith.*

a.m., Phillips began sending out the CQD with the revised position, which would be famous forever: 41° 46' north, 50° 14' west.[50]

Within a minute's time, Phillips raised the Cunard liner *Carpathia*, some fifty-eight miles away. Realizing the seriousness of the incoming *Titanic* message, *Carpathia's* Marconi Operator, Harold Cottam, notified her Captain, Arthur Rostron. Rostron immediately turned his ship around and headed toward *Titanic's* reported position at full speed. Phillips told Bride to convey this good news to Captain Smith. Bride found Smith in the Wheelhouse, and they both went back to the Marconi room. Captain Smith asked how far away she was, and must have been aghast after he worked out the distance between the two ships: it would take four hours for them to get there. There was no possibility that they would arrive before the ship sank …[51]

Meanwhile, Major Arthur Peuchen had proceeded to his room on C Deck. While there, he changed as quickly as he could, removing his formal evening attire, and then donning heavy clothes that would help to protect him against the cold. He also put on an overcoat, and then grabbed his lifebelt before leaving his room. What he saw in the Entrance on C Deck was a very sobering scene …

> In the hallway I met a great many people, ladies and gentlemen, with their life belts on, and the ladies were crying, principally, most of them. It was a very serious sight, and I commenced to realize how serious matters were.

Peuchen began making his way through this human throng. He headed up to the Boat Deck.[52]

Now that they had donned their lifebelts, First Class passengers Herbert and Carrie Chaffee were also heading back up on deck. While coming up the stairs to the Promenade Deck, they passed an officer. It was the first officer that Mrs Chaffee had seen since the collision. Although Carrie had remarked to her husband that they should stay together, the officer said something about women going to one side of the deck. Mrs Chaffee complied, separating

from her husband, and going to the port side of the Boat Deck.[53]

When First Class passengers Marguerite Frölicher and her parents left their adjoining staterooms, having fetched their lifebelts, they bumped into their own Bedroom Steward, who was standing in the hall. Days earlier, when they had boarded at Cherbourg, young Marguerite had teased the same steward for having placed a lifebelt in her cabin when the liner was so unsinkable. The whole exchange must have seemed a little ironic as she stood there with one of the same lifebelts. She remembered that the steward was 'pale as a sheet'. Yet, with typical English aplomb, he tried to reassure the young lady. 'Don't be afraid, Miss. Remember all those compartments. The ship can't sink.'

Miss Frölicher replied: 'I'm not scared, I'm just seasick.' Then she and her family went up to the Boat Deck.[54]

Since the collision, John Snyder had made three trips out on deck, all at his bride's urging, to investigate what had happened to the ship. Just as he had been about to retire once again, a steward came along. The steward told them not to be alarmed, but to dress hurriedly and go on deck. The couple took their time. Nelle Snyder recalled that with 'Jack's aid I dressed, even to putting on all my jewels.' This included four diamond rings, pins, and a jeweled vanity bag which she could carry from her arm. Once they were ready, the couple headed out on deck; apparently they just missed the order for men and women to split up and go to separate sides of the ship. They headed up towards the Boat Deck, and found that work had already begun on preparing the lifeboats.[55]

It was around this time that Norman and Bertha Chambers acquired their steamer rugs from the Deck Steward. That accomplished, they climbed the nearby port side companionway just aft of the First Class Lounge, and emerged onto the Boat Deck just forward of the No. 3 funnel.

At that point, Norman Chambers remembered that there 'did not at any time seem to be any particular group of passengers around the boats on the port side, although there were seamen there unlimbering the gear'. The scene was unbelievably noisy. In addition to the work of preparing the lifeboats for loading, there was the racket of steam blowing off from the funnels above. Whenever he needed to communicate anything to his wife, he literally had to shout in her ear over the din.[56]

Even though it was nearly an hour after the collision, the escaping steam was continuing to be a nuisance; the racket was certainly giving Marconi Operator Phillips a rough time of it. At 12:38 a.m. ship's time, Phillips was heard by the SS *Ypiranga* tapping out CQD and saying: 'Require immediate assistance. We have collision with iceberg. Sinking. Can hear nothing for noise of steam.'[57]

12:40 a.m. – 1:00 a.m.

First Class passenger Edith Rosenbaum had trudged up to the Boat Deck from the Lounge after the call came out for women and children to proceed there. However, she was not favorably impressed with the scene at the Boat Deck, recalling that there 'was so much confusion and indecision' there that she finally concluded 'the whole thing was a farce', and returned to the Lounge.[58]

Just then, Major Arthur Peuchen arrived on the Boat Deck. He was in time to pitch in as Lightoller prepared to lower Boat No. 4 to the Promenade Deck. When he got there, he saw that the port side boats 'were all ready for action; that is, the covers had been taken off of them, and the ropes cleared, ready to lower'. He was standing near Second Officer Lightoller, and Captain Smith was nearby, as well. One of the two men said: 'We will have to get these masts out of these boats, and also the sail.' Turning to Peuchen, the officer said: 'You might give us a hand.' So Peuchen hopped into the lifeboat, and the men working on the boat 'got a knife and cut the lashings of the mast, which is a very heavy mast, and also the sail, and moved it out of the boat, saying it would not be required.'[59]

Lightoller then ordered Boat No. 4 lowered to the Promenade Deck, where he believed that passengers could board more easily. There was a heavy coaling wire that ran along A Deck, and Lightoller tied No. 4 to it, 'in case the ship got a list or anything.'[60] The entire process of getting this particular boat ready and down to the Promenade Deck took quite a bit of time, as he recalled. Once the boat had drawn level with A Deck, Lightoller ordered those on the Boat Deck with him to go below and start the loading there.

Steward Joseph Wheat had been assisting passengers into their lifebelts since just after 12:15 a.m. – nearly half an hour's work. He remembered hearing an order at about this time, which he passed on, for 'all women and children [to go] on to A deck on the port side,' apparently in anticipation of loading them into Boat No. 4. Then he headed below to his cabin.[61]

Down on the port side of A Deck, Archibald Gracie was near Boat No. 4. He estimated that 'forty-five minutes' had now elapsed since the collision when Captain Smith's orders were transmitted to the crew to lower the lifeboats, loaded with women and children first.[62]

After this, Gracie recalled that a 'tall thin chap', Sixth Officer Moody,[63] stood with a number of other crewmen on the deck to bar any men passengers from getting near the boat, saying: 'No man beyond this line.'[64] Gracie could do nothing more than hand off the responsibility for Mrs Appleton, Mrs Cornell, Mrs Brown and Miss Evans directly

to Moody. He 'felt sure that they would be safely loaded in the boats' at that point.

Then Gracie noticed Isidor and Ida Straus standing nearby on the Promenade Deck:

> Then I saw Mr Straus and Mrs Straus, of whom I had seen a great deal during the voyage. I had heard them discussing that if they were going to die they would die together.[65]

He recalled that shortly after the order to begin loading the women and children in the boats came down, Mrs Straus 'shone forth heroically when she promptly and emphatically' exclaimed: 'No! I will not be separated from my husband; as we have lived, so will we die together.'

Gracie then suggested that, because of Mr Straus's 'age and helplessness, exception should be made and he be allowed to accompany his wife in the boat.'

Mr Straus replied: 'No! I do not wish any distinction in my favor which is not granted to others.' He added that he would share his fate with the rest of the men, and that he would not go beyond that. Then Gracie recalled:

> They expressed themselves as fully prepared to die, and calmly sat down in steamer chairs on the glass-enclosed Deck A, prepared to meet their fate. Further entreaties to make them change their decision were of no avail. Later they moved to the Boat Deck above, accompanying Mrs Straus's maid …[66]

Gracie saw that he could be of no further assistance with the Strauses.

Meanwhile, there was a dilemma developing. Boat No. 4 had just been lowered to the Promenade Deck, so that passengers could board from that deck rather from the open deck above. On the Boat Deck, First Class passenger Hugh Woolner later remembered hearing Captain Smith call out: 'I want all the passengers to go down on A deck, because I intend they shall go into the boats from A deck.' Bertha Chambers, who had just arrived on the port side of the Boat Deck, also saw Captain Smith come by, and she remembered his words as: 'Ladies, if you will go down to deck A I think you can get in more easily.' Carrie Chaffee, having separated from her husband, had arrived on the port side of the Boat Deck just in time to be told to go back down to A Deck, probably along with the group of others who were told to trudge down to that deck to board Boat No. 4. She stood, patiently waiting on the Promenade Deck, until No. 4 could be loaded.[67]

After hearing these orders from the Captain, Hugh Woolner decided to intervene. As he had come up on deck, he had noticed that the Promenade windows were closed, so he approached Captain Smith, gave a crisp salute, and said: 'Haven't you forgotten, sir, that all those glass windows are closed?'

'By God,' Smith said, 'you are right. Call those people back!'[68] Some of the passengers had not yet left the deck, and a number of others – doubtless exasperated – came back up. Still others apparently stayed below on the Promenade Deck.

With the enclosed windows impeding the loading of No. 4, Lightoller then gave 'two or three' stewards the order to go find the handles and crank open the windows. However, it was not going to be accomplished quickly. Hugh

Above: *This mockup demonstrates the type of window used on Olympic's B Deck, as well as along Titanic's A Deck Promenade. The cranks to open the vertically-sliding windows were removable, and the cranks were not handy when the officers made their first attempt to load Boat No. 4.*

Left: *This photograph of one of Olympic's B Deck Promenade windows, without the cranks, shows how the windows on Titanic's Promenade Deck would have appeared. Note the gears along the window tracks in both this and the preceding photo.*

Woolner remembered that one day during the crossing, he had watched the sailors 'winding them up with these spanners that are used for that purpose.' It struck him as 'being rather a slow job.'[69]

As the attempt to load No. 4 fell apart for the time being, and much of the group there dispersed, the ladies Gracie had left with Sixth Officer Moody eventually moved off to other locations. Moody himself headed back up to the Boat Deck.

First Class passenger Emily Ryerson and her husband Arthur were among the crowd that had gathered on A Deck before being ordered to the Boat Deck. Standing with them were their 21-year-old daughter Suzette, 18-year-old daughter Emily, 13-year-old son John, Emily's maid Victorine Chaudanson, and First Class passenger Grace Bowen, who was traveling with the family. Arthur Ryerson was reassuring throughout, being described as 'calm and cheerful', and when some of the women began

to get upset, he joked with them, saying: 'Don't you hear the band playing?' As they all headed up to the Boat Deck, Emily begged her husband to let her stay with him. He told her that she must obey orders, and that when they called for women and children, she must go when her turn came. 'You take a boat going to New York.' This referred to rumors circulating among the crowd that the *Olympic* and *Baltic* would soon be nearby.[70]

Bertha Chambers attributed the mistake of sending the passengers down to A Deck to 'agitation' on the Captain's part.[71] At that point, her husband Norman still felt the ship listing to starboard, and so he concluded that any lifeboats launched from the starboard side would have an easier time of clearing the ship's towering side. Thus, he led his wife up the short set of stairs and onto the roof over the Lounge, and then over to the forward boats on the starboard side. They paused just by the Gymnasium door to allow numerous passengers to emerge from the First Class Entrance onto the Boat Deck. He recalled that stewards on the deck were directing these passengers 'to the boats aft'. Chambers waited until the crowd had exited, and then they kept moving forward.[72]

Overall, Bertha Chambers was not particularly impressed with the work that the crew was doing on the lifeboats on the starboard side. 'No officer was directing, and few sailors were in sight. Things were being done, but in a haphazard, unsystematic fashion. There was no evidence of the least familiarity on the part of the crew with the routine of lowering the boats.'[73]

Back on the port side, rather than waiting around for Boat No. 4 to be ready for loading, Second Officer Lightoller moved on to Boat No. 6 to begin work on it.[74] He remembered that he was working on No. 6 about 'three quarters of an hour' after coming on deck, which places the efforts there at around 12:40–12:45 a.m.[75]

It was at about this same time – after temporarily abandoning efforts to load Boat No. 4, and while starting to work on Boat No. 6 – that Lightoller gave another order: He sent Boatswain Alfred Nichols and six other crewmen below to open the gangway doors.[76] The Second Officer did this with the intention of making it possible for the lifeboats to come alongside the ship, and take on more passengers there once afloat. The plan, however, fell by the wayside, and the men never returned from below. Lightoller had already been suffering from a certain shortage of qualified seamen; from that point on, this problem would only grow more pronounced.[77]

Below, Dr Washington Dodge had already made three trips out of his stateroom to find out what the situation was. It was only after he returned from these that he finally received word from their Bedroom Steward that the order had come down to put on their lifebelts. His wife had dressed warmly, and they had awakened and dressed their son, Master Washington – or Bobo, as he was called at the time. Later, young Washington could not remember whether it was his mother or his father who dressed him, but at some point, Dr Dodge grabbed three lifebelts from the top of their wardrobe and draped them over his arm. Once the family members were ready, they left their stateroom and climbed the forward Grand Staircase to the Boat Deck. While they were in their cabin dressing and getting their lifebelts, they missed the order, heard by others, for women and children to proceed to the port side of the ship. Thus, the family remained together.[78]

Right: *This photograph of* Olympic's *Lounge Roof during the 1920's shows the path the Chamberses took to cross over to the starboard side Boat Deck from the port side. However on* Titanic, *the lifeboat configuration was entirely different.*

Below: Titanic's *Gymnasium. A number of passengers gathered here to stay off the cold decks as lifeboats were prepared and lowered. Instructor McCawley happily demonstrated the equipment to these passengers.*

Meanwhile, Steward Etches had soon re-joined Thomas Andrews on C Deck. The two men then proceeded to the First Class Entrance and forward Grand Staircase together. Etches recalled that at that time:

> The purser [Chief Purser McElroy] was standing outside of his office, in a large group of ladies. The purser was asking them to do as he asked them, and to go back in their rooms and not to frighten themselves, but, as a preliminary caution, to put the life belts on, and the stewards would give them every attention. Mr Andrews said: 'That is exactly what I have been trying to get them to do.'

With that, Andrews left to go down the stairs to D Deck. Just then, McElroy told Etches: 'It is necessary to go up on the boat deck. Tell all the other bedroom stewards to assemble their passengers on the boat deck and stand by.' So Etches headed topside to the starboard side of the Boat Deck. Arriving there, he found that the crew was loading Boat No. 7. Etches was looking for his own lifeboat, No. 5, so he asked a Quartermaster nearby: 'Is this Boat No. 5?' The Quartermaster responded: 'No; it is the next boat.'[79]

Elsewhere, the Duff Gordons and Laura Francatelli were sticking closely together. They had found the First Class Entrance on the Boat Deck very crowded, with many people moving out onto the open Boat Deck on either side. Lucy thought some of the young American men in the crowd were making some intolerably crass wisecracks. It was so cold outside that the trio avoided going out on the deck, and instead found a spot just off the main traffic pathways.

Earlier, the stewards had come through and told passengers that they should be ready to board the lifeboats when the call came. The Duff Gordons had hardly believed their ears when they heard … was this all really happening?

They had spent some time inside the Entrance, and eventually they decided to go out onto the port Boat Deck. Things were quite crowded and struck them as very chaotic. After observing the scene there, Sir Cosmo said: 'We will go round to the starboard side. It may be better there. It can't possibly be worse.'

They then walked around to the starboard deck, and found their way into the warm, brilliantly-lit Gymnasium to wait. They sat there for a few minutes, watching events play out on the deck just beyond the room's arched windows. They also noticed that things seemed to be less crowded out there than they had been on the port side.[80]

Meanwhile, on the starboard side, First Officer Murdoch was hard at work at Boat No. 7. Lookout George Hogg, one of the two lookouts who had relieved Lookout Fleet and Lee following the collision,[81] was working with him. He had been putting the boat's plug in and completing prep work on the boat. When it came time to start loading the boat, Hogg jumped out to assist with the falls when it was ready to lower away. Murdoch had other ideas, however, and told him: 'You step in that boat.' Hogg didn't argue, saying: 'Very good, sir.'[82]

The crewmen involved in the process bundled all of the women and children standing nearby into Boat No. 7, but they quickly ran out of people willing to board. They were having trouble convincing many of the passengers just to come out on deck, particularly with the cold and noise, let alone climb into the boats. This was particularly the case because many of the passengers still did not think that there was anything wrong with the ship; *Titanic* appeared so much safer than a little wooden lifeboat in the middle of the night.

Newlyweds John and Nelle Snyder had fully dressed, and they reached the starboard Boat Deck just as the first lifeboats were being prepared. When passengers had first been told to climb aboard the boats, Nelle Snyder remembered that many persons drew back and said they would rather stay on board. But as soon as the boats were loaded, word came down for them to be lowered.[83]

Saloon Steward William Ward had turned out to No. 7, since it was his assigned boat. He remembered things were quite orderly, and that some ladies got in as well as some men. He had also noticed that most people were still treating the whole situation 'as a kind of a joke'.[84]

While most people were treating the situation lightly, Dorothy Gibson was very nervous. William Sloper recalled that she led their party along the Boat Deck toward Boat No. 7. Sloper helped her into the boat, and told her: 'Keep a stiff upper lip.' Since so many people were unwilling to board the craft, the crewmen allowed Sloper and Frederic Seward to climb in along with Dorothy and her mother. Just then, Sloper noticed that John Jacob Astor and his wife were about to board, as well. Suddenly, and quite unexpectedly, Astor drew back and pulled his wife back with him. Someone said something to Astor, but Sloper couldn't hear what it was.[85]

Philipp Mock and his sister had watched as Boat No. 7 was loaded. Mock, like others nearby, also noticed that no one 'wanted to enter the boats, even when asked to do so. They thought the ship was not going to sink and they preferred to stay by it.' However, he also recalled that the prevailing 'feeling of security, or safety among the first cabin passengers was paramount' even at that point.[86]

First Class passenger Antoinette Flegenheim had stayed on deck for some time after the collision. When the order for passengers to head up to the boats had been passed, at about 12:25 a.m., she had planned to return below to her cabin to dress. However, she had been prevented from doing so. Thus, she was on hand just as Boat No. 7 was being loaded, and found her way aboard the boat. For her, clad only in a nightgown, bathrobe, stockings, slippers, and a steamer cap, one thing was certain: it was going to be a very long, cold night.[87]

Steward Etches lent a hand at Boat No. 7, as he could see that his assigned boat, No. 5 was still being prepared for loading. He noticed Murdoch, Pitman, Ismay, the Quartermaster he had just spoken to, and two other stewards on the scene, all assisting in the effort; Etches thought that there was 'great excitement' at the time. Passengers were tripping on Boat No. 7's falls, which Etches helped to clear.

Sometime after arriving on deck, Etches saw Benjamin Guggenheim and Victor Giglio. Their appearance stunned the steward; when he had last seen them, he was sending them out of their cabin in nightclothes, a sweater and lifebelts. But now Etches saw that the two men 'were dressed in their evening clothes. They had deliberately taken off their sweaters,' and they had also removed their lifebelts. 'What's that for?' Etches asked.

'We've dressed up in our best, and are prepared to go down like gentlemen,' the millionaire replied. Somehow, they had gotten the word that the ship was mortally wounded, when most were still unaware that this was the case. Then, Guggenheim asked Etches to do him an important favor. He told Etches that he had a message for the steward to give to his wife. It was: 'If anything should happen to me, tell my wife in New York that I've done my best in doing my duty.'[88]

Etches next watched as both Guggenheim and Giglio passed from 'one lifeboat to another', obviously a reference to Boats Nos 7 and 5, 'helping the women and children. Mr Guggenheim would shout out, "Women first" '. Etches believed that the two men were of 'great assistance' to the officers.[89]

Another steward reportedly saw Guggenheim, as well, although exactly when he spotted them is unclear. Guggenheim sent another message to his wife through this steward, asking him to tell her 'that I played the game straight to the end and that no woman was left on board this ship because Ben Guggenheim was a coward. Tell her that my last thoughts will be of her and our girls.' Then the steward watched as Guggenheim 'lit a cigar and sauntered up to the boat deck to help load the life boats.'[90]

By that time, Alfred Nourney had again rejoined his friends, and they were helping to load women into Boat No. 7. After this, Nourney and his young friends were among the male passengers ordered into No. 7. Nourney, Henry Blank and William Greenfield all complied.[91] Another one of the men who boarded the boat at this time was First Class passenger James McGough. He had his back turned towards the boat when an officer, possibly Murdoch, grabbed him by the shoulder and pushed him toward No. 7 saying: 'Here, you are a big fellow; get into the boat.'[92]

Murdoch told the crewmen in the lifeboat to row away a short distance from the ship, but to stand by the gangway. The passengers in the boat, not yet realizing there was any danger, figured this was because it would only be a short time until the boats were taken back aboard *Titanic*. This incomprehension is understandable, considering the fact that early on in the sinking, First Class passenger Peter Daly heard the officers and crewmen repeatedly tell the passengers, particularly the women, that boarding the boats 'is only a precaution ... you'll be back in the morning for breakfast; there's no danger.'[93]

In reality, it seems as if early on Murdoch, like Lightoller, was thinking that more passengers could be loaded into the boats, once they were afloat, from the lower gangways. Perhaps they felt that this would be a safer option than overloading the boats while they were sitting in the davits.

It was at this point that the Dodge family arrived on the starboard Boat Deck adjacent to Boat No. 7. Dr Dodge noticed that the boat was already loading, but that there were only a few persons in it at the time. He heard 'the officer in charge' call for women and children to climb aboard, and he was having trouble getting people to fill it. However, Dr Dodge hesitated, still unsure as to whether his family would be safer on the ship or in the lifeboat. He then took the lifebelts which he had been carrying and busied himself at fastening them to his loved ones.

To young Master Dodge, the deck appeared crowded, and the racket of steam being blown off was frightening. He remembered hearing his mother remark to his father: 'Imagine, wouldn't something like this happen when his nanny isn't with us?'

Murdoch ordered Boat No. 7 away around 12:40 a.m.[94] Dr Dodge heard the order, 'Lower away' being given, and watched carefully as the boat made a safe descent to the water. Then he moved his family toward Boat No. 5, now that he had determined it would be safe for them to board the small craft.[95]

By that time, Fifth Officer Lowe had also joined in the effort to assist in lowering No. 7.[96] The lifeboat, which could hold sixty-five persons, left with about twenty-eight aboard.[97] It became the first lifeboat to leave the doomed liner. It touched down on the surface of the ocean, which was described as being 'as smooth as glass', without even as much as a ripple.

Isaac Frauenthal had also watched as Boat No. 7 was loaded and lowered away. He remembered that it …

This photograph shows Olympic's starboard side, looking aft, in 1935. It gives a wonderful idea of the perspective of passengers in the forward, starboard lifeboats as they were lowered away into the sea.

… didn't have nearly as many as it could carry comfortably, because there were not enough men on deck to fill it. I didn't hear any order given about 'women and children first', but everybody seemed to take it for granted that the women and children must have first chance at the boats.

The few that got in the first boat were laughing and joking, thinking that apparently it was foolish to ask them to go out there in the dark in a little boat when there was a great lighted ship to take care of them.

When his brother and sister-in-law had joined him, Isaac couldn't resist referring back to his set of ominous dreams and subsequent nerves when boarding the ship, for which his brother had laughed at him. 'Well, Henry,' he said, 'I wasn't so foolish, was I?'

Henry knew there was trouble, but still wasn't convinced of its severity. 'Oh,' he replied, 'the boat is too big. It can't sink.'

Isaac recalled that shortly after this, he saw Mr and Mrs Straus 'standing by the rail on the starboard side. They were a little removed from the other passengers and were calmly conversing.'[98]

Meanwhile, the Hoyts had been below in their cabin dressing warmly. As a result, they had missed both the order for passengers to put on their lifebelts, and the subsequent order for men and women to go to opposite sides of the ship. When they 'again went on deck', Jane Hoyt thought that there 'was not the slightest disorder but people were hurrying about.' At about that time, the crew was 'just getting ready to lower the first life boat. It was impossible for the officers to induce women to get in to the boat,' she recalled, as everyone still thought that the unsinkable *Titanic* was safer than a small little lifeboat.

No amount of persuasion could convince the women that it would be safer for them to get in the boats.

The first boat contained more men than it did women for this reason alone. Finally, when the women saw that the men were willing to get in the boats they began to change their minds.

I saw Mr Ismay standing with Mr Andrews when the first boat drew away and he was trying to keep order.[99]

Both Ismay and Andrews then moved on to help at Boat No. 5. They were spotted there just moments later.

Down in cabin D-28, First Class passengers Elizabeth and Mary Lines had obediently waited in their cabin for nearly an hour after the ship struck the iceberg. Their steward had told them to remain there right after the collision, but had never returned to give them further instructions. They had subsequently felt the ship come to a complete stop, and heard steam from the boilers blowing off far above. The women did not feel that they were in any immediate danger, as they had not even taken the opportunity to dress, but as time passed, they were growing concerned.

Then they heard the voice of 54-year-old Percival White, a fellow First Class passenger who was staying in adjoining cabin D-26. He was calling to his 21-year-old son Richard to head for the lifeboats. Mr White was acquaint-

Lifeboat Launch Times					
Port Side			**Starboard Side**		
Time	Boat	In Charge of Loading	Time	Boat	In Charge of Loading
12:40			12:40	7	Murdoch, Lowe
12:45			12:45	5	Murdoch, Lowe, Pitman (at 12:43)
12:47		Rockets first fired	12:47		
12:50			12:50		
12:55			12:55	3	Murdoch, Lowe
1:00	8	Lightoller, Wilde, Smith	1:00		
1:05			1:05	1	Murdoch, Lowe
1:10	6	Lightoller, Smith	1:10		
1:15			1:15		
1:20	16	Moody	1:20		
1:25	14	Lowe, Wilde, Lightoller	1:25		
1:30	12	Wilde, Lightoller	1:30	9	Murdoch, Moody
1:35			1:35	11	Murdoch
1:40			1:40	13 15	Murdoch, Moody Murdoch, Moody (at 1:41)
1:45	2	Wilde, Smith	1:45		
1:50		Rockets cease firing	1:50		
1:50	10 4	Murdoch Lightoller	1:50		
1:55			1:55		
2:00			2:00	C	Murdoch, Wilde
2:05	D	Lightoller, Wilde	2:05		
2:10			2:10		
2:15	(B)	(Lightoller) (Bridge goes under)	2:15	(A)	(Murdoch, Moody) (Bridge goes under)
2:20			2:20		

ed with the two women, and apparently noticed that their cabin light was on, so he walked down the hallway and 'pounded' on their door. When the women opened it, he must have been astonished to see that they were still inside, and still undressed at that. 'What are you doing here?' he asked. 'This ship is sinking!' He helped Elizabeth and Mary find their lifebelts. Mary later recalled that he 'was so insistent about getting us out of there' that they only had time to don their jackets, shoes, and hats. Mary also pocketed her tiny flashlight, in case it was needed.

When the women began to ascend the Grand Staircase, they came across their steward, 'sitting … at the foot of the stairs.' As they passed, Mrs Lines asked: 'You are going up on deck?'

The steward merely responded: 'No', and said good-bye.

Once they had reached the top of the stairs at the Boat Deck, they were just about to go outside when they came across an unidentified 'young officer' who began to help them into their lifebelts. As he worked at getting the belts on and tied, he said: 'We are sending you out as a matter of precaution; we hope you will be back for breakfast.' Then the two women went out on deck. Mary remembered that by the time they arrived, some of the lifeboats had already been lowered away. Yet everything was quiet and calm, and the ship still felt safe enough that many were refusing to leave in the boats …[100]

It had taken about a full hour from the time of the collision until the first boat was ready for lowering. This was in spite of the fact that Captain Smith had ordered the lifeboats uncovered as a proactive measure before he even knew the ship was sinking. This may seem like an unconscionable waste of time, yet it had taken forty or forty-five minutes before Andrews was able to tell Captain Smith that the ship was doomed. There were additional complications: the unbelievable nature of the news that the ship was sinking; the difficulties of assembling the passengers and crew in the middle of the night after many had retired – and of doing so without creating a panic when there were nowhere near enough lifeboats; and the enormity of the task of uncovering, preparing and swinging out the lifeboats on a huge ship that most of the crew were very unfamiliar with. Because of all these handicaps, it really seems a miracle that the first boat got away in just an hour's time. Once lifeboats began to leave the ship, however, the process really began to move forward quickly, each of the officers growing into his own particular style.

Just forward of Boat No. 7, Third Officer Pitman had been working on Boat No. 5. Once he had arrived, he and the men working with him had to finish stripping off the cover and getting the boat ready to swing out. While they worked, Pitman noticed a passenger standing nearby who was clad in a dressing gown and slippers. The man said to Pitman very quietly, 'There is no time to waste.' Pitman did not recognize the passenger, and mentally dismissed him as ignorant, thinking that 'he did not know anything about it at all,' and simply continued carrying on with his work.

When the time came to swing Boat No. 5 out, Third Officer Pitman was pleasantly surprised with the operation of the new style Welin davits. With the assistance of five or six seamen, the boat was swung out and lowered level with the deck in just 'two or three' minutes;[101] the Third Officer thought that these davits were a 'great improvement' over the old-fashioned radial bar davits, which took longer, and required about a dozen men on each end of the boat to lift it over the edge of deck.

It was at this point that the nearby passenger in the dressing gown again asserted himself, telling Pitman that they had better get the boat loaded with women and children. Pitman replied: 'I await the *commander's* orders.' The man replied, 'Very well.' Pitman suddenly began to realize that this passenger was most likely J. Bruce Ismay, Chairman of the White Star Line – and thus his employer. So he moved off toward the Bridge, found Captain Smith, and explained that he thought that 'Mr Ismay … wished me to get the boat away, with women and children in it.' Captain Smith said: 'Go ahead; carry on.'

Pitman returned to the boat, climbed into it, and called out to the passengers waiting nearby: 'Come along, ladies.' There was a good-sized crowd of people standing in the vicinity, and it did not take a very long time for Pitman to load the boat. He noticed that Ismay 'helped to get them along', and 'assisted in every way'.[102]

Helen Ostby, her father Engelhart, and Mr and Mrs Frank and Anna Warren all waited on the starboard side of the Boat Deck, watching as Boat No. 5 was prepared. When the time came for the women and children to begin boarding, Anna Warren moved toward the lifeboat and was helped in. Young Helen followed after her, noticing that 'there was a little gap' between the side of the boat and the edge of the deck. She thought that crossing the gap was a 'very unpleasant feeling'. Frank Warren and Engelhart

Ostby stood back, not making any attempt to board the lifeboat.[103]

Marguerite Frölicher and her parents Margaretha and Maximilian reached Boat No. 5 just as it was filling. Young Marguerite remembered 'two fat sailors' lifting her mother into a lifeboat first, and then picking her up and placing her in the boat next to her. Maximilian 'started instinctively to follow' them, as the boat was far from full. However, the sailors stopped him, saying, 'Ladies first, Sir.' He stepped back, and Marguerite could see the tears in her father's eyes as he called out to them, '*Auf weidersehen.*'[104]

The Duff Gordons and Lucy's secretary, Laura Francatelli, had stayed in the Gymnasium until a call came out for passengers to make their way to the boats. Then they headed back out to the starboard Boat Deck. Lucy watched the loading of Boat No. 5, where the orders were for women first:

> Even in that terrible moment I was filled with wonder at nearly all the American wives who were leaving their husbands without a word of protest or regret, scarce of farewell … [When] two officers came up and tried to force me into one of the boats I refused.[105]

Elsewhere, when Eleanor Cassebeer came up from her stateroom and returned to the Promenade Deck Entrance, her table companion Harry Anderson met back up with her. It looked to her as if he'd aged ten years since they had parted. Apparently he had discovered something very bad since they separated, but she didn't think too much about it at the time. Anderson led her up to the Boat Deck and out onto the starboard side, then told her in no uncertain terms to get into Boat No. 5, which the men were just about to put over the deck's edge. Here she bumped into another one of her table companions, Thomas Andrews:

> I could not hear just what he said to me at the time on account of the din, but I saw him motion me to get into the boat, which was about to be swung over the rail, 90 feet above the water [*sic*]. I asked him why he did not get in also, and he said: 'No, women and children first.'[106]

She then jumped spryly into the boat. As she climbed in, she saw her shipboard companion, Benjamin Foreman, standing at the rail not too far away. Perhaps, she thought, he had noticed that she had returned to her normal attire of severe suits. 'Come on in, there's plenty of room,' she said. He replied, 'No, it's women first.' She also noticed that Bruce Ismay had been helping to load women and children into the boat, and that he 'was dressed in pajamas and slippers, with a coat thrown over his shoulders.'[107]

Doctor Henry Frauenthal, his wife Clara, and his brother Isaac moved forward, heading toward Boat No. 5. The loading process very nearly depleted the numbers of the crowd that had been standing nearby; only two women refused to get in, and at that point, Pitman shouted out for any more ladies.

The crewmembers placed Annie Stengel into Boat No. 5. She then turned, and wanted her husband to follow her. However, Charles heard those in charge of loading say: 'No; nothing but ladies and children.' Annie heard someone say, 'No more; the boat is full.' Charles stepped back onto the deck.[108]

Passengers and crew engaging in a lifeboat drill aboard the German liner Kaiser Wilhelm der Grosse. *The scene gives an idea of how things looked during* Titanic's *evacuation.*

First Officer Murdoch, fresh from the lowering of No. 7, arrived then and also called out for more ladies, as did Ismay. A woman came up to the boat, and Ismay said: 'Come along, jump in.' She was hesitant, saying, 'I am only a stewardess.' Ismay said, 'Never mind, you are a woman, take your place,' and she climbed aboard.[109] When no more women were forthcoming, the crewmembers let a few men climb in to help fill up the boat.

Norman Chambers noticed that Boat No. 5 was quite well loaded when he and his wife came along.[110] Mrs Chambers told her husband that she was getting into that boat, and proceeded to jump in, calling after for him to join her. Chambers believed that if he didn't follow her, she would simply jump back out on the deck, so he jumped in as well. Although it was not very full, he felt that it would not have been 'sage to put very many more people in that boat'.

Edwin and Susan Kimball also made it to the deck as No. 5 was loading. So did their friends, Richard and Sarah Beckwith, along with Sarah's daughter Helen Newsom. Helen's beau, tennis player Karl Behr, also stood by. Mrs Beckwith turned to Bruce Ismay and asked if the men in their party could come in, and Karl remembered him replying: 'Why certainly.' The entire group climbed into the lifeboat and settled in.[111]

Steward Etches stood by the forward fall of No. 5. Quartermaster Alfred Olliver, who had been standing in the boat, assisting with the loading, stepped back onto the deck. He apparently did not have any intention of leaving the ship. Pitman had also jumped back onto the deck. Just then, Murdoch asked Etches: 'Are you the steward appointed to this boat?' Etches responded that he was, and the First Officer ordered him to get in the boat and assist the men with the forward fall. Pitman then called out, asking if there was a sailor in the boat. Etches looked around and told the Third Officer that there wasn't. Pitman ordered Olliver back into the boat.[112]

Still nearby, Doctor Washington Dodge moved his family toward Boat No. 5, and had them climb into it. Young Washington remembered that his mother put him into the boat, but that they had to leave his father behind, as the officer in charge had shouted that it would be 'women and children first.'[113]

At just about that point, Norman Chambers remembered hearing 'someone in authority' say: 'That is enough before lowering. We can get more in after she is in the water.' Next, First Officer Murdoch stepped up to Pitman and told him: 'You go in charge of this boat, old man, and also look after the others. Keep handy to come to the after gangway when hailed.' Pitman did not like the idea of leaving, since he still felt that he was 'better off' on the ship than in the lifeboat, but resolved to follow the order. Just then, Murdoch stuck a hand out to Pitman, and the Third Officer shook it. Murdoch said: 'Goodbye. Good luck to you,' and then moved on toward Boat No. 3. Steward Etches also had the opportunity to witness this farewell.[114]

At the time, Pitman fully expected that he would see Murdoch again, and that the lifeboats would be going back to the ship in 'perhaps two or three hours'. Later, the First Officer's manner in that moment stood out to Pitman; he concluded that Murdoch had not been expecting to see the Third Officer again. Farewell aside, Pitman had his instructions. He jumped back into Boat No. 5 and ordered: 'Lower away.'[115]

It was 12:43 a.m. As Eleanor Cassebeer looked from the lifeboat at her shipboard friend, Benjamin Foreman, he was still standing on the deck. She noticed that the small book she had lent him during the crossing was poking out from his jacket pocket.[116]

Norman Chambers recalled that just after he and his wife had gotten settled in the boat, 'a tall young officer clad in a long overcoat' came along. A clear reference to Murdoch, this officer was 'giving orders to another officer to go into our boat and take charge of the boats on our side. As a parting injunction he gave our officer (whom I later found to be a Mr Pitman) instructions to hold onto his painter and pull up alongside the gangway after the boat had reached the water.'[117]

Dr Henry Frauenthal was still unsure of exactly what had gone wrong with the ship. He had previously seen his wife Clara safely into the boat. Yet the doctor was still 'under the impression that the trouble was with the machinery and we were likely to be blown up'. This may explain the subsequent actions that he and his brother took. Right before No. 5 began descending, Isaac and Henry both leapt down into it. Elmer Taylor, a rather large man, also leaped; he landed directly on fellow First Class passenger Annie Stengel, dislocating some of her ribs.

The crewmembers were furious with the Frauenthal brothers' actions, and someone yelled out, 'Throw that man out of the boat,' but the boat had already started to lower away.[118] Just then, young Washington Dodge, sitting in the lifeboat, remembered hearing one of the officers on the scene say 'that he was going to go below decks and get his gun, if the pushing did not stop.'[119] Charles Stengel also remembered that when the Frauenthal brothers jumped into the boat, the 'officer or the man' who was in charge said: 'I will stop that. I will go down and get my gun.' Then he watched the officer leave the deck. Approximately thirty-six out of Boat No. 5's sixty-five seats were occupied.[120]

Around the time the order to lower away was given, Fifth Officer Lowe had come alongside the boat. Under

Murdoch's orders, he oversaw the lowering process, personally working one of the pair of falls. As the Fifth Officer began his work, Bruce Ismay leaned over the edge of the Boat Deck, hanging on the davit. Lowe was trying to work the slack out of the falls which were right at the Managing Director's feet. He said that Ismay was 'overanxious and was getting a trifle excited', waving his arms and shouting out, 'Lower away! Lower away! Lower Away! Lower Away!'

Lowe did not recognize Ismay at all, thinking he was just a passenger, and his patience ran thin because he felt that Ismay was interfering with his duties. In the heat of the moment, he exploded at him: 'If you will get to hell out of that I shall be able to do something!' When Ismay did not reply to this, Lowe continued: 'Do you want me to lower away quickly? You will have me drown the whole lot of them!' Without uttering another word in response, Ismay walked forward to Boat No. 3 to help with the preparations there.[121]

As No. 5 lowered, the men working at one of the davits let the falls play out more quickly than the crew manning the other davit, causing the boat to tip at a precarious angle. For a moment, the occupants felt like they would be tossed out.[122] Henry Frauenthal recalled:

In the process of being lowered, several times we thought we would be thrown into the water. When nearing the water, it was discovered that the plug in the bottom of the boat had not been safely inserted, and this was attended to. Had this been overlooked, this lifeboat would have sunk ...[123]

Helen Ostby also recalled that the trip to the water was 'very unpleasant ... Once below the boat deck, there were no lights so that it was difficult for the men on the deck, who were letting the boat down ... to keep it level. First one end would dip down, then the other, and the people in the boat would shout to them to level it off.'[124]

Marguerite Frölicher recalled that this frightful start from the deck had an unintended consequence:

Then they started to lower us, with only women in the lifeboat and still plenty of room. One end stuck and we were hanging crazily there so they pulled us up again.

I started screaming for my father and tried to get back on deck. Other women began calling to husbands and sons and suddenly a British officer said: 'Let the men in. Make haste.' I was never so happy in my life.[125]

Among the men who had been allowed into the boat was Marguerite's father, Maximilian Frölicher-Stehli. By comparison, Norman Chambers thought that the lowering process was 'very satisfactory, taking into account the apparent absolute lack of training of the rank and file of the crew.'

Finally, the boat was straightened up, but soon there came another issue. 'Halfway down', Third Officer Pitman was suddenly unsure that the plug had been put in. He blew his officer's whistle for the lowering to be halted, and then he called out loudly to one of the crewmen in the boat, asking him whether the plug was in. The crewman responded that it had been secured in place. Suddenly, a voice – probably belonging to Fifth Officer Lowe – called

down from the deck: 'It is your own blooming business to see that the plug is in, anyhow.'[126]

Shortly afterward, the boat reached the water safely. However, No. 5's troubles weren't over yet. There was difficulty in casting off the falls. Norman Chambers recalled that the 'little quartermaster had to crawl between our legs to the amidship portion of the boat in order to reach what was apparently called the "trigger", which is, I believe, a mechanism used to release both falls simultaneously.'[127]

Next the oars were unshipped and the lifeboat began to row away from the Titanic. After it had covered only a 'short distance', Henry Frauenthal asked Third Officer Pitman what had occurred. Pitman explained that they had struck an iceberg; it was the first that the doctor heard about a collision. He then asked Pitman how long it would be before they would return to the Titanic. Pitman replied that it would be 'within half an hour.'[128]

Despite this, Helen Ostby took careful note of the ship's orientation in the water as the lifeboat reached the sea. She said:

By the time we were lowered to the water, the Titanic had begun very noticeably to go down by the head. The stars were out, but it was pitch dark. The sea was calm. As we pulled away, we could see the lights of the ship, and the lighted forward portholes gradually disappearing.[129]

Saloon Steward Thomas Whiteley arrived on the Boat Deck just as Boat No. 5 was lowering away. He quickly busied himself with the loading of the other lifeboats, and assisted generally where he was needed.[130]

Philipp Mock and his sister had watched Boat No. 5 load, as well. He remembered that 'anyone could have got into' either that boat or Boat No. 7, which had left just before, as 'passengers could not be induced to get into them.' He apparently witnessed the trouble that Boat No. 5 had in lowering away, for he said:

The seamen made bad work of lowering the boats, not being familiar with handling them. Sometimes one end would be higher than the other, and other things would happen to alarm those seated in the boats.[131]

Third Class passengers Rhoda Abbott and her young sons, Eugene and Rossmore, had reached the aft decks 'just as the second life boat was being lowered'. They watched as lifeboat after lifeboat was subsequently put off, and eventually made their way to the Boat Deck.[132]

Frederick and Jane Hoyt had watched as Boats Nos 7 and 5 were loaded and lowered away. Mrs Hoyt recalled that neither boat was anywhere near full, and that the officers were having some trouble convincing passengers to leave the ship. Only later on would Mrs Hoyt begin to see lifeboats lowered with anything approaching a full load.[133]

While Second Officer Lightoller was working at the port side lifeboats, Chief Officer Wilde 'came over from the starboard side and asked, did I know where the firearms were?' Apparently Wilde had just talked to Murdoch about the subject, since the 'firearms, navigation instruments', and the like were the First Officer's responsibility. However, Murdoch had no clue where they were. This confusion harked back to the re-shuffling of senior officers at

Left to right: *Boats Nos 9, 11 and 13 aboard* Titanic.

Southampton prior to sailing; when the firearms had come aboard, Lightoller was serving in the position of First Officer, and they had been his responsibility. However, he 'had simply hove the lot, revolvers and ammunition into a locker' in his original cabin, which was now occupied by Murdoch.

Since Lightoller knew right where they were, he led Wilde, Captain Smith, and Murdoch to the First Officer's cabin, where he brought out the box of brand new Webley revolvers. Then he turned to leave. As he did, Chief Wilde 'shoved one of the revolvers' into his hands, along with a handful of ammunition, and said: 'Here you are, you may need it.' Lightoller took the whole lot and stuffed it into the pocket of his greatcoat. The Second Officer later recalled: 'The whole incident had not taken three minutes, though it seemed barely worth that precious time.'[134]

As they were heading out to the Boat Deck, Wilde said: 'I am going to put on my life-belt.' Lightoller heard this just as he was passing his own quarters. He had been too busy to think of getting his lifebelt until that point, but upon hearing the Chief Officer's comment, he 'instinctively' looked into his room, reached for the lifebelt, and put it on. Lightoller thought to himself that 'it is proverbial that the last thing a sailor will think of is a life-belt.'[135]

Then the Second Officer returned to the port side Boat Deck, and the other officers dispersed to their respective stations, as well. Charles Stengel, on the starboard Boat Deck, noticed that the same officer who had threatened to get his gun after the Frauenthal brothers jumped into Boat No. 5 'left the deck momentarily and came right back again.'[136]

Saloon Steward William Ward had been present for the loading of Boat No. 7, but had not been ordered to help man it, even though it was his assigned boat. As a result, he went aft along the deck to help prepare Boat No. 9. He 'assisted to take the canvas cover off of her', and the process continued from there.[137]

Lawrence Beesley was apparently near Boat No. 9 at the time. He remembered watching men working on that boat, as well as the other three starboard aft boats.

> Just then an officer came along from the first-class deck and shouted above the noise of escaping steam, 'All women and children get down to deck below and all men stand back from the boats.' He had apparently been off duty when the ship struck, and was lightly dressed, with a white muffler twisted hastily round his neck.[138]

As this scene played out, it began to sink in with Beesley and some others that there was real danger in the works. He watched as couples began to separate on the deck ...

Around this time, Captain Smith ordered Lamp Trimmer Hemming to make sure the boats were provided with lights. Hemming went below and began lighting the lamps, bringing them up on deck four at a time. He put the lamps into the boats that weren't already lowered away, and asked the crewmembers to pass the lamps down to the end of the falls for the boats that had already been sent down to the water.[139]

Below deck, the damage control efforts were fully under way. At 12:45 a.m., Greaser Scott and others were ordered to open up all of the watertight doors aft of the Engine Room. At that time, there was no flooding in those compartments, and the engineers wanted to bring a portable suction pipe forward, to help combat flooding in one of the forward stokeholds.

Opening only the watertight doors forward of the Engine Room was no simple task. A phone call had to be placed to the Bridge, to have them release the clutch. Only after that was done could they operate the individual doors manually.[140] After the doors had been opened, Scott watched as four men lugged the suction pipe forward.[141] Trimmer Thomas Dillon was among this group, and he remembered that the men went all the way forward into Boiler Room No. 4.[142]

Meanwhile, Steward Joseph Wheat was about to have a somewhat disconcerting experience. He had left the upper decks just minutes before in order to return to his quarters on F Deck to retrieve some personal items. These were located on the port side of the ship, directly behind watertight bulkhead F, at the bottom of the stairs which led to the Turkish Baths on the starboard side.

Wheat had previously closed the watertight door between the stairs and the Swimming Bath, forward of the bulkhead. At that time, he had seen no water in the spaces forward of the bulkhead. Even at this point, everything seemed all right as he went down. He checked to make sure everyone – all of the Turkish Bath attendants and other stewards who were housed there – had turned out. However, as he started back up the stairs to E Deck, he noticed that there was a flow of water – something between a trickle and a stream – coming down the steps. It was flowing quickly, and was just deep enough to cover the heel of his boots.

Climbing up the soggy stairs to E Deck, he noticed that water was coming from forward on the starboard side, along the First Class passage, and that it had turned the corner, entered the vestibule, and was flowing back down the stairs. Poking his nose through the open emergency door on to the port side, and looking along Scotland Road, he noticed that that corridor was still dry. He found that there were 'five or six' Third Class passengers there. They were moving aft, 'carrying and dragging boxes and bags'. Wheat started off toward the Boat Deck, going up via the aft working staircase.[143]

The water that Wheat saw coming down from E Deck on the aft side of watertight bulkhead F meant that at that point, water was collecting on the deck *above* Boiler Room No. 4. It was also accumulating above Boiler Room No. 5.

Up on deck, Fourth Officer Boxhall had certainly been one of the busiest officers in the hour after the collision; once he had finished working out the ship's position, and had given it to the Marconi operators, he had returned to the Bridge to see what the 'light' on the horizon was; he had attempted to investigate it earlier, but had been way-laid by Captain Smith. Now, looking out from the Bridge, he could clearly see the 'light'. With the aid of a pair of binoculars, he could even discern that it was actually the two masthead lights of a steamer.[144]

Boxhall decided to attempt to contact her, apparently using the Morse lamp first. Captain Smith was nearby, and saw the vessel, as well. As Boxhall made for the Morse key, Smith concurred by ordering: 'Tell him to come at once, we are sinking.'

When he got no response, Boxhall decided to go for a different tactic: He found the distress rockets that were stored on the Bridge,[145] and prepared to fire one ... surely this detonator would get the vessel's attention. He placed the rocket in the socket on the starboard Bridge wing, and then fired it off. The missile soared high into the sky above the stricken liner, leaving a faint white streak behind it as it rose. At its peak altitude of 600–800 feet, the rocket detonated with a deafening report, and 'the flash of the detonator lit up the whole deck' in a brilliant wash of illumination.[146] As it burst, white stars were thrown out, which slowly descended toward the black sea.

This distress signal got the attention of everyone on deck, and they gasped a single word in response: 'Rockets'. On the starboard Boat Deck, just after he had finished lowering Boat No. 5, Fifth Officer Lowe remembered standing next to Bruce Ismay at Boat No. 3 and seeing his face clearly in the brilliant light of the explosion.

Helen Ostby, sitting in Boat No. 5 as it was just pulling away from the ship, recalled:

> As we were sitting there watching, the first of about eight distress rockets went off, so high in the sky that they startled everyone. Everybody began to talk in the dark and wonder whether our ship had been able to send off any wireless messages.[147]

Sir Cosmo Duff Gordon pleaded with his wife to get into the lifeboats without him, but she refused. The officers had tried to snatch up Laura Francatelli, but she had stuck doggedly to her employers. As Lucy stood on the deck, she remembered watching the first rocket being launched. They continued to watch as the next boats were prepared for loading.[148]

Colonel Gracie had handed the ladies in his care off to the care of Sixth Officer Moody on the Promenade Deck. Then he had a conversation with the Strauses, who de-clared that they would not be split up, and sat down on a pair of deck chairs on the Promenade Deck. Just as Gracie was finishing his conversation with the Strauses, a stew-ard came along, rolling a small barrel out of the door from the companionway. 'What have you there?' he asked.

'Bread for the lifeboats,' came the steward's 'quick and cheery reply'.

There must have seemed little proper response to make to that somewhat incongruous scene, so Gracie simply moved inside on A Deck, and headed down for his own cabin, C-51. He wished to get some blankets there. Then he wanted to look for two of his table companions from the Dining Saloon: Edward Kent and Helen Candee. Be-fore he left the deck, Gracie believed that he saw the flash of the first rocket launched from the deck.[149]

As the Colonel passed down the staircase to C Deck, he passed Fred Wright, the instructor from the Squash Rac-quet court.

> 'Hadn't we better cancel that appointment for to-morrow morning?' I said rather jocosely to him. 'Yes', he replied, but did not stop to tell what he then must have known of the conditions in the racquet court on G Deck, which, according to other wit-nesses, had at that time become flooded. His voice was calm, without enthusiasm, and perhaps his face was a little whiter than usual.[150]

Lawrence Beesley was watching couples separate at the Boat Deck, and a vague inkling of danger was beginning to set in with him. But if there were any doubts on the point, they were erased – 'in a dramatic manner' – with the launching of the first rocket.

> Suddenly a rush of light from the forward deck, a hissing roar that made us all turn from watching the boats, and a rocket leapt upwards to where the stars blinked and twinkled above us. Up it went, higher and higher, with a sea of faces upturned to watch it, and then an explosion that seemed to split the silent night in two, and a shower of stars sank slowly down and went out one by one. And with a gasping sigh one word escaped the lips of the crowd: 'Rockets!' Anybody knows what rockets at sea mean.

Beesley stayed rooted to the spot, nearly transfixed by the 'dramatic intensity of the scene' as more rockets soon began to follow the first ...[151]

Philipp Mock was still standing on the sloping decks with his sister Emma Schabert. They had watched Boat No. 5 make its way to the sea. By that point, it was becoming clear to him that entering a lifeboat might not be such a bad idea. There were nerve-racking noises ... the steam blow-ing off from the boilers ... the officers sending up distress rockets ... meanwhile, the first lifeboats were pulling away from the ship in the water ... His sister, Emma, thought that the rocket reports 'sounded like cannons, and looked like wonderful fireworks' which gave them 'a sensation of awe'.

'With all these indications that the ship was in dire distress,' Mock thought it 'a wonder' that the passengers managed to stay so calm. 'The men were doing all that they could to help the women into the boats, and the women

First Class passenger Clarence Moore.

were accepting with wonderful courage and heroism the situation they were forced to meet.' At that point, Mock had not seen 'the slightest signs of panic' on the starboard side of the ship. He decided that he was going to attempt to approach the next lifeboat that was loading, with his sister in tow. The two promised to stick together no matter what happened.[152]

Meanwhile, Colonel Gracie had gone to his C Deck cabin to get some blankets. When he had arrived at the door to his room, he found it locked. He asked a passing steward – who was not his own steward – why this had been done. The steward replied that it was 'to prevent looting'. Gracie told him that he wanted some blankets. The steward then took him to a nearby cabin where extra blankets were stored, and gave them to Gracie. The Colonel then headed back up the stairs, perhaps via the Aft Grand Staircase.

When Gracie reached the aft part of A Deck, he began a systematic search for two of his table companions, Edward Kent and Helen Candee. He moved 'from aft, forwards, looking in every room and corner' for them. In the Smoking Room he came across a single table populated by four men. They were Archibald Butt, Clarence Moore, Frank Millet, and a fourth person who Gracie did not know. It occurred to Gracie that these four men must have known about the collision and the departing of the boats, but that they 'desired to show their entire indifference to the danger'.[153]

The four men did not stay in the Smoking Room for long, however. Just afterwards, Saloon Steward Frederick Dent Ray was headed up from helping Second Steward Dodd find a lifebelt. As he headed toward his assigned lifeboat, No. 9, he saw Clarence Moore and the same group of gentlemen – apparently including Major Butt, Frank Millet, and at least one other individual – exiting the Smoking Room.[154]

Very shortly after this, the Thayers were standing in the hallway near their C Deck staterooms; they had just finished dressing, and it was then that Marian spotted Archibald Butt passing down the corridor outside. She had gotten along famously with the Major that evening at dinner, but noticed that he had a 'strange unseeing look' on his face as he came towards them. She caught hold of his coat as he passed, and said: 'Major Butt, Major Butt, where are you going? Come with me.'

He replied: 'I have something to do first but will come then.' Mrs Thayer believed that Butt had 'gone for his letters', but he was likely on his way to check in on someone, as his cabin was located on B Deck.[155] The Thayer party proceeded up to the deck and waited for further instructions.

Jack Thayer later recalled:

We then hurried up to the lounge on 'A' deck, which was now crowded with people, some standing, some hurrying, some pushing out onto the deck. My friend Milton Long came by at that time and asked if he could stay with us. There was a great deal of noise. The band was playing lively tunes without apparently receiving much attention from the worried moving audience.

At some point, perhaps around that time, John and young Jack ran into Thomas Andrews. John Thayer asked Andrews what was going on … how bad the situation really was. Andrews replied quietly that he did not give the ship 'much over an hour to live'. The news was stunning, but Jack knew that no one would know what was really going on better than Andrews.

Jack also remembered that they did not necessarily stay in the same location all the time, mentioning that at least some of their group also 'walked around, looking at different places'. The group stayed on the cold deck for a few minutes, trying to figure out what they needed to do next. Then they returned to the 'crowded hallway where it was warm'. Next they heard the call for women to go to the port side, and for men to go to starboard. At the top of the Grand Staircase, John and Jack bade farewell to Marian and Marian's maid Margaret Fleming. Then the father and son 'went out on the starboard side' of the Boat Deck, where they walked around for a while, confident that the two ladies were in good hands. Jack noticed that at that point, none of the forward lifeboats had yet been launched on that side of the ship.[156]

Elsewhere, Ellen Toomey had been waiting in her Second Class cabin for quite some time. Her cabin companion, Elizabeth Watt, had gone on deck after the collision to investigate what was going on. She had been gone for so long that Ellen got up and decided to dress herself. As she put her clothing on, 'a steward ran by shouting, "All hands on deck" ', and as he passed, he threw her a lifebelt. Ellen was not alarmed, and it was then that Elizabeth Watt returned and got her daughter Robertha up. Elizabeth told Robertha and Ellen that 'no time should be lost'.

Ellen did not finish dressing; meanwhile, Robertha remembered being awakened at about 1:00 a.m. – although it was likely just before that. She simply put on her coat and lifebelt. Then the three went up on deck. The Second Class elevator was 'not running', and people were 'crowding up the stairway'. One of the ship's Masters-at-Arms stood with a pistol in his hand, threatening to shoot Third Class men who tried to get up into Second Class spaces.[157]

Aft, on the starboard side of the Boat Deck, Boat No. 9 was being swung out. A group that included Steward William Ward, Boatswain's Mate Haines and others was working on it at the time. When Saloon Steward Ray came up on deck and reached his assigned boat, he found that No. 9 was already uncovered, and about sixteen men were working to swing it out.

An officer – Ray wasn't sure which one, but he knew it was not Murdoch – was overseeing the work. Steward Ward remembered that Chief Purser McElroy was there.[158] However, there were only 'one or two' passengers standing nearby, and it was clear that the lifeboat was not ready to lower away. Ray 'went to the rail' just forward of the lifeboat, 'looked over and saw the first boat leaving the ship on the starboard side'. By that point, he was feeling a little cold, so he decided to go down to his room on E Deck to fetch his overcoat.[159]

At the stern Docking Bridge, Quartermaster Bright – Rowe's relief – was supposed to take over the watch at midnight, or 12:23 a.m. unadjusted ship's time, 'but time went by and no relief showed up'.[160] Following the collision, Rowe had checked the taffrail log, noting that it read 260 miles. With nothing else to do, he stood on the Docking Bridge awaiting orders through the telephone, or his relief, whichever came first.[161] He had been standing watch in the frigid night air for quite some time, and must have wondered what the delay was.

Forward, Quartermaster Bright had experienced a rude awakening. He had slept right through the accident. Not only was he awakened by Quartermaster Walter Wynn with the jarring news that the ship was going down by the head, but also with the realization that in the post-collision confusion, he somehow ended up being late in turning out to relieve Rowe. Once Bright arrived at the stern, he and Rowe stood together on the Docking Bridge, talking, apparently not sure of 'exactly what they should do'.[162] Around the time that Boat No. 5 had been lowered and the first rocket was launched from the Bridge, Quartermaster Rowe spotted Boat No. 7 in the water, just off the starboard side of the ship. It is possible that he saw it because the flash of the detonator illuminated the ocean, although this is speculation.[163] He remarked on the sighting to Bright and phoned up to the Bridge.

On the Bridge, the phone rang shortly after Boxhall had fired the first rocket, just while he was 'putting the firing lanyard inside the wheel-house'. When the phone chimed, it must have seemed a bit incongruous with the events going on around the Fourth Officer. He picked it up, however, and heard a man's voice report that one of the starboard boats had left the ship. Boxhall was surprised; he had heard no order to lower the boats. He asked if the caller was Third Officer Pitman, to which Rowe responded in the negative. Despite the confusing nature of the call, it was well-timed. Boxhall ordered Rowe to fetch the extra detonators for the distress rockets from the stern and bring them to the Bridge.[164]

Now the two Quartermasters knew exactly what they needed to do … Rowe and Bright left the aft Docking Bridge, dropped down to the Poop Deck and each picked up a box of rockets. Then they set off together and made for the Bridge.[165]

When Rowe and Bright arrived, Boxhall worked with the two Quartermasters at sending up more distress rockets, at intervals of approximately five minutes. This was in accord with international maritime regulations, which stated that rockets were to be sent up 'at short intervals' to signal distress. The men were careful to make sure that no one was on the deck nearby who could be injured if something went wrong with the firing. Boxhall chased people away from the area of Boat No. 1 with this in mind, since it was located directly aft of the Bridge wing.[166] All the while, he and Rowe continued to Morse the other vessel on the horizon. Although some believed that they saw the other ship responding, Boxhall could not make out any definite response from her, despite their desperate attempts at communication.[167]

Back below deck, shortly after receiving reassurance from a steward that the ship had struck a fishing boat and that there was no danger, Lillian Bentham had gotten into bed and fallen fast asleep. How long she was asleep she did not know, but eventually one of her friends – Albert Den-

buoy – came by and knocked on the door, waking her up. Lillian got up and opened the door. Denbuoy must have been shocked to see that she had been in bed. He informed her that people were then 'taking to the lifeboats'. She quickly threw a waterproof coat and a fur coat on, and then she hurried up on deck with her friend.[168]

Meanwhile, Saloon Steward Frederick Ray had decided to go down to his quarters for his coat, which were located on the port side of E Deck, about amidships. When he arrived, he found the room completely empty. He put his overcoat on, and then headed forward along Scotland Road. He found that …

> … the forward part of E Deck was under water. I could just manage to get through the doorway into the main stairway [First Class Grand Staircase]. I went across to the other side of the ship where the passengers' cabins were; saw nobody there. I looked to see where the water was and it was corresponding on that side of the ship to the port side.

The situation was clearly serious, but Ray turned and went up the Grand Staircase at a 'leisurely pace'.[169]

Meanwhile, Steward Wheat had made his way up to B Deck by way of the service stairs, aft of the Dining Saloon. When he arrived at B Deck, he ran across Chief Steward Andrew Latimer. Wheat noticed that Latimer 'had his big coat on with a life belt over it'. Wheat told Latimer that he should take both off, put the lifebelt back on, and then put the overcoat on over that. Otherwise 'his big coat would be no use to him'. Then Wheat started off forward, making his way toward the Grand Staircase.[170]

* * * * *

Nearby, on the Leyland liner *Californian* – prudently stopped in the ice – all was quiet. The officers who were on watch, as well as at least one off-duty crewman, all saw a number of white rockets fired from the ship to their southeast, spaced several minutes apart.[171] Captain Lord, napping fully clothed on the Chart Room settee just across from his cabin, was alerted at least once.[172] He ordered the men to signal the other ship with a Morse lamp, but never woke up his wireless operator to see what was going on, and did not even bother to go up to the Bridge himself and check on the situation.

By a little after two o'clock in the morning, the steamer that those on the *Californian* were watching with interest had disappeared from sight.[173]

* * * * *

Back on the *Titanic*, the rockets had stunned the crowds of people on deck: it was a sudden and most powerful warning of danger. Before then, all had been calm, and there had not seemed to be that much danger. But now, even the most optimistic passengers were beginning to think twice about what they needed to do. The situation was perhaps, they realized, more desperate than they had thought only minutes before.

Yet many still hesitated to commit to the lifeboats. On the port side of the Boat Deck, First Class passenger Mary Smith declined to board Boat No. 8. Her husband Lucien later forced her to separate from him and board No. 6.[174]

The forward port side lifeboats on Titanic. *No. 8 sits in the foreground, while No. 2 is visible in the distance.*

First Class Passengers Isidor and Ida Straus were alongside No. 8 as it loaded. Mrs Straus helped her maid, Ellen Bird, board the craft, before stepping onto the gunwales of the boat. She then had second thoughts, handing her maid her fur coat, saying that she would not be needing it. She stepped back onto the Boat Deck and clung to Isidor. 'We have been together all these years. Where you go I go,' she exclaimed.[175]

First Class passenger May Futrelle had just been separated from her husband when orders came through for men and women to split up. Standing on the deck right by Boat No. 8, she had also witnessed Mrs Straus clinging to her husband. She heard Ida say 'to an officer who was trying to induce her to get into a boat: "No, we are too old, we will die together." '[176]

By then, Able Bodied Seaman Thomas Jones had been ordered into No. 8. He too witnessed the Straus' refusal to separate, but couldn't hear what Mrs Straus said 'because the steam was blowing so and making such a noise'. He also remembered seeing an officer, whom he assumed was the First Officer but was almost certainly was Second Officer Lightoller, 'running around there'.[177]

Initially, First Class passengers Margaret Swift and Dr Alice Leader had no intention of leaving the ship. However, 'on second thought' the two ladies had crossed over to the port side and joined the group of women near Boat No. 8. She remembered that some of the women 'would not leave their husbands until persuaded that the men would follow later on the other boats. With this pledge the women consented to leave the ship. They all believed, as I did, that the vessel would not sink.' However Mrs Swift had watched as Mrs Straus flatly refused to be separated from her husband.[178]

On the starboard side, First Officer Murdoch placed Able Bodied Seaman George Moore in charge of Boat No.

3, since the only other sailor aboard was Able Bodied Seaman James Anderson. The crew loaded as many women and children into the boat as they could, and when no more were left nearby that were willing to board, Murdoch allowed some of the men on the scene to climb aboard.

Among the passengers put aboard No. 3 were Albert and Vera Dick. Not long before, they had received reassurances from Thomas Andrews that although the ship was badly damaged, she likely would not sink. As a result, the Dicks were 'indifferent about leaving the steamship'.[179]

Philipp Mock and his sister Emma Schabert also approached Boat No. 3 as it was loading. Philipp asked the men if they might enter the boat together, and they were told that they could not. The men urged Mrs Schabert to get in alone; she, in turn, asked if her brother could go. The officer refused, and so she declined to leave the ship. Bruce Ismay attempted to intervene and get her into the boat, but she again declined. The Chairman of the White Star Line then said to her: 'You made a great mistake not to get into that boat.' Emma replied: 'It does not matter. I prefer staying with my brother.' In total, the pair was denied access to the lifeboats four times.[180]

No. 3 began lowering away at 12:55 a.m., becoming the third lifeboat to leave the ship. Approximately thirty-two of its sixty-five seats were occupied.[181]

Back in the Marconi room, Jack Phillips was still pounding out distress signals. He had managed to reach other vessels, but the *Carpathia* was still the closest to respond. Even with the events transpiring on deck, Harold Bride saw humor in the situation and suggested that Phillips begin sending SOS, because 'it's the new call, and it may be your last chance to send it.' Phillips laughed, and at 12:57 a.m., switched to the suggested call, hoping to contact a closer ship.[182]

The First SOS?

Prior to the use of the signal SOS, the three letters CQD were used to call for assistance. CQD had been standardized by the Marconi International Marine Company in February of 1904. What did CQD mean? It has often been described as an acronym for 'Come Quickly, Distress' or other similar phrases. However, the truth of the call sign's meaning is far simpler. The first two letters, 'CQ' were typically used by wireless operators to get the attention of all stations within hearing range. The addition of the 'D' was understood to mean 'distress,' thus forming a three-letter abbreviation for: 'All stations: distress.'

However, the transmission of CQD was not without its drawbacks. First, it was easy for listeners to miss the 'D' at the end if the transmission was poor or at a great distance. Secondly, the three-letter sign was not an international standard. The distress signal SOS, for example, had been introduced in Germany in 1905. It was proposed as a replacement for CQD during the 1906 International Wireless Telegraph Convention in Berlin.

SOS was a far simpler transmission to send and understand by the receiving operator. Britain and other nations had voted to adopt the Berlin conference proposals in 1908, but wireless operators on British ships were not quick to adopt the new regulation call. They continued to use CQD for years afterward.

In the century since the disaster, popular myth has held that *Titanic* was the first ship to use the wireless distress call SOS. However, this claim has absolutely no basis in fact. SOS had been used numerous times by ships in the years prior to the *Titanic* disaster. One of the earliest reports of this distress call being sent was on August 11, 1909, when the SS *Arapahoe* of the Clyde Line broke her propeller shaft and sent out an SOS call.[183]

Despite what Bride thought, SOS was technically not new. It may have been a new-*er* call for British wireless operators in 1912, but the simple fact is that it had been proposed, adopted, and used many times before the *Titanic* sank.[184]

Far below Bride and Phillips, the battle against incoming seawater was still being fought by the ship's crewmen and engineers. Despite their valiant efforts, and in most cases completely without their knowledge, that battle was being lost irrevocably. In Boiler Room No. 5, Leading Fireman Fred Barrett and his men had just finished drawing the fires shortly before 12:55 a.m. With this accomplished, the firemen had been ordered back up out of the stokeholds. Barrett stayed behind and continued to work in Boiler Room No. 5.[185]

It was within just a few minutes, or at about 12:55 a.m., that Barrett was ordered by Junior Assistant Second Engineer Harvey to lift a manhole plate in the floor of Boiler Room No. 5. Harvey had him do this so that they could get access to valves for the pumps. Barrett did as he was asked. Because water had been thrown on the fires when they were being drawn, the compartment was thick with steam, greatly reducing visibility. Junior Assistant Second Engineer Shepherd was hurrying through the area, and not seeing the danger, fell into the manhole, breaking his leg. Unable to walk, Harvey and Barrett lifted their injured crewmate up, and carried him into the pump room.[186]

While everything seemed to be all right in that boiler room – the pumps were running, the floor plates were dry despite the list – appearances were very deceiving. Already, water was flooding aft along E Deck, snaking its way as far as the spaces above their compartment, Boiler Room No. 5, and the next compartment aft, Boiler Room No. 4. It was only a matter of time before that water found its way back down into those two boiler rooms. The battle was being lost, and the men on the front lines were not even aware of it.

Up top, Lawrence Beesley had been watching the firing of the rockets from his position aft on the Boat Deck. While no definitive word that the ship was sinking had reached him, he said that every one still knew 'without being told that we were calling for help from any one who was near enough to see'. He watched as the crew had begun to work on the aft starboard lifeboats, and soon he saw two ladies from Second Class move to the rail which separated the Second and First Class portions of the Boat Deck. They

This photo shows the railings which divided Titanic's *starboard Boat Deck into three segments. Forward, in the distance, was deck space for First Class passengers; between the two rails was the Engineers' Promenade; astern of the rails the deck was set aside for the use of Second Class passengers.*

encountered an officer there, and asked him: 'May we pass to the boats?'

'No, madam,' the officer replied politely, 'your boats are down on your own deck.' Then he pointed to the aft lifeboats, which were being worked on then.

At about the same time, Beesley heard 'a report' which circulated among the men on the starboard side of the Boat Deck. Word had it that women were to be loaded into boats from the starboard side of the ship, and that men were to be taken off on the port side. Beesley said that this report was 'acted on at once by almost all the men', who crossed over to the port side, causing the crowds on that portion of the deck to begin to swell. This left the starboard side 'almost deserted'. Beesley did not follow them, but instead decided to remain on the starboard side. A couple of others did so, as well. He wasn't sure why he stayed, but he recognized 'the necessity of being quiet and waiting in patience for some opportunity of safety to present itself'. Just after this, Beesley saw a strange sight … a bandsman – the cellist – come round the vestibule corner from the staircase entrance and run down the now deserted starboard deck, his 'cello trailing behind him, the spike dragging on the floor'. Beesley stayed on the deck, watching events unfold around him.[187]

1:00 a.m. – 1:15 a.m.

At Boat No. 9, Steward William Ward and the others had lowered the lifeboat down until it was level with the Boat Deck. After they had finished this, Ward noticed that 'a sailor came along with a bag and threw it in the boat. This man said he had been sent down to take charge of the boat by the captain.' Boatswain's Mate Haines was not about to stand for this. He ordered the man out of the boat, and the man meekly complied, and then stood nearby for several minutes.[188]

Meanwhile, forward, First Class passenger Major Arthur Peuchen had just reached the Boat Deck. There he noticed a group of about '100' stokers with their kit bags, seemingly 'crowding this whole deck in front of the boats'. Unlike many of the passengers, these men had come up from below, and knew the extent of the flooding. One of the officers – whom Peuchen described as 'powerful', and who may have been Chief Officer Wilde – came along and drove the men right out of the area. The stokers did not protest, and cooperated with the officer.[189]

Second Officer Lightoller had been very busy at the forward port boats. After lowering Boat No. 4 to the Promenade Deck level and getting held up by the closed windows there, he had decided to move on to the next two boats aft, Nos 6 and 8. Of these, Boat No. 8, loaded by Chief Officer Wilde, was to get away first. Lightoller interpreted the traditional rules of evacuation at sea to mean 'women and children only,' not simply 'first.' Yet, the ship still seemed relatively safe – safer than a lifeboat, at any rate – and he and Chief Officer Wilde did not get many volunteers.

When Lightoller arrived alongside No. 6, he noticed for the first time that the ship was 'distinctly down by the head'.[190] Mercifully, the racket from the steam blowing off had ceased while work on the forward port boats progressed. In all, after starting around 11:46 p.m., the racket had continued for over an hour.[191] Now Lightoller and the other crewmen found it much easier to communicate on the Boat Deck. Lightoller said that when the din finally

stopped, 'there was a death-like silence a thousand times more exaggerated, fore and aft the ship. It was almost startling to hear one's own voice again …'[192]

In the absence of the cacophonous venting noise, the music of the ship's band now drifted pleasantly out from inside the Boat Deck level of the First Class Entrance, not far from where Lightoller was working. They were trying to keep the passengers calm and allay panic. Lightoller noted that while he didn't like 'jazz' music as a general rule, he was glad to hear it that night.[193]

Lightoller filled Boat No. 6 while Captain Smith, Chief Officer Wilde, and other crewmembers prepared to send Boat No. 8 away. During the previous ten minutes or so, passengers had been loaded into it. Many had proved, and were still proving, reluctant to board the small boats, refusing to leave their loved ones.

Meanwhile, Emma Bucknell and her maid had proceeded onto the Boat Deck and watched as the crew had finished preparing the lifeboats for loading and lowering. She hadn't been particularly impressed with the speed of the crew's efforts, but at last, Boat No. 8 was ready to load. Finally Mrs Bucknell and her maid joined those who were boarding the craft. Emma remembered:

> Wives and husbands were separated when the women were placed in our boat. A few of the men grew seemingly desperate, and Captain Smith, who was standing by, cried out: 'Behave yourselves like men! Look at all of these women. See how splendid they are. Can't you behave like men?'
>
> All of the women were calm, though they had just been torn from their beloved ones. There was only one, a little Spanish bride [Maria Peñasco y Castellana], who cried out hysterically for her husband, who was held back by other men.
>
> Then Captain Smith himself picked up a big basket of bread and handed it across to me in the lifeboat. That was all the provisions I saw …
>
> … 'There is a light out there,' said Captain Smith to the man in charge of our lifeboat which contained thirty-five persons. 'Take the women to it and hurry back as speedily as possible.'[194]

The Countess of Rothes and her cousin, Gladys Cherry, had also climbed into Boat No. 8. They remembered that Victor Peñasco nearly had to toss his wife Maria into the arms of the ladies already into the boat, and that he then asked them to take care of her.[195]

Captain Smith called out for 'Any more ladies?' One more lady separated from her husband and boarded No. 8, as did a little girl. The lady wanted her husband to go with her, but he quietly backed away from the boat. The call for further women and children went out twice more, but none were forthcoming. At 1:00 a.m., the order to lower away was given. Captain Smith had ordered Able Bodied Seaman Thomas Jones to row for the light of the ship on the horizon, land the passengers there, and then return.[196]

After watching Mrs Straus refuse to be separated from her husband, Mrs Swift and Dr Alice Leader had changed their minds about boarding Boat No. 8. Mrs Swift decided …

> … that it would be well to go into one of the boats, too, and the officers advised us to do so.

It was a clear, starlit night. The heavens were beautiful. The boats were provisioned and in ours we had two barrels of water and some bread.

The captain, poor, dear, brave man, threw in another loaf as we pulled away. I am sorry to say that I sat with my foot on that loaf for some time. As we went the captain told us to pull for a light that was far, far away from the *Titanic*.[197]

As Boat No. 8 was lowered to the water, Gladys Cherry thought that she had done a very foolish thing to exchange the warmth and safety of the *Titanic*'s decks for the cold uncertainty of a lifeboat in the middle of the Atlantic at night.[198]

As May Futrelle watched the lifeboat lower away – at the Captain's order, she recalled – she decided that she could not leave her husband … not yet.

I was afraid, the water looked so treacherous. I ran back, threw my arms around his neck and said, 'Jack, I don't want to leave you.'

'Oh, do be calm dear', he said, and he allowed me to stay with him for a while. He said there was no great hurry and that I might remain with him a few minutes.[199]

Meanwhile, loading at Boat No. 6 continued. First Class passenger Martha Stone peered over the edge of the Boat Deck before boarding No. 6, and noticed all of the empty seats in No. 8, which had by then reached the water.[200] Boat No. 8 had left with twenty-five of its sixty-five seats occupied.[201]

First Class passenger Leila Meyer was standing on the Boat Deck with her husband Edgar. At this point, Mrs Meyer did not wish to leave her husband. She begged him to come with her onto a lifeboat, but he refused, wishing to stay behind until all of the women had been taken care of. He reminded his wife of their one-year-old daughter, who was not traveling with them at the time. This finally convinced Leila to board Boat No. 6. She was able to watch as her husband helped a number of other women into the lifeboats, and then she lost sight of him in the crowd.[202]

It was at this time that Denver socialite Margaret Brown headed toward Boat No. 6. She convinced one of her fellow passengers, Berthe Antonine Mayné, to go into the boat instead of heading back to her cabin for her money and jewels. Then Margaret started to walk away from the edge of the deck, interested in seeing what was going on with the lifeboats on the starboard side. But suddenly, there was 'a shadow, and a few seconds later I was taken hold of'. The officer told her: 'You are going, too.' Then she was dropped into the lifeboat.[203]

Down below, Mess Steward Cecil Fitzpatrick had gone back to sleep after the collision. He was only awakened again when a fireman came in to the Mess Steward's room on E Deck and tried to take a lifebelt. Fitzpatrick and the other men in the room refused to let the man have it, and the fireman then passed on word that the Chief Engineer wanted them to muster. As a result, Fitzpatrick and his mates turned out and headed topside.[204]

Meanwhile, back on the starboard side of the Boat Deck, First Officer Murdoch had been working at Emergency Boat No. 1, getting it ready for lowering. The loading of this boat was delayed, in part because Fourth Officer Box-

Olympic*'s Bridge and Bridge wing on the starboard side, with Boat No. 1 visible behind the bulwark rail. Fourth Officer Boxhall had to be careful that passengers and crew were not injured as he fired rockets while work on Boat No. 1 was under way.*

hall had to keep chasing people away from the area while he was firing the rockets. He was afraid the detonator would injure anyone standing nearby, since No. 1 was located just aft of the Bridge wing.[205]

Sir Cosmo and Lady Lucy Duff Gordon, along with Laura Francatelli, were standing right nearby. Sir Cosmo had pleaded with his wife to leave in one of the previous boats, but she and her secretary had refused to go. They were going to stick together no matter what. 'Promise me', she told him, 'that whatever you do you will not let them separate us.' Lucy recalled that after the launching of Boat No. 3 …

… everyone in the vicinity had disappeared, except for some sailors who were launching a little boat [No. 1].

… Seeing nobody else about my husband asked the officer whether we might get into it, and on receiving his permission we were helped in …[206]

In another of her accounts, she remembered the exact wording of the officer's response: 'Please do.'[207]

By this time, First Class passenger Charles Stengel had already seen his wife off in Boat No. 5. He had watched the loading of Boat No. 3, and then turned and moved forward along the deck until he reached Boat No. 1. At the time, he was feeling 'agitated somewhat'. Sir Cosmo Duff Gordon, his wife Lucy, and her secretary Laura Francatelli were already in the boat at that point. However, it was so dark that Stengel could hardly make out more than human forms in the boat. As there was no one else around, he approached Murdoch and asked if he could get into the boat.

The First Officer replied: 'Jump in.'

Stengel set out to climb in, but in clambering over the bulwark rail, he had trouble doing so. Eventually, he ended up rolling over the teak top-rail and into the boat.

Murdoch had been watching, and laughed heartily. He then said: 'That is the funniest sight I have seen to-night.'

Stengel started to feel better about the situation a little. If this officer could laugh so freely, perhaps things weren't that bad after all …

Just then Abraham Salomon, a 43-year-old New York businessman, also asked Murdoch if he could board. Murdoch told him he could, and he was soon in the boat beside Stengel and the Duff Gordon party.[208]

Once a total of twelve people – five passengers and seven members of the crew – were aboard, Murdoch ordered the boat to be lowered away.[209] The capacity of the smaller emergency boats was forty. It was about 1:05 a.m., just in between the lowering of Boats Nos 8 and 6 on the port side, when No. 1 left the deck.

On the port side, because Second Officer Lightoller had sent Boatswain Alfred Nichols and six other crewmen below to open the gangway doors, he was facing a critical shortage of manpower as he loaded Boat No. 6. It was primarily because of this shortage that the forward port boats got away from the ship quite a few minutes after the forward starboard boats had started lowering. Lightoller was also facing another issue which was delaying his work: many of the passengers still had to be coaxed into boarding the lifeboats. The *Titanic* seemed much safer than being lowered into the ocean in a tiny boat in the middle of the night. Also, as the passengers had earlier been sent down to A Deck, and then were told to go back up to the Boat Deck, there was obviously some confusion about where the passengers should even assemble.

Because the crewmen had not returned from below, Lightoller was 'reduced to sending one seaman away in a boat'. When he was ready to give the order to lower away, nobody was manning the aft davits of Boat No. 6, so Lightoller called out for 'somebody for the after-fall'. Although he had previously been ordered into the boat by the Second Officer, Lamp Trimmer Samuel Hemming realized there were no crewmembers to answer the call, and stepped back onboard, saying: 'Aye, aye, sir! All ready.'[210]

Boat No. 6 began lowering away at about 1:10 a.m.[211] Quartermaster Robert Hichens, who had been at the ship's helm when the iceberg was struck, was aboard. So was Lookout Frederick Fleet, who had spotted the iceberg from the Crow's Nest. Hichens sat at the tiller at the stern of the boat, and appointed himself in charge. By the time No. 6 began lowering away, it appears that the 5° starboard list had lessened somewhat, but the edge of the boat was still resting against the ship's side. The occupants had to 'put our hands out several times' to push it away from the *Titanic's* hull.[212] Third Officer Pitman hadn't noticed the list at all when Boat No. 5 was lowered away at 12:43 a.m.[213] This suggests that at that point, the starboard list had been slight enough that it hadn't caused Boat No. 5 to swing far enough away from the hull to interfere with the loading.

Boat No. 6 was halfway down the ship's side when it began to tip, with its bow angling downward sharply. It was very reminiscent of the earlier problems lowering Boat No. 5. Quartermaster Hichens yelled up to Lightoller to hold the bow steady, and to lower away at the stern. Then the boat evened out. Hichens also shouted up that they had no seaman to help row. Lightoller observed: 'We will have to have some more seamen here.' Then he called out: 'Any seaman there?'

Major Peuchen, then standing right near Lightoller, said: 'Can I be of any assistance? I am a yachtsman, and can handle a boat with an average man, if I can be of any use to you.'

Captain Smith was standing nearby at the time, and suggested to Peuchen: 'You had better go down below and break a window and get in through a window, into the boat.'

This proposal didn't seem feasible to Peuchen. Then Lightoller suggested to the Major: 'If you're seaman enough to get out on those falls, and get down into the boat, then you may go ahead.' This struck Peuchen as a better idea, so he reached out, grabbed the falls, and lowered himself safely into the boat.[214] Including the Major, Boat No. 6 had approximately twenty-three persons in it when it cast off. It had room for sixty-five.[215]

As soon as the boat reached the ocean, Quartermaster Hichens told Peuchen, who was then helping unhook the falls: 'Hurry up. This boat is going to founder.' The Major at first thought Hichens was referring to the lifeboat, but he soon realized the Quartermaster meant the *Titanic*, and that he was in a hurry to row away from the liner.[216] Hichens later said that he felt that Peuchen was 'not in the boat more than 10 minutes before he wanted to come and take charge of the boat.'

Margaret Brown noticed as the boat was lowered that water was entering the ship through an open porthole on D Deck. Upon looking up, she saw Captain Smith peering down at them 'like a solicitous father', ordering them 'to row to the light in the distance, and all the boats keep together.'[217]

Deep in the innards of the ship, it had been less than fifteen minutes since Junior Assistant Second Engineer Jonathan Shepherd had broken his leg in Boiler Room No. 5. Things still seemed to be relatively normal there … the pumps were working away, the fires had been drawn. Although the bunker on the forward side of the compartment was quite full of seawater, the Boiler Room itself was still dry.

At about 1:10 a.m., however, all notions of normalcy were suddenly shattered. Frederick Barrett saw a terrific rush of water coming through the pass in between the boilers. Junior Assistant Engineer Herbert Harvey ordered him up top, and Barrett did not look back. He immediately climbed up the escape ladder, only barely escaping the flood of water. Coming up to E Deck, Barrett saw water coming down the alleyway from forward of where he escaped from Boiler Room No. 5. He speculated that this might have been due to water reaching open portholes on the lower decks.[218]

Meanwhile, Third Class passenger Laura Cribb and her father arrived on the Boat Deck. Laura remembered that immediately thereafter, 'officers came up and told father to put the lifebelt on me. This he did, then telling me to get as near the lifeboats as I could.' Without a word of farewell passed between the two, she did just as her father said, separating, yet fully expecting to see him again soon.[219]

By then, Archibald Gracie had left the Smoking Room and moved forward along the Promenade Deck. He peered into every public room on the deck, looking for his table companions, with no success. Eventually, Gracie headed up toward the port side of the Boat Deck. Emerging there, he found Clinch Smith. Smith told the Colonel that their acquaintance, Helen Candee, had already departed in Boat No. 6. From that point forward, Smith and Gracie stuck together, 'part of the time on the Boat Deck, and part on the deck below it, called Deck A.'[220]

1:15 a.m. – 1:30 a.m.

After seeing flooding forward on E Deck, almost to the lowest level of the Grand Staircase, Saloon Steward Ray 'walked leisurely up to the main stairway, passed two or three people on the way, saw the two pursers in the purser's office and the clerks busy at the safe taking things out and putting them in bags.'

When on C Deck, where the Purser's Office was located, Ray bumped into First Class passenger Martin Rothschild, who he knew from a previous trip on the *Olympic*, and Ray decided to wait for him. Ray noticed that Rothschild's wife wasn't with him, so he asked where she was. Rothschild told Ray that he had already seen his wife safely away in Boat No. 6.

'This seems rather serious,' Ray remarked to Rothschild, but without telling him about the flooding he had seen below.

'I do not think there is any occasion for it,' Rothschild replied.[221]

On the forward starboard side of the Boat Deck, Fifth Officer Lowe had been assisting at Boat No. 1. As the boat lowered past B Deck, it got caught up on what was alternately described as a 'wire guy' and a 'painter', and could not be freed.[222] A crewmember was sent below to chop away this wire before the lowering continued. The lowering of a lifeboat normally took around five minutes, but this delay seems to have added an additional five minutes to the lowering. This would have prevented No. 1 from reaching the water until approximately 1:15 a.m. Once the boat touched down in the sea, the crewmembers manning it were told to 'stand off a little way and come back when called.'[223]

Lady Duff Gordon recalled that, as the boat began its descent, the water below them looked 'black and deep', and she hated the idea of leaving the big liner for their 'frail little boat'. She also recalled:

Just beside us was a man sending off rockets, and the earsplitting noise added to the horror of being suspended in mid-air while one of the lowering ropes got caught and was only released after what seemed an interminable time.[224]

Once the lowering resumed, an order was shouted down from Murdoch: 'Pull off away from the boat as quickly as possible, at least two hundred yards.' When the boat pulled off, Lady Duff Gordon could see the man sending off the rockets.[225]

As Boat No. 1 began rowing away from the ship, Lookout George Symons saw that she was down by the bow to a shocking extent. As he watched, the second row of portholes under *Titanic's* nameplate were submerging into the sea.[226]

With all four of the forward starboard boats lowered away, Murdoch and his men began to move aft. On the port side of the ship, Boat No. 4 was still in limbo; it had been lowered to A Deck but still had not been loaded because of the closed Promenade windows. For the time being, it was left to wait while the officers' attention turned to getting the aft lifeboats away.

Fifth Officer Lowe recalled why their attention was so focused on the after port quarter at that time. While he was finishing up at No. 1, a large crowd of male passengers were beginning to congregate at the aft port boats, and they were starting to get unruly. Lawrence Beesley explained why this large crowd was growing; he recalled that shortly before this, a rumor began to circulate on the starboard side that men were to be taken off on the port side, and that all the men had headed to that location as a result.[227]

Lowe immediately headed aft to assist, 'as they seemed to be busy there'.[228] Other crewmembers – such as Able Bodied Seamen Frank Evans and Edward Buley, both of whom had been working on the forward starboard boats – also turned and headed to the aft port boats.[229] The need for as many crewmen as could be assembled to assist and calm the crowds aft on the port side seems to explain the delay between the loading and lowering of the forward starboard boats and the aft starboard ones.

By about 1:15 a.m., Boats Nos 7, 5, 3, 8, 1 and 6 had left the ship. That made six boats to leave in the hour and thirty-five minutes that had elapsed since the collision, four of them on the starboard side under the careful oversight of First Officer Murdoch.

However, there was not much time left … at the bow, the water was creeping, climbing, crawling ever higher against the black steel hull plates, sliding closer to the anchor, even closer to the ship's name at the prow, and toward the forward Well Deck and Forecastle. Simultaneously, the mood aboard the liner was beginning to change. What had before been a jovial curiosity was now becoming an obvious realization that there was something significantly wrong with the ship, and that the lifeboats were not, after all, such a bad-looking place to be. Because of this, the aft lifeboats were consistently going to be the fullest boats to be launched from the stricken liner. However, even with the danger becoming apparent, some passengers were still unwilling to accept the reality of the situation, or to depart from their friends and relatives. Many of these opted to stay onboard despite the risks. Some were subsequently forced into the boats by crewmembers or their relatives and friends.

At Boat No. 14, Able Bodied Seaman Joseph Scarrott was in the midst of the 'busy' scene that Lowe had noticed. As he had finished the prep work at that boat, Chief Officer Wilde had ordered him to start loading women and children into it. He managed to get about twenty women into the boat before a group of men tried to rush the boat. He believed they were 'foreigners' because they didn't seem to understand his orders. Scarrott had to 'use a bit of persuasion' – 'persuasion' meaning that he had to use the boat's tiller on them – to force the men back and keep the situation under control.[230]

When Fifth Officer Lowe crossed over to the port side aft boats after finishing at Boat No. 1, he was headed toward the scene that Scarrott was in the thick of. On the way, Lowe ran across Sixth Officer James Moody. 'What are you doing?' he asked.

'I am getting these boats away,' Moody replied.

Lowe remarked that he had seen a number of boats leave the ship without an officer, and that he thought one of them should go in one of the two boats they were near, Nos 14 and 16. He gave Moody first choice of which of them it was to be.

'You go,' Moody replied. 'I will get in another boat.'[231] Although he was the most junior of the ship's officers and would have been completely justified in leaving the ship at that time, the Sixth Officer declined a place in the boats, opting instead to remain and assist in the evacuation effort. His selfless choice resulted in Lowe's survival, a fact which Lowe would never forget.

The two men then moved to their respective charges, Lowe to No. 14, and Moody to No. 16. The two boats began filling almost simultaneously. Lowe later recalled that Second Officer Lightoller showed up briefly at No. 14.[232]

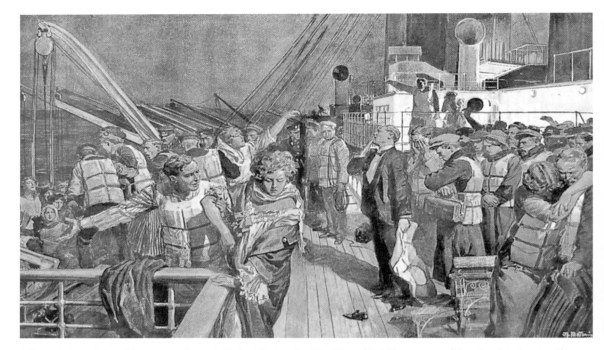

A fine artist's rendering of the scene on the port side Boat Deck as Boat No. 16 was filled. The accuracy of the artwork is stunning. Please compare with the photograph of Titanic's Boat Deck *from nearly the same perspective taken in Queenstown, seen on page 101.*

However, he didn't stay long, and soon moved on to Boat No. 12.

When the Fifth Officer first arrived at No. 14, the crewmen informed him that they had been having trouble keeping the crowds under control. With this in mind, Lowe began to oversee the effort of loading the craft.

Second Class passengers Harvey and Charlotte Collyer, and their daughter Marjorie, were standing nearby as No. 14 was loading. Charlotte thought that Fifth Officer Lowe was 'young and boyish-looking, but somehow he compelled people to obey him'. She also thought she had seen First Officer Murdoch near No. 14 early on in that boat's loading process, but by the time she boarded, she believed he had moved to another portion of the deck.[233] Boat No. 14 was about half-full when a sailor snatched up little Marjorie and put her in the boat.

Suddenly, someone shouted at Mrs Collyer: 'You, too! You're a woman. Take a seat in that boat, or it will be too late.' Mrs Collyer felt the deck's steep angle, but she clung to her husband. It took two men to tear her from him. He said: 'Go, Lotty! For God's sake be brave and go. I'll get a seat in another boat.' She was dumped into the boat, landing on her shoulder and bruising it rather badly. Rushing to her feet, she glanced back to see her husband walk steadily away into a crowd of men, where she lost sight of him.[234]

Meanwhile, Sixth Officer Moody had busied himself at Boat No. 16. Earlier, there had been a group of firemen and sailors standing around the boat with their bags, waiting to get aboard it. When Scullion John Collins arrived alongside on the scene, he thought there was 'no chance [of boarding] there', and quickly moved on.[235]

Despite the crowd, things were a bit calmer than at No. 14. However, as First Class Stewardess Violet Jessop boarded No. 16, along with her cabin-mate, she thought that

Moody looked 'weary and tired'. Even so, he gave them a cheery smile as he called out: 'Good luck!' and guided them into the boat. Moody then held up something and said: 'Look after this, will you?' Jessop reached out and was surprised to receive somebody's baby. Jessop pressed the baby to her chest and thought of how little comfort the hard cork surface of her lifebelt would provide the infant.[236]

Earlier, young Third Class passenger Anna Sjöblom had been chased out of her cabin by rising seawater. After getting on deck, she had attempted to climb up to where the lifeboats were. An 'officer of the ship' helped her up. Eventually, she made her way through a scene of confusion toward Boat No. 16, which she thought was the 'next to the last boat launched', and boarded it.[237]

At about 1:20 a.m., the men working below in the stokeholds and Engine Room were released from duty. Leading Fireman Thomas Threlfall remembered getting the order from Junior Second Engineer John Hesketh: 'We've done all we can men, get out now.'[238]

Trimmer Thomas Dillon was just headed aft from Boiler Room No. 4 to the Engine Room when he heard a similar order. He recalled that it was given 'an hour and 40 minutes' after the collision, or at about 1:20 a.m.: 'All hands on deck; put your life preservers on.'[239] For him, this order could not have come at a better time. The reason he was headed aft to the Engine Room was because he had just seen water beginning to come up from under the stokehold plates forward in Boiler Room No. 4.

Trimmer George Cavell was in Boiler Room No. 4 when the order to go up top was given. By the time he abandoned his post, the water that was coming up through the stokehold plates was over a foot deep.[240] Greaser Frederick Scott also recalled leaving the Engine Room at 'twenty past one'.[241] Scott and the others in the Engine Room were ordered up on deck by Senior Second Engineer William Farquharson.[242]

The entire group of men coming up out of the engineering spaces first made their way up to E Deck. Moving aft a short distance into an area of the ship that Scott was wholly unfamiliar with, they were provided with lifebelts and sent up on deck. Scott was only the fourth person in the group to fetch his lifebelt, and quickly made his way up the passenger stairs and to the Boat Deck.[243]

At this time, Saloon Steward Ray and First Class passenger Martin Rothschild started off from C Deck toward the Boat Deck.[244] Ray had come across Rothschild on C Deck, and had waited for him to be ready to head back above deck. The two men came up the Grand Staircase to the Boat Deck. Ray then headed aft toward his assigned lifeboat, No. 9.[245]

It was about this time that work on loading Boat No. 9 began. It had been swung out and lowered to the deck for quite some time, but there had not been any activity at loading it; this was due to the aft port boats, and many crewmembers heading there to control the crowd. Steward Ward remembered someone – either Chief Purser McElroy or First Officer Murdoch – now asking the men by No. 9: 'Are you all ready?'

Boatswain's Mate Haines replied: 'Yes.'

'Pass in the women and children that are here into that boat,' the officer ordered.

Ward noticed that there were several men nearby, and that they 'fell back, and there was quite a quantity of women and children helped into the boat'.[246]

On the port side, at around 1:20 a.m., Moody ordered No. 16 lowered away. Just before Moody gave this order, Able Bodied Seaman Frederick Clench had checked the boat's falls to make sure they were clear for lowering. He left before the boat left the deck, however, and made his way forward to Boat No. 12 to assist there.[247]

As the falls played out, the crew realized that there was only one Able Bodied Seaman and a steward aboard to man the boat, so Master-at-Arms Joseph Bailey climbed down the falls to take charge. There were approximately fifty-three persons aboard, out of sixty-five available seats.[248] As No. 16 dropped away from the Boat Deck into the beckoning darkness below, 24-year-old Sixth Officer Moody was still standing on the sloping Boat Deck; he would be the only junior officer to perish in the disaster.

At Boat No. 14, Fifth Officer Lowe was just about finished with the loading process that had been started earlier by Chief Officer Wilde. Among those who boarded this boat were Second Class passengers Elizabeth Mellinger and her daughter Madeleine.[249] Fellow Second Class passengers Esther and Eva Hart also made it into Boat No. 14. Seven-year-old Eva was placed in the boat first, and her mother followed her. As she boarded, a ...

... man who had previously tried to get in, succeeded in doing so, but was ordered out, and the officer fired his revolver into the air to let everyone see it was loaded, and shouted out, 'Stand back! I say, stand back! The next man who puts his foot in this boat, I will shoot him down like a dog.'

At this, Eva started crying, begging the officer not to shoot her daddy. Benjamin Hart had been helping women and children into the boat. He said to the officer: 'I'm not going in, but for God's sake look after my wife and child.'[250]

Mess Steward Cecil Fitzpatrick apparently arrived on the deck in time to help load Boat No. 14. He remembered that while women and children were boarding, there was a crowd 'of foreigners hanging around the lifeboat ready to leap,' and that one 'Dago' even did jump into the boat. The officer in charge of loading had to threaten all of these people with a revolver to keep them at bay, Fitzpatrick recalled.[251]

Daisy Minahan and her brother William, along with his wife Lillian, had tried to board several lifeboats together. As they traveled across the Boat Deck, they tripped 'over huge piles of bread lying on the deck' – a very curious thing to find on a ship's deck in the middle of the night. Finally they came up on Boat No. 14. She remembered: 'Officers were yelling and cursing at men to stand back and let the women get into the boats.' Daisy and Lillian were placed safely in the boat. William was unable to board.[252]

Very shortly after leaving the engineering spaces below, Leading Fireman Thomas Threlfall also arrived alongside No. 14. He was allowed to board right before Lowe climbed in and gave the order to lower away.[253] Altogether, approximately forty persons had been loaded into this boat, which had a capacity for sixty-five.[254] Lowe was so concerned about the load in the boat that he asked Scarrott: 'Do you

This artistic rendering gives some sense of what the scene surrounding the lowering of Boat No. 14 may have looked like.

think the boat will stand it?' Scarrott replied that it was hanging in the davits all right, and at 1:25 a.m., Lowe gave the order to lower away.[255]

Yet the Fifth Officer was still nervous as the boat descended. He felt that he had 'overloaded' her, and thought that the boat and the davits might not really hold the weight if any other passengers were to jump into it. When No. 14 passed the open A Deck Promenade, there was a rather large crowd of people, including some from Third Class, who had obvious intentions of jumping into the lifeboat. Lowe later described them as 'a lot of Italians' and 'Latin people', terms that were typical of period prejudices. Whatever their nationality, their intentions seemed apparent. Lowe pulled out his Browning automatic – with the chaos surrounding the loading of No. 14, he was probably very glad, in that moment, that he had thought to pick it up – and fired three shots along the ship's side to scare them back. The tactic worked.

Boat No. 14's troubles were not over, however. As the boat neared the water, one of the falls got tangled, and one end of the craft was suspended about five feet above the sea. Lowe tried to get the lines clear, but eventually just released the mechanism and let the boat drop down into the water, freeing it of the dying ocean liner.[256] Doubtlessly, this sharp drop alarmed the passengers in the boat.

By this time, Stewards Alfred Theissinger and George Brewster had come up from below and emerged onto the Boat Deck. When they did, Theissinger recalled that the water was 'only thirty feet below' the deck 'just aft of the bridge'. Both men could easily conclude that 'the vessel was doomed'.[257] He also noticed that several lifeboats had been put away,[258] and that Captain Smith was on the Bridge. He noticed large crowds of people 'running to and fro', and began to realize that he was not going to make it away from the ship up forward. He then moved aft toward the Second Class portions of the Boat Deck.[259]

While all of the excitement on the aft port Boat Deck had been playing out, Murdoch had been working hard at Boat No. 9, apparently with the assistance of Chief Purser Hugh McElroy. Boat No. 9 had been swung out earlier in the evening.[260] Work there had been delayed when, in response to rumors that men would be taken off from the aft port side, the deck near No. 9 had grown 'almost deserted'. However, the preparation and loading of this boat had eventually resumed; the efforts were intensifying as many of the officers and crew who had broken off to help calm the disorder at the aft port boats returned, now that the situation there was under control. Among the men now working at No. 9 with Murdoch and McElroy were Sixth Officer Moody and Able Bodied Seaman George McGough. McGough had just finished working at the aft falls of Boat No. 14 as it was lowered away.[261]

When Assistant Second Steward Joseph Wheat arrived alongside No. 9, Murdoch and a number of stewards and other members of the victualling department were passing women and children over from the port side to fill up the boat, since there still weren't enough passengers on the scene.[262] Steward Frederick Dent Ray was on hand, and pitched in and assisted in the loading process.[263]

Bruce Ismay also assisted at this boat, standing by the falls and helping the women and children board; however, he helped in a less obtrusive fashion than he had earlier in the night. As the minutes ticked by, a large group of men began to stand in a circle around the boat, and as women and children were passed forward through the crowd, Ismay had to shout 'make way' to them.[264]

1:30 a.m. – 1:45 a.m.

Just forward of Boat No. 14, Boat No. 12 had also been loading. Its progress was delayed by about five minutes behind work on No. 14. Able Bodied Seaman Frederick Clench was busy helping Second Officer Lightoller load the boat; both men were passing women and children into it while standing on the gunwales.

Third Class passenger Laura Cribb had been told by her father to get as close to the boats as she possibly could. Laura had thus left him and pushed her way into the crowd. She was unable to 'get into the first two boats [likely Nos 14 and 16] but was put in the third', Boat No. 12.[265]

Meanwhile, Second Class passenger Lillian Bentham had emerged on the Boat Deck by Boat No. 12. Although she was aware that passengers were being taken off in the lifeboats, she still 'did not think the *Titanic* was going to sink. It was so big, so magnificent, that I did not think it possible.' This was in spite of the fact that even then, the liner was well down at the head. However, around her there was a scene of 'alarming confusion'. There were a number of steerage passengers nearby, she remembered, and the 'men especially seemed to be crazed … They wanted to get into the boats and the officers would not let them.' She remembered that some men were yelling. An officer hurried her to the side and dropped her into the boat; although someone caught her in the boat, she somehow managed to hurt her back. In the midst of the mess, Lillian remembered hearing gunfire.[266]

Another who entered No. 12 was Stewardess Mary Sloan. She had tried returning to her cabin for some of her jewelry, but realized she did not have time to go below. One of the bell boys in the crowd recognized her, and pointing to one of the crowded boats, said: 'Miss Sloan, that's your boat!'

The stewardess replied: 'What do you know, I will wait for another.' However, she then realized time was running out, and decided that given another chance at boarding a lifeboat, she'd take it. Then due to 'a big crush' behind her, she was pushed over the deck's edge and into the boat.[267]

Second Class passenger Susan Webber also remembered there was 'a little panic' on the deck when she boarded No. 12. She remembered that in the next boat aft, No. 14, 'the ship's officers were trying excitedly' to get the boat lowered away, but it was jammed. She heard someone call out, 'Cut!' and watched as No. 14's falls were severed and the boat splashed down into the water.[268]

At about this time, Chief Officer Wilde arrived back at No. 12. He asked Able Bodied Seaman Clench how many crewmen were aboard. Clench told him, 'Only one, sir.' Wilde ordered him into the boat since there were no other seamen available. Clench also remembered that he was ordered to keep his eye 'on No. 14 boat, where Mr Lowe, the fifth officer, was, and keep all together as much as we could.'[269]

About this time, Second Class passenger Dagmar Bryhl had reached the deck with her brother Kurt and her fiancé Ingvar Enander. It is uncertain exactly which boat they reached, but Dagmar remembered that 'men and women were kissing each other farewells'. Kurt and Ingvar led her to a boat, and her fiancé lifted her into it. She recalled:

I seized his hands and wouldn't let go. 'Come with me!' I screamed as loud as I could, and still holding his hands tight. There was room in the boat. It was only half-filled, but [an] officer ran forward and clubbed [sic, clubbed] back Ingvar. This officer tore our hands apart and the lifeboat was let down. As it went down I looked up. There, leaning over the rail, stood Kurt and Ingvar side by side. I screamed to them again, but it was no use. They waved their hands and smiled. That was the last glimpse I had of them.[270]

Able Bodied Seaman Poingdestre said that the passengers near him did not behave well during the loading of No. 12, and that he had held back the men who were trying to rush the boat to the 'best of my ability'. He believed that the men 'trying to rush' the lifeboat were all Second and Third Class passengers. They 'were on the boat falls' and in the way, delaying the departure.[271] By the time they were cleared out of the way and No. 12 finally left the ship, it was 1:30 a.m.

As the lifeboat started to descend, a single male passenger – who Clench thought was a Frenchman – jumped down into the boat and hid along the bottom where no one could get to him.[272] Lillian Bentham saw the man jump into the lifeboat, but she wasn't at all sure what his nationality was.

Laura Cribb noticed that when the boat was about halfway down to the water, 'one of the pulleys got stuck', and the passengers were concerned that they would be 'overturned' into the sea. However, the pulley 'started working again just in time'.[273]

Eventually the boat reached the water safely, with approximately forty-two seats out of sixty-five occupied.[274] As her lifeboat detached from the falls, Dagmar Bryhl found herself shivering in the freezing cold air. It was going to be a long, cold night for her.

When the falls were detached, an order was shouted down for the boat to 'pull away from the ship.' Lillian Bentham heard this same order, but also remembered that the officer giving the order added that 'the *Titanic* was going down, and the suction would pull us under.'[275] Clench heard this order, but he had no idea who had shouted it down. Nevertheless he obeyed, and the boat began to make progress in leaving the *Titanic*.[276]

Elsewhere on deck was Anna Hämäläinen. Anna was a 23-year-old married woman traveling in Second Class. She was headed from Finland to Detroit, Michigan, to meet her husband, and was traveling with her infant son Viljo, then only eight months of age. She was also accompanied by another Finnish girl, 18-year-old Marta Hiltunen. Her group had not yet reached a lifeboat. Anna recalled of her experiences:

We seemed to have lots of time, especially at first, when the seriousness of the accident was not realized by most of the passengers. I went back to the cabin and put on some warmer clothes and got some for the baby. Martha was also pretty well dressed. Lots of the people waited [to dress] so long that they had only the thinnest of garments when they were put into the boat. Others were fully dressed, for they had not retired when we struck.[277]

Meanwhile, down on A Deck, Jacques and May Futrelle discovered that a large group of First Class men had congregated. Jacques began conversing with one of them, and leaned over to light his cigarette. As the glow of the flame lit their faces, May saw that the other man was Colonel Astor. The men 'weren't talking much', and 'the only thing anybody said was that we couldn't sink. Especially William T. Stead, the British editor, was sure we couldn't sink.'

As they walked along the promenade, Jacques and May peered down onto the Steerage decks at the stern of the ship, and noted that the Third Class passengers there were 'quite unexcited' at the time, and that many were not wearing lifebelts. Her husband remarked: 'Those poor devils haven't a chance.' He then added: 'I'm afraid you're not giving me a chance for my life by staying here. I might save myself in the water, but not you, too.'

Hearing this, May acquiesced, bid him farewell, and 'immediately determined to leave him and die somewhere else on the boat. I had no hope then.' As she headed up to the Boat Deck, Sixth Officer Moody noticed her and asked: 'What are you doing below, Mrs Futrelle? All the women are gone,' and led her up the steps.

May objected, telling the Sixth Officer: 'Don't pull me.'

Moody ignored her protests, however, taking her along to Boat No. 9. She was subsequently loaded aboard that lifeboat.[278]

By that point, Philipp Mock and his sister Emma Schabert had been rebuffed several times already at the lifeboats in First Class. Earlier, they had ventured aft to Second Class portions of the Boat Deck. There, they attempted to board Boat No. 9 together. However, they again met with failure. It was beginning to look unlikely that they would be allowed to board any of the lifeboats together.[279]

Among the passengers who were being shepherded into Boat No. 9 were Elizabeth and Mary Lines. The crewmen took Mrs Lines by the arms and 'swung' her from the deck into the boat. Mary was impressed by the behavior of the crew in keeping things organized, passing out blankets and reassuring everyone, not to mention the band playing and the passengers who stayed behind on the sloping decks.[280]

A pair of passengers who managed to board Boat No. 9 was First Class passengers Madame Léontine Aubart and her maid Emma Marie Sägesser. Twenty-four-year-old Aubart was the French mistress of one of *Titanic*'s most famous passengers, Benjamin Guggenheim. Reportedly, Guggenheim was on the deck nearby as the two ladies boarded the lifeboat, and said in German to Miss Sägesser, 'We will soon see each other again! It's just a repair. Tomorrow the *Titanic* will go on again.' Miss Aubart recalled that there was no commotion at all on the deck at the time, and that they were the last two women in the area. When she boarded the boat and looked back at the men on the deck, she was very impressed with their behavior:

Oh, these English! How brave, how calm, how beautiful! I, who am a patriotic Frenchwoman, say that never can I forget that group of Englishmen – every one of them a perfect gentleman – calmly puffing cigarettes and cigars and watching the women and children being placed in the boats … My last sight of the upper decks was still a group of those Englishmen, still with cigarettes in mouth, facing death so bravely that it was all the more terrible.[281]

By then, Ellen Toomey, Elizabeth Watt and her daughter Robertha had reached the port side of the Boat Deck.

Olympic's Boat No. 9 is lowered away during a test in Southampton. The scene at Titanic's Boat No. 9 would have been remarkably similar.

Upon arriving there, their shipboard friends had told them that the 'First Class lifeboats' had already been launched. Things were crowded on the port side, and Ellen remembered hearing gunfire from somewhere as events played out. Thus, the trio moved to the starboard side.

'All was hustle and bustle,' Ellen remembered. When they arrived on the starboard side of the ship, the women heard a cry of, 'All women and children this way,' and they approached Boat No. 9 as it was loading. Ellen recalled: 'Before we knew it we found ourselves in a lifeboat and being lowered.'[282]

Saloon Steward William Ward remembered having some difficulty loading No. 9. First, 'a French lady' – per-

haps Madame Aubart? – had 'fallen and hurt herself a little' as she boarded. He realized that from the edge of the deck it was 'quite a step down to the bottom of the boat, and in the dark they could not see where they were stepping.'[283] McElroy told two more men to climb into the boat to assist the ladies in. Yet the excitement in the loading process was not over yet. Next an 'old lady made a great fuss' about boarding. She let Bath Steward James Widgery and Boatswain's Mate Albert Haines take her by the hands, but then she drew away. She 'absolutely refused to get into the boat', ran back to the companionway and 'forced her way in'. One of the crewmembers attempted to go after her, but she had already gone downstairs.[284]

Sidney Collett had watched as lifeboats were filled and lowered away. He remembered that he had somehow gotten himself into the middle of a lot of foreigners just then. He watched as Boat No. 9 was filling up, and then he happened to run across his friend from Guernsey; Collett asked him if he was going to get in, but the man went over to the port side instead. At the time, there were no more women to board the boat. He recalled:

I asked the officer [Murdoch] if there was any objection to my going in that boat. He said, 'No, get in,' and I was the last one in.[285]

Quartermaster Walter Wynn, having helped at other boats, was walking by No. 9 when Sixth Officer Moody instructed him to go to his assigned boat. Evidently, Moody had stayed to assist at Boat No. 9 after he had escorted May Futrelle to it. Wynn did not know which boat he was assigned to, so the Sixth Officer told him to go in No. 9, and to take charge of it. Just as it began lowering away, Murdoch countermanded Moody's order, instructing Boatswain's Mate Albert Haines to take command of the boat. Wynn relinquished control to Haines, entered the lifeboat and took up an oar to help row.[286]

Boat No. 9 was lowered away under Murdoch's direction at about 1:30 a.m., the same time that No. 12 on the port side was lowered away. There were approximately forty people aboard the boat, which had room for sixty-five.[287] Mary Lines recalled: 'The lifeboat went down the side with a terrible jolt. I thought it was all over then, but we stayed afloat and began to row away from the ship.' Percival White and his son Richard – the shipboard acquaintances who had routed the women from their cabin and had thus saved their lives – both perished in the sinking.[288]

Meanwhile, Sidney Collett recalled:

I think it was the third from the last to go from that side. It was No. 9 and we had to get away fast. Besides other boats coming down there was danger from the sinking boat.[289]

As No. 9 began rowing away from *Titanic,* Third Class passenger Berk Pickard was frightened, thinking that it would have been better to stay on the ship, rather than to sit in the tiny lifeboat in the middle of the ocean. Since he was 'sorry at not being on the ship', he told one of the seamen in the boat that he would rather have remained aboard. The seaman laughed at him, saying: 'Do you not see we are sinking?'[290]

After Boat No. 9 was safely away, Murdoch moved on to the next boat aft, No. 11, which was taking on women and children from A Deck. Sixth Officer Moody had been ordered down to A Deck to oversee the loading of the last three aft starboard boats from there.[291]

After Philipp Mock and his sister Emma Schabert were turned away from No. 9, the pair had started to move forward to First Class regions of the deck again; however, they were prevented from doing so, and were instead sent down to A Deck. There, they found Boat No. 11 was beginning to load. 'There seemed to be very few people [present] at the time but in about two minutes there were quite a large number.'

Standing nearby, Mr Silvey told his wife Alice: 'Do just as you are told … We are under orders of the officers of the ship and must obey.' She climbed into Boat No. 11, and her husband stayed behind on the sloping deck. As the officers and crewmen were working at filling the boat, Mrs Silvey looked at them and noticed that their faces 'were white as chalk.'[292]

Steward Littlejohn had helped Able Bodied Seaman Walter Brice and others swing out No. 11, which was his assigned boat. Then he also had been ordered down to A Deck. Once he arrived there he began assisting in the process of filling it with women and children.[293]

Apparently, some men in the crowd looked poised to make an attempt at getting into the boat, and Murdoch shouted out 'women and children first.' Following the sinking, Saloon Steward Edward Wheelton, who worked at and was saved in No. 11, remarked on the First Officer's performance under pressure: 'I would like to say something about the bravery exhibited by the first officer, Mr Murdoch. He was perfectly cool and very calm.'[294]

Stewardess Annie Robinson also boarded No. 11. She remembered that as she did so, she could still hear the music of the ship's band. She also noticed that people were getting into the boat in an orderly way.[295]

Edith Rosenbaum had stayed for quite some time in the Lounge on A Deck. Finally, 'after talking with a bridge officer', she wandered outside onto the Boat Deck again. There, she ran into Bruce Ismay, Archibald Butt, and a crowd of others. When Ismay spotted her, he cried out: 'You! What the devil are you doing here? I thought all the women had left the ship!' Then he walked over, seized her by the arm, and shoved her 'none too gently' toward the stairs. She descended to A Deck, where she found herself 'between two lines of men'. Finally, she found her way aft until she was near Boat No. 11. Two men picked her up, carried her to the side of the lifeboat, and moved to toss her head-first into the craft. She recalled:

I screamed as I lurched into the craft, and at the same time lost both my slippers. I remonstrated against going out in the lifeboat, and some of the men assisted me back to the deck again, where I recovered my slippers.[296]

Almost immediately afterward, Edith ran across Philipp Mock, who had just placed his sister into the boat, and who had stayed back on the deck to help other women in. When Mock and Miss Rosenbaum met, she recalled that he persuaded her to enter the lifeboat:

'Miss,' he said gently, 'if you'll just put your foot on my knee and your arm around my neck, I'll lift you to the rail, and you can jump in by yourself.'
The dangling boat seemed so small and far away. 'All right,' I said resolutely.[297]

Even as Mock bent down to let her use his knee as a step to get up on the railing, one of the nearby sailors tore Edith's toy pig from her grasp and threw it into the lifeboat, damaging it; apparently the crewman thought it was her baby. Edith then stepped from Mock's knee to the railing, and thence into the lifeboat, landing safely within it.[298]

At that point, Mock had a decision to make. He climbed up on the rail and sat on it, looking down at the sea and the lifeboat his sister was in. The boat seemed to be quite full, and was about to lower away. Just then, one of the men in the boat sang out that there was room for one more, and asked if there were any more women. Mock looked about, and saw 'only six or seven men left' nearby. So someone in the boat called out: 'Come on, old man!' Then Mock allowed himself to be pulled into the boat, and it was lowered away.[299]

As the boat was loading, Able Bodied Seaman Brice lowered himself down the falls, and shipped the rudder. While he was occupied with this task, the boat began lowering away.[300] It was 1:35 a.m. There were approximately fifty persons aboard, making it the second most fully loaded boat up to that point.[301] As the craft reached the water, the crew encountered some problems. The after-block got jammed, and they were having trouble disconnecting it from the boat. On top of this, a heavy stream of water from the ship's condenser was being discharged just aft of where they were lowering, and the occupants had some difficulty keeping the boat from being swamped by it.[302] Philipp Mock remembered that the ropes that held the blocks needed to be cut in order to free them.[303] The boat got away safely, but this discharge would cause further difficulties during the loading of Boats Nos 13 and No. 15.

As Boat No. 11 rowed off into the night, Philipp Mock took one of the oars, and everyone 'rowed for dear life, all feeling that if the *Titanic* should go down with them any where near it they would be caught in the suction and swamped and carried down. The object was to get away from the big boat with the heavily loaded life boat.'[304]

Mrs Silvey recalled that a crowd of foreigners was still standing at the rail above, and that they looked 'ready to jump into the boats as they were being lowered'. Looking up as their boat struck the water, she remembered seeing those men being 'forced back so they could not jump upon the women and children'.[305]

Around this time, in the First Class Smoking Room aft on A Deck, Verandah Steward John Stewart looked in to see if there were any other passengers he could assist there. He found Thomas Andrews standing alone; he was staring at the painting over the fireplace, 'Plymouth Harbour', by maritime artist Norman Wilkinson. Andrews' arms were folded across his chest, his lifebelt cast aside and lying on a table near him. Apparently, the enormity of the situation had finally sunk in: the *Titanic*, his crowning achievement, was about to sink out from under him.

The ship's designer was so lost in thought that he apparently didn't realize when Stewart asked: 'Aren't you going to have a try for it, Mr Andrews?' Stewart said that Andrews never answered or moved, 'just like one stunned'. Receiving no response, the steward turned and left. Andrews stayed, still staring into nothing. Shortly after he sighted Andrews, Stewart headed to the remaining aft starboard boats which were loading from A Deck, to see if he could be of assistance there.

Author Shan Bullock speculated at what thoughts might have crossed Andrews' mind as he stood there alone, reflecting on the current situation:

> What did he see as he stood there, alone, rapt? We who know the man … can believe that before him was home and all the loved ones there, wife and child, father and mother, brothers and sister, relatives, friends … and as background to all that, swift realization of the awful tragedy ending his life, ending his ship.[306]

Below deck was Sahid Nackid, a 20-year-old Third Class passenger. He was traveling with his 19-year-old wife Waika 'Mary' Nackid, and their baby daughter Maria. The family was from Lebanon, and they were traveling to Waterbury, Connecticut. There, they planned to meet up with Sahid's mother, Josephine. Somehow, the family had managed to sleep through the collision, and much of the subsequent excitement. The first they were informed of trouble was that 'one of the officers came running thru the steerage' and told them to go on deck. Upon arriving there, they 'could see by the slope of the floor that the boat was going down'. Without bothering to dress, they rushed up on deck. They eventually managed to make their way up to the Boat Deck, and could see that 'the bow of the boat was way down in the water and the stern was sticking up at a slant.' The family moved forward along the Boat Deck.[307]

Doctor Washington Dodge had watched events play out on the starboard side Boat Deck for about, in his rough estimation, 'half or three-quarters of an hour' from the time his wife and son left in Boat No. 5. He saw one boat after another fill and lower away, but it didn't seem like the right time to climb aboard one himself. He remembered that at 'no time were there many people on the starboard side' of the Boat Deck, and although he suspected that more were on the port side, he couldn't tell for sure. This was because, as he recalled:

> We were in semi-darkness on the boat deck, and owing to the immense length and breadth of the vessel, and the fact that between the port and starboard side of the boat deck, there were officers' cabins, staterooms for passengers, a gymnasium, and innumerable immense ventilators, it would have been impossible, even in daylight, to have obtained a view of but a limited portion of this boat deck. We only knew what was going on about us within a radius of possibly forty feet.

Eventually, Dodge drifted aft along the Boat Deck toward Boats Nos 13 and 15, into what was ordinarily Second Class territory.[308]

On the aft starboard end of the Boat Deck, Assistant Saloon Steward Walter Nichols stood with a group of crewmembers, awaiting orders. Nichols' assigned boat was No. 15. He noted that the officer on the scene there had a revolver in his hand, but was calm, and was giving his orders quietly. Nichols remarked that 'we didn't know even then that anything was seriously the matter.'[309]

The officer in charge was Murdoch. After finishing at No. 11, the First Officer made his way to Boats Nos 13 and 15. Washington Dodge remembered that 'Boats Nos 13 and 15 were swung from the davits at about the same moment. I heard the officer in charge of No. 13 [Murdoch] say, "We'll lower this boat to deck 'A'." Observing a group of possibly fifty or sixty about boat 15, a small proportion of which number were women, I descended by means of a stairway close at hand to the deck below,' the Promenade Deck.[310]

Meanwhile, Bathroom Steward Samuel Rule arrived at No. 15, his assigned boat, and heard the First Officer give the order to put in the plug, as well as to ship the tiller and rudder. Next, Murdoch told the crewmen on the scene for 'some of you get into the boat.' About six men boarded, among them Nichols, John Stewart, and Trimmer George Cavell. Murdoch said 'that will do, lower away to A Deck and receive any women and children there.'[311] As No. 15 descended to the next deck, Nichols heard the *Titanic's* band playing.[312]

By this time, August Wennerström, Gunnar Tenglin, and the other Third Class passengers in their group had managed to reach the Boat Deck. They were slowly walking back and forth to keep warm. After helping 'a couple of Swedish girls' into one of the aft boats, Wennerström stood there, smoking a cigar and watching with 'eyes wide open' everything going on around them as the last boats left. Gunnar Tenglin was no longer with him, as he had apparently already boarded one of the aft boats. Wennerström found that he did not feel any sorrow or fear; instead, he felt detached, almost as if they were part of the audience of a 'wonderful dramatic play'.[313]

Wennerström then returned below deck to the Third Class quarters. While there, he ran into his friend Johan Lundahl, also from Sweden. Lundahl said, 'Goodbye friends. I am too old to fight the Atlantic's wave,' and then went to the Third Class Smoking Room, sitting down on a chair and 'awaiting his last call'. Wennerström also noticed seeing an English lady in the Smoking Room take her child on her knee, sit down at the piano, and start playing. He was under the impression that she would keep playing 'until the Atlantic's grave called them both'.[314]

Wennerström and 'a couple girls' who were with him still did not have lifebelts, and began searching for some, 'knowing now that they surely would be needed'. Eventually, their search led them into one of the First Class suites. There were 'magnificent suits, clothing thrown all over, on the table were jewels and diamonds, and on other tables champagne …' In the second room of this suite, August found a lifebelt for himself, just sitting there right next to a pitcher of water. The thought occurred to him that under ordinary circumstances, it would be instinctive to try saving all the wealth before them; however, since the ship was sinking, 'money and wealth are death [*sic*, dead] things and of no value to you, when you are face-to-face with death – you could not here buy you [*sic*, your] life or saving.'[315]

Eugene Daly, Maggie Daly, and Bertha Mulvihill had reached the Boat Deck after Boat Nos 13 and 15 had been lowered to the Promenade. They had been through quite an ordeal in getting up on deck. After Maggie had reported that her cabin was flooded out, Eugene had led the group back down to E Deck, and immediately aft along the E Deck passageway known as 'Scotland Road.' Arriving in the stern, he had asked a man for a lifebelt, since Maggie did not have one. Eugene's lifebelt was concealed by his heavy coat, and the man must have thought he was trying to take it for himself. The two began scuffling, but the man relented and gave the lifebelt to Maggie once he realized they wanted it for her.[316] Eugene's chivalrous acts did not end there. He took the time to wake up a number of women who had not yet come out of their cabins. One of these women was fellow Third Class passenger Katie Gilnagh, who was still asleep. She recalled 'the bagpipe player' from the steerage party earlier that night coming into her cabin and saying 'get up, something was wrong with the ship'.[317]

Before reaching the upper decks, the group had reached the aft Well Deck, where an expanding crowd of Third Class passengers was gathering. The passengers were kept waiting on the aft Well Decks until later in the sinking and were not allowed to proceed up to the boats, a fact which all three would bitterly complain about later. Eugene said

The Rice family, Third Class passengers.

'we were all held down in steerage which seemed to be a lifetime.' Bertha Mulvihill complained that they had been 'held below deck for the longest time', and that 'every time we went up a stair they were locked.'[318] Eventually, the crew unlocked the low lying gates at the top of the stairways leading up from the Well Deck to B Deck, and began letting passengers through. Eugene pushed the two girls through the crowds and up the stairs.

After arriving on the Boat Deck, they found 'there were no boats going off' on the aft starboard side. Bertha Mulvihill saw Margaret Rice and her five children quietly standing off to the side. She was holding her youngest child, Eugene, in her arms, while the other children clung to her skirt. That was the last time any of them saw the Rice family alive, as all six of them perished. After being told a boat was being loaded on A Deck, Eugene wasted no time in pushing through the crowd, leading Maggie and Bertha below.[319]

Elizabeth Dowdell, Virginia Emanuel and Amy Stanley had also been part of the crowd on the Well Deck which now moved toward Boats Nos 13 and 15. As they did so, Elizabeth recalled that the '*Titanic* began to list alarmingly'. Separated in the crush from Amy, Elizabeth and Virginia moved toward Boat No. 13, virtually borne along by the forward momentum of the crowd.[320]

When Boat No. 15 reached A Deck, *Titanic* was listing 'slightly' to port. The list was so subtle at that stage that it was really only obvious to the crewmen once they were standing in the lifeboat. It had not been particularly noticeable during the loading and lowering of boats that had left prior to that point.[321] Eugene Daly pushed Maggie Daly and Bertha Mulvihill towards No. 15, and helped them aboard. Several other men on the scene began pushing towards the boat, and in a moment of weakness, Eugene joined them and climbed aboard. This would not have been an issue, except that there were still women and children waiting for a place in the boat. Unlike the officers on the port side of the ship, Murdoch others officers on the starboard side were typically letting men aboard lifeboats, but only *after* there were no more women and children handy. Describing the events, Daly said the boat 'was being filled with women. Maggie and Bertha got in, and I got in. The officer called on me to go back, but I got in. Life was sweet to me and I wanted to save myself. They told me to get out but I didn't stir. Then they got hold of me and pulled me out'.[322] Eugene only attempted to save himself after ensuring that his previous vow to look after and keep Bertha Mulvihill and his cousin Maggie safe during the voyage was not broken. Both later credited him with saving their lives, and Maggie went so far as to say: 'I never would have been saved but for Eugene. He fought very hard for our lives.'[323]

Bathroom Steward Samuel Rule described these events from a different perspective. He said that when No. 15 came down to A Deck, there was a bit of a rush, and 'several of the foreign passenger men rushed for the boat.' On the Boat Deck, First Officer Murdoch shouted: 'Stand back! Women first!' The rush, minor compared to what had transpired earlier at No. 14, abated. Then Rule and the other crewmembers proceeded to take in all the women and children who were there.[324] Trimmer Cavell believed that 'most' of the passengers in No. 15 were Irish.[325]

Nearby, Dr Washington Dodge arrived on the Promenade Deck just as Boat No. 13 was drawing level with it. He and several others helped a number of women into the boat. Saloon Steward Alexander Littlejohn and other crewmembers remembered helping about '35 women and children' into the same lifeboat.[326]

Saloon Steward Frederick Dent Ray was also helping to fill the lifeboat with women and children. He had previously seen his assigned lifeboat, No. 9, loaded with women and children, and did not leave with it even though he thought that the situation was serious. Next, the steward had assisted in the loading of Boat No. 11, and also saw that boat leave without making an attempt to get in.

At Boat No. 13, Ray caught sight of Dr Dodge, but did not see his wife and son. Ray knew the Dodge family, as he served them on the *Olympic* during their east-bound passage to Europe; it was he who had helped convinced them to take return passage on the *Titanic*. The steward approached Dodge, and asked where his family was. Dodge replied that they had gone away in one of the boats. At that point, the doctor had backed away from the railing. Ray decided to do what he could to save the doctor. 'You had better get in here, then,' he called out and, getting behind him, he pushed Dodge into the boat. Then Ray followed Dodge into the lifeboat, although Dodge didn't see his table steward board.

Dodge might have been distracted because, just then, Ray was involved in a rather bizarre situation. A 'rather big woman' had come along, and Ray found himself and a few others helping her into the lifeboat. Yet, all the while, she was 'crying' and saying: 'Don't put me in the boat; I don't want to go in the boat; I have never been in an open boat in my life. Don't let me stay in.' Ray told her: 'You have got to go, and you may as well keep quiet.'[327]

Third Class passenger Elizabeth Dowdell remembered of the scene around Boats Nos 13 and 15:

It was pitiful watching the men who had to remain in absolute silence on deck, leaving their wives, sweethearts, sisters and children to face and battle with the danger without their aid. We, however, noticed in the darkness of the night – for there wasn't any moonlight – boats slipping quietly away, followed by other boats which were lowered.

Elizabeth and Virginia Emanuel were safely loaded into Boat No. 13, which Elizabeth thought was very heavily loaded.[328]

Second Class passenger Mary Hewlett had remained on the deck for quite some time. She never returned to her cabin to dress, but when she finally tore herself away from the scene to attempt doing so, she was grabbed and 'literally thrown' into Boat No. 13. She protested about being placed in the boat, and was then informed that 'the boat had been severely damaged by an iceberg'. Mary replied that she 'would rather stay on the ship', still believing – as she thought that everyone else did – that the 'monster of

the sea was unsinkable'. She didn't see any women left on the deck behind her when she boarded the boat.[329]

Around this time, Leading Fireman Frederick Barrett arrived at the Promenade Deck and 'took a walk along the deck', headed aft. His clothes soaked, the chill of the night air must have been unpleasant to say the least. Barrett saw that Boats Nos 13 and 15 were loading. No. 13 was very nearly full, and he did not see an officer at that moment. Barrett knew that the ship was in grave danger, so he simply decided to board the nearly-full lifeboat. He remembered that about three people got into the boat after him.[330]

Saloon Steward Ray might have been surprised when a small child rolled into a blanket was tossed to him in the lifeboat. Fortunately, Ray caught the bundle, and then the woman who had brought the child climbed in after it.[331]

The call went out for more women, but none were forthcoming. Sixth Officer Moody came along, and ordered Saloon Steward Littlejohn and another crewman to get in to help row the boat.[332]

Second Class passenger Lawrence Beesley was above on the starboard Boat Deck. He remembered:

Looking forward and downward, we could see several of the boats now in the water, moving slowly one by one from the side, without confusion or noise, and stealing away in the darkness which swallowed them in turn as the crew bent to the oars. An officer – I think First Officer Murdock [*sic*] – came striding along the deck, clad in a long coat, from his manner and face evidently in great agitation, but determined and resolute; he looked over the side and shouted to the boats being lowered: 'Lower away, and when afloat, row around to the gangway and wait for orders.' 'Aye, aye, sir,' was the reply; and the officer passed by and went across the ship to the port side.

Almost immediately after this, I heard a cry from below of, 'Any more ladies?' and looking over the edge of the deck, saw boat 13 swinging level with the rail of B deck [*sic*, A Deck], with the crew, some stokers, a few men passengers and the rest ladies, – the latter being about half the total number; the boat was almost full and just about to be lowered. The call for ladies was repeated twice again, but apparently there were none to be found. Just then one of the crew looked up and saw me looking over. 'Any more ladies on your deck?' he said. 'No,' I replied. 'Then you had better jump'. I sat on the edge of the deck with my feet over, threw the dressing-gown (which I had carried on my arm all of the time) into the boat, dropped, and fell in the boat near the stern.

As I picked myself up, I heard a shout: 'Wait a moment, here are two more ladies,' and they were pushed hurriedly over the side and tumbled into the boat, one into the middle and one next to me in the stern …

… As they tumbled in, the crew shouted, 'Lower away'; but before the order was obeyed, a man with his wife and baby came quickly to the side: the baby was handed to the lady in the stern, the mother got in near the middle and the father at the last moment dropped in as the boat began its journey down to the sea many feet below.[333]

Paul Mauge, Kitchen Clerk of the *à la carte* Restaurant, had made his way to the Boat Deck, along with Restaurant Chef Pierre Rousseau. They were fortunate to have made it … earlier, when they and many of the other Restaurant employees tried to leave their E Deck quarters off 'Scotland Road', they had been blocked from heading aft into Second Class by a number of stewards in the corridor. Mauge and Rousseau, who had earlier been forward looking for evidence of the collision, were fully dressed, and so they happened to look like passengers. Based on their clothing, Mauge was able to convince the stewards to let them pass, and they headed up on deck. The rest of the Restaurant staff was not allowed to proceed.[334]

When they got to the Boat Deck, Mauge saw Captain Smith attempting to convince a female passenger to enter a lifeboat. Mauge also saw at least one boat in the water. As No. 13 was on its way down the side of the ship, Mauge jumped, just as Beesley did. The lifeboat must have been at the level of A Deck, and someone still on the ship tried to pull Mauge off, back onto *Titanic*. Somehow, Mauge was able to remain in the boat, possibly due to its continued descent toward the water.

Mauge then shouted up to Rousseau several times that he should jump in. However, possibly due to his weight – Mauge said Rousseau was 'too fat' – Rousseau would not take the same leap Mauge had. No. 13 continued to lower, Rousseau was left on deck, and never managed to find his way into another lifeboat.[335]

Frederick Barrett remembered that someone called down from the Boat Deck, 'Let no more in that boat, the falls will break.'[336] Whoever gave that order, it is clear that when Murdoch had passed Beesley on his way to the port side, the First Officer felt that the situation was well under control. However with Murdoch's departure, and Moody still on A Deck, this left no officer to oversee the crewmen working the davits on the Boat Deck as Boat No. 13, and then No. 15, lowered away. Murdoch probably felt that this was a risk worth taking, as there was much work left to be done elsewhere on the ship, and precious little time to do it. The order to 'lower away' Boat No. 13 was given at 1:40 a.m.

Once the family with the baby had boarded, there were approximately fifty-five persons aboard.[337] Saloon Steward Ray recalled that 'three or four' men were left on the deck, and as No. 13 dropped away they headed aft to No. 15.[338]

Murdoch and Moody were loading the last of the aft starboard boats more heavily than previous boats which had been sent away. Boat No. 13 was nearing its capacity load, but was still shy of full by ten spaces. Boat No. 15 would end up loaded beyond its capacity as it was lowered away. The reason these boats were being loaded more fully was obvious: the ship was significantly down by the head … the officers knew time was growing short … chances of a rescue ship arriving in time to render assistance had dwindled to nearly nothing. They had to save as many as possible, and time and boats were running out fast.

Eugene Daly stopped a female passenger as she about to board No. 15; he handed her his rosary beads, two gold sovereigns he had in his pocket, and his pocket watch. He begged her to hold on to them for him, said that he would seek her out if he survived, and requested that she send them to his family if he did not make it.[339] No. 15 finished loading, and began lowering away 'thirty seconds' after No. 13.[340] Overloaded, there were approximately sixty-eight persons aboard.[341] The port list was more noticeable

as this boat lowered away, as the gunwale was 'pretty well up against' *Titanic*'s hull. However, this did not interfere with the lowering.[342] As the boat began its descent, a man jumped down from the Boat Deck, landing on Bertha Mulvihill, knocking the wind out of her, and breaking several ribs. This further aggravated the injuries to her back that she had received falling down several stairs earlier in the night.[343]

As No. 13 neared the water, it encountered the condenser discharge which had given Boat No. 11 so much difficulty just a few minutes earlier. Elizabeth Dowdell recalled:

> We were but ten feet above the water when we noticed immediately below our boat was the exhaust of the condensers. Just above the water line a huge stream of water came rushing from the ship's side. We became anxious, for we feared we would be swamped by the rush of water when we touched the level of the sea.[344]

Saloon Steward Ray recalled that …

> … two or three of us noticed a very large discharge of water coming from the ship's side, which I thought was the pumps working [*sic*]. The hole was about 2 feet wide and about a foot deep, a solid mass of water coming out from the hole. I realized that if the boat was lowered down straight away the boat would be swamped and we should all be thrown into the water. We shouted for the boat to be stopped from being lowered, and they responded promptly and stopped lowering the boat.
>
> We got oars and pushed it off from the side of the ship. It seemed impossible to lower the boat without being swamped; we pushed it out from the side of the ship and the next I knew we were in the water free from this discharge …[345]

No. 13's troubles were not over, however. The condenser discharge pushed the boat aft until its falls were pulled taut. When it stopped, No. 13 sat directly beneath Boat No. 15, which was by that point already lowering. Then a new problem presented itself: with the pin mechanism used to release the falls under tension, it failed to operate, and the boat was stuck there. Those in Boat No. 13 began to panic as they realized that Boat No. 15 was being lowered directly on top of them. They shouted to those in control of the falls to halt lowering the boat, but their cries fell on deaf ears, and the other boat kept descending.

The occupants of No. 15 heard their shouts. Once they looked down and realized what was happening, they also began shouting up to the crewmembers on the deck to stop lowering, but to no avail. Sixth Officer Moody's presence on A Deck, combined with First Officer Murdoch's departure to the port side, had left a strange vacuum of authority on the Boat Deck in the wrong place at the wrong time. This may well explain why the warnings from both boats went unheeded by the crewmembers at the falls, and why no one on deck realized what was happening.

In No. 13, the bottom of No. 15 was now so close that those in the boat began reaching up to touch it, trying to push themselves free. A 'sailor' cut the forward set of falls free. Leading Fireman Barrett leapt up and shoved two oars over the bow of the boat, trying to push it away from the *Titanic*'s side. He yelled at the others in the boat, 'Let go the after fall'. However, nobody realized what he was doing, so Barrett climbed over the passengers in the boat and began hacking at the aft falls with a knife, shouting 'One! Two!' as he cut them. No. 13 swung clear of No. 15 just as she dropped into the ocean in the space they had just occupied.[346] Disaster had been narrowly averted.

By now, Steward Alfred Theissinger had moved aft to the Second Class portion of the deck, and he eventually made his way toward Boat No. 15. He 'aided in getting her davits swung over the side of the ship, but an officer said: "There is no chance for you. I am sorry." ' Theissinger then bumped into Storekeeper Cyril Ricks, and the two men stood talking for some time; they were later joined by Steward Sidney Siebert.[347]

Third Class passengers Percival and Florence Thorneycroft had followed their orders, donning their lifebelts and proceeding to 'the second deck', apparently either a reference to the Promenade Deck, or to the Second Class portions of the Boat Deck. Exactly what lifeboat they approached is not entirely certain. However, the scene was far from orderly. Florence recalled that after she boarded the lifeboat in question, the 'men started to follow, but were ordered back in harsh terms, being told that unless they went back they would be shot'. She believed that 'the men would all be cared for later'. At the time, 'women … were being thrown into the lifeboat as if they were bundles, and if they landed on their feet all right.' Their boat was quickly lowered away and rowed off into the night.[348]

1:45 a.m. – 2:00 a.m.

Back on the port side, Murdoch had arrived at Boat No. 10, the last of the aft boats. It was still sitting in the chocks on the Boat Deck. Under Murdoch's watchful eye, progress at No. 10 was made quickly. He ordered Able Bodied Seamen Evans and Buley to swing the boat out and lower it level with the deck.[349]

As Murdoch proceeded with this task, on the Bridge, Fourth Officer Boxhall and Quartermasters Rowe and Bright were still working with the Morse key and the rockets. Their attempts to signal the ship that they could so plainly see on the horizon, but which was not answering their calls for help, were growing increasingly desperate.[350]

Just aft of the port Bridge wing, Chief Officer Wilde had begun loading Emergency Boat No. 2. A whole group of male crewmembers had managed to climb into the boat behind Wilde's back, nearly filling it up, as the Chief Officer was rounding up women and children to put into it. Captain Smith noticed this, and asked a crewmember for his megaphone. When it was handed to him, Smith called out: 'How many of the crew are in that boat? Get out of there, every man of you.' The men crawled out of the boat, and the women and children were loaded aboard.[351]

Mahala Douglas was among those shepherded into Boat No. 2. Before boarding, she asked her husband to join her, but he replied: 'No, I must be a gentleman,' and turned his face away from her. Still trying to think of something that would help his plight, she suggested: 'Try and get off with Mr Moore and Major Butt. They will surely make it.' Clarence Moore, Major Butt, and Edgar Meyer – whose wife had already left in Boat No. 6 – were all standing nearby at the time. Mrs Douglas also caught a glimpse of Arthur

Ryerson's face in the crowd, as well. Then the time arrived, and she boarded the lifeboat. As she entered, she noticed that there were already quite a number of people aboard the craft.[352]

Captain Smith stood between the Wheelhouse door and No. 2 lifeboat, keeping a close eye on the remainder of the loading process. When the loading was nearly finished and the officers were just about to lower it away, Smith turned and saw Fourth Officer Boxhall standing on the Bridge. He ordered Boxhall to 'get into that boat and go away', as the Fourth Officer recalled. Boxhall complied, got in and took charge. It was about 1:45 a.m. As the boat lowered away, he took note of the fact that there was only one other regular boat – No. 4 – visible on the port side, and that Collapsible D was still sitting on the deck. Remarkably, No. 2 left with just seventeen of its forty seats occupied.[353] Boxhall only had one sailor with him, Able Bodied Seaman Frank Osman.

Once Boat No. 2 was afloat, Boxhall worked to get the passengers organized and the oars in the water. This task was much more difficult than he might have expected, because Osman was the only crewmember aboard who was proficient at handling an oar, and who understood boat orders. The Fourth Officer had great difficulty steering the boat, since he was forced to simultaneously pull the stroke oar. Finally reaching a semblance of organization, they rowed about 100 feet out from the ship and then lay on their oars.

Back on the ship, First Class Passenger Peter Daly had been assisting the crew in loading the boats. He watched as Captain Smith looked over the port side of the ship at some of the lifeboats already in the water and shouted: 'Bring those boats back, they are only half filled.'[354] In Boat No. 2, Boxhall heard a whistle from the Boat Deck, followed by Captain Smith calling out through a megaphone for some of the boats to come back to the ship. Smith sang out to Boxhall to 'Come round to the starboard side' to the gangway doors. The Fourth Officer heeded the order immediately, and began rowing aft towards *Titanic*'s stern.[355]

Perched at the tiller of Boat No. 6, Quartermaster Hichens, who had been 'swearing a great deal, and was very disagreeable', reacted quite differently to Captain Smith's orders. Hearing the whistle, Hichens ordered everyone to stop rowing, so that he could hear the directions being shouted to them. Hichens then refused to comply with the orders, saying: 'No, we are not going back to the boat. It is our lives now, not theirs.' He insisted upon their rowing farther away. This did not sit well with the women in the boat, many of whom had left their husbands behind on the sinking ship. Understandably, they protested, but it led to nothing, as everyone felt powerless. One passenger described Hichens as 'cowardly and almost crazy with fear' at the time. Major Peuchen, already having had the one confrontation with Hichens, contemplated taking the tiller from him by force, but there were many passengers in between him and the Quartermaster, and ultimately he decided that he was not in a position to do anything.[356]

Back on the aft end of *Titanic*'s Boat Deck, Evans and Buley had swung out and lowered No. 10 until it was level with the deck. The port list had increased from a barely noticeable tilt, to approximately 10°. This complicated the loading of passengers into No. 10, as it was causing the boat to swing away from the *Titanic*'s hull somewhere between 'two feet and a half' and 'a yard and a half'.[357] After asking if he was an Able Bodied Seaman, Murdoch told Buley to 'jump in and see if you can find another seaman to give you a hand.' Buley found Evans and they both got in the boat.[358] Chief Baker Joughin stood on the Boat Deck, and was 'getting the children and chucking them into the boat'.[359] Evans stood in the bow of the boat and caught the children, also helping the women aboard as Murdoch made them leap across the gap.[360]

As he assisted, Joughin noted that all of the passengers he could see were from Third Class. Once No. 10 was about half-full, the crewmembers began having difficulty finding women who were willing to board the boat. Even at this late stage, many of them preferred the *Titanic*'s sloping decks to a small boat floating in the ocean. Many others had already abandoned the aft part of the deck; this was because there were still a few boats left forward, and since No. 10 hadn't even been swung out, much less loaded, until Murdoch arrived. Because of this, Joughin and three or four other crewmembers went down to A Deck, forcibly brought up women and children, and threw them across the gap into the boat.[361]

A seaman came running over to Imanita Shelley and her mother, who were standing near Boat No. 10, and said: 'Young lady, for God's sake get into this lifeboat they are getting ready to launch; it is the last one on board; all the rest are launched and you must not take any chances.' Isidor and Ida Straus were nearby, and seeing Imanita, they helped her to the edge of the deck. Simultaneously a seaman took hold of her mother, literally throwing her across the gap into the boat, where a crewmember caught her. Imanita was told to jump, so she quickly bade the Strauses farewell, before they helped her leap across the gap, and landed among the other passengers in the boat. Looking up, Imanita saw Mrs Straus smiling and waving on deck, and was impressed at how serene and quiet she was amid all the turmoil, 'not trying to get away and doing all to help the rest of us escape in comfort'.[362]

Second Class passenger Nora Keane was also among those who boarded Boat No. 10. Just before she climbed in, she recalled seeing 'a foreigner of some kind' – others called him 'a crazed Italian' – run and jump into No. 10. She noticed that no one seemed to notice his action. Lutie Parish did, however ... as this man jumped into the boat, he landed directly on top of Lutie, severely bruising her right side and leg, and 'crushing her foot so that it was absolutely helpless'.[363]

On a more positive note, Nora Keane said that the women were shown 'every courtesy' by the crew as they were lowered into the boats. The officers 'had perfect control of everything. There was some excitement amongst some of the people, but not what you would expect under the circumstances. Officers called out just who were to go in the boats.'

While she was waiting for her turn to board, she heard the officers calling: 'All men hold back. Give the women preference. And the men did.' In the process of boarding, Nora said that she and some of the other ladies trampled over the man who had jumped into the bottom of the boat; at the time they didn't know they were stepping on him, but he later proved to be both uninjured and of great use in rowing their lifeboat. She remembered of the scene:

First an officer and two men were put in it. The officer was then ordered out and two men, both green

hands, were put in. Later one of these was ordered out. This left one man, a stoker, whom we believed was drunk.

'What will we do if you leave us?' we asked the officer when he left the boat.

'I'll return,' he answered; but he never came back.

That stoker didn't care whether our boat kept right or not, and if it had not been for the foreigner we tramped on we would have been in a bad way.[364]

Trimmer Thomas Dillon had been among those released from the engineering spaces at about 1:20 a.m. He had eventually reached the aft Well Deck, and went to the Poop, where he noticed crewmen on the upper decks were 'chasing the women on to the port side' so that they could board a lifeboat there. Apparently, there were not enough women at hand, however; Dillon heard the crewmen sing out that this was 'the last boat', and they also called down toward Dillon: 'Any more women there?' Dillon saw some ladies on the Well Deck, so he and some others 'chased them up the ladder.' However, the men opted to remain on the Well Deck, and then moved aft to the Poop Deck.

While they were on the Poop, Dillon heard someone in the area say: 'Go to the first cabin barroom.' Dillon and several other men went there, and found that free whiskey was being served out by a steward.

'Go on, lads,' the steward exhorted; 'drink up. She is going down.'

Dillon and his companions obliged, and Dillon remembered: 'We got our share.' When they were finished, Dillon wanted to go to a First Class cabin, close it up, and try to forget about the approach of the inevitable end, but another fireman in their group convinced him not to. Instead, the group returned to the Poop Deck. One man had some cigarette paper, and another had some tobacco – just enough to make a single cigarette, which was passed around amongst the group of fifteen.[365]

While No. 10 was loading, a woman in a black dress caught her heel on the lip of the deck as she was jumping, causing her to fall in between the boat and the hull of the ship. Thankfully, somebody on A Deck caught her before she fell into the ocean, and pulled her back aboard the ship. She came back up to the Boat Deck and boarded No. 10 without further incident.[366] The boat was lowered away at around 1:50 a.m. Nora Keane thought that it was 'the fourth or fifth boat that left'.[367]

No. 10 reached the water with approximately fifty-seven persons aboard.[368] When the boat touched down, Able Bodied Seaman Evans had difficulty unhooking the falls because he couldn't get to the tripper underneath the thwart and had to release them by hand. As he did, someone shouted: 'Hurry up, the boilers may explode at any moment.'[369]

While Boat No. 10 was being loaded, Lightoller and the crewmen at the forward end of the ship had finally begun to make progress with Boat No. 4. The A Deck Promenade windows had finally been opened, and the Second Officer ordered the women and children nearby back down there. When Second Steward George Dodd relayed Lightoller's order to go below, First Class passenger Marian Thayer, frustrated, shouted out: 'Tell us where to go and we will follow. You ordered us up here and now you are taking us back.' Dodd's response was: 'Follow me.'[370]

Soon, Lightoller and other crewmen were filling No. 4 from A Deck by 'getting the women out through the

This photograph, merged from two photographs of the Olympic, *shows how* Titanic's *forward port side Promenade would have appeared. The loading of Boat No. 4 took place through the windows just forward of the expansion joint.*

windows'.[371] Lightoller's earlier decision to tie No. 4 to the coaling wire running along A Deck had paid off. The boat swung away from the side of the ship due to the port list, but not nearly as much as No. 10 had. Wooden deck chairs were used to make it easier for the passengers to step up to the windows and out into the boat, but even with this makeshift provision, some had to be tossed across. Lightoller stood at the window with one foot in No. 4, and one on the A Deck rail to assist the passengers aboard.

As the women and children were being passed into the boat, First Class passenger Emily Ryerson and her son John stepped toward the window. Lightoller saw this and attempted to prevent John from boarding, saying, 'That boy can't go.' Arthur Ryerson asserted himself saying, 'Of course, that boy goes with his mother; he is only thirteen.' Lightoller relented, but said: 'No more boys.' Emily turned and kissed her husband farewell, and then was 'flung' into the boat.[372]

First Class passengers Colonel John Jacob Astor and Colonel Archibald Gracie helped Astor's pregnant wife Madeleine aboard. Gracie lifted the young bride over the rail and through the window. Astor took her left arm as they passed her to Lightoller, who seated her in the boat. Astor also ensured that Madeleine's maid Rosalie Bidois made it into the boat. He asked for permission to board, to protect his wife in light of her 'delicate condition', but the Second Officer would make no exceptions: 'No, sir, no men are allowed in these boats until women are loaded first.' Astor did not protest. He simply kissed his wife goodbye, telling her that he would follow in another boat. Before stepping back, Astor asked Lightoller what the number of the boat was, so that he could find his wife later if he survived. Lightoller told him it was No. 4. He did not recognize Astor at the time, and assumed that he had asked for the number in order to file a complaint about him later.[373]

It seems that 11-year-old Master Elias Nicola-Yarred and his 14-year-old sister Jamilia also made it into Boat No. 4. The two children were traveling without either of their parents. The fact that they had managed to find their way up to one of the last lifeboats was truly remarkable,

but their fate was not yet certain … they were still standing there on the deck, 'frightened beyond belief, crying and looking for help'. Elias recalled watching 'a middle-aged gentleman,' help his 'very young, pregnant wife … into the lifeboat', and kiss her good-bye. Then the man turned to help the next person into the boat. Elias just happened to be standing right there, and when the gentleman 'grabbed the first person in his path', it was the young boy. His sister, also, was helped in. Master Nicola-Yarred recalled the gentlemen helped some others into the boat, as well. He was later told that his benefactor was none other than John Jacob Astor himself.[374]

Second Class passenger Anna Hämäläinen, her infant son Viljo, and their friend Marta Hiltunen were just coming along A Deck at that time. The two women had realized 'that the ship was doomed' as the sea approached the forward decks. Although the 'crowd along the rail' was thick, she remembered no sign of panic. 'Some were crying and others were perfectly calm. We were all sort of dazed. The officer who was superintending the loading [Lightoller] of that boat [No. 4] looked around and saw me with the baby in my arms,' she recalled.

'Here's a woman with a baby,' he shouted. Then he told her: 'Hurry up and get into the boat.'

Anna handed Marta her handbag, expecting that she would follow her into the boat. Then Anna was 'shoved' into the boat just as it began to lower.[375]

Marian Thayer also managed to board Boat No. 4, along with her maid Margaret Fleming. She had separated from her husband and son about an hour before, and John and Jack had assumed that the two ladies were safely away in a boat. The two men had then run across Chief Dining Saloon Steward George Dodd, who informed them that Marian and Margaret were still waiting for their boat; Dodd then reunited them with the two ladies. However, later, Jack and his parents had been separated in a crowd on the Grand Staircase, and Jack had no idea where they had gone. Assuming his parents had safely gotten into a lifeboat, he and his friend Milton Long went over to the starboard side of the Boat Deck.[376]

A few more passengers boarded, and at 1:50 a.m. – very near to the time that No. 10 began to lower from the aft end of the ship – the order to lower Boat No. 4 away was given. As it began its descent, First Class passengers Arthur Ryerson, John Thayer, Colonel Astor, and Harry Widener stood back, waving and putting on brave faces for their wives, even though they must have known that their own chances of surviving and being reunited with them were very slim. It was the last time their wives would see them.

Anna Hämäläinen recalled looking back and seeing her friend Marta still on the deck. 'The last I ever saw of her was when she stood near a group of men and women.'[377]

As No. 4 approached the water, one set of the falls caught, tipping the boat at an angle, and they had to be cut free with a knife. As the boat touched down, a seaman shouted up: 'We need another hand down here.' Lightoller asked: 'How many seamen have you?' When the crewmember responded that it was just himself, Lightoller said, 'That is not enough.' Then he sent Quartermaster Walter Perkis and another sailor down the falls and into the boat. It was Perkis who took charge.[378]

At that point, there were approximately thirty occupants aboard, out of a possible sixty-five.[379] Once Boat No. 4 was in the water, Emily Ryerson was shocked to see that the deck they just left, A Deck, was only '20 feet' from the sea. She saw water rushing in open portholes along the waterline, with the lights in the flooding rooms still blazing.[380] After releasing the falls, the boat began to row aft, parallel to the side of the dying liner.

After Boat No. 10 left, Chief Baker Joughin went below to his room and 'had a drop of liqueur'. Joughin's cabin was actually not the cabin assigned to him. He recalled: 'I was occupying, and have occupied on the 'Olympic' and the 'Teutonic', the confectioner's room because it is a better room.' This was actually the Confectioner and Second Baker's room, located just abaft of watertight bulkhead K on the port side of E Deck, directly beside the Reciprocating Engine Room hatch amidships.[381]

While he was below, Joughin saw Surgeon Dr William O'Loughlin 'and spoke to him.' Apparently around the same time, Joughin noticed that water was collecting on the floor of his cabin, and that it was deeper on the port side, underneath the closed porthole, than it was on the starboard side. He wasn't exactly sure where the water was coming from, but he believed that it was coming through the open watertight door just forward of his room, and then flowing to port.

Just as Joughin turned to leave, he saw 'two men coming and they said they were going to close' the watertight door. They were starting to do so, using a large spanner which was kept 'alongside the door in a click ready for use', but Joughin went up the stairs without waiting to see them finish the process.[382]

Since all of the aft boats were gone when he arrived on the Boat Deck, he went below again and began throwing deck chairs through the windows because he thought they would float. After throwing what he thought was 'about 50' of the chairs overboard, Joughin went to the A Deck Pantry to get a drink of water.[383]

Meanwhile, as the boats that had already been launched began rowing away from the ship, any doubts that their occupants still harbored about the seriousness of the situation vanished. In Boat No. 13, Saloon Steward Littlejohn and the others lay on their oars and looked back at the stricken liner. Littlejohn noticed that the forward portholes on E Deck were already under water. As he watched, he could see more lights further aft on E Deck going out as the ship settled lower.

When Boat No. 15 was first lowered, Assistant Saloon Steward Nichols said that 'none of us had any idea Titanic would sink.' They had heard a rumor that the Olympic was on the way to rescue them, and Nichols believed that 'she would come in the morning and pick up the boats and take off the people left on the Titanic.' As soon as Boat No. 15 got a little distance away from Titanic, Nichols must have begun to doubt this conclusion: he noticed how far down by the head the ship was, because he saw the starboard propeller sticking halfway out of the water. Also in Boat No. 15, Bertha Mulvihill leaned against the gunwale and noted that the Titanic was 'going down slowly, yet surely. I had marked in my mind's eye two portholes on the vessel. I watched the water come to them, pass them and swallow them up from sight. I was fascinated.'[384]

At about this time, Captain Smith returned to the Marconi room. He informed Jack Phillips and Harold Bride that 'she [Titanic] would not last very long,' and that the 'engine rooms were taking water and that the dynamos might not last much longer'. Coincidentally, Phillips had just re-

marked to Bride that the 'wireless was growing weaker'. Captain Smith did not release them at that point, and left to return to the scene at the port side Boat Deck.[385]

Perhaps in response to Captain Smith's visit, Phillips decided to go out on deck and have a look for himself; he turned the key over to Bride while he was out. Bride attempted to establish contact with the Baltic, but he did not think the connection was very good. He transmitted the information that Captain Smith had just given him: 'Engine room getting flooded.' The Baltic's response was simply 'We are rushing to you.' This exchange took place between 11:45–11:50 p.m. New York Time, or 1:47–1:52 a.m. Titanic time.[386]

Phillips returned from the Boat Deck rather dazed ... he said things looked 'very queer' out there, and that the 'forward well deck was awash'. He said that there was a heavy port list, which Bride had already noticed on his own.[387] Phillips said it was time that they put on their lifebelts and prepare to leave the cabin, but the Senior Operator returned to work at the key without following through on his own suggestion. He remarked to Bride that he should put on his clothes. Bride was puzzled, and it took a moment before he realized that he was still in his pajamas. Making the mental connection, he went to his cabin and dressed, and grabbed Phillips' overcoat, which he slipped over his partner as he worked. Phillips mentioned to his assistant that he was worried that they might not even be transmitting, since the electrical power was really beginning to fade; the ship's lights were even beginning to go dull. Despite his concerns, Phillips continued to work, and soon discovered that the set was still transmitting and receiving; the two men continued to work for another ten minutes ...[388]

By the time Boat No. 2 began lowering away at 1:45 a.m., work was already under way on Collapsible C on the starboard side, and Collapsible D on the port. These craft were sitting on the deck just inside the davits for Emergency Boats Nos 1 and 2. Work on C seems to have been advanced over work on D by a few minutes, but men at both sides still had a lot of work ahead of them. Fortunately, some of the work at getting these collapsibles ready for launch had already been done. After leaving his place at the ship's wheel at 12:23 a.m., Quartermaster Hichens had been ordered by Second Officer Lightoller to take the cover and grips off of Collapsible D. Able Bodied Seaman Thomas Jones had also helped get D 'ready' before leaving in No. 8.[389] It is likely that similar prep work had been done at Boat C.

Despite this, the crew still had to crank in the davits after Boats Nos 1 and 2 were lowered away, hook the collapsibles up to the falls, raise their canvas sides, and then swing them out over the water. This was a lengthy process, and far more complicated than getting the standard lifeboats ready for lowering. Colonel Gracie was working with the crew at preparing Collapsible D. He recalled:

> We had the hardest time with the Engelhardt boat, lifting and pushing it towards and over the rail. My shoulders and the whole weight of my body were used in assisting the crew at this work ... Lightoller's strong and steady voice rang out his orders in clear firm tones, inspiring confidence and obedience.[390]

After Boat No. 2 was away, Chief Officer Wilde crossed over to the starboard side to Collapsible C. He helped load

The Nackids, Third Class passengers.

passengers into the boat, then put out a call for someone to look after Boat C. Rowe recalled that in response to Wilde's call, Captain Smith told him to go help out at that boat, and to take charge of the craft. The Quartermaster fired the last rocket at about 1:50 a.m.[391]

By that time, First Officer Murdoch had moved forward along the Boat Deck and arrived at the scene surrounding Collapsible C. When he got there, he found that the collapsible was already being loaded. At about that point, Wilde left Boat C and returned to the port side, most likely by passing through the Bridge. There he got to work loading Boat D.[392]

Quartermaster Bright was only involved in the preparation work at Boat C, leaving to help with Collapsible D, before the loading process began. Rowe, who left with Boat C, described helping to fill it, while Bright did not.[393]

Around this time, Sahid Nackid came up to Collapsible C with his wife, Waika 'Mary' and their infant daughter Maria. He remembered that during the loading, the …

> … sailors saw my wife, who had only her night-gown on, and me with the baby, and motioned for her to take a seat in the boat. She did so. I helped her over the side of the boat and was going to get in with her when one of the sailors pushed me back and motioned for me to stay behind. I pointed to the baby and he took it away from me and gave it to my wife. The baby started to cry and reached out her hands for me, but even then the sailors would not let me get in.

Nackid could see, however, that there was more room in the boat. He decided to wait until the moment was just right to make his move and join them.[394]

Another Third Class passenger, Emily Badman, literally had to be carried up to the Boat Deck by her friend from Kent, England.[395] He did so after having heard a call of: 'All women and children, this way.' They had moved forward to the starboard side of the Boat Deck, and he saw her safely into Collapsible C.[396]

Third Class passenger Amy Stanley, who had become separated from Elizabeth Dowdell and little Virginia Emanuel, also found her way to Collapsible C. She was placed safely aboard.[397]

J. Bruce Ismay stood near Boat C. He had worked all during the crisis like a member of the crew, assisting women and children into the lifeboats, even getting involved to the point that he occasionally, and quite unintentionally, got underfoot … now it was clear to him that his company's greatest accomplishment was about to sink …

Indeed, the *Titanic* was dying, and dying fast; her buoyancy was beginning to fade, and her palatial First Class accommodations were beginning to disappear beneath the sea's glassy surface. To those on the deck, the end seemed to be nearer now that water was beginning to roll over the Well Deck. It would soon swamp the Forecastle, as well. The sad truth that seemed so difficult to believe just over an hour earlier was now clear to almost everyone. The *Titanic* was being inundated by the sea, the same sea which she was supposed to conquer; now she was being swallowed by it … and there wasn't much time left.

The pace of work at getting the collapsible lifeboats away was now becoming frenzied. Lightoller himself realized that 'there was not a single moment to lose' unless they wanted to suffer the ignominy of having the ship go down with lifeboats – already a precious commodity that night – still hanging in the davits. After seeing Boat No. 4 away, Lightoller had returned to the Boat Deck. When he arrived, he came across Chief Purser McElroy, Assistant Purser Barker, Surgeon Dr William O'Loughlin, and Assistant Surgeon John Simpson.

Simpson, Lightoller later recalled, was 'a noted wag', and said: 'Hello, Lights, are you warm?'

Lightoller looked at himself and realized that he was quite a sight. Despite the freezing temperatures, he had been working so hard on the lifeboats that he had long since shed both his greatcoat and the lifebelt he had donned after getting the revolvers in Murdoch's cabin earlier that night. Even then, standing in just his pajamas, with his uniform pants and a sweater thrown over them, he was 'in a bath of perspiration'.

There was not much time for the men to talk … Lightoller knew that they wouldn't 'have the ship under [them] much longer'. The small group shook hands and said their good-byes, and then Lightoller moved on to the scene at Boat D in time to begin assisting in the effort to get it ready to lower.[398]

Things were hectic at Collapsible D, as there were very few women nearby, and quite a number of men and crewmembers. When Lightoller first arrived alongside the collapsible, someone shouted that there were men in the boat. Lightoller looked over, and seeing a group of men who he described as 'Dagoes', he hopped into the boat, drew his revolver, and 'encouraged them verbally' to get out. The men promptly complied, giving the Second Officer 'the satisfaction of seeing them tumbling head over heels onto the deck, preferring the uncertain safety of the deck, to the cold lead which … they fully imagined would follow their disobedience.' Lightoller later recalled that the revolver wasn't even loaded; if true, then it was a bold bluff on his part. After this incident, the crew got the boat over the edge of the deck. It was finally ready to load. A group of crewmen established a line to block any more men from approaching the collapsible as it was being filled.[399]

Meanwhile, Jane Hoyt and her husband Frederick had watched the loading of the lifeboats, but had not separated from each other, and they still stood on the sloping decks. Jane had noticed their friend, Dr O'Loughlin, as he moved about the ship during the evacuation. She thought that he 'was one of the bravest men on the boat. His fatherly advice

Top: 001. *An early publicity illustration advertising the* Olympic *and* Titanic *for European agents.*

Middle: 002. *This illustration shows Second Class passengers enjoying* Olympic *and* Titanic's *spacious Boat Deck.*

Bottom: 003. *An illustration of the port side Verandah Café of the two liners.*

White Star Line
"Olympic" og "Titanic"
hver 45000 Tons.

Generalagent Joachim Prahl, Nyhavn 5, Kjøbenhavn K.

Top left: 004. *This photo shows the cups used in the Verandah Café, both in period illustration and in a modern day photo.*

Top right: 005. *An artist's depiction of the D Deck Reception Room.*

Center: 006. *A splendid illustration of the forward First Class Grand Staircase and A Deck Entrance.*

Left: 007. *An illustration showing patrons enjoying the Swimming Bath.*

Top left: 008. *The entrance to the White Swan Hotel in Alnwick, England, features fittings salvaged from* Titanic's *sister ship,* Olympic, *when that liner was scrapped.*

Top middle: 009. *Inside the hotel, these steps lead up into the dining room. The balustrades were from Olympic's aft Grand Staircase.*

Top right: 010. *A detail view of the balustrade from the Olympic.*

Centre: 011. *Climbing the stairs, one enters the hotel's dining room and, incredibly, finds one's self in Olympic's First Class Lounge – a near match to that found on* Titanic.

Right: 012. *This view is looking slightly to the left from the previous photograph. The windows on the right once looked out upon the Promenade Deck.*

Above: 013. *This photo shows the fireplace and mirror which once stood in the forward wall of the First Class Lounge.*

Below left: 014. *A detail view of the intricate wood carvings in the paneling.*

Below right: 015. *The craftsmanship and care with which* Olympic *and* Titanic's *First Class Lounge were produced is evidence in the breathtaking carvings from* Olympic's *Lounge.*

Opposite top left: 016. *A detail view of the fireplace and mirror.*

This page, top right: 017. *This photo was taken from the vicinity of the fireplace; visible at left is a semi-private alcove.*

This page, above right: 018. *This daytime view shows light streaming into the dining room, ex-Lounge, through the Olympic's ornate windows.*

Below left: 019. *Another view of the Olympic's Lounge paneling. It is interesting to note that because the Olympic and Titanic's interior spaces were hand made, there were subtle differences in even the pattern of wood carvings in their public rooms.*

Below right: 020. *This partition separates one of the semi-private alcoves from a nearby section of the dining room.*

This spread, top left: 021. *A rather ordinary-looking exterior view of a fire escape of the White Swan Hotel shows something unique upon closer inspection: light streaming from within one of* Olympic's *ornate windows.*

Top row, center: 022. *The hotel dining room is seen dressed for a special event. This room is one of the few places where one can get a true idea of what being aboard the* Titanic *felt like.*

Top right: 023. *A period illustration of the* Olympic *and* Titanic's à la carte *Restaurant.*

Middle left: 024. *This illustration shows a 'Bedroom B'-pattern First Class stateroom aboard the* Olympic *and* Titanic. *These rooms were specially-designed by Harland & Wolff rather than by an outside design firm.*

Inset: 025. *This is a piece of the remnant given to Frederick Dent Ray by a shipyard carpet-layer before the maiden voyage. Its shade is not entirely dissimilar to that found in the illustration of the 'Bedroom B'-pattern stateroom.*

Above right: 026. *This is a color view of the Adams-style Sitting Room, similar in appearance to* Titanic's *B-51. The actual orientation of the room is more accurate to* Olympic's *Sitting Room B-39, however.*

Bottom row, far left: 027. *A color illustration of* Olympic *and* Titanic's *Second Class Dining Saloon.*

Bottom row, left: 028. *The Second Class Library springs to life in this color illustration.*

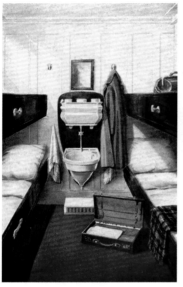

This spread, top row, left to right: 029. *An illustration of a 'Bibby-style' Second Class stateroom; a narrow passageway led from this inside stateroom down to a porthole that provided light and fresh air.*

030. *A color illustration of the Third Class Dining Saloon. Immigrants were treated to the luxury of being waited upon hand and foot by obliging stewards.*

031. *A color illustration of the Third Class Smoking Room.*

032. *Nearly identical to the Third Class Smoking Room was the General Room; in this space, however, men and women mingled freely.*

Middle row, far left: 033. *A typical view of a four-berth Third Class cabin.*

Middle row, second from left: 034. *This illustration shows a two-berth Third Class cabin, intended for single ladies or couples.*

Middle row, centre upper: 035. *A rare silk postcard of the* Titanic.

Middle row, centre lower: 036. *'Hands Across the Sea' postcards were very popular in Titanic's day. This Swedish card is for White Star vessels and headlines the* Olympic *and* Titanic. *As both vessels, as well as the* Laurentic *and* Megantic, *are listed as being under construction, the card probably dates to early 1909.*

Middle row, second from right: 037. *This rare piece of correspondence was slated to be carried on the* Titanic's *March 20, 1912 maiden voyage before that trip was canceled and rescheduled for April 10.*

Middle row, far right: 038. *This piece of IMM advertising prominently features an illustration of the* Olympic *and* Titanic.

Lower right: 039. *A colorized view of the* Titanic *leaving Belfast on April 2, 1912.*

This page, bottom right: 040. *A baggage claim ticket from aboard the* Titanic, *numbered 31438D, which included instructions for the passenger on being prepared for Customs inspections upon arrival in New York.*

Captain Smith, saving a child while the ship went down - April 15th 1912

Arrival of S. S. Carpathia after the disaster   April 15, 1912

This page, top right: 052. *A color illustration of Captain Smith rescuing a baby and bringing it to Collapsible B.*

This page, above right: 053. *A color illustration of the rescue in progress.*

This page, right: 054. *This photograph was taken for the 1980 film* Raise the Titanic. *It shows the large scale model of the ship sinking for sequences of the film which were eventually left on the cutting room floor.*

This page, bottom right: 055. *A publicity photograph for* Raise the Titanic *captures the moment when the mighty liner was raised from its watery grave.*

This page, top row, left to right: 056. *Queen's Road, Belfast, looking toward the former location of the Great Gantry, and Slips Nos 2 and 3. Compare with the photograph on page 21.*

057. *This revolving door, a near match to some of those found on Olympic and Titanic, stands in the main entrance of Harland & Wolff's offices in Belfast.*

This page, second row, left: 058. *A view of the former offices of Lord Pirrie. On the left stands a shelf full of old plans and photographs.*

This page, third row, left: 059. *A fireplace and mirror in Lord Pirrie's office.*

This page, bottom left: 060. *The gravestone of William James Pirrie.*

Opposite page, top: 061. *The Harland & Wolff Draughting Offices, where most of Olympic and Titanic's plans were drawn up, still stands.*

Opposite page, bottom: 062. *A second view of the Harland & Wolff Draughting Offices.*

Left: 063. *A view along the side of the Thompson Graving Dock, where* Olympic *and* Titanic *underwent portions of their fitting out. To grasp some concept of scale, note the size of the individuals standing on the floor of the dock.*

Below: 064. *Looking down the length of the Thompson Graving Dock, with the pump house on the left.*

Bottom left: 065. *Dunallon House, the home of the Andrews' family beginning in the summer of 1908, shortly after their marriage. The building is now the home of the Irish Football Association.*

Bottom right: 066. *The main staircase inside Dunallon House, with a commemorative model of the* Titanic *on the landing.*

was carried out in many instances where he saw opportunities for people to get a chance to save their lives, and he always went away with a "good-bye and God bless you".'

After seeing all of these things take place, the Hoyts approached the 'last collapsible life boat' on the port side, Boat D, and Frederick told Jane that she 'would have to get in'. She did not want to, however, and 'did so only after much persuasion and after we had bid each other goodbye'. She remembered that the scene at this collapsible was rather chaotic, as …

> … there was a sudden rush of steerage passengers …
> and it looked as if it [the collapsible] might be upset.
> … Chief Officer Wiley [sic, Wilde], also drowned,
> pulled his gun and ordered every man in the boat
> to get out.[400]

In Boat No. 5, approximately a hundred yards away from the ship, Third Officer Pitman sat and watched as *Titanic's* head sank deeper and deeper, and the last line of lit portholes underneath the Forecastle head disappeared. It was a sobering moment. Prior to this observation, Pitman had not yet given up hope that the ship would stay afloat.[401]

In Boat No. 2, Fourth Officer Boxhall also noticed the lines of lights going underwater as the ship settled further by the head. Following orders, Boxhall had managed to row around the stern of the *Titanic* heading for the starboard gangway doors, but it had been quite a struggle getting there, particularly with the lack of trained oarsmen. As they passed around the stern, the boat came very near the ship's propellers, which were now fully out of the water. Boxhall later said: 'I'm not certain if I didn't pass underneath them.'[402]

Boxhall reported that as No. 2 rounded the stern, it was drawn closer to the ship by what he thought was 'a little suction', and that this 'suction' was greater when the ship was settling than it was when the ship actually went down. However, Able Bodied Seaman Osman felt that there was 'no suction whatever'. They also had to avoid a rain of deck chairs and debris that was being thrown overboard for people to cling to if they took to the water.

When he got within two hundred feet of the gangway, the Fourth Officer began to feel uneasy about getting closer to the side of the ship. He then ordered the boat to pull further away from the side of the liner. Despite the fact that there were just seventeen people aboard his lifeboat, he justified this by saying that he felt that there was very little room for additional passengers in No. 2, and was worried about 'being rushed and losing everybody in the boat'.[403]

When released from duty at about 1:20 a.m. in the Engine Room, Greaser Frederick Scott had gotten a lifebelt and proceeded up to the Boat Deck. He had noticed that 'all the engineers and firemen and all that … [who] were on watch' had come up on deck right after him. About a half-hour after being released from the Engine Rooms Greaser Scott was standing on the Boat Deck with the group of engineers, trimmers and firemen.[404] They were standing up against the aft electric crane on the starboard side of the Boat Deck.[405] Among the others in the group, Scott spied Senior Second Engineer William Farquharson.[406]

At about this same time, Greaser Thomas Ranger emerged from the Fan Rooms in the deckhouse on the Boat Deck above the First Class Smoking Room. He went to the starboard-aft quarter of the deck, which was normally apportioned to Second Class passengers.[407] There he found the group of about twenty firemen, trimmers and other engineering staff, and he stopped to talk to them. They heard that 'all the boats had left the ship'. At the time, Ranger noticed that the ship had a 'slight list to port', and was down by the head, but he could not see whether the ship's bows were under water from his vantage point.[408]

All the way forward on the Boat Deck, Collapsible D was still loading. Jane Hoyt had reluctantly left her husband and boarded that boat. She recognized Mrs Irene Harris and 38-year-old Gertrude Thorne – George Rosenshine's mistress – in the collapsible with her. However, the rest of the people boarding with her seemed to be 'steerage passengers, among them several women'.[409]

2:00 a.m. – 2:20 a.m.

By this point, Greasers Thomas Ranger and Frederick Scott had separated from the other engineering staff on the starboard side of the Boat Deck, and crossed over to the port side. They looked over the edge of the deck and saw Boat No. 4 rowing aft along the port side of the ship, almost directly below them. The two greasers decided that this was their opportunity to leave the ship.

Both men climbed out on the davits. Ranger used the aft davit for Boat No. 16 – the very aft-most davit on the port side of the deck.[410] They climbed out with no little difficulty because their lifebelts were so bulky. Once they reached the end of the davits, they nimbly caught hold of the falls, where they began working their way down toward the water. Scott had only gotten halfway down, however, when he somehow lost his grip and went plunging into the icy seawater. Ranger managed to stay on the fall all the way to the water, and climbed directly into No. 4 without even getting his feet wet. Scott was pulled in within just a few minutes.[411]

Meanwhile, on the starboard side, Collapsible C was ready to lower away. The circumstances surrounding the loading of this boat are unclear, due to contradictory eyewitness testimony. Some survivors reported that there were crowds around the boat and that warning shots had to be fired to keep them back; others, mainly crewmembers, painted a picture that suggests there were few if any women and children on the scene as the boat lowered away, and that things were perfectly orderly.[412] Regardless, by that point in the process, First Officer Murdoch seems to have been having difficulty finding more women to put in, and there were no more to be found in the immediate area. Quartermaster Rowe got into the boat to work at the after fall, and Murdoch ordered the boat lowered away.[413]

White Star Chairman Bruce Ismay and William Carter, another male passenger from First Class, climbed into the boat just then.[414] Murdoch could not have helped but see them; if he did, he did not register a complaint or ask them to get back out. It was now 2:00 a.m. Quartermaster Rowe believed there were approximately thirty-nine seats occupied as the boat began to descend. After daylight broke, four 'Chinamen or Filipinos' who were stowaways came up from between the seats, meaning that Collapsible C actually had a complement of forty-three people.[415]

Rowe remembered that there was difficulty lowering the boat away, so much so that it took five minutes to reach the water, even though the sea was not far below. The liner was then listing 10° to port, causing the rubbing strake to keep 'catching on the rivets down the ship's side'. The men struggled to push it off the ship's side to free it, and to prevent damage to the fragile craft.

In the midst of this confusion, as the lifeboat was descending toward the sea, Sahid Nackid decided the time was right to make his move. He jumped into it and landed flat on his face. 'The women covered me over with their skirts,' he recalled, 'and I laid there. There had been so much confusion in casting off that the sailors did not see me jump and of course, did not see me afterwards because I was covered up.'[416]

Amy Stanley recalled:

As we were being lowered a man about 16 stone jumped into the boat almost on top of me. I heard a pistol fired – I believe it was done to frighten the men from rushing the boat. This man's excuse was that he came because of his baby. When we rowed off the child must have died had I not attended to it.[417]

The sinking of the ship was now accelerating right before the eyes of those aboard. When Collapsible C started down, Rowe observed that the Well Deck was 'awash', but that by the time the lifeboat was in the water and they cast off, the Well Deck had 'submerged'. He also recalled that the Forecastle head was not submerged at that point.[418]

Emily Badman remembered wondering, as Boat C was lowered to the water, what would become of them. She wasn't frightened at all, she later recalled. However, once the lifeboat had reached the water, she 'could see that the *Titanic* was fast sinking and the six men who were rowing pulled ... as fast as they could.' At dinner that evening, Emily had remarked to her friends that she wished she could see the *Titanic* from a small boat ... as Boat C pulled away from the dying liner, she got her wish.[419]

Sahid Nackid remembered that as soon as the boat had cast off the sailors 'started to row as fast as they could', but he remained concealed in the boat's bottom, afraid to show himself for fear of retribution for having boarded the boat without permission.[420]

Meanwhile, back on the port side at Collapsible D, time was running out to finish loading the lifeboat. Lightoller was standing in the craft, helping passengers over the bulwark at the edge of the Boat Deck. A few minutes earlier, Lightoller had looked down the stairwell just abaft the Bridge. These stairs led down to A Deck where there was a landing, and then continued down to B Deck; thus, there was a clear line of sight to that location from the Boat Deck. Alarmingly, he saw that water had already reached B Deck, and was rapidly climbing the stairs towards A Deck.[421]

Even as the icy seawater was creeping up towards their location, the crew was having 'the utmost difficulty' in finding women to board the boat. Archibald Gracie and Clinch Smith 'ran along the deck ... some distance aft shouting, "Are there any more women? Are there any more women?" ' Gracie was beginning to notice 'a very palpable list to port as if the ship was about to topple over'. No more women would be boarding the boat.

Just then the officers – Gracie heard Lightoller, but Lightoller was repeating the order from Wilde – shouted out: 'All passengers to the starboard side to straighten her up!'[422] With this order, Gracie believed that 'the final crisis had

come, with the boats all gone, and ... when we were to be precipitated into the sea.' He prayed that he might be saved, and he fell back on his training at West Point to maintain his composure. Clinch Smith urged 'immediate obedience' to Lightoller's orders, and the pair crossed over to the starboard side.

When they arrived there, Gracie thought that the list of the deck was less noticeable, but that the situation was every bit as desperate; here all the boats had gone. He saw a crowd gathered along the midships rail, and spotted John Thayer – Jack must have failed to see his father, although they were both on the same side of the deck – and George Widener in among the group. The two men were talking as if they were trying to decide what to do next. Gracie was horrified to find two of the ladies 'whom more than an hour previous I had ... consigned to the care of Sixth Officer Moody on Deck A.' Caroline Brown and Edith Evans quickly described how they had become separated from Mrs Appleton and Mrs Cornell. Gracie had not been introduced to Miss Evans before, and asked her name.[423]

In the meantime, some of the crew working at Boat D had cried out: 'Any more women and children?'

'There are no women,' was the response from someone.

Around that time, Archibald Gracie was standing on the starboard Boat Deck. He saw a crewman coming over from the port side, where they had just left, calling out that there was room for more ladies in Boat D. Gracie seized Mrs Brown and Miss Evans by the arm, and rushed them to a line of crew near amidships who said that only the women could proceed. Gracie handed them off for the second time that night and returned to the starboard side.

The two women were moved to the railing by the collapsible boat when word came back that there was room for just one more. Edith Evans insisted that Mrs Brown take the seat. 'You go first. You are married and have children.'[424]

Meanwhile, several crewmen were ordered in to man Boat D, including Quartermaster Bright. Chief Officer Wilde, noticing that no more seamen were available to man the boat, turned to the Second Officer and said: 'You go with her, Lightoller.' Lightoller looked up and said: 'Not damned likely!' Then he jumped back aboard *Titanic* in defiance of Wilde's order.[425] Chief Second Class Steward John Hardy remembered that Lightoller said he would get out and 'make room for somebody else,' and that he then asked Hardy if he could row. When Hardy said that he could, he was allowed into the boat.[426]

After being present at the loading and lowering of Collapsible C on the starboard side of the Boat Deck, First Class passengers Hugh Woolner and Mauritz Håkan Björnström-Steffansson went down to A Deck, allegedly to look for anyone there and escort them to a lifeboat. Even more likely than that, though, they had seen that Collapsible D was still not lowered on the port side, and realized it was their last chance to be rescued. They probably thought that they would have a greater chance of boarding the boat from the Promenade, since, unlike the Boat Deck, there were no crowds there, and no crewmembers were guarding entry from there. Once on A Deck, they came around the front cabins to the port side, where the collapsible would be lowering past them.

It was 2:05 a.m. when Collapsible D was ordered away. There were twenty people aboard.[427] As it descended toward the water, just ten feet below, Quartermaster Bright looked forward and saw the sea engulfing the Forecastle.

As the boat descended past A Deck, the aft fall got hung up momentarily, and Bright called out to stop lowering the forward fall, and to let out the aft one.[428]

As D was lowered away, Frederick Hoyt stood at the edge of the deck and waved goodbye to his wife. Jane noticed that at about that time, Captain Smith was giving orders through his megaphone 'here and there'. However, because of the 'general din' Jane Hoyt did not think it likely that the orders were heard at a great distance. She recalled of the lowering process:

> Seamen started to lower us but the boat suddenly gave a heavy list and the men left us hanging suspended from the air and ran to the upper side so as to save themselves. Finally one of the two men came back and completed the task of lowering us to the water.[429]

Meanwhile, Frederick Hoyt decided to approach Captain Smith; he had known the Captain for fifteen years, and approached to sympathize with him on the accident. He remarked to Smith 'on the seriousness of the situation'. The Captain replied, agreeing 'that it was "terrible".' Hoyt did not want to 'bother him with questions', as he knew that 'he had all he wanted to think of'. At the time, Hoyt 'never expected to be saved'. Captain Smith then suggested that Hoyt 'go down to A Deck and see if there were not a boat alongside.' Smith added that Hoyt would have to jump and told him that 'you had better do it soon.' It was clear that the Captain knew the end was near.

Hoyt followed the Commander's advice, and descended – probably by means of the stairway directly behind the Bridge – to the Promenade Deck. He was surprised to find Collapsible D 'still hanging on the davits,' as he was completely unaware of the delay in the lowering while he had been talking to the Captain. An idea began to form in his mind ... if he could jump overboard and swim to the boat, they might just pick him up ... He shed his overcoat, and then jumped into the water.[430]

Woolner and Björnström-Steffansson, now at the railing on A Deck, also took advantage of this temporary halt in lowering; they launched themselves out towards the collapsible, which, due to the list, swung approximately five feet away from the side of the ship as it lowered past them. Water had begun lopping over the forward bulwark rail on the port side of A Deck as Collapsible D descended past, sending a surge of green seawater rushing around the men's feet. Both had feared they would end up boxed in against the ceiling as the water rose. Steffansson tumbled head over heels into the bow of the collapsible, while Woolner came up somewhat short, and struck the gunwale with his chest. His lifebelt cushioned him, but caused him to bounce off, and nearly fall into the water. He caught himself at the last moment. As he was pulled aboard, his legs dangled in the freezing water.[431]

Jane Hoyt, in the lifeboat, was entirely unaware of her husband's leap into the sea. She recalled that as their lifeboat was 'leaving the ship's side', she could 'quite distinctly' hear the upbeat refrains of 'Alexander's Ragtime Band' being played by the ship's musicians.[432] Just as the boat was beginning to pull off, and water reached the ceiling of A Deck, just below the Boat Deck, the crewmen in the lifeboat noticed something in the water. It was a man swimming towards them, and they quickly hauled him aboard. It turned out to be Frederick Hoyt ... Hoyt's plan, the formulation of which had been aided by Captain Smith himself, had worked. As Hoyt lay shivering in the bottom of the collapsible, Rene Harris recalled that he looked up at his wife – who still had not recognized him – and called out: 'Jane'.

Jane Hoyt looked into his face, and her first response was to call out her husband's name. Then she exclaimed, 'My God! It's my husband!' One of the First Class ladies put her fur robe on the man, and Jane Hoyt tossed him her shawl to help him keep warm.[433]

Back up on the Boat Deck, Lightoller turned his attention to his next and most difficult project: Collapsible B, still sitting on the roof of the Officers' Quarters abreast of the forward funnel. A group of crewmen was now swarming over it and its counterpart, Collapsible A, on the starboard side; they must have been cursing the asinine concept of placing collapsible boats in this location, especially as time was evaporating before their very eyes ...[434] It had taken the crew quite some time to prepare both Collapsibles C and D for loading and lowering. Unfortunately, it was now obvious that there was not going to be enough time to complete the even more complicated preparation procedure of Boats A and B ...

Second Class passenger William Mellors had watched as the last boats left the ship. He later recalled that 'it was an awful sight to see the men's faces when the last boat left.'[435] Hope for rescue had begun to drain from the men still left aboard, and the increasing feelings of desperation were palpable.

Third Class passenger Rhoda Abbott and her sons Rossmore and Eugene had stuck together for a time once they had reached the Boat Deck. They had watched lifeboat after lifeboat being lowered to the sea; she had also seen men enter lifeboats that were lowered late, and without intervention by the officers. When the final boat had lowered away, there were still 'at least seven women' on the starboard side of the deck near Mrs Abbott. At some point, the ship's crew had pushed 16-year-old Rossmore back with the other men, separating him from his mother and his brother Eugene. Mrs Abbott and her sons were never able to get into the lifeboats, 'as there was no room' in them. The mother and her two sons, as well as the other women left behind from the last lifeboat, all stood near each other ...[436]

Meanwhile, Jack Thayer and his friend Milton Long were also on the starboard side of the Boat Deck, 'just a little aft of the Captain's bridge'. The pair had lost sight of Jack's father John, and his mother, some time before. His mother had subsequently been put off in Boat No. 4. The two young men had watched the crowd around 'the last boat to go on the forward part of the starboard side', and decided not to get mixed up in what was going on there. Thayer recalled that the list to port was growing very steep, and he also noticed that at about that time, people began to jump from the stern of the ship. Gathering himself, Thayer had decided to jump and slide down one of the falls, and then swim to the boats that were lying off the starboard side. Three times, however, Long convinced him to wait; even that late in the sinking, they both thought there was a possibility that *Titanic* might remain afloat.[437]

Despite the obvious time constraints, Lightoller worked feverishly at Boat B on the port side; meanwhile, First Officer Murdoch and Sixth Officer Moody toiled at Boat A on the starboard side.[438] A good group of determined crewmen and passengers assisted on both sides. Racing the sea, they hoped that they could get the boats hooked up, loaded, and lowered away before the ship sank from under their feet.

In the Marconi shack, Phillips and Bride remained at their post, even though the ship's power was fading fast and they would not be able to transmit for much longer. At some point after he had ordered Quartermaster Rowe into Collapsible C – and perhaps in response to the fact that the ship was so obviously close to sinking – Captain Smith returned to the Marconi shack for the last time, 'a very short period after' his previous visit.[439] He released the young men from their duty, telling them that they had 'done their best and could do no more', and that they 'had better take care of yourselves'. Then he was gone.[440]

Instead of getting up to leave, Phillips doggedly stuck to his work. It was 2:02 a.m. Bride remembered that he could hear what Phillips was tapping out, and thought that he was communicating with the *Frankfurt* and the *Carpathia*, perhaps in response to receiving messages from those vessels. It was difficult for him to tell, though, since Bride wasn't wearing the headphones, and couldn't hear the incoming transmissions.[441]

Bride's recollections of those final minutes were vivid. The two men could hear people rushing about out on deck. Phillips was blatantly annoyed at the *Frankfurt*'s operator, who 'persisted in calling and was interfering with Mr Phillips in reading the *Carpathia*'s message'. Phillips expressed his 'uncomplimentary opinion' of the *Frankfurt*'s operator, telling him: 'You are a fool. Keep out and do not interfere with our communication.' Then he tried to tell the *Carpathia* that they 'were abandoning the ship, or words to that effect'. Bride said that Phillips tried calling 'once or twice more, but the power was failing us', and he didn't think that they 'were getting a spark, as there were no replies'.[442]

Bride recalled with admiration his colleague's selfless work during those final minutes: 'He was a brave man. I learned to love him that night, and I suddenly felt a great reverence to see him standing there sticking to his work while everybody was raging about. I will never live to forget the work of Phillips for the last awful fifteen minutes.'[443]

Bride had already taken the time to put on his own lifebelt, but Phillips was so preoccupied with his work that Bride had to strap his colleague's lifebelt on him as he worked the key. Phillips asked Bride to get his spare money and another coat while he kept working, and when Bride looked back out, he was horrified to see that they had an uninvited guest. A stoker had come in and was quite literally slipping Phillips' lifebelt off his back. Phillips was too absorbed in his work to notice. Bride, who was very impressed with Phillips' courage, was outraged with this stoker's behavior; he knew the man had his own lifebelt and should have known where to get it.

Bride flew at him even though the stoker was a 'big man', and Bride was 'very small'. Bride's account suggests that he might have hit him with an object, as he said: 'I don't know what it was I got hold of.' Bride later admitted the feelings of rage and hatred that he directed at the thief: 'I suddenly felt a passion not to let that man die a decent sailors' death. I wished he might have stretched rope or walked a plank. I did my duty. I hope I finished him. I don't know.' Phillips and Bride promptly cleared out of the cabin, leaving the motionless stoker to his fate.[444] They emerged on the port side of the Boat Deck via the door just across from where Boat No. 4 had been. When they arrived in the cold night air, there were people 'running all over the place', and Bride heard 'the tunes of the band', coming 'from aft … It was a rag-time tune.'[445]

Around this time, a large group of Third Class passengers who had previously been somewhere else below began to emerge, via the forward First Class Grand Staircase and First Class Entrance, onto the Boat Deck. Where these passengers were coming from, and why it took them so long to reach the deck, is unknown. Many who had been working on the lifeboats had felt that the majority of women had already gotten away because there were so few to be found as they loaded Collapsibles C and D … Now they were horrified to find that there were many women and children in this new group that was swarming on deck, all of them desperately looking for a place in a lifeboat …[446]

The men on the port and starboard sides of the Boat Deck and atop the roof of the Officers' Quarters were still struggling to get the collapsibles down to the deck and ready for launch. There was a shortage of crewmembers available to help on the port side, so an officer, possibly Lightoller, crossed over the roof of the Officer's Quarters and asked: 'Are there any seaman down there among you?' Several answered the call, and crossed over to the port side. The canvas cover spars from the collapsibles were leaned up against the walls of the deck house, providing a slope that the men planned to slide the boats down on.[447] Harold Bride realized that Lightoller's group just forward and above him needed help, and he darted up to the roof to aid in the difficult effort. Phillips ran aft, and that was the last time Bride saw him alive.[448]

Lamp Trimmer Hemming had jumped out of Boat No. 6 earlier in the night in order to assist in its lowering. Now he was among the group assisting the Second Officer on the roof of the Officers' Quarters. Lightoller glanced over and saw him, asking why he hadn't gone yet. 'Oh, plenty of time yet, sir,' Hemming replied cheerfully. Lightoller was impressed – Hemming had loyally stuck with him throughout the night. The Second Officer had been concentrating so hard on getting the boats away that he hadn't even noticed him until that very moment.[449]

Just astern of where Phillips and Bride emerged on the Boat Deck, the orchestra began playing their last piece. The debate as to what the last piece was, as well as when exactly the band stopped playing, rages to this day. Some survivors claimed the band had stopped playing earlier in the night, while many others, including Harold Bride, said that they played right up until the final moments. Many later reported that the last piece played was the hymn, 'Nearer My God to Thee'. However, others who were in the area later reported that they did not play this hymn. Indeed, at least one – Colonel Gracie – felt that playing such a piece at that time would have been a tactless reminder of impending doom.[450] Harold Bride remembered that they played 'Autumn', referring either to the hymn by that name, or to the popular waltz 'Songe d'Automne', by Archibald Joyce. Interestingly, this particular piece was found in the White Star request book.[451]

Whatever it was that they played, it was a surreal moment… the strains of string music echoed across the water as the officers and crew tried to clear the last two collapsibles. Crowds began to gather around the area, particularly on the starboard side. Many of the passengers who had just arrived on deck, seeing the water so close to the deck and that there was very little chance to get to the last two collapsibles, turned toward the imagined safety of the stern, which had risen out of the water as the bow settled lower and lower. On the Poop Deck, astern, a large crowd was beginning to grow. It was comprised of people from all walks of life and levels of social status: from the humblest of immigrants to wealthy First Class passengers.

Second Class passengers Father Thomas Byles and Father Joseph Peruschitz stood together amid a ring of passengers and began granting absolutions, telling them to 'say acts of contrition and prepare themselves to meet the face of God'. Both men had assisted passengers throughout the sinking. Following the collision, Father Byles had gone through the steerage passageways with his hand uplifted, telling everyone to remain calm, and granting them his blessings and absolution. Later, both men had helped passengers into the lifeboats, 'saying prayers', and 'whispering words of comfort and encouragement to all'. Father Byles had twice refused to board a lifeboat during the night.[452]

Most people who saw the clergymen at work were struck positively by the scene. However, August Wennerström formed a different opinion of their efforts. This was based on the actions of passengers, or lack thereof, when he had seen one of the priests working with some of them earlier in the night: 'On one side of the deck laid 75 Irish in a circle with a preacher in their middle, praying, crying, asking God and Mary [sic] to help them … They just prayed and yelled, and never lifted a hand to help themselves. They had lost their own will power and were expecting God to do all the work.'[453]

Meanwhile, on the Boat Deck, Thomas Andrews was still hard at work. At around 2:10 a.m., well after Stewart had seen him during his quiet moment of reflection in the First Class Smoking Lounge, he was sighted tossing deck chairs overboard to aid the 'unfortunates' who were likely to end up struggling in the water. He was next spied carrying a lifebelt, apparently on his way to the Bridge.[454]

Despite whatever feelings of grief or impending doom were rushing through his mind, he was able to put those aside and continued working to save others until the end, just as he had done throughout the night. He would not survive the sinking; neither would any of the other members of the Harland & Wolff Guarantee Group. Engineer Thomas Millar, who had worked to build the ship at the Belfast shipyard and then signed on as a member of her crew, would also lose his life.

Captain Smith headed forward toward the Bridge of his ship, his thoughts doubtlessly moving in the direction of his wife, Sarah Eleanor, and their twelve-year-old daughter Helen. He must have known by then that he would never see them again. Even so, he did not become despondent, but stuck to his duties till the last.

At just about this time, Mess Steward Cecil Fitzpatrick was crossing from the port side to the starboard through the Bridge. He recalled that just as he was passing through …

> … I saw Capt. Smith speaking to Mr Andrews, the designer of the *Titanic*. I stopped to listen. I was still confident that the ship was unsinkable, but when I heard Capt. Smith say: 'We cannot stay any longer; she is going!' I fainted against the starboard side of the bridge entrance.[455]

Just when Bride reached Collapsible Boat B, the crew managed to push it over the edge of the Officers' Quarters.

Somehow, things went horribly awry, and the boat crashed to the deck, landing upside-down. Second Officer Lightoller was still on the roof of the Officers' Quarters, but Harold Bride seems to have 'scrambled' down onto the Boat Deck to help launch it.[456] Due to the heavy port list that had developed, water had already reached the deck on that side of the ship, and the collapsible landed in it, leaving no time for the crew to right it, much less to hook it up to the falls.[457]

On the starboard side, at about the same time, Murdoch's group was working frantically to free Collapsible A. Due to the list, the Boat Deck was still dry at this location. The First Officer had ordered the davits cranked back in so they would be ready to receive the collapsible. Hemming, having just crossed over from the port side, helped untangle the falls that had been used to lower both Boat No. 1 and Collapsible C. He then passed the block up to the men working on the roof of the Officers' Quarters. Sixth Officer Moody was among them, and he called back down: 'We don't want the block. We will leave the boat on deck.'[458]

The crew finally got Collapsible A loose, got two canvas cover spars under the bow and pushed it over the edge of the Officers' Quarters' roof. It crashed hard onto the deck, possibly damaging the canvas sides but unlike Collapsible B, it landed upright.

Just then, a stunned Fitzpatrick was regaining his composure. He realized that unless he 'got into a boat or swam for it, there would be no chance of being saved'. He headed over to join the efforts surrounding Collapsible A on the starboard side, which he found had already been moved down onto the Boat Deck.[459]

Moody's opinion that the boat should be left to float free was apparently overruled. A group of what Eugene Daly estimated to be '6 or 7' men – among them the two officers, Steward Edward Brown and Saloon Steward Thomas Whiteley, Mess Steward Fitzpatrick, Second Class passenger William Mellors, and himself – slackened and then connected the falls to the collapsible. Then they attempted to push the boat around the forward cowling that provided access to the stairway to A Deck, pushing uphill toward the davits against the port list.[460]

Despite their efforts, the boat simply could not be moved, and their progress was blocked by one of the funnel stays near the aft davit, inboard of where Collapsible C had been stored. Fitzpatrick recalled: 'When we tried to swing her [Collapsible A] in the davits, she was wedged between the winch of the davits and the spar.' He remembered hearing the 'band playing a hymn at the last moment', but he couldn't actually pick out the tune.[461]

Just then, water began gurgling up the forward hatchway onto the Boat Deck, and it was clear to those still aboard that the ship was living on borrowed time. Someone called out that they had forgotten to put the plug in the collapsible. Fireman John Thompson, despite his hands having been burned in a steam-related accident during the evacuation of the boiler rooms, had helped load the lifeboats earlier in the night. Now, he leapt into Collapsible A and unsuccessfully attempted to put the plug in.[462]

First Class passengers Colonel Archibald Gracie and Clinch Smith saw that there was no chance of the boat getting away safely, and began heading aft. As they did so, they found 'a mass of humanity several lines deep' blocking their progress. These were Third Class passengers who had just emerged from somewhere below deck.[463] Hemming estimated that there were 'one or two hundred' people in

Olympic's starboard Boat Deck, in the vicinity of Boat No. 1. Titanic's bulwark here was not planked, but was plain painted steel. However, much of the rest of this photograph is a match to Titanic's appearance in this area. It was here that a last-ditch attempt was made to get Collapsible A into the davits for Boat No. 1 so it could be launched.

the crowd.[464] Some of the women from this throng stood nearby, hoping to climb in Collapsible A when it was ready to be loaded.[465]

Hemming, realizing the attempts to launch Collapsible A were a valiant but lost cause, crossed over to the port side and headed aft, where he saw a lifeboat off the port quarter. He slid down one of the sets of falls there. Plunging into the freezing water rendered him nearly senseless. After recovering from the cold shock, Hemming immediately struck out for the boat. He wasn't wearing a lifebelt, and swam as hard as he could ...[466]

Around this time, August Wennerström and fellow Third Class passengers Edvard and Elin Lindell headed forward. They ran into a 'Swedish woman from Chicago' and her four children whom he had gotten to know during the voyage. Likely they were Alma Pålsson and her children Gösta, Paul, Stina, and Torborg. Wennerström said that she had not gotten her children dressed in time to get them up on deck and into a lifeboat before they were all gone. He and his companions attempted to push through the crowd to get the family to Collapsible A.[467]

It was then about 2:15 a.m. The surreal moments created by the juxtaposition of the frenzied activity on the ship's upper decks and the calm and peaceful refrains of the ship's band ended abruptly, for just then the bow of the ship took a 'slight but definite plunge'.[468]

Jack Thayer and Milton Long were still together on the starboard side of the Boat Deck, just aft of the Bridge. Thayer had noticed that the ship's list to port, which had been steadily increasing, had suddenly eased until the ship

was on an even keel as the ship's bow plummeted down. The two moved aft to the bulwark rail, until they were in the vicinity of the No. 2 funnel.

Jack Thayer had had enough ... it was time to go. He and Long moved to the rail, and Long climbed up on top of it, facing out with his legs dangling off into space. Thayer hesitated, and Long looked back. 'You are coming boy, aren't you?' Thayer told him to go ahead, that he would be with him in a minute. Then Long slid straight down the side of the ship. Thayer jumped out, well clear of the side, feet first, and landed in the icy water.

> The cold was terrific. The shock of the water took the breath out of my lungs. Down and down I went, spinning in all directions. Swimming as hard as I could in the direction which I thought to be away from the ship, I finally came up with my lungs bursting, but not having taken any water. The ship was in front of me, forty yards away.

Thayer and Long had jumped within seconds of each other. Yet he never saw Long – or his father – again.[469]

Brown, Daly and the others suddenly found themselves knee, and then waist deep in freezing water, and there was a frantic effort to cut the falls so that Collapsible A could float free. It turned out that Moody's plan had been the correct one. Mess Steward Fitzpatrick had only moments before believed the ship was still unsinkable ... but then the ship began 'suddenly dipping, and the waves rushing up and engulfing' him. He later told one of Thomas Andrews' friends that when the Bridge had become awash with water, he saw Captain Smith and Thomas Andrews enter the sea together.[470]

As water washed along the deck, Steward Brown leapt into Boat A and cut the aft falls. Eugene Daly, William Mellors, Mess Steward Fitzpatrick and First Class passenger Richard Norris Williams all gave accounts indicating that the Boat Deck seemed to rise slightly after its initial plunge. Mess Steward Fitzpatrick said: 'After ten seconds the *Titanic* again righted herself.'[471]

This brief recovery of the ship gave the group of men struggling around Collapsible A one last chance to cut the falls, and they took full advantage of it.[472] Eugene Daly and William Mellors, who had been clinging to the side of the collapsible, worked together to cut the aft falls. Brown said that the crowd started panicking as the water began washing around their legs, and 'there was a lot scrambled into it then … they all scrambled into the boat.'[473]

Daly said people were rushing around, and that while he was cutting the falls, 'the collapsible was crowded with people hanging upon the edges.'[474] Somehow during the scramble, Saloon Steward Whiteley's leg got tangled in a coil of rope. He was knocked into the water, and the rope cut into his skin and broke his leg; he did not feel the injury at the time, however, probably due to shock, coupled with the freezing water which numbed his extremities.[475]

Daly jumped overboard and fell into a mass of people. What happened next traumatized him for the rest of his life: 'Everything I touched seemed to be women's hair. Children crying, women screaming and their hair in my face. My God, if I could only forget those hands and faces that I touched!'[476] Daly said that the 'water was icy and for the first few minutes, I thought I could not survive the cold shock.'[477]

Mess Steward Fitzpatrick had felt the ship recover for a few seconds, but then the downward plunge resumed. He remembered, in that horrible moment, that …

> … everyone who a minute before had been attempting to lower away, except myself, had been swept into the fo'castle head. I saved myself by clinging on to the davit winch.
>
> I looked down the fo'castle, and saw the most horrible, heartrending scenes I have ever witnessed. There were women and children and firemen and stewards all fighting, shrieking for help in their death struggles. I got on the other side of the winch which was towards the after-part of the vessel, and levered myself up on the deck.
>
> Then I went to the edge of the ship and jumped into the icy water. In order to escape the suction which I surmised would be caused by the sinking of the gigantic liner, I struck out for very life. I swam from the ship as the for's'd was sinking. I did not feel any suction.[478]

As the forward end of the Boat Deck plunged under, a wave of water washed aft. Colonel Gracie and Clinch Smith were trying to reach the roof of the Officers' Quarters when it hit them. Gracie crouched and rode the wave like a crest at the beach, and he managed to grab onto the railing on top of the quarters. Clinch Smith was not so lucky. Gracie never saw him again.[479]

After unsuccessfully attempting to board Boat No. 16 earlier in the night, Scullion John Collins and another steward were pushing forward through the crowd on the starboard side of the Boat Deck, trying to help a woman and her two children into Collapsible A. Collins was carrying one of the children in his arms. Seeing that the *Titanic* 'intended to sink her bow', someone forward shouted for them to go aft, falsely claiming that a boat was being lowered there. Collins turned to head aft, and was struck by the wave as he did so, which washed him overboard. Tragically, he lost his grip on the child.[480]

Near Collapsible A, William Mellors was knocked into a stanchion by the wave, seriously injuring his ankle, and he found himself 'whizzing through the water at an awful pace'.[481] As the water hit the collapsible, Steward Brown was washed out of it and thrown into a 'whirlpool'. Brown could not swim, but fortunately was wearing his lifebelt.[482] August Wennerström and the Lindells were thrown into the water, and they landed right in front of the collapsible as it drifted further aft. During the confusion, they became separated from Alma Pålsson and her four children, and never saw them again. All five of the Pålssons perished.[483]

Further aft near the Gymnasium, First Class passenger George Rheims stood with his brother-in-law Joseph Loring. Shortly before this, Loring had grabbed his hands, saying, 'George if you survive look after my babies. If I live you will not have to worry about [your wife] Mary.' After a quick trip below, Rheims had returned, and then he and Loring stripped down to their undergarments. Suddenly, the ship began 'nosediving'. Rheims was knocked from his feet and landed in a tangle of deck chairs and ropes, still on the deck. Breaking free, Rheims spotted Loring, who said he wanted to head aft; Rheims told him it meant death if he did, and that he should instead follow him. Loring told him he couldn't swim well enough. Seeing no other choice, Rheims left Loring and leapt overboard. He never saw his brother-in-law again.[484]

Near this location, desperation set in as First Class passenger Peter Daly contemplated what to do. Just as he was about to leap overboard, a woman rushed up to him and said, 'Oh, save me! save me!' Daly replied: 'Good lady, save yourself. Only God can save you now.' The lady begged him to help her jump, so he took her by the arm and leapt overboard just as the wave hit. He was washed clear of the side of the ship. Meanwhile, on the port side, Henry Molson was last seen removing his shoes, and planning to swim for the steamer on the horizon. Molson had previously survived the sinking of the *Scotsman* in the Gulf of St Lawrence in 1899, and had swum away from the *Canada* after it collided with a collier in the St Lawrence River in 1904; he would not be as fortunate in his third shipwreck, and he was never seen again.[485]

The wave swept aft along the Boat Deck, swamping the Bridge and the crew and passengers in the vicinity. Those not immediately swept away, including Third Class passenger Carl Jansson and others on the starboard side, began running aft. The wave struck them, and Jansson went overboard.[486] Somehow, through the maelstrom, Harold Bride managed to see – or thought he saw – Captain Smith dive off the port Bridge wing into the sea.[487] Bride grabbed onto an oarlock of the upside-down collapsible. It was washed off the ship and he came up underneath it. As the Bridge submerged, Collapsible B was pushed over to the starboard side of the ship, near the base of the forward funnel, and Collapsible A was pushed aft, against a set of empty davits that had not yet submerged.[488]

Chief Baker Joughin was still inside the Deck Pantry on A Deck when the ship lurched, and he heard 'a crash as if something had buckled' that sounded 'as if the iron was parting'. Then he heard a rush of people running aft overhead. Joughin came up on deck, and got caught in the 'tail end' of a mob of people heading aft towards the Poop Deck. Joughin tried to keep out of the crowd as much as possible, and followed them down to the aft Well Deck. As he was making his way aft, Joughin transferred his watch from his front to back pocket, and noticed the time: 'a quarter past two'. The electric lights were still on.[489]

Just then, Rhoda Abbott and her son Eugene – as well as the group of ladies standing nearby – all slid off the deck into the water. Rhoda clung to her son Eugene closely, but soon they were 'drawn beneath the surface' by a whirlpool. When she returned to the surface, her son was gone. Then

ing. He struggled to get free but time and again was drawn down, and he found himself drowning. Lightoller was 'rather losing interest in things', and was about to give up when the words of the 91st Psalm popped into his mind: 'He shall give his angels charge over thee.' Then came a rush of hot air from below which spat him out and sent him sputtering up to the surface right next to capsized Collapsible B, which had no one aboard at the moment. He gratefully grabbed a rope attached to the boat and watched events unfold.[492]

Within moments, probably while Lightoller was underwater, the strains of music had faded into oblivion. Water swamped the forward First Class Entrance and Grand Staircase. The solid-oak staircase apparently broke up in the turbulent waters and parts of it floated away through the shattered wrought iron and glass dome.[493]

This tremendous view of the Olympic's Bridge and the roof of the Officers' Quarters was taken in New York during her first stay in that port. There are several differences from Titanic's appearance. However, much of what is seen here would have matched Titanic as her Bridge was about to slide under the sea. Lightoller was pinned up against the ventilator just in front of the smokestack. Interestingly, Collapsible B does not appear to be sitting in its standard position in this photo.

she was pulled under again. The second time, she was 'blown out of the water' by an explosion that burned her thighs.[490]

On the roof of the Officers' Quarters, Lightoller thought of turning aft – the natural instinct that everyone had at that time – but like Rheims, realized it would be a futile move. Instead, he walked forward to the roof of the Bridge, which was then going under, and dove into the water. Lightoller described the shock of the 28° water as being like 'a thousand knives being driven into one's body'.[491] Instinctively, he struck out toward the Crow's Nest, which was coming level with the sea; then he changed his mind, realizing that it was attached to the ship and was no refuge. Suddenly, the force of the water rushing down the intake for the stokehold ventilating fans – which was positioned on the roof of the Bridge just forward of the No. 1 funnel – sucked him back and pinned him against the fidley grat-

As the stern rose higher out of the water, Lightoller watched as people were piled into 'helpless heaps around the steep decks'. Describing the scene, he stated that there were 'many in the water by this time, some swimming, others definitely drowning … an utter nightmare of both sight and sound.'[494] Just then, the forward funnel collapsed and fell forward and towards the starboard side of the ship. The funnel crashed down, crushing a mass of people who were struggling in the water. The funnel missed Collapsible B by mere inches, washing off many who had begun to climb aboard since Lightoller reached it, and pushing it clear of the sinking ship.[495]

Richard Norris Williams had been struggling in the water, and had been separated from his father Charles Duane Williams. When they spotted each other, his father, who was about '12–15 feet' away, started swimming towards him. Richard watched as the funnel came crashing down

Labels within the image:
"The starlight night was beautiful"
Stern 2nd class Section of ship
"The Titanic looked enormous"
Boat Deck clear of boats
Every porthole & saloon was blazing with light"
"We had sixty or seventy on board"
"The bows & bridge completely under water"
Loose Floating Ice
"Sea calm as a pond – There was just a gentle heave"

An effective artistic rendering of the scene as the Titanic *began her final plunge.*

on top of his father. He said that he was transfixed, not 'because it had only missed me by a few feet ... curiously enough not because it had killed my father for whom I had a far more than normal feeling of love and attachment; but there I was transfixed wondering at the enormous size of this funnel, still belching smoke.'[496]

Fireman John Thompson had managed to stay in Collapsible A when the wave had hit, and he watched as the forward funnel collapsed. He said that the funnel 'broke loose and fell into the water with a roar, causing so great a wash that our boat was sent spinning and I was knocked violently against one of the davits.' Thompson broke his arm, and was nearly unconscious when someone hauled him back into the swamped collapsible.[497] The violent wash mentioned by Thompson helped push Collapsible A away from the sinking ship.

Eugene Daly, still struggling in the water, turned and looked over his shoulder. He said that he could see the funnels of the *Titanic* being submerged in the water. He reported that 'those poor people that covered the water were sucked down in those funnels, each of which was twenty-five feet in diameter, like flies.'[498] Daly's description is probably of the second funnel, since the first funnel fell soon after water reached its base.

August Wennerström had managed to climb aboard Collapsible A. As the stern rose higher, he looked back at the ship and saw a man lowering himself down past the rudder on what he thought was the ship's log-line.[499]

The lights of the ship still burned steadily, although they were a more dullish-red as the last gasp of the ship's power – supplied by the Emergency Dynamos – began to fade. The stern began to rear up out of the water, climbing steadily

higher to something on the order of a 30° angle. However, the exact angle could have appeared even greater than it really was to some, depending on their vantage point.[500]

Next a building and terrifying noise began to carry across the water; it sounded like breaking china to some, and continuing, rumbling explosions or thunder to many others. Many assumed that it was the ship's engines and boilers tearing loose and sliding through the hull before crashing out through the ship's nose ... the reality was far more devastating. At about 2:17 a.m.,[501] almost all of the lights suddenly snapped out as the ship broke in half just behind the third funnel.

Steward Brown, supported by his lifebelt, was struggling among the crowd near the submerged Bridge of the ship when he heard a loud report. Turning, he saw the stern of the ship give a 'tremble', and saw it going up. To him, this indicated that the 'bow had fallen off.'[502] Floating in the water, William Mellors came to his senses in time to see the 'ship part in the middle'.[503]

Saloon Steward Whiteley was about sixty feet from the *Titanic*, clinging with several other men to what he believed was an 'oak wardrobe'. He watched as the ship broke in half, and he actually saw 'all the machinery drop out of her'.[504] Sitting some distance off in Boat No. 15, Bertha Mulvihill was also able to discern this fracture; she later said that the ship 'exploded and split in half'.[505]

Steward Alfred Theissinger had been standing on the aft end of the starboard Boat Deck, talking to Storekeeper Cyril Ricks and Steward Sidney Siebert. All three men were wearing lifebelts. As they talked, 'a violent explosion suddenly shook the entire boat'. He immediately lost sight of Storekeeper Ricks, but saved himself 'from being

This period illustration shows the Titanic reaching a steeper angle than she ever did before she broke. Interestingly, however, the artist chose to depict the upper decks breaking open. The stern of the ship did eventually reach this angle, but only after the breakup.

Right: *The Titanic's stern begins to slide away into the depths. At that point, the stern section was nearly vertical, not at the relaxed angle seen here.*

thrown – God only knows where – by grabbing hold of the rail. The vessel seemed to break in two.'[506]

After the break, the angle of the stern – which had been held by the counter-balance of the flooded bow – then decreased, and it settled back into the water to nearly an even keel momentarily. The third funnel fell forward and the fourth funnel toppled backwards.[507] Just prior to the break, Richard Norris Williams watched as the *Titanic* towered over him, and then saw it settle back. Despite his feelings of horror and peril, he couldn't help feeling that it was a majestic sight.[508] Sitting in Boat No. 13, Steward Alexander Littlejohn also said that the 'stern part came down again and righted itself'.[509]

Joughin had just gotten to the Well Deck and climbed to the outside edge of the starboard side of the hull, when the stern gave a 'great list to port', throwing the 'many hundreds' of people there into a heap. Joughin hung on and managed to get to the outside of the railing on the starboard side of the Poop Deck. He did not see anyone else holding onto the rail when he got there.[510] Still on the outside of the railing, he crawled along it, toward the very aft end of the Poop Deck.

As the stern had fallen back into the water, many of those watching from the sea and from the safety of the lifeboats were fooled into thinking that the *Titanic's* final, and greatest, safety feature had sprung to life … that the stern was going to float, and that all those aboard would not, after all, be plunged into a freezing sea. However, that false hope was soon shattered.

Interestingly, some recalled that not all of the lights went out as the ship broke in half. Greaser Thomas Ranger, watching from Boat No. 4 very close to the ship, remembered that as the stern section had come back 'on a level keel', the 'lights seemed to be going out then.' He also noticed that the 'lights were right aft what were burning, on the after end what was floating', and that they were only completely extinguished 'as the aft end of the ship went under'.[511]

Slowly, the stern began rising back up into the air. As it did so, Richard Norris Williams saw it turn around in a semi-circle.[512] By that time, Eugene Daly had managed to catch the edge of the upturned Collapsible B. So many people had climbed onto the collapsible that there wasn't enough room on it for him to lift himself fully out of the water. Daly pulled himself halfway aboard, lying on the keel with water up to his hips. He was so chilled by the intense cold of the water that his senses were numbed and he was scarcely conscious of the stern of the *Titanic* looming overhead.[513] When he finally noticed the ship, he saw that 'her stern stuck up high. I thought she would fall over on us as she seemed to be swinging around, but she did not.'[514]

Steward Theissinger remembered that the stern section of the ship, where he was, 'went way up into the air and remained in that position … The lights had gradually gone out, excepting one light near where I stood. Several hundred men were gathered about me. I saw that all was over.' He turned to Steward Siebert, who was the nearest person to him, and said: 'Come we had better get away and take our chances before she sinks.' They leaped into the water, and Theissinger swam for everything he was worth, with Siebert closely behind.[515]

Cecil Fitzpatrick, the 21-year-old Mess Steward, saw *Titanic* 'stick her screws and propellers high into the air', and heard her go down 'with a swish' in 'as clean a dive as ever was made by a fish'.[516]

To many, the nearly fifteen hundred people stranded aboard the dying ship looked like swarming bees, 'clinging in clusters or bunches … only to fall in masses, pairs or singly,' as the stern rose higher.[517]

The ship's stern section continued to rise out of the water, struggling for the sky until it was completely vertical. As it stood on end, it pointed like a sinister finger, some thought, toward the heavens. There it remained for several moments, perfectly balanced and unmoving. Then cruel physics took over. As water began to flood the front end of the stern, it began to sink from sight with a building momentum.[518]

Finally, as her fantail dipped underwater for the last time, there was a slight gulp. As the ship slipped under, the surface of the water was disturbed so little that Chief Baker Joughin found himself in the sea, and did not think that his head even went under as he let go of the Poop Deck railing. In Collapsible C, Bruce Ismay, who was sitting with his back to the ship, did not turn around, as he 'did not wish to see her go down'. Indeed, he later felt glad that he had not.[519]

It was 2:20 a.m. *Titanic*, the unsinkable ship, was gone.

Chapter 6

On 'A Sea of Glass'

After the *Titanic* disappeared from sight, there was a momentary calm punctuated only by a loud, gurgling upwelling of water from where the stern had disappeared. This bubble of air coming up from below was spitting up to the surface large quantities of cork insulation,[1] wood, and other debris. A 'thin light-gray smoky vapor' clung a few feet above the water. It reminded one survivor of Dante's description of Charon and the River Lethe in Hell.[2]

Silence soon gave way to a horrifying cacophony of noise, as the fifteen hundred people who had still been aboard the ship when it made its final plunge began to scream and cry for help. It was a noise that would forever haunt those who heard it – whether they were in the sea or were listening from the safety of a lifeboat.

For those struggling for their lives among the panicked crowd in the water, the situation was horrific. First Class passenger George Rheims was one of these people, and he described the sound of the cries as 'atrociously grim, mysterious – supernatural'.[3] Second Class passenger William Mellors, also floating in the water, described the shouts as 'terrible. There were great masses of wreckage with hundreds of human beings fighting amongst hundreds of dead bodies for their lives.'[4]

As *Titanic* had plunged under, Colonel Gracie had clung to one of the ship's railings, and had been dragged underwater. When his lifebelt and his struggling brought him back to the surface, he found the surface of the water strewn with both wreckage and a great mass of humanity. He described the scene as follows:

> There arose to the sky the most horrible sounds ever heard by mortal man, except by those of us who survived this terrible tragedy. The agonizing screams of death from over a thousand throats, the wails and groans of the suffering, the shrieks of the terror-stricken and the awful gaspings for breath of those in the last throes of drowning, none of us will ever forget to our dying day. 'Help! Help! Boat ahoy! Boat ahoy!' and 'My God! My God!' were the heart-rending cries and shrieks of men, which floated to us over the surface of the dark waters continuously for the next hour, but as time went on, growing weaker and weaker until they died out entirely.[5]

Second Officer Lightoller was still clinging to the rope dangling from the upturned Collapsible B; people were struggling all around him in the water. He described the

scene simply as 'an utter nightmare of both sight and sound,' noting that to dwell on 'those heartrending, never-to-be-forgotten sounds would serve no useful purpose.'[6]

To those safe in the lifeboats, the noise coming to them across the water was nearly unbearable. Sitting in the refuge of Boat No. 1, which had 28 of its 40 seats vacant, Lady Duff Gordon recalled a moment of 'awful silence' when *Titanic* first disappeared, followed by 'a bedlam of shrieks and cries'.[7] Boat No. 1 was just 200 yards away from the ship when it sank,[8] close enough so that its occupants could hear individual cries for help from the sea. As the White Star ticket agent had told Lady Duff Gordon before she booked passage, *Titanic*'s maiden voyage had, indeed, made history in ocean travel. It just was not the sort of history that anyone wanted to make.

In Boat No. 14, Able Bodied Seaman Scarrott said 'the cries from the poor souls struggling in the water sounded terrible in the stillness of the night. It seemed to go through you like a knife.'[9] Sitting in Boat No. 13, Saloon Steward Littlejohn described the cries as 'terrible … awful and heartrending.'[10] In Boat No. 15, Saloon Steward Nichols said that 'a horrible shriek went up, cries for help and weird shouts – you can imagine what it is like if you have ever been around when they are feeding a kennel of dogs – that's the only thing I can think of that it sounded like.'[11]

Imanita Shelley said that she and the other occupants of Boat No. 10 'tried to sing, and some of the men tried to get all to shout, saying it would help us keep our bearings, but we all knew it was a kindly ruse to try and drown out that awful moaning cry, and we were unable to utter a sound. God grant that I may never hear such a sound again. No words, just an awful despairing moan, and all of them seemed to

Opposite: *In this artist's depiction, the first lifeboats pull alongside the* Carpathia.

Above: *These two photographs are of Saloon Steward Alexander Littlejohn. The photo on the left is how he appeared at the time of the* Titanic *disaster; the photo on the right, taken shortly after the sinking, shows that he had aged significantly in a span of months rather than years.*

moan in the same key, regardless of what their voices may have been. For over an hour, I resume [sic, presume], though it seemed eternity, those awful cries continued.'[12]

Heavily loaded with 55 and 68 occupants respectively, those aboard Boats Nos 13 and 15 were powerless to help any of the crowd in the icy water who were begging for help. They rowed even further away from the scene. In Boat No. 13, Leading Fireman Frederick Barrett found that while the thin work clothes he wore were appropriate for the heat of the boiler rooms, they were not adequate for the frigid night air he was being exposed to. Adding to his misery, he had been soaked to the skin during his escape from Boiler Room No. 5 as it flooded, and was so numb that he could no longer feel his limbs. Although he had been placed in charge before the boat lowered, he had to relinquish control of the tiller to another crewmember. A woman in the boat put a cloak over him, but he was so cold that afterwards he could not remember what happened next.[13]

they struggled along with only four rowers, the boat pulled even further away from the site.[16] It did not return to rescue anyone from the water.

At one point during the night, Quartermaster Walter Wynn could clearly see the red sidelight and a white light from a steamer on the horizon.[17] The occupants of Collapsible C, which contained Bruce Ismay, could also clearly see the lights of the ship on the horizon. Quartermaster Rowe ordered those rowing to pull towards the light, which they did all night, 'but seemed to get no nearer to the lights'.[18]

Back at the site of the sinking, Colonel Gracie spotted a wooden crate floating near him, and attempted in vain to straddle it; each time he tried it overturned, spilling him back into the water. Soon, he spotted Collapsible B nearby, and swam over to its side. He found that there were already about a dozen men standing on or clinging to the boat. Among them was Second Officer Lightoller, who had already pulled himself aboard, and was standing on the hull.

Nearly Unsurvivable

Expected Survival Time in Cold Water		
(Conditions as they apply to the water temperature at the time *Titanic* sank indicated in bold and with asterisk)		
Water Temperature	Exhaustion or Unconsciousness in	Expected Survival Time
70-80° F (21-27° C)	3-12 hours	3 hours-indefinitely
60-70° F (16-21° C)	2-7 hours	2-40 hours
50-60° F (10-16° C)	1-2 hours	1-6 hours
40-50° F (4-10° C)	30-60 minutes	1-3 hours
32.5-40° F (0-4° C)	15-30 minutes	30-90 minutes
*<32° F (<0 C)	*Under 15 minutes	*Under 15-45 minutes

The frigid seas, which were only 28° Fahrenheit, were taking a gruesome toll. Clinically speaking, submerged in such a hostile environment, most people could be expected to become unconscious in as little as 15 minutes; average anticipated survival times would only run from 15 to 45 minutes, although exceptions to this general rule of thumb are possible.

Initial symptoms from being submerged in such icy water typically include panic and shock, and can even cause instantaneous cardiac arrest. Breath is commonly driven from the body upon contact with water that cold, forcing an involuntary breath to be taken. Drowning is thus possible if a person lands face-first in the water.

Next, total disorientation sets in, which can last for 30 seconds or more after immersion before a person comes to their senses and can more accurately comprehend their surroundings. Limbs are quickly numbed to the point of uselessness, which makes swimming or climbing out of water difficult without outside assistance. Within minutes, severe physical pain clouds rational thought. Finally, once severe hypothermia sets in, unconsciousness and death can quickly follow.[19]

A death of this nature is not a peaceful way to go. The freezing water which those on the ship were plunged into at 2:20 a.m. was a nearly unsurvivable environment.

Boat No. 9 was just 100 yards away from the ship when it sank. Boatswain's Mate Albert Haines, in charge of the boat, asked the men whether they felt it advisable to go back. Despite having just forty people aboard, the consensus was that the boat was too overloaded, and that it would be too dangerous to return.[14] Saloon Steward William Ward said that it would have been 'madness' to return.[15] As

As soon as the Second Officer was recognized, one of the crewmembers on the boat shouted out, 'We will all obey what the officer orders.' When Colonel Gracie tried to climb aboard, he was met by a 'doubtful reception' from some of those already on the craft. Finally, they helped to lift him from the freezing water. Just then, another swimmer – who was already exhausted from the cold – came alongside. Gracie gave the man a warmer reception than he himself had received, pulling him up next to him. The man passed out face-down on the bottom of the boat for several hours.[20]

Mess Steward Cecil Fitzpatrick had swum away from the starboard Boat Deck near Collapsible A as the bow dove. He was 'a strong swimmer,' and kept afloat in the icy sea for 'quite twenty minutes' before he climbed onto Collapsible B. There, he spotted Second Officer Lightoller was already aboard.[21]

William Mellors had been in the water for five minutes, and had to fight his way through the maelstrom of panicking swimmers. A woman caught hold of his coat collar, and begged him to save her. Mellors felt that he was doomed anyway, and that the least he could do was try to keep both of them afloat. After holding the woman up for about twenty minutes, Mellors' hands began to swell so badly from the cold water that they started to resemble 'a pair of miniature boxing gloves.' He was having difficulty maintaining his grip on her. By this time, the woman was almost unconscious, but when she noticed Mellors losing his grip, she started panicking, clutching him around the throat. She was not wearing a lifebelt, and in the struggle, both were plunged underwater. When Mellors was out of breath to the point where he felt his lungs were going to burst, he was finally able to break away and come to the surface, gasping for air.

Mellors continued swimming, but no sooner had he begun than a seaman caught hold of his leg and began holding on to him 'like a leech'. Mellors' limbs were so numb that he barely noticed until he was nearly dragged underwater. He struck at the seaman. The man, hysterical from the cold and panic, only laughed and continued his attempt to pull Mellors under. Mellors next grabbed the seaman by his hair, plunging him underwater until he became 'unsensible'. He released Mellors, who tried to swim away. The man resurfaced, trying unsuccessfully to swim alongside Mellors. Suddenly, he made a noise Mellors described as a horrible 'rattle', threw his hands up, and died.[22]

Junior Marconi Operator Harold Bride was floating in the water close to where the ship had sunk; he had been washed overboard with Collapsible B at around 2:15 a.m. Initially, he had been stuck underneath the collapsible. Somehow, he had gotten separated from the upturned boat, and had been swimming ever since. Bride was so cold and exhausted that he felt like letting himself sink. Suddenly, he saw the collapsible drifting nearby, and put all his remaining strength into reaching it.

When he got alongside, he 'was all done', and was surprised to see that it was the very same collapsible that he and the others had attempted to launch. He rolled on to the cork fender of the boat, and lay there 'not caring what happened'. His feet became wedged between the slats and a man who sat on them, wrenching them. Bride was distracted by the 'terrible sight all around' of people struggling in the water near the boat, and did not have the heart to ask the man to move. By that point, the bottom of the collapsible was crowded with men. As swimmers came alongside, 'nobody gave them a hand'.[23]

In the water, the floating wreckage and deck chairs that Chief Baker Joughin and others had thrown overboard were providing refuge, albeit temporary ones, for many of the people swimming in the water. However, without being able to get the majority of one's body out of the deadly cold water, clinging to the debris was futile, and death still came swiftly.

About sixty feet from where *Titanic* sank, Saloon Steward Thomas Whiteley, buoyed up by his lifebelt, managed to catch hold of a wooden wardrobe that was floating nearby. Four other men held on to this same piece of debris with him.[24] Similarly, Saloon Steward Harold Phillimore, who leapt overboard just prior to the final plunge, clung to a piece of wreckage along with another man.[25]

As *Titanic*'s stern had risen into the air, Storekeepers Frank Prentice, Michael Kieran, and Cyril Ricks had leapt overboard. Prentice landed safely in the water, but Ricks did not. What happened to Kieran is unknown. At first, Prentice found himself among the panicking masses, but as time went on, the crowd began to thin out as the cold began to take its inexorable toll on those in the water. Prentice found his friend Ricks floating nearby, badly injured, and resolved to stay with him until the last. Prentice said Ricks 'had hurt himself, he'd hurt his legs. He'd dropped on something, and he didn't say very much. He was a great big fellow too, very good swimmer. And he died, and I … seemed to be all by myself.'[26]

Some distance away, Collapsible A was drifting amid the wreckage. Its damaged canvas sides were still down, and it was half-swamped with several feet of water sloshing around within its bottom. Not only had the collapsible been damaged in the attempt to get it down from the roof of the Officers' Quarters, but despite his best efforts Fireman John Thompson had been unsuccessful in getting the plug in place before the boat was washed overboard. As a result, water was continuing to flood into it. Only the Kapok-filled fenders of the collapsible, as well as the Kapok in the boat's bottom structure, were keeping it buoyant.[27] As a result, the craft sat low in the water, and was very unstable.

Within only a few minutes of the sinking, approximately fifteen to twenty people had struggled aboard this boat, and were forced to stand knee deep in the freezing water. Among these were First Class passenger Richard Norris Williams and Third Class passenger Carl Jansson. John Thompson, struggling back to a state of semi-consciousness, found himself lying in the water in the bottom of Boat A. Someone had hauled him aboard while he was senseless.[28]

Saloon Steward Edward Brown had never swum before in his life, and had only been saved by his decision to wear a lifebelt. Spotting a black object floating on the water in the distance, he awkwardly paddled toward it. Upon arriving, he found that it was Collapsible A, the same boat he had helped cut loose. He pulled himself aboard.[29]

Third Class passenger August Wennerström was then aboard Boat A, and he saw people in the water all around, some even hanging from its sides. As more and more clung to it, the unstable boat nearly capsized. The upset threw several people, including Wennerström, back into the water. Already dangerously chilled, he temporarily lost his senses, and when Wennerström 'got back to myself and my memory', he found himself floating interlocked with three other people. When they began to go under, he somehow found the edge of Collapsible A, and climbed back aboard.[30]

Others who climbed aboard at this time included Third Class passengers Edvard Lindell and Rhoda Abbott. Mrs Abbott had gone into the sea with her 14-year-old son Eugene, but had become separated from him when she was sucked below the surface. 'After a time', she came alongside Collapsible A and begged someone to help her aboard. No one acted, but when the boat upset, she was able to climb on, and stood in the boat to stay out of the water in the bottom.[31]

Around the same time, William Mellors had also spotted Collapsible A; he managed to swim over to it and pulled himself in. Every time people tried to climb in, the boat upset, and some of the occupants were thrown into the water. Each time this ghastly cycle played out, the people grew weaker, and each time there were fewer who were able to struggle back aboard.[32]

By the time George Rheims came alongside Collapsible A, the occupants in the boat refused to let him come aboard, probably fearing that he would cause the boat to tip again. Luckily, Rheims' pleas for help persuaded them, and he was hauled aboard. Wearing just underclothes, Rheims stood in the boat, shaking with cold.[33]

Steward Alfred Theissinger had jumped from the ship with Steward Siebert. Theissinger swam to 'a raft [Boat A] on which a few men were clinging'. He recalled:

A willing hand was extended to me and we picked up seventeen others. A woman was among these and I must give her praise. I wish I could remember her name. During those two dreary hours she laughed and sang, cheering us. The water was up to our knees.[34]

First Class passenger Peter Daly was floating on his back when he bumped into the side of Collapsible A; he called for the men in it to give him a hand. Fortunately, First Class passengers Richard Norris Williams and George Rheims answered his call, and grabbing him by his lifebelt, pulled him aboard.[35] Once August Wennerström was back aboard, he saw his friend Elin Lindell alongside in the water. The boat was overloaded that August could only take her hand, trying to hold her out of the water. Edvard Lindell was apparently unaware that his wife was by the boat.[36]

Meanwhile, the crewmembers and occupants of the lifeboats floating not far away were trying to get organized, and decide what to do. In Boat No. 10, which was approximately 150 yards away from where the ship sank,[37] Able Bodied Seamen Buley and Evans wanted to go back and pick up additional people from the water. However their boat was close to its rated capacity, with around 57 already aboard. Additionally, there were only three people in the craft to row, and one of the men, a fireman, did not know how to pull an oar. In order to assist with the rowing, Buley placed a steward at the tiller. This freed Buley up to assist with the oars, but they were still in no position to lend assistance to any of the victims in the water.[38]

In Boat No. 8, the boat furthest from the site of the sinking, Able Bodied Seaman Thomas Jones had put the Countess of Rothes in charge of the tiller. She did an admirable job of keeping the boat on course, and remained at that post through the night.[39] Stating his reasons for placing her at the tiller, Jones said: 'I was in command, but I had to row. I wanted someone at the tiller. And I saw the way she was carrying herself, and I heard the quiet, determined way she spoke to the others, and I knew she was more of a man than any we had on board.' Jones also had kind words to say for a different woman who was at one of the oars all night, saying that 'though I never learned her name, she was helping every minute.' Soon, the same woman suggested that they sing to keep their spirits up; all agreed, and they started with 'Pull for the Shore'.[40]

Ever since being lowered away at 1:00 a.m., Jones had been following Captain Smith's parting order for Boat No. 8 to row towards the steamer to the north. They could all clearly see two stationary masthead lights sitting tantalizingly on the horizon. Bedroom Steward Alfred Crawford and First Class passenger Ella White estimated the vessel was about 10 miles away.[41] Despite their best efforts, however, they did not appear to be making any significant headway toward it. When the ladies in the boat asked if they were getting any nearer, Jones said no; feeling that their efforts were futile, he had everyone lay on their oars.[42]

While the passengers in Boat No. 8 praised Jones and his conduct, several of its other crewmembers were criticized for their behavior, or for being inexperienced with rowing. The women had to assist them in their efforts. One crewmember had attempted to row without the oar in the oarlock. When First Class passenger Ella White asked him why he didn't put it in the oarlock, he responded: 'Do you put it in that hole?' Then he admitted he had never held an oar before. At least one other crewmember also confessed the same level of inexperience.

The tension was palpable. Many of the women felt that these inexperienced hands had boarded the boat under false pretenses, since they were expected to row. Additionally, not all of the crewmen took kindly to the orders and advice Jones was giving them, in spite of the fact that he was helping them row. Things devolved to the point that at least one crewman snapped at Jones: 'If you don't stop talking through that hole in your face there will be one less in the boat.'[43] It is thus no surprise that – between the generally southerly setting current in the area and the lack of trained oarsmen – making any substantial progress towards the steamer on the horizon was proving difficult.[44]

The cries from the water persisted, drifting across the water and reaching the ears of those in Boat No. 8. As it held just 25 occupants, and was making little progress toward the steamer, someone urged Jones to return to the site of the sinking. Jones agreed, saying that he wanted to 'see what we could do for the others'. He actually had the boat turned around and headed back before some of the women in the boat got frightened, at which point he relented. Jones told them, 'ladies, if any of us are saved, remember, I wanted to go back. I would rather drown with them than leave them.' He then had them resume their efforts to reach the steamer, just as Captain Smith had ordered them.[45]

In Boat No. 6, several women assisted Major Peuchen and Lookout Fleet in rowing, owing to the inadequate number of crewmembers manning the boat. First Class passenger Margaret Brown was one of the women who pitched in, having grabbed an oar as soon as the boat reached the water. Looking over the side of the boat, she noted that the sea was 'smooth as glass'.

Quartermaster Hichens continued to demonstrate questionable conduct. As the occupants of No. 6 had difficulty rowing, the boat had not gotten far away from where *Titanic* went under. The cries for help were still loud, so the women in the boat, which had just 23 seats occupied, began to plead with the Quartermaster to return and rescue some people from the water. Hichens admonished them, using the excuse that they did not have enough oarsmen, graphically describing how the 'frantic drowning victims would grapple the side of the boat and capsize it'.

The Quartermaster was unyielding, and refused to go back, saying that there were only a 'lot of stiffs there'. Needless to say, the women in the boat resented this comment greatly, for many of them had left loved ones aboard the ship. Major Peuchen told them: 'It is no use you arguing with that man, at all. It is best not to discuss matters with him.' Eventually, the occupants of the boat gave up on the idea, and tried pulling for the lights of the steamer on the horizon instead, although they did not make much progress.[46]

During this time, Hichens was sitting at the tiller 'shivering like an aspen'. He spouted a 'tirade of awful forebodings', reminding those in the boat that they were 'hundreds of miles from land, without water, without food, without protection against the cold', and that if a storm came up, they would be helpless. He told them that they were facing death by starvation or drowning. Nobody in the boat responded.

One of the ladies in the boat had a flask of brandy, and when Hichens saw it, he demanded that she give it to him, 'saying that he was frozen'. He was denied the brandy; instead, two of the women wrapped what steamer blankets they had in the boat around the Quartermaster's shoulders and legs, until he looked 'as snug as a bug in a rug'. Hichens was then asked to relieve one of the people struggling at the oars, but he refused. Instead he chose to remain at the tiller and critique the technique of those who were doing the physical labor, shouting things such as: 'Here, you fellow on the starboard side, your oar is not being put in the water at the right angle.'[47]

In Boat No. 5, the 36 occupants continued to hear 'a lot of cries and a continuous yelling and moaning' from the water.[48] First Class passenger Anna Warren, whose husband had been left behind on the ship, was momentarily distracted by the surreal view over the edge of the lifeboat: 'The sea was like glass, so smooth the stars were clearly reflected.' The beauty of this must have contrasted harshly with the horror of the cries for help.[49]

Boat No. 5 was just 200–300 yards[50] from where the ship sank when Third Officer Pitman said: 'Now men, we will pull towards the wreck.' He noted that they 'may be able to pick up a few more.' He turned the boat around to go in the directions of the cries, but the passengers immediately began protesting; they said it was a 'mad idea', that if they went back the boat would be swamped, and that any attempt to do so would be 'foolish'.[51]

Two ladies shouted out: 'Appeal to the officer not to go back. Why should we lose all of our lives in a useless attempt to save others from the ship?'[52] Nearly everyone in the boat – or at least the vocal majority – agreed, and Pitman was dissuaded from returning. Quartermaster Olliver did not express his opinion on the matter at the time. Later on, however, he said that while he was not afraid to return to rescue more passengers, he believed that doing so 'would have been endangering the lives of the people we had in the boat already'.[53]

Aboard No. 5, First Class passenger Karl Behr was rubbing Helen Newsom's wet stocking feet to keep them warm when someone nudged him. Behr straightened up, and saw the man next to him surreptitiously holding a nickel-plated revolver in his hand. The man whispered in Behr's ear: 'Should the worst come to the worst, you can use this revolver for your wife, after my wife and I have finished with it.' The calm way in which the man said this shocked Behr, and he didn't know how to respond other than to politely thank him.[54]

In Boat No. 3, which had gotten a quarter of a mile away from *Titanic* before she sank, Able Bodied Seaman George Moore made no efforts to go back at all, despite having only

about 32 people aboard. He felt that there was a danger of the boat being swamped, and believed that at the distance they were away from the wreck, by the time they rowed back, their efforts would have been for naught. He later said: 'I do not think anybody could live much more than 10 minutes in that cold water.'[55]

In Boat No. 12, which was loaded with 42 people, Able Bodied Seaman Poingdestre pulled back towards the sounds of the screams from the water. Since they had room to take on more people, nobody in his boat objected. After pulling for about 15 minutes, all they found were 'a couple of hundred deck chairs' floating in the water. There were only two seamen aboard, and both had to do the majority of the rowing. Owing to this, they were unable to get any closer than 100 yards from the cries in the water, and Poingdestre reluctantly abandoned his efforts. He began calling out, hoping to hail any other lifeboats that were in the vicinity.[56]

In the two boats that had the fewest people aboard, Boats Nos 1 and 2, similar discussions were playing out. In No. 1, Leading Fireman Charles Hendrickson was frustrated that when he proposed going back to rescue people from the water, the passengers objected. They had initially rowed toward the lights of the steamer on the horizon before *Titanic* sank, but had then given up and lain on their oars. There were screams all around them less than 200 yards away. Because of this, Hendrickson was very anxious to return and save more lives. Lady Duff Gordon expressed her fear that if they did so, the boat would be swamped, and said she didn't want to return. Rather than try to instill courage in his wife, Sir Cosmo Duff Gordon supported what she said, and also objected to going back.

Neither Lookout George Symons – who was in charge of the boat – nor the boat's other crewmembers said anything at all to back up their shipmate. This was in spite of the fact that their boat could have held 28 more people. Hendrickson later said that 'they would not listen to me,' and while he understood the risk involved, he thought that returning was the right thing to do. Able Bodied Seaman Horswill did not hear Symons propose going back, or in fact, give any other order that night. Horswill felt that 'it was inhuman' not to rescue anyone from the water, but did not feel it was his place to say so, and so he never spoke up.[57]

In Boat No. 2, Fourth Officer Boxhall periodically lit green flares. Holding them up, they pierced through a darkness which was otherwise only broken by the brilliant starlight. He had taken a box of the flares from the Bridge and put them in the boat during the loading, feeling that they would help keep all of the lifeboats together once they were afloat. More than once during the night, people were fooled into thinking these flares were an approaching ship. Sadly, when he had lit the first flare, the cries from the water got even louder, probably because the people struggling for their lives had mistaken the light for a rescue ship.

Trimmer Thomas Patrick Dillon (left) *and* Leading Fireman Charles Hendrickson (right).

Due to a lack of crewmembers to row, Boxhall had placed First Class passenger Mahala Douglas in charge of the tiller. From there she steered the craft, carefully following Boxhall's directions. With the cries from the water continuing, the Fourth Officer suggested to Able Bodied Seaman Frank Osman, the only seaman in the boat, that they go back, but ultimately he 'decided it was unwise to do so'. When Boxhall raised this idea, the women in the boat had also become very nervous. So despite the fact that the boat could hold 23 additional occupants, Boxhall had them pull as far away as possible, 'so that the women would not see and cause a panic'.[58] From time to time, the occupants in the boat could hear water lapping against the base of icebergs nearby, and when they were all quiet, Boxhall told them 'listen'.[59]

While the decision not to return may have seemed reasonable to most of the occupants of the lifeboats, everything looked very different to those on one of the half-swamped collapsibles. On top of Collapsible B, First Class passenger Jack Thayer lamented the fact that none of the lifeboats were coming back to rescue anyone from the water. Later, he expressed the following thoughts about the matter: 'The partially filled lifeboats standing by, only a few hundred yards away never came back. Why on earth they did not come back is a mystery. How could any human being fail to heed those cries?'[60]

Elsewhere, the occupants of Boat No. 4 were mercifully spared the decision of whether or not to rescue anyone from the water. Their boat, just 200 yards from Titanic when she sank, was well within sight of people standing on Titanic's deck during her final moments.[61] Because of this, several had dropped down falls or jumped overboard, reached the boat, and were quickly plucked from the water by No. 4's crew members.[62]

Amongst those who boarded Boat No. 4 in this fashion were Greasers Frederick Scott and Thomas Ranger. Both men had slid down an aft set of lifeboat falls when Boat No. 4 was still alongside Titanic, before it had begun to move further away from the dying ship. Scott had dropped into the water, and was there for just 'four to five minutes' before being pulled aboard;[63] Ranger had dropped down the falls into the boat without even getting wet.[64]

Lamp Trimmer Hemming swam to this boat just before Titanic sank, but after it had begun rowing away from the ship's side. Hemming was not wearing a lifebelt, and had swum furiously through the frigid water after dropping down a set of falls. Arriving alongside, he clung to one of the boat's lifelines. Pulling his head above the gunwale, he saw his friend, Storekeeper Jack Foley, standing in the boat. 'Give us a hand in, Jack,' he said. Foley asked 'Is that you, Sam?' Hemming replied in the affirmative, and was quickly hauled aboard.[65]

After Titanic had disappeared below the surface, Quartermaster Perkis ordered No. 4 rowed back towards the cries in the water. They were able to rescue seven or eight additional men,[66] among them Greaser Alfred White,[67] Able Bodied Seaman William Lyons,[68] Trimmer Thomas Dillon,[69] Bedroom Stewards Sidney Siebert[70] and Andrew Cunningham[71] – who had left the ship together – as well as Storekeeper Frank Prentice,[72] and possibly one or two passengers.

After his friend Ricks had died, Prentice had swum away, and eventually found himself alone. He noticed that the 'cries [for] help, prayers and all subsided, and everything

was quiet.'[73] By the time Boat No. 4 picked him up, there were few cries coming from the water nearby. The frigid temperature of the sea was beginning to claim more and more people. Things were becoming silent and eerily calm in the nearly pitch-black night.

Trimmer Dillon had been in the sea for approximately 20 minutes, and had seen 'about one thousand people in the water' during his swim to Boat No. 4. By the time he reached it, he was exhausted. Right after being pulled aboard, Dillon fell unconscious, clearly suffering from hypothermia.[74] The icy water was so deadly that despite having been in the water for less than half an hour, at least two of the men pulled into the boat later died, including Seaman Lyons, and Bedroom Steward Siebert.[75] Lyons and Siebert had lain down in the stern of the boat after being pulled aboard, and never woke up. First Class passenger Emily Ryerson's recollections were even more disturbing. She noticed that some of the men who had been pulled from the water 'were raving and delirious most of the time' from the cold.[76]

Later, when Dillon finally came to, he 'was not properly right'. This was because he found himself in the bottom of the boat with two dead bodies – those of Seaman Lyons and a man who he thought was a passenger – lying on top of him.[77] One of the crewmembers who had been pulled aboard, Frank Prentice, took a bottle of brandy from his pocket, and attempted to take a drink of it for its warming sensation. Quartermaster Perkis promptly took it away and threw it overboard, then tossed the man into the bottom of the boat and covered him with a blanket.[78]

In the water, Saloon Steward Harold Phillimore was still lying on top of a piece of floating wreckage. The man hanging on alongside him had grown steadily weaker. Finally the man had said, 'What a night', rolled off into the water, and died.[79] Elsewhere, Thomas Whiteley was still clinging to the wardrobe that had proven to be a temporary sanctuary for him, shivering uncontrollably. He had kept his circulation going by beating his hands and feet in a steady motion. As time went on, the four other men sharing the wardrobe slowly dropped off, one by one, and soon Whiteley was alone.[80] Seeing a white object in the water nearby, Whiteley cast off and swam for it.

The object turned out to be the upturned Collapsible B, which now had over 30 people standing on top of or clinging to it. When Whiteley tried to climb aboard, Second Officer Lightoller refused to let him, saying 'It's thirty-one lives against yours. You can't come aboard. There's not room.' Whiteley pleaded with them in vain; then, in desperation, he found himself praying that somebody might die, so that he could take their place. Ashamed of this thought after the sinking, Whiteley explained his feelings, saying that 'it was only human' given the circumstances. Soon, someone did die and was rolled off the raft; Whiteley was let aboard.[81]

Eugene Daly, shivering and with his hands blue-tinged and cramping, was still half in the water and half on Collapsible B; his soaked overcoat was preserving some of his body heat, but it was also weighing him down. When another person passed away and dropped into the water, Daly was hauled fully aboard.[82]

As the collapsible got even more overloaded, its occupants feared it would sink, and they had good reason to worry as it sank lower and lower under the weight. Harold Bride lay on the bottom of the boat; his feet, which were now sitting two feet under water, were still being jammed against the cork fender by the man sitting on top of them. First Class passenger Jack Thayer was kneeling behind Bride, barely able to maintain his hold on the hull. Another man clung to Thayer, kneeling on his legs and with his hands on the 17-year-old's shoulders; in turn, a third man was clinging to the person Thayer was forced to support. Nobody on the boat moved for fear of pitching everyone into the sea.[83]

Fireman Harry Senior met an even harsher reception than Whiteley did when he tried to climb aboard Collapsible B: 'I tried to board her, but some chap hit me over the head with an oar. There were too many in [sic, on] her. I got around the other side of the boat and climbed in.' Right after Senior boarded, another man was hauled aboard, but he 'died just after he was pulled over the side'. Senior said: 'I saw any amount of drowning and dead around us.'[84]

Chief Baker Joughin had been swimming around since riding the stern down into the sea. Supported by his life-belt, he paddled alongside Collapsible B; there he saw the occupants standing on top of the boat, clinging to each other's shoulders to keep their balance. When Joughin tried to climb on, he was pushed off. However, he wisely stayed as close as he could to the boat, and eventually went around to the other side. Once there, Entrée Cook Isaac Maynard recognized him, and offered Joughin his hand. The baker grabbed a hold of his hand and hung on to it; he also held on to the side of the boat, but his legs and feet remained in the water.[85]

The men began using the remaining oars and wooden planks as paddles, in an attempt to propel the upturned boat away from the remaining swimmers in the water. One man with a powerful voice came alongside, encouraging the men, saying: 'Hello boys, keep calm, boys.' Then he asked for assistance. When told that one more aboard might sink them all, the man, despite being in such a vulnerable state, bravely responded: 'All right, boys; good luck and God bless you.' Then he swam along for about two minutes before becoming still in the water.[86] Some believed that this man was Captain Smith.[87]

Meanwhile, the occupants of Collapsible A were experiencing a similar situation. With about twenty people aboard the swamped boat, it wallowed through the water, and the Kapok was barely keeping the craft afloat. George Rheims stood in his underclothes, 'shaking with cold.' His suffering was so intense that on two occasions, he had thought of throwing himself into the water and ending things. Both times, thoughts of his wife Mary brought him back to his senses. The occupants 'had to push back about 10 poor people who wanted to climb aboard'.[88]

August Wennerström had been holding onto Elin Lindell's hand for about half an hour when he finally lost his grip on her. She had apparently passed away without him noticing, and immediately sank 'down under the water to her ocean grave'. Wennerström reluctantly turned to her husband Edvard to tell him the news, and saw that his appearance had changed from that of a 36-year-old man, to 'something like 90 or 100'. His face had sunk in, his mustache was gray from frost, and his eyes were open, but fixed and unmoving. He lay in the bottom of the boat, with water up to his chest, and never responded or said a word. Wennerström then realized that he too had passed away.[89]

Boat No. 4 had already rescued a handful of men from the water; then Quartermaster Perkis and the other occupants in the boat rowed about, trying to find anyone else

Above: *Third Class passengers Edvard and Elin Lindell.*

Left: *Fireman Harry Senior.*

nearby. He was amazed that throughout the sinking, the crewmembers had 'conducted themselves the same as they would if it were an ordinary everyday occurrence'.[90] Soon, they sighted a light from another lifeboat in the water.[91] This boat proved to be No. 12, and as they began making for it, Able Bodied Seaman Poingdestre started hailing them. The occupants in No. 4 responded, and Poingdestre and Perkis had the two boats tie together.[92]

Nearby, several of the women in Boat No. 14 began to sob, realizing that a reunion with the husbands they had left on the ship was unlikely. Second Class passenger Esther Hart was one of those who reached this conclusion: 'I knew … that I had seen the last of my Ben [Benjamin Hart], and that I had lost the best and truest friend, the kindest and most thoughtful husband that ever woman had.'

Fifth Officer Lowe, a sailor through and through, attempted to console the women in the boat; unfortunately, it came off in a rather rough fashion: 'Don't cry, please don't cry,' he said. 'You'll have something else to do than cry; some of you will have to handle the oars. For God's sake stop crying. If I had not the responsibility of looking after you I would put a bullet through my brain.'[93] Continuing, Lowe suggested that the occupants in the boat should sing to get their minds off things, saying: 'A good song to sing would be, "Throw Out the Life Line". ' He also suggested: 'I think the best thing for you women to do is to take a nap.'[94]

After Boat No. 14 had lowered away from *Titanic*, Lowe had the occupants row approximately 150 yards away from the ship. Then he had them stop and lay on the oars. He wanted to remain close enough to the scene of the wreck to rescue people from the water if they had the opportunity. However, his boat was rather full. Seeing several other lifeboats nearby, he hailed them. Finding no officer in any of them, Lowe told them: 'All right consider the whole of you are under my orders; remain with me.' An idea was forming in his mind, and he explained that if the boats 'are tied together and keep all together, if there is any passing steamer they will see a large object like that on the water quicker than they would a small one.' Soon he had herded together Boat No. 10 and Collapsible D, as well as Boats Nos 4 and 12, tying them all up to his own. Doing so formed a sort of mini flotilla.[95]

In Boat No. 10, one of the crewmembers explained to Imanita Shelley that this was being done simply for 'safety's sake'. She felt that the boats sticking together was a good idea. However, she was concerned that the boats could be damaged as, despite the calm sea, their hulls kept bumping into each other, and there was also a lot of wreckage around them in the water.[96]

As soon as the boats were assembled, Lowe asked if there were any seamen present. When the answer was yes, the Fifth Officer said: 'All right; you will have to distribute these passengers [in No. 14] among these boats. Tie them all together and come into my boat to go over into the wreckage and pick up anyone that is alive there.'[97] Lowe wanted to go rescue any survivors, but was waiting to do so 'until it quieted down', and 'until the drowning people had thinned out'. The Fifth Officer felt that to row back into a crowd of struggling people in the water would have been 'suicidal', believing that 'the whole lot of us would have been swamped and then nobody would have been saved.'[98] With the cries from those in the water continuing, some of the women in the boat implored Lowe to go back and rescue people right away. Lowe told them: 'You ought to be damn glad you are here and have got your own life.'[99]

At around 3:00 a.m., the twelve occupants of Boat No. 1 saw a light on the water, and had begun rowing towards it. With the cries for help having largely ceased by then, the realization of what had happened was finally beginning to set in. With poor timing, Lady Duff Gordon turned to her secretary Laura Francatelli and said: 'There is your beautiful nightdress, gone.'

Fireman Robert Pusey rebuked her, saying, 'Never mind about your nightdress madam, as long as you have got your life.' He then turned to Sir Cosmo, saying: 'I suppose you have lost everything?'

Sir Cosmo said: 'Yes.'

The fireman responded: 'But you can get some more?'

'Yes,' the wealthy sportsman acknowledged.

Pusey then said: 'Well, we have lost our kits and the company won't give us anymore, and what is more our pay stops from tonight. All they will do is send us back to London.'

Sir Cosmo said to them: 'You fellows need not worry about that; I will give you a fiver [£5 sterling draft] each to start a new kit.'

Later, this incident gave rise to false rumors that the Duff Gordons had bribed the crewmembers not to return to the site of the wreck to rescue swimmers. Although the conversation, in retrospect, looked very bad, this offer does not appear to have been a direct bribe.[100]

Back at the flotilla of lifeboats, Fifth Officer Lowe had been busy transferring approximately 33 people out of Boat No. 14 into the other boats. He wanted to make more room in his boat so that he could return to the site of the sinking without jeopardizing the lives of passengers. Around twelve people were transferred to Collapsible D, while No. 4 received ten additional occupants, and No. 12 picked up the remaining eleven. After the transfers were complete, Collapsible D had about 35 occupants aboard, Boat No. 4 had approximately 48, and Boat No. 12 had about 53. It does not appear as if any passengers were transferred into Boat No. 10, which was already rather heavily loaded with 57 persons.[101]

While the passengers from No. 14 were being distributed among the other boats, Lowe used some very emphatic language, cursing regularly; he was obviously in a hurry. When First Class passenger Daisy Minahan went to climb into another boat, he yelled: 'Jump, God damn you, jump.' He had been so 'blasphemous' that a few of the women wondered whether he was under the influence of alcohol.[102] In fact, however, Lowe was a teetotaler.[103] It seems probable that some of the society women in his care were simply unaccustomed to hearing the common language of sailors, and thus took particular offense with him.

While Minahan had negative things to say about the Fifth Officer, other women in the boat were very impressed with his conduct and work; included among the latter group was First Class passenger Sara Compton. She said that 'Mr Lowe's manly bearing gave us all confidence … [and] he seems to me to personify the best traditions of the British sailor.'[104]

During the transfer process, Lowe found one woman with a shawl over her face who seemed to be in too much of a hurry to get in the other boat. Suspicious, Lowe ripped the shawl away, and discovered that the woman was in fact a man, whom he believed to be an 'Italian'. So disgusted that he couldn't speak, Lowe caught hold of the man, and tossed him into the other boat.[105]

By 3:20 a.m., with his passengers transferred out and nearly all the cries from the water subsided, Lowe decided it was safe to make a rescue attempt.[106] The Fifth Officer took on additional crewmembers until he had about eight or nine men in the boat, himself included;[107] all were prepared to go back to the wreck site to look for survivors. The other men aboard included Able Bodied Seamen Buley,[108] Evans,[109] and Scarrott,[110] Saloon Steward George Crowe,[111] Bathroom Steward Frank Morris,[112] Steward Alfred Pugh,[113] Leading Fireman Thomas Threlfall,[114] and Second Class passenger Charles Williams,[115] who volunteered to stay in No. 14 to help row. Lowe ordered the other boats in the flotilla to lie on their oars and stick together, and then he steered No. 14 back towards the wreck. Evans and Buley were transferred from Boat No. 10, which had 55 people aboard after their departure.

Once Boat No. 14 reached the disaster site, the men were confronted with a horrific sight; it was immediately clear that they had waited too long to return. Among all the floating debris in the still water, there were literally hundreds of bodies around them, suspended by their lifejackets. Some had their heads laid back, while others had their faces in the water. All was quiet and still. There were so many bodies that they could not be counted. The water was so thick with them that it proved difficult just to row. Evans could not even bring himself to look over the side for fear that he was going to break down. As they continued their search, Buley and the others reached over the gunwale and turned over several of the people to see if any were alive. All of them were dead, and Buley said that it 'looked as though none of them were drowned. They looked as though they were frozen.'[116]

Suddenly, the men heard moaning. Without anything other than starlight to guide them,[117] they pushed through the flotsam and bodies, rowing towards the source of the noise. Soon they discovered a passenger who was still alive, First Class passenger William Hoyt of New York. He was 'a large, fleshy man', and it took the efforts of everyone aboard to haul him into the boat. Hoyt was bleeding from his mouth and from his nose, so Lowe propped him up in the stern. The men took his collar off and loosened his shirt to help him breathe, and a steward moved his limbs and chafed his arms, but to no avail. Sadly, Hoyt was too far gone, and

First Class passenger William Hoyt

never recovered. He died shortly after being taken aboard.[118]

Going further into the wreckage, the men in No. 14 heard a voice calling for help. They spotted a man kneeling on a piece of wreckage that looked like a staircase. He looked 'as if he was praying, and at the same time he was calling for help'. Despite being just twenty yards away, it took the men in Boat No. 14 nearly half an hour to get close enough to rescue him. The bodies in the water were so thick that they could not row, and they had to push the deceased out of the way in order to force their way to him. When they got close enough, Steward Alfred Pugh extended an oar to the man, who turned out to be Saloon Steward Phillimore. Phillimore grasped the oar long enough to be pulled to the side of the boat, but his hands were so numb that he had to be hauled aboard by his lifebelt. In his own words, he felt 'frozen stiff'.[119]

Homing in on the last of the shouts, the men in No. 14 were able to find one more survivor, Third Class passenger Fang Lang of Hong Kong. Lang was a sailor with the Donaldson Line, and he was extremely fortunate; he had managed to find and then climb on top of a sideboard or table which had kept him largely out of the water. After being taken into the boat he quickly recovered; he even went to work at rowing, in order to keep warm.[120] Fifth Officer Lowe and the other men continued shouting out and searching for survivors, but in vain. As the occupants of No. 14 began rowing away, Able Bodied Seaman Scarrott noticed how all of the bodies they passed seemed to have perished from cold, as their limbs were all cramped up. Describing their departure from the area, he said: 'As we left that awful scene we gave way to tears. It was enough to break the stoutest heart.'[121]

Meanwhile, in Boat No. 7, several of the occupants began yelling out, hoping to attract the attention of the other boats. Soon, Third Officer Pitman in No. 5 saw No. 7 approaching and hailed it. He had the two boats lashed together in order to be more visible to a rescue ship if one 'hove in sight before daylight', as well as for stability. The Third Officer and the other crewmembers transferred about six people from Boat No. 5 into Boat No. 7 to 'even them up a bit.' After the transfers, No. 5 had approximately 30 people in it, while No. 7 had 34.[122]

Around that time, First Class passenger Alfred Nourney, sitting in Boat No. 7, saw one of the green flares that Boxhall was periodically sending up from Boat No. 2. Thinking it was a rescue ship, he fired off all the cartridges in his revolver into the air, hoping to attract their attention.

Third Officer Pitman shouted over to him: 'You had better save all your revolver shots, you had better save all your matches, and save everything. It may be the means of saving your life.'[123]

In Boat No. 6, Quartermaster Hichens had a similar idea to that which Pitman and Lowe had. As morning was drawing close, another boat was rowing along nearby. Hichens raised his voice and shouted for them to pull alongside, and to tie up

with his boat. The other boat, which turned out to be No. 16, immediately obeyed Hichens' direction. Seeing that No. 16 had more crewmembers to row than No. 6 did, they asked: 'Surely you can spare us one man, if you have so many.'

Master-at-Arms Joseph A. Bailey accordingly sent over a fireman to help row. This fireman was covered in coal dust and dressed in a thin set of work jumpers. Margaret Brown thus took her sable stole and wrapped it around his legs to help keep him warm. The two boats remained lashed together for about fifteen minutes, and Hichens had them lay on the oars. The boats knocked together, and at Major Peuchen's suggestion, lifebelts were put in between the boats to cushion them.

After this, Hichens resigned the helm, and settled down to rest. One person in their boat was a boy with an arm injury who was physically unable to row, and the occupants suggested that in light of this, he be allowed to take control of the tiller. They also suggested that the two boats be cut loose from one another, and asked that Hichens help them row. The Quartermaster refused, even after several of the women in the boat tried to goad him into action.

The passengers in the boat wanted to resume rowing in order to keep their circulation going and stay warm, but Hichens was adamantly against it. When Margaret Brown told a passenger, who was clothed only in pajamas, to go ahead and cut the two boats loose anyway, Hichens moved to prevent it. At this, Margaret Brown told the Quartermaster that if he did, he would be thrown overboard. Seeing how angry she was, someone laid a hand on her shoulder to calm her down, but her threat had worked: Hichens was said to be so paralyzed with fright that had she moved in his direction, 'he would have tumbled into the sea'.

Hichens spoke so uncivilly to the women in the boat during this period that the fireman who transferred over exclaimed in a thick cockney accent: 'Oi sy, don't you know you are talking to a lidy?'

Hichens responded: 'I know who I am speaking to, and I am commanding this boat.'

Despite this verbal assault, Mrs Brown's chastisement had temporarily worked. With the two boats separated, the occupants of No. 6, including Margaret Brown, began rowing again.[124]

Now that the screams of those in the water had ended, an eerie quiet settled over those in the lifeboats, a silence broken only by the occasional remark, or the sobs of those who were beginning to realize the awful reality of what had happened. In heavily-loaded Boat No. 15, several women 'wept and moaned'.

Besides the emotional impact of the disaster, many of those in the boats were also beginning to feel the physical strain of the events. Bertha Mulvihill began to fully notice the effects of her rib and back injuries, and there was nothing more that Maggie Daly or anyone else in the boat could do to assist her. Bertha felt worse and worse as morning approached; every breath hurt. Feeling faint, she leaned over the gunwale of the boat, with her hair dangling into the water. By morning, strands of her hair had frozen together.[125] In Boat No. 10, Lutie Parrish was also suffering from injuries to her leg and ankle where the man had landed on top of her during the lowering of the boat. Imanita Shelley tried to keep her mother comfortable, but the swelling had increased, and was making her uncomfortable.[126]

The stars were still shining brilliantly, but as it got closer and closer to dawn, a breeze began to pick up, and the sea, which had been smooth as glass, began to develop a swell. The flotilla that Lowe had assembled earlier had begun to separate. In Collapsible D, Quartermaster Bright and the other occupants were having difficulty rowing, because they lacked crewmen to pull the oars. Despite being chilled to the bone from jumping into the water before he was pulled into Collapsible D, Frederick Hoyt sat next to Chief Second Class Steward Hardy, dutifully helping to row.[127]

Not far away, sometime between 3:30 and 4:00 in the morning, those in Boat No. 14 discontinued their search for survivors. As they rowed away, they continued their looking, but found nothing. With the first signs of morning just beginning to show on the horizon, Lowe felt 'quite satisfied that I had a real good look around, and that there was nothing left'. Just then, they sighted the glow of lights on the horizon, which looked to be from a steamer; this brought a great sense of relief.[128]

With the breeze continuing to pick up, Lowe and the crewmembers erected the sail in No. 14, and soon were 'bowling along very nicely' at several knots. In a testament to his skills as a sailor, Lowe was the only crewmember to assemble and utilize his lifeboat's sail.

As Boat No. 14 came across Collapsible D, Lowe felt that it looked 'sorry', and saw they were having trouble rowing through the waves. He sailed down to the collapsible, where he found Quartermaster Bright in command. Lowe had the two boats hooked together, and took her in tow, continuing to sail along as the sky began to lighten.[129]

* * * * *

The Cunard liner *Carpathia* had raced through the night toward the distress coordinates, steaming as fast as possible through the darkness. At around 2:40 a.m., Rostron saw a green signal flare about half a point on the port bow; he remarked that *Titanic* must still be afloat, since the *Carpathia* was still a long way from the distress coordinates, and the flare seemed to be high up on the horizon. However, that hope soon began to fade.

Within just a few minutes, at 2:45 a.m., there were more pressing things to occupy Rostron's mind. An iceberg loomed up about a point on the port bow; Rostron spotted it by the reflection of a star off its face, and had to port the *Carpathia* to keep it clear of the ice. He thus narrowly avoided the same fate that had befallen *Titanic*. Knowing that *Titanic* had struck ice, Rostron had posted additional lookouts on the bow, and everyone kept a sharp watch. Beginning at 2:45 a.m., Rostron also had his crewmen fire off rockets and company signals every 15 minutes, to reassure *Titanic* that they were coming. An hour later, at 3:45 a.m., Rostron was informed that his long list of orders had been carried out, and that everything was in a state of readiness for the rescue attempt.[130]

On the Bridge of the small vessel, as the clock ticked on with no sign of the stricken liner, Captain Arthur Rostron had begun to lose hope. It was 3:30 a.m., and no wireless signals had been heard from *Titanic* in well over an hour. As they got closer and closer to the distress coordinates, they should have seen *something* of her; yet they could detect no sign of *Titanic*.

* * * * *

Around this time, people in *Titanic*'s lifeboats saw a low-lying flash of light on the southern horizon. In Boat No. 6,

Second Cashier Mabel Martin – who was one of the women helping to row – exclaimed: 'There is a flash of lightning.' Quartermaster Hichens disagreed, saying: 'It is a falling star.' Soon, like the men in Boat No. 14, Hichens saw a glow of light begin to pierce the horizon, and he became convinced that it was a ship.[131] On Collapsible B, 'shortly before four o'clock,' Jack Thayer saw the masthead light of the steamer come over the horizon, to which they all 'gave a thankful cheer'. Unfortunately, their ordeal was not yet over.[132]

In Collapsible A, August Wennerström scanned the horizon, which was becoming gray, followed by orange, as dawn approached. He saw a dim light, and rejoiced to discern that it was a steamer. A moment later, the light was no longer visible to them. For one man in the boat who was barely clinging to life, this disappointment seemed to be too much: 'We will not be saved, we must die here,' he exclaimed. Less than a minute later he expired, and his body was rolled out to lighten the boat. Soon, the light on the horizon became visible again; first one masthead light appeared, followed by a second, and later, a green sidelight. George Rheims believed he 'saw her lights probably at four o'clock in the morning.'[133]

In Boat No. 15, the waves were beginning to raise havoc on the overloaded boat when the occupants noticed the steamer approaching. Bertha Mulvihill described the scene:

> It was awfully cold. The water every once in a while slapped up over the bow of the boat and covered us with spray. None of us had more than nightclothes, with a scant covering over those … Dawn was just breaking when I saw a light off in the distance. I spoke to the nearest sailor about it, and asked if it possibly could be a vessel coming to help us. He said it must be a ship's light, but someone spoke up and said it was probably a boat's light. Then two big green [sic] lights broke through … [and] we knew it was a ship coming to rescue us. We cheered and cheered and cheered. Some cried. I just sat still and offered up a little prayer.[134]

* * * * *

Back on board the *Carpathia*, by 4:00 a.m., Captain Rostron determined that he had to be 'somewhere in the vicinity' of the distress coordinates, and almost up to where they had seen the green signal flares. As a result, he ordered the engines stopped. Rostron was unaware that the distress coordinates worked up by Fourth Officer Boxhall, and transmitted to the *Carpathia* earlier that night, had been wrong; they indicated a position some 13 miles to the west of where *Titanic* actually sank.[135]

Ironically, Boxhall was responsible for both the miscalculation of the distress position, and the *Carpathia* finding the survivors anyway. He was the one who worked up the second set of distress coordinates at Captain Smith's request before they were transmitted by wireless; but it was also his green flares that had guided *Carpathia* to the actual position of the lifeboats throughout the night. If Boxhall had not tossed the box of flares into Boat No. 2 as it loaded – almost as an afterthought – then *Carpathia* may well have completely missed seeing the lifeboats in the dark; she could easily have steamed right past them and proceeded to the position that was transmitted, ending up 13 miles away. This could have ended up costing more lives before the actual position of the survivors had been pinpointed.

At around 4:05 a.m., Rostron saw another flare, closer this time. It was at this point that the awful realization set in, and he 'knew really it was a boat and not the ship herself'. Rostron planned on picking up the lifeboat on *Carpathia*'s port side, thus offering the leeward side of the ship where the seas would be calmer. However, the ship had not yet ceased its forward momentum, and suddenly, an iceberg appeared right in their path. None of the lookouts or officers had been able to see it until the last possible second. Since it was so near, Rostron said: 'I had to port my helm hard-a-starboard and put her head round quick and pick up the boat on the starboard side.' Disaster was averted, but the whole thing was a little too close for comfort. By 4:10 a.m. the Cunarder had stopped, and the lifeboat that had been signaling them began rowing towards their side.[136]

* * * * *

Even as the lights of the *Carpathia* were becoming visible to those in the lifeboats, the lights of the other ship – the one which had been visible to the north of *Titanic* throughout the night – were still visible to many. Those boats that were rowing towards that vessel, such as Boat No. 8, had never seemed to draw any closer, even by the time dawn approached. The ship never responded to *Titanic*'s distress signals, despite the fact that they could not have helped but see them.

With the appearance of *Carpathia* on the horizon, Boat No. 8 and the other lifeboats gave up, turned around, and began to head towards the closer vessel as she approached them.[137] Collapsible C headed toward the green flares coming from Boat No. 2.[138]

Elsewhere, for those on top of Collapsible B, the situation had deteriorated further. As waves continued to kick up, Collapsible B shifted from side to side, causing air to leak out from under the boat. As a result, it continued to settle lower and lower. Soon, water began washing over Harold Bride's face as he reclined on the hull, and he had to breathe when he could.

As the men continued desperately scanning the horizon for signs of a rescue ship, a crewmember on the boat said: 'Don't the rest of you think we ought to pray?' He asked what religion everyone was, and a quick survey revealed that there were Catholics, Methodists, and Presbyterians alike. The men decided the Lord's Prayer was the most appropriate, and recited it, with the crewmember who suggested it leading the rest of them.

As waves began to wash over the hull of the upturned boat more and more, the water reached the waists of those sitting in a reclined position. Colonel Gracie, who had not noticed the icy temperature of the water while he was struggling in it earlier in the night, was by now 'suffering severely from cold and exposure,' and his teeth were chattering. Eugene Daly likewise shivered uncontrollably, huddling under his soaked-through overcoat. As the breeze continued to pick up, Daly found that his clothes had frozen 'as stiff as boards'. Two men on the stern of the boat, 'unable to stand the exposure and strain, gave up the struggle and fell off'. Several others who had clung to the collapsible earlier in the night had already passed away.

Second Officer Lightoller had all the men who were physically able stand in two rows, facing forward, holding on to one another by their lifebelts, or any way they could. To keep the collapsible's buoyancy, he tried to keep the capsized boat level by calling out for everyone to lean first in the opposite direction of that which the boat was rolling, and then in the other direction as the boat shifted back.

Harold Bride was unable to stand, his feet both crushed and frostbitten, so Thayer and the others tried to hold him up out of the water as much as possible. Each man supported the man next to him, and they supported the person next to them in turn. In an attempt to hail any boats that were nearby, Lightoller said, 'Now boys, all together,' and had them repeatedly yell: 'Boat ahoy! Boat ahoy!' This was kept up for a while, but when no responses were forthcoming, Lightoller decided that it would be best for everyone to save their strength.

Earlier in the night, when Lightoller had discovered Bride's presence on the boat, he had begun calling out questions to the Junior Marconi Operator regarding who they had been in communication with prior to the sinking. In order to keep everyone's hopes up, Bride told everyone repeatedly that they had been able to contact the *Baltic*, *Olympic* and *Carpathia*. He also said that the *Carpathia* was coming up as fast as she could, and that he expected to 'see her lights at about four or a little after'. The men began scanning the brightening horizon even more closely looking for any vessels. They had been fooled several times by the green flares Boxhall was lighting in Boat No. 2. However, just as Bride had predicted, they saw the lights of a steamer appear on the horizon right about four o'clock.[139]

With the coming of dawn, the men atop Collapsible B were surprised to see the small flotilla of lifeboats approximately half a mile away. They had not seen any lights from other boats in that direction during the night, and nobody had responded to their earlier hails. With the sea continuing to get rougher, the men on the boat were 'right glad' at the discovery. It was not a minute too soon. Second Officer Lightoller was finally able to find his whistle; he put it up to his cold lips and 'blew a shrill blast' on it twice, attracting the attention of the other boats' occupants. He yelled: 'Come over and take us off.'

To this, Able Bodied Seaman Frederick Clench in Boat No. 12 responded: 'Aye, aye; I am coming over.' Then he separated his boat from the flotilla.[140]

Boat No. 4 also separated, and both immediately began heading over to the upturned collapsible. Just before the lifeboats arrived alongside, Lightoller ordered the 28 men who were still alive not to scramble onto the other boats, but to take their time and wait their turn, so as to not endanger all of their lives. They all obeyed, climbing hand over foot into the other two boats. Approximately 16 climbed into Boat No. 12, and about 12 managed to clamber into No. 4. This led to these two boats being very heavily loaded with 69 and 60 aboard respectively.[141]

Some of the men had to be helped into the other boats. Harold Bride was in such bad shape by that point that he had to be carried off the collapsible. Jack Thayer thought Bride 'would have slipped off the bottom … if several of us had not held onto him for the last half hour.' Similarly, Eugene Daly was shivering uncontrollably, and was 'dragged' into one of the boats. Describing the situation, he said: 'My sufferings in the lifeboat were intense until we reached the *Carpathia*, where I was made comfortable.' Daly, who had been able to remain conscious up to that point, passed out before his boat reached the Cunarder.[142]

Colonel Gracie climbed into Boat No. 12, where he was glad to see 'young Thayer' sitting in the middle of the boat. He was unaware up to that point that Thayer had even been aboard the collapsible with him. In an odd twist of fate, Marian Thayer, in Boat No. 4, thought she recognized her son as he climbed into Boat No. 12, but was not certain that it was him until they were reunited on the *Carpathia*.

Cecil Fitzpatrick, the young Mess Steward, had somehow also managed to survive the night on Collapsible B. He climbed gratefully into Boat No. 12, and then remembered being rowed toward the *Carpathia* – and safety.[143]

Second Officer Lightoller stayed on top of Collapsible B until every other man had been taken off. Then he lifted a lifeless body into Boat No. 12, and then climbed into the same boat himself. Colonel Gracie did not know who the man was whose body Lightoller had brought aboard, but he was dressed like a member of the crew. The Colonel worked over the body for some time, rubbing the temples and wrists in an attempt to revive the man. It was futile. The man's neck was stiff; rigor mortis had already set in. With so many people aboard No. 12, Gracie was forced to sit on top of the body until they reached *Carpathia*.

Steamer blankets were distributed to the men who had been brought aboard from the collapsible, and they huddled together underneath them to keep warm. Once on board No. 12, Lightoller took command, standing at the tiller. He then had those at the oars begin rowing towards the ship on the horizon. Collapsible B was abandoned at the scene.[144]

In swamped Collapsible A, the situation was not any better than it had been on Collapsible B. The waves were causing water to slosh around inside the boat. Nearly everyone was standing, in order to keep as much of their bodies out of the icy sea water as possible. Fireman John Thompson had been standing too, but as his injuries and the cold water took their toll, he eventually collapsed and fell into the bottom of the boat.[145] William Mellors stood, supporting another man. Mellors, chilled and utterly exhausted, lost his grip on him, and the man fell, landing next to the five or six dead bodies lying in the bottom of the boat. Fortunately, he recovered and survived.[146]

Richard Norris Williams asked one man in the boat for his hat, so that he could help him bail. The man said no. Another man asked if it was all right to put his arm around Williams' neck, as he felt so cold and tired. Williams replied: 'Sure.' Williams felt the man's grip tighten and slacken several times, before loosening all the way. The man's body lifelessly slid into the water and drifted away. As the collapsible settled further in the water, the occupants were forced to roll some of the other bodies overboard in an attempt to lighten the boat.[147]

Rhoda Abbott, who had chunks of cork in her hair, was still managing to stand and help the other survivors, despite the horrific loss of her two teenage sons. George Rheims was very impressed with her stoicism, and said: 'Mrs Abbott is the most courageous woman I ever saw. She worked with the men to balance the boat, remaining on her feet all the time.'[148]

August Wennerström was completely numb from limb to limb. He said: 'If we want [*sic*, wanted] to know if we still had the legs or any other [body] part left, we had to feel with the hand.'[149] Saloon Steward Edward Brown's feet were so swollen from the 28° water that they had burst his boots. His hands were also very swollen.[150]

As the sky continued to lighten, Fifth Officer Lowe and the others in Boat No. 14 noticed Collapsible A in the distance, sitting very low in the water, and looking as if it was about to sink. Lowe immediately began sailing towards the boat. As the waves were kicking up, and towing Collapsible D was slowing his forward progress, the Fifth Officer contemplated cutting Boat D adrift, so that he could travel faster. He was worried because Collapsible A looked to be 'in a worse plight than this one I had in tow.' He then decided that he could manage things, and worked his way over to the other boat.

The occupants in Collapsible A had been shouting all night in an attempt to get the attention of any boats nearby, but when none came, they had given up. They didn't know anyone had seen them until they spotted Boat No. 14's sail as it approached. As Boat No. 14 drew within 150 yards of the collapsible, Lowe, worried that the survivors might rush their boat and capsize it, pulled his Browning automatic out of his pocket, and fired four or five warning shots into the water, saying that 'they must not rush the boat.'[151]

Arriving alongside the swamped collapsible, Lowe found just thirteen people still alive out of the approximately twenty who had originally climbed aboard. There were also three corpses left in the bottom of the boat.[152] Lowe immediately began transferring the survivors into Boat No. 14, where they were covered with blankets and every attempt was made to keep them warm. Several of the occupant's hands and legs were so frostbitten that they needed assistance to board the other boat. John Thompson, still unconscious, was carried into No. 14. Leading Fireman Threlfall held Rhoda Abbott in his arms until they reached the *Carpathia*.[153] Later, Mrs Abbott had kind things to say about Fifth Officer Lowe: 'Had it not been for Officer Lowe I would have been drowned. I was nearly exhausted when he lifted me into his lifeboat. It would have been impossible for an officer to show more courtesy and many of the criticisms that have been made against this man are very unjust.'[154]

Steward Alfred Theissinger was also on Collapsible A, and recalled that the water had been up to the occupants' knees through the night. However, 'before daylight a lifeboat came near' to them, and he remembered that they were all taken aboard.[155]

August Wennerström perhaps best described the feeling of being rescued after such a long ordeal:

> Think of yourself in the middle of the ocean, standing in icy water for … hours, and during those hours seeing 1,000 go under, and nothing in sight to save your own life, and [then] so unexpected, a hand be [*sic*, is] reached out to you.[156]

The survivors from Boat A told Lowe that the three men in the bottom of the collapsible were dead; Lowe wanted to make absolutely certain. He checked them carefully, and was forced to conclude that they were gone. He decided to leave them in the boat, as he was there 'to save life', and not to 'worry about bodies'.[157] Lifebelts were placed over the faces of the three victims, and then the boat was abandoned. Lowe sailed away with Collapsible D still in tow.

In Boat No. 2, Fourth Officer Boxhall sat at the tiller, and the occupants laboriously made their way toward the *Carpathia*'s side. The breeze was making the boat drift towards the ship, and Captain Rostron could see that they did not have full control of the boat. Arriving near the side of the ship at 4:10 a.m., Boxhall saw some of *Carpathia*'s crewmembers peering down from the Bridge wing. He sung up to them: 'Shut down your engines and take us aboard. I have only one sailor.'

At that point, Mahala Douglas shouted out: '*Titanic* has gone down with everyone on board!'

The Carpathia.

Boxhall brusquely told her to shut up. Realizing that she should not have said anything, Mrs Douglas felt 'he was perfectly right' in doing so.[158]

Upon hearing Boxhall's plea for assistance, Captain Rostron turned to *Carpathia's* Second Officer, James Bisset. He told him to 'go overside with two quartermasters, and board her as she comes alongside. Fend her off so that she doesn't bump, and be careful that she doesn't capsize.'

Bisset and two seamen headed to the rail of *Carpathia's* foredeck, where rope ladders were hung over the side. As Boxhall maneuvered Boat No. 2 beside the ship's hull, Bisset and the seaman climbed down into the boat, and helped guide it astern to an open gangway on C Deck. There they made the boat fast with some lines that had been lowered.[159]

Since some of the occupants were not in fit condition to climb safely up the short Jacob's ladder to the gangway, bosun's chairs and canvas bags were lowered, to help haul aboard the adults and children who couldn't climb. It was breaking day as the first survivors were being taken aboard, and there was an impressive orange, yellow and red glow to the sky.

With daylight's arrival, those on *Carpathia* and in *Titanic's* lifeboats could see icebergs all around them. Under less tragic circumstances, it would have been called a beautiful and inspirational morning. Captain Rostron described the icebergs that surrounded them, saying: 'There were about 20 icebergs that would be anywhere from about 150 to 200 feet high and numerous smaller bergs; also numerous what we call 'growlers.' You would not call them bergs. They were anywhere from 10 to 12 feet high and 10 to 15 feet long above the water.'[160]

As one female passenger from Boxhall's boat was hauled up to the *Carpathia* in a bosun's chair, she held something beneath her coat, which Bisset and the *Carpathia's* crew-members believed was a baby. Suddenly, she exclaimed: 'Be careful of my doggie!' Somehow this passenger had managed to rescue her dog, in a boat which had just 17 of its 40 seats occupied.

Sometime around 4:20 a.m., once every other occupant of Boat No. 2 had been taken aboard *Carpathia*, Boxhall climbed aboard and was led to the Bridge by Second Officer Bisset. There he came across Captain Arthur Rostron. Although the question was rhetorical, Rostron asked him: 'Where is the *Titanic?*'

Boxhall replied: 'Gone! She sank at 2:20 a.m.' A moment of stunned silence followed, even though everyone on *Carpathia's* Bridge had to have suspected the worst. Boxhall added 'in a voice of desperation' that *Titanic* 'was hoodoo'd from the beginning...'

Rostron gently took him by the arm and said in a quiet voice: 'Never mind that, my son. Tell me, were all her boats got away safely?'

Boxhall replied that he believed so, but that it was hard to see. He added that the ship struck the berg at 11:40, and that the 'boats were launched from 12:45 onwards.' As he continued giving details, he lamented that many of the boats were lowered half full, as nobody then believed the ship would sink.

Rostron asked: 'Were many people left on board when she sank?'

Boxhall, a calm and consummate professional all through the tragedy, finally broke down as the weight of the tragedy hit him head on: 'Hundreds and hundreds! Perhaps a thousand! Perhaps more!' he shouted, his voice cracking with emotion. 'My God, sir, they've gone down with her. They couldn't live in this icy cold water.' Among other details, he added that there had been room for a dozen more people in his boat, but they didn't pick up any swimmers.

Since those on the *Carpathia* had not yet sighted any of the other lifeboats, Boxhall told Rostron that 'the other boats are somewhere near.' Indeed, as morning broke, many of the occupants in the other boats saw the *Carpathia* sitting on the horizon. She was a most welcome sight indeed, and they began rowing towards her, waiting for their turn to get picked up.

Rostron thanked *Titanic's* Fourth Officer, and told him to 'go below and get some coffee, and try to get warm.' Boxhall's report was the first confirmation to anyone from the outside world of the tragic news: *Titanic* had sunk with great loss of life.[161]

CHAPTER 7

IN THE WAKE OF A LEGEND

By the time Boat No. 2 was unloaded, and Fourth Officer Boxhall had reported to Captain Rostron, other lifeboats were nearing *Carpathia*. Each, in turn, queued up, ready to discharge their human cargo; the wait must have seemed like an eternity.

First to arrive after Boat No. 2 was Boat No. 1, with its small load of only twelve crew and passengers, at around 4:45 a.m. By now, *Carpathia*'s crewmembers were fully engaged in the rescue efforts. Curious passengers had crowded along the rails of the rescue ship, looking down from the decks as the lifeboats approached; some even took photographs of history as it played out.

As the occupants of Boat No. 1 climbed aboard *Carpathia*, Leading Fireman Hendrickson grabbed Sir Cosmo Duff Gordon's jacket from the bottom of the boat, and brought it aboard. Sir Cosmo told Hendrickson: 'If you will get the men's names I will see that they get some money in a few days or give them a cheque shortly.' Sir Cosmo went to Captain Rostron, to let him know of his intentions to make good on his word, and give £5 to each of the crewmembers of Boat No. 1 for a new kit. Rostron told him that would be 'quite unnecessary', but Sir Cosmo laughed, saying: 'I promised it; so I have got to give it them.'[1]

During the voyage to New York, Sir Cosmo saw Hendrickson on a deck below the Smoking Room, and asked him to have the crewmen from Boat No. 1 assemble. Once they came on deck, he asked each man what his name was, and handed him a £5 check. Afterwards, Sir Cosmo and Lady Duff Gordon posed with the crewmembers and other occupants of Boat No. 1, wearing their lifebelts, while *Carpathia* passenger Dr Frank Blackmarr snapped several pictures. The Duff Gordons also had the crewmembers sign their lifebelts.[2]

Following the unloading of Boats Nos 2 and 1, there was a gap of time before the next boat came in. Collapsible C, under the command of Quartermaster Rowe, pulled up at 5:45 a.m.[3] One of the 42 other people in Collapsible C with Rowe was J. Bruce Ismay. Once Ismay reached the deck, he stood off to the side with his back up against a bulkhead, obviously in shock from the tragedy.

Dr Frank McGee, *Carpathia*'s surgeon, asked White Star's Chairman: 'Will you not go into the saloon and get some soup, or something to drink?'

Ismay said: 'No, I really do not want anything at all.'

Dr McGee insisted: 'Do go and get something.'

Ismay again refused, saying: 'If you will leave me alone I will be very much happier here.' Then he added: 'If you will get me in some room where I can be quiet, I wish you would.'

The doctor advised him to 'go in the saloon and get something hot', but when Ismay refused once again, McGee found a room for him to stay in.[4]

Ismay stayed in that room for the remainder of the voyage to New York, never leaving it. Devastated by what had happened, he ate nothing but soup, as he 'did not want very much of anything'. Ismay was 'obsessed with the idea, and kept repeating, that he ought to have gone down with the ship because he found that women had gone down.'

Two of the very few visitors the Chairman received during the subsequent voyage were Second Officer Lightoller and Jack Thayer. Lightoller and Dr McGee had tried convincing Ismay, to no avail, to 'get the idea out of his head' that he should have stayed on the ship. McGee brought Thayer to Ismay's room later that morning, to see if he could cheer him up and get him to eat something. Young Thayer and his father had spoken with Ismay frequently while aboard *Titanic*. When he came into the room, Ismay, who was sitting in pajamas, barely responded to Jack, and was staring straight ahead, in a very nervous state. Thayer had breakfast in the cabin, and told Ismay that 'he had a perfect right to take the last boat.' Despite this, Ismay did not respond.[5]

Since *Titanic* had been pointing north immediately before she sank, and since *Carpathia* came up from the south-south-east, in general the odd-numbered starboard lifeboats were closer to the rescue ship than the port boats. No. 2, which was a port boat, had rowed around the stern of *Titanic* just before she sank, onto her starboard side. This explains her early arrival.

Boat No. 5, carrying Third Officer Pitman and Quartermaster Olliver, was next in, arriving at around 6:00 a.m. Third Officer Pitman stated that it was daylight as they waited to be picked up, and that their boat was a half mile or

Above: *The occupants of Boat No. 1 pose together on* Carpathia's *deck.*

Opposite: *Boat No. 11 off-loads its human cargo to the* Carpathia.

less from six icebergs. At least one of these icebergs towered 100 to 150 feet above the sea. Once Pitman was aboard the Cunarder, he helped with the rescue efforts, lending a hand where one was needed. He spent the remainder of the journey to New York assisting where he could, and comparing notes with Lightoller, Colonel Gracie, and a small group of other survivors on their experiences.[6]

Shortly after No. 5 was picked up, Boat No. 7 approached, arriving around 6:15 a.m. The two boats had remained near each other even after cutting their ties. When Alfred Nourney climbed aboard Carpathia, he wasted no time in taking advantage of the hospitality of the ship's crewmembers. After lunch, the would-be 'Baron' engaged in some extremely ungentlemanly behavior. He went to the Smoking Room, and lay down on top of a pile of blankets, monopolizing them for himself to use as a bed. The blankets were intended for survivors as they were brought aboard, and Nourney refused to move when a woman asked for them.

The lady, disgusted, nearly spat out the words: 'To think of it: the like of you saved and women left to drown; shame on you.' She could scarcely restrain the urge to grab Nourney by the collar and toss him into the sea. She yanked away the top blanket underneath Nourney, causing him to roll on to the floor. People jeered him and, thoroughly shamed, he beat a hasty retreat from the room.[7]

Closely following Boat No. 7 was Boat No. 9. When the occupants of this boat had first seen Carpathia, they had started rowing towards it 'like we were pulling for gold'. Once alongside, Able Bodied Seaman George McGough helped the women up the Jacob's ladder that had been lowered. One woman started up, but was exhausted and slipped, hanging there 'fully 10 minutes before they got her aboard'. Some of the women were afraid of heights, and didn't want to go up the ladder, causing further delay. Once the occupants of No. 9 were aboard, Sidney Collett said that 'we were nearly frantic, everybody was asking each other, "Did you see so-and-so", or "Do you know anything about such and such a person?"'[8]

It was at around 6:30 a.m. that Boat No. 13, with Leading Fireman Barrett aboard, arrived. By that point, Barrett had recovered somewhat from the cold. Lawrence Beesley noticed the quiet and stillness that both the survivors and the people on Carpathia displayed: 'There was very little excitement on either side: just the quiet demeanor of people who are in the presence of something too big as yet to lie within their mental grasp, and which they cannot discuss.'

Beesley recalled that after the survivors were aboard, they were informed that passengers could send Marconigrams to their relatives free of charge, and telegraph forms were passed around liberally. Beesley wrote a message to some friends in England, but after the disaster, he discovered that it had not been received, and as a result his friends and family believed he was dead; this unfortunate impression was rectified only after he contacted them, or when they saw his press account in the papers. His name had accidentally been left off the list of those saved which the Carpathia had transmitted to shore, and there were even obituary notices of him in the British papers. With the massive number of wireless messages that were written and waiting to be transmitted, not all of them could be sent.[9]

Boat No. 16 – which carried Master-at-Arms Bailey and Stewardess Violet Jessop – was picked up at 6:45 a.m. As the occupants came aboard, Carpathia's crewmembers gave them drinks of brandy, which Jessop said went down 'like

molten fire'. As she stood there, she still clutched to her chest the infant which Sixth Officer Moody had handed her just before Boat No. 16 lowered away. Just then a woman rushed up, snatched the baby away, and ran off with it.

Jessop, still numb from the cold, wondered why the mother had 'not expressed one word of gratitude for her baby's life'. The stewardess then started the sad search for her friends amongst the survivors; she found a pathetic few. In vain, she searched for 'our dear Tommy Andrews, for the good doctor, for the boys that made life aboard easier for us, for good friends in all departments. But they were all among the missing when the roll was called'.[10]

Boat No. 11 came in around 7:00 a.m. … Then, at around 7:15 a.m., Boat No. 14 – commanded by Fifth Officer Lowe – came sailing up, with Collapsible D in tow. While the occupants of Boat No. 14 were being picked up, Fireman John Thompson was still unconscious in the bottom of the boat. When he woke up, he was safely onboard the Carpathia. He was suffering from a broken arm, frostbite, and burns to his hands. On top of this, his jaw was locked from the cold.[11]

George Rheims had to be lifted aboard the ship, as he couldn't walk or climb the ladder at all. He was carried down to one of the ship's hospitals, and spent the rest of the day and night being treated there.[12] Peter Daly suffered similar injuries, and was taken to the hospital as well. While there, he and Rheims exchanged addresses. Since Rheims had saved him, Daly asked if he could send a picture of himself 'with a dedication fit for the King of England'.[13]

When Richard Norris Williams climbed up the ladder to Carpathia, his legs felt alright. He was immediately taken inside, where he was helped to dry off. He then warmed himself in between an oven and the galley wall. However, in the coming days, his frostbite was found to be so bad that the ship's doctors felt his legs might need to be amputated. Fortunately, Williams refused, and gradually made a full recovery.[14]

Leading Fireman Threlfall, who had held Rhoda Abbott since her rescue from Collapsible A, helped get her aboard. She was in a poor state, and was carried to one of the ship's hospitals, where she was treated for hypothermia, leg contusions, burns, frostbite, and shock.[15] William Mellors was in a similar condition when assistance reached him. Doctor Washington Dodge, who came aboard from Boat No. 13, noted that Mellors was 'very much exhausted'. Dodge took him to the stateroom he had been staying in, and gave Mellors medicine and medical attention.[16] One dead body, that of William Hoyt, was brought aboard Carpathia from the bottom of Boat No. 14.

By that point, lifeboats were starting to arrive several at a time. At 7:30 a.m., Boats Nos 3, 8, and 15 came in and started unloading their passengers. As Boat No. 8 was rowing towards Carpathia, the Countess of Rothes was still at the tiller, aided by her cousin Gladys Cherry. With the swells increasing, and fatigue setting in, it was getting 'very difficult to steer'. Several passengers in No. 8 had to be lifted up to the gangway by a hoist. The Countess later stated: 'I was not at all frightened. Everybody was saying as we left the ship that "she was good for twelve hours yet" and I was too numb to realize the terror of it all until we were safe on board the Carpathia.'[17]

Once the survivors came aboard, the Cunarders' crew took them down to the Dining Saloon for warm drinks and stimulants. Gladys Cherry remarked that 'the women came in unconscious, some hysterical and all more or less collapsed.' Regarding the Carpathia's crew, she said that 'they

Top: *Boat No. 14 sails toward rescue.*

Middle: *Boat No. 14 tows Collapsible D toward* Carpathia.

Bottom: *Collapsible D approaches the Cunard liner.*

were wonderful [with] all they did for us.'[18] Able Bodied Seaman Thomas Jones was extremely complimentary of the Countess of Rothes' hard work in Boat No. 8. As a token of his appreciation, he presented her with the brass number plate from their boat.

It was a case of mutual admiration, and despite having come from two completely separate worlds, the two kept in touch after the disaster, writing to each other periodically. In one letter, the Countess lamented that Jones, an unnamed 'American lady', her cousin Gladys, and she had been the only ones in their boat who wanted to row back to rescue people from the water. She reassured Jones, saying: 'You did all you could, and being my own countryman, I wanted to tell you this.'[19]

When it came time for Maggie Daly and Bertha Mulvihill to board the ship from Boat No. 15, Maggie was only able to climb up the Jacob's ladder with assistance. By then, Bertha, who was in a good deal of pain, was delirious. It had been several hours since *Carpathia* arrived on the scene, but it took a lot of time for all of the boats to be picked up. Bertha could remember just one thing distinctly from the time she was waiting: She watched an ice cake, real or imagined, that was bumping into the side of the boat. 'I watched it, and once, I remember, I laughed when another cake of ice pushed between it and the boat. I must have been ill then.'[20]

Bertha was too weak to climb the ladder, so a sling was lowered and tied around her, and she was hoisted aboard. This brought fresh agony, as the process irritated her rib and back injuries. Once she had gained the deck, Bertha said that *Carpathia*'s crewmembers could not have been any kinder. She was given blankets, food and hot drinks, and

Boat No. 6, with Quartermaster Hichens standing at the tiller, approaches the Carpathia.

a doctor came to check on her. A passenger had offered to give her the use of his cabin, but because of her injuries, she spent most of the voyage to New York laying flat on her back on the deck, which helped alleviate her pain.[21]

Assistant Saloon Steward Walter Nichols said that aboard the *Carpathia*, 'things were pretty crowded … Many of the women stayed in their rooms the whole trip. I heard that Mr Ismay stayed in his cabin all the time.'[22]

Boat No. 4 came in next at around 8:00 a.m., with approximately 60 people aboard. Besides the survivors, the bodies of Able Bodied Seaman William Lyons and Bedroom Steward Sidney Siebert were also removed from the boat and taken aboard *Carpathia*.[23] Trimmer Patrick Dillon was in bad shape when picked up; he, along with some of the other crewmembers who had been fished from the sea, spent a good deal of time in one of the ship's hospitals after being brought onboard.[24] Emily Ryerson later remarked that the 'kindness and the efficience [*sic*, efficiency] of all the arrangements on the *Carpathia* can never be too highly praised'.[25]

Boats Nos 6 and 10 arrived around 8:00 a.m., close to when the occupants of No. 4 were picked up. Shortly after coming aboard, Margaret Brown went to the Dining Saloon; there she saw Quartermaster Hichens in the corner, surrounded by a cluster of people. He was playing the role of the 'brave and heroic seaman', gesticulating wildly, and telling all those present 'what difficulty he had in maintaining discipline among the occupants of the boat'. Looking up, he noticed Margaret and some of the other survivors from Boat No. 6 standing nearby, and 'made a hasty retreat'.[26]

While waiting for Boat No. 10 to get picked up, Second Class passenger Imanita Shelley noticed that the lips of several passengers in the boat were cracked and bleeding. Her initial thoughts were that they had some sort of disease, before touching her hands to her own mouth, and finding that her own lips were bleeding as well. Apparently, the icy temperatures and spray of water had caused their lips to chap and crack. Shelley and some of the others were hoisted aboard via a sling, while some of the babies and small children were hauled up to *Carpathia* in burlap sacks.

Shelley's mother Lutie Parrish had to be taken below to have her injured leg and foot examined in the 'steerage hospital.' Shelley complained that there were a lot of 'foreigners' there, and that a strong smell of antiseptic permeated every-

thing. She was much more positive about the doctors aboard the ship, and 'how hard they worked, unceasingly to do for us.' Shortly after boarding, Shelley went to the wireless cabin and wrote out a message to be delivered to her husband, in order to let him know that she and her mother were all right. Much like what happened to Lawrence Beesley, her message was never sent, probably owing to the large volume of messages that were waiting to be sent.[27] Shelley was bothered by this oversight, as she had paid £1 to have her message sent home, unlike Beesley, who was not charged for his message.

Last in, at around 8:15 a.m., and most heavily loaded of all with around 70 occupants, was lifeboat No. 12. The boat was so overloaded that the *Carpathia*'s crew had some difficulty maneuvering the boat alongside her hull to offload its human cargo. Harold Bride, one of several survivors from Collapsible B who were aboard this boat, attempted to climb the Jacob's ladder. Although his feet pained him terribly, he got to the top, saw hands reaching out to him, and promptly passed out. The next thing Bride knew, he was in a cabin on the ship, and a woman was leaning over him, waving back his hair and rubbing his face. He felt someone at his feet, and also the warm jolt of a shot of liquor as it was administered; then he was carried down to the ship's hospital, where he stayed for a time.[28]

Second Officer Lightoller, who had taken command of No. 12 when he transferred from Collapsible B, saw all the survivors and the apparently dead body out of the lifeboat. Only then did he climb aboard the *Carpathia* himself.[29] The senior surviving officer of the lost *Titanic* was the last survivor to be taken aboard the Cunarder. Immediately afterwards, he met with Captain Rostron.

After speaking with Rostron, Lightoller was taken to a room, where he stripped off his wet clothes so that they could be dried, and climbed into a bunk. He remained there for only half an hour before turning out; thereafter, he wasn't in a bunk or bed again until after the arrival in New York. Lightoller assisted *Carpathia*'s crew and aided the survivors however he could. He had in-depth discussions about the sinking with his fellow surviving officers and Colonel Gracie, among others.[30]

Chief Second Class Steward John Hardy was shocked when he saw Lightoller aboard *Carpathia* the following day. The last time he had seen the Second Officer was when Lightoller had jumped back aboard *Titanic* after being ordered into Collapsible D by Chief Officer Wilde. Up to that moment, Hardy had assumed Lightoller perished.[31]

Besides Harold Bride, several of the other survivors who had been rescued from Collapsible B were also suffering from severe hypothermia. Eugene Daly was unconscious when brought aboard. Several crewmembers carried him to the cabin of Dr Frank Blackmarr, who had volunteered his services and the use of his cabin in aiding the survivors, and placed him in one of the berths. Blackmarr administered stimulants and hot drinks, and slowly Daly came around. As he did, he told the doctor his story in an emotional dumping of thoughts and details. Several times during the retelling, Daly fell back on his pillow 'sobbing and moaning', and saying: 'My God, if I could only forget!' When Daly was feeling better, he was given a heavy blanket in which armholes had been cut to use as clothing until his own clothes were dried out, and he was taken down to the ship's engine room to warm up.[32]

Another survivor who was in poor shape was Saloon Steward Thomas Whiteley. After being brought aboard

Carpathia, Whiteley passed out, and was unconscious for the next two days. While being given medical treatment in one of the ship's hospitals, it was discovered that Whiteley had broken a bone in his leg, had lacerated feet, and was suffering from hypothermia. He remained in the hospital until the arrival in New York.[33] Chief Baker Charles Joughin was in somewhat better shape, although his feet were so swollen that he had to climb up the ladder to *Carpathia* on his knees.[34]

As the lifeboats came in one by one, *Titanic* passengers lined *Carpathia*'s rail, anxiously searching for and desperately hoping to see friends and family coming in the next lifeboat. As he was waiting his turn to board the ship, Colonel Gracie looked up and noticed the faces of several acquaintances and friends who had survived, and he waved at them. Despite being very cold, Gracie had been able to climb up the Jacob's ladder by himself. Once aboard, he went to the Second Class 'dispensary', where he was given a warm reception, and was handed a hot drink. Gracie then went to the Dining Saloon, where his wet clothes were taken to be sent down to the bake oven for drying out. Waiting for his clothes' return, Gracie lay down on the lounge in the corner, underneath a mound of rugs and blankets. He said that 'nothing could exceed the kindness of the ladies, who did everything possible for my comfort.'[35]

In many cases, *Titanic* survivors who were still waiting for their loved ones to be brought aboard would be disappointed; for many wives looking for their husbands came the sad truth that their husbands had gone down with the ship. August Wennerström said that the 'shrieks and cries of the rescued after coming up on *Carpathia* were horrible'. He noticed that some of the women were clothed in robes and wrappers. 'Most of them believed that their husbands had been picked up in some other boat. Mothers called for their children, and children cried for their lost playthings, not understanding that their dads also were gone.'[36]

First Class passenger Alice Silvey was among those who had not grasped the entirety of the situation until aboard the rescue ship. She said that her foremost thought was for the 'poor stokers … I did not think for a moment that any passengers had remained on the ship. I thought the men far down in the hold must have been the only ones to go down.' Only after she was aboard the *Carpathia* did she realize that there had been a great loss of life, including her husband, William. Up until then, she had fully expected that he had been rescued in another lifeboat.[37]

When Jack Thayer had climbed the last rung of the *Carpathia*'s ladder, his mother Marian was standing nearby, and she was 'overjoyed' to see him. Unfortunately, her joy quickly turned to sadness as she realized that her husband John was not with her son, as she had assumed he would be. In fact, Jack hadn't seen his father since being separated from his parents during the sinking.[38]

While some of the survivors still clung to the false hope that another ship had picked up their loved ones, for most the truth really began to sink in. Wennerström, Thayer, and the others who had struggled for their lives in the water, and on the collapsibles, were all too aware of the horrible reality of what had happened. As Wennerström put it, 'we few, who had went down with *Titanic* and had been around the place during the whole night and with our own eyes saw them all die, knew that no other boat had been around and that all who were saved was [*sic*] on the *Carpathia* – but we never said it, we let them keep the hope. Many never knew the truth before they landed in New York.'[39]

Thanks to Captain Rostron's quick-witted orders to his own crew, the *Carpathia*'s crew had been fully prepared to care for the *Titanic*'s survivors. The Cunarder's crew tried to get survivors off the deck and herd them below into the Dining Saloons, to give them food and drink, and then to find warm sleeping quarters. Many of the generous *Carpathia* passengers offered to share their cabins with survivors, and some even completely gave over the use of their cabins to the survivors; they chose instead to sleep on steamer chairs in the Smoking Room.[40] Rostron's orders had specified that *Carpathia*'s own Third Class passengers were to be grouped together, to make as much room for the survivors as possible. Even so, many of *Titanic*'s passengers had to find places to sleep in the *Carpathia*'s common rooms.[41]

Complicating matters, however, was the fact that due to immigration laws, the survivors would have to be separated by class, just as they had been on *Titanic*. Yet some exceptions were made when passengers of different classes had to be berthed together in the hospitals for medical treatment. Such was the case with Lutie Parrish, a Second Class passenger on *Titanic*, who was given a bed in the hospital for *Carpathia*'s Third Class passengers. Once everyone was aboard, Saloon Steward Alexander Littlejohn said that he and other surviving stewards 'set to work looking after the passengers as though on our own ship'.[42]

Captain Rostron later remarked at the stoicism of *Titanic*'s survivors as they were brought aboard: 'As each boat came alongside everyone was calm, and they kept perfectly still in their boats. They were quiet and orderly, and each person came up the ladder, or was pulled up, in turn as they were told off. There was no confusion whatever among the passengers. They behaved magnificently – every one of them.'[43]

After all the boats were unloaded, Captain Rostron lowered the ship's falls, and hauled seven of *Titanic*'s lifeboats aboard using the davits. The crew used the forward cargo cranes to haul six more boats on to the Forecastle, making a total of thirteen boats recovered. Of the boats that came alongside *Carpathia*, five were set adrift – Boat Nos 4, 14, and 15, as well as Collapsibles C and D. These boats joined Collapsibles A and B, which had been set adrift earlier after their occupants were rescued by other *Titanic* lifeboats.[44]

As this process was being completed, the Leyland Line ship *Californian* arrived on the scene, having cut through the ice field to the west. Once in communication, Rostron 'gave them the notes' via semaphore about *Titanic* having sunk. Owing to some confusion, Rostron and some of his crew were unsure whether all of *Titanic*'s lifeboats had been accounted for; Rostron thus told Captain Lord: 'Think one boat still unaccounted for.' Lord asked if he should search around, and Rostron replied, 'Yes, please.'[45] However, all of the work had already been done, and there was no one left to rescue from the water.

By 8:30 a.m., all of the survivors had been taken aboard. Captain Rostron called for his Purser. After consulting with Bruce Ismay – who 'left everything in my hands' – Rostron told the Purser to hold a service, 'a short prayer of thankfulness for those rescued and a short burial service for those who were lost'. Rostron asked one of *Carpathia*'s passengers, who was an Episcopal clergyman, to lead the service, which he did willingly.[46]

While this service was being performed, Rostron maneuvered his ship around the wreck site, double checking for any more survivors. He spotted nothing except for debris, and a lone body floating approximately 100 yards off,

Hoisting one of the lifeboats aboard the deck.

held up by a life preserver. The person bore the appearance of being a crewmember, and he was lying on his side, with his head awash. The body was not recovered, as Rostron did not want to cause any more excitement or hysteria among the survivors than was absolutely necessary. No other bodies were visible to *Carpathia,* or the *Californian* for that matter; they had apparently drifted away from the wreckage due to the local current and the wind which had sprung up that morning.[47]

Rostron continued his search for approximately a half hour.[48] He then asked the *Californian* to continue the search for any survivors on rafts or wreckage, and turned his ship to the southwest. He sailed on for some 56 miles before being able to get around the ice, and then he turned and headed west for New York.

Rostron stopped in to speak with Bruce Ismay in his cabin, and suggested that Ismay contact White Star to notify them about the disaster. Ismay wrote on a scrap of paper:

> Deeply regret advise you *Titanic* sank this morning after collision with iceberg, resulting in serious loss of life. Full particulars later. Bruce Ismay.[49]

Captain Rostron took the message to the Marconi office, and had Harold Cottam transmit it to New York. Cottam had been on duty since the previous night, and despite being fatigued, showed no signs of wanting to turn in. There were many critical messages to be sent and received, and

more were piling up as time went on – including those from survivors trying to let their relatives know they were alive.

Ismay was extremely eager for *Titanic's* surviving crewmembers to be sent back to England as soon as possible after arriving in New York. He sent several wireless messages to Phillip Albright Small Franklin, Vice-President and General Manager of International Mercantile Marine, on April 17. Through the course of these messages, he used the rather obvious code name of 'Yamsi,' or Ismay spelled backwards, to convey the following directive:

> Very important you should hold *Cedric* daylight Friday for *Titanic's* crew. Answer. YAMSI.[50]

Later that same day, Ismay sent an additional wireless to Franklin, which made it clear that he personally intended to return to England early in the morning of April 19, following *Carpathia's* projected late arrival on the night of April 18:

> Most desirable *Titanic* crew aboard *Carpathia* should be returned home earliest moment possible. Suggest you hold *Cedric,* sailing her daylight Friday, unless you see any reason contrary. Propose returning in her myself. Please send outfit of clothes, including shoes, for me to *Cedric.* Have nothing of my own. Please reply. YAMSI.[51]

Several other messages repeating this request were sent. Franklin responded by wireless to Ismay, saying that they had arranged for *Titanic's* crew to sail home aboard the *Lapland* on that Saturday, and that they all considered it 'most unwise' to delay the *Cedric* given the circumstances.

Following the sinking, Ismay was criticized, as it appeared that he had planned to flee the United States and hurry the surviving crewmembers out of the country before a formal inquiry into the sinking could be organized there. Ismay himself denied that was ever his intention, saying he was unaware that there would even be an inquiry held in the United States. Ismay did know that an inquiry was sure to be held by the British Board of Trade, however, and wanted to be back in England for it.[52]

When Second Officer Lightoller testified in the Senate Inquiry, he claimed that it was his idea that the *Cedric* be delayed to take the survivors back to England as quickly as possible, and that he suggested this to Ismay. According to him, the thought was to get them back to their families, to where an inquiry was sure to be held, and to where new jobs would be available. Whether Lightoller's claim was truthful, or simply an attempt to protect his employer, is unknown.[53]

Rostron had one last sad task to perform. While recovering the lifeboats earlier in the day, the bodies of three or four dead men had been brought aboard from the boats. Reportedly, one of the four men may have been alive when brought aboard, but that he subsequently succumbed to hypothermia. At around 4:00 p.m., these four individuals were buried at sea from the deck.[54]

Lists of the *Titanic* survivors were prepared by the *Carpathia's* officers; they were assisted in this effort by *Titanic's* Second Officer Lightoller and Steward John Hardy; they also helped prepare the list of *Titanic's* surviving crew. When these lists were circulated, Imanita Shelley was greatly disturbed to see that her stewardess from aboard *Titanic* was among the missing.[55]

Icebergs photographed from the Carpathia *that morning.*

The lists of survivors were taken to Cottam, who was still on duty in the Marconi Room, for transmission. However, Cottam had then been up for over 24 hours straight, and was close to collapse, even though he continued sending messages. Captain Rostron appealed to Harold Bride for help, saying that Cottam was getting 'queer'. Bride was still recuperating from his injuries in *Carpathia*'s hospital. Despite this, he readily agreed to help, but had to be carried to the Marconi Shack. He assisted Cottam until *Carpathia* reached New York.

Cottam had been extremely busy. He had worked the wireless all day and night Sunday, all day and night Monday, and all day Tuesday; he finally fell asleep at the instrument for a mere three hours late Tuesday night. Waking up in the same uncomfortable position early Wednesday morning, he immediately resumed sending messages until Bride relieved him late Wednesday afternoon. All told, Cottam believed he only got eight to ten hours of sleep between the time the *Carpathia* arrived at the scene of the wreck, and the time she arrived in New York on Thursday, April 18.[56]

The number of messages that Cottam and Bride had to deal with was staggering. In addition to sending out the 712 survivor names, one by one, there were service messages going out from Captain Rostron; there were also incoming inquiries from dozens of newspapers, and from friends and relatives of the dead and the survivors, asking for details; there were also outgoing personal messages from the survivors themselves, telling their friends and families that they were safe. In this tremendous crush, an incoming message from United States President William Howard Taft, asking for information about his military aide, Archibald Butt, was received. According to *Carpathia*'s Chief Purser Ernest Brown, the response was a Marconigram stating simply: 'Not on board'. Captain Rostron's instruction to the Marconi operators was that transmitting the survivor lists, and the personal messages from survivors, were to take priority.

On her way west, *Carpathia* ran into rainy and stormy weather, followed by a thick fog on Wednesday, April 18. This forced her to slow down for safety purposes. During the voyage, *Titanic*'s survivors – cramped into small spaces aboard the rescuing liner – had nothing to do but discuss their lot. As a result, a number of wild – and a few not so wild – rumors began to circulate: that Captain Smith, Chief Of-

ficer Wilde, First Officer Murdoch, or Chief Engineer Bell had shot themselves;[57] that the lookouts had sighted several icebergs before the one they actually struck, and that the ship still had not slowed down;[58] and that Major Butt had entered into a pact with Colonel Astor and George Widener to shoot them, and then himself, before the ship sank.[59]

Some of the survivors – led by Dr Henry Frauenthal, Margaret Brown, and Martha Stone – formed a committee to honor the brave crewmen of the *Carpathia* who had saved them. They collected funds from the survivors, and by the time they reached New York, over $4,000 was raised and distributed among the crew. Captain Rostron was given $500, and the rest of the officers and crewmembers were given amounts ranging from $5 to $100 – even $5 was a significant amount of money at the time. Once in port, the fund eventually raised over $15,000, and was turned over to J. P. Morgan & Company for safekeeping.[60]

* * * * *

As could have been expected, once the news that the *Titanic* had sunk hit the United States and Great Britain, the newspapers picked it up. They splashed the story all over their front pages in giant block text. The first reports were hopeful, and instilled a false sense of relief. One newspaper, for example, dedicated its entire first page to the 'near disaster', announcing: 'All *Titanic* Passengers are Safe.' They claimed that everyone was transferred aboard the *Virginian* by lifeboat. This paper also claimed that the *Virginian* was 'Towing Great Disabled Liner Into Halifax.'[61] Another paper had headlines declaring: '*Titanic*'s Passengers are Transhipped.' Also: 'All Saved from *Titanic* after Collision.'[62]

Other papers described this imaginary North Atlantic version of a Chinese Fire Drill in even greater detail, claiming that all the passengers were safe. Inconsistently, some papers claimed that the passengers had, in fact, been transferred to the *Carpathia* or *Parisian*, not the *Virginian*. Since a passenger train had already been dispatched to pick up survivors who were expected to land in Halifax, it was forced to turn around and head back to New York, where those two ships were due to arrive. The confusion and worry these rumors must have caused passengers' families is unimaginable. It added to the uncertainty, and eventually

to the sadness, as many had believed their loved ones were safe before learning the truth.

Initially, *The New York Times* was the only paper to run an accurate headline about the situation, reporting: 'New Liner *Titanic* Hits Iceberg; Sinking By Bow At Midnight.'[63] Their first headline met with heavy criticism from the other papers, which did not believe *Titanic* had sunk. Only later did the rest catch up and begin reporting the reality of the disaster. More dreary headlines, such as: 'Hope for more *Titanic* Survivors Faint' and, 'Only about 800 Rescued from *Titanic*', began to run from the presses.[64]

Captain Haddock of the *Olympic* was of the opinion that these false rumors were attributable to garbled wireless messages. He fervently denied that his ship sent or received any misleading or false reports stating *Titanic* was safe.

Haddock noted that at 1:35 p.m. on April 15, *Olympic* had received a wireless message asking: 'Are all *Titanic* passengers safe?' Two hours earlier, they had received a wireless message from the ship *Asian,* mentioning that they had heard *Titanic* signaling Cape Race, then later sending SOS calls; the message also passed along *Titanic*'s distress coordinates and reported that the *Asian* was west of *Titanic,* and was then towing an oil tanker to Halifax. Somehow in the rush of messages, Haddock believed amateur wireless operators had confused the information from these messages, leading to the false headlines.[65]

Even White Star Line officials had not been immune to the false headlines and reports. By 10:30 a.m. on Monday morning, Phillip A. S. Franklin, Vice-President and General Manager of International Mercantile Marine, was

---

Top: *Survivors on* Carpathia's *forward deck.*

Above left: *Survivors on deck, braced against the cold in steamer rugs.*

Above right: *Looking down on survivors from* Carpathia's *upper decks. In the upper right hand corner, the survivors from Boat No. 1 can be seen posing for their group photograph.*

overwhelmed with visitors and phone calls to the White Star Line office in New York City. Believing the reassuring reports in the press, Franklin was optimistic. He stated that rumors *Titanic* had sunk were preposterous ... that the cessation of the ship's wireless signals was not uncommon ... that the situation was due to nothing more than 'atmospheric interference'. He stated that the White Star Line placed 'absolute confidence in the *Titanic*. We believe the boat is unsinkable.'

Franklin continued to stay optimistic throughout the day, despite a growing list of reasons to believe that the situation was not as positive as he insisted. The office was continuously swamped with callers and visitors. Franklin admitted that *Carpathia* might have had some of *Titanic's* passengers aboard, but that they had not yet heard from the *Parisian*, which he felt may also have rescued some survivors.

out to control the situation. Franklin later admitted that he held back on the news because it was 'discouraging'.[69] People in the crowd were weeping. Relatives of passengers on the ship were storming the White Star Line offices *en masse*, hoping to get news regarding their loved ones.

Vincent Astor – Colonel Astor's son – accompanied by A. J. Biddle, was one of the earliest to arrive. After speaking with White Star Line officials, he came out and 'buried his face in his hands and sobbed'. He had been told that his stepmother Madeleine Astor was known to be among the saved, but that the worst was feared for his father, whose name was missing from the list of survivors sent from *Carpathia*. Another visitor at the offices was a White House attaché, who had been dispatched by President Taft to get news of the President's military aide and close friend, Major Archibald Butt. He too left with doubtful news.[70]

Crowds gather outside the Manhattan offices of the International Mercantile Marine and White Star Line at 9 Broadway, across from Bowling Green Park. Although the revolving door has been replaced, this building still stands, and as of this writing houses an electronics store.

As reporters continued to press him, the beleaguered Vice-President finally admitted that there had been 'a terrible loss of life'. At 4:35 p.m., a wireless operator atop Wanamaker's Department Store at the corner of 9th Avenue and Broadway finally overheard a wireless message from the *Olympic*. It was earth-shatteringly clear, stating that *Titanic* had sunk with great loss of life, and that 675 survivors were aboard *Carpathia*.[66]

Despite this news, Franklin continued to hold out hope, saying: 'We are hopeful that the rumors which reached us by telegraph from Halifax that there are passengers aboard the *Virginian* and *Parisian* will prove to be true. It is the loss of life that makes this thing so awful. We can replace the money loss but not the lives of those who went down.' Then, at 8:20 p.m., he acknowledged that it was likely that the only survivors were those aboard *Carpathia*.[67]

By midnight, Franklin wept openly. He said: 'I thought her unsinkable, and I based my opinion on the best expert advice. I do not understand it.'[68]

Later, as the size of the 'excited' crowds outside of the White Star Line office grew, police officers were called

As news of the true scope of the disaster spread around the globe, family members and friends continued to clamor for any news on the fate of their loved ones. Huge crowds grew outside the White Star Line office in London, clamoring for the latest information, and the crowd outside the company's New York offices continued to grow. Names of survivors were posted as they were received. Many families had already seen their relatives' names on the lists of survivors that were being sent by telegraph from *Carpathia* and which were then published in the papers. However, these lists were rife with errors; some individuals who had perished, such as Sixth Officer James Moody, were actually at first listed as survivors;[71] others, who actually survived, were listed as victims. It must have been a tortuous few days as all awaited confirmation. In a cruel trick of fate, some were given false hopes.

Margaret Brown's brother, Daniel Tobin of Denver, Colorado, had traveled to Chicago when word of the *Titanic* disaster hit the papers. He kept a constant vigil outside of the White Star Line offices there. When a report came in that his sister's name was on the list of passengers taken on

Top left: *Crowds also gather outside White Star's Southampton offices, anxious for news of survivors.*

Top right: *Outside the London offices of the White Star Line, newsboys try to sell papers featuring the story of the disaster.*

Left: *Edith Gracie, daughter of Archibald Gracie.*

and resolve, writing a heartfelt letter of condolence to the family members and friends of the other victims. On April 18, her message was posted outside of the White Star Line offices in London:

> To my poor fellow sufferers: My heart overflows with grief for you all and is laden with sorrow that you are weighed down with this terrible burden that has been thrust upon us. May God be with us and comfort us all. Yours in deep sympathy, Eleanor Smith.[75]

* * * * *

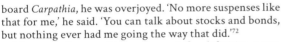

board *Carpathia*, he was overjoyed. 'No more suspenses like that for me,' he said. 'You can talk about stocks and bonds, but nothing ever had me going the way that did.'[72]

Many relatives would have to wait for definitive news. What Colonel Gracie's daughter Edith had heard so far was positive, but it was not definitive. She said: 'I am hoping that what they told me is true, and that father is safe, but I am not sure yet whether it is true. The message I received concerning father's safety said he was probably one of the survivors. It did not state decidedly that he was saved. Therefore, I am hoping for the best, but have been in constant fear that something has happened to him and will be until I see him.' She proceeded to New York to wait for the *Carpathia* to come in. Her mother – who was said to be close to a nervous breakdown – and other relatives would meet up with her there.[73]

At the offices of the *Chicago Daily News*, G. Woodward, Charles Joughin's brother-in-law, made inquiries about his relative's fate. Like so many others, he was forced to wait for reliable news. He was told that the names of crewmembers who had lost their lives had not yet been made public. Woodward remarked that 'my brother-in-law has been in the White Star service for fifteen years. About two weeks ago I received a letter from him saying he had been sent from the *Olympic* to the *Titanic*. His home is in Southampton, England, and he has a wife and two children there.'[74] Eventually, he would receive the joyous news of Charles' survival.

Other survivors had not received good news. A grief-stricken Eleanor Smith already knew that her husband, Captain Smith, was not among those picked up by *Carpathia*. Despite this, she demonstrated extraordinary strength

Back aboard the *Carpathia* the weather had turned bad, and the ship had to sail through a storm and rather rough seas. Bertha Mulvihill was terrified that the *Carpathia* might sink, and a number of other survivors were similarly alarmed.[76] Down in the 'steerage hospital', Imanita Shelley and her mother Lutie Parrish both had similar concerns, and tried to ward off 'awful nausea which began to take hold of us, for after the *Carpathia* had picked us up we had the worst kind of weather, the sea devils evidently mad at the idea of any of us escaping their clutches.'[77]

Weather was not the worst of what Imanita Shelley and her mother had experienced while aboard the *Carpathia*. During the first night aboard, one female survivor in the ship's Third Class hospital, apparently hysterical, tried to throw herself overboard. She was prevented from doing so by several people nearby. Angry, she stood at the foot of Lutie Parrish's bed with an improvised club, and announced that she was going to kill her. Mrs Parrish was helpless to defend herself due to her injured foot and leg. Seeing no one nearby to help her mother, Imanita tried to distract the woman. She turned and said: 'You are another one that won't let me dies [sic], and I'll fix you, too.'

Shelley responded as best she could: 'No, I want to help you. If you want to commit suicide, you have a perfect right to.'

The woman immediately changed her attitude, telling Shelley how glad she was that at least one person onboard the *Carpathia* was her friend. Shelley told her that if she wanted to jump overboard, then she 'ought to do it in a ladylike manner, and that no lady would try to jump overboard without an escort'. The woman agreed, begging her to find

Above: Carpathia *steams past her own pier to that which would have been used by* Titanic, *had she not sunk. There, she offloads the thirteen lifeboats she picked up from the wreck site.*

Right: Titanic's *lifeboats in Pier 59, with* Carpathia's *hull in the background.*

a man to assist her in this task. Shelley 'at once called the steward and he in turn called another man and they escorted her to the doctor's, and we never saw her any more'.

For the remainder of the voyage, Shelley assisted her mother and others who were in the hospital. Shelley fancied herself a translator, claiming that since so few of the Steerage passengers in the Third Class hospital spoke English, a stewardess had come to her, begging for help in making herself understood. Shelley, who only spoke English, claimed that she could make the 'foreigners' understand her simply by 'pitching' her voice, using the 'inflect and accent' of the person that she was trying to speak to, and imitating their manner of speech. She claimed that she was able to make the Spanish, Italian, Hungarian, and French speaking steerage passengers alike all understand her by using this method. She also claimed that 'if one were able to get *en rapport* with the spirit of any language it was not necessary to know the actual words.' Somehow, it seems more likely that the individuals to which she referred actually spoke some English, and that her 'ingenious' method was not quite as intelligent as it appeared to be.[78]

By the time the *Carpathia* passed Ambrose Lightship on the approach to New York Harbor late on Thursday, April 18, it was raining. Many small boats surrounded the single-funnel steamship, carrying reporters who eagerly hunted for any stories they could get from the survivors. They shouted up to the *Titanic* survivors lining the railings, asking for information. Using flares to light the sky, they attempted to get photographs of them too. Some reporters had even bribed their way aboard the pilot vessel *New York* and attempted to climb the ladder up to the *Carpathia*'s deck, but were turned back by *Carpathia*'s officers. One reporter

did actually make it on board, but was corralled by the crew, taken to Captain Rostron, and detained on the bridge until *Carpathia* tied up at the dock.[79]

While these reporters were prevented from boarding *Carpathia*, by a strange coincidence, there were already some aboard. Carlos Hurd, one of *Carpathia*'s passengers, just happened to be a reporter for the *St. Louis Post Dispatch*. Captain Rostron attempted to protect the privacy of the survivors by preventing communication between them and either Hurd or his wife. Despite this, Hurd managed to conduct several dozen interviews. As the *Carpathia* was entering New York Harbor, Hurd wrapped up his interview notes in a makeshift waterproof package, and then threw it down to a boat that had come alongside. His notes were rushed to the office of the *New York World*, where they were among the earliest published stories that featured actual eyewitness information.[80]

Once inside New York Harbor, the *Carpathia* passed the Battery at Manhattan's southern tip ... it was mobbed by a throng of over 10,000 people who stood in the rain to catch their first glimpse of the tiny Cunarder. *Carpathia* surprised everyone by passing her own pier, No. 54, and continued up the North River to the White Star piers, 59 and 60. There she offloaded the thirteen lifeboats she had recovered from the scene of the disaster. This was an unimaginably eerie sight, and one filled with tragic meaning. They were all that remained of the great ship ... of everything she had

Crowds gathered in lower Manhattan by the Cunard Line docks, awaiting the Carpathia's *arrival.*

been, these little boats were all that had completed the voyage.[81]

For hours before the *Carpathia* arrived, crowds had been gathering at the Cunard pier at the end of Fourteenth Street. Some of these people were there to find family or friends who survived the sinking ... some were just there to see what they could see ... others were newspapermen, looking for a good story. In anticipation of the large crowds, New York Mayor Gaynor and Police Commissioner Waldo arranged for a heavy police presence at and near the pier. They appointed Inspector George McClusky to take charge of crowd control, and assigned him 200 policemen, including a dozen mounted police and a number of officers in civilian clothing. Police cordons were set up hours in advance of the anticipated arrival, in preparation to control the crowds that were sure to show up, and to keep out those who did not bear passes from either the government or the Cunard Line.[82]

All possible preparations had been made to aid the survivors. The Municipal Lodging House, which could accommodate 700 people, agreed to provide food and lodging to the survivors for as long as they needed it. The Red Cross and Salvation Army were also prepared to help survivors in this regard. Eva Booth, director of the Salvation Army, waited at the pier to personally oversee things. When all was said and done, Mayor Gaynor estimated that more than 5,000 persons could be accommodated in the lodgings that were offered up, far in excess of what was needed. R. H. Farley, head of the White Star Line's Third Class Department, said that the line would provide all the steerage passengers with railroad tickets to their intended destinations.[83]

By the time the *Carpathia* finished unloading *Titanic's* lifeboats, and returned to her own berth, the crowd at Pier 54 was estimated to have swelled to over 30,000 people. None of them were deterred by the rain and poor weather. There was a long line of automobiles waiting on the pier. Besides family members of survivors who were waiting to drive their relatives home, the Waldorf-Astoria had sent over eight limousines to take the following survivors, among others, back to the hotel: Mary Fortune and her three daughters, Mary Smith, Ella White, Orian Davidson, Mahala Douglas, Eleanor Widener and her maid Amalie Gieger, Mary Wick and her daughter Mary, Caroline Bonnell, Emily Ryerson and her children, John and Mary Snyder, and Dickinson and Helen Bishop.

At one point, there were 35 ambulances outside the Cunard pier, representing every hospital in Manhattan, Brooklyn, and the Bronx. St Vincent's Hospital sent the largest number, eight in total, and St Luke's had also sent several. Similarly, Mrs Virginia Fair Vanderbilt had convinced her friends to lend their automobiles to be used to meet the *Carpathia*, and help transport survivors who needed medical treatment. Through her efforts alone, multiple limousines and all the Fifth Avenue and Riverside Drive automobile buses were waiting near the pier.[84]

By 9:30 p.m. the liner was docked, and the forward and aft gangways were put out. Reporters hurried to get their cameras and equipment set up, in order to take photographs of the scene. Some of the survivors who were in poor condition were hurried down the gangway first, and into waiting ambulances. One of these was Thomas Whiteley, who was carried down the gangway in pajamas, and whisked off.[85]

Among the first passengers down the gangway to shore were survivors from First Class.

Dr Isaac Frauenthal and his wife were immediately taken into an automobile to leave the pier. As they were hurrying toward the vehicle, a reporter eager to settle a rumor which had been circulating asked Dr Frauenthal if Madeleine Astor had indeed died aboard the ship. 'That is not true,' the doctor responded. 'Mrs Astor was well yesterday.'

Next down the gangway were Mrs Malvina Cornell and her sisters, Charlotte Appleton and Caroline Brown. They were met by Mr Cornell, who bundled them away. Soon afterwards, Madeleine Astor, who was wearing a white sweater, was escorted to the pier by two of the *Carpathia's* officers. William A. Dobbyn, Colonel Astor's personal secretary, had been waiting on the pier all evening, and spotted her. Also waiting for her were her stepson Vincent Astor – her *senior* by about a year and a half – as well as her sister Katherine Force, some friends, and two physicians, including Dr Kimball. Preparations had been made to take her back to Colonel Astor's house at 840 Fifth Avenue.[86]

After greeting his stepmother, Vincent sprinted toward his automobile. It was a large, black limousine sitting at the front of the line of cars; two other automobiles, driven to the pier by other members of their group, sat nearby as escorts. Astor cranked the engine to start it and jumped into the driver's seat. As he did so, a reporter asked how Madeleine was. 'I am delighted to say that she is far better than I expected to find her,' was his response. When asked if he had heard any other good news, he said: 'I have not yet dared to ask Mrs Astor any questions.' Someone asked if there had been any news of Colonel Astor, to which he said 'no'.

Meanwhile, Madeleine was emotionally overwhelmed. She was alternately described as 'hysterical' and 'upon the point of collapse'. Her sister was forced to support her, and helped her to a bench inside the building. Katherine was overheard asking: 'Have you heard from anyone else?' Madeleine said no, and then began weeping again. It took her five minutes to regain her composure, at which point she said she was ready to be taken to the waiting limousine. Once she had climbed in, she was driven off. Later, reporters were told that she wasn't suffering from a serious condition, but 'was suffering greatly from shock and grief'.[87] Following this nearly carnival scene, the Duff Gordons were spotted leaving *Carpathia*.

A bit later, the Second Class passengers left the ship and the pier. Lutie Parrish was carried to a waiting ambulance that was headed to Mount Sinai Hospital; her daughter Imanita Shelley also climbed in. Acquiescing to their begging, the driver let the women stop at the King Edward Hotel first – to allow Shelley to pick up letters from her husband – before taking Mrs Parrish to the hospital. Fortunately, it was discovered that Mrs Parrish's foot and leg were not broken, but just very badly bruised. With rest, she would make a full recovery.[88]

It was around 11:00 p.m. before the Third Class passengers began to disembark. Eugene Daly had to be helped off the ship due to his frostbitten feet. As the Third Class passengers started down the gangway, Bertha Mulvihill was told that she was to be taken to the hospital. She didn't want to go … all she wanted was to see her family. She got off the ship and ran into the crowd on the pier, not knowing if any of her family was there. Since her return to America was a surprise, she didn't think that her fiancé Henry knew she was coming. However, by a quirk of fate, her family had

Two female passengers descend the gangplank and reach shore for the first time since leaving Europe a week before.

found out that she was aboard, and both her fiancé and her brother-in-law Ted were waiting for her when she came ashore.

Bertha's sister Mary described the circumstances in which the family had discovered she was on the ill-fated ship: 'We didn't know she was aboard at all until Henry read her name among those saved in the *Evening Bulletin* Tuesday night … He was reading the list of those on the boat when his eyes came up Bert's [Bertha's nickname] name. He nearly fainted. Then he rushed over to my house … [and] told my husband and me that Bert was on the *Titanic*.'

When Bertha saw her two loved ones waiting for her, she was overcome with joy. After a joyous greeting, they rushed her over to Grand Central Station to start the journey back to Providence, Rhode Island. During the trip home, Bertha broke down crying as she recounted her experiences. Once home, a doctor from Providence City Hospital treated her injuries, and told her she must eat sparingly and only liquid foods. He wouldn't allow her to sleep right away 'for fear that during her sleep she would review the scenes of the disaster, and upon waking, would not be right in the mind.' Bertha's sister sent a cablegram home to their mother in Ireland on April 19, 1912, conveying the simple message: 'Bertha safe – Mary.'[89]

Finally, the *Titanic's* crew were taken off the *Carpathia*. They were put aboard the U.S. Immigration Service Tender *George Starr*, to be taken north to Pier 60. Debarking there, they were put aboard the Red Star Line's *Lapland* as Phillip A. S. Franklin had arranged, and were assigned cabins, in preparation for being sent back home to Britain.[90]

Before all the crew and passengers of the *Titanic* had left the rescue ship, several purposeful-looking men boarded *Carpathia*. Senator William Alden Smith and Senator Francis G. Newlands were directed to the cabin where White Star Chairman Bruce Ismay had been in seclusion for the entire trip back to New York. Captain Rostron had only escorted Phillip A. S. Franklin down to Ismay's room about ten minutes before news reached him that Senator Smith was aboard.[91] Ismay had already attempted to make arrangements to leave the United States aboard the *Cedric* shortly after they were due to arrive in New York; additionally, in many of the newspapers, Ismay had come off as the scapegoat of the disaster. Senator Smith wanted to make sure that Ismay, and the crew of *Titanic*, were questioned before they could leave the country. Left with no choice in the matter, Ismay agreed to Smith's demand that he and the other witnesses would remain and give evidence.

One of the first things Ismay did after arriving in New York was to issue instructions that no International Mercantile Marine ships were to leave port without a sufficient number of boats to accommodate every person on board.[92] The other major shipping companies had also voluntarily decided to provide enough boats for everyone aboard their ships, and did so without any rulings by the British Board of Trade. The decision by the companies was announced by Sydney Buxton in the House of Commons on April 23, 1912.[93]

The next men to board *Carpathia* were the head of the Marconi International Marine Communication Company, Guglielmo Marconi, and Jim Speers, a reporter from *The New York Times*. Both men were there to speak with Harold Bride. Shortly before *Carpathia* docked at the Cunard pier, Harold Bride and Harold Cottam had received wireless messages sent from Seagate Station, at the Narrows, New York Harbor. These had been sent by Frederick M. Sammis, Chief Engineer of the Marconi Company. The first message said: 'Say, old man, Marconi Co. taking good care of you. Keep your mouth shut and hold your story. It is fixed for you so you will get big money. Do your best to clear [the remaining messages].' Guglielmo Marconi himself had agreed that Bride and Cottam should be allowed to sell the exclusive report of their personal experiences. It was known that the two Marconi operators were exhausted, and it was thought that if they were given this news, 'maybe it will spur them on and make them feel better.' Shortly after the first message, another wireless message was received, telling the men: 'Arranged for your exclusive story for dollars in four figures. Mr Marconi agreeing. Say nothing until you see me …' The exact amount being offered was $1,000 overall for both men's stories.[94]

After Marconi and Speers boarded *Carpathia,* they found Bride sitting in the wireless room with his bandaged and injured feet propped up. He was still transmitting messages, trying to help Harold Cottam clear the large mass of them which had built up during the *Carpathia's* voyage to New York. Cottam himself had already left the ship at Mr Sammis' request, and would subsequently meet him at the Strand Hotel, presumably to dictate his story to a *New York Times* reporter there. Bride was so absorbed in his work that he didn't even notice the two men come in. His skin was drawn so tightly over his face that the bones in his face protruded, and his eyes appeared sunken-in. To Speers, Bride's face looked 'spiritual, one which might be expected in a painting'. Marconi listened to what Bride was sending for a moment, before saying: 'That's hardly worth sending now, boy.'

Bride looked up, and immediately recognized the famous inventor, who was a personal hero of sorts. He held out his hand, which Marconi grasped and held warmly. Bride said: 'Mr Marconi, Phillips is dead. He's gone.' Marconi offered some words of comfort, and in addition to congratulating Bride on his survival and thanking him for his hard work and assistance, he told Bride that if he was offered money for his story, he should take it. The Marconi Company, not White Star, were the employers of Bride. Speers, taking out his notepad and pencil, confirmed that the *New York Times*

was willing to pay Bride $500 for his story. Bride agreed, dictating the story of his survival. When published on April 19, 1912, Bride's account filled five columns on the front page of the *New York Times*.[95]

That night, the crowds eventually dispersed. Pier 54 finally became nearly deserted. Only a few people were left behind to clear up the debris and dirt from the near mob-scene. Crowd control gates were removed and stored away. Soon, all tell-tale traces of the epic scene which had played out on the new Cunard pier had been removed. It was almost as if nothing unusual had ever occurred there …

The *Carpathia's* own passengers, who along with the crew had been so helpful to the *Titanic's* survivors during the preceding four days, were encouraged to go ashore while the *Carpathia* was cleaned and loaded with supplies. By 4:00 p.m. on April 19, the plucky little Cunarder was headed back to sea to complete her voyage to the Mediterranean, a voyage which had been so unimaginably interrupted by the disaster. There were a 'small army of sightseers' at the pier to see *Carpathia* off, and they cheered the ship as she got under way. The vessel's flag was at half mast, as were all the flags visible from the pier.[96]

Shortly before *Carpathia* headed back to sea, there was still one member of *Titanic's* crew who had not yet left: Harold Bride, who had continued working the wireless due to the backlog of messages. Because of Bride's badly sprained ankle and frostbitten feet, he had to be carried ashore on the shoulders of two of *Carpathia's* officers.

According to press reports, over 140 of the survivors were transported to area hospitals for treatment, after their arrival in New York. Most of these survivors had very minor injuries, or had suffered from exposure or shock, and all were expected to recover.[97] Very few were seriously injured enough that a lengthy hospital stay was required, but over 100 had been taken to St Vincent's Hospital.[98] Among these were Harold Bride, Fireman John Thompson, Trimmer William McIntyre, Saloon Steward Thomas Whiteley, First Class passenger Peter Daly, Second Class passenger Emilio Pallas y Castillo, as well as Third Class passengers Rhoda Abbott, Thomas McCormack, and Anna Kelly. Several other survivors, including George Rheims and Bertha Mulvihill, were supposed to have been taken to the hospital, but instead sought medical care from family doctors or practitioners elsewhere.

While the survivors were resting and recovering in St Vincent's Hospital, Cardinal John Farley canceled any celebrations of his seventieth birthday, which was on April 20, in order to visit those who were hospitalized. He spent over an hour comforting the survivors, and for 'each he had a word of consolation'. Afterwards, the Cardinal returned to his home, where it was said 'it was evident that he was greatly saddened.'

He remarked that 'it was indeed an appalling disaster and one that is hard to look back on,' and paid tribute to the men and women who had died, saying that 'the splendid bravery which they showed was something that the world will never cease to admire … especially the men who gave up their lives that women might be rescued … There were the women who refused to go into the lifeboats too, who preferred to remain and face death with their husbands. These are some of the cases which should prove an inspiration to the world. The resignation with which they awaited death was truly Christian. There was no panic, no wild despair. They felt that they were in the hands of God, and

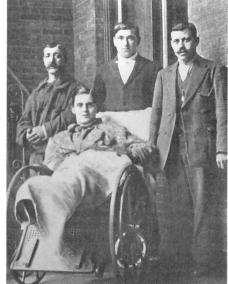

Top left: *Harold Bride is carried off the* Carpathia, *his badly frozen feet wrapped in thick bandages.*

Top right: *Fireman John Thompson, Saloon Steward Thomas Whiteley, Trimmer William McIntyre, and Second Class passenger Emilio Pallas y Castillo at St Vincent's Hospital following the sinking.*

Right: *Survivors on the forward deck of the* Carpathia *as she sat at Pier 54 in Manhattan.*

were resigned to their fate. That is the way it will be looked upon when this great disaster becomes history.'[99]

* * * * *

Around the world, memorial services were organized in remembrance of the victims of the *Titanic* disaster. In London on Friday, April 19, a large memorial service was held in St Paul's Cathedral. Over 5,000 people attended, including Alexander Carlisle, one of *Titanic*'s designers. Nearly twice that number of people had crowded outside of the cathedral, hoping to get in. The service, culminating with the 'Dead March' from Händel's 'Saul', was described as highly emotional and touching, with many of the attendants openly crying or sobbing. People who attended described it as a 'congregation truly representative of the grief of the nation, and, indeed, of many nations, whose citizens are among the roll of the missing.' Carlisle, who occupied a seat in the choir, 'appeared deeply affected,' and fainted, falling back into his chair. Help was summoned, and an ambulance soon arrived, but by then Carlisle had recovered sufficiently to be driven home.'[100]

While efforts to memorialize and remember those lost were taking place, other efforts were underway to aid the living. In the days immediately following the disaster, New York Mayor Gaynor and the Red Cross established a relief fund, to help aid the survivors and families of those lost following their ordeal. By April 21, 1912, the relief fund had already received over $77,342.75 in donations. Many people gave small donations, but one of the biggest contributors was Vincent Astor, who donated $10,000 to the fund, with the message: 'Will you please accept the enclosed check as a contribution from me to the fund for the needy survivors of the *Titanic* disaster?' Mayor Gaynor wrote a very complimentary thank you letter for the donation:

Dear Mr Astor:
Your generous contribution to the fund for the relief of the survivors of the *Titanic* disaster and of the dependents of those who lost their lives is at hand.

Permit me to express to Mrs Astor and to the whole family through you my sympathy with you all in the great loss which you have sustained. My acquaintance with your father was a most agreeable one, and the oftener I met him the more his gener-

In Memoriam

WALLACE H. HARTLEY,

AGED 33 YEARS.

Bandmaster of the S.S. "Titanic,"

WHO LOST HIS LIFE IN THE DISASTER

APRIL 15TH, 1912.

INTERRED AT COLNE CEMETERY MAY 18TH, 1912.

A program for Wallace Hartley's memorial service, May 18, 1912.

ous, superior, democratic qualities grew on me. He was a man among men. The heroic way in which he met his death, disregarding himself and looking to the safety of others, is exactly what every one well acquainted with him knew to be the case even before authentic accounts were received.

Sincerely yours,

W. J. Gaynor, Mayor[101]

* * * * *

After *Carpathia* resumed her voyage to Europe, another survivors' committee was formed to recognize her crew. This committee, headed by Mr Frederic Steward, supplemented the previously donated funds, and used them to purchase a silver loving cup for Captain Rostron, as well as special medals for all 320 of *Carpathia's* crewmen. *Carpathia* arrived back in New York again on May 29, and Margaret Brown presented the cup and medals to Rostron and the crew who were still aboard the ship at that time. Sixty medals were mailed to the crewmembers who had left the *Carpathia* since the sinking.

* * * * *

For the crew and passengers of *Titanic*, though the danger to life was over, they all still had to put their lives back together. For one *Titanic* survivor, there was still some important unfinished business. On April 19, Bedroom Steward Henry Etches fulfilled the promise that he had made to Benjamin Guggenheim: he delivered the dictated message from the deceased millionaire to his widow, Florence Seligman. Calling on the family at the St Regis Motel, Etches insisted that he had to deliver the message to Mrs Guggenheim in person.

The family, including Benjamin's brother Robert, had been hoping for news of their loved one, whom the press had reported was among the missing prior to *Carpathia's* arrival in New York. That terrible piece of news had been confirmed by a wireless dispatch sent from *Carpathia* and received late on April 18.[102] After relating how Benjamin had been one of his charges during the voyage, Etches told them about their relative's chivalrous actions, and of the final favor Guggenheim had asked of him. Etches, producing the note and handing it to the widow, reported: 'That's all he said, there wasn't time for more.' The family was very grateful for the news and visit.[103]

For most of the crew, the most important thing was to get back to work, as their pay stopped the moment the *Titanic* sank beneath the waves. Some of these crew members were kept in New York, so they could testify at the American Inquiry; however, many went back to Britain on the *Lapland*, which left on April 20. One crewman, Leading Fireman Frederick Barrett, returned to work right away despite his ordeal; he got a berth on the *Olympic* fairly rapidly once he got home, and was back in New York on May 25. On that day, Senator Smith of the Senate Inquiry interviewed him in one of the *Olympic's* boiler rooms.

For many wives and mothers who had lost husbands, things looked grim. They had no money, and they had little reason to continue on to where the family had intended to go. However, some cases had a happy ending. Two little French boys had been saved in Collapsible D, and were being cared for in America by survivor Margaret Hays. The boys, Michel and Edmond, did not speak English; they had been placed in the lifeboat by their father, Michel Navratil, who had then stepped back onto the deck and perished. Navratil, who was estranged from his wife, had kidnapped the children and was fleeing to America. Since the boys couldn't speak English, no one knew who they were. In the aftermath of the sinking and rescue, photos of the two unknown '*Titanic* Orphans' were published in papers around the world, and their mother, still in Southern France, saw and recognized them. The White Star Line made arrangements, and Mrs Navratil came to America, where she was reunited with her children on May 16. The family then returned to France.[104]

* * * * *

The fallout from the *Titanic* disaster was both immediate and dramatic. While shipping companies had previously been loathe to carry enough boats for all on board, they quickly changed their tune – even before any laws or regulations mandated such a drastic, but long overdue, move. This was done partially out of legitimate concern that another similar disaster could occur, and also to reassure potential passengers, many of whom were then reluctant to travel aboard crack ships in light of the disaster. The decision by the companies led to a rush to supplement the number of lifeboats aboard the vessels, and one of the quickest solutions was to place additional collapsible boats aboard the ships from other vessels, or storage.

Such was the case with *Titanic's* sister ship *Olympic,* which was due to set sail from Southampton on April 24, 1912. The nearly-identical sister to *Titanic*, she was then facing an enormous stigma, and it turned out that a few collapsibles was not sufficient to erase these doubts.

Concerns over the seaworthiness and quality of the forty second-hand collapsibles that were taken from troopships and rushed onto the *Olympic* led to significant problems. Following a morning lifeboat drill where the boats passed inspection by the British Board of Trade, the firemen and greasers aboard the ship expressed concern with the safety

Top: *A group of* Carpathia's *officers pose with Captain Rostron.*

Above right: *Margaret Brown presents Captain Rostron with a silver loving cup.*

Left: *A* Carpathia *menu from 1913.*

of the boats. Nothing could pacify them, and they decided to strike, refusing to sail unless the collapsibles in question were replaced by regulation lifeboats.

Among their complaints against the collapsibles were the concerns that some could not be opened up easily because they had many thick layers of paint on them; that they were old boats that had not been opened up in years and were in poor condition; that they took too long to lower; that one of the collapsibles shipped a small amount of water during the drill. Additionally, in one instance, a fireman was easily able to put his thumb through the canvas side of one of the boats while examining it.

Left: *Loading extra collapsible lifeboats aboard the* Olympic *in Southampton, in preparation for her first post-*Titanic *crossing.*

Above: *Discontent with the new collapsible lifeboats, some of* Olympic's *firemen go on strike minutes before the sailing.*

Five minutes prior to sailing, all of the stokers and greasers grabbed their kits, and marched down the gangways and off the ship. All of the passengers were already aboard the *Olympic*, and this development must have been humiliating for the White Star Line, which was already reeling from the *Titanic* disaster. The strikers had called out to the sailors and other members of the Deck Department, hoping that they would join them in the strike, but Captain Haddock had the gangways to shore removed before the other men had a chance to leave.

After the strikers had disembarked, a deputation of five firemen and five greasers met with Mr Curry, the local manager of the White Star Line. In the presence of Commander Blake, the Emigration Officer, they said that they were not satisfied with the collapsible boats. Blake responded that he had examined the boats, and that he was perfectly satisfied with them. He offered to take the *Olympic* down to Cowes, to let the men select any boats that they pleased, and to give a demonstration of their seaworthiness. Members of the deputation refused, fearing that if the crewmen returned to the ship, they would not be allowed to leave. Curry told them that they had five minutes to decide, and the spokesmen held an impromptu meeting on the quay with their fellow strikers, who unanimously decided not to return to the ship.

Rather than trying to negotiate further, the White Star Line looked for volunteers among the crowds of men on the quay to work as replacement firemen. Only about twenty men took the offer. After the delay in *Olympic*'s departure

reached a full hour, the ship was towed down Southampton Water, where she would stay until additional firemen could be found to work the voyage. At 9:00 p.m., a tug boat brought forty non-union firemen aboard. The striking firemen and greasers left the dock 'in procession'. Leading Stoker Gregory, one of the spokesmen for the strikers, said that he himself didn't care about the lifeboats, as he was unmarried, but many of the men had wives and families, and their lives were as valuable as any First Class passenger. Meanwhile, passengers who were supposed to have boarded the *Olympic* in Cherbourg that evening decided to wait there overnight, hoping that the vessel would arrive the following morning, but it did not.

By April 25, a deputation from the strikers' union arrived on the scene, and observed a demonstration of the seaworthiness of the collapsible boats. The demonstration was quite satisfactory. The deputation stated that they would recommend a return to work, provided that one of the collapsibles, which had leaked during the test, was replaced. However, the strikers were still wary, and during the lifeboat demonstration, seamen had noticed a rent in one of the boats, which shook their confidence.

Despite the near-resolution of the strike, the situation again worsened when it was discovered that around midnight, the White Star Line had used a tugboat to bring groups of non-union firemen aboard *Olympic*. Learning of the presence of these strikebreakers, a large group of seamen and Quartermasters objected to the decision. Captain Haddock then told the men that if 'anybody wanted to go ashore they could go', clearly anticipating that most would stay. The men took a ballot, and after discussion, decided that they would all go ashore.

Early in the morning of April 26, 53 men – mostly seamen and Quartermasters – deserted, jumping into the tug that had dropped off the replacement firemen. They stated that they would not sail with a 'scratch crew', their term for a group of highly untrained individuals and substitutes, many of whom could not provide documentation that they had ever been to sea as firemen. The deserters said that they were not going to 'risk their lives with men in the stokehold who knew nothing about their work'. Because of the lack of crew aboard *Olympic,* even some stewards were to have been sent down to help stoke the ship during the voyage, a job which they were not qualified for.

Captain Haddock was furious, and when the seamen failed to heed his orders to return to the ship, he signaled the cruiser HMS *Cochrane.* The commander of the cruiser, Captain Goodenough, went aboard *Olympic* and told the strikers that their action was 'virtually a mutinous one'. When his words had no effect, the police were fetched from Portsmouth. All 53 seamen and Quartermasters were taken into custody, and charged in court at Portsmouth Town Hall with 'unlawfully disobeying the commands of the captain'. They were remanded on bail, pending a hearing on the following Tuesday.

Due to this humiliating setback, the White Star Line had to cancel *Olympic's* voyage, and ordered the ship back to Southampton. The passengers aboard the liner were indignant over the whole affair. The White Star Line issued an official statement to the public expressing their regret about the situation, and imploring the public's 'support in efforts we intend making, to secure the proper punishment of the crew's mutinous behavior, as unless firmness is shown now we despair of restoring discipline and maintain sailings.' The decision to cancel the voyage distressed Southampton greatly. The shipping lines were the port's lifeblood, and people were anxious about the possible fallout from the strike.

It was reported on April 29, 1912, that the local branch of the Seamen and Firemen's Union decided that from that day forward, seamen and firemen on every ship leaving Liverpool would insist upon the right of inspection of lifeboat accommodations by accredited representatives from the union; they also demanded an increase of wages to £4 10s per month for seamen, and £5 per month for firemen. The press also reported that the people waiting to embark on *Olympic* in Cherbourg, France, had booked on other liners when the voyage was cancelled; many had climbed the gangplanks of ships belonging to rival passenger lines. This was only to be expected, but it certainly was stinging news to White Star officials.

On April 30, 1912, the 53 seamen and Quartermasters were back in court in Portsmouth, and all pleaded 'not guilty' to the charges against them. Mr Raeburn, the prosecutor, made the case that the crewmembers in question had blatantly disregarded Captain Haddock's orders. Mr Emanuel, the defense lawyer, argued that the men were placed under arrest before any warrant was issued, and therefore had been seized illegally. When *Olympic's* Purser, George Borradaile, was asked whether he could identify any of the men in court with the offenders listed in *Olympic's* log, he pointed at one or two people. As the accused men were about to reply, Mr Emanuel told them: 'Don't say anything at all. Take no notice whatever.' Purser Borradaile turned and 'found himself facing a double row of smiling seamen's faces'. All of the men refused to speak, and the case was adjourned until May 4, 1912.

Eventually, on May 6, the 53 deserters were found guilty of having refused Captain Haddock's orders, but they were allowed to go free unpunished. The Bench felt that the *Titanic* disaster was fresh on the defendants' minds, and that the men had done something they would not have done under ordinary circumstances. Therefore, they took action under the Probation of Offenders Act, and dismissed the information without giving any punishment. With the *Olympic* firemen's strike concluded, the men were free to return to work, and

the ship was able to resume its transatlantic crossings. As she sailed from Southampton on May 15, 1912, it was a great relief to everyone involved.[105]

* * * * *

Even before the *Carpathia* had docked in New York and offloaded its cargo of human survivors, the White Star Line realized that they had another problem to deal with, and it was a time-sensitive one, at that. With a total of 1,496 victims from the disaster, it was clear that hundreds of bodies were still afloat on the open North Atlantic. It would be important to recover as many of these as possible and return them to their grieving families. Accordingly, White Star made arrangements for a ship and a team of undertakers. The ship would be provided by the Commercial Cable Company of Halifax, Nova Scotia. John Snow & Company, Ltd – the largest undertaking firm in the province – was engaged to recover and embalm the bodies.

By early on Wednesday, April 17, the cable ship *Mackay-Bennett* left Halifax en route to the sinking coordinates. In a wireless dated Saturday, April 20, the vessel reported that they had been contacted by the North German Lloyd Liner *Rhein*; the German vessel had passed wreckage and bodies to the northeast of the disaster site, and the *Mackay-Bennett* accordingly made for that position, expecting to arrive at 8:00 p.m. that night. She was also contacted by the *Bremen*, which reported spotting debris and well over a hundred bodies at nearly the same location on April 20.

After receiving these messages, Bruce Ismay issued the following statement:

> The cable ship *Mackay-Bennett* has been chartered by the White Star Line and ordered to proceed to the scene of the disaster and do all she could to recover the bodies and glean all information possible.
>
> Every effort will be made to identify bodies recovered, and any news will be sent through immediately by wireless. In addition to any such message as these, the *Mackay-Bennett* will make a report of its activities each morning by wireless, and such reports will be made public at the offices of the White Star Line.
>
> The cable ship has orders to remain on the scene of the wreck for at least a week, but should a large number of bodies be recovered before that time she will return to Halifax with them. The search for bodies will not be abandoned until not a vestige of hope remains for any more recoveries.
>
> The *Mackay-Bennett* will not make any soundings, as they would not serve any useful purpose, because the depth where the *Titanic* sank is more than 2000 fathoms.

When the *Bremen* arrived back in port, her officers reported to the public that from the Bridge, they had seen over a hundred bodies floating in the sea, as well as the upturned and adrift Collapsible B, small pieces of wood, steamer chairs, and other wreckage. Since the *Mackay-Bennett* was nearby, and since *Bremen* did not have the facilities or supplies needed to deal with the bodies, they did not retrieve any of the corpses.

While *Bremen's* officers did not care to talk in further detail about the tragic spectacle they had witnessed, Jo-

Collapsible B was found adrift by the crew of the cable ship Mackay-Bennett *while they were on their mission to recover bodies of the* Titanic *victims.*

hanna Steinke, a First Class passenger aboard *Bremen*, described the scene in graphic detail:

> … our ship sighted an iceberg off the bow to the starboard. As we drew nearer, and could make out small dots floating around in the sea, a feeling of awe and sadness crept over everyone on the ship.
>
> We passed within a hundred feet of the southernmost drift of the wreckage, and looking down over the rail we distinctly saw a number of bodies so clearly that we could make out what they were wearing and whether they were men or women.
>
> We saw one woman in her night dress, with a baby clasped closely to her breast. Several women passengers screamed and left the rail in a fainting condition. There was another woman, fully dressed, with her arms tight around the body of a shaggy dog.
>
> The bodies of three men in a group, all clinging to one steamship chair, floated near by, and just beyond them were a dozen bodies of men, all of them encased in life-preservers, clinging together as though in a last desperate struggle for life. We couldn't see, but imagined that under them was some bit of wreckage to which they all clung when the ship went down, and which didn't have buoyancy enough to support them.
>
> Those were the only bodies we passed near enough to distinguish, but we could see the white life-preservers of many more dotting the sea, all the way to the iceberg. The officers told us that was probably the berg hit by the *Titanic*, and that the bodies and ice had drifted along together.

Mrs Steinke reported that a number of passengers demanded that the *Bremen* stop and pick up the bodies, but the officers assured them that the *Mackay-Bennett* was only two hours away, and was heading towards the scene for that exact purpose.[106]

In the meanwhile, numerous other ships also began reporting this floating graveyard. For example, the *Winifredian* reported seeing a body floating about 25 miles from the reported position of *Titanic*'s sinking.[107]

By Sunday, April 21, the *Mackay-Bennett* had reached the area reported by *Bremen*, and immediately began picking up bodies. They recovered 51 persons on that day, 26 on April 22, 128 more on April 23, 87 on April 25, and 14 more on April 26. Some bodies were recovered over 170 miles from the scene of the wreck. Captain F. H. Lardner then had the ship turned around, and headed back to Halifax. When they arrived in port on Tuesday, April 30, they were able to report that they had found 306 bodies in all. Some 116 were buried at sea, while 190 were brought back to land.

Among the more prominent passengers whose bodies were recovered were Colonel Astor and Isidor Straus. Purser McElroy's body was also recovered.[108] As a general rule, all identifiable bodies of First Class passengers were embalmed and brought back to shore no matter what their condition. On the other hand, bodies of passengers from Second and Third Class, and those of crew members, were recovered and embalmed based on condition.

Those that were to be taken back to Halifax were packed in ice until Undertaker John Snow, Jr could do his work. Bodies that were mangled, deteriorated, or unidentifiable were sealed in weighted canvas bags, given impromptu funerals, and buried at sea. The words recited during these burial services were: 'I am the resurrection and the life, with the Lord; he that believeth in me, tho' he were dead, yet shall he live, and whosover liveth and believeth in me shall never die.' When the time for the committal came, the following words were recited over each body before they slid overboard:

> For as much as it hath pleased Almighty God to take unto Himself the soul of our dear brother departed, we therefore commit his body to the deep to be turned to corruption, looking for the resurrection of the body (when the sea shall give up her dead) and the life of the world to come, through Jesus Christ, our Lord, who shall change our vile body, that it may be like unto His glorious body, according to the mighty working whereby He is able to subdue all things to himself.

The same services and verses were read over and over again. Most of the bodies that were recovered were in decent condition. Nearly all appeared to have frozen to death, with very few having drowned. Some had been mangled during the liner's violent break-up and sinking, but most of the bodies were floating with serene looks on their faces, as if they were sleeping. All but one of the bodies, that of a 2-year-old boy, were recovered wearing lifebelts. Besides bodies, several floating deck chairs, and multiple pieces of floating wooden debris were recovered as mementoes by *Mackay-Bennett*'s crew.[109]

While the *Mackay-Bennett* was still at the disaster site, a second cable ship, the *Minia*, was chartered to assist in the recovery of bodies. The *Minia* departed Halifax on Monday, April 22, and body recovery started on Friday, April 26. Eleven bodies were found and picked up that day, and one each was found on April 27, 28, 29, and 30. After picking up two more bodies on Wednesday, May 1, the *Minia* sailed for Halifax. She reached port on May 6 with 15 bodies, as two of those recovered had been buried at sea.

Top left: The body of a Titanic *victim being recovered by crewmen from the* Minia *three weeks after the disaster.*

*Top right: *Titanic's *lifeboats tied up between Piers 59 and 60.*

Below right: This rare view inside two of Titanic's *recovered lifeboats shows that they were littered with discarded oars and lifebelts.*

*Bottom right: *Collapsible A *was found adrift and was recovered by the crew of the White Star Line's* Oceanic *one month after the disaster. Three bodies were still aboard.*

The *Montmagny* left Halifax that same day, Monday, May 6. Arriving at the site on Thursday, May 9, she was only able to find one body before that day was out, and three more on Friday, May 10. She returned to Halifax on Monday, May 13.

The fourth and final ship chartered and sent out to the wreck site was the sealer *Algerine*. She was dispatched from St Johns, Nova Scotia, on May 16, and recovered only one body. The victim was returned to St Johns on June 8, and was subsequently transshipped to Halifax.

A total of 209 bodies were brought back to Halifax, and were stored in a curling rink. People from all over the United States, and elsewhere, made the sad trip to claim them there. President Taft, hoping that Major Archibald Butt's body had been recovered, sent a member of the War Department to investigate. Sadly, he returned empty handed. Of the recovered bodies, 59 were shipped on to other points at the request of the victims' families. The remaining 150 were laid to rest in three Halifax cemeteries: Fairview, Mount Olivet, and Baron von Hirsch.[110]

Unfortunately, despite the best efforts of the crew of the *Mackay-Bennett*, not all of the bodies could be found. Many continued to drift on the currents, held afloat by their lifebelts, and were scattered over a wide area. One particularly sad incident involving these bodies was told by some Scandinavian immigrants en route to Minnesota, who related how 'in several instances, bodies were struck by our boat and knocked from the water several feet into the air'. The incident was so disturbing that a transcription of the account was sent to President Taft.[111]

On May 13, the White Star liner *Oceanic* found *Titanic's* Collapsible A still afloat, and drifting in the North Atlantic. On board the collapsible, they found the three bodies Fifth Officer Lowe had left behind on the morning of April 15. The bodies were those of two unidentified crewmen – a sailor and a fireman – and also First Class passenger Thom-

son Beattie. All three were buried at sea from the *Oceanic*. Collapsible A itself was hauled aboard and taken to New York; there it joined the thirteen other *Titanic* lifeboats in the loft above Piers 58 and 59.

One of the items found in the bottom of the boat included a ring reported as having the names 'Edward and Gerda' on it. It apparently belonged to Edvard and Elin Lindell, as Elin's middle name was Gerda. It seems that the ring had slipped off and fallen into the boat as August Wennerström clutched Elin's hand, struggling to keep her afloat while they awaited rescue. Additionally, Richard Norris Williams' fur coat was found in the bottom of the boat, and later returned to him.[112]

On June 6, the body of Saloon Steward William Thomas Kerley was found and buried at sea by the *Ottawa*.[113] Just two days later, the eastbound freighter *Illford* discovered

Carpathia, Senator Smith revealed his plans for the investigation.

In a startling display of bureaucratic efficiency, the Senate Inquiry convened the very next day, Friday, April 19, at the Waldorf-Astoria Hotel in New York. The inquiry proceeded under the direct supervision of Senator Smith. There would be a veritable parade of witnesses, and the

the body of *Titanic* steward W. F. Cheverton. The body was recommitted to the sea.[114]

In all, 712 people survived the sinking. Four people were buried at sea from the *Carpathia*. The four 'funeral ships' listed above found a combined total of 328 bodies; the *Oceanic*, *Ottawa* and *Illford* retrieved an additional five. In sum, about 337 bodies were accounted for; when one adds the number of survivors, the total accounted for is 1,049 of the 2,208 people *Titanic* carried when she left her last port of call, Queenstown. Some 1,159 bodies were never accounted for. These were either never found on the surface of the North Atlantic, or had sunk with the ship.[115]

* * * * *

Even before the *Carpathia* docked in New York, United States authorities were preparing to detain and interrogate survivors. Their goal was to ascertain the circumstances surrounding the disaster and determine who – if anyone – was to blame for the loss of so many lives, many of whom had been American citizens.

The desire to detain the survivors was urgent since it was known to these authorities that Bruce Ismay was attempting to arrange a swift return to England for he and the surviving crew members. Senator William Alden Smith had appointed to chair a committee to investigate the sinking. During his visit to Ismay aboard the

This collapsible lifeboat was recovered by an Elders & Fyffes ship in the Bahamas a year and a half after the disaster. It was thought to have been one of Titanic's *collapsible boats, having drifted on with the currents, but it is difficult to tell with certainty.*

first called to testify was Bruce Ismay himself. The Inquiry lasted eighteen days, continuing until May 25. The first two days' sessions were held at the Waldorf-Astoria in New York. Beginning on the third day of testimony, April 22, the witnesses and assessors were moved to Washington, D.C. for further investigation.

A total of 82 witnesses testified over the course of the Inquiry, and almost two dozen statements from other survivors and knowledgeable parties were entered into the record. In addition to Bruce Ismay, all four of the *Titanic's* surviving officers testified. So did many crew members – including those involved with working in the boiler and engine rooms, and those who helped evacuate passengers and lower the lifeboats. Also of note, many passengers of all classes gave evidence. Other key witnesses who had been involved in the story were also called, including Captain Arthur Rostron and Marconi Operator Harold Cottam of the Cunarder *Carpathia*, who gave the details of their rescue efforts. Captain Stanley Lord of the Leyland liner *Californian* also appeared to answer allegations that his ship had been the one visible to *Titanic* throughout the sinking, and

Top right: *Friday, April 19, 1912. J. Bruce Ismay giving testimony at the American Inquiry. The proceedings were being held in the ballroom of the Waldorf-Astoria Hotel.*

Middle right: *Saturday, April 20, 1912. Harold Bride gives testimony to the American Inquiry.*

Bottom right: *Stewards F. Dent Ray* (left) *and William Burke* (right) *with another surviving* Titanic *crewman. The photo was taken at the American Inquiry in Washington, D.C. on Saturday, April 27, 1912. By the process of elimination, the unidentified man in this photo has to be either Andrew Cunningham or Alfred Crawford; this is because the only other crewmen who testified that day were Henry Etches and Arthur Bright, who had mustaches at the time, and Second Officer Lightoller.*

that the crew had neglected to respond to *Titanic*'s distress signals the night of the sinking. Over 1,150 pages of testimony and affidavits were taken, covering many aspects of the disaster and providing a valuable body of testimony.

The final report of the Senate Inquiry was released on May 28, 1912. Its findings were:

> The steamship *Californian* had been closer to *Titanic* than the 19 miles reported by her Captain, Stanley Lord; that *Titanic*'s distress signals were observed by the *Californian*, and that the officers and crew failed to respond properly to them.
>
> *Titanic* was equipped with lifeboat capacity for 1,178 persons, but carried well over that number in passengers and crew. Only a few of the lifeboats were fully loaded upon lowering, thereby saving only 706. [This was an erroneous number, as more recent research has proven there were actually 712 survivors.]
>
> There was no apparent distinction or discrimination in how passengers were saved, whether First, Second, or Third Class.
>
> Marconi coverage was inadequate.

Recommendations for future revisions to safety guidelines, laws, and regulations were also given:

- Sufficient lifeboats for accommodating all crew and passengers aboard ships should be provided.
- No less than four trained crewmembers were to be assigned to each lifeboat, with drills being carried out at least twice a month.
- Passengers and crew members should be assigned to each lifeboat.
- Ocean steamships of over 100 passengers should be required to carry two electric searchlights.
- A Marconi operator should be required to be on duty at all times. Direct communication between the Marconi office and the Bridge should also be required, so that a Marconi operator does not have to leave his station to send important communications to the Bridge. Legislation was also recommended to prevent interference by amateurs. Auxiliary power was needed for the Marconi apparatus.
- Firing of rockets at sea for any purpose other than for distress should be a misdemeanor.

- Watertight bulkheads should continue up to the uppermost continuous structural deck, and then that deck itself should be watertight.[116]

Left: *Third Officer Herbert Pitman, with relatives, after arriving back home in England aboard the* Adriatic.

Below left: *Lord Mersey* (right), *who chaired the Board of Trade Inquiry into the sinking.*

may testified again, along with Rostron and Cottam from the *Carpathia*, Captain Lord and several of the officers of the *Californian*, and a number of other ship captains – over 100 witnesses in total. One very glaring omission was that no passengers testified at the British Inquiry, with the exception of First Class passengers Sir Cosmo and Lady Duff Gordon and Bruce Ismay, who had technically been a passenger on the ship.

The Wreck Commission presented their findings in a report on July 30. The report of the British Inquiry found:

> *Titanic* was built according to the rules and policies of the Merchant Shipping Acts, 1894–1906. The lifeboat capacity complied with these rules. [In fact, *Titanic* exceeded the regulations in terms of lifeboat capacity at the time of the sinking.]
> *Titanic* had been provided with sufficient officers and crew.
> The cause of the loss of the *Titanic* was due to: 1) Collision with an iceberg; 2) The ship *Californian* seeing the rockets fired from *Titanic*, but making no rescue attempt.
> There was no structural reason that any class of passenger had less of an opportunity than those from another class to reach the deck and lifeboats.

Like the Senate Inquiry Final Report, the British Inquiry final report also made several recommendations for the future:

- Bulkheads and watertight sub-divisions should be enhanced.
- Lifeboat capacity should be increased to provide space for all persons aboard a vessel.
- Adequate crewmen should be trained in lifeboat lowering and rowing. A boat drill should be held as soon as practical after a vessel leaves port.
- Marconi operations should be worked by a sufficient number of operators to allow for 24-hour service.
- Company regulations should specify that ships should proceed at a moderate speed in an ice region.
- Captains should be instructed that it is a misdemeanor to fail to go to the relief of a vessel in distress.[118]

On the other side of the Atlantic, the British Board of Trade had started planning their own Inquiry nearly immediately after hearing word of the disaster. Wishing to act promptly, on April 22, 1912, Sydney Buxton – the President of the British Board of Trade – had requested that a Wreck Commissioner be appointed to investigate the disaster. On April 24, while being questioned in the House of Commons, Buxton discussed the urgency with which revisions to regulations would need to be made in light of the disaster. He said: 'There will not be a moment's delay in preparing and issuing revised regulations with regard to the number of boats and lifesaving appliances, but it is desirable to act in the light of the fullest information and the best expert advice.'[117] That is one of the main reasons why expert witnesses were called during the British Inquiry.

Under Wreck Commissioner Lord Mersey, the British Inquiry convened at the Drill Hall of the London Scottish Regiment at Buckingham Gate on May 1. Testimony continued over 36 days, and ended on July 3, with the final session being transplanted to London's Caxton Hall. Many of the crew who testified in the United States were also questioned in London, including the four surviving officers. Bruce Is-

The Inquiries had shown that the then-standing Board of Trade regulations were hopelessly out of date, and did not adequately address the realities of shipping in 1912. The findings of the two Inquiries were taken to heart very quickly, and changes were soon made on both sides of the Atlantic. As a result, shipping firms started providing lifeboats for all. For ships then under construction, watertight subdivision and bulkheads were improved. These changes affected all liners, particularly the *Titanic*'s two sisters, *Olympic* and *Britannic*.[119]

Above: *Sir Cosmo Duff Gordon testifying at the British Inquiry on either Friday, May 17 or Monday, May 20, 1912.*

Right: *Harold Bride* (middle) *pausing for a smoke with his father* (left) *after arriving back in England.*

In direct response to the sinking, a new organization charged with monitoring the presence of icebergs in the Atlantic and Arctic Oceans was formed. Known as the International Ice Patrol, this body was established in 1914 as an arm of the United States Coast Guard. Though a part of the Coast Guard, the Patrol is financed by thirteen nations interested in trans-Atlantic navigation.[120]

* * * * *

Although the Inquiries addressed issues that needed attention regarding the building and sailing of ocean-going vessels, it did not address one major issue: the survivors who lost family members and, in many cases, almost everything they owned. What would become of family members left at home, who had lost the breadwinners of the family, and were now in serious financial difficulties? This question was addressed by the Limitation of Liability Hearings of 1912 to 1915.

When potential claimants in Britain heard that the Board of Trade Inquiry had not found the White Star Line at fault, they moved quickly to file their claims in the United States. Since the *Titanic* was sailing toward New York, and as the White Star Line was an American-owned company, the case was brought against them in the Southern District Court of New York State.

Claimants came forward seeking restitution for both loss of property and loss of life; they filed claims or depositions, or in some cases both. The claims filed totaled a staggering $16,804,112.00. Under American law, the White Star Line's liability was limited to the salvage value of the *Titanic*. This was determined by the value of the lifeboats, with deductions for the costs associated with board and travel for the survivors after they landed. These costs amounted to only $97,772.02.

The court's responsibility was to verify the claims, and determine if they had any legal validity. Assuming they did, the court was to apportion payment of each claim from any

monies available. The proceedings suffered from a number of delays due to issues relating to contacting the claimants. The process of recording depositions in the case began in September of 1912, and continued through June of 1915. However, the formal testimony in the U.S. District Court before Judge Julius M. Meyer did not begin until June of 1915.[121]

At an early stage of the hearings, Judge Holt of the District Court stated that British law applied in this case. This meant that the entire amount of claims, $16,804,112.00, had to be divided among the claimants. In December of 1915, a tentative settlement was agreed to by both the claimants and White Star. By July of 1916, the case was settled, and $665,000 was divided *pro rata* among the claimants. This meant that most survivors received far less compensation than they had been seeking, and all future legal action was barred.[122]

With all of these thorny legal and financial questions sorted out, one might have expected the *Titanic* to slowly fade from public attention. Survivors attempted to piece their lives back together and move on; many refused to speak of their experiences, simply trying to bury their memories. Between 1914 and 1945, the horrors of the Great War, the unbridled optimism of the 'Roaring Twenties,' the bleak years of the Great Depression, and finally the Second World War filled headlines and gripped the world's attention. Yet during the second half of the twentieth century and on into the twenty-first, interest in the *Titanic* would experience an astounding resurgence.

CHAPTER 8

THE ETERNAL ECHOES

The world has changed so significantly from *Titanic's* era that it is difficult to comprehend from a century's remove what life in 1912 was like. 17-year-old Jack Thayer described it this way:

These were ordinary days, and into them had crept only gradually the telephone, the talking machine, the automobile. The airplane ... was only a few years old, and the radio as known today, was still in the scientific laboratory ... Upon rising in the morning, we looked forward to a normal day of customary business progress. The conservative morning paper seldom had headlines larger than half an inch in height. Upon reaching the breakfast table, our perusal of the morning paper was slow and deliberate. We did not nervously clutch for it, and rapidly scan the glaring headlines, as we are inclined to do today. Nothing was revealed in the morning, the trend of which was not known the night before ... These days were peaceful and ruled by economic theory and practice built up over years of slow and hardly perceptible change. There was peace, and the world had an even tenor to its ways.

A dollar could be exchanged for four shillings, four marks, or five francs. In exchange for a five-dollar gold piece or a five-dollar bill, one could pocket a pound note or a gold sovereign ...

In those days one could freely circulate around the world, in both a physical and an economic sense, and definitely plan for the future, unhampered by class, nationality, or government ...

Today the individual has to be contented with rapidity of motion, nervous emotion, and economic insecurity.[1]

Certainly, this description – penned in 1940 – of a society filled with rushed, nervous, people filled with economic uncertainty has continued to intensify in the first years of the twenty-first century.

Jack Thayer attributed this tremendous change to the sinking of the *Titanic*, and the sentiment is thoroughly understandable; it was an earth-shattering period for the young man, as he lost his father in the sinking and suffered tremendously – both physically and mentally – from its effects. In reality, the sinking of the White Star liner was not the pivotal moment in human history that it has frequently been made out to be; to some extent, its role in the shift toward a more uncertain reality has been overblown. This change really had far more to do with the effects of the 'Great War', now known as World War I. That ghastly conflict stripped much of the world's 'even tenor' away, and set the stage for tremendously devastating events later on ... the Great Depression, the rise of the Nazi party in Germany, World War II, and many other things.

Yet the loss of the *Titanic* did cause a complacent world to sit up and reassess its position. Advancing technology was then considered a potential cure-all for man's ills; great confidence was placed in the technological marvels of the day, such as the *Titanic* ... if these great works could be felled in a single night from a brush with an iceberg, what else could go wrong? It was certainly a portent of things to come.

The disaster was indeed tremendous news until the outbreak of the Great War. Many books were released on the subject in the months after the sinking. Barely a month after the tragedy, survivor Dorothy Gibson even starred in a silent film, *Saved from the Titanic*, which was largely based upon her personal experiences that night. However, the sinking of the *Titanic* was overshadowed to a large extent by the outbreak of the Great War, scarcely twenty-eight months after her loss.

During the 'Roaring Twenties', people looked forward rather than behind; during the Great Depression, most were too concerned about putting food on their tables to worry about a long-lost ocean liner. Then came World War II, a devastating six-year conflict that ended with the uncertainty of the Nuclear Age and the Cold War.

It was not until the 1950s, then, that the public in general was ready to look back upon the loss of the *Titanic*. Things seem to have really started in 1953, with the release of the 20th Century Fox motion picture *Titanic*. The movie starred Clifton Webb and Barbara Stanwyck as a fictional couple whose marriage was literally at the breaking point and who, together with their two children, found themselves directly in the middle of the tragedy. While the film openly claimed a high level of accuracy based on the transcripts of the two Inquiries into the sinking, it fell far short of that. A majority of the events portrayed were either dramatically embellished or simply inaccurate. However, the film's stunning visual effects really captured the imagination, and the film did recreate in some ways the *feel* of being aboard the liner.

The historical record of the *Titanic* disaster took a tremendous leap forward with the publication of the book *A Night to Remember* in 1955. Written by Walter Lord, the book was simultaneously ground-breaking and eminently readable; it was nearly impossible to put down. Lord had spent a great deal of time reading the transcripts of the official inquiries into the disaster and discussing the night's events with still-living survivors. The volume quickly became an international best-seller.

Left: *Joseph Boxhall* (middle) *and Herbert Pitman* (right) *at the premiere of* A Night to Remember.

Below: *A publicity photo for* Raise the Titanic. *The photo shows the enormous scale model of the ship, which has only a few inaccurate details. Were it not for the fact that, five years after the movie was released, the ship was found broken in half, one could nearly believe that this was a photo of the real ship, raised from the sea floor.*

Two and a half years after the book's release, a film of the same title hit theaters. Starring British actor Kenneth More as Second Officer Lightoller, and directed by Roy Ward Baker, the movie was a gripping portrayal of the sinking of the *Titanic*. The film's score was written by British composer William Alwyn, and had a truly noteworthy primary theme.

While largely acclaimed as the most accurate film about the disaster, *A Night to Remember* did contain some inaccuracies. The opening sequence, where a bottle of champagne was broken over the liner's prow and she was formally christened was one example. The film was also clearly intended as a vehicle for its star, Kenneth More, who portrayed Second Officer Lightoller; throughout the sinking, Lightoller is shown personally loading nearly every lifeboat. Many actions that were in reality taken by other officers were acted out by More's Lightoller; the portrayal of Thomas Andrews, played by British actor Michael Goodliffe, was eminently believable ... yet his accent was British instead of Irish. The same could be said of First Officer Murdoch, a Scotsman, and at least some others. Recent research has also highlighted a number of other historical errors in the film. It could

also be said that its special effects were not quite on a par with the 1953 American film.

On the other hand, the 1958 film stood as a tremendous improvement in the historical portrayal over its immediate predecessor. Joseph Boxhall, *Titanic*'s Fourth Officer, served as a technical guide, and an obvious attempt was made to correctly recreate many of the liner's interior features. Much of the dialogue was reconstructed from survivors' original statements. A number of survivors, including Edith Russell – known as Edith Rosenbaum in 1912 – and Lawrence Beesley visited the set during filming. Edith Russell met the actress portraying her 1912 self, and Charles Lightoller's widow and son carefully coached Kenneth More on how to accurately portray the liner's Second Officer. When the real Captain Smith's daughter, Helen, visited the set and met Laurence Naismith, who was portraying her father, she found the striking physical resemblance between the two men almost too much to bear. The film was also a masterpiece in that it did not use a fictional plot and primary characters to draw audiences in; instead, it primarily relied upon historical figures and showed them in such a way that audiences cared about what happened to them.

In September of 1979, another film on the disaster was released to United States audiences. Produced by EMI Films, and entitled *S.O.S. Titanic*, it was a fascinating re-enactment based at least in part on Lawrence Beesley's book, *The Loss of the S.S. Titanic, Its Stories and Its Lessons*. While *A Night to Remember* had focused almost entirely on the night of the disaster, this film explored what life was like on board the *Titanic* before she sank. The film starred an incredible cast: Ian Holm as Bruce Ismay; David Janssen as Colonel John Jacob Astor, David Warner as Lawrence Beesley, a young Helen Mirren as Stewardess Mary Sloan, Scottish actor Paul Young as First Officer Murdoch, Cloris Leachman as Margaret Brown, and many others.

It is very difficult to conceive of better portrayals of many of these historical characters – Murdoch with a Scottish accent; a feisty Margaret Brown quipping with her friend Emma Bucknell; an authentically Irish group of shipboard acquaintances in Third Class, with the men in the group all riveted by the beauty of another girl traveling on the ship with them; the friendship between Thomas Andrews and Mary Sloan; the trials of Colonel Astor and his young bride as they sought to maintain a reputable position in society; Irene Harris slipping and falling down the Grand Staircase; a feisty Harold Lowe cussing out Bruce Ismay as Boat No. 5 is lowered ... the film really was quite stunning. It was also overlaid by a tremendous score by Howard Blake, filled with period music such as 'I'm Falling in Love with Some-one', 'The Irish Emigrant',[2] and a number of well-known pieces – such as 'Bethena' and 'Elite Syncopations' – by American Ragtime composer Scott Joplin.[3]

Directed by William Hale, the film, as it originally aired on ABC Network in the United States, also sported a bold and very effective method of telling the tragic story: through a flashback. The film's opening sequences showed the dramatic rescue of *Titanic*'s survivors by the liner *Carpathia*, before flashing back to the voyage and finally returning to the bewildered survivors as the *Carpathia* steamed for New York.

The film also had a number of historical inaccuracies. Nearly every public room on the ship was inaccurately portrayed, as much of the movie was filmed onboard the *Queen Mary* or at existing locations rather than on set re-creations of the liner; the date given for that Sunday is inaccurate; Lawrence Beesley was portrayed as hesitantly involved in a romantic interest with a fictional character, Leigh Goodwin, played by Susan Saint James[4]; mysterious jets of water shoot over passengers and crew struggling on the Boat Deck toward the end of the sinking; the promi-nent use of Margaret Brown's nickname 'Molly' long before it became used, and a number of other things.

Following the movie's full-length release on American television, a second and much shorter version was released theatrically for British and other audiences. In the extreme editing, the flashback-style storytelling – so ahead of its time in 1979 – was removed, and many other of the film's finest moments were lost entirely. While the shorter version received a commercial DVD release, showing the film in its stunning visual quality, the full-length version has become almost entirely lost.

On August 1, 1980, ITC released the film *Raise the Titanic* in the United States.[5] Based on the best-selling book by ad-venture author Clive Cussler, the film starred Richard Jordan as Dirk Pitt, Cussler's serial hero. Co-stars included Jason Ro-bards as Pitt's boss, Admiral James Sandecker; David Selby as Dr Gene Seagram; Anne Archer as Seagram's wife Dana; and a cameo appearance by legendary actor Alec Guinness, who played a fictional surviving *Titanic* crew member named John Bigalow. The film centered upon a Cold War plot to make nuclear warfare obsolete, with the key 'ingredient' in this plot being a rare mineral that sank in the hold of the *Titanic*.

The movie was tremendously expensive to make, and featured excellent visual special effects. A spectacular score for the film was composed by John Barry, the composer for numerous movies, including many of the James Bond films between 1963 and 1987. Despite the big budget, special ef-fects, and dramatic score, the film was not the best-possible adaptation of the novel, and was a tremendous box office disaster. Novelist Clive Cussler was dismayed and vowed never to have another one of his novels adapted for the big screen.[6] The stunning score for the film was almost entire-ly lost.[7] Due to its popularity, however, it was subsequently reconstructed by conductor, orchestrator and arranger Nic Raine, re-recorded and released on compact disc.[8]

In November of 1996, a miniseries named *Titanic* was aired on American television. The film starred Catherine Zeta-Jones in one of her first major roles,[9] Peter Gallagher, Eva Marie Saint and Tim Curry as fictional characters. Some of the historical characters were portrayed by George C. Scott as Captain Smith; Roger Rees as J. Bruce Ismay; Marilu Henner as Margaret Brown and Kavan Smith as Fifth Officer Lowe, among others. While much of the film centered upon the fictional story, it did have a few histori-cal highlights, such as an interesting portrayal of the Alli-son family and Alice Cleaver. It was also ground-breaking in that it was the first cinematic portrayal which showed the ship breaking in half as she sank – all films made prior to the wreck's discovery in 1985 held to the traditional de-piction that she had sunk intact.[10] Its low points included a disturbing rape scene and numerous historical errors.

This miniseries was only a prelude to a much more lavish production by director James Cameron, which was released in the United States on December 19, 1997. It was backed by two major motion picture companies, Twentieth Century Fox and Paramount Pictures, and it was the most expensive film made up to that time, with a budget of some $200 mil-lion.[11] An enormous new film studio was constructed in Ro-sarito, Mexico, in which a nearly full-size replica of the liner's exterior was built.[12] The forward portion of this set was built so that it could be lowered into a large tank of water for scenes where the ship takes its 'slight but definite plunge' forward.

Large sets were also constructed to represent the ship's interior spaces, and special attention was given to repro-ducing these as faithfully as possible for the film. Enormous scale models of the ship were built for use in the special effects sequences showing the ship at sea, and digital tech-nology was used to help put the scale-model on the open sea, populated with passengers and crew, and to help 'sink' the liner. Director James Cameron even led an expedition to the wreck of the ship in 1995, during which he shot footage for use in the film; this marked the first time that footage of the actual liner's wreck was included in any motion picture film on the subject.

The movie starred Kate Winslet, Leonardo DiCaprio, Billy Zane, Frances Fisher and David Warner[13] as a set of fictional characters involved in a developing love story. Glo-ria Stuart portrayed the modern-day, aged version of Kate Winslet's character, and Bill Paxton played an underwater explorer in search of a fictional diamond necklace that would supposedly have been worth more than the Hope Diamond.

In an attempt to keep the historical details accurate, Cameron brought in *Titanic* historians Don Lynch and Ken Marschall to consult – both before the film started production and during the shoot. In fact, some of Marschall's paintings served as 'storyboards' for certain scenes of the finished film. Don Lynch actually appeared on screen during the film, playing Frederick Spedden as he watched his son spin a top on the aft A Deck.[14] Also making a cameo in the film were Ed and Karen Kamuda, Ed being the President of the Titanic Historical Society.

Historical figures shown in the film included Bernard Hill as an eminently enjoyable Captain Smith; Victor Garber in perhaps one of the most endearing portrayals of Thomas Andrews to date; Jonathan Hyde as J. Bruce Ismay, Kathy Bates as Margaret Brown and many, many other famous passengers and crew, such as Archibald Gracie,[15] John and Madeleine Astor, Benjamin Guggenheim and Madame Aubart, Bandmaster Wallace Hartley, among others. Most of the cast was selected specifically for a resemblance to the original historical person they were portraying.[16]

Much of the romantic story was wound around historic events which were known to have occurred, and in some cases, the fictional characters could be seen shaping the historical events. However, some of the filmmakers' decisions on depictions of events during the voyage drew criticism: Ismay pressuring Captain Smith to drive the ship faster against his will; passengers being shot; and Murdoch both taking a bribe and committing suicide, among other things.[17]

Still, the film was in many ways a tremendous step forward in cinematic depictions of the voyage and sinking. Accompanied by a wonderfully moving score provided by James Horner, the movie literally brought the *Titanic* back to life as never before. Although its opening weekend was a rather small $28.6 million in domestic U.S. gross, the film became a juggernaut, retaining a top position at the box office for 17 weeks in American theaters. It wound up taking in over $600 million in the United States, the U.S. box office record for the time, and an additional $114 million in the United Kingdom, steaming toward a grand total of $1.84 *billion* in worldwide gross.[18] It was nominated for fourteen Oscars and swept the year, taking eleven of these.

In the years since its initial release, the film has predictably become a proverbial whipping-boy. Many men simply roll their eyes at the idea of watching a period romance; *Titanic* 'rivet counters' can't resist finding every technical mistake made with the full-size sets and scale models; special effects enthusiasts can't resist showing how dated the computer graphics look compared to newer films; yet in many ways the film marked an enormous step forward in cinematic depictions of the disaster. While many facts turned up after the film's release that showed historical or technical errors in the movie, it should be remembered that many of these revelations were only the result of the wave of interest in the ship which swept the world after the film's release.[19]

A 3-D version of the movie was released in theaters on April 4 (UK) and April 6 (USA), 2012 – just days before the centennial of the liner's maiden voyage. As James Cameron said:

There's a whole generation that's never seen 'Titanic' as it was meant to be seen, on the big screen. And this will be 'Titanic' as you've never seen it before, digitally re-mastered at 4K and painstakingly converted to 3D. With the emotional power intact and the images more powerful than ever, this will be an epic experience for fans and newcomers alike.[20]

To mark the centennial anniversary of the sinking, not one but two new productions were filmed. One of these, entitled *Titanic: Blood and Steel*, was a 12-part miniseries focusing on the construction of the ship. An article reported prior to its release that it would 'focus on the design and construction of the luxury liner, with the drama set against the class-bound backdrop of Edwardian Belfast ..., where financial pressures may have led to fatal compromises.'[21]

The miniseries proved to be more of a soap opera than anything else. While the producers managed to get some historical details correct, the majority of the 'facts' it contained were gross distortions of history. The construction timeline of the *Olympic* and *Titanic* was badly mangled; *Titanic* was consistently shown under construction in *Olympic*'s slip; blueprints shown throughout the series were actually of the *Lusitania*; much of the plot was based on the fallacy that financial pressures led to 'fatal compromises' in the construction quality of the two ships. This is but a short list of the many serious errors which historians were shocked to find; they were particularly inexcusable since some of the actual facts presented demonstrated that the producers had access to a large amount of good information when putting the series together, yet decided to present a more 'marketable' production filled with historical errors.

The second production was simply called *Titanic*, and it was a four-part miniseries on the disaster by Julian Fellowes, the creator of the period drama *Downton Abbey*. It was said that this miniseries would 'focus on the lives of the passengers and crew on the famous ship and will feature stories of romance and mystery. Both fictional and historical characters will be included in the drama.'[22]

Fellowes claimed that his production would right some of the historical errors of James Cameron's *Titanic*, but he actually made more than a few mistakes of his own. The ship's officers, including Captain Smith, were placed in wrong locations before and during the collision. In fact, many of the historical characters show up in places they shouldn't be; as one example, Mrs Astor is shown entering Boat No. 5, when she actually entered No. 4 over an hour later. Collapsible B was shown floating off the starboard side of the Boat Deck rather than the port; not to mention *Titanic* was depicted as apparently steaming backwards at one point, and was also shown as sinking on an almost even keel. Fellowes obviously chose not to adhere too closely to the commonly accepted facts of the sinking, regardless of his claims for accuracy.

Over the years, many documentaries regarding the sinking of the *Titanic* have also been produced. These have ranged the gamut from superb – some of the best including A&E's *Titanic: Death of a Dream* and *Titanic: The Legend Lives On*, as well as James Cameron's *Ghosts of the Abyss* – to the downright laughable. Some have helped to bring the ship and its story back to life, portraying facts and offering background information in a way that no cinematic portrayal really could. However, at times, it has been clear that the portrayal of so-called 'facts' is nothing of the sort.

The recent profusion of the latter type of documentary is a particularly unwelcome development for historians interested in preserving history, rather than having history distorted. While films portraying the disaster are clearly entertainment no matter how well put together, or how closely they adhered to the historical record, documentaries purport to represent facts in a historical way. It is important that those interested in history for history's sake compare evidence before simply placing stock in what is presented in a televised broadcast.

At the time of this writing, it remains to be seen whether any new miniseries, films or documentaries will remain true to the historic record, rather than relying on speculative and overly-dramatic or poorly researched interpretations in an attempt to help sell them commercially. Although the latter method is generally applied in the production of most recent works, this choice is absolutely inexcusable in light of the abundance of readily-available historic facts. Whatever the eventual content of future productions, public fascination with the liner is sure to remain intense in the years to come.

On-screen depictions aside, the actual *history* of the *Titanic* also continues to develop. Since the discovery of the liner's wreck in the early hours of September 1, 1985, by Dr Robert Ballard and a team of scientists and researchers, a valuable record of the liner's condition on the sea floor has been made.

Ballard was not the first person to search for the remains of the great ship. Indeed, there are indications that his may not actually have been the first team to find the wreck's location. It is known that during the Cold War, navies from both sides were performing extensive and highly detailed sonar mapping projects of the floor of the Atlantic. This was done as a means both to support submarine operations, and to support anti-submarine detection and warfare. Tantalizing hints and clues have emerged over the years that a large object or objects were located during the course of these mapping efforts. It is also reported that some involved with these expeditions believed that the objects could only have been the wreck of the liner.

However, these have always been second- and third-hand reports; government files on the projects were – and remain – classified, as much of the technology used and some of the information gleaned was of a secret nature, and in some cases may remain pertinent to today's naval operations. Additionally, some of the rumors on the subject have begun to border on a 'conspiracy-theory' level of absurdity. Inconveniently, many of those who claim to have been involved with these 'early discoveries' of the wreck can not easily produce documentation to back up their claims. Without tangible evidence – either from Government records or from those actually involved – the entire subject must remain something of a debatable point.[23] At the very least, such widespread rumors go to show that it is not easy for large projects or endeavors of any sort to remain a secret, particularly with the passage of time. This is something that proponents of the *Titanic/Olympic* 'switch' conspiracy would do well to remember.

What can be stated with certainty was that Ballard's 1985 team from Woods Hole Oceanographic Institute was the first to locate and photograph the wreck and present the information to the public. Ballard had been involved in secret work for the United States Government in locating and exploring the remains of two of their lost nuclear submarines, the USS *Scorpion* and the USS *Thresher*. However, Ballard – who had always dreamed of finding the lost liner – realized that much of the equipment used in those projects could easily be used to find the *Titanic*. He was granted permission by the US Navy to use the equipment in that endeavor once he had finished his other projects. His expedition was a joint venture with the French oceanographic institute IFREMER; the team had been running out of both time and money, having searched the area for what seemed an eternity before stumbling onto the wreck.

The world once again went wild over the *Titanic*. Interest in the ship was stirred to new, unprecedented levels. Further expeditions to the site in the years since have resulted in a remarkable photographic record of the ship as it is today, and many artifacts have been recovered and placed in exhibits traveling the world, allowing people to connect firsthand with the disaster, with the ship, and with the people who were aboard her during her last voyage.

Sadly, the salvage efforts have resulted in a bitter dispute within the *Titanic* community. Some feel that it is blatantly immoral to recover objects from what they consider to be a grave site; some survivors who were still alive after the wreck was found were of this opinion. Others feel that recovering and preserving artifacts from the wreck site provides an incredible advance in our understanding of those who were aboard the ship, and claim that they are attempting to preserve the memory of those lost. While most people cannot afford to visit the wreck site in person, it is much easier for some to visit traveling expeditions which feature the recovered artifacts.

Admittedly, it is difficult to stand in front of these objects and not feel the sudden, pressing *reality* of the *Titanic* and the tragedy of her loss. As something that a majority of the world's population have never personally laid eyes on, it is easy to begin to see the *Titanic* as this sort of mythical creature and the people who were aboard her as sort of half-real characters in her story … in other words real, but never really so as one stares at two-dimensional black-and-white, badly deteriorated photographs. But to suddenly see in person items from the ship – a recovered davit, porthole, personal effects, or even the tremendous 'Big Piece' of the ship's hull – is an experience that is hardly describable.

As the years have passed since 1985, the last survivors of the disaster – and with them, the living memories linking us to the ship – have passed away. Her legacy now rests in the hands of historians and researchers. At times, that future seems doubtful; as the direct human connections to the tragedy have been lost, it is easier for many to take license with the ship's history in order to sell new and demonstrably false ideas on an unsuspecting public. The media eagerly spreads 'new theories' and 'new facts' because they know that *Titanic* stories *sell*; however, they are loathe to reprint retractions even when researchers can clearly demonstrate facts to the contrary. Phrases like 'brittle steel', 'bad rivets', 'cost-cutting' and 'conspiracy' have become common catch-phrases in the media, and are frequently mentioned in discussion among those with a passing interest in the ship; such things do not represent the historical record, however, and it is easy for the public to begin to lose historical perspective.

Artifacts recovered from the ship are also, sadly, susceptible to theft. In late 2011, for example, it was reported that a gold-plated necklace thought to have belonged to Eleanor Widener was stolen from a Denmark artifact exhibition. The necklace was insured for £14,000, but it was felt that it was so easily identified that it would probably never turn up beyond the black market.[24]

More happily, public fascination with the lost ship has ensured many expeditions to the wreck of the liner for the purpose of photographing and exploring her. Through these, many facts about the ship and her construction have been revealed; previously undocumented areas of the liner's interior – previously known only through photographs of her sister ship, *Olympic* – have been photographed and at least some of this material has been shared with the public.

In fact, some of the details unearthed on the *Titanic* have provided historians with insight into lost features of the *Olympic*'s design ... a rather unusual reversal from previous discoveries, where information about the *Titanic* and her design was typically extrapolated from the design of the *Olympic*. These have also produced interesting information on some of the previously unknown differences between the two liners ... differences in the pattern on the gates of her elevators ... the first photographs of the *Titanic*'s Turkish Baths – not seen since Steward Wheat looked in on them at about 12:45 in the morning of Monday, April 15, 1912 – proved the variations in the rooms' configuration from that found on the *Olympic* in 1911 ... the presence of special gates just inside the shell doors of the D Deck First Class Entrance ... an upright drinking glass on the washstand of cabin D-27 ... a bowler hat apparently belonging to Henry S. Harper in his cabin, D-33 ... that the windows of the First Class Dining Saloon (backlit by portholes during the day, and electric lighting at night) were virtually identical to those photographed on the *Olympic* ... the list goes on and on.

There have been numerous expeditions to the wreck of the liner since her 1985 discovery. The first was by Dr Robert Ballard in 1986;[25] then followed expeditions by the salvage company RMS Titanic, Inc., in 1987, 1993, 1994, 1996, 1998, 2000, 2004 and 2010;[26] an expedition to film the wreck in IMAX in 1991;[27] commercial dives by Deep Ocean Expeditions in 1998, 1999, 2000, and 2003; expeditions headed by James Cameron in 1995, 2001 and 2005;[28] a dive for a new documentary by The History Channel in 2005;[29] and also Ballard's return trip to the lost liner in 2004.[30]

Perhaps future expeditions will be able to turn up more information of interest ... a sub-bottom profiler sonar survey of the stern might confirm that the wreck's central propeller really had three blades, rather than *Olympic*'s four ... perhaps the piano on the port side of the Boat Deck First Class Entrance could be reached and photographed? ... perhaps further areas deep within the wreck could be photographed ... maybe sections of the mangled stern's interior could be further explored ... perhaps a portion of a funnel's outer skin could be retrieved and studied for the purposes of confirming the ship's actual shade of 'White Star buff.' As much as is known about the great liner, there will always be more to learn.

Unfortunately, the expeditions to the wreck have confirmed that the *Titanic* is deteriorating. It has become abundantly clear that the sea is slowly consuming the wreck; iron-eating bacteria are eating the ship's steel, and there are signs that portions of the wreck – particularly in the more lightly-constructed superstructure – are even beginning to collapse. Many of the windows on the forward half of the Promenade Deck – added only about a month before the maiden voyage – are beginning to come loose and slide away. Eventually, the wreck's condition will deteriorate to the point that the ship will hardly be identifiable.

Despite the bleakness of the wreck's future, the liner's legacy still lives on today. After the enormous popularity of the 1997 film, the cruise industry began to see a significant up-tick in traffic. While during the 1970s and 1980s, it seemed as if the heyday of the great ships had seen its conclusion, cruising's popularity has actually led to a new round of competition between cruise companies. The 70,000-gross registered ton mega-ships of the 1990s gave way to vessels of 100,000 gross registered tons. Eventually, Cunard – which

had merged with the White Star Line in 1934 – set out to build the world's largest passenger ship. Intended as a glorious successor to the *Queen Elizabeth 2*, the new ship was named *Queen Mary 2*. At 1,132 feet in length and boasting a gross tonnage of 151,400, her interior volume was over three and a quarter times that of the *Titanic*. Slated as a tough-built trans-Atlantic liner that could double as a cruise ship during the winter months, many industry analysts scoffed that she was too big and too expensive to turn a profit.

This seems to be far from the truth. In fact, the *Queen Mary 2* only stood as the 'world's largest passenger ship' for a brief time. The Royal Caribbean Cruise Line, one of Cunard's greatest rivals at the time of this writing, have placed into service five 137,000-ton and three 154,000-ton cruise ships; these were followed by two behemoths – named *Oasis of the Seas* and *Allure of the Seas* – of some 225,000 gross tons each. Each of these is roughly four-and-three-quarters times larger than the *Titanic* in measured interior volume. While some endlessly debate the cruise ships as worthy successors to the passenger liners of the early twentieth century – these frequently quip that the new ships are too big, too crowded, or that their sterns are too ugly and box-like, and so on – the popularity of new tonnage has proven one thing: big ships are still here to stay.

The loss of the *Titanic*, though tragic, also helped to save the lives of many others during the last century. How many other great sea disasters were prevented through the actions of the International Ice Patrol? How many disasters which did take place had a smaller death toll because there were lifeboats for everyone aboard? How many calls for help in the middle of the night were heard because of a 24-hour radio watch? Yet, the sea has long proved a worthy adversary to the best that man can build. The sinking of the *Costa Concordia* on January 13, 2012, with the loss of 32 lives, is a powerful reminder that no ship is unsinkable. The specter of the *Titanic* should never be far from the minds of the officers on today's cruise ships. Her loss is a constant reminder of the need for vigilance. It is hoped that never again will a great ocean liner find its way onto an iceberg in the middle of the night, taking the lives of hundreds or thousands.

In the century since the *Titanic* plunged to an icy grave, the world has changed in many ways; yet she was the epitome of what man was capable of building during the Edwardian Era. Had she survived her maiden voyage and World War I, she most likely would have found great success during the 1920s and early 1930s, even as her sister *Olympic* did. Ironically, one is forced to ask: if she had found a quiet, ignominious end being scrapped in Jarrow, Northumberland, or Rosyth, Scotland, in the 1930s, would she be remembered with such fondness? The answer is simple: probably not. Sinking as a new ship in the spring of 1912, she now stands as this sort of moment 'frozen in time'. As a result, we of an uncertain twenty-first century can nostalgically look back and glimpse what life was like a hundred years ago.

The *Titanic* may have passed from living memory. Yet her history, her legacy, and the remembrance of all the people who set sail aboard her infamous maiden voyage will never, ever be forgotten. The entire concept of the proud and brilliantly-lit ocean liner, settling into a sea of glass in the middle of the night on the North Atlantic, with the haunting refrains of 'Alexander's Ragtime Band' echoing through the still, icy air fires the imagination as very few other subjects in history ever have ... or ever will.

Titanic's final chapter is not yet written.

APPENDICES

Appendix A: *Titanic*'s Technical Specifications & Some Common Misconceptions

PRIMARY PARTICULARS

Overall Length:	882 feet, 9 inches
Length Between Perpendiculars:	850 feet, 0 inches
Maximum Breadth:	92 feet, 6 inches
Draught forward:	34 feet, 6 inches
Draught aft:	34 feet, 7 inches
Displacement:	52,310 tons at 34 feet, 7 inches draught and ditto 143.8 tons per inch draught
Gross Registered Tonnage:	46,328.54 tons
Height From Keel to Navigating Bridge:	104 feet, 0 inches

Further Particulars & Common Technical Misconceptions Regarding *Titanic*

It is worth noting that, contrary to numerous reports in second-hand sources, all three of the *Olympic*-class ships bore an identical length between perpendiculars and length overall. The numbering and spacing of all their frames was identical as well.

Also of interest is the *Titanic*'s given displacement, which was a measurement of the ship's actual weight. Frequently, a displacement of some 66,000 tons is cited for the *Titanic*. However, to achieve 66,000 tons of displacement, she would have needed to draw just over 42 feet 6 inches – about eight feet greater than her registered draught and deeper than the boot-topping paint applied to her hull. Under no circumstances would the ship ever have been loaded that deeply.

In point of fact, the *Titanic*'s displacement could range from a light displacement of 40,806 tons at a draught of 27 feet, 11 inches (this condition would have meant the ship would have been completely devoid of all stores, fuel and fresh water) up to the displacement cited above (52,310 tons at 34 feet 7 inches) and beyond to nearly 54,755 tons at 36 feet of draught. Notably, the *Olympic* and the *Titanic* displaced the same amount of water at identical draughts.[1] Also of interest is that this measurement of weight was given in Imperial Tons, which is comprised of some 2,240 pounds. In modern tons of 2,000 pounds, the ship's weight at a draught of 34 feet 7 inches (approximately 117,174,400 pounds) would amount to just over 58,587 tons. At her maximum registered draught of 36 feet, she would weigh 61,325 modern tons.[2]

Another area of interest to researchers has to do with the gross registered tonnage of the *Titanic*. Frequently, this measurement is cited as the liner's weight. In reality, however, this was a measurement of enclosed volume, not weight. At this measurement, the *Titanic* was roughly half again as large in enclosed space as Cunard's *Lusitania*, which measured some 31,550.47 tons, and their *Mauretania*, which measured 31,937.69 tons. Although the *Olympic* and *Titanic* had started life identically, due to certain alterations in her accommodations during fitting out, the *Titanic*'s final gross registered tonnage was some 1,004 tons greater than her sister's.[3]

In this one area of measurement alone, then, did the *Titanic* have bragging rights over her sister as the 'world's largest ship', and at that the difference was really only on paper. Interestingly, the *Olympic* underwent a number of modifications during her career, and was later measured at a maximum of 46,439.48 gross registered tons – some 111 tons greater than *Titanic*. This shows just how small the differences between the two ships really were, and how flexible the measuring of internal volume was.

All of *Titanic*'s roughly fifty thousand tons of weight needed a tremendous motive power in order to drive the ship through the sea. The powerplant of the *Titanic* was of a hybrid type that would prove most economical. She and her sister were each endowed with a pair of reciprocating engines; these four monsters, two to each vessel, were the largest of their kind ever built, and each produced some 15,000 nominal horsepower. Each of these engines was geared to its own propeller. The marvel of the design, however, came next. The waste steam from these reciprocating engines was then channeled into a low-pressure turbine, which provided some 16,000 horsepower to drive a third propeller, and which was placed along the liners' centerline.

With no additional fuel consumption, the *Olympic* and *Titanic* were thus given more than a 50 per cent increase in power. The total nominal horsepower of some 46,000 was more than enough to allow them to comfortably attain a 21-knot service speed. Although not quite as fast as the Cunard liners, the *Titanic* – and her similarly endowed sister – would certainly prove quite competitive. At the same time, *Titanic* also offered potential passengers a much more comfortable sea voyage to make up for the few extra hours they would spend in transit. There were many times during the career of the *Olympic* when she managed to prove faster than her projected 21-knot service speed, and Bruce Ismay believed that due to some minor improvements in the *Titanic*'s machinery, they were justified in expecting that she would prove marginally faster than her sister.[4]

What kind of minor improvements? Frustratingly, there are a lot of details regarding changes from the *Olympic* to the *Titanic* that are still unknown to modern researchers, simply because there was very little opportunity for documentation on the changes to *Titanic*. Yet every now and then a new bit of information surfaces. For years, it has been well documented that the *Olympic* had two wing propellers, each of which had three blades, and sported a diameter of 23 feet 6 inches, and that her four-bladed center propeller was some 16 feet 6 inches in diameter. There are many photographs of the *Olympic* prior to her maiden voyage that showed this configuration, and many of these photographs have been used to illustrate the configuration thought to be installed on *Titanic*.

However, recently a notebook retained by Harland & Wolff, which gives the engineering particulars of the propelling machinery of the vessels they built, came to light. It clearly indicates that the *Titanic's* central propeller had three blades, rather than four. This original document shows that the *Titanic's* center propeller was slated to be a three-bladed prop with a diameter of 17 feet 0 inches. The same document also shows that the pitch of the blades on both the center prop and the wing props on the *Titanic* was different than those originally fitted to the *Olympic*.

Such an alteration was by no means peculiar; indeed, it is known that in the spring of 1913, the *Olympic* was given a three-bladed center propeller. However, after the First World War, that propeller was replaced with a four-bladed one. Minor changes to the pitch of *Olympic's* propellers were not unusual throughout her career, and demonstrate that propeller science was constantly evolving; naval architects at the yard were tinkering and tweaking in order to derive the best speed and efficiency from the *Olympic's* powerplant. Although the concept that the *Titanic* actually sank with a three-bladed center propeller is rather earth-shattering, it should come as no surprise that there were such alterations to the *Titanic* based on early service experience with her sister. This single series of changes most likely explains why Bruce Ismay testified that he was expecting a minor improvement in the *Titanic's* speed over that of the *Olympic*.[5]

Beyond the incredible powerplant of the *Titanic*, the great liner was, ironically, a very safe ship as well. She was designed with a total of sixteen major watertight compartments, separated by fifteen transverse watertight bulkheads. These bulkheads rose to the base of E Deck forward of Boiler Room No. 1, and up to the base of D Deck aft of Boiler Room No. 1. None of the bulkheads reached up to C Deck, which was the highest watertight deck that ran the full length of the ship, but all of them rose well above the waterline.

For ease of movement between the compartments, the bulkheads were pierced in various locations to interconnect them via hatchways Each hatchway was provided with a watertight door. The doors in question were of the vertically operating type, and had a friction clutch that normally kept them in the raised, or open, position. In the event of an emergency, they could be closed in any of four ways: (1) the Captain or Officer of the Watch could close the important ones from a switch on the Bridge; (2) crewmen in the compartment could also close any of the individual doors by simply tripping a lever next to the door which operated the friction clutch; an alarm would be sounded, normally for about twenty to thirty seconds, before the door was fully closed; (3) the doors could also close themselves, in that a float mechanism mounted beneath the floor would rise with any incoming seawater, and cause the door to lower; and finally, (4) a hand gear was also fitted on the bulkhead deck above, allowing an operator to raise or lower the doors without being present in the actual compartment.

The *Titanic* was theoretically a 'two compartment' ship. This meant that she was designed so that any two adjoining watertight compartments – even the massive Turbine and Reciprocating Engine Rooms – could be flooded without posing any real danger to the ship itself. Alternately, in the event of a head-on collision, any three of her first five watertight compartments, or the first four starting from the bow, could be flooded without really endangering her floatability.[6] Any damage beyond this simply seemed implausible. Even by modern standards the watertight subdivision of the *Titanic* was very safe. Indeed, had the *Lusitania* struck an iceberg in the same manner as the *Titanic*, opening damage along her side, it is quite likely that she would have foundered much more quickly and dramatically than did the *Titanic*.

Much has been made over the years of the fact that the *Olympic* and *Titanic* were called 'unsinkable'. This term was famously used by *The Shipbuilder* magazine; in the course of its special issue on the superliners, it called them 'practically unsinkable'. For a long time, it was believed that the White Star Line itself had perpetuated the idea that they were unsinkable; later generations of researchers pinned the phrase down to the press, however, and some even claimed that White Star never used the term in any of its publicity.

However, the fact is that the White Star Line *did* use that exact word in a late summer of 1910 special brochure on the new steamers. After a discussion of much of the technical details of these great wonder ships, White Star copywriters pointed out that 'as far as it is possible to do so, these two wonderful vessels are designed to be unsinkable'. While not stated as an absolute, it was at the very least a comparable phrase to that used by *The Shipbuilder*. The word 'unsinkable' also seems to have been picked up and used by publicity and ticket agents, as well as some White Star personnel, in conversations with passengers who had booked on *Titanic's* maiden voyage. In the course of such conversations the idea typically conveyed was simply that the liner was unsinkable, without any qualifiers.

In point of fact, however, using such terminology at the time was not considered extraordinary by any means. Indeed some four years earlier, *The Shipbuilder* magazine

The foregoing particulars apply of course to the "TITANIC" as well, and this steamer should take the water a few months after the launch of her sister ship "OLYMPIC." It is anticipated that the latter will make her maiden voyage to New York about July, 1911; and as far as it is possible to do so, these two wonderful vessels are designed to be unsinkable.

This paragraph from a White Star publicity brochure uses the word 'unsinkable'.

had called the *Lusitania* and *Mauretania*, not 'practically unsinkable', but simply 'unsinkable'. The qualifying word 'practically', or other words to that effect, was simply not to be found in that discussion. Use of the word 'unsinkable' in advertising copy, trade journals and the press merely reflected common public opinion that crack trans-Atlantic liners of the day were safe to the point that the ships were really considered lifeboats in and of themselves. Fears of disaster, particularly on the part of nervous passengers unaccustomed to braving the elements on the rugged North Atlantic, could be laid to rest.

Even after the *Titanic* made her maiden voyage, use of this label – or terms like it – did not cease. Once *Olympic* had undergone an extensive series of improvements in her watertight subdivision, during the winter of 1912–1913, confidence again ran high; the press said of the *Olympic* that her builders believed that they had 'realized the quest of an unsinkable ship'.[7] The *Britannic*, third ship of the class, was likewise said to have been so safe that the danger of foundering had been reduced 'to the lowest point, and absolute safety [was] as nearly assured as human skill and foresight can make possible'.[8] Other ships during the twentieth century were also deemed unsinkable, or nearly so. So the use of this term, as it was applied to the *Titanic*, was nothing out of the ordinary and, in fact, was quite common. The term merely garnished attention later on since its application to the *Titanic* was so incredibly ironic.

It has also been implied, over the years, that the quality of the rivets or the hull plates used on the *Titanic* was inferior – either by neglect or in a deliberate cost-saving measure. It has even been suggested that the structures of the *Olympic* and *Titanic* were designed poorly, and that in essence they were very weak ships … disasters just waiting to happen. Further, it has been implied that the structural modifications made to the *Olympic* after the *Titanic* disaster were intended to address these grievous weaknesses in a form of cover-up.

However, the facts really belie these claims. It is true that modern metallurgy tests have proven that the quality of some of *Titanic*'s rivets was sporadic, primarily the soft iron rivets used in certain sections of the hull, as opposed to the steel rivets used elsewhere in her form. However, the quality of all the rivets was generally consistent with the standard shipbuilding practices of the time. There is no evidence of cost-saving at the expense of overall safety. Indeed, only modern analyses of the materials have shown the occasional defects; at the time of *Titanic*'s construction, the British Board of Trade inspector was able to say in a detailed report of the riveting: 'The workmanship is of the highest class throughout.' What, if any, difference better rivets might have made during the actual collision is endlessly debatable, but recent scientific tests have shown her hull was very resistant to damage from collisions like the one she was involved in that night. Beyond that, even with the most modern welded hull, significant damage would have resulted.[9]

As far as the strength of the ship's steel plates, these were thoroughly tested to the satisfaction of the British Board of Trade long before they were ever installed on the side of the ship.[10] Recent investigations have reaffirmed that the quality of their manufacture was not substandard, but rather was quite in line with the steel-making capabilities of the day.

Finally, as regards the strength of the *Titanic*'s hull design, we know that the *Olympic*'s strength, both prior to the *Titanic* disaster and after her post-*Titanic* modifications, was unquestionable. During January of 1912, the ship fought her way through a tremendous gale while west-bound for New York. Captain Smith remembered it as the worst storm he had ever seen during his career. In enormous seas, rails along the Forecastle were torn off, the No. 1 Hatch cover – which weighed five tons – was ripped from its mount and thrown onto the Well Deck, and the steam winch and anchor windlass were loosened. Despite this brutal punishment, there was no sign of weakness in the *Olympic*'s structure, which was comparable to *Titanic*'s on her maiden voyage. Other than some discomfort to a few seasick or nervous passengers, and that it all made for a good story for the papers, the whole storm was something of a non-event. By comparison, during *Titanic*'s initial crossing, the weather was smooth and calm.

Only at the very end, when the *Titanic*'s flooded bow began to drop beneath the sea and her stern section was raised above it, did her structure succumb and begin to fail. Even this final failure, however, is noteworthy, since at the time she was being subjected to forces far greater than her designers had ever built her to withstand; these were far greater than any forces she would ever have encountered during her career. And it is in this final area that another detail of the ship's structural strength has been called into question: the design of *Titanic*'s expansion joints.

Two of these expansion joints were incorporated into the design of the ship's superstructure, which rested atop the main portion of her load-bearing hull. They were designed to allow the superstructure – B Deck, A Deck, and the Boat Deck – to flex as the hull beneath 'worked' at sea. The concept of expansion joints was a relatively new technique adopted by ship designers working in previously uncharted territory. There would be subsequent improvements in handling these stresses on the ship's structure as time went on.

However, as far as the *Titanic* herself went, the expansion joints did not affect the strength of the ship's hull structure, specifically because they were features of the superstructure only. Thus they were not load-bearing elements. By the time the ship was under enough strain to begin its eventual breakup, the hull itself was already beyond designed tolerances; she would have broken up with or without the presence of the expansion joints in the superstructure, and their presence had no bearing upon the actual sinking of the ship.

Indeed the *Titanic* was a strong enough ship that she survived for nearly three hours after a collision which produced damage far beyond her originally-designed tolerances. Right up until the final few minutes of the sinking, she provided a relatively stable platform from which to launch the lifeboats and to send calls for assistance – calls which were answered and resulted, finally, in the rescue of her lifeboats' precious human cargo.

Could the design of the *Titanic* have been better? Certainly in hindsight, there was room for improvement, and such improvements were incorporated into both of her sister vessels. However, there is no direct or indirect evidence to suggest that her owners or builders tried to cut corners at the risk of the vessel's safety, or that the ship was of an inherently poor design. At the time of her construction, she was a very strong ship and one that her builders, her owners, and the people who stepped aboard her decks could rightly have expected would deliver them in perfect safety to the opposite side of the North Atlantic.

Appendix B: From Southampton to Cherbourg

There has always been some vagueness over exactly what times on April 10, 1912 certain events transpired. The ship was scheduled to depart at 12:00 noon, but there is some disparity of evidence on what time she actually cast off. Once the lines had been let go, the escorting tugs moved the ship ahead and turned her to port, until she was pointing down the River Test. Once the *Titanic* engaged her engines, she quickly became entangled in the *New York* incident, which by all reckoning delayed her departure. But by how long? Some estimates put the delay at about an hour. Yet primary references on the point are quite scarce. So is there any way to confirm that length of time, or to find evidence that it may have been shorter or longer?

First, let's start at Cherbourg, France, where the ship was due to make her first port of call that evening. Frustratingly, some passengers recalled that the *Titanic* was due in Cherbourg at 5:00 p.m., while others recalled that she was due at 6:00 p.m. Whatever time they felt that the ship was due, all of the passengers waiting in Cherbourg to board the liner remembered being told that they faced a likely delay of an hour or more. A number of passengers on the *Nomadic* recalled that they boarded the *Titanic* at 7:00 p.m.[1] Margaret Brown recalled that it had taken the *Nomadic* about a half hour to reach the ship once she had anchored. We also know from several sources, including period newspaper accounts, that the ship dropped anchor inside the Cherbourg breakwater at 6:30–6:35 p.m. Paris Mean Time, or 6:20–6:25 p.m. Greenwich Mean Time.[2] It would have taken some minutes of low-speed maneuvering for the ship to enter the harbor, but Margaret Brown said that the process took only 'a few minutes' from her first appearance outside the breakwater.[3]

We also know the approximate distance between the Nab Light – where the Southampton pilot would normally disembark and where the *Titanic* began the open water cross-Channel passage – and the Cherbourg breakwater: 66 nautical miles. Additionally, we know precisely how fast the ship made the cross-Channel trip: 68 revolutions on the reciprocating engines, indicating a speed through the water of 20.2 knots.[4] Thus it would seem that the cross-Channel passage in open water took about three hours and fifteen minutes.[5]

Now let us return to the times for the departure from Southampton. There is actually quite a bit of disagreement over what time the *Titanic* cast off from the dock. She was scheduled to sail at noon sharp. However, those present on the occasion disagreed as to what time the departure actually began:

- 'She left Southampton at 12 o'clock.'[6]
- 'Twelve.'[7]
- 'It sailed at noon on the 10th instant.'[8]
- 'Just after twelve.'[9]
- 'I think a little after 12; a little after noon.'[10]
- 'We left Southampton at about 12:05 p.m.'[11]
- 'We left the dock at 12.15.'[12]
- 'The ship started at about 12.15.'[13]
- ' … a quarter past twelve.'[14]

It would seem from this disparity in statements that the departure came somewhere between 12:00 and 12:15 p.m.

Indeed, if the actual time she cast off nearly split the difference between those two extremes in recollections, that would nicely explain the three categories of estimates: 'Noon', as in precisely; 'just after', but apparently not quite a quarter past; and 'about 12.15' to '12:15'. However it is difficult to be dogmatic on the point in lieu of firmer, and elusive, evidence. For the sake of this discussion, we will place the departure at 12:15 p.m., although it should be recognized that it may have occurred several minutes earlier than that.

Yet all of this discusses merely the time when *Titanic* cast off from the dock. 'Departing Southampton' was not a simple, definable 'moment' in time. There was the time that the liner cast off from her berth, to be sure, but there was also the point at which she entered the main channel and began her course down-river toward open water. Additionally, the journey to open water – along a twisting route of approximately twenty-five or more land miles, or about twenty-two nautical miles – would have taken quite some time. It had to be negotiated carefully. This was particularly true of the 'reverse-S' maneuver to enter the Solent, the final and relatively straight cut of water that would take the ship down toward Portsmouth, and eventually open water. All of this would seem to complicate an estimate of the amount of time that it should have taken for *Titanic* to reach open water, and thence connect with our estimates both of the time she dropped anchor in Cherbourg, and the length of time it would have taken for her to cross the Channel through open water.

Fortunately, we can find some assistance in estimating just how long the voyage to the mouth of the Solent would have taken the *Titanic* on Wednesday, April 10. Where does this aid come from? When her older sister *Olympic* – of nearly identical size and maneuvering capabilities – departed Southampton on September 20, 1911, she had just made it to the mouth of the Solent when she collided with the Admiralty cruiser HMS *Hawke*. Although a terrible incident in and of itself, the ensuing legal entanglements provided an opportunity for the minutes from *Olympic*'s logbook on that day to be read into evidence. We thus know precisely how long it took from when the ship cast off from the dock until she collided with the *Hawke*. Since weather conditions were relatively similar on September 20, 1911 and April 10, 1912 – without unusually high winds or reduced visibility – and since the two departures were made under the same Pilot and same Captain, the comparability increases to a close approximation. Knowing how long it took *Olympic* to make it to the mouth of the Solent should tell us how long it should have taken *Titanic* to reach the same point, had the *New York* incident *not* interfered.

On the morning of September 20, 1911, the *Olympic* cast off at 11:10 a.m. Proceeding down the River Test, she reached Black Jack Buoy at 12:30 p.m., and began the 'reverse-S' maneuver to enter the Solent at 12:34 p.m. That maneuver encompassed some ten minutes' time, ending at 12:44 p.m. At that point, the *Olympic* had entered the main channel, and her engines had been returned to 'Full Ahead'. This order on the telegraphs had also engaged her turbine engine. She was accelerating to a speed of 20 knots for the trip down the Solent. She collided with the *Hawke* at 12:46 p.m., before she had reached her intended speed. This means that, in total, it took the *Olympic* 1 hour and 34 minutes to enter the Solent and set her engines to 'Full Ahead'. The Solent was largely a straight cut of water with a run of about 14–15 nautical miles; covered at an average speed of 20 knots, passage through the Solent would have encompassed about three-quarters of an hour's steaming time. Had the *Olympic* not collided with the *Hawke*, she likely would have reached the Nab about 2 hours and 20 minutes after casting off from the dock, or at about 1:35 p.m.

By comparison, the *Titanic* cast off from the same dock at about 12:15 p.m. Without the interference of the *New York* affair, she most likely would have reached the Nab at about 2:35 p.m. that afternoon. Ordinarily, at that point the ship would have needed to stop her engines, and the Pilot would have disembarked to the waiting pilot boat by Jacob's ladder. Only once the smaller boat was clear would the ship have re-engaged her engines. This step was well-rehearsed and in good weather would have taken but a short time if everything went smoothly. In general terms, one period reference book described a departure from New York Harbor – fairly representative of the procedure in any major port – in this manner:

> The trip down the bay is, of course, always interesting, even to New Yorkers. Ellis Island, the Statue of Liberty, Staten Island, and Coney Island, are all soon left behind. In the meantime the sailors have been getting out the sea ladder for the pilot's descent; at last the steamer is abaft the pilot boat ... looking not unlike a private yacht. A rowboat is put off from the steam pilot boat and the sailors throw the rowers the rope and the boat is trailed alongside and brought underneath the sea ladder. There is a sharp clank-clank in the engine-room of the signals and the machinery stops, while the pilot with his little bag of mail shakes hands with the captain and disappears over the rail. He reaches the rowboat, the rope is cast off, and as soon as it is a safe distance from the ship, clank-clank goes the engine signal from the bridge, and the machinery is not usually stopped again until a foreign port is reached.[15]

From this general description we can surmise that with an experienced pilot like George Bowyer, a familiar port, and good weather, the entire process of dropping the pilot could have taken as little as 10–15 minutes. The trip down to the Cherbourg breakwater would have encompassed about 3 hours and 15 minutes time from the Nab Light. Thus, without the *New York* incident, and including a pilot drop-off at the Nab, the timing of the departure would appear to be thus:

12:15 – Casts off from White Star Dock.
1:50 – Emerges from 'reverse-S' curve, enters the Solent with all engines engaged for 20 knots.
2:35 – Arrives at the Nab, stops to disembark Pilot Bowyer.
2:45–2:50 – Re-engages engines (68 revolutions/20.2 knots) bound for Cherbourg.
6:00–6:05 – Arrives at entrance to Cherbourg Harbor.

This gives us a good approximation of the time that the *Titanic* would have reached the Cherbourg breakwater, had the *New York* affair not have intervened: about 6:00–6:05 p.m. Greenwich Mean Time. If it took the liner 'a few minutes' to enter Cherbourg Harbor and drop anchor, then she most likely would have finished at about 6:10–

6:15 p.m.[16] Keeping in mind that the ship apparently cast off from the White Star Dock about fifteen minutes late, this careful reconstruction of the timeline would indicate that passengers who recalled that the ship was due to arrive in Cherbourg at 6:00 p.m. were accurate, as opposed to those who felt the ship would arrive at 5:00 p.m.

This arrival estimate is further backed up by the timing of *Olympic*'s maiden voyage departure – also made in good, clear weather. Having cast off from the dock, it took quite some time for the accompanying tugs to maneuver the ship out into the main channel. Once this had been accomplished, the tugs departed at 12:45 p.m., and the ship was solidly under way by 1:00 p.m. She arrived at Cherbourg, without any further delays, at 7:00 p.m., some six-and-a-quarter hours after the tugs cast off from her side in Southampton. It was reported that the liner's speed across the Channel was not pushed, despite the delay in departure.[17] Without the delay in entering the main channel, which was reported to have taken about an hour, it seems quite likely *Olympic* would have made Cherbourg around 6:00 p.m.

An anticipated arrival time for the *Titanic* of around 6:00 p.m. in Cherbourg seems even more likely since French clocks were not set to Greenwich Mean Time. Although France had accepted Greenwich, England as 'Longitude 0' in 1911, it still had not accepted the standard world time zones by the following spring. A period guidebook said:

> A number of European countries have not accepted *Standard Time* based on the meridian of Greenwich, but base their time on a meridian of their own. France, for instance, uses the local mean time of Paris, which is 9 minutes and 21 seconds faster than *Greenwich Time*. This is the time that appears outside of railroad stations, but the clocks inside by which the trains are operated are five minutes slower.[18]

Based upon Paris Mean Time, France continued to define legal time as GMT plus nine minutes and 21 seconds until August of 1978. So on April 10, 1912, French clocks were running 9 minutes and 21 seconds ahead of British clocks. According to Paris Mean Time, then, the *Titanic* was originally to drop anchor at about 6:10 p.m. Her late departure from the dock would have delayed that time to anchoring to as late as 6:25–6:30 p.m. Paris Mean Time. So although the *Titanic*'s clocks were running according to Greenwich Mean Time all that afternoon and evening, we must allow for the possibility of a ten-minute discrepancy from ship's time for those who awaited the ship in Cherbourg, depending on what time zone the timepieces they used were set to.

What is even more interesting is that our primary sources for the anchoring time of 6:30–6:35 p.m. come from French papers, and it is doubtful that they would have recorded that time in Greenwich Mean Time just because the ship's clocks were set to that time. So for that time estimate, subtract about ten minutes, meaning that the ship apparently dropped anchor in Cherbourg at 6:20–6:25 p.m. GMT. This is roughly 10–15 minutes after she should have dropped anchor, had there been no *New York* incident. So up to this point, it would appear that the *New York* incident only delayed the *Titanic*'s arrival in Cherbourg by 10–15 minutes. However, several things are not yet factored in.

First, it is interesting to note that there is evidence that the *New York* incident was not the only delay experienced by *Titanic* in clearing Southampton. One of the First Class passengers bound for Queenstown, 31-year-old theological student Francis M. Browne, watched the departure with great interest. He later wrote that the delay whereby the *New York* was brought out ahead of the *Titanic*'s bows was 'but for a moment, and then we slowly forged ahead down Southampton Water with the Channel open and free before us'. Yet he also recalled that there was, very shortly afterward, a second delay: 'A tug came to take ashore the workmen and navvies who had been arranging the luggage in the storerooms, and we were fully off.'[19]

So it would appear that there were really three separate delays in leaving port: the initial delay in casting off, of perhaps as much as 15 minutes, the delay to allow the *New York* to clear the *Titanic*'s bows, and the delay to allow a few stragglers to disembark by tug. It would be ludicrous to suggest that the latter two delays would have postponed the ship's arrival in Cherbourg by only 10–15 minutes. So how could the *Titanic* have made up for lost time?

It seems that the key may lie with Trinity House Pilot George Bowyer. There is some evidence which suggests that Bowyer remained aboard the *Titanic* during the entire voyage down to Cherbourg.[20] Why would Bowyer have stayed with the ship? From time to time, Harbor Pilots were forced to stay with the vessels they took out of port, particularly if bad weather made a transfer to the pilot boat extraordinarily dangerous. Yet on that Wednesday afternoon, the weather was ideal. It would seem that there is only one logical explanation: omitting a stop at the Nab Light to disembark Bowyer would have saved about 10–15 minutes and helped to get the liner back on schedule.[21]

This means that the *New York* incident as well as the pause to disembark a few crewmen who had stayed aboard too long to a nearby tug could now total a more believable 20–30 minutes. If the ship cast off from her dock before 12:15, then any of those minutes would have to be added back in to that delay. This means that the delays from the two pauses *together* – not just the *New York* incident, but also the stop to offload the navvies to the tug – might have totaled a maximum of 35–45 minutes, depending on the exact time that the ship had cast off.

Although all of these estimates are just that – carefully reconstructed estimates – it would seem that the *New York* incident did not delay the ship's arrival in Cherbourg by a full hour's time. So why were so many told that the incident with the *New York* had taken a full hour? One must remember that the ship had left her dock late, perhaps up to fifteen minutes late. Thus, it is easy to see why passengers waiting in Cherbourg were told that the ship had been delayed by an hour. When a 20–30-minute delay from the two separate pauses was combined with being as much as 15 minutes late in casting off from the dock, it all added up to a delay of about three quarters of an hour, some of which seems to have been made up by omitting the stop to disembark Pilot Bowyer at the Nab. In Cherbourg, White Star and other local officials were probably completely uninformed that some of that delay may have been caused by a late departure from the dock; all they – and passengers there waiting to board – knew was that the ship arrived about an hour late. With the amount of time the ship was delayed from casting off and the second pause being somewhat forgotten through the pages of history, the impression which has

been given was that the delay caused by the *New York* incident took more time than it really did.

Still, one might ask: is there any eyewitness evidence that could back up a shorter delay by the *New York* incident? Major Peuchen later recalled: 'I should think we were delayed probably three-quarters of an hour by this trouble.'[22] Third Officer Pitman recalled that the delay was not serious, but rather set the ship back by 'about half an hour'.[23] So after careful consideration, it seems that the *New York* incident and the subsequent stop to offload a few stragglers to the nearby tug delayed the *Titanic*'s departure by at most three-quarters of an hour.

Appendix C: The Question of Binoculars

In the years since the *Titanic* sank, much has been made of the fact that the lookouts were not supplied with binoculars, or 'glasses', as they were frequently termed at the time. It has been intimated that because Lookouts Frederick Fleet and Reginald Lee were not given a set on that cold, dark night, they were not able to spot the iceberg in time, with disastrous results. But where did this concept originally come from, and does it stand intense scrutiny?

In part, this story may have originally sprung from Frederick Fleet himself. At the American Inquiry, Senator Smith asked Fleet whether he could have spotted the iceberg at 'a greater distance' if he had been provided binoculars. Fleet replied: 'We could have seen it a bit sooner.' When pressed, 'How much sooner?' Fleet responded: 'Well, enough to get out of the way.'[1] At the British Inquiry, Fleet made a similar implication, stating that if he had a pair of binoculars handy, then he 'certainly' could have seen the iceberg sooner, and in 'time for the ship to get out of the way.'[2]

In point of fact, despite all of the rush and haste to get the *Titanic* ready for her departure from Belfast, a supply of 'Theatre, Marine and field' glasses, or binoculars, were supplied for each of the ship's officers, as well as a pair for the Captain and another pair – typically called pilot glasses – which were to be left on the Bridge.[3] When the lookouts in the Crow's Nest found that they did not have any glasses upon leaving Belfast, Second Officer Blair had lent them a pair. He gave Lookout George A. Hogg – who would stay with the ship through the maiden voyage – his own set of glasses, which were marked, 'Second Officer, S.S. "Titanic".[4] However, Hogg remembered that when the ship arrived in Southampton, Blair came up to the Nest and told him 'to lock them up in his cabin and return him the keys.'[5] Blair gave this order even though there was a storage box in the Crow's Nest to keep them in, located in the port-aft corner.[6] Hogg did as directed, proceeded to the Second Officer's cabin, and locked the glasses up. Before he could return Blair's keys, he was tapped for some sort of work on the Forecastle, and he passed the keys on to Seaman William Weller, who had also come down from Belfast, so that he could give them to Blair.[7]

However odd it might initially sound, there really was nothing unusual about this procedure. Seaman Jones said that in his experience, the binoculars were not left in the Crow's Nest while the ship was in port, as they could get stolen. As a result, lookouts would 'go to the office and get them when we left port' and bring them up to the Nest.

The glasses would remain there for the trip but then, 'upon arriving at port again, [the lookouts would] take them into the office.'[8] Fred Fleet also remembered that the glasses he used aboard the *Oceanic* were not kept in the Crow's Nest while the ship was in port; at the end of each voyage, they were taken back to the Second Officer.[9]

Thus, it does not seem that there was anything particularly unusual about the lookouts needing to go find a pair of binoculars when the time came to leave port. Accordingly, at some point on the day of the liner's departure from Southampton, Lookout George Symons had gone to Second Officer Lightoller[10] in the hopes of obtaining a set of glasses.

'What is it, Symons?' Lightoller asked.

'We have no look-out glasses in the crow's nest,' Symons replied.

Lightoller responded with an: 'All right,' and proceeded to Chief Officer Wilde's room. 'There are no look-out glasses for the crow's nest,' he told the Chief Officer. Wilde responded that he was aware of the fact, and that he 'had the matter in hand,' but that there were no glasses for the lookouts. Lightoller returned to the waiting lookout man, and told him: 'Symons, there are no glasses for you.'[11]

With that, Symons left and informed the other lookouts of the fact.[12] This may have been the point when Lookout Lee remembered a discussion among himself, Symons, Fleet, Hogg, and Evans on the subject. However, that did not mean that the lookouts gave up in asking for them. Lookout George Hogg remembered that he had also asked Lightoller for glasses after departing Queenstown. 'Where is our look-out glasses, sir?' Although he didn't exactly catch Lightoller's response, he recalled that it was something like, 'Get them later.' Whatever the precise wording of Lightoller's answer, Hogg had no more success in procuring a set than Symons had.[13] The lookouts were simply going to have to make do without them during the trip.[14]

Having a set of glasses available to lookouts was not entirely uncommon on ships of the period. Archie Jewell recalled having a pair on seven or eight voyages on the *Oceanic* prior to the *Titanic*'s maiden voyage.[15] George Symons had been with the *Oceanic* as lookout for three years, and similarly remembered having binoculars on that liner.[16] Fred Fleet also recalled having a single pair of glasses for the lookouts' use on every trip he made aboard the *Oceanic*. However, he also remembered that they were 'very poor', and that he could hardly see much of anything with them.[17] Seaman John Poingdestre, who also had transferred from the *Oceanic*, said that he knew that binoculars had been supplied to lookouts on other liners, and had used them personally.[18] Seaman Thomas Jones had served as a lookout on the *Majestic* for twelve months, and subsequently on the *Oceanic*. He went so far as to say that he had never known a Crow's Nest to be without glasses.[19]

However, such a provision was far from universal. Lookout Reginald Lee had just transferred from the *Olympic*, but he had been at sea for fifteen or more years. Generally speaking, he was not aware of glasses being supplied to the lookouts. On those occasions when he did have them for use, he was unsure as to whether they were supplied by the company or privately owned.[20] Quartermaster Walter Wynn also said that while he knew that glasses had been provided for the lookouts on the *Oceanic*, he did not think that it was the typical practice on other ships unless the weather was foggy.[21] Lookout George Hogg said that he 'always had night glasses in the White Star boats',[22] but his experience as a lookout with the White Star Line was limited to a single round-trip voyage on the *Adriatic*. When he had served as a lookout with ships of other steamship companies, he had never been supplied with binoculars.[23]

The lack of consistency in the provision of glasses for lookouts may have stemmed from differing opinions on their use. Not everyone felt that binoculars were necessary or, indeed, even useful for lookouts in the Crow's Nest to have. Some thought that they could actually be detrimental to the lookouts' job, as the glasses might allow them to fix their attention in one small area of the horizon for too long. Indeed, using them all the time would have cut a lookout's field of vision dramatically; if he was not focused in the right area at the right time, he could easily miss something important. Even for those who felt binoculars were useful to the lookouts, it was thought that they were best used only *after spotting* an object, as an aid in identifying the object seen, and obtaining further useful information about it.

For example, Archie Jewell said that glasses for the lookouts were 'very useful'[24] and that when they were available, he used them 'very often'.[25] Reginald Lee agreed with Jewell, saying that having and using glasses was 'better than the ordinary eyesight'.[26] However, he did admit: 'If you have got good eyesight it is not necessary to have them perhaps.'[27] George Symons said that he found glasses 'very useful'.[28] Yet by the same token, he said that a lookout would use his 'own eyes as regards picking up anything', and the glasses would only be used afterward to 'make certain of that object' and examine it for further information.[29]

Frederick Fleet also said that while glasses were handy, he would only use them if the lookouts 'fancied we saw anything on the horizon', and that he would depend upon his naked eye first to sight objects, and then use the glasses.[30] Interestingly, he contradicted himself later on when he said that he would use glasses 'constantly' when on a 'sharp lookout' such as he was on the night of April 14.[31] Shortly thereafter he reversed himself again, agreeing that he would use his naked eyes alone to detect an object, and then use the glasses to make sure of it.[32]

Lookout George Hogg said that he trusted his eyesight first in detecting objects; only then would he use binoculars. Personally speaking, he felt that the glasses were not really meant to detect objects, but rather to study them once sighted.[33] Seaman Thomas Jones, who had served as a lookout on previous voyages, felt that glasses would not be 'much of a help to pick anything up; but to make it out afterwards, they were'. He also felt that at night they were 'not of any use at all', and that he would prefer his own eyesight rather than glasses.[34]

Captain Stanley Lord of the *Californian* said that he 'would never think of giving a man in the lookout a pair of glasses'.[35] He said that he simply did 'not see any necessity for it', as once the lookout reported the presence of an object or light, 'it has nothing to do with him what it is afterwards'.[36] Although the *Oceanic* was widely reported to carry binoculars for her lookouts, her Captain, Bertram Fox Hayes, later said that binoculars 'spoil the look-out', and that it wasn't the lookouts' business to find out what the object he sighted was, which way it was going and so forth. That, he said, was the officer's business. White Star's Marine Superintendent, Benjamin Steele, said that he didn't even believe in using them.[38] Captain Richard Jones of the Dominion liner *Canada* – an IMM ship – said that he did not think it desirable to have lookouts use glasses, because 'in the first place, it is very difficult to focus the glasses, and if the glasses are not properly focused the man might as well have a blank tube to look through'.[39] Even famed explorer Ernest Shackleton said that he did not believe in 'any look-out man having glasses at all'.[40] Captain Moore of the Canadian Pacific liner *Mount Temple* said that he 'never' had glasses used by his lookouts, but that every one of his officers had his own glasses, and they were used from the Bridge.[41]

Second Officer Charles Lightoller was asked about whether glasses would have been used only after detecting an object. He replied: 'Each man uses them as he wishes. Different men have different ideas of the glasses, and of using them. Some keep them glued to their eyes altogether. I consider that very detrimental.'[42] He personally liked to have glasses in hand when he was on watch on the Bridge, but would only put them up to his eyes occasionally.[43] In his personal experience, he said that he had always seen an iceberg first with his eyes, and then examined it through glasses.[44] Lightoller also agreed with Captain Lord in that the officers didn't want lookouts to identify what an object was, but instead merely to report its location to the Bridge.[45] With regard to spotting a derelict, iceberg, or other item that was close to the ship, the lookout man 'must not hesitate a moment, and on the first suspicion, before he has time to put his hand to the glasses or anything, one, two, or three bells must be immediately struck, and then he can go ahead with his glasses and do what he likes, but he must report first on suspicion'. Only for an item much further out did Lightoller feel that a lookout should investigate the object with his glasses before reporting it.[46]

Bruce Ismay was asked about White Star's policy of supplying glasses to lookouts. He responded: 'I believe up to the year 1895 we used to supply look-out glasses to the look-out men, and since that date I think it has been left to the discretion of the commander whether he gives them look-out glasses or not.' He also acknowledged that there were then some considerable differences of view prevalent about having lookouts use binoculars. However, if a certain ship's Captain wanted glasses, White Star would make provision of them.[47] Harold Sanderson said that he thought Ismay believed in binoculars' usefulness more than he personally did.[48]

It seems that although a good supply of glasses was brought aboard the *Titanic* for the use of her senior officers, no provision was made for the lookouts to receive glasses. Whether this was an oversight – an item lost or misplaced in the haste of those last days in Southampton before she departed on her maiden voyage – or whether they were simply deemed unnecessary is unclear. Even Lightoller, who was so connected with the lookouts' request for binoculars, claimed that he could not say whether any glasses had been specifically supplied for the use of the lookouts on that voyage, and if not, why.[49]

The binoculars which were initially made available to the lookouts on the trip down from Belfast were the same set assigned to then-Second Officer Blair, and were subsequently returned to his cabin. When Blair left the ship, and Lightoller became Second Officer in his place, the glasses were probably utilized by Lightoller through the subsequent voyage. That means that the glasses Lightoller recalled using on his watch during the night of April 14 were most likely – although not certainly – the same pair which had been used by the lookouts on the trip down from Belfast. The decision by Blair to share his set of glasses with the lookouts seems to have been a personal one; it seems not to have occurred to Lightoller to repeat the offering despite the lookouts' requests.

As far as the lookouts were concerned, it is clear that they seemed to like having binoculars handy; in spite of the varying opinions on their use, after the disaster lookouts began to raise a 'popular cry' to be supplied with them. As a result, Harold Sanderson said that the White Star Line had decided to provide binoculars for lookouts on their ships.[50] However, testimony at the inquiries was relatively unanimous in agreeing that having them was unnecessary for use in initially spotting objects such as icebergs, and the British Inquiry saw no need to recommend that they be supplied to all lookouts. In fact, modern tests have been made with binoculars on dark nights on open water; the tests demonstrated that using such glasses to detect objects is highly ineffective, and borderline pointless.[51]

Of far greater consequence was a factor that absolutely no one had control over: the elements. In the cold air that night, as the ship moved forward through the atmosphere, this produced an icy 'wind' that cut into the faces of the lookouts in the Crow's Nest. Their unprotected eyes stinging and tearing, the lookouts would have squinted into the night, braced for the duration of their watch. Although these elements were not unknown to lookouts on the Atlantic in cold temperatures, it is possible that they reduced the ability of Fleet and Lee to identify the iceberg in time to avoid a collision.

Blaming the disaster, even in small part, on 'mysteriously missing' binoculars certainly makes for a good – not-to-mention oft-repeated – story. However, after a careful consideration of the evidence, we are left to conclude that their absence had little or no effect on the outcome of the collision.

Appendix D: What Time Is It?

Over the years, considerable controversy has existed over what time *Titanic*'s clocks were keeping when she struck the iceberg at 11:40 p.m., April 14, 1912. This time, termed 'Apparent Time Ship' (ATS), was changed daily as ships moved east or west, in order to proportionately account for the difference in time between European and American ports. On east-bound trips, the days were shortened and clocks were set ahead. On west-bound trips, the days were lengthened, and the clocks were set back.

Each of the three formal investigations into the sinking reached a separate conclusion on the *Titanic*'s ATS after the accident, and each of these conclusions differed from the other two. The American Senate Inquiry concluded she was 1 hour and 33 minutes ahead of New York Time; the British Inquiry concluded she was 1 hour and 50 minutes ahead of New York Time; and the Limitation of Liability Hearings in 1913 concluded that she was 1 hour and 39 minutes ahead of New York Time. Obviously, all of these conclusions couldn't be right. So, the simplest thing to do is to compare the evidence and follow it through to its natural conclusion. For the sake of simplicity, the present authors will only refer to west-bound crossings; the same principles would apply to east-bound crossings.

On the *Titanic*, during a west-bound crossing, the ship's clocks were set back each night so that at local apparent noon[1] the following day, the clocks would read 12:00; setting them back at night while the passengers slept would no doubt have made for an easier adjustment on passengers' body-clocks. A 1924 brochure for the *Olympic's* passengers stated:

It is necessary to put the clock back every 24 hours. The alteration in time is made at about midnight, and the clock is usually put back from 35 to 45 minutes on each occasion, the exact amount of time depending upon the distance the ship is estimated to make by noon the next day. During the first 24 hours, however, owing to the change from mean time to apparent time, the alteration is likely to be considerably more than 45 minutes.[2]

That this alteration was usually made at midnight aboard the *Titanic* herself is confirmed by the evidence of Second Officer Lightoller and Third Officer Pitman. Pitman's testimony is revealing:

Senator SMITH: When were the ship's clocks set; do you know?
Mr. PITMAN: They are set at midnight every night.
Senator SMITH: They were set at midnight?
Mr. PITMAN: Every night.

Pitman continued: 'They are corrected in the forenoon, perhaps half a minute or a minute; that is all.' Then Second Officer Lightoller added: 'The clocks are set at midnight, but that is for the approximate noon position of the following day. Therefore [at noon the next day] the clocks will be accurate.'[3]

However, every time the clocks were adjusted, this resulted in a lengthening of the night watches. If all of this was placed into a single watch, crewmen could rightly have complained. However, it is known that the time shift was carried out among the two night watches for the crew. The adjustment was split roughly equally, with the first half being carried out at 12:00 midnight, and the second being carried out at 4:00 a.m. Both of these adjustments would thus be after all public rooms had closed, and after passengers were supposed to be in bed.

Beyond this, it can be established that no adjustment had been made to the *Titanic's* clocks up to midnight on Sunday, April 14. How? Third Officer Pitman was asked: 'Were they set at midnight Sunday night?' Pitman replied: 'No; we had something else to think of.'

Quartermaster George Rowe was on duty at the time of the collision. He later said that his 'watch should have ended at 12:22 but time went by and no relief turned up,' a clear reference to unadjusted ship's time.[4] Frederick Fleet also said that he and Lee, on duty in the Crow's Nest at the time of the collision, were to have a watch that was 'about 2 hours and 20 minutes' in length.[5] Quartermaster Hichens, at the ship's helm, was also relieved at 12:23 a.m. by Quartermaster Perkis.[6] Obviously, all of these survivors, on duty at the time of the collision, could not have been wrong about expecting a clock adjustment at midnight that night.

It is also clear that the adjustment was never carried out. When Hichens was relieved, he also specifically noted that

it was at 12:23 a.m., not 12:00 as the clock would read if the ship's clocks had already been adjusted. That being the case, why weren't the clocks set back as was expected? As Pitman said, after the collision, 'we had something else to think of'.[7]

Some have postulated that the first of the two clock setbacks actually occurred at 10:00 p.m. on the evening of April 14. However, there is evidence to the contrary. First, there is the testimony of Quartermaster Hichens at the American Inquiry, which does not seem to allow for such a possibility. How so?

Hichens was on duty from 8–12 p.m. He clearly stated that his watch that night was to total four hours' time, 'two hours standby and two hours at the wheel'. He was also clear in saying that he was not relieved until 12:23 a.m. unadjusted time.[8] If an adjustment had been made to the ship's clocks at 10:00 p.m., and another was due again at midnight, then Hichens would have been on duty for 4 hours and 47 minutes – nearly five hours, not the 'four hours' Hichens referred to. Starting at 8:00 and running until 10:00, Hichens was the Standby Quartermaster while Olliver had the helm; then he took the wheel from Olliver at 10:00 p.m., at which point Olliver became the Standby Quartermaster. From their 10:00 p.m. switch until the collision, Hichens said he was on duty at the wheel for 'one hour and forty minutes'.[9]

In addition to Hichens' statements, if half of the adjustment was made while some passengers were still awake, and others were asleep in their rooms, one could expect a wide variation in the recollections of passengers and crew as to when the ship hit the iceberg, and when it sank. Yet, the large majority of survivor evidence points to the collision having occurred at about 11:40 p.m. and the sinking occurring at 2:20 a.m. Finally, it should be pointed out that no actual evidence has been presented to the effect that the ship's clocks were adjusted in any way before midnight, at a time such as 10:00 p.m. The midnight adjustment was to be the first of the night, and the second adjustment, amounting to some 24 minutes, would have been made at 4:00 a.m. on the morning of April 15.[10]

As a result of this, it can be seen that all through the day of Sunday, April 14, *Titanic's* clocks were running at the estimated position of that ship for noon of that same day. What time was that? Based upon navigational evidence, this would amount to 2 hours and 2 minutes ahead of New York Time, and 2 hours and 58 minutes behind Greenwich Mean Time, based upon her noon position of 43° 02' N 44° 31' W.[11]

This navigational evidence is supported by evidence from Harold Bride.

Senator SMITH: Did you have a watch or clock in your room?
Mr. BRIDE: We had two clocks, sir.
Senator SMITH: Were they both running?
Mr. BRIDE: Yes sir, one was keeping New York time and the other was keeping ship's time.
Senator FLETCHER: The difference was about 1 hour and 55 minutes?
Mr. BRIDE: There was about two hours' difference between the two.[12]

During his testimony, Bride obviously felt it necessary to correct Senator Fletcher in showing that ship's time was then running about two hours ahead of New York Time, not 1 hour and 55 minutes. His testimony is particularly important since the clock in the Marconi Room keeping ship's time was tied into the Magneta circuit, which was a slave clock to the master clocks on the Bridge.[13] It was obviously important for the Marconi Operators to be able to record transmission and reception times in New York Time.

Unfortunately, the matter has recently become a subject of contention among some *Titanic* researchers because the 2 hour and 2 minute time difference places the clocks of the *Titanic* and the *Californian* only about twelve minutes apart. This is inconvenient for some of the *Californian's* staunchest defenders, as it happens to support some of the evidence that the *Californian* saw the *Titanic's* distress rockets.

However, it should be stressed that this information was first turned up by a defender of Captain Lord, Leslie Harrison, and is supported by firm navigational and eye-witness evidence. Although a number of erroneous time estimates for ship's time have been advocated – beginning with the three formal inquiries into the disaster – the 2 hour and 2 minute time is the only one that is backed up by a broad spectrum of data and fits in with the known speeds and locations of the ship right from when she left Southampton.

Appendix E: Taking Evasive Action

Ever since 1912, the often-repeated story of the collision goes something along these lines:

> … At a little before 11.40, one of the look-outs in the crow's nest struck three blows on the gong, (Hichens, 969) which was the accepted warning for something ahead, following this immediately afterwards by a telephone message to the bridge 'Iceberg right ahead.' Almost simultaneously with the three gong signal Mr. Murdoch, the officer of the watch, gave the order 'Hard-a-starboard', and immediately telegraphed down to the engine room 'Stop. Full speed astern.' (Boxhall, 15346) The helm was already 'hard over', and the ship's head had fallen off about two points to port, when she collided with an iceberg well forward on her starboard side.
>
> Mr. Murdoch at the same time pulled the lever over which closed the watertight doors in the engine and boiler rooms. (15352) …
>
> … From the evidence given it appears that the '*Titanic*' had turned about two points to port before the collision occurred. From various experiments subsequently made with the s.s. '*Olympic*', a sister ship to the '*Titanic*', it was found that travelling at the same rate as the '*Titanic*', about 37 seconds would be required for the ship to change her course to this extent after the helm had been put hard-a-starboard. In this time the ship would travel about 466 yards, and allowing for the few seconds that would be necessary for the order to be given, it may be assumed that 500 yards was about the distance at which the iceberg was sighted either from the bridge or crow's-nest.[1]

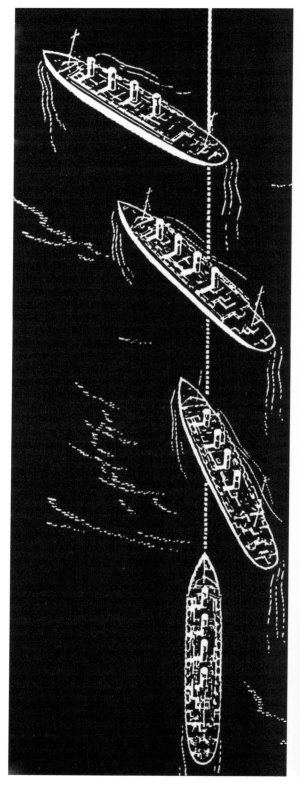

A period illustration of how Olympic *and* Titanic *turned.*

However convincing this may sound, the reality is that the Court's conclusions were wrong in certain fundamental respects.

Thirty-Seven Seconds?

For starters, let's take the 37-second portion of their conclusion. Where did this estimate come from? Edward Wilding testified:

> Since the accident, we have tried the 'Olympic' to see how long it took her to turn two points, which was referred to in some of the early evidence. She was running at about 74 revolutions, that corresponds to about 21-and-a-half knots, and from the time the order was given to put the helm hard over till the vessel had turned two points was 37 seconds.[2]

While the data in itself is very useful information, how does it compare with the situation the *Titanic* was in as Murdoch took evasive action to avoid the iceberg? Certainly, the *Olympic* and *Titanic* maneuvered very comparably because of their identical size, weight,[3] and rudders, as well as the close parallel between their machinery. However, the *Titanic* was cutting through the water at almost precisely 22.5 knots, not 21.5 knots. Although the difference might seem inconsequential, the one-knot difference would have introduced significant variables in the maneuvering characteristics of the vessels.

Also, it should be noted that the time being estimated was from the time that the officer gave the order to turn *Olympic*'s wheel to the time that she had achieved a turn of two points. One point equaled 11.25°, so two points equaled 22.5°. But why was this time measurement taken only to a turn of that degree? Apparently, this was based on the testimony of Quartermaster Hichens, who said that the *Titanic* had 'just swung about two points when she struck' the iceberg.[4]

Yet, the *Titanic* may not have turned quite that far when she first made contact with the iceberg. Lookout Fleet thought that she had not turned quite that much. He said that she had turned only 'a little over a point, or two points' before the collision.[5] We also know from Quartermaster Olliver that Murdoch reversed his turn as the iceberg passed the Bridge, ordering: 'Hard to port!'[6]

Some have argued that despite Olliver's testimony, this order never took place. These critics typically cite the evidence of Quartermaster Hichens, who was at the wheel at the time, and who said nothing about the matter in his testimonies in the two inquiries. However, *Carpathia* passenger Howard Chapin interviewed Hichens while they were both on the *Carpathia*, just a day or so after the sinking. In this account, Hichens plainly related that a 'hard-a-port' order was given just seconds after the 'hard-a-starboard' order.[7] It is unknown why Hichens did not mention this in the inquiries.

However, the basic truth is that since the *Titanic* was steered from the rudder at her stern, if she was allowed to continue under the port turn without alteration, significant damage would have taken place over a much greater length of the starboard side than actually happened. The only thing that explains the lack of any hull damage aft of midships along the ship's side is that Murdoch reversed his turn when the bow began to swing to port. Such a maneu-

ver would also explain Quartermaster Rowe's testimony that when the ship stopped her 'head was facing north'.[8]

From all of this, it seems likely that the two full points Hichens was referring to was the maximum swing of the bow before the 'hard to port' order began to take effect and the ship began to turn the other way. In other words, the collision most likely began *before* the ship's swing had reached two full points. All of this means it is nearly certain that less than thirty-seven seconds elapsed from the time that Murdoch gave the 'hard to starboard' order until the first moment of the collision.

Additionally, the court concluded rather speciously that Murdoch's order to turn to starboard came 'almost simultaneously' with the sounding of the bell. However, Fleet had phoned down to and conversed with Moody after sounding the warning bell. Then Moody had relayed the warning to Murdoch. All of this happened *before* Murdoch's order to turn was given. Both Hichens and Fleet agreed that about a half a minute elapsed during that time before Murdoch's order to turn was given.[9] Lastly, even Boxhall indicated that the evasive action was taken only very shortly before the collision, saying that Murdoch's spoken 'hard to starboard' order was given 'just a moment before' the collision.[10]

A Bungled Maneuver?

Another detail regarding the evasive action which needs addressing has to do with Hichens' actions at the wheel, and a theory which has recently received widespread media attention. Before presenting the details of this theory, it is important to understand the typical confusion which has surrounded the helm orders given by First Officer Murdoch: in a holdover from the days when tillers were used to control ship's direction, in 1912 an order for 'hard to starboard' literally meant to turn the ship's bow to port. This was because pushing the tiller to starboard would have turned the rudder – and thus the ship – in the opposite direction.

With this in mind, according to this theory, while most ships of the time had the 'reversed' helm, the *Titanic*'s helm was of a new style, where a starboard order meant just that. In the heat of the moment, the story goes, Hichens bungled the steering maneuver, panicking and turning the wrong way.[11] It is alleged that these precious lost seconds doomed the ship to strike the iceberg, thus making Hichens the man responsible for sinking the *Titanic*. This purported blunder was allegedly covered up by everyone involved, but Lightoller himself is supposed to have passed the details on to his wife, Sylvia, before he died.

While this theory received a great deal of media attention, the 'facts' as presented simply do not add up. For starters, Lightoller was not even present when the evasive action was taken, and was instead asleep in his berth at the time. Supposedly, the information was relayed to him by those present, during a conference between the four senior officers shortly after the collision. However, one has to wonder: when did this alleged confab take place? None of the other officers ever formally informed Lightoller that the ship was sinking, so when would they have had time to convey such a blunder by the helmsman to him?

Even if such a conference did take place, and the information was passed on directly to Lightoller, the theory as it was revealed to the public did not even come directly from Lightoller. Rather, it was supposedly presented by the senior officers to Lightoller, then to Lightoller's wife

Sylvia, and then from Sylvia to other members of their family. Basing such a startling revision of history upon a single source – let alone a fourth-hand one at that – is not a particularly good place to start.

Finally, even the simple premise that the story is based on – namely, that *Titanic*'s helm was set up differently from other ships of the era – is not based in fact. We know from evidence presented in the *Olympic/Hawke* inquiry that *Olympic*'s helm adhered to the 'reversed' design which was standard in 1912. The Brown's Patent Telemotors that the wheels were attached to, and which relayed commands hydraulically to the rudder, were of a single patented design. Their use was common not only to the *Olympic* and *Titanic*, but also on other famous ships such as the *Lusitania*, *Mauretania*, and later the *Aquitania*. In other words, all of the ships whose helms were controlled by Brown's Patent Telemotors functioned identically – whether they were ships built shortly before or shortly after the *Titanic*.[12]

While the helms were rigged identically on various British liners of the period, is it possible that the orders were misunderstood somehow? The answer is again negative. In the 1913–1914 International Conference on Safety of Life at Sea, the Conference recommended that 'in view of the diversity of practice and opinion the … different countries, the question of the adoption of a uniform system of helm orders should be considered'. Such confusion was thus the result of various nations having different and non-uniform systems of giving and interpreting helm orders. However, no formal international rule was laid out by that Conference, and neither was such a rule made in the 1929 International Conference on Safety of Life at Sea. In 1931, one reason for the lack of such a rule was given by W. Graham, President of the Board of Trade, in June of 1931:

> The reluctance of British seamen to change their traditional system, and the misgiving which some of them feel as to possible danger in the event of a change of their system, were fully stated by the British delegates [at the 1929 Conference].[13]

So even as late as 1929, British seamen were opposed to changing their method of giving helm orders from the traditional system which was in use aboard *Titanic* in 1912, and which had been in use for something like three hundred years. It was not until 1935 that all maritime nations informally agreed that the direction of a turn should be referenced by the direction of the rudder rather than the direction of the helm or tiller.

One last straw which some might grasp at on this subject is: the *Titanic* was an American-owned ship. Is it not possible that this in some way opened the way for the alleged confusion? In a word, no. The *Titanic* may have been American-owned, but she was built to British Board of Trade specifications as a British-flagged vessel. Additionally, the officers and men on the Bridge that night were to a man British seamen – the same stock of British seamen who, in 1929, were noted to be opposed to the changing their long-standing tradition of helm orders. In short, there is no basis to believe that there was any confusion about the intended direction of turn on the night in question. Murdoch's helm orders were promptly and correctly carried out by Quartermaster Hichens under the watchful eye of Sixth Officer Moody.

Were the Engines Reversed?

Finally, we come upon the subject of the order to reverse the ship's engines. Fourth Officer Boxhall is the only person who testified that Murdoch ordered 'Full Astern' on the telegraphs prior to the collision. Although the exact details given vary, Firemen Frederick Barrett and George Beauchamp, Trimmer Patrick Dillon, and Greasers Thomas Ranger and Frederick Scott – who were down in the Engine and Boiler Rooms – all testified to having received the order of 'Stop' either just prior to the collision or right after the collision, or to having seen the engines stop. None testified as to having received a 'Full Astern' order prior to the collision.[14]

Back on the Bridge, while Hichens, Olliver and Boxhall all recalled the conversation between Captain Smith and First Officer Murdoch, only Boxhall included the segment of having 'run the engines full astern'. According to Hichens at the American Inquiry:

> The skipper came rushing out of his room – Capt. Smith – and asked, 'What is that?' Mr. Murdoch said, 'An iceberg.' … Capt. Smith [said] to Mr. Murdoch: 'Close the emergency doors.' Mr. Murdoch replied, 'The doors are already closed.'[15]

Hichens recalled at the British Inquiry that 'about a minute … after the collision the Captain rushed out of his room and asked Mr. Murdoch what was that and he said, "An iceberg, Sir", and he said, "Close the watertight door." … [Murdoch said], "They are already closed."'[16]

Olliver recalled that as he entered the Bridge, he watched as Murdoch 'turned the lever over and closed' the watertight doors. Then, 'just after she struck', he overheard Murdoch report 'to the captain that they [the watertight doors] were closed'. Again, there was no mention of reversing the engines; in fact, Olliver said that the engines were not reversed while he was on the Bridge, although he did remember Captain Smith subsequently telegraphing 'Half Ahead'.[17] However, he also said that the ship had 'almost stopped' when the engines were put at 'Half Ahead'. Knowing that, he agreed with Senator Burton's conclusion that 'he must have backed the engines, then'.

Of the three, Boxhall alone recalled the same exchange, but with the added detail:

> The captain said, 'What have we struck?' Mr. Murdoch, the first officer, said, 'We have struck an iceberg. … I put her hard astarboard and run the engines full astern, but it was too close; she hit it.' … Mr. Murdoch also said, 'I intended to port around it. … But she hit it before I could do any more.' … Mr. Murdoch continued to say, 'The water-tight doors are closed, sir.' … [And] the captain asked him if he had rung the warning bell. … [Murdoch] said, 'Yes, sir.'[18]

At the British Inquiry, Boxhall's recollection was nearly identical:

> The Captain was alongside of me when I turned round. … [He] asked [Murdoch] what we had struck. … The first officer said, 'An iceberg, Sir. I hard-a-starboarded and reversed the engines, and I was going to hard-a-port round it but she was too

close. I could not do any more. I have closed the watertight doors.' The commander asked him if he had rung the warning bell, and he said, 'Yes.'

We do know that the ship's engines were engaged in reverse *shortly after* the collision. Trimmer Thomas Dillon recalled that the engine order telegraph had rung only 'two seconds' before the ship struck the berg. The engines then stopped about 'a minute and a half' after the collision, and then about 'a half a minute' later, they 'went slow astern' for about 'two minutes'. Subsequently he recalled them going forward again, which would match up quite nicely with Quartermaster Olliver's evidence that Captain Smith had re-started the engines at 'Half Ahead' shortly after the collision.[19]

The testimony of Trimmer Dillon is at least partially reinforced by the recollections of Quartermaster Rowe. He said that following the collision, as the iceberg passed along the side of the ship, he felt vibrations on the stern from the engines reversing, and pulled the taffrail log in to prevent the line from fouling the propellers.[20] Although he wasn't on the Bridge at the time, Third Officer Pitman also testified that he was told that the ship went full astern *after* the collision, not before.[21]

Similarly, Charles Stengel recalled hearing the engines stop 'two or three minutes' after the impact, and that they next 'started again just slightly; just started to move again'.[22] Mrs Hoyt recalled hearing a 'noise ... which seemed to indicate that the engines of the ship had reversed'.[23]

So when did Murdoch order the engines reversed? It is difficult to say.[24] From several different lines of evidence, it seems most likely that less than thirty seconds had elapsed from the time when Murdoch gave his order on the engine order telegraphs – whatever order that was – to the time of the impact. Thus, even if Murdoch had initially rung down an order for 'Full Speed Astern' on the engines, it is very unlikely that the engines would have been reversed before the collision. Why?

If such an order had been rung down, the engineers would have faced a complex process: the throttles to the two main engines needed to be closed, and their rotations allowed to slow until they were nearly stopped; only then could the reversing levers be thrown over and the throttles opened back up. It has been estimated:

> Under the best of circumstances, with engineers standing by to receive orders via the telegraphs, reciprocating engines of the size and type on *Titanic* could be stopped and reversed within 30 seconds, with another 50 to 60 seconds elapsing before the engines would be backing hard. On the night of April 14th, however, an emergency Full Astern order would have caught the engineering watch completely by surprise, so additional reaction time would have to be factored in.[25]

So whatever Murdoch's initial order at the telegraph was, due to the mechanical design of the ship, the speed with which her engines were being operated, and the short period of time between the sighting of the berg and the impact, it is quite clear that the engines could not have been brought down from full speed and then reversed before the collision was felt. As the engines did not affect the overall evasive maneuver, the exact order Murdoch gave actually played no part in the collision. Coincidentally, this fact clears the cloud which has hovered over Murdoch's reputation – perpetuated after the fact – which intimates that his maneuver had actually doomed the ship.

Another question arises, looking at the sequence of events afresh: what was Murdoch doing during the roughly thirty seconds between the time that the warning was rung down on the bell and the time he gave the order to starboard the helm and he ran to the engine order telegraphs? Murdoch very likely spotted the iceberg concurrent with the lookouts, particularly since he was lower to the water, and the iceberg would likely have blotted out more of the stars from the horizon than it would have from the lookouts' position.

Perhaps Murdoch was carefully ascertaining the berg's extremities in the darkness, whether the ship was actually on a collision course with the berg, and – once he realized it was – which direction and what course of action seemed best. Only once he had gone through these three steps would he have given the orders to take evasive action.

As even a cursory examination of the actual testimony by the eyewitnesses shows, events played out rather differently than has been commonly accepted over the years. Even the evasive action taken did not happen as is commonly represented in books, documentaries and films on the subject.

Appendix F: The Iceberg Damage

For many years, the common perception was that the *Titanic*'s hull was torn open like tinfoil by the collision with the iceberg, opening a gash along almost three hundred feet of her length. The simple fact is, however, that the *Titanic* would have sunk very quickly had her hull been shredded in such a manner. Even as early as the British Inquiry, this legend was laid to rest on good authority.

After listening to the eyewitness evidence on the levels of the water, and what time those were observed after the collision, Harland & Wolff's Edward Wilding was able to estimate how much water had entered the vessel in so many minutes; these calculations allowed him to compute the approximate size of the actual iceberg damage. He related:

> I cannot believe that the wound was absolutely continuous the whole way. I believe that it was in a series of steps, and that ... it was the end of one of the series of wounds which flooded the different spaces [Boiler Rooms Nos. 6 and 5].
>
> My estimate for the size of the hole required (and making some allowance for the obstruction due to the presence of decks and other things.), is that the total area through which water was entering the ship, was somewhere about 12 square feet. The extent of the damage fore and aft, that is from the foremost puncture to the aftermost puncture in the cross bunker at the forward end of No. 5 boiler room, is about 500 [*sic*] feet, and the average width of the hole extending the whole way is only about three-quarters of an inch. That was my reason for stating ... that I believe it must have been in places, that is, not a continuous rip. A hole three-

quarters of an inch wide and 200 feet long does not seem to describe to me the probable damage, but it must have averaged about that amount. ... It can only have been a comparatively short length, and the aggregate of the holes must have been somewhere about 12 square feet. One cannot put it any better than that.[1]

By and large, Wilding's conclusions about the nature of the iceberg damage were entirely forgotten by the public, who imagined that only a giant rent in the hull could have felled the greatest ship in the world.

However, while well supported, Wilding's calculations lacked direct evidence to confirm them. When the wreck was discovered in 1985, hopes were high that the original iceberg damage could be found and photographed. Unfortunately, when the bow made contact with the soft sediments of the sea floor, it had buried itself nearly up to the anchors at the bow. This effectively hid all of the forward damage from visibility. However, when Ballard explored the wreck in 1986, he was able to explore the lower starboard side

hull in the vicinity of Boiler Rooms Nos 5 and 6, where the sediment was not as deeply piled up. Since Frederick Barrett had given clear testimony of side damage running along the starboard hull in this vicinity, this seemed to be the only area where such original testimony might be confirmed.

Exactly as expected, some of the hull plates along the starboard hull – right in the vicinity of Boiler Room No. 6 – were clearly damaged. Ballard reported that the ...

... damage we were able to observe and photograph seemed quite minor: a number of separated and horizontally creased hull plates, the openings ranging from less than an inch to six inches in width. On the bases of the portion of the damaged hull we were able to see – from a point just aft of the Well Deck to its furthest aft point a couple of feet into boiler room No. 5 (roughly between hull frames 58 and 80 forward) – Wilding's hypothesis that the damage was intermittent seems to be supported.[2]

These two images show the iceberg damage locations reported by Paul Matthias' sonar survey. The upper image shows the damage along the shell of the hull, while the lower one shows the various compartments breached. The aft-most segment of damage, which stretches for about forty-five feet, is still visible on the wreck. This final segment of damage is the one which sealed Titanic's fate.

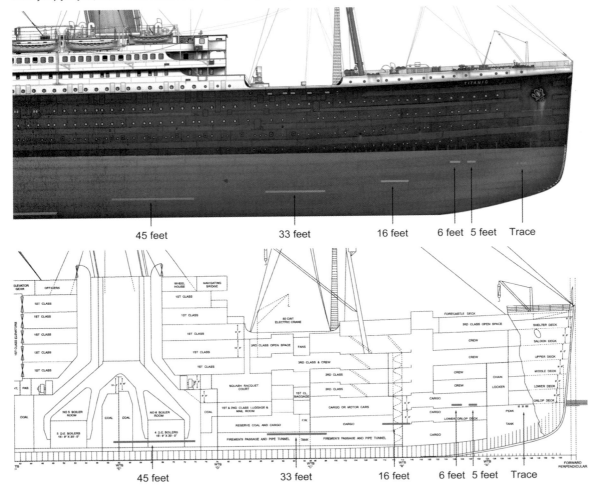

45 feet   33 feet   16 feet   6 feet 5 feet   Trace

45 feet   33 feet   16 feet   6 feet 5 feet   Trace

While such damage might be attributable to the impact with the sea floor, this was damage *directly where* Barrett's eyewitness testimony placed it. Instead of being viewed from the inside of the damaged Boiler Room, it was instead being seen from the outside for the very first time.

In 1996, sonar specialist Paul Matthias, in cooperation with RMS Titanic, Inc., did a survey of the mud-covered regions of the bow. He reported finding six sections of iceberg damage-related deformations in the hull, including the one visible along the side of Boiler Room No. 6. His findings seemed to closely match the reported damage done to the ship. Critics of his work point out that Matthias found much more damage which he did not choose to report, including damage on the port side of the hull, thus negating the usefulness of any of his findings. However, as the damage pattern so closely harmonizes with the known extent of the damage done to the ship, it should not be so quickly dismissed.

One thing that Matthias did not claim to be able to do is discern the *width* of these deformations in the hull; however, as their width could have been affected when the ship impacted with the sea floor, that fact does not negate the value of knowing the locations of the deformations, which were spread out over a length of roughly 230 feet.[3] Interestingly, even the trace damage Matthias reported in the Forepeak harmonizes with the damage pattern reported by Hemming and others, in that it was below the top of the Peak Tank.

In other words, intermittent contact with the iceberg caused a number of openings in the hull of the ship along the starboard side. Each of these was rather small in nature and on their own would have posed no threat to the ship's safety. However, spread out over the length of the ship, they were enough to doom the liner.

Opening the Watertight Doors?

While the subject of the iceberg damage and subsequent flooding is being discussed, a brief mention might be made of an often-repeated bit of criticism against the ship's officers and crew. It has been suggested that the ship's watertight doors should have been opened after the collision, allowing water to flow aft along the bottom of the ship. This, it is proclaimed, would have allowed the ship to settle evenly into the water, and to have stayed afloat for far longer.

This theory is entirely implausible. It fails to take into account the fact that if this had been done, the ship would have lost her longitudinal stability, and thus her ability to remain upright in the water; this means that she would have listed at a steep angle, before rolling over and sinking. It is estimated that this would have happened about a half hour sooner than she sank in reality. Beyond that, she also would have lost power sooner than actually happened, plunging everyone into darkness, interfering with the lifeboat loading and ability to send distress calls, and ultimately causing panic and more deaths among those still aboard.[4] More people would likely have died before *Carpathia* arrived as well.

Also complicating this theory is the fact that no watertight doors interconnected the forward four watertight compartments (Forepeak through Cargo Hold No. 3); this means that the majority of the damaged areas were not accessible to compartments aft by the opening of watertight doors. Finally, even if the crew had opened the watertight doors between the remaining compartments, the flotation

mechanisms built in to the doors would have closed them as soon as incoming seawater lifted them.

Appendix G: The Duff Gordon Affair

Perhaps no incident on the night of the sinking is more mysterious to modern researchers than the events that transpired in Boat No. 1 after it left the *Titanic*'s Boat Deck, and before it tied up alongside the *Carpathia*.

On the night that the *Carpathia* docked in New York, Lady Lucy and Sir Cosmo Duff Gordon dined with a few of their friends, including Abraham Merritt, the editor of the *New York American*. Lady Duff Gordon freely gave her account to her friends.

About a half hour after Mr Merritt left, he called her on the telephone. 'Mr. Hurst has just rung me up,' he said, 'and must have your story of the "*Titanic*" wreck for tomorrow morning's newspaper. May I tell your story as I have heard it?' She gave her permission, and the story went to press the next morning, first appearing in the *New York American* of Friday, April 19, 1912.[1] The account was quite vivid, and gave some interesting details about the sinking. It was also worded in the 'first person' manner, suggesting to the lay reader that it was a direct quotation rather than a later summation by a reporter.

However, when called to testify at the British Inquiry, Lady Duff Gordon flatly denied many of the details of the account as it subsequently appeared in the *London Daily News*, and claimed that many of the details were an 'invention' by the reporter.[2]

When one goes back to read the paper's story, however, the modern researcher is more or less left scratching his or her head. Many of the details in that newspaper account harmonize beautifully with Sir Cosmo Duff Gordon's testimony at the British Inquiry, and also with original private letters written by Lady Duff Gordon to family and acquaintances.[3] Many of the details also agree closely with those given in her personal autobiography, written in 1932.[4] Included among these was that she awoke her husband after the collision, that after more than one investigation he ascertained their need to dress and head up to the Boat Deck, and even the fact that Boat No. 1 was about 200 yards away from the ship when the ship sank – something that is nearly unanimously agreed upon by occupants of the boat who touched on the point.

Nevertheless, at the Inquiry Lucy took exception to a large portion of the newspaper account attributed to her, calling it 'rather inventive'.[5] In particular, she denied some of the events on the Boat Deck, as they were about to board Boat No. 1, that the newspaper account had detailed. She denied that an officer had asked if she was ready to board,[6] that she had said to her husband that they might as well board the boat, even though it would be 'a little pleasure excursion until the morning',[7] the terminology of referring to Boat No. 1 as 'the captain's special boat',[8] and so forth. She also took exception to statements in the article concerning specific details of the final moments of the ship, and whether she heard any cries for assistance after the sinking. She specifically stated that the occupants of her boat were nearly silent throughout the sinking. She also said very definitely that after the *Titanic* sank, she 'never heard a cry', although she heard 'terrible cries' be-

Sir Cosmo Duff Gordon testifies at the British Inquiry.

fore the ship sank. 'My impression,' she recalled of the time after the sinking, 'was that there was absolute silence.'[9]

Where does the truth lie? What is clear today is that the boat did not return to aid swimmers in the water, even though it was only about 200 yards away from the site, and many of the boat's occupants recalled hearing the pleas for assistance clearly. Leading Fireman Charles Hendrickson said that he suggested going back, but the passengers – particularly Sir Cosmo and the two female occupants, Lady Duff Gordon and her secretary, Laura Francatelli[10] – objected that they would be swamped if they did so. It is also quite clear that about twenty to thirty minutes after the *Titanic* sank, Sir Cosmo offered £5 to each of the crewmen in his boat, ostensibly to start a new kit.[11] Once aboard the *Carpathia*, this gesture was in fact paid – apparently in the form of a £5 order.[12] From other evidence, it is quite clear that the cries in the water went on for quite some time after the sinking, gradually diminishing; in other words, according to Sir Cosmo's own recollections, his offer of £5 was made concurrent with the time that many other survivors said the cries for assistance were still audible. Whether the offer was made in innocence or not, it certainly looked *very* suspicious.

To an unjustifiable extent, any male survivor of the wreck had a lot of explaining to do to a very irate public. However, all of the occupants of Boat No. 1 seemed destined to particular scrutiny, as it only carried twelve occupants – about one-quarter its full capacity. As the Duff Gordons steamed east from New York to Europe aboard the *Lusita-*

nia, the press had a field day with their story. They openly stated that Sir Cosmo had, in an act of cowardice, bribed the crew into not returning and helping those in the water. When the couple disembarked the *Lusitania* in Liverpool upon their arrival in England, they went to catch the Boat Train to London. At the station, newsboys ran by shouting, 'Read about the *Titanic* coward!' Nearby placards advertising newspaper stories read, 'Baronet and Wife Row Away from the Drowning', and, 'Sir Cosmo Duff Gordon Safe and Sound While Women Go Down on *Titanic*'. Lucy recalled her husband's face was stricken. When they reached home, they found a barrage of letters; some supportive from friends, others filled with hate.[13]

The actual truth of what happened and – more importantly – why it happened may never be known. Yet it is quite clear, from her private correspondence with Mrs Asquith, that Lady Duff Gordon was worried about her husband. The direct assaults on their reputation weighed heavily upon him – and with good reason. Whether or not the attacks were true on any level, the Duff Gordons had a reputation to uphold and social circles of the day were loathe to forgive even perceived mistakes; the stories could have ended Lady Duff Gordon's career. They could quickly have found themselves ostracized from proper society.

No matter whether the offer of £5 had been made as a generous gift or as a direct or implied bribe, the whole affair simply looked bad. Thus, it becomes very clear why Lady Duff Gordon was so adamant that they had never heard the cries for assistance. Although there is a consensus that after the *Titanic* sank she became violently ill – whether due to shock and fear or due to seasickness – there is little reason to believe that she could not have heard such a clamor from a distance of only 200 yards in the still of night and in an open boat.

On this subject, Lady Duff Gordon's account from the newspaper story is far more believable than her story at the Inquiry. This begs the question: What else from that newspaper story – given among good friends immediately after landing in New York, and before things got ugly in the press – was accurate, and what was not? Obviously, some portions of it were very inconvenient in light of the controversy that engulfed the couple upon returning to England. Was it true, as Lady Duff Gordon asserted at the British Inquiry, that the newspaper editor sent along his rough comments, and then they were later worked up by a clever writer? Or was the story something that was more carefully transcribed and published, but which Lady Duff Gordon was forced to deny because it had started a terrible wave of controversy? Is it possible that the essence of the story was accurate, but that certain portions of it were not transcribed completely accurately, giving Lady Duff Gordon the opportunity to pick it apart from the witness stand?

If any portion of her newspaper account agrees with statements that she made in her personal letters, or in her testimony, or in her autobiography, or is in harmony with the general evidence given by others, then it is most likely accurate and has been included in the narrative as such. Where the accounts differ, it is likely that the exact truth will never be known.

A staged reenactment of an officer shooting steerage passengers on the Titanic. *The re-enactment was photographed on the* Mauretania.

Appendix H: Incidents of Gunfire During the Sinking

Of all the mysteries relating to the sinking of the *Titanic*, incidents of gunfire remain one of the most controversial. Three instances of shots fired prior to the sinking were discussed in the inquiries, and can be documented to varying degrees by sources other than the testimony.

The most thoroughly documented shooting event took place during the lowering of Boat No. 14, when the crowd began to get unruly and attempted to rush the boat. Fifth Officer Lowe testified that as his boat was lowering past A Deck, he saw a group of 'Italians' preparing to jump into it, and fired three shots along the side of the ship to warn them off. Lowe felt that he had overloaded No. 14, and that the sudden jerk of someone jumping down into the boat might cause it to buckle. Lowe stated emphatically that the shots were aimed at no one in particular, and that nobody was hit.[1]

Lowe's version of events is backed up by, among others, the accounts of Able Bodied Seaman Joseph Scarrott, Saloon Steward George Crowe, and First Class passenger Sara Compton, who all stated that he fired warning shots;[2] First Class passenger Daisy Minahan, who said Lowe threatened to shoot any man who tried jumping into the boat,[3] and Second Class passenger Charlotte Collyer, who claimed Lowe only threatened men with a revolver.[4]

Another incident of gunfire that was documented in the inquiries, albeit by one eyewitness, relates to warning shots fired during the launch of Collapsible C. This event is very controversial, because this is the boat that J. Bruce Ismay, the Managing Director of the White Star Line, was rescued in. Ismay himself testified that there was no

struggle on the part of the men to get into boats, and that when he stepped aboard Collapsible C, there were no passengers left on deck.[5]

Quartermaster George Rowe's testimony partially corroborates Ismay's claim, indicating that while there were still crewmembers on deck as the collapsible lowered, there were no women and children or passengers.[6] Barber August Weikman said that there were no women in the vicinity when Ismay boarded the boat,[7] as did Third Class Pantry Steward Albert Pearcey,[8] and First Class passenger William Carter.[9] None mentioned gunfire or panic. Carter did qualify his statement, claiming that he heard no shooting while he was on the Titanic, but could not say what happened after he left the ship.[10]

First Class passenger Hugh Woolner's testimony in the Senate Inquiry contradicts what the crewmembers and Ismay had to say about the conditions surrounding the launch of Collapsible C. Woolner testified that he and fellow First Class passenger Mauritz Håkan Björnström-Steffansson were helping load Collapsible D on the port side when they heard shouting on the starboard side of the ship. Curious, they crossed over in enough time to see two flashes of a pistol in the air, and First Officer Murdoch shouting at men who had been 'swarming' into the collapsible there to get out of the boat.[11] Björnström-Steffansson confirmed Woolner's versions of events, saying that he saw one of the officers 'fire his revolver into the air twice'.[12]

First Class passenger Jack Thayer claimed to have seen Ismay 'push' his way into the last lifeboat. Thayer agreed that two shots were fired to stop men from boarding the boats, but believed that the person who fired them was Purser Hugh McElroy, not Murdoch.[13] Fireman Harry Senior said that he saw the 'first officer' produce a revolver and fire what he took to be warning shots aimed over the heads of two or three men who were trying to rush the boats.[14] Among others, Third Class passengers Emily Goldsmith and her son Frankie Goldsmith gave additional supporting evidence. They independently claimed that as Collapsible C was about to lower away, men tried rushing the boat, and that an officer had to fire warning shots in the air to keep them back.[15] Second Class passenger William Mellors stated that he saw an officer threaten men with a revolver to prevent them from entering the boat as it lowered.[16] While the exact details of what happened are not clear, it is difficult to reconcile the accounts that describe no crowds or panic at that boat with those that indicate that warning shots were fired.

The only other incident of shots being fired prior to the sinking that is mentioned in the Inquiries comes from Colonel Archibald Gracie. Gracie testified that Second Officer Lightoller told him that he had to fire a pistol to prevent Steerage passengers from rushing the last boat on the port side, presumably Collapsible D. Gracie stated that this was hearsay, as he did not see or hear this himself.[17] In his book, Gracie told a slightly different story. He said that Lightoller told him that he drew his pistol and threatened the men who rushed the last port boat, but mentions nothing about shots actually being fired.[18] In his own book, Lightoller claimed that he had to force men out of the 'emergency boat' by brandishing his 'unloaded' revolver.[19]

While the evidence of gunfire at Collapsible D is hazy, it is clear that there was some form of gunplay at that boat, possibly involving both Lightoller and Chief Officer Wilde. First Class passenger Jane Hoyt stated that when Collapsible D was partly filled with women and children, there was a rush of 'steerage passengers' on the boat, and it 'looked as if it might be upset'. She said that Wilde pulled out his gun and 'ordered every man in the boat to get out'.[20]

These are the only incidents of gunplay prior to the sinking that are documented in the Inquiries. Eyewitness accounts from survivors who were never called to testify indicate the possibility that there were additional incidents; among these, there are even accounts which suggest that one of the Titanic's officers may have fired on passengers and then killed himself. While the details are all rather hazy, it is clear that the events that played out as the ship sank were not as calm as popular myth suggests, particularly in the latter stages of the sinking.[21]

Appendix I: The Loss of Deck Crew on the Titanic Over Time

As early as 1:00 a.m., during the loading of Lifeboat No. 6, Second Officer Lightoller was lamenting the lack of seamen available to launch and man the lowering lifeboats.[1] This is remarkable because, at that time, only four lifeboats had left the ship (Nos 7, 5, 3 on the starboard side, and No. 8 on the port side). Was Lightoller's assessment that few seamen were available accurate, and if so, why were more not available to help during the evacuation? What happened to them?

Since the following analysis discusses professional seamen who were available to help launch the lifeboats, and man them once afloat, more than just the Able Bodied Seamen have to be considered. It would be necessary to include the other members of the Deck Department who would have been called trained sailors, or fit the general description of 'seaman', 'sailor', 'deckhand', etc. This includes the six Quartermasters, all of whom left in lifeboats, and who in most cases were in charge of the boat they were in. We must also include the officers themselves, since we know that Captain Smith and all of the senior and junior officers supervised, or took part in, the loading and lowering of the boats. Furthermore, several of these – Lightoller, Boxhall, Pitman, and Lowe – eventually took charge of lifeboats after they left the ship. Of the sixty-six listed members of the Deck Department Crew, forty-three survived.[2]

We also know that Boatswain Alfred Nichols and six crewmen – very likely all of whom were Able Bodied Seamen[3] – had been sent below by Second Officer Lightoller during the loading of Lifeboat No. 6, at around 1:00 a.m. He had instructed them to try and open the D Deck Reception Room doors, with the idea of making it possible for the lifeboats to come alongside and take on additional passengers from those locations. Nichols and the six men were never seen again after going below. Lightoller speculated that they may have been trapped by rising water, but this cannot be confirmed.[4]

In most cases, we know which Deck Department members got off in which lifeboat with certainty. The table and graph on the following page give details regarding the lifeboats and who got off in each:

Time	Life-boats on Board	Lifeboat Gone	Deck Crew Left On Board	# of Deck Crew Gone	Crewmembers Who Have Left the Ship
					Loss of Deck Crew on _Titanic_ Over Time
12:30	20		66	0	
12:35	20		66	0	
12:40	19	7	63	3	Hogg,[5] Jewell,[6] Weller [7]
12:45	18	5	61	2	Pitman,[8] Olliver [9]
12:50	18		61	0	
12:55	17	3	59	2	Moore,[10] Anderson[11]
1:00	16	8	50	9	Jones,[12] Pascoe[13] (Nichols and six other seamen sent below to open the gangways at this time and did not return.)
1:05	15	1	48	2	Symons,[14] Horswill[15]
1:10	14	6	46	2	Hichens,[16] Fleet[17]
1:15	14		46	0	
1:20	13	16	43	3	Bailey,[18] Archer,[19] Forward[20]
1:25	12	14	40	3	Lowe,[21] Scarrott,[22] Harder[23]
1:30	10	9, 12	34	6	Haines,[24] Wynn,[25] McGough[26] & Peters[27] (No. 9); Clench[28] & Poingdestre[29] (No. 12)
1:35	9	11	32	2	Brice,[30] Humphreys[31]
1:40	7	13, 15	28	4	Lee,[32] Hopkins[33] & Vigott[34] (No. 13); A. Evans[35] (No. 15)
1:45	6	2	26	2	Boxhall,[36] Osman[37]
1:50	4	4, 10	21	5	Perkis,[38] McCarthy[39] & Foley[40] (No. 4); F. Evans[41] & Buley[42] (No. 10)
1:55	4		21	0	
2:00	3	C	20	1	Rowe[43]
2:05	2	D	18	2	Bright,[44] Lucas[45]
2:10	2		18	0	
2:15	0	A, B	16	2	Lightoller,[46] Hemming[47]
2:20	0		16	0	

Turning the information in the table above into a graph, we see:

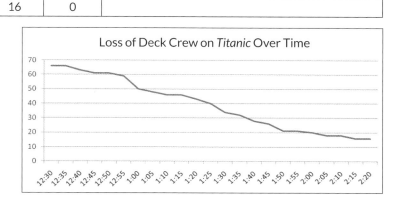

Loss of Deck Crew on _Titanic_ Over Time

It may be that, since the readying and loading of the lifeboats started earlier on the starboard side under First Officer Murdoch, there may have been more crew available there than on the port side. However, there is no way of proving that, beyond Lightoller's recollection that he was shorthanded. We do know that of the lookouts, five out of the six were on the starboard side and boarded lifeboats there. This may be indicative of more seamen in general having been on that side.

If fewer members of the Deck Department were available on the port side of the ship, and Lightoller lost seven more after sending some below to the gangway, he could very easily have been short of crew. This helps to explain his offer to Major Arthur Peuchen to help man lifeboat No. 6, after Lamp Trimmer Hemming had to step out of the boat to man one of the sets of falls because there were not enough seamen nearby. Also, by the time No. 6 was being loaded, passengers were starting to congregate around the aft port lifeboats, and the situation there began to get disorderly; as discussed in the narrative, the ruckus at the aft port boats drew crewmen from other parts of the Boat Deck, such as Fifth Officer Lowe, Seamen Evans and Buley, and quite a few others, all of whom came from working on the forward starboard boats.

The above tables show that there were sixteen members of the Deck Department still available on the *Titanic* when she sank at 2:20 a.m. This number does not include the seven crewmembers who went below to the gangway and never returned. Of these sixteen who remained until the end, four of them were officers: Captain Smith, Chief Officer Wilde, First Officer Murdoch, and Sixth Officer Moody, and two were Surgeons: Dr O'Loughlin, and Dr Simpson. The remaining ten cannot be identified with certainty, since we do not know which six seamen went below with Boatswain Nichols and never returned; regardless, among those left would have been a number of Able Bodied Seamen, as well as other Deck Department crewmen.

Obviously, as time went on, it became harder and harder to find crewmembers to load and lower the lifeboats. And even then, some of the remaining crew had to be ordered into the lifeboats rather than entering them on their own; among these were Boxhall, Rowe, and Bright, who felt their first duty was to help save others' lives over their own. The evidence does support Lightoller's claim that he was shorthanded on the port side, and this situation grew worse as members of the Deck Department were sent away to man the boats. When one examines this evidence, it is even more remarkable that all of the boats save Collapsibles A and B were safely lowered away.

Appendix J: The Music of the *Titanic*'s Band
By George Behe

[Note: This 'guest appendix' is based on an essay that George Behe wrote for the Titanic Historical Society in 1983. This present essay has been footnoted, and the book's authors have asked George to supplement it with additional information that he has uncovered since he wrote the original version. We would like to thank George for granting us permission to reproduce his complete, updated essay here.]

Ever since the *Titanic* went down in 1912 there has been controversy about which musical selections were played by the ship's gallant bandsmen during the sinking. Legend has always had it that – after playing ragtime to bolster the passengers' spirits – the bandsmen played 'Nearer My God to Thee' in the final moments before the great vessel foundered.

Walter Lord's seminal work, *A Night to Remember* (published in 1955) was responsible for a general change of opinion regarding the accuracy of the above 'legend'. Mr Lord's book focused attention on an interview granted by Junior Marconi Operator Harold Bride, who stated that – as he swam away from the dying ship – he clearly heard the band playing 'Autumn'.[1] (This idea was supported in 1913 by survivor Margaret Hays, who reported that the bandsmen performed popular selections until right before the final plunge, at which time they played 'that old familiar hymn, "Autumn" '.[2]) *Titanic* researchers generally followed Walter Lord's lead and accepted Harold Bride's statement as being the last word on the subject, and they subsequently dismissed the possibility that 'Nearer My God to Thee' was ever played by the bandsmen that night.

This mindset reigned supreme until 1986, at which point Walter Lord published his book *The Night Lives On* and discussed the possibility that Harold Bride had been misunderstood in 1912 when he told of having heard *Titanic*'s band play 'Autumn'. Whereas it had always been assumed that Bride was referring to the Episcopal hymn of that name, Lord suggested that Bride had actually been referring to 'Songe d'Automne', a waltz by Archibald Joyce that was popular at the time of the *Titanic*'s sinking. Indeed, at least one period White Star music booklet does list 'Songe d'Automne' among the musical selections that the Line's bandsmen were prepared to play for their passengers.

Interestingly, it seems at least possible that Joyce's 'Songe d'Automne' might not have been the song that Harold Bride was referring to when he spoke of 'Autumn', since it has been reported that French composer Cecile Chaminde's similarly-titled syncopated dance 'Automne' – Opus 35, Number 2 – was also a well known tune in 1912. It has also been suggested that Bride might have been talking about W. B. Bradbury's 1864 hymn 'Aughton' (also known as 'He Leadeth Me') and that the newspaper reporter who recorded Bride's story might have misunderstood the Englishman's pronunciation of the hymn's title.[3]

At any rate, researchers' attention was once again diverted from the possibility that there might be any truth to the old legend that 'Nearer My God to Thee' was played on board the *Titanic*. Several researchers have even gone one step beyond Walter Lord by suggesting that, at the very end, *Titanic*'s bandsmen were not playing any music *at all*; these researchers quote First Class passengers Archibald Gracie's[4] and A. H. Barkworth's[5] observations that the *Titanic*'s bandsmen put their instruments down some little time before the actual sinking – thereby inferring that all music being played on board the ship must necessarily have ceased at that time.

In actuality, though, the above inference may not be accurate. So many survivors reported hearing music being played just before the *Titanic* foundered[6] that one wonders if the bandsmen might have stopped playing their instruments only *temporarily* at the time Gracie and Barkworth made their observations. If this was indeed the case, we must of course wonder *why* the musicians would have interrupted their playing and abandoned their instruments for a short period of time.

The answer to the above question might be as simple as this: the bandsmen may have set their instruments aside in order to go down to their cabins and retrieve their lifebelts. Indeed, observations made by two different *Titanic* survivors lend credence to the likelihood that this was actually the case.

The first observation pertaining to this issue was made by First Class passenger Pierre Maréchal, who related it to Secretary Williams of the Amalgamated Musicians' Union. Secretary Williams later wrote:

> Maréchal declared that the musicians received an order to play all the time without stopping, so as to avoid a panic. They were placed on the deck, that is to say, between the decks [on A Deck]. Maréchal specially noticed that none of them had lifebelts, he being convinced that in giving them these orders their lives were to be sacrificed to avoid disorder on board.[7]

Pierre Maréchal took a seat in Boat No. 7 before it lowered at 12:40 a.m., and his observation that the ship's bandsmen were not in possession of their lifebelts at that time is straightforward. However, a separate observation was made by Stewardess Katherine Gold shortly before she took her place in Boat No. 11 at 1:35 a.m.,[8] by which time the situation with the bandsmen had changed. According to Mrs Gold:

> When we left the ship men were sitting on A deck, smoking cigarettes and tapping time with their feet to the music of the band. These passengers and the bandsmen, too, had their lifebelts beside them, and I was specially struck by a glimpse of a violinist playing steadily with a great lifebelt in front of him. The music was ragtime just then.[9]

It seems quite possible, then, that – after retrieving their lifebelts from their cabins – the *Titanic*'s musicians returned to A Deck and continued playing their music where they had left off shortly before.

It was reported by many survivors that, soon after the collision, the *Titanic*'s band sought to reassure the ship's passengers by playing ragtime and other cheerful music. There is no question about the truth of these reports, and the names of a number of the tunes that were played have been preserved for posterity. One such song was Irving Berlin's 'Alexander's Ragtime Band', which was mentioned by at least four First Class survivors: Major Arthur Peuchen,[10] Lily Futrelle,[11] Marjorie Newell[12] and George Brereton.[13] Another lively song, Ayer and Brown's 'Oh, You Beautiful Doll', was mentioned by Geoffrey Marcus in his book *The Maiden Voyage*, but the original source of Marcus' information is unknown. In *The Night Lives On* author Walter Lord mentions that Melville Ellis's 1911 London hit, 'In the Shadows', was played by the bandsmen, but, like Marcus, Lord did not reveal his source. In addition to hearing 'Alexander's Ragtime Band', Marjorie Newell is also said to have heard the band play Irving Berlin's 'One O'clock in the Morning I Get Lonesome', the American folk song 'Turkey in the Straw', and Franz Lehár's 'The Merry Widow'.[14] *Titanic* survivors on board the *Carpathia* told First Class passenger John Snyder that they heard the *Titanic*'s bandsmen playing the old sentimental favorite, 'Home, Sweet Home'.[15] Last but not least, Richard O'Connor, in his 1956 book *Down to Eter-*

nity, mentions that 'The Londonderry Air' was played that night, although – again – O'Connor's source of information is unknown.[16]

Saloon Steward Edward Wheelton recalled the bandsmen playing 'selections from the opera and the latest popular melodies of England and America',[17] but he did not specify the titles of these musical pieces. We know that the band played at least one waltz during the sinking (in later years Second Class passenger Edwina Troutt could even hum the melody), but the title of this waltz must remain forever unknown.

Despite the playing of these popular tunes, though, it has always seemed unlikely to the present author that the *Titanic*'s band continued to play lighthearted music right up until the time the ship foundered. Indeed, there would have been little need for ragtime and other cheerful music during the final half-hour before the sinking; most of the boats were gone by then, and the peril would have been obvious to those people who remained on board the ship. Instead of attempting to lull the passengers' fears with gay tunes at that point, it seems more likely that the bandsmen would have used their music to instill courage in those individuals who needed it.

Some people found that patriotism added steel to their backbones; indeed, Captain Smith is reported to have appealed to his crew to 'Be British!' It appears that the bandsmen were thinking along similar lines, because from Boat No. 5 First Class passenger George Harder plainly heard the strains of 'The Star Spangled Banner' drifting over the water.[18] Other survivors told *Carpathia* passengers Reverend Henry Burke and Reverend Daniel McCarthy about hearing this same song as well as other patriotic music.[19] In this same vein, Edwina Troutt wrote to a friend right after the disaster and told about having heard the bandsmen playing 'The Land of Hope' (one of Elgar's Pomp and Circumstance Marches which the British public adopted as an anthem called 'The Land of Hope and Glory'.)[20]

Instead of relying solely on patriotism, though, some people looked to their religion as a source of inspiration and courage in the face of what was about to happen. The bandsmen knew this, and their choice of music seems to have reflected that knowledge. Interestingly, a male passenger who was picked up from the sea after the sinking told survivor Bertha Watt that the Reverend Ernest Carter and his wife (both of whom were lost) suggested to the bandsmen that it might be appropriate if they played a hymn.[21] The possibility therefore exists that, during the final half-hour before the vessel sank, the bandsmen chose to forego their repertoire of popular and patriotic music and concentrate instead on playing inspiring hymns to instill courage in those people who might derive benefit from them.

This of course raises a crucial question: are *Titanic* researchers really justified in dismissing the 'Nearer My God to Thee' story as mere legend? The present author doesn't think so; indeed, in recent years more than one long-discredited 'legend' about the *Titanic* disaster has been shown to have a basis in fact (e.g. the so-called 'legend' of a man who donned woman's clothing in order to get into a lifeboat).[22] That being the case, perhaps it will be worthwhile for us to re-examine the evidence pertaining to the hymns that are reported to have been played by the *Titanic*'s bandsmen while the vessel was sinking.

First Class passenger Emma Schabert said that, after playing ragtime for a while, the band began playing religious music. 'When we Meet Beyond' was one of the first hymns they chose, followed by others.[23] First Class passenger Dr Washington Dodge reported from Boat No. 13 that he heard the band play 'Lead, Kindly Light'.[24] While Boat No. 14 was being lowered at about 1:25 a.m., survivor Edith Brown reported that the band was playing an unnamed hymn.[25] A group of *Titanic* crewmen reported hearing the band play 'Abide With Me' and 'Eternal Father, Strong To Save', as well as other hymns. And finally, we have Junior Marconi Operator Harold Bride's previously mentioned account of 'Autumn' being played while he struggled in the water.

As has been already discussed, author Walter Lord gave special emphasis to Harold Bride's 'Autumn' story, explaining that Bride's account 'somehow stands out' from many other conflicting stories. That is true (as far as it goes), but – over the years – later writers and researchers have become rigid in their thinking about 'Autumn' (or 'Songe d'Automne'), maintaining that this was *undoubtedly* the last song played on the *Titanic* and that the 'Nearer My God to Thee' story is only a myth concocted by sensation-hungry newspaper reporters. Indeed, this notion seems to have become 'truer' with each repetition until it is now accepted as absolute fact.

It is true that many questionable stories about the *Titanic* disaster were concocted by reporters in the days immediately following the disaster. It is also clear, however, that many of these so-called 'questionable' stories were not invented by reporters at all, but originated instead with actual *Titanic* survivors who discussed their experiences while they were still on board the *Carpathia*. The 'Nearer My God to Thee' story is one of these, since Reverend Burke and Reverend McCarthy, both *Carpathia* passengers, were told about the hymn by survivors while the rescue ship was still at sea.

It seems clear that, besides ragtime and patriotic music, a considerable number of hymns were played by the *Titanic's* bandsmen during the latter stages of the sinking. Nobody knows the names of all the hymns that were played, the order they were played in, or which was the final hymn that was selected by bandmaster Wallace Hartley that night. Many survivors claimed to have heard 'Nearer My God to Thee' played before the ship foundered; indeed, Edwina Troutt mentioned having heard that hymn when she wrote a letter to a friend mere days after the sinking.[26] Saloon Steward Edward Wheelton agreed with Miss Troutt, telling a reporter that – before the final plunge – the bandsmen changed the cheerful character of their musical program and played the hymn 'Nearer My God to Thee'.[27] Another Saloon Steward, Jacob Gibbons, was adamant that this was indeed the case. According to Gibbons:

> The cries of those on board were terrible, and I doubt whether the memory of them will ever leave me during my lifetime. It has been denied by many that the band was playing, but it was doing so and the strains of 'Nearer My God to Thee' came clearly over the water with a solemnity so awful that words cannot express it.[28]

In light of the information we have just examined, is there any further evidence to suggest that the above hymn might have been played on board the *Titanic* that night? The present author believes there is. Elwand Moody, a well-known Leeds musician, was a close friend of Wallace Hartley and had just completed twenty-two Atlantic crossings with him on the *Mauretania*. In fact, Hartley had asked Moody to accompany him on the *Titanic*, but Moody had declined.

Not long before the *Titanic's* maiden voyage, Moody asked Hartley, 'What would you do if you were ever on a ship that was sinking?' Hartley looked thoughtful for a moment and replied:

> I don't think I could do better than play 'O God, Our Help In Ages Past' or 'Nearer My God to Thee'.[29]

Later, after the disaster, Moody said, 'When I read the statement in the papers that he had gone to his death leading the band in 'Nearer My God to Thee,' I believed it. If it had been some other hymn I might not have done so, but as it is I can quite believe it. It is just what he would do.'

Lewis Cross, bass viol player on the *Celtic*, was another friend of Wallace Hartley who once spoke with him about the possibility of a shipwreck. Hartley smiled and said:

> Well, I don't suppose it will ever happen, but you know music is a bigger weapon than a gun in a big emergency, and I think that a band could do more to calm passengers than all the officers.[30]

The present author believes that Wallace Hartley proved his point on the night the *Titanic* went down. I do not know if 'Nearer My God to Thee' was the *final* hymn played by the *Titanic's* band, but I believe the evidence shows that the hymn *was* played that night.

* * * * *

Note: The authors of this book agree with George Behe's assessment that 'Nearer My God to Thee' was likely played the night *Titanic* sank, but that it cannot be proven that it was the *last* song played. The story that 'Nearer My God to Thee' was played was circulating onboard the *Carpathia* before the ship reached New York, proving the story did not originate in the yellow press.

Complicating matters, 'Nearer My God to Thee' can be set to three different melodies, and is often played differently on both sides of the Atlantic. In his book *The Night Lives On*, Walter Lord speculated that since American and British survivors alike claim that this hymn was played, that 'more than half of those who remembered the hymn must have been mistaken'. This was in fact a misunderstanding on Lord's part. Not every melody that 'Nearer My God to Thee' is set to is exclusive to one side of the Atlantic, as Lord suggested. For instance, the American version of the hymn, which is set to the melody of 'Bethany', is the only version that is played in Scandinavia. As such, it is possible that many Europeans would have been familiar with the American version of 'Nearer My God to Thee', and vice versa.

Additionally, besides Elwand Moody's story that Wallace Hartley said he would play 'Nearer My God to Thee' if he was on a sinking ship, there is additional evidence that *Titanic's* bandmaster had a special affinity for this hymn: Hartley, a Methodist, attended services with his family at Bethel Independent Methodist Chapel, where his father Albion was the choirmaster and Sunday School Superintendent. Hartley himself is said to have introduced 'Nearer My God to Thee' to the congregation.[31]

If Hartley did indeed choose to play this hymn during the sinking, it seems possible that he could have picked the version set to 'Propior Deo', preferred by Methodists, and allegedly Hartley's favorite version of the hymn.[32] It is also possible that they could have played the version of the hymn set to 'Horbury', which was traditionally played by Episcopalians. Church services on Atlantic liners tended to be styled after the Church of England, and this version of the hymn would have been familiar to many aboard. However, it has to be noted that the White Star songbook says that the bandsmen were prepared to play 'hymns of all nations', so the band would have been equally capable of playing 'Bethany', as well as the other two versions of the hymn.

The sheer volume of claims that 'Nearer My God to Thee' was played highly suggests that there is at least a kernel of truth to the stories, as it is hard to envision *all* of the literally dozens of witnesses being wrong, or having fabricated the stories. The proof is not conclusive, but is strongly suggestive.

Additionally, the present authors believe that there is the strong possibility that both 'Autumn', (whether it be the hymn by this name or Joyce's 'Songe d'Automne') *and* 'Nearer My God to Thee' were indeed played that night, regardless of the order. Second Class passenger Susan Webber said that the band was still playing 'on the bridge' near the end, and that across the waters, she heard the strains of 'Autumn'.[33] First Class passenger Helen Candee, in her account of the sinking, raises the possibility that both of these songs were indeed played by the band during the sinking:

> And over them trembled the last strains of the orchestra's message: 'Autumn' first, then 'Nearer, my God, to Thee'.[34]

Appendix K: Shots in the Dark: Did an Officer Commit Suicide on the *Titanic?*[1]

Even as the rescue ship *Carpathia* was heading towards New York Harbor, rumors were circulating on board that an officer had shot himself as *Titanic* sank. These rumors first began appearing in the newspapers as early as April 18, 1912, the day the *Carpathia* arrived in New York.

Carlos Hurd, one of the *Carpathia*'s passengers, just happened to be a reporter for the *St. Louis Post Dispatch*. Captain Rostron attempted to protect the privacy of the survivors by preventing communication between them and Hurd or his wife. Despite this, Hurd managed to obtain several dozen interviews. As the *Carpathia* entered New York Harbor, he wrapped up the notes from his interviews in a makeshift waterproof package and threw it down to a boat that came alongside the ship. Parts of the notes, which included mention of the rumors of an officer suicide, were rushed to the office of the *New York Morning World*, where they were published that same day.

> Revolver shots heard shortly before the *Titanic* went down caused many rumors, one that Captain Smith had shot himself, another that First Officer Murdoch had ended his life, but members of the crew discredit these rumors.[2]

By the time the following day's *New York Times* was published, additional reports were circulating. These included stories to the effect that an officer had shot two men who attempted to rush a lifeboat, before turning the gun on himself. James Cameron's *Titanic* portrayed First Officer Murdoch committing suicide after attempting to launch Collapsible A from the Boat Deck. Though little mentioned, the CBS miniseries *Titanic* (1996) also showed Murdoch shooting himself. But, what did the survivors themselves actually see and say about a suicide? This appendix is an attempt to bring together and analyze the accounts and information relating to this subject in a comprehensive manner.

During the course of our research, quite a few accounts were found that referred to shots being fired during the lifeboat loading. Given the purpose of this appendix, we have not included many of the accounts which do not specifically refer to an officer shooting himself, or to other events surrounding an alleged officer suicide. Other incidents of gunfire during the sinking are discussed in Appendix H. We have also chosen not to include accounts of survivors who were in the general vicinity of alleged shooting incidents, but who gave no specific information that would confirm or refute the allegation that a shooting/suicide occurred, since non-statements add little to the case either way. The spelling in the survivor accounts is kept as it appeared in original documents.

Primary Accounts of an Officer's Suicide

The following primary accounts are taken from survivors' own letters, diaries, and private narratives, or their testimony at the Senate or British Inquiries, or at the Limitation of Liability Hearings of 1912–1915. In these cases, there is very little doubt that the survivors really said what they are quoted as saying, unlike press accounts of the day. Since many survivors gave multiple accounts of the same incident, some secondary accounts may be mixed in with the primary, in an effort to keep a person's statements together.

Third Class passenger Eugene Daly: Eugene Daly was rescued from the upturned Collapsible B. He was brought aboard the *Carpathia* unconscious, and was carried to the cabin of Dr Frank Blackmarr. Upon awakening, Daly related his experiences. As he spoke, Blackmarr wrote down Daly's story in his personal scrapbook. Daly said:

> After the accident we were all held down in steerage. Finally, some of the women and children were let up, but we had quite a number of hot-headed Italians and other peoples who got crazy and made for the stairs. These men tried to rush the stairway, pushing and crowding and pulling the women down. ... I saw two dagos shot and some that took punishment from the officers ... I finally got up to the top deck and made for the front. The water was just covering the upper deck at the bridge and it was easy to slide because she had such a tip.[3]

Daly then goes on to describe his help in cutting the ropes on a collapsible boat that was crowded with people hanging from its edges. The ship plunged suddenly, water reached their hips, and then the ship rose again slightly. They cut the collapsible free, and then ended up in the water. Due to Blackmarr's notes, which recorded Daly's emotional dumping of the events he experienced (Daly broke down crying several times during the recollections), it is unclear if the shooting he refers to occurred below or up on deck. Black-marr's notes also do not include mention of an officer sui-cide. However, a later interview with Dr Blackmarr makes it clear that Daly had indeed told him about this, and that the shooting incident referred to above, and the suicide, were one in the same:

> The only panic at the beginning, as I understand it, was in the steerage, where there were many persons who lacked self-control. There was no shooting, as I learn, except that a steerage passenger told me he saw an officer trying to control the maddened rush by shooting two persons. The same officer shot himself a minute later.[4]

Daly later wrote a letter to his younger sister in Ireland describing his experiences. The letter is undated, but was apparently written sometime between April 18 and April 21, 1912. This letter was later published in several British newspapers:

> We afterwards went to the second cabin deck … and the two girls and myself got into a boat. An of-ficer called on me to go back, but I would not stir. They then got hold of me and pulled me out.
>
> At the first cabin when a boat was being lowered an officer pointed a revolver and said if any man tried to get in, he would shoot him on the spot. I saw the officer shoot two men dead because they tried to get in the boat. Afterwards there was an-other shot, and I saw the officer himself lying on the deck. They told me he shot himself, but I did not see him. I was up to my knees in the water at the time. Everyone was rushing around, and there were no more boats. I then dived overboard.[5]

This version is apparently an abridged version of Daly's letter to his sister. A more complete version of this letter was published in another paper, a reprint of the *New York Herald*:

> We went to the deck, but there were no boats going off. Then we went to the second cabin deck. A boat was being lowered there. It was being filled with women. Maggie and Bertha got in, and I got in. The officer called on me to go back, but I got in. Life was sweet to me and I wanted to save myself. They told me to get out, but I didn't stir. Then they got hold of me and pulled me out. Then the boat was lowered and went off.
>
> There was another boat there, but I went to the first cabin. The steerage people and second cabin people went to the first cabin of the ship. They were getting women into the boats there. There was a terrible crowd standing about. The officer in charge pointed a revolver and waved his hand and said that if any man tried to get in he would shoot him on the spot. Two men tried to break through and he shot them both. I saw him shoot them. I saw them lying there after they were shot. One seemed to be dead. The other was trying to pull himself up at the side of the deck, but he could not. I tried to get

to the boat also, but was afraid I would be shot and stayed back. Afterwards there was another shot and I saw the officer himself lying on the deck. They told me he shot himself, but I did not see him.

> Then I rushed across the deck, and there was a sort of canvas craft there. I tried with six or seven men to get it out, but we could not. It was stuck un-der a wire stay which ran up to the mast. The water was then washing across the deck. The ship lurched and the water washed the canvas craft off the deck into the ocean. I was up to my knees in water at the time. Everyone was rushing around, but there were no boats. Then I dived overboard.[6]

Daly repeated this story at the home of Mayor Gaynor of New York when he visited to ask for assistance from the Mayor's Relief Fund.[7] Daly filed a claim for lost property and personal injury in 1913 as part of the Limitation of Li-ability hearings, then testified in front of Judge Julius M. Meyer in the United States District Court on June 25, 1915. He stated under oath that he had seen two men shot.[8]

Daly also told his family and daughter Mary about this incident numerous times over the years:

> … [The] ship's officer in charge of overseeing the boats held him back at gunpoint. My dad retreated, afraid of being shot, but other men rushed forward. The ship's officer shot down two of them right be-fore my father's eyes. There was utter confusion. Then my dad heard another shot ring out, and he couldn't see what was happening, but he was told by the people around him, that the officer who had shot the two men a few minutes before, had put the gun to his own head, and shot himself. I'm sure he did it in despair for what he had to do. My dad later saw his body on the deck, it was a terrible night.[9]

In several of Daly's accounts, it is difficult to determine the timing of the shooting incident he described. His account to Dr Blackmarr makes it unclear as to whether the shooting occurred above or below decks, although his later accounts make it clear that it was above deck. The abridged version of the letter to his sister suggests the shooting happened during the attempted launch of Collapsible A, since Daly said that he was up to his knees in water at the time. While writing *The Night Lives On*, Walter Lord noticed this detail and how it matched Saloon Steward Edward Brown's de-scription of water reaching his legs during the attempted launch of Collapsible A. For this reason, he speculated that the incident may have happened at that boat.

However, the unabridged version of Daly's letter reveals more specific details. It indicates that the shooting did not happen as the water was rushing across the deck, which is the impression given by the abridged version of Daly's letter, but rather sometime as a boat was lowering, prior to both the attempted launch of Collapsible A, and prior to water reaching the deck.

In the full letter, Daly stated that he, Maggie Daly, Ber-tha Mulvihill, all got into a lifeboat at the 'second cabin deck'. He was thrown out, with the boat being lowered af-terwards. He said that there was another boat nearby, but that he went to the 'first cabin' instead. It can be established that Daly's cousin and Bertha Mulvihill left in Boat No. 15. In Mulvihill's own accounts, she stated that only two boats were left, and that the boat she boarded was the last boat.[10] In another account, Daly said the boat he was thrown out of was 'the last boat'.[11] Boats No. 13 and No. 15 began lowering within 30 seconds of each other, with No. 15 leaving last.[12]

Daly appears to have referred to A Deck as the 'second cabin'. The loading of No. 13 and No. 15 largely took place from A Deck. It can also be established that there was a slight rush at No. 15, with the men being told to stand back, matching Daly's claim.[13] Finally, in his account to Dr Blackmarr, Daly said that he had to climb up a set of falls to the top deck, because 'the stairs were so crowded that I could not get through', strongly suggesting that he had been on A Deck.[14]

Daly's account to Dr Blackmarr states that after he reached the top deck, he 'made for the front'. In his letter to his sister, Daly stated that the Steerage and Second Class passengers went there, that they were loading women into the boats, and that there was a 'terrible crowd standing about'. It was at this time that the officer warned the men, and then shot two who attempted to break through and board the boat. One of these men was still alive, 'trying to pull himself up at the side of the deck'. This description fits the areas forward where Boat No. 1 and Collapsible C were launched on the starboard side, and Boat No. 2 and Collapsible D on the port side. There was a solid bulwark at the edge of the deck, which may be what the wounded man was trying to pull himself up on. The boats listed above could only be boarded by climbing over these solid bulwarks just aft of the Bridge. There were no railings anywhere else on the edge of the Boat Deck that were also in the vicinity of lifeboats.

After the shooting and suicide, Daly stated that he 'rushed across the deck', and that there was 'a sort of canvas craft there'. He describes the efforts to get this boat launched, and said it was stuck under a wire stay. Daly told Dr Frank Blackmarr that passengers clung to the edges of this collapsible as they were working on it, and that they had to cut ropes to free it as water reached the deck where he was located. In the full version of his letter to his sister, he also says the water reached the deck while they were trying to free the collapsible. These details match Collapsible A and that boat only. Collapsible B was never hooked up to the falls, and did not have people hanging on its edges as it was being freed.

Complicating matters is the fact that Daly believed that he helped free the same boat he was later saved on, Collapsible B. However, he was unaware of how the boat he was rescued on came to be upside down; if he had, indeed, worked at Collapsible B, he would certainly have known this, since it fell to the Boat Deck upside down as the men tried to free it. No wire stays prevented Collapsible B from being pushed off the roof of the Officers' Quarters. However, these details do match Collapsible A. There was a wire funnel stay directly inboard of the aft davit which launched Boat No. 1 and Collapsible C, and which had then been cranked back in for Boat A. This, coupled with having to push the collapsible uphill against the port list, and the bow of it around the structure surrounding the stairway down to A Deck, would have impeded the efforts to launch it. Daly was likely confused since Collapsible B ended up on the starboard side of the forward funnel as *Titanic* sank, but it is clear that his 'canvas craft' was indeed Collapsible A.

The identity of which boat Daly was saying the shooting occurred at would seem to hinge on what he meant by 'rushed across the deck' after the shooting. If he meant literally from one side of the ship to the other after the shooting, then that may mean the incident occurred at Collapsible D on the port side. On the other hand, if he meant that he rushed from the edge of the Boat Deck, where the mystery boat was loading, to nearer the deck house on the same side of the ship, then he may have been referring to gunfire at Collapsible C. In any event, it appears as if Daly's shooting occurred forward, and sometime during the launch/attempted launches of the forward collapsible boats, and fairly close to the end. The evidence Daly gave may allow for the possibility, however, that this shooting took place shortly before the attempted launch of Collapsible A, which has been the previously accepted timing of this incident.

While the location of the events Daly witnessed appears to be in question, the credibility of him as a witness appears impeccable. Whatever the truth, there is no doubt that he was absolutely convinced of what he had seen. He mentioned it to a *Carpathia* passenger, to his sister in a letter home, to the Mayor of New York, under oath in a court of law, and to his family.

First Class passenger Laura Francatelli: Miss Francatelli, Lady Duff Gordon's secretary, was rescued in Boat No. 1. She wrote a private letter to someone named 'Marion' on April 18, 1912, which describes a suicide:

> The dear brave officer gave orders to row away from the sinking boat at least 200 yards, he afterwards poor dear brave fellow, shot himself. We saw the whole thing, and watched that tremendous thing quickly sink...[15]

The wording of Miss Francatelli's letter makes it difficult to tell whether she was referring to the officer shooting himself, or to the ship sinking when she said that she 'saw the whole thing'. If she was referring to the suicide, it is difficult to tell how clearly she could have seen events unfolding on a sinking ship at night from a lifeboat.

If Francatelli was referring to the same event that Eugene Daly claimed to have witnessed, then it is possible, however unlikely, that she could have seen events unfolding on the Boat Deck from hundreds of feet away. The forward portion of the Boat Deck would have been nearly level with the water and on a straight line of sight with Miss Francatelli at the time, and No. 1 did not row far away from the starboard side of the ship. If Miss Francatelli was not referring to the suicide when she said that she 'saw the whole thing', then she may have just been repeating something that she heard from someone else.

In any event, since her description was written on April 18, 1912, the day *Carpathia* reached New York, it seems to support the fact that suicide rumors were circulating onboard the rescue ship before the arrival, rather than originating afterwards in the yellow press.

First Class passenger George Rheims: George Rheims was rescued aboard the swamped Collapsible A. He wrote a private letter to his wife in France on April 19, 1912 which describes the following incident:

> While the last boat was leaving, I saw an officer with a revolver fire a shot and kill a man who was trying

to climb into it. As there remained nothing more to do, the officer told us, 'Gentlemen, each man for himself, good-bye.' He gave a military salute and then fired a bullet into his head. That's what I call a man!'[16]

On the same day that he wrote the letter to his wife, Rheims was interviewed by a reporter from the *New York Herald*. Published the following day, this account confirms the details in the letter to his wife:

> The majority of men passengers did not attempt to get in the boats. The men assisted the women. But when the boats began to be lowered some men lost their heads. From the lower deck men jumped into crowded boats and others slid down ropes. One officer shot a man who attempted to get into a crowded boat. Immediately afterward the officer said:-'Well, goodby [*sic*],' and killed himself.[17]

With the exception of Rheims belief that one man was shot while Daly believed two were shot, the accounts given by Rheims are strikingly similar to those given by Daly. So similar, in fact, that it is reasonable to assume that they had witnessed the same incident. The timing of the alleged suicide is not as easy to deduce from Rheims' accounts as it is from Daly's. However, Rheims' letter seems to indicate that the shooting happened as a boat was being lowered away, which Collapsible A never was, unless he meant 'loading' when he said 'lowering'.

Like Daly's account, this may support the conclusion that the shooting, if it occurred, happened at either Collapsible C or D, the last two boats lowered away. In his letter, Rheims says that after the shooting, he had time to briefly converse with his brother-in-law, go down to his cabin for 'one minute' to retrieve a photograph, and come back on deck and undress, before the ship began 'nosediving' – a reference to the Boat Deck submerging at 2:15 a.m. He and his brother-in-law then bid farewell, and Rheims leapt overboard.

Rheims was berthed in cabin A-21 on the starboard side of A Deck, just below the Boat Deck. It would not have taken him long to get to his cabin and then return to the Boat Deck. Rheims indicates that he jumped overboard on the starboard side near the Gymnasium.[18] As such, it appears that the events he described in the latter-stages of the sinking took place on the starboard side.

Rheims also filed a deposition in the Limitation of Liability hearings. Unfortunately, in it, he did not mention the suicide, nor was he asked about it. In fact, the only reference to gunfire came when he was asked generally: 'Did you hear any particular noises?' Rheims replied that he heard 'two pistol shots'. When asked how long that was before the ship sank, he said: 'About 40 minutes before she sank.'[19]

Some have expressed the opinion that because Rheims did not mention the shooting and suicide at the hearings, he must have made the whole thing up. Others say that since he heard gunshots early in the sinking, Rheims must have heard Fifth Officer Lowe's warning shots at No. 14, and either mistook, or guessed, what really happened.

However, several things run counter to this logic. First, in the hearings, Rheims was never asked whether he saw what happened when he heard the gunshots, and in fact,

no follow-up questions of any kind about the gunfire were asked. Whether or not there were any shootings was beyond the scope of the hearings, the sole purpose of which were to determine whether White Star Line was legally liable in the sinking, and how much compensation for the survivors and families they were responsible for. The purpose of the hearings was not to root out the truth on unrelated issues for the historical record.

Second, the critics are assuming that the gunfire Rheims reported hearing '40 minutes' before the ship sank were one and the same with the shooting and suicide he claimed to have witnessed elsewhere. Rheims outlined the events of the suicide in great detail in the private letter to his wife; that letter was not seen publicly until 1981. In writing this letter, there was no apparent motive to lie, or to do anything other than tell the truth as he knew it. Rheims also repeated the same story to a reporter on the day he wrote the letter to his wife.

In both instances, Rheims states that he saw the incident first-hand. In the letter to his wife, it is plain that the timing of the shooting he witnessed was very shortly before Rheims leapt overboard, and not forty minutes before the end. It also seems improbable that Rheims would have described an incident so closely matching the description given by Daly, whether he actually witnessed it or not, when there is no evidence the men ever met to compare notes on their experiences. This is particularly true since First and Third Class passengers were kept segregated, even onboard *Carpathia*.

Rheims appears to be a reliable witness, with no motive or reason for lying. The fact that he did not mention the incident in the Limitation of Liability deposition cannot, and should not, be construed as proof that it did not happen, particularly in light of his other accounts of the sinking which describe the incident. After all, there are other details of Rheims' ordeal, both during and following the sinking, that he relayed in the letter to his wife which were not brought up in the Limitation of Liability hearings. Few would make the argument that those details were made up simply because he did not mention them in the hearings. However, that standard is often applied when researchers examine the gunfire issue, simply because it is a controversial point; most have a preconceived notion about whether it happened or not, rather than letting the evidence guide their conclusions.

First Class passenger Richard Norris Williams: R. N. Williams and his father were on the forward starboard Boat Deck as the Bridge dipped under. Swept into the water, Williams' father was crushed by the falling forward funnel. Williams survived by reaching Collapsible A. He wrote a personal account of his experiences during the sinking for his family; it was later published. He described the following events as transpiring immediately after seeing Captain Smith near the Bridge with a seaman. The seaman went off on an errand. Williams and his father heard a curious noise and turned to see water pouring over the Bridge rail. They immediately began heading aft:

> I heard the crack of a revolver shot from the direction where I had left Captain Smith. I did not look around. ... The ship seemed to give a slight lurch. I turned towards the bow. I saw nothing but water with just a mast sticking out of it. I don't remember the shock of the cold water, I only remember think-

ing, 'suction,' and my efforts to swim in the direction of the starboard rail to get away from the ship...[20]

In a letter to one of the present authors, Quincy Norris Williams, the son of Richard Norris Williams, confirmed that his father talked about hearing gunfire near the Bridge as water began reaching their location. When asked if his father had ever elaborated on this incident, his son said no. He said that his father was not the sort to speculate about things that might have happened, but that he did not see personally. He heard gunfire, but just as he said in his private account, Williams and his father did not turn around to see what had happened. They were too busy heading aft to escape the approaching water. Williams' account supports that there was indeed gunfire on the forward starboard side of the ship, shortly before the Boat Deck submerged. If such an incident occurred, he was in a position to see or hear it, and that is exactly what he reported.

Primary Accounts, No Officer Suicide

The following section details the first-hand accounts of those who specifically state or give evidence that an officer suicide did not occur.

Junior Marconi Operator Harold Bride: Harold Bride survived by clinging to the upturned Collapsible B. He was on the port side of the ship when the bow plunged under. His accounts lend some insight into the fate of Captain Smith.

I now assisted in pushing off a collapsible lifeboat, which was on the port side of the forward funnel, onto the boat deck. Just as the boat fell I noticed Capt. Smith dive from the bridge into the sea. Then followed a general scramble down on the boat deck, but no sooner had we got there than the sea washed over. I managed to catch hold of the boat we had previously fixed up and was swept overboard with her.[21]

Bride repeated this claim in his famous *New York Times* account.[22] If Bride really saw Captain Smith jump into the sea at the last moment, then it would seem to eliminate the possibility of him having committed suicide.[23]

First Class passenger Colonel Archibald Gracie: Colonel Gracie and his friend, Clinch Smith, helped to get Collapsible A down from the roof of the Officers' Quarters, then headed aft as water began reaching the Boat Deck. He was rescued aboard Collapsible B. In his book, Gracie specifically addresses the rumors of an officer committing suicide:

Did either the Captain or the First Officer shoot himself? Not withstanding all the current rumors and newspaper statements answering this question affirmatively, I have been unable to find any passenger or member of the crew cited as authority for the statement that either Captain Smith or First Officer Murdoch did anything of the sort. On the contrary, so far as relates to Captain Smith, there are several witnesses, including Harold S. Bride, the Junior Marconi operator, who saw him at the last on the bridge of his ship, and later, when sinking and struggling in the water. Neither can I discover any

authentic testimony about First Officer Murdoch's shooting himself. On the contrary, I find fully sufficient evidence that he did not. He was a brave and efficient officer and no sufficient motive for self-destruction can be advanced. He performed his full duty under difficult circumstances, and was entitled to praise and honor. During the last fifteen minutes before the ship sank, I was located at that quarter forward on the boat deck, starboard side, where Murdoch was in command and where the crew under him were engaged in the vain attempt of launching the Engelhard boat. The report of a pistol shot during this interval ringing in my ears within a few feet of me would certainly have attracted my attention, and later, when I moved astern, the distance was not so great as to prevent my hearing it.[24]

Gracie was in the appropriate area of the ship to see or hear gunfire if the alleged incident occurred at Collapsible A, and was adamant that he heard nothing of the sort. Earlier, however, Gracie had led two First Class passengers – Caroline Brown and Edith Evans – towards Collapsible D on the port side. There he encountered a cordon of crewmembers with linked arms, all trying to prevent men from rushing the boat, and he was forced to leave the ladies.[25] Gracie testified that Lightoller told him that Steerage passengers had tried to rush Collapsible D, and that he had to fire off shots to make them get out. Gracie said that he did not hear this gunfire.[26]

Gracie also did not mention hearing shots fired at Collapsible C. Yet First Class passengers Hugh Woolner, Mauritz Håkan Björnström-Steffansson and Jack Thayer, as well as Third Class passengers Emily and Frank Goldsmith, among others, all said that they saw warning shots fired to keep passengers from rushing that boat.[27]

If Gracie did not mention, or claimed not to have heard, the warning shots we know were fired during the loading of Collapsibles C and D, then we must ask: Could he have missed additional gunshots if the suicide incident occurred at either of these boats as they lowered away, or later at Collapsible A? Gracie argued that this could not be the case. However, if shots were indeed fired at Collapsible A, then it is possible that he was unaware of them. First, Gracie had gotten as far aft as the cul-de-sac where the Officers' Quarters intersected the First Class Entrance, and was just forward of the railing separating the crew deck space from the forward First Class Promenade when he was struck by the wave. That distance, when combined with the noise from the crowd of steerage passengers then surrounding him, could have muffled such gunshots, or prevented them from registering in his mind.[28] However, this does not explain how he did not hear shots fired at Collapsible C and D earlier.

Complicating matters is the fact that at the time of the incident, Colonel Gracie did not know the identity of the officer who he saw on the scene, and thus could not say for certain who he saw and when. This is confirmed by the following passage from his book:

My friend, Clinch Smith, urged immediate obedience to Lightoller's orders, and, with other men passengers, we crossed over to the starboard quarter of the ship, forward on the same Boat Deck where, as I afterwards learned, the officer in command was First Officer Murdoch who had also done noble work, and was soon thereafter to lose his life.[29]

Lamp Trimmer Samuel Hemming stated that Sixth Officer Moody was also on the scene, helping to get Collapsible A off the roof of the Officers' Quarters.[30] In his own testimony, Gracie admitted that Second Officer Lightoller had later told him that Murdoch was working near his location, which is why the Colonel believed the officer he saw working was Murdoch.[31] Gracie and Lightoller had lengthy conversations about the sinking aboard the *Carpathia*.

Second Officer Charles Lightoller: Lightoller survived by reaching Collapsible B after leaping overboard from the roof of the Bridge. Lightoller had helped get Collapsible B down from the roof of the Officers' Quarters and then crossed over to the starboard side to see if he could be of any help there. From that location, Lightoller would have been in a perfect position to see what was happening near Collapsible A, and to comment on the fate of the officers working there. In both the Senate and British Inquiries, Lightoller mentioned seeing First Officer Murdoch working on the falls. He did not mention seeing Chief Officer Wilde, or Sixth Officer Moody. In response to rumors in the press, Lightoller wrote a letter to Murdoch's widow Ada that refuted the stories about him committing suicide. The letter was signed by all of the *Titanic*'s surviving officers:

Hotel Continental,
Washington.
April 24th, 1912.

Dear Mrs. Murdoch,

I am writing on behalf of the surviving officers to express our deep sympathy in this, your awful loss. Words cannot convey our feelings, – much less a letter.

I deeply regret that I missed communicating with you by last mail to refute the reports that were spread in the newspapers. I was practically the last man, and certainly the last officer, to see Mr. Murdoch. He was then endeavouring to launch the starboard forward collapsible boat. I had already got mine from off the top of our quarters. You will understand when I say that I was working the port side of the ship, and Mr. Murdoch was principally engaged on the starboard side of the ship, filling and launching the boats. Having got my boat down off the top of the house, and there being no time to open it, I left it and ran across to the starboard side, still on top of the quarters. I was then practically looking down on your husband and his men. He was working hard, personally assisting, overhauling the forward boat's fall. At this moment the ship dived, and we were all in the water. Other reports as to the ending are absolutely false. Mr. Murdoch died like a man, doing his duty. Call on us without hesitation for anything we can do for you.

Yours very sincerely,
(Signed)

C.H. Lightoller, 2d Officer;
J. Grove Boxhall, 4th Officer;
H.J. Pitman, 3d Officer;
H.G. Lowe, 5th Officer.[32]

If Lightoller's account is accurate, then it seems to eliminate the possibility that Murdoch could have been the officer who shot himself, if anyone did; it would also eliminate the possibility that a shooting happened at Collapsible A. However, more recent information that has been uncovered suggests that Lightoller might not have been telling the whole story.

During her research into the disaster, author Diana Bristow came into contact with James O. McGiffin, son of Captain James McGiffin. Captain McGiffin was the Marine Superintendent of the White Star Line in Queenstown, and a close friend of First Officer Murdoch. He served with both Murdoch and Lightoller on the SS *Medic*. McGiffin said that when Lightoller saw his father, he told him all about the disaster. He told Captain McGiffin that Murdoch had been forced to shoot a crewman who was leading a rush on a lifeboat, and who had tried to push ahead of women and children. He stated that the bullet struck the man's jaw.[33] This account is very similar to a story that was circulating in 1912:

'Stand back,' shouted the officers who were manning the boat. 'The women come first,' ... men continued their pushing and shoving ... Shots rang out. One big fellow fell over the railing into the water. Another dropped to the deck, moaning. His jaw had been shot away. This was the story told by bystanders afterwards on the pier.[34]

The information provided by James O. McGiffin is tantalizing, and the similarity to the above 1912 story and Daly's account of one of the victims still being alive after being shot is apparent. However, more information is needed before any real conclusions are drawn. If this report is accurate, then it suggests that Lightoller may not have told the whole story, perhaps in order to console his friend's grieving widow. If Lightoller's letter to Ada Murdoch is accurate, then it suggests that First Officer Murdoch could not have committed suicide.

Secondary Accounts of an Officer's Suicide

The following information is taken from secondary accounts of survivors who claimed to have seen a suicide. Since these accounts are taken mainly from press interviews and 1912 books and cannot be confirmed elsewhere, their reliability may not be as good as primary accounts which state that a suicide did or did not occur. In these cases, we cannot be certain that the survivor actually said what they are quoted as saying.

Second Class passenger Charlotte Collyer: Mrs Collyer was rescued in Boat No. 14. She reported:

He [Murdoch] was a masterful man, astoundingly brave and cool. I had met him the day before, when he was inspecting the second-cabin quarters, and thought him a bull-dog of a man who would not be afraid of anything. This proved true; he kept order to the last, and died at his post. They say he shot himself. I do not know.[35]

Mrs Collyer did not witness the alleged suicide herself and did not state who told her about it, so the reliability of this account cannot be determined.

Second Class passenger Mary Davis: Miss Davis was rescued in Boat No. 13. A press article quoted her as saying that she 'told of seeing First Officer Murdoch commit suicide by shooting'.[36] These are the only details given, and no actual quote from her was provided. Since Miss Davis was in No. 13, which was launched from the aft starboard part of the Boat Deck around 1:40 a.m., it may have been very difficult for her to see anyone or anything happening on the forward end of the Boat Deck near the end, even if her lifeboat did not get very far away before the sinking.

It is possible that Davis could have witnessed a separate incident entirely, or it could indicate that the suicide actually happened at the aft boats. In either case, First Officer Murdoch was seen at Boats Nos 15 and 10, as well as Collapsibles C and A after the lowering of No. 13.

Third Class passenger Edward Dorking: Dorking was saved by leaping overboard at the last second and reaching Collapsible B. He claimed to have witnessed shootings and a suicide:

> An officer stood beside the life-boats as they were being manned and with a pistol in hand, threatened to kill the first man who got into a boat without orders. The rule of 'women first' was rigidly enforced. Two stewards hustled into a lifeboat that was being launched. They were commanded to get out by the officers and on refusing to obey the command, were shot down.[37]

Dorking told more of the story in another interview:

> Almost at the moment I climbed on the raft I could hear pistol shots sounding from the *Titanic*. The sounds of shots had been distinct during all my swim. I don't know how many were fired, but they kept on during all the time I was within hearing distance. I saw an officer, it may have been the captain or it may not, shoot himself before I got away from the ship.[38]

There are differing details between these accounts, but because the quotes come from newspapers, it is difficult to say whether this is a result of ambiguity on Dorking's part, or the inaccurate reporting of the day. Dorking tentatively identifies the officer that committed suicide as Captain Smith, but makes it clear that he was far from certain in this identification. Dorking was on the ship until the end, but unless primary accounts from him that mention this incident are uncovered, it is difficult to know how reliable these newspaper quotes really are.

Third Class passenger Edward Dorking.

What is interesting is that Dorking says the men were shot during the launching of a boat, which appears consistent with Daly and Rheims.

Third Class passenger Soloman Abraham Hyman: Hyman was probably rescued in Boat No. 13, since his *New York Herald* account details how his lifeboat was the second to last launched in his section of the ship, and that it was nearly swamped while being lowered by water rushing out of the condenser. He claimed to have witnessed a shooting:

> The officer who was standing at the rope had a pistol in his hand, and he ordered everybody to keep back. First, one women screamed and then another, and one man (I think he was an Italian) pushed toward the boat and the officer fired at him.[39]

Another press account, entitled 'Saw Chief Officer Wilde End His Life With Pistol', attributes statements to Hyman to the effect that he saw an officer fire on passengers and then kill himself. He is extensively quoted in the remainder of the article, but curiously, no actual quote from him about this incident was provided:

> According to some of the passengers Chief Officer Wilde shot himself when he saw the *Titanic* was doomed. He had spent his last hour struggling with the third class passengers, and it is said had to use violence to quiet them and keep them from stampeding the first and second cabin sections. Abraham Hyman, of Manchester, England, who was coming to this country to join a brother in Paterson, N.J., is one of the passengers who told about seeing Chief Officer Wilde rushing around with a revolver in his hand. There was not much panic before he left the *Titanic*, he said, except when the chief officer fired into a belligerent group of third class passengers. A man standing next to him had his chin shot off, he said.[40]

Since no actual quote attributed to Hyman is provided, the reliability of this report is unknown. Both accounts quote him as saying that he saw an officer fire on passengers.

Of interest is the fact that Chief Officer Wilde is specifically mentioned as the officer who shot himself. It is also noteworthy that we have here yet another mention of a passenger being shot in the chin.

However, we cannot say whether Hyman himself mentioned Wilde by name, or only said 'the chief officer'. It is possible that detail was added by a reporter. There is definite evidence of Murdoch at No. 13, but none that Wilde was involved in the loading of any of the aft starboard boats. It is improbable that Hyman could have witnessed an incident happening on the forward part of the Boat Deck from his location near Boat No. 13.

However, it is possible that he may have witnessed a separate incident since Miss Davis, also rescued in No. 13, reportedly claimed to have witnessed a suicide as well. Of note, Chief Officer Wilde was seen after the launch of No. 13, working on Boat No. 2, as well as Collapsibles C and D.

Third Class passenger Carl Jansson: Jansson remained on the ship until the end, and was washed overboard as she sank. He was rescued in Collapsible A. Jansson was on the starboard forward section of the Boat Deck as the Bridge began to submerge:

> Suddenly I heard shrieks and cries amidship, and the sharp report of several shots. People began to run by me toward the stern of the ship, and as I started to run I realized that the boat was beginning to go down very rapidly, and there was quite a decline noticeable in the deck, showing that her nose was being buried. A wave struck me and I went overboard.[41]

Another press account attributed quotes to Jansson that suggest he saw an officer commit suicide. While the article claims that Jansson saw 'Chief Officer Murdock [sic] shoot himself', the actual quote provided from him does not mention Murdoch's name:

> Shortly before the last boat was launched I glanced toward the bridge and saw the chief officer place a revolver in his mouth and shoot himself. His body toppled overboard.[42]

This account is very similar to another report that appeared in papers the day after the *Carpathia* reached New York:

> Passengers declare they saw Chief Officer Wilde shoot himself and that his body fell into the sea.[43]

If Jansson claimed to have witnessed a suicide as the one interview suggests, then it seems likely that he was one of the sources for the above statement. The account attributed to Jansson states that the 'chief officer' shot himself, but does not specifically mention Wilde's name. That may have been an extrapolation by a reporter. Two things about this alleged suicide account stand out. First, Jansson only claimed to have heard shots fired in the first interview, and did not specifically say he saw a suicide. Second, other than the timing, the suicide account attributed to him does not agree with the details of a possible suicide which are found in the primary eyewitness accounts. Thus, it seems reasonable to believe that the second account is an exaggeration or twisting of his words to make the story more dramatic, unless Jansson had witnessed another incident entirely.

If Jansson did indeed hear or see shots fired just before the last boat was launched, then this would corroborate the other accounts that place an incident at the forward end of the Boat Deck near the end, during the loading of Collapsible C or D. Reporters seem to have interpreted his claim that it was the 'chief officer' in different ways, with one newspaper interpreting this to mean Murdoch, and another to mean Wilde. Unfortunately, due to uncertainness about the reliability of the quotes attributed to Jansson, no firm conclusions can be drawn about them.

Able-Bodied Seaman George McGough: A press account attributes the following quotes to McGough:

> Both Captain Smith and Junior Chief Officer Murdoch were now together on the bridge, the water being up to their armpits. The next I saw of Captain Smith was in the water holding a child in his arms. He swam to the raft on which was Second Officer

Lightoller and gave the child to the mate. That was the last. He and the ship went down, and Murdoch -- God help me; don't ask me what I saw.[44]

McGough may have been referring to a suicide with his statement of 'God help me, don't ask me what I saw'. However, having boarded Boat No. 9 fifty minutes before the ship sank, McGough would not have been in a position to see either Smith or Murdoch at the end. Second Officer Lightoller did not report seeing Smith in the water, much less receiving a child from him.

Third Class passenger Oscar Olsson: Olsson was rescued in Collapsible A. He gave some accounts using the name Oskar Johann or Oscar Johansson. He claimed to have heard gunfire in the last moments as the Bridge was plunging under:

> We saw the water come up and up until it almost reached him [Murdoch]. Then we heard a pistol shot. Many people thought he had shot himself.[45]

This account seems to indicate that Olsson did not actually see the suicide. If accurate, it would be yet another account from someone who was near the forward end of the Boat Deck as the ship sank, and who heard gunfire.

Third Class passenger Anna Sjöblom: Anna Sjöblom seems to have been rescued in Boat No. 16, the first of the aft port boats lowered, around 1:20 a.m. She met with the press at the home of her aunt and uncle following the disaster, and gave the following account:

> When we rowed away from the *Titanic*, my face was toward the sinking steamship and the things I saw I will never forget. I saw an officer shoot himself through the temple with a revolver.[46]

Since Sjöblom left in a boat from the aft port side, it is unlikely that she could have witnessed a shooting or suicide on the forward half of the Boat Deck after she left, if that is where it happened. She could have witnessed an incident at the aft boats, or a separate incident entirely. Davis and Hyman may have reported shooting near Boat No. 13, which was launched on the aft starboard side; yet that was over twenty minutes after Sjöblom left the ship, making it unlikely that she could have witnessed an event at that location either.

Given the limited information, all that can be said for the accuracy of Sjöblom's statements is that two separate reporters who visited her at her home quoted her as saying the same thing regarding a suicide, suggesting she actually made the claim.

Third Class passenger Victor Sunderland: Sunderland claimed to be near Collapsible A with Second Officer Lightoller when the Boat Deck began to submerge, and that he was following Lightoller when he leapt over the port side. Lightoller's own accounts contradict this; he never said that he worked at Collapsible A, but rather that he jumped from the roof of the Officers' Quarters. Sunderland was rescued aboard Collapsible B. He claimed to have seen shots fired:

> In one boat, partly filled with women, a man sat - I think he was a Russian. An officer told him to get

out, but he wouldn't. The officer fired his revolver one or twice and still the man sat there. The officer then shot him and he dropped back in his seat. He was lifted up and dropped overboard.[47]

Sunderland gave another interview in which he mentioned shots being fired:

> I saw an officer fire his revolver once or twice, killing a man. ... I started heading towards the stern of the ship and heard another shot. I asked what had happened, and a gentleman told me that an officer had shot himself. Seeing that I could not secure a spot in a lifeboat, I leapt from the ship and into the water just a few feet below.[48]

Sunderland was near the forward area of the Boat Deck, where other accounts suggest shots were fired, and claims to have witnessed just that. The first account does not mention a suicide, and the second makes it clear that he did not witness it himself. Since no private accounts in which he mentions this incident have yet been uncovered, the reliability of the quotes attributed to him are unknown.

Of note, Sunderland places the incident with the 'Russian' being shot sometime before water reached the Boat Deck, at a regular boat that was loading from the deck.

Barber August Weikman: Weikman was washed overboard from the forward starboard side of the Boat Deck and reached Collapsible A. He claimed to have seen First Officer Murdoch fire on a passenger:

> They put the women and the children in the lifeboats and then they started to put in the crew with them. One man to every five women. When no women were near the boats they took the men, whether they were passengers or crew, anybody who stood nearest, and this accounts for the three Chinamen who were taken off. First Officer Murdock [sic] shot a foreigner who tried to climb over the rail into a boat. ... While this was going on I was on the upper deck assisting the passengers to the boats. I had a life belt on, and when the forward part of the ship listed I was washed overboard by a huge wave. Looking backward, I could see Captain Smith, who had been standing on the bridge, swimming back to the place where he had stood, having been washed off the *Titanic* by the same wave that had washed me from the ship into the water.[49]

In his affidavit for the Senate Inquiry, Weikman mentioned nothing about seeing Murdoch shoot anyone, nor did he mention seeing Captain Smith swimming in the water.[50] It is possible that he omitted these details, or that the quotes were fabricated by a reporter. If Weikman did see Captain Smith in the water, however, it agrees with Bride's and Mellors' stories of the Captain's fate.

Of note, the quotes attributed to Weikman place the shooting at a boat where passengers had to climb over a rail. The only boats where this was necessary were the foreword-most boats on both sides of the ship, where there was a solid bulwark that had to be climbed over to board them. Boats launched from these davits included Nos 1 and 2, as well as Collapsibles C and D.

Second Class passenger Charles Whilems: Whilems was rescued in Boat No. 9. He gave the following account:

> Mr. Wilhelms [sic] declared that he had heard several shots fired on the *Titanic* after he left the ship, and that several of his companions told him they had seen Murdock [sic], one of the officers, shoot himself. Other survivors, he said, told him that several passengers had been shot by officers in trying to force their way into the lifeboats.[51]

Unfortunately, both the origins and the timing of the shots Whilems heard are unknown. Also frustrating is that the identities of his 'companions' can not be established. The reliability of his statements thus cannot be determined.

Saloon Steward Thomas Whiteley: Whiteley was swept overboard as the ship sank, and was rescued aboard Collapsible B. He gave the following account:

> Murdoch shot one man – I did not see this, but three others did – and then shot himself.[52]

Unfortunately, Whiteley did not mention who these 'three others' were, so there is no way of checking the veracity of his statements. In another account, Whiteley claimed that he overheard two of the *Titanic*'s lookouts say 'no wonder Mr. Murdoch shot himself', while they were discussing alleged ignored warnings from the Crow's Nest.[53] However, in all of his *Titanic* lectures, given after the sinking, Whiteley never mentioned that he personally witnessed any shootings.[54]

Since Whiteley's statements about the suicide appear to be based on hearsay, they must be weighed with caution. However, they do support the fact that stories of an officer shooting someone, and then killing himself, were widely circulating long before the *Carpathia* reached New York.

First Class passenger Eleanor Widener: Mrs Widener was rescued in Boat No. 4. She claimed to have witnessed the following:

> As the boat pulled away from the *Titanic* I saw one of the officers shoot himself in the head, and a few minutes later saw Capt. Smith jump from the bridge into the sea.[55]

Another press article suggests that Mrs Widener did not witness the alleged suicide herself, but was of the opinion that it had happened due to information she heard from someone else.[56] The first interview may be an extrapolation of her words by a reporter.

Boat No. 4, lowered at 1:50 a.m., was relatively close to the ship when it sank; it was close enough that its occupants were able to pull several people from the water who had jumped overboard and swam to the boat. Conceivably, then, she could have witnessed events unfolding on the deck. However, since no reliable statements from others known to have been rescued in No. 4 have been found to corroborate her account, this all seems unlikely – particularly since No. 4 had rowed aft. It also seems unlikely that she actually witnessed Captain Smith jumping overboard, even though that statement agrees with what Harold Bride and several other witnesses saw.

Secondary Accounts, No Officer Suicide

J. Bruce Ismay, Managing Director of the White Star Line: Ismay was rescued in Collapsible C. When a reporter asked what Captain Smith was doing when he last saw him, Ismay said that he was 'standing on the bridge'. He was then asked if it was true that he committed suicide. Ismay said that no, he had 'heard nothing of it'.[57] Ismay did not actually see what happened to Captain Smith.

Second Class passenger William Mellors: Mellors was rescued in Collapsible A, and was on the ship until the end. He said that 'Captain Smith … did not shoot himself', but that he 'jumped from the bridge'.[58] He did not say anything regarding the fates of the other officers.[59]

Fireman Harry Senior: Senior was rescued aboard Collapsible B. He claimed to have seen Captain Smith leap overboard as the ship plunged under. This agrees with what Bride and Mellors stated. However, Senior also claimed that Captain Smith was carrying a baby at the time and handed it to someone on Collapsible B.[60] Entrée Cook Isaac Maynard, it was later claimed, was the man who took the baby from Captain Smith.[61] However, the reliability of these statements is unknown.[62]

Carpathia Passengers, White Star Line Personnel

The following information comes from statements by *Carpathia* passengers and crewmembers, or from statements by White Star Line employees who were not onboard the *Carpathia*, but who spoke with survivors and heard reports of a shooting and/or suicide. These accounts again indicate that the stories were circulating before the *Carpathia* even reached New York.

First Class *Carpathia* passenger May Birkhead: Ms Birkhead wrote a news story detailing the discussions she had with *Titanic* survivors on the *Carpathia*. She was told that Captain Smith shot himself with a pistol as the ship was sinking.[63] Unfortunately, she does not list her source for this statement.

First Class *Carpathia* passenger Dr Frank Blackmarr: As mentioned previously, Dr Blackmarr was told by Eugene Daly that an unnamed officer shot two men then killed himself. This was the only report of shootings that Blackmarr heard.

Second Class *Carpathia* passenger Carlos F. Hurd: As mentioned previously, while interviewing passengers, Hurd was told there had been gunfire during the sinking. He also heard rumors that Captain Smith or First Officer Murdoch committed suicide as the ship sank. He did not reveal his sources.

***Carpathia* passenger Dr J. F. Kemp:** Doctor Kemp claimed to have heard the following story from a survivor:

> A boy and one of the last children to be taken from the *Titanic* told me that he saw Capt. Smith put a pistol to his head and then fall down.[64]

Kemp went on to say that he didn't know if the story was true, but that he found it hard to believe that the child

would have made it up. He also stated that a 'number of passengers' spoke of the use of pistols and shots being fired, but that they were all too busy helping the survivors to follow up on the claims.

The only 'boys' who left late enough to have seen this would be either Jack Thayer, who escaped on Collapsible B or William Carter Jr, who left in No. 4. Thayer never made any early claims about witnessing a shooting; Carter's press account of April 21 1912 in the *Brooklyn Eagle* mentions an officer shooting a passenger.

***Carpathia* Surgeon Dr Arpad Lengyel:** A survivor of the *Titanic* reportedly told Dr Lengyel that some of the survivors in the boat he was rescued in saw Captain Smith shoot down two men who tried to climb into a lifeboat.[65] Since this story is third-hand at best – and from a press account – the accuracy of the quotes attributed to Dr Lengyel are questionable.

***Carpathia* Captain Arthur Rostron:** Captain Rostron spoke with reporters following the disaster and was adamant that Captain Smith did not commit suicide:

> 'I wish you would deny in as strong language as permissable this persistent report send out by some press concern that Capt. Smith killed himself when he realised that the *Titanic* was doomed,' said Capt. Rostron. 'I have it from the lips of members of his crew who tried to save his life that he did not commit suicide. He stuck to the ship until he was washed from the bridge. Then some of his men caught him in the swirling waters and landed him safely on the edge of a lifeboat, but he tumbled back into the ocean and went down.'[66]

Unfortunately, Captain Rostron did not mention who told him of Captain Smith's fate.

White Star Line Assistant to the Vice-President Fred Toppin: Toppin spoke with the *Titanic*'s surviving officers, and with some of her crewmembers following the *Carpathia*'s arrival in New York. Many years later, Toppin was interviewed by researcher Ernie Robinson, who knew him between 1934–1941. Toppin told Robinson that he thought two officers had shot themselves, and that this was the result of conversations with 'senior surviving crew' and others at the pier when they arrived.[67]

Toppin did not mention which officers he believed had shot themselves, or who specifically had told him this. This information must be taken with caution, since Toppin was recalling from memory words spoken to him many years earlier.

Refuted or False Accounts and Accounts of Unknown Reliability

These accounts of an officer's suicide are ones which were refuted by the survivors whose names the words are attributed to, are known to have been made up, or in which no survivor name is given. Thus, it is impossible to determine the reliability of the accounts.

First Class passenger Paul Chevré: Chevré was rescued in Boat No. 7. A press account quoted him as saying that he saw Captain Smith shoot himself.[68] On April 22, 1912 he stormed into the office of *Le Presse* in Quebec, and demanded that a story be run saying that the entire account was a lie.[69]

First Class passenger Robert Williams Daniel:

I saw the captain holding the bridge after the ship had sunk to the level of the sea. Then he went overboard.[70]

Daniel also claimed that he knew that First Officer Murdoch committed suicide because he was 'not more than ten feet away' at the time.[71] However, a press interview with Trimmer Thomas Patrick Dillon, who was on the Poop Deck when the ship went under, places Daniel at the stern, jumping overboard as the ship plunged under.[72] Dillon subsequently boarded Boat No. 4. There is evidence that suggests Daniel may have leapt overboard from the stern, and perhaps also reached Boat No. 4. However, Colonel Archibald Gracie believed he was rescued in Boat No. 7, and an unpublished private letter from First Class passenger Orian Davidson describes him as being in Boat No. 3 with her, helping to row.[73] Whichever version of his escape is true, Daniel would not have been in a position to see what was happening on the forward portion of the Boat Deck near the end.

First Class passenger Dr Washington Dodge: Dodge was rescued in Boat No. 13. One account quoted him as saying that he saw an officer gun down two men then shoot himself.[74] In a public address given in San Francisco, Dr Dodge denied having seen any shootings, and said that most of the accounts attributed to him in the press were 'wholly unfounded'.[75]

First Class passenger Lady Lucy Duff Gordon: Lady Duff Gordon was rescued in Boat No. 1. One account quoted her as saying that she heard shots as the Boat Deck began to submerge.[76] Another account had her saying that she saw an officer shoot a male passenger, and that his body fell into her lifeboat.[77]

Although these accounts are interesting in light of Laura Francatelli's account of a suicide, at the British Inquiry, Lady Duff Gordon denied most of the quotes attributed to her in the press.[78] Nobody reported a passenger being shot near No. 1, and no body was recovered from that boat.

Fireman Frederick Harris: Harris was probably one of the men transferred out of Boat No. 14 by Fifth Officer Lowe once it was afloat. A press account attributed to him says that he saw Captain Smith leap overboard with a child, and that he believed First Officer Murdoch was the one who committed suicide.[79] If he was indeed rescued in Boat No. 14, there is no way he would have been in a position to see Captain Smith at the end.

First Class passenger James McGough: McGough was rescued in Boat No. 7. A press account quotes McGough as saying that he heard shots fired as the bow of the ship went under, that he was told that Captain Smith committed suicide, and that several men were shot for pushing ahead of women and children.[80] McGough specifically denied hearing shots fired in his affidavit for the Senate Inquiry.[81]

Quartermaster J. R. Moody: Someone calling himself 'Quartermaster Moody' gave sensational accounts in which he claimed to have seen First Officer Murdoch shoot himself.[82] Other portions of 'Quartermaster Moody's' account claim that he was on the Bridge at the helm when the ship struck the iceberg. There were no Quartermasters with that name onboard *Titanic*.

If Moody was a real person who had been at or near the ship's helm during the collision, he would either have to have been Sixth Officer Moody – an impossibility, since he did not survive – or Quartermaster Hichens, who left the ship at 1:10 a.m. in Boat No. 6. This boat rowed swiftly away from the sinking ship, so Hichens could not have seen anything on deck at the end. No quotes from Hichens alleging anything resembling the 'Moody' quotes have been discovered.

Steward Albert Smith: Someone calling himself Albert Smith, who claimed to have been rescued in Boat No. 11, said he saw First Officer Murdoch shoot himself after all the lifeboats had been launched.[83] Nobody by the name of Albert Smith appears on the crew list.

Second Class passenger Charles Eugene Williams: While speaking to a reporter, Charles Williams' friend George E. Standing made some interesting assertions about Williams' experiences. Standing claimed that Williams had seen Captain Smith swim up to his lifeboat and hand over a child; when he was told that First Officer Murdoch had killed himself, Standing's story went, Captain Smith then pushed away from the boat.[84]

In reality, Williams was not in contact with the water and would not have been in a position to see the events his friend described. Fifth Officer Lowe testified in the Senate Inquiry that he had taken Williams into Boat No. 14 to help row.[85]

Able Bodied Seaman Jack Williams: Someone using the name Jack Williams claimed that he and fellow crewmember William French saw Murdoch shoot himself as the ship sank, and that Captain Smith did not commit suicide.[86] No crewmembers by the name of Jack Williams or William French were aboard the *Titanic*.

Accounts from unknown sources[87]

Chief Officer Wilde stood on the bridge after the collision. He raised his arm and shot himself. He dropped where he stood. – *No name attributed.*[88]

Murdock [*sic*] was splendid, too; but I fear it is true that he did shoot himself. He did not do so, however, until the very end, when he had done everything he could for others. – *An unknown 'steward in the first-class saloon'.*[89]

Mr. Murdoch calmly pulled out his revolver and blew out his brains. – *No name attributed.*[90]

[One] or two Italians tried to rush the boats, but the chief officer kept them back, and finally fired at them, whether he killed them he could not say. Then the officer shot himself. – *Anonymous crewmember leaving the SS Lapland.*[91]

Other Information Relating to a Suicide

1) Which officers would have had guns? – Answering the question of whether an officer could have committed suicide must, by necessity, involve ascertaining which officers would have had access to a firearm in the first place. While Second Officer Lightoller worked on the forward port lifeboats, Chief Officer Wilde approached him and requested that he direct them to the ship's firearms. This may have been in response to events at Boat No. 5, or the crowds of passengers beginning to mass at the aft port boats. Captain Smith, Chief Officer Wilde, First Officer Murdoch and Second Officer Lightoller all went to the arms locker in the First Officer's cabin and received Webley revolvers.[92] Lightoller was the only officer among them to survive. It appears that the other officers (Moody, Lowe, Boxhall, and Pitman) were not present at this time, although Chief Officer Wilde could have taken extra revolvers (if there were any) with him to hand out to them later. However, there is absolutely no evidence to suggest that this happened.

Sixth Officer Moody was the only officer who perished that was not present when the firearms were handed out. Fifth Officer Lowe had his own personal weapon, a Browning automatic, in his cabin; he used this weapon to fire warning shots during the lowering of Boat No. 14. Thus, it is conceivable that some of the other officers may have had personal firearms as well, including Moody. Again, even though this is a possibility, there is no evidence at all to indicate that this was the case.

Many years after the sinking, First Class passenger Jack Thayer described Chief Purser Hugh McElroy as having fired a revolver during the lowering of Collapsible C.[93] Not a single other eyewitness corroborates Thayer on this point; in fact, the other witnesses believed that Murdoch fired those shots, not McElroy.[94] Even if McElroy had fired shots, where he had obtained a revolver is unknown, since it is unlikely that his position as Purser would have required him to have one in his possession. Yet like Lowe, it is possible that he could have carried a personal firearm.

It has been suggested that the Masters-at-Arms may have had firearms, but again, there is no evidence for it. Of the two Masters-at-Arms, one – Thomas W. King – perished. There is at least some evidence that a few of the Able Bodied Seamen and other crewmembers may have had guns aboard the ship; however these would likely have been personally-owned firearms, rather than ones issued to them as part of their job. Second Class passenger Imanita Shelley claimed that 'the sailor in charge of the boat' she was in, Boat No. 10, threatened a man with a revolver after he had jumped down into it as it lowered away – an act which had injured at least one woman in the boat, and angered the crewmembers aboard.[95] Able Bodied Seaman Buley was in charge of this boat, and Able Bodied Seaman Evans was also aboard, so it is likely that she was referring to one of these two individuals as the one she thought was armed.

Among passengers, it appears as though many may have had firearms in their possession: Second Class passenger Alfred Nourney, traveling under the title 'Baron Alfred von Drachstedt', fired off a revolver in Boat No. 7 in an attempt to call for help;[96] First Class passenger Norman Chambers admitted to having an automatic pistol with him during the sinking;[97] and Second Class passenger Michel Navratil's body was recovered with a loaded revolver on it.[98] Some reports of questionable reliability suggest that First Class passenger Major Archibald Butt may have had a firearm on his person as well.[99] It is impossible to tell exactly how many other passengers had firearms aboard the ship, but based on this small sampling, it appears that it was common.

In summary, of the officers lost that night (Smith, Wilde, Murdoch and Moody), the senior three were known to be in a position to have received a pistol. There is no direct evidence that Moody had a gun that night, although we cannot say for certain that he did not. There is only Thayer's report – made 28 years after the sinking – that McElroy fired a gun; still, it is questionable whether the Purser would even have had one in the first place. There is evidence that numerous passengers were armed. By this evidence alone, we can say for certain who *had* a firearm in their possession, but we cannot say for certain who *did not* have one.

2) Why were officers sometimes misidentified? – In short, this seems most attributable to the officer re-shuffle at Southampton, where Chief Officer Wilde was brought aboard temporarily, and Murdoch and Lightoller were reduced in rank a step, with former Second Officer Blair leaving the ship. This apparently caused great confusion. It can be established from photographic evidence that Lightoller did not change his uniform insignia before the ship left Southampton; it would seem that this may also have applied to Murdoch.

During both the Senate and British Inquiry, some crewmen specifically identified Wilde as the Chief Officer, but other crew members specifically referred to Murdoch as the 'chief officer'.[100] Other members of the crew used the term 'chief officer' without a name attached, and in many cases there is no way to tell exactly which of these men they were referring to.

Able Bodied Seaman Joseph Scarrott had this to say about the lifeboat drill at the dock in Southampton on the morning of sailing:

> The boat turned out; we were told to put our lifebelts on, so many men, there were both watches there, an officer there, junior officers, and two chief officers.[101]

It is unknown whether Scarrott really meant to say senior officers instead of two chiefs, or if he was being specific as to what he saw. If Murdoch did not change his uniform, it would easily explain many of the misidentifications the night of the sinking.

The lighting on the deck, or lack thereof, is another factor one has to consider regarding the difficulty in identifications. The Boat Deck and other decks were not nearly as well lit as they are portrayed in movies of the disaster. Saloon Steward William Ward testified about this factor:

> I think it was Chief Officer Murdoch [who called out for the women to get into Boat No. 9]. I would not be sure whether it was him or the purser. They were both tall men, and I would not be sure which one it was. It was dark, you know.[102]

Obviously, it was easy to confuse people during the lifeboat loading, and the differences in the uniforms did not help him to discover if it was Murdoch or McElroy that he saw.

Since passengers and officers typically did not mingle on White Star Line ships, it is likely that many of the passengers would not have been able to tell Murdoch from Wilde. As described earlier, even Colonel Gracie did not know which officer was which until someone told him who was who after the sinking.

However, there are some cases when passengers knew officers. Second Class passenger Charlotte Collyer's account tells of having met First Officer Murdoch, and reveals one way in which a passenger might come to know an officer:

> I had met him [Murdoch] the day before, when he was inspecting the second-cabin quarters.[103]

In addition, the Hoyt family was said to have known Captain Smith,[104] and the Speddens were said to be acquainted with First Officer Murdoch.[105] These factors illustrate the difficulty that most passengers and even crewmembers may have had in identifying the officers, factors which further complicate the question of which officer may have shot himself, if anyone did.

Final Analysis

As can be seen from the accounts presented in this article, much of the 'evidence' of an officer committing suicide is of dubious nature. Many of the survivor accounts disagree with each other, and some of the survivors probably would not have been in a position, either on the ship or close enough to it, to see what stories run in the newspapers quoted them as saying. Further complicating matters, many accounts of an officer's suicide were fabricated by reporters or later refuted by the people they were attributed to.

With all of the sensational press stories and rumors, it seems impossible to say for certain what actually happened, other than that some sort of event must have spawned the rumors that circulated onboard the *Carpathia*. However, among all of the flotsam and jetsam, we do start to see some consistency.

There is some evidence from passengers saved in Boat No. 13 (Davis and Hyman) that may suggest a suicide occurred near that boat, because both witnesses claimed to have seen a shooting or suicide. However, with the exception of a private letter written by Third Class passenger Karl Albert Midtsjø – in which he states that 'someone was shot when they tried to push their way into the boats'[106] – no other evidence has been found that suggests that gunfire, much less a suicide, occurred during the loading of the aft starboard boats. The existing evidence is not very convincing, since there are no direct quotes from Davis or Hyman about the alleged incident, and Midtsjø may have been referring to something that he did not even witness for himself.

Several of the accounts examined refer to gunfire on the forward end of the Boat Deck, apparently very late in the loading process of a boat, and just before it lowered away. Based on the descriptions given, it appears likely that this boat was either Collapsible C or D, since these accounts describe the boat lowering, and then go on to describe water reaching the deck, or the ship plunging shortly after the shooting/suicide.

Even more convincing is that there are two eyewitnesses whose words are taken from primary sources, and who gave multiple accounts of a suicide or shots fired at that time and area of the ship (Daly and Rheims). There seems to be no motive for lying, since some of their statements were made privately in letters, statements to family

members or, in Daly's case, a court of law. There is no evidence that Daly and Rheims ever met each other, yet both described seeing nearly the same thing.

Their statements, coupled with the secondary accounts of those who claimed to have witnessed a suicide or to have heard gunfire as one of the last boats was loading or lowering (Dorking, Jansson, Sunderland, and Weikman), and were in the correct position to have witnessed or heard it, strongly suggests that the shooting and suicide story may indeed have a basis in fact. Other witnesses (R. N. Williams and Olsson) also describe a suicide, but apparently place it a few minutes later, during the attempted launch of Collapsible A, since they describe water having reached the Boat Deck at the time.

One additional witness, Saloon Steward Walter Nichols, may lend further credence to the story of shots fired at this later time and location on the starboard side. Sitting some distance off the starboard side in Boat No. 15, he described the following in a private letter to his sister in New York City, Mrs James Openshaw:

> I could see that she was down a good deal by the head because the propeller was sticking half way out of the water. When we were a couple hundred feet away from the ship I saw two flashes and heard two revolver reports from near the bridge. All the boats had been lowered and I did not know what the shots meant.[107]

Locations, Motivations and Means

In this section, the possible motivation of the various 'suspects' for having committed suicide is addressed. Please keep in mind that all of the comments in this section are merely speculative, as there is no way to actually 'know' what was going through these men's minds in the final stages of the sinking. People can react very differently under the same circumstances during a crisis situation. Certain motivations were common to all these men – the imminent sinking of the ship, and the impending death of most of those still on it, including the officer himself. Also – was this unknown officer involved in passengers being shot to prevent them from rushing a lifeboat, as some of the accounts say? If so, the suicide could have been overcome by the shock of those events.

Captain Edward Smith: As shown above in some of the accounts themselves, Captain Smith was the subject of several stories that he shot himself. Many of the early press accounts and headlines of the disaster claimed that he did so, and these rumors were widespread enough that Captain Rostron felt the need to refute them. Some of the papers printed headline stories stating that he killed himself,[108] and one even went as far as to commission an artist to draw a scene of him shooting himself.[109] Smith's body was not recovered.

Possible Motivation: Captain Smith was the man ultimately responsible for the *Titanic* – and those aboard her – regardless of whether he was on the Bridge during the collision. Even though he was due to retire soon, the sinking of the *Titanic* and the subsequent loss of life would be a very large blemish on his reputation.

Location: A number of accounts place Smith on the forward area of the Boat Deck, near the Bridge, not long before it dipped under. Bride's and Mellors' accounts seem credible,

A period newspaper illustration of Captain Smith's last moments.

and both describe him diving off the Bridge as it began to submerge. There are numerous other accounts that indicate that Smith jumped overboard, and was seen in the water following the sinking.[110] If these accounts are correct, they eliminate the possibility of Smith having committed suicide.

The only evidence besides wild rumors which indicates Smith could have shot himself is 1) the account of Richard Norris Williams, who heard gunfire near the spot where he and his father last saw Captain Smith, and 2) the account from Dorking, where he tentatively names Smith as the officer he saw shoot himself – even though he was far from certain in this identification. Onboard the *Carpathia*, Dr Kemp heard an unnamed boy say that he saw Smith shoot himself, but without a name attached to the account, there is no way to determine its veracity.

The Means: Captain Smith was one of the officers who went to the Chief Officer's cabin when the revolvers were brought out and distributed.

Chief Officer Henry Wilde: While less numerous than headlines claiming Captain Smith or First Officer Murdoch shot themselves, there were numerous stories in the press claiming that Wilde killed himself. However, the rumors and references naming Wilde as the officer who committed suicide are not very convincing, in and of themselves. The account by 'unknown' could easily have been a fabrication by a reporter, and the mention of Wilde in the Hyman account may also be a reporter's fabrication, as he himself did not mention Wilde. The term 'Chief Officer' is used in a number of accounts, but as detailed earlier, not all survivors actually meant Wilde when they referred to that rank. Any references to the Chief Officer shooting himself,

without the provision of a name, would apply equally well to Murdoch as they would to Wilde. Wilde's body was not recovered.

Possible Motivation: It has been suggested that Wilde could have been despondent over the death of his wife and two sons, which occurred about a year and a half before the maiden voyage, and that the disaster could have pushed him over the edge into suicide. An acquaintance of Wilde's claimed that when speaking about his wife, he had heard Wilde say that 'he didn't care particularly how he went or how soon he joined her'.[111]

However, it is impossible to say whether Wilde still felt this way during the maiden voyage or not. Second Officer Lightoller remembered seeing Chief Officer Wilde during the sinking. He recalled: '[I] was on my way back on deck again when I heard Wilde say, "I am going to put on my life-belt". '[112] At that point in time, right after the revolvers were handed out, it did not appear that Wilde was suicidal; it seems that, to the contrary, he was still thinking about survival – although this certainly could have changed later in the sinking.

Others have suggested that Wilde was despondent over some sort of career setback, and yet it is known that he was slated to receive his own command. His trip on the *Titanic* would most likely have been a single round-trip voyage, and then he most likely would have taken command of one of the White Star liners which had been laid up due to the coal strike. This was what his fellow officers said was the case; even if they were mistaken, being brought aboard the newest liner in the fleet could not have been considered a demotion by any means.

Location: Wilde's whereabouts very late in the sinking are curiously absent from survivor accounts. The last confirmed place that he was seen was during the loading of Collapsible D. Lightoller was vague about where Wilde may have gone after he sighted him there. Wilde appears to have at least threatened men rushing Collapsible D with a gun;[113] shots may have been fired at that boat (See Appendix H), and there is no known evidence that Wilde was seen after the loading of that boat. Collapsible D is where Lightoller told Colonel Gracie that he had been forced to fire warning shots, and where crewmembers linked arms to prevent men from rushing the boat again. After the sinking, Saloon Steward Littlejohn was asked if there was 'any actual shooting'. He responded that the 'chief officer I think it was, shot one of the Italian waiters belonging to the restaurant because he got into a boat and would not come out of it when he was told to'.[114] It is unclear whether Littlejohn saw this incident himself, or was told about it by someone else. Littlejohn had previously served with Wilde and Murdoch onboard the *Olympic*, so while he – or his source of information – could have been referring to Murdoch by that mistaken rank, this account leaves open the real possibility that Wilde was indeed involved in some sort of gunplay.

Details about Wilde's despondent attitude prior to the voyage, as well as the details in eyewitness accounts that suggest a shooting or suicide may have occurred at either Collapsible C or D are intriguing. However, they are far from conclusive.

What is certain is that Lightoller did not mention seeing Wilde near Collapsible A; on the other hand, he was specific about having seen Murdoch there, and denied that the latter officer shot himself. Lightoller did not write to Wilde's family issuing a similar denial. Allegedly, later in life, while he was living in Hertfordshire, Lightoller admitted to an acquaintance that he 'knew someone who committed suicide that night', but he didn't specify who.[115]

One press article claimed that Wilde was last seen on the Bridge smoking a cigarette, and that he waved goodbye to Lightoller as the ship sank.[116] Lightoller himself never claimed this in his testimony, only allowing that he had last seen Wilde 'quite a long time before the ship went down'.[117] *The Means:* Wilde was one of the officers who received a revolver from the First Officer's cabin. In fact, according to Lightoller, he was the one who asked for them to be brought out, although there is circumstantial evidence that Murdoch may have asked for the revolvers prior to Wilde's having done so.[118]

First Officer William Murdoch: Many of the early rumors specifically mention Murdoch as the officer who committed suicide. When examining rumors of who may have shot himself as the ship sank, it is Murdoch who is most often mentioned, and by name, not just rank. Yet this in itself does not *prove* it was Murdoch, since none of the primary accounts of the alleged suicide specifically identify him.

However, Miss Francatelli's account indicated her belief that an officer who had lowered her boat shot himself. Only two officers directly assisted in the loading of Boat No. 1: Murdoch and Fifth Officer Lowe. Lowe survived.

According to the testimony of Hugh Woolner and others, Murdoch had previously fired warning shots at Collapsible C during the loading process, and before the boat began lowering away. This demonstrates that he was willing to use his revolver if necessary to prevent a rush on a boat that could potentially cost lives. Murdoch's body was not recovered. *Possible Motivation:* Murdoch was the officer directly in charge of the *Titanic* in the hours leading up to the collision with the iceberg. As such, he was responsible for the ship and all its passengers during that time, and may have felt responsible for being unable to avert the collision. *Location:* Murdoch was right where many of the primary accounts of a suicide place the shooting: working at Collapsible C, and then trying to get Collapsible A launched. Lightoller told Murdoch's widow that he saw her husband swept into the sea while working on the falls to Collapsible A.

Lightoller may later have told James McGiffin, the Marine Superintendent of the White Star Line in Queenstown, that he saw Murdoch shoot a man, although that is not certain at this time. If Lightoller's account to Ada Murdoch is accurate, then he could not be the officer who committed suicide. If his account to McGiffin is accurate, then he may have been lying to Mrs Murdoch about what really happened, in order to spare her feelings.

It is interesting to note that of the officers mentioned in press accounts, Lightoller only felt the need to write a letter denying the rumors to Murdoch's widow. There were many rumors circulating about Smith and a few, although not nearly as many, about Wilde as well. This opens an intriguing possibility: Did Lightoller write the denial because he knew her husband *was* involved in the rumored event? Possibly. Equally likely, however, is that he personally knew that Murdoch did not commit suicide, and that he did not write denials regarding the others because he did not have personal knowledge of the fates of the other officers.

It is interesting to note that Lightoller is the only survivor to definitively claim that Murdoch worked at Collapsible A. As discussed earlier, Colonel Gracie did not know

which officer he had seen and when, until told about it after the sinking. He said that Lightoller told him Murdoch was the officer he saw at that scene. Lamp Trimmer Hemming saw Sixth Officer Moody at Collapsible A giving orders, but did not see Murdoch. This could simply be due to the fact that so few people who were aboard that late in the sinking lived to tell the tale, or it could mean that Murdoch was not at Collapsible A when Lightoller said he was. *The Means:* Murdoch was one of the officers who received a revolver when they were passed out in the First Officer's cabin earlier that evening. In fact, there is circumstantial evidence suggesting he may have been the officer who initially asked for the revolvers to be brought out, although Lightoller said that Wilde was the officer who asked for them.[119]

Sixth Officer James Moody: The only reason to consider Moody a 'suspect' for having committed suicide is that he was last seen by Samuel Hemming working at Collapsible A, near the area where shots may have been fired. Moody's body was not recovered. *Possible Motivation:* No specific motivation can be determined. *Location:* Moody was last seen helping to lower Collapsible A from the roof of the Officers' Quarters, and telling the men working there that he didn't want the block, but would prefer to leave the boat on the deck. Lightoller did not see him working on the falls to Collapsible A, although he was specific about having seen First Officer Murdoch on the scene. *The Means:* There is no evidence that Moody had a firearm, although he could have been handed one by another officer. Another possibility is that, like Fifth Officer Lowe, he owned a personal firearm.

Chief Purser Hugh McElroy: In 1940, Jack Thayer said that he saw McElroy fire warning shots with a revolver at Collapsible C. However, this account was given many years after the sinking, and is contradicted by other witnesses who believe Murdoch fired those shots. Other than Thayer's account, there is no reason to suspect that McElroy had a revolver, much less shot himself. McElroy's body was recovered, and no mention of gunshot wounds was noted.[120] *Possible Motivation:* No specific motivation can be determined. *Location:* Second Officer Lightoller last saw McElroy quietly standing off to the side with the Assistant Purser and Senior and Junior Surgeon sometime after No. 4 was lowered away on the port side at 1:50 a.m.[121] McElroy wasn't actively involved in the loading of the boats at that time, although there is evidence that he had been involved in the loading earlier in the night.[122] This calls into question Thayer's account of McElroy playing so prominent a role in the loading and launch of Collapsible C, lowered just ten minutes later, particularly since that boat was likely loading at the very time Lightoller saw McElroy standing quietly off to the side. *The Means:* Other than Thayer's account 28 years after the sinking, there is little reason to suspect that McElroy would have had a revolver. It is unlikely that his position would have required him to have had one.

Chief Engineer Joseph Bell: There is absolutely no reason to consider Bell a 'suspect' as the person who committed suicide, other than press accounts mentioning that he was rumored to have shot himself. The source of these allegations was not given.[123] Bell's body was not recovered.

Possible Motivation: No specific motivation can be determined.

Location: The last sighting of Bell may have been by Second Officer Lightoller, after Boat No. 4 was lowered away at 1:50 a.m. Writing 28 years after the disaster, Lightoller said that he saw all of the engineers after they came up on deck. They had been released from their duty so that they could take their chances up on deck.[124] This would mesh pretty well with other available statements about men from the Engineering Department and at least one engineer being seen on the deck by other survivors.[125] However, this clashes with Lightoller's 1912 testimony, in which he specifically denied having seen the engineers on deck.[126]

The Means: Other than the rumors in the press, there is absolutely no reason to believe that Chief Engineer Bell had a firearm, or that he shot himself. No actual eyewitness accounts claiming that he shot himself have surfaced.

Master-at-Arms Thomas W. King: Some researchers have suggested that it might have been King who committed suicide. There is absolutely no evidence to suggest this. His body was not recovered.

Possible Motivation: No specific motivation can be determined.

Location: King's location during the loading of the collapsibles and during the sinking in general is unknown.

The Means: It is unknown whether or not King's position as Master-at-Arms would have required him to have a firearm.

First Class passenger Major Archibald Butt: One of the more wild press rumors was that Major Butt had entered into an agreement with fellow First Class passengers George Widener, Colonel Astor, and Isidor Straus to kill them first, then shoot himself before the boat sank, and that this act had been carried out.[127] Butt and Widener's bodies were not recovered, but Astor's and Straus's were. There is no mention that either body bore gunshot wounds.[128]

Quotes attributed to a male Second Class passenger, most likely Albert Caldwell,[129] and to Mrs Irene Harris,[130] claim that Major Butt helped keep men from rushing the lifeboats at gunpoint; according to the former, Butt may even have opened fired on them. Mrs Harris later denied that Major Butt had fired a shot.[131] Caldwell was rescued in Boat No. 13 along with his wife and 10-month-old son, and Mrs Harris was rescued in Collapsible D. It is plausible that if Major Butt was wearing his military uniform, that he could have been mistaken for an officer.

Possible Motivation: No specific motivation can be determined.

Location: Archibald Butt appears to have been last seen during the launching of Collapsible D around 2:05 a.m., where shots may have been fired; it is also one of the locations where a suicide could potentially have taken place, based on the eyewitness accounts.

The Means: Besides the questionable newspaper accounts, there is no reason to suspect that Major Butt had a firearm or committed suicide.

One very important thing to remember when considering this subject is that there is no solid evidence whatsoever

that any bodies were recovered with gunshot wounds. In a 1912 press account, an unnamed *Carpathia* passenger stated that one of the bodies brought onboard the ship after the survivors were rescued was a fireman who had been 'shot by one of the officers for disobeying orders' and pushing into the last boat ahead of the women and children. There is absolutely no eyewitness testimony which backs up this claim.

There are also stories that John Snow, Jr, a Halifax undertaker who worked on some of the *Titanic* victims, may have seen evidence of gunshot wounds on some of the recovered victims.[132] This report cannot be substantiated, however, and is second- or third-hand at best. Even if there were passengers who were shot, or even if an officer committed suicide, the odds that their bodies were recovered are highly unlikely. Only 337 out of the 1,496 victims' bodies were recovered (23%).[133] Captain Lardner of the *Mackay-Bennett,* the ship that recovered the bodies, stated that 'not one of the bodies that were recovered had any pistol shots'.[134]

Alternative Explanations?

Some *Titanic* researchers have theorized that nobody shot anyone or committed suicide, but that there is another way of explaining the eyewitness accounts: when *Titanic*'s forward funnel fell, the wire stays supporting it snapped, sounded like gunshots, and the flying wires cut passengers down, fooling nearby witnesses into believing that the victims had been shot.

While this is an interesting theory and could explain the accounts of those who merely heard noises that they believed were gunfire, it does not explain the accounts of passengers such as Eugene Daly, George Rheims and others who were nearby and claim to have *seen* the shooting occur during the loading and lowering of a lifeboat. If Richard Norris Williams' account is accurate, it would seem to make the snapping funnel stay theory even less likely, since the gunfire that he heard occurred well before his father was killed by the falling forward funnel.

Another theory that has been put forward is that witnesses saw or heard Fifth Officer Lowe fire warning shots at Boat No. 14, and due to the confusion, believed that passengers were actually being fired upon. However, this does not explain the accounts of those who heard shots fired shortly before, or right as the Boat Deck plunged under. Boat No. 14 was launched at 1:25 a.m., while the Boat Deck plunged under fifty minutes later, around 2:15 a.m.

This theory also does not adequately explain the accounts of those who said they actually *saw* a shooting right near them, or who like Daly, saw the bodies lying on the deck. The timing of the shots at No. 14 does not match that of the gunfire described by witnesses, many of whom place the alleged shooting/suicide late in the loading and lowering of either Collapsibles C or D, or during the attempted launch of Collapsible A.

Conclusions

Did an officer shoot men before committing suicide in the final stages of *Titanic*'s sinking? If so, what was the identity of this officer? Unless more eyewitness information is uncovered and made public, the matter is unlikely to be settled with finality. As of this writing, there simply is not enough hard, factual, reliable data available to make any concrete determinations about the incident, much less about who may have been involved. Many of the people who would have witnessed the suicide, if it occurred, or who saw how the officers met their fate, perished in the disaster. Very few that were on the ship during the loading and lowering/attempted lowering of the collapsible boats lived to tell their story.

One does not envy the situation of the crewmembers who were scrambling around Collapsibles C and D, and later Collapsible A: as they worked, it was clear that their time was nearly up. Water was rapidly approaching the Boat Deck, and over a thousand people were still on board. Collapsible C got away from the starboard side just fifteen minutes before the Boat Deck plunged under, and when Collapsible D was lowered away five minutes later, the Boat Deck on the port side was just ten feet above the water, due to the 10° port list which had developed. During the attempted launch of Collapsible A, between 2:00 to 2:15 a.m., the water approached and then consumed the Boat Deck.

At Collapsible C on the starboard side, it is reported that there had been a rush of men during the loading, that First Officer Murdoch had to fire shots to control the situation, that the men were then pulled out, and only then were women and children loaded aboard. Although the exact circumstances are unclear, Chief Officer Wilde and Second Officer Lightoller may have had to do the same when men pushed their way into Collapsible D, and the crewmembers then linked arms to prevent another rush on the boat ahead of the remaining women and children.

According to Colonel Gracie's account, there was a mass of humanity, most likely Steerage passengers, which came up from below deck at the last minute, only to find the sea near, and nearly all of the boats gone. This crowd included women and children. Scullion John Collins agreed with Gracie, and testified in the Senate Inquiry that there were 'hundreds on the starboard side' during the attempted launch of Collapsible A.[135] Saloon Steward Edward Brown testified in the British Inquiry that there were four or five women waiting to get into that last collapsible, and that as the water came onto the Boat Deck, there was a 'scramble' among the passengers to get into the boat.[136]

One can easily imagine how the situation at any of these three boats could have escalated to the point where shots needed to be fired to prevent the women and children from being crowded out, and to ensure that the boats could be lowered away safely; in the case of Collapsible A, such a threat might have been required to prevent people from getting in the way of the efforts to cut the falls that fastened the collapsible to the sinking ship. By the time these boats were being loaded, it was abundantly clear that the end would come in minutes, as the water came up and up. There is no way of telling for certain whether a shooting/suicide happened. What is certain is that if Collapsibles C and D had not been lowered, or if Collapsible A had not been freed, more people would have died in the sinking.

In the opinion of the authors, all of the men examined above were heroes to the end – regardless of whether any of them were forced to open fire on passengers in an attempt to restore order and to save the lives of others including women and children, and regardless of whether they did or did not take their own life. Despite any human failings that may have led to the collision itself, there is documented evidence that all of the officers helped load the lifeboats and saved many people – people who would have otherwise lost their lives. The officers and crewmembers of the *Titanic* did their duty until their final moments, when they could do no more.

Appendix L: Thomas Andrews' Fate

One of the more poignant images of the *Titanic* disaster is that of Thomas Andrews, standing by the fireplace in the First Class Smoking Room moments before the final plunge, staring at the painting 'Plymouth Harbor', accepting his fate with quiet resignation. This image has been accepted as the truth, and has been perpetuated in many books and films about the disaster, including James Cameron's blockbuster film. But did Thomas Andrews really meet his fate in this way? To answer that question, we must first find the origin of this story.

This well-known portrait of Thomas Andrews comes from the account of Verandah Café Steward John Stewart. It was quoted in part in Shan Bullock's 1912 book *Thomas Andrews: Shipbuilder*. Bullock placed Stewart's sighting of Andrews sometime after 2:05 a.m., approximately 15 minutes before *Titanic* sank. Interestingly, Bullock himself did not claim this was the last time Andrews was seen. Yet this is the popular belief that has continued through the years. Apparently it is the result of simply drawing a line between the report of Andrews in that location, and Bullock's statement that the sighting was after an event which he had placed at 2:05 a.m.

Yet the timing of Stewart's sighting, as put forward by Bullock, was likely a guess on that author's part. No quote from Stewart is provided, giving either the exact time or an estimate, although it would seem that the steward spotted Andrews shortly before leaving the ship. All of this is rather dissatisfying from a scholarly perspective. Yet, the manner in which the witness in question was rescued should provide some clue as to when the shipbuilder was seen.

Stewart did not elaborate on his method of rescue in the above-mentioned account. Yet, Able Bodied Seaman Frank Evans may have provided a clue during his Senate Inquiry testimony. Evans was one of the crewmembers that returned to the site of the sinking in Boat No. 14 when Fifth Officer Lowe returned to search for survivors. Evans thought a total of four men were pulled from the water, two of whom he recognized. One of these was 'the steward, young Stewart'.[1]

No follow-up questions about 'Stewart' were asked, and it has been assumed that Evans was referring to John Stewart, since he was the only crewmember aboard with that last name. How familiar Evans – as a member of the Deck Department – would have been with members of the Victualling Department is unknown. However both men had previously served on the *Olympic*, so it is at least possible that they would have known or recognized each other. Another question is whether Evans, 27-years-old at the time of the disaster, would have referred to Stewart, also aged 27 at the time of the sinking, as 'young Stewart'.

This has led to speculation by some *Titanic* researchers that Evans actually said 'the steward, young steward', and that somehow it was mistaken as 'Stewart' in the transcript. How they could have thought he was referring to a specific crewmember if he indeed said 'steward' is unknown, and there is no definitive proof either way. Colonel Archibald Gracie, in his 1913 book *The Truth About the 'Titanic'*, lists Stewart as having been rescued in No. 14 and quotes Evans as saying that 'another picked up was named J. Stewart, a steward'. This wording is not reflected in the existing transcripts of the inquiry. If Stewart was pulled from the water, then it is possible that he was aboard the ship until the end and did see Andrews right before the ship sank.

However, is there any evidence that suggests Stewart was rescued in a boat other than No. 14? During the British Inquiry, Bathroom Steward Samuel Rule was asked if he knew who took charge of Boat No. 15, the boat he was rescued in. Rule said that it was a 'man called Jack Stewart', and that he was 'a steward; he was a steward called Stewart'. Rule stated that the man was still alive, and when asked, stated that he saw him after the sinking, although not since he had left Southampton the Tuesday prior to testifying.

In response, the Attorney-General stated that he had not heard his name before. As mentioned previously, Stewart's name was allegedly brought up in the previous Senate Inquiry in relation to Boat No. 14, but the commission appeared unaware of this. This is somewhat odd, since the questioners had reviewed the statements of the witnesses from that inquiry, and in several cases, asked for clarification when contradictory statements were given in the British Inquiry. Both the Commissioner and Attorney-General expressed interest in seeing Stewart to clear up some questions that they had regarding Boat No. 15, but for some reason, he was never called to give testimony.[2]

It seems probable that Rule, as a fellow steward and a fellow member of the Victualling Department, would have been more likely to know and recognize Stewart than Evans would have been. There is also some corroborating evidence that supports Rule's assertion that Stewart was rescued in No. 15 and not pulled from the water. Stewart himself doesn't appear to have left a public account stating how he was rescued. However, in a *Titanic* documentary, Molly Adams, Stewart's daughter, stated that her father 'came off on the last lifeboat'.[3] So her father told her he was rescued in a lifeboat, not that he was pulled from the water. Boat No. 15 was the last of the aft starboard boats lowered away, which provides circumstantial evidence supporting Rule's claim that Stewart was in that boat.

In the end, it appears that John Stewart was rescued in Boat No. 15, and was not one of the men pulled from the water into No. 14. There is no reason to doubt that Stewart actually saw Thomas Andrews standing alone in the First Class Smoking Room before he departed the ship. However, this reassessment of the evidence concerning his rescue, and the conclusion that the evidence leads us to, does change the commonly accepted timing of their encounter. This is the case because Boat No. 15 was lowered away around 1:40 a.m., meaning that Stewart's sighting must have taken place prior to that time, and not after 2:05 a.m.

This conclusion also leaves open the very real possibility that Stewart was not the last person to see Thomas Andrews, and that the shipbuilder did not meet his end staring catatonically into space below deck. In fact, in *Thomas Andrews: Shipbuilder*, author Shan Bullock never suggested or presented the case that this was the final known location of Andrews. Indeed, he wrote just the opposite. After discussing Stewart's sighting, Bullock wrote:

> But whatever he saw, in that quiet lonely minute, it did not hold or unman him. Work – work – he must work to the bitter end.

Then Bullock discussed several other very late sightings of Andrews. He cited an unnamed survivor as saying that they saw Andrews 'a few minutes before the end, on the Boat deck, our final and grandest sight of him, throwing deck chairs overboard to the unfortunates struggling in the water below'.

Interestingly, Bullock also added that another person saw Andrews, 'bareheaded and carrying a lifebelt, on his way to the bridge perhaps to bid the Captain goodbye'. Although Bullock placed this sentence before Stewart's sighting, he does not give any evidence for placing it in that location. This single sentence is also interesting in that it mentions him carrying a lifebelt; Stewart's sighting also had Andrews with a lifebelt, which at the time was draped over a nearby chair.

What about Bullock's placement of this sighting of Andrews moving forward to the Bridge? It is possible that this sighting was very late in the disaster, after he threw the deck chairs overboard. Why might this be suspected? Because Thomas Andrews was reportedly on the Bridge with Captain Smith just before the ship took its final plunge. This detail comes from 21-year-old Mess Steward Cecil William N. Fitzpatrick.[4] Fitzpatrick's account appeared in two different papers, one of which was extremely shortened, but the other of which survives intact. He said:

> I then went for'w'd on the port side, and I was passing through the bridge when I saw Capt. Smith speaking to Mr. Andrews, the designer of the *Titanic*. I stopped to listen. I was still confident that the ship was unsinkable, but when I heard Capt. Smith say: 'We cannot stay any longer; she is going!' I fainted against the starboard side of the bridge entrance.
>
> After some minutes I recovered sufficiently to realize that unless I got into a boat or swam for it, there would be no chance of being saved.
>
> I then went to launch one of the collapsible boats which had been eased down off the top decks on the starboard side [Collapsible A]. We found, when we tried to swing her in the davits, that she was wedged between the winch of the davits and the spar…
>
> … The next thing I remember was the ship suddenly dipping, and the waves rushing up and engulfing me. After ten seconds the *Titanic* again righted herself, but then I saw that everyone who a minute before had been attempting to lower away, except myself, had been swept into the fo'castle head. I saved myself by clinging on to the davit winch.[5]

This sighting places both Captain Smith and Thomas Andrews together on the Bridge just before the end, since the Captain told Andrews that the ship was 'going'. This account is very much in harmony with the known movements of Captain Smith as reported by numerous other survivors, who said that the Captain returned to the Bridge just minutes or even moments before the end.[6] Fitzpatrick was subsequently rescued from Collapsible B by Boat No. 12. This gives confirmation that he was on board the ship until the end, which means he could have been in a position to see Andrews in the final moments before the sinking.[7]

Fitzpatrick's account also lines up very nicely with several other individuals who said that after the ship made her plunge downward, she recovered before diving again. Clearly, this account deserves attention. Since Fitzpatrick's sighting came just before he assisted at Collapsible A and jumped into the sea, it places Andrews and Smith on the Bridge together just moments before 2:15 a.m., when the ship made the 'slight but definite plunge' referred to by Second Officer Lightoller.

This newspaper account is further corroborated – and expanded upon – by a completely different line of evidence: a private letter written by Andrews' good friend David Galloway to Andrews' uncle, Lord Pirrie on April 27, 1912. Galloway traveled from New York to Southampton aboard the *Lapland,* along with members of the *Titanic's* crew who had just given testimony in the Senate Inquiry. Galloway interviewed the crewmembers to see if they had any information on his friend's fate, and he included the reports in the letter to Lord Pirrie.

Galloway said that an officer, unfortunately unnamed, claimed Andrews was last seen throwing deck chairs and other objects into the water, and that 'his chief concern seemed to be the safety of others rather than his own'. Instantly, the account catches attention… Perhaps this officer was the same source for Bullock's conclusion that Andrews was last seen throwing deck chairs overboard?

Galloway also reported to Pirrie that near the end, a 'young mess-boy' saw Andrews and Captain Smith on the Bridge. Both men put on lifebelts, and then the witness heard Smith say: 'It's no use waiting any longer.' When water reached the Bridge, both men entered the sea together.[8] While Galloway did not name the survivor, the only likely candidate is Mess Steward Cecil Fitzpatrick. No other surviving crewmember fits Galloway's description of being both 'young' and a 'mess-boy'.

In the press interview in question, Fitzpatrick does not mention seeing Andrews go overboard with the Captain, but this is perhaps not surprising. While Andrews was mentioned in some press accounts following the sinking, he was not famous with the general public yet, and his fate did not become legendary until some time after the disaster. Most reporters, as they conducted their interviews, were clamoring for news about any of the deceased officers, or regarding the most famous First Class passengers; few of these would have cared about, or pursued questioning regarding, the fate of someone who was then a little-known passenger. The published press articles reflect this: front pages of the papers were literally plastered with headlines and claims about how Captain Smith and the other officers had died.

If Fitzpatrick was on the starboard side of the Boat Deck, however, one might wonder: how could he have seen the two men dive from the *port* side of the Bridge, the location where many reported Captain Smith had left the ship as the Bridge became awash. The answer is quite simple: working at Collapsible A on the forward extremity of the Boat Deck, Fitzpatrick could easily have seen through the open Bridge and at least a portion of the port side wing would likely have been visible to him.

We know Fitzpatrick was on the *Titanic's* forward Boat Deck late in the sinking, and in a position to see Smith and Andrews near the end. In addition to his own account above, there is the account of Second Class Passenger Lillian Bentham, who was rescued in Lifeboat No. 12. She mentions Fitzpatrick, by name, as having been pulled into her lifeboat from an overturned boat.[9] This places Fitzpatrick as one of the survivors aboard Collapsible B, having been washed overboard at the last, just as he stated in his own account.

After a careful review of the evidence, then, the age-old tale of Thomas Andrews meeting his fate in a state of shock in the Smoking Room, as the ship sank under him, falls by the wayside. It seems to be nothing more than an oft-repeated, if erroneous conclusion based on some very scanty evidence. While there is no way to know for certain, it appears that Thomas Andrews took some time in the Smoking Room to gather his thoughts, probably just before 1:40 a.m. Then he continued doing what he had done for much of the evacuation: assisting the crew, and attempting to save the lives of others. It appears that he kept this work up till the very end, with little regard for his own safety, and only left the ship at the last moment along with Captain Smith.

Appendix M: Down With the Ship? Captain Smith's Fate[1]

Of the unknowns surrounding the sinking of the *Titanic,* one of the most tantalizing remains how Captain Smith met his end. Legend holds that the Captain went down with his ship, and met his end heroically, in a way that any Edwardian sailor or gentleman would have envied. This legend has been sustained by portrayals of his death in books and movies, including *A Night to Remember* and James Cameron's *Titanic.*

Most survivor accounts do not shed any light on Captain Smith's fate. Given the small number of survivors who remained onboard the ship until the end and also survived, this is not at all surprising. When one considers how few of this already small number of survivors would have been in a position to see Captain Smith at the end, it is even less so. Those who did broach the subject often gave conflicting evidence, which adds to the confusion. This appendix is an attempt to critically and objectively examine the evidence relating to the Captain's fate, to see if any conclusions can be reached. Please note that the spelling in the survivor accounts is retained from the original documents.

Introduction
The stories and rumors surrounding Captain Smith's end, as provided by survivors, are both varied and contradictory. A reporter from the *New York Times* noted:

> How different were the impressions made on different persons was illustrated by the many versions, told by witnesses, of how Captain Smith died …[2]

The eyewitness accounts and versions of Smith's end can be divided into four general categories: 1) death by suicide; 2) staying on the Bridge/going down with the ship; 3) leaping overboard near the end; and 4) death by drowning or hypothermia. Each of these versions of the Captain's end will be examined individually, then in conjunction to see if any of them are related, particularly in the case of the latter two versions of his death.

Death By Suicide
Among the most widely circulated rumors concerning Captain Smith's fate, following the *Carpathia's* arrival in New York, were those to the effect that he had committed

suicide. The papers published headlines such as: 'Captain Smith and Chief Engineer Kill Themselves', and: 'The *Titanic*'s Captain Shot Himself as the Ship Went Down, With Band Playing'.[3] May Birkhead, a passenger on the *Carpathia*, wrote a news story in which she reported a rumor that Captain Smith had shot himself; Carlos Hurd, another *Carpathia* passenger, made a similar report.[4] Miss Birkhead did not report the source of this story, and Hurd stated that surviving crewmembers denied the rumors. Another person aboard the *Carpathia* who reported these rumors was Dr J. F. Kemp, who wrote that one of the last children to leave the *Titanic* told him that he saw 'Captain Smith put a pistol to his head and then fall down'.[5] The only 'children' to leave the ship late enough to have witnessed such a scene were Jack Thayer and William Carter Jr; however, neither made such a claim in their own accounts about Captain Smith.

The majority of the stories in the press did not list their sources. Many of those that were attributed to a specific survivor later proved to be false, or of questionable reliability. First Class passenger Paul Chevré is a prime example of this. An account quoted him as saying that he saw Captain Smith commit suicide.[6] Chevré was rescued in Boat No. 7, the first lifeboat lowered away; he was furious about the story when he saw it in the papers, and publicly refuted the whole account.[7] The rumors about the Captain were widespread enough, however, that Captain Rostron felt the need to issue a statement refuting them, based on what he had heard from surviving *Titanic* crewmembers.[8]

Despite all of the stories, little evidence to support them has ever been uncovered. Numerous accounts do place Captain Smith on the forward area of the Boat Deck, near the Bridge, shortly before it dipped under. This is where a suicide is alleged to have taken place.

Yet, the only two accounts which lend anything like support to the tales of Captain Smith killing himself come from First Class passenger Richard Norris Williams and Third Class passenger Edward Dorking; both men were on the ship until the last. Williams said that he and his father saw Captain Smith near the Bridge at the same time the Boat Deck began to submerge; as they turned to flee from the approaching water, they heard gunfire from the direction where the Captain had been.[9] Yet it must be emphasized that Williams did not turn around, and clearly stated that he did not see what happened. The second account comes from Dorking; therein, he claimed that just before he jumped overboard, he saw an officer shoot himself.[10] He speculated that it may have been the Captain, but was far from certain in this identification. Dorking's account also comes from a press interview of unknown reliability.

Captain Smith was one of the officers who went to the First Officer's cabin when the revolvers were distributed at Chief Officer Wilde's request, so he probably had the means to commit suicide.[11] However, several reliable eyewitness accounts, which will be examined later, describe the Captain jumping overboard near the end; several others even describe seeing him in the water after the ship sank. When combined with the lack of evidence to support the rumors of a suicide, these accounts tend to eliminate the possibility of him having done so.

Captain Smith's prominent white beard would have made him readily identifiable, and it is likely that more eyewitnesses would have reported that he shot himself, if that is actually what happened. An examination of the eyewitness accounts indicate that most claiming that an officer committed suicide did not name the officer, which further indicates that the Captain did not kill himself. This being the case, an important question arises: Why were there so many stories about Captain Smith having ended his own life? Perhaps overzealous reporters and editors in the yellow press were responsible, since they had a tendency to alter eyewitness accounts, in order to make them more dramatic. Also, since pocket recorders did not exist in 1912, most press interviews were written down in notes or taken in shorthand. Transcription errors when the stories went to print were frequent.

Reporters were also very well aware that *Titanic*'s collision with the iceberg and subsequent sinking was the second serious accident of his career in the space of seven months. With the collision between the *Olympic* and the *Hawke* only seven months past, it is very likely that reporters speculated that Captain Smith would have been despondent after he discovered his ship was doomed, his career ending in ignominy. When stories that an officer shot himself began to circulate, they may have had a logical reason to believe Smith was the one involved, despite the lack of eyewitness evidence indicating this. It would have been tempting for them to imagine him feeling so disgraced and anguished about the accident and pending disaster that he shot himself in order to avoid the embarrassment that a second serious accident, and the possible loss of his certificate, would bring him and his family if he survived.

This apparent jump in logic is more understandable when one considers that several Captains had shot themselves in the years prior to the *Titanic* disaster, and for exactly this reason. According to a press article, one was Captain H. Brunswig. He went to his cabin and shot himself, reportedly out of fear that he was going to lose his certificate, after his Hamburg-American line vessel the *Prinzessin Victoria Luise* ran aground off Port Royal, Jamaica, on December 16, 1906; another was Captain Giuseppe Paradi, who shot himself for feelings of responsibility after his Italian steamship *Sirio* wrecked on rocks near Hormigas Island on August 2, 1906.

In addition to this, the article in question describes the following Captains as having lost their certificates as a result of accidents of varying seriousness: Captain Inman Sealby was dismissed from his position with the White Star Line after his vessel, the *Republic*, was rammed by the Lloyd Italiano Line steamship *Florida* on January 23, 1909. His ship sank the following night; Captain Frederick Watkins lost his certificate after his American Line steamship *City of Paris* grounded on the British coast; and Captain Le Horn's career ended after his Peninsular and Oriental steamship *China* ran aground in the Red Sea in 1897.[12] This newspaper article provides one possible explanation of why Captain Smith was rumored to have shot himself; however, in Smith's case, these rumors appear to have absolutely no basis in fact.

Staying on the Bridge/Going Down with the Ship

Rumors that Captain Smith went down with the ship are one of the more popular images that spring to mind when someone thinks of the *Titanic* disaster. This scenario has certainly had more staying power than the rumors that he shot himself, since they have persisted for more than a century following his death. But, is there any actual evidence to support the stories?

Before analyzing other survivor accounts, the testimony given by the *Titanic*'s surviving officers and crewmembers in the disaster inquiries will be examined to see if they said anything indicating that Smith went down with his ship. Not only would crewmembers have been the most likely to recognize the Captain, but since the accounts given in the inquiries are first-hand, we can be certain that the words are those actually spoken by the witness. The same cannot be said regarding press accounts of the day. Some of the more relevant testimonies that directly relate to the question of whether Captain Smith went down with his ship include those given by Second Officer Lightoller, Lamp Trimmer Samuel Hemming, and Saloon Steward Edward Brown.

Second Officer Lightoller gave some relevant testimony in the Senate Inquiry. The last time that he saw Captain Smith was when he caught a glimpse of him crossing from the starboard to port side of the Bridge.[13] Unfortunately, Lightoller did not indicate how long before the sinking this sighting took place. As such, it does not prove or disprove the story about Smith going down with the ship; all it does prove the he was in the vicinity of the Bridge when the Second Officer last saw him.

Lamp Trimmer Samuel Hemming assisted with Collapsible A until water neared the Bridge. Realizing their efforts were hopeless, he crossed over to the port side and leapt overboard. His testimony is relevant to the question of what happened to Captain Smith:

Senator Smith: Did you see him [Captain Smith] at any time on the bridge?
Mr. Hemming: Yes, sir.
Senator Smith: When?
Mr. Hemming: The last time I saw the captain, sir, was just as I was coming down off the house.
Senator Smith: Just as you came down from the house? You mean by that the top of the officers' quarters?
Mr. Hemming: Yes, sir.
Senator Smith: Where this collapsible boat [A] was?
Mr. Hemming: Yes, sir.
Senator Smith: You saw what?
Mr. Hemming: The captain was there, and he sung out: 'Everyone over to the starboard side, to keep the ship up as long as possible.'

And then later in the questioning, Hemming indicated that he saw the Captain about a half hour before leaving the ship, and that Smith was alone at the time.[14] Hemming's testimony places the Captain on the Bridge during the attempted launch of Collapsible A, shortly before the water reached that area of the ship, washing Collapsibles A and B overboard. His testimony matches details subsequently given by Steward Edward Brown in his British Inquiry testimony:

10585. ... Whilst you were working down the last collapsible boat [A] from the top of the officers' quarters to the deck, did you notice Captain Smith? – Yes, the Captain came past us while we were trying to get this boat away with a megaphone in his hand, and he spoke to us.
10586. What did he say? – He said, 'Well, boys, do your best for the women and children, and look out for yourselves.' He walked on the bridge.
10587. He then returned to the bridge? – Yes.
10588. And about that moment of time the ship took her last plunge? – Yes, a very few seconds after that.[15]

While working on Collapsible A, Brown saw Captain Smith on the Bridge at roughly the same time and from the same general location as Hemming. This was right before the Bridge plunged under. The timing was confirmed by the account of Steward Alexander Littlejohn, who was 'a great friend' of Brown, indicating that the timing he described was not the result of leading questions. Brown told his friend the following, which leaves the impression that he himself believed Captain Smith went down with the ship:

He told me he was washed off the bridge as the forward funnel dipped and that the captain was on the bridge at the time and said to the other stewards around him, 'Do what you can for yourselves boys.'[16]

There is further corroboration of Smith's presence on the starboard side near the Bridge just before the Boat Deck submerged. Fireman Harry Senior claimed to have seen Captain Smith shortly after helping free Collapsible A from the roof of the Officers' Quarters:

He [Senior] went on to describe how the boats were lowered, and said that after all the ordinary boats had been launched he and others ascended to the hurricane deck and threw down a number of collapsible boats. 'While we were preparing to lower these,' he went on, 'we heard the captain shout "Every man for himself." I had seen the captain on the bridge. When he shouted his last command the ship was sinking fast. I dived over the side, and by good luck I found myself in the water near one of the collapsible boats. '
It had either been thrown or had fallen over the side, and was floating bottom upwards.'[17]

Trimmer Eustace Snow was assisting in the effort to launch Collapsible A, and last saw Captain Smith at this time as well. He claimed that Smith said, '[W]ait till the boat takes to the water, then every man for himself.'[18] First Class passenger Richard Norris Williams' previously-mentioned account of the disaster provides yet another account placing Captain Smith near the starboard side of the Bridge right before the Boat Deck submerged. At this time, he and Williams' father saw Captain Smith near the Bridge with a seaman. The seaman went off on an errand, and then there was a curious noise, and then Williams and his father turned to see water pouring over the Bridge rail. They immediately began heading aft.[19]

When all of the above evidence is taken into account, it provides strong indication that the Captain was indeed near the starboard side of the Bridge of the *Titanic* right before it plunged under. However, none of the witnesses actually saw him go down with the ship, so other than providing strong indication of his presence on the Bridge just before the final plunge, no other conclusion can be drawn from them. There are many accounts from survivors who claimed to have seen Captain Smith after this, including Fireman Senior, who stated that he saw him in the water, after having seen him on the Bridge. These accounts will be examined later in this appendix.

Given the lack of Inquiry testimony that would conclusively prove that Captain Smith went down with his ship, are there any accounts that support that claim? Yes, although since they are from press accounts, the reliability of them is unknown. One of these accounts comes from Greaser Alfred White, who remained on board the ship until the end. White claimed that sometime after 1:30 a.m., he was released from the Engine Room to find out how serious the situation was.[20] White stated that the ship was down alarmingly by the head, and that he made his way up on deck via a ladder in the 'escape funnel'. Sometime after arriving on deck, White headed forward and said that he 'found Captain Smith standing on the bridge knee deep in water'. All the lifeboats were gone, so White headed aft and let himself down into the water on a set of falls. He was picked up by Boat No. 4.[21] It must be noted that while White gives the impression that Smith went down with the ship, he did not actually see this happen.

Another survivor who is often cited as having seen Captain Smith go down with the ship is First Class passenger Robert Daniel. Daniel claimed to have last seen the Captain standing on the Bridge, shouting through a megaphone. He also claimed that Smith remained on the Bridge, 'trying to make himself heard', and that he was still there when Daniel last saw him.[22] It must be noted that while it has been interpreted that way, Daniel never actually claimed that he saw Captain Smith go down with the ship. He only says that the Captain was near the Bridge when he last saw him. According to other evidence, it is clear that Daniel was nowhere near the Bridge as it dipped under, and that he would not have been in a position to see what happened to Captain Smith at the end. Thus, his accounts do not shed any light on the matter one way or another.[23]

One survivor who actually claimed to have witnessed Captain Smith go down with the ship was First Class passenger and professional card sharp George Andrew Brereton, who gave accounts using the alias 'George A. Braden', 'G. A. Brayton', and the like. Brereton claimed to have leapt overboard, and to have witnessed the following while being held afloat by his lifebelt:

> I saw Capt. Smith while [I was] in the water. He was standing on the deck all alone. He was swept down by the water, but got to his feet. Then, as the boat sank, he was again swept from his feet, and this time he was drowned.[24]

Brereton was never in the water, having left the ship in a lifeboat some time before the sinking. Therefore, he would not have been in any position to see Captain Smith at the end as claimed.

Ship's Barber August Weikman was also quoted in a press interview as saying that he saw Captain Smith go down with his ship:

> I was on the upper deck assisting the passengers to the boats. I had a life belt on, and when the forward part of the ship listed I was washed overboard by a huge wave. Looking backward, I could see Captain Smith, who had been standing on the bridge, swimming back to the place where he had stood, having been washed off the *Titanic* by the same wave that had washed me from the ship into the water.[25]

In his affidavit for the Senate Inquiry, Weikman did not mention seeing Captain Smith swimming in the water. It is possible that he omitted these details, or that the quotes were fabricated by a reporter.

Another survivor, First Class passenger Caroline Brown, was quoted as saying that the Captain stood on Bridge until water covered the ship, and that he was offered assistance to get into one of the lifeboats, but he refused.[26] Other versions of this account have Mrs Brown claiming that the occupants of her lifeboat were the ones who offered the Captain assistance. Mrs Brown had been escorted to Collapsible D by Colonel Archibald Gracie. This boat left around 2:05 a.m., before water reached the Boat Deck, so she could not have witnessed this event herself, although it is possible that she was relating something that another witness told her.

With the apparent lack of reliable accounts supporting the conclusion that the Captain went down with the ship, we are left with the question of why so many rumors and press stories assumed that this is what happened. Although there is strong evidence that Captain Smith was seen near the starboard side of the Bridge shortly before the end, there is no real evidence to suggest that he actually went down with her. Part of this question might be answered by some of the statements Captain Smith made in the years prior to the *Titanic* disaster, hinting or indicating that some of the crew would bravely go down with the ship if they ever faced such a situation:

> Dr. Williams, a friend of Capt. Smith of the *Titanic*, relates a conversation he had with Capt. Smith when the latter commanded the *Adriatic*. ... Dr. Williams pointed out the inadequacy of the *Adriatic*'s lifeboats, and asked Capt. Smith what would happen if the *Adriatic* struck a concealed reef of ice and was badly damaged. Capt. Smith replied: 'Some of us would go to the bottom with the ship.'[27]

And:

> Mr. Kempster, managing director of Harland and Wolff, the builders of the *Titanic*, stated that before the ship left Belfast Captain Smith was asked if courage and fearlessness in [the] face of death existed among seamen as of old. Captain Smith declared if any disaster like that to *Birkenhead* happened they would go down as those men went down.[28]

Besides Captain Smith's own statements, there was the overall sense in Edwardian times that the chivalrous thing for a gentleman to do would be to go down with a sinking ship rather than be rescued ahead of women and children. A newspaper article published after the disaster illustrates this attitude:

> The voice of chivalry rang out over the wireless across the water wastes and the answer to that cry was 'women and children first.' Chivalry lives today unselfish and noble and those brave heroes, actuated by chivalry, that went down with the ship will be raised to immortality.[29]

One reporter wrote that 'everything connected with the death of Captain Smith reveals him in the character of one who maintained the best traditions of the sea'. Another reporter wrote that 'from the known character of Captain Smith ... it is believed that he went down with the ship, and also other officers'.[30] This quote was given at least a full day prior to the *Carpathia* reaching New York, before any actual eyewitness testimony was available to reporters.

When the general public learned of Captain Smith's death, some who knew him held similar sentiments. William Jones, a boyhood friend of Smith, had the following to say about his fate:

> Ted Smith passed away just as he would have loved to do. To stand on the bridge of his vessel and go down with her was characteristic of all his actions when we were boys together. … I cannot express my contempt for those who so cowardly reported that he committed suicide. … Ted Smith commit suicide in the face of danger? His whole life as I know it, and especially when he and I were boys together, gives the lie direct to such a report…if any man had dared to predict face to face with Ted Smith that if at any time he should be faced with such an emergency … and had suggested that he would take his life that man would be minus a few teeth before the words were well out of his mouth.[31]

Later, when it became known that several witnesses had last seen Captain Smith near the Bridge, the attitudes and beliefs about Edwardian gentlemen may have made it easy for people to picture the charismatic, tough and popular Captain going down with his ship, despite the lack of actual eyewitness evidence to bear this out.

Leaping Overboard

If he didn't go down with his ship, where did Captain Smith go after he was seen re-entering the Bridge during the attempted launch of Collapsible A on the starboard side? Aboard the *Carpathia*, reporter Carlos Hurd had interviewed several survivors, and his notes were among the first eyewitness accounts of the disaster to be published after the arrival in New York. He related the following story, given to him by an unnamed *Titanic* survivor:

> Captain Smith remained on the bridge until just before the ship sank, leaping only after those on the deck had been washed away.[32]

Based on what he had been told by fellow survivors, Second Class passenger Lawrence Beesley believed that Captain Smith stayed on the Bridge until the water reached his location, then 'quietly leapt overboard'.[33]

Do any first-hand statements support these assertions? Junior Marconi Operator Harold Bride was on the port side of the ship right before the Boat Deck began to submerge. Bride's report to the Marconi Company of his experiences sheds some light on Captain Smith's actions, subsequent to crossing over from the starboard side of the ship:

> Leaving the [wireless] cabin, we climbed down on top of the house comprising the officers' quarters and our own, and here I saw the last of Mr. Phillips, for he disappeared walking aft. I now assisted in pushing off a collapsible lifeboat, which was on the port side of the forward funnel, onto the boat deck. Just as the boat fell I noticed Captain Smith dive from the bridge into the sea. Then followed a general scramble down on the boat deck, but no sooner had we got there than the sea washed over.

> I managed to catch hold of the boat we had previously fixed up and was swept overboard with her.[34]

Bride's testimony at the American Inquiry agrees with his report to the Marconi Company. It also expands upon the details in that report, including his uncertainty of whether the Captain had been wearing a lifebelt:

> Mr. Bride: The last I saw of the captain of the *Titanic*, he went overboard from the Bridge about, I should think, three minutes before I left it myself.
> Senator Smith: Did he have a life preserver on?
> Mr. Bride: I could not say, sir.
> Senator Smith: You said in New York the other day that he did not. Do you want to correct that?
> Mr. Bride: Yes, I want to correct it. He had not a life preserver on the whole of the time when we were working, when he came into the cabin at frequent intervals. We had not a life preserver on.
> Senator Smith: How long was that before the ship sank?
> Mr. Bride: That was from the beginning of the catastrophe to the end.[35]

Unfortunately, Harold Bride was not the most consistent witness, and gave differing descriptions of how close to the end it was when he helped push Collapsible B off the roof of the Officers' Quarters. In his report to the Marconi Company, he specifically mentioned that he saw Captain Smith jump overboard at nearly the same time they managed to push Collapsible B down to the Boat Deck, and his testimony indicates a similar time frame. He also says that the water had already reached the deck. The ship was listing approximately 10° to port at the time, so water reached this side of the Boat Deck before it got to the Boat Deck on the starboard side. Obviously, if Bride did see Captain Smith jump overboard from the port side of the Bridge, it had to be after Steward Brown saw him reenter the Bridge from the starboard side.

However, in his famous press interview, Bride had given a different timeline of events, and didn't mention seeing Captain Smith jump overboard. In that version of the story, Bride stated that after he helped get Collapsible B down from the roof of the Officers' Quarters, he returned to the wireless cabin, and that Captain Smith released Jack Phillips and him from their duty. He then stated that he looked out from the wireless cabin, saw the Boat Deck awash, and that Phillips continued sending for 'ten minutes, or maybe fifteen minutes' after this. He claimed that water then entered their cabin. After this, he said that he and Phillips had a scuffle with a stoker who tried to steal the former's lifebelt, and that only then did they exit the cabin. Phillips next disappeared aft, and the water swept the raft overboard.[36]

These discrepancies do little to instill confidence that Bride was accurately remembering the timeline or details of events as they actually happened. Fortunately, portions of Bride's account given to the Marconi Company – which is a first-hand account, and not subject to misinterpretation or alteration of details by a reporter as the *New York Times* account may have been – can be corroborated by Second Officer Lightoller's accounts. As detailed previously, Lightoller did not see Captain Smith at the end, although he was on the scene as Collapsible B was pushed down from the roof of the Officers' Quarters, and would have been in a position to confirm the timing of this event, anchoring in time when Bride may have seen Captain Smith. Lightoller's testimony reveals some helpful details:

> 14035. Had you time to do anything more after you got that collapsible boat [Collapsible D] afloat? – I called for men to go up on the deck of the quarters for the collapsible boat up there. The afterend of the boat was underneath the funnel guy. I told them to swing the afterend up. There was no time to open her up and cut the lashings adrift. Hemming was the man with me there, and they then swung her round over the edge of the coamings to the upper deck, and then let her down on to the boat deck. That is the last I saw of her for a little while.
> 14036. There was no time to open her up at all? – No, the water was then on the boat deck.[37]

Lightoller, in his book, gave additional confirmation that water had already reached the port side of the Boat Deck when Collapsible B was pushed down from the roof of the Officers' Quarters:

> We had just time to tip the boat [Collapsible B] over, and let her drop into the water that was now above the boat deck, in the hope that some few would be able to scramble on to her as she floated off.[38]

As Lightoller indicated, Samuel Hemming also helped push Collapsible B off the roof of the Officers' Quarters. Hemming testified that after helping Lightoller launch Collapsible D, he helped push Collapsible B over, before crossing over to the starboard side to assist at Collapsible A. The Boat Deck on the starboard side, probably owing to the list to port at the time, was still dry. Hemming assisted just long enough to help with the falls and see that 'there was no chance of the boat being cleared away'. It was then that Hemming said he went to the Bridge and looked over, and saw the water was 'climbing upon the bridge' near the starboard side where he was located.[39]

All of this indicates that as soon as Collapsible B was freed from the roof, water had already reached the port side of the Boat Deck, just as Bride said in his Marconi report and indicated in his testimony. This is also when he claims to have seen Captain Smith dive overboard. The details in Bride's *New York Times* interview do not match the timing as given in Bride's Marconi report or testimony, and by the other eyewitnesses who were on the scene.

Given the varying details given by Bride, are there any other accounts which confirm his story of seeing Captain Smith jump overboard? Second Class passenger William Mellors had been on the starboard side of the ship prior to the Boat Deck plunging under, and helped with Collapsible C and the attempt to launch Collapsible A. Like Steward Brown, Fireman Senior and the other witnesses at that location, he saw Captain Smith giving orders. His subsequent account tends to support the details given by Bride:

> I was not far from where Captain Smith stood on the bridge, giving full orders to his men. ... He did not shoot himself. He jumped from the bridge when he had done all he could ... [and] his last words were[:] 'You have done your duty, boys. Now every man for himself.' ... Then came a grinding noise. ...

> I was hurled into the deep ... waves engulfed me, but I was not drawn towards the ship...[40]

The wording Mellors used makes it unclear whether he actually saw Captain Smith jump overboard, or if he was simply repeating something that he had been told. Mellors was washed overboard from the starboard side of the ship, and did not cross to the port side in the final moments.[41] However, Smith may have been visible to Mellors from his vantage point on the starboard side, if he was standing near the starboard Bridge wing or near the entrance to the Bridge and looking across to the port side.

Partial corroboration of Mellors' account comes from Mess Steward Cecil Fitzpatrick. Fitzpatrick was crossing through the Bridge, and saw Captain Smith talking with Thomas Andrews. He overheard the Captain say, 'We cannot stay any longer; she is going!'[42]

A friend of Thomas Andrews, David Galloway, sailed from New York to Southampton on the *Lapland* with many of *Titanic*'s surviving crewmembers. In trying to discover what had happened to his friend, Galloway spoke with many of the survivors, including 'a young mess-boy'. Fitzpatrick is the only crewmember who fits Galloway's description, and who was aboard the *Titanic* that late in the sinking. Galloway wrote that near the end, this 'mess-boy' saw Andrews and Smith on the Bridge. Both men put on lifebelts, and Smith told Andrews, 'It's no use waiting any longer.' The witness also recalled that when the Bridge became awash, he saw both Smith and Andrews enter the water.[43] The evidence and consistency between the details supports that Galloway's witness was indeed Fitzpatrick.

Fitzpatrick saw Smith and Andrews donning lifebelts before he went to help with Collapsible A.[44] Fitzpatrick's account gives the impression that he was only working at Collapsible A for a few minutes at most before the Boat Deck submerged; he said that the 'next thing I remember' was the ship dipping suddenly and waves engulfing him, right after he discussed the attempts to get Collapsible A into the davits.[45] Steward Brown estimated that Collapsible A was gotten down from the roof of the Officers' Quarters 'about 10 or 12 minutes' after Collapsible C lowered away.[46] Collapsible C was lowered away at 2:00 a.m., which means that according to Brown's estimate, Collapsible A was down on the Boat Deck by approximately 2:10–2:12 a.m. This would have left little time to do anything other than push the boat towards the davits and hook up the falls before the Boat Deck submerged at 2:15 a.m.

Since Collapsible A was already on the deck when Fitzpatrick arrived on the scene, this places him on the starboard side forward sometime in between 2:10–2:15 a.m., when work commenced on that boat. William Mellors also worked on this boat, and as such, would have been located near Fitzpatrick when the Boat Deck submerged. Perhaps not coincidentally, both men claimed to have seen Captain Smith jump overboard. If Smith did leap from the port side as Bride indicates, then this serves as potential corroboration of his version of events, and also confirmation that from their location near the Bridge, Fitzpatrick and Mellors could have looked across and seen Smith.

Other survivors also claimed that Captain Smith jumped overboard, although the reliability of these accounts appears to vary widely. Fireman Harry Senior, as related previously, helped free Collapsible A from the roof of the Officers' Quarters, and had been on hand to hear Captain

Smith give his last orders to the men on the starboard side as he stood near the Bridge. A different press account claimed that after Senior jumped overboard and reached the upturned Collapsible B, 'Captain Smith jumped into the sea from the promenade deck of the *Titanic* with an infant clutched tenderly in his arms'.[47] The story that Captain Smith attempted to save a child, as well as possible sightings of him in the water following the sinking, will be examined in detail later. This press account does not give an actual quote from Senior; in Senior's other accounts where he is quoted in depth, he does not mention seeing Smith leap overboard, although he did claim to see the Captain in the water. It is possible that he guessed that Smith leapt overboard, rather than actually having witnessed it.

Another crew member who allegedly saw Captain Smith jump from the ship was Trimmer James McGann. McGann claimed that the Captain and he tried to save two children who were near the Bridge as the water reached the Boat Deck. McGann's account places him on the port side during the attempted launch of Collapsible B, at the same time and location where Bride claimed Captain Smith jumped overboard:

I had gone to the bridge deck to assist in lowering a collapsible boat. The water was then coming over the bridge, and we were unable to launch the boat properly. It was overturned and was used as a liferaft.... He [Captain Smith] turned to the men lowering the boat and shouted 'Well, boys, it's every man for himself.' He then took one of the children standing by him on the bridge and jumped into the sea.[48]

First Class passenger Mrs George Widener claimed to have witnessed the following:

I went on deck and was put into a life boat. As the boat pulled away from the *Titanic* I saw one of the officers shoot himself in the head, and a few minutes later saw Capt. Smith jump from the bridge into the sea.[49]

Another press article seems to suggest that Mrs Widener may not have witnessed these events for herself, but was only of the opinion that it happened because of information she heard from someone else.[50] The first interview may be an extrapolation of her words by a reporter. Mrs Widener was rescued in Boat No. 4, which was lowered away around 1:50 a.m. This boat was close to the ship when it sank, so conceivably she could have witnessed events unfolding on the deck. However, since no reliable statements from others known to have been rescued in No. 4 have been found to corroborate her account, it seems highly unlikely, particularly given the dim Boat Deck lighting and the fact that she was not right there on the deck to witness such events.

Someone calling himself 'Quartermaster J.H. Moody' gave accounts in the papers following the disaster, and claimed to have been the crewmember who was at the helm when the *Titanic* struck the iceberg. This would mean that unless the entire account was fabricated by a reporter, it must have been given by Quartermaster Robert Hichens, who was at the helm when the accident occurred. The only other person in the Wheelhouse then, Sixth Officer James Moody, perished in the disaster. 'Quartermaster Moody' gave sensationalized details about the disaster, and claimed

that Captain Smith was on the Bridge until the last and 'leaped into the sea after the decks had been washed away'.[51] Given the sensational details found in his accounts, and that the real identity of the alleged eyewitness cannot be ascertained, little weight can be given to his statements. If Quartermaster Hichens gave the account, it is very unlikely he could have seen Captain Smith at the end, since he left the ship early in the sinking, in Boat No. 6. This boat was lowered away at 1:10 a.m., and according to Hichens, was approximately a mile away when the ship sank.

Another passenger who claimed to have witnessed Captain Smith jump overboard was Second Class passenger Charles Williams. Williams gave several press interviews after the disaster. In one account, he was quoted as saying that he 'saw the captain holding the bridge after the ship had sunk to the level of the sea. Then he went overboard'.[52] In other accounts, Williams said that he was saved in one of the collapsible lifeboats, and also claimed to have seen Captain Smith in the water, but he never said that he saw him jump overboard. During the Senate Inquiry, Fifth Officer Lowe testified that Williams was one of the men he took aboard Boat No. 14 to help row.[53] Boat No. 14 was lowered away around 1:25 a.m., long before the Boat Deck submerged, making it extremely unlikely that Williams could have seen Captain Smith as the Bridge dipped under.

Given all of the information examined above, it seems likely that after giving final orders to the men working on Collapsible A, Captain Smith crossed over to the port side of the Boat Deck. Steward Brown and others saw him near the Bridge or saw him re-enter the Bridge from the starboard side during the attempts to launch Collapsible A. Based on the accounts of Harold Bride, Mellors, Fitzpatrick, and McGann, it seems likely that Captain Smith re-emerged on the port side of the Boat Deck, and gave final orders to the men working there.

Shortly after this, Collapsible B was pushed off the roof of the Officers' Quarters and landed upside down on the Boat Deck. Due to the port list, water had just begun to reach the port side of the Boat Deck, either from coming over the Bridge rail, or from coming up the stairway down to A Deck. The eyewitness accounts strongly suggest that with nothing left to do, Captain Smith did not go down with his ship, but rather, turned and jumped overboard. He likely did so with Thomas Andrews.

Unfortunately, due to inconsistent details and blatantly falsified or fabricated accounts, the exact circumstances and details are far from clear. However, the bulk of evidence does suggest that the myth that the Captain went down with his ship has no basis in fact, and that in all probability, he jumped overboard from the Bridge.

Sightings in the Water?

If Captain Smith did indeed jump overboard from the Bridge, what happened to him? Did any survivors see him in the water following those final chaotic moments on the Boat Deck? Several accounts of Captain Smith being seen in the water circulated in the press immediately following the *Carpathia*'s arrival in New York. During an interview, D. W. McMillan, the brother of First Class passenger Elisabeth W. Robert, summarized a letter that his sister had written:

My sister, Georgette [Madill] and Miss [Elisabeth] Allen were taken off in one of the last boats with the fourth officer in charge, following his being commanded by Captain Smith to take charge of the boat. There was room for about two or three more persons in the boat and Captain Smith called for the boat to come back. The officer ordered the boat turned, but as they started back they saw the stern of the *Titanic* rising in the air, and didn't dare to go near for fear it was going to sink. Shortly afterward the boat went down before them and they say the shrieks of the steerage passengers were awful and heart rending. Captain Smith went down with the ship and came up again, but sank before they could reach him with the boat.[54]

Fourth Officer Joseph Boxhall was rescued in Boat No. 2, which was launched around 1:45 a.m. During the Inquiries or in known private letters, none of the survivors in this lifeboat mentioned seeing Captain Smith in the water. It is possible that McMillan's sister had been mentioning something that she hadn't witnessed herself, but was instead told by a fellow survivor. Unfortunately, the actual text of the letter is not provided in the article. Lookout George Hogg was another survivor who supposedly stated that he saw Captain Smith in the water. Hogg was rescued in Boat No. 7, which was the first lifeboat lowered away, around 12:40 a.m. He was quoted as saying the following:

After launching the boat [No. 7], we rowed away about 200 yards. When we rowed back again towards the steamship an upturned boat with several men clinging to it drifted across to our bow. I noticed Capt. Smith clinging to it. He looked much exhausted. Just then the efforts of two men clinging to the boat cut off my view of the captain. When the range was clear again the captain was missing.[55]

In the Senate Inquiry, Hogg claimed that the crew in Boat No. 7 pulled around for some time after the sinking, but found no survivors, and then rowed away. He did not mention seeing Captain Smith in the water, and existing evidence indicates that No. 7 never came near the upturned Collapsible B during the night. This makes the entire account questionable, although it is possible that Hogg was simply relating something he had been told by a fellow survivor, and that the reporter or editor altered this or mistook it to mean that Hogg himself had seen it. One compelling detail is that he specifically mentions the Captain clinging to Collapsible B. Additional reliable evidence, which will be examined later, suggests that Smith may indeed have been sighted near that lifeboat.

First Class passenger Mrs Ruth Dodge was another survivor quoted as saying that she saw Captain Smith in the water:

Then I saw a man who I am sure was Captain Smith. He was being pushed onto a life raft. He flung his arms about and struggled like a mad man. It was easy to see he did not want to go. But the men who pushed him [probably the remaining ship's officers] insisted and at length got him onto the raft. He looked wildly about for a moment, waving his arms in despair and supplication. Then he leaped off the raft into the ice-caked sea which closed over his head forever.[56]

Mrs Dodge and her son were rescued in Boat No. 5, which was lowered around 12:45 a.m. She would have been too far away from the ship at the end to see Captain Smith. Mrs Dodge's husband, Dr Washington Dodge, gave an address about the *Titanic* disaster at the Commonwealth Club in San Francisco on May 11, 1912. During the address, Dodge addressed some of the purported press interviews attributed to he and his wife:

My wife had never given an interview, and had made none of the statements attributed to her. With one exception, all of the interviews attributed to me were wholly unfounded.

Apparently, the entire interview with Mrs Dodge was wrongly attributed to her, or was fabricated out of rumors the reporters had heard.

Another dramatic, and perhaps equally questionable account, was told by Second Class passenger Charles Williams. As mentioned earlier, Williams claimed in some accounts that he had seen Captain Smith dive overboard; he also claimed to have stood knee-deep in water on a collapsible lifeboat all night, despite the fact that he was actually taken in Boat No. 14 by Fifth Officer Lowe to help row. In this version of events, Williams allegedly stated the following about Captain Smith's fate, although no direct quotes from him were provided:

Charles Williams ... was equally positive that he saw the captain swimming in the water with the child in his arms, and afterwards saw him pass the infant into a small boat which a few minutes before had picked Williams up after he jumped overboard. 'What happened to First Officer Murdock?' Williams said the Captain asked. He was told that the officer had shot himself, and then, Williams says, Capt. Smith pushed himself away from the lifeboat, freed the life belt which supported him, and dropped out of sight. He never rose to the surface, though the lifeboat lingered many minutes over the spot.[57]

Boat No. 14 left *Titanic* at 1:25 a.m., and Williams would not have been close enough to the scene to see Captain Smith at the end. One of Williams' friends, George E. Standing, repeated this tale to a reporter of the *New York World*, and it later appeared in British newspapers such as the *Daily Sketch*.[58] Many details of Williams' accounts are inconsistent and can be proven false. Of note, Williams repeated the story that Captain Smith saved a child, so he may have been repeating rumors that he had heard, and that this was embellished in the printed version. In any event, little credence can be given to Williams' accounts as they appeared in the papers.

Fireman Frederick Harris supposedly told a reporter that he 'saw the captain jump into the water and grasp a child, which he placed on one of the rafts, of which there were all too few. He did not see the captain afterwards.'[59] Harris was one of the men transferred out of Boat No. 14 by Fifth Officer Lowe during the night, and therefore he probably did not see this for himself. No actual quote from Harris is provided in the article. The description attributed to Harris does not indicate that this event occurred at No. 14. None of the surviving crewmembers from this lifeboat who testified in the inquiries described seeing the Captain in the water.

Carpathia passenger Fred Beachler claimed that he was told the following by an informant whom he considered to be reliable, since the source was 'an officer of the *Titanic*':

> I also learn on the same reliable authority, verified by others, that Captain Smith … was in the water with a child in his arms, which he succeeded in placing in one of the boats. He was begged to come aboard himself, but refused and turned back as though to aid others, and was not seen again.[60]

Beachler did not reveal the identity of the officer who allegedly told him this information, so the accuracy of his claims cannot be determined. None of *Titanic*'s surviving officers ever went on record as saying they knew anything definitive about Captain Smith's fate. Able Bodied Seaman George McGough allegedly repeated some of the same rumors as Beachler in a press interview:

> Both Captain Smith and Junior Chief Officer Murdoch were now together on the bridge, the water being up to their armpits. The next I saw of Captain Smith was in the water holding a child in his arms. He swam to the raft on which was Second Officer Lightoller and gave the child to the mate. That was the last. He and the ship went down…[61]

This account is somewhat suspect, as McGough was rescued aboard Boat No. 9, which was lowered away around 1:30 a.m. Therefore, he would not have been in a position to see Captain Smith at the end. However, it is possible that McGough was repeating a story or rumors that he had heard. The quote is interesting because it repeats the rumor that Captain Smith attempted to save a baby, as allegedly reported by Harry Senior, James McGann, Beachler, and others. It expands upon this by inferring that the lifeboat which he supposedly swam to was the same one Second Officer Lightoller was saved on, Collapsible B. Lightoller himself never claimed to have seen Captain Smith in the water, much less to have been handed a baby by him. With this in mind, is there any credible information to suggest that Captain Smith actually reached Collapsible B after the sinking?

Second Class passenger Charlotte Collyer claimed that she had been told that Captain Smith reached one of the collapsibles after this sinking, although she doesn't specify Collapsible B:

> I was told afterwards by more than one trustworthy person that Captain E.J. Smith of the *Titanic* was washed against a collapsible boat and held on to it for a few moments. A member of the crew assured me that he tried to pull the Captain on board … he shook his head, cast himself off, and sank out of sight.[62]

Collyer did not name the crewmembers who told her this story. Captain Arthur Henry Rostron of the *Carpathia,* in issuing a statement denying the rumors that Smith had committed suicide, also claimed that the Captain had reached Collapsible B:

> I have it from the lips of members of the crew who tried to save his life that he did not commit suicide

> … he was washed from the bridge … some of his men caught him … and landed him safely on the edge of a lifeboat, but he tumbled back into the ocean and went down. He had been too weakened by hard knocks while being tossed about the sinking *Titanic* to hold on to anything. The buffeting he encountered on the wrecked ship undoubtedly had dazed him and left him in no condition to exert even his remaining strength.[63]

Unfortunately, Captain Rostron did not name the survivors who told him of Captain Smith's fate. It is known that he spoke with *Titanic*'s surviving officers onboard the *Carpathia*, so it is possible that one of them relayed this information to him, although this is just speculation. He could have heard the story from any number of surviving crewmembers. If the information related to Captain Rostron is accurate, it suggests that Captain Smith may have approached Collapsible B, but was so weakened by the cold water or injuries sustained during the final plunge and breakup of the ship, that he did not survive. Saloon Steward Arthur McMicken suggested just such a scenario in a press interview:

> The Captain was seen not far from where the *Titanic* went down. He wore oilskins, which weighed him down, and he seemed so exhausted he could barely keep afloat.[64]

McMicken was rescued in Boat No. 11, which was lowered away around 1:35 a.m. Nobody in his lifeboat reported seeing Captain Smith in the water, which makes it unlikely that he saw this for himself. It was probably based on information related to him by another source.

Did any of the men who took refuge aboard the upturned Collapsible B claim to see Captain Smith approach their lifeboat? Saloon Steward Thomas Whiteley, rescued aboard Collapsible B, claimed to have seen Captain Smith save a baby by placing it 'in one of the lifeboats crowded with people', before pushing away.[65] However, Whiteley's statements do not seem consistent with Collapsible B, since he does not indicate that the lifeboat was overturned, and he mentions several women being in the lifeboat. No women were saved aboard Collapsible B. First Class passenger Jack Thayer had the following to say in his account of the disaster, which provides some possible confirmation of Captain Smith being sighted at Collapsible B:

> We prayed and sang hymns. A great many of the men seemed to know each other intimately. Questions and answers were called around-who was on board, and who was lost, or what they had been seen doing? One call that came around was, 'Is the Chief aboard?' Whether they mean Mr. Wilde, the Chief Officer, or the Chief Engineer, or Captain Smith, I do not know. I do know that one of the circular life rings from the bridge was there when we got off in the morning. It may be that Captain Smith was on board with us for a while. Nobody knew where the 'Chief' was.[66]

While Thayer did not actually see Captain Smith, his account verifies that some survivors discussed the possibility of Captain Smith being seen at Collapsible B as the events of that night were playing out. His mention of the life ring from the Bridge is significant for reasons that will be discussed later. In his book, Colonel Archibald Gracie provided useful information about Captain Smith:

> After we had left the danger zone in the vicinity of the wreck, conversation between us first developed, and I heard the men aft of me discussing the fate of the Captain. At least two of them, according to their statements made at the time, had seen him on this craft of ours shortly after it was floated from the ship. In the interviews already referred to Harry Senior, the fireman, referring to the same overturned boat, said: 'The Captain had been able to reach this boat. They had pulled him on, but he slipped off again.' Still another witness, the entrée cook of the *Titanic*, J. Maynard, who was on our boat, corroborates what I heard said at the time about the inability of the Captain to keep his hold on the boat. From several sources, I have the information about the falling of the funnel, the splash of which swept from the upturned boat several who were first clinging thereto, and among the number possibly was the Captain.[67]

Gracie's comments are interesting, because they confirm that on the actual night of the sinking, some of the survivors who were on Collapsible B believed that Captain Smith had reached their lifeboat. Thayer and his accounts also indicate that these stories did not originate in the press after the fact. Gracie's mention of 'J. Maynard', who was actually Entrée Cook Isaac Maynard, being aboard Collapsible B takes on added significance when one considers the following rumor that reporter Carlos Hurd was told by survivors onboard the *Carpathia*:

> It is also related that when a cook later sought to pull him [Captain Smith] aboard a lifeboat he exclaimed 'Let me go,' and jerking away, went down.[68]

It is likely that this unnamed cook was Maynard, given the similarities to what Gracie reports Maynard as saying. Chief Baker Charles Joughin testified that Maynard was aboard Collapsible B with him.[69]

As mentioned previously, a press article alleged that Fireman Harry Senior had seen Captain Smith jump overboard with a baby near the end. This same article claimed the following:

> It only took a few strokes to bring him [Smith] to the upturned life boat, where a dozen hands were stretched out to take the little child from his arms and drag him to safety. 'Captain Smith was dragged on the upturned boat,' said the fireman, 'he had on a life buoy and a life preserver. He clung there a moment and then he slid off again. For a second time he was dragged from the icy water. Then he took off his life preserver, tossed the life buoy on the inky waters, and slipped into the water again with the words: 'I will follow the ship.''[70]

Harry Senior repeated this story with less detail to the British press.[71] Of note, Senior claims that Captain Smith had a lifebelt and a 'life buoy' with him when he approached Collapsible B. If Senior was referring to a life ring when he said 'life buoy', this takes on added significance, since Jack Thayer claimed that a life ring from the vicinity of the Bridge was spotted alongside Collapsible B in the morning.

As detailed earlier, Trimmer James McGann claimed to have seen Captain Smith jump overboard from the port side of the Boat Deck with a child as water reached their location. McGann claimed that he tried to help another child himself:

> Taking refuge on the bridge of the ill fated *Titanic*, two little children remained by the side of Capt. Smith until that portion of the big ship had been swept by water. Survivors of the crew who went down with the *Titanic*, but were saved by clinging to an overturned lifeboat, today told of their gallant commander's efforts to save the life of one of the children. He died a sailor's death and the little girl who had entrusted her life to his care died with him. 'He held the little girl under one arm,' said James McGann, a fireman, 'as he jumped into the sea and endeavored to reach the nearest lifeboat with the child. I took the other child into my arms as I was swept from the bridge deck. When I was plunged into the cold water I was compelled to release my hold on the child, and I am satisfied the same thing happened to Capt. Smith.'

Elsewhere in the article, McGann stated the following:

> He endeavored to reach the overturned boat, but did not succeed. That was the last I saw of Capt. Smith.[72]

McGann was saved by clinging to Collapsible B. He suggests that Captain Smith was unsuccessful at saving the child he had allegedly jumped overboard with. McGann believed that Smith lost his grip on the child in the cold water, just as McGann did with the child he tried to save. If there really was an attempt to save a child, this scenario is at least somewhat plausible. The same thing happened to Scullion John Collins, who claimed that he had a baby washed from his arms by the wave produced as the Boat Deck of *Titanic* dipped under.[73]

One of the biggest questions that crops up over these stories that Captain Smith attempted to save a child, besides their seemingly melodramatic elements, are that if he did, why isn't there more eyewitness evidence to back up the claims? Surely, if a crying baby had been handed to one of the men aboard Collapsible B, more of the survivors would have mentioned this after the fact. It would have been hard to miss. Many of the survivors from this collapsible did give accounts later, and few outside of Senior and McGann claimed that Captain Smith attempted to save a baby. Several other survivors claimed that Captain Smith attempted to save a child, but their statements are either questionable or second-hand, because they were not aboard the upturned boat. It is possible that Senior and McGann themselves were the source of these rumors. Newspapers did print pictures of Entrée Cook Isaac Maynard, claiming that he was the 'steward who took the baby from Captain Smith's arms'.[74]

Maynard was aboard Collapsible B, but no definitive statements from him that would confirm or deny the allegations about the child have been discovered. Doreen Bartram,

Isaac Maynard's niece, reported that 'mother used to say Uncle Ike saved the baby from the captain's arms as the *Titanic* sank', and that 'mum was always very proud of him. … She always used to talk about him'. While this does not prove anything either way, it does indicate that the tradition of Maynard being handed a baby by Captain Smith exists in his family.[75]

One grim possibility is that if a child was rescued, it was either unconscious, or never made it to Collapsible B alive. McGann suggests this in his account, where he assumed that Captain Smith lost his grip on the child in the water. One story attributed to Able Bodied Seaman Albert Horswill states that 'Horswell [sic] saw Captain Smith swimming about with the dead body of a child in his arms'.[76] Horswill was one of the twelve survivors who were rescued in Boat No. 1, which was lowered away at 1:05 a.m. He wasn't near enough to the ship when it sank to see this for himself. Horswill testified in the British Inquiry, and did not mention this story. If the quotes attributed to him are actually his, then he had to be relating information that he heard from someone else.

Another press account related a similar story about the Captain to 'crewman Cyril Handy' and 'Steward Charles Collins'. Neither of these names appear on the crew list, although it is possible that 'Handy' could have been Chief Second Class Steward John Hardy, and that 'Charles Collins' could have been Scullion John Collins. Yet neither of these men ever made any statements like those attributed to the similarly-named crewmembers in the account. According to the story, Captain Smith was seen swimming in the water with a woman and child. The woman and child were both taken aboard a lifeboat, but the baby died within a few minutes and was put overboard. Captain Smith himself refused to be rescued. The woman who had been swimming with the Captain was said to be an unmarried second class passenger. 'Collins' claimed that she passed out, but was revived in the morning. When he questioned her, she said that she knew nothing about the child.[77]

Even though this account is highly detailed, the problems with it are obvious. The names of the alleged eyewitnesses do not appear on the crew list. Even if the men to whom the quotes were attributed were actually John Hardy and John Collins, the story is still problematic. Hardy was rescued in Collapsible D, launched at 2:05 a.m. There is no record of a woman from second class being pulled from the water by Collapsible D. Collins was rescued aboard Collapsible B, but did not mention seeing Captain Smith or the baby in his detailed Senate Inquiry testimony. There is no record of a woman being saved aboard this lifeboat either. The details in the press account indicate that the lifeboat Smith was allegedly seen at was a regular lifeboat, filled with women and children. Given the problems with the account, it is likely that it was based on rumors, or fabricated entirely, and cannot be relied upon.

An account which seems more reliable may provide stronger evidence as to why so few of the survivors mentioned Captain Smith rescuing a child, if this actually happened. Second Class passenger Elizabeth Nye gave a press interview in which she reported speaking with a crewmember who had been rescued on Collapsible B. She said that one of the men 'who was on the raft' told her that 'the girl whom the Captain saved died half an hour later'.[78]

While one shudders to consider the possibility, if Captain Smith did attempt to save a child, it may have been unconscious from the cold, and expired shortly after being handed to Maynard, or another crewmember on Collapsible B. This, combined with the darkness and lack of lighting that night, would provide an explanation for why more survivors on Collapsible B did not mention the event, if it indeed happened. Those who did witness it may have felt it was too grim to mention or discuss after the fact.

Another possibility is that Senior or McGann mistook Captain Smith's attempts to hand a lifebelt or other object to the men on Collapsible B as an attempt to save a baby; yet this explanation does not adequately explain the detailed descriptions attributed to these two men, particularly in McGann's case. Harold Bride did not see Captain Smith with a child, or holding an object when he leapt overboard, which is at odds with these stories. However, it is possible that Bride might not have been able to see this from his viewing angle, as it was presumably above and behind him.

At least one *Titanic* researcher has suggested that Captain Smith was actually seen handing a bag containing the ship's log to one of the men on Collapsible B, and that in the darkness, this was mistaken for him attempting to save a child. This scenario is not backed up by any eyewitness evidence at all, and seems to be nothing more than far-fetched speculation, since no crewmembers ever claimed that the log was saved. It is equally likely that while Captain Smith was seen in the water, that he never attempted to save a child at all, but that these stories can be attributed to rumors that began on the *Carpathia,* and later exploded in the press. As one anonymous *Titanic* crewmember told the press in New York, he had been given $250 for 'as fine a cock-and-bull story as a sailor ever spun', so it can be established that some false stories were being spread.[79]

One would have more confidence in the stories attributed to Senior and McGann, if first-hand correspondence or depositions mentioning the story, rather than press accounts attributed to these two men, were discovered. However, in the case of Senior, there is reason to believe that he actually did tell the story about Captain Smith, and that it did not originate in the press. Weeks after the disaster and following his original press interviews, Senior gave a separate interview in which he repeated the story about seeing Captain Smith and the baby.[80] While this does not prove that the story is true, it does give strong indication that the story originated with Senior himself, rather than with an over-zealous reporter.

Despite the doubt about the authenticity of the stories of Captain Smith saving a child, there is considerable evidence that he was sighted at Collapsible B, as has already been demonstrated. Additional confirmation that an officer, possibly Captain Smith, reached Collapsible B comes from Third Class passenger Edward Dorking, who was saved aboard that boat. Dorking was not familiar with the officers of the *Titanic* and did not know them by sight, as demonstrated by his claims to have witnessed an officer who 'may have been the captain or it may not' shoot himself in the final moments aboard the ship. Dorking relates that after he jumped overboard, and as he was swimming to Collapsible B, a 'man who wore an officer's uniform' was swimming behind him in the water. He claimed that the following happened after they reached the collapsible:

> The officer was so exhausted he became unconscious. In ten minutes after he struggled over the side of the raft and was safe he was dead.[81]

Since Dorking apparently could not recognize the officers by sight, it is possible that this man was Captain Smith; this, then, could agree with the other evidence that Smith reached Collapsible B before dying.

One final eyewitness provides convincing first-hand evidence that Captain Smith may have reached Collapsible B. Fireman Walter Hurst was rescued on the upturned boat. Author Walter Lord wrote the following:

> Another swimmer kept cheering them on: 'Good boy! Good lads!' He had the voice of authority and never climbed aboard. Even though they were dangerously overcrowded, Walter Hurst couldn't resist holding out an oar. But the man was too far gone. An oar touched him, he spun about like a cork and was silent. To this day Hurst thinks it was Captain Smith.[82]

In his actual correspondence with Walter Lord in the 1950s, Hurst provided more detail, denying that Captain Smith actually climbed aboard Collapsible B, but confirming his long-standing thoughts that Captain Smith was alongside them in the water:

> I can state definitively that Captain Smith did not meet the raft but I always had the idea he was the man that spoke to us in the water but I could not be sure … there was one man quite near us he had the voice of authority kept cheering us ['Good Boy Good Lads']. I reached the oar out to help him but he was too far gone as it touched him he turned about like a cork and was silent.[83]

Owing to the darkness and difficulty in seeing at the time, Hurst was not certain that the man in the water was Captain Smith, although he maintained throughout the rest of his life that it was. Third Class passenger Eugene Daly, also rescued aboard Collapsible B, recalled this same man:

> One man was alongside and asked if he could get upon it. We told him that if he did, we would all go down. His reply was[:] 'God Bless You. Goodbye.'[84]

Saloon Steward Arthur McMicken related a story that he had heard which indicated that Captain Smith approached a raft, but that 'it was seen that to take the Captain into the boat would endanger the lives of all aboard'. McMicken was told that Smith did not climb aboard, and that several men did reach out for him, but it was too late.[85] This corresponds well with Hurst's recollections. Colonel Archibald Gracie recalled this same swimmer in the water, as did several other survivors aboard Collapsible B:

> There was one transcendent piece of heroism that will remain fixed in my memory as the most sublime and coolest exhibition of courage and cheerful resignation of fate and fearlessness of death. This was when a reluctant refusal of assistance met with ringing response in the deep manly voice of a powerful man, who, in his extremity, replied: 'All right boys; good luck and God bless you.' I have often wished that the identity of this hero might be established and an individual tribute to his memory preserved.

> He was not an acquaintance of mine, for the tones of his voice would have enabled me to recognize him.[86]

Colonel Gracie was not sure who the man in the water was, and from both Hurst and his accounts, it can be inferred that it was difficult to see at the time, since it was very dark. Gracie offered no opinion as to whether he believed this swimmer was Captain Smith. He was probably unaware that others felt it was, since he did not address this question in his book. Compounding the issue is that Gracie made it clear that he did not know which officer he was seeing and when, until 'he afterwards learned' their identities.

Despite this, Gracie would have been able to identify Captain Smith by sight, not just because of Smith's distinctive beard, but also because he was present at the Sunday church service in the Dining Saloon which Captain Smith presided over. It is difficult to tell how familiar Gracie would have been with Smith's voice from hearing it at that service, but this is a factor worth considering. Additionally, Second Officer Lightoller did not report hearing Smith's voice while aboard Collapsible B, although it is possible that he could have missed it between the noise of survivors in the water, and those struggling aboard the collapsible.

Conclusions

When all of the evidence relating to Captain Smith's fate is examined critically and objectively, it is easy to see why the mystery surrounding his death has endured for an entire century. Many survivors claimed to have knowledge of how the Captain died, and their stories range from plausible to completely absurd.[87] Only by sifting through and examining the evidence as a whole can some conclusions be drawn.

One of the most widely published stories following the disaster, and perhaps the most forgotten, was that Captain Smith committed suicide. There is virtually no evidence to indicate that this actually occurred. Many accounts claiming that he shot himself had no eyewitness names attached to them. All but one or two of those that do can be proven to be false or at least second-hand, and are therefore questionable. Accounts do place Captain Smith near the Bridge before the Boat Deck plunged under, near where an officer suicide, if it occurred, may have happened. Beyond that, there is nothing to suggest that Captain Smith met his end by his own hand. In the years prior to the *Titanic* disaster, several Captains had lost their certificates due to accidents involving their ships, and several Captains shot themselves after their vessels foundered. Once rumors that an officer shot himself began circulating in the wake of the disaster, it is easy to see why some may have assumed Captain Smith was the officer to do so.

The story that Captain Smith stuck to the Bridge and bravely went down with his ship is one of the more iconic images associated with the disaster, and has been perpetuated by film portrayals and books about the sinking. The evidence that he was near the Bridge at the end is solid. Several surviving crewmembers stated that they last saw Captain Smith giving orders to the men trying to launch Collapsible A, on the starboard side of the Boat Deck, during the attempted launch of that boat. Some indicate that Smith re-entered the Bridge shortly before water reached the deck, but no credible accounts state that they actually saw him go down with the ship.

Even before survivor accounts were available to the press, newspapers were already speculating that Captain Smith went down with his ship. During the Edwardian era, this would have been considered an extremely honorable and heroic death. Captain Smith himself allegedly made statements hinting that he would go down with his ship if he was ever confronted with a disaster. These factors help explain why so many assumed this is how the Captain met his end, even though the eyewitness evidence does not prove it. If Smith wore a lifebelt as some eyewitnesses claim, it is difficult to imagine that it was his intent to remain aboard.

Several other eyewitnesses indicate that after being seen on the starboard side, Captain Smith crossed over to the port side of the Boat Deck near the Bridge, at the same time as the attempt to free Collapsible B from the roof of the Officers' Quarters was taking place. Accounts suggest that as the Boat Deck began to submerge a few minutes later, the Captain turned and jumped into the ocean. The evidence conflicts as to the exact details, but strongly indicates that Smith did not go down with the ship. Multiple witnesses claim that the Captain was later seen in the water. Some of these accounts are second hand, and many are false or inaccurate, because the eyewitness claiming to have seen the events was too far away from the ship at the time, or were not rescued in the way that they claimed.

Several survivors who were rescued by clinging to the upturned Collapsible B claimed that Captain Smith reached their lifeboat shortly after the sinking. Some of them claimed that Smith's last act was to save a baby, although the details vary and the truth behind the tale, if any, is unknown. All that can be said is that at least one of the survivors aboard Collapsible B repeatedly claimed that the Captain saved a child, indicating that the story was not invented by a reporter, although it was certainly spread by the press. Those who claim that Smith reached this lifeboat state that the Captain was either injured during the sinking, or simply too exhausted to be saved, or that there wasn't enough room for him to board the collapsible. Descriptions from other survivors rescued indicate that during the night, those onboard Collapsible B discussed the possibility that Captain Smith had been aboard, as the events were playing out. The stories that he reached this collapsible did not originate after the fact. Colonel Archibald Gracie and Jack Thayer verify this, as do other survivors.

When all is said and done, it appears that Captain Smith did not commit suicide, or go down with the ship as legend claims. The most credible evidence suggests that he leapt overboard, and at some point shortly after the sinking, reached Collapsible B. Starlight would have been the only light source that eyewitnesses could use to see; while we know from the testimony of survivors that identification of others was possible that night, it made positive identifications difficult.

Colonel Gracie speculated that if Captain Smith had been aboard the upturned collapsible, he may have been washed off during the collapse of the forward funnel. It is possible that the Captain was either killed or injured at this time. If he wasn't, he would have been extremely weakened or rendered unconscious after 10–20 minutes in the 28° water, perhaps less if he had been hurt during the breakup or sinking. Fireman Hurst maintained throughout his life that Captain Smith did indeed come alongside Collapsible B, encouraging the men aboard. By the time Hurst tried to assist the man he believed was the Captain, he had already succumbed to hypothermia. Jack Thayer saw a life ring from the Bridge floating near Collapsible B in the morning. If Captain Smith had indeed been alongside Collapsible B, this life ring may have marked the very spot where he met his end.[88]

Appendix N: The Breakup

For over seventy-three years, the generally accepted wisdom was that the *Titanic* sank with her hull completely intact. This was recounted in numerous books written on the subject, and was seen in film portrayals such as the 1953 film *Titanic*, 1958's *A Night to Remember*, and 1979's *S.O.S. Titanic*. The typical picture painted of the sinking was that the ship swung up to a nearly vertical position; that a loud noise sounded, caused by the crashing of every movable object aboard the ship – including machinery, engines and boilers – down to the bow; that the boilers most likely tore their way through the bow plates of the ship; that, once relieved of this weight, the ship eased back slightly in the water, and then sank at that angle with a growing momentum. As Walter Lord wrote in *The Night Lives On*, this view 'became accepted as gospel. To question it amounted to heresy'. But then there came a tremendous surprise.

In 1985, when Dr Robert Ballard discovered the wreck on the sea floor, he and his team were shocked to find that the stern portion of the ship had broken away from the bow; the distance between the two halves suggested that the break had occurred at, or on, the surface. Yet, this left the lingering question: shouldn't there have been survivors who described a breakup if it had happened on the surface? In point of fact, there *were* survivor accounts that *did* clearly describe a breakup before the final plunge... and not just a few. There were a great many of them.

But if there really were a large number of survivor accounts that mentioned a breakup, how did the accepted version of history, cherished for three quarters of a century, become that of a non-break scenario? Well, Second Officer Lightoller and Third Officer Pitman – considered experts in their profession – were so forceful in their statements at the inquiries that those conducting the proceedings, none of whom were seafaring men, decided to take their word for it.

At the British Inquiry, for example, witness after witness had clearly alluded to the ship breaking up – or at least to the stern settling back toward an even keel, clear evidence of a breakup – before she took her final plunge. However, when Lightoller took the stand, he denied all such testimony and asserted that the ship sank intact. At that point, Lord Mersey was reminded by the Solicitor-General: 'Your Lordship knows a lot of Witnesses have said their impression was the afterpart settled on the water.'

Mersey concurred, saying: 'I have heard that over and over again.' Turning to Lightoller, Mersey asked: 'That you say is not true?'

Lightoller responded: 'That is not true, My Lord. I was watching her keenly the whole time.'

Lord Mersey's response was telling. 'I had difficulty in realising how it could possibly be that the afterpart of the ship righted itself for a moment.' So, because Mersey and others of the committee had trouble understanding the testimony regarding a breakup, they had great difficulty in grasping the mechanics involved in what they were hearing from eyewitnesses. When Lightoller – the senior surviving officer of the ship and thus someone who carried great clout with the committee – categorically denied all such reports, they were rather pre-disposed to accept his version of the sinking.[1]

The conclusion that the ship had sunk intact was published with the court's findings and was subsequently disseminated to the public at large. That conclusion was further reinforced by two of the earliest publications rushed to press after the disaster. Penned by survivors Archibald Gracie and Lawrence Beesley, both authors were clear that the ship had sunk in one piece – even though Gracie was under water and had not personally seen the sinking. Lightoller later penned a written account of the disaster, in which he again reiterated that the ship had not broken.

The picture that Lightoller, Pitman, Gracie and Beesley painted all seemed logical, coherent, and well thought-out. Yet, it was completely and wholly inaccurate. In not paying enough attention to the *majority* of survivor evidence, researchers, authors, historians – and thus the public who relied upon their conclusions – were all duped into believing that things happened differently than they really had.

Survivor Accounts – What They Said They Saw

So, having identified how an inaccurate conclusion came to be commonly accepted, we are left with the question: how many of the survivor accounts available to historians today stated that the ship broke? How many said the ship sank intact? How many referred to events which, without exactly mentioning a breakup, in retrospect gave clear evidence of such? How many simply hadn't seen the event, or didn't refer at all to specifics in their accounts?

After extensive research, we have studied a total of 149 survivors' statements – nearly 21% of the 712 survivors.[2] A good number of these descriptions came from the formal inquiries. Others were accounts given by survivors specifically for publication in newspapers; most of these went to press within the first weeks or months after the disaster. Still others have turned up over the years in the form of personal letters written by survivors to family or friends, and many of these were written very shortly after the disaster.

Of these 149 survivors, nine specifically said they did not see the ship sink or did not know what had happened. A further 51 eyewitnesses simply did not say whether they saw the ship break or not; among these were accounts that very briefly mentioned the ship sinking but gave no specifics, as well as accounts that gave only general movements of the ship in the final moments. A further 24 eyewitnesses spoke of frightening sounds, one or more explosions, what they assumed were bulkheads giving way, and more – all without specifically mentioning a breakup. One of these eyewitnesses spoke of an explosion that ripped out the ship's bottom, but did not specifically mention a breakup.[3] After tallying the figures, it turns out that 84 of the 149 accounts studied came from survivors who either had not seen the ship sink, or who mentioned no specifics on the subject. However, none of the survivors we have placed in this category said anything that would specifically *exclude* a breakup at the surface.

Of the remaining 65 accounts studied, 53 survivors specifically said that the ship broke or split as it was sinking, and many of these provided further details in their accounts. Sometimes more than one account was available

from these survivors, and the consistency between them is very encouraging.

Two further women, who were in Boat No. 4, did not see a break-up firsthand. However, as the ship was sinking, they did hear a person in their lifeboat say, 'She's broken'; in their account, they reported that statement, and at the same time they did not disagree with it.[4] Another survivor, young Frank Goldsmith, Jr, recalled someone in his lifeboat yelling: 'Oh, she's going to float!'[5] While not a specific statement of a break, this exclamation was almost certainly a reference to the gyrations of the ship during and immediately after the breakup, which were referred to by at least some of the fifty-three other eyewitnesses who described the ship rending. For that reason, this statement should also be counted as second-hand evidence of a breakup.

A further survivor who gave a direct account shortly after the sinking, Sidney Collett, said that he heard terrible noises as the ship sank, and said that they 'may have been bursting of the boilers or the vessel breaking in two. I don't know'.[6] Although he was unsure of which of these two explanations was true, he did not dismiss the concept of a breakup as impossible. Since we today know that none of the boilers exploded, this leaves Collett's account sounding more like – in retrospect, at least – it was describing a breakup. One other survivor, Karen Abelseth, said that the ship resurfaced after it sank, overturned twice, and then sank again.[7] Although initially coming off as a rather bizarre description of those final minutes, one has to allow for the possibility that she was describing in a very nontechnical manner at least some of the motions of the ship during and after the breakup.

In summary, eighty-four persons who gave accounts did not say anything for or against a breakup; another fifty-three specifically said the ship broke up, three heard statements as the ship sank referring to a breakup, another allowed for the possibility, and still one more described something unusual that may have been referring to the way the ship moved after the breakup.

Compared with all of these numbers, only seven of the 149 eyewitness accounts that we studied stated for certain that the ship *did not* break, but rather sank intact. These individuals were Second Officer Charles Lightoller – in his inquiry testimony and in his later book and other accounts; Third Officer Herbert Pitman in his inquiry testimony; Trimmer Thomas Dillon at the British Inquiry; First Class Passenger Hugh Woolner at the U.S. Inquiry; First Class Passenger Elisabeth Allen;[8] First Class Passenger Caroline Bonnell;[9] and Second Class Passenger Lawrence Beesley. They represent less than five per cent of the total.[10] It is clear that the number of persons who stated emphatically that the ship sank intact were by far in the minority.[11] It is unfortunate that for many years, the majority of survivor accounts were ignored and historians were thus led to a spurious explanation of the ship's sinking, one that was only challenged when presented with hard evidence in the form of twisted, rent steel.

Cinematic Depictions

Today, people are most familiar with the depiction of the breakup from the James Cameron film *Titanic* of 1997. This portrayal was the first big-screen depiction of those horrible moments during the ship's end, and is certainly the best known. It also looked *tremendously real* – much more so than previous silver-screen portrayals where the 'ship' was obvi-

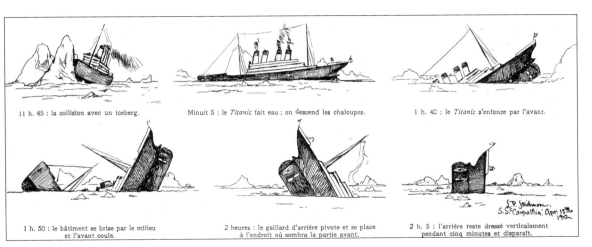

11 h. 45 : la collision avec un iceberg.

Minuit 5 : le *Titanic* fait eau ; on descend les chaloupes.

1 h. 40 : le *Titanic* s'enfonce par l'avant.

1 h. 50 : le bâtiment se brise par le milieu et l'avant coule.

2 heures : le gaillard d'arrière pivote et se place à l'endroit où sombra la partie avant.

2 h. 5 : l'arrière reste dressé verticalement pendant cinq minutes et disparaît.

This illustration was done aboard the Carpathia *by L. D. Skidmore, a passenger of that vessel. Although purportedly based upon Jack Thayer's eyewitness recollections, it is obvious that the liner did not break in this manner.*

ously a miniature. In the 1997 film, the ship's bow plunges and her stern rises to a visible angle of about 40–42°.[12] As the power fails, the shell plating begins to bulge outward, the ship's structure gives way cleanly at the upper decks just behind the No. 3 funnel, and the ship splits down the side shell plating to the keel. Unrestrained, the stern crashes mightily back into the sea, sending out a tremendous wave as it does.[13] Still connected to the flooded bow by the keel, the stern is pulled back upright as the bow slides away. The keel then detaches, and the stern is left poised vertically, pausing before sliding under the sea with building momentum.

The final sinking sequences, showing the breakup and sinking, were achieved using a 7 1/2-ton 1/8-scale model of the stern half of the liner. Placed in a large tank, the model was then set at a 45° angle and mounted on a rig so that when a primary hydraulic pin was pulled, the stern half would be allowed to simply drop back into the water. To ensure that the model would break in the appropriate places, decks and interior miniatures were pre-scored; a slight twist was even engineered into the drop so that the ship would not break entirely symmetrically. In the area where the break was set to occur, aluminum hull plates were installed along the impending break line, to simulate tearing and shearing stresses on the hull plating for scale effect. Within the model, a mechanism was also installed that would begin to bulge the hull outwards at the same time the decks began to give way. Artificially bulging the hull outwards in this manner was included to show that the bottom of the ship was pushing up as the vessel was breaking – something that could not otherwise be seen since the bottom of the hull was underwater at the time. From this review, it can be seen that certain elements of the model's behavior – and thus the depiction in the film – could easily have departed from the actual physics of the breakup and sinking.[14]

So the lingering question remains: silver-screen depictions aside, how did the breakup actually play out, technically speaking?

Forensic Investigations
– The Good, the Challenges, and the Unknown

True nuts and bolts investigators – real 'rivet counters' in the form of historians, enthusiasts, and even marine fo-

rensic experts – would like nothing better than to be able to do a thorough forensic analysis of the wreck. Closely connected with a physical on-site forensic investigation would be another – and tremendously powerful – modern engineering tool: the computer. In modern engineering programs, programmers can recreate three-dimensional representations of the *Titanic* in digital form. Then, harnessing the number-crunching power of computers, strong or weak areas of the *Titanic*'s hull, the locations of stress-concentrations under various load scenarios, and areas of the vessel where structural failures were most likely to take place under certain situations can all be quickly identified. However, each of these unique modern tools is susceptible to its own Achilles' heels.

For example, a forensic analysis on the wreck itself might have been easy if, when the wreck was discovered, there were just two large sections and those two components fit together at a seam in the middle. However, that simply is not the case. Instead, there is a large amount of material missing from the two major sections. This list includes a length of double bottom from the aft end of Boiler Room No. 2 through the forward section of the Reciprocating Engine Room; it also includes, at the Boat Deck level, everything from the casing for the No. 3 funnel all the way aft to the area around the No. 4 funnel. While the tear at the aft end of the bow seemed to be clean and nearly vertical in nature, from keel to Boat Deck, the stern section showed a much more destructive pattern. There, the damage expands aft as it ascends from the keel and double bottom. Most of the missing material from between the perimeters of the two major sections of ship was spread throughout a vast debris field on the seafloor, between the two halves of the wreck. This included the five single-ended boilers from Boiler Room No. 1, which had originally been attached to the now missing segments of double bottom.

Still, some may object that forensic investigations of wrecks such as that of TWA Flight 800 have been performed successfully, turning up evidence that has most likely pinpointed the cause of the disaster. Unfortunately, comparing these to similar investigations on the wreck of the *Titanic* would be like comparing apples to oranges. The wreckage of TWA Flight 800 rested at a depth of between

115 and 130 feet, and was accessible to divers. After an exhausting effort in limited and sometimes nil visibility, over 95% of the original plane was recovered. Brought back to a leased hanger on Long Island, New York, the small pieces were reconstructed on a wire frame until the pertinent portions of the original airplane's shredded form looked more or less complete again. Investigators were then able to do a detailed, in person, and up-close examination of the wreckage – without significant time restraints. Their findings then led them to conclusions on the process that led to the plane's demise.[15]

However, in *Titanic's* case, the wreck lies in over 12,000 feet of water. The major portions of the wreck are completely unrecoverable, and are completely inaccessible to all but a handful of deep-diving submersibles. And whereas TWA Flight 800 had been resting in the sea for only a very short time, *Titanic* had been suffering from the effects of deterioration and decay for three-quarters of a century before *any* photographic record of her remains could be made. Without being able to recover the major portions of the ship's hull, an on-bottom investigation is the only alternative, and it is one fraught with all sorts of complications. Without being able to study each piece close-up in good lighting for extended periods of time, it is nearly impossible to identify where each piece of wreckage, large or small, came from – something crucial to good forensic examination.

Even on the larger bow and stern hull segments, the investigation is by no means simple. On the stern, the hull is literally shredded, with vast portions of hull plating peeled away from the hull and twisted out of kilter. At the stern of the bow section, in the area of the First Class Lounge, decks were pancaked sharply down and bits of side plating are also twisted out of place. Finally, the clock is always running against on-site investigations – dive-time is limited to what the submersibles and their human occupants can withstand, and expensive expedition time is limited by funding.

This begs the all-important question: of the damage visible on the wreck and debris pieces today, what of that damage was sustained in the breakup and sinking, and what of it was introduced into the wreckage during the descent and impact with the bottom, permanently tainting any forensic investigation?

Naturally, with all of these complications – including the post-break damage that was done to the wreck during descent to, and impact with, the sea floor – any team must be extremely cautious and careful in proceeding with a forensic investigation. In the first place, researchers must go into the investigation with a fresh mind, looking for evidence to lead to conclusions instead of looking for evidence to support a pre-existing theory. Beyond that, their conclusions should ideally be verifiable through another form of evidence and, where it is not, it should not contradict other known and reliable evidence.

Computer Recreations as an Investigative Tool

The second modern-day forensic tool, computer-based recreations of the *Titanic*, can also fall prey to weaknesses. Foremost among these is a term that has been used in the computer world for decades: 'GIGO'. This acronym stands for the phrase 'Garbage In, Garbage Out'. The meaning is that the results obtained through computer studies are only as good as the information programmed into them. In

order to identify stresses and weaknesses within the hull, the recreation must be an exact – or nearly exact – representation of the *Titanic's* original physical form. Where differences from the original are built into the model, calculations must be made to show whether those differences might taint the findings.

Unfortunately, while the basics of her construction are well documented, certain details of *Titanic's* structure are still unknown or questionable, and more information is always coming to light on points both minor and major. Plans used must be accurate to the *Titanic*, not her sister ship *Olympic*, since there were a number of alterations incorporated into the *Titanic* from her sister ship.

To take but one example, on *Titanic*, a crew staircase that did originally exist on *Olympic* just astern of the No. 3 funnel uptake, amidships, and which ran from the Promenade Deck to E Deck, was altered on *Titanic*.[16] The openings in the decks were enlarged in their transverse direction rather late in the *Titanic's* fitting out, widened by a foot. The staircase was also extended until it ran up to *Titanic's* Boat Deck. The alteration, while small in and of itself, must be considered in any computer models because it was within the general area of the breakup, and was built directly adjacent to the large funnel uptake and ventilation shafts. Just astern of this area, there were also large deck openings for the aft First Class Grand Staircase. While the upper levels of that staircase were contained within the superstructure – and thus did not take up the strain of the hull as it worked in a seaway or under the hogging stresses it suffered that night – the well of that staircase did pass through the plating of the strength deck, B Deck, before the staircase itself terminated on C Deck. In other known cases of structural failure in ocean liners, it was not a single opening in the deck which produced structural weakness, but rather the interaction between several openings which were in close proximity. So we can see how even minor alterations in a vital area of the ship, if not factored into a computer model, could cause a change from reality when stress tolerances of that entire region are being calculated.

Beyond being accurate to *Titanic's* finished form as we know it, there would be an additional level of authenticity that one would want to account for, whenever possible, taking into account a margin of error for the unknown. The main questions would be: did the ship's strength in the area under scrutiny match, exceed, or fall short of design tolerances? For example, were rivets in one portion of the hull under study driven in hydraulically, or by hand? The strength of the joint could be affected by this difference. Additionally, what was the likely slag content and thus the tensile strength of those particular rivets? How did any and all of such potential differences, though each might seem minor, 'add up'? Could they materially affect the entire model and resulting calculations, and if so, by how much? Finally, does the computer model encompass enough area of the ship's form to identify a starting point for the fractures, or is it possible that the area being studied is too small?

Without delving into such minutiae, there are larger and more basic aspects of the ship's design where a close approximation to reality would probably provide a 'good enough' result in computer modeling, albeit with a margin of error. But in computer modeling, everything always comes down to an accurate representation of the ship's form, strengths and weaknesses in the area of the break. At a remove of a century, with some original archival material still unavailable to all researchers or missing altogether, there are certain lingering questions about the details. As a result, any strength and weakness calculations made from a computer must always be treated with at least some level of suspicion. As with physical forensic investigations, if the results obtained fly in the face of other evidence, or do not make a great deal of sense, then it's time to go back to the drawing board.

Survivor Accounts as an Investigative Tool
The third line of investigative research has to do with a careful analysis of what survivors said they saw. As researchers previously discovered, ignoring survivor accounts – even those that might initially seem preposterous – can be a disastrous pitfall. Even so, survivor accounts are far from infallible. Personal perception, faulty memories, emotional reaction to life-threatening situations, exaggeration, or outright dishonesty can quickly throw a monkey wrench into the works of an investigation relying solely on first-hand accounts.

For example, while the majority said that the ship broke, a very few said with certainty that it did not. Still others mentioned great explosions, horrible noises, or gyrations of the ship without mentioning a break. So what should be believed? Putting together the pieces of the general picture painted by the survivors is fraught with problems. Quite often, such survivor accounts were not given exactly chronologically, or were given in the course of a question-and-answer session at one of the inquiries, where the subject changed back and forth and can be difficult to follow. So misreading an account, or not reading an entire account, can prove to be its own quagmire.

Terminology that was used at the time, but is little understood today, can pose a problem; even the background of the witness – were they individuals familiar with technological structures and general principles of physics, or were they not of a technical mind? – should be taken into account wherever possible. As with both previous forms of investigation, it is vitally important to follow evidence to a conclusion, rather than to start with a theory and look for evidence to support it. Finally, only an investigation that uses *all* of the tools available to researchers today and arrives at a conclusion that is best supported by a *preponderance* – or overwhelming majority – of evidence can be considered a viable conclusion.

The Investigation Begins
Thus it is time for us to become a twenty-first century maritime equivalent of Sherlock Holmes. We must interview eyewitnesses – in this instance, since all survivors of the *Titanic* disaster have passed away – through the use of any and all existing accounts. These can be gleaned from first-hand interviews made with the survivors over the years for documentaries and what-not; they can also be taken from letters by the survivors to others; finally, newspapers – both in 1912 and in the years since – have carried a great number of survivor stories, and must be carefully searched for clues. However, one must be very careful in using newspaper accounts to make sure that the survivor's statements are clear and hold up under close scrutiny; the most desirable use direct quotations, and are not paraphrased statements made by the writer. Whatever adds up to the majority should be followed, and then compared, with physical forensic and

computer modeled investigations to ensure harmony before any conclusions can be drawn.

Our investigation must begin at a point before the actual break witnessed by survivors. Based upon the most detailed analysis of the sinking from 11:40 p.m. to 2:15 a.m., certain details about the ship's position in the water can be clearly ascertained, giving us an excellent starting point. At about 2:05 a.m., the ship was about 7° down by the head with an approximate 10° list to port. The port forward corner of the Promenade Deck bulwark was close to slipping beneath the waves at the time; simultaneously, Collapsible D was being launched from the port side, and First Class passengers Steffansson and Woolner were about to leap into the boat. The ship was continuing to increase her forward trim. Her apparent flotation pivot point was approximately in line with the forward edge of her No. 4 funnel. Everything forward of that point was moving down, while everything aft of that point was moving up.[17]

Although the ship had settled slowly since the collision, the more deeply the ship sank into the sea, the faster she was beginning to slip away. Over the next ten minutes, the ship's trim seems to have increased from 7° to about 10°, while also maintaining her list to port. As water was coming up on the port Boat Deck, the starboard side of the deck was still above the surface of the sea. Collapsible B, having landed on the port Boat Deck upside-down, began to float free. On the starboard side, there was a frenzy of activity around Collapsible A, in an attempt to get it to the falls from Boat No. 1; alas, time had run out.

The 'Slight But Definite Plunge'
Now that the stage is set, it is time to consider what eyewitnesses said about the moments which immediately followed:[18]

Joseph Scarrott, AB: She was sinking by the head. … Very slow it appeared to be. As the water seemed to get above the bridge she increased her rate of going down … When the port bow light [the red port side light] disappeared she seemed to go faster.[19]

Emily Ryerson, First Class passenger: I … turned to see the great ship take a plunge toward the bow…[20]

William Ward, Saloon Steward: She went very gradually for a while … She did not appear to be going fast, and I was … still of the opinion she would float … [Then] she gave a kind of sudden lurch forward …[21]

Alexander Littlejohn, Saloon Steward: We watched her like this for some time, and then suddenly she gave a plunge forward …[22]

Anne Caton, Turkish Bath Attendant: … [She] appeared to be settling rapidly, with the bows and bridge completely under water.[23]

Second Officer Lightoller: We had just time to tip the boat [Collapsible B] over, and let her drop into the water that was now above the boat deck … Hemming and I then … went over to the starboard side…

Just then the ship took a slight but definite plunge – probably a bulkhead went – and the sea came rolling up in a wave, over the steel-fronted bridge, along the deck below us, washing the people back in a dreadful, huddled mass. Those that didn't disappear under the water right away, instinctively

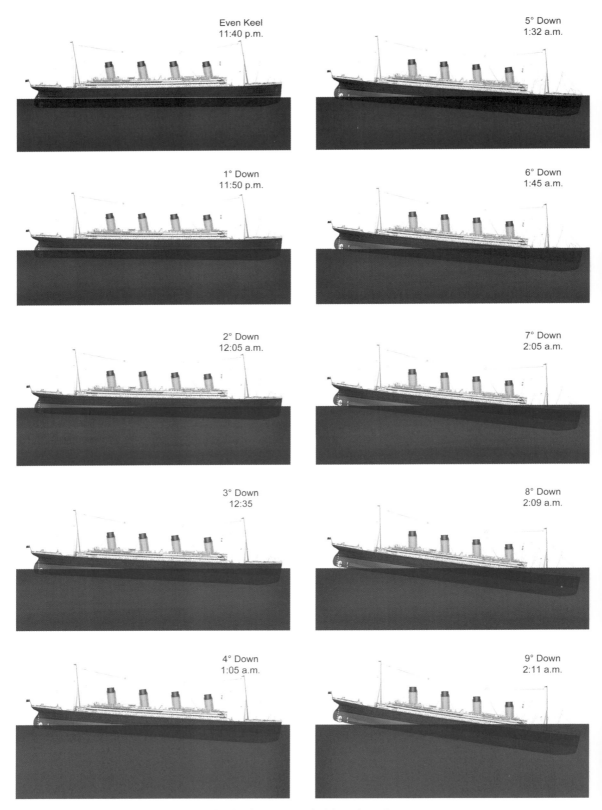

Even Keel
11:40 p.m.

5° Down
1:32 a.m.

1° Down
11:50 p.m.

6° Down
1:45 a.m.

2° Down
12:05 a.m.

7° Down
2:05 a.m.

3° Down
12:35

8° Down
2:09 a.m.

4° Down
1:05 a.m.

9° Down
2:11 a.m.

This and following two images: *The various angles that the* Titanic *reached during her sinking.*

10° Down
2:14 a.m.

15° Down

11° Down
2:15 a.m.

16° Down

12° Down

17° Down

13° Down

18° Down

14° Down

19° Down

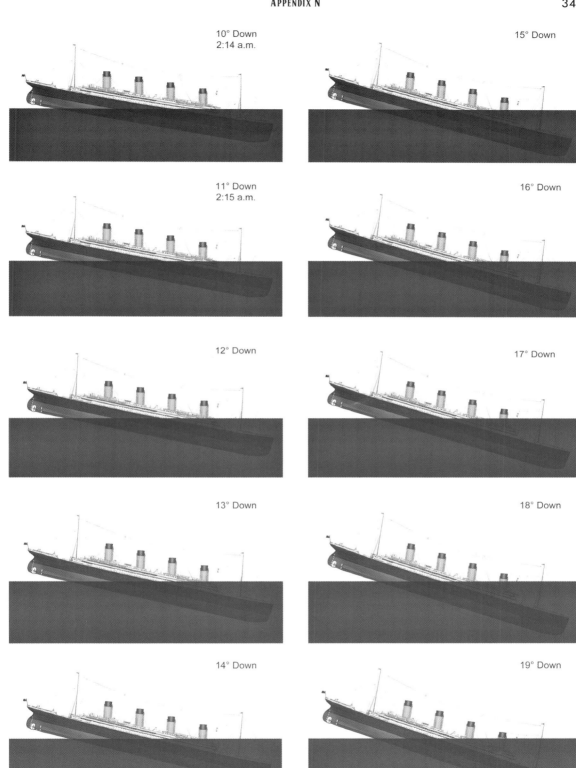

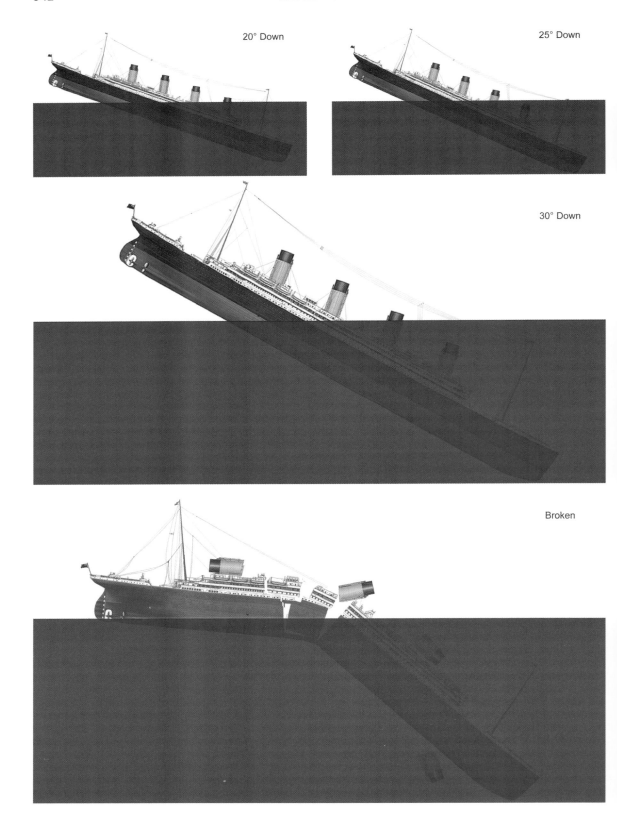

20° Down

25° Down

30° Down

Broken

started to clamber up that part of the deck still out of the water, and work their way towards the stern, which was rising steadily out of the water as the bow went down. A few of the more agile leapt up on top of the officers' quarters where Hemming and I were at the moment ... turning to the fore part of the bridge, I took a header.[24]

Jack Thayer, First Class passenger: [Milton Long] and I stood by the davits of one of the boats that had left [on the starboard side] ... just a little aft of the Captain's Bridge.

The list to port had been growing greater all the time.

... I got a sight on a rope between the davits and a star and noticed that she was gradually sinking. About this time she straightened up on an even keel and started to go down fairly fast ...[25]

William Mellors, Second Class passenger: We were trying to fix up a collapsible boat [Boat A] when she gave the first signs of going under. There seemed to be a tremble run through the whole of the ship and the next thing we heard were loud reports inside which I think were the water-tight doors giving way and before you could say Jack Robinson there seemed to be mountains of water rushing through the doors, and I was swept away from where I was right against the collapsible boat, and I simply clung on for all I was worth, whilst all this was going on she was going under water ... when suddenly her nose on which I was seemed to suddenly rise from underneath the water and I and a few more that were close by cut the ropes that held the boat to the falls.[26]

Cecil William Fitzpatrick, Mess Steward: I then went to launch one of the collapsible boats [Boat A] ... The next thing I remember was the ship suddenly dipping, and the waves rushing up and engulfing me. After ten seconds the *Titanic* again righted herself, but then I saw that everyone who a minute before had been attempting to lower away, except myself, had been swept into the fo'castle head. I saved myself by clinging on to the davit winch.[27]

Here we see a close consensus of survivor testimony. Just at the point that the port boat deck was becoming awash, the ship 'trembled', 'lurched', and 'plunged' under the surface, swamping the forward Boat Deck. The exact cause of this plunge forward is unknown. One likely possibility is that a bulkhead – perhaps not even one that was meant to be watertight – had collapsed or overtopped down in the bowels of the ship, and the sudden shift changed the vessel's center of gravity, driving the bow down. Lightoller suggested a potential explanation along those lines, and it still seems to be the most likely cause for the sudden shift.

Whatever caused the plunge, the effect on the deck was immediate and rapid: everyone forward, just behind the Bridge on the port and starboard sides, and on the roof of the Officers' Quarters, was washed off the deck. Moments later, however, it is reported that the bow recovered slightly, bobbing back up just a little. What caused this effect? At the time, the ship was balanced like a see-saw, with buoyant stern sections being counteracted by flooded bow sections. It seems likely that the water flowing into the newly-flooded area – which had caused the slight plunge – also shifted

the ship's center of gravity slightly aft as it moved. The ship then temporarily found her equilibrium, recovering very slightly before the sheer amount of water flooding her internal spaces took back over and resumed the downward thrust of her forward end.[28] In the meanwhile, from numerous lines of evidence, a large crowd of people on the Boat Deck turned to rush aft for the imagined safety of the stern.

But time was fast slipping away. When the bow began to dive again, it did so with gusto. Let's pick up the survivor testimony once again:

Charles Joughin, Chief Baker: I went to the deck pantry [probably the Lounge Deck Pantry, in the vicinity of the No. 3 funnel on A Deck], and while I was in there I thought I would take a drink of water, and while I was getting the drink of water I heard a kind of crash as if something had buckled, as if part of the ship had buckled, and then I heard a rush overhead ... It was not an explosion or anything like that. It was like as if the iron was parting.29

Colonel Archibald Gracie, First Class passenger: Clinch Smith and I instantly saw that we could make no progress ahead, and with the water following us behind over the deck, we were in a desperate place. I can never forget the exact point on the ship where he and I were located, viz., at the opening of the angle made by the walls of the officers' house and only a short distance abaft the *Titanic's* forward 'expansion joint.' Clinch Smith was immediately on my left, nearer the apex of the angle, and our backs were turned toward the ship's rail and the sea. Looking up toward the roof of the officers' house I saw a man to the right of me and above lying on his stomach on the roof, and I promptly followed. The efforts of both of us failed ... As I came down, the water struck my right side. I crouched down into it preparatory to jumping with it, and rose as if on the crest of a wave on the seashore ... I was able to reach the roof and the iron railing that is along the edge of it, and pulled myself over on top of the officers' house on my stomach near the base of the second funnel...

... My holding on to the iron railing just when I did prevented my being knocked unconscious. I pulled myself over on the roof on my stomach, but before I could get to my feet I was in a whirlpool of water, swirling round and round, as I still tried to cling to the railing as the ship plunged to the depths below. Down, down, I went: it seemed a great distance. There was a very noticeable pressure upon my ears ...[30]

Charlotte Collyer, Second Class passenger: I shall never forget the terrible beauty of the *Titanic* at that moment. She was tilted forward, head down, with her first funnel partly under water. To me she looked like an enormous glow worm, for she was alight from the rising water line clear to the stern – electric lights blazing in every cabin on all the decks and lights at her mast heads ...[31]

Caroline Bonnell, First Class passenger: After a while when we were a considerable distance away, a whole deck of lights, the lowest deck, was suddenly snuffed out. At the same time the mast light dropped a little further down in the star pointed sky. After this the tragedy moved with a relentless swiftness.

Deck by deck we watched the lights go out as the boat dropped lower and lower into the sea.

At last but four rows of lights were left …[32]

Lawrence Beesley, Second Class passenger: She slowly tilted straight on end with the stern vertically upwards …[33] [She] tilted slowly up, revolving apparently about a center of gravity just astern of amidships …[34]

Eugene Daly, Third Class passenger: Her stern went up and she gradually sunk forward. Her stern stuck up high.[35]

Joseph Scarrott, AB: As the water got above the bridge she started to go down faster … This part of the ship [the stern] was right up in the air. You could see her propeller right clear, and you could see underneath the keel; you could see part of her keel …[36]

George Symons, Lookout: [Her] forecastle head was well under water then… You could see her starboard sidelight …, and her stern was well up in the air … [You] could not see her keel … You could just see the propellers … I stood and watched it till I heard two sharp explosions in the ship … Then she suddenly took a top cant, her stern came well out of the water then …[37]

John Poingdestre, AB: … [The] propeller and everything was quite clear.[38]

Emily Ryerson, First Class passenger: Then suddenly, when we still seemed very near, we saw the ship was sinking rapidly. I … turned to see the great ship take a plunge toward the bow, and two forward funnels seemed to lean…[39]

Jack Thayer, First Class passenger: I came up facing the ship … I was trying to get away from the ship. I looked back and the second funnel fell and missed me by about ten yards. This funnel … made a tremendous additional wash and suction. I was drawn down again.[40]

Charles Lightoller, Second Officer: The forward funnel was still there – all the funnels were above water … [when] I first came up [to the surface] … After the [forward] funnel fell there was some little time elapsed. I do not know exactly what came or went, but the next thing I remember I was alongside this collapsible boat again, and there were about half a dozen standing on it. I climbed on it, and then turned my attention to the ship. The third if not the second funnel was still visible, certainly the third funnel was still visible. The stern was then clear of the water … and she was gradually raising her stern out of the water. Even at that time I think the propellers were clear of the water.

… Only the forward [funnel had broken away, *sic*]. I am not sure whether [the second one] was below water or not … [The] second funnel was immersed.

Well, I daresay [that the stern must have been very well up in the air]; it would be. [And the propellers all visible, yes] clear of the water. That is my impression … [Some] part of the [third funnel was visible]. As a matter of fact, I am rather under the impression that the whole of the third funnel was visible.[41]

George Crowe, Saloon Steward: After getting clear of the ship the lights were still burning very

bright, but as we got away she seemed to go lower and lower, and she almost stood up perpendicular …[42]

Arthur Bright, Quartermaster: All at once she seemed to go up on end … [Subsequently asked by Senator Bourne, 'The ship went down by her bow first and you could see the stern, and see the keel on the stern, could you?' Bright responded:] Yes, sir.[43]

John Podesta, Fireman: Then all of a sudden, she swerved and her bow went under, her stern rose up in the air.[44]

Henry Etches, Bedroom Steward: She seemed to raise once as though she was going to take a violent dive …[45]

Alfred Crawford, Bedroom Steward: We saw her at a distance … It seemed as if her bow was going down first … We saw all the lights going out on the forward part of her [and still burning on the after part] … There was a good bit of the stern part out of water … [she] seemed all clear right from amidships to aft.[46]

Edward Buley, AB: First of all you could see her propellers and everything. Her rudder was clear out of the water.[47]

Major Arthur Peuchen, First Class passenger: I kept my eyes watching the lights, as long as possible [from about five-eighths of a mile away in Boat No. 6] … While the lights were burning, I saw her bow pointing down and the stern up; not in a perpendicular position, but considerable … I should think an angle of not as much as 45°.[48]

Elmer Taylor, First Class passenger: The ship was going down by the bow. The first row of port holes was below the water line, then another row, while aft, the glowing port holes were lifted higher and higher until the screws were silhouetted, well out of water … [As] a background, I ask you to visualize a steel structure that if stood on end beside the Eiffel Tower, Paris, the top of the structure would be about level with the topmost platform … and almost twice as high as the Washington Monument in Washington, D.C.[49]

… When the *Titanic* settled by the bow, the stern was lifted in midair, and this went on until about half of the ship was out of water at an angle of about 30 degrees.[50]

Amelia 'Mildred' Brown, Second Class passenger: [We] stopped to watch her go down … It went [down] in the front until it was standing like this [here Miss Brown drew a line that was raised from the horizontal at an angle of thirty degrees] …[51]

Here we have a broad range of eyewitness accounts on the next few moments of the sinking. By this point, the ship had taken its initial plunge, the list to port had begun to flatten out, the ship's forward plunge had checked itself for a moment, and then the head-long plunge had resumed. The ship's lights, although dimming as steam pressure supplied by the boilers diminished, were still burning in all areas of the ship not already under water.

The plunge created a large wave which washed aft with significant momentum, picking Gracie up and depositing him on the roof near the base of the second funnel. His exact location is a little unclear, as he also speaks of landing on the roof of the Officers' Quarters. However, as he mentioned that the rail of the Boat Deck was then nearby, and also that he was just a little aft of the expansion joint, he may initially have been as far forward as the deck just forward of the Entrance deckhouse. His careful mention of landing on the roof 'near the base of the second funnel' seems to indicate that he landed as far aft as the roof of the First Class Gymnasium or Entrance, rather than on the roof of the Officers' Quarters themselves. Some room for interpretation in his location should be allowed for, however.

The Collapse of the Forward Funnels

It was during this plunge that mention is made of the forward two funnels falling. At this point, the question naturally arises: what caused these two funnels to fall? Lightoller wrote in his autobiography that in those moments, the 'terrific strain of bringing the after-end of that huge hull clear out of the water, caused the expansion joint abaft No. 1 funnel to open up. … The fact that the two wire stays to this funnel, on the after-part, led over and abaft the expansion joint, threw on them an extraordinary strain, eventually carrying away the port wire guy, to be followed almost immediately by the starboard one'.[52] Indeed, today on the sea floor, the ship's forward expansion joint has been opened, initially leading to suspicions that what Lightoller described might have been what actually happened.

However, several things might suggest otherwise. First of all, Lightoller did not mention the expansion joint at all in his testimony at either inquiry; his only mention of it was years later. While not definite evidence *against* his statement, there is very little to support it. No other eyewitnesses, as far as we can ascertain, mentioned any such opening of the expansion joint. Again, while not proof that it didn't happen, a single account given over twenty years after the fact is a rather thin place to start. As far as the wide open condition of the expansion joint on the wreck, we know that the bow section suffered tremendous damage upon impact with the sea floor. Plowing into the mud at an angle of forward trim, when the prow came to rest, the rest of the ship still carried momentum forward and downward. There is actually some visible evidence that the deckhouses on the Boat Deck, on either side of the expansion joint, probably came together at the top, causing some damage, before the joint re-opened to its current condition. The picture painted is that when the bow suddenly stopped, the physics created a stubbed-toe effect. This caused the superstructure aft of the expansion joint to continue moving, until the two segments of superstructure slammed together. With the forward motion dissipated, the unsupported aft end of the bow then began to bend downward. As the lower hull bent until the double bottom came to rest on the sea floor, this process also separated the two portions of the superstructure resting upon the hull, until the two segments ended up as we see them today.

Additionally, there is excellent reason to believe that the guy wires which stretched aft from the No. 1 funnel were not even under any form of extreme tension at the time the funnel collapsed. The funnels were raked at about an 80° angle from horizontal (or about 10° astern of vertical) when the ship was sitting flat on the water. At the time that the base of the No. 1 funnel was submerging, the ship's forward trim would have been something like 14°. In other words, the funnels would only have been tipped forward from complete vertical by about 4°. During *Olympic*'s career, at no point did her funnels ever threaten to dismount, no matter how strong the storm, no matter what the trim or roll, so it is hard to imagine this angle alone causing the funnels to dismount and collapse. Also suggestive of the concept that the ship's forward trim had little to do with the collapse is that while the forward two funnels were collapsing, the after funnels stayed firmly in place through that moment of the sinking; they remained in place until after the lights went out. If aft funnels could stand at an even greater angle without difficulty, then there is little reason to believe that the loss of two guy wires on the forward funnel at a point when it was nearly perfectly balanced in a vertical position would have caused it to simply tear loose and come crashing down toward the sea. Obviously, Lightoller's latter-day 'expansion joint theory' for the collapse of the forward funnel is wanting as a plausible explanation.

Another, and far more likely explanation, was actually given by Harland & Wolff's Edward Wilding. At the British Inquiry, he listened to much of the survivor evidence given, taking careful note of testimony that had a bearing on technical matters. When called to the stand, he was asked what might have accounted for the funnels' collapse. He replied:

> The funnels are carried from the casings in the way of the comparatively light upper decks – that is, the boat deck and A deck. When these decks became submerged and the water got inside the house, the water would rise outside much faster than inside, and the excessive pressure on the comparatively light casings which are not made to take a pressure of that kind would cause the casing to collapse; would take the seating from under the funnel and bring the funnel down.[53]

Looking at the remains of the base of the No. 1 funnel on the wreck, there do seem to be signs in the tattered remnants of shredded metal which support Wilding's conclusions. In short, the structural failure of the forward funnel likely had little to do with a parting of guy wires. Indeed, it is more likely that it was the collapse of the funnel that caused the guy wires to part, rather than the reverse. Most likely, the collapse began on the starboard side of the funnel, which is what caused it to swing slightly to starboard of the ship's centerline as it came down.

When the No. 2 funnel began to slide under the surface, the ship would most likely have already been approaching a 20° angle. Very shortly thereafter, it collapsed in a similar way that the collapse of the No. 1 funnel had played out. Of note, its failure transpired even though none of its guy wires were stretched across the forward expansion joint, adding further evidence to the concept that the guy wires of the funnels parted as a result of their collapse, and not *vice versa*. It seems likely that although the ship's downward angle had increased somewhat from the point when the No. 1 funnel fell, the collapse of the No. 2 funnel – witnessed so clearly by Thayer – likely had to do with a similar reason to that which caused the No. 1 funnel to fall, namely water pressure as the casing flooded. This is particularly true since the Nos 3 and 4 funnels continued to remain standing even after both forward funnels had collapsed. The only factor present at both forward funnels – a factor that was also then absent at the after funnels – was the flooding and movement of water around them. Only this difference could explain why both forward funnels failed as their bases submerged, while the after funnels stayed with the ship as the downward plunge progressed to an even greater angle.

The Downward Plunge Continues

It is at this point that we come upon an oft-debated question regarding the breakup: what angle did the ship reach before she broke? This is a tremendously thorny question. Fortunately, a lot of detail was provided by the witnesses quoted in this appendix. They were located in a variety of vantage points and at varying distances, and they all said that the stern of the ship was well clear of the water before the lights went out. How 'well clear'?

Lookout George Symons was in Boat No. 1, which was launched at 1:05 a.m. The boat rowed out some distance from the ship's side, and then they paused. He compared her position in that moment with her position after she took her plunge toward the bow. Referring to the earlier condition, he said that one could 'just see the propellers', but that one 'could not see her keel'. This would seem to place his observation at roughly 1:30 a.m. or perhaps a little later. When the ship took her plunge, however, he said that 'her stern came well out of the water then'. The difference between the two positions was obviously quite a large one.

Other witnesses used phrases like 'her stern stuck up high', 'the stern [was] vertically upwards', 'the propeller and everything was quite clear', that she 'almost stood up perpendicular', and that both the propellers and the rudder were 'clear out of the water'. Another said that the stern 'was right up in the air. You could see her propeller right clear, and you could see underneath the keel; you could see part of her keel'. Alfred Crawford said that while the lights were still on, the ship 'seemed all clear right from amidships to aft'.

However, such statements do not necessarily give us a precise picture. Even at an angle as shallow as 11°, which was about the ship's position as the ship took her 'slight but definite plunge' and the bow was swamped, the propellers would all have been clear out of the water, and at least a portion of the keel and double bottom would have been visible.

Further details are badly needed, and they are quickly found. Colonel Gracie, who was pulled under water in the vicinity of the roof over the Officers' Quarters/First Class Entrance – or possibly as far aft as the Gymnasium – resurfaced only after the ship had completely sunk. He was apparently submerged when the ship was attaining an angle of about 16–19° – a range, it should be reiterated, that would depend entirely on how far aft the wave had washed him before depositing him. As a direct observation, he said: 'From my personal viewpoint I also know that the *Titanic*'s decks were intact at the time she sank, and when I sank with her, there was over seven-sixteenths of the ship already under water, and there was no indication then of any impending break of the deck or ship.'[54] So this would seem to be our minimum range for the angle that the ship attained before breaking up.

At the opposite end of the spectrum, we have the evidence of Lightoller. When asked if the stern 'must have been very well up in the air' at that point, he agreed. He said that the angle was then steep enough to have submerged or nearly submerged the second funnel while leaving most, or all, of the third funnel clear out of the water; although by that point the second funnel had already fallen, this means that Lightoller must have thought the angle consid-

erable. More specifically, he clearly stated that the ship had 'reached an angle of 50 or 60 degrees, or something about that' *before* the 'rumbling sound' which we know was an audible symptom of the failure of the ship's hull.[55] This would seem to be the highest-end of the angle estimates.

Yet Lightoller might not have been in the best location to estimate her angle at that moment. Even so, a number of others gave further – and highly specific – information on the point. Peuchen said that while the 'lights were burning, I saw her bow pointing down and the stern up; not in a perpendicular position, but considerable … I should think an angle of not as much as 45°'. Amelia 'Mildred' Brown indicated with gestures an angle of 30°. Elmer Taylor gave an unbelievably detailed account, and said that as the bow settled, 'the stern was lifted in midair' until 'about half of the ship was out of water at an angle of about 30 degrees'.

Survivors were thus all quite clear that the ship's stern rose to a significant angle. We are left with a rather broad range of angles to consider – from a minimum of about 16° up to a maximum less than 45°. What are we, at this remove, to make of this? First of all, visual estimation of angles and trim is highly subjective. When viewing the ship as a three-dimensional object in the water, the first thing that needs to be realized is that the portion above water was not continuous in shape. While the Promenade and Boat Decks were clearly box-shaped, the bottom of the ship astern of the bilge keels narrowed toward a point at the rudder. If some witnesses used the bottom of the ship, rather than the top, to estimate the ship's forward trim prior to the break, this may have exaggerated the angle to a certain extent. Perspective – the tendency for three-dimensional objects to disappear to a common vanishing point as they recede into the distance – should also be taken into account. Thus, if the ship's stern was farther away from the viewer then the bow and midship areas – such as the case with Lightoller, who was very close to the ship and literally floating over her forward portions – this could also have exaggerated the perception of angle.

However, one can not wholly discount perception of angle, either. Simultaneously, descriptions of what portions of the ship were above water and what places were thought to be below water are also helpful in resolving these various perceptions. Knowing the precise point at which the ship was pivoting throughout the sinking, and combining this into the mix is also helpful.

A 20° trim would have just barely covered the entire base of the No. 2 funnel, while a 25° trim would have submerged the funnel to roughly half its height above the deck. Something between the two angles, then, would certainly have brought the No. 2 funnel low enough in the water to allow the process that Wilding suggested to play out, causing it to fall and narrowly miss Jack Thayer. However, a 30° forward trim would have produced a position in the water even more similar to what Lightoller outlined, particularly if he had somehow missed the collapse of the No. 2 funnel and only thought that it was then completely submerged, while the No. 3 funnel was still above the water. A 30° angle would also be very much in harmony with the impressions conveyed by Amelia Brown, Elmer Taylor, and Major Peuchen. An angle of about 25–30° would also harmonize with Crawford's statement that the ship 'seemed all clear right from midships to aft' at that time. So far, survivor consensus – while initially seeming disparate – is actually relatively consistent.

Forensically speaking: at what point would the stresses upon the ship's structure have been the greatest? Interestingly, the stresses imposed on the ship's form – by lifting the stern section of the vessel out of the water – would have risen to their highest peak at about the time that the ship attained a forward trim of 15°. As the ship's trim increased from that point, the stresses would actually have decreased slightly but with a gradually-steepening curve until they were virtually nonexistent at a wholly perpendicular 90° angle. Had the ship remained intact up to a completely 90° angle, the weight of her stern would have been well-balanced, with its weight bearing directly down on the flooded bow.

Looking simply at the stresses imposed on the ship's form, a forward trim of 15° would seem to be the point at which the hull would naturally have succumbed and her structure failed. Some have thus suggested that the break occurred at just such a shallow angle. However, as we have seen, the angles necessary to submerge the ship enough to even remotely match statements by Lightoller, Amelia Brown, Elmer Taylor, Major Peuchen and others would seem to indicate a higher-angle break. So how can these two disparate lines of research – survivor recollections and forensic stress calculations – be reconciled logically?

One of the survivors may hold the key to the entire thing. Chief Baker Charles Joughin recalled:

> I went to the deck Pantry [almost certainly the Lounge Deck pantry, in the vicinity of the No. 3 funnel on A Deck], and while I was in there I thought I would take a drink of water, and while I was getting the drink of water I heard a kind of crash as if something had buckled, as if part of the ship had buckled, and then I heard a rush [of people] overhead [on the Boat Deck] … It was not an explosion or anything like that. It was like as if the iron was parting.[56]

The 'rush' that Joughin referred to 'overhead on the deck'[57] may be the same one referred to by Gracie:

> Clinch Smith made the proposition that we should leave and go toward the stern, still on the starboard side, so he started and I followed immediately after him. We had taken but a few steps in the direction indicated when there arose before us from the decks below, a mass of humanity several lines deep, covering the Boat Deck, facing us, and completely blocking our passage toward the stern.
> There were women in the crowd, as well as men, and they seemed to be steerage passengers who had just come up from the decks below. Instantly, when they saw us and the water on the deck chasing us from behind, they turned in the opposite direction towards the stern. This brought them at that point plumb against the iron fence and railing which divide the first and second cabin passengers…[58]

Gracie's description of the crowd being halted in their aft progress by a railing dividing the First and Second Class passengers is a little misleading, although certainly unintentionally. There actually was no railing directly separating First and Second Class portions of the Boat Deck on the starboard side. Instead, there was a short stretch of Boat Deck set aside specifically as an Engineers' Promenade between the First and Second Class decks, just astern of the No. 3 funnel. What Gracie was most likely referring to, then, was the railing separating the First Class Boat Deck from the Engineers' Promenade portion of the Boat Deck; if this conclusion is correct, then the pile of passengers scrambling to get aft would have been located almost directly above Joughin in the A Deck Lounge Pantry. It was a very short time, perhaps only a few seconds, after this that the bow made its first plunge to the depths, at about 2:15 a.m.

Thus, the noise that Joughin was referring to – 'a kind of crash as if … part of the ship had buckled … as if iron was parting' – happened at about the same time that the ship made her plunge by the bow. In other words, that sound apparently occurred when the ship was still at rather a shallow angle of forward trim. What exactly produced this sound we will probably never know with certainty. Steel structures under stress do tend to produce unusual groans and other noises; it could thus be that the sound Joughin heard was not a significant failure within the vessel's hull, and that it sounded more serious to him than it really was. However, one has to allow for the possibility that the sound was produced by the same failure in the ship's structure that led to her 'slight but definite plunge'. It is also possible that it was an early sign of the process leading to the ship's eventual breakup.

The history of structural failures shows us that if a certain load-bearing element of a structure gives way, the redundant strength in other portions of that structure will take up the load if it is strong enough to do so without failing itself. A case in point would be the structural failure of the World Trade Center towers on September 11, 2001. Although a number of load-bearing portions of the towers' structures were compromised upon initial impact from the airliners, the remaining portions of the structure took up the strain. In the end, the remaining strength of the structure was compromised by the heat from the ensuing fire. The final structural failures of each tower, the result of an ongoing and irreversible process, were sudden and quite visible.

In the same manner, it seems more than likely that certain elements within the *Titanic*'s hull were beginning to give way as the ship's bow took its plunge. These failures, while invisible to anyone on the decks or in the lifeboats, began an irreversible cascade effect. As the ship's stern continued swinging higher out of the water, other elements of the ship's hull began to take up that strain. Their load may have been temporarily aided by the fact that the stresses were beginning to diminish as the angle of the stern's ascent increased past 15°, when forensic calculations suggest that the stresses had peaked. There may even have been a number of internal structural failures coming one after another in a domino-like fashion, while remaining portions of the hull took up the strain.

As this process played out, there could have been enough time for the ship to attain a greater angle of forward trim than that which forensic calculation alone would suggest – one that would more closely match eyewitness testimony. If correct, it would appear that eventually a point was reached where so much of the ship's structural strength had been compromised that she simply could not hold herself together any longer. Another possibility is that as the ship's weight shifted in the water with her stern rearing up, the strain began to increase on a slightly different, and possibly slightly weaker, portion of her structure that simply could not take the load.

In short, viewing the breakup as an ongoing process which may have extended through two or more minutes (the time from when the bow plunged deeper into the sea through the time of the visible breakup at the time the primary lights failed), the survivor evidence and forensic stress calculations would actually seem to go hand in hand rather than being wholly contradictory. To completely ignore the main body of eyewitness accounts is a mistake that, it should be remembered, was made once before by *Titanic* researchers – and that mistake swayed popular opinion in an incorrect direction for nearly three-quarters of a century.

This having been said, it is doubtless that further evidence – forensic and otherwise – on the point will be brought up, debated, and theorized over for years or decades to come. While we are not prepared to set ourselves up as giving some sort of 'final word' on this subject, we do feel that this wide-angle perspective of aggregate evidence from a variety of survivor and forensic sources suggests that the outward and visible break transpired when the ship had arrived at roughly a 30° angle of forward trim, give or take a little.

The Breakup

What happened next was positively astounding to all of those who witnessed the event. The spectacular and highly prominent failure of the ship's structure, which appears to have occurred at about 2:17 a.m., was merely the *grande finale* of an ongoing process. Let us resume with the survivor evidence to let them tell us exactly what happened next.

Lawrence Beesley, Second Class passenger: She slowly tilted straight on end with the stern vertically upwards, and as she did, the lights in the cabins and saloons which had not flickered for a moment since we left, died out, came on again for a single flash, and finally went out altogether. At the same time the machinery roared down through the vessel with a rattle and a groaning that could be heard for miles …[59] It was partly a roar, partly a groan, partly a rattle, and partly a smash, and it was not a sudden roar as an explosion would be: it went on successively for some seconds, possibly fifteen to twenty … [it] was stupefying, stupendous … It was as if all the heavy things one could think of had been thrown downstairs from the top of a house, smashing each other and the stairs and everything in the way.[60]

C. E. Henry Stengel, First Class passenger: … [All] of a sudden there were four sharp explosions … and then she dipped and the stern stood up in the air. … I should judge it would be a battery of boilers going. …; they were quite hard explosions. She dipped, then, forward, and all you could see was the stern sticking up.[61]

Hugh Woolner, First Class passenger: Lights were burning and she settled forward still further, then stopped for about thirty seconds. Suddenly with a terrific roar, like thousands of tons of rocks rumbling down a metal chute, she plunged bodily down, head first. Every light went out and the roaring went on for about a minute.[62]

Lady Lucy Duff Gordon: I turned and saw the remaining lights of the *Titanic* burning with steady brilliance, but only for a moment and they were gone. A dull explosion shook the air. From the doomed vessel there arose an indescribable clamor. A louder explosion followed and the stern of the great ship shot out of the water. For a few seconds she stayed motionless while agonized cries from her decks grew in intensity. Then, with one downward rush, she plunged to her grave and the air was rent with awful shrieks.[63]

Helen Ostby, First Class passenger: As the ship began to stand on end, we heard a big rumbling, rattling noise as if everything was being torn from its moorings inside the ship. All of a sudden that stopped, and she stood on end very quietly for a minute, then went down like an arrow.[64]

Martha Stephenson, First Class passenger: The lights on the ship burned till just before she went. When the call came that she was going I covered my face and then heard someone call, 'She's broken.' After what seemed a long time I turned my head only to see the stern almost perpendicular in the air so that the full outline of the blades of the propeller showed above the water. She then gave her final plunge…[65]

Lily Potter, First Class passenger: After the lights went out, some ten minutes before the end, she was like some great living thing who made a last superhuman effort to right herself and then, failing, dove bow forward to the unfathomable depths below.[66]

George Rheims, First Class passenger: She went down straight; I saw the screws out of the water in the air; she went down perfectly straight; put her nose in the water.[67]

Henry Harper, First Class passenger: [The] lights of the *Titanic* suddenly went out and we began to think her end could not be very far away. I have heard a lot of talk about explosions in the *Titanic*; that her boilers blew up and tore her body apart. I certainly heard nothing that sounded like an explosion. I did hear a great roar mingled with hissing coming from the direction of the ship. … Very slowly the giant black hull began to diminish against the skyline. It was a frightful thing to feel that the ship was going, faster and faster, and that we could do nothing for the people on her…[68]

John Podesta, Fireman: … [*Titanic's*] stern rose up in the air. Out went all her lights and the rumbling noise was terrible. It must have been her boilers and engines as well as her bulkheads, all giving way. Then she disappeared altogether.[69]

Archie Jewell, Lookout: As she went away by the head so the lights went out, and we heard some explosions as she was going down. But all the lights went out and we could only see a black object in front of us. … As the stern stood up in the air so all the lights went out.[70]

William Sloper, First Class passenger: Suddenly the lights dimmed … in a minute the lights went out entirely and then the stern seemed to rise perpendicularly in the air. There were two loud explosions, a grinding crash and the big ship plunged out of sight.[71]

William Ward, Saloon Steward: She gave a kind of sudden lurch forward, and I heard a couple of reports, reports more like a volley of musketry than anything else. You would not call them a heavy explosion. It did not seem to me like an explosion at all.[72]

Susan Webber, Second Class passenger: We couldn't hear the explosion when it came, but the boat was torn apart near the middle.[73]

Emily Badman, Third Class passenger: We had gone about a mile when there were two big explosions and the *Titanic* split in two. The front end went down at once and the back stood up so that it was almost straight and then went out of sight.[74]

Lillian Bentham, Second Class passenger: We had just moved a few yards from the giant ship when she was broken by the explosion of her boilers and sank in two sections.[75]

Kate Buss, Second Class passenger: It was a grand sight at sea, and with every light she was a picture. She parted right in halves, the forward part went down first, and the aft seemed to stand upright. There was a terrific explosion.[76]

Major Arthur Peuchen, First Class passenger: We heard a sort of a rumbling sound and the lights were still on at the rumbling sound, as far as my memory serves me; then a sort of an explosion, then another. It seemed to be one, two, or three rumbling sounds, then the lights went out. ... I saw it when the lights went out. You could not tell very much after the lights went out. ... I could only see the outline of the boat, you might say. ... It was intact at that time ... I heard the explosions ... [it was] a sort of rumbling sound. It was not a sharp sound – more of a rumbling kind of a sound, but still sharp at the same time. It would not be as loud as a clap of thunder, or anything that way, or like a boiler explosion, I should not think. ... I imagined that the decks had blown up with the pressure, pulling the boat down, bow on, this heavyweight, and the air between the decks; that is my theory of the explosion. I do not know whether it is correct or not, but I do not think it was the boilers. I think it was the pressure, that heavy weight shoving that down, the water rushing up, and the air coming between the decks; something had to go.[77]

Kornelia Andrews, First Class passenger: We watched the ship go down. At last came a mighty crash, the boilers had exploded, and then in a moment the ship seemed to break in pieces or rather in half; the bow going down first and then all the lights went out and in a short time nothing more was to be seen ...[78]

Laura Cribb, Third Class passenger: ... suddenly the lights of the ship went out. Immediately there was a terrific explosion mingled with the shrieks and moans from the helpless and doomed passengers who were left on the wreck of the great ship. The explosion caused the ship to split in half, the stern straight up in the air, and then it sank rapidly.[79]

Nellie Becker, Second Class passenger: She seemed to break right in the middle, and the middle to fall in. It was terrible beyond words. I shall never forget that sound.[80]

Ruth Becker, Second Class passenger: We could see the port lights go under one by one until there was an awful explosion of the boilers bursting. And then the ship seemed to break right down the middle ... and after a bit, go down.[81]

Charlotte Collyer, Second Class passenger: The end ... came with a deafening roar that stunned me. Something in the very bowels of the *Titanic* exploded, and millions of sparks shot up to the sky, like rockets in a park on the night of a summer holiday. This red spurt was fan-shaped as it went up, but the sparks descended in every direction in the shape of a fountain of fire. Two other explosions followed, dull and heavy, as if below the surface. The *Titanic* broke in two before my eyes. The fore part was already partly under the water. It wallowed over and disappeared instantly. The stern reared straight on end and poised on the ocean for many seconds – they seemed minutes to me.

It was only then that the electric lights on board went out ... I turned my face away, but looked around the next instant and saw the second half of the great boat slip below the surface as casually as a pebble in a pond.[82]

Charles Dahl, Third Class passenger: By this time the water was up to the bridge of the doomed vessel. The bow settled long before the stern. Suddenly we heard an explosion, and in about two minutes a second followed.

All the lights then went out. She seemed to break in two. The stern went down. There was no trouble for us to see it. There seemed to be a black cloud come up as the head went down. There were terrible noises as of the crushing of timber.[83]

Washington Dodge, First Class passenger: Suddenly, while I was looking at the dark outline of the steamer, I saw her stern rise high from the water, and then the vessel was seen to completely disappear from sight with startling rapidity. A series of loud explosions, three or four in number, were then heard, due, as we all believed, to bursting boilers ... My idea is, that when the stern of the ship was lifted high out of the water by the bursting of the water-tight compartments, in the forward end of the vessel, that the vast weight of the machinery caused the framework and the plates of the ship to give way, thus allowing the great inrush of waters to complete her destruction.[84]

Frank Dymond, Fireman: The *Titanic* broke in two, and her boilers blew up. The sound of the machinery as it ran out of her was plainly heard when she went down.[85]

Esther Hart, Second Class passenger: The front portion of her was pointing downwards and she appeared to be breaking in halves. Then with a mighty and tearing sob, as of some gigantic thing instinct with life, the front portion of her dived, for that is the only word I can use properly to describe it, dived into the sea, and the after part with a heavy list, also disappeared. ... For a few moments we could see everything that was happening, for, as the vessel sank, millions and millions of sparks flew up and lit everything around us.[86]

Bertha Lehmann, Second Class passenger: All at once there were three loud reports, they sounded like a very loud crash of thunder when it strikes very close to you. We all looked at the *Titanic*. It had broken apart! The front part of the boat went under first. The helm of the front half sank and then the middle.[87]

William Mellors, Second Class passenger: ... [She] was going under water and it seemed as if thousands of men were dragging me under with her... There was suddenly an explosion and I found myself whizzing through the water at an awful pace, having been blown away by the explosion. When I came to my senses a few minutes after I looked round and suddenly saw the ship part in the middle with the stern standing several hundred feet out of the water ...[88]

Walter Nichols, Saloon Steward: The ship sank slowly and steadily and then we heard a little explosion that must have been the first boiler. After that the lights began to go out in different parts of the ship. Then came a big explosion. We could see a mass of black smoke. The boat seemed to lift right up out of the water and tilt up on end, and then seemed to break and drop back. For one moment she was right up in the air standing on her nose. ... There was no other sound – just the crying of the people.[89]

Emily Ryerson, First Class passenger: [The] two forward funnels seemed to lean and then she seemed to break in half as if cut with a knife, and as the bow went under the lights went out; the stern stood up for several minutes, black against the stars, and then that, too plunged down ...[90]

Joseph Scarrott, AB: When the third funnel had nearly disappeared I heard four explosions, which I took to be the bursting of the boilers. The ship was right up on end then.

Suddenly she broke in two between the third and fourth funnel. The after part of the ship came down on the water in its normal position and seemed as if it was going to remain afloat, but it only remained a minute or two and then sank. The lights were burning right up till she broke in two.[91]

* * * * *

... you could hear the breaking up of things in the ship, and then followed four explosions.[92]

Eugene Daly, Third Class passenger: Her stern stuck up high. I thought she would fall on us as she seemed to be swinging around, but she did not.[93]

John Thayer, Jr., First Class passenger:[94] I saw the ship in a sort of red glare, and it seemed to me that she broke in two just in front of the third funnel ... At this time I was sucked down, and as I came up I was pushed out again and twisted around by a large wave. When I got on [an overturned life boat] I was facing the ship. The stern then seemed to rise in the air and stopped at about an angle of 60 degrees. It seemed to hold there for a time and then with a hissing sound it shot right down out of sight with people jumping from the stern. The stern either pivoted around towards our boat, or we were sucked toward it ...[95]

* * * * *

The *Titanic* seemed to hang and with the roar of boilers and engines breaking loose in the hold slipping to the forward part of the ship the stern bulkheads held and the ship, pivoting and moving in an almost perpendicular position, was sticking up in the air almost 300 feet.

The ship then corkscrewed around so that the propeller, rudder and all seemed to go right over the heads of us on the upturned boat. Of course the lights now were all out. The ship seemed to hang in this position for minutes. Then with a dive and final plunge, the *Titanic* went under the water with very little apparent suction or noise.[96]

* * * * *

The water was over the base of the first funnel ... Suddenly the whole superstructure of the ship appeared to split, well forward to midships, and bow or buckle upwards. The second funnel ... seemed to be lifted off, emitting a cloud of sparks ... There was the gigantic mass, about fifty or sixty yards away. The forward motion had stopped. She was pivoting on a point just abaft of midship. Her stern was gradually rising into the air, seemingly in no hurry, just slowly and deliberately...

[The] great after part of the ship, two hundred and fifty feet of it, rose into the sky, till it reached a sixty-five or seventy degree angle. Here it seemed to pause and just hung, for what felt like minutes. Gradually she turned her deck away from us ... Then, with the deadened noise of the bursting of her last few gallant bulkheads, she slid quietly away from us into the sea.[97]

George Symons, Lookout: She took a heavy cant and her bow went down clear ... Head down, and that is the time when I saw her lights go out, all her lights. The next thing I saw was her poop. As she went down like that so her poop righted itself and I thought to myself, 'The poop is going to float.' It could not have been more than two or three minutes after that that her poop went up as straight as anything; there was a sound like steady thunder as you hear on an ordinary night at a distance, and soon she disappeared from view ...

... Her head was going well down ... her stern was well out of the water ... It righted itself without the bow; in my estimation she must have broken in half. I should think myself it was abaft the after expansion plate ... about abeam of the after funnel, or a little forward. ... I saw the poop right itself ... then it went up and disappeared from view.[98]

John Poingdestre, AB: I thought when I looked that the ship broke at the foremost funnel ... [because] I had seen that part disappear. ... She was short; the afterpart righted itself after the foremost part had disappeared. ... It uprighted itself, as if nothing had happened ... straight on the water again ... [The afterpart did not float on the water for] above a couple of minutes.[99]

Thomas Dillon, Trimmer: [*Titanic*] took one final plunge and righted herself again ... [before] I left the ship. [*Authors' note:* Dillon was then on the Poop Deck.] ... [The aftermost] funnel seemed to cant up towards me ...; it seemed to fall up this way.[100]

Frederick Scott, Greaser: [Lifeboat No. 4] had just got at the stern of her when she started breaking up ...; she broke off at the after-funnel, and when she broke off her stern end came up in the air and came down on a level keel and disappeared. ... [She broke at] the after-funnel. From the after-funnel to the stern of her… just aft of the last funnel.[101]

Charles Lightoller, Second Officer: After she reached an angle of 50 or 60 degrees, or something about that, there was this rumbling sound, which I attributed to the boilers leaving their beds and crushing down on or through the bulkheads. The ship at that time was becoming more perpendicular, until finally she attained the absolute perpendicular … and then went slowly down. She went down very slowly until the end, and then, after she got [to] … the afterpart of the second cabin deck, she, of course, went down much quicker.[102]

* * * * *

The fore part, and up to the second funnel was by this time completely submerged, and as we watched this terribly awe-inspiring sight, suddenly all the lights went out and the huge bulk was left in black darkness, but clearly silhouetted against the bright sky. Then, the next moment, the massive boilers left their beds and went thundering down with a hollow rumbling roar, through the bulkheads, carrying everything with them that stood in their way. … [The] ship slowly but surely reared herself on end and brought rudder and propellers clear of the water, till, at last, she assumed *an absolute perpendicular position.* In this amazing attitude she remained for the space of half a minute. Then with impressive majesty and ever-increasing momentum she silently took her last tragic dive …[103]

Frank Osman, AB: After she got to a certain angle she exploded, broke in halves, and it seemed to me as if all the engines and everything that was in the after part slid out into the forward part, and the after part came right up again, and as soon as it came up right down it went again.[104]

George Crowe, Saloon Steward: … [She] almost stood up perpendicular, and her lights went dim, and presently she broke clean in two, probably two-thirds of the length of the ship. … Two-thirds in the water, one-third of the aft funnel sticking up. … She broke, and the after part floated back. … [The] bow part, two-thirds of the ship, sank. … [Then] there was an explosion, and the aft part turned on end and sank. … There were several explosions. … A kind of muffled explosion. It seemed to be an explosion at a very great distance, although we were not very far away.[105]

John Collins, Scullion: Just as I came up to the surface… Her bow was in the water. She had not exploded then. Her bow was in the water, and I just looked around and saw the lights. … She exploded once in the water, and her stern end was up out of the water; and with the explosion out of the water it blew her stern up. … I am sure it floated for at least a minute. … [The] lights was [sic] out.[106]

Frederick Clench, AB: I heard two explosions … [Before] the ship had sunk there was one explosion … I should say a matter of 10 minutes before she went under. … The lights went out after the second explosion. Then she gradually sank down into the water very slowly.[107]

Arthur Bright, QM: She broke in two. All at once she seemed to go up on end, you know, and come down about half way, and then the afterpart righted, [sic, spurious comma] itself again and the forepart had disappeared. A few seconds the after part did the same thing and went down. I could distinctly see the propellers – everything – out of the water. … I heard something, but I would not call it an explosion. It was like a rattling of chain, more than anything else. … [When asked to confirm that the ship went down by her bow first, and that he could see the stern and the keel on the stern, Bright responded in the affirmative, then added:] Then that righted itself again, got on an even keel again after that. … It settled down in the water on an even keel. [When asked if he saw any lights on the stern after she settled, he responded in the affirmative:] … until she finally disappeared underneath the water. … [She broke] as near the middle as anything, I should say; but it was dark.[108]

May Futrelle, First Class passenger: [All of] a sudden the lights snapped out. There was a terrible creaking noise, the *Titanic* seemed to break in two. There was a tremendous explosion.

For a fraction of a second she arose in the air and was plainly visible in the light caused from the blowing up of the boilers …[109]

* * * * *

She began to settle by the nose. Then came two dull explosions. We saw her break in two. The bow, which had been pointing downward, dipped, turned up again, writhed and sank with the stern – exactly as though one had stepped on a worm.[110]

Ida Hippach, First Class passenger: When we had rowed about 150 yards away from the *Titanic* we heard a fearful explosion. I saw the ship split open. At the same time the ship's bow rose up in the air as the steamer sank towards the center.[111]

Edward Buley, AB: She went down as far as the afterfunnel, and then there was a little roar, as though the engines had rushed forward, and she snapped in two, and the bow part went down and the afterpart came up and staid up five minutes before it went down. … [We] could see the afterpart afloat, and there was no forepart to it. I think she must have parted where the bunkers were. She parted at the last, because the afterpart of her settled out of the water horizontally after the other part went down. First of all you could see her propellers and everything. Her rudder was clear out of the water. You could hear the rush of machinery, and she parted in two, and the afterpart settled down again, and we thought the afterpart would float altogether. … She uprighted herself for about five minutes, and then tipped over and disappeared. … [The afterpart] went down headforemost. … You could see she went in two, because we were quite near to her and could see her quite plainly. … The lights were all out.[112]

Frank Evans, AB: You could see her when the lights were clear, and then until she gave the final plunge. … She parted between the third and fourth funnels … The foremost part was gone, and it seemed as if the engines were all gone out. [When asked if the stern 'came up and was horizontal with the surface of the water' after the break, Evans replied in the affirmative.] ... From the after funnel to the ensign mast [came up]. ... I should say about 200 feet was afloat; that is, of the stern part. ... You could see that in the outline. Then she made a sudden plunge [forward], and the stern went right up.[113]

Alexander Littlejohn, Saloon Steward: Her stern went right up in the air. There were two or three explosions and it appeared ... that the stern part came down and righted itself.[114]

Harold Lowe, Fifth Officer: She went down head first and inclined at an angle. That is, when she took her final plunge she was inclined at an angle of about 75°. ... Pretty well [perpendicular]. ... I heard explosions ... I should say about four.[115]

Thomas Whiteley, Saloon Steward: When I got the rope on my leg off I came to the top, made for some wreckage which I hung on to, just in time to see the *Titanic* blow her sides away. She broke in the middle, her forward end went down. The after end righted itself, went right up into the air and disappeared.[116]

Carrie Chaffee, First Class passenger: Just before going down it seemed to writhe, breaking into three parts into which it was divided. First the middle seemed to go down, lifting the bow and stern into the air. Then it twisted the other way, throwing the middle up. Finally the bow went under, and it plunged, stern last.[117]

Elmer Taylor, First Class passenger: Instead of all the inside fittings of the ship breaking loose from their moorings, the excessive weight of the stern dangled in mid-air, broke the back of the ship at one of the expansion joints.

The crashing sound, quite audible a quarter of a mile away, was due, in my opinion, to tearing the ship's plates apart, or that part of the hull below the expansion joints, thus breaking the back at a point almost mid-way the length of the ship, or about through the Music Room.[118]

Thomas Ranger, Greaser: The forward end of the ship went underneath and seemed to break off, and the afterpart came back on a level keel. ... [Then it] turned up and went down steadily. ... She just slowly turned up and went down. You could see the propellers in the air.[119] ... The lights gradually went out as the aft end of the ship went under.

[Asked if when he had come up on deck the only portion lighted was the stern, Ranger responded, 'Yes.' When asked if, when the forward end of the boat had broken off, the after end had 'come back suddenly or slowly on to a level keel', Ranger responded: 'She came back slowly.'[120]]

The Sounds of the Breakup

Passenger after passenger told the same, or nearly the same story: the lights burned as the ship's stern reared up higher out of the water. At almost the same exact time that the lights went out, a terrible sound began. Most of those who described the ship splitting placed the timing of that event concurrent with that of the horrible sounds and the failure of the lights. The sound was invariably described as 'explosion[s]', a 'terrific roar', a 'terrible' 'rumbling noise', a 'mighty crash', a 'deafening roar', 'reports', 'reports more like a volley of musketry', a 'sound like steady thunder ... at a distance', a 'rattling of chain', and so forth.

At the time most attributed these sounds to boilers exploding, or to all of the ship's boilers and machinery breaking loose and crashing down through the ship; a few attributed them to failures of the ship's watertight bulkheads. Some, like Peuchen and Taylor, thought that the great sound had to do with failures of the ship's hull or decks. Today, we know that none of the ship's boilers exploded. The boilers in Boiler Room No. 2 are all intact and visible at the aft end of the bow section, still in their mounts; all five single-ended boilers from Boiler Room No. 1 are in the debris field, intact. No other boilers have been found in the debris field. So this terrible noise must have been caused by the failure of the ship's hull.

Is it possible that the parting of the hull could have sounded like 'reports', 'a volley of musketry', or 'explosions'? From a broader maritime perspective, the answer would be absolutely, yes. During the 1920s, the two largest ships in the world – the *Leviathan* and the *Majestic* – both suffered significant failures of their primary hulls while they were at sea. Although both ships survived, those aboard the two vessels variously described the structural failure as sounding like a naval gun being fired, a 'cannon shot', 'a loud retort', and '[a] bang! A sharp snapping crack sound!'[121] The similarities to the descriptions of the noises during *Titanic*'s breakup are quite impressive. While there seems to have been only one sound on each of the German-built vessels, eyewitnesses who saw the *Titanic* break mentioned anywhere from one to four of these frightful noises, with the most common numerical estimate being three or four. It seems most likely that the quick series of reports had to do with the most significant failures of portions of the ship's structure.

One possible reason for the disparity in the number of reports mentioned is suggested by Charlotte Collyer's recollection. In mentioning three separate sounds, she described the first sound as being 'in the very bowels of the *Titanic*', and throwing sparks up and out in a fan shape, like a 'fountain of fire'. She described the second pair of sounds quite differently than the first, saying that they were 'dull and heavy, as if below the surface'. Concurrent with the second set of sounds, she said that the '*Titanic* broke in two before my eyes'. It thus seems likely that the first structural failure sounded louder to her ears, while still being well internal to the ship from her perspective. The other two sounds were audibly duller and sounded from below the surface.

Also noteworthy is Saloon Steward George Crowe's recollection that after the stern had 'floated back' into the water, and after the bow had sunk, then 'there was an explosion, and the aft part turned on end and sank. ... There were several explosions ... A kind of muffled explosion. It seemed to be an explosion at a very great distance, although we were not very far away'. This would seem to indicate that the final report heard by Crowe came immediately before the stern section's forward dive to a vertical or near-vertical position in the water. Also interesting is that this report apparently sounded muffled, as if at a great distance, to Crowe, a similar description to Charlotte Collyer's.

It is possible that, to some eyewitnesses, the duller sounds were either drowned out by the louder sound of the first report, or did not impress themselves as forcefully on the minds of some. Some of the reports may even have been very close together in nature, sounding more like a single report than two separate sounds. Only those with the clearest memories, the best hearing, or the best possible position in the water to hear clearly may have been able to sort through the overwhelming nature of what was happening at that time.

It is interesting to note, however, that there were three major separation points in the double bottom; a major separation – or perhaps more than one – also happened at the top and sides of the ship's hull structure. Most likely, then, the sounds described by the passengers were the sounds of the ship's main structural failures transpiring. Accompanying the large reports seems to have been an ongoing groaning, roaring, metallic clattering sound that continued throughout the hull failure and which, according to most accounts, did not continue as the stern section itself made its final vertical dive. This would tend to indicate that they, also, had to do with the structural failure of the ship.

Whatever actually caused those sounds, they must have been absolutely appalling to hear, and when combined with the ghastly human chorus of terrified people riding the ship through its final gyrations, the aural picture of utter chaos and fright is revealed in all its horror.

The Stern 'Settles Back'
A good number of the survivors quoted above also described the ship as partially righting itself, or were very clear that the stern came back down on something of an even keel, immediately after the break. How do their recollections mesh with cinematic depictions of the stern's violent collapse onto the surface of the sea? Thomas Ranger said that she 'came back on a level keel … slowly',

while others used words or phrases such as that the stern 'floated' back, 'settled down again', or 'came down'. None of these descriptions bring to mind a picture of a startling crash with a large ensuing wave. Only one, Saloon Steward Walter Nichols, used a term that could be interpreted as a violent crash, when he said that the ship 'seemed to break and *drop* [Authors' emphasis] back'. Most likely, the stern settled back at a slower pace than previously thought, perhaps due to an ongoing series of structural failures that progressively separated the two halves.

When Did the Lights Fail?
As an interesting aside, several of the witnesses seemed to indicate that at least some of the ship's lights stayed on *after* the ship broke. Foremost among these was Greaser Thomas Ranger; although he was very specific about the ship breaking up, his testimony on the lights is at odds with the general sequence:

> 4114. When you say the forward end seemed to break off, and the afterpart came back on a level keel, and then you say the lights were going out. When she came back like that on a level keel were there any lights? – Right aft. The lights were right aft what were burning, on the afterend what was floating.[122]

Elizabeth Shute also made a reference to a light in those final moments. She wrote that as the liner was 'fast, fast

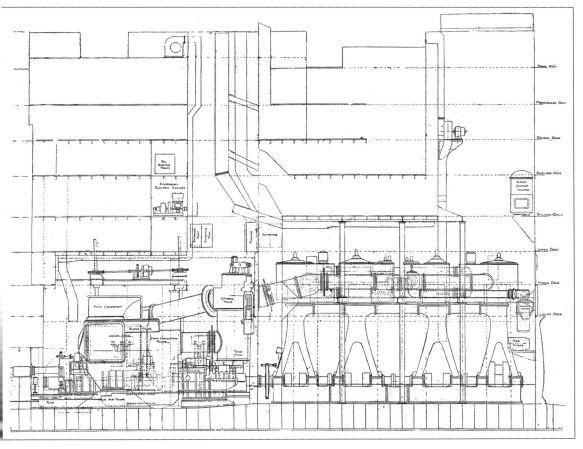

This period plan of Olympic *and* Titanic *shows the location of the emergency dynamo.*

disappearing', there was only 'one tiny light' remaining, 'a powerless little spark, a lantern attached to the mast'.[123] Quartermaster Bright said that he saw the lights still burning after the ship had broken. Frank Prentice, who was aboard the ship as she sank, said that the ship 'seemed to break in two', and that the stern, where he was, 'went way up into the air and remained in that position. ... The lights had gradually gone out, excepting one light near where I stood'.[124] August Wennerström recalled that his last sighting of the ship was 'the electric light, still burning when she was under the water'.[125] Charles Joughin also said that when he was hanging on the outside rail waiting for the ship to take her final plunge, he checked his watch, noted the time at 2:15 a.m., and then placed the watch in his back pocket. He said that even then – certainly well after the ship had broken, since the ship was about to take her final plunge – there was an electric light burning. 'The electric lights were burning right to the very last.' When asked if there was 'never a time when you were on that ship when there was not electric light where you were', he responded: 'Right to the very finish that I saw.'[126]

Thomas Ranger had said that as he was 'coming up the dummy funnel' to the deck, the 'emergency light engine was running'.[127] He was almost certainly referring to the emergency generating sets, which consisted of two 30-kilowatt dynamos located above the waterline on D Deck in the Turbine Engine Casing. Built to be fed by steam from Boiler Rooms Nos 2, 3, or 5, it seems most likely that the former boiler room was supplying the steam in those last minutes. The emergency sets, though weak by comparison to the quartet of 400-kilowatt dynamos comprising the main set, were capable of providing quite a bit of illumination. It was connected to an emergency lighting circuit that could provide limited lighting throughout the ship even if the primary electrical-generating set was inoperative; the emergency circuit could also power the Marconi set, the ship's mandatory running lights, telegraph and compass lights, and a number of other vital areas. One of the ship's primary electrical circuits supplied only the after section of the liner, and powered elements of the Docking Bridge and equipment, as well as the stern light – which was possibly the one referred to by Wennerström in his account.[128]

Interestingly, three of the six witnesses who referred to the lights burning even at this late stage were either still aboard the ship, or were swimming for their lives in the water very close to the ship. Ranger was in Boat No. 4, which was still very close to the liner as she sank. Quartermaster Bright was in Collapsible D, also not very far from the ship; of this group, only Elizabeth Shute – in Boat No. 3 – was quite a distance from the dying vessel. If the 'tiny... powerless ... lantern' she referred to was a lamp on the mainmast – optional according to Board of Trade regulations at the time – then it may have been an oil lamp, not connected to the other references of certain electrical lights operating even after the break. On the other hand, it could potentially have been another light – perhaps even the extreme aft light by the jackstaff on the Poop – that she was referring to, and she believed that it was on the mast because it was so high above the water.

It should be remembered that a majority of eyewitnesses said that the failure of the lights was catastrophic and complete, and that it happened very suddenly. However, it does seem possible that, one way or another, a 'last gasp' of electricity was supplied to the after section of the vessel even after the breakup, powering a few meager lights that the majority either did not notice, or did not refer to in their statements.

A Top-Down Break...? Or A Bottom-Up Break...?

For years, it has been generally assumed that the ship broke from the top down, giving way first at her upper decks, with the failure continuing down to her keel. This was generally what eyewitnesses seemed to have been describing. It is also a theory that seemed to make sense because at the time, the ship was under hogging stress (downward stress upon both extreme ends of the ship) rather than sagging stress (downward stress upon the center of the ship). Hogging stress would produce tension at the ship's upper section, while tending to compress her lower hull. The ship's keel and double bottom were also designed to be the strongest portions of the hull, and thus seemed least likely to be the culprit of the initial failure. Additionally, if the keel of the ship had remained inter-connected with both the bow and stern sections, it was believed that the eventual descent of the bow could have been the force which pulled the then un-flooded stern down headfirst until it was standing in the air, thus dooming the stern to follow the bow of the ship.

More recently, however, some have theorized that the ship's keel and double bottom failed first, and that only after the double bottom had failed did the upper decks begin to give way. Much of this theory has been based upon new forensic investigations and analyses of crucial pieces of physical evidence at the wreck site. In 2005 two very large segments of the Titanic's double-bottom and keel were explored and thoroughly documented by an expedition to the site. While the pieces had been discovered during previous expeditions, their importance does not seem to have been fully realized at the time.[129]

These two enormous chunks of wreckage proved to be interconnecting, full-width and intact sections of the ship's double bottom structure, with the bilge keels still connected. They also connected nearly perfectly with the aft end of the double bottom found on the bow section, and with the forward end of the double bottom on the stern section. This means that the entirety of the ship's double bottom has now been accounted for. Obviously, tremendous forces were involved in causing these two immensely strong pieces of the ship to detach from the rest of the structure and from each other.

These two segments of double bottom are not the only noteworthy forensic evidence available, however. Another large piece of the ship which has been identified and recovered is what became known as 'The Big Piece'. Although much smaller than the double-bottom portions of the ship on the sea floor, this piece is very interesting as it formed part of the ship's starboard shell plating along C and D Decks, in the vicinity of cabins C-79 and C-81 and their interconnecting bathroom. 'The big piece' was located at the top edge of the hull proper, as the floor of B Deck, just above, formed the top of the hull girder.

Not only is this directly in the area referred to by many survivors as being involved in the breakup, but the piece itself is also noteworthy, as it became detached from the rest of the vessel in a manner that could only have transpired during the breakup. As it broke free, the separation from the C Deck plates seems quite grisly; a section of the floor of C Deck, (on Frame 32 Aft, in line with the bulkhead separating stateroom C-79 from its adjoining bath room) tore away from the decking in the vicinity of the outboard edge. The beam bracket connecting the frame to the deck remained in place, and the decking beyond tore through, leaving behind a jagged and ugly edge.

Meanwhile, the steel plating of the hull plates which eventually formed 'the big piece' were also detaching from the surrounding hull plating on all sides. Most telling of all, most of the places where the plates gave way were not at the joints *between* plates, but instead were tears *right through* the plating. This is especially stunning because much of the plating in this area had been given special 'doubling' plates, tremendously increasing the thickness and strength of the hull. Whatever force had caused this 'big piece' to shred away from the other portions of those same, enormously strong hull plates had to have been profound – almost beyond imagination.

So what can survivor testimony, available physical evidence – including the double bottom segments and 'the big piece' – as well as modern forensic tools such as computer analysis all tell us about the progressive order of the ship's hull failure? Let us first turn to the survivors for a starting point and to get some idea of how the ship actually moved during those moments.

While many of those who said the ship broke were silent on what happened to the bow during and after the break, a few were very specific on the point. May Futrelle, in one account, said that when the ship broke in two, the bow, 'which had been pointing downward, dipped, turned up again, writhed and sank with the stern, exactly as though one had stepped on a worm'. Ida Hippach said that she 'saw the ship split open. At the same time the ship's bow rose up in the air as the steamer sank towards the center'. Carrie Chaffee said that, 'Just before going down it seemed to writhe, breaking into three parts into which it was divided. First the middle seemed to go down, lifting the bow and stern into the air. Then it twisted the other way, throwing the middle up. Finally the bow went under, and it plunged stern last.'

These three accounts, taken on their own, might seem to indicate that the ship broke with her middle moving in a downward direction, in response thrusting the previously-sunken bow back upwards. However, certain details of the accounts would seem to defy basic physics, particularly since the bow section was at that time so thoroughly flooded. It also does not match the accounts of some survivors who were swimming in the water over the bow portions of the ship; none of these said that the ship itself rose up again out of the depths underneath their feet once it had fully submerged.

At the same time, several other accounts were very specific in stating that something else had transpired. Charlotte Collyer's account spoke of millions of sparks shooting up to the sky in a fan shape, indicating an expanding opening in the upper decks or upper portions of the ship early on during the break. She was even more specific when she said that the fore part, which was 'already partly under the water … wallowed over and disappeared instantly'. Esther Hart said that when the ship appeared to be breaking in halves, the 'front portion of her dived … into the sea'. Bertha Lehmann said: 'It had broken apart! The front part of the boat went under first. The helm of the front half sank and then the middle.' Jack Thayer recalled that 'the whole superstructure of the ship appeared to split, well forward to midships, and bow or buckle upwards'. Frank Osman similarly seemed to describe seeing a large opening in the ship, for he thought that he saw the 'engines and everything that was in the after part' slide out 'into the forward part'. Arthur Bright said that when the ship's stern section tipped to the bow and sank in its final throes, it was doing 'the same thing' as the bow had done just after the break. Thomas Whiteley, swimming in the water, said that he saw '*Titanic* blow her sides away. She broke in the middle, her forward end went down…'

So how can these apparently dichotomous accounts be reconciled? Carrie Chaffee's account may hold the key, as she specifically said that the ship had broken 'into three parts'. This brings us to an interesting point – *where precisely* did survivors say the ship had broken? Here we have great disparity – some said that it was close to midships, i.e., in the vicinity of the First Class Lounge on the Boat Deck. Jack Thayer, in one of his accounts, said that she had broken just in front of the No. 3 funnel, while in another he said that it was more in the vicinity of midships. At the opposite extreme, some, such as Frederick Scott, said that the break occurred as far aft as *behind* the No. 4 funnel. Meanwhile some, like Frank Evans, were very specific that they saw the ship break 'between the third and fourth funnels'. At first glance, these statements once again seem completely irreconcilable.

However, a quick look at the physical evidence on the wreck shows how these varying statements *could all* be correct. The cleanest section of split seems to be at the aft end of the bow section, and runs in a more or less – although not perfectly – vertical line in the vicinity of Frame Numbers 12–13 Aft in the after portion of the No. 2 Boiler Room. At the bottom of the ship, this is where the double bottom broke, and where the front end of the detached forward double bottom segment interconnected with the bow of the ship. At the top of the ship, at the Boat Deck, the superstructure seems to have parted in just about the same area, around the forward portion of the No. 3 funnel casing, and in the extreme after segment of the First Class Lounge where it wrapped around the funnel casing. This split would very clearly mesh with those who mentioned a forward break.

At the stern, the picture is a little different. At the forward half of the stern section, the double bottom parted in the Reciprocating Engine Room, in the vicinity of Frames 35–37 Aft. This was directly beneath the forward portion of each of the reciprocating engines, and the break literally snapped the forward cylinders off of each engine; each of these portions of engine eventually ended up in the debris field. From the known damage and separation of the reciprocating engines, Frank Osman's statement about seeing the engines slide out of the stern into the bow section – while at first seeming ludicrous – actually begins to sound plausible. Where the stern section's double bottom broke, the aft portion of the stern segment of detached double bottom interconnects rather nicely. Meanwhile, at the top of the stern section, very little is left above the now-exposed stern three-quarters of each reciprocating engine. At the Boat Deck level, only from the area of the Second Class Entrance deckhouse – abaft the No. 4 funnel – and on towards the stern does anything become even remotely recognizable. Forward of that point, very little is identifiable, particularly above D Deck. This damage pattern would seem to mesh well with those statements that said the ship broke aft of the No. 4 funnel.

Meanwhile, the double bottom between the forward and stern halves of the wreck also broke apart into two large segments. This occurred in the vicinity of Frames 24–26, underneath the single-ended boilers in Boiler Room No. 1.

Finally, at the top, starboard side, the forces causing the ship to break up also caused 'the big piece' to literally shred away from the surrounding portions of the hull and the C Deck plating. In addition, a small 'tail' of the outer hull plating – pointed downward from the main body of 'the big piece' like a knife and shaped very much like a blade – was detached from the rest of the ship and came off with 'the big piece'. This blade-shaped 'tail' originally formed a narrow portion of the outer shell of the First Class Pantry on D Deck.

Everything above the floor of B Deck was part of the superstructure – lightly constructed, and not of any real material strength to the hull itself. The forward and aft expansion joints separated those upper decks into three distinct segments, allowing them to flex and work in a seaway as the primary hull flexed below, all without imposing excessive load-bearing strain on the lightweight construction of the superstructure. Although in recent years these expansion joints have been targeted as a 'weak spot' in the structure of the ship as a whole, in reality they had nothing to do with the ship's primary hull. They were merely stress-relieving joints for the superstructure. As such, the after expansion joint should not be considered to have played a significant role in the failure of the ship's primary hull during the breakup.

However, there are some points regarding the after expansion joints that are worth noting. If the ship had broken cleanly in the vicinity of the No. 3 funnel, the stresses and strains imposed on the superstructure aft of the aft expansion joint should have been relieved by that feature of the ship's design. Yet, the location of 'the big piece' was below and astern of the expansion joint. This means that the catastrophic failure of the *Titanic*'s primary hull was ongoing over quite some distance – even abaft the location of the expansion joint. The failures of the hull in this area, beneath portions of the superstructure decks that would otherwise not have been suffering from strain, apparently transferred tremendous stresses onto those sections of the superstructure, as well.

A hull failure forward, near the No. 3 funnel, and another one aft, in the area of the reciprocating engine hatch and 'the big piece', would have produced three distinct sections of the ship, exactly as Carrie Chaffee said in her account. It is also quite possible that this would account for some of the disparity in statements made by other survivors. In this sort of scenario, the bow section – from the vicinity of the No. 3 funnel forward – would have continued to plunge down and forward, disappearing nearly immediately after the break as some witnesses described. Meanwhile, the third and central section of the vessel, in the area of the reciprocating engine hatch, would have been suffering its own ghastly finale. It would seem that it was this portion of the hull that some survivors saw 'fall in', or move in a downward direction, particularly if they had been watching the superstructure decks collapse as the hull beneath them was compromised and failed.

Finally, as the stern section came back on a more or less even keel, this could easily have produced the reverse effect mentioned by some, pushing that third, central segment of collapsing hull back up before it finally detached from the

stern, crumbling, and went into the sea. This third section of the ship would most likely have torn itself to shreds at the surface and during the subsequent plunge to the sea floor. Some of this section's pieces could have been quite large, while others ended up being much smaller.

The statements regarding a break in the vicinity of the No. 4 funnel, particularly Frederick Scott's statement that it was abaft of that towering structure, were probably referring to visible failures of the superstructure just forward of the Second Class Entrance. This makes sense since sections of the superstructure aft of the Entrance remain, while others just forward of that point are a nearly-unrecognizable mess, particularly above D Deck. Significant failures of the superstructure in the vicinity of the No. 4 funnel would also explain why that funnel toppled, as its base would have been significantly compromised and not strong enough to withstand the gyrations of the ship as the stern settled back onto the sea.

After careful examination of seemingly disparate accounts, it thus seems that the cumulative statements of eyewitnesses as to the nature of the breakup really mesh quite well with the damage patterns seen on the wreck. It would appear that the actual failure of the ship was far more involved, infinitely messier, and much more destructive than many had previously thought. It also means that much of the 'missing' portions of the ship once located between the bow and stern probably separated at the surface during the breakup.

So far we have considered how the eyewitnesses described the events, and we have carefully constructed various scenarios as to how their evidence fits in with forensic evidence and damage patterns seen on the wreck today. However, we have not so far ascertained whether the break had most likely started at the top of the vessel or at the bottom. This question is particularly complicated to answer, as it means accounting for an incredible number of factors.

Recent forensic examinations by the most technically knowledgeable historians of the *Titanic* have produced some interesting results. A computer model representing a small segment of the ship's original structure was built; calculations were then performed to see where stresses were concentrated. It was calculated that the stresses on the ship's keel were only about 83 per cent of the stresses imposed on the strength deck. However, it was also found that the joints in the bottom structure in the area that they studied may only have had 42–56 per cent of the strength of the side shell plates, which aided in the material strength of the top portion of the hull. This suggested that strains would have exceeded material strength first in the area of the double bottom, rather than at the strength deck, implying that the double bottom may have been the first segment of the hull to fail.[130]

However, the report was not a complete study of the entire area in question. The detailed digital model itself focused only on a 42-foot length of double bottom in the region of Boiler Room No. 1. There was a slight extension aft of Watertight Bulkhead K (Frame 30 Aft), which separated Boiler Room No. 1 from the Reciprocating Engine Room. However, the extension of the model astern of that bulkhead was only included to better model events as they played out beneath Boiler Room No. 1, and did not give any data concerning events in the Reciprocating Engine Room. That area of the ship was involved in the breakup because it was there that one of the separations of the double bottom actually occurred. The model also terminated at Watertight Bulkhead J (Frame 18 Aft), which separated Boiler

Room No. 1 from Boiler Room No. 2, forward. As such, events in Boiler Room No. 2 were not modeled. Again, this may be of importance as the separation of the double bottom from the bow section was located about five to six frame spaces forward of that bulkhead, within Boiler Room No. 2. Also of great importance, the model did not represent the full width of the liner, but instead was only about 20 feet in width.[131] This may be noteworthy since, as we shall soon see, the break does not appear to have been simultaneous across the entire width of the ship.

This specific swath of structure was chosen for scrutiny because it was in this area that a discontinuity in the depth of the double bottom (gradually increasing its depth from 63 inches to 76 inches between Frames 25–29 Aft) indicated a potential weakness. According to strength calculations made by the panel, the double bottom could not have buckled in any other location because of its great strength. Conceivably, however, the construction of a complete digital structure of the vessel in the region in question – from the forward section of Boiler Room No. 2 through the Reciprocating Engine Room, and from the strength deck down to the keel and double bottom – may have produced different results if tested under a variety of conditions.

None of the foregoing is intended to diminish the importance of the panel's research or findings; since so much hard work and careful research was put into the study, it should not be ignored or casually swept aside. However the findings should be considered preliminary rather than final; the forensic research is an ongoing and ever-evolving process which is ever improving. As this study was light years ahead of previous computer models of the ship – some of which inaccurately included the superstructure as part of the load-bearing hull, thus contaminating the results – so further studies in the future may either support or augment the findings from this particular study.

If it is accurate that the break began at the double bottom of the ship, then the failure may first have occurred between Frames 25–26 Aft, where the split between the two halves of the once-missing portions of double bottom is seen today. The marine forensics panel describes this break as a failure in the ship's bottom plating, which then successively progressed to other portions of the structure. Next, the downward pull by the bow section – still attached to the stern by way of the strength deck and upper side shell plating – began to place extreme tension upon the interconnecting portions of the upper works. This would seem a potential candidate for explaining why so much of the upper decks and superstructure, both fore and aft of the expansion joint in the superstructure, failed in such a terrifically messy process. However, there could be other explanations for all of this that turn up in the future.

Indeed, a second and independent research team, working with additional forensic data from the wreck site and even more data at their disposal, recently tackled the same subject. They came up with a completely different scenario, in which the original top-down break theory seemed to best explain the damage patterns seen on the wreck today.

Looking at forensic investigation on the structural failures of other vessels might also be of aid to researchers. The hulls of the *Leviathan* and *Vaterland* both gave way under hogging conditions, as their forward hulls smashed down upon large waves and their stern sections were left unsupported in the air. In both situations, it was the upper strength decks of each vessel that gave way first, and the

failure then spread to the shell plating on one side of the ship before the stresses were relieved and the tears stopped. Certainly, these vessels were not of the same construction as the *Titanic*. For example, their divided uptakes, as well as the proximity of other openings in the deck to those uptakes, have long been a suspect area of weakness. However – particularly in the *Leviathan*'s case – special strengthening and re-structuring had taken place to better combat the stresses, and the hull failure occurred anyway. A comparison of these incidents to the sinking of the *Titanic* may provide some useful data for investigators.

Beyond comparisons to other near-disasters, there is another element to the breakup of the *Titanic* that has not been factored into any forensic investigation to date, save the most recent one that came up with the 'top-down' explanation: namely, that the breakup does not seem to have been perfectly simultaneous across the entire width of the ship. Among the survivor statements quoted above, there is some evidence of this. Saloon Steward Percy Keen said that he saw 'the fore part of the ship break away up to the foremost funnel, and it appeared to us that when the ship had listed heavily to port the engines fell out and crashed through the side'. Although he did not mention the list to port, Saloon Steward Thomas Whiteley mentioned a similar phenomenon when he said that he got to some wreckage 'just in time to see the *Titanic* blow her sides away. She broke in the middle, her forward end went down'.

It is also possible that Esther Hart may have referred to this when she said that 'the after part with a heavy list, [*sic*, comma placement] also disappeared'. Since in technical maritime terminology 'trim' refers to a fore-aft angle, and 'list' would more aptly refer to a port–starboard angle, at first glance it would seem that she was referring to a side-to-side tip by the stern. However, we should be careful about assuming that this is definite evidence on the point, since Mrs Hart was a passenger and could have been unfamiliar with the correct terminology.

Another survivor, Charles Joughin, was much clearer on the point. He said that just as he got 'practically on the side' of the aft Well Deck as he worked his way aft, 'she gave a great list over to port and threw everybody in a bunch except myself'. In that moment, he 'clambered on the [starboard] side'. He was also very clear that it was not a matter of the starboard side going up and the port side going down; rather, the starboard side 'was not going up, but the other [port] side was going down'. He also said that the ship 'did not return' from this list to port. This would indicate that the stern section of the ship lost support on the port side first, in one manner or another, causing the port side of the stern to drop further than the starboard.

Looking at the remains of the wreck, there may be some forensic evidence to support this concept. First, the detached pieces of the double bottom do not appear to have split entirely straight across from port to starboard. The break point of the stern segment of the aft piece appears to move further aft on the extreme port side than it does on the starboard side. Similarly the middle break, from the vicinity of Frames 25–26 Aft, while remaining nearly perfectly consistent for much of the ship's width, juts forward an extra frame for the width of two strakes of shell plating (strakes C and D), just to starboard of the keel.

Closely related to this subject, two survivors who went into the water from the forward regions of the starboard Boat Deck – Eugene Daly and Jack Thayer – also gave detailed information about some movements of the stern in those final moments that seemed to have gone unnoticed by many others. Both men specifically referred to a point after the break, when the stern was rearing back up to something like perpendicular. Daly said: 'Her stern stuck up high. I thought she would fall on us as she seemed to be swinging around, but she did not.' Thayer said, repeating through the course of three different accounts, that the stern had 'pivoted' around, 'corkscrewed' and 'turned' and that the 'propeller, rudder, and all seemed to go right over the heads of us'. Since both men had left the ship's starboard side forward, for the ship to turn to such an extent that the propellers seemed to be above them would require nearly a 180° directional rotation by the stern, most likely in a port (or counter-clockwise, if viewing the ship from above) direction. Since most of those who survived did not mention such a rotation, it very likely did not happen until the stern was nearing its greatest angle – nearly perpendicular – in the water. At that point, such a rotation would have been less noticeable in the dark than if it had taken place when she was sitting at a shallower angle.

Is this rotation at the surface before the final plunge forensically supported on the wreck? In point of fact, it is, for the stern section is turned roughly 180° out of alignment with the bow section. While on its own this could have been explained by other events, the two lines of evidence actually seem to fit together very nicely.

It is also noteworthy to consider that if the stern section was rotating, some powerful force must have caused that rotation. Simultaneously, there has to be an explanation for the relatively quick manner in which the stern stood up on end in those final minutes. Flooding alone would not have done so, since any open watertight doors aft of the Reciprocating Engine Room would almost certainly have closed themselves when incoming seawater lifted their float mechanisms, which were designed to allow the doors to close themselves under their own weight. However, investigators exploring the stern section have seen at least one watertight door at the aft end of the Reciprocating Engine Room still open. In the carnage of the breakup, the bulkhead could easily have been distorted to the point that the door didn't close properly; it is also possible that debris blocked the path of the door's travel, stopping it from closing properly. Even so, with one or more watertight doors still open in the stern section, it would still have taken time for water to propagate throughout the Reciprocating Engine Room and into spaces further aft.

It is also unlikely that the weight of the broken and shattered reciprocating engines, the majority of which still remained seated at the very forward end of the stern section, would on its own have so dramatically caused the stern section to stand on end; their weight would certainly have been a factor in the physics at work, but it does not seem enough to completely explain the rapid way in which the stern again stood on end after it had temporarily settled back onto the sea's surface.

So what would account for both the rotation as well as the quick forward dive of the stern section? It is possible that some component of the ship's structure was still attached to the bow. Proponents of a top-down break would suggest the keel and double bottom would be a likely candidate, while those who believe the ship broke from the bottom up would suggest it might have been components of the upper side shell plating and/or strength deck.

Of note, the detachment points at the stern of the bow section seem to be slightly further aft on the starboard side than on the port. Finally, much of the hull plating on the starboard side of the stern section is peeled away from the internal decks and splayed out on the seafloor, whereas more of the port hull remains closely attached to the inner decks. 'The big piece' was also a portion of the starboard hull.

All of this, combined with the previously considered evidence that the port side structure of the hull gave way first, could indicate that elements of the ship's starboard structure were holding the two primary halves of the vessel together even after the ship suffered its primary and visible hull failure. This could also have aided in producing the 'three-piece' breakup, as tension would have continued throughout the region. As the bow sank away from the surface, if any elements of the two primary halves were connected, they would naturally have pulled on the stern section. A connection on the starboard side would explain the rotation, and the downward pull of the bow. When combined with the forward weight of the reciprocating engines and the flooding of the Reciprocating Engine Room from the ship's break, all of these factors could easily have pushed the forward half of the stern section down. From there, it is most likely that whatever components of the ship's structure were holding the two halves together finally parted. At that point, the stern section was doomed to sinking as soon as the flooding forces overwhelmed what was left of the stern's positive buoyancy.

It is even possible that for this portion of the scenario – the late-stage connection point between the two halves – we may have a bit of supporting testimony. This evidence came from Saloon Steward George Crowe's previously mentioned account, where he said that 'there was an explosion, and the aft part turned on end and sank'. Although not a certainty by any means, it is possible that the close timing of this 'explosion' sound to the stern's up-ending motion might be evidence of a late connection between the halves straining or parting.

Even though we do not have all the answers, certain recent theories can be laid to rest with finality. Some ideas have cropped up that the ship sank more quickly as a result of the breakup, and that it affected to a large degree the number of survivors. Yet an open-minded investigation shows clearly that the breakup was a result of the final moments of the sinking process. One way or another, that ship was plunging to the seafloor within just a few minutes of that 'slight but definite plunge' and the swamping of the Bridge. The end had arrived.... Had the ship's hull failed to part, the stern would doubtless have simply continued to swing up until the flooded bow section pulled the entire ship under. There is no real reason to believe that the breakup affected the timing of the ship's demise, or that any more lives were lost or saved because of it. Another concept, namely that the bottom-up break would explain why none of the engineers survived, is also a tremendous stretch. Anyone left so deep within the ship at that point would have faced certain death no matter how things played out from the moment of the break. Even if the ship had remained intact as it sank, they would most likely have been trapped inside until the spaces flooded or imploded. No matter how events played out, their fates were already sealed.

Another point begins to emerge with startling clarity: that the breakup was not evidence of some sort of inherent flaw in the ship's design or construction. The expansion joints themselves clearly played no significant part in the strength of Titanic's hull or its failure. Indeed, the fact that the liner remained complete as long as she did while being subjected to tremendous stresses is remarkable evidence of great strength rather than substandard weakness. The ship clearly did not sink because it was breaking up, as some have postulated; rather, the ship broke up because she was sinking – and quickly at that.

As International Marine Engineering said in a preliminary report of the disaster in its May, 1912 issue:

> … It is evident, therefore, that the hull structure of the Titanic was of exceptional strength.
>
> Without further information, however…, no accurate assumption can be made as to the longitudinal bending stresses or the shearing stresses at any section of the hull. The first reports from the survivors even indicated that there was a breakage or partial rupture, or bending of the hull, at a point aft of the 'midship section … In modern ship design the maximum shearing and longitudinal stresses are proportioned for cases as extreme, if not more extreme, than that in which the Titanic was placed, although the Titanic was in about the worst condition as far as the stresses are concerned that a ship can be placed.[132]

Although at the time they had only the vaguest reports available to work from, they were still able to conclude that not only was the vessel in very nearly the worst imaginable situation at the time, but that her hull structure 'was of exceptional strength'.

So at this time, we are left with a remarkably good, and simultaneously gnawingly incomplete picture of the ship's final moments. Questions such as the exact angle that the ship assumed before it broke, and whether the ship broke from the bottom up or the top down, are not necessarily thoroughly answered. Further analysis – both of the historical record and of forensic evidence – is certainly in order. Hopefully, the research produced in this appendix will enlighten readers with as much information as we have available to us at this time. It is also hoped that the information presented here can be used as a tool for the use of other researchers who will in the future attempt to discover exactly how those horrifying final ten minutes of the Titanic's maiden voyage played out, answering questions to which we, at this time, seem to have only incomplete answers.

Appendix O: 'J. "Brute" Ismay'?

In the decades since the Titanic's sinking, White Star Chairman Joseph Bruce Ismay's role in the disaster has been clouded in myth, speculation, distortion and falsehood. It is natural human tendency, perhaps, to look to assign blame to one or more individuals for unspeakable tragedy. At times, criticism of a person's, or persons', actions seems to be justified. Yet all too frequently – particularly in the case of the Titanic – individuals have been singled out for disproportionate blame or censure. Such is the case with J. Bruce Ismay.

Any male passenger who had the audacity to survive the sinking of the liner faced a certain stigma upon their return home. In an era of chivalry, when one of the worst insults that could be hurled at a man was to call his behavior 'ungentlemanly', how could surviving men justify climbing into a lifeboat when women and children were left behind on the ship? It was easy to draw a comparison between their survival and the behavior of notables such as John Jacob Astor or Major Archie Butt, who were not saved.

Yet in most cases, this criticism was simply unwarranted. In many of the situations where male passengers saved themselves, the circumstances surrounding their departure would lead a reasonable researcher to conclude that if a certain man had not taken a particular opportunity presented to him, then his life would simply have been added to the list of the lost. Simultaneously in many of those cases, the action to save his own life did not apparently cause the loss of another person. In such situations, simply deciding to seize the opportunity, when it did not cost anyone else their life, would not seem to be an arguably immoral one.

However, the survival of one man was seen, by many, to be both unconscionable and unforgivable: that of J. Bruce Ismay, Chairman of the White Star Line. As the company's Chairman, many felt that Ismay simply should have let himself perish that night. This conclusion seemed to be reinforced when Ismay's wireless messages from the Carpathia gave the impression that the Chairman was trying to 'slip away' from American authorities and make a safe return to England. Things got worse when it became clear, during the formal Inquiries, just how well-informed Ismay had been of the ship's navigation during the voyage, and of the proximity of ice on the day of the disaster. Ismay's own attempts to downplay his knowledge of the ship's navigation, of ice in the area, and of certain other matters backfired badly. It was a bad situation, and it got worse.

The press was quick to pounce upon Ismay as the real villain of the Titanic disaster. Such condemnation of Ismay seemed particularly in evidence within the papers under the control of William Randolph Hearst. Things got ugly, and quickly … it even got to the point where some of the press cleverly transformed his name into 'J. Brute Ismay', perhaps one of the worst insults in an entire string of horrendous personal attacks.

Ismay's public reputation never recovered from the events of that voyage. In some films and documentaries, and even some books on the subject, Ismay has at times been portrayed accurately, but is often presented very badly. When the portrayals are bad, they run the gamut from simply 'oily' to 'nearly villainous'. The less overt of these negative portrayals show Ismay as sitting more or less in the background, prodding others on in decisions they weren't comfortable with; from these one can almost see Ismay twisting the corners of his mustache in a generally slimy way – the stereotypical sneaky, nefarious businessman out to make a profit even if it risked lives. From the worst of these, one can nearly envision Ismay up on Captain Smith's shoulders like some enraged baboon, pummeling the Commander's head while screaming for him to go faster, faster … faster! Some have even suggested that the decision to move the ship forward after the collision was entirely at Ismay's behest, and that his pressure to continue was partially to blame for the speed with which the ship sank.

However, it is vitally important to consider the facts at hand instead of rushing to judgment. First, let's consider Ismay's actions prior to the collision to see where criticism may or may not be warranted.

When the *Olympic* and *Titanic* were being built, did Ismay or anyone else in the White Star Line attempt to cut corners in the provision of lifeboats or in the quality and safety of the ships' construction in order to turn a better profit? While frequently implied, not a single shred of evidence has ever been presented to support such an allegation. Indeed, the opposite would seem to be true. For example, Ismay was perfectly willing to include newly-designed davits capable of holding more lifesaving craft, in case the British Board of Trade increased lifeboat regulations. When the Board of Trade reached its decisions not to change the regulations, there was simply no need to go beyond those rules by what might have seemed a perfectly ridiculous amount – at least, by what might have seemed perfectly ridiculous *before* the sinking of the *Titanic*.[1]

Regarding the construction-quality of the *Olympic* and *Titanic*, it is absolutely laughable to imply that Ismay was trying to shave so close to the bone with the liners' construction costs that he had them built to a deficient standard. Everyone from both White Star and Harland & Wolff knew at the project's outset that each of these new ships would be examined down to the minutest detail by Board of Trade surveyors. Those surveyors would visit the ships literally hundreds of times during construction. They, and the Government body they represented, had great authority in improving the ships' design or build-quality in any places where they conceivably might have believed them deficient. Long before the first rivet was even driven, the Board had to approve every plan for the liners' design.

In other words Ismay and Lord Pirrie would almost certainly have known that any collusion between them to deceive the Board of Trade and its surveyors by using slipshod materials or substandard designs could, and probably would, have backfired badly and very publicly. This would have resulted in additional expenses and delays to rectify the problems – as well as a great deal of negative publicity for the prestigious companies and the men at the helm of these companies.

The short of it is this: the two companies were in business to make money. If Harland & Wolff had been exposed as a slipshod construction firm, their business quite simply would have dried up. Orders would have gone to other shipyards. If Ismay or the White Star Line had been exposed for colluding with the builders to build defective ships, passengers would take other ships. Why would Ismay have risked being exposed in a scandal over such a small percentage of the overall expense, if indeed he even had the clout to have attempted to do so? It simply makes no sense. No, that would have been a terrible, unjustifiable, risk to take for the saving of a few thousand pounds here and there.

Finally, the North Atlantic was a frightening place to venture in even the best-built craft. Indeed, the toughness of the *Olympic* was well proven during at least two violent storms in 1912, and during her collision with the *Hawke* in 1911. This was at a point when her hull design and watertight subdivision were nearly identical to that of the *Titanic*, and did not reflect post-disaster modifications and upgrades. She was not built as a substandard ship. For his own part, Ismay seemed content to leave most of the technical matters in the capable hands of the shipbuilding company, and was far more content burying himself in the intricate details of the ship's proposed amenities and comforts.

If Ismay had any question on the safety of his ships, he would not have entrusted his life to the *Titanic* on its maiden voyage, and neither would he have entrusted the safety of his family to the *Olympic* the year before. All of this really goes to show that during the phases of design and construction, Ismay was not involved in some sort of conspiracy to build super-fragile vessels that could fall apart at the drop of a hat.

Finally, the White Star Line was financing the ships through the issuance of bonds; contrary to popular belief the *Olympic* and *Titanic* venture was not being bankrolled by J. P. Morgan's deep pockets.[2] Due to the methods through which they were financed, it was vitally important to the company that the liners remain profitably employed on the North Atlantic; the discovery of any structural deficiencies would have required lengthy and expensive shipyard refits, during which time the liners would not be earning revenue.[3]

What about during the voyage? Was there any evidence of wrongdoing by Ismay during the trip? It was apparently perfectly normal for Ismay to be kept informed of how his liners were doing while he was aboard; especially during the maiden voyages of each new ship would he have been particularly anxious to ensure that they met, or exceeded, expectations on all fronts. Ismay did admit to talking to Chief Engineer Bell when the ship was at Queenstown. They discussed how much coal *Titanic* had on board, the need to economize it, and when the ship would dock in New York. They also discussed "driving her at full speed" for a few hours sometime on Monday or Tuesday.[4]

After the fact, Ismay clearly felt that minimizing his personal knowledge of the ship's performance during the crossing would help his public image. However, that in itself is no evidence of wrongdoing on his part during the voyage. This was more of an attempt at after-the-fact 'spin control', and it ended up failing miserably.

What of the conversation reported by Elizabeth Lines, held between Ismay and Captain Smith on Saturday, April 13? While many have scoffed at or downplayed Lines' account in an attempt to justify Ismay, is such a rabid defense really called for? Nothing in her recollections of the conversation seem to be evidence of anything really Machiavellian on Ismay's part. Rather her report seemed to describe an enthusiastic monologue by the Chairman to the Captain on how well the ship was doing. The machinery was proving itself well, the boilers were bearing the steam pressure, and the ship would make it into New York ahead of schedule, Ismay concluded. Nowhere is there a shred of evidence that Ismay was trying to force Captain Smith to drive his ship at a speed the Captain was uncomfortable with. At sea, the Captain is the absolute authority; Captain Smith had nothing to fear from Ismay, particularly since he was so close to retirement. Lines merely recalled that he nodded in affirmation of Ismay's statements. Indeed, if Ismay had chosen to exert any untoward pressure on the Captain, why would he have done so in a public room in front of passengers, and in rather unguarded tones at that?

As far as the question of whether there was an attempt to beat a record or not, the answer depends entirely on what record it is implied they were trying to break. As far as taking the Blue Riband, that was entirely out of the question. The *Titanic* simply was not capable of taking the prize from the *Lusitania* or *Mauretania*. From Ismay's words about 'beating the *Olympic*', however, it seems quite clear that Ismay was hoping that they would make a faster trip than the *Olympic* did on her maiden voyage, getting into New York on Tuesday evening rather than Wednesday morning. Yet the potential for a Tuesday night arrival was well-known to many passengers and crew even at the time of the ship's departure and through the voyage, and was recorded in personal correspondence even before the disaster.[5] While the possibility was reportedly in doubt to some extent after Saturday's run was posted, Ismay remained confident of it on Saturday, and that hope was revived in others after Sunday's run was posted. Passengers like the Thayers and Wideners heard directly from Ismay that the ship's speed would be increased during the remainder of the voyage; this really went a long way toward proving that Ismay had a certain level of 'inside information' about the progress that the ship was making.

Whether there was hope of breaking *Olympic's* record or not, and no matter how much Ismay knew, driving a ship at full speed in good weather was entirely common for both Captain Smith and any other Captain then on the Atlantic.[6] Looking at the service records of numerous other liners, both before and after, it is clear that whenever possible, Commanders were eager to make the best possible speed, especially in case poor weather delayed other portions of their voyage. The final approach to New York, off the Grand Banks, was frequently foggy, and conceivably fog could have forced a reduction in the ship's speed on Monday or Tuesday. Despite the high speed of the *Titanic* on Sunday, April 14, we know that the she was not even making her maximum speed up to the time of the collision. Her five auxiliary boilers had not yet been lit, let alone applied to the engines. She was traveling faster than at any other point in the voyage, but the speed she was then making was not her maximum.

On Sunday, it is clear that Captain Smith and his officers took the warnings of ice rather seriously. They kept the lookouts well-informed on what to look out for and when; the Captain and officers were also thoroughly prepared to slow the ship at the slightest deterioration in visibility. There is also good circumstantial evidence that Captain Smith did not fully retire before the collision, as he was apparently dressed when he arrived on the Bridge very shortly after the impact. Perhaps he might have been involved in something in his personal Chart Room, or was in his cabin resting without retiring. It is possible that he intended to be close at hand during the night, in case there was any deterioration in visibility or if ice fields were spotted and he was needed on the Bridge.

The fact that Smith showed the *Baltic's* warning to Ismay is also well established. However, if Smith was hesitant to maintain his speed despite the warnings, and Ismay pressured him to do so, no clear evidence of this has ever come to light. While the absence of evidence is not enough to say for certain that Ismay did not make some sort of suggestion or recommendation that the ship's high speed be maintained, historians must be careful not to jump to that conclusion. There is no evidence of 'Ismay the Terrible' peering over Smith's shoulder all that afternoon and evening, careful to make sure there was no reduction in speed and threatening to fire him at the least hesitation or objection. Instead, Ismay spent time socializing with fellow passengers all day on the decks, in the Smoking Room, in the Restaurant, and in the Restaurant Reception Room; he and Captain Smith both seemed wholly confident.

What about Ismay's actions after the collision? To begin with, there is no evidence that Ismay exerted undue influence on Captain Smith to re-start the engines after the collision. In fact, the timing of things seemed to indicate that Ismay arrived on the Bridge at about the time that the engines were rung off for good, not at the time that they were re-started. Ismay did meet up with Chief Engineer Bell on the Grand Staircase, but it was a brief conversation, held after the engines had stopped, and the two men parted company headed in different directions.

Subsequently, Ismay was seen with the Captain and other senior personnel on the Grand Staircase. Once the order to load the lifeboats had been given, Ismay toiled to help convince passengers to board them, and he also tried to instill a sense of urgency in members of the crew. Many who may not otherwise have been saved boarded lifeboats through the persuasion of Ismay. He was so thoroughly engaged in this effort that he never returned to his stateroom during the loading of the boats. He was still on the deck when Collapsible C was being filled, just a short time before the ship took her final plunge.

Up to that point, none of Ismay's decisions seem to have been openly reprehensible. But what of his decision, in the end, to save his own life in Collapsible C? Ismay was absolved of any wrongdoing in preserving his own life at the formal inquiries into the disaster. The typical portrayal of events surrounding the loading of that boat is a quiet one. However, there is some evidence that things at Boat C may have been more chaotic, and in the end more violent, than is commonly accepted. For example, Jack Thayer – then standing on the starboard Boat Deck – recalled:

> There was some disturbance in loading the last two forward starboard boats. A large crowd of men was pressing to get into them. No women were around as far as I could see. I saw Ismay, who had been assisting in the loading of the last boat, push his way into it. It was really every man for himself.[7]

However in his early account, dated April 20, 1912, Thayer only mentioned a crowd in the vicinity of that collapsible. He did not recount seeing Ismay 'push his way' into the boat. This could have been merely an omission in his early recollections, or it could have been a mistake in his later one. Obviously, if Ismay had pushed his way into Collapsible C, his testimony about the scene at the time could not be considered trustworthy.[8]

Whatever the truth, Ismay *did* find his way into Collapsible C.[9] Yet, so did four stowaways and First Class passenger William Carter. There is nothing in the historical record that shows that any officer registered a complaint about Carter or Ismay boarding. Indeed, it seems that at that point they were having difficulty finding women to place in the craft, and it was lowered away. Murdoch seems to have had no problem in allowing male passengers to leave the ship in the lifeboats he was filling.[10] If he or any of the other officers had any feelings upon seeing Ismay board the collapsible, their emotions were not recorded and can only be speculated on. What seems a likely conclusion is that no one died *because* Ismay boarded the Collapsible. The court was actually much harder on William Carter – and unfairly so – for his boarding the collapsible at the same time as Ismay.

If it did no harm for Ismay to save himself, did it do any good? Certainly his wife and children would have thought so upon hearing of his rescue. While Ismay may have regretted the way his reputation was assailed after the disaster, he was able to continue with his life and his eventual death was mourned by many.[11]

Appendix P: Buried at Sea

One of the most confusing aspects of *Carpathia's* rescue of the *Titanic* survivors involves the burials conducted from her while she was at sea. *Carpathia* lacked the facilities to preserve and store the bodies until the arrival in New York, necessitating this sad task. But how many individuals were actually buried at sea, and who were they?

The eyewitnesses estimated that anywhere from four to eight victims underwent this service. Rostron testified that three bodies had been brought aboard, with another dying a few hours later, and that those four individuals were buried at sea.[1] Survivor Lawrence Beesley believed that four bodies had been taken from the boats, with four additional men dying during the day, for a total of eight being buried at sea.[2] But who was correct?

Beesley's numbers appear to be more of an estimate, while Rostron seemed certain that just four individuals were buried at sea. He testified that three dead men were taken from the boats, and that another man was brought aboard alive, but that he died at 10:00 a.m. on April 15. Rostron said that the four bodies were buried at sea around 4:00 p.m. that same day. It is true that Rostron's testimony varied slightly from the Senate Inquiry to the British Inquiry. In the former he said, 'I think he [the man who died] was one of the crew', while in the latter, he stated that the body was that of 'a passenger we took up from the boat'. Yet Rostron insisted at both inquiries that it was four men who were buried at sea, and that they had a list bearing their names. Unfortunately, he did not have the list with him when he testified.[3]

Supporting evidence for Rostron's count of four comes from Carpathia's Chief Purser Ernest Brown, who stated that four bodies were buried at sea.[4] Carpathia passenger Fred Beachler stated that two bodies had been brought aboard, as well as a survivor who died after a few minutes aboard the rescue ship, with all three being buried at sea on April 15. He also said that a fourth died and was buried at sea the following day.[5] James Bisset, Carpathia's Second Officer, concurred, although he said that they had picked up 'four men who had died of exposure in the lifeboats', and that all four were buried at sea at 4:00 a.m. on Tuesday, April 16. Bisset may simply have confused the time, as Rostron said the men were buried at 4:00 p.m. on April 15, not 4:00 a.m. the following morning.[6]

While Rostron's inquiry testimony varies slightly, and the accounts from the other witnesses all vary somewhat in detail, each of these individuals agreed that four men were buried at sea. Furthermore, there is strong evidence that three were dead when brought aboard, and that a fourth – near death when recovered – perished a few hours later. In his recollections, Rostron varied as to whether this man was a crewman or passenger.

Can the four individuals who were buried at sea be identified? A press account from an unnamed source published soon after the disaster said that the three dead bodies brought aboard were those of First Class passenger William Hoyt, Third Class passenger David Livshin [traveling under the alias Abraham Harmer], and Bedroom Steward Sidney Siebert, and that all three were buried at sea the morning of April 15. The man said to have died aboard Carpathia and been buried at sea the following morning was Able Bodied Seaman William Lyons.[7]

The details in Fred Beachler's account differ from this unnamed source, but he did agree on the names of the individuals buried at sea. He said that two of the men were already dead when brought aboard, and that another was still alive, but died a few minutes later. He listed these individuals as William Hoyt, David Livshin, and Sidney

Siebert, and said that all three were buried at sea the morning of April 15. Beachler also claimed that William Lyons was alive when brought aboard, before dying, and being buried at sea the following day.[8]

An unnamed Carpathia steward gave an interview following the arrival in New York, and was yet another person who specifically identified these same four individuals as the ones who were buried at sea. However, there are still more variations in the time and details relating to the burial, as the steward claims all four were buried at sea Tuesday, April 16; he also claimed that Siebert and Lyons were dead when brought aboard, while Hoyt and Livshin were alive, and 'lived but a few minutes after'.[9]

If those four men were indeed the individuals buried at sea from Carpathia, an examination of the eyewitness accounts should reveal who – if anyone – was the individual who died aboard the rescue ship. First, Fifth Officer Lowe stated multiple times in the course of his testimony that William Hoyt, who he had rescued from the water, died in Boat No. 14. He also said that he 'landed' everyone, including Hoyt's body, safely on Carpathia. Hoyt was in a bad state when pulled from the water, bleeding from his nose and mouth.[10] There seems to be little doubt that Hoyt had actually died in the lifeboat, as Able Bodied Seamen Joseph Scarrott, Frank Evans, and Saloon Steward George Crowe all concurred with Lowe's statements regarding this.[11]

Bedroom Steward Sidney Siebert and Able Bodied Seaman William Lyons were among the men pulled from the water into Boat No. 4. First Class passengers Emily Ryerson and Marian Thayer both said that two men died aboard this boat after being pulled from the water.[12] Elizabeth Eustis and Martha Stephenson, in an account shared with Colonel Gracie, stated that two men pulled into the stern of Boat No. 4 died, and their bodies were taken aboard Carpathia.[13]

Quartermaster Perkis' testimony concurs with this, as he said that two men pulled from the water died in the boat, although he believed that they were a fireman and a steward.[14] Lamp Trimmer Samuel Hemming said that two men died in Boat No. 4, specifically identifying one as Lyons, and the other as either 'a steward or a fireman'.[15] Trimmer Dillon testified that when he regained consciousness in Boat No. 4, 'Lyons [was] lying on top of me, a seaman, and a passenger lying on top of me dead.'[16] Bedroom Steward Cunningham testified that he and 'a mate' – a reference to Siebert – leapt overboard at the same time, and that his mate had died right after being pulled aboard No. 4. He stated that two dead bodies were taken aboard Carpathia.[17] When all the evidence is considered, it seems clear that two men died aboard Boat No. 4, that these two men were indeed Able Bodied Seaman Lyons, and Bedroom Steward Siebert, and that their bodies were taken aboard Carpathia.

Another body was said to have been taken aboard Carpathia, from Boat No. 12. Colonel Gracie testified that when the survivors atop Collapsible B were picked up by No. 12, Lightoller transferred a 'lifeless body' into the latter. Gracie said that he tried to revive the man, 'rubbing the temples and the wrists', but that when he tried turning the man's neck, it was stiff, and rigor mortis had set in. Gracie believed that this man was dressed like a member of the crew, but didn't say why, and recalled that he had gray woolen socks. Boat No. 12 was so crowded after rescuing some of the men from Collapsible B that Gracie was forced to sit on top of the body until Carpathia picked them up.[18] Lamp Trimmer Hemming provides some confirmation of this, as he testified that he was told that there was a dead body atop Collapsible B when Boats Nos 4 and 12 rescued the survivors from it, although he did not see this for himself.[19]

The identity of the body taken from the upturned Collapsible and aboard *Carpathia* is open to question. Colonel Gracie, for unknown reasons, felt that the man was dressed like a member of the crew. In his famous *New York Times* interview, Harold Bride said that one man taken from Collapsible B was dead, and that as he went to climb aboard *Carpathia* up the Jacob's ladder lowered to Boat No. 12, he saw that the 'dead man was Phillips'.[20] However, Bride, when testifying in the Senate Inquiry, changed his story, saying that he had only been told that Senior Marconi Operator Jack Phillips died on Collapsible B, and was later buried at sea from *Carpathia*, and had not witnessed this for himself.[21]

In his book, Colonel Gracie states that the body he tried to revive while in Boat No. 12 was definitely not that of Phillips. He reported that when speaking with Lightoller, the Second Officer agreed with him that the body was not that of the Senior Marconi Operator.[22] In Lightoller's Senate Inquiry testimony, he says that Bride told him that Phillips had been aboard and died on the boat, but it is clear that Lightoller never saw this for himself.[23] In his 1935 book, Lightoller's memory must have been becoming faulty, or he was altering facts for dramatic effect, as he vividly describes Jack Phillips being aboard Collapsible B, and telling everyone the position of the various ships they had contacted by wireless, and when they could expect a rescue, before succumbing to the cold and dying. He also claims that Phillips' body was taken aboard Boat No. 12 at his insistence.[24]

It is clear from Gracie, and the other 1912 evidence, that the man on Collapsible B who called out which ships were on their way was Harold Bride, not Phillips. Lightoller's 1912 testimony contradicts his latter-day statements that he saw Phillips aboard Collapsible B, and that the body transferred off that boat was Phillips. Lightoller's later statements are clearly unreliable in that regard.

There is little to no evidence that Jack Phillips' body was ever aboard Collapsible B, or recovered. In fact, the only first-hand evidence that suggests that he was comes from Saloon Steward Thomas Whiteley, who may have been Bride's source for this story. In a press interview, Whiteley claimed that Phillips had been aboard Collapsible B with him, that he died, and was taken aboard *Carpathia*, where they 'tried to revive him with brandy and all that, but it was too late'. Whiteley claims that four bodies were buried at sea from *Carpathia*, including 'one sailor, two firemen, and Phillipee [*sic*]'. The reporter noted: 'It was first believed that this man was a cabin passenger, but Whitley [*sic*] declares it was Phillipee [*sic*].'[25] There is not a single other witness who in 1912 claimed Phillips' body was recovered, and his name was never mentioned by any source aboard *Carpathia* as being one of the four bodies buried at sea. It seems reasonable to conclude that Whiteley was simply mistaken in his identification, or that if Phillips had been aboard Collapsible B, his body was not recovered.[26]

If the body recovered from Collapsible B was not Jack Phillips, then who was it? The article containing the interview with Whiteley states that the body in question was believed to be that of a 'cabin passenger', until Whiteley suggested otherwise. Of the four persons named by *Carpathia* witnesses as having been buried at sea: William Hoyt, Sidney Siebert, William Lyons, and David Livshin, aka Abraham Harmer, only Livshin is unaccounted for.

There is no credible evidence from *Titanic* survivors of any more than four bodies being taken aboard *Carpathia* from the lifeboats.

Since there is strong evidence that a body was taken aboard the rescue ship from Boat No. 12, after it had been transferred into it from atop Collapsible B, it is reasonable to assume that the body in question was that of David Livshin. Unfortunately, few specific details about how Livshin died are known. Given the strong evidence from those in Boats Nos 14 and 4 to suggest that William Hoyt, Sidney Siebert, and William Lyons were all dead when taken aboard *Carpathia*, it would seem logical to conclude that if any of the four individuals buried at sea were alive when taken aboard the ship, that it would have to have been Livshin.

However, Colonel Gracie's efforts to revive the individual taken from Collapsible B into Boat No. 12, saying that rigor mortis had already set in, and subsequently having sat on the body until *Carpathia* picked them up, runs counter to this assumption. Captain Rostron varied on whether the man he said died aboard his ship was a crewmember or passenger, but in the British Inquiry, he did state it was a passenger.[27] In the press account with Thomas Whiteley where he claims Jack Phillips was on Collapsible B, it is also mentioned that the man that *Carpathia*'s crew attempted to revive was thought to be a 'cabin passenger'.[28] Both of these tidbits could support Livshin being the man who died onboard the ship, but only if Gracie was somehow mistaken when stating he was dead. One must wonder though, if the body taken aboard *Carpathia* was clearly dead as Gracie claimed, why would the crew have attempted to revive the man with brandy as Whiteley said they did?

Another person who, it is sometimes claimed, had been taken aboard and buried at sea from *Carpathia* is Third Class passenger Edvard Lindell.[29] Lindell died in Collapsible A, as witnessed by August Wennerström, and as described in the narrative. Like the claim that Jack Phillips was buried at sea from *Carpathia*, this claim also runs counter to the evidence. In his account and notes on the disaster, Wennerström says nothing to suggest that any of the victims from Collapsible A were taken aboard Boat No. 14 when it picked up the surviving occupants in that boat. In fact, his account suggests that most of the people who died in the boat were rolled overboard to lighten the load, as it was thought the boat was sinking.[30] It is likely that Lindell was among those tossed into the ocean; his body was not in the collapsible when it was found adrift nearly a month after the disaster, although a ring inscribed with the names of both he and his wife was found in the bottom of the boat.[31] Similarly, neither Fifth Officer Lowe, nor any of the occupants of Boat No. 14 said anything about taking on bodies from the swamped collapsible when the survivors were transferred out. Lowe himself said: 'I am not here to worry about bodies; I am here for life, to save life, and not to bother about bodies'[32] There is absolutely no evidence that Lindell's body was taken aboard *Carpathia*.

When all the evidence is examined, it strongly suggests that four bodies were buried at sea from *Carpathia*, and that those individuals were Hoyt, Siebert, Lyons, and Livshin. However, aside from the number buried at sea, the exact details and circumstances become cloudy. Examining the evidence reveals a large number of inconsistencies and striking contradictions regarding which of these four men were still alive when taken aboard the ship, if any of them were, and even as to what time of day the burial at sea was conducted, whether they were all buried at the same time, etc.

For example, it was alternately claimed that:

- Hoyt, Livshin, and Siebert were dead when brought aboard, and that Lyons died on the *Carpathia* later;
- that Hoyt and Livshin were dead when brought aboard, and that Siebert and Lyons died at varying times after being brought aboard;
- and that Siebert and Lyons were dead before being brought aboard, and that Hoyt and Livshin were the ones who died after being brought aboard.

Claims relating to the burials at sea are equally contradictory:

- All four men were buried at 4:00 p.m. on April 15;
- all four men were buried at sea at 4:00 a.m. on April 16;
- three men were buried on April 15, with one being buried the following day;
- and all four were buried on April 16.

Keeping this in mind, all that can be safely concluded is that four men were buried at sea from *Carpathia,* and that one may or may not have been alive when brought aboard, dying shortly afterwards. While this individual is frequently identified as Able Bodied Seaman Lyons in published works, the evidence does not allow for any conclusive statements to that effect. In fact, the witnesses in Boat No. 4 strongly support that Lyons was dead before being taken aboard the rescue ship. The evidence relating to Siebert being dead in Boat No. 4 is not as strong as it is for Lyons, but then again, nobody in the boat claimed he was alive when they were rescued. William Hoyt certainly appears to have died in Boat No. 14, and the evidence relating to this is persuasive. That leaves David Livshin, but if Colonel Gracie's account is accurate, it is hard to see how he could have been alive when taken aboard *Carpathia.*

Eyewitness accounts could have been further confused due to the fact that coincidentally, one *Carpathia* passenger, Franz Willwerth, died while aboard the ship. It is unclear whether Willwerth, who was being deported from the United States, died on the outbound portion of *Carpathia*'s voyage, or during the return to New York with the survivors. It is also unclear whether he was buried at sea, although it seems probable that he would have been. If so, it is possible that at least some witnesses believed he was a *Titanic* victim, which further confused the numbers and details of who was buried at sea, and when.[33]

In the end, the existing evidence supports the conclusion that only four bodies were taken aboard *Carpathia* from the lifeboats and later buried at sea. The evidence also allows for the identification of those four victims. However, the evidence does not allow for any definitive statements regarding which of these individuals, if any, were still alive when brought aboard, or for the exact details of the burial (or burials) to be determined. Unless further evidence is uncovered, the exact details of the burials at sea will remain a mystery.

Appendix Q: Trapped 'Like Rats?'

Over the years, one of the most horrifying and oft-told stories regarding the sinking of the *Titanic* was that many of her Third Class passengers were deliberately locked below

and left to die a horrifying death. However, how close do these tales come to reality?

To begin with, one must understand that the entire liner was carefully sub-divided to keep passengers of any given class from entering areas set aside for passengers of another class. Particularly important was keeping Third Class passengers separate from Second and First, in accord with immigration laws intended to prevent the spread of infectious disease. There were a series of printed notices or signs to deter passengers from leaving their own designated sections of the ship. On the open decks, there was also a series of railings with low, hinged gates, which kept passengers within their allotted space.[1] Within the ship, there also seem to have been some tall Bostwick gates subdividing lower deck passenger sections. As much of the accommodations deeper within the ship were interchangeable between First and Second, or between Second and Third classes, these gates may have been useful in helping to maintain delineation among these accommodations.[2]

There were a number of reports from surviving Third Class passengers of being kept behind locked gates, preventing access to the lifeboats; these included accounts from Daniel Buckley and Olaus Abelseth. However, their reports almost universally give very little indication of where these incidents occurred. It can not be over-emphasized that all Third Class passengers had easy access to certain open decks, such as the forward Well Deck, the aft Well Deck, and the Poop Deck. Common areas like the General Room and Smoking Room were located aft on C Deck, just a few steps away from the open Well Deck, and many Third Class passengers were no doubt easily aware of how to get to these locations. The working passageway on E Deck, termed Scotland Road, was regularly used by both crew and Third Class passengers.[3] On the night of the disaster, large numbers of Third Class passengers housed forward were seen moving aft along Scotland Road, and many subsequently made their way to the aft Well Deck and Poop Deck.

In light of all this information, many of the reported incidents of Steerage passengers being kept behind locked gates may actually have taken place on the open decks separating the aft Well Deck from the Second Class deck, rather than within the ship. A few accounts do seem to indicate locked gates within the ship, and these accounts are not easily dismissed as exaggerations or newspaper reporters' inventions. However, situations such as these seem to have been few and far between, and by and large they would not have seemed to prevent the vast majority of Third Class passengers from reaching the open decks.

Far more dangerous to Third Class passengers was the rather complex layout of the ship's lower decks. According to Seaman Poingdestre, there were no signs or notations for Third Class passengers that would have told them what direction they should go to get to the upper decks and lifeboats.[4] Even worse, many of those aboard the ship could not speak or read English. As a result, if Third Class passengers became disoriented or their typical routes for movement through the ship's inner compartments were in some way or another unavailable, they may have had a difficult time escaping the ship's interior spaces; however, it must be remembered that such situations were not necessarily evidence of deliberate attempts to keep them below. In fact, a number of accounts have survived which indicate stewards who came across bewildered Third Class passengers and led them out of the ship's interior via alternate routes.

Thus, it seems very unlikely that many of the ship's Steerage passengers were deliberately locked down within the ship's lower decks and left to drown 'like rats', as the saying goes. However, once they reached the aft Well Deck and Poop Deck areas, Third Class passengers did face a very real hurdle: getting up *to the lifeboats*, which were in First and Second Class portions of the Boat Deck. Evidence indicates that many of them managed to find their way toward the lifeboats, particularly during the last hour of the disaster; indeed, crowds of Third Class passengers were reported in those areas of the ship. Some of these passengers no doubt survived because they took the initiative to pass barriers and ignore notices on the open decks. Others seem to have been perfectly content to stay in their portions of the ship and wait to see what happened.

Interestingly, there is some evidence that a good-sized group of Second Class or Steerage passengers made a last-ditch effort to get out of their own portions of the ship and into First Class regions, perhaps in an attempt to reach the last collapsible lifeboats as they were loading. Archibald Gracie, then forward on the starboard Boat Deck, recalled:

> In five minutes the water from the deck below reached the boat deck on which we stood, and the sailors seemed not to have time to launch the boat; so Mr. [Clinch] Smith and I decided to hurry toward the stern; but we had only gone a few paces when, to our amazement, we saw men and women in a solid mass come up from the decks below, steerage or second class perhaps, facing toward us. But even here there was no panic, though appalling death was evident in the near future.[5]

Based upon Gracie's position on the Boat Deck, it is clear that this human wave of Second or Third Class passengers had come up from below via the First Class Entrance and forward Grand Staircase. But this leaves the question: where did they come from *before that*? Obviously, not from still further below, as everything below the Boat Deck and Promenade Deck in the vicinity of the forward First Class Grand Staircase was then flooded. Very likely, many of these passengers had come through barriers astern, and then moved forward along the Promenade Deck – either along the outer deck or within the public rooms – before climbing to the top level of the Grand Staircase. In other words, their presence on the forward Boat Deck at that late stage seems to be less evidence of their having been trapped *below* as it was an attempt to make their way toward the last-remaining lifeboats from locations *aft*.

Wherever they had come from, their prospects at that time were quite bleak, and most of them turned and headed aft again along the Boat Deck, piling up against the rails separating the First Class spaces from the Engineers' Promenade and Second Class areas aft. Most of them would have been plunged into the sea when the ship made her bow-first plunge moments later. Even for these hapless individuals, at least they were spared the horror of being trapped within the ship as it sank.[6]

It is thus clear that most of the Steerage passengers had the opportunity to at least make it to the open deck before the liner sank. Many – either assisted by crew members, or forging forth on their own – made a break for the lifeboats, and at least some of these did so in time to save themselves. Others remained behind, not willing to venture away from their des-

ignated areas, or were kept back by a few crewmen who felt it was their duty to keep them away from the lifeboats. The simple fact that the lifeboats were located only in First and Second Class regions of the ship, and that many of the Steerage passengers did not speak English and could not understand verbal instructions, seems to have been enough to do the rest of the job. One of the *Titanic*'s legacies would be that lifeboats would be provided for all of those aboard subsequent liners.[7]

Consequently, there is a lot of evidence that the majority of Third Class passengers did make it on deck before the ship sank. However, an analysis of the bodies that were recovered after the disaster shows that a lesser percentage of Third Class [Steerage] passenger bodies were found than those of other groups that can be shown to have been on deck at the end. Of the people who died in the sinking, 23% of the bodies were recovered. Of the First Class passengers, most of whom were likely on deck at the end, 32% of the bodies were recovered. Third Class bodies were only recovered at a rate of 14%. This could be explained by at least a certain percentage of them not being able to reach the outside decks at the end.[8] It could also simply mean that fewer of them had accessed or actually wore lifebelts.

But, the simple fact is that there is no evidence of a systematic 'extermination' of Steerage passengers in the historical record. There simply was not enough time, organization, or lifeboats, and Third Class passengers bore the brunt of the effects from these circumstances. Legends of locked gates and ideas of crewmen shooting passengers below decks have been long overblown. While the historical record clearly shows some unfortunate incidents, these were apparently few and far between.

Appendix R: The *Californian* Affair

Over the years, the subject of the Leyland Line steamship *Californian* and its proximity – or lack thereof – to the *Titanic* has become one of the most hotly debated topics within the *Titanic* community. It is not within the purview of this volume to delve deeply into this emotionally charged subject; however, the present authors feel that this volume would be lacking if at least some of the facts were not touched upon. One of the greatest problems surrounding the *Californian* incident is its great complexity. Here we will attempt to boil the controversy down to its essence.

The Basics
As the *Titanic* was foundering, some of her officers, crew and passengers recalled seeing the lights of another vessel on the horizon; while their descriptions of what sort of ship they thought it was differed, most agreed that the ship was off the port-bow quarter of the *Titanic*. According to Quartermaster Rowe and Fifth Officer Lowe, the *Titanic* stopped with her bow facing in a generally north-northwest to north direction. In an attempt to contact the other vessel, those on the *Titanic* used Morse lamps and a number of distress rockets;[1] by and large, these were described as white distress rockets by those aboard the White Star liner.

According to then-standing Regulations for Preventing Collisions at Sea, Article 31, Number 3, distress rockets were defined as: 'Rockets or shells, throwing stars of any colour or description, fired one at a time, at short intervals.' By all accounts, the *Titanic*'s rockets and the manner of their firing complied with that regulation. Sadly, *Titanic*'s officers were not able to make out any definitive reply, and the attempts were abandoned about the time that Fourth Officer Boxhall left in Boat No. 2, and Quartermaster Rowe turned out to render assistance at Collapsible C.

The *Californian* was stopped in the ice for the night. Her Captain, Stanley Lord, had made the prudent decision not to try to pick his way through the danger until daylight. During the night, the officers standing watch on the *Californian* saw a liner approach from a generally easterly direction, and then appear to shut out some of her lights and stop. A while later, some of those aboard the Leyland liner saw the ship fire about eight rockets – one of them, Apprentice James Gibson, specifically said that as he watched through binoculars, he 'observed a white flash apparently on her deck, followed by a faint streak towards the sky which then burst into white stars'.[2]

Captain Lord had by that point gone to nap on the Chart Room settee, and was informed that the other vessel had fired a number of 'white rockets'.[3] Lord told his men to try to contact the other ship via Morse lamp, but did not ask the wireless operator to be awakened to investigate the situation further. The men on the Bridge discussed this mysterious liner; they watched, commenting on the ship's appearance and feeling that she looked rather odd – Officer of the Watch Stone even remarked to Apprentice Gibson that the ship looked 'queer', and that she seemed to 'have a big side out of the water'.[4] Eventually, the other ship disappeared from the horizon.

A little while later, the men on the *Californian* saw three white rockets to the south, which they believed were coming from a different vessel than the one which they had observed and which had subsequently disappeared from

sight.[5] Chief Officer Stewart came on duty at 4:00 a.m.; a half-hour later, he had a discussion with Captain Lord on the subject of what had transpired during the night. Lord told Stewart to wake up the Marconi Operator, and the news was quickly received that the *Titanic* had sunk. The *Californian* later arrived at the scene where the *Carpathia* was recovering *Titanic*'s lifeboats, but by that point the work had already been done, and the Leyland liner eventually resumed course for Boston, Massachusetts.

Subsequently, men from the *Californian* were questioned at the American and British Inquiries into the disaster. The investigators concluded that the Leyland liner could have easily pushed through the ice and helped to rescue the *Titanic*'s passengers and crew, had she started out with the firing of the first rockets. Captain Lord eventually lost his position with the Leyland Line, although he was subsequently able to find employment with other steamship companies.

Conclusions

From the basic facts, it seems apparent that the men on the *Californian* saw the *Titanic* and the rockets that she fired. It seems that even on the night of the disaster, there was some question in the minds of a number of the participants as to what sort of signals they were, however. Later, when Captain Lord was asked if – on that night – he felt that the rockets were distress calls, or company signals, Lord made it very clear that he had not been sure, and that he had been awaiting confirmation on the point from his officers.[6]

As long as there was some doubt that they might not be company signals, however, someone should have done *something* to try to determine which of the two they were.

The Californian *on the morning of April 15, 1912.*

Waking up the *Californian*'s wireless operator would have been the simplest thing to do, and would likely have quickly resulted in the reception of some of *Titanic*'s distress signals – the two ships were well within wireless range of each other, and there is no reason to believe that if the set was turned on, they would not have heard them. However, nothing of the sort was done.

Without bringing in the question of whether or not the *Californian* itself could have reached the *Titanic* in time to help save any lives – which is a debatable question – one thing stands out above anything else. According to the Merchant Shipping Act of 1906, it was a misdemeanor to fail to respond to distress signals; if there was any question as to whether the rockets were distress rockets or company signals, a thorough investigation by someone should have been made. The failure to completely investigate the situation was a misdemeanor in and of itself.

Because of this simple fact, those who attempt to defend the *Californian*'s inaction like to imply that there were other, so-called 'mystery' ships in the vicinity or in between the two vessels that night, and many candidates to fill this role have been advanced over the years. A complicated ballet of three or four – why not ten? – ships has been expounded in defense of the *Californian*'s inaction. Despite the astronomical odds against these theories, and a complete lack of proof that identifies any particular ship as having been the alleged interloper, defenders of the Leyland liner and her Captain rabidly defend the concept. Yet even if one were to accept this extraordinary proposition, the simple fact remains: rockets, beyond a doubt *Titanic*'s, were seen by those on the *Californian*, and were not investigated.

Attempts have also been made to obfuscate the timeline of events aboard the *Titanic*, and the amount of time which separated the two vessels' clocks. All of this has been done to help 'prove' that the rockets seen by those on the *Californian* did not belong to the *Titanic*, and/or that the timing of events observed by witnesses on each ship respectively do not line up. In doing so, attempts have been made to snatch at any little thread which might indicate a non-traditional timeline of events aboard the *Titanic*. This evidence has been carefully compiled and presented in the pages of books, trade journals and web sites; however, while these claims may sound somewhat convincing when considered on their own, the larger body of evidence on the subject shows a very different picture.

The simple fact is that it is known about how long it took for the *Titanic* disaster to play out. With little exception, it seems that the collision took place at 11:40 p.m. and that she sank at about 2:20 a.m. – a time of about 2 hours and 40 minutes. Many survivor accounts are startlingly incomplete; if one attempts to push events too far up in the timeline, this tends to create gaps – in many cases large ones – later on in the disaster. At times, where more than one account from a single survivor is available, the recollections change with each telling. It seems more likely that these variations are most often the result of omissions in certain accounts. One must carefully study all the available accounts from a single survivor before jumping to any conclusions.

It is far more important to attempt to objectively reconstruct a timeline without any pre-conceived notions and to let the pieces fall where the evidence places them. That is how the timeline in this volume was prepared: a careful balance of *everything* … survivor time estimates … the level of flooding reported by survivors at certain times …

reported changes in the trim and heel of the ship … and the like. The difference between the clocks of the *Titanic* and *Californian* had nothing to do with our independent analysis. Once we finished constructing the *Titanic* timeline, however, we then went back and compared notes with what was reported about the *Californian*, and the correlation was startlingly close.

It is clear that at the time of the collision and throughout the sinking, the *Titanic*'s clocks were running 2 hours and 2 minutes ahead of New York Time, and 2 hours and 58 minutes behind Greenwich Mean Time. This is supported by both navigational evidence and survivor testimony; it was also first suggested by perhaps the strongest and most prominent defender of Captain Lord.[7] As far as the time that *Californian*'s clocks were keeping, this was based on her position at noon that day, 47° 25' W.[8] Her clocks were running 1 hour and 50 minutes ahead of New York Time, or 3 hours and 10 minutes behind Greenwich Mean Time.[9] In other words, there was a difference of about 12 minutes between clocks on the *Californian* and clocks on the *Titanic*, with the *Californian*'s clocks being behind those on the *Titanic*.

With this time difference in mind, the similarity between the times of the *Titanic*'s collision, the time she started and finished firing her rockets, and the time that she sank all appear to be a close match to the times that those on the *Californian* saw the steamer they were watching stop, fire rockets, and eventually disappear. As a result, the present authors feel that there is good reason to suspect that the *Titanic* and *Californian* were watching each other directly, without the presence of a 'mystery steamer' or 'mystery steamers' in between them.

However, there is a tremendous caveat. Could the *Californian* have reached the *Titanic* before the *Titanic* sank? Could she have saved more lives because of her close proximity to the scene? By any reckoning she was far closer than the *Carpathia* and any of the other ships who attempted to respond to *Titanic*'s distress calls. Yet, *Californian*'s lifeboats could only hold 218 people.[10] Given the startlingly short amount of time that people could survive in the icy water, the presence of ice in the vicinity which may have blocked direct access to the *Titanic,* and the likely amount of steaming time the Leyland vessel would have needed to reach the White Star liner, it seems likely that her efforts would not have been able to save everyone aboard, if anyone. However, if even one additional life had been saved – or even if the *Californian* had simply attempted to carry out a rescue without success – then those efforts would have been worthwhile and would have cleared her officers of any reproach. In the end, we will never know for sure how many might have been saved, simply because no attempt was made.[11]

It is regrettable that Captain Lord has unjustly served as a scapegoat over the years, when the responsibility for the actual accident cannot in any way be placed on him. Perhaps more questionable than any mistakes in judgment or lack of action by Captain Lord and his crew, however, are their obfuscations and attempts at covering up that they had seen rockets or been near *Titanic* after the *Californian* arrived in Boston. In the end, there are no villains in the *Titanic*'s story as a whole, or in the story of the *Californian*; only humans in unusual circumstances who made mistakes as they tried to pick their way through the disaster. However, the simple fact that *Titanic*'s rockets were sighted by the *Californian*, and that further action should have been taken, is an unavoidable one.

POSTSCRIPT

Rhoda Abbott was hospitalized following the *Carpathia*'s arrival in New York, and she was one of the last survivors discharged from St Vincent's Hospital. Physically and mentally taxed, and suffering from burns to her thighs,[1] contusions on her legs,[2] and frostbite to her hands and feet, it took a significant period of time for her to recover. She suffered from respiratory problems and asthma for the rest of her life. Rhoda was the sole female survivor to be rescued from Collapsibles A and B, or from the water.

Rhoda struggled with grief and feelings of loss following the death of her teenaged sons Rossmore and Eugene in the sinking. She felt that she no longer had any purpose in life. She frequently wrote to Emily Goldsmith, whom she had befriended during the maiden voyage. In a letter she wrote in 1914, Rhoda spoke of Eugene, saying: 'I know he is safe in God's keeping, but I miss him so much'. On a postcard sent that same year, she said: 'I have so envied you with Frankie [surviving], and me losing both mine, but I trust that they are better off out of this hard world'.

Abbott, who had separated from her husband prior to the *Titanic* disaster, married her lifelong friend George Williams in December 1912. By all accounts, her marriage was one of convenience, rather than being born out of any great love. The couple decided to move to Jacksonville, Florida, since they believed the warmer climate would ease her respiratory problems. In 1928, despite Rhoda's fear of the ocean, the couple undertook a sea voyage in moving to London, so that her husband could settle his late father's estate. They planned to return to the United States when this family business was concluded.

While in London, George suffered a massive disabling stroke, but Rhoda remained faithfully by his side. She cared for him until his death in 1938. After his passing, Rhoda wanted to return to the United States; she had become an American citizen when her husband was granted citizenship in 1919, had been issued a U.S. passport, and planned to return home as soon as she could sell her husband's property in London.

Unfortunately, with the outbreak of World War II, Great Britain passed the Financial Restriction Act, which made it impossible for her to move her assets out of England during the war. Rhoda periodically renewed her passport, but the financial situation, and a desire not to 'travel during war time conditions', prevented her from returning to America. She eventually gave up on her dream of returning to the U.S. and spending her final years there with her friends; she instead remained in England until her death in 1946. Her closest living relative at the time of her passing was a niece, who she was not close to.

Researcher Robert Bracken noted that following the sinking, Rhoda appeared to have developed a 'fatalistic' attitude that prevented her from enjoying life beyond the disaster; he also noted that she led an unfulfilled and sad life after the loss of her sons.[3]

* * * * *

After Colonel John Jacob Astor's death, **Madeleine Astor** inherited an annual $300,000 income from his $5 million trust fund, and was allowed the use of his mansions – the first on the corner of 65th Street and Fifth Avenue in New York,[4] and the second his estate in Newport, R.I. – under the condition that she forfeit her inheritance and usage if she remarried.[5] Colonel Astor left his oldest son Vincent the majority of his fortune, with a sizeable trust fund going to his daughter Ava. Both children were the product of his first marriage, which ended in divorce in 1909.

Madeleine gave birth to a son on August 14, 1912, four months to the day from when *Titanic* struck the iceberg. She named him John Jacob Astor, after his father.[6] Madeleine married her childhood friend, William K. Dick, on June 22, 1918, in Bar Harbor, Maine. Her remarriage attracted a lot of attention. Dick was a banker, Vice President of the Manufacturers Trust Company, and part owner of the *Brooklyn Times*. As per Colonel Astor's will, Madeleine was forced to forfeit all of her inheritance from him after the wedding. However, her son John still received a $3 million trust that was held until he turned 21.[7]

Madeleine and William Dick had two sons before divorcing on July 21, 1933, in Reno, Nevada. Madeleine was no stranger to controversy or scandal, since she was just 18 when she had married 47-year-old Colonel Astor. Her divorce from Dick created another scandal, not just because she married for a third time quickly afterwards, but also because she had apparently been having a relationship with 'Italian middleweight pugilist' Enzo Fiermonte prior to her divorce. Fiermonte and Madeleine married on November 27, 1933, just four months after her divorce from Dick. After a rocky marriage involving multiple separations, Madeleine and Enzo divorced on June 11, 1938, 'on the grounds

Madeleine Astor and her son John Jacob Astor V in late 1925.

of extreme cruelty'. Madeleine passed away from a heart condition on March 27, 1940. She was just 46 years old.[8]

* * * * *

Following his ordeal, **Frederick Barrett** signed on to the *Olympic* as a fireman. On May 25, 1912, Senator William Alden Smith was given a tour of *Titanic's* sister ship by Captain Herbert Haddock, as part of the Senate Inquiry. Captain Haddock happened to mention that one of the firemen aboard had been on *Titanic*, and Senator Smith, who was chairing the inquiry, went to see him in one of the boiler rooms; he wanted to gain a better understanding of what the conditions had been below deck when the collision occurred. Barrett's testimony was taken down at this time.[9] He testified in more depth at the British Inquiry.

Upon returning home, Barrett made it a priority to visit his sister in the Potteries. Unlike some of the other survivors who had been thronged by well-wishers and bystanders when they returned home, Barrett received a quiet reception. At that time, people in the town were completely unaware of the role he played in the *Titanic* disaster.[10]

* * * * *

Joseph Boxhall suffered from pleurisy in the wake of the disaster. He testified in both the Senate and British Inquiries. Soon after returning to England, Boxhall joined the *Adriatic*, serving as Fourth Officer. He joined the Royal Navy Reserve as a Sub-Lieutenant, and in 1915, was promoted to Lieutenant. During World War I, he was commissioned to serve aboard the battleship *Commonwealth*, and was then dispatched to Gibraltar, where he commanded a torpedo boat. After World War I, Boxhall was promoted to the rank of Lieutenant Commander.

Boxhall married his fiancée Marjory in 1919, but the couple never had children. In May 1919, he returned to the merchant service with the White Star Line, serving as Second Officer on the *Olympic*. During the 1920s, he served aboard a number of vessels sailing to Australia, as well as the United States, and Canada. Following the Cunard-White Star merger, Boxhall, by then a senior officer, served aboard *Berengaria*, *Aquitania*, *Ausonia*, *Scythia*, *Antonia* and *Franconia*.

Boxhall had been promoted as high as Chief Officer by the end of his career, but despite years of loyalty and exemplary service, he was never given his own command in the merchant service. Boxhall decided to retire in 1940, after four decades at sea.

Despite his reluctance to speak about *Titanic*, Boxhall served as technical adviser for the film version of *A Night to Remember*. He and Herbert Pitman both attended the premiere of the movie. Boxhall also got reacquainted with Walter Nichols at the premiere, who he had known both before and after *Titanic*.

In the 1960s, Boxhall's health began to fail. Despite this and the fact that he was soft spoken and did not like talking about the disaster, in 1962, he granted a radio interview to the BBC discussing the sinking.[11] The last of *Titanic's* surviving officers, Boxhall passed away in 1967 at the age of 83. As per his last wishes, Boxhall was cremated, and his ashes were scattered over the location of his distress coordinates, 41° 46 N, 50° 14 W, which is where he always maintained *Titanic* had sunk. Clearly, *Titanic* had remained a major part of his life, even more than 50 years later.

* * * * *

After the disaster, **Margaret Brown** helped establish the *Titanic* Survivor's Committee, which she personally chaired. On May 29, 1912, she presented *Carpathia's* Captain Rostron with a silver loving cup, and every crew member still on board the Cunarder with a medal. This was done on behalf of the survivors in commemoration of the ship and crew's exemplary rescue efforts.

Margaret wrote detailed press accounts relating her experiences during the sinking; these were published in newspapers in New York, Denver, and Paris. Her exploits and the strong character she displayed in Boat No. 6 gained her some publicity and notoriety, which she used to her advantage. She was deeply invested in women's rights, labor and workforce issues, promoting literacy and education for children, and preserving historical sites. In 1914, Brown was named as a candidate for a Senate seat for the second time, but stopped campaigning when her sister married a German baron. Anti-German feelings were high in the lead-up to, and during, World War I; she felt her sister's marriage would generate undue controversy.

After the outbreak of World War I, Brown worked with the American Committee for Devastated France to rebuild areas behind the front lines which had been devastated in the fighting, and aided wounded soldiers. Margaret was awarded the French Legion of Honour for her good citizenship, including activism and philanthropy, in the United States. Near the end of her life, Brown became an actress, and performed in stage productions.

When Margaret's husband, James Joseph 'J.J.' Brown, died in 1922, the couple had been separated for a number of years. 'J.J.' did not have a will. Margaret and her two children subsequently entered into a long and bitter five-year dispute, before her husband's estate was finally settled. Brown did not communicate with her children following the disagreement. Ironically, due to lavish spending, when 'J.J.' Brown died, he did not have as much of his fortune left to pass on as one might have expected.

At one point, Brown announced that she was engaged to Duke Charto of France. Less than 48 hours later, she recanted, saying: 'Me marry that old geezer – never. Give me every time the rugged men of the West, the men of Europe – why, in France there are only perfumed and unbathed Continental gallants – in England only brandy-soaked British gents.' She then proceeded to go on a world tour.

Margaret Brown died of a brain tumor on October 16, 1932 in New York, where she had been working with young actresses. She was 65. Contrary to popular myth, Margaret Brown was not an outcast among members of upper class society, and was accepted more than is commonly portrayed. For example, Vincent Astor and his family were 'intimates' of Margaret, 'whom she entertained at her 76-room New York home'. Nearly all portrayals of her in plays and movies are inaccurate, and do not reflect the real life Margaret Brown.

Brown became more famous following her death than she ever had been in life. In the 1930s, *Denver Post* reporter Gene Fowler penned a folk tale loosely based on her life. This tale led to a highly fictionalized story about her being written for a romance magazine. This story led to radio broadcasts in the 1940s, and eventually to the Broadway play *The Unsinkable Molly Brown*, which was made into a movie by MGM in 1964.

These stories perpetuated myths about Margaret, although by all accounts she was a larger-than-life personality in reality. Brown actually gave herself her nickname, when she remarked to a reporter following the *Titanic* disaster that the reason for her survival was 'Brown luck … I'm the unsinkable Mrs. J.J. Brown'. The name has stuck to this day.[12]

* * * * *

After the arrival in New York, **Harold Bride** was taken to the hospital; he later went to the home of Walter E. Jarvis, his uncle, so that he could spend time with his family while he convalesced. During his stay, Bride had the opportunity to get some bed rest, which aided the healing of his frostbitten foot, and sprained ankle. While he was at his uncle's house, Bride was visited by Marconi Operator Harold Cottam, whom he had befriended aboard the Cunard liner as they worked the key together on the way to New York. Bride was surprised to discover how well received the account he wrote and sold to the *New York Times* was. The article had led to him being considered one of the heroes of the sinking, a notion Bride was not comfortable with.

Bride's family had gotten word of his survival, and a *New York Times* reporter came to his uncle's house. The newspaperman bore a message from the Marconi Operator's father, via their London correspondent. He found Bride sitting in a chair enjoying a cigarette, with both feet bandaged. Bride's parents had sent their love, and said they were proud of him. Bride told the reporter: 'I'm glad that they have heard I'm safe. It's awfully good of you to bring this message up here to me.'

The reporter told him that the *New York Times* would gladly transmit any reply he wanted to send, and Bride laughed, saying: 'Tell the *Times* that I am very grateful. I would like to send a message, or rather two messages, if I may be permitted.'

His relatives laughed. They knew that the second message he alluded to would be for Mabel Ludlow, the young nurse who Bride – just 22-years-old at the time – was engaged to. The reporter agreed, and Bride dictated a message to his father: 'Quite safe. Uncle Walter and Aunt Millie and Esther looking after me. One foot badly sprained, the other frostbitten. Both improving. Am leaving for Washington for Senatorial Inquiry Monday morning. Home as soon as possible. Love to all. HAROLD.' Next, Bride dictated a message to Mabel: 'Safe and well. One ankle sprained. Home as soon as possible. Fondest love. HAROLD.'[13]

Bride testified in both the Senate and British Inquiries, and often gave contradictory stories between the two hearings. Whether this was due to any intentional evasiveness on Bride's part, or genuine difficulty with his memory – common after traumatic events – is unknown. During the Senate Inquiry, Bride was so physically exhausted that he had to be propped up in a chair with pillows, with his legs elevated.

After returning to England and recovering, Bride fell for another woman, Lucy Downie, and broke off his engagement to Mabel. His first job after the sinking was as a telegraphist in a London post office. Bride finally returned to sea as a Marconi Operator aboard the *Medina* in August

1912, the *German* in December 1912, and the *Dover* and *Namur* during January and February 1913. Bride was assigned to a relay station on the coast of Scotland in 1914.

Bride left the employ of the Marconi Company sometime during 1916. Between 1918 and 1919, Bride ended up serving as the wireless operator aboard the ship HMS *Mona's Isle*. Harold and Lucy were married on April 10, 1920, and the couple eventually had three children. Bride retired from the sea for good in 1922. His final assignment had been to serve as a wireless operator aboard the Cross-Channel Ferry.

Bride sought obscurity from that point on, and rarely discussed *Titanic*. The whole experience had been extremely traumatic, and Bride's thoughts often dwelled on Jack Phillips, whose loss he felt deeply. Eventually, the publicity and recognition that went with being a well-known *Titanic* survivor got to Bride, and he moved his family to Scotland to avoid unwanted attention. People who remember the family from their days in Scotland described Bride and his wife as being extremely private.

Bride quietly lived out the remainder of his days working as pharmacist in Scotland, before working as a traveling salesman for a London pharmaceutical company. A heavy smoker, he died of lung cancer on April 29, 1956, at the age of 66. Bride's niece stated that her uncle was an avid ham radio operator in his later years, staying up late, and contacting operators all over the world.[14]

* * * * *

Eugene Daly suffered frostbite to his feet and legs in the disaster. He credited his overcoat with having helped keep him warm enough to survive the night, and thereafter refused to travel without it.[15]

When Daly reached New York, he sent home a very brief letter to his mother Catherine in Ireland, letting her know that he and his cousin were safe. The correspondence was a mastery in understatement: 'Dear mother; got here safe. Had a narrow escape but please God, I am all right, also Maggie. I think the disaster caused you to fret, but things could have been worse than what they were.'[16]

Having lost everything in the sinking, Daly called on New York City's Mayor Gaynor on April 22, 1912 to plead for assistance from the Red Cross Relief Fund. Eugene recovered sufficiently enough to take part in the war pipes competition in Celtic Park, Queens on May 19, 1912, although he didn't win. Music remained an important part of his life after the sinking.[17]

Daly filed a claim in the Limitation of Liability hearings on January 4, 1913, seeking damages of $10,600 for his

Eugene Daly in later life.

lost property, and for 'personal injuries to the lower half of my person, which injuries are of a permanent nature'. He testified in front of Judge Julius M. Mayer in the United States District Court as part of the same hearings on June 25, 1915. As with all the survivors seeking compensation from the White Star Line,

Daly was not awarded the amount of money he sought.[18] Daly lived and worked in New York and New Jersey following the disaster, and continued to help financially support his younger sister Maggie and his family in Ireland. He was drafted into the military during World War I, marrying his fiancée Lillian prior to leaving. The couple later had one child, Marion. Eugene returned to Ireland in 1921 because his mother was ill, and thought to be dying. While aboard the ship, Daly was in a 'state of extreme panic'. He was unable to eat or sleep, and constantly paced the decks. His mother recovered, but Daly, too afraid of going back on a ship, decided that he and his wife would remain in Ireland.[19]

Daly stayed in his homeland until his wife passed away. Eventually he moved back to the United States, flying this time, and subsequently lived with his daughter and her husband in the Bronx. He remained friends with Bertha Mulvihill, although they had a falling out shortly after the sinking over false rumors that Daly had received money to speak publicly about the disaster. Daly reacted indignantly, feelings were hurt, and the two stopped speaking to each other. A few years later, Daly and his wife were in Providence, and tried to visit Bertha, but she would not see him.[20] Daly passed away on October 30, 1965. He was 82 years old.

* * * * *

After the disaster, **Frederick Fleet** testified in both the Senate and British Inquiries. He appeared to have been extremely uncomfortable while testifying, had difficulty articulating his responses, and reacted defensively to many of the questions, at one point asking: 'Is there any more likes to have a go at me?' The examiners commented that they felt sorry for him, and told him: 'You have given your evidence very well, although you seem to distrust us all.'[21]

Fleet returned to the sea, serving as both a Lookout and Able Bodied Seaman. He served aboard the *Olympic,* but eventually left the White Star Line and worked for other companies, including the Union Castle Line. Evidently, he returned to the White Star Line again at some point, as he related that 'the *Olympic* was my last ship...' Fleet left the sea for good in 1936; this was during the Depression years, when the passenger trade was hit hard, and jobs on the liners were hard to come by. He found employment at the Harland & Wolff shipyards, which had built *Titanic* and her sisters. Later, he worked as a shore Master-at-Arms for the Union Castle Line.

In his later years, Fleet sold newspapers on Pound Tree Road in Southampton for the *Southampton Echo,* where many people remember him. He said that he sold papers 'to while away the time'. In the 1960s, Sylvia Lightoller – Charles Lightoller's widow – met Fleet in the park, and the two reminisced.[22] During this time period, Fleet and Ed Kamuda, the future President of the Titanic Historical Society, began corresponding with each other via letters, and became good friends. Fleet remarked at how he had been poor most of his life, saying that 'from the time I started ...

I was no better off, pay in those days was very poor, I was always without money, always in debt'.

At the time, Fleet and his wife Eva lived in a house with her brother. Tragically, when Eva passed away on December 28, 1964, Fleet's brother-in-law evicted him. In his last letter to Kamuda, Fleet sounded desperate: 'My dear friend. Just a few lines to let you know I am in deep trouble. I have lost my wife, also I am leaving my house, the place where I have been living. There is only my brother in law and myself, we cannot agree. From yours sincerely, Fred Fleet.'[23]

Despondent and severely depressed, Frederick Fleet hanged himself on January 10, 1965. He was 76 years old.[24] Fleet was buried in a pauper's grave in Holly Cemetery, but the Titanic Historical Society was able to raise enough donations to place a headstone in his memory in 1993.

* * * * *

Following the arrival in New York, **Sir Cosmo and Lady Duff Gordon** began receiving criticism for surviving in a lifeboat that had just 12 persons aboard, while making no attempt to return and rescue anyone else. When it was discovered that Sir Cosmo had paid each of the crewmembers in the boat £5 to replace their kits, it gave rise to rumors that the Duff Gordons had either bribed their way into the boat, or bribed the crewmembers into not returning. There is no evidence to support either accusation. Regardless of this, the couple's reputation suffered as a result, Sir Cosmo's even more so.

Both testified in the British Inquiry, and in so doing were the only passengers to give evidence to the court. At the inquiry, Lord Mersey had a balanced approach to the Duff Gordon situation, lambasting the false rumors that were being spread and some of the lines of questioning that Sir Cosmo had been subjected to, while still pointing out that the occupants in Boat No. 1 did nothing to rescue people from the water:

> The very gross charge against Sir Cosmo Duff Gordon that, having got into No. 1 boat he bribed the men in it to row away from the drowning people is unfounded. I have said that the members of the crew in that boat might have made some attempt to save the people in the water, and that such an attempt would probably have been successful; but I do not believe that the men were deterred from making the attempt by any act of Sir Cosmo Duff Gordon's. At the same time I think that if he had encouraged to the men to return to the position where the 'Titanic' had foundered they would probably have made an effort to do so and could have saved some lives.[25]

Following the British Inquiry, the couple returned to their business; over time, things regained a sense of normalcy. Lady Duff Gordon continued to find success as a dress and lingerie designer, creating styles under the professional name of 'Lucile, Ltd'. She was called a 'genius', and her gowns were pronounced the 'final dictum of fashionable attire on the Continent and in the United States'. She was well-known among high society in London, Paris, and New York, and was a celebrity of sorts.

Despite his wife's successes, Sir Cosmo rarely accompanied her on business. He was described as 'a handsome but reserved Scotsman who ... detested reporters and especially loathed the tabloid coverage her Ladyship attracted'.[26] Some of his wife's fashion designs were considered risqué, and generated a lot of attention and followers.

Lucy had shops in New York, Paris, and an establishment in Hanover Square, London, which largely attracted a clientele of British nobility. She was widely credited with revolutionizing the dress of Englishwomen, advocating shorter skirts and more revealing, yet tasteful, designs.[27]

In 1922, the couple was forced to close Lucy's London and Paris establishments, due to difficulty keeping up with the growing competition. Sir Cosmo passed away in London on April 20, 1931, after an extended illness. He was 69 years old. In 1932, Lady Duff Gordon completed and released her memoirs *Discretions and Indiscretions.* Between 1932 and 1935, Lucy's business collapsed, and she fell on hard times. She was living in a nursing home when she passed away from pneumonia on April 20, 1935, exactly four years to the day after her husband died.[28] She was 72 years old.

* * * * *

Prior to the disaster, **Colonel Archibald Gracie**, a published historian, had spent 7 years researching and writing *The Truth About Chickamauga.* This book was about the Civil War battle his father had fought in. While he found the experience of writing the book rewarding, it was mentally and physically taxing. He journeyed alone, leaving his wife Constance and their daughter Edith at home. Gracie claimed that he had taken his subsequent trip to Europe to 'gain much-needed rest', and 'get it off my mind', but that was only part of the story. In fact, Gracie had gone to Europe at the urging of a medical specialist, who had seen him approximately six weeks prior to the disaster, and thought that the rest and relaxation would be beneficial for his well being.[29] Gracie, a diabetic, was experiencing health concerns. He had minor surgery shortly before the sinking, and was 'not in thoroughly restored health' at the beginning of the maiden voyage.[30] The Colonel liked to stay physically active while traveling, but owing to his exhaustion and ongoing recovery from surgery, he spent most of his time during the voyage socializing and reading.

Despite his traumatic experiences and having suffered from hypothermia, Gracie experienced relatively few immediate aftereffects. Unlike some of his fellow survivors saved from Collapsible B, he did not suffer from frostbite. However, once aboard *Carpathia*, Gracie discovered that he had received a blow on top of his head while struggling in the water; he also found inflamed cuts on both of his legs, as well as bruises on his knees. He did not feel any of these injuries prior to being rescued. His whole body was sore to the touch for several days.

Since Gracie was an amateur historian, he spent a good deal of the *Carpathia*'s voyage to New York City discussing the sinking with survivors, and had in-depth conversations with Second Officer Lightoller and some of the other officers. Following the arrival in America, Gracie gave a detailed and accurate account which was widely published in the press.[31] Once he was safely home, the Colonel wasted no time in beginning to write about his own experiences, and the disaster in general. He spent the spring, summer, and fall of 1912 corresponding with as many *Titanic* survivors as he could, and compiling a manuscript for publica-

tion. Gracie hoped to set the record straight about the true events of the sinking. The result of his labors is one of the most detailed accounts written by a *Titanic* survivor.

By December 1912, Gracie had largely completed his book. He planned to continue correcting the proofs of the manuscript, and to write a final chapter dealing with the causes of the disaster and the lessons it taught.[32] Sadly, Colonel Gracie never had an opportunity to put the finishing touches on the volume, as his health took a sharp turn for the worse. Gracie was reported to have been 'haunted by his memories of the wreck of the *Titanic* and never completely recovered from the shock of his experiences in that disaster'. His wife and daughter were said to have been very 'fearful for him for some weeks past'. However, it was reported that Gracie was well enough to be up and about until shortly before his death; as late as Thanksgiving 1912, he attended a reception at the Hotel Gotham which his wife and he gave to introduce their daughter, Edith Temple Gracie.

On December 2, 1912, Colonel Gracie fell into a diabetic coma, passing away on December 4, at the age of 54. During his final hours, *Titanic* still weighed heavily on Gracie's mind, and his last words were reportedly 'we must get them all in the boats'. While his death was caused by his disease, his family members and physicians felt that the true 'cause was the shock he suffered last April when he went down with the ship and was rescued later after long hours on a half-submerged raft'.[33] Even though his book wasn't completed, it was published posthumously as *The Truth About the Titanic* in May 1913. Like any book, the text contains some mistakes, but Gracie's work is still considered a classic and essential read, and an excellent reference for students of the *Titanic* disaster.[34]

* * * * *

Robert Hichens testified in the Senate Inquiry, where he denied stories regarding some of his reported behavior and conduct in Boat No. 6. He specifically denied that he was asked to return to rescue people struggling in the water.[35] He later testified in the British Inquiry.

Hichens and his wife Florence, living in Southampton, had six children between 1908 and 1925. Contrasting with the unflattering portrait painted of him by other survivors, Hichens' family loved him dearly. They were so worried when they heard that *Titanic* sank that it was feared his wife, who was then pregnant, would miscarry. Hichens' father wrote a letter reflecting on the family's grief, until they had learned of his survival: 'Oh the tears that has [sic] been shed here only God knows. No rest only from this morning then the tears of joy.'

Margaret Brown was not held in high regard by the family. Hichens remarked that Brown 'could have walked into any lifeboat. ...Why oh why did she have to walk into mine?' Hichens returned to sea, and work often kept him away from home. His life following *Titanic* was so shrouded in mystery that many of his own children did not know the details, and his grandchildren were initially unaware of his role in the *Titanic* disaster.

Researcher Phil Gowan, with much effort, was able to piece together Hichens' post-sinking life. He apparently spent time in Durban and Johannesburg, and was rumored to have received remuneration from the White Star Line. During World War I, Hichens served in the Royal Navy

Reserve, and then served on smaller ships for the next two decades. He spent time in China and Hong Kong in the 1920s, and family stories suggest his activities there may have included gun running and piracy.

Hichens fell onto hard times in his later years, and was away from his family during much of the 1930s. In late 1933, he had a disagreement with an acquaintance over the sale of a motor vessel, and blamed him for the woes he was then experiencing. Drunk, Hichens went to the man's house. After an argument, the two got into a physical scuffle, and Hichens attempted to shoot and kill the man, and then himself. Fortunately, the other man was only slightly wounded, and Hichens' attempt to end his own life was unsuccessful. He was arrested, and a letter on his person proved that he had been planning to shoot his acquaintance, and then kill himself. He attempted to cut his wrists while in custody, and then served several years in prison, being released in 1937.

When his wife became ill in 1939, Hichens finally returned home, staying until her death. By 1940, he was back at sea, serving on the *English Trader*. Hard living finally caught up with him, and his health began to fail. On Sept. 23, 1940, Hichens fell into a coma while at sea, and passed away. Because he had been out of touch with many family members for so many years, even his own children never learned the full circumstances of his passing. Until his true fate was uncovered, many false rumors of his end had persisted.[36]

* * * * *

Just after the arrival in New York, **Joseph Bruce Ismay** issued instructions that no International Mercantile Marine ships were to leave port without a sufficient number of boats to accommodate every person on board.[37] Upon hearing that an inquiry was being set up to look into the causes of the accident, Ismay issued an official statement to the press:

> In the presence of and under the shadow of a catastrophe so overwhelming my feelings are too deep for expression in words. I can only say that the White Star Line and its officers and employees will do everything possible to elleviate [sic] the sufferings and the sorrow of the survivors and their relatives and friends. The *Titanic* was the last word in shipbuilding, and every requirement prescribed by the British Board of Trade had been lived up to. The master, officers, and seamen were the most efficient in the British service. I am informed a committee of the United States Senate has been appointed to investigate the wreck. I heartily welcome an exhaustive inquiry, and any aid that I or my associates or navigators can render is at the service of the public and the Governments of the United States and Great Britain. Under these circumstances I must respectfully defer making further statement at this time.

Ismay donated $50,000 to the pension fund for widows of seamen on the *Titanic* shortly after the disaster.[38] He also testified at both the Senate and British Inquiries.

Yet Ismay was the subject of much controversy, and personal attacks on his reputation, simply for having survived

the sinking. The fact that Ismay helped load a good number of boats during the disaster, and attempted to assist the officers and crew in general has often been overlooked, or outright ignored, by historians.[39]

In the British Inquiry, Clement Edwards personally attacked Ismay during his questioning, expressing the opinion that 'having regard to his position, it was his duty to remain upon that ship until she went to the bottom'. When Lord Mersey sought to clarify what Edwards was saying, the latter said, 'I do not flinch from it a little bit.[40]

In the Final Report at the British Inquiry, Lord Mersey argued against Edwards' position, saying an 'attack was made in the course of the Enquiry on the moral conduct of two of the passengers, namely, Sir Cosmo Duff Gordon and Mr. Bruce Ismay. It is no part of the business of the Court to enquire into such matters, and I should pass them by in silence if I did not fear that my silence might been misunderstood'. Mersey also said: 'As to the attack on Mr. Bruce Ismay, it resolved itself into the suggestion that, occupying the position of Managing Director of the Steamship Company, some moral duty was imposed upon him to wait on board until the vessel foundered. I do not agree. Mr. Ismay, after rendering assistance to many passengers, found 'C' collapsible, the last boat on the starboard side, actually being lowered. No other people were there at the time. There was room for him and he jumped in. Had he not jumped in he would merely have added one more life, namely, his own, to the number of those lost.[41]

Ismay had wanted to argue publicly against the accusations being made against him, but was dissuaded from doing so by the directors of the White Star Line, who believed it would only draw additional negative attention to the company. In 1913, Ismay left the International Mercantile Marine Company. However, this was in accordance with an arrangement that had long since been made; Ismay had given International Mercantile Marine notice of his pending resignation a month *prior* to the sinking. In October 1912, Ismay apparently had a change of heart, writing a letter expressing his desire to retain at least his position of Chairman of the White Star Line. He was refused, and subsequently resigned both the Presidency of International Mercantile Marine, and his Chairmanship of the White Star Line on June 30, 1913.[42]

After Ismay's resignation, he spent considerably less time in London, and less time at the Liverpool offices of the White Star Line. He began dividing his time between London and Ireland; when in Ireland, he would stay at Costelloe Lodge, in County Galway, in a state of partial retirement. Rumors held that Ismay became a virtual recluse following the *Titanic* disaster, never to be heard from again, but these are not at all accurate. Although he withdrew from certain social circles, and was semi-retired, he continued to remain active in his business interests. These ranged from being Chairman of the Asiatic Steam Navigation Company; Director of the London, Midland & Scottish Railway; the Liverpool & London and Globe Insurance Company; the Sea Insurance Company; and the Birmingham Canal Navigation. He was also chairman of the Liverpool Steamship Owners' Protection Association, the Liverpool & London War Risks Association, and the Delta Insurance Company.

Ismay's business acumen was touted in his obituary: 'In business Ismay was accounted an austere man. He was certainly taciturn by nature, but could be a charming host. He had an extraordinary memory; his success was due to his industry, integrity, and acumen, qualities which he inherited from his father.'

Ismay was also very active in charity work. Some of his accomplishments included inaugurating the *Mersey*, a cadet ship, for the training of officers for the merchant navy, as well as giving £11,000 to found a fund for widows of seamen. In 1919, he gave £25,000 to set up a fund to recognize the contributions of merchantmen in World War I. In 1924, he inaugurated the National Mercantile Marine fund with a gift of $125,000.

In 1936, Ismay's health began to fail, and he was forced to withdraw from most of his business activities. He had been diagnosed with diabetes earlier in the 1930s, and his health had taken a turn for the worse. Eventually, part of his right leg had to be amputated. Ismay returned to England, buying a small home near Liverpool. He passed away in London on October 17, 1937, at the age of 74. He was survived by his wife Julia, two sons, and two daughters. Following Ismay's passing, his son George Bruce Ismay continued to be associated with the passenger trade via Cunard White Star, Limited.[43]

* * * * *

During World War I, **Violet Jessop** served as a nurse for the British Red Cross. In that work, she served aboard the HMHS *Britannic*, the sister ship to *Titanic* and *Olympic*, which had been converted into a hospital ship for war duty. Her voyage on that ship was cut short when the converted liner struck a mine and sank off the Greek island of Kea on November 21, 1916. In this posting, Jessop had the unfortunate distinction of having been aboard both *Titanic* and *Britannic* when they sank. Jessop had also been serving as a stewardess on *Olympic* when she collided with the British warship HMS *Hawke* on September 20, 1911, when both vessels sustained significant damage.

Perhaps Jessop's closest shave was when the *Britannic* was sinking. That liner's propellers continued to churn as the disaster took place, and Jessop was forced to jump out of the lifeboat she was in to avoid being drawn into them. She was sucked underwater, hitting her head on the keel of a lifeboat, before someone pulled her into another boat. She said: 'Years later when I went to my doctor because of a lot of headaches, he discovered I had once sustained a fracture of the skull!' She credited her thick auburn hair and hairdo with cushioning the blow, and preventing an even worse injury.

After World War I ended, Jessop returned to the White Star Line, serving on the *Olympic* and *Majestic*. Eventually she joined the Red Star Line, where she served mostly aboard *Belgenland*; she also completed some voyages aboard the *Lapland* and *Westernland*. Violet said that the *Belgenland* had the highest crew morale of any ship she had ever served on. Later she worked for the Royal Mail Line, aboard the *Alcantara* and *Andes*.[44]

On October 29, 1923, when she was 36 years old, Violet married fellow White Star Line employee John James Lewis; Lewis was substantially her senior. Few people attended their wedding. The marriage was a failure and the couple separated, but did not divorce. Jessop considered it a great mistake that they ever wed, and being a stringent Catholic, was ashamed at the failure, and felt she could never marry again. The reason for the failed marriage is

unclear, as Jessop never spoke of the circumstances, and rarely even mentioned the wedding.[45]

In 1950, Violet retired to Suffolk, where she lived in a sixteenth-century thatched cottage. She raised hens and tended her garden. A few years after her retirement, Jessop received a bizarre middle-of-the-night phone call from a lady regarding the *Titanic*. She asked Violet if she saved a baby during the sinking, to which Violet responded: 'Yes.' The mysterious caller said: 'Well, I was that baby,' laughed, and hung up on her. Jessop later mentioned this story to biographer John Maxtone-Graham, who told her it was likely a prank call. Jessop disagreed, telling him that it couldn't have been a prank, because 'I had never told that story to anyone before I told you now'.

Violet granted some interviews when the movie version of *A Night to Remember* was released in 1958. She passed away in 1971 at the age of 83.[46]

* * * * *

Charles Joughin made a full and complete recovery from his experiences – quite remarkable considering the amount of time he had spent in the water that night. He testified at the British Inquiry. He soon returned to the sea, serving as Chief Baker on a number of vessels, including a stint with the American Export Lines, as well as troop transports during World War II. He retired around 1944. Joughin was reported to have survived another shipwreck, as he was aboard the SS *Oregon* when it sank in Boston Harbor. His wife Nellie preceded him in death. Joughin passed away in 1956, leaving behind a daughter and step-daughter.[47]

* * * * *

Charles Lightoller testified at both inquiries following the sinking. He was indignant at some of the questions asked of him, such as whether the falling funnel hurt anyone when it crashed down on the masses in the water. Lightoller did not want the British Board of Trade, the White Star Line, Captain Smith, or any of his fellow crewmembers to shoulder the blame for the disaster, and admitted that 'it was very necessary to keep one's hand on the whitewash brush', particularly at the British Inquiry.[48] As the only surviving senior officer from *Titanic*, Lightoller's word was trusted on a number of issues by the examiners, even in cases where the majority of eyewitness evidence contradicted him: this was true, for example, of his claim that the ship sank intact.

As he was a Lieutenant in the Royal Navy Reserve, Lightoller was called to duty in the Royal Navy during World War I. In that service he again served aboard the *Oceanic*, which had been converted to an armed merchant cruiser during the war. On September 8, 1914, Lightoller was aboard when the ship ran aground and had to be abandoned. He once again had to lead an evacuation effort, loading and lowering lifeboats.

In 1915, Lightoller was given command of a torpedo boat, HMTB *117*, winning the Distinguished Service Cross for engaging a Zeppelin in combat. Following this, he was given command of the torpedo boat cruiser *Falcon*. On April 1, 1918, Lightoller was asleep in his bunk when the vessel collided with a trawler and sank while escorting a convoy in the North Sea.

Lightoller was next given command of the destroyer *Garry*, and on July 19, 1918, the ship rammed and sank German submarine *UB-110*. The ship's bow was badly damaged, and they had to limp back to port in reverse to relieve stress on the bulkheads. For these actions, Lightoller received a bar on his Distinguished Service Cross, and was promoted to Lieutenant Commander.

By the time Lightoller came out of the Royal Navy in 1918, he held the rank of Commander. He returned to the White Star Line, serving as Chief Officer on *Celtic*, before being passed over for a promotion to the *Olympic*. It was clear that White Star management was not going to give him his own command. Lightoller did not want to remain a Chief Officer for the remainder of his career, so he decided to retire shortly thereafter. Despite his twenty years of loyal service to White Star Line, when he told them the news, the stunning response was: 'Oh, you are leaving us, are you. Well, Good-bye.' None of *Titanic*'s surviving officers were ever given their own command by the company.

Following his retirement, Lightoller and his wife Sylvia engaged in a variety of jobs such as running an inn, raising chickens, and engaging in property speculation. In 1936, Lightoller gave a radio interview for the BBC, in which he described how *Titanic* sank.[49]

In May 1940, when Lightoller was 66 years old, he and his oldest son Roger used his 58-foot motor yacht *Sundowner* to aide in the evacuation of the British Expeditionary Force and Allied troops from Dunkirk, France. They rescued 130 men while Luftwaffe planes made bombing and strafing runs at them as they sailed back to Ramsgate, England. Lightoller and his wife had five children, but sadly two of his sons, Brian and Roger, were killed during World War II. Lightoller ran a boatyard in his later years, building motor launches for river police, and passed away in 1952.[50]

* * * * *

Harold Lowe testified in both the Senate and British Inquiries following the sinking. Several false rumors regarding him were brought up during his testimony in America. First, it was rumored that he had been drunk during the sinking, probably due to his use of harsh language. In fact, Lowe was an abstainer.[51] There were also thorny questions about his firing of warning shots between the ship's side and Boat No. 14 as it was lowered; how had he managed to avoid hitting anyone? While nearly all the eyewitness accounts agree that Lowe fired warning shots only, the Michigan Minutemen had heard several seamen gossiping that he fired directly into the crowd. This may explain why Senator Smith questioned him so thoroughly on this point, while never directly bringing up the allegations.[52]

Lowe gained a certain level of fame for his actions in Boat No. 14, saving at least three people from the sea, as well as assisting other lifeboats full of survivors. When he returned to his home in Barmouth, over 1,300 people attended a reception held in his honor at the Picture Pavillion. He was presented with an inscribed gold watch, which read: 'Presented to Harold Godfrey Lowe, 5th officer R.M.S. *Titanic* by his friends in Barmouth and elsewhere in recognition and appreciation of his gallant services at the foundering of the *Titanic* 15th April 1912.'[53]

Lowe married Ellen Whitehouse in 1913, and the couple eventually had a son and daughter. He resumed his career as an officer, but like Lightoller, Pitman, and Boxhall, was never given a command of his own while in the merchant service. Lowe served in the Royal Navy Reserve during World War I, and was promoted to the rank of Commander. He retired to Deganwy in North Wales with his family. When World War II broke out, Lowe volunteered his house for use as a sector post, and despite failing health, carried out his duties to his fullest. Harold Lowe passed away in 1944. He was 61 years old. His friends and neighbors eulogized him as 'a man who made up his mind what his duty was and did it regardless of personal consequences'.[54]

* * * * *

Following the sinking, **William Mellors**' hands and feet were badly frostbitten, and it took him some time to fully recover. When he wrote his mother on April 22, 1912, he apologized for the poor handwriting, saying that 'my nerves are shattered'. When he wrote a letter to his friend Dorothy Ockenden on May 9, 1912, he mentioned that he still had not regained all the feeling in his hands.[55] Luckily, Mellors was eventually able to make a full and complete recovery, but it took months to regain the full use of his fingers, legs, and feet.

Mellors filed a claim in the Limitation of Liability hearings seeking $148 for lost property, and $5,000 because he had 'received severe bodily injuries, and was frozen in the legs, feet and arms and other parts of his body, by reason of the exposure to the water and cold, and suffered illness and sustained permanent injuries and incurred expenses for medical treatment, and was incapacitated entirely from work for several months after April 14, 1912, and was partly incapacitated from work thereafter'. Mellors testified in front of Judge Julius M. Mayer as part of those hearings on June 26, 1915.[56] Despite his injuries, Mellors was not awarded the full amount of compensation he was asking for.

After recovering, Mellors went to work at the Richmond County Country Club on Staten Island, and served as a valet in New York City until 1915. In 1916, he traveled and worked as a social entertainer. During World War I, Mellors enlisted in the military, and following the war, he was naturalized as a U.S. citizen due to his record of exemplary service. Mellors spent the next 15 years working as a salesman. Mellors married his wife Juanita in 1920, and the couple eventually had a daughter.

In 1935, Mellors became the associate editor of the *National Republic* magazine in Michigan. By the end of World

William Mellors in 1925.

Left: *Bertha Mulvihill in her later years.*

Below: *Walter Nichols* (left) *and Joseph Boxhall* (right) *together at the premier of* A Night to Remember.

The couple had a very happy marriage, eventually having five children. They christened their first child Mary, because Bertha had prayed while in the lifeboat, and promised the Virgin Mary if she survived, she would name her first daughter after her.

Bertha spoke to reporters immediately following the sinking, but thereafter, she rarely spoke of her experiences. The subject was taboo in her home or at family gatherings. She led a happy life, but due to the disaster, she had headaches and nightmares, and would wake up crying, and would even hide in a closet during thunderstorms due to the noise. Despite her strong desire to see her family in Ireland again, she never returned home, for fear of crossing the ocean again. Sadly, she never again saw her brother Brian, who was just an infant when she left home. Her fear of the ocean was so strong that during family outings, she could not even bring herself to stay at the family beach house at Bonnet Shore on Narragansett Bay.

In her later years, Bertha was finally able to open up about the disaster, talking to her family about it, and even making the occasional public comment about it following the publication of *A Night to Remember* and the subsequent film. She enjoyed spending as much time with her grandchildren and family as she could, even when her health began to fail. Bertha and Eugene Daly remained friends following the sinking, but they soon had a falling out when she heard false rumors that he was speaking publicly about the disaster in a vaudeville circuit. Several years later, Daly tried to visit, but Bertha wouldn't see him, feeling that their differences had never been reconciled. Despite this, she always credited him with her survival. Bertha passed away on October 15, 1959. She was 73 years old.

* * * * *

War II, Mellors was promoted to full editor. During the Second Red Scare – which lasted from 1947 to 1957 – *National Republic* furnished the Dies Committee[57] with a large amount of documents and evidence that they allegedly used in their investigations. Mellors, supposedly a gifted speaker, traveled around the country, trying to rouse crowds of 'loyal Americans' against hidden communists in the United States.

Around this time, Mellors' health began to decline, and he died in 1948. He was just 54 years old. Following his death, the *National Republic* declined in popularity, and by the end of the 1950s, was no longer being published.[58]

* * * * *

Bertha Mulvihill spent some time in a hospital in Rhode Island following the disaster, and another several months recovering from her rib and back injuries. These injuries caused her lingering pain for the rest of her life, particularly in her later years. On April 19, 1912, her sister Mary sent an extremely brief cablegram home to their family in Ireland. Two words were all that was needed to disclose the happy news: 'Bertha safe – Mary.'[59]

Bertha married her fiancé Henry Noon on August 12, 1912. Her association with the disaster made her a local celebrity of sorts in the Providence area, and a crowd of local press members and well-wishers mobbed the wedding dinner at her sister's house. The newly married couple had to sneak out a back window. The couple discussed going to Ireland for their honeymoon, but Bertha could not bring herself to set foot on a ship again.

Upon reaching New York, **Walter Nichols** discovered that his family believed he was dead, so he sent a message home as quickly as he could. He was penniless, however, and needed to raise money for his return trip home to England. As a result, he sold his story to the press, along with a copy of the vivid personal letter he wrote to his sister which described his experiences.

Nichols, one of a number of crewmembers who had signed on to *Titanic* from the SS *St. Paul,* which had been laid up due to the coal strike, lamented the loss of so many of his former shipmates.[60] Nichols believed that, of the twenty men from the *St. Paul* who had joined the *Titanic* when he had, he was the only survivor.

Nichols returned to sea at the beginning of World War I, working aboard Canadian Pacific Steamships, sailing aboard troopships from Halifax, Nova Scotia and Quebec, to Avonmouth, Bristol, United Kingdom. He made several crossings on the SS *Prince Edwards,* which was later torpedoed off Gallipoli. He also sailed from Canada to Liverpool on the SS *Principello,* SS *Avon,* and SS *Lake Michigan.* Nichols' last recorded sailing during this period was in 1915. His whereabouts until the fall of 1918 are unknown, and even his family is not sure where he was during those years.

In October 1918, Nichols served aboard the HMHS *Panama,* a hospital ship out of Southampton, via the ports of Trieste and the Dardanelles in Turkey. Nichols served on this vessel for over nine months before returning to Southampton. After that period, the destination of the ship's next voyage is unclear, although Nichols' family believes that it was engaged in taking ANZAC troops home to New Zealand and Australia.

Once Nichols returned from this voyage, he served aboard the SS *Czar*, a former Russian American liner; on August 28, 1919, Nichols accompanied the ship on a 58-day voyage to Murmansk, in North Russia. The ship was taking men and supplies to support the White movement in the Russian Civil War. Nichols made three round trips aboard this vessel. He then joined the Royal Mail Steam Packet Company as a steward, and between 1920 and 1926, once again completed round trips across the Atlantic from Southampton to New York aboard SS *Orduna* and SS *Orbita*. Nichols was transferred to the RMS *Alcantara* for its maiden voyage, and served aboard her for the next two years, until he retired from the sea in 1928. At the time of his retirement, Nichols had been at sea for a total of 38 years.

Nichols then resided in the village of West Moors, Dorset, which was where his wife Florence's family lived. There he took a job at the post office. Their two sons ran businesses from their large backyard. By the time World War II broke out, Nichols had retired from full-time work, living beside the sea in the town of Swanage, Dorset, and working part-time in the Grosvenor Hotel restaurant. One of his sons served in the Merchant Navy during the war, while his other son served with the Fire Brigades, in which service he suffered several traumatic experiences. Nichols, by then an elderly man, worked at the Admiralty Ordinance Factory at Holton Heath near Poole, where torpedo research was conducted. He lived on site, and was eventually transferred to Red Barracks, Weymouth, near the Navy base of Portland.

After the war, Nichols returned to his home in Swanage and continued working at the Grosvenor Hotel. In 1951, Florence and he celebrated their fiftieth wedding anniversary. Sadly, in 1953, Florence passed away, and the couple's only daughter followed in short order. Instead of living alone, Nichols moved in with his son and grandson Howard back in West Moors. Nichols was interviewed during the making of *A Night to Remember*, and due to this, was invited to the premier of the film. There he was reintroduced to Joseph Boxhall, whom he had known before and after *Titanic*. Nichols passed away in 1961, following a short illness. He was 85 years old.[61]

* * * * *

As a surviving officer, **Herbert Pitman** was called to testify at both the Senate and British Inquiries. In May 1912, he rejoined his previous ship, *Oceanic*, where he served as Third Officer.

In September 1912, Pitman underwent what was supposed to be a routine reexamination of his vision, based on White Star Line and Board of Trade regulations that their Captains and officers get their vision tested periodically. Pitman's vision had been tested seven times previously, and he passed the British Board of Trade requirements on each occasion. However, since his previous examination, regulations had been changed, and the vision tests used had been revised; these made it much more difficult for even a mildly color blind person like Pitman to pass. The Board of Trade was concerned that color blind officers would be unable to distinguish the colors of a ship's lights at night, and thus not know which direction they were sailing in.

Pitman failed the new examination. Despite his years of service as an officer without any difficulties, he was ruled incompetent and was asked to surrender his certificate. The White Star Line assisted Pitman, however, transferring him to their Purser Department. Although it has previously been suggested that Pitman's vision was deteriorating, and that he switched to a less demanding position as a result, this was not the case.[62] Pitman ended up serving on *Titanic*'s sister ship *Olympic*, but as a purser, rather than as an officer.

In the early 1920s, Pitman left the White Star Line, and began working for Shaw, Savill and Albion Company, Ltd. He married his fiancée Mildred in 1922. Pitman continued to serve aboard vessels as a purser, and during World War II, he served in that capacity aboard *Mataroa*. He retired from the Merchant Navy in 1946, after more than fifty years at sea. Prior to his retirement, Pitman was awarded membership in the Most Excellent Order of the British Empire (MBE), for his long and meritorious service at sea and in hazardous waters during World War II.[63]

Sadly, Pitman was preceded in death by his wife; he spent his later years living with his niece in Pitcombe, and passed away in 1961. Pitman briefly corresponded with author Walter Lord, prior to the publication of *A Night to Remember* in 1955. However it appears that he was reluctant to discuss the disaster in detail, referring to it as the '*Titanic* affair'.[64] Pitman was reunited with his former shipmate Joseph Boxhall during the 1958 film premiere of *A Night to Remember*. By that point, these two men were the only surviving officers of the ship.

* * * * *

George Rheims suffered significant injuries during the sinking. By the time he and the other survivors arrived in New York City, his feet were swollen up and very black. After the arrival, Rheims did not go to St Vincent's or another hospital, as so many of the other injured survivors did. Instead he was taken to his New York residence at Hotel Plaza, where a doctor called on him, and confined him to bed for two weeks. Rheims had frostbite, and developed gangrene in two of his toes. He had to be carried everywhere he went, and his medical bills began to add up.

After he was well enough to return to Paris, Rheims had to walk on crutches for another week, and was still not well enough to return to work for three additional weeks. Rheims suffered 'quite a lot of pain' during his recovery, and noted that his memory was somewhat impaired following the disaster. While Rheims eventually recovered, he said that 'when it is cold now I suffer with my feet'.

He had a happy reunion with his wife Mary following the disaster, and resumed work related to his importing company in Paris, including his two overseas trips a year. Rheims filed a deposition and claim in the Limitation of Liability hearings on November 14, 1913 for over $6,418 in lost property and valuables, as well as for his injuries and subsequent doctor bills. Despite his injuries, he lived a full life, passing away in 1962.[65]

* * * * *

Following her mother Lutie Parrish's recovery from her injuries, **Imanita Shelley** was reunited with her father Samuel Parrish, and husband William. At the time of the disaster, Imanita had been living in Deer Lodge, Montana, and her mother was living in Woodford County, Kentucky.

Shelley frequently moved around the country, and at various times lived in Kentucky, Montana, Missouri, Oregon, Washington, Hawaii, and California. Imanita and her mother had the reputation of being 'social climbers', and despite the traumatic affects of the disaster, the two soon resumed their extensive travels. In addition to many locations in Europe, they journeyed to such far-flung places as Egypt, India, Hong Kong, Java, Japan, and China. While they toured the world, it appears that they routinely left their husbands behind for extended periods of time. At least one census from this period indicates that their husbands, Samuel Parrish and William Shelley, were living together, and were listed as the sole residents of their house. This suggests that Imanita and her mother may have been traveling and away from their husbands on a somewhat permanent basis.

After Imanita's mother fell ill and died in 1930, the family – which had been living in Hawaii – moved yet again. Lutie Parrish was left in a solitary grave there. Throughout their lives, Shelley and her mother did not form many close friendships due to their frequent relocations and travels; they also did not leave behind much money, as they spent so much on their travels. Later in her life, Imanita moved to California, passing away in 1954.[66]

* * * * *

Following the death of his father, and of his shipboard acquaintance Milton Long, in the sinking, **Jack Thayer** went through a natural process of grieving. However, he was able to rebuild his life and complete his education. In a few years, Thayer graduated from the College of Arts and Sciences at the University of Pennsylvania. His family had long been 'active in the affairs' of the university. While in college, Thayer had taken part in sports and worked on undergraduate publications.

Thayer appeared at the Limitation of Liability hearings, testifying in the U.S. District Court Annex in the Woolworth Building in New York on June 24, 1915. During his testimony, he vividly described his experiences. He claimed that he and his father 'were constantly in the company of', and spoke with Bruce Ismay during the maiden voyage. He recalled that prior to the collision, Ismay indicated that they were increasing the ship's speed, and that additional boilers were even to be lit.[67] Throughout his life, Thayer was haunted by the memory of the *Titanic* disaster. In 1940, he had published a pamphlet regarding his experiences entitled *The Sinking of the S.S. Titanic*.

During World War I, Thayer served as an artillery captain in the 79th Division, and was an honorary member of the First Troop, Philadelphia Cavalry. Thayer was eventually married to Lois Cassatt, and the couple eventually had six children.

In 1919, Thayer entered the employ of Lee, Higginson & Co., Bankers, and was put in charge of their Philadelphia office. In 1932, he left the firm to become a partner in Yarnall & Co., where he worked until 1937. Eventually, Thayer went on to be the Director of the Academy of the Fine Arts, as well as Chairman of the Board of Trustees of the Haverford School, of which he was a graduate. He was president of the Philadelphia Skating Club and Humane Society, and his hobby was figure skating. He was also an avid racquetball player.

On October 2, 1939, Thayer became treasurer of the University of Pennsylvania, his *alma mater*. He served as a director of the bicentennial celebration at the university in 1940. In February, 1944, Thayer was appointed to the newly created office of Financial Vice President.

Two of Thayer's sons served in World War II. Tragically, his son Edward was killed while serving in the Pacific in October 1944. Thayer had difficulty putting his life back together after his son's death, and suffered from bouts of depression. Thayer's lifelong friend, Lieutenant Governor John Bell, said that in September 1945, Thayer suffered a nervous breakdown, due to 'worrying about the death of his son, Edward C. Thayer, who was killed in the service'.

Jack Thayer was reported missing by Bell, and Thayer's brother Frederick, after he failed to return home from work on September 18, 1945. A few days prior, Thayer was said to have been suffering from amnesia. His body was found in a parked car on September 22 with his wrists and throat cut, apparently having taken his own life. He was just 50 years old.[68] Thayer's wife Lois outlived him, remaining active in community affairs and clubs, and living to the age of 83.[69]

* * * * *

After the arrival in New York, and while he was recovering from his ordeal, **August Wennerström** sought assistance from the Salvation Army; the organization provided him with temporary shelter, $25, and a train ticket to Chicago. He also received assistance from the Red Cross.

While August was at the Salvation Army in Chicago, he met his future wife Naomi, who was also of Swedish background. The couple eventually moved to Culver, Indiana, where Wennerström became superintendent of buildings and grounds at Culver Military Academy. His wife and he had six sons and one daughter. Until his death in 1950, August gave presentations to clubs locally and in Sweden about the sinking of the *Titanic*, lecturing from his typed notes on the disaster.[70]

* * * * *

Following his recovery from frostbite, lacerated feet, and his broken leg, **Thomas Whiteley** was released from St Vincent's Hospital in New York City. His story of survival attracted reporters, and Whiteley granted numerous interviews. He was eventually paid to give public lectures regarding his experiences, and spoke to sold-out crowds.

Whiteley attempted to sue the White Star Line in 1914 due to his injuries, alleging that there was negligent steering, and that *Titanic* was not seaworthy. His legal council stated that a number of nautical witnesses would need to attend the proceedings, and a hearing date of March 2, 1914 was set.[71] However, it appears that the case never went to trial. It has been speculated that the White Star Line settled with Whiteley. Even Whiteley's descendants are unaware of the exact details.

In February 1916, when he was just 21 years old, Whiteley enlisted in the Royal Flying Corps, and was shipped to France, where he served in World War I. Whiteley was transferred to the Royal Air Force in April, 1918. When he first enlisted, he held the rank of Air Mechanic 2nd Class, and was an RAF Corporal Mechanic by the time his service was complete. Whiteley was wounded in action, receiving bullet wounds behind his left ear, on his scalp and the right side of his face, and to his lower right abdomen. He was able to make a full and complete recovery.

In May 1924, Whiteley worked his passage to New York City aboard the *Celtic,* but deserted and received no pay. He subsequently began a stage career. Between 1924 and 1927, he appeared in productions on Broadway and in Atlantic City, Philadelphia, and Chicago, such as *Ziegfield Follies*, *Sky High*, and *The Nightingale*, among others. He subsequently moved to Hollywood, working at the Lupino Lane Comedies Educational Studios from 1927 to 1928, before appearing in the film adaptation of the World War I stage play *Journey's End*. Following this, Whiteley wrote scenarios for *Won by a Neck* in 1930, and *Pleasure* in 1931. He also played small roles in MGM films during this time period.

Whiteley eventually returned to England, marrying his fiancée Isabel, and the couple subsequently had two daughters. In 1939, Whiteley held an advisory role in the Max Miller comedy *The Good Old Days*. However, Whiteley began to seek alternative ways of supporting his family, as the jobs he was qualified for did not pay well. He worked in a variety of capacities, before reenlisting in the RAF on March 22, 1939; he was initially stationed near enough to visit his family regularly. He was eventually promoted to Warrant Officer, and was able to send money home.

In 1942, Whiteley was deployed with 87 Squadron, and ended up serving in Gibraltar, North Africa, and Italy during World War II. He wrote home as frequently as he could. On October 11, 1944, Whiteley experienced cardiac problems, and died en route to a hospital. He was 50 years old.[72]

* * * * *

The time had arrived. About one hundred and fifty nautical miles south of the *Titanic*'s wreck, nearly a month after the disaster, there came the jangling of telegraph bells; the steady whine of a liner's turbine engines ceased, and the sound of her form cutting through the sea began to fade as her momentum slowed. It was a quarter to seven in the evening of Friday, May 10, 1912. Captain Daniel Dow of the Cunard steamship *Carmania* was making an unusual stop on his liner's westbound passage. Although far south of the location where the *Titanic* foundered, he and his officers sighted many icebergs in the area, a silent menace and frightful reminder of the White Star liner's recent fate.

A First Class steward was dispatched to the cabin of one of Dow's passengers. The lady, Henrietta Loring, had made a special request to be informed when the liner reached the longitude of the *Titanic*'s wreck. Most passengers were then headed in to dinner, so the scene on the liner's decks was very quiet as Mrs Loring approached the rail. Not far behind her was her personal stewardess and another gentleman, Eric Rose, who had been her late husband's partner in the London stock brokerage firm of Rose, Van Custen & Company.

Joseph Loring, Henrietta's husband, had not planned to travel on the *Titanic* the previous month. He had instead been planning to take the *Carmania* – the very ship his wife now stood upon. However, his brother-in-law, George Rheims, had convinced him to take the *Titanic* instead; what was to have been an exciting passage on the world's greatest ship had turned into a tragedy of epic proportions. Loring's body had not been recovered.

This location was the closest that Henrietta Loring could get to the place where he had died. It seemed an appropriate location. She had brought with her several boxes of flowers and a special wreath of immortelles – a flower noted for its longevity, and frequently used in funerals at the time. The small group cast the flowers and wreath into the sea; overcome with emotion, Henrietta Loring was eased away from the rail and aided back to her stateroom, leaving the decks quiet and all but empty. The flowers bobbed in silent memoriam as the *Carmania* steamed off into the fading sunlight, just as the *Titanic* had on the evening of Sunday, April 14, 1912, nearly four weeks before … the smell of fine cuisine wafting from her galleys … lights flickering to life from within her public rooms and cabins … full of life and dreams of a bright and happy future.[73]

ENDNOTES

PROLOGUE:

1. American Inquiry, pg. 97. (Henceforth Amer.)
2. British Inquiry, Questions 17085–17102 (Henceforth Br.); Amer. 100–103.
3. Br. Report, Section 7.
4. Br. 25388.
5. Amer. 19.
6. *Tramps and Ladies*, Sir James Bisset, (Angus & Robertson, 1959) Chapter 22. Rostron testified in 1912 (Amer. 20–21) that this took place in his cabin; Bisset recalled that it was in the Chart Room. The current authors feel that Rostron's earlier memories are probably more accurate, but either could be true.
7. Amer. 20–21.
8. *Tramps and Ladies*, Sir James Bisset, (Angus & Robertson, 1959) Chapter 22.

CHAPTER 1: A LEGEND IS BORN

1. For further information on the *Lusitania* and *Mauretania*, please see: *Lusitania: An Illustrated Biography* (Amberley, 2010) and *The Edwardian Superliners: A Trio of Trios* (Amberley, 2012) both by J. Kent Layton.
2. Three old slipways were demolished to make way for the two new ones. Work on this got under way in late 1906. Work on the graving dock, eventually named the Thompson Graving Dock, began as early as 1904.
3. Günter Bäbler, 'The Dinner at Lord Pirrie's in Summer 1907: Just a Legend?' (*Titanic Post*, Swiss Titanic Society, 2000.) The entire story of this dinner party seems to have come only from Wilton Oldham's book *The Ismay Line* in 1961; it has been picked up and repeated many times since then, but apparently all of these retellings are based upon Oldham's book. Many older works, including Shan Bullock's *Thomas Andrews, Shipbuilder* do not include the story.
   As is the case with most legends, there may be kernels of truth in the story of the dinner party. Perhaps the idea to build two new and unprecedented White Star liners had first come to the fore at a dinner party at the Pirries' home. Speculatively speaking, is it feasible that the dinner party took place during the summer of 1906, then, instead of the summer of 1907? Conceivably, but it is unlikely that White Star would wait until the following spring to ask Harland & Wolff to produce initial plans for the liners. If there is any truth to the legend at all, it is probably only the location of a preliminary discussion between Ismay and Pirrie on the subject.
4. It is very important to note that the first keel plate was laid on the date cited above, namely March 31, 1909. Some books have cited this date as March 22; however, the work that started on that date was the laying of wooden keel blocks on the slipway, and not the laying of the ship's first keel plate.
5. For a fuller discussion of the new liners' technical specifications and a number of common misconceptions in this area, please see Appendix A: *Titanic's* Technical Specifications & Some Common Misconceptions.
6. *Titanic: Belfast's Own*, Stephen Cameron (Wolfhound Press, 1998) pgs 11–14 gives greater detail on hiring practices and day-to-day life of the workers. (Henceforth cited as *Belfast's Own*.)
7. Thanks Stephen Cameron of the Belfast Titanic Society for his offering his personal insights into some of the details of Belfast connections to the *Titanic*.
8. Baron Pirrie from 1906, Lord Lieutenant of Belfast from 1911, and Viscount Pirrie from 1921. All three of these titles were held by him from his appointment until his death on June 6, 1924.
9. Not only was Pirrie highly experienced in the craft of shipbuilding and draughting, but he was also very much a 'hands-on' Chairman, frequently to the point where he became overbearing with his subordinates. Pirrie's close involvement in the planning was confirmed by the testimony of Alexander Carlisle (Br. 21269). Carlisle said that 'they were entirely designed practically by Lord Pirrie'. While this may have been a slight exaggeration, as others such as Carlisle and Thomas Andrews were also heavily involved in the designs, Carlisle's testimony shows just how involved Pirrie really was.
10. From an interview of Carlisle by Mrs Cecil Chesterton, quoted in *Belfast's Own*, pgs 28, 29.

11. Carlisle's testimony to the Board of Trade put much of the design work for the two ships on Lord Pirrie. However, it is clear that he had a great deal of say in the formulation of designs for both vessels.
12. Br. 21322.
13. Andrews suffered from varicose veins in his legs. According to Violet Jessop, a First Class Stewardess on the *Olympic* and *Titanic* who knew Andrews rather well, during the maiden voyage of the *Olympic* some members of the crew – primarily those among the Victualling Department – presented him with a very handsome walking stick. The crew was very grateful for his ongoing efforts in making their accommodations more comfortable. She even felt that, in some way, Andrews managed to impart some of his positive personality into the ships he had designed and helped build. *Titanic Survivor: The Newly Discovered Memoirs of Violet Jessop…* Introduced, Edited and Annotated by John Maxtone-Graham, (Sheridan House, 1997) pg. 103. (Henceforth cited as *Titanic Survivor*.)
14. When the *Olympic's* keel was laid on December 16, 1908, Andrews was just thirty-five. Andrews was married slightly less than six months before this event. When *Titanic's* keel was laid on March 31, 1909, he had just turned thirty-six. At the time of *Titanic's* launch on May 31, 1911, he was thirty-eight. When the *Titanic* departed Belfast for the first time and subsequently set out on her maiden voyage from Southampton, Andrews was thirty-nine.
15. The new Belfast City Hall was completed in 1906.
16. The information of his residence here can be found in the 1901 National Census of Ireland, which can be found at http://www.census.nationalarchives.ie. The other residents in the household was one Jane Scott, aged 50, then the 'Head of Family', and her sister, 43-year-old Hannah Scott. The house was able to support a single on-site servant, namely 53-year-old Hannah Callan.
17. Position according to his 1901 Census record.
18. *Belfast's Own*, pg. 92.
19. Rumor had it that Andrews was being groomed to head Harland & Wolff once Lord Pirrie passed away. The uncle/nephew relationship was especially close since Pirrie had no children. However, there is no definite evidence one way or another on this point.
20. In the 1911 Census, Andrews gave his profession as 'Shipbuilder'. It is also interesting to note in that same census, he gave his religion as 'Unitarian', a point which is affirmed in Shan Bullock's book, *Thomas Andrews, Shipbuilder* (1912). (Henceforth cited as Bullock.) His wife, however, gave her religion as 'Church of Ireland'. All information in this end note is taken from the 1901 and 1911 Irish Census Records, which are viewable at: http://www.census.nationalarchives.ie.
21. Dunallon is the house name. In the 1911 census, the house number was given as 12. Today, the house is Number 20, and it houses the Irish Football Association. Also of interest is that the street name is often misspelled in second-hand sources as 'Windsow' Avenue. The house's name seems to be misspelled occasionally in similar accounts, as well. However it is clearly given as Windsor in the 1911 census records.
22. 1911 Irish Census records, viewable at: http://www.census.nationalarchives.ie. The servants were: Cook Helon Lee (Presbyterian, aged 52); Housemaid Margaret Jones (Church of Ireland, aged 39); Parlourmaid Mary Boyle (Church of Ireland, aged 41); General Servant Lizzie Scott (Church of Ireland, aged 14).
23. Quotations from fuller references to his character by his workmates contained in Bullock. Reading through Shan Bullock's book commemorating Mr Andrews, one gets the impression that the picture painted of Andrews' personality and life might be a bit 'rosy', as it were. However, much of the information contained in the book was collected shortly after the sinking, and directly from people who knew Andrews – friends, family, and co-workers – so many of the references therein should be taken with great weight.
    It is easy to picture the easy-going, mild-mannered Thomas Andrews from many of the portrayals in books and films through the years. It is less easy to picture Andrews giving shipyard employees the 'rough side of his tongue', or, upon finding a yard worker trying to conceal some mistake, his anger blazing, as specifically described in Bullock's book. However, it seems that there was never any unfairness, bias or malice behind such incidents of chastisement. In a dangerous, fast-paced environment like that of Harland & Wolff, one can easily

imagine why at times Andrews might have needed to sharply correct an errant or indolent worker.

24. By the time of the 1911 census, one Bessie Abernathy (Church of Ireland, aged 44) was employed in the home as a nurse for young Elizabeth.

25. The names of the servants come from the 1911 census. The actual date of Wilding's marriage to Marion is not known to the authors at the date of this writing, but according to the 1911 census, taken on Sunday, April 2 of that year, the wedding had taken place less than a full year previously.

26. Br. 23853–23856, 23872.

27. According to the 1911 Census, taken on Sunday, April 2, Carruthers was then aged 50, his wife was aged 50, and their son was aged 16. At that time, Francis and Mary had been married for 27 years. They had four children, one of whom had died, and the other two were apparently not then living with their parents. The household also had a servant, 23-year-old Agnes Mawha.

28. Br. 23975.

29. Br. 23889–23905. The original correspondence on the subject, dated 25 April 1910 through 2 June 1911, can be found at the National Archives, MT 9/920H, 1128–1135. This is only a single example of many contained in the correspondence on that same file.

30. Br. 23978, 23970–23971.

31. Br. 23963–23967. Carruthers' conclusion on the quality of the bulkhead work is worth noting here. When asked if he found any of the bulkheads not watertight (23965), his response was, 'No, I found them all very good indeed.'

32. Some books on the *Titanic* point out that Carruthers personally visited the ship some 2,000–3,000 times during her construction. However, this does not appear to be the case. When Carruthers was asked directly (Br. 23975): 'Were you very frequently on the *Titanic*?' his response was: 'Yes, about every day.' Even if he visited the ship once every day from the time her keel was laid on March 31, 1909 until she left Belfast on April 2, 1912, the total number of visits could number no more than 1,099 times; even at that, the wording of his testimony leaves room for the probability that he did not visit her every single day. It would appear that these 2,000–3,000 visits tallied up during the British Inquiry were divided among *three or four separate* BOT Surveyors, and are not attributable solely to Carruthers. See also Br. 20872–20876, and 21422–21423.

33. *Cumberland News*, April 20, 1912.

34. Amer. 957.

35. The color of the *Olympic*'s hull is frequently cited as a light grey; however, the exact shade looks very light in period photos, and the description of 'virgin white' (*The Olympic Class Ships*, Mark Chirnside, 2011, pg. 35; henceforth cited as *Olympic Class* [yr]) also indicates a very light color.

36. PRONI D2805/C1/1; *Belfast's Own*, pgs 43–44.

37. *Belfast's Own*, pg. 24; Public Record Office, Belfast, D2805/MIN/A/2.

38. *The Belfast Newsletter*, June 1, 1911.

39. *Ibid.*

40. *Ibid.*

41. *Ibid.*

42. *Titanic: The Ship Magnificent*, Bruce Beveridge, et. al., (The History Press, 2008) Vol. 2, pg. 204. Henceforth cited as *TTSM*, followed by volume number and page number.

43. *TTSM*, Vol. 1, 520.

44. All of the pianos supplied to the *Olympic* and *Titanic* were apparently Steinways. Further details can be found in *TTSM*, Vol. 1, 130–135. By way of comparison, Cunard had specified Broadwood pianos for the *Lusitania*. For reasons of space, descriptions of the *Olympic* and *Titanic*'s interior public rooms are kept brief in this narrative. Anyone wanting further particulars on any of these spaces should refer to Volume 2 of *Titanic: The Ship Magnificent*.

45. The color of *Titanic*'s Dining Saloon tiles is known because some were recovered from the wreck. The *Olympic*'s Saloon 'lino' tiles were of a different color altogether, and her Dining Saloon chairs were padded in green leather. This all raises some doubt as to whether *Titanic*'s Dining Saloon chairs were actually padded in green leather, since that color would clearly have clashed with tile of a predominantly red, ocher and blue. However, to date no evidence on the color of the leather on these chairs has ever surfaced.

    Interestingly, Extra Third Baker Charles Burgess of the *Titanic* told Walter Lord that while *Olympic*'s Saloon did not have carpeting, *Titanic*'s Saloon was carpeted, and 'you sank in it up to your knees'. Ernest Townley, a Londoner who visited the *Titanic* on the morning she sailed, also made a specific reference to a thick-pile carpet in the Dining Saloon.

46. *RMS Olympic: Titanic's Sister*, by Mark Chirnside (The History Press, 2004) Appendix V. Henceforth cited as *RMS Olympic*.

47. Indeed, during the 1920s the fixed swiveling chairs were removed from the *Mauretania*'s First Class Dining Saloon and replaced with more mobile ones.

48. On ship's plans from the period, the facility was simply called 'Restaurant'. However – perhaps to avoid confusion for unseasoned trans-Atlantic travelers not used to using the term 'saloon' – the room was cited in period literature as an *à la carte* Restaurant, and was frequently referred to either as 'the Restaurant', or 'the *à la carte* Restaurant'.

49. Sources disagree on Gatti's place of employment immediately before joining *Titanic*. While some cite Ritz's 'Gatti's Adelphi', and 'Gatti's Strand' as his previous employment, an annotated White Star First Class Deck Plan for the *Titanic* (dated December, 1911) said: 'The Restaurant is under the management of the Company, who have appointed Mr. L. Gatti, late of Oddenino's Imperial Restaurant, London, as Manager.' Frank Browne, First Class passenger on the trip to Queenstown, saved one copy of this deck plan (it can be seen in *The Last Days of the Titanic*, by E. E. O'Donnell, pgs. 30-32). Another copy was preserved by Steward F. Dent Ray, and bears the same information. As this plan was apparently still in circulation on board the ship, the current authors tend to trust this citation in favor of others. Oddenino's Imperial was located at 60–62 Regent Street, Westminster, London. However, this does not preclude the possibility that Gatti had previously worked for Ritz establishments in London, as is mentioned in other sources.

50. According to the ship's First Class Plan of Accommodation, and the 'Notes for First Class Passengers' from March 1910, the use of the equipment was free of charge.

51. Some references on the *Titanic* cite his age at 36. However, he is recorded as 34 in two original source documents, PRONI 2A/45/381 H (Particulars of Engagement) and National Archives (UK) MT9-920.

52. *Titanic* First Class Plan of Accommodation, December 1911; *TTSM*, Vol. 2, 416. Unfortunately, the exact times of day when the baths were open for free use by ladies has not survived, or at least have not been found. According to records for the *Olympic*'s first three voyages, however, it is clear that this offering was made available to them.

53. *Titanic* First Class Plan of Accommodation, December 1911.

54. *Ibid.*

55. *Notes for First Class Passengers on Board Steamers of the White Star Line*, March 1910 Edition.

56. *TTSM*, Vol. 2, 241.

57. *TTSM*, Vol. 2, 245–246. These tiles have been recovered from the wreck site, proving their original color. By way of comparison, the *Olympic*'s Smoking Room floor tiles were buff and gray in color, perhaps more palatable to modern sensibilities of interior décor. In an interesting twist, it is quite possible that the leather covering the furniture in *Titanic*'s Smoking Room was red or burgundy in color, as opposed to the green leather used in *Olympic*'s Smoking Room. There is little or no evidence on this point, however – beyond the basic consideration of how ghastly green leather would have looked against mahogany walls and blue and red floor tiles.

58. *Notes for First Class Passengers on Board Steamers of the White Star Line*, March 1910 Edition.

59. *RMS Olympic*, 51.

60. *The Shipbuilder*. Midsummer, 1911 Special Number.

61. *TTSM*, Vol. 2, 27.

62. *Olympic* was launched on October 20, 1910, and sailed on her maiden voyage seven months and three weeks later, on June 14, 1911. However, of that near eight-month period, about two weeks at the end were consumed with the ship's trials, a publicity visit to Liverpool, and public inspections at both Belfast and Southampton. Thus, actual work of completing the *Olympic* took about 7½ months.

63. From notes by Bruce Ismay, contained in *The Ismay Line*, by W. J. Oldham (1961); also based upon selected notes by Thomas Andrews made during the maiden voyage, some of which are available online through Mark Chirnside's web site.

64. The authors would like to thank Daniel Klistorner, author of *Titanic in Photographs* (The History Press, 2011, henceforth cited as *Photographs*) for sharing his research on this subject with us so that it could be included in this volume. For a full breakdown on the facts behind Mr Klistorner's discovery, please refer to that volume.

65. The name for this particular space, Café Parisien, has been spelled in every conceivable way, including 'Café Parisian' and 'Café Parisienne'. However, extensive research by Art Braunschweiger of the TRMA has revealed that the spelling used here, Café Parisien, is the proper spelling as it was used in the First Class Plans of Accommodations issued by the White Star Line just before the maiden voyage.

66. Two copies of these plans, dated December of 1911, showed the new B Deck cabins outboard, and the enlarged Entrance on B Deck for the Restaurant Reception Room, but did not show cabins A-36 or A-37. Exactly how late it was decided to include these two cabins is unclear, but it must have been within the last few months of work.

67. *The Shipbuilder*. Midsummer 1911, Special Number.

68. *TTSM*, Vol. 2, 365.

69. Please see *The Titanic Commutator*, Vol. 27 No. 164, 232–234.

70. For further information on this conspiracy theory, and why the evidence does not support it, please see the following references: *Titanic or Olympic: Which Ship Sank? The Truth Behind the Conspiracy*, by Steve Hall and Bruce Beveridge (The History Press, 2012); 'Olympic & Titanic – An Analysis of the Robin Gardiner Conspiracy Theory', by Mark Chirnside (available at http://www.markchirnside.co.uk/Conspiracy_Dissertation.pdf).

71. Many of *Titanic*'s 37 inch x 31 inch B Deck windows had been replaced with 37 inch x 21 inch windows in preparation for the new B

Deck staterooms. However, a number of the original 37 inch x 31 inch windows remained along *Titanic*'s B Deck in the vicinity of the Private Promenades and the Café Parisien.

72. Br. 21275–21277.
73. Br. 21393. The details of these two meetings are primarily reconstructed from Carlisle's thorough testimony on the subject. During the course of the British Inquiry, Sanderson and Ismay were asked about the meetings, as well. However they had little or nothing to add – and in Ismay's case, considerably less to offer – beyond what Carlisle testified to.
74. Br. 21394.
75. Br. 21400, 21401.
76. Br. 21402. Since Carlisle said that Ismay 'agreed' with the statement, it must have been made originally by Pirrie, who did all or nearly all of the talking for Harland & Wolff at the meeting.
77. Br. 21396, 21404–21406. Carlisle's testimony is difficult to decipher, as to begin with he was discussing events from both meetings at the same time. Then he was walked carefully through the events, and questioned about each meeting separately, and he was much clearer in his statements as to what happened at which meeting.
78. Br. 21408.
79. Br. 21293–21295.
80. Br. 21411–21414.
81. Br. 21418.
82. Br. 21375–21377.
83. Br. 21379–21384.
84. National Archives, MT15/114, pg. 19.
85. Br. 21415, 21416, 21421.
86. Br. 21316–21322.
87. Br. 21345–21349.
88. Br. 21328–23330.
89. Br. 21514–21516.
90. Br. 21520–21524.
91. These figures are based on the 'Report of Survey of an Emigrant Ship', dated April 4 and April 12, 1912 (National Archives, MT/9-920H, 475). Frustratingly for modern researchers, in 1912 there was a long list of complicated rules and exceptions to measuring lifeboat capacities. This meant that in some other contemporary source documents (such as 'Declaration of Survey of a Passenger Steam Ship', dated April 3, 1912, MT/9-920H, 479), these same boats' capacity was measured differently. In this report, the same twenty boats could only accommodate 1,167 persons, broken down so that the fourteen primary boats carried 915, the two cutters carried 64 (32 each), and the collapsibles 188 persons. The discrepancy was discussed at length on Day 17 (Br.), during the testimony of Harold Sanderson. It is also referred to in *TTSM*, Vol. 1, 573–575.
    Because of these discrepancies, the round load plates for the fourteen primary lifeboats would have stated their capacity at sixty-four persons, and the two emergency cutters' round load plates would have put their capacity at thirty-three persons each. It seems that the collapsible boats did not have load plates attached. Since the 1,178 capacity was accepted by the builders, the Board of Trade under certain rules of computation, and was used in period references such as *The Shipbuilder*, this is the set of figures that will be used throughout this text.
92. National Archives, MT9/920H 484.
93. Br. 20490.
94. Br. 24040, 24041.
95. Br. 24044.
96. Br. 24047–24049.
97. Br. 24052–24058.
98. Br. 24052. His calculations were given in hundredweight (cwt) at the British Inquiry. These were Imperial measures equaling 112 pounds each. 2 Imperial cwt = 224 pounds. 2¼ Imperial cwt = 252 pounds.
99. PRO MT9-920A-1, pg. 151.
100. PRO MT15/114 pgs 12–13.
101. An Imperial hundredweight (cwt) = 112 pounds, so a half-hundredweight weight would have weighed 56 pounds.
102. Br. 20491.
103. PRO MT9-920A-1, 151.
104. Story told by McRoberts' son-in-law Brian Millar to Stephen Cameron. The direct quotation can be found in *Belfast's Own*, pgs 21–22.
105. There would appear to be photographic evidence of the *Olympic*'s port propeller, still attached to the ship in drydock, (H&W photo H-1707) with the missing blade about to be replaced with the other. When *Olympic* arrived in Belfast, *Titanic* had not yet been removed from drydock despite advance notice of her impending presence; this indicates that *Titanic* may have remained in drydock while one of the blades from her port propeller was removed. It is also possible that *Titanic*'s entire port prop was removed, if the full level of damage was unknown prior to *Olympic*'s arrival and a thorough inspection, and that only the one blade was subsequently utilized as a replacement.
106. National Archives, MT9-920A-1, 151.
107. It took longer to build the *Titanic* than the *Olympic* during all stages of construction. Harland & Wolff built the *Olympic*'s hull in one year and ten months, whereas *Titanic*'s took two years and two months. The fitting out of the *Olympic* took a little over seven months, while the same

process on the *Titanic* took just over ten months. Although later delays can be blamed on *Olympic*'s early-service mishaps, even before that point modifications to the *Titanic*'s design from the *Olympic*, as well as perhaps a focusing of effort on finishing the first liner for entry into service all helped to contribute to a longer build time for the *Titanic*. In total, *Olympic*'s build time (from the laying of the keel to delivery) took 2 years, 5½ months; *Titanic* took just a shade over three full years.
108. *Titanic & Other Ships*, C. H. Lightoller, 1935.
109. In his autobiography, Lightoller stated that he and Blair were transferring together from the *Oceanic*. However, first-hand documentation shows that when signing on to the *Titanic*, Blair gave his previous ship as the *Teutonic* (PRO, Belfast, TRANS 2A/45/381A). Lightoller frequently misnamed ships in his autobiography. The *New York* incident, for example, somehow became the *St. Paul* incident. It is thus not surprising that he misremembered where Blair had been before the three men joined *Titanic* in Belfast.
110. *The Odyssey of C.H. Lightoller*, by Patrick Stenson, 1984.
111. The story, although there are some factual discrepancies in it, is contained in *The New York Times* of March 23, 1911.
112. *Titanic & Other Ships*, C. H. Lightoller, 1935. Lightoller does not name Haddock directly. However, Haddock was in command of the *Oceanic* from April of 1907 through to March of 1912, concurrent with Lightoller's service on that ship.
113. *Titanic & Other Ships*, C. H. Lightoller, 1935.
114. *The Maiden Voyage*, by Geoffrey Marcus, 1969 (Henceforth cited as *The Maiden Voyage*); *Of Ships and Men*, by Alan Villiers, 1962.
115. PRO, Belfast, TRANS 2A/45/381A
116. Amer. 371.
117. Amer. 260. The inquiry transcript reports Pitman testified that his last ship was the 'Dolphin'. However, no White Star Line ship by that name appears in the Lloyd's Shipping Registry in the years preceding the *Titanic* disaster. It appears likely that he actually served aboard the *Delphic*, and that this was an error in the Inquiry transcript. A 1909 crew roster for the *Delphic* lists a 'Fourth Officer W. H. Pitman' as serving aboard her. While the initials don't match, the rank is correct, and it lists this crewmember as being 31 at the time, and his home as Somerset, both of which match Herbert Pitman. The November 10, 1910 edition of *Auckland's Evening Post* lists a 'Mr. J. Pitman' as serving as the *Delphic*'s Fourth Officer. While not certain, both of these references support the conclusion that Herbert Pitman served aboard the *Delphic*, and not a vessel named *Dolphin*; thus the ship's name is given as the *Delphic* in the primary text.
118. Amer. 209.
119. This information was turned up by *Titanic* researcher Inger Sheil, after consultation with Lowe's family. For further information on Harold Lowe, please see Inger Sheil's *Titanic Valour: The Life of Fifth Officer Harold Lowe* (The History Press, 2012).
120. Amer. 369.
121. Amer. 386.
122. Amer. 373, 376.
123. Recalled by Dr Beaumont. *Titanic Voices: Memories from the Fateful Voyage*, by Donald Hyslop, Alastair Forsyth and Sheila Jemima, (St. Martin's Press, 1994) 90. (Henceforth cited as *Voices*.) One is left to wonder when this conversation took place, since O'Loughlin and Smith were both serving on the *Olympic* before transferring to *Titanic*. He reported aboard the *Titanic* at Belfast on March 24. However, Captain Smith had taken the *Olympic* out of Southampton for New York on March 13; the liner arrived in the American port and departed from there on March 23, 1912. So obviously this conversation took place before Smith's final round-trip voyage on the *Olympic*. The question is: how much earlier? Beaumont did not elaborate.
124. *A Night to Remember*, Walter Lord, 1976 Edition, pg. 53. (Henceforth *A Night to Remember*.)
125. *Titanic Survivor*, 123.
126. It should be noted that the Marconi Company was not a single entity, but was rather comprised of various corporations, including the British Marconi Company, the Marconi International Marine Communications Company, and the Marconi Wireless Telegraph Company of America. Phillips and Bride were employed by the Marconi International Marine Communications Company. (Br. 16020, 16025)
127. Amer. 134.
128. Amer. 133.
129. In addition to the 5-kw primary set, *Titanic* was also fitted with an older-style 1 1/2-kw emergency set.
130. For a thorough breakdown on the *Titanic*'s Marconi set, please see *TTSM*, Volume 1, Chapter 24.
131. Br. 16026–16037.
132. Amer. 144.
133. Br. 16350.
134. Naturally, the reference to a 24-hour day is an average, as five hours separated Southampton and New York times. West-bound, the *Titanic*'s clocks were adjusted backward each night, producing a nearly 25-hour day, while east-bound the process was reversed, producing a day slightly longer than 23 hours.
135. As the official ship's time was customarily changed in two stages (at midnight and again at four o'clock in the morning) through the night,

136. Br. 16333–16339.
137. Amer. 135. Apparently, the Marconi Co. engineers were working right up to a point very close to the departure from Belfast.
138. Br. 15770–15776.
139. Br. 14621, 14627.
140. Br. 23963.
141. Br. 14630, 14631.
142. This weight is again given in Imperial, or Long, tons of 2,240 pounds. 15.75 Imperial tons would amount to 35,280 pounds, or 17.64 modern tons of 2,000 pounds each.
143. Br. 14629.
144. Haddock took command of the *Oceanic* for her April 1907 west-bound crossing to New York. (The *Oceanic*'s manifest upon arrival in New York on April 17, 1907, was signed by Captain Haddock.) It is known that Haddock was still in command of the *Oceanic* on January 6, 1910. On that date he appeared before the Southampton Harbour Board deputation along with other White Star high-ups, as they lobbied for improvements in Southampton waters in order to accommodate the *Olympic* and *Titanic*. (*Voices*, 29) When he signed on the *Titanic*, he gave his last ship as the *Oceanic*. (PRO Belfast, TRANS 2A/45/381A)
145. This refers to the first White Star ship to bear the name, of 1874. *Titanic*'s younger sister would eventually be named *Britannic*, while a third vessel of the name, the motorship *Britannic*, would be launched in 1929.
146. Some sources (such as National Archives BT100-259, pg. 112) cite Bell's age as 51, but apparently he was born in May of 1861, which means that he would only have turned 51 shortly *after* the *Titanic* sank. When he signed aboard the ship on April 2, he gave his age as 50.
147. Robert Fleming would eventually serve as Chief Engineer aboard the *Britannic*, third of the *Olympic*-class liners.
148. Amer. 957.
149. *Ibid*.
150. When he signed on to the *Titanic*, he gave his last ship of service as being the *Gothland*. Here we run into a bit of an interesting story. The 7,755-gross ton *Gothland* referred to was originally built as the SS *Gothic*, intended for the White Star-Shaw Savill & Albion Co.'s joint service to Australia and New Zealand. She began her maiden voyage to New Zealand in late 1893. In June of 1906, she had a serious fire on board, and was subsequently refitted and transferred to the Red Star Line, another IMM company, and renamed *Gothland*. She was recorded arriving in New York under that name in January and February of 1911, and again in July.

It seems that the vessel was thereafter transferred again, chartered for service on the Australian run in early December of 1911 by the Aberdeen Line. In this transfer, her name was changed again to *Gothic*. She remained under that name and stayed with Aberdeen through the first part of 1913. Later she was transferred back to Red Star, and once more named *Gothland*. So if Millar served on the vessel before December of 1911, then she would indeed have been known as the *Gothland*. If he was with the ship on her Australian run after December of 1911, then he should properly have been called *Gothic*. The exact dates of Millar's service with the vessel are unclear, however, so further research into the matter is called for at a future time.
151. See further information on this at http://www.belfast-titanic.com, under the article 'Two Pennies', a recollection by Millar's son. The family still cherishes the two pennies that Millar's son recalled receiving from him before he left on the ill-fated voyage.
152. Special thanks to Daniel Klistorner, who passed on this particular nugget to the present authors after he had discovered it for his own book, *Titanic In Photographs* (The History Press, 2011).
153. White Star had done away with the official position of Commodore in 1882, and would not reinstate that until Captain Hayes took command of the new flagship *Majestic* in 1922. This did not stop most people from referring to Captain E. J. Smith as 'Commodore', since he was the undisputed senior Captain of the line.
154. *Titanic & Other Ships*, C. H. Lightoller, 1935.
155. These times were specified in the sign-on sheets.
156. *The Belfast Newsletter*, April 2, 1912.
157. Ray must have brought the carpet fragment ashore with him when the *Titanic* arrived in Southampton. This would suggest that he may have returned to his home during the ship's layover in Southampton; he then lived at 56 Palmer Park Avenue, Reading, Berkshire, just over forty miles from the *Titanic*'s berth.
158. *Voices*, 24–25.
159. Despite popular belief and misidentification, all known photographs of 'Honour and Glory Crowning Time' and the Grand Staircase are actually of the same location on the *Olympic*. Consequently, there is no way to verify Wilson's information, or indeed of knowing whether the clock was perhaps installed during the stay in Southampton instead, or if the mirror remained steadfastly in place through the maiden voyage.

Based upon the technical design of the Magneta circuit, it would not seem that having one 'slave' clock missing on the circuit, such as the one in the Grand Staircase, would have impeded the other 'slave'

clocks in the system. In fact, junction boxes were left available so that extra clocks could be added to the system, should the need arise. (*TTSM*, Vol. 1, 520)
160. Chisholm had reportedly designed the *Titanic*'s lifeboats.
161. PRO MT9-920A-1, 151; also Br. 23988–23998.
162. Br. 25291, 25295, 25296.
163. Lowe's deposition to the British Inquiry, courtesy John Creamer. The entire text of Lowe's deposition can be found in George Behe's *On Board R.M.S. Titanic: Memories of the Maiden Voyage* (Lulu Press, 2011), pgs 351–354. (Henceforth cited as *On Board*, Behe).
164. Amer. 135. Interestingly, Bride recalled that the trials took place on Monday, rather than Tuesday, as they actually did.
165. Amer. 135.
166. *Ibid*.
167. Bullock, Chapter 7.
168. *Belfast's Own*, 70.
169. PRO MT9-920A-1, 151, 152.
170. Recalled by First Class Stewardess Mary Sloan, contained in Shan Bullock's *Thomas Andrews, Shipbuilder*, Chapter 7.
171. Bullock, Chapter 7.
172. Amer. 51.
173. Mr Van der Hoeff was mentioned in *The Belfast Newsletter*, but his name was misspelled in some sources as Wyckoff Derholf.
174. Amer. 210.
175. Amer. 137.
176. Amer. 135.
177. Amer. 210–211.
178. Deposition of Edward Wilding, Limitation of Liability Hearings.
179. *Ibid*.
180. Bullock, Chapter 7.
181. Amer. 801.
182. According to the *Hampshire Independent*, the two vessels passed each other 'a short distance somewhere off Portland'. (*Voices*, 36). However, the *Olympic* was bound for Cherbourg, requiring a trip to the south-southwest, while *Titanic* was east-bound toward Southampton water some distance to the west. It seems unlikely that the two ships actually came within sight of each other, although the spectacle of the two largest liners in the world passing at sea would have been an incredible one.
183. In his memoirs, Bowyer took much time discussing the *Olympic*, but avoided any mention of the *Titanic*. That he piloted the ship in to Southampton that night is an educated assumption, based on the fact that White Star seemed to prefer his pilotage to that of others, the fact that he most likely had taken the *Olympic* out earlier in the day, and a host of other factors. However at this point, the present authors can not say for certain that it was Bowyer; hence the careful wording in the text.
184. Amer. 261. The distance cited in the text is an approximation.
185. Br. 17501–17503. For more information on the binoculars, please see Appendix C: The Question of Binoculars.
186. *The New York Times*, April 7, 1912.
187. *Trenton True American*, March 27, 1912.
188. *The New York Times*, April 5 and April 7, 1912.
189. *The New York Times*, April 7, 1912.
190. *Titanic Survivor*, pg. 103.
191. Bullock, Chapter 7.
192. An excellent description of this facility, and its history, can be found in *Voices*, 20–22.
193. Bullock, Chapter 7.
194. *Ibid*.
195. *Ibid*. Apparently these details are based on certain correspondence available to Bullock. Some of the problem items identified aboard *Titanic* were discovered in Southampton. Bullock wrote that it was in one of Andrews' 'last letters' that he mentioned the hot press in the Restaurant Galley, and the number of screws in the hat hooks. The color of the pebble dashing, as well as the plans to stain the wicker furniture green on one side of the ship, came from correspondence of 'another earlier date'.
196. *Anaconda Standard*, May 6, 1912. This story is a reprint of Imanita Shelley's account that she wrote for the *Powell County Post* in Deer Lodge, Montana. Courtesy Mike Poirier.
197. *TTSM*, Vol. 1, 497–500.
198. *Voices*, 44; *TTSM*, Vol. 1, 500.
199. The figures of coal taken on, consumed, etc., come from documents contained in the British National Archives which were filled out to clear the ship. The specific document in question can be seen in *Titanic: Triumph & Tragedy*, pgs 64–65. Clearly, the *Titanic* was not short of coal, as has been alleged. Please see Appendix 7, '... Short of Coal?', of *Olympic Class* [2011].
200. *The Titanic Commutator*, No. 161, 22. 'Titanic At Southampton', by Stanley Lehrer.
201. This information was contained in a post card which he sent off to his sister, Elsie, on April 6. He did not state therein whether Bride accompanied him or if he traveled independently.
202. Amer. 211–12.
203. *Christian Science Journal*, October 1912. Recalled by Charles Lightoller. Full text available in *On Board*, Behe, 348–351. Which ship was

being referred to is entirely unclear; it could have been either the *Oceanic* or the *Majestic*, as both ships were laid up in Southampton at the time.

204. This postcard was transcribed and the entire text appeared in *Voices*, 36. A photo of the card appeared along with several news stories when the card went to auction, and the transcription from *Voices* has been confirmed as correct. Although Blair made a single-quote mark around the name *Titanic*, he did not do so around the name of her sister ship, *Olympic*, and that difference has been retained in this quotation. Additionally, he underlined the word 'very' in 'very disappointed', and that also has been retained in this quotation. The card in question went to auction by Henry Aldridge in late 2007, and was purchased by an undisclosed bidder.

205. Amer. 212.

206. *Northern Constitution*, May 1912.

207. Researcher Geoffrey Marcus discovered that Wilde had been hesitant to accept the appointment to the *Titanic* until his friends told him that he would be 'mad to refuse' the opportunity, so he had accepted the posting. (*The Maiden Voyage*)

208. Amer. 429.

209. *Titanic & Other Ships*, C. H. Lightoller, 1935.

210. *Cork Examiner*, April 1912. A photograph taken from one of the passenger tenders at Queenstown and appearing in this paper shows Second Officer Lightoller and First Officer Murdoch in the gangway doors. Not only is it the last known photograph of Murdoch before the sinking, but it reveals that Lightoller was still wearing the stripes indicating his previous rank of First Officer.

211. Amer. 54, 55.

212. *Titanic & Other Ships*, C. H. Lightoller, 1935.

213. Amer. 53.

214. Amer. 53, 54.

215. Recalled by Blair's daughter Nancy, *Voices*, 85.

216. Recollection of Eileen Lenox Conyingham. *Voices*, 51.

217. In 1924, for example, the Prince of Wales took passage on the *Berengaria*; the ballroom was given a fresh coat of paint, and voluminous quantities of flowers were brought in to disguise the paint's aroma.

218. A great deal of information about the Bealings' connections to the White Star Line and *Titanic* can be found in *Voices*, 49–51.

219. Bullock, Chapter 7. It has been assumed that this letter was written in the evening, and this may be correct. However, Andrews' secretary said that Andrews was in the offices both in the morning and evening, so it is possible that the letter was written earlier on in the day, as well. A timestamp on the original letter, if available, would settle the question rather nicely.

220. It has been said that when he left the ship, he accidentally came away with the key to the Crow's Nest telephone lock-box. Just such a key has recently turned up at auction and sold for a hefty sum. However, some historians are unsure as to whether the key in question really belonged to *Titanic*. The key's authenticity seems to be unsettled at this point, and certainly made no difference in the subsequent disaster, since the lookouts had no trouble accessing the telephone when they reported the iceberg. If the key in question really did belong to the *Titanic*, it had nothing to do with the binocular story, and the two are frequently mashed together in the re-telling.

221. Amer. 211.

222. Amer. 135.

CHAPTER 2: AN AUSPICIOUS CROSSING

1. Some books have cited sunrise time in Southampton that morning as being 5:18 a.m., but without direct reference to how that time was calculated. Southampton's city center is listed as being located at 50° 46' N, 1° 23' W. *Titanic* was berthed about one mile southwest of that precise position. The National Oceanic and Atmospheric Association (NOAA) sunrise/sunset calculator places local time sunrise for that location, on that date in history, at 5:23 a.m. The difference is on the whole small, but is worth noting.

2. First Class passenger Adolphe Saalfeld described the morning as 'calm and fine, the sky overcast' that day. (*On Board*, Behe, 83–84.) There are photos held in private collections that show the ship tied up that morning, with a brilliant beam of sunlight illuminating the ship's Forecastle and Bridge, while the rest of the ship is shielded from the sun by clouds. (See *The Titanic Commutator*, No. 161, pgs 20–21.)

   Assistant Electrician Albert Ervine attributed the near-collision with the *New York* to 'high winds'. However, it is clear that it was caused by the suction of the *Titanic*'s propellers, not wind. Indeed, it would have required a tremendously strong wind to break the *New York* from her moorings; photographic evidence of the departure shows variable moderate winds – enough to make the flags flutter from *Titanic*'s masts, but not enough to flatten smoke emitting from the tugboats.

3. Amer. 378.

4. Photos clearly show the White Star house flag, as well as the British ensign, flying from the ship that morning, and on previous days while in port. Further details on the liner's flags can be found in Art Braunschweiger's 'Flags of RMS *Olympic* and RMS *Titanic*', available online through the Titanic Research & Modeling Association; also *TTSM*, Vol. 1, Chapter 22.

5. Bullock, Chapter 7.

6. Amer. 674.

7. Recalled by Albert Benham, *Voices*, 92.

8. *Olympic* normally flew the Blue Ensign during her career, as well. Further details on the liner's flags can be found in Art Braunschweiger's 'Flags of RMS *Olympic* and RMS *Titanic*', available online through the Titanic Research & Modeling Association; also *TTSM*, Vol. 1, Chapter 22.

9. Br. 24106.

10. Amer. 212.

11. Br. 24094, 24095, 24126; Amer. 376; Amer. 674. Times for the muster were given as 8:00, 8:30, etc., and this can look very confusing until you consider the breakup of the crew on various decks, and the fact that Fireman John Podesta mentioned that the muster 'usually takes about an hour'. (*Titanic Commutator*, December 1964.)

12. Third Officer Pitman said (Amer. 263) that the entire Deck Department was called out for this drill. However, Seaman Jones said (Amer. 559, 567) that he supposed that everybody was there, about thirty or forty individuals. His numerical estimate is a bit shy of the full complement of the department.

   There may have been some from the department – such as the Ship's Surgeons – who were exempted from being present on this occasion. It is known that Fourth Officer Boxhall was not directly in the middle of the drill; that rather, he was in some location watching, and did not see the boats lowered or raised back up – he only saw them in the water being rowed around.

13. Amer. 376.

14. Amer. 262; Amer. 214. This comes from Boxhall's testimony, and the wording is slightly confusing. When asked if he was present for this boat drill, Boxhall replied that he was not, and that he did not see the boats lowered. However he did say that he saw the boats in the water, after they had been lowered, from his location 'in another part of the ship'. He was then asked who was officer of the watch that day, to which he replied that 'all officers were on duty'. Next, he was asked: 'Did you see Mr. Murdoch there at this time?' Apparently, although not certainly, the question referred specifically to the lifeboat drill, as Boxhall never did reveal his exact location during the boat drill. Boxhall replied: 'Yes; and Mr. Wilde, the chief officer.' Lightoller included himself in references to the Boat Drill that morning, and was aware of the number of seamen put in the boats for testing purposes. (Br. 14451–14455.)

15. Amer., 375–376, Lowe recalled his boat during the drill as No. 11. (Br. 503–513), AB Seaman Joseph Scarrott affirmed three times that he was in Boat No. 13 during the drill. Some books cite Boats Nos 11 and 15, while others cite Boats Nos 13 and 15. However, everyone agreed that only two boats were employed, and these are the only specific references the current authors have found to which boats were used during the drill. The only possible conclusion, then, is that it was Boats Nos 11 and 13 which were employed in the drill.

16. Br. 21952.

17. Br. 509; Amer. 263.

18. Br. 21954.

19. Amer. 376.

20. Amer. 376–377.

21. Amer. 376.

22. The train times from Waterloo to Southampton are listed in the 1910 reference *The Scientific American Handbook of Travel* at 1 hour 44 minutes (page 319). A first-hand account of the same passage on June 8, 1911 put the duration at 'about 90 minutes'. (*Railway and Travel Monthly*, July 1911, pg. 61.)

23. Francis Browne is apparently the only one who took the First Class Boat Train and later recalled its departure time from Waterloo at 9:45. All other First Class passenger accounts the current authors have seen refer to its departure at 8:00 a.m. Some books and other histories have recounted that the Second and Third Class Boat Train from Waterloo was the early one, while the First Class Boat Train was the later of the two. However, it has proven difficult to find any first-hand references to this, despite the seemingly logical explanation frequently given for this timing. All we have to go by is the time estimates given by passengers, and the known duration of the transit. Further evidence on this point may come to light later.

24. *Jigsaw Picture Puzzle of People Whom I have Known And Sundry Experiences From 1864 to 1949*, by Elmer Zebley Taylor. (Henceforth cited as *Jigsaw*, Taylor)

25. According to some reference works discussing Mr Browne, he was born on January 3, 1880, while others cite his birthday as July 3, 1880. While the former seems to be best documented at the time of this writing, it is possible that he was born in July, which would have meant that he was 31 at the time he boarded the *Titanic*.

26. Browne is exhaustively referred to as 'Father' Browne in many books on the *Titanic*. The truth is that, although he did become a Jesuit priest on July 31, 1915, he was not a priest in April of 1912, and that title will not be applied to him through the remainder of this text.

27. According to one source, this two-day passage was a gift to Francis Browne from his Uncle Robert; according to other sources, he was traveling at the invitation of his friend, Mrs Odell. According to White Star ticketing records, the Odell/May group, Francis Browne,

(cross-Channel to Queenstown) and the Dennis and Eileen Lenox-Conyngham (cross-Channel to Cherbourg) were all on the same group of tickets. Perhaps Browne accepted the invitation and then his uncle had purchased the ticket for him. Francis Browne's ticket was forwarded to him directly by post, sent on April 3 and arriving on April 4.

28. Originally, Browne identified a solitary figure in this photo as 'Astor', having come down to see them off. Many assumed that it was John Jacob Astor IV, who would be aboard the *Titanic*. However, Astor was boarding from Cherbourg, France, not London, and it would have been a physical impossibility for him to be present. Others have stated that the figure was J. J. Astor's cousin, William Waldorf Astor, but the man bears no resemblance to that Astor, either. Thus, the identity of the tall figure remains unknown.

It has recently been mentioned that one of the partially obscured figures on the right in this same photo might have been J. Bruce Ismay, and the portion of the man's head visible does bear something of a resemblance. However, Bruce Ismay was reportedly rather tall, some six inches taller than the average Briton of the time, and this figure is decidedly more average in height. It has been suggested that the man seen talking with this obscure figure is a reporter, and a photographer – purportedly the reporter's cohort – stands nearby with a camera, having just snapped a figure of the legendary White Star Chairman. Allegedly, only an important person such as Ismay would have drawn both a reporter and a photographer, and thus, it is alleged, the man must be Ismay.

However, there is no definitive evidence in the photo to suggest a connection between the photographer (not even necessarily a professional) and the man talking with 'Ismay'. No photos have ever surfaced taken of Ismay that morning at the Waterloo Station, and no other reports of his departure from that station have ever turned up. Both the 'reporter' and the photographer are dressed just as well as the others at the platform, and the 'reporter' is not seen holding anything such as a notebook with which to take notes for his 'story'.

While a woman – possibly, it is thought, Ismay's wife, but then again not Ismay's wife if it is not convenient to the theory – is present, there is no sign of Ismay's children, two of whom were reportedly with him when they boarded the ship. Perhaps Ismay was detained, and his family traveled ahead? Perhaps. The whole supposition, while possible, seems to be built on something of a 'house of cards' of conclusions to which there seems very little evidence. Thus, the identity of the partially obscure figure should remain in the decidedly 'unidentified' category at this point. Perhaps future evidence on the point will surface.

29. A great deal of biographical information on the Crosbys may be found in *On Board*, Behe 462–464.

30. *Jigsaw*, Taylor.

31. Amer. 3.

32. *The Ismay Line*, Wilton Oldham, pg. 186. Recently, Oldham's facts have been called into question with suggestions that at the very least Bruce Ismay remained behind in London and was photographed on the Waterloo Platform by Francis M. Browne on the morning of April 10. However, the photographic evidence and surrounding arguments do not at this time sustain the assertion as fact. More evidence would have to be presented on the matter before this story from Oldham's book could be discounted. Please see Endnote 28 for further information.

33. *Jigsaw*, Taylor.

34. The details of the pier-side sheds were given in *Railway and Travel Monthly*, July 1911, 61–63.

35. *The Belvederian*, (Belvedere College Yearbook) 1912 Edition. (Henceforth cited as *Belvederian*.)

36. *On Board*, Behe, 504.

37. These plans had been updated by the March, 1912 printing.

38. *Belvederian*.

39. *Amsterdam Evening Recorder*, April 23, 1912. Courtesy Mike Poirier.

40. *Philadelphia Evening Bulletin*, April 1912. Quoted in full in *On Board*, Behe, 299–308. Unfortunately, it is impossible to precisely pinpoint what cabin the Futrelles were booked into with the data at hand.

41. The Hallet & Davis Piano Company was absorbed into the Aeolian American Corporation after The Great Depression. The Hallet & Davis name was later acquired by an overseas piano company. In an interesting twist, Hallet & Davis was one of the piano manufacturers who supplied pianos for the well-known W. W. Kimball Piano Company of Chicago.

42. *The Auburn Citizen*, April 23, 1912.

43. *Maidenhead Advertiser*, April 29, 1912. The account is available in full in *On Board*, Behe, 419–422.

44. Letter written to Byles' housekeeper, Miss Field, from on board the *Titanic* while the liner was in Cherbourg Harbor. The original letter, in whole, can be read at: http://www.encyclopedia-titanica.org/letter-frbyles-miss-field.html. The letter is in the collection of Joan Barry, Byles' great niece.

45. *Evening Banner*, April 26, 1912.

46. *Anaconda Standard*, May 6, 1912. This story is a reprint of Shelley's account that she wrote for the *Powell County Post* in Deer Lodge, Montana. Courtesy Mike Poirier.

47. *Ilford Graphic*, May 10, 1912. Mrs Hart's full account is available in *On Board*, Behe, 323–328.

48. *The Loss of the S. S. "Titanic"*, Ch. 1, by Lawrence Beesley, 1912. (Henceforth cited as Beesley.)

49. *The Hartford Courant*, April 20, 1931.

50. *The Indianapolis Star*, April 23, 1912. Courtesy Mike Poirier.

51. Miss Dowdell's account is compiled from her accounts in *The Hudson Dispatch*, April 20, 1912; *The Jersey Journal*, April 20, 1912; *The Hudson Observer*, April 20, 1912. The Amy Stanley portion of the story is compiled from *The Oxford Times*, May 18, 1912 (full account available in *On Board*, Behe, 402–403).

52. *A Brush With Life*, Norman Wilkinson, 1969. Quoted in *Voices*, 94.

53. Townley's entire account was published in the London *Daily Express* of April 16, 1912. It can be read in *On Board*, Behe, 67–69. Noteworthy in this account is Townley's specific reference to thick pile carpet in his description of the Dining Saloon. This statement harmonizes with what Extra Third Baker Charles Burgess told Walter Lord, as recorded in *A Night to Remember*. Burgess said that *Titanic* was more elaborate than the *Olympic*, and cited an example: 'Take the dining saloon – *Olympic* didn't even have a carpet but the *Titanic* – ah, you sank in it up to your knees.'

Could both individuals be completely wrong? It is known that the Saloon was fitted with 'lino' tiles, which have been recovered from the wreck. On the other hand, did Townley actually make it in to the Saloon, or did he just look into it from the carpeted Reception Room? One later-day recollection of carpeting in the Saloon is easily dismissed; a second one does raise an eyebrow on the point, however. This point is certainly worthy of further investigation.

54. *The Irish Times*, April 16, 1912, quoted in full in *On Board*, Behe, 69–70. The name of the correspondent remains unknown. As an interesting aside, it is conceivable that this newspaper correspondent was in the Gymnasium at the same time as Beesley and his friends; however, there were many people coming in and out of the Gym that morning, and without firmer evidence, it should only be considered a possibility.

55. *Titanic: Triumph & Tragedy*, 64–65 contains a reproduction of this document.

56. *Titanic & Other Ships*, C. H. Lightoller, 1935.

57. Amer. 332.

58. Amer. 330–332.

59. Bullock, Chapter 7.

60. Br. 1390.

61. Fellow Second Class passenger Kate Buss explained the relationship in a letter that she wrote on board the *Titanic* on April 11: Collett was a nephew of 'the old Huntleys, of Huntley Palmer'. Miss Wright's mother was one of the Huntleys, as well. Miss Buss' full letter may be read in full in *On Board*, Behe, 94–95.

62. *The Auburn Citizen*, April 23, 1912.

63. This information was given from a 'private source' to Geoffrey Marcus for his book, *The Maiden Voyage*. Researcher Mark Chirnside has independently found references to the officers' stations on board the *Olympic* in 1911 and 1920, and the assignments line up quite well. There is some variance as to the assignment of the Fifth Officer (some departures had that officer assigned to the Compass Platform amidships, while others had him on the Bridge wing.) However, none of that evidence would seem to preclude the information provided by Marcus' 'private source', and it is thus included here as it was published in his book. Also of interest is the fact that Wilde and Lightoller were paired up, while Murdoch and Pitman were also paired up. These same pairs of officers were assigned to the port and starboard side lifeboats, respectively, on the night of April 14–15th.

64. *Southern Daily Echo*, April 17, 1962. Quoted in full in *Voices*, pgs 98–99.

65. Beesley, Ch. 2.

66. There is some apparent conflict in the recollections of eyewitnesses to this event. Podesta recalled (quoted in *Titanic: Triumph & Tragedy*, 75) that when the Slades and Penney arrived, the gangway had already been lowered from the ship's sides. Beesley, watching from above, seemed to indicate that the gangway was still connected, as he said that after the argument it was 'dragged back'. However, his wording is not entirely clear; it leaves room for the interpretation that the gangway had already been brought back a bit, but there were perhaps a pause while the decision was made not to allow the men to board, and then it was dragged away completely.

Another interesting piece of information that Beesley relates is that the 'petty officer' he referred to was at the shore end of the gangway. Almost universally, it has been assumed that Sixth Officer Moody was the 'petty officer' in question, since he was assigned to the after gangway. However, if the gangplank had been disconnected already, Moody would already have been on the ship, not standing on the shore end. It is thus possible that this 'petty officer' was not Moody, but rather someone else connected with the shore staff. Even if this had been the case, it is likely that Moody was involved in the decision not to allow the men aboard.

Clearly the gangway had to be re-connected once for R. C. Lawrence to disembark; perhaps the gangway had been disconnected again when the Slades and Penney arrived. Or perhaps Moody was simply fed up with the last-minute delays and had to make an executive decision on the point. So what is the most likely explanation for all of this?

It seems apparent that the gangway was either still connected, or had just been disconnected for the second time and not yet pulled back completely. If so, then Moody may have confronted the tardy crewmen on the gangplank before re-boarding the ship, after which the gangplank was pulled back all the way. However, there is some room for interpretation in lieu of further evidence.

67. *Jigsaw*, Taylor.
68. *Barrier Miner*, May 4, 1934.
69. Beesley, Ch. 2.
70. *Olympic Class* [2011], 145–146.
71. *London Daily Express* of April 16, 1915. Quoted in full in *On Board*, Behe, 67–69.
72. *Birkenhead News* (unknown date).
73. *Titanic Survivor*, 121.
74. The Straus name is correctly spelled with only a single 's' at the end. Interestingly Colonel Gracie claimed, in his book *The Truth About the Titanic*, that he and *both* Strauses were then together on the deck. However, Mrs Straus wrote a letter to a friend that day in which she explained that her husband later had to describe the entire *New York* incident for her after the fact. Please see *On Board*, Behe, 86–87.
75. *The Tacoma Times*, December 5, 1911.
76. *On Board*, Behe, 477–478; *The New York Times*, April 16, 1912; *The Evening News*, December 6, 1911; *The New York American*, April 29, 1912.
77. This company was not directly related to Levi Strauss & Co., the jeans company founded in 1869 by Levi Strauss. The two families were not directly related, either; in addition to the different spelling, Isidor's family hailed from Otterberg, Germany, and Levi Strauss's family was from Buttenheim, in Bavaria, Germany.
78. It is frequently said that Straus was a 'co-founder' of Macy's; however, the company had been founded *before* he was affiliated with it. Yet by the time he took passage on the *Titanic*, Straus was the owner of the company.
79. Some of this information can be found in *The Truth About Titanic*, Ch. 1; and *On Board*, Behe, 537–8.
80. *The Truth About the Titanic*, Ch. 1.
81. Account by May Futrelle, recorded in the *Philadelphia Evening Bulletin*, April (29?), 1912. Account is available in full in *On Board*, Behe, 301. Mrs. Futrelle's recollection of a band playing from shore is at variance with other evidence. No band was engaged to play from shore that morning, as had been done with the *Olympic*'s maiden sailing the previous year. What she was referring to is unknown, and further investigation on this point is in order at a future date.
82. The turbine was only engaged at speeds of 'Half Ahead' or better on the engine order telegraphs.
83. *Jigsaw*, Taylor.
84. *The Irish Times*, April 16, 1912, quoted in full in *On Board*, Behe, 69–70.
85. Beesley, Ch. 2.
86. Account by May Futrelle, recorded in the *Philadelphia Evening Bulletin*, April (29?), 1912. Account is available in full in *On Board*, Behe, 301.
87. Amer. 332.
88. *Titanic & Other Ships*, C. H. Lightoller, 1935.
89. Account by May Futrelle, recorded in the *Philadelphia Evening Bulletin*, April (29?), 1912. Account is available in full in *On Board*, Behe, 301.
90. Bullock, Chapter 7.
91. Sentiment expressed by Butterworth in a letter that he wrote while the ship was on her way to Queenstown. It can be read in its entirety in *On Board*, Behe, 95.
92. Amer. 332.
93. *London Daily Express* of April 16, 1915. Quoted in full in *On Board*, Behe, 67–69.
94. *On Board*, Behe, 237.
95. *On Board*, Behe, 247.
96. Account by May Futrelle, recorded in the *Philadelphia Evening Bulletin*, April (29?), 1912. Account is available in full in *On Board*, Behe, 301.
97. *Jigsaw*, Taylor.
98. It should be noted that the courses and speeds referred to in this section are derived from the detailed navigational data of the *Olympic*'s September 20, 1911 departure from Southampton over the same course. These figures and records were carefully recorded in her log, and were later used as evidence in the legal cases resulting from that action. Additionally, the weather conditions on the day that the *Olympic* collided with the *Hawke* were relatively similar – clear, relatively calm and in daytime – and thus are comparable. *Olympic* collided with the *Hawke* shortly after completing this 'reverse-S' curve and ringing her engines back up to 'Full Ahead' (about 20 knots) for the trip down the Solent to open water. These should thus be regarded as estimations of the *Titanic*'s course and navigation; however, the confined spaces of the Southampton waters and similar weather conditions would have produced a near-duplication of the course run and times by the *Olympic* the previous September.

Olympic departed White Star Dock at 11:10 a.m. on September 20, and entered the 'reverse-S' turn at Calshot Spit at 12:34 p.m., 1 hour and 24 minutes later. It took her 10 minutes to make the turn, and she re-engaged her engines for 'Full Ahead' at 12:44 p.m., 1 hour and 34 minutes after departure.

On April 10, 1912, it seems to have taken about 15 minutes to get the *Titanic* into the main channel once she cast off from the pier, and she cast off at approximately 12:00 noon. (Please see Appendix B: From Southampton to Cherbourg for further details on this portion of the ship's voyage.) If the *New York* incident had not transpired, it is very likely that the *Titanic* would have entered this 'reverse-S' turn at about 1:24 p.m., exiting the turn ten minutes thereafter.

99. *Belvederian*.
100. These courses, such as South 65° West, were based upon the layout of the magnetic compass card in use at the time. The graduation by degrees on the card began at due North and due South (modern 360° and 180°, respectively), and ran to the right or left – east or west – by 90° to either side. So South 90° West would have equated to due west or 270°, while South 90° East would have equated to east or 090°. Thus, a course of South 65° West would have equated to a course of west-southwest, or 245°.
101. Course 121°.
102. This is based upon a length of that passage estimated at approximately 14.5 nautical miles, covered at an average speed of 20 knots, which is the speed that *Olympic* was accelerating to for her passage down the Solent when she collided with the *Hawke*. To cover 14.5 nm at 20 knots would have taken roughly 43 minutes, and as an approximation only, a few minutes should be allowed for in either direction. Thus, the text states a relatively generic 'about three-quarters of an hour'.
103. Beesley, Ch. 2.
104. *Belvederian*.
105. The *Titanic* did not drop anchor in Cherbourg until about 6:30 p.m., but she had left her berth shortly after about 12:00 p.m. This amount of time would seem an inordinately long stretch for her to have taken between the two points, and some have thus estimated that her speed must have been much lower than that stated in this text – something on the order of 15–16 knots.

However, Bruce Ismay specifically testified at both inquiries (Amer., 3; Br. 18368–18370) that the engines were run at 68 revolutions between Southampton and Cherbourg. Although a full slip table was never completed for the *Titanic*, (see testimony of Fifth Officer Lowe, Amer. 385) research by Sam Halpern shows that 68 revolutions works out to an approximate speed of 20.2 knots. The turbine would have been engaged only above 50 revolutions, or 'Half Ahead' on the engine order telegraphs. Please see Halpern's article, 'Speed and Revolutions' (Revised January, 1911) online at his web site: http://www.titanicology.com/Titanica/SpeedAndRevolutions.htm.

For more information on the delays experienced in clearing Southampton waters, please see the Appendix B: From Southampton to Cherbourg.

The larger picture on the timing of events that afternoon gives a clear indication that the *Titanic* was not slouching at 15–16 knots during the trip through open water between the two ports. Rather, it seems that she was making about 20.2 knots through the water.
106. *Belvederian*.
107. Passenger's name unknown; account printed in the *Belfast Evening Telegraph*, April 15, 1912. Published in its entirety in *On Board*, Behe, 110–111.
108. *Belvederian*.
109. Our thanks to George Behe for identifying Taylor's 'Williams' with the correct identity, Fletcher Fellows Lambert-Williams. Beyond these Williams, there were only two Williams traveling in First Class: Charles D. Williams (aged 51) and his son, tennis star Richard Norris Williams (aged 21). Neither man would fit the description, but Fletcher Lambert-Williams does, especially as he was traveling alone, one of the details that Taylor did give on his acquaintance. If Lambert-Williams' friend called him 'Williams', then the current authors feel it best to refer to him as Williams in this text, as well.
110. *The Band That Played On*, by Steve Turner (2011, Thomas Nelson), Chapter 5. Brailey's father's name was Ronald.
111. Some sources cite his age as thirty. *The Band That Played On*, pg. 105, gives his date of birth as July 28, 1883, which would have made him just twenty-eight at the time of the *Titanic*'s maiden voyage.
112. Some sources cite his age as 30; *The Band That Played On*, pg. 91, gives his date of birth as August 9, 1890, which would have made him 21 at the time of *Titanic*'s maiden voyage.
113. While some sources cite his age as 32, *The Band That Played On*, pg. 102, lists his date of birth as March 20, 1872, which would have made him just 30 while on board the *Titanic*.
114. *On Board*, Behe, pg. 104.
115. *Titanic Survivor*, Violet Jessop (Sheridan House, 1997), pg. 124 This reference has caused much consternation among *Titanic* historians, leading some to even conclude that it happened on a different day than Sunday. However, the concept that Hume led the less prestigious tea concert on Sunday may solve the riddle permanently. Supporting it is the fact that Jessop mentioned this conversation before she mentioned the evening and sunset. When the tea-time per-

formance ended at 5:00, that certainly would have been considered "evening." However, this is merely the best-supported hypothesis available at this time.

116. Further biographical details on each member of the *Titanic*'s band can be found in *The Band That Played On*, by Steve Turner (2011, Thomas Nelson.)

117. The original transcription of this statement contained the word 'you' instead of 'your', as seen in the main text. However, from the context, it is quite clear what was actually said that day, and has been corrected for this telling.

118. *Jigsaw*, Taylor.

119. Please see Appendix C: The Question of Binoculars.

120. Br. 2308.

121. Br. 2332; Leading Fireman Charles Hendrickson said that it was not a common occurrence (Br. 5233–5237). However, the phenomenon was well known to Barrett. Even the United States Navy, in 1898, had acknowledged that bunker coal kept near a hot bulkhead would 'run a great chance of igniting within a few days'. (*What Really Sank the Titanic?* McCarty/Foecke, 2008, 178.)

122. Br. 5239.

123. Br. 2296–2302.

124. Br. 2338–2340.

125. *The Scientific American Handbook of Travel*, Munn & Co., 1910, pg. 281.

126. *Ibid.*

127. Edith Rosenbaum changed her last name to Russell in 1918. At the time of the *Titanic*'s maiden voyage, she was still known as Edith Rosenbaum. Although she is well known to *Titanic* enthusiasts as Edith Russell, the name Rosenbaum will be used throughout this text as it was correct for 1912.

128. Edith Rosenbaum left numerous accounts of her experiences on the *Titanic*. Including among these was a 1934 account which she attempted to have published unsuccessfully, as well numerous newspaper and magazine interviews. Many of these accounts were kindly provided to the authors by Mike Poirier.

129. First Class passenger Margaret Brown recalled that the ship's bugler sounded the call to dinner a half hour after she had boarded, but not many people responded (*On Board*, Behe, 217). However others, such as Francis Browne, recalled the bugle call to dinner sounding earlier, that they were already seated while other passengers were boarding from the tender, and that they were still seated when the ship departed Cherbourg at 8:10. It would seem that Mrs Brown was mistaken in her recollections. Another possibility is that a second call for dinner was sounded for those who had only just arrived from Cherbourg.

130. *Awake!* October 22, 1981, 3–7.

131. *Newport Herald*, May 28–29, 1912. For the full account, please see *On Board*, Behe, 217–226.

132. Account provided by Mike Poirier.

133. [old 137] *Providence Daily Journal*, April 15, 1962. Courtesy Mike Poirier.

134. [old 40] Miss Laura Mabel Francatelli's age is a subject of some debate, ranging from 30 up to 32, depending on which source is consulted. When the *Carpathia*'s manifest was filed in New York, listing *Titanic*'s survivors, she was recorded as Mabel Francatelli, and her age was set at 30.

135. [old 41] *The Oxford Magazine,* Volume 19 (March 23, 1901), pg. 272.

136. [old 42] *Discretions and Indiscretions*, Lady Lucy Duff Gordon, 163–4. Text provided by Mike Poirier. (Henceforth cited as *Indiscretions*)

137. [old 43] *Indiscretions*, 164.

138. Deposition of George Rheims given in U.S. District Court during the Limitation of Liability hearings, November 14, 1913; *The Sun*, May 13, 1912.

139. *The New York Times*, April 9, 1912, April 17, 1912.

140. *The Globe-Democrat*, April 19, 1912. Courtesy Mike Poirier.

141. *Jigsaw*, Taylor.

142. *Belvederian*.

143. In one televised interview, Miss Rosenbaum said that the Lift Attendant in question had told her he was fourteen years of age. According to the ship's crew list, there were four Lift Stewards: 17-year-old Frederick Allen; 31-year-old William Carney; 18-year-old Alfred King; 17-year-old Reginald Pacey. While it seems most likely that the conversation was had with one of the three younger Lift Stewards, none of the four were as young as fourteen. Apparently, Miss Rosenbaum's memory failed her on this point.

144. Bullock, Chapter 7.

145. *Belvederian*.

146. The Harpers were in stateroom D-33; D-33 was on a side companion which gave onto four rooms: D-31, D-37 and D-35. According to the list found on Steward Cave's body (known as the Cave List), all three of these other rooms were already filled. However, nearby D-27, D-29 and D-49 were all unoccupied according to the same list, and emerge as potential candidates.

   Interestingly, one of James Cameron's expeditions to the wreck managed to obtain access to D-27, and found an upright double washstand with an upright drinking glass still on the side in its rack. Some period photographs suggest that stewards placed these drink-

ing glasses upside-down on the rack; it thus seems possible that the room was actually occupied on the trip, and that a passenger had taken a drink from that glass, placing it in the upright position on the rack before the sinking. Please see *Ghosts of the Abyss*, 100–101; *The Titanic Commutator*, Vol. 27, No. 164, 234–235.

147. *Binghamton Press*, April 29, 1912. Mrs Cassebeer's account can be read in full in *On Board*, Behe, 235–237. Also an account by Mrs Hoyt given in the *Amsterdam Evening Recorder*, April 23, 1912. Additional private accounts also provided by NMM/Mike Poirier Collection.

148. Amer. 1100.

149. *Salford Reporter*, May 23, 1912.

150. Passenger's name unknown; account printed in the *Belfast Evening Telegraph*, April 15, 1912. Published in its entirety in *On Board*, Behe, 110–111.

151. Amer. 3; Br. 18373. See also Sam Halpern's article, 'Speed and Revolutions', available through his web site at: http://www.titanicology.com/Titanica/SpeedAndRevolutions.htm.

152. Br. 2203, 2204. Twenty of the ship's twenty-four main boilers were lit at the time. One more main boiler would be lit Friday, April 12, and the final three Sunday morning. Apparently, the final five auxiliary boilers were never lit.

153. *Titanic: A Centennial Reappraisal*, Sam Halpern et al., (2011, The History Press) Section 5. (Henceforth cited as *Centennial Reappraisal*.)

154. This is a rough approximation based on the following evidence. First, the latitude and longitude of a mid-position between Land's End and the Scilly Isles: 49° 59' North, 5° 59' West; it should be remembered that *Titanic*'s actual position may have been slightly different. Second, the ship's estimated overnight speed of about 20.7 knots through the water since leaving Cherbourg. Although her precise course is not known, the general course would have encompassed approximately 192 nautical miles before the *Titanic* entered open water without either Land's End or the Scilly Isles on either side. Without accounting for any effects of wind or current, at 20.7 knots this would have taken the ship about 9.3 hours. Finally, the ship had weighed anchor and resumed her journey from Cherbourg at 8:10 p.m. It would have taken a few minutes or her to clear the breakwater and build up speed. This is a generalization, and should be given a margin of error, but it gives a fairly accurate representation.

155. *Belfast Evening Telegraph*, April 15, 1912. Full account contained in *On Board*, Behe, 110–111.

156. *Ibid.*

157. Beesley, Ch. 4.

158. *Philadelphia Evening Bulletin*, April 1912. Quoted in *On Board*, Behe, 299–308.

159. *Jigsaw*, Taylor.

160. Account provided by Mike Poirier.

161. *The Evening Sentinel*, April 24, 1912. Courtesy Mike Poirier.

162. *The Brooklyn Daily Eagle*, April 19, 1912. Courtesy Mike Poirier.

163. Beesley, Ch. 2.

164. *On Board*, Behe, 91-92.

165. *The Maiden Voyage*.

166. Beesley, Ch. 2.

167. This time would have amounted to about 11:55 a.m. GMT.

168. Beesley, Ch. 2.

169. *The Hartford Courant*, April 20, 1931. Courtesy Mike Poirier.

170. Daly – an Irishman – is mentioned as playing a set of bagpipes as the *Titanic* departed Queenstown. Technically, there are many different types of bagpipes; included among these are the Great Highland Bagpipe, which is Scottish in origin, and the uilleann (pronounced 'illawn') pipes, which are Irish in origin. While stating that Daly played a bagpipe would thus be broadly correct – as the uilleann pipes are a form of bagpipe – it is more accurate to say that he played the Irish uilleann pipes.

171. Information courtesy of the Daly family; Emergency and Relief booklet by the American Red Cross, 1913; *Irish American*, May 4, 1912; *The Irish Sunday Press*, June/July 1956, courtesy of Geoff Whitfield; *Cork Examiner*, May 9, 1912.

172. Information courtesy of Mark Petteruti and the Mulvihill family; *Providence Journal*, April 20, 1912.

173. Private letter from Margaret Rice to a friend in Spokane, Washington. Neither Eugene Daly nor Bertha Mulvihill mention traveling with Margaret Rice in their accounts, but Margaret mentioned that she was traveling with them to America in a private letter sent shortly before the disaster.

174. *Belvederian*.

175. This information was compiled after exhaustive research on the part of Lester Mitcham. The complete crew and passenger list compiled by Mitcham can be found in *Centennial Reappraisal*, Appendices A–F.

176. *Cork Examiner*, April 13, 1912; *Cork Examiner*, May 9, 1912; information courtesy of Mark Petteruti and the Mulvihill family.

177. Beesley, Ch. 2.

178. Amer. 3; Br. 18367. Looking carefully at Ismay's testimony, it would seem that the speed of the reciprocating engines was upped from 70 directly after leaving Queenstown to 72 the next day. For further information on this, please see *Centennial Reappraisal*, Chapter 5.

179. *Indianapolis Star*, April 23, 1912. Courtesy Mike Poirier. In this interview, Thompson was also reported to have said that they 'were

to beat all records' on the maiden trip. Obviously, the ship could not have taken the Blue Riband; perhaps he was referring to the record speed of the *Olympic*'s maiden voyage. From other evidence, it is clear that the furnaces which had been lit up to the time of the collision were being fired hard, as Thompson recalled. Thus, it is not as if Thompson's entire account is questionable.

180. In her personal account, Mrs Shelley said that this occurred 'after leaving Queenstown the next day'. Although there is some room for interpretation on the timing of this event, it seems that she was referring to 'the next day' after they boarded, and that Mrs Parrish's trip to the Purser occurred directly after leaving Queenstown.

181. 2:55 p.m. Greenwich Mean Time (GMT); 9:55 a.m. New York Time (NYT). From this point forward in the primary text, the time of events aboard the *Titanic* will be given in Apparent Time Ship (ATS) unless otherwise noted.

182. 'Keeping Track of a Maiden Voyage', by Sam Halpern; *Centennial Reappraisal*, Chaps 5 and 13.

183. *The Auburn Citizen*, April 23, 1912. Courtesy Mike Poirier.

184. Beesley, Ch. 2.

185. The five-man orchestra played before dinner between 5:00 and 6:00 p.m. in the Second Class foyer on C Deck, and resumed playing at 8:00 p.m., after dinner, in the First Class Reception Room. (*TTSM*, Beveridge et. al., Vol. 2, pg. 27.)

186. *East Kent Gazette*, May 4, 1912. Letter quoted in full *On Board*, Behe, 94–95.

187. A very detailed breakdown of the various watches and other events during *Titanic*'s maiden voyage has been compiled by Sam Halpern, and is available on his web site at: http://www.titanicology.com/WatchTablesFile.htm.

188. *Jigsaw*, Taylor.

189. The accounts by Mrs Cassebeer and Mrs Hoyt fill in almost all of the spaces at this table. The information for her assignment to Purser McElroy's table comes from private accounts by Mrs Cassebeer. Shan Bullock adds Mr and Mrs Dick. Unless one of these accounts is mistaken, it would appear that the current authors have identified ten occupants at this table. Only three tables in the Saloon accommodated more than eight people – two held ten each, and the third held twelve. If this was, indeed, Purser McElroy's table as Mrs Cassebeer clearly related, then this would explain why the table was such a large one. The Chief Purser's table was nearly as coveted as that of the Captain.

190. *Binghamton Press*, April 29, 1912. Mrs Cassebeer's account can be read in full in *On Board*, Behe, 235–237. Also an account by Mrs Hoyt given in the *Amsterdam Evening Recorder*, April 23, 1912. Courtesy Mike Poirier.

191. Account provided by Mike Poirier.

192. As Miss Frölicher was frequently called Marguerite, she will be referred to by that name throughout this text.

193. *The Evening Sentinel*, April 24, 1912. Courtesy Mike Poirier. In her account, Marguerite said that this occurred on the first night out, which one would initially assume would refer to Wednesday night. However, her mother had written a letter late Wednesday night mentioning that they had no trace of seasickness within the family. Because the family had boarded in Cherbourg, it is likely that Marguerite was referring to Thursday's meal, rather than Wednesday's.

194. *Anaconda Standard*, May 6, 1912. This story is a reprint of Shelley's account that she wrote for the *Powell County Post* in Deer Lodge, Montana. Courtesy Mike Poirier.

195. Br. 10304–10316.

196. Amer. 811–812.

197. *Titanic Survivor*, pg. 123.

198. Amer. 294. Third Officer Pitman was asked directly: 'When were the ship's clocks set; do you know?' He responded: 'They are set at midnight every night.' When asked: 'They were set at midnight?' he reaffirmed: 'Every night.'

199. During the entirety of Friday, April 12, the ship's clocks (Apparent Time Ship, or ATS) were running 3 hours and 36 minutes ahead of New York Time (NYT), and 1 hour and 24 minutes behind Greenwich Mean Time (GMT).

200. *Indiscretions*, 164.

201. *The Anaconda Standard*, May 6, 1912. Courtesy Mike Poirier.

202. *Ibid*. This account was told by Mrs Shelley, and may have been something she personally witnessed, but the exact day this happened was not specified.

203. Beesley, Ch. 3.

204. Br. 2203, 2204; Amer. 3. Barrett did not specify exactly when on Friday this boiler was lit up, but Ismay recalled that the revolutions had increased on the second day. It is possible that the boiler was fired up overnight or early on Friday morning, and that the steam pressure was applied later in the day.

205. 'Keeping Track of a Maiden Voyage', Sam Halpern; *Centennial Reappraisal*, Chapter 13.

206. Account provided by Mike Poirier.

207. *Providence Daily Journal*, April 15, 1962. Courtesy Mike Poirier.

208. *Binghamton Press*, April 29, 1912. Mrs Cassebeer's account can be read in full in *On Board*, Behe, 235–237. Also an account by Mrs Hoyt given in the *Amsterdam Evening Recorder*, April 23, 1912. Additional private accounts also provided by NMM/Mike Poirier Collection.

209. George Behe identified these girls as Louise and Simonne Laroche, daughters of Joseph and Juliette Laroche. Joseph Laroche was from Haiti, not Japan; he was black – and is thought to be the only individual of that race aboard the ship. However his rather exotic facial features, and those of his daughters – Mrs Laroche was Caucasian – may have fooled Kate Buss into believing that the little girls were Japanese.

210. *East Kent Gazette*, May 4, 1912. Quoted in full in *On Board*, Behe 115–116.

211. 5:46 p.m. Apparent Time Ship (ATS); 2:10 p.m. New York Time (NYT); 7:10 p.m. Greenwich Mean Time (GMT).

212. Br. 16059, 16060.

213. Br. 16061.

214. 6:21 p.m. ATS; 2:45 p.m. NYT; 7:45 p.m. GMT.

215. Br. 16065.

216. Amer. 460–461.

217. Br. 14801. In answering this question, Lightoller said that it was the duty of the First Officer of White Star ships to draw up the boat list. Although the list was posted on Thursday, April 11, there is no reason to believe that Lightoller drew up the list before the ship departed Southampton and before Lightoller's official position was demoted to Second Officer. (Chief Officer Wilde did not formally come aboard until the night before departure, and the officers held their original ranks through the stay at Southampton until the evening of April 9.) Lightoller subsequently said that he 'did not examine it, in absolute detail and check it by the [crew] list'. (Br. 14803.) Clearly, this list was drawn up by Murdoch after departing Southampton, and it was only ready by some point on Thursday.

218. Br. 69.

219. Br. 11328–11330.

220. Br. 5221–5224.

221. Br. 5290–5293.

222. Br. 6423–6429.

223. Br. 6013–6019.

224. *The Evening Sentinel*, April 24, 1912. Courtesy Mike Poirier.

225. Bullock, Chapter 7.

226. *Jigsaw*, Taylor.

227. *Indiscretions*, 164–165. Lady Duff Gordon did not give the name of her stewardess, but did give a clue in saying that she was Irish. This could point to Mary Sloan, who was from Belfast. Another possibility is that it was Sarah Stap. This possibility emerges from an interview with Stewardess Sarah Stap for the *Birkenhead News*, wherein it is said that she had care of both the Duff Gordons and the Astors. Miss Stap was born at sea, and so it is possible that she had an Irish accent. However, the Astors were slated for cabins C-17 and C-21, while the Duff Gordons were on A Deck. It thus seems likely that the newspaper article is incorrect in the statement that she had care of both families. Mary Sloan's personal account does not specifically mention the Duff Gordons, but neither does it specifically exclude them as being in her care.

228. Amer. 948.

229. 'Keeping Track of a Maiden Voyage', Sam Halpern, available at his web site, www.titanicology.com. *Centennial Reappraisal*, Chapters 5 and 13.

230. *East Kent Gazette*, May 4, 1912. Quoted in full in *On Board*, Behe, 119–120.

231. Beesley, Ch. 2.

232. Br. 2206–2215.

233. Amer. 3, 954; Br. 18374–18377.

234. Recalled by Mrs Lines during her testimony at the Limitation of Liability Hearings.

235. Recent research by Sam Halpern and Mark Chirnside has resolved the question of what time the *Olympic* began her maiden crossing of the Atlantic. She had passed Daunt's Rock at 4:22 p.m. of the first day, while *Titanic* had started at 2:20 p.m. on her first day, approximately two hours earlier than the time of her sister.

Looking strictly at the mileage estimates for each day's runs, the *Titanic*, by noon on Saturday, had a 41-mile lead over her sister, a lead that would only increase at Sunday's noon location, and the gap would continue to widen as *Titanic*'s speed was increased Sunday evening and into Monday.

However, now that the question of what time *Olympic* started her trip has been resolved with certainty, it can be said that although *Titanic* was ahead of her sister, it was not due to increased speed over her sister up to noon on Sunday. *Olympic* had run 962 miles to local apparent noon on day two of her maiden voyage, in 45.8 hours at an average speed of 21.00 knots; *Titanic* had run 1,003 miles to noon on her second day, in 47.89 hours at an average speed of 20.94 knots. By noon on her third day, *Olympic* had covered 1,504 miles in 70.57 hours at an average speed of 21.31 knots; By noon on her third day, *Titanic* had covered 1,549 miles in 72.64 hours for an average speed of 21.32 knots – in other words, to noon on Sunday, the two vessels' average speeds had been a near match to about 1/100 of a knot in average speed.

Because the *Titanic* had cleared Daunt's Rock two hours ahead of the *Olympic*'s maiden voyage, however, Bruce Ismay clearly felt that they were making better time than the *Olympic* had, and this is true in the strictest sense of the wording. After noon on Sunday, the *Titanic*'s speed increased as more boilers were brought on line and hooked into the engines.

It is quite clear from all available evidence that *Titanic* was slated to arrive in New York late on Tuesday evening and begin her docking process. Since the *Olympic* had arrived at the Ambrose Lightship at 2:24 a.m., as the *Titanic* had gotten a two-hour head start on her sister in departing Queenstown, and since the *Titanic*'s speed was increased on Sunday evening (intended through Monday), a Tuesday night arrival was almost a certainty, unless weather factors (or, in the event, a collision with an iceberg) interfered.

236. Please see Appendix O: 'J. "Brute" Ismay?' for further details on Ismay's presence and behavior during the crossing. Simply put, however, Captain Smith did not show any discord of thought with Ismay's thinking during this Saturday conversation. If he held any inward reservations about continuing at an ever-increasing speed, the Commander did not feel strongly enough on the subject to use his authority to slow the ship down. It seems that he simply trusted his ship, his officers, and his lookouts to avoid any danger that might lie ahead, as was frequently the case with North Atlantic skippers of the era.

237. Br. 5244.

238. Br. 5245.

239. Br. 2304–2305.

240. Br. 5246–5251. It has been suggested over the years that this coal bunker fire heated the steel of the bulkhead to the point that its structural integrity was compromised. It has further been suggested that that weakness played a part – significant or otherwise – in the loss of the liner on the following night. It was this particular coal bunker where the iceberg damage crossed the watertight bulkhead separating Boiler Room No. 6 from Boiler Room No. 5. It was in this same area of the ship that Frederick Barrett recalled something giving way which brought a quick flooding of Boiler Room No. 5 during the sinking.

Of interest, no one claimed that they actually saw the bulkhead heated to the point where it was 'red hot'. Hendrickson only said that he could see where he *thought* it had been red hot. Given the strength of the steel used in the *Titanic*'s bulkheads, and the temperatures at which coal burns, it is very unlikely that the fire caused any significant weakening of the bulkhead in question. For further details on this, please see *What Really Sank the Titanic?* 175–180.

241. Amer. 1100.

242. *The Truth About the Titanic*, Ch. 1.

243. *Jigsaw*, Taylor.

244. *Liberty* magazine, April 23, 1932. Account text provided by Daniel Klistorner.; also the *Philadelphia Evening Bulletin*, April 1912. Account available in full in *On Board*, Behe, 299–308.

245. *Binghamton Press*, April 29, 1912. Mrs Cassebeer's account can be read in full in *On Board*, Behe, 235–237. Also an account by Mrs Hoyt given in the *Amsterdam Evening Recorder*, April 23, 1912. Additional private accounts provided by NMM/Mike Poirier Collection.

246. *Jigsaw*, Taylor. In his recollection, Taylor placed this event on Sunday evening. However, the specific reference to Captain Smith being in the Reception Room after dinner does not fit in with the known movements of Captain Smith on Sunday night. According to many, Smith was in the First Class Restaurant and then headed directly to the Bridge. This means that the event must have occurred on a previous night during the crossing.

247. Account provided by Mike Poirier.

248. Beesley, Ch. 2.

249. *Ibid*.

250. It has often been repeated that the *Rappahannock* signaled the *Titanic* with an ice warning, but Dave Gittens turned up some excellent research on this point in his online article at: http://users.senet.com.au/~gittins/rappahannock.html

According to the April 26, 1912 article in *The New York Times*, quoted in the narrative, the *Rappahannock* had sustained damage while traversing an 'ice field', but Chief Smith did not report sighting any icebergs, nor did he at the time mention anything about a warning to the *Titanic*. This was reported later in *The Maiden Voyage* by Geoffrey Marcus after an interview with Smith, and also in a letter published in *The Daily Telegraph* on April 7, 1962. The current authors believe it is certainly plausible that the *Rappahannock* sighted the *Titanic* on the night of Saturday, April 13, which is why it is included in the narrative. Anything beyond that would be past the purview of this volume.

251. Amer., 1052; Br. 16788–16794. The apparatus failed at about 11:00 p.m. Saturday night, and was operating by 4:30–5:00 the following morning according to Bride. Bride also said that it was not working for 'five and a half to six hours'. This adds up until one accounts for the fact that at midnight, the ship's public-room clocks were put back by 45 minutes to 11:15 p.m. Again, as was the ordinary custom, the Bridge clocks were put back in two stages – 23 minutes in the first watch, and 22 in the second watch. This means that from 11:00 p.m. to 4:30–5:00 a.m. was really a span of 6¼–6¾ hours, not the 5½–6 hours Bride recalled.

Bride was even mistaken on exactly which *night* the wireless failed, later saying that it was operating again by 4:30–5:00 a.m. 'Saturday morning'. Bride was obviously exhausted that night. It is not really

surprising that he made an error in his recollections of about 45 minutes in the telling of this part of their experiences later on.

The fact that this event took place Saturday night–Sunday morning, rather than Friday night–Saturday morning, is borne out by the fact that the two operators were so exhausted on Sunday, and also why Bride had agreed to start his Sunday night–Monday morning shift early, in order to help Phillips get caught up on his rest. Additionally, the two men had not managed to catch up on their workload until late Sunday night.

252. 'Keeping Track of a Maiden Voyage', Sam Halpern, available at his web site, www.titanicology.com. *Centennial Reappraisal*, Chapters 5 and 13.

253. *The Ilford Graphic*, May 10, 1912. Account contained in full in *On Board*, Behe, 323–328.

254. *Jigsaw*, Taylor.

255. One Third Class passenger, Jakob Johansson, wrote in his diary that everyone had to stay inside because it was raining on Sunday. However, he did not specify the time of the rain, nor did he give any other details. (*On Board*, Behe, 124.) On the other hand, a number of others – including Lady Duff Gordon –reported that the day was fair and sunny right from early that morning.

256. *The Truth About the Titanic*, Ch. 1.

257. *The Sinking of the S.S. Titanic*, Jack Thayer, 1940. (Henceforth cited as Thayer, 1940.)

258. Please see Sam Halpern's article, 'Keeping Track of a Maiden Voyage', available through his web site, http://www.titanicology.com.

259. *The Truth About the Titanic*, Ch. 1.

260. *The Ilford Graphic*, May 10, 1912. Account contained in full in *On Board*, Behe, 323–328.

261. Br. 16097–16099.

262. *Titanic – Signals of Disaster*, Booth and Coughlan.

263. *Jigsaw*, Taylor.

264. *The Truth About the Titanic*, Ch. 1.

265. TTSM, Vol. 2, 366. This is a 'typical' ending time for these Sunday services, and some room for variance should be allowed.

266. *The Hartford Courant*, April 20, 1931. Courtesy Mike Poirier.

267. *The Auburn Citizen*, April 23, 1912. Courtesy Mike Poirier.

268. *Titanic – Signals of Disaster*, Booth and Coughlan.

269. *Providence Daily Journal*, April 15, 1962. Courtesy Mike Poirier.

270. *Titanic – Signals of Disaster*, Booth and Coughlan.

271. Amer. 3–4; Br. 18386–18398.

272. Amer. 64.

273. Amer. 385.

274. Br. 3708–3792, testimony of Trimmer Thomas Dillon. Leading Fireman Frederick Barrett agreed with Dillon (Br. 2202–2359) that the boilers in Boiler Room No. 1 remained unlit. Fireman Alfred Shiers, on the other hand, said that the auxiliary boilers *were* lit (1913 Limitation of Liability testimony). It makes little difference, as whether the boilers were lit or not, they would not yet have been applied to the engines by midnight that night. However, Dillon was assigned to work in Boiler Room No. 1, and was on duty just before midnight. As there was nothing to do in Boiler Room No. 1 at the time, he and his men had been sent into the Reciprocating Engine Room to 'assist in cleaning the gear'. (Br. 3714) On this point, Barrett and Dillon – both of whom were on duty late on Sunday night – seem to be more reliable than Shiers. However, Shiers' other testimony – to the effect that the engines' speed was increased at 7:00 p.m. Sunday night – seems to harmonize well with aggregate evidence from many others.

275. Amer. 970–971.

276. Beesley, Ch. 2.

277. Account provided by Mike Poirier.

278. *The Patriot*, April 20, 1912. Courtesy Mike Poirier.

279. Amer. 378.

280. Lawrence Beesley, in *The Loss of the S.S. Titanic*, recalled: '... going on deck after lunch we found such a change in temperature that not many cared to remain to face the bitter wind, – an artificial wind created mainly, if not entirely, by the ship's rapid motion through the chilly atmosphere. I should judge there was no wind blowing at the time...'

Yet Lookout Archie Jewell said (Br. 277) that a 'strong breeze [was] blowing all that day'. Lightoller also lamented to Captain Smith, between 8:55 and 9:25 p.m., over the calming of the breeze from earlier in the day. Beesley seemed to base his supposition on the fact that when the ship had been coming into Queenstown, he had felt a similar breeze, which had died off as the ship came to anchor. However, it seems from the aggregate evidence that Beesley was quite mistaken in attributing this wind solely to the forward motion of the ship through the atmosphere.

281. Beesley, Ch. 2.

282. *Ibid*.

283. *The Ilford Graphic*, May 10, 1912. Account contained in full in *On Board*, Behe, 323–328.

284. *Providence Daily Journal*, April 15, 1962. Courtesy Mike Poirier.

285. *Jigsaw*, Taylor.

286. Accounts provided by Mike Poirier.

287. *Newport Herald*, May 28, 29, 1912. Full account available in *On Board*, Behe, 217–226.

288. *The Brooklyn Daily Eagle*, Friday, April 19, 1912. Courtesy Mike Poirier.

289. Br. 13448–13474.

290. Br. 16129–16131.

291. Br. 16122. The 'DC' in Washington, D.C. is quoted as 'DS' at the inquiry, but it is an obvious transcription error that has been corrected in the main text.

292. Br. 16176.

293. Br. 18327–18337.

294. Br. 16178.

295. Amer. 1144.

296. *Indiscretions*, pg. 165.

297. Amer. 1100.

298. *Seattle Daily Times*, April 22–23, 1912. Quoted in full in *On Board*, Behe, 287–299. Mrs Futrelle's observations about everyone expecting to arrive on Wednesday do not harmonize with her next statement, that everyone was 'certain' that the *Titanic* would 'make her trip in record time'. Most likely, she confused the two days; thus the bracketed 'sic' and correction.

299. Thayer, 1940.

300. Testimony at the Limitation of Liability Hearings. *The New York Times*, June 25, 1915.

301. *The Auburn Citizen*, April 23, 1912.

302. Beesley, Ch. 2.

303. Amer. 1147.

304. Miss Dowdell's account is compiled from her accounts in *The Hudson Dispatch*, April 20, 1912; *The Jersey Journal*, April 20, 1912; *The Hudson Observer*, April 20, 1912. The Amy Stanley portion of the story is compiled from *The Oxford Times*, May 18, 1912 (full account available in *On Board*, Behe, 402–403).

305. Br. 246–264; 272–277.

306. *Pageant*, October 1953. Courtesy Mike Poirier.

307. *On Board*, Behe, 404. The clocks were to be set back 47 minutes at midnight of Sunday, April 14. Thus, from noon of April 14 to noon of April 15, when the run would be calculated, was some 24.78 hours of steaming time. 580 miles, divided by 24.78 hours, creates an average speed of 23.4 knots. Such a speed was very high. However, it was not entirely impossible for an *Olympic*-class liner under favorable circumstances. During an east-bound crossing in 1924, the *Olympic* turned in a 550-mile run, made on a 23 1/4-hour day. This meant that she had averaged over 23.5 knots during that period. (*Olympic* Class [2011], 111.) However, this was when *Olympic* was operating on oil fuel. A 34-mile gain – from the *Titanic*'s 546-mile run on Sunday to 580 on Monday – seems like a high number. Yet the steward's expectation does show that he was expecting the liner's speed to be increased significantly over the previous run.

308. The conversation between Bruce Ismay, Emily Ryerson, and Marian Thayer was clearly recounted by Mrs Ryerson during her deposition at the Limitation of Liability Hearings into the disaster. The information on Ismay's personality comes from his 1937 obituary in *The Times*, as well as some other *Times* articles: August 23, 1937, October 21, 1937, and October 23, 1937. The information on whether or not the passengers could remain on board the ship overnight if the steamer docked late is excerpted from White Star Line printed material made available to passengers on board the ship; this was a longstanding company policy.

309. Br. 15110–15117. Although Pitman could not remember the ship's name, the message's contents were clearly those of the message from the *Caronia*. Pitman could not recall the contents of the second message, or what ship it had come from.

310. Br. 16879–16880.

311. Br. 16911–16913. Boxhall had forgotten that he did this until after Lowe testified to having seen the note on the *Officers'* Chart Room table. Either Boxhall made two copies, and placed a note on each of the two charts, or he forgot leaving it in the Officers' Chart Room as opposed to the Captain's personal Chart Room. It is also possible that Boxhall took it to the Captain's Chart Room, and that Captain Smith brought it back before Lowe sighted it 'shortly after 6' o'clock.

312. Br. 13700, 14834, 14835.

313. There is a difference between speed through the water and speed made good. A ship's actual geographic progress is affected by wind and currents. In *Titanic*'s case, the currents were working somewhat against her, so that while she was making one speed through the water, she was making an average geographic speed of 22.12 knots from noon to 11:40 p.m. that night.

314. Please see the box: 'Did They Turn the Corner Late?' for further information on this point. It also seems that although the officers were planning to steer a course of 265° true toward New York, Boxhall later discovered that the ship had actually been making 266° true since turning the corner, due to compass deviation. Further details on this can be seen in Sam Halpern's article 'A Minute of Time', published in *The Titanic Commutator*, Nos 171, 172. Additional information can be found in his article 'Keeping Track of A Maiden Voyage', published in *White Star Journal*, Vol. 14, No. 2.

315. Amer. 381.

316. The transcripts of the American Inquiry give Lowe as saying that it was 162 miles from the ship's noontime position to the corner. It's either a transcription error, or Lowe accidentally reversed the last two digits

317. Br. 15664.

318. Researcher Sam Halpern deserves full credit for working out the finer points of the *Titanic*'s navigation throughout the voyage, and in particular the finer points of the ship's navigation during the afternoon and evening of Sunday, April 14. For a fuller explanation of how these estimates were reached, we suggest that readers refer to *Centennial Reappraisal*, Chapters 5 and 13, as well as the following articles by Sam Halpern: 'Keeping Track of a Maiden Voyage' (available online at: http://www.encyclopedia-titanica.org/keeping_track.html); 'Collision Point' (available online at: http://www.glts.org/articles/halpern/collision_point.html), and other articles available online through Mr Halpern's web site: www.titanicology.com.

319. Sworn statement by Lowe to the British Consulate in New York. Held in the collection of John Creamer and cited with permission; Amer. 378.

320. Amer. 414–417; Br. 15777–15785; Sworn statement by Lowe to the British Consulate in New York, held in the collection of John Creamer (available in full in *On Board*, Behe, 351–354). Between his American and British testimony, there would seem to be some minor discrepancy over exactly what frame this piece of note paper was stuck into – whether it was the frame of the notice board over the table, or whether it was on the frame of the table itself. Looking at his testimony, his wording seems to be better composed and thought out at the British Inquiry, where he said it was on the Chart Room table. His statement given to the British Consulate in New York agrees with his testimony at the British Inquiry. Thus, the current authors have selected this statement to represent his experience. Readers should keep in mind, however, that either statement could be the accurate representation of what happened that afternoon.

321. Br. 15128–15130, 15135–15139.

322. This approximation is based on the known positions of the ship at 5:50 p.m. (41° 56.5' N, 47° 04' W) and 7:30 p.m. (41° 52.5' N, 47° 53' W), as well as the average speed she made between those two points. As the ship moved westward between those two positions, literally chasing the sun as it set, this would have introduced a slight lengthening of the day. Based upon the known movements of the sun in that latitude for that date, it would seem that a maximum three-minute range (6:50–6:53 p.m.) should be allowed for, with the highest probability – mathematically, navigationally, and astronomically – falling at an exact sunset time of about 6:52 p.m. Naturally, a small margin for error should be allowed for on the use of this particular time, and thus the word 'about' is included in the primary text.

Our thanks to Sam Halpern, not only for his original research in tracking down the movements of the ship during the entire maiden voyage, but also in helping to confirm our calculations on this point. These calculations also very closely approximate Second Officer Charles Lightoller's recollections at the British Inquiry:

13662. What time was it dark on this night?
- I think about half-past six, between half-past six and seven.
323. Br. 13601.
324. Br. 277–280.
325. Br. 13586.

CHAPTER 3: THE EVE OF DISASTER

1. Amer., 948; *Amsterdam Evening Recorder*, April 23, 1912. Courtesy Mike Poirier.

2. Br. 18452.

3. Br. 18454, 18455.

4. Br. 18458.

5. Limitation of Liability Hearings, Deposition by Alfred Shiers.

6. Br. 17704–17710.

7. 5:20 p.m. New York Time.

8. 5:35 p.m. New York Time. Information in this paragraph taken from several different sources: the testimony of Bride at both the US and British Inquiries, the testimony of *Californian*'s operator, Cyril Evans at the British Inquiry, and the testimony of Marconi International Marine Communication Co.'s Deputy-Manager in London, George E. Turnbull at the British Inquiry.

Bride mentioned that there were two transmissions, the first of which was directed to the *Titanic* which he heard but ignored, and the second, sent to the *Antillian*, which he acknowledged and took to the bridge. He was quite fuzzy on the times of the two transmissions, and the time that separated them, however.

However the New York time of each message was clearly stated in Turnbull's testimony. The first was sent at 5:20 p.m. (7:22 p.m. *Titanic* apparent time) and the second at 5:35 p.m. (7:37 p.m., *Titanic* apparent time). During the proceedings, the court 'roughed in' that the 5:35 message would have been 'about 7:30' *Titanic* time, but it is clear that *Titanic*'s clocks were 2 hours 2 minutes ahead of New York that evening. Many books which discuss this message say that it arrived 'at 7:30', but it appears to have come in about seven minutes later than that.

9. Br. 16197.

10. Br. 16406; 16428–16432. If Bride's estimate is correct, this means that he gave the slip to the Officer of the Watch at about 7:39 p.m.

In his testimony at the British Inquiry Lightoller put his return to the bridge at 7:35 p.m. However, Lightoller did not recall the delivery of the 7:37 p.m. message from the *Californian* while he was on watch. Based on the evidence in hand, there are a couple of possibilities: the first is that Lightoller came up a few minutes after 7:35, allowing time for the report to be handed to Murdoch while he was serving as temporary Officer of the Watch, instead of to Lightoller directly; the second is that Lightoller did receive the warning right from Bride's hand, but that he later either did not recall getting it, or that he merely claimed not to have seen it. Based on the evidence in hand, we tend to believe the former possibility more than the latter. A final possibility is that Bride handed the note to Pitman at about 7:40 p.m. after the third officer had finished taking the sights with Lightoller, at the time that Pitman went into the Chart Room to begin the sight reduction process, although Pitman either did not recall such an event or never seems to have mentioned it.

Lightoller's reappearance on the Bridge, Murdoch's departure, the stellar observations by Lightoller and Pitman, and Bride's delivery of the *Californian's* wireless message – all of these things took place in a very short space of time, leaving room for something to get over-looked or forgotten along the way by those who survived.

11. Amer. 720–721.
12. Br. 13605–13606.
13. Br. 14670.
14. Br. 25060.
15. Br. 25062.
16. Br. 25063.
17. Br. 25112–25113.
18. Br. 25114.
19. Br. 25238, 25239.
20. Br. 25610, 25611.
21. Br. 25614.
22. Br. 276–280; Amer. 720. Captain Lord of the *Californian* testified at the American Inquiry that from noon to 10:00 p.m., he experienced a north wind on that Sunday. As the two ships were then converging on opposite courses, it is very likely that the north winds reported by Captain Lord were the same ones that were reported by those on the *Titanic*, including Archie Jewell.
23. These weather details are rather important, as they helped to set the stage for the disaster which followed. This is because as the breeze fell away, there was a decided lack of any whitecaps or wave action which could have helped the lookouts spot the iceberg in time to avoid it. Lightoller pointed that out to Captain Smith in their conversation on the Bridge between 8:55 and 9:25 p.m. The information on these weather conditions has been pieced together from testimony such as Lightoller's, Jewell's, Captain Lord's (of the *Californian*), as well as from other sources. Please also see '*Titanic*: Changing Reality' by Mark Chirnside and Sam Halpern (available at: http://www.mark-chirnside.co.uk/TitanicChangingReality.html); see endnote 17 of their article for further references.
24. Amer. 340.
25. Bullock, Chapter 7.
26. Amer. 1101.
27. Amer. 948.
28. *Washington Herald*, April 21, 1912.
29. In her deposition to the American Inquiry, Daisy Minahan said that she spotted 'Mr. and Mrs. Harris' dining in the Restaurant with them on the evening of Sunday, April 14. First-hand accounts from May Futrelle show clearly that they were dining with the Harrises, and from reading her accounts without any other information from Miss Minahan, one would initially believe that they were dining in the D Deck Saloon, as she used the term 'saloon' rather than 'restaurant'.

However, a closer inspection of her accounts gives a few clues. During her dinner account, she said that one had to look out the portholes to realize that they were at sea. This would have been impossible in the D Deck Saloon, as the portholes were covered with decorative backlit glass. On the other hand, the B Deck Restaurant had windows, not portholes. However, she also said that the orchestra played during dinner; the five-man orchestra only began playing in the Reception Room, not the Dining Saloon, at 8:00 p.m. Meanwhile, the trio in the Restaurant did play all through dinner. Additionally, she called their dining area as the 'luxurious saloon after-deck', which might better indicate a saloon located aft, which the *à la carte* Restaurant was.

While there may be room for interpretation in either direction, at this point it seems best to place them in the B Deck Restaurant than in the D Deck Saloon. However, further information on the point may come to light either way.
30. These quotations come from Mrs Futrelle's account, found in the *Seattle Daily Times* of April 22, 23, 1912. The account, in its entirety, can be read in *On Board*, Behe, 287–299.
31. *Ibid.*
32. May Futrelle's account, *Philadelphia Evening Bulletin*, perhaps of April 29, 1912 (the date is unclear). The full account can be read in *On Board*, Behe, 300–308.
33. Amer. 948.
34. Interestingly, nearly every second-hand reference to this dinner party states that it was held in Captain Smith's honor. However, first-hand evidence on this seems rather scant, so it may be apocryphal.
35. *Washington Herald*, April 21, 1912. Luis Klein, allegedly an Able Bodied Seaman on *Titanic*, made unsubstantiated claims that Captain Smith and other officers had been drunk at the time of the sinking, and that one of the lookouts on watch was asleep at the time of the collision (*Cleveland Plain Dealer*, April 23, 1912). Klein was cross-examined by the Marshall's office in Cleveland, who found his story credible. He claimed that he was willing to repeat everything he had said in the Senate Inquiry. However, when he was subpoenaed and brought to New York, he fled from his hotel the night before he was to be called to testify (Amer. 516). Klein's claims were discredited when it was discovered that he was not listed on any of the crew lists, and there was no evidence that he had ever been aboard the ship at all.
36. Account provided by Mike Poirier.
37. Smith's presence and visibility were mentioned by Bruce Ismay (Amer. 948), as well as many of the other passengers who left recollections of the dinner in the Restaurant that night. However, Ismay could not see Major Butt, apparently because he was seated within the alcove.
38. Letter by Mrs Thayer to President Taft, located in the William H. Taft papers, Library of Congress. Available in full in *On Board*, Behe, 414–416.
39. Testimony of Charles Stengel, (Amer. 980), reporting Gertrude Thorne's statement to him. It is possible that the couple was at the Widener's dinner party, for they were known by sight to both May Futrelle and Irene Harris, both among the upper echelon of *Titanic*'s First Class passengers. However, it is also possible that they were only eating nearby in the Restaurant, and that they saw Captain Smith at a table near their own.
40. Amer. 1151.
41. *The New York Times*, April 13, 1912.
42. The phrase 'Darby and Joan' is typically used to described a happily married older couple. The term is typically used to describe such couples who live in humble circumstances, so the sarcasm in applying the term to the Strauses is obvious. The phrase's origins go back to the early 1700s, at least.
43. *Indiscretions*, 165–166.
44. Amer. 1149.
45. Amer. 1100–1101.
46. Mrs Futrelle's story is compiled from the two accounts she gave (*Seattle Daily Times*, April 22/23, 1912; *Philadelphia Evening Bulletin* date unknown). Both accounts are contained in their entirety within *On Board*, Behe.
47. Amer. 273.
48. Amer. 272.
49. Amer. 275.
50. *Ibid.*
51. Amer. 223.
52. Amer. 458.
53. *Jigsaw*, Taylor.
54. *The Evening Sentinel*, April 24, 1912. Courtesy Mike Poirier.
55. *Binghamton Press*, April 29, 1912. Mrs Cassebeer's account can be read in full in *On Board*, Behe, 235–237. Also an account by Mrs Hoyt given in the *Amsterdam Evening Recorder*, April 23, 1912. Additional private accounts also provided by NMM/Mike Poirier Collection.
56. Vera Dick (née Gillespie) was born on June 12, 1894.
57. Bullock, Chapter 7.
58. F. Dent Ray's testimony at the US Inquiry (pages 800–801) is very clear that he last saw Mr and Mrs Clark at Sunday's lunch. Mr Clark was lost in the disaster, and accounts from Mrs Clark about dinner that evening seem to be nonexistent. Either the couple skipped their dinner that night, or they dined in the Restaurant.
59. Thayer, 1940.
60. This account is quoted in *On Board*, Behe, 404–409.
61. *The Oregonian*, April 27, 1912.
62. Amer. 332.
63. *The Coshocton Tribune*, April 19, 1962. Courtesy Mike Poirier.
64. *On Board*, Behe, 148.
65. *On Board*, Behe, 404.
66. Amer. 332.
67. *The Truth About the Titanic*, Ch. 7.
68. *The Syracuse Herald*, April 23, 1912. Courtesy Mike Poirier.
69. Beesley, Ch. 2.
70. *Rochester Democrat and Chronicle*, April 21, 1912. Courtesy Mike Poirier. Lillian Bentham had been born in Holley, New York; while she had been traveling in Europe, her family had moved to Rochester.
71. *The Auburn Citizen*, April 23, 1912.
72. Br. 16450, 16451.
73. Br. 16409–10.
74. Br. 16457–16469.
75. Br. 16470–16475.
76. Br. 16482.
77. Amer. 1149. Mrs Smith said that there was 'a coffee room directly outside the café, in which people sat and listened to the music and

drank coffee and cordials after dinner... I stayed up until 10.30, and then went to bed. I passed through the coffee room, and Mr. Ismay and his party were still there'. Although her account leaves some room for interpretation, it does not seem that Ismay had gone to the Café Parisien, as Mrs Smith had. Instead, it seems that she was referring to the Restaurant Reception Room, at the base of the Aft First Class Grand Staircase.

78. Amer. 1149.

79. Amer. 980.

80. Clearly Captain Smith did not leave the Restaurant before 8:45, according to Mrs Smith; it is also clear that Daisy Minahan's time estimates for that evening are a rather mixed bag of accurate and inaccurate. Miss Minahan was very clear that they entered the Restaurant at 7:15 p.m. according to the ship's clocks. However, she was apparently basing her 9:25 and 9:45 p.m. estimates off another watch, perhaps her brother's, which seems to have been inaccurate by about 45 minutes. From the larger picture, it is very clear that by 8:45, things were really beginning to wind down in the Restaurant. It is most logical to conclude that very shortly after Mrs Smith saw the Captain at the Widener's table at 8:45, he departed and headed directly to the Bridge, where he met with Second Officer Lightoller by 8:55 p.m. It was Miss Minahan who remembered Captain Smith having a cup of coffee just prior to his departure.

81. Amer. 66. This is based on Lightoller's recollection: 'Probably one of us said "Good evening".' Some variation should be allowed for between the event and Lightoller's apparently fuzzy recollection in his testimony.

82. Amer. 67; Br. 14421.

83. Amer. 67, Br. 13635. Lightoller allowed for a range of times for his conversation with the Captain to end, in his aggregate testimony between both Inquiries. Since his order to the lookouts came at about 9:30, however, and it was given a few minutes after the Captain left, it seems likely that the Captain parted from Lightoller at about 9:25 p.m. However, it should be noted that this is an estimate and could be off by a couple of minutes in either direction.

84. Amer. 226–227.

85. Br. 17–29; Br. 925–932; Amer. 450; Br. 11334–11339; Br. 13656–13661. Standby Quartermaster Hichens heard Lightoller give this order to Moody shortly after returning from taking a message to the Carpenter about the fresh water tanks. Lookouts George Symons and Archie Jewell both remembered the message and passed it on. The timing of this order is confirmed by Lightoller, Jewell, and Symons. Hichens did not give an exact time for it, but his testimony does fit well with the 9:30 p.m. estimate. This is because he said that the phone order to the lookouts occurred a 'couple of minutes' after he returned from his trip to the Carpenter. He also said that he was thereafter ordered to make another excursion, and that he returned in time to call out First Officer Murdoch at 9:45 p.m.

86. Br. 13667–13671.

87. Br. 11339–11341.

88. Br. 13676, 14289–14291. According to Lightoller (14325–14328) there was a pair of glasses for each senior officer and one for the Captain, as well as a pair of pilot glasses – all available. Thus, Lightoller felt that at any point during the crossing, a pair would have been available on the Bridge.

89. Amer. 450.

90. Bullock, Chapter 7.

91. Thayer, 1940.

92. Account provided by Mike Poirier.

93. *The Evening World*, April 22, 1912; Notes of Walter Lord's interview with Katie Manning, née Gilnagh; conducted on 07/20/55. Courtesy of Paul Lee. Note that Katie Gilnagh's full name was Mary Katherine Gilnagh.

94. *Anaconda Standard*, May 6, 1912. This story is a reprint of Shelley's account that she wrote for the *Powell County Post* in Deer Lodge, Montana. Courtesy Mike Poirier.

95. *Amsterdam Evening Recorder*, April 23, 1912. Courtesy Mike Poirier.

96. *Indiscretions*, 167.

97. Amer. 332.

98. *A Night to Remember*, 1976 Edition, pg. 203. The Countess of Rothes gave this information directly to Walter Lord. Unfortunately, in the telling and retellings over the last half-century, it seems that the Countess' recollections have become garbled, leading to an apparent impossibility.

   The Countess told Lord that 'while dining out with friends a year after the disaster – she suddenly experienced the awful feeling of cold and intense horror she always associated with the *Titanic*. For an instant she couldn't imagine why. Then she realized the orchestra was playing 'The Tales of Hoffman', the last piece of after-dinner music played that fateful Sunday night'.

   In the years since then, this has somehow become garbled into the Countess saying that *Barcarolle* was the final piece played at dinner that night. However, she did not say that the piece was played 'at dinner', but rather it was 'the last piece of *after*-dinner music'. Then again, she did not even specify *Barcarolle* as the piece in question; *The Tales of Hoffman*, by Jacques Offenbach, was an opera in three acts (*Barcarolle* was featured in the Second Act), so the piece in

question – while probably the famous *Barcarolle* (which was listed in the White Star Line Songbook that Hartley and the other musicians worked from) – may have been another piece from the same opera.

99. *On Board*, Behe, 404.

100. *The Truth About the Titanic*, Chs 1–2. Although Gracie did not say the time he retired, he did say that he was awakened at around midnight, and that by that point he had gotten 'nearly three hours of invigorating sleep'.

101. Br. 15735.

102. Br. 4383–4399.

103. Br. 15445–15551; Amer. 226–227. Boxhall remained on duty after Lightoller handed the watch over to Murdoch at 10:00 p.m. In this stretch of testimony, he remembered seeing the Captain '[o]n and off, [for] most of the watch', from about 9:00 p.m. on. He also remembered that Smith was 'frequently' in the Wheelhouse. However, Lightoller did not mention seeing him again after they parted company on the main Bridge at about 9:25. He said: 'If he [Captain Smith] had been actually on the bridge, yes, I should have seen him.' (Amer. 66) However, the statement seemed to leave open the possibility that the Captain could have appeared in the Chart Room or the enclosed Wheelhouse before he left his watch. Lightoller believed that the Captain would not have gone to bed under those conditions, but would rather have remained in his personal Navigating Room – the forward-most room of his suite, which had a window facing forward to the starboard Bridge wing – 'where he would be handy to pop out on the bridge'. (Br. 13772)

   When pieced together, Boxhall's recollections could suggest that Captain Smith occasionally ventured out during Murdoch's watch, after 10:00 p.m. If so, it is possible that the Captain was checking to make sure that weather conditions were not deteriorating at all. This suggests that Captain Smith's involvement with the ship's navigation during the last 2½ hours of the voyage, leading up to the collision, was greater than is generally presumed. This could be why he was so quick to arrive on the Bridge immediately after the collision, fully dressed, although it is probable that he had been in his room (Br. 1025–1027) at the actual time that the iceberg was sighted and the collision took place. However, as he was fully dressed when he appeared on the Bridge following the collision, it is very likely he had not turned in for bed even up to that point. Possibly this was due to a heightened sense of the need for diligence from around 11:00 p.m. on, when it was expected they would reach the ice reported by wireless.

104. For information on whether the ship's clocks were adjusted at 10:00 p.m., please see the Appendix D: What Time Is It?

105. Amer. 450. Murdoch would have arrived on the Bridge at 10:00 p.m. exactly, or possibly just before 10:00. The conversation with Lightoller seems to have run on for a few minutes while Murdoch's night vision became adjusted; meanwhile, the change of Quartermasters at the helm seems to have been something that would have been very quick to carry out, since night vision was not required in the enclosed Wheelhouse.

   It would thus seem that the course was called out to the officers on the Bridge while they conversed. Hichens was not clear on which of the two officers Quartermaster Olliver had reported the course to, and received a response from, as he naturally could not see outside the Wheelhouse. It would seem that this routine course-check was carried out while Lightoller and Murdoch conversed prior to Lightoller's departure.

106. Amer. 458.

107. Br. 965–966.

108. Amer. 68.

109. *Titanic & Other Ships*, C. H. Lightoller, 1935.

110. *Ibid.* Lightoller and other officers did not give much information on what the rounds consisted of in their testimony at the formal Inquiries. Lightoller did mention (Amer. 89) that it did bring him into contact with the passengers, although he did not necessarily encounter passengers every time he made the rounds.

111. Br. 17579, 17580.

112. Amer. 971.

113. Account provided by Mike Poirier.

114. *Jigsaw*, Taylor.

115. *On Board*, Behe, 148.

116. Mrs Futrelle's story is compiled from the two accounts she gave (*Seattle Daily Times*, April 22/23, 1912; *Philadelphia Evening Bulletin* date unknown); both accounts are contained in *On Board*, Behe.

117. *The Brooklyn Daily Eagle*, April 19, 1912. Courtesy Mike Poirier.

118. *The Hartford Courant*, April 20, 1931. Courtesy Mike Poirier.

119. *The Auburn Citizen*, April 23, 1912.

120. *The Hartford Courant*, April 20, 1931. Courtesy Mike Poirier.

121. *On Board*, Behe, 404.

122. Amer. 1101.

123. Bruce Ismay's account to the *Berkshire Evening Eagle*, April 22, 1912. Ismay did not mention spending time in the Restaurant Reception Room, as Mrs Smith so clearly recalled him doing. However, this was more of an omission than some sort of deception; the Restaurant Reception Room was adjacent to the Restaurant itself, and it was quite natural for passengers to view the after-dinner socializing in the adjacent Reception Room as being connected to the meal.

124. *The Auburn Citizen*, April 23, 1912.
125. Amer. 332.
126. Deposition of George Rheims given in U.S. District Court during the Limitation of Liability hearings, November 14, 1913. Rheims doesn't mention Latimer by name, but describes the steward in question as 'the Commodore Steward, because I think he is the oldest steward'.
127. Thayer, 1940.
128. 9:05 p.m. New York Time.
129. Amer. 735.
130. Quartermaster Rowe first mentioned these 'whiskers' to *Titanic* author Walter Lord in June of 1953, while Lord was researching his book, *A Night to Remember*. The first letter Rowe sent (available through Paul Lee's web site at http://www.paullee.com/titanic/ gtrowe.html) only mentioned the phenomenon. Further details were apparently supplied to Lord after a subsequent query to Rowe. Lord then included this information in *A Night to Remember*, 33.
131. *Titanic Survivor*, 124–125.
132. Amer. 332.
133. *The Brooklyn Daily Eagle*, April 19, 1912. Courtesy Mike Poirier.
134. *The Duluth News Tribune*, May 2, 1912. Courtesy Mike Poirier.
135. *The Hartford Times*, April 19, 1912. Account available in full in *On Board*, Behe, 174–177.
136. *The Auburn Citizen*, April 23, 1912. Courtesy Mike Poirier.
137. *Washington Herald*, April 19, 1912.
138. Amer. 649.
139. Amer. 1142.
140. Amer. 332–333.
141. *The Hartford Times*, April 19, 1912. Account available in full in *On Board*, Behe, 174–177.
142. April 20, 1912 account by Jack Thayer. George Behe collection. Account in full available in *On Board*, Behe, 412–414; also Thayer, 1940.
143. Mrs Futrelle's story is compiled from the two accounts she gave (*Seattle Daily Times*, April 22/23, 1912; *Philadelphia Evening Bulletin* date unknown; both accounts are contained in *On Board*, Behe.
144. Account provided by Mike Poirier.
145. Miss Dowdell's account is compiled from her accounts in *The Hudson Dispatch*, April 20, 1912; *The Jersey Journal*, April 20, 1912; *The Hudson Observer*, April 20, 1912. The Amy Stanley portion of the story is compiled from *The Oxford Times*, May 18, 1912 (full account available in *On Board*, Behe, 402–403).
146. Amer. 526.
147. Amer. 736. *Californian*'s clocks were adjusted about 12 minutes ahead of *Titanic*'s time (See Appendices D, R), and Evans recalled overhearing Phillips at work with Cape Race between 11:25 and 11:30 p.m. – more specifically, 'two or three minutes before the half hour ship's time', or 11:27–11:28. This would have equated to 11:39–11:40 by the time kept aboard *Titanic*.
148. This is the average speed which the liner had maintained in actual geographical movement. Her actual speed through the water was higher, but her forward progress was being slowed by the currents.
149. BBC radio interview with Commander Joseph Boxhall, first broadcast on October 22, 1962. The recording of this interview is available online at http://www.bbc.co.uk/archive/titanic/5049.shtml. Boxhall's later admission of being in his cabin drinking tea at the time of the warning from the Crow's Nest is stunning if true, because it means Boxhall was in his cabin while he supposed to be on watch.
In his 1912 testimony, Boxhall only said that he was coming out of the Officers' Quarters when he heard the bells, but he offered no explanation of what he had been doing there. Boxhall is known to have suffered from pleurisy right after the sinking. Symptoms of pleurisy can include stabbing pains in the chest, shortness of breath, coughing, fever or chills, etc. If Boxhall was feeling ill during the maiden voyage, it may offer an explanation for why he would have been drinking tea in his cabin while on duty that night. To leave his post, logically it would only have been with First Officer Murdoch's express permission.
150. For more information on the intended clock setback that night, please see Appendix D: What Time Is It?
151. Br. 17391.
152. Br. 2435.

CHAPTER 4: RENDEZVOUS WITH DESTINY

1.   Amer. 526.
2.   Amer. 450.
3.   Amer. 318. Fleet's recollection of the timing is at a sharp variance with the depiction in the 1997 film, which shows Fleet ringing down for some seconds, frustrated that no one is answering, and shows Moody rounding a corner from the port side aft and heading over to the phone before answering it.
4.   Amer. 318.
5.   Amer. 450; Amer. 318. In the testimony given about this statement, a period is usually used to end the quotation. However, on the night in question it was almost certainly a more imperative statement, particularly considering the need to relay the order clearly through the telephone without repeating it if, say, a more soft-spoken word was not distinctly heard by Moody. Thus the present authors have supplied an exclamation mark.
6.   Amer. 318.
7.   Admittedly, it is speculation that Murdoch had spotted the iceberg by that point, but it would seem to be logical, as Murdoch was lower to the water and thus in an even better position to spot the berg than the lookouts were, having a more direct line-of-sight to the horizon.
     As simple as the 'right ahead' part of the bell warning might seem, an object 'right ahead' might actually be only partially obstructing the ship's path, and might extend more to port than to starboard, or vice versa.
8.   Amer. 450; Br. 986.
9.   Amer. 318; Amer. 456–457.
10. Br. 973.
11. *TTSM*, Vol. 1, 523–524.
12. Amer. 450.
13. From the door on the starboard side of the Officers' Quarters to the Bridge was a distance of about sixty feet. In his testimony, Boxhall said that he heard the warning bell just as he was coming out of the Officers' Quarters. (Br. 15343, 15344) However, he also said that he felt the collision 'only a moment or two after that'. (Br. 15345). Walking from that doorway to the Bridge should not have taken the entire time that it took from warning to evasive action to collision. The timing of Boxhall's testimony simply doesn't add up. It thus seems more likely that he was still in his cabin having tea when the warning came, and that he left in response to hearing the warning bell.
14. Amer. 361–362.
15. Br. 2425.
16. A thorough analysis of this point by Captain Charles B. Weeks, Jr, was placed in the article, 'Was the *Titanic*'s Rudder Large Enough?', now available on the Encyclopedia Titanica site at http://www.encyclopediatitanica.org/titanic-rudder.html.
17. Br. 942. It might be argued that if anyone had motive to under-estimate the turning characteristics of the *Titanic*, it was the man at the wheel during the collision. Yet even Hichens was willing to say that the *Titanic* handled well.
18. Please see Appendix F: The Iceberg Damage for further information.
19. Amer. 527–528. Please see Appendix E: Taking Evasive Action for further details on this subject.
20. Br. 15350.
21. Br. 15349–15355; Amer. 531.
22. Amer. 531. It is established that the *Lusitania* and *Mauretania* had such equipment on their Bridge, and that when the light was illuminated, the door was recorded as being open; that, when the door was closed, the light went off. Perhaps this was due to the different systems of door operation, or perhaps it was only included on the Cunarders because they were built to meet Admiralty requirements. Whatever the case, no such indicator panel seems to have been installed on the *Titanic*.
23. Amer. 456–457.
24. *New York Herald*, April 20, 1912.
25. Br. 4201–4203.
26. Br. 1860–1916.
27. Br. 661a–686.
28. Amer. 521–523; Br. 17600–17608; letters from George Rowe to Titanic Historical Society President Ed Kamuda, dated 1963, and published in *The Titanic Commutator*, No 156.
29. Br. 13739–13746; Amer. 58–59.
30. Br. 14930–14933; Amer. 275–276.
31. *Pageant*, October, 1953. Courtesy Mike Poirier. Interestingly, Miss Rosenbaum's recollections of the collision are stronger than most from that area of the ship. It is quite likely that if she was thrown off balance, it was because she was not well-planted on her feet at that particular moment. It is also possible that she was giving a slightly embellished version of the collision for readers in this account, given forty-one years after that night. However, it does not seem outlandish enough to exclude from the narrative; readers should place it in the context of what other passengers recalled.
     The reference to the floor of her room seeming tilted does not seem to indicate an immediate list from flooding – which would have been reported by others simultaneous to the impact and stopping of the engines – but rather to the heel the ship took as she responded to the 'hard to port' maneuver that First Officer Murdoch had given.
32. Deposition of George Rheims given in U.S. District Court during the Limitation of Liability hearings, November 14, 1913.
33. *The Amsterdam Evening Recorder*, April 23, 1912. Courtesy Mike Poirier.
34. *Chicago Evening Post*, April 23, 1912. Account reproduced in *On Board*, Behe, 344.
35. *Indiscretions*, 167; second newspaper account provided by Mike Poirier. Some additional details, but not quotes, from *On Board*, Behe, 280–283.
36. *The Loss of the Titanic*, Washington Dodge. Address delivered by Dr Dodge to San Francisco's Commonwealth Club. Account contained in *On Board*, Behe, 264–277.
37. *Providence Daily Journal*, April 15, 1962. Courtesy Mike Poirier.
38. *The Coshocton Tribune*, April 19, 1962. Courtesy Mike Poirier.
39. *Minneapolis World*, (date unknown). Courtesy Mike Poirier. Additional details (but not quotes) were found in John Snyder's account of April 24, 1912, which can be read in *On Board*, Behe, 401–402.

40. *The Berkshire Evening Eagle*, April 22, 1912. Account available in full in *On Board*, Behe, 332–335; Br. 18505; Amer. 3.
41. *On Board*, Behe, 148–150.
42. April 20, 1912 account by Jack Thayer. George Behe collection. Account in full in *On Board*, Behe, 412–414; also Thayer, 1940.
43. Amer. 333.
44. Amer. 971.
45. *Jigsaw*, Taylor.
46. *The Brooklyn Daily Eagle*, April 19, 1912. Account reproduced in *On Board*, Behe, 208–209.
47. Mrs Futrelle's story is compiled from the two accounts she gave (*Seattle Daily Times*, April 22/23, 1912; *Philadelphia Evening Bulletin* date unknown); both accounts are contained in *On Board*, Behe.
48. Account provided by Mike Poirier.
49. *Ibid.*
50. *The Brooklyn Daily Eagle*, April 19, 1912. Courtesy Mike Poirier.
51. Deposition of Elizabeth Lines, given as part of the Limitation of Liability hearings, November 24, 1913; *Boston Traveler*, April 15, 1966; unknown newspaper, August 6, 1975; letter from Miss Mary Lines to her friend Miss Helen Iselin, April 16, 1912, as published in *On Board*, Behe. The progressing story of Mrs Lines and her daughter Mary are taken from the above sources. The authors would like to thank Mike Poirier for providing us with copies of the Lines' newspaper articles from his collection.
52. *The Binghamton Press*, April 29, 1912. Courtesy Mike Poirier. In other and much later accounts, also provided by NMM/Mike Poirier Collection, she mentioned tying her long stockings with lingerie ribbons and putting on a pair of high-button shoes, but her different accounts give some minor variations, so the current authors are deciding to go with the earliest account on this point, closest to the time of the sinking.
53. Accounts provided by Mike Poirier. One question that arises: what cabins were Emma Schabert and Philipp Mock assigned to? Neither names appear on the 'Cave List', which contained the cabin assignments for many First Class passengers.
    It has been speculated that Emma Schabert had a C Deck cabin, one of her accounts suggests that her room was both on the starboard side of the ship and that it was numbered '28'. Only E Deck cabins on the starboard side would have had an even number. Most likely, Mrs Schabert was in cabin E-28, although this is merely speculation based on the evidence in hand. This conclusion was first suggested by Craig Stringer and included in an article written by Mike Poirier on Philipp Mock and Emma Schabert. Up to the date of this writing, no evidence has been presented that cabin E-28 was occupied by a passenger other than Mrs Schabert.
    Philipp Mock's cabin is uncertain, but it was apparently very close to Emma Schabert's, as he met her immediately after the shock of the collision.
54. *The Evening Tribune*, April 23, 1912. Courtesy Mike Poirier.
55. *The Duluth Herald*, May 1, 1912. Courtesy Mike Poirier.
56. *Newport Herald*, May 28, 29, 1912. Full account available in *On Board*, Behe, 217–226.
57. Account provided by Mike Poirier (April 24, 1912); Amer. 1041–1042. In Bertha Chambers' account of April 24, 1912, she did not mention her husband's solo trip top-side before returning, collecting her, and heading back up together.
58. *Newburgh Daily News*, April 26, 1912. Courtesy Mike Poirier.
59. *The Hartford Times*, April 19, 1912. Account available in full *On Board*, Behe, 174–177.
60. Amer. 883.
61. *The Auburn Citizen*, April 23, 1912. Courtesy Mike Poirier.
62. *The Stars and Stripes*, April 16, 1955. Courtesy Mike Poirier.
63. *Rochester Democrat & Chronicle*, April 21, 1912. Courtesy Mike Poirier.
64. *The Auburn Citizen*, April 23, 1912. Courtesy Mike Poirier.
65. *The Toronto World*, April 19, 1912. Available in *On Board*, Behe, 157; Beesley, Ch. 3.
66. *The Hartford Courant*, April 20, 1931. Courtesy Mike Poirier.
67. *The Patriot*, April 20, 1912. Courtesy Mike Poirier.
68. *The Indianapolis Star*, April 23, 1912. Courtesy Mike Poirier.
69. *The Rockford Republic*, April 25, 1912.
70. Private letter from William Mellors to Dorothy Ockenden written on May 9, 1912, courtesy of Brian Ticehurst.
71. *Palladium Times*, September 1, 1985. Courtesy Mike Poirier.
72. *The Ilford Graphic*, May 10, 1912. Account contained in full in *On Board*, Behe, 323–328.
73. *The Fort Wayne Sentinel*, April 29, 1912. Courtesy Mike Poirier.
74. *Washington Post Semi-Monthly Magazine*, May 26, 1912. Full account available in *On Board*, Behe, 246–254.
75. *Anaconda Standard*, May 6, 1912. Courtesy Mike Poirier.
76. *The Syracuse Herald*, April 23, 1912. Courtesy Mike Poirier.
77. Account provided by Mike Poirier.
78. *Pawtucket Times*, May 22, 1912. Courtesy Mike Poirier.
79. Miss Dowdell's account is compiled from her accounts in *The Hudson Dispatch*, April 20, 1912; *The Jersey Journal*, April 20, 1912; *The Hudson Observer*, April 20, 1912. The Amy Stanley portion of the story is compiled from *The Oxford Times*, May 18, 1912 (available in *On Board*, Behe 402–403).

80. *Awake!* October 22, 1981, pgs 3–7.
81. *Palladium Times*, September 11, 1985. Courtesy Mike Poirier.
82. In a letter home to his younger sister Maggie Daly which was published in several newspapers, Daly stated that he was in 'compartment 23, Deck C, steerage'. However, there were no steerage accommodations on C Deck. It is possible that he meant cabin C-23 on F Deck, just aft of Watertight Bulkhead B. However, on deck plans, this cabin is listed as having only two berths, and in his letter, Daly plainly states that he shared his cabin with two other men. A later account may clear up the mystery. In a press interview given decades after the sinking, Daly stated that he was berthed in cabin Q-43 with two other men, towards the bow, and that his ticket was marked 'Cabin Q-43'. Again, there is a problem. There was no cabin 43 in section Q. However, an analysis of the details in Daly's accounts indicates that he was likely berthed in cabin F-43, near the bunker hatch and watertight bulkhead C, on F Deck. Unlike cabin C-23 on F Deck, deck plans show that this cabin had four berths. Regardless of which of these two cabins he was in, the noise and impact of the collision would have been tremendous. The authors would like to thank Sam Halpern for helping them interpret the evidence relating to Daly's cabin.
83. *The Irish Sunday Press*, June/July 1956, courtesy of Geoff Whitfield; *East Galway Democrat*, May 11, 1912.
84. *Utica Herald-Dispatch*, April 30, 1912. Courtesy Mike Poirier.
85. Amer. 577.
86. Amer. 649–650.
87. *Titanic Survivor*, Ch. 20. Unfortunately, Jessop used pseudonyms for most of the other people that she came into contact with during the *Titanic*'s voyage; in her memoirs she called her cabin-mate 'Ann Turnbull', but there was no Ann Turnbull signed on for the trip, leading one to question who her cabin-mate was. It is known that Jessop and her cabin-mate were rescued in the same boat, which was Boat No. 16. Some have speculated that Stewardess Elizabeth Leather, who also left in No. 16, was her cabin-mate. However, according to Leather's testimony at the British Inquiry, she was asleep for half-an-hour to three-quarters of an hour after the time of the collision, which is at odds with Jessop's account. It is possible that Jessop's account is flawed, but another possibility is that the stewardess in question was Evelyn Marsden, who was also picked up in Boat No. 16.
88. *The Brooklyn Daily Eagle*, April 19, 1912. Courtesy Mike Poirier.
89. Amer. 802.
90. Amer. 596.
91. *Liverpool Journal of Commerce*, April 30, 1912. Account supplied by George Behe; *Western Daily Mercury*, April 29, 1912. Account supplied by Ioannis Georgiou.
92. *The Washington Herald*, April 19, 1912; *Cleveland Plain Dealer*, April 21, 1912 (Courtesy Mike Poirier).
93. Amer. 883.
94. *The Auburn Citizen*, April 23, 1912. Courtesy Mike Poirier.
95. *The Stars and Stripes*, April 16, 1955. Courtesy Mike Poirier.
96. *The Auburn Citizen*, April 23, 1912. Courtesy Mike Poirier
97. *The Hartford Times*, April 19, 1912. Account available in full in *On Board*, Behe, 174–177.
98. Br. 15353.
99. Amer. 229
100. Br. 1025–1036; Amer. 450; 531; 533.
101. Br. 15355; Amer. 230.
102. The fact that these three officers went out on to the starboard wing in order to spot the iceberg immediately after the collision lends weight to other existing evidence that Murdoch had reversed his turn to 'port around' the iceberg. If the ship had remained under starboard helm (turning her bow to port) then the natural place to go in order to see the iceberg would have been the port side wing. Instead, all three men first went to the starboard side.
103. In his October 1962 BBC radio interview, Boxhall stated that nobody told him to go below, but that he did this on his own. If this later recollection is correct, it is still likely that Boxhall would have needed to ask Captain Smith for permission to leave the Bridge.
104. *The Berkshire Evening Eagle*, April 22, 1912. Account available in *On Board*, Behe, 332–335; Br. 18506–18509; Amer. 3.
105. *The Loss of the Titanic*, Washington Dodge. Address delivered by Dr Dodge to San Francisco's Commonwealth Club. Account contained in *On Board*, Behe, 264–277.
106. Amer. 333.
107. *The Loss of the S.S. Titanic*, Lawrence Beesley, 1912, Ch. 3.
108. *The Auburn Citizen*, April 23, 1912. Courtesy Mike Poirier.
109. *The Fort Wayne Sentinel*, April 29, 1912. Courtesy Mike Poirier.
110. *Rochester Democrat & Chronicle*, April 21, 1912. Courtesy Mike Poirier.
111. *The Evening Sentinel*, April 24, 1912. Courtesy Mike Poirier; additional details also supplied by Mike Poirier.
112 *Providence Daily Journal*, April 15, 1962. Courtesy Mike Poirier.
113. *The Duluth Herald*, May 1, 1912. Courtesy Mike Poirier.
114. Br. 4002–4005.
115. *The Binghamton Press*, April 29, 1912. Courtesy Mike Poirier. Andrews' movements in the minutes immediately following the collision have been a source of speculation over the years. However, this sighting may help to lay much of that speculation to rest. Miss

Cassebeer's location can be surmised through her statement that they were at 'the bow of the boat'. Obviously, they could not have been standing at the Forecastle, which was off-limits to passengers; they were also looking down upon the ice on the Well Deck. This could not have been done from the forward edge of the Boat Deck, which was off-limits to passengers. However, it could have been done at the forward end of the Promenade Deck or the walkway below on B Deck. Most likely, it was on A Deck, as a group is known to have gathered there and Andrews' cabin was also on A Deck.

It likely took Cassebeer less than five minutes to reach this location from her D Deck stateroom. While the pair were standing there, Andrews met them, unaccompanied by any of the ship's officers. This suggests that Andrews felt the collision and immediately went out on deck to investigate for himself, moving forward along A Deck, until he met up with Miss Cassebeer. From there, he may have gone up to the Bridge to talk to Captain Smith; alternatively, he may have gone aft to the Entrance, and thence down the forward Grand Staircase to the lower decks for a damage inspection. Miss Cassebeer's account is almost certainly the first post-collision sighting of Andrews.

116. *The New York Herald*, April 19 & 20, 1912.
117. Amer. 333.
118. *Pageant*, October 1953. Courtesy Mike Poirier. It seems that Miss Rosenbaum, Mr Stead, and Mr Millet were all part of the group referred to by Mrs Cassebeer when Thomas Andrews came by.
119. *On Board*, Behe.
120. Account provided by Mike Poirier.
121. *Chicago Evening Post*, April 23, 1912. See *On Board*, Behe, 344.
122. *On Board*, Behe.
123. Limitation of Liability Deposition by Rheims.
124. Amer. 577.
125. Scarrott's account and quotations are taken from his testimony at the British Inquiry, Br. 335–347; also *The Sphere* (quoted in *Voices*, 142).
126. Amer. 526–537. Many theories have been presented as to why Smith ordered the ship 'Slow Ahead' after the collision when he did not yet know the extent of the damage. Some of these theories are highly speculative, such as Ismay somehow pressuring Smith to continue ahead since they were trying to break the *Olympic*'s crossing record, and the Captain trying to reach the vessel on the horizon. While dramatic, neither of these theories stand up to scrutiny, particularly the one regarding the nearby ship, since there is no evidence anyone had yet spotted it. It is more likely that after Murdoch's 'Stop' order prior to the collision, Smith was simply trying to maintain the vessel's forward motion, to get a safe distance away from the iceberg it had just struck, before stopping for good.
127. Br. 3716–3729.
128. Throughout this chapter, the timeline and chronology of events following the collision will be as detailed and reported in *Centennial Reappraisal*, Chapters 7 and 13. Chapter 13 contains a highly detailed chronology of the *Titanic*'s sinking, with all information referenced for further research.

Details on the post collision actions, inspections, etc., as well as the lifeboat launching chronology are contained in Chapter 7 of the aforementioned book, and in substantially more detail in the article, '*Titanic*: The Lifeboat Launching Sequence Re-Examined', by Bill Wormstedt, Tad Fitch and George Behe, with contributions by Sam Halpern and J. Kent Layton. The original version of this article was published in edited form in *The Titanic Commutator*, No. 155, 2001; a revised and unabridged version of this article was released online in 2006, and continues to be revised as additional evidence is brought to light. This article is available at the following URL: http://www.wormstedt.com/Titanic/lifeboats/lifeboats.htm.
129. Beesley, Ch. 3.
130. *The Indianapolis Star*, April 23, 1912. Courtesy Mike Poirier.
131. *Palladium Times*, September 11, 1985. Courtesy Mike Poirier.
132. *The Brooklyn Daily Eagle*, April 19, 1912. Account reproduced in full in *On Board*, Behe, 208–249.
133. *Newport Herald*, May 28, 29, 1912. Full account available in *On Board*, Behe 217–226.
134. Br. 17116. Hemming's statement might at first seem to imply that they descended to the Tank Top – the level of the boilers and engines. However, the top of the Tank was actually on the Orlop Deck. Hemming apparently meant that they descended to the top of the tank, not the Tank Top.
135. Amer. 656, 664; Br. 17710–17733. Hemming and Haines each gave slightly different recollections of the conversation. The wording given in the text is stitched together from each of these recollections, and represents the most likely way the conversation played out.
136. Br. 13753–13756. In his British Inquiry testimony, Lightoller mentioned that he saw Murdoch on the port wing before he crossed back over to the starboard side, where he saw Captain Smith. There, from his other testimony, it seems clear that he saw Captain Smith peering into the darkness astern. And yet, Boxhall had testified that he, Murdoch and Smith went on the starboard wing right after the collision. It appears that after Boxhall left the Bridge, Murdoch moved off toward the port Bridge wing, and Captain Smith remained on the starboard wing just long enough for Lightoller to spot him when he stuck his nose out the door on that side.

137. Br. 13753–13758. Lightoller had noticed that the engines were stopped while he was lying in his bunk, but by the time he went out on deck, the ship was proceeding slowly ahead again, which confirms the observations of Quartermaster Olliver, Trimmer Dillon, Lawrence Beesley, etc.
138. Amer. 58–60; Br. 13761. Lightoller testified that he emerged on the port Boat Deck 2–3 minutes after the collision, where he bumped into Pitman. The two men 'conferred' for some unspecified time. Apparently it was after Pitman returned to his cabin that Lightoller crossed over to the starboard side and peered out the door toward the Bridge. He did not mention seeing anyone else on the Bridge with them; Boxhall must thus have already left on his initial inspection by that point.
139. Amer. 450–45. In the British Inquiry, Hichens gave a vaguer description of these events, and makes it sound as if Smith noted the 5° list after he gave the order to swing the lifeboats out, and begin serving the lifebelts to the passengers. However, in the Senate Inquiry, Hichens gave a more detailed description of this event, and was explicit that the timing was 5 minutes after the collision.
140. Br. 18503–18514; *The Berkshire Evening Eagle*, April 22, 1912. Full account contained in *On Board*, Behe 332–335.
141. Since Murdoch ordered the ship 'hard to port' following the collision in order to swing the stern away from the iceberg, the *Titanic* started turning to starboard, and when the speed ran down, she would have ended up pointing north-northwest. Both Fifth Officer Lowe and Quartermaster Rowe confirm that the ship was indeed pointing north as it sank (Deposition of H. G. Lowe before the British Consulate General in New York, May 1912; Br. 17671). Confirming this, the bow section of the *Titanic* sits on the ocean floor pointing northward, where it fell after planing away from the surface. Tests conducted in water tanks by the Discovery Channel in the 1990s with a model of the *Titanic*'s bow section indicate that it would have remained facing roughly in the direction it was facing when it sank, rather than spiraling or twisting on the way to the ocean floor. Further clarification of this point is available in Sam Halpern's article 'Collision Point' at http://www.glts.org/articles/halpern/collision_point.html.
142. *TTSM*, Vol. 1, 297. After studying dozens of survivor accounts of the timing between the collision and subsequent events, the current authors have been led to conclude that the ship's engines were rung off very shortly after the collision, probably at around 11:46, and that the steam began to blow off very quickly after that point – likely even before 11:50. This makes sense, as the ship's steam-generating system was under very high pressure that evening, and it would not have taken long for that pressure to pop the safeties.
143. *Titanic & Other Ships*, C. H. Lightoller.
144. Deposition of Elizabeth Lines, given as part of the Limitation of Liability hearings, November 24, 1913; *Boston Traveler*, April 15, 1966; unknown newspaper, August 6, 1975; letter from Miss Mary Lines to her friend Miss Helen Iselin, April 16, 1912, as published in *On Board*, Behe. The progressing story of Mrs Lines and her daughter Mary are taken from the above sources. The authors would like to thank Mike Poirier for providing us with copies of the Lines newspaper articles from his collection.
145. *The Hartford Times*, April 19, 1912. Account available in full in *On Board*, Behe, 174–177.
146. *Washington Post Semi-Monthly Magazine*, May 26, 1912. Full account available in *On Board*, Behe, 246–254.
147. Amer. 577. Hogg was very precise in saying that he was awakened 'at 20 minutes to 12' and then he had gone out on deck. However, when he returned to his room, he felt the need to ask Evans what time it was. The two men were due to go on duty at 12:23 a.m., unadjusted ship's time, or midnight precisely once the clocks had been reset.

If Evans was then working off adjusted ship's time (i.e., 11:45 plus 23 minutes = 12:08 a.m.) then a number of problems become evident with the timing of Hogg's account. Hogg left in Boat No. 7, which was lowered away at about 12:40 a.m. According to his testimony, Evans and he went on duty 'at 12 o'clock'. Then they stayed in the nest for 'about twenty minutes'. Then he went down to the Boat Deck and began helping to uncover the lifeboats. He was also sent to fetch a Jacob's ladder, and had only just returned from that when he was ordered away in Boat No. 7.

If Evans was working from adjusted time when he told Hogg that it was 11:45 p.m., this would have been 12:08 a.m. unadjusted time; after dressing, it would have taken a few minutes to dress and make their way to the nest, and they would not have left the nest before 12:30 at the earliest. Thereafter, it would have taken several minutes at least for Hogg to reach the Boat Deck; yet Hogg said that when he got to the Boat Deck, he 'assisted in *starting* [authors' emphasis] to uncover the boats'. This timing simply would not work out.

On the other hand, if Evans was working from adjusted ship's time, then this would also create a large gap between the time of the collision (11:40–11:45 by nearly all accounts) and the time that Hogg returned to talk to Evans. The only plausible explanation is that at 11:45, Evans decided that since they were already awake, they should go up and relieve Fleet and Lee a few minutes early. In doing so, perhaps they would even be able to find out some particulars on exactly what had happened.

Lookouts Fleet and Lee support Hogg's testimony that he relieved them at midnight. Fleet testified that Lee and he were up in the Crow's Nest until being relieved 'a quarter of an hour to 20 minutes after' the collision. (Amer. 319) Lee also testified that he was relieved at 12:00 a.m. (Br. 2454), and that he was below deck when he heard the Boatswain give the order to begin uncovering the boats. He knew it was about midnight because the off-duty watch had just come below when this order came down. (Br. 2488a–2493) The testimony of Hogg, Fleet and Lee agree closely with each other, and support a 12:40 a.m. launch time for Boat No. 7 – the first lifeboat lowered.

148. Br. 11347–11351.

149. Amer. 1107.

150. *Indiscretions*, pgs 167–168; second newspaper account provided by Mike Poirier. Some additional details, but not quotes, from *On Board*, Behe, 280–283.

151. *The Truth About the Titanic*, Ch. 2; supplementary quotations from Amer. 989–998; see also *On Board*, Behe, 311–314.

152. Thayer, 1940.

153. *The Binghamton Press*, April 29, 1912.

154. *On Board*, Behe, 148–150.

155. *Providence Daily Journal*, April 15, 1962. Courtesy Mike Poirier.

156. Mrs. Futrelle's story is compiled from the two accounts she gave (*Seattle Daily Times*, April 22/23, 1912; *Philadelphia Evening Bulletin* date unknown; both accounts are contained in *On Board*, Behe.)

157. *The Rockford Republic*, April 25, 1912.

158. *Anaconda Standard*, May 6, 1912. This story is a reprint of Shelley's account that she wrote for the *Powell County Post* in Deer Lodge, Montana. Courtesy Mike Poirier.

159. *Utica Herald-Dispatch*, April 30, 1912. Courtesy Mike Poirier.

160. *Liverpool Journal of Commerce*, April 30, 1912. Account supplied by George Behe; *Western Daily Mercury*, April 29, 1912. Account supplied by Ioannis Georgiou.

161. *The Brooklyn Daily Eagle*, April 19, 1912. Courtesy Mike Poirier.

162. Amer. 971.

163. Br. 18515–18519. This conversation with Bell had to have taken place prior to midnight, because Ismay states that it was before he heard Smith give the order to 'lower' or 'get the boats out'. It can be established that Captain Smith gave the order to uncover and clear the boats as a precautionary measure around 12:00 a.m., even before the extent of the damage was known.

It is also possible that Ismay encountered Bell while he was going down the staircase and the engineer was headed up, and that he turned and came back up the staircase with Bell – so as not to delay him in getting to the Bridge, perhaps – and then they parted at the top of the stairs. Although Gracie's sighting of Ismay with a crewmember is not specific to Bell, his timing seems to fit very closely with the other details given by Ismay.

164. Amer. 333.

165. *Indiscretions*, 167; second newspaper account provided by Mike Poirier. Some additional details, but not quotes, from *On Board*, Behe, 280–283. In her autobiography, Lady Duff Gordon clearly recalled the engines stopping *twice* ... Once immediately after the collision, and again once she had completed her brief investigation on deck.

166. Amer. 657. It is nearly impossible to tell how low Haines went, but he specifically used the word 'down'.

167. Amer. 607.

168. Br. 661a–686.

169. Br. 1917–1969.

170. Br. 15266.

171. Amer. 232.

172. Amer. 533–534.

173. *The New York Herald*, April 19/20, 1912.

174. James Johnstone's name has proved a source of consternation for historians. At the British Inquiry, his name was recorded as James Johnson. On some of the printed crew lists, it is also recorded as James Johnson. However, on every list where he personally had to sign his name, he signed it 'Johnstone', with a 't' and ending with an 'e'. He did so even on lists where his name was recorded as 'Johnson' on the printed side of the list. (PRO BT 100/259 pgs. 297–298, 398; PRONI 2A/45/381 H.) A thorough examination of UK census records is hampered not only by the common occurrence of both his first and last names, but also by the lack of a middle name or initial, varying ages given on all of the crew lists, as well as varying places of birth cited. At this time, the name is best documented as James Johnstone.

175. Br. 3363–3366. Johnstone did not know White, but found out who he was afterwards, although he was not certain in his identity.

176. Br. 3367–3374. There is some question regarding whether Captain Smith sent for Andrews, asked him to come to the Bridge, and upon his arrival, asked him to make an inspection below for damage; whether Andrews proceeded to the Bridge of his own accord; or whether Andrews started off on his own to go below from his cabin.

The timing and location of Andrews' appearance in the D Deck Reception Room on the forward Grand Staircase suggests that it is possible that Andrews went to the Bridge at the Captain's request and started below from there. If Andrews had felt the collision and started off on his own from his cabin, he would most likely have appeared on the staircase sooner; he may also have used a different route to get

to the engine spaces from that location. (One very direct route would have been down the aft staircase to C Deck, then forward to the Maid's & Valet's Pantry, thence down to E Deck and Scotland Road on E Deck.)

The present authors' conclusion from the existing evidence is that Andrews proceeded directly to the Bridge from his cabin, stopping briefly at the forward end of A Deck; we suspect that once Andrews arrived on the Bridge, that Captain Smith asked him to go below and look into the damage. Once the shipbuilder left the Bridge, it appears that Captain Smith detoured to go to the Marconi Room, and then he followed Andrews below.

177. Br. 3400–3401, Br. 3588. Extrapolated from Johnstone's testimony. It appears that the quotation that Johnstone remembered from Andrews, namely 'All right', was part of a larger reassurance to the crowd, and that perhaps just that portion of it was directed at Johnstone. Johnstone's testimony on this aspect seems a bit incomplete.

178. Amer. 810–817; *Cleveland Plain Dealer*, April 21, 1912 (Courtesy Mike Poirier); *The Washington Post*, April 20, 1912; *The Washington Times*, April 20, 1912. It should be noted that Etches' stretch of testimony at the American Inquiry is quite disjointed. Only by piecing that account together with his newspaper accounts and the larger overall timeline can one even begin to understand the timing of his movements.

It seems relatively clear that the Boatswain in question was Alfred Nichols, as Boatswain's Mate Haines was concurrently seeing evidence of flooding in the No. 1 Cargo Hold, and subsequently headed up to the Bridge.

179. *The Weekly Telegraph*, May 10, 1912.

180. *The Brooklyn Daily Eagle*, April 23, 1912; *Stars and Stripes*, April 16, 1955. Courtesy Mike Poirier.

181. *Minneapolis World*, (date unknown). Courtesy Mike Poirier. Additional details (but not quotes) can be found in John Snyder's account of April 24, 1912, in *On Board*, Behe, 401–402.

182. *The Brooklyn Daily Eagle*, April 19, 1912. Account reproduced in *On Board*, Behe, 208–209.

183. *The Duluth Herald*, May 1, 1912. Courtesy Mike Poirier.

184. *Jigsaw*, Taylor.

185. *The Brooklyn Daily Eagle*, April 19, 1912. Courtesy Mike Poirier.

186. Account provided by Mike Poirier.

187. *On Board*, Behe.

188. *Ibid*.

189. *Washington Post Semi-Monthly Magazine*, May 26, 1912. Full account available *On Board*, Behe, 246–254.

190. Miss Dowdell's account is compiled from her accounts in *The Hudson Dispatch*, April 20, 1912; *The Jersey Journal*, April 20, 1912; *The Hudson Observer*, April 20, 1912. The Amy Stanley portion of the story is compiled from *The Oxford Times*, May 18, 1912. Full account available in *On Board*, Behe, 402–403.

191. *The Irish Sunday Press*, June/July 1956, Courtesy of Geoff Whitfield; *East Galway Democrat*, May 11, 1912.

192. *New York Times*, June 26, 1915. This account draws from Daly's 1915 testimony in U.S. District Court as part of the Limitation of Liability hearings.

193. From the typed notes of August Wennerström used in his talks about the disaster, preserved by the Wennerström family. Courtesy of Jerry Wennerström and Mike Herbold.

August Wennerström's actual name was August Andersson. A journalist and socialist activist, he authored a widely-read publication in 1905 criticizing King Oscar II of Sweden. Arrested and later acquitted, he subsequently decided to emigrate to the United States. He took the Wennerström name from a similarly-spelled friend's name, in order to hide his identity. Similarly, Carl Jansson was a socialist activist in Sweden, and emigrated without permission.

194. Amer. 1041–1042. In Bertha Chambers' account of April 24, 1912, she did not mention her husband's solo trip top-side before returning, collecting her, and heading back up together.

195. *The Auburn Citizen*, April 23, 1912. Courtesy Mike Poirier. Collett mentioned Captain Smith in conjunction with this order, but in this particular instance, it does not seem likely that Collett actually saw Captain Smith. Collett was in the Second Class places, and the Captain was then between the Bridge and an inspection trip below.

196. From his accounts, one could initially get the impression that Thayer left his room moments after the collision. However, he specifically referenced hearing the engines stop, then re-start, and then stop again. This presents two possibilities: that he was hearing the engines slip into reverse for a few throbs, and then stop, and that he left his room before Captain Smith re-started the engines briefly. The other possibility – one backed up by his hearing a number of people turn out onto the deck while he was still in his cabin – is that he stayed in his room through the Captain's brief attempt to move the ship forward between 11:43 and 11:46 p.m. The latter seems more likely as it fits better with other passengers who said that there was a period of silence after the engines stopped; it also allows time for him to have heard people moving about while he was still in his cabin.

A word on Thayer's deck designations is also in order. He consistently seems to have been suffering from the sort of 'deck letter confusion' that many other passengers suffered from that night. In his account, he said that on this trip, he went up to '"A" deck on the port side'. This could easily refer to the Promenade Deck. However, he also remembered being in the 'hallway or lounge' with his father there, where he saw Ismay, Andrews, and some of the ship's officers pass. He said that his family next hurried to the 'lounge on "A" deck, which was then crowded with people, some standing, some hurrying, some pushing out onto the deck'. His later references to B Deck would actually indicate to a thorough student of the ship's design that the first location was the Boat Deck, and the second the Promenade Deck.

    For example: Why would his parents have descended to *Titanic*'s B Deck in the hopes of getting off in a lifeboat...? How could he have been in the Lounge on the Promenade Deck and seen Ismay, Andrews and officers hurrying by...? How could passengers have been hurrying out onto the deck directly from the Lounge on the Promenade Deck, as his wording indicates...? His use of the term 'hallway or lounge' is a key to understanding his use of the terminology. Cunarders like *Lusitania* and *Mauretania* had their Boat Decks labeled 'A' Deck, their Promenade Decks labeled 'B' Deck, and so on. Very likely, Jack – a seasoned traveler – was simply mislabeling the deck letters. So in his accounts, a reference to A Deck could be read 'Boat Deck', B Deck could be read 'Promenade Deck', and the 'lounge' could probably be translated into the First Class Entrance at the top of the Grand Staircase.

    At the same time, he recalled correctly in both 1912 and 1940 that their rooms were on the port side of C Deck; if he did have his deck designations confused, it may have been inconsistent or his reference to C Deck could be the only correct designation that he gave.

197. If it is correct that Jack Thayer had his deck letters confused, and this confusion was consistent, then he may have first arrived on the Boat Deck, and then descended to A Deck and walked forward to the rail; there was no passenger access to the forward edge of the Boat Deck by the Bridge to overlook the forward Well Deck. Thayer does seem to separate the locations, but gives no sense of vertical orientation in the statement.

198. April 20, 1912 account by Jack Thayer, George Behe collection. Account available in *On Board*, Behe, 412–414; also Thayer, 1940. In his 1940 account, Thayer said that his father joined him on deck; in his 1912 account, he said that he returned to his stateroom and that both of his parents came out on the deck with him. In his 1940 account, he spoke only of being with his father there, and said that they subsequently returned to their cabin and found his mother and her maid dressed. How can all of this be reconciled?

    Not easily. Earliest accounts are usually the best ones to trust, before a passenger has had time to over-analyze and perhaps distort perceptions, actions, and movements. Yet both of Thayer's accounts are equally believable. It's impossible to say with certainty how his night played out, only to reconstruct a most likely sequence.

    Most likely, Jack's recollection of returning to his stateroom is correct and that both of his parents did go up on deck; his mother was still awake at the time of the collision. Perhaps his mother returned to her room – because of the cold and after realizing that the ship was damaged in some manner; while she began to dress, Jack and John stayed on the deck, finding further information; then when the men returned to their rooms, they found his mother and her maid nearly dressed, Jack dressed fully, and they all then went out on deck together. This, however, would merely seem to be the simplest way of reconciling all the different details without claiming that his recollection was mistaken. ... It is more likely that Jack omitted a detail about his mother returning to her cabin than to believe his very good 1912 account is completely mistaken on the point.

199. If young Jack Thayer's deck letter recollections were mistaken, then Thayer could easily have been the young lad that Gracie spotted on the port side of the Boat Deck. Gracie knew John Thayer, Jack's father, but would he immediately have recognized Jack on the deck in that moment? Probably, since in his book, he mentions recognizing Jack Thayer during the rescue. ... While conjecture, the idea is intriguing, as it would seem that the pair were on the same deck at just about the same time. Yet it could also have been any of the other young men in First Class, as well.

200. *The Truth About the Titanic*, Ch. 2; supplementary quotations from Amer. 989–998; see also *On Board*, Behe, 311–314. Only Gracie's account in *The Truth About the Titanic* mentions his trip aft along the Boat Deck. However, it does not conflict with his other accounts, and is thus considered supplementary rather than contradictory.

201. Amer. 232.

202. Br. 15371–15377.

203. *The New York Herald*, April 19, 1912; *The New York Herald*, April 20, 1912.

204. Br. 3377–3396; Br. 10696–10697. Mackay's estimate of this sighting transpiring 20 minutes after the collision seems to be too long, in light of the established times of other, related events.

205. *The Washington Herald*, April 19, 1912; *Cleveland Plain Dealer*, April 21, 1912. Courtesy Mike Poirier.

206. Br. 1957–1961.

207. Br. 3986–4016. Greaser Frederick Scott also claimed that he felt the collision, before he heard telegraph bells and saw the 'Stop' order for the main engines. (Br. 5513–5546) Scott's account is questionable, though, because by his own admission, he was in the Turbine Engine

Room when the collision came and the watertight doors closed. The telegraphs on which he claimed to have seen the orders given were located at the forward end of the Reciprocating Engine Room, on the Starting Platform. The watertight door between the Turbine Engine Room and this location was closed, so there is no way Scott could have seen the 'Stop' orders on the telegraph as claimed. A number of other details from Scott's testimony are questionable. For example, he claimed that the orders on the telegraph he couldn't see following the collision were: 'Stop' for 10–15 minutes, 'Slow Ahead' for 10 minutes, followed by 'Stop' again for 4–5 minutes, 'Slow Astern' for 5 minutes, and finally 'Stop'. (Br. 5624–5626) Not a single other witness supports this sequence of events, and by his own timeline, this would mean that *Titanic*'s engines continued to operate on-and-off until sometime between 12:09 a.m. and 12:15 a.m., which is patently absurd. For these and other reasons, Scott's testimony relating to the telegraph orders has been discounted.

208. Amer. 657.

209. *American Medicine*, May 1912. 'My Experience in the Wreck of the *Titanic*', by Henry Frauenthal. Account available online at: http://www.archive.org/stream/americanmedicine18newyuoft/american-medicine18newyuoft_djvu.txt.

210. Account provided by Mike Poirier.

211. Apparently, this was not yet an official order; however, the precise timing of the event was not given by Mrs Chaffee in her account, and there is some room for interpretation.

212. *Evening Tribune*, April 23, 1912. Courtesy Mike Poirier.

213. *Amsterdam Evening Recorder*, April 23, 1912. Courtesy Mike Poirier.

214. *Indiscretions*, 167; second newspaper account provided by Mike Poirier. Some additional details, but not quotes, from *On Board*, Behe, 280–283.

215. *The Syracuse Herald*, April 23, 1912. Courtesy Mike Poirier. There seem to be some gaps in Badman's account, as she does not mention dressing at all after the collision. She also did not mention what her cabin-mates did in the first few minutes.

    However, we do know that Third Class passengers moved up from their forward sections, and then aft along Scotland Road, when they were chased out by rising water. Her sighting of at least part of this group moving up and aft means that flooding had already occurred there, causing the mass exodus, which helps us to fix the approximate time. When she said that she went to one of the 'upper decks', this could refer to the forward General Room on D Deck, or even to the open Well Deck just above – she did not specify whether it was inside or outside. In either case, it would not have taken her long to go back to her cabin.

216. *The Washington Herald*, April 19, 1912; *Cleveland Plain Dealer*, April 21, 1912. Courtesy Mike Poirier.

217. *The Brooklyn Daily Eagle*, April 19, 1912. Courtesy Mike Poirier.

218. Account provided by Mike Poirier.

219. In both accounts, Thayer said that the ship was first listing to starboard, and then listing to port. However, there is a good deal of evidence that the ship was actually listing only to starboard at that point. Some time later, the ship did list over to port, and it is possible that Thayer was confused on the timing when he gave his accounts.

220. April 20, 1912 account by Jack Thayer, George Behe collection. Account in *On Board*, Behe, 412–414; also Thayer, 1940.

221. Br. 18517–18518; *On Board*, Behe, 334.

222. *The Truth About the Titanic*, Ch. 2; supplementary quotations from Amer. 989–998; see also *On Board*, Behe 311–314. There are plenty of photos of Ismay wearing a hat when ashore. However, it seems that it was his custom not to wear one while he was at sea.

223. Beesley, Ch. 3; *The Toronto World*, April 19, 1912 (*On Board*, Behe, 157–162). In his book, Beesley recalled that the ship was still moving ahead slowly when he reached the Boat Deck; in his other account, however, Beesley said that the engines had already stopped before he headed up, causing the consternation of those in the passageways. It is difficult to say just how long the ship drifted forward after Captain Smith stopped the engines, but this goes to show that relying on a single account from a survivor rather than multiple accounts (where available) can lead to mis-timings of events.

224. Br. 11352–11354.

225. Br. 11352–11416.

226. Br. 3377–3396; Br. 10696–10697. Mackay's estimate of this sighting transpiring 20 minutes after the collision seems to be too long, in light of the established times of other, related events.

227. Br. 3397–3399; Br. 10893–10901. This entire stretch of the story is pieced together from the testimony of both Johnstone and Wheat. Whereas Wheat thought it was about 10–15 minutes after the collision, Johnstone thought it was about 25; based on the overall timeline of events that had transpired up to that point, it would seem that Wheat's estimate was the more accurate one.

228. *Chicago Evening Post*, April 23, 1912. See *On Board*, Behe, 344.

229. *On Board*, Behe, 148–150.

230. *The Evening Sentinel*, April 24, 1912. Courtesy Mike Poirier; additional details also supplied by Mike Poirier.

231. Mrs Futrelle's story is compiled from the two accounts she gave (*Seattle Daily Times*, April 22/23, 1912; *Philadelphia Evening Bulletin* date unknown; both accounts are contained in *On Board*, Behe.

232. Amer. 534.

233. *The Loss of the Titanic*, Washington Dodge. Address delivered by Dr Dodge to San Francisco's Commonwealth Club. Account contained in *On Board*, Behe, 264–277.

234. Although the three spaces were within the same watertight compartment, the Squash Racquet Court player's area on G Deck was only accessible by a single staircase from the Spectator's Court above on F Deck. It was partitioned off from the Post Office on its starboard side, as well as the First Class Baggage Room and No. 3 hatch.

235. *The Brooklyn Daily Eagle*, April 23, 1912; *Stars and Stripes*, April 16, 1955. Courtesy Mike Poirier. In his 1912 account, Nourney mentioned three feet of water, in his 1955 account, he mentioned six feet of water.

236. *On Board*, Behe; also deposition of George Rheims given in U.S. District Court during the Limitation of Liability hearings, November 14, 1913. In his early account, Rheims said that the information came through a quarter-hour after the shock, and that shortly afterward – an unspecified amount of time – he met Loring. In his early account, Rheims placed the collision at 11:00 p.m. and the order to put on lifebelts at 11:30, some 30 minutes after the collision (or 12:10 a.m., if one accounts for the 40-minute discrepancy in Rheims' timing of the collision). In 1913, however, Rheims said he went out on the deck 10–15 minutes after the shock, and that it was 'about 25 minutes' after the collision that he went to the Boat Deck. Only after that (and comparing his testimony to his original account allows for quite some gap of time) did he see the first boat was lowered.

237. *The Auburn Citizen*, April 23, 1912. Courtesy Mike Poirier.

238. Amer. 1042; April 24, 1912 account (unknown paper) provided by Mike Poirier.

239. Private letter from William Mellors to Dorothy Ockenden written on May 9, 1912, courtesy of Brian Ticehurst.

240. *The Hartford Courant*, April 20, 1931. Courtesy Mike Poirier.

241. Amer. 634–635; Br. 10697–10700; Br. 2488a–2493; Br. 13800. The general timing of when the 'all hands' order was given can be fixed to within a few minutes of midnight by several lines of evidence. Able Bodied Seaman Frederick Clench testified that following the collision, he went under the Forecastle Head, where he looked under the hatchway, saw the tarpaulin bulging up, and heard water rushing in. He believed this was sometime around 11:50 p.m. Clench had time to return to his quarters, change, and have a smoke before all hands were called to the Boat Deck. This suggests that the order was given very close to midnight.

   Lookout Reginald Lee testified that the order for the crewmembers to turn out and get the boats ready for turning out was given just after 12:00 a.m. He said that he knew this, because the off-duty watch had just gone below when the order came down.

   Steward Mackay testified that the 'all hands' order came down very shortly after he saw Captain Smith heading back on deck from his first trip below, which would also place this order around 12:00 a.m. Several other lines of evidence confirm that Smith was back on the Bridge from his initial trip below around midnight, that he ordered the lifeboats uncovered at that time, and also ordered Boxhall to wake the off-duty officers. Second Officer Lightoller testified that Chief Officer Wilde told him that 'all hands' had already been called when he came out on deck after being roused around midnight. (See Endnote 246 below for further details on the timing of Boxhall's trip to wake the officers.) It is important to note that the 'all hands' order probably took a few minutes to filter down to all of the crewmembers below decks, so precisely when various crewmembers received the order likely depended on their location.

242. Br. 18519. *The Berkshire Evening Eagle*, April 22, 1912. Full Account contained in *On Board*, Behe 332–335.

243. Amer. 233; Br. 15379–15380; Br. 15584–15588. In the Senate inquiry, Boxhall said that Smith's reply to his news was 'All right', while in the British Inquiry, he claimed that Smith said nothing that was fixed in his memory. Boxhall clearly remembered at the Senate Inquiry that right after he returned from his inspection below, the Captain gave the order to uncover and clear the boats.

244. Amer. 604. Buley was referring to Murdoch according to his original ranking of 'Chief Officer', but it seems clear that he was definitely referring to Murdoch, as he used his name. He also referred to this same 'Chief Officer Murdoch' as working on Boat No. 10 later in the night.

245. Amer. 536.

246. Br. 15378–15379; Br. 13781–13785; BI 14949. Lightoller gave estimates of between 15 and 30 minutes after the collision for when Boxhall woke him. Pitman testified that it was 20 minutes after the collision, in agreement with these estimates; he also confirmed that when he went out on deck, the crew had already been called out, and were beginning to uncover the lifeboats. (Br. 14951–14952) Lowe must have fallen back asleep after Boxhall roused him, as he testified that the first he knew of the accident was when he was awakened by voices around his cabin, and found there were passengers wearing lifebelts on deck.

247. *The New York Herald*, April 19, 1912; *The New York Herald*, April 20, 1912.

248. Account provided by Mike Poirier.

249. *Indiscretions*, pg. 168.

250. *Providence Daily Journal*, April 15, 1962. Courtesy Mike Poirier. In this story, Helen Ostby seems to have recalled that she saw the Captain coming down the stairs when they were on their way up after putting on their lifebelts. However, that would have been too late for the Captain to have been on his way below for a damage inspection. More likely, she spotted Smith on the stairs at this point, and simply recalled it later in her account because she mentioned that they were going up that same staircase.

251. Amer. 1109.

252. *The Coshocton Tribune*, April 19, 1962. Courtesy Mike Poirier. In the original quotation, the name is spelled Freulichen. The family name was spelled that way consistently throughout the article; however, there is great evidence that the name was spelled Frölicher, at least in 1912. As such, the current authors have altered the quotation to reflect the apparent proper name that this Swiss banker would have used to address her. It is conceivable that there is another explanation, but most likely the name was simply misspelled in the original article.

253. Br. 2001–2036.

254. It is important to remember that *Olympic* and *Titanic* differed in their internal structure in the vicinity of the Turkish Baths, both in the layout of the baths and in the entry to them. In 2005, when James Cameron led an expedition into the Turkish Baths, they were able to use the non-watertight door leading directly from the stairs into the Baths to gain access to the Cooling Room, which they found to be in a fantastic state of preservation. Wheat's actions would not have cut off access to anyone in the Turkish Baths at the time.

255. Br. 10920–10941. Wheat does not say how long this process took. He apparently quit watching the Mail Room flood at about 11:55 (ascertained from the water level he described when he left). It must have been about 12:00 a.m. that he began to close these watertight doors, and this effort in total probably took a few minutes. The next event he described, running into Purser McElroy on the stairs between C and D Decks, seems to have occurred at approximately 12:15 a.m.

256. Amer. 577–578; Amer. 317, 319. Fred Fleet was very clear in his testimony that when they came on watch at 10:00 p.m., they were to have a watch of 'about 2 hours and 20 minutes' (actually 2 hours and 23 minutes, with the setback planned for just before 12:00 a.m.). The conclusion of this watch would have been at 12:23 a.m. unadjusted ship's time. However, he also stated that he was relieved by Hogg and Evans about 'a quarter of an hour to 20 minutes after ... the accident'. Hogg and Evans also believed that they arrived in the Crow's Nest 'at 12 o'clock'. (Amer. 578.)

257. Br. 11352–11416; Br. 2473–2493/2514–2520.

258. Amer. 810–817; *Cleveland Plain Dealer*, April 21, 1912 (Courtesy Mike Poirier); *The Washington Post*, April 20, 1912; *The Washington Times*, April 20, 1912.

259. Amer. 596.

260. Br. 13789–13791.

261. *Titanic & Other Ships*, C. H. Lightoller, 1935.

262. Amer. 71.

263. *The Auburn Citizen*, April 23, 1912. Courtesy Mike Poirier.

264. *Washington Post Semi-Monthly Magazine*, May 26, 1912. Full account available in *On Board*, Behe, 246–254.

265. *The Washington Herald*, April 19, 1912; *Cleveland Plain Dealer*, April 21, 1912 (Courtesy Mike Poirier).

266. *The Truth About the Titanic*, Ch. 2; supplementary quotations from Amer. 989–998; see also *On Board*, Behe, 311–314. In all of his accounts of the disaster, Gracie was remarkably specific that his watch read 12:00 midnight when the collision occurred and when the ship began blowing off steam. However, from many, many other lines of evidence, it is clear that the collision happened at 11:40 (some accounts say as late as 11:43, but this is still close enough to 11:40 to prove the ship's clocks had not been adjusted by the time of the collision). Gracie admitted in one account that he had not adjusted his watch since before midnight the previous night, so it is possible that it was not well-adjusted to ship's time even though it read midnight. Gracie himself seemed to allow for this possibility. In his book, Gracie said that he felt that correct ship's time would then have been 'about 11.45'.

267. Amer. 275–276; Br. 14930–14948.

268. *The Brooklyn Daily Eagle*, April 23, 1912; *Stars and Stripes*, April 16, 1955. Courtesy Mike Poirier.

269. *The Hartford Times*, April 19, 1912. Account available in *On Board*, Behe, 174–177.

270. *Amsterdam Evening Recorder*, April 23, 1912. Courtesy Mike Poirier. Although there is no specific time recorded for this conversation, the time when the Squash Racquet Court was flooding is known; it would have required a minimum of 3–5 minutes for this information to get up to the Doctor, and for him to then rejoin the Hoyts and pass the news on to Frederick. It is also worth noting that the report did not specify just how full the Court was at the time the observance was made. However, it seems clear that the Doctor had told the Hoyts that he was unsure of how bad the damage was, left them, found out that the Racquet Court was flooding, and then subsequently rejoined them, when he passed this new information on. Mrs Hoyt does not

help us to pin down the timing of their movements any further, but the overall picture is that they waited for a number of minutes before returning to their stateroom.

271. Amer. 333.

272. April 20, 1912 account by Jack Thayer. George Behe collection. Account in full available in *On Board*, Behe 412–414; also Thayer, 1940. Here we come across another apparent discrepancy in Thayer's two accounts. In 1912, he said that after noticing the list increasing, his family decided to return to their rooms to dress. In 1940, Jack said that he and his father alone were on deck until 12:15, when they heard the order for lifebelts, and that upon returning to their rooms, they found Mrs Thayer fully dressed.

　　The most likely way of explaining the discrepancies is that Mrs Thayer went up with her husband and son at first, and she then decided to go back below to dress; after waiting a few more minutes, the father and son team heard the order to don lifebelts, and they followed after her, where they found that she and her maid were fully dressed.

　　Interestingly, Jack Thayer never specifically mentioned seeing Captain Smith pass by, while a number of others clearly spotted him several times.

273. *Jigsaw*, Taylor.

274. Account provided by Mike Poirier.

275. There are interesting disparities, as well as interesting parallels, between Henry and Isaac's accounts. Isaac clearly remembered two trips to his brother's stateroom. In the first, he did not say that his brother came to the door, but rather that he had refused to get up. After this, Isaac said that he had gone up on deck, where he heard the conversation between Captain Smith and Colonel Astor. Then he returned to his brother's cabin, finally getting him up.

　　According to Henry, Isaac made only one visit, at 'about twelve o'clock', and he got up during that visit. Shortly after they got on deck, the first boat was being lowered. Isaac recalled that when they got on deck, the stewards were having trouble getting passengers on deck, and that shortly thereafter the first boat was sent away. What is one to take from this?

　　It seems that Henry remembered only the second visit, and that when Isaac woke them up at 'about twelve o'clock', it was actually just after midnight. Clearly, Captain Smith had left the Bridge at about midnight, and Frauenthal apparently encountered him on deck just as he was leaving. This would place Isaac Frauenthal's second visit to Henry's cabin just a few minutes after midnight, or at 'about twelve o'clock'.

276. It would seem that Dr Henry Frauenthal left his cabin after this warning, somewhere around 12:10 a.m. (*American Medicine*, May 1912; 'My Experience in the Wreck of the *Titanic*', by Henry Frauenthal. Account available online at: http://www.archive.org/stream/americanmedicine18newyuoft/americanmedicine18newyuoft_djvu.txt.).

277. *Chicago Evening Post*, April 23, 1912. See *On Board*, Behe, 344.

278. Ibid.

279. *The Brooklyn Daily Eagle*, April 19, 1912. Account reproduced in *On Board*, Behe, 208–209.

280. *The Brooklyn Daily Eagle*, April 19, 1912. Courtesy Mike Poirier. In this portion of her account, Mrs Swift did not specify what got her back up out of bed. The current authors suspect that it was the voice which Emma Bucknell heard calling out as the man passed, saying that 'everyone should dress immediately and go on deck', but that is only one possibility. It also seems very likely that this voice came from Edwin Kimball, who had been told by the Mail Clerk who was 'wet to the knees' that he should 'advise women to dress, as they might have to go on deck'. Kimball said he informed a number of people, including 'a number of women who were traveling alone' that they needed to get dressed and up on deck.

281. This seems to have been Edwin Kimball, whose cabin was right nearby.

282. These two women may have been none other than Mrs Margaret Swift and her companion Dr Alice Leader, as they shared the same side-passageway. How could this be the case? In Mrs Swift's account, it is possible that the use of the male pronoun 'his' in 'his hand' was a misquote on the reporter's part, and that the two ladies learned their information from Mrs Bucknell in the hallway first. More likely, they did have a male visitor – possibly even Frederick Kenyon, their traveling companion – but he first talked to only to Mrs Swift at the door. In this scenario, Mrs Swift would have been the woman seen by Mrs Bucknell trying to convince Dr Leader that it really was an iceberg. As far as the age, Mrs Bucknell said that the two ladies were young women. Mrs Bucknell was about 60 at the time, while Mrs Swift and Dr Leader were 46 and 49 respectively. The accounts line up so closely that it would be very difficult not to see a connection between them. However, it is merely a theory at this point.

283. The portion about the valuables comes from *The Detroit Free Press*, April 21, 1912; courtesy Mike Poirier. The remainder of this portion of her story comes from an account provided by Mike Poirier.

284. Amer. 1042; April 24, 1912 account by Mrs Chambers (newspaper unknown), account provided by Mike Poirier.

285. Amer. 276; Br. 14954–14957.

286. Br. 13800–13804.

287. *The Auburn Citizen*, April 23, 1912. Courtesy Mike Poirier.

288. Beesley, Ch. 3; *The Toronto World*, April 19, 1912. *On Board*, Behe, 157–162.

289. *The Ilford Graphic*, May 10, 1912. Account contained in *On Board*, Behe, 323–328.

290. *Utica Herald-Dispatch*, April 30, 1912. Courtesy Mike Poirier.

291. *Awake!* October 22, 1981, pgs 3–7.

292. In his account – which was apparently given a single time and reprinted in various newspapers as it came through the wires, with certain snatches missing from some of them – Theissinger said: 'I was detailed to C deck and when we started over I had charge of staterooms occupied by some of the most noted people on board.' He listed his charges: Mr and Mrs Straus, Benjamin Guggenheim, Howard Case, H. F. Julian, the Taussig family, and Arthur Gee. He gave Gee's stateroom number as 'No. 63', and the Taussigs' as '67 and 68'. He gave the Strauses' room number as 'No. 50'. So far so good (According to research by Daniel Klistorner, Gee later switched to E-66).

　　The trouble is that Guggenheim was in B-84, and was under the care of Henry Etches. Etches woke Guggenheim up, even though Theissinger claimed to. There is some evidence that Madame Aubart and Emma Sägesser took an initial trip to Guggenheim's cabin shortly after the collision, and made contact with Victor Giglio; if this is accurate, it may explain why Etches found Guggenheim so wide-awake when he knocked on his cabin door. Additionally, the Strauses were listed as being in C-55–57. Meanwhile, Julian, the Taussigs, and Gee were on E Deck (E-60/E-67 and E-68/and E-66, respectively). Did Theissinger really tell the reporter that he had a section on 'E Deck', and the reporter heard or miswrote it as 'C Deck'? Did he really rush to the staterooms of Guggenheim and the Strauses? Is it possible that he had night duty on B or C Deck, and thus had become acquainted with them, so that he rushed to their rooms in addition to his main section on E Deck? Or was Theissinger merely 'overinflating' the importance of the passengers in his care and of his actions that night? It is difficult to say where the truth lies. Admittedly, his story of waking the Strauses seems more likely than his story about waking up Benjamin Guggenheim. Why? Because he specifically mentions being at the Purser's Office at one point, and the Strauses cabin was directly next-door to the Purser's Office, just next to the First Class Entrance. Based on his known movements, then, his story about the Strauses is at least possible. Thus, the current authors will include the Straus portion of his account in the narrative in the order he suggests; the current authors will leave out the Guggenheim portion because there seems to be evidence against it. However, it should be remembered that it is possible that he did go to Guggenheim's cabin between the time Etches made his first and second calls to that cabin.

293. *The Washington Herald*, April 19, 1912; *Cleveland Plain Dealer*, April 21, 1912. Courtesy Mike Poirier.

294. *Indiscretions*, 167; second newspaper account provided by Mike Poirier. Some additional details, but not quotes, from *On Board*, Behe, 280–283.

295. Mrs Futrelle's story is compiled from the two accounts she gave (*Seattle Daily Times*, April 22/23, 1912; *Philadelphia Evening Bulletin* date unknown; both accounts are contained in *On Board*, Behe.

296. *The Brooklyn Daily Eagle*, April 19, 1912. Courtesy Mike Poirier. In her account, Mrs Swift added that she also said that they should 'get into the boats'. However, this is not what Mrs Bucknell and her maid were told at about the same time. It is possible that the 'officer' said something about the boats, or getting into the boats, but it would seem a little early for that here. The other possibility is that Mrs Swift and Dr Leader were delayed more than Emma Bucknell and her maid. Mrs Bucknell, when she left her cabin, stayed for quite a while on the deck before boarding No. 8. Mrs Leader may have left some of that detail out of her account.

297. Account provided by Mike Poirier.

298. *Newport Herald*, May 28, 29, 1912. Full account available in *On Board*, Behe, 217–226.

299. Amer. 1109.

300. Br. 13277–13283; Bullock, 1912. Bullock attributes the 'three have gone already' quote to an unnamed stewardess, but from the details given, and comparing this account with her inquiry testimony, it is clear that the witness in question was Annie Robinson. Robinson places her sighting 'about half-an-hour' after the collision, or at approximately 12:10 a.m.

301. Amer. 1042. First Class Passenger Norman Chambers looked in on the group of 'officers' conducting the inspection as they observed the Mail Room; he overheard the remark that the ship was 'not making any more water'. The initial flooding rate was quite fast; however, the rate at which the water rose would have seemed to decelerate as the water inside the ship equalized with the outside waterline.

　　There is also evidence that Captain Smith and Thomas Andrews came across Chief Engineer Bell while they were below; if this is the case, Bell doubtless would have informed them of some flooding in Boiler Room No. 6, as well... however, the electric lights had been out in the stokeholds previously, which may have impeded the inspection of damage, and the damage control efforts themselves. It thus seems possible that when Smith headed backup, the full extent of the flooding in No. 6 was not known.

All in all, it seems that whatever he had seen and personally witnessed while below, when Captain Smith turned to head topside, he apparently thought the situation was serious, but coming under control.

302. Br. 10696.

303. *Newburgh Daily News*, April 26, 1912. Courtesy Mike Poirier.

304. The exact phraseology used by Ray needs some clarification. There were many 'Saloon Stewards' on the *Titanic*, and Ray was one of them. However, Ray used the word 'the' *before* the term 'saloon steward'. This would indicate that in this instance, he was using the word 'saloon' to refer to First Dining Saloon Steward William Moss – who was sighted nearby at around the same time by William Ward.

305. Amer. 802.

306. Amer. 596.

307. *The Brooklyn Daily Eagle*, April 19, 1912. Courtesy Mike Poirier. It would seem likely that Ray and Nichols were called out by Dodd within just a couple of minutes of each other. When Ray gave his estimation of the time that he was awakened, he said: 'As near as I could make out, it was about 20 minutes [after the collision.] It was around about 12 o'clock.' However, he was sleeping at the time and apparently had little point of reference; Nichols thought that when Dodd came through their quarters, it had been 'I should say three-quarters of an hour' after the collision. It is likely that if both men were referring to Dodd, then Nichols' would be the more reliable estimate, as he was up and fully oriented about what was happening, not just getting up from a groggy sleep. However, it seems likely that both timings were just that: estimates. They should not be relied upon too closely against other evidence. Indeed, Nichols' account does bear some other inconsistencies, so perhaps the best thing to do is to compare the accounts of Ray and Nichols and to average the estimates out, and then to place them in a timeline based on more solid and reliable estimates.

There is good evidence, for example, that Captain Smith – while on the Bridge – had given a preliminary order to call out all hands at midnight; it seems likely that it would have taken a few minutes for the order to filter down to E Deck, particularly as Dodd would have been stopping at each room to awaken the stewards.

308. *Titanic Survivor*, Ch. 21. In her memoirs, Jessop did not name the group of men, but she later gave author John Maxtone-Graham their identities. She also did not give the exact time, but she did give a sequence of events to work from: she saw men working at the boats, then came back inside, saw a rather relaxed Captain Smith, and then saw the members of the orchestra on their way to play. The evidence indicates that this segment of her recollections was quite early in the event, probably around 12:15–12:20 a.m. This seems to confirm other evidence that at that time, Captain Smith felt that the damage was not as serious as first indications might have suggested.

309. Amer. 971; the Wideners were in cabin C-82. If it was the Wideners, then they would not have been returning to their rooms if they were headed up the stairs at the Promenade Deck.

310. Amer. 276; Br. 14954–14969. It would seem that this expedition by Pitman took a period of time. Remember that he encountered Moody on the port-side aft quarter of the Boat Deck, apparently at about 12:05 a.m. He did not specify precisely where Moody was when they met up, but Beesley saw Moody working on Boat No. 16 at about 12:05, so the Sixth Officer may have been all the way aft on the deck.

Pitman then would have needed to walk forward on the Boat Deck and descend to the forward Well Deck, perhaps by means of the emergency staircase on the port side of the Bridge. Once there, he said that he went 'to the forecastle head', but could see no sign of danger. On his return, 'before emerging from near the forecastle head', he saw the stokers coming up. Then he went to the No. 1 hatch and saw the flooding. After this, he returned to the Boat Deck, and made for Boat No. 5.

Pitman's round-trip after he left Moody thus conservatively involved a walk forward of approximately 400 feet (give or take, depending on precisely where Moody was when they talked), and a descent of three decks; on the return, Pitman needed to move aft from the No. 1 hatch to Boat No. 5 on the starboard side, a fore-aft distance of about 125 feet, and have climbed from C Deck back to the Boat Deck. Pitman also encountered some crew members, and thus time needs to be allowed for his conversation with them. All told, it seems that Pitman would not have arrived back at Boat No. 5 until about 12:20 – which is precisely his estimate of when he returned and began to work on that lifeboat. (Br. 14992) and the timing of work at No. 5 would seem to be supported by other evidence.

311. Br. 1041–1043; Hichens stated that this order came down sometime after midnight. Since Hichens stated he was at the helm until 12:23 a.m., this means the order to swing out the boats and begin getting the passengers on deck was given sometime between 12:00 and 12:23 a.m. Imanita Shelley testified that the order to begin getting the passengers up on deck was given about three-quarters of an hour after the collision, or 12:25 a.m. (Amer. 1147) Steward Joseph Wheat was more specific, stating that the stewards were ordered to get lifebelts on the passengers, and get them on deck by Chief Purser McElroy around 12:15 a.m. (Br. 13229) After the order was given by

Smith, it would have taken a few minutes to filter down to all the crewmembers in different parts of the ship.

312. There are two possible times Captain Smith could have worked up his initial dead reckoning (DR) position. The first opportunity would have been while Boxhall was below on his second inspection after 11:50 p.m., and after the Carpenter and mail clerk had made their respective reports to Smith. It would only have taken Smith a few minutes to have done this. The second option is that it was after Captain Smith had arrived back on the Bridge from his second trip below around 12:12 a.m., and after Smith went to the Marconi operators at 12:15 a.m., telling them to be prepared to transmit a call for distress, but before 12:25 a.m., when Andrews told him the ship was sinking. Understandably, there is a shortage of direct eyewitness testimony on the matter; clearly Smith's DR position was worked up by the time the first distress call was sent, and that Boxhall's refined second DR position went to the wireless operators about 10 minutes after the first call went out. The present authors feel it is probable that Captain Smith made his DR estimate after arriving on deck following his own inspection below decks, having dicovered that the ship was substantially damaged, but before Thomas Andrews discovered the ship was doomed; however, the evidence could be interpreted either way.

313. *The New York Times*, April 19, 1912. Harold Bride said that Smith came back approximately 10 minutes later, telling the men to begin sending CQD A 12:15 a.m. time for Smith having first visiting the Marconi room to tell them to prepare to send a distress call is in line with Bride's estimate of him returning 10 minutes later at 12:25 a.m. with the order to begin sending the distress call. The first distress call was received at 10:25 p.m. New York Time, as it was picked up and recorded at the Cape Race station. Since how far ahead of New York time the *Titanic*'s clocks were has been established – namely, 2 hours and 2 minutes – it can be extrapolated that the first distress call was sent at about 12:27 a.m. *Titanic* time. This is in keeping with Smith initially visiting the Marconi room at 12:15 a.m., and with Bride's timeline of events.

Conclusive evidence regarding the 2 hour and 2 minute time difference, which was first noted by researcher Leslie Harrison, is detailed in the article 'Time and Time Again', by researcher Sam Halpern. This article is available at the following URL: http://www.titanicology.com/Californian/TimeandTimeAgain.pdf.

314. Amer. 333.

315. Amer. 971.

316. *On Board*, Behe, 148–150.

317. *The Brooklyn Daily Eagle*, April 19, 1912. Account reproduced in *On Board*, Behe, 208–209.

318. *The Binghamton Press*, April 29, 1912. Additional later accounts also provided by NMM/Mike Poirier Collection. Her identification of Purser McElroy comes from these later accounts, but the identification does not contradict the statement from her 1912 account; rather, this information is considered supplementary.

319. Br. 10942–10952.

320. There are certain inconsistencies in the different accounts of Marian and Jack Thayer. Jack mentioned, in his 1940 account, that at 12:15 a.m. the stewards passed word for everyone to go below and dress in warm clothing, and to put their lifebelts on. Marian Thayer said that as they finished dressing and left their rooms, she saw Major Butt in the hallway outside, but placed that sighting at 'about 12:10', – five minutes before Jack said they started down to get dressed and put on their lifebelts. Thayer also said that he and his father encountered Thomas Andrews, who told them that the ship didn't have more than an hour to live – however, the placement indicates that this occurred *before* the order for passengers to dress and don their lifebelts ... which simply doesn't make sense.

Most likely, Jack and John Thayer remained on deck until word came down at about 12:15 a.m. for passengers to don their lifebelts, or perhaps even later than this – otherwise, why would they all have put on their lifebelts during this expedition to their cabins? It seems that they were in their staterooms for some time preparing, for Marian saw Colonel Butt as they left, perhaps as late as 12:45 a.m. (Witnesses placed Butt during the early stages of the sinking, and Saloon Steward Ray saw Moore and the group he had been sitting with, including Butt, exit the Smoking Room, prior to the lowering away of Boat No. 7. That boat left the deck at 12:40 a.m. Given the timing, Marian's sighting likely came after Butt left the Smoking Room.) The Thayers likely came across Andrews sometime after he had broken the bad news to Captain Smith, which was around 12:25 a.m. Alternatively, they may have encountered Andrews as they headed up to the Lounge since they were there at about the time that Andrews came up from his inspection. It is simply impossible to say with certainty exactly what order things happened in for the Thayer family, and the current authors have simply placed their amalgamated story in the most likely sequence and timing. Some variations should be allowed for.

321. *The Hartford Times*, April 19, 1912. Account available in *On Board*, Behe, 174–177.

322. *The Brooklyn Daily Eagle*, April 19, 1912. Courtesy Mike Poirier. In this account, Mrs Swift indicates that the officer went away and came back shortly thereafter with the order to go up on deck and get into

the lifeboats. This would have placed their arrival on deck after that of Mrs Bucknell and her maid, who did not hear this order and left independently before that point. Mrs Bucknell also remembered being on the deck for quite some time, while Mrs Swift says nothing about being on deck for a long time.

323. *Chicago Evening Post*, April 23, 1912. See *On Board*, Behe, 344.
324. *The Brooklyn Daily Eagle*, April 19, 1912. Account reproduced in *On Board*, Behe, 208–209.
325. Mrs Futrelle's story is compiled from the two accounts she gave: *Seattle Daily Times*, April 22/23, 1912; *Philadelphia Evening Bulletin* date unknown; both accounts are contained in *On Board*, Behe.
326. *The Truth About the Titanic*, Ch. 2.
327. *American Medicine*, May 1912. 'My Experience in the Wreck of the *Titanic*', by Henry Frauenthal. Account available online at: http://www.archive.org/stream/americanmedicine18newyuoft/americanmedicine18newyuoft_djvu.txt.
328. *The Coshocton Tribune*, April 19, 1962. Courtesy Mike Poirier.
329. *Minneapolis World*, (date unknown). Courtesy Mike Poirier. Additional details (but not quotes) in John Snyder's account of April 24, 1912, in *On Board*, Behe, 401–402.
330. *The Daily Mirror*, May 13, 1912. Courtesy Mike Poirier.
331. There were two stewards named Stone: Edward Thomas Stone and Edmond J. Stone. Neither man survived, and Etches did not specify which of the two the steward he spoke to was.
332. Amer. 810–817; *Cleveland Plain Dealer*, April 21, 1912 (Courtesy Mike Poirier); *The Washington Post*, April 20, 1912; *The Washington Times*, April 20, 1912. This portion of Etches' account is important, as it seems to indicate that he had no access to the correct time by means of a personal time-piece at that point. This likely means that his subsequent timing of events are simply estimates, and should not be relied upon in building a timeline.
333. *The Evening Sentinel*, April 24, 1912. Courtesy Mike Poirier. In this account, Mock thought the order came down at 12:05 a.m., but it seems that this order was actually passed about ten minutes later than that.
334. The Washington Roebling on board the *Titanic* was Washington Roebling II, aged 31. He was the grandson of John Roebling, who had begun the Brooklyn Bridge. John Roebling's son Washington had finished the project despite serious health issues. John Roebling's other son, Charles G. Roebling, was the father of the *Titanic* passenger Washington Roebling II. The young man was named in honor of his uncle, the man who completed the Brooklyn Bridge.
335. *Pageant*, October 1953. Courtesy Mike Poirier.
336. *The Brooklyn Daily Eagle*, April 23, 1912; *Stars and Stripes*, April 16, 1955. Courtesy Mike Poirier.
337. *The Duluth Herald*, May 1, 1912; *The Duluth News Tribune*, May 2, 1912. Courtesy Mike Poirier.
338. *Providence Daily Journal*, April 15, 1962. Courtesy Mike Poirier.
339. Amer. 1042.
340. *The Rockford Republic*, April 25, 1912. Bryhl's story is rather difficult to piece together. When her fiancé returned, it was obvious that he had heard no order to go to the lifeboats. The order to load the boats came immediately after Captain Smith learned the ship was sinking; it is most likely that Enander was working on a hunch, and had heard nothing official about the ship being in a sinking condition.
   Dagmar also remembered that Enander's second visit had not been long after his first. However, according to this account, when they reached the deck the lifeboats were lowering. Not just the *first* boats, but the scenes she reported actually sound more like the scenes reported at the aft lifeboats, which were lowered later – including emotional farewells, as well as 'awful' screaming and yelling. This would not represent the scene at the forward boats which were lowered early on. So it seems almost certain that something in her account is simply missing. Perhaps once they got on deck they waited for a period before approaching the lifeboat. This single account does not answer all of the questions that it raises.
341. *The Syracuse Herald*, April 23, 1912. Courtesy Mike Poirier.
342. *Pawtucket Times*, May 22, 1912. Courtesy Mike Poirier.
343. Miss Dowdell's account is compiled from her accounts in *The Hudson Dispatch*, April 20, 1912; *The Jersey Journal*, April 20, 1912; *The Hudson Observer*, April 20, 1912. The Amy Stanley portion of the story is compiled from *The Oxford Times*, May 18, 1912 (full account available in *On Board*, Behe, 402–403). In two of her accounts, Elizabeth recalled quite a scene of congestion, confusion and panic in getting up on deck. In her other account, she is quoted as saying that 'there was no great excitement'. It is possible that the newspaper reporters were 'tarting up' her account in the re-telling, or it is possible that they encountered some congestion as they left the deck. It is difficult to say with accuracy. One way or another, however, all three made it to the open decks without any problem.
344. *Palladium Times*, September 11, 1985. Courtesy Mike Poirier.
345. *Indiscretions*, 167; second newspaper account provided by Mike Poirier. Some additional details, but not quotes, from *On Board*, Behe, 280–283.
346. *The Truth About the Titanic*, Ch. 2. Where exactly Gracie ran into Cullen is open to speculation ... was it in the Entrance? Was it after he returned to his cabin from the Entrance? If it was in the Entrance that
they met, did Cullen follow Gracie back to his cabin, or did Gracie find him again in the Entrance? Gracie simply does not say.
347. Br. 5919–5936; Br. 5978–5980.
348. Amer. 276; Br. 14951–14974; Br. 14991–14993. The 12:20 a.m. time estimate of Pitman's arrival at No. 5 is his own estimate. Fireman Alfred Shiers also testified at the British Inquiry (Br. 4709–4710) that he did not arrive at Boat No. 5 until 'about three quarters of an hour' after the collision, or 12:25 a.m.
349. *Titanic & Other Ships*, C. H. Lightoller, 1935.
350. *American Medicine*, May 1912. 'My Experience in the Wreck of the *Titanic*', by Henry Frauenthal. Account available online at: http://www.archive.org/stream/americanmedicine18newyuoft/americanmedicine18newyuoft_djvu.txt.
351. *The Evening Tribune*, April 23, 1912. Courtesy Mike Poirier.
352. *The Loss of the Titanic*, Washington Dodge. Address delivered by Dr Dodge to San Francisco's Commonwealth Club. Account contained in *On Board*, Behe, 264–277.
353. Amer. 802.
354. Amer. 1043.
355. Amer. 810–817; *Cleveland Plain Dealer*, April 21, 1912 (Courtesy Mike Poirier); *The Washington Post*, April 20, 1912; *The Washington Times*, April 20, 1912. It should be recalled that placing this portion of Etches' account so late in unadjusted ship's time should not be construed as evidence that he was late in reporting to his post. As the clocks were supposed to have been put back at midnight, Etches would have been due to arrive at that location at 12:23 a.m. unadjusted ship's time, which *Titanic* was still keeping.
356. *The Auburn Citizen*, April 23, 1912. Courtesy Mike Poirier.
357. *Amsterdam Evening Recorder*, April 23, 1912. Courtesy Mike Poirier.
358. *On Board*, Behe 148–150.
359. *Newport Herald*, May 28, 29, 1912. Full account available in *On Board*, Behe, 217–226.
360. *The Brooklyn Daily Eagle*, April 19, 1912. Courtesy Mike Poirier.
361. *The Truth About the Titanic*, Ch. 2.
362. This information was conveyed by Maréchal to Secretary Williams of the Amalgamated Musicians' Union, and was subsequently passed on by Williams.
363. *Birkenhead News* (date unknown).
364. The time is clearly known because she also spotted Captain Smith there, after his second trip below, and before Thomas Andrews came back up to inform him that the ship was doomed. The facts also show that Smith returned to the Bridge at about 12:12 a.m., and shortly thereafter issued orders for passengers to don their lifebelts. In her account, Jessop gives no details of her activity between the time she saw Smith on the stairs, the time she saw the band, and the time she saw officers loading the lifeboats. Gracie missed the order for passengers to don their lifebelts, given at about 12:15, because he was in his cabin packing his bags. When he came back out, he found people putting on their lifebelts; only then did he return to his cabin, put his lifebelt on, and then return to the Promenade Deck. It was at that point, he recalled, that he began to hear the music. Most likely, Gracie came out just after the lifebelt order had been passed at about 12:15, and could have taken about five minutes to return to his stateroom, fetch the belt, have his steward fasten it, and return to the Promenade Deck.
   If the order of Gracie's recollections is correct, then it seems unlikely that they began playing before 12:20 a.m. However, of Gracie's three primary accounts, the detail about when the band began to play only comes from one source, *The Truth About the Titanic*. It is possible that he was slightly off in where he placed that statement – for example, if the band began to play as he was coming back up instead of when he was on the Promenade Deck. At the other end of things, Jessop may have omitted something between her sighting of Smith and the musicians, or between her sighting of the musicians and of hearing the music begin. One way or another, 12:15–12:20 emerges as the most likely candidate for when the musicians began to play.
365. Please see Appendix J: The Last Song.
366. *The Evening Banner*, April 26, 1912.
367. Beesley, Ch. 3.
368. *Titanic & Other Ships*, C. H. Lightoller, 1935.
369. Account provided by Mike Poirier.
370. A number of passengers called the First Class Reception Room on D Deck 'the lounge' in their accounts. Some remembered the musicians playing in the evenings in the 'lounge'. However, the orchestra played according to a regular schedule, and they were never scheduled to play in the Lounge on A Deck; No piano was even supplied to that room on either *Olympic* or *Titanic*. A number of others also used the term 'lounge' to describe the various Entrance Foyers above D Deck. As such, one should be careful about interpreting the word 'lounge' strictly to refer to the First Class Lounge on A Deck.
   Jack Thayer's recollections about seeing the band in the 'lounge on "A" Deck' are complicated by his apparent inconsistency in lettering the decks, and by his similar reference to passengers pushing out onto the deck from that location. ... This is because there was no direct access to the Promenade Deck from the Lounge. He could just as easily have been referring to the Entrance Foyer, which is precisely where a number of others, including Maréchal, spotted the band early in their playing.

371. It is possible that the bandsmen had gone below to fetch their lifebelts just then.

372. *New York Times*, May 31, 1912.

373. *Daily Mirror*, April 30, 1912.

374. *On Board*, Behe, 305

375. Private letter from Elizabeth Nye to Walter Lord.

376. Br. 10800.

377. One of the three co-authors works in a family-operated business that performs piano tuning and restoration. In the course of this line of work, he has moved many pianos through the years, including large uprights of the dimensions and weights of the Steinway Model R that was in *Titanic*'s Entrance. Pianos of that model weighed nearly 800 pounds, and were also a bit top-heavy during any maneuvering. Without the use of tools, a dolly, and a team familiar with piano-moving, dismounting the piano, moving it through the vestibule door, around a 90° turn in the vestibule, and then over the coaming at the doorway to the deck seems more likely to have gotten someone wedged than anything else. It also would have inhibited the free flow of passenger and crew traffic in and out of the port side Entrance during the entire time of the move.

378. Br. 10585–10593.

379. Beesley, Ch. 3.

380. Amer. 577–578.

381. Br. 5554–5564, 5576–5583; Br. 19923–19925; Scott's testimony does not seem to imply that the man in the tunnel was injured or caught in one of the watertight doors. Bedroom Steward Theissinger gave a newspaper account in which he said: 'The watertight doors were shut immediately upon the first notice of the crash. ... In the engine room one unfortunate, an engineer, had his leg caught as a door swung to. It was crushed and he was held as in a vise. Before leaving the *Titanic* I was told how he had begged to be shot to end his agony. His wish was complied with, but this is the only shot I know of.' (*Cleveland Plain Dealer*, April 21, 1912. Courtesy Mike Poirier. The story also ran in *The Washington Herald* on April 19, 1912, and is a very close match with that from the *Cleveland Plain Dealer*.) However, Theissinger said that the man was an engineer, and that the event took place in the Engine Room; Scott spoke of a greaser in the after tunnel. Theissinger did not see the event first-hand, and there does not seem to be any other available evidence of anyone being caught in a watertight door or caught and subsequently shot. It is quite possible that his story was 'tarted up' by the reporter taking the story down before it went to the wires, or that Theissinger had misheard the report, or it may simply have been an unfounded rumor. The current authors simply cannot say where this story came from and whether there is any truth to it or not.

382. *Portland Oregonian*, 1912; *The Life and Times of Andrew Jackson Sloper* by William Sloper, 1949. Mrs Warren referred to Andrews as 'Mr. Perry, one of the designers of the vessel'. The time estimate of seeing Andrews about 45 minutes after the collision is her own, and closely matches where the present authors have concluded the sighting took place (about 12:22, or 42 minutes after the collision). Thanks go to George Behe for providing the authors with the above accounts. Thanks are also due to Sam Halpern and George Behe, for helping to piece together the exact sequence and timing of events in the first hour or so after the collision.

383. *The New York Herald*, April 19/20, 1912.

384. Br. 2840–2874. The time estimate for when Poingdestre was in the Seamen's Quarters is his own.

385. The concept that Smith and Andrews went to the Bridge is an interpretation of evidence in hand; most likely, Andrews would have wanted to discuss the matter with the Captain in a quiet place out of earshot of other passengers, to avoid spreading alarm. As evidenced previously, Smith was already on deck by this point, and the Bridge and Chart Room would not have been far away.

386. Br. 15610.

387. Second Officer Lightoller thought it took 45 minutes from the time of the collision until the orders to fill the boats came down, or 12:25 a.m. (Amer. 431). Colonel Gracie also concluded from his own observations 'and those of others', that it was 45 minutes after the collision when this order was given. (*The Truth About Titanic*, Ch. 2) Seaman John Poingdestre's testimony provides supporting evidence. After spending some time uncovering a few boats, Poingdestre went below into the Forecastle to get his boots. When a nearby wooden bulkhead collapsed, flooding his quarters and nearly washing him away, he quickly returned to the upper decks. Once there, he overheard Captain Smith give the order to 'start putting the women and children into the boats'. He estimated that it was about three-quarters of an hour after collision when the bulkhead collapsed, or 12:25 a.m., and that he got out within half a minute. (Br. 2843–2846; Br. 2870–2874) All of this is consistent with the evidence of First Class passenger Albert Dick, who stated that it was 'fully an hour after the vessel struck that the lifeboats were launched'. (*The Waterloo Times Tribune*, April 19, 1912) First Class passenger Dickinson Bishop also said the time that the first boat was launched was 'about a quarter to 1'. (Amer. 1003) 388. Br. 2840–2874.

389. *Titanic & Other Ships*, C. H. Lightoller, 1935.

390. *New York Times*, April 28, 1912. Why did Smith wait to send a call for assistance until this point? Prior to 12:25 a.m., he had personally gone below deck twice, and between his own observations and damage reported to him on the Bridge by the Carpenter, the Mail Clerk, etc., he was convinced that some significant damage had been done to the vessel – enough to wake up the rest of the officers and prepare the lifeboats. However, he did not know at that point that the ship was doomed; nor did he learn this fact until Andrews broke the news to him some 45 minutes after the collision. It would have made no sense for Captain Smith to pull the proverbial fire alarm on getting assistance from other vessels until he was sure that they needed it. His conversation with Thomas Andrews, after they had both come up from below, would have been the first time that he was sure that the ship was doomed; it is thus the first point that Smith would have known that calling for assistance was absolutely necessary.

That it took 47 minutes for the first distress call to be sent may seem surprising, but it took nearly half an hour to discern that there was serious damage done to the ship – including two inspection trips below by Boxhall, inspections by Andrews and Captain Smith, a conference on the Bridge, Boxhall being sent to wake the other officers, and also to work out their position.

Harold Bride's testimony and recollections of what was going on in the Marconi room paint a very slow-moving picture, as well. He was not awakened by the collision, but woke up afterward; he listened to Phillips working at the key for some time; at about 11:55 p.m. (Amer. 144) he rose and talked to Phillips; then he got dressed to relieve the Senior Operator; he had taken over the key and Phillips had closed the curtain to the sleeping berth when Captain Smith came in. After Smith arrived, the distress call was sent very quickly; but obviously quite a bit of time elapsed between the collision and Captain Smith's appearance with the orders to send the call for distress. Bride admitted he could not estimate exact times of certain events on the stand at the U.S. Inquiry, and seemed confused when presented with evidence that the first distress call went out at 10:25 p.m. NYT.

Another point to keep in mind is that in his story presented to *The New York Times* upon arriving in New York, Bride said that Captain Smith came to the Marconi office and warned them to be ready to send a distress call, but not to send it yet. He also stated in that article that the Captain returned 10 minutes later and told them to send the call. He did not discuss this early visit during his testimony; however, as discussed previously, Smith's known movements, the timeline for when he returned from his inspection tour below, and when the first distress signal was sent, all tend to support Bride's story about a 10 minute gap between two visits, with the order to send the call coming during the second.

391. The first distress calls sent from the ship had a longitude of 50° 24' W; these were sent for 10 minutes before the position changed to 50° 14' W. The initial position was apparently derived by Captain Smith before he had asked Boxhall to do a second dead reckoning fix of their position. For further information on this, see Sam Halpern's article, 'It's A CQD OM', Parts 1 & 2 (TIS' *Voyage* Nos 64 & 65).

CHAPTER 5: THE LOSING BATTLE

1. It is very fortunate that Captain Smith took the proactive measures of ordering the crew to uncover and clear the lifeboats, and to have the off-duty officers awakened before he began his inspection below; by making the decision to prepare the boats early, much time was saved in getting them away later.

Many have speculated on what caused the apparent breakdown in communication between Captain Smith and his officers over what to do once the boats were ready to load. This may actually have been because Captain Smith had taken the precautionary measure of having the boats uncovered before he knew that the ship was doomed, and before he knew that the boats would actually need to be used. By the time of that discovery, the officers and men were, to a large extent, spread out across the length of both sides of the Boat Deck; calling them all back to give orders would have caused a delay in the work when a time crunch was foremost in Captain Smith's mind.

It is the present authors' feelings that this combination of circumstances may have caused the subsequent breakdown in communication. It would also explain why some of the officers did not believe the ship's wounds to be mortal for so long after Captain Smith discovered the fact.

2. Br. 15385–15386.

3. October 1962 BBC radio interview; Sam Halpern, 'It's A CQD, Old Man', available through his web site, www.titanicology.com.

4. Br. 15610.

5. Br. Inquiry Report – List of Communications. Since times on this document are all given in New York time, the times given in this narrative have been adjusted forward by 2 hours and 2 minutes to represent accurate Apparent Time Ship during the sinking.

6. *Pageant*, October 1953. Courtesy Mike Poirier.

7. *The Duluth Herald*, May 1, 1912; *The Duluth News Tribune*, May 2, 1912. Courtesy Mike Poirier.

8. *Providence Daily Journal*, April 15, 1962. Courtesy Mike Poirier.

9. Mrs Futrelle's story is compiled from the two accounts she gave (*Seattle Daily Times*, April 22/23, 1912); *Philadelphia Evening Bulletin* date unknown; both accounts are contained in *On Board*, Behe.

10. Account provided by Mike Poirier.

11. *On Board*, Behe; also deposition of George Rheims given in U.S. District Court during the Limitation of Liability hearings, November 14, 1913. It is important to look at both of Rheims' accounts, as his Limitation of Liability testimony omits certain details such as his return to his stateroom – where he dressed warmly and donned a lifebelt – before going back to the Boat Deck. In Rheims' early account, he said it was 'an officer' who gave them the order to put on their lifebelts; in his Limitation of Liability testimony, he said it was Thomas Andrews. As his later testimony is more detailed on the point, the present authors believe it is probably the more accurate identification.

12. Br. 13288–13291; 13304, 13305, 13311. Interestingly, she believed that this conversation occurred 'three-quarters of an hour' after the collision, or around 12:25 a.m.; this very nicely lines up with other estimates of the timing of events during the first hour after the collision, and was about fifteen minutes after she had seen Andrews below deck.

13. Bullock. Please also see Mary Sloan's letter to her sister, reprinted in *On Board*, Behe, 395–397.

14. *Jigsaw*, Taylor.

15. Private letter from William Mellors to Dorothy Ockenden written on May 9, 1912, courtesy of Brian Ticehurst.

16. From the typed notes of August Wennerström used in his talks about the disaster, preserved by the Wennerström family. Courtesy of Jerry Wennerström and Mike Herbold. If this detail is true, it displays an enormous lack of situational awareness on the part of the Third Class stewards, even after it was apparent that the flooding in the forward cabins was significant. One must wonder whether any of these passengers ended up putting their lifebelts on again later, and if not, if this false sense of security instilled by the stewards cost additional lives.

17. *The Weekly Telegraph*, May 10, 1912.

18. *New York Times*, April 19, 1912.

19. Account of Daly, written down by Dr Frank Blackmarr onboard the *Carpathia*, and signed by Daly. Reproduced in "Dr. Frank Blackmarr's Remarkable Scrapbook," *Titanic Commutator*, 3rd Quarter 1998; *Titanic Story* by Mary Daly Joyce, Eugene Daly's daughter. This account is available on the *St. Louis Today* website at http://images.stltoday.com/stltoday/resources/titanicstory.pdf

20. Information courtesy of Bertha Mulvihill's family.

21. Br. 9921–9929.

22. *Palladium Times*, September 11, 1985. Courtesy Mike Poirier.

23. Information courtesy of Bertha Mulvihill's family; *The Irish Sunday Press*, June/July 1956, courtesy of Geoff Whitfield. While it has often been stated that all the single Third Class male passengers or men traveling alone on the ship were berthed in the bow of the ship, and that all the single women, women traveling alone, and families were berthed in the stern, there is reason to question whether this was universally true.

   In a letter to his sister describing his ordeal, Eugene Daly describes going up on deck following the collision, presumably to the forward Well Deck, and recalled that he next 'went down and went to the room where Maggie Daly and Bertha Mulvihill were.' It doesn't sound as if he went aft; in fact, later in his letter he says that after waking the two girls, he went for a 'lifebuoy', (or lifebelt) in the stern, and that the girls came with him. This sounds as if they went aft with him, not that they were already aft.

   Bertha Mulvihill's private accounts to her family indicate that she was nearly thrown from her bed by the collision, which would not have been the case had she been berthed in the stern, where the collision was not felt so strongly. Furthermore, she claimed her cabin was located near one of the ship's boiler rooms, and that a 'fireman' knocked her down the stairs when they were trying to go up on deck. The boiler rooms were located from below the third funnel forward. The stern Third Class cabins were located well aft of the boiler rooms.

   Bertha also told her family that water came into the passageway outside her door not long after the collision. Additionally, Margaret Daly's descriptions of her cabin being 'under five feet of water' when she attempted to return to it makes little sense if they were berthed in the stern Third Class cabins, directly below the Poop Deck – spaces which did not flood prior to the ship breaking in half. On the other hand, her description *does* match the testimony of fellow Irish Third Class passenger Daniel Buckley, who was berthed in the bow, and described similar flooding. He said there was some water outside his cabin shortly after the collision, and that he went up on deck before returning below to get a lifebelt. He was blocked from doing so by a rush of water at the bottom of the staircase, which covered the bottom three or four stairs (Amer. 1019).

   Contrast Margaret Daly's description of the flooding with the known rate of flooding as reported by crewmembers below deck, and in compartments well forward of the stern Third Class cabins. The ship's boiler rooms were numbered 1 through 6, with Boiler Room No. 1 being furthest aft, and Boiler Room No. 6 furthest forward. Leading Fireman Frederick Barrett reported that there was a rush of water in the pass between the boilers in Boiler Room No. 5 at 1:10 a.m. (Br. 2348–2349) Boiler Room No. 5 was below the forward funnel. That location was just beginning to flood at 1:10 a.m.

   According to Trimmer Thomas Dillon, water was just coming up over the forward stokehold plates in Boiler Room No. 4, aft of Boiler Room No. 5, when he was ordered up on deck around 1:20 a.m. He said that at that time, water had not yet reached the boiler rooms further aft, Nos 3, 2 and 1 (Br. 3811; Br. 3913). The boiler rooms only extended as far aft as the third funnel, far forward of where the Third Class cabins were located under the Poop Deck. This is strong evidence that at least some women were indeed berthed in the bow. Perhaps Bertha and Margaret were berthed forward due to being in the charge of Daly?

   An analysis of all the evidence suggests that the two girls may have been berthed in one of the two-person Third Class cabins located in the bow on E Deck, aft of watertight bulkhead B. Neither girl mentioned anyone else having been in their cabin with them, and the Third Class cabins on F and G Deck appear to have been for single men only. Their cabin being located on E Deck corresponds with the aforementioned testimony of Seaman Poingdestre, who indicated that the wooden bulkhead separating the Seamen's Quarters on E Deck from the Third Class passenger space there collapsed around 12:25 a.m., flooding the compartment with 3 feet of water. Since the water that collapsed the bulkhead came from the Third Class side of the deck, it appears that at that point, water had already flooded Third Class berths on E Deck several feet deep at least.

   Corroborating evidence for at least some of the steerage women being berthed in the bow of the ship comes from the accounts of Third Class survivors Emily Badman and Anna Sjöblom. Both girls also felt the collision strongly, and were woken up by it. Emily Badman stated that her berth was 'up near the front on the right hand of the *Titanic*'. She describes having a porthole in her cabin, and there being four girls total, including herself, berthed in the room. (*The Syracuse Herald*, April 23, 1912) Anna Sjöblom did not explicitly state that her room was in the bow as Badman did, but like Mulvihill, she said: 'Water began coming up where I was in a short time, and I fought my way to get above it.' (unknown newspaper and date) This would only have been possible if her cabin was in the bow, since the stern cabins did not flood that early.

   Like Mulvihill and Daly's cabin, Badman's room could very well have been on E Deck. Blueprints of the ship indicate a four-person cabin with a porthole forward on the starboard side of E Deck, aft of watertight bulkhead B, and near the staircase up to D Deck, very near one of the cabins that Mulvihill and Daly may have occupied. Sjöblom's account doesn't give enough detail to narrow down a specific cabin, but it must have been located near Maggie Daly's in order to have begun flooding so early.

   The present authors would like to thank Sam Halpern for sharing his thoughts on the possible location of the girls' cabins, and Mike Poirier for sending the Badman and Sjöblom accounts to us.

24. *Anaconda Standard*, May 6, 1912. Courtesy Mike Poirier.

25. In his account, Nichols said that A Deck was the deck he was headed for, which on *Titanic* would have referred to the Promenade Deck. However, Nichols also said that the deck he was headed for was 'where the lifeboats are'. This can only mean the Boat Deck. Other ships of the period, such as the *Lusitania* and *Mauretania*, labeled their Boat Deck 'A Deck', and thus at times when passengers or crew referred to A Deck, they were actually referring to the Boat Deck.

26. *The Brooklyn Daily Eagle*, April 19, 1912. Courtesy Mike Poirier. At a casual glance, Nichols' account might seem to suggest a very, very early lowering of multiple boats on the starboard side. However, this is not necessarily the case.

   Nichols said that he had been called out about 45 minutes after the collision, or 12:25. A leisurely walk up to the Boat Deck from E Deck might have taken at most five minutes. When he got up on deck, at about 12:30 by this reckoning, he saw passengers in the Gymnasium. Then he spoke about his assigned boats, aft, and said that boat crews were working on Nos 11 and 13. He also mentioned that when he looked down, he could see 'several of the boats were already in the water'. But this would mean that at least Boats Nos 3, 5 and 7 (the first three boats to leave the starboard side) – and possibly a fourth, No. 1, as 'several' usually refers to three or four – had already been lowered away by 12:30 a.m. Under even the best of circumstances, this was impossibly good performance at prepping, loading and lowering those 3–4 boats, and is at odds with the general timing presented by numerous other lines of evidence. This includes an overwhelming amount of evidence that the boats did not even start loading until 12:25 a.m.

   So how does this account fit into the larger picture? By his own words, it can be easily established that Nichols was on deck when Boats Nos 11 through 15 were swung out from the deck. Doctor Washington Dodge had put his wife and son into Boat No. 5. That boat was lowered away at 12:45 a.m. Dodge then waited, by his own estimation, 'half or three-quarters of an hour' before seeing Boats Nos 13 and 15 swung out and lowered simultaneously to A Deck. Nos 13 and 15 were subsequently lowered to the water at 1:40 a.m., some 55 minutes after No. 5 was lowered. Nichols remembered that 'it took us about twenty minutes to fill our lifeboat and get away'. So this portion of Nichols' account, and Dodge's estimation of the timing seem to fit together rather nicely.

It seems from all available information that Boats Nos 13 and 15 were not swung out and lowered down to the deck until shortly before they were lowered down to A Deck to fill, although they had almost certainly been uncovered and prepared before that point. With this in mind, notice the pertinent and otherwise confusing portion of Nichols' account:

> No. 15, my boat, was the after boat on the starboard side. All the odd numbered boats are on one side of the ship and the even numbered boats on the other. There were ten of us to man the boat, which is a big one, holding about seventy to eighty persons. When I got on deck it was still dark, but I could hear the wireless machine sputter. I didn't see any icebergs or anything. Up on Deck A, which is the boat deck, [sic] there were only the boat crews. At least that is all I could see. *I saw them working away at Boat No. 11 and Boat No. 13. When I looked down I saw that several of the boats were already in the water.* [Authors' emphasis.] The ship was brightly lit, and I could see the boats, with people in them, floating about in the reflection of the light of the ship.
>   *The officer in charge of the boats on that part of the deck had a revolver in his hand.* [Authors' emphasis.] He gave his orders quietly and we didn't realize even then that anything serious was the matter. The ship was down in the water a little forward but you couldn't notice it much from where I was.

So Nichols seems to indicate in this account that he saw the boats in the water when he saw work at Nos 11 and 13. He also indicates that he saw an officer with a revolver in his hands (apparently, but not certainly, this was not a reference to Murdoch, since he named Murdoch later and not here). His reference to seeing lifeboats in the water is thus sandwiched directly between work on Nos 11 and 13 and seeing an officer at the aft boats with a revolver.

Additionally, there are a few odd things mentioned in his account. The first oddity is that he recalled that he 'could hear the wireless machine sputter'. This is an utter impossibility, as the set itself was housed in a soundproof room within the structure of the Officers' Quarters, forward of his position.

Nichols shortly thereafter named 'First Officer Murdock' as the officer in charge of loading on 'Deck B' (meaning the A Deck Promenade). However, there is no other evidence to suggest that Murdoch was at the A Deck Promenade at that time; instead, the evidence indicates that he stayed on the Boat Deck. Most likely, Nichols was referring to the time when Murdoch was prepping the lifeboat at the Boat Deck before sending it down the Promenade Deck to complete loading; however, if this is the case, this would seem to be another apparent inconsistency in Nichols' account.

Finally, and perhaps most stunning, Nichols reportedly saw John Jacob Astor 'kiss his wife goodby [sic]'. This was not a claim that someone else had seen them part, and that it was reported to him. This was a claim of a direct sighting, as Nichols said he recognized them because the Colonel 'had been pointed out' to him in the Saloon. Yet Astor did not bid a final farewell to his wife until Boat No. 4, which left well after Nichols did by all accounts.

Additionally, Nichols was 'just forward of the Engine Room' in his quarters on E Deck. His assigned lifeboat (No. 15) was the furthest aft on the starboard side. If he had wished to go directly to his lifeboat from his quarters, he almost certainly would have used the working staircase just forward of the Engine Room, which on *Titanic* (in a change from the *Olympic*'s 1911 design) ran all the way up to the Boat Deck. After being aboard the ship that long, it is utterly inconceivable that Nichols would not have been thoroughly familiar with the fastest route up to No. 15. Despite this, he mentions the Gymnasium, off the forward Grand Staircase, next in his account.

From this, the current authors can establish a couple of theories as to why this apparent disparity exists. The first possibility is that he went up the forward Grand Staircase in order to see if he could be of any assistance as he went up, and was perhaps delayed in reaching the deck. Another possibility is that he went to No. 15 immediately – whatever route he took – and then found that work was not being done there at the time; at that point he, not unlike Steward Ray with Boat No. 9 when he found it was not ready for him, may have moved on to other areas where he thought he could be more useful.

Most likely, Nichols gave his account slightly out of order, jumping back and forth to fill in details; it is also possible that some errors may have crept in as the reporter was taking notes and later transcribing them. Whatever happened to him between the time he started topside and the time No. 13 was eventually lowered, what can be ascertained is that Nichols account is problematic. It is filled with dubious details and inconsistencies even when compared to itself, let alone when compared to other accounts or timelines. Because of

these issues, this account does not on its own necessitate a shift of the timing of the lowering for the first lifeboats.

If anything the pertinent portion of his account, with the sighting of lifeboats in the water sandwiched between the swinging-out of the after boats and seeing an officer there with a gun in his hand, is supplementary, not directly contradictory, to the timeline suggested by the larger body of evidence. Evidence indicates that this sighting simply happened later than a simple read-through of his account would at first indicate. It is simply impossible to be dogmatic about the timing of events based on this account.

27. Amer. 971.
28. Amer. 577–578.
29. Amer. 596.
30. Etches estimated that he saw Andrews on B Deck 'about 20 minutes past 12'. (Amer. 812) However, this cannot be correct. As has already been established, Andrews was conducting his inspection of the damage below decks at that time, and did not rush back to the Bridge until 12:25 a.m. Interestingly, when Etches was speaking to Steward Stone on E Deck, before heading up to A Deck, he recalled asking Stone: 'What is the time?' Stone replied: 'Never mind about that.' This may indicate that Etches was estimating the times he recalled, and that he may not even have had a timepiece on him when he turned out of his cabin. If this is true, then this would certainly explain why he mis-estimated the time that he met Andrews.
    Etches' sighting of Andrews likely occurred sometime shortly after his estimated time of 12:20 a.m. Very likely it was just after Andrews had been on A Deck and ordered Annie Robinson to get her lifebelt on.
31. Amer. 810–817; *Cleveland Plain Dealer*, April 21, 1912 (Courtesy Mike Poirier); *The Washington Post*, April 20, 1912; *The Washington Times*, April 20, 1912.
32. There was one Boatswain, Alfred Nichols, and one Boatswain's Mate, Albert Haines. It seems that Hogg was referring to Nichols, although it is nearly impossible to be certain. However, if it was Nichols, then it might fit in well with the fact that he had been ordered by Second Officer Lightoller to open the gangway doors in order to help load the lifeboats from there. Perhaps the Jacob's ladder was for that endeavor? While speculation, the whole effort went by the wayside, and the Jacob's ladder was never delivered to the Boatswain.
33. Amer. 577–578.
34. Amer. 388. Lowe later estimated that the head was down 12–15 degrees at that moment. According to research conducted by Sam Halpern, in the article, '*Titanic*'s Sinking: Angles of Trim and Heel', published in *The Titanic Commutator*, No. 174, the forward trim at this point would have been about 3°. However it is easy, for someone standing on a canted deck, to feel that the trim or list is greater than it actually is.
35. Amer. 387–388; Br. 15790–15810.
36. Br. 13872–13875. Able Bodied Seaman Poingdestre testified that he heard Captain Smith himself order the crew to begin putting the women and children into the boats. (Br. 2874) The fact that Lightoller had to ask the Captain for permission to begin preparing, and then again to load the boats is often cited as an example of Smith being an ineffective commander during the sinking. In fact, it seems that work in this area was only then catching up to the proactive orders that Captain Smith had already given to Poingdestre and the other crewmen.
37. Account provided by Mike Poirier.
38. Amer. 971.
39. *The Brooklyn Daily Eagle*, April 19, 1912. Account reproduced in *On Board*, Behe, 208–209.
40. *Chicago Evening Post*, April 23, 1912. See *On Board*, Behe, 344.
41. Amer. 802.
42. Amer. 596.
43. *Binghamton Press*, April 29, 1912. Mrs Cassebeer's account can be read in *On Board*, Behe, 235–237; also the account by Mrs Hoyt given in the *Amsterdam Evening Recorder*, April 23, 1912. Additional private accounts also provided by NMM/Mike Poirier Collection.
44. *The Hartford Courant*, April 20, 1931. Courtesy Mike Poirier.
45. *The Patriot*, April 20, 1912. Courtesy Mike Poirier.
46. Beesley, Ch. 3. *The Toronto World*, April 19, 1912 (*On Board*, Behe, 157–162).
    A quick read of Beesley's book account might suggest that the Second Class boats were nearly ready to load by 12:20. However, the time he gave was 'about 12:20'. He did not give any time estimates in his written newspaper accounts. This would suggest that he was only estimating the times much later when writing the book, in order to expand on his first account. The possibility of an error in this estimation is clear, but should be placed as close to the estimate as other events will allow. Another thing to keep in mind is that Beesley also mentioned that time at the *outset* of the work being done on the boats. It is obvious that this effort took some time, as the covers were still on the boats and they had to be thoroughly prepared.
    Beesley said that the first boat on the starboard side to receive attention was Boat No. 9. It is also known that Steward Ray found that No. 9 was just being cranked out at about 12:45 a.m., when Boat No. 7 was lowered.

47. *The Washington Herald*, April 19, 1912; *Cleveland Plain Dealer*, April 21, 1912 (Courtesy Mike Poirier). The wording of Theissinger's account suggests that he went from C Deck down to D Deck, met with Brewster there, and then the pair passed back up the staircase through the C Deck entrance. Theissinger does not say what, if any time, he spent with Brewster on D Deck, or where they met, so it is difficult to judge just how long he was below on D Deck before coming back up.

48. *The Truth About the Titanic*, Ch. 2. This recollection only appeared in Gracie's book, and not in his Senate Inquiry testimony or in his April 1912 written account. In the book, it is sandwiched between other details which are included in those other accounts.

Where does this bit fit in with the rest of Gracie's account? Clearly, the order had not yet been passed for ladies to proceed toward Boat No. 4, and so Gracie was able to use this information to reassure the ladies that help was on the way. The exact time of *Titanic*'s first wireless distress call is also known: 10:25 p.m. New York Time, or 12:27 a.m. *Titanic* time, when the correct 2 hour, 2 minute time difference is accounted for. So this had to have occurred after 12:27 a.m. ship's time, and before word was passed to proceed to the lifeboats. Interestingly, Gracie placed this very close to the time which he gave as his sighting of the ship off the *Titanic*'s port bow. This harmonizes very well with the timing of Boxhall's spotting of the same light on the horizon.

Although Gracie placed the word of wireless traffic coming down *before* the sighting of the light, his testimony at the Senate Inquiry (page 990) indicates that this sighting happened very shortly after he came across the ladies on the Promenade Deck. It is possible that the two events occurred so closely to one another that the order was reversed when he inserted the detail into the text of *The Truth About the Titanic*. No matter which one of the two events occurred first in reality, it is clear that the sighting of the light and subsequent conversation with Astor would not have taken very long. Thus, the present authors have placed both incidents in the order in which Gracie mentioned them.

Wireless contact with other vessels was established immediately at 12:27 a.m. ship's time, and the word apparently traveled quickly down to Gracie and others on the Promenade Deck, arriving there by no later than about 12:40 (when word came down for the ladies to move toward Boat No. 4 on the Promenade Deck). Also note that this statement is nonspecific; it was not based upon the *Carpathia*'s 12:49 a.m. (10:47 p.m. NYT) message that she was headed to the *Titanic*'s assistance. Rather this news – as it reached Gracie – was probably based on the early wireless responses which Phillips and Bride received, which the officers seem to have relayed to passengers as certain word of a rescue ship's coming.

49. *The Truth About the Titanic*, Ch. 2.
50. Amer. 233. According to Boxhall, when he had finished calculating the position, he reported to Captain Smith, who ordered him to take it to the Marconi operators.

With the position of the ship's wreck site established, it is now known that Boxhall's famous position was off by approximately 13 miles, and Captain Smith's initial estimate was equally flawed; both were the product of a miscalculation in their dead reckoning and/or their calculations. *Titanic* researcher Sam Halpern has made a very well-reasoned case that 41° 45.5′ N, 49° 55′ W was the actual site of the collision with the iceberg. The actual location of the *Titanic*'s wreck, as measured from the center of the boiler field, which likely dropped right to the ocean floor, is 41° 43.5′ N, 49° 56.8′ W. Refer to his articles 'Collision Point' (at the Great Lakes Titanic Society's site http://www.glts.org/articles/halpern/collision_point.html), and 'It's A CQD OM' Parts 1 & 2 (TIS' *Voyage* Nos 64 & 64).

51. Amer. 148–149.
52. Amer. 333–334.
53. *The Evening Tribune*, April 23, 1912. Courtesy Mike Poirier.
54. *The Coshocton Tribune*, April 19, 1962. Courtesy Mike Poirier; *A Night to Remember* 67.
55. *Minneapolis World*, (date unknown). Courtesy Mike Poirier. Additional details (but not quotes) can be found in John Snyder's account of April 24, 1912, published in *On Board*, Behe, 401–402.
56. Amer. 1043; April 24, 1912 account by Mrs Chambers (unknown newspaper), provided by Mike Poirier.
57. This communication, as well as its New York time of 10:36 p.m., was fixed at the British Inquiry in the final report.
58. *Pageant*, October 1953. Courtesy Mike Poirier.
59. Amer. 334. Peuchen was later rather confused about how the boats were numbered, and there is some room for interpretation in his statements. From the overall timing of his story, it seems certain that he reached the Boat Deck in time to clear the masts out of Boat No. 4 before it was lowered to the Promenade Deck. Based on his description of events, it appears that he subsequently loaded No. 8 before leaving in Boat No. 6.
60. Br. 13834; Amer. 81.
61. Br. 10953–10956.
62. *The Truth About the Titanic*, Ch. 2. Gracie determined that the order to load the boats came down 45 minutes after the collision based upon his 'own conclusions, and those of others', in agreement with

other estimates of when this order was given. In his earlier testimony at the Senate Inquiry, Gracie described events on the Promenade Deck. He referred specifically to his conversation with John Jacob Astor, and then he said: 'Some time elapsed, I should say from three-quarters of an hour to an hour before we were ordered to the boats.' It would seem that by the time Gracie had written his book, after corresponding with other survivors, he determined that the order had been given closer to forty-five minutes after the collision, rather than an hour.

Only one lifeboat, No. 4, reached the forward port quarter of the Promenade Deck for direct loading. It seems that the order sending the women and children down to A Deck to board the lifeboat from that location was given before the crew realized that the windows needed to be opened and that the cranks were missing; the loading was subsequently halted and delayed so long that No. 4 did not begin lowering away until 1:50 a.m. Gracie may have believed that the other boats were being lowered to the Promenade Deck because he saw them descending from the Boat Deck; however, these other port boats were never lowered to A Deck.

63. When Gracie's account is examined for timing and placed in the proper location in the timeline, it sheds light on Sixth Officer Moody's whereabouts between being seen uncovering the aft port boats very shortly after midnight by Third Officer Pitman, and his subsequent involvement in the loading of Boat No. 16, which lowered away at 1:20 a.m. Previously, his whereabouts during that stretch of time had been unknown.

64. Amer. 990 .
65. *Ibid*.
66. *The Truth About the Titanic*, Ch. 2. It is important to note that this entire exchange occurred on the Promenade Deck, not on the Boat Deck, and was a prelude to the Strauses' final near- (and then non-) parting at Boat 8.
67. *The Evening Tribune*, April 23, 1912. Courtesy Mike Poirier.
68. Amer. 882–883.
69. Amer. 882.
70. Amer. 665.
71. Mrs Chambers' account, April 24, 1912 (unknown newspaper). Courtesy Mike Poirier.
72. Amer. 1043.
73. Mrs Chambers' account, April 24, 1912 (unknown newspaper). Courtesy Mike Poirier.
74. Br. 13834.
75. Br. 13858–13859.
76. Br. 13906; *Titanic & Other Ships*, C. H. Lightoller, 1935.
77. Please see Appendix I: The Loss of *Titanic*'s Deck Crew Over Time, for further information on this crew shortage.
78. *The Loss of the Titanic*, Washington Dodge. Address delivered by Dr Dodge to San Francisco's Commonwealth Club. Account contained in *On Board*, Behe, 264–277.
79. Amer. 810–817; *Cleveland Plain Dealer*, April 21, 1912 (Courtesy Mike Poirier); *The Washington Post*, April 20, 1912; *The Washington Times*, April 20, 1912. It seems that Etches made only a single trip to his section on B Deck, awakening Guggenheim and Giglio, and being intercepted by Andrews and discovering that the rest of his passengers were already up. In his testimony, he said that he had told Guggenheim that he would return; however, the exact wording of his testimony – when taken in context and not excerpted 'close to the bone' in the form of a single sentence – seems to indicate that he saw Guggenheim and Giglio depart their cabins before he left the section with Andrews and went down to C Deck. This would explain why, when he saw the two men on the Boat Deck during the loading of Boats Nos 5 and 7, he was surprised to find that they had returned to their staterooms after he had left them, and that the two men had fully dressed, also apparently removing their lifebelts in the process. While there is some room for interpretation in Etches' testimony, this seems to be the most straightforward and simple explanation for his movements during the period.
80. *Indiscretions*, 167; second newspaper account provided by Mike Poirier. Some additional details, but not quotes, from *On Board*, Behe, 280–283.
81. As described earlier in the narrative, Lookouts Hogg and Alfred Evans relieved their shipmates in the Crow's Nest at midnight, and after 20 minutes, they saw 'people running about with lifebelts on' down on the Boat Deck. (Amer. 577–588). This is consistent with the order for passengers to begin coming up on deck with lifebelts on being given between 12:10–12:20 a.m., as previously discussed.

Obviously, when Hogg and Evans relieved Fleet and Lee at midnight, they were ahead of the normal 12:23 a.m. change of shift that Quartermasters Hichens and Rowe testified about. It seems most likely that when the ship's crew were ordered to turn out at 12:00 a.m., instead of going up on deck to help clear the lifeboats, they went to relieve their mates in the Crow's Nest.

Lookouts Fleet and Lee support Hogg's testimony. Fleet testified that he and Lee were relieved in the Crow's Nest 'a quarter of an hour to 20 minutes after' the collision. (Amer. 319) Lee also testified that he was relieved at 12:00 a.m. (Br. 2454), and that he was below deck when he heard the Boatswain give the order to begin uncovering the boats. He knew it was about midnight because the off-duty watch had just come below when this order came down. (Br. 2488a–2493).

82. Amer. 578.
83. *Minneapolis World* (date unknown). Courtesy Mike Poirier. Additional details can be found in John Snyder's account of April 24, 1912, which can be found in *On Board*, Behe, 401–402.
84. Amer. 596–597.
85. *The Hartford Times*, April 19, 1912. Account available in *On Board*, Behe, 174–177. The concept that the Astors were so close to boarding No. 7 together is quite an astounding one. Whatever the motive for their decision, it was to prove very costly to them both.
86. *The Evening Sentinel*, April 24, 1912. Courtesy Mike Poirier.
87. *Newburgh Daily News*, April 26, 1912. Courtesy Mike Poirier. It should be remembered that this account of Mrs Flegenheim's experiences was given second-hand by her friends, Mr and Mrs William Walker, of New Windsor, New York. If one were to read her account without studying the larger picture of the timing of certain events, one could twist it into proof that the boats started lowering much earlier than they actually did. However, using this account to support such a timeline would be an unscholarly approach to the affair, as it was second-hand. There are clear gaps in her story of what happened, as presented in this account. As this seems to be one of the few accounts given by Mrs Flegenheim of her experiences that night, however, it – such as it is – has been included.

    Additionally, it seems to have been assumed over the years that Mrs Flegenheim departed in Boat No. 7; there may be room for interpretation on the point, as it seems she never said it was No. 7, but rather that it was 'the first boat' to leave. Many passengers said that they were in the 'first' or 'last' boat to leave, and yet their recollections are clearly far from accurate. However, placing her at Boat No. 7 does seem to fit with the overall timeline, so at this point the current authors have concluded that she most likely did board No. 7.
88. *The Washington Times*, April 20, 1912. Popular myth holds that this conversation took place shortly before the sinking. In reality, it had to have taken place prior to Etches' departure from the ship in Boat No. 5, sometime around 12:43 a.m.
89. *The Washington Post*, April 20, 1912; *Cleveland Plain Dealer*, April 21, 1912. Courtesy Mike Poirier.
90. *Newburgh Daily News*, April 20, 1912. Courtesy Mike Poirier. The identity of this steward is a little unclear. The newspaper account lists the source as a 'room steward' named 'John Johnson'. The only problem is that there was no such person. Steward James Johnstone gave an account on April 19, published in the April 20, 1912 edition of the *Worcester Evening Gazette*. In that article, he was listed as 'John Johnson'. It is possible that Johnstone – whose name was frequently misspelled and misheard as Johnson – gave a second interview subsequently published in the *Newburgh Daily News*. Because this is a speculative identification, however, the present authors have left the names out of the description in the narrative.
91. *The Brooklyn Daily Eagle*, April 23, 1912; *Stars and Stripes*, April 16, 1955. Courtesy Mike Poirier.
92. Amer. 1143.
93. *New York Times*, April 22, 1912.
94. Throughout this chapter, lifeboat launch times will be noted in accord with the previously mentioned article, '*Titanic*: The Lifeboat Launching Sequence Re-Examined', by Bill Wormstedt, Tad Fitch and George Behe, with contributions by Sam Halpern and J. Kent Layton. The lifeboat launch table contained in this chapter is also from this article.

    This table represents the present best attempts of the present authors, as well as George Behe and Sam Halpern, to build an objective and accurate timeline and lifeboat launch sequence from the ground up. We have worked objectively from all available eyewitness and forensic evidence, starting from scratch, and letting the evidence guide our conclusions. Pre-existing notions regarding the lifeboat launch times were tossed out. The findings of previously published timelines – many of which bear flaws or conflict with eyewitness accounts – were not the basis for the authors' conclusions.

    In another recent examination of the evidence by Senan Molony ('Resetting *Titanic*'s Chronology: Early Boats, Early Rockets', published simultaneously in the British Titanic Society's *Atlantic Daily Bulletin* and in the Titanic International Society's *Voyage* No. 62), the author attempted to prove that the time when the distress rockets began to be launched was earlier than is currently accepted. In doing so, Molony concluded that the first lifeboat to leave, No. 7, was lowered at 12:25 a.m. – about fifteen minutes before the time the present authors concluded in their article, and twenty minutes earlier than the launch time the British Inquiry stated in its final report. However, a thorough and objective examination of all the evidence indicates that Molony's conclusions do not accurately represent the sequence and timing of events that night.

    Evidence discussed earlier in the narrative indicates that the order to uncover and clear the boats was proactively given by Captain Smith around 12:00 a.m., before he went below deck for the second time to begin his inspection tour, and before he knew that the ship was sinking. Molony's claim that the lifeboats could have began lowering away as early 12:25 a.m. is not consistent with this evidence. Second Officer Lightoller estimated that it took 15–20 minutes to uncover

a lifeboat (Br. 13855). Fifth Officer Lowe estimated it would take 20 minutes to get a boat uncovered, swung out, and into the water (Amer. 406). However, Lowe's estimate does not include the time needed to load passengers into the boats. As he said, 'it was not the launching of the boats that took the time. We got the whole boat out and in the water in less than ten minutes. It was getting the people together that took the time.' (Amer. 277). With the order to uncover the boats not coming until 12:00 a.m., these estimates by two seasoned officers indicate that the boats would not have been uncovered or even ready to start loading until around 12:20 a.m., much less filling them and then lowering away.

    Furthermore, as detailed previously, Captain Smith did not know that the ship was doomed until around 12:25 a.m., when Thomas Andrews was seen by two eyewitnesses rushing up the Grand Staircase to deliver that news. Prior to that time, there was no reason for Smith to order the boats loaded. Molony's conclusions would have us believe that the lifeboats were being lowered *before* the evidence suggests the Captain even knew the ship was mortally wounded. Additionally, as shown earlier in the narrative, there is ample evidence that the order to swing out the boats and begin getting the passengers on deck with their lifebelts on wasn't given until sometime between 12:10–12:25 a.m., and that the order to begin loading women and children into the boats wasn't given until 12:25 a.m. At that point, time still would have been needed to load the boats with passengers – passengers who were very apprehensive to board the boats at that point. This makes a 12:40 a.m. departure the most plausible conclusion.

    The aforementioned article by Bill Wormstedt, Tad Fitch and George Behe, with contributions by Sam Halpern and J. Kent Layton, goes into the evidence supporting a launch time of 12:40 a.m. for Boat No. 7 in significantly more detail. All sources are footnoted and listed.
95. *The Loss of the Titanic*, Washington Dodge. Address delivered by Dr Dodge to San Francisco's Commonwealth Club. Account contained in *On Board*, Behe, 264–277; also an article named '60 Years Ago The *Titanic* Went Down' (paper unknown) containing an interview with young Washington Dodge, account courtesy of Mike Poirier.
96. Br. 15809–15811.
97. Throughout this and the subsequent chapters, the estimated number of occupants in each boat when it was lowered, as well as details pertaining to persons transferred between boats once afloat, those rescued from the water, etc., will be drawn from the online article '*Titanic* Lifeboat Occupancy Totals', by Bill Wormstedt and Tad Fitch, 2011. This article examines in depth the eyewitness accounts and forensic evidence related to the issue of the number of people who were rescued in each boat, with all sources documented and footnoted; it is available online at the following URL: http://wormstedt.com/titanic/lifeboats/occupancy.pdf
98. Account provided by Mike Poirier.
99. *Amsterdam Evening Recorder*, April 23, 1912. Courtesy Mike Poirier.
100. Deposition of Elizabeth Lines, given as part of the Limitation of Liability hearings, November 24, 1913; *Boston Traveler*, April 15, 1966; unknown newspaper, August 6, 1975. These two newspaper articles are courtesy of Mike Poirier.
101. Amer. 277. Some researchers have concluded that this reference to 'two or three minutes' referred to the entire process of stripping the cover, prepping the boat, swinging it out and lowering it down to the deck level. However, studying the context of Pitman's testimony, it is clear that he was only referring to the operation of the davits. The entire process of preparing the boat for loading would therefore have taken more than two or three minutes.
102. Amer. 276–277.
103. *Providence Daily Journal*, April 15, 1962. Courtesy Mike Poirier.
104. *The Coshocton Tribune*, April 19, 1962. Courtesy Mike Poirier.
105. *Indiscretions*, 167; second newspaper account provided by Mike Poirier. Some additional details, but not quotes, *On Board*, Behe, 280–283.
106. *The Binghamton Press*, April 29, 1912. Additional private accounts also provided by NMM/Mike Poirier Collection.
107. *The Binghamton Press*, April 29, 1912. Courtesy Mike Poirier. Additional later accounts by Mrs Cassebeer also supplied by NMM/Mike Poirier Collection. This sighting is interesting, as one of Ismay's own accounts suggests that he returned to his stateroom and put on a suit – apparently over his pajamas – directly after speaking to Chief Engineer Bell. It seems that Ismay did not take the time to remove his pajamas or put on a proper shirt during that trip to his stateroom. In his haste, he may also have neglected to put on more formal footwear.
108. Amer. 971; *The Truth About the Titanic*, Ch. 7.
109. Amer. 816–817.
110. Although Norman Chambers recalled that this was Boat No. 7, his description of events and other evidence – particularly his wife's account of April 24, 1912 – actually matches Boat No. 5. Colonel Gracie also believed that the Chambers made it into No. 5.
111. *The Brooklyn Daily Eagle*, April 19, 1912. Account reproduced in *On Board*, Behe, 208–209.
112. Amer. 816–817.
113. *The Loss of the Titanic*, Washington Dodge. Address delivered by Dr Dodge to San Francisco's Commonwealth Club. Account contained in

On Board, Behe, 264–277; also article named '60 Years Ago The *Titanic* Went Down' (paper unknown) containing interview with young Washington Dodge, account provided by Mike Poirier.

114. Amer. 817.

115. Amer. 277–278; Amer. 282; Br. 15016–15021; Br. 15034–15035. Pitman's testimony at both Inquiries gave several variations for Murdoch's exact words here. This conversation is reconstructed as best as the evidence allows from a comparison of Pitman's testimony, but the authors' acknowledge that the exact quotations could have been slightly different.

116. Private account supplied by NMM/Mike Poirier Collection.

117. Amer. 1043.

118. Amer. 817; *The Truth About The Titanic*, Ch. 7.

119. *The Loss of the Titanic*, Washington Dodge. Address delivered by Dr Dodge to San Francisco's Commonwealth Club. Account contained in *On Board*, Behe, 264–277; also article named '60 Years Ago The *Titanic* Went Down' (paper unknown) containing interview with young Washington Dodge, account provided by Mike Poirier.

120. '*Titanic* Lifeboat Occupancy Totals', by Bill Wormstedt and Tad Fitch, 2011, available at: http://wormstedt.com/titanic/lifeboats/occupancy.pdf.

121. Amer. 389–390.

122. Amer. 1030–1031.

123. *American Medicine*, May 1912. 'My Experience in the Wreck of the *Titanic*', by Henry Frauenthal. Interestingly, Henry never made mention of his jumping into the lifeboat in his account. It could be that he was so embarrassed by it that he decided to 'gloss over' that point. Interestingly, according to his account, when his brother and he jumped in, he did not believe that the ship was going to sink. Account available online at: http://www.archive.org/stream/americanmedicine18newyuoft/americanmedicine18newyuoft_djvu.txt.

124. *Providence Daily Journal*, April 15, 1962. Courtesy Mike Poirier.

125. *The Coshocton Tribune*, April 19, 1962. Courtesy Mike Poirier.

126. Amer. 1044; April 24, 1912 account (unknown paper) supplied by Mike Poirier.

127. Amer. 1044.

128. *American Medicine*, May 1912. 'My Experience in the Wreck of the *Titanic*', by Henry Frauenthal. Account available online at: http://www.archive.org/stream/americanmedicine18newyuoft/americanmedicine18newyuoft_djvu.txt.

129. *Providence Daily Journal*, April 15, 1912. Courtesy Mike Poirier.

130. Details are from Thomas Whiteley's *Titanic* lecture, originally published in the Pawtucket, Rhode Island newspaper.

131. *The Evening Sentinel*, April 24, 1912. Courtesy Mike Poirier; additional information also supplied by Mike Poirier.

132. *Pawtucket Times*, May 22, 1912. Courtesy Mike Poirier. There is very little way of telling exactly when Rhoda and her sons reached the deck, as her account is missing many details. Did she mean that she saw Boat No. 5 lowered? Or was she speaking only of the second of the aft group of lifeboats? Did she manage to make it all the way to the Boat Deck? Probably not at first, as she instead referred to the 'after-deck'; this was almost certainly a reference to the Aft Well Deck or Poop Deck, where Third Class passengers were initially held back. Eventually, however, it seems that she did make it to the Boat Deck, since she mentioned that there were women left behind on the deck when the last lifeboat was lowered, but some men got into late boats without any protest. She could only have been in a position to see these details if she had reached the Boat Deck.

133. *Amsterdam Evening Recorder*, April 23, 1912. Courtesy Mike Poirier.

134. *Titanic & Other Ships*, C. H. Lightoller, 1935. For further details on the timing of this incident, please see Endnote 136.

135. *The Christian Science Journal*, Vol. XXX, October 1912, No. 7.

136. Amer. 975. Lightoller mentioned this excursion to Murdoch's cabin two separate times. The first was made in his account published in *The Christian Science Journal*, October 1912. In that account, he seems to have placed the timing just before Collapsible B was brought down from the top of the Officers' Quarters, very near the end of the disaster. He was also very careful to avoid mentioning what the officers were going to get: guns and ammunition. In the second account where he mentioned this trip (*Titanic & Other Ships*, C. H. Lightoller, 1935), he seems to have connected it with the lowering of Boat No. 6 and Peuchen's boarding of that boat. However, even here the present authors cannot be certain of when the trip took place, since he merely mentioned the Peuchen story and then connected it to the trip to Murdoch's cabin with the words: 'It was about this time...'
   Lightoller gave conflicting evidence on the order of lowering for Boats Nos 6 and 8 (Br. 13841–13842; Amer. 80). Lightoller also gave conflicting information on when this trip to Murdoch's cabin occurred (after Boat No. 6 or just before Collapsible B, depending on the account). Thus, the current authors feel that his evidence on the timing of the event may not be entirely reliable.
   To this, one has to add the testimony of Charles Stengel and the recollections of young Washington Dodge, as stated in the narrative. It is clear that at Boat No. 5, the initial order was for 'women and children' or 'women first'; possibly this was because Murdoch was not at No. 5 during much of the loading, and its loading was instead overseen by Third Officer Pitman (Bruce Ismay and Thomas Andrews were report-

edly nearby assisting in the loading, repeating the order, as well). Murdoch customarily had no problem allowing women and children into the boats. Another established fact is that Murdoch came along, ordered Pitman into the boat, and then reportedly moved on to the next boat.
   Based on the evidence presented, the Frauenthal brothers jumped in just as the lifeboat was starting from the deck, with Fifth Officer Lowe helping to lower away. Their action prompted an officer to call out that he was going to get his gun. However, this officer would not seem to have been Lowe, since Lowe had already brought his gun from his cabin when he came on deck. It's possible that the officer could have threatened to get it simply to help keep order, but Stengel also said that the officer who threatened to get the gun actually left the deck and returned shortly thereafter. Lowe does not appear to have left the deck, but instead continued helping lower No. 5.
   It would seem that Murdoch was most likely the officer at hand just as the Frauenthals jumped in; it is also possible that Wilde may have crossed over to the starboard side to ask Murdoch where the revolvers were, and could have been the officer in question. Interestingly, Lightoller thought that when Wilde approached him, he had just come from the starboard side. Yet Pitman – in Boat No. 5 at that point – specifically said that he did not remember seeing Wilde at any point after the collision, (Amer. 296) although it is possible that he may have missed seeing him. In either case, since Wilde didn't know where the revolvers were, he approached Lightoller and asked for them to be brought out.
   Why would Murdoch or Wilde have had such a strong reaction to the Frauenthal brothers' actions? While Murdoch clearly had no issue allowing men into the boats throughout that night, this action – especially the injury to Mrs Stengel – may have crossed the line in his mind, or in the mind of Wilde if he was at hand. The Frauenthals' action also clearly hinted at the possibility of further – and perhaps worse – trouble ahead.
   Wilde told Lightoller that he had asked Murdoch about the location of the firearms, and that Murdoch did not know where they were. Wilde seems to have been the only one to approach Lightoller, but somehow Wilde and Lightoller met Murdoch and the Captain at Murdoch's cabin. Perhaps Murdoch suspected they were either somewhere in his cabin, or in Lightoller's (which adjoined his own) and while Wilde was fetching Lightoller, the First Officer set off to meet them in the corridor outside their cabins to save time. Perhaps Lightoller had previously told Murdoch that the weapons were in Murdoch's cabin, but Murdoch did not know precisely where they were and he didn't want to waste time looking for them; indeed, Lightoller said that the locker he stuffed the firearms case into was 'of little use owing to its inaccessibility'. The present authors simply cannot say for sure.
   However, the absence of Murdoch, Wilde and Captain Smith anywhere near Boat No. 5 – apparently while they were getting the ammunition – might very well explain why no one interceded when Lowe erupted at Ismay, his employer, during the lowering of No. 5. This vacuum of officer presence may even explain why Ismay felt the need to 'step up' and 'take charge' of the lowering in the way he attempted to. It is also quite possible that this excursion, and the lack of officer presence, would explain at least in part why there was a slightly longer gap between the lowering of Boats Nos 3 and 5 and the gap which separated Nos 5 and 7.
   Lightoller also clearly remembered that it was on his way back from this trip to fetch ammunition that he encountered the Strauses, who so famously refused to board the next lifeboat Lightoller lowered, No. 8. While it is not conclusive evidence of this event transpiring at the time indicated in the narrative, that portion of Lightoller's recollection sets the stage for that scene rather nicely once the moment is moved to this point rather than after No. 6 lowered away.
   Finally, Stengel recalled that the officer who left the deck to get his gun returned very shortly thereafter. Lightoller recalled that the entire excursion 'had not taken three minutes'. So even this seems to fit well with the timing of Stengel's recollections; it also indicates that the officer Stengel was referring to was Murdoch, rather than Wilde, since the latter did not help load any of the starboard boats except Collapsible C.
   While the present authors leave open the possibility for this event having occurred later, perhaps after the lowering of Boat No. 6, we feel that the evidence available at this time best supports this placement in the timeline rather than a later one. We also feel that Murdoch emerges as the most likely candidate for the officer who made the threat at No. 5. Should further evidence on the point to the contrary come to light, however, some adjustment may be required down the road.

137. Amer. 597.

138. Beesley, Ch. 3. Beesley did not state how long he watched the crew work. He only gave the start time and a description of events, and said that shortly thereafter he saw the first rocket launched. It is thus obvious that the scene played out over a number of minutes, beginning at 'about 12:20'.

139. Amer. 665.

140. Br. 3801–3804.

141. Br. 5570–5605.
142. Br. 3738–3794.
143. Br. 10957–11069.
144. Br. 15385–15393. Boxhall's testimony is a bit disjointed, and there is some room for interpretation on what he did and when. Boxhall recalled hearing about the 'light' while the boats were being uncovered. It appears that he then went to the Bridge to investigate, but when he got there, Captain Smith spotted him and ordered him to work out their position, subsequently ordering him to take the position to the Marconi Room. It seems that Boxhall did not get a good look at the vessel and did not attempt to signal her until after his trip to the Marconi Room with the revised position. The present authors would like to thank Samuel Halpern and George Behe for taking the time to give their input on Boxhall's actions.
145. Apparently twelve distress rockets were kept on the Bridge, with another twenty-four kept astern. These should technically be called 'distress socket signals', but as many referred to them as 'rockets' or 'distress rockets', they will be referred to as such throughout the running narrative.
146. Amer. 401.
147. *Providence Daily Journal*, April 15, 1962. Courtesy Mike Poirier.
148. *Discretions*, pg. 167; second newspaper account provided by Mike Poirier. Some additional details, but not quotes, from *On Board*, Behe, 280–283.
149. Between his two different written accounts, Gracie gave two distinct times and two separate places where he was when the first rocket was fired. In his book (*The Truth About the Titanic*, Ch. 2), he thought that the first rocket was fired while he was on the Boat Deck after Boat No. 6 had been lowered away. However, in his April 1912 written account (*On Board*, Behe 312) he placed the firing of the first rocket while his placing of the ladies into the officers' care on the Promenade Deck. This shows how with different retellings, a single survivor's story can change, and independently could be used to support different arguments.

It is possible that Gracie missed the firing of the first rocket while he was below, and that the rocket he saw from the Boat Deck after No. 6 left was not actually the first rocket. However, if Gracie's other account is correct, which seems equally likely, then it would seem that he did see the first rocket go up at some point before leaving the Promenade Deck to go below. Exactly when that occurred in the chain of incidents mentioned between his various accounts is impossible to say, however.
150. *The Truth About the Titanic*, Chs 1–2. In the book, this account is broken up between two completely disparate stretches of text, and Gracie even supplies two slightly different estimates of how long after the collision this occurred. In the later segment, he reported that the order to load the boats had come about three-quarters of an hour after the collision; the events which he described after the order came through – the handing off of his ladies to Moody, the Straus conversation, and the incident with the steward and the barrel could have taken 2–3 minutes. To proceed into the companionway and down to C Deck might have taken another 2–3 minutes. However when introducing this conversation Gracie said that it took place '*within* [Authors' emphasis] three-quarters of an hour after the collision'. Worse yet, recall that in his other accounts he allowed for it to have been longer than three-quarters of an hour after the collision when the order to load the boats had come through. Obviously, there is some variance in Gracie's estimates of when certain events occurred.
151. Beesley, Ch. 3.
152. *The Evening Sentinel*, April 24, 1912. Courtesy Mike Poirier; additional information also supplied by Mike Poirier.
153. *The Truth About the Titanic*, Ch. 2; supplementary quotations from Amer. 989–998; see also *On Board*, Behe.

Gracie's cabin, C-51, was forward of the Forward Grand Staircase. Gracie was explicit, however, in his statements that he walked the length of the Promenade Deck from aft to forward. So unless he walked aft along the deck and then back forward on the deck, he must have come up the Aft Grand Staircase. From Gracie's cabin, if he wished to begin a systematic search of A Deck for his table companions starting from the stern, then he would have needed to ascend from a point far aft of the Forward First Class Grand Staircase; the Aft Grand Staircase is as good candidate as any, although it should be treated as a hypothesis rather than a plain fact.

His account given in *The Truth About the Titanic* appears, in this instance, to be an expansion of his April 1912 written account, and of his testimony at the Senate Inquiry. In neither of those accounts did he mention the trip to his cabin to get blankets.

There is another example of the evolution of Gracie's story, as told through different accounts. In his Senate Inquiry testimony and his April 1912 written account, Gracie said that the fourth man with Butt, Moore, and Millet was Arthur Ryerson, although he only ascertained this after the fact. By the time he penned *The Truth About the Titanic*, however, he was only able to say that this fourth man was 'a stranger, whom I therefore cannot identify'. Perhaps when Gracie learned that Ryerson's family had not yet left when he came through the Smoking Room, he decided that his earlier identification of the fourth man was incorrect. However, this cannot be stated with certainty.

154. Amer. 801. Ray described seeing Moore leave the Smoking Room with the table companions he had been sitting with there. While he doesn't mention Major Butt or Frank Millet by name, it can safely be assumed that these were the other individuals with Moore, as they were seen sitting together in the Smoking Room by several witnesses. Ray saw the group in question leaving the Smoking Room before he headed to his assigned boat, No. 9, and saw Boat No. 7 being lowered away; this places the time of his sighting of Moore and his group sometime between 12:40 and 12:45 a.m.
155. William H. Taft papers, Library of Congress, *On Board*, Behe, 414–416.
156. *On Board*, Behe, 412–414; Thayer, 1940. Because of certain inconsistencies in Thayer's accounts, it's nearly impossible to tell exactly when he allegedly saw Thomas Andrews. However, it had to be after Andrews discovered that the ship was sinking. Andrews was sighted by others heading up the Grand Staircase shortly before 12:25 a.m.; he may have bumped into the Thayers then, even before he got to Captain Smith. However, based on other accounts, Andrews was clearly not interested in stopping as he came up, and he ignored most other queries. More likely, Andrews came across the Thayers in the location where the present authors have placed the account, after coming back from his conversation with Captain Smith.

In his earliest account, Thayer said that they 'walked around, looking at different places', while in his later account, Thayer said that they went to the Lounge. Perhaps they went to the Lounge first, and then he and his father or all three walked around. This would make allowance for coming across Thomas Andrews, who was known to be in the area of the Grand Staircase at about this time.
157. *The Indianapolis Star*, April 23, 1912. Courtesy Mike Poirier; Robertha Watt's account can be found in *On Board*, Behe 422–423. Robertha's time estimate seemed to be just that: an estimate. It seems likely that she was awakened at around 12:45, in the general area where we have placed the account.
158. Amer. 597. Ward also mentioned Murdoch and Ismay, but he specifically mentioned them in connection with the loading, not necessarily the preparation work. Since Ray said Murdoch wasn't there at that point, Murdoch must have arrived at that location after the preparation work was finished. Ray, a fellow member of the Victualling Department, would almost certainly have known McElroy by sight, so this suggests that there may have been another deck officer present during the preparation process.
159. Amer. 802–803. The estimated number of men working on Boat No. 9 comes from Ray's testimony. He said there were two sailors at *each* davit, (or 'at the winding arrangement to wind the boat up', in his words) and 'about a dozen other men' nearby. Later, Senator Smith repeated the number back in a question, but he misremembered the number which Ray had just given him, which clearly totaled about sixteen, and which is included as such in the narrative.
160. *The Titanic Commutator*, #156. The testimony and evidence shows that Quartermaster Rowe's relief was due to arrive at about 12:23 a.m., according to unadjusted ship's time, or 12:00 a.m., if all the clocks had been put back around midnight as intended. Rowe, in a letter to Ed Kamuda of the Titanic Historical Society in 1963, said that his 'watch should have ended at 12:22 but time went by and no relief turned up', a clear reference to unadjusted ship's time.

According to research done by Sam Halpern, this clock change would most likely would have taken place just before midnight, meaning that if the clocks went back at 11:59 p.m., for example, then they would have gone back to 11:36 p.m., thus delaying the ringing of eight bells until midnight adjusted time, or 12:23 a.m. unadjusted ship's time. No matter what the procedure was intended to be, the ship's clocks were not officially put back due to the accident.

Bright had slept right through the collision, and was not awakened until one of his mates returned to their quarters and awoke him, saying the 'ship is going down by the head'. He specifically said (Amer. 832) that he was late in relieving Rowe; just how late he was he did not specify. He did say that once he arrived, that he and Rowe talked for 'some moments' before spotting a lifeboat in the water. Depending on how one interprets 'some moments', this could leave Bright's arrival on the aft Docking Bridge anywhere from just a few minutes late (i.e., Bright's verbal emphasis was 'some moments', as in quite a while between his arrival and spotting the boat), or that he had just shown up when this transpired (i.e., Bright's statement was a flat 'some moments', as in not a long period). Rowe's comments about time going by and his relief not showing up, as well as Bright's mate informing him the ship was going down by the head when he was awakened, tend to indicate the Bright was more than just a few minutes late in arriving at the stern.

The evidence from Rowe and Bright do not in any way preclude a 12:40 a.m. departure of Boat No. 7, and in fact, the sum total of the evidence at hand (from both these men and others) supports this conclusion.
161. Amer. 521–523; Br. 17603–17607.
162. Amer. 832.
163. Rowe's testimony in 1912 and his later accounts given during the 1960s vary wildly on different points. These variances include what events he saw at what point, and the exact timing of various events. (For specifics, see 'The Distress Rockets and Quartermaster Rowe',

and 'The Launch Time of the First Lifeboat' in the previously mentioned URL: http://www.wormstedt.com/Titanic/lifeboats/lifeboats.htm) However, the timing of Rowe's next action is fixed clearly by Boxhall's testimony about receiving a phone call just after he was returning the firing lanyard to the Wheelhouse, just after launching the first rocket.

164. Br. 15593. Rowe's testimony is contradictory regarding the timing of some events. In June 1963, 51 years after the disaster, when speaking to J. Powell of the Mercantile Marine Services, Rowe said that he did not set his watch back the 23 minutes to keep pace with the expected time change around midnight. (The letter from Powell citing this can be seen in Senan Molony's article, 'Early Boats, Early Rockets'.) However, there are a couple of things that contradict that statement.

First, Rowe put the timing of seeing the first boat in the water at 12:25 a.m., (Amer. 519) which flies in the face of an overwhelming preponderance of evidence that the lifeboats were launched later, at the times indicated in this text. (In 1963, he also said that this same event happened at 1:00 a.m., and also at 12:30 a.m., contradicting his other accounts.) However, if Rowe set his watch back – or if he didn't physically set his watch back, but realized that the clocks were due to be set back around midnight and was *thinking* in adjusted time – then adding 23 minutes to his 12:25 a.m. estimate brings the timing of seeing the first boat in the water to 12:48 a.m. This is much closer to the timing of this event as supported by the majority of the evidence. Not coincidentally, this timing is right after the time that the first rocket was sent up, around 12:47 a.m. (Read the section of the present authors' aforementioned lifeboat launch article entitled 'The Distress Rockets and Quartermaster Rowe', which delves into this topic in more detail, and which is available at http://www.wormstedt.com/Titanic/lifeboats/lifeboats.htm).

It is also important to note that Rowe testified that it was 1:25 a.m. when he left the Bridge to get in Collapsible C; in his next breath, however, he said that the ship sank 'Twenty minutes, I believe' after he left (Amer. 524). Since the ship sank at 2:20 a.m., his 1:25 a.m. time is clearly mistaken; even if one used the British Inquiry launch time of 1:40 a.m. for that boat, and concluded that Rowe spent 15 minutes working there before the boat was lowered away, his statements would place the ship's sinking at 2:00, not 2:20. Additionally, Rowe said that when Collapsible C began lowering, the forward Well Deck was awash, but that in the 5 minutes it took the boat to lower to the sea, the Well Deck had submerged. Quartermaster Bright testified that the Forecastle was just going under when Collapsible D lowered away (Amer. 837). In order for the Well Deck to submerge and not just be awash, the physical design of the ship and angles she assumed while sinking dictate that the Forecastle head would also have to have gone under, which was just happening as Collapsible D lowered away at 2:05 a.m.; this is strong evidence that Collapsibles C and D left within minutes of each other, not 25 minutes or more apart. This clearly contradicts Rowe's 1:25 a.m. time for leaving the Bridge, but supports his statement that the collapsible left around 20 minutes before the ship sank.

Another possibility is that Rowe's later memory of not setting his watch back was correct, but that he just did not have a terrific grasp of overall timing. However, while being interviewed by J. Powell on March 2, 1963, Rowe gave some completely contradictory information: he said that the first lifeboat launched was No. 13, at 1:00 a.m., and that it was the second from aft. No. 13 was the second boat from aft on the starboard side, but it was one of the last boats lowered on that side of the ship. When asked if he had estimated the 1:00 a.m. time, or if he had looked at his watch, Rowe responded that he '*did not think of or about a watch*' (authors' italics). Rowe also estimated in the same interview that he went to the Bridge at 12:25, and that it took him 10 minutes to get there. He also said that he did not know where Boxhall was during the firing of the rockets, indeed that he hadn't seen him after the first two rockets went up. (The authors thank Paul Lee and Samuel Halpern for providing access to this report.) This blatantly contradicts Boxhall's 1912 testimony about overseeing the firing of the distress rockets until being ordered into Boat No. 2. Other letters, written to Ed Kamuda during 1963 and 1968 and reprinted in *The Titanic Commutator*, No. 156, also seem at variance with what Rowe wrote to Mr Powell, even though they were written within months of each other. For example, he claimed to Powell on June 11, 1963 that rockets were fired while he was still on the Poop Deck; he told Ed Kamuda on September 3, 1963 that he fired the first rocket, i.e., that none were fired before he reached the Bridge.

Obviously, by 1963, Rowe's memories were fading, vague and contradictory. Thus, his statements regarding the timing of events cannot be relied upon independent of other data. The majority of evidence points to a later launching of the first lifeboat, No. 7, around 12:40 a.m., and that the first rocket went up between the lowering of Boats Nos 5 and 3, after No. 7 was away. The fine points of this are endlessly debatable, but this is a logical conclusion based on numerous lines of evidence.

165. Bright clearly testified that he and Rowe each took a box of rockets to the Bridge; oddly, Rowe never alluded to Bright's participation in

bringing the rockets up to the Bridge, or to his subsequent assistance in firing them.

166. Amer. 239.

167. Amer. 934.

168. *Rochester Democrat & Chronicle*, April 21, 1912. Courtesy Mike Poirier.

169. Amer. 803. Ray's statement about going up the Grand Staircase at a 'leisurely pace' may indicate that he stopped during the ascent to care for other tasks; if he were to go directly down the stairs to E Deck, and then back up to the Boat Deck via the forward Grand Staircase, this may have taken less than ten minutes.

From following the indicated water levels, it would seem that Ray saw the water on E Deck at about 12:50 a.m. However, Ray's next detail was meeting up with a passenger named Rothschild, who had just sent his wife away in Boat No. 6, which began lowering away at 1:10 a.m. At the early end of his account, he had been at No. 9 at about the time that No. 7 was launched, or 12:40 a.m. If No. 7 had been lowered away any earlier, then this would only tend to exacerbate the gap in his story. It would seem that Ray either stayed below for a few minutes on E Deck aft, or watched the flooding forward briefly, or handled a number of other tasks while below before bumping into Rothschild.

170. Br. 11069–11071.

171. Even more startling is the fact that the approximate times that they saw these rockets correspond very well with the timing of the rocket-firing sequence aboard the *Titanic*, once you account for the 12-minute difference in the two vessels' clocks. Second Officer Stone on the *Californian* saw a rocket (not necessarily the first) at about 12:45 a.m. *Californian* time, or about 12:57 a.m. *Titanic* time, and saw another one shortly afterward. (Affidavit of Herbert Stone, written for Captain Lord on April 18, 1912, while the *Californian* was still at sea. Stone's full affidavit and a wealth of other information on this topic are available on Dave Billnitzer's website 'The *Titanic* and the Mystery Ship' at the following URL: http://home.earthlink.net/~dnitzer/Frameset.html) Stone had gone to the speaking tube at 12:35 a.m. *Californian* time, after Captain Lord whistled up to ask if the steamer on the horizon had moved. 12:35 a.m. *Californian* time corresponds to 12:47 a.m. *Titanic* time, precisely the time that the first rocket was sent up, which means that Stone likely missed seeing the initial rocket.

Third Officer Groves thought that he had stayed on the Bridge until approximately 12:10–12:15 a.m. (12:22–12:27 a.m. *Titanic* time), and he did not see any rockets during that period (Br. 8493–8494). There was no clock on the upper Bridge of the *Californian*, but the officers would most likely have had a pretty good idea of what time it was from their own timepieces adjusted to ship's time.

Apprentice James Gibson had a good look at the ship at 'about a quarter or twenty past twelve', or 12:27–12:32 a.m. *Titanic* time, and thought he saw her signaling via Morse lamp, but could not discern any message (Br. 7708–7718). He had not seen any rockets at that point. Gibson left the Bridge at 12:25 a.m., or 12:37 a.m. *Titanic* time, still not having seen any rockets. (*Note*: he also affirmed that he left the Bridge at twenty-five to one, but that was in response to a question; both times he spoke of his own accord, he said he left the Bridge at 12:25 a.m.) When he came back on the Bridge at 12:55 a.m., or 1:07 a.m. *Titanic* time, Second Officer Stone told him that he had seen five rockets. They saw another three together. Stone said that the last rocket was fired at 'about 1:40 a.m.', or 1:52 a.m. *Titanic* time. This is in line with Fourth Officer Boxhall's estimate of being sent to Boat No. 2 about half an hour before the ship sank, and with Quartermaster Rowe being ordered to stop firing rockets and being sent to Collapsible C by Captain Smith in time to finish loading it and leave about 20 minutes before the ship sank.

According to Apprentice Gibson, at 2:05 a.m., or 2:17 a.m. *Titanic* time, the lights of the steamer he and Stone were watching disappeared. (Br. 7789) This is the very time when the *Titanic*'s lights went out, just prior to her breaking in half and sinking at 2:20 a.m. (See Sam Halpern's article 'Rockets, Lifeboats, and Time Changes', which delves into this topic in detail, and which is available at the following URL: http://www.encyclopedia-titanica.org/rockets-lifeboats-and-timechanges.html#_ednref43)

172. Note Sam Halpern's article, 'A Captain Accused', available via this URL: http://www.encyclopedia-titanica.org/item/4622/)

173. For further information, please see Appendix R: The *Californian* Affair.

174. *New York Tribune*, April 20, 1912; *The Cincinnati Enquirer*, April 20, 1912.

175. Amer. 112; Amer. 827; *The Sinking of the Titanic*, Ch. 17, by Jay Henry Mowbray, 1912. Bedroom Steward Alfred Crawford said that Mrs Straus handed her maid a rug at No. 8. He was mistaken. Ellen Bird said that Mrs Straus had actually given her the fur coat she was wearing. After the sinking, Ellen tried to return the fur coat to Mrs Straus' family, but they refused, saying she should keep it, since Ida had given it to her. The refusal of Mrs Straus to leave her husband has become a legendary part of the sinking. Crawford's testimony on the subject seems credible since it was given at the Senate Inquiry, as does Ellen Bird's, since she was Ida Straus' maid, and was in a position to see the couple part. It is worth noting that many more people claimed

to have seen the old married couple refuse to part than could have witnessed it in reality.

In his 1935 book, Second Officer Lightoller claimed that after Boat No. 6 left, and after coming back from retrieving the firearms from First Officer Murdoch's cabin, he saw Mr and Mrs Straus up against the deck house, chatting cheerily, and that he stopped and asked Mrs Straus if he could help her to a boat. She said, 'I think I'll stay here for the present.' Mr Straus asked, 'Why don't you go along with him dear?' She declined, saying, 'No, not yet.' To some, this may suggest that No. 8 left after No. 6, since Crawford and Bird both say Mrs Straus refused to leave her husband at the former boat, and Lightoller describes her declining his assistance sometime after No. 6 left. However, Lightoller must be describing a later separate incident if it even happened at all (there are a few instances where he adds details to his 1935 account which contradict what he said in 1912, such as alleged interactions with Jack Phillips on Collapsible B, claiming to have seen the engineers up on deck, when he denied seeing them in 1912, etc.). This is particularly true since Crawford and Bird said the Strauses refused to part alongside No. 8, which Ellen Bird called 'the first boat'. Lightoller said he saw Mr and Mrs Straus leaning up against the deck house, and his version of what they said does not match what Crawford and Bird describe. Furthermore, Crawford says that Captain Smith and Chief Officer Wilde were assisting at No. 8 when the couple refused to part, and does not mention Lightoller being present. In his own accounts, Lightoller does not claim to have been involved in the loading of No. 8 at that point.

176. Mrs Futrelle's story is compiled from the two accounts she gave (*Seattle Daily Times*, April 22/23, 1912; *Philadelphia Evening Bulletin* date unknown; both accounts are contained in *On Board*, Behe.

177. Amer. 571. Jones said that he knew Chief Officer Wilde, but was unable to name this 'first officer'. Since photographic evidence indicates that Lightoller had not had the opportunity to change his uniform to that of a Second Officer's ranking prior to the voyage, Jones probably just mistook Lightoller for the First Officer.

178. *The Brooklyn Daily Eagle*, April 19, 1912. Courtesy Mike Poirier. Mrs Swift placed the time of the collision at 11:45 p.m., and the departure of her lifeboat as 'between 1 and 1:30 o'clock'. She also mentioned that hers was 'the second boat that left the vessel. I might have gone in the first, but I did not believe that there was any real danger, and I hesitated to get down in an open boat at 1 o'clock in the morning when our own ship seemed to be perfectly safe'.

This could be taken to mean that she saw Boat No. 6 leave before No. 8; or it could be a reference to the lowering of Boat No. 4 to the Promenade Deck. Since she said that she had just come over from the starboard side when she joined the ladies waiting for Boat No. 8, it is also possible that she saw one of the boats on the starboard side leave before she crossed over to port.

179. *The New York Herald*, April 19, 20, 1912.

180. *The Evening Sentinel*, April 24, 1912. Courtesy Mike Poirier; additional information also provided by Mike Poirier.

181. 'Titanic Lifeboat Occupancy Totals', by Bill Wormstedt and Tad Fitch, 2011. (http://wormstedt.com/titanic/lifeboats/occupancy.pdf)

182. *New York Times*, April 28, 1912. In his press account, Bride seems to have confused the timing of his joke about the SOS. Bride says that he made this joke 'five minutes' after Phillips began sending CQD, which was at 12:27 a.m. *Titanic* time. However, an SOS was not heard by other ships – or at least, was not documented as having been received by anyone – until 10:55 a.m. New York Time, or 12:57 a.m. *Titanic* time. At 10:55 NYT, this SOS call was recorded in the *Mount Temple*'s PV as 'MGY calling SOS', and '*Titanic*' calls '*Olympic*' SOS, as recorded in Lord Mersey's final report. (http://www.titanicinquiry. org/BOTInq/BOTReport/BOTRepWireless.php; note the British Inquiry's mistaken belief that *Titanic* time was 1 hour and 50 minutes ahead of New York Time, rather than 2 hours and 2 minutes.)

183. *New York Times*, August 11, 1909.

184. The article, titled '"S.O.S." – The Ambulance Call of the Seas', (*New York Times*, February 13, 1910) details the origin of SOS as a distress call, and several instances of its uses in the years prior to the *Titanic* disaster.

185. Br. 2006–2023.

186. Br. 2024–2037.

187. Beesley, Ch. 3. In his book, Beesley thought that he saw this cellist at 'about 12.40'. Beesley seems to have been roughly estimating this, as he prefaced the statement with 'this must have been'. He clearly stated that he saw a number of things begin at about the same time, including work on Boat No. 9 and the boats just astern. Frustratingly, Beesley does not give any estimates of time (other than the collision) in his *Toronto World* account of April 19, 1912; nor does he mention this sighting of the cellist or the incident about the ladies at the rail asking to be let up to First Class regions.

While Beesley's account makes it sound as if all of the boats on the starboard aft quarter were lowered to A Deck and loaded from there, not all the evidence agrees with these statements; for example No. 9 was loaded from the Boat Deck. So at least part of Beesley's statement would be incorrect if he was applying it to all of the boats. Most likely, he was simply compressing his impressions of efforts which

took some time – beginning at No. 9 – into a single statement. He stayed there on the deck, watching the events as they continued to unfold, over a period of time.

188. Amer. 597.

189. Amer. 335. This officer was likely Chief Officer Wilde, who was at the forward port boats at the time, and who assisted in the loading of Boat No. 8. Additionally, Chief Officer Wilde was described as a big man by Second Officer Lightoller. Peuchen's testimony makes it clear that he knew Captain Smith and Second Officer Lightoller, so Wilde is the most likely candidate, since Murdoch was occupied on the opposite side of the ship. In a letter to Colonel Archibald Gracie, First Class passenger Helen Churchill Candee also mentions this incident, and praised the conduct of the firemen for not protesting when the officer forced them to leave.

190. Br. 13852.

191. Amer. 314. Pitman said: 'She was blowing off steam for three-quarters of an hour, I think...' By nearly all accounts, this racket began very shortly after the ship came to its final stop around 11:46 p.m., after she briefly steamed 'slow ahead' following the collision. Colonel Gracie testified that the steam began blowing off just after he awoke, at midnight by his watch. (Amer. 989) However, while Gracie stated that the collision happened at midnight according to his watch, in his book he went on to specify: 'Correct ship's time would make it about 11.45.' (*The Truth About the Titanic*, Ch. 2) This indicates that the time his watch was keeping was not correct ship's time, and possibly that he was not awakened by the collision as he believed he had been, but a few minutes later.

Placing the start of the steam venting so close to the collision, rather than at midnight, is much more in keeping with the bulk of the evidence on the matter. Remember that the steam-generating plant was operating at high pressure prior to the collision; once the engines were stopped, the safeties would have popped quite quickly.

If the steam began venting at 11:46 p.m., then by Pitman's estimate, it would have ceased sometime around 12:31 a.m. – precisely when the earliest boats were being prepared and loaded, as mentioned in the narrative. In his book, Lightoller states that the steam was still venting when Captain Smith gave the order to begin loading women and children into the boats. Lightoller recalled that following this order, he was helping lower 'the first boat' – which had apparently already been swung out, level with the Boat Deck in preparation for loading – when the steam venting stopped. (*Titanic & Other Ships*, C. H. Lightoller, 1935)

The steam evidence does not fit the first boats lowering away as early as 12:25 a.m. Why? In order for the boats to have started lowering that early on, prep work would have to have been completed by about midnight, and the order to load them given around that time, in order to leave enough time for them to be loaded and start off at that time. Yet, this is wholly incompatible with the evidence Lightoller and Pitman gave on how long the steam vented and what stage work on the boats had reached when it stopped. However, this same evidence is exactly in line with a 12:25 a.m. time for the order to begin loading the lifeboats, and with a 12:40 a.m. departure time for the first lifeboat.

192. *Titanic & Other Ships*, C. H. Lightoller, 1935.

193. *Ibid.*

194. Account provided by Mike Poirier.

195. *On Board*, Behe, 148–150.

196. Amer. 570.

197. *The Brooklyn Daily Eagle*, April 19, 1912. Courtesy Mike Poirier.

198. *On Board*, Behe, 148–150.

199. Mrs Futrelle's story is compiled from the two accounts she gave (*Seattle Daily Times*, April 22/23, 1912; and *Philadelphia Evening Bulletin*, date unknown; both accounts are contained in *On Board*, Behe.).

200. *New York Tribune*, April 20, 1912.

201. 'Titanic Lifeboat Occupancy Totals', by Bill Wormstedt and Tad Fitch, 2011, at http://wormstedt.com/titanic/lifeboats/occupancy.pdf

202. *New York Tribune*, April 19, 1912.

203. *Newport Herald*, May 28, 29, 1912. Full account available in *On Board*, Behe, 217–226. Berthe Antonine Mayné booked her trip on *Titanic* using the name Madame de Villiers.

204. *Liverpool Journal of Commerce*, April 30, 1912. Account supplied by George Behe; *Western Daily Mercury*, April 29, 1912. Account supplied by Ioannis Georgiou. There is simply no way of telling how long Fitzpatrick slept after the collision. However, he did offer a clue in that he recalled the ship listing to port when he got on deck, and that he described events most likely relating to the lowering of Boat No. 14.

205. Amer. 239.

206. *Indiscretions*, 171. It is clear that the officer she asked was Murdoch.

207. *On Board*, Behe, 282.

208. Amer. 971–972.

209. 'Titanic Lifeboat Occupancy Totals', by Bill Wormstedt and Tad Fitch, 2011. (http://wormstedt.com/titanic/lifeboats/occupancy.pdf)

210. Amer. 80; *Titanic & Other Ships*, C. H. Lightoller, 1935. Lightoller was not exaggerating when he claimed that there was a shortage of seamen to assist in the loading of the boats from this point on. See Appendix I: The Loss of Deck Crew on the *Titanic* Over Time, for further details.

11. Most lifeboat launch timelines, including the timeline constructed during the British Inquiry, indicate that Boat No. 6 left before No. 8. However, there is substantial evidence that Boat No. 8 was lowered away first. Colonel Archibald Gracie, a *Titanic* survivor, first reached this conclusion after examining the evidence and talking to eyewitnesses while writing his book, *The Truth About the Titanic*, published in 1913. The independent research of *Titanic* historian Paul Quinn and Mike Findlay also supports this same conclusion. An exhaustive examination of the eyewitness evidence, which supports No. 8 leaving first, is presented in the previously mentioned article, '*Titanic*: The Lifeboat Launching Sequence Re-examined', by: Bill Wormstedt, Tad Fitch, and George Behe, with contributions by Sam Halpern and J. Kent Layton. (http://www.wormstedt.com/Titanic/lifeboats/lifeboats.htm)

12. Br. 1375–1377.

13. Br. 15233–15239.

14. Br. 1172–1175; *Titanic & Other Ships*, C. H. Lightoller, 1935; Amer. 336. The exact dialogue has been reconstructed from these three sources. Lightoller's later recollection did not include Peuchen's early comments that Captain Smith was present, or his suggestion; however, there is no reason to think that this was anything other than an omission in an account given years after the sinking. Thus the present authors have pieced the account together to form a more complete whole. Some variations in the exact dialogue should be allowed for.

15. '*Titanic* Lifeboat Occupancy Totals', by Bill Wormstedt and Tad Fitch, 2011. (http://wormstedt.com/titanic/lifeboats/occupancy.pdf)

16. Amer. 452; Amer. 336.

17. *Newport Herald*, May 28, 29, 1912. Full account available in *On Board*, Behe, 217–226.

18. Br. 2006–2036, Br. 2053–2075; Br. 2348–2352. This catastrophic flooding of Boiler Room No. 5 has led some to speculate that a coal fire in that same starboard bunker, just aft of the primary bulkhead between Boiler Rooms Nos 6 and 5, weakened the bulkhead to the point where it gave way under the weight of the water which had flooded Boiler Room No. 6. This bunker fire had burned ever since the ship had left Belfast, but was by no means uncommon for the period. A thorough forensic analysis of the incident by Dr Tim Foecke and Dr Jennifer Hooper McCarty was published in their book, *What Really Sank the Titanic?* (Citadel Press, 2008) The conclusion that they reached is that the coal bunker fire had little or no effect on the sinking. Indeed, it is most likely that this rush of water came when the lighter-weight coal bunker's bulkheads (not the primary bulkhead between BR's 6 and 5) gave way. The timing of the event is fixed with relative certainty by the evidence of Barrett; he said that he saw the rush of water around 1:10 a.m. (Br. 2348–2349.)

At first, it may seem impossible for Barrett to have escaped from Boiler Room No. 5 up to Scotland Road on E Deck some 25 minutes after Steward Wheat saw water flooding down to E Deck from E Deck by the Turkish Baths. By that point, wouldn't Barrett's escape have been cut off? If one goes back and considers the nature of the flooding on F Deck, the water had apparently come up the starboard passageway at the time, but Scotland Road was noted to be perfectly dry. As more water came up the starboard side, it would have flooded the space by the Turkish Baths before spreading over to the port side – particularly as the ship was then listing over to starboard. However, at this point the ship's list to starboard was beginning to ease, and would eventually shift over to port. Only as that list eased – perhaps due to the complete flooding of F Deck in the vicinity of the Turkish Baths as water filled the space from E Deck – would water have crept up Scotland Road on the port side, where the escape door from Boiler Room No. 5 was located.

As the water crept up Scotland Road on the port side of E Deck, it would have started to pour down the staircase to F Deck (the stairs were located on the port side of Scotland Road, by the Steward's Lavatory, and went down to the Linen Drying Room on F Deck). As it descended the stairs, it would have begun to flood those sections before making its way into the Swimming Bath on the starboard side. Initial flooding on the port side of this compartment – above No. 5 Boiler Room – might have accounted for the first signs of the ship starting to list over to the port side.

19. *Palladium Times*, September 11, 1985. Courtesy Mike Poirier.

20. *The Truth About the Titanic*, Ch. 2; supplementary quotations from Amer. 989–998; see also *On Board*, Behe, 311–314.

It is wholly impossible to be certain of all Gracie's movements. It can be determined that he worked at the lifeboats on the forward port side. He remembered helping to load 'about two boats, at least two boats' from the Boat Deck in addition to No. 4, but he also does not mention which ones. It can safely be assumed that he helped to load Boat No. 2, just before No. 4. He is also clear that he helped to get Boat D into lowering position after working at No. 4. This would fulfill his recollection of working at two boats on the Boat Deck. He was not present during the loading of Boat No. 6, however, because he missed the boarding of his acquaintances Helen Candee and Major Peuchen in that boat; his recollections of Peuchen's boarding that boat were also drawn from Lightoller's testimony, not his own memories.

Gracie himself alluded to a gap in his recollections while working on the boats. He said that his 'energies were so concentrated upon this work of loading the boats at this quarter that lapse of time, sense of

sight and sense of hearing recorded no impressions during this interval until the last boat was loaded'. (*The Truth About the Titanic*, Ch. 2)

The next event which Gracie describes in any detail is the loading of Boat No. 4; although it seems clear that he was involved in the loading of other boats forward on the port side, which ones they were the present authors can not say with certainty.

221. Amer. 803.

222. Br. 11454; *Newark Star*, April 19, 1912.

223. Br. 5011; Br. 6453. It is likely that Murdoch or Lowe gave this order, but the officer's name is not given in the testimony.

224. *Indiscretions*, 171–172.

225. *Ibid.*

226. Br. 11490–11495.

227. Beesley, Ch. 3.

228. Amer. 406, Br. 15828–15830.

229. Amer. 675; Amer. 604.

230. Br. 383–386.

231. Br. 15837.

232. Amer. 406. When explaining where he thought Lightoller went, Lowe said that he 'must have gone to the second boat forward'. Admittedly, this could be a reference to Boat No. 2, or to the 'second boat' from the front, No. 4, which was still in limbo. Most likely, however, it was a reference to the 'second boat' from the front of the after-port quarter of boats: No. 12, where Lightoller was spotted shortly thereafter. Because of other evidence that Lightoller proceeded directly to Boat No. 12, the present authors have included that conclusion in the narrative.

233. Is this another instance of Second Officer Lightoller being mistaken for First Officer Murdoch due to their uniform insignia? Mrs Collyer referred to Murdoch a number of times in her account, so it does not seem likely; yet the possibility cannot be entirely ruled out. She does not say how she identified the officer as Murdoch, but she took the trouble to spell his name correctly in her account; perhaps they had met at some point during the crossing as she claimed in her account, or even after the collision. If Murdoch did stop by at No. 14 briefly, then this would explain his delay in reaching Boat No. 9 and starting the loading process there. Perhaps he went to that quarter of the deck briefly to make sure that the crowd was well under control? It is simply impossible to say.

234. *Washington Post Semi-Monthly Magazine*, May 26, 1912. This full account is available in *On Board*, Behe, 246–254.

235. Amer. 628.

236. *Titanic Survivor*, Ch. 21. Jessop, who disguised most of the *Titanic* crewmember and passenger names in her memoirs, referred to this officer as 'Mason', but it is obvious she was referring to Moody, who was the officer in charge of loading No. 16.

237. Account provided by Mike Poirier.

238. *The Bridgewater Mercury*, May 1912. Although Threlfall was non-specific about his location at the time, he did mention that he was engaged in drawing the fires. This most likely places him in Boiler Room No. 3 or Boiler Room No. 4. The fires in Boiler Room No. 2 were most likely needed to continue supplying steam to the Emergency Dynamos on D Deck until the end. (Br. 20918)

239. Br. 3806–3828. Dillon initially testified that this order was given at 'An hour and 40 minutes' after the collision, or 1:20 a.m. (Br. 3810–3811); then he agreed with the examiner that this would have made it 'a quarter-past one'. (Br. 3812–3813) Later in his testimony, Dillon again stated that it was 'About an hour and forty minutes' after the collision, or at 1:20 a.m., when he came back into the Engine Room from Boiler Room No. 4 (Br. 3913). Both times he spoke of his own volition, rather than simply agreeing with an examiner's statement, he indicated a time of 'an hour and forty minutes' after the collision, or 1:20 a.m. This is in agreement with the times given by Scott and Threlfall.

240. Br. 4252–4267. The flooding in Boiler Room No. 4 has been a source of persistent speculation over the years. It seems to have started too early to have been part of the 'bulkhead-topping' sequence. Working from this, some have suggested that it was bottom damage, or in other words, evidence of a grounding. However, this kind of significant damage would have produced far greater quantities of water before 1:20 a.m.

At about 12:10 a.m. (an estimated time built on his testimony), Trimmer Thomas Dillon noticed a very small quantity of water coming up through the stokehold plates of Boiler Room No. 4, long before Boiler Room No. 5 experienced its disastrous flooding at around 1:10 a.m. According to research done by Samuel Halpern, it is possible that this was evidence of a single strake of plating between two frames having popped open during the collision. For further details, please see his article at the following URL: http://www.titanicology.com/FloodingInBR4.html.

Another possibility was that by about 1:20 a.m. – when Trimmer George Cavell eventually abandoned his post – the water descending into the Turkish baths, (seen by Steward Wheat at about 12:45 a.m., and noticed by F. Dent Ray near the E Deck level of the First Class Grand Staircase at about the same time) had found its way back down into the compartment as well.

241. Br. 5838–5839.

242. Br. 5723–5727.

243. Scott had no idea what portion of the ship he was in, just that it was only a little way aft of the Engine Room exit which he had come up through. When he got his lifebelt, Scott believed he was in Third Class deck spaces, and that he ascended to the deck via the Third Class stairs. However, the Third Class stairs were quite a distance aft. It seems quite possible that Scott – as he was in such an unfamiliar portion of the ship – might actually have been in Second Class areas of the ship, and that he proceeded up to the Boat Deck via the Second Class stairs. However, it is nearly impossible to say for certain where these lifebelts were. Only one thing is sure: Scott said that it took him about 'five minutes' to get up to the Boat Deck. (Br. 5775)

244. Ray specifically said 'A deck'. However, he also said that it was 'the open deck', also. From other sources, it seems that most – if not all – of the loading of Boat No. 9 took place from the Boat Deck. Here we have another probable example of deck-letter confusion.

245. Amer. 803.

246. Amer. 597.

247. Amer. 635–636.

248. 'Titanic Lifeboat Occupancy Totals', by Bill Wormstedt and Tad Fitch, 2011. (http://wormstedt.com/titanic/lifeboats/occupancy.pdf)

249. Account provided by Mike Poirier.

250. The Ilford Graphic, May 10, 1912. Account contained in On Board, Behe, 323–328. While Lightoller was portrayed as shouting this order in the 1997 film Titanic, it seems most reasonable to conclude that it was Fifth Officer Lowe who gave this shout. Greaser Scott also claimed to have heard an officer threaten any man that 'I will shoot him like a dog', if they tried to board No. 14 (Br. 5657), although there are significant problems with his testimony, and despite his claim to have witnessed this himself, Scott may have been repeating information related to him by another witness. See the subsection titled 'The Stern Port Boats' in the aforementioned article 'Titanic: The Lifeboat Launch Sequence Re-Examined', by Bill Wormstedt, Tad Fitch, and George Behe, at the following URL for additional details relating to Scott: http://www.wormstedt.com/Titanic/lifeboats/lifeboats.htm

251. Liverpool Journal of Commerce, April 30, 1912. Account supplied by George Behe; Western Daily Mercury, April 29, 1912. Account supplied by Ioannis Georgiou. In both of the above accounts, Fitzpatrick said that the man who tried to jump into the boat was shot dead. Other portions of his accounts suggest clearly that this was Boat No. 14. Perhaps with all of the gunfire surrounding the launch of this boat, Fitzpatrick only thought he saw a man shot. Or perhaps the reporter was 'jazzing the story up' a bit. It is nearly impossible to say.

252. Amer. 1109.

253. Br. 5640, 5707, 5841; Br. 3810–3811; The Bridgewater Mercury, May 1912.

254. 'Titanic Lifeboat Occupancy Totals', by Bill Wormstedt and Tad Fitch, 2011. (http://wormstedt.com/titanic/lifeboats/occupancy.pdf)

255. Amer. 615; Br. 387–393.

256. Amer. 417–419; Br. 15840–15851. Lowe's description of these men as 'Italians' and 'Latin people' met with a lot of criticism, particularly from Cusani, the Royal Ambassador of Italy. On April 30, 1912, Lowe made a statement in his presence apologizing for his statements, saying that he canceled the word 'Italian', and instead substituted the words 'immigrants belonging to Latin races'. He also stated that he 'did not intend to cast any reflection on the Italian nation'. This statement was entered into the inquiry evidence. While offensive by today's standards, Lowe's statements were not unusual, and tend to reveal a common prejudice of the day. Even a quick perusal of Titanic survivors' statements reveals that many automatically equated passengers who were acting unruly during the sinking were from steerage, and that they were 'Latin peoples', 'Italians', or 'dagoes'.

257. Here we have a perfect illustration of the danger of relying on survivors' timing estimates as opposed to following the level of flooding and the speed with which the ship was settling. When he came out on deck, Theissinger said that 'it was 12:30 ... and we saw the vessel was doomed'. However, he was also very clear not only about the three boats he saw in the water, but also about how far up the water had come – 'only thirty feet below the topmost deck'. Such a timing estimate is thoroughly unconvincing, as there is no way that he could have believed that the water would be that high at 12:30 a.m. Nor would it make sense that he could conclude from the water level that 'the vessel was doomed' at 12:30.

If one starts with the water level, however, it becomes apparent that Theissinger made this observation well after 12:30 a.m. It wasn't until nearly 1:30 a.m. that the water level had approached that height along the ship's sides. Also interesting is that Theissinger did not say where he got the time from... a personal time piece? If so, had he assumed that the clocks had been adjusted at midnight, as was the usual custom? That could help to explain the difference. Was he just estimating the time? Possibly. Because of his clear indication of the ship's orientation at the time he arrived on deck, the present authors have placed his arrival there a little later than he believed that it was.

258. Theissinger said that: 'Boats 1, 2 and 3 were already in the water.' However, Boat No. 2 was on the port side, while Boats 1 and 3 were on the starboard side. It is possible that he emerged on the port Boat Deck, and not the starboard, or that he was on both sides and noticed three boats gone in total. There is simply too much detail missing

from this portion of his account to make any conclusion with certainty. Wherever he was when they reached the deck, he eventually headed aft and found his way to the starboard side.

259. The Washington Herald, April 19, 1912; Cleveland Plain Dealer, April 21, 1912 (account provided by Mike Poirier). It is possible that the events Theissinger subsequently witnessed – with women and children filling boats and men being 'told off' – happened at No. 11, but his wording leaves room for some doubts on the point. The present authors will therefore resume his account at Boat No. 15, his next definite location and sighting.

260. Amer. 803. Saloon Steward F. Dent Ray knew Murdoch by sight, but did not know any of the other officers. He was very clear in the testimony cited that when No. 9 was swung out earlier in the night, Murdoch was not the officer in charge there. Ray, who was assigned to No. 9, said that when his boat was being swung out, he went to the rail and 'saw the first boat leaving the ship on the starboard side', which indicates the timing he was speaking of. 'Feeling rather cold', Ray had returned to his room for his overcoat at that time. This suggests that Murdoch worked at No. 9 only later in the sinking, once it actually began loading.

261. Br. 395; Amer. 657. Able Bodied Seaman Joseph Scarrott saw George McGough standing by the aft falls as No. 14 lowered away, and Boatswain's Mate Albert Haines testified that he left the ship in No. 9, which is backed up by other evidence. All three men knew each other well, having served in the same watch deck crew under Fourth Officer Boxhall. This evidence is important to the understanding of the timing of lowering of the aft port boats in relation to the aft starboard ones. This essentially proves that No. 14 left the ship prior to No. 9, contrary to the lifeboat timings published by the British Inquiry. See 'Titanic: The Lifeboat Launching Sequence Re-Examined', by Bill Wormstedt, Tad Fitch and George Behe, with contributions by Sam Halpern and J. Kent Layton at the previously mentioned URL: http://wormstedt.com/Titanic/lifeboats/lifeboats.htm

262. Br. 13187–13189.

263. Amer. 804.

264. Amer. 545.

265. Palladium Times, September 11, 1985. Courtesy Mike Poirier.

266. Rochester Democrat & Chronicle, April 21, 1912 and April 15, 1931. Courtesy Mike Poirier. The 1912 article mentions the gunfire and people being shot, while the 1931 article does not. However, the 1912 account was provided to reporters by Miss Bentham's brother, and not first-hand. It is possible that Miss Bentham was referring to the gunfire at Boat No. 14 while it was being lowered nearby, and that in the second-hand retelling it somehow was blown out of proportion.

What's also interesting is that in the 1912 article, her brother said that it was the 'first officer' who placed her in the boat. Clearly Second Officer Lightoller was working at No. 12 at the time, but photographic evidence shows that he most likely had not changed his uniform insignia with the officer re-shuffle at Southampton. Is it possible that this was actually a reference to Lightoller, and that his rank was mistaken as being that of the First Officer? The concept, while by no means a certainty, is intriguing.

267. Mary Sloan's letter to her sister, reprinted in full available in On Board, Behe, 395–397.

268. The Hartford Courant, April 20, 1931. Courtesy Mike Poirier. Her account is riddled with a number of errors, which have to be deftly fielded. First, she said that she left in Boat No. 13; initially one might construe the event she referred to as the mess between Nos. 13 and 15. However, in that instance, it would have been her boat which had the falls cut, not the other. What about the trouble No. 11 experienced? There is no evidence that No. 11's falls were cut while part or all of the boat was still above the air. Rather, No. 11's falls were cut once it was in the water. It seems much more plausible that she was in Boat No. 12, and saw the preceding boat which had left – No. 14 – smack the water when Lowe cut the falls. This is just one piece of evidence that supports her being in No. 12. When the correct timeline for the aft port boats was discovered, placing the launch of No. 14 before No. 12, then this account seems to fall nicely into place in the timeline.

269. Amer. 636.

270. The Rockford Republic, April 25, 1912. Courtesy Mike Poirier. It has been suggested that Dagmar escaped in Boat No. 12, but that theory – right or wrong – seems to have little first-hand evidence from her own written and newspaper accounts. The present authors decided to place this account here, in the vicinity of No. 12, but without making a definite connection to No. 12, since the extant evidence does not at this point allow for any conclusive statements about what boat she was rescued in.

271. Br. 2965–2972.

272. Amer. 637.

273. Palladium Times, September 11, 1985. Courtesy Mike Poirier.

274. 'Titanic Lifeboat Occupancy Totals', by Bill Wormstedt and Tad Fitch, 2011. (http://wormstedt.com/titanic/lifeboats/occupancy.pdf)

275. Rochester Democrat & Chronicle, April 21, 1912 and April 15, 1931. Courtesy Mike Poirier.

276. Amer. 636.

277. Detroit Free Press, April 21, 1912. Courtesy Mike Poirier.

78. *Daily Boston Globe*, April 17, 1932. Courtesy of George Behe and Mike Poirier. It has frequently been concluded that May Futrelle was rescued in Collapsible D. However, this is incorrect. In the above newspaper, Futrelle herself states that she was rescued in Boat No. 9, and alludes to the Lines ladies, who were also saved in No. 9. She refers to them as a mother and daughter, 'Boston women' who were coming to America to see the son graduate from Harvard. (In fact, Elizabeth Lines' son was graduating from Dartmouth College.) Futrelle also mentions 'an able seaman named Paddy' being in charge of the boat, a reference to Able Bodied Seaman George McGough, who in other accounts, is also referred to as 'Paddy McGough'. Several witnesses said that McGough was in charge of No. 9, likely because he sat at the tiller.

79. *The Evening Sentinel*, April 24, 1912. Courtesy Mike Poirier. Although Mock did not specifically reference the number of this boat, he said it was 'the boat aft'. This was apparently a reference to No. 9's location aft in Second Class regions of the deck. When the pair attempted to move forward again, they were prevented and diverted toward Boat No. 11.

80. Deposition of Elizabeth Lines, given as part of the Limitation of Liability hearings, November 24, 1913; *Boston Traveler*, April 15, 1966; unknown newspaper, August 6, 1975. The two newspaper articles are courtesy Mike Poirier.

81. *The Daily Mirror*, May 13, 1912. Courtesy Mike Poirier.

82. *The Indianapolis Star*, April 23, 1912. Courtesy Mike Poirier; Robertha Watt's account can be found in *On Board*, Behe, 422–423. Ellen's recollection of gunfire is probably on the port side at Boat No. 14, even though the wording of her account seems a little out of place. Yet Robertha Watt's account mentions nothing of gunfire at Boat No. 9.

83. Amer. 597.

84. Amer. 597; Amer. 602.

85. *The Auburn Citizen*, April 23, 1912. Courtesy Mike Poirier.

86. Br. 13322–13328. Many occupants in Boat No. 9 claimed that Able Bodied Seaman George McGough was in charge of Boat No. 9. However, this appears to be a mistake based on the fact that he was sitting at the tiller.

287. 'Titanic Lifeboat Occupancy Totals', by Bill Wormstedt and Tad Fitch, 2011. (http://wormstedt.com/titanic/lifeboats/occupancy.pdf)

288. Deposition of Elizabeth Lines, given as part of the Limitation of Liability hearings, November 24, 1913; *Boston Traveler*, April 15, 1966; unknown newspaper, August 6, 1975. The two newspaper articles are courtesy Mike Poirier.

289. *The Auburn Citizen*, April 23, 1912. Courtesy Mike Poirier.

290. Amer. 1055.

291. *The Weekly Telegraph*, May 10, 1912; Br. 6497–6498; Br. 2527–2528. Sixth Officer Moody is not mentioned by name as being the officer who was ordered down to A Deck and who supervised the loading there, but his identity is made clear by the evidence. Steward Littlejohn mentioned an unnamed officer being down on A Deck during the loading of No. 13. This officer may also have been on hand for the loading of boat No. 11 on the same deck, although Littlejohn's description doesn't specify this for certain. Steward Rule also seems to confirm the presence of an officer on A Deck during the loading of No. 15, saying that he ordered them to get all the women and children into the boat that they could find.

Lookout Lee testified that the officer in charge on A Deck at No. 13 was either the Fifth or Sixth Officer, that he was drowned, was six feet tall, thin, and with a light complexion. Of all the officers, this description fits Moody alone both in physical terms and in terms of his fate. Captain Smith and Chief Officer Wilde were engaged elsewhere at the time and do not even remotely fit that physical description. Likewise, Lightoller was engaged on the port side nearly exclusively, and Murdoch remained on the Boat Deck. Third Officer Pitman had already left the ship, and Fourth Officer Boxhall was forward and never assisted on A Deck aft. Fifth Officer Lowe had already left the ship in No. 14 by this time, and wasn't involved in the loading and lowering of the aft starboard boats. Moody is the only plausible option.

292. *The Duluth Herald*, May 1, 1912. Courtesy Mike Poirier.

293. Amer. 651; *The Weekly Telegraph*, May 10, 1912.

294. Amer. 549.

295. Br. 13301, 13312–13314.

296. *The New York Times*, April 23, 1912. Courtesy Mike Poirier.

297. *Pageant*, October 1953. Courtesy Mike Poirier.

298. Ibid.

299. *The Evening Sentinel*, April 24, 1912. Courtesy Mike Poirier.

300. Amer. 651.

301. 'Titanic Lifeboat Occupancy Totals', by Bill Wormstedt and Tad Fitch, 2011. (http://wormstedt.com/titanic/lifeboats/occupancy.pdf)

302. Amer. 544; Amer. 651.

303. *The Evening Sentinel*, April 24, 1912. Courtesy Mike Poirier.

304. Ibid.

305. *The Duluth Herald*, May 1, 1912. Courtesy Mike Poirier.

306. *Thomas Andrews: Shipbuilder*, Shan Bullock, 1912. Bullock's source for this story is not named in the text, but he can be identified as Steward John Stewart. Please see Appendix L: Thomas Andrews' Fate, for further details on this subject.

307. *Waterbury Republican*, April 25, 1912. Courtesy Mike Poirier.

308. *The Loss of the Titanic*, Washington Dodge. Address delivered by Dr Dodge to San Francisco's Commonwealth Club. Account contained in its entirety in *On Board*, Behe 264–277.

309. *New York Times*, April 22, 1912.

310. *The Loss of the Titanic*, Washington Dodge. Address delivered by Dr Dodge to San Francisco's Commonwealth Club. Account contained in *On Board*, Behe, 264–277.

311. Br. 6490–6493; 6596–6599.

312. *New York Times*, April 22, 1912.

313. From the typed notes of August Wennerström used in his talks about the disaster, preserved by the Wennerström family. Courtesy of Jerry Wennerström and Mike Herbold. Gunnar Tenglin later gave newspaper interviews claiming to have been rescued in Collapsible A. However, this is contradicted by his private accounts of his survival, and other comments he made about the sinking, claiming that he boarded the 'next-to-last' lifeboat aft.

314. Ibid. Wennerström appears to have been guessing that this lady stayed below deck after he left.

315. Ibid.

316. *East Galway Democrat*, May 11, 1912.

317. Notes of Walter Lord's interview with Katie Manning, née Gilnagh; conducted on 07/20/55. Courtesy of Paul Lee.

318. Account of Daly, written down by Dr Frank Blackmarr, and signed by Daly. Reproduced in 'Dr. Frank Blackmarr's Remarkable Scrapbook', *Titanic Commutator*, 3rd Quarter 1998; information from a private account by Bertha Mulvihill to her family; *Centennial Reappraisal*, Appendix J.

319. *Daily Sketch*, May 4, 1912; *Providence Journal*, April 20, 1912; information courtesy of Bertha Mulvihill's family, based on accounts of the disaster given to them after the sinking. The aforementioned interview with Bertha Mulvihill that appeared in the *Providence Journal* is based on a real interview given by Bertha Mulvihill, and does contain some accurate information. However, it also contains many inaccuracies and embellishments that she later complained about. Amongst others, these include her allegedly becoming friends with Quartermaster Hichens during the voyage, seeing Captain Smith wielding a gun, and supposedly hearing 'Nearer My God to Thee' as the ship sank, all details that she denied. The article also refers to Eugene Daly as 'Eugene Ryan'. This account mentions Bertha's sighting of the Rice family, but claims the reason that the family perished was because Margaret Rice's husband wasn't allowed to enter the boats by the officers, and that she wouldn't leave without him. While Bertha really did see the Rice family, Mrs Rice's husband was killed in an accident well before the *Titanic* sank, and was never aboard.

320. Miss Dowdell's account is compiled from her accounts in *The Hudson Dispatch*, April 20, 1912; *The Jersey Journal*, April 20, 1912; *The Hudson Observer*, April 20, 1912. The Amy Stanley portion of the story is compiled from *The Oxford Times*, May 18, 1912 (full account available in *On Board*, Behe, 402–403).

321. Br. 6501–6505.

322. *East Galway Democrat*, May 11, 1912. There is some evidence to suggest that Daly was beaten during the struggle to remove him from the boat. According to the May 4, 1912 issue of the weekly New York paper *Irish World*, Daly 'bore the marks on his face of blows from sailors who fought with him against entering the last boat as it was lowered with many vacant seats'. No. 15 was not the last boat as the article claimed, but was the last of the aft starboard boats lowered. There apparently were seats open when Eugene was pulled out of the boat, although No. 15 ended up being one of the most heavily loaded boats that night when all was said and done; all of the seats were filled by the time it was lowered, and it wasn't lowered away half empty as the article suggests.

323. *Cork Examiner*, May 7, 1912. This quote comes from a letter to Maggie's sister Mary that was published by the newspaper.

324. Br. 6537; 6587–6590; 6648–6658.

325. Br. 4461–4470.

326. *The Weekly Telegraph*, May 10, 1912.

327. Amer. 804.

328. Miss Dowdell's account is compiled from her accounts in *The Hudson Dispatch*, April 20, 1912; *The Jersey Journal*, April 20, 1912; *The Hudson Observer*, April 20, 1912. The Amy Stanley portion of the story is compiled from *The Oxford Times*, May 18, 1912 (full account available in *On Board*, Behe, 402–403).

329. The Fort Wayne Sentinel, April 29, 1912. Courtesy Mike Poirier. Mrs Hewlett's account has a wonderful beginning and an interesting end, but the mid-portion of it leaves much detail out. At the end point of the account, it is very interesting to note that she was one of the last women who entered the boat, and that she admitted to protesting boarding the craft. Is she the same woman that Steward Ray had to argue with? While merely speculative, this presents itself as a tantalizing possibility.

330. Br. 2115–2156.

331. Amer. 804.

332. *The Weekly Telegraph*, May 10, 1912.

333. Beesley, Ch. 3.

334. Br 20128–20133.

335. Br 20161–20180. Mauge was only one of three *à la carte* Restaurant employees to survive. The others were Miss Ruth Bowker, 1st Cashier, and Miss Mabel Martin, 2nd Cashier.

336. Br. 2156–2167. Barrett's testimony seems confused in this particular stretch, but it seems that this is the best interpretation of the evidence as regards the timing of the order. Murdoch would have known that the lifeboats were safe to fill with 65–70 passengers, because he was present during weight tests in Belfast. It seems likely that this order was given by someone other than Murdoch, particularly since Beesley did not recall hearing the officer who passed him by say anything like that. The order recalled by Barrett could have been given by someone else – one less informed on the capacity of the boats – who happened by after Murdoch had departed; however, this is pure speculation.

337. 'Titanic Lifeboat Occupancy Totals', by Bill Wormstedt and Tad Fitch, 2011. (http://wormstedt.com/titanic/lifeboats/occupancy.pdf)

338. Amer. 804.

339. *The Irish Sunday Press*, June/July 1956, courtesy of Geoff Whitfield. Unfortunately, the identity of the female passenger is unknown. It may have been Maggie Daly, Bertha Mulvihill, or someone whom Daly simply recognized. Many passengers in No. 15 were Irish Third Class passengers, some of whom had gotten to know each other during the voyage. In the latter-day interview with Daly, this female passenger is referred to simply as a 'woman who had been put into one of the lifeboats', while Maggie Daly is referred to by name elsewhere in the article. Mary Daly Joyce, Daly's daughter, states in an article for the St. Louis Today website that he had entrusted these items 'to the girls (i.e. Maggie and Bertha) to send home'. However, Bertha's private accounts to her family don't mention him giving them any personal affects. It is possible that she neglected to mention this, but the truth cannot be ascertained at this time.

340. Br. 2170.

341. 'Titanic Lifeboat Occupancy Totals', by Bill Wormstedt and Tad Fitch, 2011. (http://wormstedt.com/titanic/lifeboats/occupancy.pdf) Fireman Frank Dymond took charge of No. 15 once it reached the water. (Br. 4374) There was some confusion about who was in charge of this boat. Steward Rule believed that Steward Stewart was in command. (Br. 6596) It is possible that Stewart was put in charge before Dymond boarded, and subsequently relinquished control to him. Oddly, Rule also testified that there was an Able-Bodied Seaman aboard. (Br. 9621–9623) This crewmember was likely Lookout Evans, but for some reason, despite being a member of the Deck Department, he did not assume command of the boat. Please see Appendix I: The Loss of Deck Crew on the *Titanic* Over Time, for additional evidence relating to Evans in No. 15.

342. Br. 6503.

343. Information courtesy of Bertha Mulvihill's family.

344. Miss Dowdell's account is compiled from her accounts in *The Hudson Dispatch*, April 20, 1912; *The Jersey Journal*, April 20, 1912; *The Hudson Observer*, April 20, 1912. The Amy Stanley portion of the story is compiled from *The Oxford Times*, May 18, 1912 (full account available *On Board*, Behe, 402–403).

345. Amer. 804.

346. Br. 743a; Br. 2170–2174; Beesley, Ch. 3.

347. *The Washington Herald*, April 19, 1912; *Cleveland Plain Dealer*, April 21, 1912. Courtesy Mike Poirier. Immediately after this, Theissinger's account mentions standing talking to Storekeeper Cyril Ricks while staring at the iceberg which they had run into. He estimated that it was 300 feet high. While he probably did talk to Storekeeper Ricks after No. 15 was lowered, the entire portion of his account about the iceberg seems to be a complete fabrication, either on the part of Theissinger or the journalist who wrote the article.

348. *Utica Herald-Dispatch*, April 30, 1912. Courtesy Mike Poirier. There has been speculation that the couple boarded Boat No. 10, discussed later in the text. However, it isn't entirely clear as of this writing where that idea came from. The concept of holding the men back while women boarded does not seem to fit well with Murdoch's style, either, and it can be established that he was involved in the loading of Boat No. 10. Because of this, the present authors have chosen to place this portion of their account in the general vicinity of Boat No. 10, but without drawing a definite connection to that boat. Some interpretation on the point should be allowed for.

349. Amer. 604; Amer. 612–613; Amer. 675–676.

350. Bright later testified (Amer. 832) that he did not actually send any Morse signals himself; his participation was limited to the rocket-firing.

351. Amer. 1101.

352. *Ibid*.

353. 'Titanic Lifeboat Occupancy Totals', by Bill Wormstedt and Tad Fitch, 2011. (http://wormstedt.com/titanic/lifeboats/occupancy.pdf) It is interesting to note that Boat No. 1 gets so much attention for having contained just twelve occupants; meanwhile Boat No. 2 – launched much closer to the end, when it was known that the ship was doomed – left with only a small number more, but has garnered virtually no attention for having so many vacant seats. The names of seventeen occupants of this boat can be established.

354. *New York Times*, April 22, 1912.

355. Br. 15450–15453. In his testimony, Boxhall says he wasn't sure who it was that was calling out. In his 1962 radio interview, Boxhall said that it was Captain Smith. His latter-day comment is backed up by 1912 accounts from other survivors such as Peter Daly, who said Captain Smith was the one who ordered the boats to come back to the ship.

356. Amer. 337; *The Truth About The Titanic*, Ch. 6. The quote about Hichens being crazed with fear during these events comes from the private account of First Class passenger Helen Churchill Candee, which was published in part in Colonel Gracie's book.

357. Amer. 676; Br. 5987.

358. Amer. 604.

359. Joughin was the sole witness to claim that Lifeboat No. 10 was the first of the aft port boats to leave the *Titanic*. However, the British Assessors chose to believe his account over the accounts of Evans and Buley, both of whom testified that No. 10 was the last of the aft port boats to be lowered. Other passengers, who did not testify at either Inquiry, also said No. 10 left last; among these were Nellie O'Dwyer, Imanita Shelley, Gretchen Longley, Kornelia Andrews, Anna Hogeboom and Ada Ball. See 'Titanic: The Lifeboat Launching Sequence Re-Examined', by Bill Wormstedt, Tad Fitch and George Behe, for additional details.

360. Amer. 676.

361. Br. 5954–5957; 5981–5987; Amer. 604. Buley confirms Joughin's version of events. He said that the women were reluctant to board No. 10, even though it was the last lifeboat to be lowered from that part of the deck, and they 'threw them in' because they 'didn't like the idea of coming in'.

362. *Anaconda Standard*, May 6, 1912. Courtesy Mike Poirier. Boat No. 10 was the last of the aft port boats lowered, not the last boat overall; however, the seaman in question must have believed it was the last one to leave the ship. Imanita Shelley and Lutie Parrish are sometimes listed as having been saved in Boat No. 12. However, there is a good deal of evidence against this. In his book, Colonel Gracie concluded – based on correspondence with survivors – that these two ladies were in Boat No. 10. There is a lot of evidence to support his conclusion.

The lifeboat Shelley left in hung away from the ship's side 'between 4 and 5 feet' due to the port list. During the loading of the aft boats, the port list was only this severe while Boat No. 10 was being loaded. During the loading of Boats Nos 16, 14 and 12, either no list was described, or a slight list to port was mentioned. (See 'Titanic: The Lifeboat Launching Sequence Re-Examined', by Bill Wormstedt, Tad Fitch and George Behe, for additional details on the list and how it relates to the lifeboat timeline.) Shelley's mother had to be thrown into the boat and she had to jump across the gap, also conditions that suggest Boat No. 10, where Joughin and others had to chuck passengers and children across the gap into the boat. Shelley indicated in her Senate Inquiry affidavit (Amer. 1147) that she was told her boat was the last boat. The majority of eyewitnesses said No. 10 was the last of the aft port boats.

Additionally, according to her affidavit, the ship's baker (Joughin) was manning Shelley's boat at the time of its lowering just as Joughin himself testified (Br. 6007). Joughin was not involved in the loading of Boat No. 12, which he did not even see leave the ship. (Br. 6009) Shelley also indicated that a man jumped down into her lifeboat as it was lowering, injuring Lutie Parrish, and that there was trouble getting to the tripper and freeing the falls once her lifeboat touched down in the water. Seaman Frank Evans mentioned both of these incidents in his testimony, saying that they happened in No. 10 (Amer. 676); others from No. 10 mention a man jumping into it and landing on a woman as it lowered away. All of these facts support Gracie's conclusion that Shelley was in boat No. 10. The only point counter to this evidence is Shelley's claim that her boat rescued the survivors off Collapsible B, which Boats No. 4 and No. 12 did. It is possible that Shelley was embellishing her account in this regard, as none of the other details she mentions account for Boat No. 12. It is also possible that she was transferred to Boat No. 12 by Fifth Officer Lowe when he redistributed passengers between the boats in his makeshift flotilla after *Titanic* sank, although Shelley doesn't describe that happening.

363. Amer. 1147; Amer. 676; *Anaconda Standard*, May 6, 1912. Courtesy Mike Poirier. Imanita Shelley says that this man jumped from the deck into the boat just as it reached the water. Able Bodied Seaman Evans speculated that this man must have jumped from A Deck, since First Officer Murdoch was overseeing things on the Boat Deck at that point.

364. *The Patriot*, April 20/23, 1912. Courtesy Mike Poirier. One is forced to wonder if the 'drunk stoker' she referred to wasn't Baker Joughin, who had been drinking that night. Also intriguing is the mention of an officer who was placed in the boat and then ordered back out. Is it possible that this was Sixth Officer Moody? Although conjecture, the possibility that Moody had been so close to surviving in Boat No. 10 is quite an interesting one. Whoever it was that ordered the officer out must have been Murdoch, who was supervising the loading process.

365. Br. 3828–3856; *Winston-Salem Journal*, July 23, 1912. Dillon was entirely unsure of what boat was being loaded, but did know that it was on the port side.

366. Amer. 676.

367. *The Patriot*, April 20, 1912. Courtesy Mike Poirier.

368. 'Titanic Lifeboat Occupancy Totals', by Bill Wormstedt and Tad Fitch, 2011. (http://wormstedt.com/titanic/lifeboats/occupancy.pdf)

369. Amer. 677; Anaconda Standard, May 6, 1912. Courtesy Mike Poirier. Shelley supports Evans' description of the difficulty they had in releasing the falls at No. 10.

370. Private account of Martha Stephenson & Elizabeth Eustis, 1912; The Truth About The Titanic, Ch. 2.

371. Amer. 81.

372. Amer. 1107. Lightoller isn't identified by name in Emily Ryerson's affidavit, but it is clear that he was the officer in question, since he was in charge of the loading of No. 4. She refers to him as 'an officer at the (A Deck) window'. In her 1915 Limitation of Liability testimony, Ryerson identified Second Steward Dodd as the crewman who tried to prevent her son from boarding the boat. However, in her 1912 affidavit filed in the Senate Inquiry, she stated that 'I only remember the second steward at the head of the stairs', and that he told them where to go on the boat deck. She didn't mention Dodd in connection with Boat No. 4.

373. Private account of Martha Stephenson & Elizabeth Eustis, 1912; The Truth About The Titanic, Ch. 2.

374. Awake! magazine, 10/22/1981. Master Nicola-Yarred's account of benefiting from the assistance of a man he later learned was John Jacob Astor seems quite authentic, as there were not many obviously-pregnant ladies traveling with middle-aged husbands in First Class on the ship. This account would thus place the two children at Boat No. 4, which would certainly have appeared to be 'the last boat,' as Master Nicola-Yarred recalled, from their particular vantage point on A Deck.

Others have speculated that the children departed in Boat C, since Jamilia recalled that their boat caught on the ship's side as it went down and the ship was still listing to port. However, since Boat No. 4 was tied off to the coaling wire by Lightoller earlier that night – to prevent it from swinging away from the ship's side if a list began to develop – and needed to be cut free in order to be lowered, it could have given some of its occupants the impression that the boat got hung up on ship's side. Because of this, Jamilia's recollections do not necessarily support that they were in Boat C. The children survived the sinking and were safely united with their family. Their names were eventually 'Americanized' to Louis and Amelia Garrett. Louis turned 12 on April 16, 1912.

375. Detroit Free Press, April 21, 1912 (courtesy Mike Poirier); also unknown, undated newspaper account (courtesy of Peter Engberg-Klarström).

376. April 20, 1912 account by Jack Thayer. George Behe collection. Account in full available in On Board, Behe, 412–414; also Thayer, 1940.

377. Detroit Free Press, April 21, 1912 (courtesy Mike Poirier); also unknown, undated newspaper account courtesy of Peter Engberg-Klarström.

378. Amer. 581; Amer. 1107–1108.

379. 'Titanic Lifeboat Occupancy Totals', by Bill Wormstedt and Tad Fitch, 2011. (http://wormstedt.com/titanic/lifeboats/occupancy.pdf)

380. Amer. 1107.

381. Br. 6305–6309.

382. Br. 6020–6021, 6211–6223, 6226–6231, 6290–6304. For Joughin to have seen water in this location, he must have been in his cabin quite late in the sinking.

383. Br. 6020–6039. It is clear that Joughin's account has some significant timing issues. Considering the half-tumbler of liquor he consumed during the disaster, it is likely that his timing estimates – and perhaps, in some cases, the order in which he did things – should be taken with a grain of salt.

For example, although he said that he went from the Boat Deck down to B Deck to throw chairs overboard, there was no location on B Deck for him to do this from. He also did not say that he then had to go back up to the deck pantry, which would have been required if he went from B Deck up to A Deck. It seems almost certain that he was instead on the Promenade Deck the whole time.

384. The Weekly Telegraph, May 10, 1912; New York Times, April 22, 1912; Providence Journal, April 20, 1912.

385. Br. 16533; New York Times, April 19, 1912.

386. Br. 16540–16547; British Wreck Commissioner's Inquiry Report. The Titanic's end of the Baltic/Titanic exchange was recalled by Bride. He remembered sending this message himself while Phillips was out on deck checking on the situation. The New York time of this exchange was fixed in the British Inquiry final report, using wireless logs: (http://www.titanicinquiry.org/BOTInq/BOTReport/BOTRepWireless.php)

387. Br. 16549–16533. This particular detail is very important. Phillips found the Well Deck awash sometime during or after Bride's 1:47–1:52 a.m. exchange with the Baltic. This shows that QM Rowe's Senate Inquiry estimate that he stopped firing rockets and left the Bridge at 1:25 a.m., leaving soon thereafter in Collapsible C, is far too early. What Phillips said he saw can be correlated with Rowe's observances. The latter said the Well Deck was awash when Collapsible C left the ship, and that in the 5 minutes it took to lower the boat due to the port list, the Well Deck had submerged. Coupled with Rowe's testimony that Collapsible C left 20 minutes before the ship sank, and the timing of Phillips' trip on deck, this indicates that the rocket firing

ceased much later than 1:25 a.m., and that the collapsible left closer to 2:00 a.m.

388. Amer. 159; New York Times, April 28, 1912. Although Bride said that at that time (around 1:50 a.m.) they were concerned about whether they were getting a spark, the wireless log in the British Inquiry shows that their signals were picked up during the next ten minutes by the Mt. Temple, the Caronia, and the Carpathia. However, it was clear to those operators that in the minutes leading up to 2:00 a.m. (Titanic time), their power was fading and their signals were getting harder to read.

389. Br. 1053–1055; Br. 1082–1089; Amer. 570.

390. The Truth About the Titanic, Ch. 2.

391. Amer. 519. It appears that Quartermaster Rowe may have been the person to send up the last rocket. Rowe stated that he asked Captain Smith, and not Boxhall, if he should fire another rocket, and Smith said, 'No, get into that boat.' (Amer. 51) Though Rowe did not say he fired a rocket then, it does show that Captain Smith, and not Boxhall, was in charge of rocket firing at this time, as the Fourth Officer had previously left in Boat No. 2.

There is other evidence of rockets being fired after Boxhall left the Bridge. Chief Steward John Hardy said he had last seen Captain Smith while he was on the Bridge 'superintending the rockets, calling out to the quartermaster about the rockets'. (Amer. 601) First Class passenger Mahala Douglas, who left the Titanic with Boxhall in No. 2, said goodbye to her husband as the boat was lowering away. 'That was the last word I ever spoke to him. They were putting off rockets on the deck as we got away.' (New York Herald, April 20, 1912)

Assuming Rowe was the person sending up the last rocket, it would have occurred around 1:50 a.m. Boxhall left the ship around 1:45 a.m., and Captain Smith began supervising the rockets at that time. Hardy and Douglas both indicate at least one rocket was fired after the Fourth Officer left, before Smith ordered Rowe to desist and help out at Collapsible C. After firing this last rocket (or rockets) at around 1:50 a.m., Rowe would have had around 10 minutes to help out at the starboard collapsible before it started lowering away at 2:00 a.m.

392. Amer. 886, 889–890; Br. 10391–10394. Some have claimed that Wilde was the only officer who helped at Collapsible C. However, this ignores the eyewitness accounts which indicate that both officers were present at different points. First Class passenger Hugh Woolner said that Murdoch stopped a rush at the collapsible with warning shots from his revolver, and oversaw the last stages of the loading. It is unlikely that Woolner misidentified Murdoch's identity, as he specified Murdoch's name and rank, and said that he recognized the First Officer's voice. Murdoch was the ship's only Scottish officer, and his voice would have been easily distinguishable.

Third Class Pantry Steward Albert Pearcey also specified Murdoch's role in the loading of this boat, having been ordered into it by him. Pearcey has previously served with Murdoch on the Olympic. Both of these men are backed up by Fireman Harry Senior, who stated that the 'first officer' worked at Collapsible C. Senior's account matches Woolner's regarding the First Officer's actions at the boat.

Wilde probably left and went to the port side, because progress on Boat C was somewhat advanced over that on Boat D. Murdoch's arrival on the scene likely coincided with Wilde's departure, in that Wilde saw that the First Officer could look after the situation if he left to work on Boat D.

393. Amer. 519–520; Amer. 832–833. Another bit of evidence that supports a later timeline for the firing of the rockets and the lowering of the boats than some claim comes from QM Bright in his testimony at the American Inquiry. He said that he worked along with Boxhall and Rowe at firing the rockets; he thought they fired a half-dozen rockets at intervals. When asked how long the intervals were, he could not seem to remember, explaining:

I could not say. After we would fire one we would go and help clear the boats away, and then we would come back again.

When asked how long the entire process of firing the rockets continued, he estimated that it took 'probably half an hour'. Interestingly, Rowe also felt that their work on the Bridge firing the rockets took a relatively short time, about forty minutes, as he recalled in the British Inquiry:

17684. How long do you think it was from the time you commenced firing the rockets till you finished firing the rockets? - From about a quarter to one to about 1.25 [i.e., 40 minutes].

Note here, not the exact times that Rowe gives, since those are clearly on the early side, but rather the duration he speaks of: forty minutes. The period that Bright and Rowe were referring to would have been the period that the three men worked together on the Bridge. It would not have included the period from when Rowe placed the call to the Bridge until he and Bright arrived there, or the period before his phone call, when Boxhall fired at least one rocket, as supported by the Fourth Officer's inquiry evidence. Working backward from the time that the last rocket was fired should thus give us a pretty good idea of when the process started.

When Boxhall departed in No. 2, at 1:45 a.m., work had already begun on both Collapsibles C and D. Shortly after Captain Smith ordered Boxhall into No. 2, he ordered Rowe to take charge of Collapsible C. Rowe's testimony at the American Inquiry is that the Captain told him not to fire any more rockets before getting into C; in later letters and interviews during the 1960s (previously referred to) discussing the same moment, he says that Smith ordered him to fire that last rocket and then go. Either way, it is clear that the rocket-firing stopped around 1:50 a.m., give or take a few minutes. Working backwards from that time by thirty minutes (Bright) would place Rowe and Bright's arrival on the Bridge around 1:20 a.m.; working backwards by forty minutes (Rowe) would place their arrival around 1:10 a.m.

To the 1:10–1:20 a.m. estimate of Rowe and Bright arriving on the Bridge, one would have to add time for the two men to walk from the Poop Deck up to the Bridge, as well as the time it took them to collect the rockets from the locker, and to descend to that locker from the aft Docking Bridge after their phone call to Boxhall. But that trip would certainly not have taken half an hour or longer. But just how long would it have taken? In his March 2, 1963 interview with J. Powell, Rowe said that this trip took only 10 minutes. Thus, from the time Rowe first placed his call to the Bridge to the time he and Bright arrived there would most likely have encompassed no more than 15 minutes. This would place his call to the Bridge – based on the 30–40 minute estimates, a trip to the Bridge which reportedly took about 10 minutes, and the time to make the call and pick up the rockets from the locker – between 12:55 to 1:05 a.m., which fits *very well* with a 12:40 a.m. departure of Boat No. 7, giving it enough time to slide just far enough out from the hull for Rowe to spot it.

Working backward from about 1:50 a.m., arriving at 12:55-1:05 a.m. by using these estimates by Rowe and Bright of how long the work took and how long it took them to get there, suddenly brings something else to one's attention. Rowe said (Amer. 519), that he spotted the first lifeboat to leave the ship at 12:25 a.m. Endnote 164 discusses the possibility that Rowe had set his watch back by 23 minutes at midnight, assuming that the ship's clocks had also been set back as anticipated. If he *had* set his watch back, and you add 23 minutes to 12:25 a.m., you arrive at a time of 12:48 a.m. when he spotted that boat. This is a mere seven minutes' difference from the early time that we arrive at when working backward from the end-point of firing the rockets. In other words, working from the ends to the middle of his accounts creates a near-perfect match.

Furthermore, if one throws a 23-minute adjustment to his watch into his estimate of when he left the Bridge, this also begins to look much closer to the timeline suggested by many other lines of evidence. To say that Rowe was a problematic witness over the course of his testimony, interviews and letters spanning over fifty years would be an understatement of epic proportions. However, by looking at his evidence in the light of other events and the testimony of other witnesses, a pretty clear picture of how events played out emerges.

One final line of evidence that confirms a later sequence for the firing rockets comes from the *Californian*. The last rocket that her officers noticed went up at about 1:40 a.m. according to their ship's time; since the *Titanic*'s clocks were about 12 minutes ahead of the *Californian*'s, this puts the last rocket that they saw *after* Boxhall's known departure time, and close to the estimated 1:50 a.m. time our timeline built independently. If correct, the 1:40 sighting by the *Californian*'s men would place the last rocket launched at 1:52 a.m., *Titanic* time.

394. *Waterbury Republican*, April 25, 1912. Courtesy Mike Poirier.
395. Unfortunately, Miss Badman's friend from Kent, England was unnamed in her accounts. She later claimed that it was Edward Lockyer, but there is no evidence to confirm this identification at the time of this writing.
396. *The Syracuse Herald*, April 23, 1912. Courtesy Mike Poirier. In Miss Badman's account, she remembered seeing two shootings on the Boat Deck, but she did not mention the location or time of these events. She only said that the first shooting was of a steward who refused to help with the boats. The second was of an Italian man who jumped into the boat on top of women and children as it was being lowered away. The boat was then hoisted back up, the man brought out on the deck, and shot.

Miss Badman's account is sorely lacking in details. The cry of 'All women and children, this way', had obviously been given some time before 2:00 a.m. However, their location at the time is unknown; the time the order was given is unknown; who gave the order is unknown; how long they were on the Boat Deck is unknown. Thus, the present authors have skipped trying to run her account into the chronological narrative and have instead 'caught up' with her at the loading of Boat C. To delve more fully into the timing of events for her would seem to be no more than guesswork.
397. *The Oxford Times*, May 18, 1912. Full account available in *On Board*, Behe, 402–403.

398. *Titanic & Other Ships*, C. H. Lightoller, 1935. In his book, published over twenty years after the disaster, Lightoller wrote that he worked on Boat No. 4, and also on Boat No. 2, and Boat D. However, in his testimony at the American Inquiry, Lightoller stated that another officer had lowered No. 2 while he worked at Boat No. 4. Colonel Gracie noted this when he wrote his 1913 book, *The Truth About the Titanic*. The conclusion that Lightoller worked at Boat No. 4, and then came up to help at Boat D is in harmony with the timing of the two boats' launch, as fixed by numerous other lines of evidence. Lightoller's later recollections on this point must have been colored by the passage of time.
399. *Titanic & Other Ships*, C. H. Lightoller, 1935; *The Truth About The Titanic*, Ch. 2. In his 1935 account, Lightoller says that this incident happened at the 'emergency boat', which could be taken to mean Boat No. 2. However, as noted above, Lightoller said in 1912 that he had nothing to do with the loading of this boat. It is likely that Lightoller meant Collapsible D, or that he simply confused the details over the years; in his 1913 book, Colonel Gracie says that Lightoller told him personally that men rushed Collapsible D, and that he had to threaten to shoot them.
400. *Amsterdam Evening Recorder*, April 23, 1912. Courtesy Mike Poirier.
401. Br. 15039–15040.
402. BBC radio interview with Commander Joseph Boxhall, first broadcast on October 22, 1962.
403. Amer. 242–243; Amer. 540; Br. 15472–15478; BBC radio interview with Commander Joseph Boxhall, October 22, 1962. In his testimony in the British Inquiry, Boxhall said: 'I do not remember any gangway doors being open.' However, in his 1962 BBC radio interview, Boxhall said that when he rowed around to the starboard side, he 'found that there was such a mob standing in the gangway doors...I daren't to go alongside because if they'd jumped they'd swamp the boat...I daren't go along the side again, and I pulled off and laid off...I pulled away about a quarter of a mile...'

In his testimony, Boxhall claimed suction was one of the reasons he didn't go alongside the ship, while Able Bodied Seaman Osman said there was no suction, and that they 'could not get to the starboard side because it was listing too far'. At the inquiries, no one said that the gangway doors had actually been open when No. 2 came around the stern. However, it would be understandable if, at the time, the survivors were reluctant to admit that the doors had been opened and that they had not come alongside to take on any additional passengers.

If Boxhall wasn't mistaking details in his mind 50 years after the sinking, it would mean that the officers' plan, mentioned by Lowe in the inquiries, for the boats launched at less than full capacity to take on more men from the gangways once afloat, had nearly been successful after all. Recall that Lightoller had sent men below earlier in the night to open gangway doors, and those men were never seen again. Perhaps the plan of the officers came closer to succeeding than previous histories of the events have acknowledged.
404. Br. 5706–5709. Scott also testified that he left the deck 'between a quarter of an hour and twenty minutes' after coming on the deck at 'about twenty to two'. (Br. 5841–5842) Since it is clear the difference between the lowering times of Boats Nos 14 and 4 was greater than that, so by any reckoning, this second estimate of timing is flawed. Scott himself said that once he had gotten his lifebelt he was able to make it up to the deck in about five minutes. (Br. 5775) Overall it seems that his first estimates on the timing of events were more correct than his second estimates.
405. Br. 5685–5693. Scott testified that he noticed these engineers about a half-hour after coming on deck. (Br. 5795) This would have been at about 1:50–1:55 a.m.

Scott's observation runs counter to the myth that the engineers stayed below deck until the ship sank, never abandoning their posts. It is not surprising that the engineers were released to come on deck just after the other men working below deck. With the flooding being as advanced as it was by 1:20 a.m., there was nothing further that they could do below deck.
406. Br. 5710.
407. Ranger seemed to indicate that he was actually on B Deck, near the Second Class Smoking Room. However, he and Greaser Scott climbed up the davits for Boat No. 16 from the Boat Deck. Scott also mentioned that there was a group of engineers, firemen 'and all that' who were on the starboard side aft of the Boat Deck. It is nearly impossible to imagine two similarly-sized groups of engineering staff on the aft-starboard sides of the Boat Deck *and* B Deck nearly simultaneously, so it seems almost certain that Ranger was still on the Boat Deck. This is particularly true since Scott had just switched off the fans over the First Class Smoking Room just above the Boat Deck. While the present authors leave open the possibility that Ranger went down to B Deck before coming back up, this does not seem to be the most likely explanation.
408. Br. 4033–4062.
409. *Amsterdam Evening Recorder*, April 23, 1912. Courtesy Mike Poirier.
410. Br. 4088–4089. Ranger did not say that the two men went out on the same davit, so the present authors really can't conclude whether they shared the same davit or used adjacent davits.

11. Br. 5669–5673, 5695–5698, 6514; Br. 4054, 4067–4073.

12. See Paul Lee's article 'Ismay's Escape: Did He Jump or Was He Pushed?' This article discusses the circumstances under which Ismay boarded Collapsible C, as well as the conditions surrounding the loading of that boat in general. It is available at the following URL: http://www.paullee.com/titanic/ismaysescape.html.

13. Please see Appendix H: Incidents of Gunfire During the Sinking for further details.

14. William Carter boarded this boat; his family had just left in Boat No. 4 on the port side at 1:50 a.m., some ten minutes earlier. Because the Mersey Inquiry Report incorrectly placed the lowering of Collapsible C at 1:40 a.m., instead of its actual departure time of 2:00 a.m., they assumed that Mr Carter had abandoned his family to save himself, with Carter's family boarding No. 4 after he had left the ship. However, Mr Carter did state that he had seen his family off first, and his wife later confirmed this as fact. This detail is added in an attempt to help correct a longstanding misconception regarding Mr Carter's conduct that night.

15. Amer. 520; 'Titanic Lifeboat Occupancy Totals', by Bill Wormstedt and Tad Fitch, 2011. (http://wormstedt.com/titanic/lifeboats/occupancy.pdf)

16. Waterbury Republican, April 25, 1912. Courtesy Mike Poirier.

17. The Oxford Times, May 18, 1912. Full account available in On Board, Behe, 402–403.

18. Amer. 524; Br. 17688.

19. The Syracuse Herald, April 23, 1912. Courtesy Mike Poirier.

20. Waterbury Republican, April 25, 1912. Courtesy Mike Poirier.

21. Br. 14020–14027. Lightoller stated in his testimony that before Collapsible D lowered, 'I could see it [water] climbing up the stairway', i.e. from B Deck. He also stated that D only had to be lowered 10 feet to reach the water. A Deck was 9 feet 6 inches below the Boat Deck, so the water would have been close to the level of A Deck as the crew started to lower the collapsible. Lightoller said that once D was finally lowered, 'A Deck was under water', and that 'almost immediately afterwards' he saw water coming up the stairway onto the Boat Deck. The authors are thankful to Sam Halpern for his observations regarding the technical details and physical layout of the ship as it relates to Lightoller's testimony.

22. Amer. 74. Lightoller's recollection adds the 'to straighten her up' portion.

23. Truth About the Titanic, Ch, 2.

24. Cleveland Plain Dealer, April 21, 1912; The Truth About the Titanic, Ch. 2.

25. Amer. 81; Titanic & Other Ships, C. H. Lightoller, 1935.

26. Amer. 588.

27. 'Titanic Lifeboat Occupancy Totals', by Bill Wormstedt and Tad Fitch, 2011. (http://wormstedt.com/titanic/lifeboats/occupancy.pdf) A picture taken of Collapsible D as it approached Carpathia is clear enough to allow a rough count, which looks to be approximately thirty-five occupants.

However, Collapsible D picked up three people from the water (including Woolner and Björnström-Steffansson), and around twelve people when Lifeboat No. 14 was transferring people prior to going back into the wreckage looking for survivors. The most accurate estimate of the number of occupants in Collapsible D as it lowered appears to be around twenty.

28. Br. 14019–14020; Amer. 839. Quartermaster Bright's observation that the Forecastle was submerging as Collapsible D lowered, when correlated with Quartermaster Rowe's testimony, is further proof that Collapsible C and D left at most five minutes apart, and that the former left close to 2:00 a.m., and not 1:40 a.m. as the British Inquiry concluded. Rowe's description of the forward Well Deck being 'awash' as Collapsible C began lowering, and being 'submerged' five minutes later when it reached the water is telling, as the physical layout of the ship dictates that the Forecastle head had to be submerging or submerged in order for the Well Deck to be submerged. Bright indicates this was happening as Collapsible D began lowering.

29. Amsterdam Evening Recorder, April 23, 1912. Courtesy Mike Poirier.

30. Ibid; The Truth About the Titanic, Ch. 6. Other details of Frederick Hoyt's experiences were supplied by him in a letter to Colonel Archibald Gracie; Paterson Morning Call, April 23, 1912.

31. Amer. 887–888. Woolner estimated that he and Steffansson had to jump nine feet to reach Collapsible D. With a 10° port list (the degree supported by eyewitness accounts at the time) the edge of the collapsible would have swung five feet away from Titanic's side, and it would have been approximately nine feet to the middle of the boat when they jumped.

32. Amsterdam Evening Recorder, April 23, 1912. Courtesy Mike Poirier; The Truth About the Titanic, Ch. 6. Other details of Frederick Hoyt's experiences were supplied by him in a letter to Colonel Archibald Gracie.

33. Paterson Morning Call, April 23, 1912; also account by Irene Harris in New York Evening Journal, May 11, 1912. Her account is contained in full in On Board, Behe, 320–323.

34. There were actual provisions to assist the crew in getting Boats A and B down to the Boat Deck; the two funnel stays that ran to the deck outboard of the collapsibles were fitted with links so that tackles could be connected to hoist the boats off the roof and on down to the Boat Deck. The problem that night was that no one seemed to be aware of that provision, and no one seemed to know where the tackles were stored, either. If anyone did, they did not have time to fetch them. The authors would like to thank Art Braunschweiger for providing these technical details.

435. Private letter from William Mellors to Dorothy Ockenden written on May 9, 1912, courtesy of Brian Ticehurst. Mellors' testimony in the Limitation of Liability hearings in June 1915 in the U.S. District Court confirms that he was near Collapsible C as it lowered.

436. Pawtucket Times, May 22, 1912. Courtesy Mike Poirier. This 'last boat' lowered from the rail may be a reference to Collapsible C. If that is the case, the fact that Boat A was being prepped for departure nearby afterwards would have tended to keep Mrs Abbott and the other women nearby, hoping that they could board the craft.

437. April 20, 1912 account by Jack Thayer. George Behe collection. Account in full available in On Board, Behe, 412–414; also Thayer, 1940.

438. Chief Officer Wilde's whereabouts after helping get Collapsible D away have not been established.

439. Amer. 159

440. New York Times, April 28, 1912; Amer. 159–160. Captain Smith's quote is a paraphrase from the lengthy and rambling quotation that Bride gave in his story to The New York Times, supplemented with information from his Senate Inquiry testimony.

441. It was the Caronia that heard Phillips' transmitting to the Titanic at midnight New York time, or 2:02 a.m. Titanic time. (Established at the British Inquiry and shown at: http://www.titanicinquiry.org/BOTInq/BOTReport/BOTRepWireless.php) The Caronia's operator did not report hearing Phillips' response, which is in harmony with the fact that the wireless set's last gasp of power was then giving out.

442. Amer. 151–153; Br. 16561–16566. When Bride and Phillips appeared on the Boat Deck, all boats except Collapsibles A and B had gone. The last boat to depart prior to this was Collapsible D on the port side, which left at 2:05 a.m. They obviously arrived on the Boat Deck just before the 2:15 a.m. final plunge.

At 11:58 p.m. New York time (2:00 a.m. Titanic time), the Asian heard a transmission from the Titanic, reportedly an 'SOS.' When the Asian answered Titanic, she received no further communication. Interestingly, at 12:00 midnight New York time, or 2:02 a.m. Titanic time, the Caronia's operator heard the Frankfurt call up the Titanic, saying that they were 172 miles away at the time of the first SOS.

The Ypiranga heard Frankfurt calling Titanic around this same time. Although Bride said that Phillips told Frankfurt's operator that he was a 'fool', Phillips' response was recorded simply as 'Stdbi, stdbi, stdbi!' (i.e. 'Stand by.') in Ypiranga's PV.

The Virginian's operator heard from Cape Race at 12:05 a.m. New York time, or 2:07 a.m. Titanic time, that they had not heard from the Titanic 'for about half an hour. His power may be gone'. At 12:10 a.m. New York time, or 2:12 a.m. Titanic time, the Virginian's operator thought that he heard Titanic calling 'very faintly, his power being greatly reduced'. Again, at 12:20 a.m. New York time, or 2:22 a.m. Titanic time (after the ship had already sunk), the Virginian's operator heard two faint 'v's', thought that it sounded like Titanic, and believed that her operator was adjusting his spark. However, the fact that no one picked up Phillips' response to the 2:02 a.m. Frankfurt message demonstrates that at least the later of these two of the transmissions picked up by the Virginian's operator came from another wireless set, perhaps even an amateur set a long distance away.

However, it is known that the Titanic was the only ship on the Atlantic at the time with a rotary spark gap, which emitted a distinctive tone instead of a rasping spark. Some have used this detail to argue that the Titanic's clocks were not 2 hours and 2 minutes ahead of New York time. ('Titanic Time: Tested by Wireless', Senan Molony, Voyage No. 63.) However, the later transmissions could have come from any shore-based station with a rotary spark gap. Is this a stretch to believe? No. Why?

This is because at 1:58 a.m. New York time, or 4:00 a.m. Titanic time (by the 2 hrs 2 min estimate, or 3:31 a.m. Titanic time by the 1 hr 33 minute estimate that is advocated by some), the Mt. Temple's operator reported that the Birma's operator thought that he heard the Titanic transmitting, and so sent: 'Steaming full speed to you; shall arrive you 6 in the morning. Hope you are safe. We are only 50 miles now.' This was unquestionably after the Titanic had sunk by any estimate of time, and yet operators were still thinking that they heard the Titanic's Marconi set in operation. So if they were mistaken at 4:00 a.m., (Titanic time) it was certainly possible that they were mistaken at 2:22 a.m. (Titanic time).

So it is very clear, in view of the overall timeline, that the Virginian's operator was mistaken in thinking that it was the Titanic calling at 2:22 a.m. Titanic time. It is also possible that the earlier 2:10 a.m. transmission (Titanic time) may not have come from the Titanic, although Phillips and Bride clearly worked the key to about that time. So which of these two – the 2:00 a.m. transmission picked up by the Asian and Ypiranga, or the 2:10 a.m. transmission picked up by the Virginian – was the last call sent by the Titanic may never be known for sure. In either case, Phillips and Bride continued to work the key until just about 2:10 a.m., whether the set was still transmitting their messages or not.

443. *New York Times*, April 28, 1912.

444. *Ibid*.; Amer. 160. Bride changed his story by the time he testified in the British Inquiry. By that point, he was claiming that he forced the stoker away from Phillips as he attempted to steal the lifebelt, and then Phillips noticed and came to help. In this version, Bride only held the man, while Phillips beat him unconscious. Bride's reluctance to admit to the examiners his role in the potential killing of a fellow crewmember, justified or not, is understandable; however, the contradiction did not escape the examiners, who pointed out that this version of events was different from what he initially said in America. This is but one example of several contradictions between Bride's various accounts. Some details of his testimony given between the American and British Inquiry differed so widely that the Solicitor-General said he would like to be 'satisfied we had got hold of the same gentleman who gave evidence in America'.
   In a blatantly distasteful example of embellishment in the yellow press, the story of Bride and the stoker was repeated in newspapers following the sinking, but with the story altered to the point where the stoker was a 'negro', and was shot with a rifle.

445. *New York Times*, April 28, 1912. Bride's quote about the band is important, because it seems they were still playing in the vicinity of the First Class Entrance when the operators left their cabin. That location was still 'aft' of where Phillips and Bride emerged on to the deck.

446. *The Truth About The Titanic*, Ch. 2.

447. *The Truth About The Titanic*, Ch. 2. The quote from the officer comes from Gracie's book. Gracie didn't specify that this officer on the roof of the Officer's Quarters who asked for assistance was Lightoller; indeed he didn't seem to know who it had been. However, it makes sense that it was the Second Officer, since he was in charge of the group working at Collapsible B, and there is no evidence that another officer was involved there.
   It's been said repeatedly that the crew tried to use oars to slide the boats down to the Boat Deck. This is incorrect. They were instead using the canvas cover spars which were installed longitudinally in the collapsibles to keep their canvas sides elevated. The authors would like to thank Bruce Beveridge of the TRMA for helping the present authors get this detail right.

448. *New York Times*, April 28, 1912.

449. *Titanic & Other Ships*, C. H. Lightoller, 1935.

450. *The Truth About The Titanic*, Ch. 2.

451. Please see Appendix J: The Last Song.

452. *Washington Post*, April 23, 1912. Details of Father Byles' and Father Peruschitz's actions earlier in the night come from the account of Third Class Passenger Ellen Mockler, and from the Catholic magazine *America*.

453. From the typed notes of August Wennerström used in his talks about the disaster, preserved by the Wennerström family. Courtesy of Jerry Wennerström and Mike Herbold.

454. Bullock, 1912. Bullock's source for this story was a survivor's account in his possession, but unfortunately, he did not mention the name.

455. *Liverpool Journal of Commerce*, April 30, 1912. Account supplied by George Behe; *Western Daily Mercury*, April 29, 1912. Account supplied by Ioannis Georgiou. If it seems surprising that Fitzpatrick could have thought the ship would still float even that late, it must be remembered that Jack Thayer and Milton Long, just a little aft of the Bridge on the starboard side, still thought the same thing.

456. Amer. 160–161.

457. Br. 14035–14036; *Titanic & Other Ships*, C. H. Lightoller, 1935.

458. Amer. 666.

459. *Liverpool Journal of Commerce*, April 30, 1912. Account supplied by George Behe; *Western Daily Mercury*, April 29, 1912. Account supplied by Ioannis Georgiou.

460. Br. 10530; *East Galway Democrat*, May 11, 1912. This article contains the contents of a letter Daly wrote to his younger sister Maggie, still in Ireland; the letter was penned sometime between April 18 and 21, 1912. Daly believed that he helped free Collapsible B, the boat he was later saved on. However, he was unaware of how this boat came to be upside down. As Lightoller and others described, Collapsible B fell into the water on the Boat Deck upside down as they freed it, and there 'was no time to open her up at all'. If Daly actually freed that boat, he would have known those details.
   Daly also describes the collapsible he worked on as getting stuck under a wire stay. This description makes no sense if he was referring to Collapsible B, since no wire stays would have prevented it from being pushed off the roof of the Officers' Quarters. However, Daly's description makes perfect sense if he was describing Collapsible A, since there was a wire funnel stay directly inboard of the aft davit used to launch Boat No. 1 and Collapsible C. That same set of davits had been cranked back in to receive Collapsible A. This, coupled with having to push the collapsible uphill against the port list, and trying to maneuver its bow around the structure surrounding the stairway down to A Deck, would have impeded the efforts to launch it.
   Onboard the *Carpathia*, Daly told Dr Frank Blackmarr that passengers clung to the edges of the collapsible he worked at as it was being freed, and that they had to cut ropes to free it as water reached

the deck where he was located; these details do not match what happened at Collapsible B. All of this indicates that the boat he helped with was Collapsible A on the starboard side, and not Collapsible B as he believed. As detailed by Lightoller, Collapsible B somehow ended up on the starboard side near the funnel as the Bridge plunged under, so Daly's confusion about this is understandable. Other passengers who were near Collapsible A when it was washed overboard, and who later reached Collapsible B, also thought they were in Boat A.

461. *Liverpool Journal of Commerce*, April 30, 1912. Account supplied by George Behe; *Western Daily Mercury*, April 29, 1912. Account supplied by Ioannis Georgiou; *Titanic: Belfast's Own*, by Stephen Cameron (1998), pg. 93. This latter account was forwarded to Lord Pirrie by Andrews' friend David Galloway. For further information, please see Appendix L: Thomas Andrews' Fate.

462. *New York Herald*, April 20, 1912.

463. *The Truth About The Titanic*, Ch. 2.

464. Amer. 671.

465. Br. 10534.

466. Amer. 666.

467. From the typed notes of August Wennerström used in his talks about the disaster. Courtesy of Jerry Wennerström and Mike Herbold.

468. *Titanic & Other Ships*, C. H. Lightoller, 1935.

469. April 20, 1912 account by Jack Thayer. George Behe collection. Account in *On Board*, Behe, 412–414; also Thayer, 1940.

470. *Liverpool Journal of Commerce*, April 30, 1912. Account supplied by George Behe; *Western Daily Mercury*, April 29, 1912. Account supplied by Ioannis Georgiou; *Titanic: Belfast's Own*, by Stephen Cameron, 1998, pg. 93.

471. *Liverpool Journal of Commerce*, April 30, 1912. Account supplied by George Behe; *Western Daily Mercury*, April 29, 1912. Account supplied by Ioannis Georgiou.

472. Account of Daly, written down by Dr Frank Blackmarr, and signed by Daly. Reproduced in 'Dr. Frank Blackmarr's Remarkable Scrapbook', *Titanic Commutator*, 3rd Quarter 1998; private letter from William Mellors to Dorothy Ockenden written on May 9, 1912, courtesy of Brian Ticehurst; *Main Line Life*, May 11, 1997. All three men describe the Boat Deck rising up slightly after the initial plunge. For full details on this, please see Appendix N: The Breakup.

473. Br. 10652.

474. 'Dr. Frank Blackmarr's Remarkable Scrapbook', *Titanic Commutator*, 3rd Quarter 1998.

475. *Bangor Daily Commercial*, April 19, 1912; *Chicago Daily Tribune*, April 21, 1912.

476. 'Dr. Frank Blackmarr's Remarkable Scrapbook', *Titanic Commutator*, 3rd Quarter 1998.

477. *The Evening World*, April 22, 1912.

478. *Liverpool Journal of Commerce*, April 30, 1912. Account supplied by George Behe; *Western Daily Mercury*, April 29, 1912. Account supplied by Ioannis Georgiou.

479. *The Truth About The Titanic*, Ch. 2.

480. Amer. 628.

481. *Evening Banner*, April 26, 1912; Private letter from William Mellors to Dorothy Ockenden written on May 9, 1912, courtesy of Brian Ticehurst.

482. Br. 10542–10548.

483. From the typed notes of August Wennerström used in his talks about the disaster. Courtesy of Jerry Wennerström and Mike Herbold.

484. Private letter from George Rheims to his wife, April 19, 1912. Rheims' deposition – filed in the Limitation of Liability hearings on November 14, 1913 – indicates that he leapt overboard near the Gymnasium.

485. *New York Times*, April 22, 1912; *Titanic: The Canadian Story*, Alan Hustak, 1999.

486. *New York Times*, April 19, 1912.

487. Amer. 164. Please see Appendix M: Down With the Ship? Captain Smith's Fate, for further information.

488. Amer. 91–92; *Titanic & Other Ships*, C. H. Lightoller, 1935; *New York Herald*, April 20, 1912.

489. Br. 6040–6052; Br. 6359–6364. It seems likely that Joughin was hearing the very early stages of the breakup of the ship, as the stresses on the hull and keel increased.

490. *Pawtucket Times*, May 22, 1912. Courtesy Mike Poirier.

491. *Titanic & Other Ships*, C. H. Lightoller, 1935.

492. *Titanic & Other Ships*, C. H. Lightoller, 1935; *The Christian Science Journal*, Vol. XXX, October 1912, No. 7. Exactly what caused this rush of hot air is debatable. But there still seems to be evidence on the wreck of a tremendous force having pushed the air intake apart from inside, partially verifying Lightoller's story.

493. The effect of a huge amount of water crashing over and around the forward Grand Staircase was not fully understood until film director James Cameron went to re-create the moment for his 1997 blockbuster, *Titanic*. The staircase set was built very much like the original ship's staircase, and should approximate very closely the original's strength. When the set was lowered quickly into the tank and a large volume of water was sent crashing down through the dome from above, the staircase quite literally broke up and floated out. After this incident, *Titanic* researchers began to see that this startling re-creation may be the explanation for the nearly complete

absence of the staircase's remains on the wreck. Only the steel framing for the lowest portions of the staircase are still in place today.

494. *Titanic & Other Ships*, C. H. Lightoller, 1935.
495. *Ibid*.
496. *Main Line Life*, May 11, 1997.
497. *New York Herald*, April 20, 1912.
498. 'Dr. Frank Blackmarr's Remarkable Scrapbook', *Titanic Commutator*, 3rd Quarter 1998.
499. From the typed notes of August Wennerström used in his talks about the disaster. Courtesy of Jerry Wennerström and Mike Herbold. Wennerström believed that this man was later picked up and rescued from the water, but does not give his name. In a letter to Ed Kamuda of the Titanic Historical Society in 1963, Quartermaster George Rowe claimed that he had pulled in the log-line of the ship while he was still on the stern Docking Bridge earlier in the night, to prevent it from fouling the propellers. If this is true, the man Wennerström saw might have been climbing down a rope or fall rather than the actual log-line.
500. Please see Appendix N: The Breakup, for all pertinent information on the angles reached before the break.
501. 2:17 a.m. is logical, especially since the plunge at the bow started at about 2:15 a.m. Also interesting is that Apprentice Gibson on the *Californian* saw the lights of the steamer he was watching disappear at 2:05 a.m. by their clocks. Adding the 12-minute time difference between the two ships comes right out to about 2:17 a.m., the same time that the *Titanic*'s lights snapped out. These two completely disparate lines of evidence (along with all the other evidence already presented) really go a long way toward demonstrating that the ship that Stone and Gibson were watching from the Bridge of the *Californian* was the *Titanic*.
502. Br. 10553–10557.
503. Private letter from William Mellors to Dorothy Ockenden written on May 9, 1912, courtesy of Brian Ticehurst.
504. *Chicago Daily Tribune*, April 21, 1912; *Bangor Daily Commercial*, April 19, 1912.
505. Information courtesy of Bertha Mulvihill's relatives. Bertha always told the family that she had broken in half.
506. *The Washington Herald*, April 19, 1912; *Cleveland Plain Dealer*, April 21, 1912. Courtesy Mike Poirier.
507. Br. 3861–3868. Trimmer Thomas Dillon, standing on the Poop Deck, said that the aft funnel 'seemed to cant up towards me'. When questioned further on the point, he agreed with the statement that it 'seemed to fall aft'. This would have been after the break, and the funnel stays to the forward side of the funnel broke, tipping the funnel aft.
508. Private notes from an interview conducted by Walter Lord with Richard and Norris Williams, dated April 27, 1962. Notes are contained in 'The Lord/Pellegrino Communications Files' collection, and are available online at: http://www.charlespellegrino.com/passengers/r_n_williams_11.htm.
509. *The Weekly Telegraph*, May 10, 1912.
510. Br. 6052–6073.
511. Br. 4094–4119. Please see Appendix N: The Breakup (subheading When Did The Lights Fail?) for further information. To many of those acquainted with the basics of the *Titanic*'s history, this is a rather startling bit of information. However, it was noted by more than one survivor.
512. For more information on this rotation of the stern section as it sank, please see Appendix N: The Breakup.
513. *The Evening World*, April 22, 1912; *The Irish Sunday Press*, June/July 1956, courtesy of Geoff Whitfield.
514. *East Galway Democrat*, May 11, 1912. First Class passenger Jack Thayer, also saved on Collapsible B, recalled the same thing in his 1940 book *The Sinking of S.S. Titanic*. Describing the scene, he stated that Collapsible B had been 'gradually sucked in toward the great pivoting mass … we were right underneath the three enormous propellers. For an instant, I thought they were sure to come down right on top of us'. For more information on this rotation of the stern section as it sank, please see Appendix N: The Breakup.
515. *The Washington Herald*, April 19, 1912; *Cleveland Plain Dealer*, April 21, 1912. Courtesy Mike Poirier.
516. Liverpool Journal of Commerce, April 30, 1912. Account supplied by George Behe; *Western Daily Mercury*, April 29, 1912. Account supplied by Ioannis Georgiou.
517. Thayer, 1940.
518. Please see Appendix N: The Breakup, for all available information on the details regarding the breakup.
519. Br. 6074–6076; Amer. 13

CHAPTER 6: ON 'A SEA OF GLASS'

1. Amer. 349. During the inquiries, there were several times when it was mentioned that large quantities of cork had been seen among the floating debris. It was speculated that the cork was from lifebelts; in fact, it was from cork used as insulation inside the ship, freed as she broke apart.
2. *The Truth About the Titanic*, Ch. 4.
3. Private letter from George Rheims to his wife Mary, April 19, 1912.
4. Private letter from William Mellors to Dorothy Ockenden written on May 9, 1912, courtesy of Brian Ticehurst.
5. *The Truth About the Titanic*, Ch. 4.
6. *Titanic & Other Ships*, C. H. Lightoller, 1935.
7. Unknown newspaper, dated April 20, 1912. Courtesy Mike Poirier.
8. Br. 5022; Br. 13098.
9. *Sphere*, May 25, 1912.
10. *The Weekly Telegraph*, May 10, 1912.
11. *New York Times*, April 22, 1912.
12. *Anaconda Standard*, May 6, 1912. Courtesy Mike Poirier.
13. Br. 2176.
14. Amer. 657.
15. Amer. 599.
16. Amer. 598; Amer. 657.
17. Br. 13336–13351.
18. Amer. 520.
19. The information and table are based on information published online by the United States Search and Rescue Task Force. See 'Cold Water Survival' page at the following URL for additional information: http://www.ussartf.org/cold_water_survival.htm.
20. *The Truth About the Titanic*, Chapters 4–5.
21. *Liverpool Journal of Commerce*, April 30, 1912. Account supplied by George Behe; *Western Daily Mercury*, April 29, 1912. Account supplied by Ioannis Georgiou.
22. Private letter from William Mellors to Dorothy Ockenden written on May 9, 1912, courtesy of Brian Ticehurst.
23. *New York Times*, April 19, 1912.
24. Thomas Whiteley's *Titanic* lecture.
25. Letter from Harold Phillimore to Ed Kamuda, June 12, 1964. Courtesy of Don Lynch.
26. Interview with Frank Prentice recorded for *Titanic: A Question of Murder*, TVS, 1982.
27. Kapok was a buoyant filling made of vegetable fiber. It was packed into sacks and attached to the collapsibles' fenders, and it was also inserted between the mid-keel, the side keels and the outer planking. The bow and stern sections of the floating body were also filled with buoyant cork. For further information, please see *TTSM*, Vol. 1, 571.
28. *New York Herald*, April 20, 1912.
29. Br. 10563–10570.
30. From the typed notes of August Wennerström used in his talks about the disaster, preserved by the Wennerström family. Courtesy of Jerry Wennerström and Mike Herbold.
31. *Pawtucket Times*, May 22, 1912. Courtesy Mike Poirier.
32. Private letter from William Mellors to Dorothy Ockenden written on May 9, 1912, courtesy of Brian Ticehurst.
33. Private letter from George Rheims to his wife Mary, April 19, 1912.
34. *The Washington Herald*, April 19, 1912; *Cleveland Plain Dealer*, April 21, 1912 (Courtesy Mike Poirier).
35. *New York Times*, April 22, 1912.
36. From the typed notes of August Wennerström used in his talks about the disaster, preserved by the Wennerström family. Courtesy of Jerry Wennerström and Mike Herbold.
37. *Anaconda Standard*, May 6, 1912. Courtesy Mike Poirier.
38. Amer. 606.
39. Amer. 572; Amer. 827.
40. *New York Times*, April 20, 1912.
41. Amer. 827; Amer. 1008.
42. Amer. 570; Amer. 827.
43. Amer. 1007–1010.
44. For evidence that there was a southerly setting current of 196.7° that night, see Sam Halpern's article 'Collision Point', available at the following URL: http://www.glts.org/articles/halpern/collision_point.html.
45. Amer. 570; Amer. 1008; letter from the Countess of Rothes to Thomas Jones, courtesy of Geoff Whitfield.
46. Amer. 338; Additional details are from the accounts of First Class passengers Helen Candee and Margaret Brown, as recorded in *The Truth About Titanic*, Ch. 6.
47. *Ibid*.
48. Amer. 1032.
49. Account of Anna Warren, as recorded in *The Truth About Titanic*, Ch. 7.
50. Amer. 530; *Hartford Times*, April 19, 1912.
51. Amer. 282; Amer. 530; Amer. 1032.
52. Amer. 818.
53. Amer. 530.
54. *Titanic Disaster*, by Karl Behr, reprinted in *Titanic Commutator*, No. 176, 2006.
55. Amer. 563.
56. Br. 2992–3029; Amer. 636. It must be noted that Able Bodied Seaman Frederick Clench's testimony only partially confirms Poingdestre's, although Clench was not the most detailed witness in some regards. Clench does not mention Boat No. 12 rowing back toward the ship to look for survivors, only saying that they rowed a quarter of a mile away from the ship and lay on the oars, never seeing any wreckage. When asked 'what did you do after you resumed rowing', i.e. after the ship sank, Clench replied: 'We was rowing up there', but he never elaborated. (Amer. 636–638)

57. Amer. 973; Br. 12387–12393; Br. 5047–5057; Br. 12375–12378.
58. Br. 15469–15472; Amer. 541; Amer. 1101.
59. Br. 3513.
60. Thayer, 1940.
61. Amer. 666.
62. Amer. 581–582.
63. Br. 5669.
64. Br. 4085–4086.
65. Amer. 666.
66. Br. 4104; Br. 5843; Amer. 582; Amer. 667.
67. *The Sinking of the Titanic*, (Jay Henry Mowbray, 1912) Ch. 18. White does not specifically identify the boat that rescued him as No. 4. However, the details in his account make it clear that he was pulled into this boat: White slid down a set of falls, and was pulled into a nearby boat which contained 'five firemen in her as a crew, forty-nine women and sixteen children. There was no officer'. While these details are not 100% correct, they do come close to describing Boat No. 4; Boats Nos. 4 and 14 were the only ones to row back and pick up passengers from the water after the ship sank, and White's details more closely match the composition of occupants of the former.
68. Amer. 667.
69. Br. 3886.
70. Amer. 795. Bedroom Steward Siebert is the 'mate' Cunningham refers to as leaving the ship with him, and says that he died right after being pulled into the boat.
71. Amer. 795. Another person possibly pulled from the water into Boat No. 4 was Assistant Pantryman Steward F. Smith. This possibility is raised in the testimony of Bedroom Steward Cunningham, who says that 'there was a fireman there', named 'F. Smith'. It seems likely that Cunningham mistakenly referred to Smith as a fireman during his testimony, as Smith was a steward, and there were no other crewmembers named 'F. Smith' aboard the ship. There was a Trimmer named Ernest Smith, but the name doesn't match. Whoever Cunningham was referring to, it does not appear that an F. Smith was ever aboard No. 4: he did not survive the disaster, and only two men (Lyons and Siebert) died in Boat No. 4.
72. Amer. 796.
73. Interview with Frank Prentice recorded for *Titanic: A Question of Murder*, TVS, 1982.
74. Br. 3877–3881; Br. 3890.
75. Amer. 795.
76. Amer. 1108.
77. Br. 3932–3934. It seems possible that Dillon was mistaking Siebert for a passenger, since the majority of testimony indicates that only two men died aboard this boat (Amer. 582; Amer. 668; Amer. 1108), and both have been identified: Siebert and Lyons.
78. *Titanic: Our Story* by Martha Stephenson and Elizabeth Eustis, from *On Board*, Behe; Prentice's account in *The Southern Evening Echo*, April 15, 1982.
79. Letter from Harold Phillimore to Ed Kamuda, June 12, 1964. Courtesy of Don Lynch.
80. Thomas Whiteley's *Titanic* lecture.
81. *Chicago Daily Tribune*, April 21, 1912.
82. *The Irish Sunday Press*, June/July 1956.
83. Thayer, 1940.
84. *New York Times*, April 19, 1912.
85. Br. 6093–6104. Joughin claimed that he was 'practically' in the water for 2½ hours (Br. 6109) prior to being pulled into one of the lifeboats – either Boat No. 4 or No. 12 – that rescued people from Collapsible B. It is physically impossible for a person to have survived that long completely submerged in 28° water; but a careful reading of Joughin's account suggests that at least the upper-half of his body was out of the water as he hung on to Maynard and the boat, with just his legs and feet in the water. It has also been suggested, erroneously, that the liquor Joughin had consumed that night somehow protected him in the water. While alcohol does give a warming feeling and could dull the senses to the point where someone might not feel the cold as much, it actually constricts blood vessels, which would lead to lessened blood flow to the extremities. This would cause a person to pass away much more quickly than they would if they not had anything to drink. All in all, it seems likely that Joughin was not in the water for 2½ hours, that he survived from not being completely submerged during his ordeal, and that alcohol had little or nothing to do with his survival.
86. *The Truth About the Titanic*, Ch. 5; Amer. 632. Colonel Gracie, Scullion John Collins (Amer. 633), Eugene Daly (account to Dr Blackmarr), and Fireman Walter Hurst (correspondence with Walter Lord) all mention this swimmer in their accounts. It was an incident that stuck with those who witnessed it.
87. See Appendix M: Down With the Ship? Captain Smith's Fate, for more details.
88. Private letter from George Rheims to his wife Mary, April 19, 1912.
89. From the typed notes of August Wennerström used in his talks about the disaster, preserved by the Wennerström family. Courtesy of Jerry Wennerström and Mike Herbold.
90. Amer. 582.
91. Amer. 668.
92. Br. 3029–3048.
93. *Ilford Graphic*, May 10, 1912.
94. Amer. 1009.
95. Br. 410; Amer. 407–410; Br. 439.
96. *Anaconda Standard*, May 6, 1912. Courtesy Mike Poirier.
97. Amer. 677.
98. Amer. 409.
99. Amer. 1109.
100. Br. 13117–13119; Br. 12586. This conversation is reconstructed from the inquiry testimony of Pusey and Sir Cosmo Duff Gordon. For further information on this subject, please see Appendix G: The Duff Gordon Affair.
101. Details on the transfers and evidence relating to it are detailed in 'Titanic Lifeboat Occupancy Totals', by Bill Wormstedt and Tad Fitch, 2011 This article is available online at the following URL: http://wormstedt.com/titanic/lifeboats/occupancy.pdf.
102. Amer. 1109.
103. Amer. 386.
104. *The Truth About the Titanic*, Ch. 6.
105. Amer. 407–408. For many years, the story of a man dressing as a woman in order to board a lifeboat was believed to be a legend. In fact, Lowe's testimony and other conclusive pieces of evidence prove that this incident actually occurred. See George Behe's online article 'The Man Who Dressed As A Woman' at the following URL for further details: http://home.comcast.net/~georgebehe/titanic/page4.htm.
106. Amer. 410; Amer. 606; Amer. 678. Estimates all seem to place the time when Lowe went back for survivors between an hour and an hour and a half after the sinking. Given the time that the *Carpathia* arrived on the scene, 4:00 a.m., (Amer. 21) and all that Lowe did after rowing back to the site but before being rescued, the shorter estimate, or a time of around 3:20 a.m., seems more likely.
107. Amer. 677.
108. Amer. 605.
109. Amer. 677.
110. Br. 439.
111. Amer. 616.
112. Br. 5341.
113. Letter from Harold Phillimore to Ed Kamuda, June 12, 1964. Courtesy of Don Lynch.
114. *Bridgewater Mercury*, April 1912; *Herts Advertiser & St. Albans Times*, May 4, 1912.
115. Amer. 406; Amer. 621.
116. Amer. 678; 605.
117. In the 1997 film *Titanic*, Fifth Officer Lowe is shown using a flashlight to help guide them in their work. Director James Cameron said: 'One of the problems with these scenes photographically is that historically there was absolutely no light other than starlight. ... The stars were certainly brilliant, but what we've created is what I call the "light of the mind," a subtle, shadow-less illumination that allows us to see action and emotion and photograph it unobtrusively. It's a tough call because you don't really know how far you can push it before the audience begins to question it. I've also added flashlights to some of the lifeboats. It's one of our few historical inaccuracies but we have to light the scenes somehow.' (*James Cameron's Titanic*, Ed. W. Marsh, 1997, pgs. 163–165.)
    Some have criticized the scenes, saying that flashlights had not been invented by 1912. In point of fact, they had ... the Lines, for example, carried one in their lifeboat. However, it does not seem that those in Fifth Officer Lowe's boat were actually equipped with flashlights as they searched the waters.
118. *New York Times*, April 27, 1912; Amer. 408; Amer. 616; Amer. 678–679; Br. 441.
119. Br. 441; *Sphere*, May 25, 1912; Letter from Harold Phillimore to Ed Kamuda, June 12, 1964. Courtesy of Don Lynch.
120. Amer. 616; *American Semi Monthly Magazine*, May 1912. The exact number of people rescued from the water by Boat No. 14 is up for debate. Lowe believed that four men were rescued, with one dying (Amer. 410), and Buley (Amer. 605), Evans (Amer. 677–678), and Scarrott (Br. 439) all concurred with his numbers. Threlfall believed four were rescued, but gave no additional details (*Bridgewater Mercury*, April 1912).
    However, Crowe (Amer. 616) and Morris (Br. 5349) both believed there were three men rescued, with one dying. Crowe gave the most detailed description of the three men rescued, and seemed certain in his count. Evans' count of four mistakenly includes Verandah Steward John Stewart, who was not rescued in Boat No. 14, but in Boat No. 15. (Please see Appendix L: Thomas Andrews' Fate, for more details on Stewart's rescue.) The identities of Hoyt, Phillimore, and Lang are established as three of the survivors who Lowe rescued. If there was a fourth, his identity has not yet been determined.
121. *The Sphere*, May 25, 1912.
122. Amer. 299–300. Further details on the transfer of occupants between No. 5 and No. 7 are detailed in 'Titanic Lifeboat Occupancy Totals', by Bill Wormstedt and Tad Fitch, 2011. URL: http://wormstedt.com/titanic/lifeboats/occupancy.pdf.
123. *The Times*, April 20, 1912; Amer. 975. Pitman isn't mentioned by name as the one who told Nourney to save his ammunition. However, 'the man in charge' of the small flotilla of No. 5 and No. 7 was indeed the Third Officer.

124. Amer. 341; *The Truth About The Titanic*, Ch. 6. These events in Boat No. 6 are reconstructed from Major Peuchen's testimony, as well as the accounts of Helen Candee and Margaret Brown, which were given to Colonel Gracie.
125. The 1997 film *Titanic* has at times been criticized for depicting the bodies in the water with frozen features. However, these accounts should make it clear that such a depiction was very accurate.
126. Information courtesy of the family of Bertha Mulvihill; *Anaconda Standard*, May 6, 1912. Courtesy Mike Poirier.
127. Amer. 590–591.
128. Amer. 409; *The Sphere*, May 25, 1912.
129. Amer. 409.
130. Amer. 20–21; Br. 25401.
131. *The Truth About the Titanic*, Ch. 6. Based on account of Margaret Brown to Colonel Gracie. The woman identified as Miss Norton was actually Miss Martin.
132. Thayer, 1940.
133. From the typed notes of August Wennerström used in his talks about the disaster, preserved by the Wennerström family. Courtesy of Jerry Wennerström and Mike Herbold; George Rheims deposition in the Limitation of Liability hearings, given on November 14, 1913.
134. *The Providence Journal*, April 20, 1912.
135. The fact that Boxhall's distress coordinates were off by 13 miles was unknown until the position of *Titanic*'s wreck was discovered in 1985. For additional details on how this error may have been made, see Sam Halpern's article 'It's A CQD Old Man: 41.46 North, 50.14 West', available online at http://www.encyclopedia-titanica.org/its-a-cqd-old-man-4146-north-5014-west.html.
136. Amer. 21–22; Br. 25401–25405; *Tramps and Ladies*, Ch. 23, by Sir James Bisset, 1959.
137. Amer. 570; Amer. 829.
138. Amer. 520.
139. *New York Times*, April 28, 1912; *The Truth About the Titanic*, Ch. 5; *The Irish Sunday Press*, June/July 1956. The events aboard Collapsible B described in the preceding paragraphs are reconstructed from these sources.
140. Amer. 639; *The Truth About the Titanic*, Ch. 5.
141. *The Truth About the Titanic*, Ch. 5; specific details on the transfer of occupants into boat Nos 4 and 12 are detailed in '*Titanic* Lifeboat Occupancy Totals', by Bill Wormstedt and Tad Fitch, 2011. URL: http://wormstedt.com/titanic/lifeboats/occupancy.pdf
142. Thayer, 1940; *The Evening World*, April 22, 1912; account of Daly, written down by Dr Frank Blackmarr onboard the *Carpathia*, and signed by Daly. Reproduced in 'Dr. Frank Blackmarr's Remarkable Scrapbook', *Titanic Commutator*, 3rd Quarter 1998.
143. *Liverpool Journal of Commerce*, April 30, 1912. Account supplied by George Behe; *Western Daily Mercury*, April 29, 1912. Account supplied by Ioannis Georgiou.
144. *The Truth About the Titanic*, Ch. 5; Thayer, 1940.
145. *New York Herald*, April 20, 1912.
146. Private letter from William Mellors to Dorothy Ockenden written on May 9, 1912, courtesy of Brian Ticehurst.
147. Private notes from an interview conducted by Walter Lord with Richard Norris Williams, dated April 27, 1962. The notes are contained in 'The Lord/Pellegrino Communications Files' collection, and are available online at: http://www.charlespellegrino.com/passengers/r_n_williams_11.htm.
148. *The Washington Post*, April 20, 1912.
149. From the typed notes of August Wennerström used in his talks about the disaster, preserved by the Wennerström family. Courtesy of Jerry Wennerström and Mike Herbold.
150. Br. 10666.
151. Amer. 679; Amer. 751; Br. 586.
152. '*Titanic* Lifeboat Occupancy Totals', by Bill Wormstedt and Tad Fitch, 2011. URL: http://wormstedt.com/titanic/lifeboats/occupancy.pdf.
153. *New York Herald*, April 20, 1912; *Bridgewater Mercury*, April 1912.
154. *Pawtucket Times*, May 22, 1912. Courtesy Mike Poirier.
155. *The Washington Herald*, April 19, 1912; *Cleveland Plain Dealer*, April 21, 1912 (account provided by Mike Poirier).
156. From the typed notes of August Wennerström used in his talks about the disaster, preserved by the Wennerström family. Courtesy of Jerry Wennerström and Mike Herbold.
157. Amer. 412.
158. Amer. 22; Amer. 1102; *Tramps and Ladies*, Ch. 23.
159. *Tramps and Ladies*, Ch. 23.
160. Amer. 22; *Tramps and Ladies*, Ch. 23.
161. *Ibid*.

CHAPTER 7: IN THE WAKE OF A LEGEND

1. Br. 12588–12591; Br. 12827.
2. Br. 12844; *Indiscretions*, page 183.
3. All lifeboat recovery times taken from research by historian George Behe, in *Centennial Reappraisal*, Appendix I.
4. Amer. 961.
5. Amer. 426; Amer. 961; Thayer, 1940. Jack Thayer's account of visiting Ismay in his room is confirmed by Ismay's inquiry testimony. Thayer's 1915 Limitation of Liability testimony supports the conclusion that he

and his father spoke with Ismay frequently aboard *Titanic*. However, Thayer claimed that Ismay's hair had turned completely white in the short time since the disaster; however, this clearly didn't happen, as there are many pictures of Ismay at the inquiries and afterwards that do not show his hair white, or any grayer than is normal for a man of his age.
6. Amer. 266; Amer. 270; Amer. 299; Amer. 331.
7. *Albany Times-Union*, April 19, 1912; *Rochester Democrat and Chronicle*, April 21, 1912. Both of these accounts are reproduced in full in *The Carpathia and the Titanic: Rescue at Sea*, by George Behe, Lulu Press, 2011. (Henceforth cited as *Carpathia*, Behe.)
8. *The Auburn Citizen*, April 23, 1912. Courtesy Mike Poirier.
9. Beesley, Ch. 7.
10. *Titanic Survivor*, Ch. 22.
11. *New York Herald*, April 20, 1912; *Worcestershire Chronicle*, April 27, 1912.
12. George Rheims' deposition in the Limitation of Liability hearings, given on November 14, 1913.
13. Private letter from George Rheims to his wife, April 19, 1912. Rheims doesn't name Peter Daly as the one who asked for his photograph with a dedication, but it is clear from his description that it was Daly. He says the man in question was the father of nine, while Daly and his wife eventually had ten children. No other Collapsible A survivor fits that description. Furthermore, Daly credited Rheims and Richard Norris Williams with saving his life (*New York Times*, April 22, 1912).
14. Private notes from an interview conducted by Walter Lord with Richard Norris Williams, dated April 27, 1962. Notes are contained in 'The Lord/Pellegrino Communications Files' collection, and are available online at: http://www.charlespellegrino.com/passengers/r_n_williams_11.htm.
15. *Worcester Telegram*, April 20, 1912.
16. *The Truth About the Titanic*, Ch. 7. Letter from Dr Dodge to Colonel Gracie.
17. *New York Herald*, April 21, 1912; the entire Cherry account is published in *Carpathia*, Behe.
18. *On Board*, Behe, 149.
19. Letter from the Countess of Rothes to Thomas Jones, courtesy of Geoff Whitfield.
20. *The Providence Journal*, April 20, 1912.
21. Information courtesy of the family of Bertha Mulvihill.
22. *New York Times*, April 22, 1912.
23. Amer. 795; Amer. 668.
24. Br. 3935.
25. Amer. 1108.
26. Details from the account of First Class passenger Margaret Brown, as recorded in *The Truth About Titanic*, Ch. 6.
27. *Anaconda Standard*, May 6, 1912. Courtesy Mike Poirier.
28. *New York Times*, April 19, 1912.
29. The identity of the body recovered from No. 12 remains unknown. It had been brought aboard the lifeboat from overturned collapsible B, and was thought to have been First Marconi operator Jack Phillips. However, research by George Behe has shown that the body was probably not Phillips. See 'The Fate of Jack Phillips' at http://home.comcast.net/~georgebehe/titanic/Page13.htm for details.
30. *The Christian Science Journal*, Vol. XXX, October 1912, No. 7; *The Truth About the Titanic*, Ch. 6. In his Senate Inquiry testimony Gracie mentioned that he and Lightoller discussed the details of the disaster aboard *Carpathia* several times. Lightoller also alluded to this in his testimony from the same inquiry (Amer. 73; Amer. 93).
31. Amer. 589.
32. 'Dr. Frank Blackmarr's Remarkable Scrapbook', *Titanic Commutator*, 3rd Quarter 1998; *The Irish Sunday Press*, June/July 1956, courtesy of Geoff Whitfield.
33. Thomas Whiteley's *Titanic* lecture.
34. Br. 6271–6273.
35. *The Truth About the Titanic*, Chapters 5–6.
36. From the typed notes of August Wennerström used in his talks about the disaster, preserved by the Wennerström family. Courtesy of Jerry Wennerström and Mike Herbold.
37. *The Duluth Herald*, May 1, 1912. Courtesy Mike Poirier.
38. Thayer, 1940.
39. From the typed notes of August Wennerström used in his talks about the disaster, preserved by the Wennerström family. Courtesy of Jerry Wennerström and Mike Herbold.
40. *Ibid*.
41. Amer. 20–21.
42. *The Weekly Telegraph*, May 10, 1912.
43. Amer. 23.
44. Amer. 24.
45. Amer. 23.
46. Amer. 22.
47. See Sam Halpern's article 'We Could Not See One Body', published in *The Titanic Commutator*, Vol. 32, No. 181 for an examination of why the bodies of *Titanic*'s victims were not visible to the *Carpathia* or *Californian*, and why they separated from the floating wreckage.
48. Amer. 22–23; Amer. 25.

49. Amer. 952.
50. Ibid.
51. Ibid.
52. Amer. 952–954.
53. Amer. 926; Amer. 936.
54. Amer. 23. Please see Appendix P: Buried at Sea, for further details on this matter.
55. Anaconda Standard, May 6, 1912. Courtesy Mike Poirier.
56. New York Times, April 19, 1912; Amer. 125–126.
57. New York Times, April 19, 1912; New York Herald, April 19, 1912.
58. Titanic: Safety, Speed and Sacrifice, by George Behe, 1997.
59. New York Times, April 19, 1912.
60. Titanic: Triumph and Tragedy, by John Eaton & Charles Haas, 1995. (Henceforth cited as Triumph & Tragedy.)
61. Baltimore Sun, April 15, 1912.
62. New York Sun, April 15, 1912.
63. New York Times, April 15, 1912.
64. The Titanic, End of a Dream, Ch. 3, by Wyn Craig Wade, 1979. (Henceforth cited was Wade.)
65. New York Times, April 21, 1912.
66. Legend has it that this message was received by David Sarnoff, who went on to helm RCA. Sarnoff himself fed into the story, but there is a decided lack of first-hand evidence available on the matter. As there is no certain proof that Sarnoff was personally involved in the event, the current authors have omitted mention of his name in the primary text. Further research into this matter may be of use in determining the facts one way or another.
67. New York Times, April 16, 1912.
68. The details and quotes relating to Franklin in this, and the preceding two paragraphs are, unless otherwise noted, from Wade, Ch. 3.
69. New York Times, April 17, 1912.
70. New York Times, April 17, 1912; New York Times, December 1, 1996.
71. Daily Sketch, April 19, 1912.
72. Chicago Daily News, April 16, 1912.
73. Washington Times, April 17, 1912.
74. Chicago Daily News, April 19, 1912.
75. Washington Post, April 19, 1912.
76. Information courtesy of the family of Bertha Mulvihill.
77. Anaconda Standard, May 6, 1912. Courtesy Mike Poirier.
78. Ibid.
79. The Maiden Voyage, by Geoffrey Marcus, 1991.
80. New York Morning World, April 18, 1912.
81. Research by historian George Behe has shown that the lifeboats picked up by the Carpathia, and offloaded at Piers 59 and 60, were lifeboats: 1, 2, 3, 5, 6, 7, 8, 9, 10, 11, 12, 13, and 16 – thirteen in all. See Appendix I of Centennial Reappraisal for additional details on the lifeboats recovered.
82. The Sinking of Titanic and Great Sea Disasters, by Logan Marshall, 1912.
83. Ibid.
84. Ibid.
85. Thomas Whiteley's Titanic lecture.
86. The Daily Banner, April 19, 1912. According to the April 19, 1912 edition of the Washington Herald, Madeleine's destination was her parents' home, and not Colonel Astor's home.
87. Washington Herald, April 19, 1912.
88. Anaconda Standard, May 6, 1912. Courtesy Mike Poirier.
89. The Providence Journal, April 20, 1912; Westmeath Independent, April 20, 1912; Additional information courtesy of the family of Bertha Mulvihill.
90. The Maiden Voyage; Triumph & Tragedy.
91. Amer. 183.
92. Amer. 959.
93. Daily Sketch, April 24, 1912.
94. Amer. 861–862.
95. Wade, Ch. 4. Details of Marconi's and Speer's meeting with Bride are as reported in this book.
96. New York Times, April 20, 1912.
97. Washington Post, April 20, 1912; The Daily Banner, April 19, 1912.
98. New York Times, April 21, 1912.
99. Ibid.
100. New York Times, April 20, 1912.
101. New York Times, April 21, 1912.
102. Daily Sketch, April 19, 1912. This dispatch, reportedly sent by Captain Rostron, was received in New York via Sagaponack shortly before 11:00 p.m. on April 18.
103. The Washington Post, April 20, 1912; Chicago Record Herald, April 21, 1912.
104. Michel Navratil's body was recovered by the Mackay-Bennett (body #15) on April 21, the first day of the recovery effort; he had a loaded firearm on him. His body was taken to Halifax, where it was interred at the Baron De Hirsch Cemetery. The cemetery is designated as Jewish, and Navratil was mistakenly buried here, based on his assumed name of Louis Hoffman.
105. Daily Sketch, April 25, 1912 through May 6, 1912. The issues of this paper in this range of dates chronicle the Olympic strike, and discuss it in great detail.
106. The Sinking of the Titanic and Great Sea Disasters, Ch. 21, by Logan Marshall, 1912. The preceding details about the Mackay-Bennett, Bremen, and body recovery are drawn from this source.
107. Wade, Ch. 17.
108. Bodies #124, #96, and #157 recovered by the Mackay-Bennett respectively. Astor's body was rumored to have been crushed and soot-covered when recovered, indicating he was killed by the falling forward funnel. In fact, this is not true. Astor's body was in good condition when recovered, and there is no evidence that he was killed by the funnel. See George Behe's article 'The Two Deaths of John Jacob Astor' at the following URL for further details: http://home.comcast.net/~georgebehe/titanic/page12.htm.
109. These details have been gleaned from various eyewitness accounts contained in Carpathia, Behe.
110. Wade, Ch. 17.
111. Ibid.
112. Cork Examiner, May 16, 1912; The Truth About the Titanic, Ch. 7. Further details on the body recovery can be found in Triumph & Tragedy, Ch. 16; and Titanic Remembered: The Unsinkable Ship and Halifax, by Alan Ruffman, 2000.
113. Encyclopedia Titanica, biography of William Thomas Kerley, http://www.encyclopedia-titanica.org/titanic-biography/william-thomas-kerley.html.
114. Personal communication from George Behe, July 11, 1999.
115. Bill Wormstedt's 'An Analysis of the Bodies Recovered from the Titanic' at http://wormstedt.com/titanic/analysis.html.
116. Recommendations as given in the Final Report of the Senate Inquiry.
117. Daily Sketch, April 25, 1912.
118. Recommendations as given in the Final Report of the British Inquiry.
119. For further details on the modifications made to the Olympic and Britannic in light of the Titanic disaster, please see The Edwardian Superliners: A Trio of Trios, (2012, Amberley Books) by J. Kent Layton, Chapters 5 and 7.
120. http://en.wikipedia.org/wiki/International_Ice_Patrol.
121. Unfortunately, much of the testimony taken at the Limitation of Liabilities hearings is not currently available. Many of the claims and depositions from the 1913 portion of the case are housed in the National Archives in New York, but for some reason, the transcripts of the testimony given in U.S. District Court in June 1915 appears to be missing; this includes the testimony of survivors such as Jack Thayer, Eugene Daly, William Mellors, and others, none of whom were called to testify in the American or British inquiries. Copies of the 1915 testimonies, if they still exist, would be a great find for researchers, perhaps revealing new aspects of the sinking. Details of what they testified about can be gleaned from the June 1915 New York newspapers, who covered the court sessions. If anyone has any information on the whereabouts of the 1915 testimonies, please contact the present authors. The Titanic Inquiry web-site, at http://www.titanicinquiry.org/, does have a section pertaining to the Limitation of Liability hearings, and the web-master is adding more testimonies as they become available.
122. New York Times, January 28, 1916; New York Times, July 29, 1916. Additional details on the Limitation of Liability hearings are from Triumph & Tragedy.

CHAPTER 8: THE ETERNAL ECHOES

1. Thayer, 1940.
2. Startlingly, a post card with the lyrics to 'The Irish Emigrant' – one of a set of four, apparently – was mailed by Third Class passenger Patrick Dooley before boarding the liner in Queenstown. Dooley died in the sinking. It was thus apparently well-known to at least some of those aboard Titanic, and makes the depiction in the 1979 film seem – in retrospect – like a startlingly good choice. Please see Titanic: Legacy of the World's Greatest Ocean Liner, by Susan Wels, (Time Life Books/Tehabi Books, 1997) pg. 91.
3. The 1970s were a time of great revival for Scott Joplin's music, particularly beginning with the release of the film The Sting in 1973. In 1912, Joplin's music was still considered socially unacceptable within certain society circles, and some have criticized the inclusion of Joplin's works in dramatic re-enactments of the voyage or sinking.

   However, ragtime was extremely popular music in 1912, despite the stigma some attached to it; it was particularly popular among the younger generation of the period – people of Jack Thayer or Milton Long's generation.

   It is quite likely that Joplin's works were very well-known to the Titanic's bandsmen, as they had to be prepared for popular requests – and many of these would have come from American passengers familiar with Joplin's works. It is very likely that they would have known precisely how to play at least some Joplin works during the Titanic's maiden voyage.

   A Joplin waltz, such as 'Bethena', would have been nearly impossible for anyone to have complained about. Furthermore, many passengers recalled hearing the band playing ragtime as the ship went down – not just a single piece, but a number of them, apparently. While Joplin was not the only ragtime composer, he was the most popular and best-known of them. It is thus very likely that some of Joplin's work was heard aboard the Titanic.

An official soundtrack was not released until 2013. As many of the period pieces played in the film are not listed in the credits, the music contained in the film has become something of a legend in the *Titanic* community. We managed to identify many of the pieces contained in the full version of the film prior to the soundtrack release:

- 'Waltz from Eugene Onegin'
  (Pyotr Ilyich Tchaikovsky, 1878)
- 'Rule, Britannia' (traditional)
- 'Eternal Father, Strong to Save'
  (William Whiting/John B. Dykes, 1860–1861)
- 'The Irish Emigrant' (Irish traditional)
- 'The Irish Washerwoman' (Irish traditional)
- 'The Father O'Flynn Jig' (Irish traditional)
- 'Isn't It Grand, Boys?' (Irish traditional)
- 'Elite Syncopations' (Scott Joplin, 1902)
- 'Bethena – A Concert Waltz' (Scott Joplin, 1905)
- 'A Breeze From Alabama' (Scott Joplin, 1902)
- 'The Easy Winners' (Scott Joplin, 1901)
- 'I'm Falling in Love with Someone' (Victor Herbert, 1910,
  from the operetta *Naughty Marietta*)
- 'Roses From the South' (Johann Strauss II, 1880)
- 'For He's A Jolly Good Fellow' (traditional)
- 'Turn Off Your Light, Mr. Moon Man'
  (Music by Fred Barnes and R. P. Weston/Lyrics by
  Fred Barnes and R. P. Weston; from the 1911 Broad
  way musical *Little Miss Fix-It*. First performed by Nora
  Bayes and Jack Norworth)

Another piece, which was played during the dance between Martin Gallagher and 'The Irish Beauty', has been identified as 'The Connemara Waltz'. There is a traditional Irish piece known as 'The Queen of Connemara', written in waltz-time. However, as of this writing we can find no recordings of that piece which clearly correlate with the piece heard in the film. The soundtrack contained the piece, but only as it was initially heard during boarding at Queenstown, not during the dance.

4. The introduction of the Leigh Goodwin character, though not historically accurate, did give Lawrence Beesley someone to talk to, and articulate some of the things he said in his book.
5. The film was subsequently released in international markets over the following nine months.
6. In 2005, a second 'Dirk Pitt' adventure film – *Sahara* – was released. The intention was to 're-boot' the franchise with a series of adaptations of the Cussler books. Starring Matthew McConaughey as Dirk Pitt, Steve Zahn as his sidekick Al Giordino (Giordino was given only the briefest of screen-time in *Raise the Titanic*), William H. Macy as Admiral James Sandecker and Penelope Cruz as Dr Eva Rojas, *Sahara* was a much better adaptation of the original novel than *Raise the Titanic*. Many Cussler fans were critical of it, though, and the rights to sequel films became bogged down in protracted legal squabbling between Cussler and the motion picture company behind the film. As of this writing, it does not appear that further Dirk Pitt movies will be produced.
7. According to Producer James Fitzpatrick, all that had been found of the original recordings, up until 1999, were the film's non-dialogue 'Music & Effects' tracks.
8. Silva Screen Records, 1999.
9. It is said that Director Steven Spielberg first noticed her in this role, and recommended her to Director Martin Campbell for the role of Elena in *The Mask of Zorro*.
10. Even though this was the first depiction of the *Titanic* breaking apart, the filmmakers did not make good use of the opportunity. Instead, they used a series of 'quick cuts' during the break-up sequence, which prevented the audience from actually seeing the break-up with any clarity.
11. The *Titanic*'s original build price, of approximately £1.5 million in 1911, would have translated out to roughly $188 million 1997 USD. If this year-to-year conversion is anything like accurate, this would mean that the film cost more money to make than the original ship. There are varying estimates for the actual budget of the film, with some ranging as high as $220 million.
12. It is worth noting, since it is a subject of much debate and misinformation, that the set itself was actually built at full scale. However, to save costs, certain sections of the exterior set were removed; this included the entire Forecastle, as well as a number of segments from the length in the remaining portion of the set. This had the effect of making the entire set somewhat shorter in overall length than the real ship was. To offset the fore-shortened length, certain prominent features of the ship – such as the funnels – were scaled down slightly so that she would not appear too tall in relation to length. This decision also turned the familiar two groups of windows forward on *Titanic*'s A Deck Promenade into four smaller groups. Later, Cameron reportedly said that he regretted not constructing the Forecastle portion of the ship, as it only made more work in post-production.
13. David Warner played Lawrence Beesley in the 1979 film *S.O.S. Titanic*.
14. The scene was based upon the famous Frank Browne photo, filmed from almost the identical perspective, and with only very minor variations.

15. In this film, Gracie was portrayed by Bernard Fox, who had played Lookout Frederick Fleet in the 1958 film *A Night to Remember*.
16. Historian Don Lynch said that during the shooting of some of the film's scenes, it was quite easy for him to walk through the cast and correctly identify the characters being played.
17. For information on Ismay's involvement with the voyage, please see Appendix O: 'J. "Brute" Ismay'? For information on incidents of gunfire and the possibility of officer suicides, please see Appendix H: Incidents of Gunfire During the Sinking, and Appendix K: Shots in the Dark: Did an Officer Commit Suicide on the *Titanic*?
    It should be pointed out that filmmakers only have a single option to use in their portrayal of historical events. On the other hand, the historical record offers more than one possibility.
18. As of the Second Edition printing of this book, (following the 3-D re-release in April of 2012), *Titanic* stands as the No. 2 grossing film worldwide, with an aggregate $2.18 billion take. It was finally topped by James Cameron's film *Avatar* (2009) which took in $2.7 billion worldwide.
    If one adjusts for inflation, *Titanic* currently sits in the No. 5 spot. In descending order, the first four places on this list are occupied by *Gone With the Wind* (1939), *Star Wars* (1977), *The Sound of Music* (1965), and *E.T.: The Extra-Terrestrial* (1982). During its theatrical re-release in 2012, it moved up on this list from sixth place to fifth, taking the No. 5 spot from *The Ten Commandments* (1956). Interestingly, if one accounts for inflation, *Avatar* is still below *Titanic*, at the No. 14 spot.
19. It would be beyond the scope of this text to discuss every historical error in the film, or to try to show which of these 'errors' were actual errors, which were perhaps exaggerations for dramatic effect, and which were really only selections from a historical record that presented multiple possibilities. The best thing to do is to familiarize one's self with the best research on the liner.
20. CNN, May 20, 2011, 'Titanic 3-D to be released in 2012'.
21. AolTV, 'Battle of the "Titanic" TV Series: Chris Noth and Neve Campbell Join "Blood and Steel"', by Catherine Lawson, August 31, 2011.
22. *Digital Spy*, '"Titanic" drama begins filming', May 10, 2011, by Catriona Wightman.
23. A very interesting series of reports by researcher Dr Paul Lee can be found on his web site, at: http://www.paullee.com/titanic/titanic-found.html.
24. BBC News, '*Titanic* necklace stolen from Denmark exhibition', September 19, 2011. Available at: http://www.bbc.co.uk/news/world-europe-14979008.
25. The 1985 and 1986 expeditions were subsequently covered in Ballard's books, *The Discovery of the Titanic, Exploring the Titanic*, and *Lost Liners*; the 1987 documentary *Secrets of the Titanic* also covered the expeditions.
26. At times, the RMS Titanic, Inc. expeditions have provided intense media scrutiny and documentary coverage. Among these was the 1997 documentary *Titanic: Anatomy of a Disaster*.
27. This expedition eventually resulted in the IMAX documentary *Titanica*.
28. Footage from the 1995 dives were used in the 1997 film; footage from 2001 was released in the documentary *Ghosts of the Abyss*; the 2005 expedition was used in conjunction with The Discovery Channel for the special *Last Mysteries of the Titanic*.
29. This expedition led up to The History Channel documentary *Titanic's Final Moments: Missing Pieces*.
30. This expedition resulted in the Ballard book *Titanic: The Last Great Images*, and a documentary entitled *Titanic Revealed*.

APPENDIX A: *TITANIC*'S TECHNICAL SPECIFICATIONS & SOME COMMON MISCONCEPTIONS

1. Edward Wilding, of Harland & Wolff, testified (Br. 19796–19800) to the *Titanic*'s displacement at the draught specified as given above. This figure matched the known measurements of the *Olympic*'s weight.
2. The fallacy of the 66,000-ton displacement was first recorded by Mark Chirnside's article, 'The 66,000 Ton Myth', published in the Irish Titanic Historical Society's *White Star Journal* (2007, Volume 15 Number 3, pages 20–21).
3. *Olympic*'s gross registered tonnage in 1911 was 45,323.82. The *Titanic* was some 1,004.72 tons greater in measured enclosed space, to be precise.
4. Br. 19051–19053. Edward Wildling, who worked side by side with Thomas Andrews during the design and construction of the *Olympic* and *Titanic*, said at the British Inquiry that he fully expected *Titanic*'s top speed could be as high as 23¼ knots. (Br. 20923) In 1914, the *Olympic* managed to briefly exceed 25 knots during a mad dash for the safety of port after the outbreak of the First World War. There is every reason to believe that *Titanic* could have done just as good, if not slightly better under similar circumstances.
5. This revelation was originally uncovered by maritime researcher and author Mark Chirnside in late 2007. His article on the subject, 'The Mystery of *Titanic*'s Central Propeller' can be found online at http://www.encyclopedia-titanica.org/mystery-titanic-central-propeller.

html. The original archival document in question is from the Public Record Office of Northern Ireland (D2805/SHIP/8A-E). Therein, it is specified that the pitch of *Titanic*'s wing propellers was upped to 35 ft 0 in. This was increased from *Olympic*'s original wing propeller pitch of 33 ft 0 inches, which itself was increased to 34 ft 6 inches during her post-*Hawke* repairs. The third ship of the class, *Britannic*, was given a four-bladed center propeller.

Unfortunately, there are no known period photographs of the *Titanic* with its central propeller installed. Today, *Titanic*'s center propeller is completely buried under the mud of the sea floor. It will take a thorough on-site investigation with sub-bottom profiling sonar in order to prove (or potentially disprove) this original documentation with finality. However, as of this writing, this original document is the best source of information on the exact design and configuration of the *Titanic*'s propellers.

6. Br. 20820.
7. A wireless dispatch from Belfast to *The New York Times*, published March 13, 1913.
8. *The Machinists' Monthly Journal*, Vol. XXVI, No. 4, (Washington, D.C., April, 1914), pgs. 336, 337.
9. PRO MT15/212, 'Riveting', signed by Board of Trade Surveyor Francis Carruthers on 22/2/1912. The most fascinating investigations into the hull's strength were performed for the documentary *Titanic at 100: Mystery Solved*. Under even the most rigorous stress tests, replica hull plates and rivets held up far better than might have been anticipated.
10. PRO MT15/212 shows correspondence relating to the full testing of *Titanic*'s shell plating, including the desired range of tensile strength in tons per square inch (29–33 tsi for the plates, 28 tsi for the butt straps), and the complete results of all tests performed on the steel. Harland & Wolff was able to report that the steel used had been tested and passed by Lloyd's.
    PRO 9-920H, starting at page 1054, shows a rather lengthy list of correspondence between Board of Trade surveyors in Belfast, Harland & Wolff personnel, and Board of Trade officials in London on a variety of subjects; these include the collision bulkheads, and how the freeboard of the sister ships was arrived at. There is much discussion, in this correspondence, on the general strength and safety of the ships. These missives provide a great deal of information on how closely the Board of Trade was keeping an eye on the construction of these unprecedented vessels to assure their final safety.

APPENDIX B: SOUTHAMPTON TO CHERBOURG

1. For example, in a letter written on board, Second Class passenger Elizabeth Watt wrote that at 7:05 p.m., they had just taken on passengers from Cherbourg. Quoted in *On Board*, Behe, 87.
2. The 6:30–6:35 p.m. times are from *Le Réveil*, April 1912; *L'Illustration*, April 27, 1912. If Margaret Brown was correct that the journey by the *Nomadic* to the *Titanic* took about a half-hour, and passengers embarked at about 7:00 p.m., then this would also reinforce an anchor-time of about 6:30. Please continue reading for an explanation of the difference between GMT and PMT.
3. *Newport Herald*, May 28/29, 1912. Full account available in *On Board*, Behe, 217–226.
4. Bruce Ismay specifically testified at both inquiries (Amer. 3; Br. 18368–18370) that the engines were run at 68 revolutions between Southampton and Cherbourg. Although a full slip table was never completed for the *Titanic*, (see testimony of Fifth Officer Lowe, Amer. 385) research by Sam Halpern shows that 68 revolutions works out to an approximate speed of 20.2 knots. (Please see Halpern's article, 'Speed and Revolutions' (Revised January, 1911) online at his web site: http://www.titanicology.com/Titanica/SpeedAndRevolutions. htm.)
5. 66 nautical miles divided by 20.2 knots' speed = 3.267 hours, or 3 hours 16 minutes precisely.
6. Bruce Ismay, Amer. 3.
7. George Beauchamp, Br. 874.
8. Fifth Officer Lowe, Amer. 375.
9. William Lucas, Br. 1390–1392.
10. Major Peuchen, Amer. 329.
11. Deposition of Fifth Officer Lowe to the British Consulate, May, 1912. Used with permission of John Creamer. Full text available in *On Board*, Behe, 351–354.
12. Third Officer Pitman, Amer. 261.
13. Letter from 11-year-old Eileen Lenox-Conyngham (cross-Channel passenger to Cherbourg, First Class) to her nanny, Louisa Sterling. *Voices*, 108.
14. *Belvederian*.
15. *The Scientific American Handbook of Travel*, 96–97.
16. Naturally, the actual amount of time that 'a few minutes' encompassed could vary from person to person, and should be perceived as a rough estimate rather than a precise 3–4 minutes as a strict definition would imply. There were two openings in the Cherbourg breakwater, and it would seem that the *Titanic* entered through the western of the two, turning to port and presenting her starboard side to shore, or to the south. No matter how well-rehearsed the maneuver was, caution was called for in any confined waters, and 'several minutes' may have been as long as 10–15 minutes in reality.

17. *RMS Olympic: Titanic's Sister* (Chirnside, 2004) pg. 72.
18. *The Scientific American Handbook of Travel*.
19. *Belvederian*.
20. This detail is passed on by descendents of Bowyer.
21. If correct, then Bowyer would most likely have taken return passage to Southampton on another vessel, and it probably would have been done at the expense of the White Star Line. In his *Titanic* photo album, Francis Browne included a photo of 'the pilot boat coming to take the pilot'. However, a close examination of the photo shows that the ship is still under way, and no evidence of a transfer seems obvious within the photo itself. Yet it does show that Browne had the concept in his mind; was it something that he mis-captioned later on? At this point, evidence from Bowyer's family and the caption from the Browne photographs are not directly at odds; even if they were, they would seem to have an equal chance of being correct. Documentation must be turned up to prove the point one way or another.
22. Amer. 332.
23. Amer. 261.

APPENDIX C: THE QUESTION OF BINOCULARS

1. Amer. 324.
2. Br. 17401–17403.
3. Br. 14325–14328.
4. Br. 17494–17500; 17377–17378. Apparently, the marking along the side, namely, 'Theatre, Marine and field', referred to three levels of magnification; if other similarly marked glasses from the era are comparable to these, then they may have referred to 3x, 4x, and 9x magnification. Hogg said that 'you worked them as you wanted to use them', possibly indicating the operation of the magnification mechanism. As these glasses were marked, 'Second Officer, S.S. "Titanic"', this means that the glasses were supplied for specific officers aboard the *Titanic*, and were not personally owned by Blair.
5. Br. 17501.
6. Br. 11325, 11326. This was a better arrangement than on the *Oceanic*, where the glasses were kept in a canvas bag. (Br. 11320.)
7. Br. 17502, 17503.
8. Amer. 568.
9. Br. 17372.
10. Between those involved, there is a difference of opinion as to exactly when and where this happened. On the matter of when, Symons said it was right after clearing the Nab, while Lightoller did not say whether it was before or after the ship had left her dock. Lookout Fleet added to the confusion, when he said that the request had been made by 'the station lookout men ... Hogg and Evans'. (Amer. 323–324.) Oddly, he also recalled that 'we' – not specifying who but obviously referring to the lookouts as a group – 'asked for [glasses] before we left Southampton', but were told that there were 'none intended for them'. (Amer. 364)
    There is also an apparent contradiction over where the request took place. Symons said that he found Lightoller in the Officers' Mess, while Lightoller said that he was in his room and heard Symons outside his quarters, apparently meaning in the hallway outside of his cabin. Since both men agreed that Lightoller subsequently went to a nearby room belonging to another officer (Symons thought it was Murdoch's, Lightoller said it was Wilde's), it would seem that the event occurred in the Officers' Quarters as Lightoller said it did. However, this placement also poses a problem: if this occurred *after* the ship had cleared Southampton water, why wouldn't Symons have gone to the Bridge, to whoever was on duty? It is possible that those on the Bridge had referred Symons to Lightoller and sent him to the Officers' Quarters; it is equally possible that it was because the event actually took place on April 10, but before the ship departed, at a time when fewer people would have been on the Bridge.
    Either way, the details of this conversation simply don't seem to add up, and it is very difficult to conclude when and where it actually happened from the evidence in hand.
11. Br. 14485; 11324. The final quotation is a merger of two different recollections made as to what Lightoller's response to Symons was. Symons recalled that Lightoller had said: 'Symons, there are none.' Lightoller said that his exact response was: 'There are no glasses for you.' While there is very little difference between the wording, it seems logical that Lightoller would have used Symons' last name when he returned; thus, Symons' recollection of the use of his name is added to Lightoller's more expansive wording. However, a slight variation should be allowed for in this quotation.
12. Br. 11324. Interestingly, Lookout Fleet recalled the same request was made of Second Officer Lightoller, but he recalled that it had been made before the ship departed. This begs the question: if the lookouts had made a request for binoculars before leaving Southampton, and were told that there were none intended for their use, why would they ask again immediately after clearing Southampton waters?
13. Amer. 583; Br. 17507–17511.
14. Br. 2647–2656.
15. Br. 209–211; 218–224.
16. Br. 11312, 11317–11322.
17. Amer. 323.
18. Br. 3161–3165.

19. Amer. 568.
20. Br. 2364–2371.
21. Br. 13374–13381.
22. Amer. 583.
23. Br. 17487; 17513–17516.
24. Br. 216.
25. Br. 221.
26. Br. 2372.
27. Br. 2657.
28. Br. 11323.
29. Br. 11986–11988.
30. Amer. 360–361; Br. 11994.
31. Br. 17404–17407.
32. Br. 17441–17445.
33. Amer. 584–585; Br. 17517–17524.
34. Amer. 568.
35. Amer. 721; Br. 7271.
36. Amer. 727.
37. Br. 21846–21848.
38. Br. 21975.
39. Br. 23712–23713.
40. Br. 25058–25059.
41. Amer. 766.
42. Amer. 424.
43. Br. 13682–13689; 14289, 14290.
44. Br. 13690; 14291.
45. Br. 14293.
46. Br. 14300.
47. Br. 18603–18607; 18947–18950.
48. Br. 19341.
49. Br. 14322–14324.
50. Br. 19356, 19357.
51. This demonstration was carried out for the 2008 documentary *Seconds From Disaster: The Sinking of the Titanic*, which aired in the U.S. on the National Geographic Channel.

APPENDIX D: WHAT TIME IS IT?

1. Local apparent noon is a term applied to the time when the sun reaches its highest altitude in the sky – this point is thus precisely the middle of the daylight hours at that location, or local apparent noon. Every location on earth has a different local apparent noon.
2. Brochure held in researcher Mark Chirnside's collection.
3. Amer. 294.
4. *The Titanic Commutator*, No. 156, letters from Rowe to Ed Kamuda of the Titanic Historical Society in 1963.
5 Amer. 317.
6. Br. 1017–1018.
7. Amer. 294.
8. While Hichens did not refer to 'adjusted time' or 'unadjusted time', and did not notice a change to the clocks after the collision, he was very specific in saying that his relief showed up at 23 minutes after the hour – the precise amount of time of one of the two intended clock setbacks. It would be absurd to suppose that Perkis was late by the *precise* amount of time of one of the two clock setbacks, and that if it did happen, that Hichens did not mention his relief was tardy in either of his stretches of testimony.
9. Amer. 449–451.
10. Amer. 451.
11. This information was first uncovered in the 1960s by Leslie Harrison, an advocate for, and friend of, Captain Stanley Lord of the *Californian*. The data was again analyzed by researcher Sam Halpern, and re-affirmed. Further, Mr Halpern was able to run through a complete navigational track of the *Titanic*'s voyage through the Atlantic, including daily noon positions and time alterations. All of this information is contained in Mr Halpern's article, 'Keeping Track of a Maiden Voyage', which was published in the Irish Titanic Society's *White Star Journal* during 2006. Further information is also available in *Centennial Reappraisal*.
12. Amer. 906.
13. For an explanation of slave/master clocks on the Magneta circuit, please see Chapter 1.

APPENDIX E: TAKING EVASIVE ACTION

1. Report of the British Inquiry, 'The Collision'.
2. Br. 25292.
3. *Titanic*'s displacement at 34 feet 7 inches was noted to be 52,310 long tons (Br. 19796–19767). This was identical to *Olympic*'s displacement despite the minor modifications made to the *Titanic*.
4. Br. 949.
5. Amer. 362.
6. Amer. 527–528.
7. The Chapin/Hichens account is available in *Carpathia*, Behe.
8. Br. 17671.
9. Amer. 361; Br. 973.
10. Br. 15347. Boxhall also stated (Br. 15345) that the shock came only 'a moment or two' after he heard the crow's nest bell sound, but it is likely that Boxhall was truncating the timetable to some extent from

when he heard the bell, possibly because he had been inside having tea instead of on the Bridge during this crucial moment.
11. This claim first surfaced in a novel, *Good as Gold* (2010, Quercus), authored by Louise Patten, grand-daughter of Second Officer Lightoller. While the appearance of such a claim in a novel might not at first seem important, the claim subsequently received wide attention in the press and the claim was reiterated in interviews which the author gave. For example, *The Daily Telegraph*, '*Titanic* Sunk By Steering Blunder, New Book Claims', by Richard Alleyne (available online at: http://www.telegraph.co.uk/culture/books/booknews/8016752/Titanic-sunk-by-steering-blunder-new-book-claims.html) and 'The "Truth" Behind The Sinking Of *Titanic*', Sky News article, September 22, 2010, by Alison Chung (available online at: http://news.sky.com/home/uk-news/article/15738121).
12. For further details on the *Titanic*'s steering and telemotors, please see *TTSM*, Vol. 1, 522–528.
13. June of 1931 Commons Sitting, Mercantile Marine.
14. Br. 1860–1866; Br. 661–668; Br. 3715–3721; Br. 3995–4003; Br. 5521–5544.
15. Amer. 450.
16. Br. 1025–1030.
17. Amer. 531–532.
18. Amer. 229–230. Portions of Boxhall's testimony between the quotations were removed for ease of comparison.
19. Br. 3719–3729.
20. Letters from George Rowe to Titanic Historical Society President Ed Kamuda, dated 1963, and published in *The Titanic Commutator*, No. 156. At times, Quartermaster Rowe's later recollections were unreliable and even contradictory. However in this instance, it seems that there is no evidence to the contrary. Indeed, Rowe testified at both inquiries that he rushed to the taffrail log and read it immediately after the impact. The detail thus seems supplementary, rather than contradictory, to his formal testimony.
21. Amer. 313.
22. Amer. 974–975.
23. *Amsterdam Evening Recorder*, April 23, 1912.
24. *Titanic* researcher Sam Halpern has speculated that First Officer Murdoch did indeed order 'Stop' and 'Full Astern' before the collision, just as Boxhall testified. However, he believes that given the unexpected nature of the orders, and how little time there was between the sighting of the berg and the collision, that the reverse order wasn't carried out prior to the collision; furthermore, he feels it is possible that the engines did not start to reverse until a minute or two after the crash, after they had initially stopped, as per Dillon's testimony. By the time the engines reversed, Boxhall had already headed below deck, so it is plausible that he could simply have seen the Engine Room telegraphs set to 'Full Astern' prior to exiting the Bridge, thus leading to the confusion. The authors would like to thank Sam Halpern for sharing his thoughts on this matter.
25. 'On *Titanic*'s Bridge', by Art Braunschweiger. (*Voyage* No. 71)

APPENDIX F: THE ICEBERG DAMAGE

1. Br. 20347, 20422–20423. Recent research by Sam Halpern indicates that Wilding may have come in at a slightly high figure in estimating his twelve square feet; Halpern's calculations indicate an aggregate closer to ten square feet. However, in his 1915 testimony (Limitation of Liability Hearings) Wilding did allow for some 25% interpretation either way on that figure. In other words, when this margin for error is accounted for, Wilding's calculations are still very close to what even the most modern research produces. For further information please refer to *Centennial Reappraisal*, Ch. 6.
2. *The Discovery of the Titanic*, Dr Robert Ballard (Warner Books, 1987), pg. 196.
3. Taking careful note of the frame numbers at the start and end of the disclosed damage (Frames 59–149 forward), as well as the spacing between these frames, gives us a close approximation of the overall length of the damage patterns.
4. 'The Sinking of the S.S. *Titanic* – Investigated by Modern Techniques', March 26, 1996/December 10, 1996, Bedford and Hacket.

APPENDIX G: THE DUFF GORDON AFFAIR

1. Br. 12965, 12966. This story was repeated in various newspapers on both sides of the Atlantic, with some minor variations. The account was picked up by the *London Daily News* and printed in their April 20 edition; it was this version of the story that Lady Duff Gordon was presented with during her presence on the stand at the British Inquiry. Most of the published versions are, in the whole, relatively consistent, but do contain a number of inaccuracies. None of these, however, directly contradict her statements regarding the ship's final gyrations, pertinent to our investigation.
2. Br. 12935–12948. Although Lady Duff Gordon did not use the word 'invention' personally, she agreed with the word when it was used twice by her examiner, Mr Clement Edwards.
3. Two letters in particular stand out for scrutiny. Both are contained in *On Board*, Behe, 280–283. The first is a letter by Lady Duff Gordon to her sister; the second is a letter from Lady Duff Gordon to Margot Asquith, wife of Britain's then Prime Minister, Herbert Henry Asquith.

The second letter is dated Thursday, May 16, 1912. Sir Cosmo would take the stand on Friday, May 17 and Monday, May 20, while Lady Lucy would take the stand on Monday, May 20.

4. Her autobiography, *Discretions and Indiscretions* (1932), contained three chapters pertinent to the *Titanic* disaster. Although the present authors have procured a copy from Mike Poirier, the book is not commonly available to the public. However, the full text of the *Titanic*-related portions can be read online at http://www.encyclopedia-titanica.org/i-was-saved-from-the-titanic-lady-duff-gordon~chapter-0~part-1.html.
5. Br. 12923.
6. Br. 12935, 12936.
7. Br. 12937.
8. Br. 12938.
9. Br. 12906–12911.
10. Br. 11163, 11164; 5025–5033; Hendrickson did not know Ms Fran-catelli's name or her exact connection to the Duff Gordons, but there were only two female occupants of the boat, and Hendrickson clearly stated that it was 'the women [who] objected' to the idea of going back to help anyone else.
11. Br. 12586.
12. Br. 5188–5216; 11830–11848; 12243–44; 12291–12302; 12586–12591; 12592–12668.
13. *Indiscretions*, 192.

APPENDIX H:
INCIDENTS OF GUNFIRE DURING THE SINKING
1. Amer. 417–419.
2. Br. 383–393; Amer. 617; *The Truth About the Titanic* Ch. 6.
3. Amer. 1109.
4. *American Semi-Monthly Magazine*, May 1912.
5. Amer. 11.
6. Br. 17627–17640.
7. Amer. 1099.
8. Br. 10431–10437.
9. *Washington Times*, April 22, 1912.
10. *Washington Post*, April 20, 1912.
11. Amer. 886. Woolner mentioned this incident, in the same terms, in a private letter that was written aboard the *Carpathia* on April 19, 1912. Steffansson gave accounts that corroborate Woolner's story.
12. *New York Tribune*, April 19, 1912.
13. Thayer, 1940. Thayer says that this incident happened 'on "A" deck, just under the boat deck'. On the face of it, this seems problematic. Collapsible C did not load from A Deck. However, earlier in his account, Thayer describes seeing the boats uncovered on '"A" deck', then later going to the deck below, i.e. the 'lounge on "B" Deck'. The First Class lounge was on A Deck, not B Deck. It appears that Thayer was mistakenly referring to the Boat Deck as A Deck, and was referring to A Deck as B Deck. What he called the 'boat deck' must have been the roof of the Officers' Quarters.
14. *Daily Sketch*, April 29, 1912. While Senior does not specify that the shots were fired at Collapsible C, the facts strongly suggest this. Senior helped load the boats, and describes having 'thrown down' a collapsible boat from the Officer's Quarters after all the other boats were gone. This boat was Collapsible A, which establishes Senior's presence on the starboard side. Senior was unaware of how Collapsible B came to be upside-down when he climbed aboard it later. If Collapsible B was the boat he freed, he would have known how that happened, since Lightoller and Bride said this boat landed upside down on the boat deck after being pushed off the roof of the Officers' Quarters. The details Senior gave also closely match Hugh Woolner's testimony about the circumstances surrounding the loading of Collapsible C.
15. *Detroit News*, April 24, 1912; *Echoes in the Night*, Frank Goldsmith, 1991; Audio recording of a talk given by Frank Goldsmith, transcription generously provided by Bob Godfrey. After initially telling researchers he was rescued from the starboard side, later in his life, Frank Goldsmith claimed to have been rescued in Collapsible D. However, details in accounts given by both he and his mother prove they were rescued in Collapsible C. Both mention their boat getting caught on rivets as it was being lowered, and that the occupants had to keep pushing it away from the ship's side. Due to the 10° list to port, Collapsible D swung away from the ship's side, while Collapsible C hung up against it. Mrs Goldsmith also remembered four Chinese stowaways in her boat. Quartermaster Rowe and Bruce Ismay also placed these same four stowaways in Collapsible C. There were approximately eight oriental passengers on the *Titanic*: two perished, one was rescued from the water by Boat No. 14, one was rescued in Boat No. 13, and four were rescued in Collapsible C.
16. *New York Times*, June 27, 1915; *New York Herald*, June 27, 1915. During the Limitation of Liability proceedings, Mellors testified about this incident in front of Judge Julius Meyer in the United States District Court. Mellors said this happened at the 'last boat'. His own accounts suggest that he was on the starboard side at the end. Bob Bracken's article on Mellors at the Encyclopedia Titanica website contains information from Second Class survivor Bertha Watt; it confirms Mellors was near Collapsible C when it lowered, then helped with Collapsible

A. Bracken's article is available at http://www.encyclopediatitanica.org/william-mellors.html.
17. Amer. 991–992.
18. *The Truth About the Titanic*, Ch. 2.
19. *Titanic & Other Ships*, C. H. Lightoller, 1935.
20. *Amsterdam Evening Recorder*, April 23, 1912. Mrs Hoyt refers to Wilde as 'Chief Officer Wiley' in this article. Courtesy Mike Poirier.
21. For further information on possible officer suicides, please see Appendix K: Shots in the Dark: Did An Officer Commit Suicide on the *Titanic*?

APPENDIX I: THE LOSS OF DECK CREW ON THE *TITANIC* OVER TIME
1. Amer. 80; *Titanic & Other Ships*, C. H. Lightoller, 1935.
2. *Centennial Reappraisal*. See Lester Mitcham's crew and passenger listings in Appendix D of that book for specific details on those lost and saved amongst the Deck Department, as well as a listing of every passenger and crewmember that was aboard for the maiden voyage.
3. Lightoller doesn't specify that the other men were seamen. However, in the inquiries, Lightoller explains that the lack of seamen available to help him on the port side was the result of the Boatswain taking the men below to open the gangways; this clearly indicates that those men were seamen. (Amer. 85) In his book, Lightoller refers to the men Nichols took below as 'hands', i.e. deckhands/sailors.
4. The area of the gangway doors on D Deck was not flooded by 1:00 a.m. Leading Stoker Barrett described water coming onto E Deck, one deck below D Deck, from forward just after 1:10 a.m. It is possible that Nichols and the other six crewmembers remained below until later in the sinking, and at some point well after that time they were overwhelmed by the flooding, or simply never made it back up on deck. Fourth Officer Boxhall was in Boat No. 2, which was lowered away at 1:45 a.m. Fifty years after the sinking, he recalled that when Boat No. 2 rowed around the stern to the starboard side, the gangway doors there were open. (1962 BBC radio interview) Perhaps the crewmembers in question remained below all that time trying to organize passengers at the gangway doors. Another possibility is that the men came back up on deck at some point after they opened the doors, were given new orders, and thereafter were engaged exclusively on the starboard side; thus, Lightoller may not have seen them, and simply assumed they died below.
5. Amer. 578.
6. Br. 88–112.
7. Br. 97–98.
8. Amer. 277.
9. Amer. 528.
10. Amer. 560.
11. James Anderson is not mentioned by name as having been in No. 3. However, Moore's testimony shows that there was another seaman in that boat with him (Amer. 561). Since all the other surviving members of the Deck Department can be placed in other boats by the evidence, the process of elimination makes it likely that he was the unnamed seaman in this boat.
12. Amer. 570.
13. Pascoe does not mention his boat number in his account of the sinking. However, he does say that there 'was room for forty more in the boat in which he had left'. (*Western Morning News*, April 29, 1912) From Jones' testimony it is clear that there was another 'sailor' besides himself in No. 8, although he does not name him. Boat No. 8 left the ship with twenty-five people aboard, leaving forty seats unoccupied. Pascoe's description fits this boat.
14. Amer. 574.
15. Br. 12321–12326.
16. Amer. 451.
17. Amer. 324.
18. Amer. 645. Bailey is not mentioned by name, but as the 'master-at-arms'.
19. Br. 18115.
20. Forward isn't mentioned by name as having been in this boat. Archer testified that there was another 'able seaman' in No. 16 with him, (Br. 18117), and refers to this man several times as his 'mate'. (Amer. 645). Of the surviving members of the Deck Department who cannot be placed in another boat, Forward is the only one who Archer would have called 'mate'; both men were in the same watch.
21. Amer. 399.
22. Amer. 403.
23. Br. 403–404. Harder is not mentioned by his name as having been in this boat, but is identified as 'a window-cleaner'.
24. Amer. 657.
25. Br. 13316.
26. Amer. 657.
27. *Ibid*.
28. Amer. 636.
29. Br. 2775.
30. Amer. 652.
31. *Ibid*.
32. Br. 2509.
33. Br. 2535–2536.

34. *Morning News*, May 21st, 1912. Courtesy of Peter Engberg-Klarström.
35. Steward Samuel Rule testified that there was a 'deckhand' in No. 15, and when asked to clarify, he agreed that he was either an Able-Bodied Seaman, or 'an ordinary seaman'. (Br. 9621–9623) This sailor is not mentioned by name, but by the process of elimination, appears to have been Lookout Alfred Evans. According to Evans' family, he stated he was in the 'last boat lowered'. No. 15 wasn't the last boat lowered, but was the last of the aft starboard boats, and did have an unidentified seaman in it, fitting Evans' details. Information courtesy of Peter Engberg-Klarström.
36. Br. 15423.
37. Amer. 538.
38. Amer. 581.
39. Amer. 666.
40. *Ibid*.
41. Amer. 675.
42. Amer. 604.
43. Amer. 519.
44. Amer. 833–834.
45. Br. 1515–1518.
46. Amer. 91.
47. Amer. 666. Lamp Trimmer Hemming was rescued in Boat No. 4, but did not board it at 1:50 a.m. He stayed and worked on the ship until just before water reached the Boat Deck around 2:15 a.m.; he then lowered himself down a fall, and swam '200 yards' to No. 4, where he was pulled in.

APPENDIX J: THE MUSIC OF THE *TITANIC*'S BAND

1. *New York Times*, April 19, 1912.
2. *Riverside Daily Press*, January 23, 1913. However, one can't help but wonder if Miss Hays was familiar with Harold Bride's widely-reported newspaper reference to 'Autumn' and decided to incorporate that song into her own story.
3. A discussion of Chaminde's 'Automne' appears in *Early Radio: In Marconi's Footsteps 1894 to 1920*, by Peter Jensen, Kangaroo Press, 1995. A discussion of Bradbury's 'Aughton' appears in *The Musical Times*, Vol. 116, No. 1589 (July 1975), page 625, letters to the editor, 'The *Titanic* Hymn', by Ronald Johnson. (Indeed, composer Gavin Bryars subscribed to this viewpoint when he incorporated 'Aughton' as 'Hymn IV' in his classical composition, 'The Sinking of the *Titanic*'.)
4. During a talk given at the University Club in Washington on November 23, 1912, Colonel Gracie claimed that the band stopped playing an hour and a half before the ship sank. Curiously, he mentions nothing about this in his book, only noting his belief that the band played cheerful music, and not hymns.
5. *Evening Banner*, April 26, 1912.
6. *New York Times*, April 19, 1912, Br. 10589. Both Bride and Saloon Steward Edward Brown are among these witnesses. Brown, who remained on board the ship until the Boat Deck submerged, was asked whether the bandsmen were playing at the last, and he replied: 'I do not remember hearing them stop playing.' By that time the bandsmen had ascended from A Deck to the Boat Deck and were playing at the companionway located between the ship's first and second funnel.
7. *New York Times*, May 31, 1912.
8. *Western Daily Mercury*, April 30, 1912.
9. *Daily Mirror*, April 30, 1912.
10. *The Toronto World*, April 20, 1912.
11. *Seattle Daily Times*, April 22 & 23, 1912.
12. Account written by Marjorie Newell for Walter Lord, available at the following website: http://www.charlespellegrino.com/passengers/marjorie_robb.htm
13. *New York Evening World*, April 23, 1912.
14. Account written by Marjorie Newell for Walter Lord, available at the following website: http://www.charlespellegrino.com/passengers/marjorie_robb.htm
15. *Minneapolis Tribune*, April 22, 1912.
16. It should be noted that 'Londonderry Air' was performed by the ship's band in the Clifton Webb film *Titanic*, which came out three years before Richard O'Connor's book was published. It seems at least possible that O'Connor might have borrowed that tune from the film without researching the subject himself.
17. *Daily Sketch*, April 20, 1912.
18. *Brooklyn Daily Eagle*, April 19, 1912.
19. *Scranton Times*, April 20, 1912.
20. Private letter from Edwina Troutt to her friend Annie Webbers, April 19, 1912, reproduced in *On Board*, Behe.
21. *The Spectrum*, April 1914. The full text of this memoir is reproduced in *On Board*, Behe.
22. See the online article 'The Man Who Dressed as a Woman', by George Behe at the following URL for more details: http://home.comcast.net/~georgebehe/titanic/page4.htm.
23. *New York Sun*, April 19, 1912.
24. *The Bulletin*, April 19, 1912.
25. *Seattle Daily Times*, April 27, 1912.
26. Private letter from Edwina Troutt to her friend Annie Webbers, April 19, 1912, reproduced in *On Board*, Behe.
27. *Daily Sketch*, April 20, 1912.
28. *Daily Sketch*, May 1, 1912.
29. *Manchester Guardian*, April 22, 1912.
30. *New York Evening Journal*, April 22, 1912.
31. See the online article 'Did faith drive *Titanic*'s musicians?' by Joey Butler, April 15, 2011. This article is available online at the following URL: http://www.umc.org/site/apps/nlnet/content3.aspx?c=lwL4KnN1LtH&b=5259669&ct=9353535
32. *The Night Lives On*, Ch. 11, by Walter Lord, 1986.
33. *The Hartford Courant*, April 20, 1931. Since this account was given 19 years after the sinking, it is possible that Ms Webber was incorporating details into her account that she read in the press; this may have included Bride's mention, in his famous 1912 *New York Times* account, of 'Autumn' being played.
34. *Collier's Weekly*, May 4, 1912.

APPENDIX K: SHOTS IN THE DARK: DID AN OFFICER COMMIT SUICIDE ON THE *TITANIC*?

1. This appendix is an updated, revised, and expanded version of the article 'Shedding Light on the Controversy: Did an Officer Commit Suicide on the *Titanic*?' by Bill Wormstedt and Tad Fitch, published in *The Titanic Commutator* No. 173, 2006. An online version of this article is available online at: http://wormstedt.com/Titanic/shots/shots.htm
2. *New York Morning World*, April 18, 1912.
3. The entire Daly account is contained in James Harper's article, 'Dr. Frank Blackmarr's Remarkable Scrapbook', published in the *Titanic Commutator*, 3rd Quarter 1998, and is also available online at: http://wormstedt.com/Titanic/shots/shots.htm.
4. *Chicago Daily Tribune*, April 20, 1912.
5. *London Daily Telegraph*, May 4, 1912.
6. *Daily Sketch*, May 4, 1912.
7. *Washington Post*, April 22, 1912.
8. *New York Times*, June 26, 1915.
9. Mary Daly Joyce, Eugene Daly's daughter, recalled this during a speech at the Missouri *Titanic* monument dedication at the Dickey House in Marshfield, Missouri, on April 26, 2008.
10. *The Providence Journal*, April 20, 1912.
11. *Irish World*, May 4, 1912.
12. Br. 2131; 2170–2171. Besides the description of the launch sequence and the deck the boats loaded from, another detail supports the conclusion that Maggie Daly and Bertha Mulvihill were in Boat No. 15: Bertha recalled that her boat was so heavily loaded that the gunwale was barely above the water. No. 15, with sixty-eight aboard, was the most heavily loaded boat that night. ('*Titanic* Lifeboat Occupancy Totals', by Bill Wormstedt and Tad Fitch, at http://wormstedt.com/titanic/lifeboats/occupancy.pdf.) Bertha's description is supported by Steward Rule, also rescued in No. 15, who said that the boat was down in the water 'right to the gunwales'. (Br. 6618; Br. 6621)

Bertha also told her family that there was a lot of shouting from the boat launched prior to theirs, and also a great hurry to cut the ropes; this sounds very much like the situation as Boat No. 15 nearly came down on top of No. 13. Neither Bertha nor Maggie Daly mentioned gunfire at or near their boat, which should have been the case if they were rescued in any of the aft port boats. Neither claimed to have been rescued in a collapsible, and Daly's letter does not indicate that it was a collapsible, either.

Additionally, Trimmer Cavell testified that the majority of those saved in No. 15 were Third Class women, (Br. 4369) and that there were a lot of 'Irish girls' in the boat. (Br. 4371)

Since the first printing of this book, the presence of Bertha and Maggie in this boat has been confirmed. Bertha stated in a private account that 'we climbed ... to crowd into boat 15', and also "the people ... saw boat 15 lowering by their deck and ... jumped into the boat ... [they] fell on me ... I had broken ribs from it'.
13. Br. 6537; 6587–6590; 6648–6658.
14. 'Dr. Frank Blackmarr's Remarkable Scrapbook', published in the *Titanic Commutator*, 3rd Quarter 1998.
15. Private letter written by Laura Francatelli on April 18, 1912. The full text of the letter is available online at http://wormstedt.com/Titanic/shots/Francatelli.html.
16. Private letter written by George Rheims on April 19, 1912. The full text of this letter is available online at http://wormstedt.com/Titanic/shots/rheims.html.
17. *New York Herald*, April 20, 1912.
18. Deposition of George Rheims given in the Limitation of Liability hearings on November 14, 1913.
19. *Ibid*.
20. *Main Line Life*, May 11, 1997.
21. Written report of Harold Bride to the Marconi Company, written on April 27, 1912, and entered into evidence on Day 4 of the Senate Inquiry.
22. *New York Times*, April 19, 1912.
23. Please see Appendix M: Down With the Ship? Captain Smith's Fate for further evidence on what happened to the Captain.
24. *The Truth About The Titanic*, Ch. 3.
25. *The Truth About The Titanic*, Ch. 2.
26. Amer. 991–992.

27. Please see Appendix H: Incidents of Gunfire During the Sinking, for more details on this subject.
28. Amer. 993.
29. *The Truth About The Titanic*, Ch. 2.
30. Amer. 666.
31. Amer. 994.
32. *Dumfries & Galloway Standard and Advertiser*, May 11, 1912.
33. *Titanic: Sinking the Myths*, by Diana E. Bristow, 1995.
34. *The Sinking of the Titanic*, by Logan Marshall, 1912.
35. *The Semi-Monthly Magazine*, May 1912.
36. *Evening Star*, April 22, 1912. The full newspaper article is available online at: http://wormstedt.com/Titanic/shots/davis.html.
37. *Bureau County Republican*, May 2, 1912.
38. *New York Herald*, April 19, 1912.
39. *The Complete Titanic*, by Steven Spignesi, 1998.
40. *New York Herald*, April 19, 1912. The entire article is available online at: http://wormstedt.com/Titanic/shots/hyman.html.
41. *New York Times*, April 19, 1912.
42. *Chicago American*, April 25, 1912.
43. *New York Herald*, April 19, 1912.
44. *New York Evening World*, April 20, 1912.
45. *Nearer My God to Thee: The Story of the Titanic*, 1912.
46. *The Tacoma Tribune*, April 30, 1912; *The Seattle Daily Times*, April 30, 1912.
47. *Cleveland Plain Dealer*, April 26, 1912.
48. Unknown British newspaper, May 1912. The word 'started', supplied in the quotation, is a guess based on the sentence structure; the original copy has a mark over the word, making it nearly illegible. Some room for interpretation should be allowed on this word's inclusion.
49. *Daily Enterprise*, April 20, 1912.
50. Amer. 1099.
51. *New York Times*, April 21, 1912.
52. *Washington Post*, April 20, 1912.
53. *New York Herald*, April 21, 1912.
54. Thomas Whiteley's *Titanic* lecture.
55. *New York Times*, April 20, 1912.
56. *Milwaukee Journal Sentinel*, April 20, 1912.
57. *New York Herald*, April 19, 1912.
58. *Sinking of the Titanic and Great Sea Disasters*, by Logan Marshall, 1912.
59. For further details on Mellors' account, please see Appendix M: Down With the Ship? Captain Smith's Fate.
60. *New York Times*, April 19, 1912.
61. *Daily Sketch*, April 29, 1912.
62. Please see Appendix M: Down With the Ship? Captain Smith's Fate.
63. *New York Herald*, April 19, 1912.
64. *New York Times*, April 19, 1912. The full account is available online at: http://wormstedt.com/Titanic/shots/kemp.htm.
65. *Ibid.*
66. *Cleveland Plain Dealer*, April 20, 1912.
67. This information can be found online at the following URL: http://www.dalbeattie.com/titanic/tihbride.htm#newinfo.
68. *New York Herald*, April 21, 1912.
69. *Titanic: The Canadian Story*, by Alan Hustak, 1998.
70. *Washington Times*, April 19, 1912.
71. *New York Times*, April 20, 1912.
72. Br. 3855–3857.
73. *The Truth About The Titanic*, Ch. 7; Information on the Daniel mention in the Davidson letter is courtesy of Peter Engberg-Klarström.
74. *New York Tribune*, April 19, 1912.
75. Dr Dodge's address at the Commonwealth Club, May 11, 1912.
76. *Denver Post*, April 19, 1912.
77. *Daily Sketch*, April 20, 1912.
78. Br. 12920–12970. For more information on the veracity of the Lady Duff Gordon's accounts, please see Appendix G: The Duff Gordon Affair.
79. *Western Daily Mercury*, April 29, 1912. For the full account, see http://wormstedt.com/Titanic/shots/harris.html.
80. *The Sinking of the Titanic*, by Logan Marshall, 1912.
81. Amer. 1143.
82. *The Sinking of the Titanic*, by Jay Henry Mowbray, 1912. The 'QM Moody' accounts are available online at http://wormstedt.com/Titanic/shots/moody.html.
83. *Atlanta Journal*, April 21, 1912.
84. *Daily Sketch*, April 30, 1912.
85. Amer. 406–407.
86. *Sinking of the Titanic and Great Sea Disasters*, by Logan Marshall, 1912; *The Sinking of the Titanic*, by Logan Marshall, 1912.
87. Since the names of the witnesses who gave these accounts is unknown, their reliability cannot be established.
88. *News of the World*, April 21, 1912.
89. *Liverpool Echo*, April 29, 1912.
90. *Western Daily Mercury*, April 29, 1912. The full account of this unknown crewmember is available online at http://wormstedt.com/Titanic/shots/unknown1.html.
91. *Western Morning News*, April 29, 1912. The full account is available online at http://wormstedt.com/Titanic/shots/unknown2.html.
92. *Titanic & Other Ships*, C. H. Lightoller, 1935.
93. Thayer, 1940.
94. See Appendix H: Incidents of Gunfire During the Sinking, for more details.
95. *Anaconda Standard*, May 6, 1912. Courtesy Mike Poirier.
96. Amer. 975; *The Times*, April 20, 1912.
97. Amer. 1042.
98. *Record of Bodies and Effects: Passengers and Crew, S.S. Titanic*, No. 15, Public Archives of Nova Scotia.
99. *Denver Post*, April 19, 1912.
100. Amer. 604; Amer. 675.
101. Br. 509.
102. Amer. 600.
103. *The Semi-Monthly Magazine*, May, 1912.
104. *Paterson Morning Call*, April 23, 1912.
105. *Titanic Commutator*, Vol. 16, No. 3, November 1992. Extracts from First Class passenger Margaretta Spedden's diary are reproduced in this issue.
106. Private letter from Midtsjø to his brother, April 19, 1912.
107. *New York Times*, April 22, 1912.
108. *New York Herald*, April 19, 1912.
109. *L'Excelsior*, April 20, 1912.
110. Please see Appendix M: Down With the Ship? Captain Smith's Fate.
111. *Northern Constitution*, May 11, 1912.
112. *The Christian Science Journal*, Vol. XXX, October 1912, No. 7.
113. *Amsterdam Evening Recorder*, April 23, 1912. Courtesy Mike Poirier.
114. *The Weekly Telegraph*, May 10, 1912.
115. Information courtesy of Susanne Störmer. This subject was discussed during the 1997 Irish Titanic Historical Society convention.
116. *Cornish Post*, May 2, 1912.
117. Br. 14766.
118. See Chapter 5 and endnotes for further details.
119. See Chapter 5 and endnotes for further details.
120. *Record of Bodies and Effects: Passengers and Crew, S.S. Titanic*, No. 157, Public Archives of Nova Scotia.
121. Amer. 445; *Titanic & Other Ships*, C. H. Lightoller, 1935.
122. Amer. 597.
123. *New York Times*, April 19, 1912; *New York Herald*, April 19, 1912.
124. *Titanic & Other Ships*, C. H. Lightoller, 1935.
125. Please see Chapter 5 and endnotes for details on these sightings.
126. Br. 14565–14568.
127. *New York Times*, April 19, 1912.
128. *Record of Bodies and Effects: Passengers and Crew, S.S. Titanic*, Nos 124 & 96, Public Archives of Nova Scotia.
129. *New York Herald*, April 19, 1912.
130. *The Sinking of the Titanic*, by Logan Marshall, 1912.
131. *Omaha Daily News*, April 21, 1912.
132. *Titanic: Touchstones of a Tragedy: The Timeless Human Drama Revisited through Period Artifacts and Memorabilia*, by Steve Santini, 2000.
133. See Bill Wormstedt's article 'An Analysis of the Bodies Recovered from *Titanic*', which is available at the following URL: http://www.wormstedt.com/Titanic/analysis.html.
134. *The Sinking of the Titanic*, by Jay Henry Mowbray, 1912.
135. Amer. 631.
136. Br. 10628; Br. 10650–10652.

APPENDIX L: THOMAS ANDREWS' FATE

1. Amer. 750.
2. Br. 6596–6600; 6642–6644; Despite Rule's claim that Stewart was in charge of No. 15, Fireman Frank Dymond appears to have assumed command of the boat once it reached the water.
3. *Titanic Remembered*, Madacy Entertainment, 1998. Thank you to Peter Engberg-Klarström for pointing out this account to the authors.
4. Several sources list his name as 'Charles W.N. Fitzpatrick'. However, Fitzpatrick was born in Kilkenny, Ireland, and Irish census records specifically state that his first name was 'Cecil'. (http://www.census.nationalarchives.ie/reels/nai000882528/)
5. *Western Daily Mercury*, April 29, 1912. Account supplied by Ioannis Georgiou.
6. Please see Appendix M: Down With the Ship? Captain Smith's Fate. The portion of Fitzpatrick's account where he says he 'fainted' does not necessarily mean that he lost consciousness, but could instead imply that he was stunned and felt weak in a moment of shock, and that it took him a bit to recover. Whatever he meant, he was not stunned for a long period; it is clear that Captain Smith would not have told Andrews that the ship was 'going' if he did not think that she really was about to.
7. *Liverpool Journal of Commerce*, April 30, 1912.
8. *Belfast's Own*. The details concerning Galloway's letter to Pirrie are contained in this book. The authors extend their appreciation to Stephen Cameron for giving permission to reference this information.
9. Lillian W. Bentham, *Times-Tribune*, 1962. Available online Encyclopedia Titanica at: http://www.encyclopedia-titanica.org/50-years-after-memory-titanic.html.

APPENDIX M: DOWN WITH THE SHIP? CAPTAIN SMITH'S FATE

1. Authors' Note: This appendix is an expanded and revised version of the article: 'Down with the Ship: The Fate of Captain Smith, Parts 1 &

2', by Tad Fitch, published in *The Titanic Commutator*, Nos 183 and 184, 2008.

2. *New York Times*, April 20, 1912.
3. *The Cleveland Leader*, April 19, 1912; *The New York Herald*, April 19, 1912.
4. *New York Herald*, April 19, 1912; *The Chicago Daily Tribune*, April 19, 1912.
5. *New York Times*, April 19, 1912.
6. *New York Herald*, April 21, 1912.
7. *Titanic: The Canadian Story*, Alan Hustak, 1998.
8. *Cleveland Plain Dealer*, April 20, 1912.
9. *Main Line Life*, May 11, 1997. The article in this magazine contains excerpts from Williams' detailed private account written for his family.
10. *New York Herald*, April 19, 1912.
11. *Titanic & Other Ships*, C. H. Lightoller, 1935.
12. *New York Herald*, April 21, 1912. Details of the other Captains and disasters in this section are as reported in the original article.
13. Amer. 69–70.
14. Amer. 671–672.
15. Br. 10585–10588.
16. *The Weekly Telegraph*, May 10, 1912.
17. *Daily Sketch*, April 29, 1912. While Senior did not specify Collapsible A by name, the identity of the craft can be established since he was unaware of how Collapsible B came to be upside-down. If he had helped free Collapsible B, he would have known this, since Lightoller and Bride say this boat landed upside down on the Boat Deck after being pushed off the roof. Furthermore, Senior described seeing First Officer Murdoch fire warning shots in the air while the boats were loading, an incident First Class Passenger Hugh Woolner described in his Senate Inquiry testimony as having happened at Collapsible C. All of this strongly suggests that Senior was on the starboard side at the time.
18. Deposition of Eustace Philip Snow, filed during the British Board of Trade Inquiry. Snow was never called to testify. His deposition still exists and was recently auctioned off. Snow was saved aboard Collapsible B. The words 'takes to' are an extrapolation based on context; the actual word(s) are illegible due to a blemish on the copy presented to us for consideration. Some room for interpretation should be allowed on the reconstruction of these two words.
19. *Main Line Life*, May 11, 1997.
20. Others said that they were released from the Boiler and Engine Rooms at 1:20 a.m. The current authors have retained White's original estimation even though we feel it is outweighed by other eyewitnesses' testimony.
21. *Cleveland Press*, April 20, 1912. White told this story in several press accounts. However, by the time he wrote a private letter to the brother-in-law of the late Harland & Wolff Guarantee Group member William Henry Marsh Parr on June 21, 1912, White's story had changed. In the letter, he claimed that he was *in* the fourth funnel when the ship split in half, and that he fell into the ocean with the funnel. This is completely at odds with his earlier statements. White gave a deposition as part of the British Board of Trade Inquiry, but was never called to testify. His deposition is missing and may no longer be extant.
22. *The Cleveland Leader*, April 19, 1912.
23. There is a good deal of contradictory evidence relating to Robert Daniel's method of escape. First Class passenger Orian Davidson wrote a private letter where she mentions that he was in her boat, No. 3. Colonel Gracie believed Daniel was saved in Boat No. 7. Daniel himself claimed to have been rescued from the water, and other lines of evidence support his assertion. Trimmer Patrick Dillon gave a press interview where he claimed that he and Daniel jumped overboard from the stern. No matter which of these scenarios are accurate, Daniel would not have been near the Bridge at the end, and would thus not have been in a position to witness Captain Smith's fate.
24. *New York Times*, April 19, 1912; *Cleveland Press*, April 19, 1912.
25. *Daily Enterprise*, April 20, 1912.
26. *New York Herald*, April 19, 1912.
27. *New York Times*, April 19, 1912.
28. *Daily Sketch*, April 22, 1912. The HMS *Birkenhead* was a British troopship which struck an uncharted rock off Simon's Bay, South Africa, and sank on February 26, 1852. A large number of the crew and soldiers went down with the ship, and were said to have done so in a brave and stoic manner.
29. Unidentified New York newspaper, April 20, 1912.
30. *New York Herald*, April 20, 1912; *Daily Sketch*, April 17, 1912.
31. *Daily Sketch*, April 25, 1912.
32. *The Chicago Daily Tribune*, April 19, 1912.
33. *Cleveland Press*, April 19, 1912.
34. April 27, 1912 report of Junior Marconi Operator Harold Sidney Bride to the Marconi Company, entered into evidence on Day 4 of the United States Senate Inquiry.
35. Amer. 897.
36. *New York Times*, April 28, 1912.
37. Br. 14035–14036.
38. *Titanic & Other Ships*, C. H. Lightoller, 1935.
39. Amer. 666.
40. *Sinking of the Titanic and Great Sea Disasters*, Logan Marshall, 1912.
41. *New York Times*, June 27, 1915; Private letter from William Mellors to Dorothy Ockenden written on May 9, 1912, courtesy of Brian Ticehurst. Mellors testified in the Limitation of Liability hearings before Judge

Julius M. Meyer in the United States District Court on June 26, 1915. Press summaries indicate that he gave detailed accounts of the events at the end. Unfortunately, the transcripts of his testimony, which could confirm the details relating to Smith, are lost and may no longer exist.
42. *Western Daily Mercury*, April 29, 1912. Courtesy of Ioannis Georgiou.
43. *Belfast's Own*.
44. *Western Daily Mercury*, April 29, 1912. Courtesy of Ioannis Georgiou.
45. *Ibid.*
46. Br. 10630.
47. *New York Times*, April 19, 1912. Senior gave a deposition detailing his experiences as part of the British Inquiry, but unfortunately was never called to testify. Senior's deposition is missing and may no longer be extant.
48. *Cleveland Leader*, April 21, 1912. McGann was rescued aboard Collapsible B. McGann gave a deposition for the British Inquiry, but he was not called to testify, and the deposition is missing.
49. *New York Times*, April 20, 1912.
50. *Milwaukee Journal Sentinel*, April 20, 1912.
51. *Chicago Daily Tribune*, April 19, 1912.
52. *Washington Times*, April 19, 1912.
53. Amer. 406–407.
54. *Atlantic City Daily Press*, April 23, 1912.
55. *Cleveland Plain Dealer*, April 19, 1912.
56. *Washington Times*, April 19, 1912.
57. *New York Times*, April 20, 1912.
58. *Daily Sketch*, April 30, 1912.
59. *Western Daily Mercury*, April 29, 1912.
60. *New York Herald*, April 19, 1912.
61. *New York Evening World*, April 20, 1912.
62. *American Semi-Monthly Magazine*, May 1912.
63. *Cleveland Plain Dealer*, April 20, 1912.
64. *New York Herald*, April 20, 1912.
65. *Washington Herald*, April 21, 1912.
66. Thayer, 1940.
67. *The Truth About Titanic*, Colonel Archibald Gracie, 1913, Ch. 5.
68. *Chicago Daily Tribune*, April 19, 1912.
69. Br. 6099. Maynard gave a deposition as part of the British Inquiry, but was not called to give testimony. The whereabouts of his deposition, if it still exists, is unknown.
70. *New York Times*, April 19, 1912.
71. *Daily Sketch*, April 29, 1912.
72. *Chicago Daily Tribune*, April 21, 1912.
73. Amer. 628.
74. *Daily Sketch*, April 30, 1912.
75. *Shoreman Herald*, July 25, 2009.
76. *Western Morning News*, April 29, 1912.
77. *New York Evening World*, April 20, 1912.
78. *New York Herald*, April 20, 1912.
79. *New York Times*, April 21, 1912.
80. *London Daily Telegraph*, April 29, 1912.
81. *New York Herald*, April 19, 1912.
82. *A Night to Remember*.
83. Private correspondence between Walter Hurst and Walter Lord, currently housed with Walter Lord's collection in the National Maritime Museum in Greenwich. Courtesy of Paul Lee.
84. 'Steerage Story' from the diary of *Carpathia* passenger Doctor Frank Blackmarr. The entire Daly account is contained in James Harper's article, 'Dr. Frank Blackmarr's Remarkable Scrapbook', published in the *Titanic Commutator*, 3rd Quarter 1998.
85. *New York Herald*, April 20, 1912. McMicken did not witness these events himself, having left in a lifeboat, possibly No. 11, sometime before the sinking.
86. *The Truth About the Titanic*, Ch. 5.
87. *New York Times*, July 21, 1912. Captain Peter Pryal claimed that he saw Captain Smith in Baltimore several months after the disaster. Pryal served with Smith on the *Majestic*, and said that there was no possibility that he was mistaken in his identification. Pryal claimed that after a brief conversation, Smith bid him farewell, bought a ticket to Washington, and passed through the gate of the railway station. Whether this account was a joke or if Pryal actually believed it is unknown.
88. Unless otherwise stated, the lifeboat launch times and information on which officer aided in loading which boat are taken from '*Titanic*: The Lifeboat Launch Sequence Re-Examined' by Bill Wormstedt, Tad Fitch and George Behe, with contributions by Sam Halpern and J. Kent Layton, originally published in first form in *The Titanic Commutator*, No. 155, 2001. A revised and expanded version of this article was released online in 2006, with the most recent revisions being added in 2010. It is available at the following URL: http://www.wormstedt.com/Titanic/lifeboats/lifeboats.htm.

APPENDIX N: THE BREAKUP

1. Br. 14094.
2. Although it would admittedly be better to find accounts from every survivor, that simply would not seem to be a realistic or realizable achievement. The accounts about to be considered are taken from

passengers of every class, and crew of every station aboard the ship, both men and women alike; they are also drawn from those who were close to or aboard the ship, as well as those much farther away from the ship, in those final minutes. As the present authors went through the collection process, turned up additional accounts, and rolled them into the mathematical calculations we are about to present, we noticed something about the numbers: the comparable percentages of who said what happened during the sinking (broke, didn't break, etc.) did not alter widely. For these two reasons, we believe that this unprecedented collection of survivor evidence is a very representative and fair collection of the entire body of survivors.

3. This last reference is drawn from the typed notes of August Wennerström used in his talks about the disaster, preserved by the Wennerström family. Courtesy of Jerry Wennerström and Mike Herbold.

4. These two women were sisters, Miss Elizabeth Eustis and Mrs Martha (Walter B.) Stephenson. Their joint account was given directly to Col. Archibald Gracie for publication in his 1913 book, *The Truth About the Titanic*. The reference to 'She's broken' can be found on page 196 of the 1913 edition.

5. *The Titanic: End of a Dream*, Wyn Craig Wade (Rawson, Wade, 1979), pg. 228.

6. *The Auburn Citizen*, April 18, 1912 (Courtesy Mike Poirier).

7. Described in a letter written to her father after she arrived in New York following the disaster. The full contents of the letter can be found in *On Board*, Behe, 159. Originally published in *Sondmoorsposten*, May 28, 1912.

8. *The Truth About the Titanic*, Chs 3, 6.

9. Caroline Bonnell began to pen her account before the *Carpathia* arrived in New York, and she completed it shortly thereafter. It can be read in its entirety in *On Board*, Behe, 209–213. Originally published in *The Decatur Review*, April 19, 1912.

10. 4.69%, to be exact. The accounts of Second Class Passenger Lawrence Beesley are interesting. His earliest published account, given in the *Toronto World* of April 19, 1912 (contained in *On Board*, Behe, 157–162), and many of his subsequent early accounts (contained in *On Board*, Behe, 194–208) do not say anything about a breakup either way. However, in his 1912 book, *The Loss of the S.S. Titanic*, Beesley said that he was aware of accounts of explosions and that the ship broke in half. He said that he had heard of such accounts even while aboard the *Carpathia*. While much of the personal narrative in his book is based heavily on his early account published in the *Toronto World*, he paused in the middle of the account to tackle the reports of a breakup. He wrote:

> No phenomenon like that pictured in some American and English papers occurred—that of the ship breaking in two, and the two ends being raised above the surface. I saw these drawings in preparation on board the *Carpathia*, and said at the time that they bore no resemblance to what actually happened.

It seems most likely that the 'drawings' he referred to were the famous drawings made by L. D. Skidmore after listening to Jack Thayer's description of the sinking. It is obvious that those drawings – which showed the ship's prow bursting up from beneath the surface during the breakup – were inaccurate by any measure. It was this inaccurate portrayal of events which seemed to have stood out so negatively to Beesley, and for good reason.

11. Fifth Officer Lowe, at both inquiries, gave some relatively detailed evidence about the sinking. At the American Inquiry, he described her as rearing up to about a 75° angle and then sinking. When asked at the British Inquiry if the ship had righted herself near the end, Lowe stated that she did not. However, he was not specifically asked whether or not the ship broke, and thus never clearly went on the record on the point. For this reason, the current authors have placed Lowe in the 'didn't specifically say' category; even if he specifically believed that the ship had sunk intact, however, it does not materially affect the overall sum of evidence on the point. In not including him as saying that the '*Titanic* sank intact', we seem to be in good company; even Walter Lord, in *The Night Lives On*, did not list Lowe with Lightoller, Pitman, Gracie and Beesley.

12. It was said by those working on the set that the model used to depict the breakup scene was placed at a 45° angle. A careful study of the angle depicted in the scene where the ship's lights fail, immediately before the breakup and where the horizon is visible for a reference, shows an angle slightly less than that. There are a number of good sight lines to read the angle from, including the waterline, the edges of the Boat and Promenade Decks, etc.

    Due to the perspective of viewing a three-dimensional object, the angles do alter toward the perceived vanishing point. They range from a minimum of about 37° at the Boat Deck up to a maximum of 49° at the turn of the bilge; if one does not count the bilge line, which was slightly tapered as the hull narrowed and probably adds to the POV angle visible in the scene, then the average shown on film is almost precisely 40°. In the split second between when the lights begin to fail until just before the scene cut, the angle visibly increases by about one further degree.

In a view of the side of the ship during the break, where no horizon is visible, the angle seems greater – up to an average over 48° – but without a visible horizon, there is no reference point. The next cut, a true 'side on' and close perspective showing the hull tearing apart, seems to show the ship remaining at about the 41° angle shown in the moment after the lights fail. The final cut, immediately following, returns to a perspective quite similar to that shown during the light failure sequence, and shows the bow forward of the break increasing steadily from about a 42° angle. Thus, in finished scenes from the movie, all sightlines with a visible horizon seem to depict a maximum 42° angle as the ship's structure is failing.

13. The wave depicted in that scene is one of the details most often complained about by those with a critical eye. While releasing the model in such an unrestrained manner certainly caused a large wave upon final impact (in the area of the rudder and screws), the exaggerated, enormous, frothy wave flying out from under the forward end of stern section seems to have been more the result of cinematic special effects. We will soon be delving more deeply into the question of a wave, or lack thereof – and why or why not it would have existed – in the narrative.

14. Details of the model used for the breakup and final sinking sequences, the methods of filming, etc., can be found in *Cinefex* No. 72, pgs 118–122.

15. It should be noted that although the conclusions from that particular investigation are widely accepted, not everyone finds them satisfactory.

16. On the vessels' Iron Plans, the staircase is clearly picked out with the handwritten notation: 'New stairway opening 401 [*Titanic*] 26/9/11 [Sept. 26, 1911]'.

17. 'Angles of Trim and Heel', by Sam Halpern (*The Titanic Commutator*, Issue 174, pgs 104–112; 'Finding the Apparent Floatation Pivot Point (AFPP)', by Sam Halpern (available online at: http://www.titanicology.com/Titanica/Finding_the_AFPP.pdf).

18. As the reader proceeds in reading the survivor recollections contained in this appendix, it will quickly become obvious that it has been necessary, in some cases, to piece accounts back together from lengthy stretches of testimony or accounts that were not given entirely in a chronological manner. In so doing, it has at times been necessary to insert bracketed words or phrases to make the sentences complete and understandable. This was done for two primary reasons: first, to save space, as quoting the back and forth of testimony and questions would have taken up a great deal of room; second, this was done to try to show clearly all of the points that any given eyewitness gave about events in any given stage of the ship's sinking in a condensed area, so that their full import becomes obvious. In putting the accounts together in this manner, the present authors have very carefully studied the context of all statements, and we have referenced the accounts back to their primary sources. This is done so a reader may independently verify that the quotations are accurate, in context, and have not been deliberately 'forced' into saying something that the original witness did not actually refer to.

The current authors also have not included every statement from every eyewitness account that we considered in the course of this project. Many of them are repetitive in nature, or are held in private collections. We believe that those included are a very good representation of the overall picture.

19. Br. 413–419.

20. Amer. 1108.

21. Amer. 599.

22. This account was quoted in *The Breakup of Titanic: A Progress Report from the Marine Forensics Panel* (SD-7), by Roy F. Mengot & Richard T. Woytowich.

23. *Barrier Miner*, May 4, 1934. Courtesy Mike Poirier.

24. *Titanic & Other Ships*, C. H. Lightoller, 1935.

25. From an account of his experiences dictated by Thayer on April 20, 1912. Held in the collection of George Behe. Account reproduced in *On Board*, Behe, 412–414.

26. This quote comes from a letter by Mellors to Dorothy Ockenden dated May 12, 1912. Permission to quote from this letter was kindly given by Brian Ticehurst, and his permission is greatly appreciated. The full text of the letter, from beginning to end, can also be found in *On Board*, Behe, 359–361.

27. *Western Daily Mercury*, April 29, 1912.

28. This theory has been arrived at after consultation with a number of *Titanic* researchers, including Sam Halpern and Scott Andrews, whose input is greatly valued. After some discussion, this consensus emerged as the most likely candidate. While the way the ship moved in those moments is known, it should be remembered that the explanation for this chain of events is merely an educated guess; further evidence may come to light in the future that suggests an alternative explanation.

29. Br. 6040–6051. Joughin had admittedly consumed a large amount of alcohol during the sinking; it is even possible that the 'drink of water' he referred to in his testimony here was further consumption of alcohol. Interestingly, his testimony about events in those final minutes seems to be remarkably clear-headed. However, his inebriated state should be taken into account when reading his testimony.

30. *The Truth About the Titanic*, Chs 2, 4. The personal narrative was interrupted at the end of Chapter 2 for some perspective from other eyewitnesses in Chapter 3, before resuming in Chapter 4.
31. *Washington Post Semi-Monthly Magazine*, May 26, 1912, available in full in *On Board*, Behe, 246–254.
32. Miss Bonnell's account appeared in the *Decatur Review*, April 19, 1912, and appears in *On Board*, Behe, 209–213.
33. From Beesley's account published in the *Toronto World* of April 19, 1912. The account was penned by Beesley before landing in New York from the *Carpathia*. The entire account can be read in *On Board*, Behe, 157–163.
34. Beesley, Ch. 4.
35. *Westmouth Independent* (1912, date unknown), available in *On Board*, Behe, 259–260.
36. Br. 418, 422.
37. Br. 11502–11511.
38. Br. 3114.
39. Amer. 1108.
40. From two separate accounts given by Thayer. The first sentence comes from an account of his experiences dictated by Thayer on April 20, 1912. Held in the collection of George Behe. Account reproduced in *On Board*, Behe, 412–414. The remainder of the quotation comes from *The Evening Bulletin*, April 14, 1932.
41. Br. 14072–14084. Instead of copying whole sections of question-and-answer testimony for this section, certain words or phrases from the original questions are included in brackets to complete the sentences in this quotation. This has been done primarily to show the statements without interruption, in harmony with the format of other survivor accounts quoted in this appendix which were not taken from the inquiries.
42. Amer. 620.
43. Amer. 841.
44. *Voices*, 161.
45. Amer. 818.
46. Amer. 116.
47. Amer. 610.
48. Amer. 339.
49. For clarification: the Washington Monument stands 555 feet tall, about 63% of the *Titanic*'s length overall. The Eiffel Tower's top observation deck stands some 902 feet above ground, only twenty feet higher than the *Titanic*'s length overall.
50. *Jigsaw*, Taylor.
51. Account text provided by George Behe.
52. *Titanic & Other Ships*, C. H. Lightoller, 1935.
53. Br. 20921.
54. *The Truth About the Titanic*, Ch. 3.
55. Br. 14097.
56. Br. 6040–6051. Joughin's inebriated state should be taken into account when reading his testimony.
57. Br. 6041.
58. *The Truth About the Titanic*, Ch. 2.
59. From Beesley's account published in the *Toronto World* of April 19, 1912. The account was penned by Beesley before landing in New York from the *Carpathia*. The entire account can be read in *On Board*, Behe, 157–163.
60. Beesley, Ch. 4.
61. Amer. 980.
62. *New York Sun*, April 19, 1912. Available in full in *On Board*, Behe, 179–182.
63. *Indiscretions*.
64. *Rhode Island Sunday Magazine*, April 15, 1962. Courtesy Mike Poirier.
65. *On Board*, Behe, 406.
66. *The Truth About the Titanic*, Ch. 7.
67. From Rheims' Limitation of Liability Hearings Deposition.
68. *Harper's Weekly*, April 27, 1912. Available in *On Board*, Behe, 317–319.
69. *Voices*, 161.
70. Br. 175–177.
71. *New Britain Herald*, April 19, 1912. Available in *On Board*, Behe, 175.
72. Amer. 599.
73. *The Hartford Courant*, April 20, 1931. Courtesy Mike Poirier.
74. *Syracuse Herald*, April 23, 1912. Courtesy Mike Poirier.
75. *Democrat & Chronicle*, April 15, 1931. Courtesy Mike Poirier.
76. *East Kent Gazette*, May 4, 1912. Available in *On Board*, Behe, 132–134.
77. Amer. 339.
78. *Hudson Evening Register*, April 20, 1912. Available in *On Board*, Behe, 143–144.
79. Account published in *The Times* in 1932, re-printed in 1985, provided by Mike Poirier.
80. Account from Nellie Becker published in the *The Madras* [India] *Mail*, (1868–1981), May 22, 1912
81. *St. Nicholas Magazine*, 1913. Text available in *On Board*, Behe, 191–193.
82. *Washington Post Semi-Monthly Magazine*, May 26, 1912. Text available in *On Board*, Behe, 246–254.
83. *Manitoba Free Press*, April 29, 1912. Available in *On Board*, Behe, 258–259.
84. Washington Dodge, *The Loss of the Titanic*. Text available in *On Board*, Behe, 264–277.
85. *Hampshire Telegraph*, May 3, 1912. Text available in *On Board*, Behe, 284.
86. *Ilford Graphic*, May 10, 1912. Text available in *On Board*, Behe, 327.
87. *Brainerd Daily Dispatch*, December 2, 1937. Text available in *On Board*, Behe, 347.
88. Private letter from William Mellors to Dorothy Ockenden written on May 9, 1912, courtesy of Brian Ticehurst.
89. *Brooklyn Daily Eagle*, April 19, 1912. Text available in *On Board*, Behe, 367.
90. Amer. 1108.
91. From Scarrott's account published in *The Sphere* of May 25, 1912. Text available in *On Board*, Behe, 386.
92. Br. 426.
93. *Westmeath Independent*, 1912 (unknown date). Text available in *On Board*, Behe, 259–260.
94. It should be noted that portions of three accounts from John Thayer, Jr are given here. Each is referenced separately. The first account was taken very shortly after the disaster, while the second two were published in 1932 and 1940, respectively. While overall quite complementary, there are a few variations between them. As with all survivor accounts, without a good reason to suspect otherwise the present authors tend to view the earlier ones as less susceptible to errors or mistakes; the same would hold true of Thayer's accounts. One deviation is that in his 1940 recollections, the fall of the second funnel sounds as if it is connected with the breakup of the ship, and the location of the break seems to be further forward than given in his previous accounts. According to his 1912 account, it seems that the No. 2 funnel fell just before the breakup occurred, but he does not necessarily connect the two events as he seemed to in his 1940 account. Either way, it seems that the No. 2 funnel fell very close to the time of the ship's visible breakup.
95. Jack Thayer's private account, April 20, 1912. Courtesy George Behe. Available in *On Board*, Behe, 413–414.
96. *The Evening Bulletin*, April 14, 1932.
97. Thayer, 1940.
98. Br. 11501–11525.
99. Br. 3108–3119.
100. Br. 3858–3869.
101. Br. 5674–5682. When asked pointedly if the ship had broken 'between the third and fourth funnels', Scott replied in the negative, and very specifically stated that she had broken *behind* the No. 4 ventilating funnel.
102. Br. 14097.
103. *Titanic & Other Ships*, C. H. Lightoller, 1935.
104. Amer. 541.
105. Amer. 621.
106. Amer. 630.
107. Amer. 638.
108. Amer. 839–841.
109. *Seattle Daily Times*, April 22, 23, 1912. Text available in *On Board*, Behe, 287–299.
110. *Philadelphia Evening Bulletin*, April (29?), 1912. Account available in *On Board*, Behe, 305.
111. *Chicago Tribune*, April 22, 1912.
112. Amer. 609–610.
113. Amer. 753.
114. This account was quoted in *The Breakup of Titanic: A Progress Report from the Marine Forensics Panel* (SD-7), by Roy F. Mengot & Richard T. Woytowich.
115. Amer. 410–411.
116. From a lecture given by Whiteley, available on Encyclopedia Titanica at: http://www.encyclopedia-titanica.org/thomas-whiteleys-titanic-lecture.html.
117. *The Evening Tribune*, April 23, 1912. Courtesy Mike Poirier.
118. *Jigsaw*, Taylor.
119. Br. 4094–4102.
120. Br. 4154, 4174, 4175.
121. *The Edwardian Superliners*, 361–362 and 382–383. *Leviathan*, Frank O. Braynard, Vol. 4, pg. 363–365.
122. Br. 4114.
123. Account contained in *The Truth About the Titanic*.
124. *The Washington Herald*, April 19, 1912.
125. From the typed notes of August Wennerström used in his talks about the disaster, preserved by the Wennerström family. Courtesy of Jerry Wennerström and Mike Herbold.
126. Br. 6359–6365.
127. Br. 4109.
128. All of this technical information has been gleaned from *TTSM*, Vol. 1, Chapter 17.
129. The question of who discovered these pieces first created an ugly outburst within the *Titanic* community. The simple truth of the matter is that expeditions prior to 2005 had identified the pieces of hull; however, no full investigation was made of their importance and how they may have fit into the knowledge of the ship's breakup. The 2005 expedition, which had failed to meet some of its initial goals, seems to

have shifted its concentration to these large pieces of double bottom in order to make the most productive use of their trip.

130. *The Breakup of Titanic: A Progress Report from the Marine Forensics Panel* (SD-7), by Roy F. Mengot, UGS, and Richard T. Woytowich, NYC College of Technology (Joint Meeting April 16, 2009), pg. 5.

131. *The Breakup of Titanic*, pg. 5–6.

132. *International Marine Engineering*, May 1912, Volume 17, pgs 198–200.

APPENDIX O: 'J. "BRUTE" ISMAY'?

1. There is also no evidence that Ismay or others connected with him attempted to exert undue influence on the Board's process of deliberating whether or not to raise the regulations.

2. This is a particularly important consideration, and one that runs counter to oft-repeated legends. For further information on how the ships were financed, and the long-term liability that they incurred to the company, please see *Olympic Class* [2011], Appendix Five: 'Financing the *Olympic* Class'.

3. It is also important to remember that each of the ships cost approximately £1.5 million to build, and each carried insurance of only £1 million, with the remaining risk on each being carried by the company's own insurance fund. In other words, if either ship was lost or considered unsalvageable, the company would only receive partial financial compensation for that loss. Damage to the company's reputation and the inability to operate an effective weekly service while replacement tonnage was financed, constructed and placed in service would have produced further damage to the line.

4. Br. 18387-18395. Ismay had taken the maiden voyage of the *Olympic* the year before, and of many other White Star liners before that. Some of his testimony about their conversation does not meet facts: the ship was not short of coal, and based on her location at the time of the collision and the admission Ismay made that they might run her at top speed on Monday or Tuesday, it is clear that she would easily have arrived in New York on Tuesday evening; Ismay may have been trying to 'rewrite history' by downplaying any question of the ship's speed during the voyage, even though Captain Smith was only steaming according to general practice of the time.

5. Many pieces of personal correspondence written *before* the ship sank mentioned the possibility of arriving on Tuesday. These were later corroborated by survivors such as Elizabeth Lines, Lawrence Beesley, and others. To see some of these accounts, please see *On Board*, Behe.

   It is clear that the potential for, even probability of, a Tuesday night arrival was not something concocted after the sinking to try to prove culpability on the part of Ismay or the White Star Line. All evidence from this correspondence also indicates that the potential for a Tuesday night arrival was a welcome concept to both passengers and crew.

6. The 1997 James Cameron film, *Titanic*, portrayed the Saturday afternoon conversation between Ismay and Smith for the first time. An actress can even be spotted in the background in the scene, visibly taking note of their discussion; while no actress is credited as portraying Mrs Lines in the film's credits, the Fox special *Breaking New Ground* clearly highlighted the attention to detail behind the scene, and showed the actress in a close-up while discussing Mrs. Lines' observations. That being said, the content of the conversation in the film does not seem to closely parallel Mrs Lines' accounts. Ismay is portrayed as clearly pushing the Captain to do something that he did not feel comfortable doing; yet there is no historical indication that Ismay was pushing Smith — merely that Ismay was pleased by the information on the ship's progress and enthusiastic about their prospects for beating the *Olympic*'s maiden voyage record.

   In the scene where Captain Smith visits Lightoller on the Bridge a couple of hours before the collision, Lightoller offers a hesitant warning; Smith pauses to reflect – perhaps weighing Ismay's pressure to go faster? Yet Smith decides to maintain speed. Again, since there is no historical evidence that Captain Smith was uncomfortable with the ship's speed, Ismay's purported influence seems blown out of proportion.

7. Thayer, 1940.

8. For more information on the events surrounding the loading of these boats, please see Appendix H and Appendix K.

9. In portraying the moment Ismay stepped aboard, the three most recognized films on the disaster show nearby officers looking on in almost universal disgust and contempt. In *S.O.S. Titanic*, Captain Smith gazes from the Bridge wing, clearly enraged, as his officers look on in surprise; in *A Night to Remember*, a stunned Murdoch halts the lowering before reversing his decision and telling the men at the falls to continue; in Cameron's *Titanic*, Ismay leaps aboard seconds before the lowering begins, Murdoch is surprised but simply orders the craft to be lowered away. It is quite likely that these portrayals are not far from the truth, but from a historical perspective there is no supporting direct evidence.

10. It would seem that Murdoch did draw the line, however, when people attempted to sneak into the boats and their actions caused potential risk to passengers. It would seem that Murdoch had earlier threatened to get his gun when the Frauenthal brothers jumped into Boat No. 5; Amy Stanley also believed that someone jumped into Collapsible C as it was being lowered away, drawing a round of gunfire in protest. However, that man was not Ismay, as Amy believed the man had a baby aboard the boat.

11. Please see the Postscript for details on Ismay's life after the disaster.

APPENDIX P: BURIED AT SEA

1. Amer. 23.

2. Beesley, Ch. 7.

3. Amer. 23; Br. 25485.

4. Information on Brown's account courtesy of Chris Dohany.

5. *Daily Sketch*, May 6, 1912. This account is reproduced in *Carpathia*, Behe.

6. *Tramps and Ladies*, Ch. 23.

7. *The Sinking of Titanic and Great Sea Disasters*, by Logan Marshall, 1912.

8. *Daily Sketch*, May 6, 1912. Account is reproduced in full in *Carpathia*, Behe.

9. *New York Sun*, April 19, 1912. Account is contained in *Carpathia*, Behe.

10. Amer. 408; Amer. 412.

11. *New York Times*, April 27, 1912; Br. 441; Amer. 616; Amer. 678–679.

12. Amer. 1108; *The Truth About the Titanic*, Ch. 6.

13. *The Truth About the Titanic*, Ch. 6.

14. Amer. 582.

15. Amer. 668.

16. Br. 3933–3934.

17. Amer. 794–797. Cunningham doesn't mention Siebert by name, but both men were Bedroom Stewards, and served together. Given the evidence that Siebert's body was taken aboard *Carpathia*, and that he died in Boat No. 4, it seems reasonable to conclude that he was the 'mate' referred to in Cunningham's testimony.

18. *The Truth About the Titanic*, Ch. 5.

19. Amer. 670.

20. *New York Times*, April 19, 1912.

21. Amer. 162.

22. *The Truth About the Titanic*, Ch. 5.

23. Amer. 73.

24. *Titanic & Other Ships*, C. H. Lightoller, 1935.

25. *Bangor Daily Commercial*, April 19, 1912.

26. See George Behe's article 'The Fate of Jack Phillips', for an in-depth examination of the evidence, or lack thereof, that Phillips died on Collapsible B and was buried at sea from *Carpathia*. This article is available online at the following URL: http://home.comcast.net/~georgebehe/titanic/Page13.htm.

27. Br. 25485.

28. *Bangor Daily Commercial*, April 19, 1912.

29. *Triumph & Tragedy*. It is claimed in this book that Lindell's body was recovered and buried at sea from *Carpathia*.

30. From the typed notes of August Wennerström used in his talks about the disaster, preserved by the Wennerström family. Courtesy of Jerry Wennerström and Mike Herbold.

31. *Cork Examiner*, May 16, 1912.

32. Amer. 412.

33. Private communication with George Behe, October 18, 2011. Information relating to Willwerth is contained in immigration papers.

APPENDIX Q: TRAPPED 'LIKE RATS'?

1. Archibald Gracie, writing of one such rail and gate (*The Truth About the Titanic*, Ch. 2), said that he easily vaulted over these.

2. Such Bostwick gates were not included in the *Titanic*'s original plans. However, such gates were not always included in plans for her sisters where gates were known to exist. If they existed, the location of these gates can only be speculated upon. Exploration within the wreck of the liner show no gates along accessible portions of Scotland Road on E Deck.

3. Br. 19949.

4. Br. 3288.

5. *On Board*, Behe 313.

6. It is conceivable that there were yet others within the Entrance at the time who did not have time to make it on the deck by the time the ship took her head-first plunge. This is apparently the basis for the scenes in the 1997 film, where crew and Third Class passengers alike are trapped within the Grand Staircase and Entrance as the water floods into the area. The historical possibility that others were still within the Entrance at the time of the plunge makes the scene in the film even more devastating to watch.

7. Although there is not enough room for all of the passenger accounts touching upon this subject to be included here, some of them are found within the narrative of Chapters 4 and 5. The present authors would recommend that the reader refer to Appendix J: The Question of Locked Gates, of *Centennial Reappraisal* for further details on the subject.

8. See Bill Wormstedt's article 'An Analysis of the Bodies Recovered from the *Titanic*', for the full breakdown of the bodies recovered, online at http://wormstedt.com/Titanic/analysis.html.

APPENDIX R: THE *CALIFORNIAN* AFFAIR

1. The exact number reported by those on the *Titanic* varies, but the generally accepted number would fall somewhere between six and twelve.

2. Signed statement by Apprentice James Gibson to Captain Lord, April 18, 1912.

3. Br. 7829.

4. Br. 7650, 7651.

5. Br. 7579; 8008–8012. While Second Officer Stone would not state with certainty that the lights were rockets, Apprentice James Gibson thought that they were.

6. Br. 6931–6948.
7. Please see Appendix D: What Time Is It? for further details.
8. Amer. 715.
9. Amer. 720. Both the position and time estimates were offered into evidence by Captain Lord himself.
10. *Olympic Class* [2011], Appendix 8.
11. For further information on the *Californian/Titanic* incident, please see *Olympic Class*, [2011], Appendix 8; *Centennial Reappraisal*, Chapter 10; articles by Sam Halpern available through his web site, www.titanicology.com.

POSTSCRIPT:

1. *Pawtucket Times*, May 22, 1912. Courtesy Mike Poirier.
2. *Worcester Telegram*, April 20, 1912.
3. All of the details relating to Abbott's post-sinking life are as presented in the article 'The Mystery of Rhoda Abbott Revealed, Unraveling a *Titanic* Enigma', by Robert Bracken, 2004. This article is available online at the following URL: http://www.encyclopedia-titanica.org/rhoda-abbott.html.
4. 840 Fifth Avenue, across from Central Park.
5. *New York Times*, March 28, 1940.
6. *New York Times*, August 15, 1912
7. *Ibid*.
8. *New York Times*, March 28, 1940.
9. Amer. 1140–1141.
10. *City's Unsung Titanic Hero*, by Fred Leigh, February 26, 1987. This article is located online at the following URL: http://www.encyclopedia-titanica.org/citys-unsung-titanic-hero.html
11. The entire interview is available online: http://www.bbc.co.uk/archive/titanic/5049.shtml.
12. *Denver Post*, October 28, 1932; *Molly Brown: Unraveling the Myth. The True Life Story of the Titanic's Most Famous Survivor*, by Kristen Iversen, 1999.
13. *New York Times*, April 21, 1912.
14. *Harold Sidney Bride Research Summary*, by Scott Anderson, 1999. This summary, with a good amount of detail about Bride's post-*Titanic* career and life is available at the following URL: http://www.hf.ro/harry_snk.htm.
15. *Southern Star*, February 7, 1998.
16. *Cork Examiner*, May 7, 1912.
17. *The Evening World*, April 22, 1912; *Irish American*, May 4, 1912.
18. Claim filed in the Limitation of Liability hearings, January 4, 1913; *New York Times*, June 26, 1915.
19. Booklet of the American Red Cross Relief Fund, Case Number 99, 1913; *Eugene Daly – By His Daughter*, by Marion K. Joyce. This entire article is on the Encyclopedia-Titanica website at the following URL: http://www.encyclopedia-titanica.org/eugene-daly-his-daughter.html.
20. Information courtesy of the family of Bertha Mulvihill.
21. Br. 17479–17480.
22. *Southampton Echo*, January 11, 1965; *New York Times*, January 12, 1965; *Voices*.
23. *Voices*. Portions of the Fleet letters are reproduced in the book cited above, and are published in full in the article 'Remembering Frederick Fleet', *The Titanic Commutator*, Vol. 17, No. 1, 1993.
24. *Southampton Echo*, January 11, 1965; *New York Times*, January 12, 1965.
25. Final Report of the British Inquiry.
26. Information courtesy of Randy Bryan Bigham.
27. *New York American*, April 22, 1935.
28. Information courtesy of Randy Bryan Bigham.
29. *Washington Times*, April 18, 1912.
30. *New York Times*, December 5, 1912.
31. *The Times*, April 20, 1912.
32. *New York Times*, May 4, 1913.
33. *New York Times*, December 5, 1912. Gracie's death certificate lists the cause of death as a diabetic coma, and reports its duration.
34. Additional information in this section is as reported in *The Truth About the Titanic*.
35. Amer. 451–453.
36. Unless otherwise noted, all details of Hichens' post-sinking life are drawn from Phil Gowan's article 'Whatever Happened to Robert Hichens?' This article is available at the following URL: www.titanic-titanic.com/article_phil_gowan_bio_robert_hichens.shtml.
37. Amer. 959.
38. *New York Times*, April 19, 1912; *New York Times*, October 19, 1937.
39. For more details on this portion of Ismay's life, please see Appendix O: 'J. "Brute" Ismay'?

40. Br. 18866–18867.
41. Final Report of the British Inquiry.
42. *The Times*, October 18, 1937; Wade, Ch. 'Feuilleton'.
43. *The Times*, October 18, 1937; *New York Times*, October 19, 1937; Wade, Ch. 'Feuilleton'.
44. *Titanic Survivor*, Ch. 20.
45. 'Violet's Barren White Star Wedding', by Senan Molony, 2011. This article is available at the following URL: http://www.encyclopediatitanica.org/violets-barren-white-star-wedding.html.
46 *Titanic Survivor*, Ch. 20.
47. *Paterson Evening News*, December 10, 1956.
48. *Titanic & Other Ships*, C. H. Lightoller, 1935.
49. This interview is available online at: http://www.bbc.co.uk/archive/titanic/5047.shtml.
50. The remainder of the information relating to Lightoller's life is drawn from: *Titanic & Other Ships*, C. H. Lightoller, 1935; *The Odyssey of C.H. Lightoller*, by Patrick Stenson, 1984; and information courtesy of the Royal Navy Museum, and Inger Sheil.
51. Amer. 386.
52. Wade, Ch. 13.
53. The description of this event and the engraving on Lowe's watch are gleaned from the profile of Lowe on the BBC North West Wales Public Life website, which can be found at the following URL: http://www.bbc.co.uk/wales/northwest/halloffame/public_life/captainlowe.shtml.
54. Wade, Ch. 'Feuilleton'.
55. Private letter from William Mellors to Dorothy Ockenden written on May 9, 1912, courtesy of Brian Ticehurst.
56. *New York Times*, June 26, 1915.
57. The forerunner of the U.S. House of Representatives Un-American Activities Committee.
58. Unless otherwise noted, the remainder of the details of Mellors' post-sinking life are drawn from Robert Bracken's article 'William J. Mellors, A Survivor Emerges From the Mists of Time'. This article is available at the following URL: http://www.encyclopedia-titanica.org/william-mellors.html.
59. *Westmeath Independent*, April 20, 1912.
60. 'Uncle Walter Survives *Titanic*', by David Cowin, 2010. This article by one of Nichols' nephews is available online at the following URL: http://www.hardscrabble.ca/?q=node/289.
61. Unless otherwise noted, all information since the previous endnote citation in the main text is courtesy of Howard Nichols, the only grandson of Walter Nichols. The authors would like to express their gratitude to Howard for generously sharing his wealth of knowledge about his grandfather's life and career with us, and for allowing us to include this information in our book. Howard, a retired Occupational Skills Trainer – both as a Paramedic Instructor with the NHS Ambulance Service and then as a Mobile Training Unit Instructor with the RNLI Lifeboats – has travelled to over 100 countries. He is currently a professional 'after dinner' speaker, covering most of the southern United Kingdom. He gives highly interesting talks on a variety of topics, including his travels, and an excellent presentation on his grandfather entitled 'The Mysterious Life of Walter Henry'. Interested parties are encouraged to contact him at speaker@howard-nichols.me.uk, and to visit his website at the following URL: http://www.howard-nichols.me.uk/
62. 'Pitman's Own Private Iceberg', by Senan Molony. This article is available at the following URL: http://www.encyclopedia-titanica.org/pitmantitanic-iceberg.html.
63. Information courtesy of Brian Ticehurst.
64. Letter from Pitman to Walter Lord, April 7, 1955, courtesy of Paul Lee.
65. Deposition of George Rheims in the Limitation of Liability hearings, submitted November 14, 1913.
66. The information on Imanita Shelley and Lutie Parrish's post-disaster lives is drawn from the bio entries of both ladies submitted by Phil Gowan to the Encyclopedia-Titanica website; information uncovered by, and posted on the ET message boards by Phil Gowan; information courtesy of Arne Mjaland; and on information posted on Genealogy.com.
67. *New York Times*, June 25, 1915.
68. *Philadelphia Inquirer*, September 23, 1945.
69. *Philadelphia Inquirer*, June 26, 1977.
70. *The South Bend Tribune*, April 19, 1998; additional information courtesy of Jerry Wennerström.
71. *The Times*, January 17, 1914.
72. All additional details are as per information on the official website about Whiteley, which is maintained and run by his descendants. The URL is: http://tomwhiteley.info/index.html.
73. *The Sun*, May 13, 1912; *The New York Times*, May 13, 1912; *The San Francisco Call*, May 13, 1912.

ACKNOWLEDGMENTS

No book – particularly one this complex – is simply the result of the person or persons listed on its cover. Literally dozens of individuals connected with the *Titanic* took the time to help us put this project together. Without their assistance, it would not be what it is now.

First, special thanks are due to George Behe, who has researched the *Titanic* and the people aboard her for many years, and who served as a past Vice-President of the Titanic Historical Society. Not only was he kind enough to supply us with research materials that so few have ever had access to before, but he was ever-available to help us as we went along, and to offer insights and suggestions into improving the historical narrative. He was also kind enough to supply a wonderful Introduction for the book for us. George, we owe you a case of Mountain Dew.

Special mention and thanks should also be given to Mike Poirier, a maritime researcher for many years who has generously provided us with dozens of first-hand survivor accounts – and photographs – to use in this volume. We were positively staggered at the treasure-trove of material he was willing and able to provide us with, and without his help, this book's pages would be far less interesting and fresh.

We would also like to give special thanks to Sam Halpern, who has done so much to bring the history of the *Titanic* – particularly on navigational and timing matters – into clear focus. Not only did he share his research with us to help us get things just right, but he was also always available so that we could bounce ideas off of him. Behind the scenes, we have written volumes of correspondence in trying to sort out where all the pieces of this puzzle lie. Sam was always quite happy to have us play 'devil's advocate' and argue against our first conclusions, all for the sake of making sure that we were all moving on the right track. Also a special thanks for suggesting the book's title!

Bruce Beveridge and Scott Andrews, the most widely acknowledged technical researchers of the *Titanic*, were always available to guide us through thorny technical issues. Daniel Klistorner was kind enough to share some of his more significant discoveries of the ship's history with us, including those from his own book, *Titanic in Photographs*, before that book hit shelves. His generosity and assistance are greatly valued. Mark Chirnside was also ever-ready to share information and thoughts with us.

Mark Petteruti deserves a special thank you for his help and generosity over the years, and for being willing to share photographs and information relating to his grandmother Bertha Mulvihill. We owe Mark, his brother Joe Petteruti, and their entire family thanks for their assistance. Thanks are also owed to Howard Nichols, for generously providing images and information relating to his grandfather Walter Nichols' life and career.

Thanks are owed to our Editor at Amberley, Campbell McCutcheon, for considering yet another *Titanic* book for publication, and for generously providing photographs and assistance with the book.

Many others supplied us with additional accounts or photographs for use. These include (in alphabetical order of their last names): Henry Aho, Jonas Anderssén, Mark Baber, Fiona Nitschke Beckwith, Randy Bryan Bigham, Dave Billnitzer, Bob Bracken, Stephen Cameron, Peter Davies-Garner, Shelley Dziedzic, Richard Edkins, Peter Engberg-Klarström, John Feeney, Dave Fredericks, Paul Fryer, Ioannis Georgiou, Bob Godfrey, Phil Gowan, James Harper, Mike Herbold, Paul Lee, Don Lynch, Arne Mjaland, Ron Moody, Samuel Scott Murdoch, Daniel Parkes, Parks Stephenson, Inger Sheil, Jonathan Smith, Brian Ticehurst, Jerry Wennerström, Geoff Whitfield, and Quincy Norris Williams. A special thanks to Don Lynch for his comprehensive list of suggestions on our first edition.

Tad Fitch would like to thank: I would like to thank my co-authors for all of their hard work on this volume, and for making the experience of working on and putting the manuscript together a pleasurable one. A good deal of thanks are owed to my wife Jackie for her patience as I spent many hours and long nights with another lady, *Titanic*, over the past few years, as I worked on this project. A special thank you to my father Jerry Fitch, brother Jason, and friend Marty Beauchamp for encouraging my interest in history and writing over the years. A general thank you to the rest of my family and friends for their support as well.

J. Kent Layton would like to thank: My dad for trusting me with his treasured copy of *A Night to Remember* and buying a 1/350-scale model of the great liner to build with me – both when I was only four years old. He truly started a lifelong obsession; my mom for giving me the writing skills and for all the proofreading over the years; Elyse for her general support; for my buddies Andrew (and now Yeni, too!), Craig (and Amy & the little tyke), and Aaron (and Mic & fam); all of my family and friends; to James Cameron and James Horner for helping bring *Titanic* back to life (although I still haven't met Kate Winslet, unfortunately). Thanks to Tad and Bill for making this an enjoyable team effort. Finally: in memory of Ed Thompson, Thomas Earl Stott, and Barb Withers, who passed away while work on the First Edition of this book was in progress; and to composer John Barry, who fired my imagination through his score for *Raise the Titanic* and so many other wonderful films.

Bill Wormstedt would like to thank: First I would like to thank George Behe, for years ago instructing me on the right way on doing research into the *Titanic*... and the wrong way to avoid! Thanks to my dad, for giving me an interest in the sea, and in 1957, showing me around his Coast Guard ship, the *Escanaba* (WHEC 64) in New Bedford, Mass. Thanks also to Kent and Tad, for helping make this project a reality. And finally, thanks to my wife Nancy for accepting my *Titanic* hobby, and giving up time with me while I worked on it.

If you contributed to this volume, and somehow in this great mix your name his slipped through the cracks of our list of acknowledgments, we do apologize. If you kindly re-

mind us of the omission, then we will certainly add your name to the list in future editions.

Finally, although we have attempted to present the most accurate history of the *Titanic* yet written, we are sure that some mistakes managed to slip through the cracks. These mistakes are ours and ours alone, and should be attributed to no one else.

PHOTO CREDITS

Authors' Collection: 6, 13, 16 (all except lower left), 17, 22, 27 (top left), 28 (top right), 29 (lower left), 34 (top right), 37 (btm left), 40, 42 (left), 43 (middle), 44 (btm left), 46 (right), 47 (lower left), 52 (top left), 54, 59 (top right), 64 (middle left), 67 (right), 70 (top left and right), 74 (top and lower right), 76, 78 (map by J. Kent Layton), 79, 80 (map by J. Kent Layton), 81 (top), 83 (top left, third row), 86 (btm, map by J. Kent Layton), 87 (top left, map by J. Kent Layton), 90 (top), 91 (second row, center), 92 (top and center), 93 (top left), 93 (btm), 95 (second row, map by J. Kent Layton, and btm), 98 (btm left), 101 (btm row), 102 (btm left), 108 (right), 111 (upper right), 117 (top left), 122 (map by J. Kent Layton), 125 (btm right), 129 (top row, second from right and right), 139 (right), 141 (upper), 142 (right), 145, 152 (right), 157, 167, 174 (left), 175 (top), 184 (btm left), 185 (btm right), 186 (btm left), 188, 190, 193 (btm left), 202, 214, 217, 224, 232, 241, 243 (right), 245, 251, 253 (btm), 254, 258 (btm right), 260 (lower left), 263, 265 (btm right), 268 (right), 271 (all except top left), 274 (top left), 275, 278 (btm), 292, 299, 311, 318, 370

Bruce Beveridge Collection: 8, 19 (Plans Copyright Bruce Beveridge), 26 (top left), 27 (top right), 31 (lower), 37 (right), 38 (right), 42 (right), 44 (third row), 57 (lower right and btm left), 58 (all except top left), 59 (top left), 60 (top left), 62, 64 (top), 68 (top), 78 (btm left), 81 (btm), 82, 84 (top right), 87 (top right), 97 (top left), 98 (top right), 100 (top and btm left), 101 (top right, second row), 102 (top right and btm right), 144 (btm), 176 (lower), 184-185 (with details by J. Kent Layton), 200, 204, 205, (296 lower, with modifications by J. Kent Layton), 379, 442-447 (Plans Copyright Bruce Beveridge)

J&C McCutcheon Collection: 2 (restoration by J. Kent Layton), 4, 18 (top right), 21 (top left), 23, 24 (lower right), 30 (btm left), 32 (center), 33 (btm right), 34 (top left and btm right), 35, 36 (right), 38 (left), 41, 43 (top), 47 (top right), 50 (lower), 52 (btm left), 57 (top left and right), 60 (top right), 72, 78 (restoration by J. Kent Layton), 78 (btm right), 83 (2nd row, left), 84 (top left, 2nd row), 85 (btm), 86 (top), 88 (2nd and 3rd rows, second from right), 95 (top), 108 (left), 140, 149 (top), 181, 186 (top right), 195, 211, 234, 236, 250, 253 (top and middle), 256, 261 (top), 266, 267 (top), 272, 276, 337, 435 (btm)

Jonathan Smith Collection: 14, 21 (btm right), 24 (top right), 25 (lower), 26 (top right), 27 (all except top left and top right), 28 (all except top right), 29 (all except lower left), 30 (top right), 33 (all except btm right), 36 (left), 37 (top left), 43 (btm), 44 (top, second row, and btm right), 47 (center), 51, 52 (center), 58 (top left), 60 (btm left and right), 64 (left), 65, 66 (top left and right), 67 (left), 68 (btm), 69 (btm), 77, 80 (btm), 83 (top right, second row right), 84 (btm left), 85 (top row), 86 (middle), 87 (btm left), 91 (top), 97 (all except top left), 98 (top left), 99 (middle and btm), 101 (top left), 103, 121, 163, 170 (right), 174 (right), 175 (btm), 186 (top left), 210, 233, 235, 236, 260 (top left and right), 268 (left), 270, 274 (center), 284, 298, 435 (top)

Daniel Klistorner Collection: 31 (top), 32 (all except center), 34 (btm left), 64 (middle right), 95 (second from btm), 104 (top right), 105 (top), 111 (btm left), 120 (left), 124, 128 (top), 131 (left), 135, 141 (lower), 142 (left), 149 (btm row), 192, 207, 222 (modification by J. Kent Layton), 230

George Behe Collection: 66 (lower right), 70 (btm right), 88 (top left), 104 (top left), 110, 113, 120 (right), 128 (btm), 132, 143 (btm left), 162 (left), 173 (left), 176 (top), 249, 258 (btm left), 261 (btm), 265 (top right), 267 (btm left)

Ioannis Georgiou Collection: 21 (top right), 25 (top), 46 (all except left, second from right and right), 47 (top left), 50 (top), 52 (top right), 71 (right), 83 (btm left), 88 (2nd & 3rd rows, all except second from right), 92 (btm), 93 (top right), 94 (top row, left, second from left, and second from right), 114, 116, 129 (top row, left and second from left), 143 (btm right), 151, 155, 158, 170 (left), 243 (left)

Library of Congress, Prints & Photographs Division: 12, 16 (lower left), 24 (top left), 30 (top left, top center, and lower left / Daniel Klistorner Collection), 39, 70 (btm left), 91 (second row, left and right), 94 (second row), 112, 125 (btm left), 126, 129 (btm left), 131 (right), 139 (left), 143 (top), 144 (top), 156, 169 (Courtesy Daniel Klistorner), 193 (top right), 257, 258 (top), 259, 262, 265 (top left), 267 (btm right), 273, 368

Mike Poirier Collection: 89, 90 (btm), 94 (top row, right), 95 (btm), 105 (btm); National Archives, Courtesy Mike Poirier: 46 (left), 46 (second from right); National Archives and Records Administration, Courtesy Mike Poirier: 69 (top left and right), 71 (left), 96, 98 (btm right), 99 (top), 111 (btm right), 117 (right two), 118, 129 (btm right), 138 (left, center), 152 (left)

Arne Mjaland Collection, Courtesy George Behe: 104 (lower right)

Georgiou/Klistorner/Chirnside/Layton Collection: 18 (top left), 20, 73, 198, 353

Chirnside/Klistorner/Layton Collection: 59 (btm left), 441

National Archives & Records Administration: 66 (lower left), 366

Courtesy Ron Moody: 59 (top center)

Courtesy Phil Gowan: 71 (center), 162 (right)

Courtesy Shelley Dziedzic: 173 (right), 278 (top), 375

Courtesy Public Archives of Nova Scotia: 271 (top left)

Courtesy Howard Nichols: 376 (btm)

Courtesy Cyril Codus: 296 (top, with modifications by J. Kent Layton), 340-342 (with modifications by J. Kent Layton)

Courtesy Dave Fredericks: 138 (right)

Mark Petteruti Collection: 102 (top left), 376 (top)

Painting by Robert Lloyd: Cover, 182

Color Section:

Jonathan Smith Collection: 001, 027-034, 039, 054; **Authors' Collection:** 002, 003, 005-007, 023, 024, 026, 041, 055; **Daniel Klistorner Collection:** 004 (inset J&C McCutcheon Collection); **Courtesy Henri Aho:** 008-010, 014-017, 020, 021; **Courtesy Jonas Anderssén:** 011-013; **Courtesy White Swan Hotel:** 018, 019, 022; **George Behe Collection:** 025, 035-038, 044, 047, 050-053; **Courtesy Cyril Codus:** 043; **Courtesy Peter Davies-Garner:** 042, 056; **J&C McCutcheon Collection:** 045; **Trevor Powell Collection:** 046, 048; **National Archives & Records Administration:** 040; **Painting by Robert Lloyd:** 049; **Courtesy Paul Fryer:** 057-066

INDEX

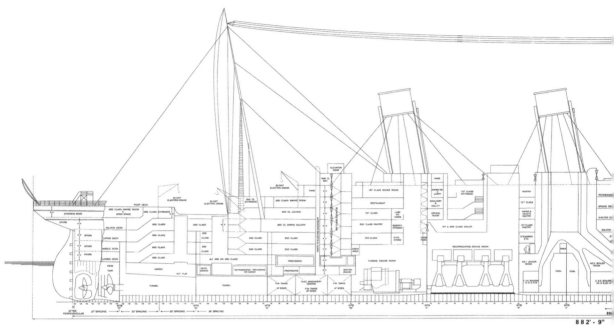

88 2' - 9"

Yard number	401
Registration number	131,428
Length over all	882ft. 9in.
Length between perpendiculars	850ft.
Breath extreme	92ft. 6in.
Depth molded to Shelter Deck	64ft. 3in.
Depth molded to Bridge Deck	73ft. 3in.
Total height from keel to Navigating Bridge	104ft.
Load draft	34ft. 7in.
Displacement at load draft	52,310 tons
Gross tonnage	46,328.54 tons
Net register tonnage	21,831.34 tons
Indicated horsepower of reciprocating engines	30,000

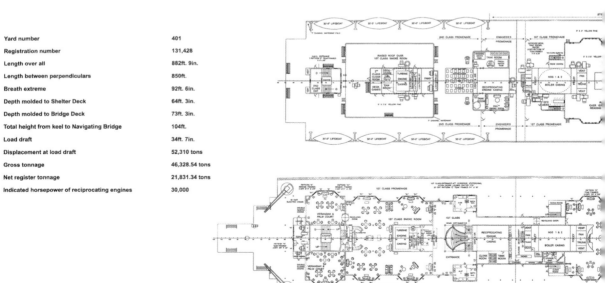

This and following pages: *General arrangement plans of the* Titanic, *drawn by Bruce Beveridge.*

E SCREW STEAMER

TANIC

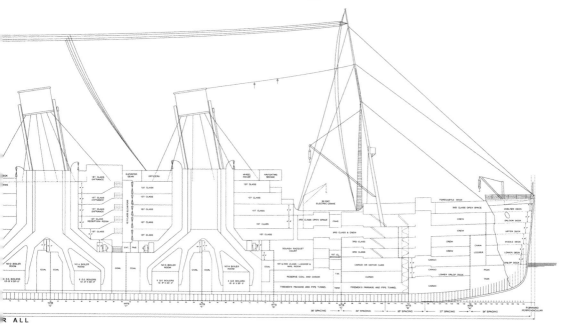

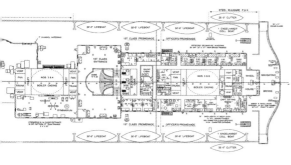

BOAT DECK

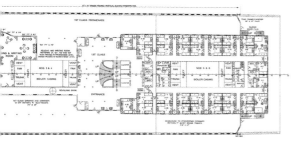

A - DECK

ALL UPPER BERTHS (NO.2) IN ROOMS ON THIS DECK WERE
PULLMAN BERTHS AND FOLDED UP.

ROOMS A 5, 6, 7, 8, 9, 10, 11, 12, 14, 15, 16, 17, 18, 19, 20, 21,
22, 23, 24, 25, 26, 27, 29, 30, 31, 32 AND 33, WERE SO FITTED
THAT A SOFA BERTH FOR AN EXTRA PASSENGER COULD
BE PROVIDED WHEN REQUIRED.

ROOMS A 5, 6, 9, 10, 14, 15, 18, 19, 22, 23, 26, 27, 30 AND 31,
WERE LIGHTED AND VENTILATED FROM THE DECK ABOVE (BOAT DECK)
INDICATED BY A DASHED CIRCLE.

AE -	ASH EJECTOR
B -	BUNK
BR -	BAG RACK
CS -	COAL SHUTE
D -	CHEST OF DRAWERS
DC -	DIRECT CONTACT
DT -	DRESSING TABLE
DRES -	DRESSER
DRS (NUMB) -	DRAWERS
DP on TANK TOP -	DRAIN POT
FE -	FIREMAN'S ESCAPE
FL -	FOLDING LAVATORY
FW -	FRESH WATER
GI -	GALVANIZED IRON
H -	HEATER
H -	HOIST
HP -	HOT PRESS
L on LK -	LOCKER
LAA -	LIGHT & AIR
MP -	MOORING PIPE
PT -	PIPE TUNNEL
P on TANK TOP -	PLATE OVER MAN HOLE
S on FOREPEAKS -	SCUTTLE
S on BOAT DECK -	SKID LIGHT
SB -	SIDE BOARD
T on TE -	TUNNEL ESCAPE
TV -	TUNNEL VENT
V -	UTLEY'S VENTILATING PORTHOLE
V -	VENT
W -	WARDROBE
WP -	WASH PORT
WT -	WATERTIGHT
WTB -	WATERTIGHT BULKHEAD
WTD -	WATERTIGHT DOOR
WR -	WARDROBE ROOM
WT -	WRITING TABLE
	DUTCH DOOR
	LAVATORY SINK
	SINK
	UPHOLSTERY
	URINALS
	WALL SEAT TEAK
	WALL SEAT UPHOLSTERED
	WASH BASIN
	WATER CLOSET

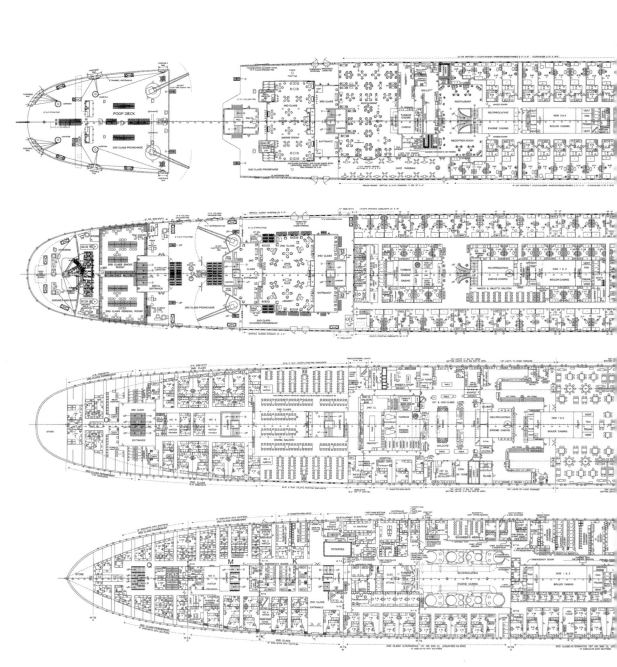

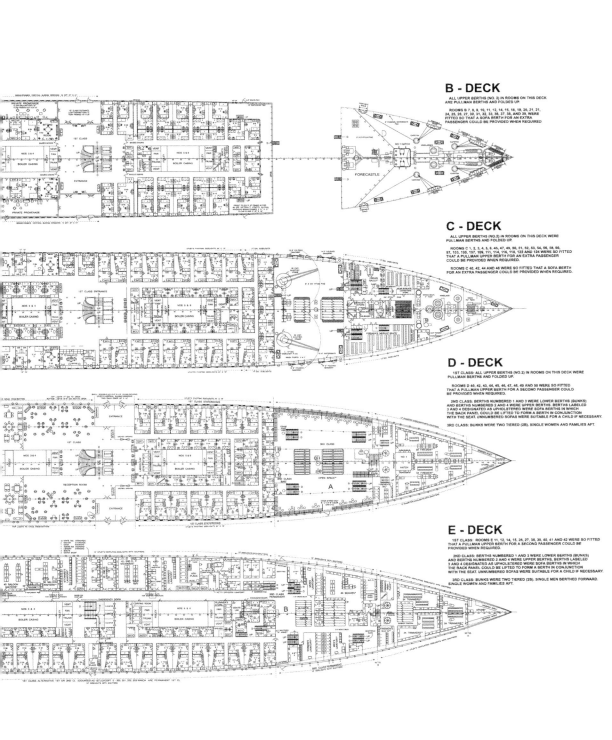

B - DECK

ALL UPPER BERTHS (NO.2) IN ROOMS ON THIS DECK
ARE PULLMAN BERTHS AND FOLDED UP.

ROOMS B 7, 8, 9, 10, 11, 12, 14, 15, 18, 19, 20, 21, 21,
24, 25, 26, 27, 30, 31, 32, 33, 36, 37, 38, AND 39, WERE
FITTED SO THAT A SOFA BERTH FOR AN EXTRA
PASSENGER COULD BE PROVIDED WHEN REQUIRED

C - DECK

ALL UPPER BERTHS (NO.2) IN ROOMS ON THIS DECK WERE
PULLMAN BERTHS AND FOLDED UP.

ROOMS C 1, 2, 3, 4, 5, 6, 45, 47, 49, 50, 51, 52, 53, 54, 56, 58, 59,
97, 103, 105, 107, 109, 111, 114, 116, 118, 122 AND 124 WERE SO FITTED
THAT A PULLMAN UPPER BERTH FOR AN EXTRA PASSENGER
COULD BE PROVIDED WHEN REQUIRED.

ROOMS C 40, 42, 44 AND 46 WERE SO FITTED THAT A SOFA BERTH
FOR AN EXTRA PASSENGER COULD BE PROVIDED WHEN REQUIRED.

D - DECK

1ST CLASS: ALL UPPER BERTHS (NO.2) IN ROOMS ON THIS DECK WERE
PULLMAN BERTHS AND FOLDED UP.

ROOMS D 40, 42, 43, 44, 45, 46, 47, 48, 49 AND 50 WERE SO FITTED
THAT A PULLMAN UPPER BERTH FOR A SECOND PASSENGER COULD
BE PROVIDED WHEN REQUIRED.

2ND CLASS: BERTHS NUMBERED 1 AND 3 WERE LOWER BERTHS (BUNKS)
AND BERTHS NUMBERED 2 AND 4 WERE UPPER BERTHS. BERTHS LABELED
3 AND 4 DESIGNATED AS UPHOLSTERED WERE SOFA BERTHS IN WHICH
THE BACK PANEL COULD BE LIFTED TO FORM A BERTH IN CONJUNCTION
WITH THE SEAT. UNNUMBERED SOFAS WERE SUITABLE FOR A CHILD IF NECESSARY.

3RD CLASS: BUNKS WERE TWO TIERED (2B). SINGLE WOMEN AND FAMILIES AFT.

E - DECK

1ST CLASS: ROOMS E 11, 12, 14, 15, 26, 27, 38, 39, 40, 41 AND 42 WERE SO FITTED
THAT A PULLMAN UPPER BERTH FOR A SECOND PASSENGER COULD BE
PROVIDED WHEN REQUIRED.

2ND CLASS: BERTHS NUMBERED 1 AND 3 WERE LOWER BERTHS (BUNKS)
AND BERTHS NUMBERED 2 AND 4 WERE UPPER BERTHS. BERTHS LABELED
3 AND 4 DESIGNATED AS UPHOLSTERED WERE SOFA BERTHS IN WHICH
THE BACK PANEL COULD BE LIFTED TO FORM A BERTH IN CONJUNCTION
WITH THE SEAT. UNNUMBERED SOFAS WERE SUITABLE FOR A CHILD IF NECESSARY.

3RD CLASS: BUNKS WERE TWO TIERED (2B). SINGLE MEN BERTHED FORWARD.
SINGLE WOMEN AND FAMILIES AFT.

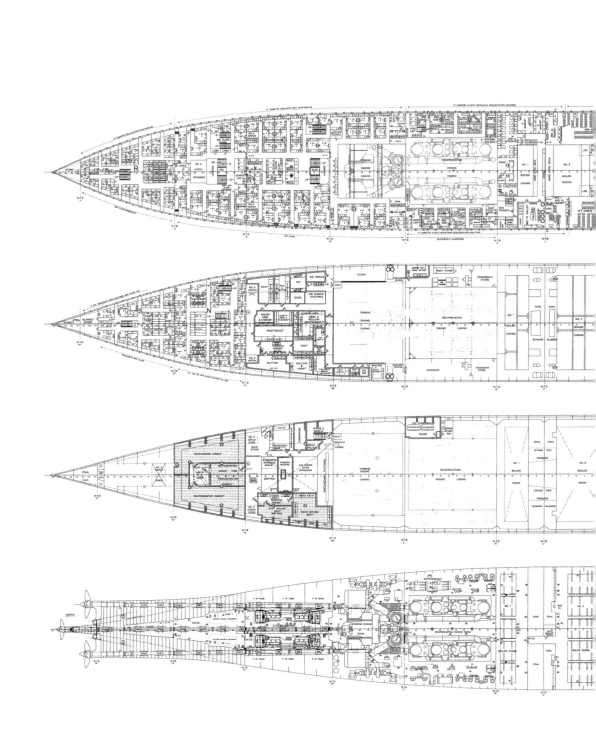

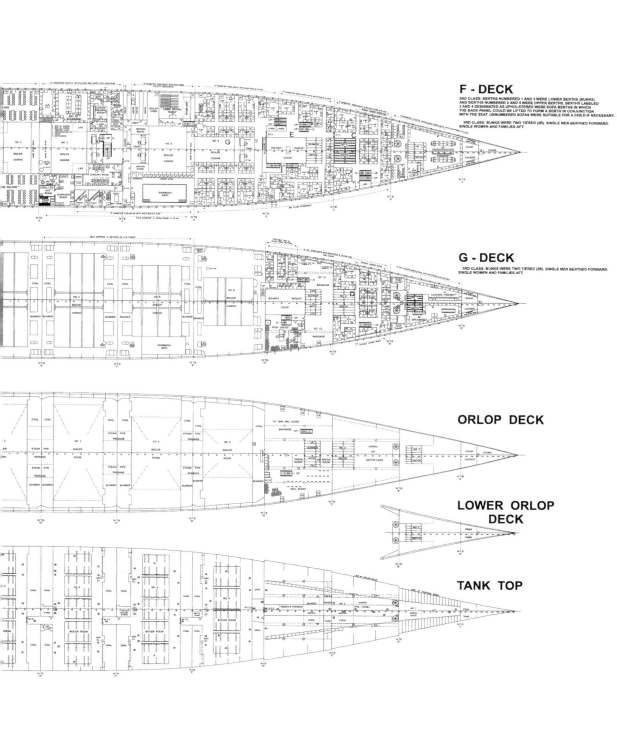

F - DECK

2ND CLASS: BERTHS NUMBERED 1 AND 3 WERE LOWER BERTHS (BUNKS) AND BERTHS NUMBERED 2 AND 4 WERE UPPER BERTHS. BERTHS LABELED 3 AND 4 DESIGNATED AS UPHOLSTERED WERE SOFA BERTHS IN WHICH THE BACK PANEL COULD BE LIFTED TO FORM A BERTH IN CONJUNCTION WITH THE SEAT. UNNUMBERED SOFAS WERE SUITABLE FOR A CHILD IF NECESSARY.

3RD CLASS: BUNKS WERE TWO TIERED (2B). SINGLE MEN BERTHED FORWARD. SINGLE WOMEN AND FAMILIES AFT.

G - DECK

3RD CLASS: BUNKS WERE TWO TIERED (2B). SINGLE MEN BERTHED FORWARD. SINGLE WOMEN AND FAMILIES AFT.

ORLOP DECK

LOWER ORLOP DECK

TANK TOP

J. KENT LAYTON became fascinated with the *Titanic* when he was first learning to read. His fascination with the subject never waned, and what was once a hobby soon became a serious study and analysis of the history of the *Titanic* and other great Atlantic liners. His experience in the field now totals over two decades. He has authored critically acclaimed books such as *Lusitania: An Illustrated Biography*, *The Edwardian Superliners: A Trio of Trios*, *Transatlantic Liners*; his next work is the forthcoming *The Unseen Mauretania (1907): The Ship in Rare Illustrations*. He lives in the Finger Lakes region of Central New York, and divides his time between his writing and his work as a piano tuner.

TAD FITCH has researched the *Titanic* and maritime history for over two decades. He has written numerous articles related to *Titanic* that have been published in the Titanic Historical Society's journal *The Titanic Commutator*, and online at *Bill Wormstedt's Titanic* and *Encyclopedia Titanica*. He, along with George Behe and Bill Wormstedt, co-authored the landmark article, "*Titanic*: The Lifeboat Launching Sequence Re-Examined". He was a co-author of *Report Into the Loss of SS Titanic: A Centennial Reappraisal* and the recently published *Into the Danger Zone: Sea Crossings of the First World War*. Tad was born in northeast Ohio, and works in the field of psychology. When not writing, he enjoys scuba diving and traveling.

BILL WORMSTEDT first became interested in the *Titanic* after reading Walter Lord's *A Night to Remember* in junior high school. He discovered the online *Titanic* community in 1995, and soon started commenting and writing about the *Titanic*. His articles have been published in THS's *The Titanic Commutator*, *Encyclopedia Titanica*, and his own web site, *Bill Wormstedt's Titanic*. With Tad Fitch and George Behe, he co-wrote *The Lifeboat Launching Sequence Re-Examined*, and is one of eleven co-authors of *Report Into the Loss of SS Titanic: A Centennial Reappraisal*. Bill is a retired computer programmer who resides in Seattle, Washington.